MW01618177

Psychology Applied to Work®

THIRTEENTH EDITION

An Introduction to Industrial and Organizational Psychology

Satoris S. Howes
Paul M. Muchinsky

Hypergraphic Press

Hypergraphic Press

Psychology Applied to Work®: An Introduction to Industrial and Organizational Psychology, **Thirteenth Edition**

Satoris S. Howes
Paul M. Muchinsky

Design and Layout: SHS Design
Cover and Interior Design Image: karandaev/iStock
Printer: Signature Book Printing

Printed in the United States of America
1 2 3 4 5 6 21 20 19 18 17 16

Library of Congress Control Number: 2021921515

ISBN: 978-0-9749345-5-6

Hypergraphic Press, Inc.
P.O. Box 470
Northfield, MN 55057

From Satoris (Tori) Howes:

Dedicated to my mom, Renee Youngcourt, who would have read every word in this book if she were still here; my dad, Bean Youngcourt, who may not read a single page, but will put it on display in his house and tell me he's proud of me; and my grandmother, Mary Bruneau, who thanked me when I said she wouldn't have to actually read the previous edition — and would be just as thankful to not have to read this one if she were still here.

About the Authors

Satoris "Tori" Howes was born and raised a "military brat," spending her formative years in North Dakota and Missouri. She earned her B.S. degree in psychology and public relations from the University of Central Missouri, her M.S. degree in industrial and organizational (I-O) psychology from Missouri State University, and her Ph.D. in I-O psychology from Texas A&M University. At the end of her graduate studies, she worked as a consultant in the Chicago branch of a global leadership solutions consulting firm. She then transitioned back into academia, working for a year at the University of Wisconsin - River Falls before joining the faculty in the Department of Psychological Sciences at Kansas State University. There, she received the College of Arts and Sciences William L. Stamey Teaching Award in 2012. She later transitioned to the Department of Management in the College of Business Administration at Kansas State University, where she was awarded the Ralph E. Reitz Outstanding Teaching Award and the Outstanding Contributions in Research Award, both in 2015. Dr. Howes is currently a Professor in the College of Business at Oregon State University, where she was awarded the Scholarship and Creative Activity Award in 2018, the Breaking Barriers in Research diversity award in 2019, and the Prominent Scholar Award in 2021. Her main research interests include the employment interview, performance appraisal and feedback, work-family issues, and judgment and decision making, areas in which she has authored and coauthored numerous journal articles and chapters in edited volumes. Dr. Howes is a Fellow of the Society for Industrial and Organizational Psychology (SIOP) and the American Psychological Association (APA), as well as an active member of the Academy of Management and the Society for Human Resource Management (SHRM). She was the 2016 recipient of SIOP's prestigious Distinguished Teaching Contributions Award and is the Editor of *Industrial and Organizational Psychology: Perspectives on Science and Practice*. In addition to her role as an academic, Dr. Howes is a leadership coach for the Professional Development Academy. She resides in Bend, Oregon, and enjoys running, golfing, playing board games, and spending time with her husband (John) and their four children (Rook, Audrey, Matthew, and Ryan). She can be reached at satoris.howes@gmail.com.

Paul M. Muchinsky was born and raised in Connecticut. He received his B.A. degree in psychology from Gettysburg College, his M.S. degree in psychology from Kansas State University, and his Ph.D. degree in industrial/organizational psychology from Purdue University. He was a faculty member of Iowa State University for twenty years. In 1993, he was appointed the Joseph M. Bryan Distinguished Professor of Business at The University of North Carolina at Greensboro. In 2004, Dr. Muchinsky was the inaugural recipient of the Distinguished Teaching Contribution Award from the Society for Industrial and Organizational Psychology for his outstanding educational contributions to the field. In 2008, Dr. Muchinsky was awarded the honorary Doctor of Science (D.Sc.) degree from Gettysburg College. He was a Fellow of four divisions of the American Psychological Association: the Society for Industrial and Organizational Psychology; the Society for the Teaching of Psychology; the Society of Consulting Psychology, and the Society of Counseling Psychology. He was a Diplomate of the American Board of Professional Psychology (in industrial and organizational psychology). Many of the cases and examples of concepts presented in this book came directly from his professional experiences.

Dr. Muchinsky passed away in 2015, but he would be proud that his life's work continues with the updating of *Psychology Applied to Work*® by the professor and author that he respected and admired, Dr. Satoris Howes.

Brief Contents

1 Overview and Historical Background of I-O Psychology 1

2 Research Methods in I-O Psychology 25

3 The Context of Work 59

4 Criteria: Standards for Decision Making 87

5 Predictors: Psychological Assessments 119

6 Organizational Strategy and Staffing 165

7 Organizational Learning 193

8 Performance Management 229

9 Culture and Organizational Change and Development 263

10 Teams and Teamwork 291

11 Affect, Attitudes, and Behavior at Work 323

12 Workplace Health and Well-Being 359

13 Work Motivation 391

14 Leadership 425

15 Union/Management Relations 457

Contents

Chapter 1 **Overview and Historical Background of I-O Psychology** 1

I-O Psychology—What it Is, and Isn't 2

The Lighter Side of I-O Psychology: *I vs. O* 4

The History of I-O Psychology 4

The Early Years (1900–1916) 5

World War I (1917–1918) 8

Between the Wars (1919–1940) 9

World War II (1941–1945) 12

Toward Specialization (1946–1963) 13

Government Intervention (1964–1993) 14

The Information Age (1994–2018) 15

Social Media and I-O Psychology: *Web 2.0 and the World of Work* 16

The Experience Age (2019–Present) 17

The Science and Practice of I-O Psychology Today 18

The Scientist-Practitioner Model 18

COVID-19 and I-O Psychology: *Rethinking Business as Usual* 19

Professional Affiliations 21

Licensing of I-O Psychologists 22

The Mandate of I-O Psychology 23

Chapter Review 24

Chapter 2 **Research Methods in I-O Psychology** 25

Statement of Research Problem 27

Design of the Research Study 28

Social Media and I-O Psychology: *Getting Past the WEIRD Participants* 29

Primary Research Methods 30

True Experiment 30

Quasi-Experiment 32

Non-Experiment 33

Secondary Research Methods 34

Archival Research 34

Meta-Analysis 35

Data Mining 36

Faces of I-O Psychology: *Alexis A. Fink* 38

Qualitative Research 39

Methods/Sources of Data Collection 41

Organizational Records 41

Questionnaires 42

Observation 43
Interviews/Focus Groups 44
Organizational Neuroscience 45
Measurement and Analysis 46
Measurement of Variables 46
The Correlation Coefficient 47
Determining Causality 49
The Lighter Side of I-O Psychology: *Spurious Correlations* 51
Conclusions from Research 51
COVID-19 and I-O Psychology: *The Need for Holistic Research* 52
Ethical Issues in Research 53
Chapter Review 56

Chapter 3 **The Context of Work** **59**
The Structural Context 60
The Social Context 62
Humanitarian Work Psychology 62
Diversity, Equity, and Inclusion 64
Social Media and I-O Psychology: *Slacktivism or Activism?* 66
The Environmental Context 67
Cross-Cultural Considerations 67
Sustainability Concerns 68
The Legal Context 69
Workplace Discrimination 70
The Lighter Side of I-O Psychology: *Plans for Breeding?* 71
Faces of I-O Psychology: *Eric M. Dunleavy* 77
Workplace Health and Safety 82
Family and Medical Leave 82
COVID-19 and I-O Psychology: *Families First Coronavirus Response Act* 83
Child Labor 84
Chapter Review 85

Chapter 4 **Criteria: Standards for Decision Making** **87**
Social Media and I-O Psychology: *Criteria for "5 Star" Organizations* 89
Conceptual Versus Actual Criteria 89
Criterion Deficiency, Relevance, and Contamination 91
Work Analysis 93
Sources of Work Information 94
The Lighter Side of I-O Psychology: *Don't Be a Sucker* 95
Work Analytic Procedures 96
How to Collect Work Analytic Information 99
Managerial Work Analysis 103
Uses of Work Analytic Information 103
Evaluating Work Analytic Methods 104
Competency Modeling 104

Performance Criteria 105
Major Performance Criteria 106
COVID-19 and I-O Psychology: *Working While Sick* 108
Faces of I-O Psychology: *Lawrence Houston III* 111
Dynamic Performance Criteria 115
Chapter Review 116

Chapter 5 Predictors: Psychological Assessments 119

Assessing the Quality of Predictors 121
Reliability 121
Validity 123
The Interplay Between Reliability and Validity 129
Predictor Development 130
The Lighter Side of I-O Psychology: *The Poetry of Prediction* 131
Ability Tests 132
Cognitive Ability 132
Physical Ability 134
Psychomotor Ability 135
Sensory/Perceptual Ability 135
Personality Inventories 136
Faking in Personality Assessment 140
Social Media and I-O Psychology: *Assessing Personality via Facebook* 142
Integrity Tests 142
Situational Judgment Tests 144
Biodata Inventories 145
Drug Testing 147
Computerized Adaptive Testing 148
Online Testing 149
Faces of I-O Psychology: *John C. Scott* 150
Interviews 151
Degree of Structure 152
Interview Formats 152
Work Samples and Situational Exercises 154
Work Samples 154
Situational Exercises 156
Assessment Centers 157
Letters of Recommendation 158
Overview and Evaluation of Predictors 158
COVID-19 and I-O Psychology: *Unanswered Questions* 161
Chapter Review 162

Chapter 6 Organizational Strategy and Staffing 165

Recruitment 168
Social Media and I-O Psychology: *Social Recruitment* 168
The Lighter Side of I-O Psychology: *Responses to Rejection Letters* 171

Personnel Selection 172
Selection Decisions 176
Personnel Selection from a Human Perspective 179
COVID-19 and I-O Psychology: *College Admissions Amid COVID-19* 184
Validity Generalization 184
Determination of the Cutoff Score 186
Test Utility and Organizational Efficiency 188
Faces of I-O Psychology: *Joshua Brenner* 189
Placement and Classification 190
Chapter Review 191

Chapter 7 Organizational Learning 193
Formal Versus Informal Organizational Learning 195
Learning and Task Performance 197
Assessing Training Needs 199
Methods and Techniques of Training 201
Computer-Based Training 201
COVID-19 and I-O Psychology: *Returning to "Normal" or Not?* 202
Non–Computer-Based Training 204
Active Learning Approaches 206
Error-Management Training 207
Self-Regulatory Training 208
Special Training Topics 210
Diversity Training 210
Expatriate Training 212
Sexual Harassment Training 214
Management Development Issues 215
Social Media and I-O Psychology: *Workplace Romances, Social Media, and Sexual Harassment Concerns* 216
Mentoring 217
Faces of I-O Psychology: *Sandra L. Lee* 218
Executive Coaching 221
The Lighter Side of I-O Psychology: *We Need Coaching, Too!* 222
Transfer of Training 223
Evaluation Criteria of Training Programs 224
Chapter Review 226

Chapter 8 Performance Management 229
The Performance Management Process 231
COVID-19 and I-O Psychology: *Performance Management Challenges* 233
Purposes of Performance Management Systems 234
Faces of I-O Psychology: *Steven T. Hunt* 235
Performance Appraisal and the Law 237
Performance Rating Scales 239
Rating Errors and Biases 244

Rater Training 246
Rater Motivation 247
Peer and Self-Assessments 249
Peer Assessments 249
Self-Assessments 251
360° Feedback 252
Feedback in Performance Management Contexts 254
Giving Feedback 254
Seeking Feedback 255
Reactions to Feedback 256
The Lighter Side of I-O Psychology: *You Rock!* 257
Reactions to Performance Appraisals 258
Future of Performance Management 259
Social Media and I-O Psychology: *The Crowdsourced Performance Review* 260
Chapter Review 261

Chapter 9 **Culture and Organizational Change and Development** **263**
Culture 264
National Culture 264
Organizational Climate and Culture 269
Social Media and I-O Psychology: *The New Water Cooler* 273
Perceptions of Fit 276
COVID-19 and I-O Psychology: *Fit Disruption or Fit Enhancement?* 277
Organizational Change 278
Faces of I-O Psychology: *Mark G. Ehrhart* 280
Downsizing, Outsourcing, and Offshoring 282
The Lighter Side of I-O Psychology: *The Man Who Outsourced His Job* 283
Mergers and Acquisitions 286
Organization Development 287
Leadership Development as OD 288
Team Building as OD 288
Survey Feedback as OD 288
Chapter Review 289

Chapter 10 **Teams and Teamwork** **291**
Level of Analysis 292
Defining Characteristics of Work Teams 294
Types of Teams 295
Social Media and I-O Psychology: *Social Media Teams* 296
COVID-19 and I-O Psychology: *Virtually All Virtual* 298
Team Life Cycle 299
Team Structure and Composition 302
Faces of I-O Psychology: *Suzanne T. Bell* 304
Team Processes 305
Transition Processes 305

Action Processes 306
Interpersonal Processes 307
Team Cognition 310
Shared Mental Models 310
Decision Making in Teams 313
Personnel Selection for Teams 314
The Lighter Side of I-O Psychology: *Collective Nouns* 316
Training for Teams 316
Performance Appraisal in Teams 317
Concluding Comments 319
Chapter Review 320

Chapter 11 **Affect, Attitudes, and Behavior at Work** **323**
Affect, Moods, and Emotions 325
Broaden-and-Build Theory of Positive Emotions 329
The Lighter Side of I-O Psychology: *Working From Home* 330
Job Attitudes 331
Job Satisfaction 331
Work Commitment 335
Employee Engagement 338
Organizational Justice 339
Faces of I-O Psychology: *John C. Howes* 340
Behaviors 343
Organizational Citizenship Behavior 343
Counterproductive Work Behavior 345
Organizational Politics 348
Social Media and I-O Psychology: *The Cyberbully's Blog* 349
The Psychological Contract 351
COVID-19 and I-O Psychology: *Health and Safety Psychological Contracts* 352
Violations of the Psychological Contract 354
Chapter Review 356

Chapter 12 **Workplace Health and Well-Being** **359**
Physical Stressors 361
Task-Related Stressors 363
Role Stressors 364
Social Stressors 366
Social Media and I-O Psychology: *The Stress Potential of Social Media at Work* 367
Work Schedule-Related Stressors 367
Shift Work 367
Flexible Work Arrangements 369
Career-Related Stressors 372
Traumatic Events 374

Stressful Change Processes 375
Stress-Management Interventions and Wellness Programs 376
Balancing Work and Nonwork 377
Faces of I-O Psychology: *YoungAh Park* 378
Work-Family Conflict 378
Work-Family Enrichment 380
The Lighter Side of I-O Psychology: *Mesearch Research* 381
Work-Family Interventions 382
The Stigma of Dirty Work 383
COVID-19 and I-O Psychology: *Pandemic Taint* 386
Alcohol and Drug Abuse in the Workplace 387
Chapter Review 389

Chapter 13 **Work Motivation 391**

Work Motivation Theories 394
Biological-Based Theory 394
Maslow's Hierarchy of Needs 395
Two-Factor Theory 397
Flow Theory 398
Self-Determination Theory 399
Equity Theory 401
Expectancy Theory 403
Goal-Setting Theory 406
Job Characteristics Model 410
Synthesis and Application of Work Motivation Theories 412
The Lighter Side of I-O Psychology: *Dear Desperate* 412
The Impact of Time on Work Motivation 416
Social Media and I-O Psychology: *Cyberloafing* 417
Overqualification and Work Motivation 419
COVID-19 and I-O Psychology: *A Blessing for the Overqualified?* 420
Fun and Games of Work Motivation 421
Faces of I-O Psychology: *David R. Earnest* 422
Chapter Review 423

Chapter 14 **Leadership 425**

Theoretical Approaches to Leadership 427
The Trait Approach 427
Faces of I-O Psychology: *Melissa Wolfe* 428
The Behavioral Approach 430
Social Media and I-O Psychology: *Follow the Leader (on Twitter)* 431
The Power and Influence Approach 431
The Contingency Approach 433
COVID-19 and I-O Psychology: *Leading in a Pandemic* 434
Leader-Member Exchange Theory 435

Full-Range Leadership Theory 436
Authentic Leadership 441
Servant Leadership 441
The Lighter Side of I-O Psychology: *An Authentic Political Leader?* 442
Strategic Leadership 443
Implicit Leadership Theory 443
Substitutes for Leadership 444
Points of Convergence Among Approaches 445
Dark Side of Leadership 446
Leadership in Teams 448
Cross-Cultural Issues in Leadership 449
Diversity Issues in Leadership 451
Entrepreneurship 453
Concluding Comments 454
Chapter Review 455

Chapter 15 Union/Management Relations 457
What Is a Union? 459
Unions as Organizations 461
The Formation of a Union 463
The Labor Contract 465
Social Media and I-O Psychology: *Members Unite… Online* 466
Collective Bargaining and Impasse Resolution 466
Responses to Impasse 469
Grievances 472
Influence of Unions on Non-Unionized Companies 474
Behavioral Research on Union/Management Relations 475
Employee Support for Unions 475
Union Influence 476
Dispute Settlement 477
Commitment to the Union 478
I-O Psychology and Labor Relations 480
What Is the Future of Labor Unions? 484
COVID-19 and I-O Psychology: *Union Impact During the Pandemic* 485
Chapter Review 487

Endnotes 489

Image Credits 561

Author Index 565

Subject Index 585

Preface

Years ago, when Paul asked me to join him on chronicling the advancements of I-O psychology and bringing the field to life through this text, I was honored, confused, and worried. I was honored for the obvious reasons. I was also confused. Why me? Why now? Why me? All right, so I already asked that last question, but I assure you I asked it many more times than that. But mostly, I was worried that he was going to figure out I wasn't the right person to ask and yank the opportunity away. (Imposter syndrome was at an all-time high, no doubt.)

I recall sitting with Paul and his wife, Kay, at a table following our conference the year he "proposed." I use that term because that's the term Paul used. He said that me joining him as a coauthor was like a marriage and we were now in this together. Talk about a strange conversation, with his wife sitting there while he talked about our new union! When Paul excused himself, Kay looked at me and said, "You have no idea how big of a deal this is. For Paul to ask you to join him on his book means he really trusts you and you must be good." Great. Cue imposter syndrome and sweat.

Not long after, we began working on the 11th edition. Every word I changed, deletion I made, and paragraph I added, I cringed as he gritted his teeth and grunted. I kept expecting him to announce this was a huge mistake and we were getting a coauthor divorce. Instead, he would growl, "Fine. If that's what you want." This isn't to say he was happy with everything I wrote. "Tori!" he said one day, "If you use 'That is' one more time I'm going to fly out to Kansas to throw the book at you. And I mean the whole book!" I'm likely paraphrasing as I believe he used more colorful terms, but I digress.

When we were finally putting the finishing touches on the 11th edition, Paul said to me, "I hear you've been asking why I chose you as my coauthor. You want to know?" I don't know that I actually said yes, but it wouldn't have mattered. He had a speech, and he was going to give it. "I read one of your papers and you had a sentence in there that was pure magic. I read it and my jaw dropped. It was perfect." He told me what paper and what sentence it was. I said, "I didn't write that. My coauthor, Allen, did." Sigh. Paul said, "Oh. Well, his writing is perfect. You say, 'that is' a lot, but I still made the right choice."

Paul passed away in 2015, not long after having me sign in blood that I would continue his legacy. OK, there was no blood. Or sweat. But there were tears, as his passing left a huge hole in the world of I-O psychology. I vowed to make him proud with my continuation of Psychology Applied to Work, and I believe he would be. This edition does exactly what Paul entrusted me to do. It shares the most current story of I-O psychology in an easy-to-understand way. The science and practice of the field are intertwined in the examples throughout the book. Most importantly, I had fun while working on this revision as I sought ways to make the subject matter more meaningful and personal.

I believe you will find the material within this book to be applicable to many aspects of your life, not just work. I welcome any feedback you may have. Enjoy!

Satoris (Tori) S. Howes

The chapter-by-chapter revisions for the 13th edition include the following:

- **Chapter 1** (Overview and Historical Background of I-O Psychology): Introduction of the Experience Age (2019-Present) in the history of I-O psychology. Updates in the timeline of major world events and I-O psychology, the growth in I-O psychology, salaries paid in the field, and the future of I-O psychology. Two *Consider This* reflection points added to increase critical thinking.
- **Chapter 2** (Research Methods in I-O Psychology): Updates and expansion of information on archival research, data mining, and organizational neuroscience. New sections on HARKing and study preregistration as ethical considerations. Six *Consider This* reflection points added to increase critical thinking.
- **Chapter 3** (The Context of Work; new chapter this edition): Material on structural, social, environmental, and legal contexts of work previously covered in other chapters, now together to provide a better understanding of the issues impacting I-O psychological research and practice. Structural context has new information on the six elements of organizational structure. Social context has substantial new material on diversity, equity, and inclusion as well as updates on humanitarian work psychology. Environmental context includes updates to cross-cultural and sustainability considerations. Updates and new detail added to the legal context, with new material provided on workplace health and safety, family and medical leave, and child labor. Eight *Consider This* reflection points included to increase critical thinking.
- **Chapter 4** (Criteria: Standards for Decision Making; previously Chapter 3): Expanded material on emotional labor. New material on presenteeism to counter absenteeism. Six *Consider This* reflection points added to increase critical thinking.
- **Chapter 5** (Predictors: Psychological Assessments; previously Chapter 4): Expanded discussion regarding controversy of cognitive ability tests as predictors. New sections on psychomotor ability and sensory/perceptual ability. Greater detail on the Big Five personality traits and biodata inventories as predictors. Eight *Consider This* reflection points added to increase critical thinking.
- **Chapter 6** (Organizational Strategy and Staffing; previously Chapter 5): Greater detail on the role of predictor validity, selection ratios, and base rates in determining the quality of personnel selection decisions. Five *Consider This* reflection points added to increase critical thinking.
- **Chapter 7** (Organizational Learning; previously Chapter 6): Additional content on organizational socialization. Updates to sexual harassment training, diversity training, and expatriate training. Eight *Consider This* reflection points added to increase critical thinking.
- **Chapter 8** (Performance Management; previously Chapter 7): New material on behavioral observation training and the Dunning-Kruger effect. Seven *Consider This* reflection points added to increase critical thinking.

- **Chapter 9** (Culture and Organizational Change and Development; previously Chapter 8): Removal of outdated material. Considerable update and expansion to national and organizational culture. Real-world examples added for Competing Values Framework. Additional detail on perceptions of fit. Six *Consider This* reflection points added to increase critical thinking.
- **Chapter 10** (Teams and Teamwork; previously Chapter 9): More detailed discussion of faultlines and team cohesion. Six *Consider This* reflection points added to increase critical thinking.
- **Chapter 11** (Affect, Attitudes, and Behavior at Work; previously Chapter 10): New material on specific emotions, including the dual threshold model of workplace anger. Six *Consider This* reflection points added to increase critical thinking.
- **Chapter 12** (Workplace Health and Well-Being; previously Chapter 11): New sections with substantial expanded coverage of work stressors. New material on workplace safety, traumatic events at work, and boundary theory. Seven *Consider This* reflection points added to increase critical thinking.
- **Chapter 13** (Work Motivation; previously Chapter 12): New sections on Maslow's hierarchy, the two-factor theory of motivation, and fun and games of work motivation. New coverage of the Genetic Information Nondiscrimination Act of 2008. Expanded detail of equity theory and expectancy theory. Eight *Consider This* reflection points added to increase critical thinking.
- **Chapter 14** (Leadership; previously Chapter 13): Updates to research findings throughout. Six *Consider This* reflection points added to increase critical thinking.
- **Chapter 15** (Union/Management Relations; previously Chapter 14): Updated information on right-to-work laws. Additional information added on legality of labor strikes. Five *Consider This* reflection points added to increase critical thinking.

In addition to the changes noted above, all chapters were revised to enhance readability, with citations now provided as endnotes (with references found at the back of the book) rather than within the text. Each chapter concludes with a list of the key terms from the chapter and questions to aid in the review of the material. Lastly, there are four special features that appear throughout the book, two of which are new to this edition. The first two special features, *Social Media and I-O Psychology* and *COVID-19 and I-O Psychology*, offer exciting new insights into how the field of I-O psychology is evolving in response to social changes, with the latter of these two being new to this edition. The last two special features, *Faces of I-O Psychology* and *The Lighter Side of I-O Psychology*, provide a glimpse into the non-technical side of I-O psychology, introducing readers to professionals in the field and presenting some amusing content relevant to each chapter, with the latter of these two also being new to this edition.

I (SSH) would like to express my gratitude to several people for helping to make the 13th edition of *Psychology Applied to Work*® a reality. First, a huge thank you to Natalie Marfleet, who may be a machine under her human-like exterior. If things are easy to understand, it is because of her editing skills and ability to call me out when I was being too technical or obtuse. If things are difficult to understand, it is because I was stubborn and should have listened to her. Thank you also to Brian Muchinsky, Paul's son, who has allowed me to bounce ideas off him and has been a perpetual motivator as I've continued his dad's work. Although Brian didn't follow in Paul's footsteps as an I-O psychologist (gasp!), he is a spectacular attorney who offers mediation services in employment and other issues relevant to I-O psychology, so I still like him. I would be remiss if I didn't also thank each of the contributors to the *Faces of I-O Psychology* feature (Alexis Fink, Eric Dunleavy, Lawrence Houston III, John Scott, Josh Brenner, Sandra Lee, Steven Hunt, Mark Ehrhart, Suzanne Bell, John Howes, YoungAh Park, David Earnest, and Missie Wolfe). Their willingness to help share the field with the future of I-O psychology is much appreciated. And finally, a massive thank you to my extraordinarily supportive family. John, thank you for your encouragement, patience, sense of humor, adaptability, adventurous spirit, and most importantly, your love and friendship. Sorry ladies, he's taken. To Rook, Audrey, Matthew, and Ryan, thank you for being you. I am a better person because each of you is in my life. Also, if any of you reads this book, you'll be my favorite. Love you all so much!

Ancillaries for Instructors and Students

For Instructors

Instructor's Manual with Test Bank. The *Instructor's Manual with Test Bank* is electronically downloadable and is available to every registered instructor. It includes case studies, chapter outlines, learning objectives, test items (true/false, multiple choice, short answer, and essay), instructional tips, and web links. PowerPoint slides are provided for each chapter that summarize the main points of the text, the content of which can be modified for individual instructor customization. Instructors should register online at www.PsychologyAppliedtoWork.com to access the *Instructor's Manual with Test Bank*.

For Students

Student Study Guide. The *Student Study Guide* is electronically downloadable and is available at no cost to students. Its purpose is to provide additional assistance in understanding industrial/organizational psychology. The free *Student Study Guide* can be accessed at www.psychologyappliedtowork.com/student-resources/

CHAPTER 1

Overview and Historical Background of I-O Psychology

Chapter Outline

I-O Psychology—What it Is, and Isn't

The Lighter Side of I-O Psychology: *I vs. O*

The History of I-O Psychology

The Early Years (1900–1916)

World War I (1917–1918)

Between the Wars (1919–1940)

World War II (1941–1945)

Toward Specialization (1946–1963)

Government Intervention (1964–1993)

The Information Age (1994–2018)

Social Media and I-O Psychology: *Web 2.0 and the World of Work*

The Experience Age (2019–Present)

The Science and Practice of I-O Psychology Today

The Scientist-Practitioner Model

COVID-19 and I-O Psychology: *Rethinking Business as Usual*

Professional Affiliations

Licensing of I-O Psychologists

The Mandate of I-O Psychology

Chapter Review

Learning Objectives

- Explain how I-O psychology relates to the profession of psychology as a whole.
- Compare and contrast I-O psychology with similar fields in psychology and business.
- Describe the history of I-O psychology, including major people, events, and eras.
- Describe the scientist-practitioner model and its importance to I-O psychology.
- Discuss how and why psychologists are licensed.

What comes to mind when you hear the term "Industrial and Organizational Psychology?" Considering you're reading the first chapter in a book devoted to the field, there is the chance that you have a basic understanding of what it is. But it could also be the case that you just stumbled upon this book and were curious about its contents. Or perhaps you are reading it as part of a course that simply filled a degree requirement (or fit into a nice slot in your schedule), and you don't actually have a good idea of what you've gotten yourself into. Regardless of your level of current understanding of industrial and organizational (I-O) psychology, you are definitely in for a treat, as you're about to explore a field of study that has become increasingly popular and, as you'll learn, has direct relevance for many aspects of your life.

In this chapter, you'll find an overview of what I-O psychology is—and isn't—before diving deeper into the separate topics. In addition, we provide a brief history of the field in order to provide context on how we've gotten to where we are today. Finally, we discuss some specialty topics within I-O psychology that have garnered more attention in recent years.

I-O Psychology—What it Is, and Isn't

The first thing that likely stands out to people when they hear "I-O psychology" is the word "psychology." I-O psychology is a specialty area of psychology, and as such, it is important to have an understanding of what psychology entails. Psychology is the scientific study of thinking and behavior. It is a science because psychologists use the same rigorous methods of research found in other areas of scientific investigation. Some of their research is more biological in nature (such as the effects of brain lesions on food consumption); other research is more social in nature (such as identifying the factors that lead to bystander apathy). Because psychology covers such a broad spectrum of content areas, it is difficult to have a clear and accurate image of what a psychologist does. Many people think that every psychologist "is a shrink," "has a black couch," "likes to discover what makes people tick," and so on. In fact, these descriptions usually refer to the specialty of clinical psychology—the diagnosis and treatment of mental illness or abnormal behavior. Most psychologists do not treat mental disorders, nor do they practice psychotherapy. In reality, psychologists are a very diversified lot with many specialized interests.

"...the mere mention of 'psychology' often evokes images of Freud, couches, and psychoanalysis, not to mention sex therapy."[1]

—Zickar & Gibby 2007, p. 76

Approximately 6% of all psychologists work in the I-O area. Our relatively small representation in the total population of psychologists probably explains why some people are unaware of the I-O area. The general public is not as aware of I-O psychology as, for example, clinical psychology. Even within psychology departments at universities, I-O psychology has not received as much attention as other areas. For example, every year approximately 1.5 million students in the United States enroll in an introductory psychology course.[2] Although students presumably learn about the various areas of psychology in an introductory course, only 49% of instructors who taught introductory psychology courses reported covering I-O psychology in their classes, and only 16% covered I-O psychology as its own section.[3]

Much of psychology is organized around processes (such as sensation and cognition) and explanatory concepts (such as intelligence and personality), not major life activities, like work.[4] Thus, there is the perception that I-O psychology is dissimilar to traditional academic psychology. In addition, I-O psychology is often misperceived by those outside of the field, in part because it is associated with ideas about psychology that don't reflect I-O psychology's focus.[5] After decades of professional obscurity (especially compared to the healthcare areas of psychology), I-O psychology is currently experiencing growth in visibility and recognized value.

I-O psychology An area of scientific study and professional practice that addresses psychological concepts and principles in the work world.

So what exactly is **I-O psychology**? Put simply, I-O psychology is the scientific study and professional practice that addresses psychological concepts in the world of work. Much like other fields of psychology, I-O psychology shares a strong focus on the scientific method in seeking to find answers to research questions. In the same manner that a cognitive psychologist might approach questions concerning the sensation and perception of vision by establishing hypotheses and testing theories in a systematic fashion, an I-O psychologist will establish hypotheses about a topic relevant to the workplace, and test it in much the same manner—systematically and with good scientific practices. In addition, the various applications of psychology are often directed toward enhancing the welfare of an individual or an institution (such as a school or business organization).[6] Clinical psychology, for example, is directed toward enhancing the lives of individuals. I-O psychology strives to enhance both the institution and the individual, but the image of the field is often perceived as more aligned with institutional welfare.

I-O psychology also shares some overlap with fields outside of psychology. With its clear focus on application to business, it is not surprising that there is convergence with human resource management, organizational behavior, and organization development. In many ways, the "industrial" side of I-O psychology aligns with topics typically covered in a human resource management class (such as selection, training, and performance management), and the "organizational" side of I-O psychology aligns with topics covered in an organizational behavior course (such as leadership, motivation, and job attitudes). An individual specializing in organization development will take many classes and engage in activities similar to those of I-O psychologists specializing in organizational change, teams, and culture and climate issues. Of course, the distinction between the "I" side and the "O" side is not always clear-cut, as many I-O psychologists find themselves engaged in both industrial and organizational topics (see The Lighter Side of I-O Psychology: *I vs. O*).

Despite its overlap with other fields, I-O psychology is distinct from them. Within psychology, I-O psychology is considered to be a form of applied psychology, with the application of the principles being of utmost importance. As a result, I-O researchers strive to have their research be useful for practitioners, and will make a concerted effort to highlight the practical application of their findings. Compared to individuals focused on human resource management, I-O psychologists do not typically study compensation (outside of its relationship to motivation), and are often more aware of and interested in the individual differences that workers bring to the job that impact their performance and well-being. I-O psychologists also tend to take a more "micro" view of organizations, focusing on individuals, as opposed to a "macro" perspective that focuses on organizational systems. In this way, they differ somewhat from organization development and strategic management specialists. Of course, some I-O psychologists are well versed in compensation and macro theories, which affords them the ability to work seamlessly with others in those fields, or work in those fields themselves. It is its similarities with other specialties, combined with its unique characteristics, that make I-O psychology so valuable within the workplace, and similarly what makes I-O psychologists so marketable (a point discussed later in this chapter).

The Lighter Side of I-O Psychology: *I vs. O*

While it isn't always true, many I-O psychologists identify with one side of the field over the other. If we are interested in such topics as leadership, teams, or motivation, then we say we are more "O," whereas if we're more interested in topics such as recruitment, selection, or performance management, then we say we are more on the "I" side. The distinction, however, is rather silly in some ways. Although we often separate topics or classes on the basis of their overall categories of "I" or "O," we rarely do anything in isolation. If teams are "O" and performance management is "I," then what is it when we manage the performance of teams? If selection is "I" and leadership is "O," then what is it when we select for leadership positions in organizations? Plus, what are you if you are interested in two completely different areas? In 2002, Paul (one of the authors of this textbook) wrote a satirical piece that poked fun at our tendency as I-O psychologists to dichotomize ourselves into "I" and "O" camps. In the column, which can be found online for those interested in reading the full piece, he provided some "quotes" from "Society for Industrial and Organizational Psychology" (SIOP) members on how they saw themselves. Of course, as a satirical piece, the quotes were fake and talked of experimentation with the "other" orientations during grad school, of the "other" side being "perverse and unclean," and of hiding their appreciation of and interest in the "other" side for fear of being discovered. Of course, the point of the column was to just be ourselves—in every way—and to be open-minded to others regardless of their orientations and/or proclivities. As one fake quote said, "Why is it we must be either an *I* or an *O*? What is wrong with being both? When I'm with *I*'s, I am an *I*. When I'm with *O*'s, I'm an *O*. I feel totally at ease being bicategorical. It is the mark of a mature and sophisticated person to exhibit flexibility in orientation. I consider myself to be such a person... I am the hyphen between the *I* and the *O*. I love the *I*'s, the *O*'s, and fellow hyphens" (Muchinsky 2002, p. 58).[7]

The History of I-O Psychology

To fully appreciate where we are today with the field, it is important to look at our historical roots. That said, it is always difficult to write *the* history of anything; there are different perspectives with different emphases. It is also a challenge to divide the historical evolution of a discipline into units of time. In some cases, time itself is a convenient watershed (decades or centuries); in others, major events serve as landmarks. In the case of I-O psychology, the two world wars were major catalysts for changing the discipline and therefore feature prominently in our review of the history of the field.

The historical overview that we present will show how the field of I-O psychology came to be what it is and how some key individuals and events helped shape it. It is important to observe that many notable psychologists are not included in this history, including Wilhelm Wundt and Edward Titchener. Although they certainly play a role in the development of I-O psychology (or of I-O psychologists, rather, as many I-O psychologists can trace their academic lineage to these individuals[8]), their specific contributions to the field are not as clear or explicit as the individuals described below. Similarly, individuals who have a connection to the field but did not directly contribute to its history are omitted from this history. For example, while some consider Thomas Edison to be a pioneer of I-O psychology because of a strict employment test he created and used in 1921,[9] his connection was more superficial than those profiled here.

The Early Years (1900–1916)

Fun fact:
The term *industrial psychology* was apparently used for the first time in Bryan's 1904 article. Ironically, it appeared in print only as a typographical error. Bryan was quoting a sentence he had written five years earlier, in which he spoke of the need for more research in individual psychology. Instead, Bryan wrote "industrial" psychology and did not catch his mistake.[10]

In its beginnings, what we know today as I-O psychology didn't even have a name; it was a merging of two forces that gathered momentum before 1900. One force was the pragmatic nature of some basic psychological research. Most psychologists at this time were strictly scientific and deliberately avoided studying problems that strayed outside the boundaries of pure research. However, the psychologist W. L. Bryan published a paper about how professional telegraphers develop skill in sending and receiving Morse code.[11] A few years later in 1903, Bryan's presidential address to the American Psychological Association (APA) touched on having psychologists study "concrete activities and functions as they appear in everyday life" (Bryan 1904, p. 80).[12] Bryan did not advocate studying problems found in industry per se, but he emphasized examining real skills as a base upon which to develop scientific psychology. Bryan is not considered the father of I-O psychology, but rather a precursor.

The second major force in the evolution of the discipline came from the desire of industrial engineers to improve efficiency. They were concerned mainly with the economics of manufacturing and thus the productivity of industrial employees. Industrial engineers developed "time and motion" studies to prescribe the most efficient body motions per unit of time to perform a particular work task. For example, by arranging parts to be assembled in a certain pattern, a worker could affix a nut to a bolt every 6 seconds, or 10 per minute.

The merging of psychology with applied interests and concern for increasing industrial efficiency was the impetus for the emergence of I-O psychology. In the late 19th century, American society was undergoing rapid changes and developments because of industrialization, immigration, a high birth rate, education, and urban growth.[13] A drive for social reform prevailed, Americans were ready for the useful, and society looked toward science for practical solutions. These societal demands forced psychologists to popularize their science and demonstrate the value of psychology in solving problems and helping society. I-O psychology took its place upon the social stage to help improve the quality of work, thereby ultimately improving the quality of life.[14] By 1910, "industrial psychology" (the "organizational" appendage did not become official until over 60 years later) was a legitimate specialty area of psychology.

Four individuals stand out as the founding figures of I-O psychology in the United States. They worked independently of one another, and their major contributions deserve a brief review.

Walter Dill Scott

Walter Dill Scott. Scott, a psychologist, was persuaded to give a talk to some Chicago business leaders on the need for applying psychology to advertising. His talk was well received and led to the publication of two books: *The Theory of Advertising* (1903) and *The Psychology of Advertising* (1908). The first book dealt with suggestion and argument as means of influencing people. The second book was aimed at improving human efficiency with such tactics as imitation, competition, loyalty, and concentration. By 1911, Scott had expanded his areas of interest and published two more books: *Influencing Men in Business* and *Increasing Human Efficiency in Business*. During World War I, Scott was instrumental in the application of personnel procedures in the army. Scott has been described as the consummate scientist–practitioner who was highly respected in both spheres of professional activity.[15] Scott had a substantial influence on increasing public awareness and the credibility of industrial psychology.

Frederick W. Taylor

Frederick W. Taylor. Taylor was an engineer by profession. His formal schooling was limited, but through experience and self-training in engineering he went on to obtain many patents. As he worked himself up through one company as a worker, supervisor, and finally plant manager, Taylor realized the value of redesigning work to achieve both higher output for the company and a higher wage for the worker. His best-known work is his book *The Principles of Scientific Management* (1911). These principles are: (1) science over rule of thumb, (2) scientific selection and training, (3) cooperation over individualism, and (4) equal division of work best suited to management and employees.[16] In perhaps the most famous example of his methods, Taylor showed that workers who handled heavy iron ingots (pig iron) could be more productive if they had work rests. Training employees when to work and when to rest increased average worker productivity from 12.5 to 47.0 tons moved per day (with less reported fatigue), which resulted in increased wages for them. The company also drastically increased efficiency by reducing costs from 9.2 cents to 3.9 cents per ton.

As a consequence of this method, it was charged that Taylor inhumanely exploited workers for a higher wage and that great numbers of workers would be unemployed because fewer were needed. Because unemployment was rampant at this time, the attacks on Taylor were virulent. His methods were eventually investigated by the Interstate Commerce Commission (ICC) and the U.S. House of Representatives. Taylor replied that increased efficiency led to greater, not less, prosperity and that workers not hired for one job would be placed in another that would better suit their potential. The arguments were never really resolved; World War I broke out and the controversy faded.

Fun fact: Vladimir Lenin advocated for scientific management in post-revolutionary Russia (though it may have just been political rhetoric to make himself look progressive).[17]

Lillian Moller Gilbreth

Fun fact:
Gilbreth invented the shelves inside refrigerator doors and the foot-pedal trash can![22]

Lillian Moller Gilbreth. Lillian Gilbreth was one of several female psychologists who made substantial contributions in the early era of I-O psychology.[18] Along with her husband, Frank Gilbreth, she pioneered industrial management techniques that are still used. Her husband was more concerned with the technical aspects of worker efficiency, while she was more concerned with the human aspects of time management. Lillian Gilbreth was among the first to recognize the effects of stress and fatigue on workers. Gilbreth made a historic speech at a meeting of industrial engineers in 1908. She was asked for her opinion because she was the only woman at the meeting. According to historical accounts,[19] Gilbreth

> . . . rose to her feet and remarked that the human being, of course, was the most important element in industry, and that it seemed to her this element had not been receiving the attention it warranted. The engineer's scientific training, she said, was all for the handling of inanimate objects. She called attention to the fact that psychology was fast becoming a science and that it had much to offer that was being ignored by management engineers. The plea in her impromptu remarks was for the new profession of scientific management to open its eyes to the necessary place psychology had in any program industrial engineers worked out (Koppes 1997, p. 511).[20]

The mother of 12 children, Gilbreth combined a career and family, and was called by a leading publication, "a genius in the art of living" (California Magazine 1944).[21] Two of her children wrote a book about her life, *Cheaper by the Dozen*, which was made into a motion picture in 1950 and remade in 2003. In 1984, the United States Postal Service commemorated Gilbreth with a postage stamp in her honor.

Hugo Münsterberg

Hugo Münsterberg. Münsterberg was a German psychologist with traditional academic training. The noted American psychologist William James invited Münsterberg to Harvard University, where he applied his experimental methods to a variety of problems, including perception and attention. He was a popular figure in American education, a gifted public speaker, and a personal friend of President Theodore Roosevelt. That said, he was also described as condescending and overly sensitive to criticism, with responses to criticism often being sarcastic, lengthy, and contemptuous.[23] Nevertheless, he was a respected voice of authority, advocating strongly for the necessary role of psychology in business and everyday life.[24] Münsterberg was interested in applying traditional psychological methods to practical industrial problems. His book, *Psychology and Industrial Efficiency* (1913), was divided into three parts: selecting workers, designing work, and using psychology in sales. One of Münsterberg's most renowned studies involved determining what makes a safe trolley car operator. He systematically studied all aspects of the job, developed an ingenious laboratory simulation of a trolley car, and concluded that a good operator could comprehend simultaneously all of the influences that bear on the car's progress.

When World War I broke out in Europe, Münsterberg supported the German cause. He was ostracized for his allegiance, and the emotional strain probably contributed to his death in 1916. Münsterberg's influence in the history of the field is well evidenced by the coterie of I-O psychologists who were guided by his teachings. As one scholar has

Fun fact:
One of Münsterberg's students was William Marston, the creator of the comic strip character Wonder Woman![26]

concluded, Münsterberg is a reminder that it is not necessary to like someone to respect their contributions, as he clearly had a significant impact on the development of I-O psychology despite being an individual who would likely "be the butt of many jokes and the object of much derision" if he were alive today (Landy 1992, p. 801).[25]

Only the U.S. involvement in the war gave some unity to the profession. The primary emphasis of the early work in I-O psychology was on the economic gains that could be accrued by applying the ideas and methods of psychology to problems in business and industry. Business leaders began to employ psychologists, and some psychologists entered applied research. However, World War I caused a shift in the direction of industrial psychological research. Figure 1-1 shows a running timeline from 1900 to the present of major events in I-O psychology and major events in world history.

Robert Yerkes

World War I (1917–1918)

World War I was a potent impetus to psychology's rise to respectability. Psychologists believed they could provide a valuable service to the nation, and some saw the war as a means of accelerating the profession's progress. Robert Yerkes was the psychologist most instrumental in involving psychology in the war. As president of the APA, he maneuvered the profession into assignments in the war effort. The APA made many proposals, including ways of screening recruits for mental deficiency and of assigning selected recruits to jobs in the army. Committees of psychologists investigated soldier motivation and morale, psychological problems of physical incapacity, and discipline. Yerkes continued to press his point that psychology could be of great help to the United States in wartime.

The army, in turn, was somewhat skeptical of the psychologists' claims. It eventually approved only a modest number of proposals, mostly those involving the assessment of recruits. Yerkes and other psychologists reviewed a series of general intelligence tests and eventually developed one that they called the **Army Alpha**. When they discovered that 30% of the recruits were illiterate, they developed the **Army Beta**, a special test for those who couldn't read English. Many military recruits in WWI were foreign-born and had limited capacity to read and write English. The Army Beta was used to assess such recruits, and contained information presented in the form of pictures and graphics.[27] Meanwhile, Walter Dill Scott was conducting research on the best placement of soldiers in the army. He classified and placed enlisted soldiers, conducted performance ratings of officers, and developed and prepared job duties and qualifications for more than 500 jobs.

Army Alpha
An intelligence test developed during World War I by I-O psychologists for the selection and placement of military personnel.

Army Beta
A nonverbal intelligence test developed during World War I by I-O psychologists to assess illiterate recruits.

Plans for testing recruits proceeded at a slow pace. The army built special testing sites at its camps and ordered all officers, officer candidates, and newly drafted recruits to be tested. Both the Army Alpha and Army Beta group intelligence tests were used, as were a few individual tests. The final order authorizing the testing program came from the Adjutant General's office in August, 1918. However, the war ended just three months later, and testing was terminated just as it was finally organized and authorized. As a result, the intelligence testing program didn't contribute as much to the war as Yerkes had hoped. Even though 1,726,000 individuals were ultimately tested in the program, actual use of the results was minimal.

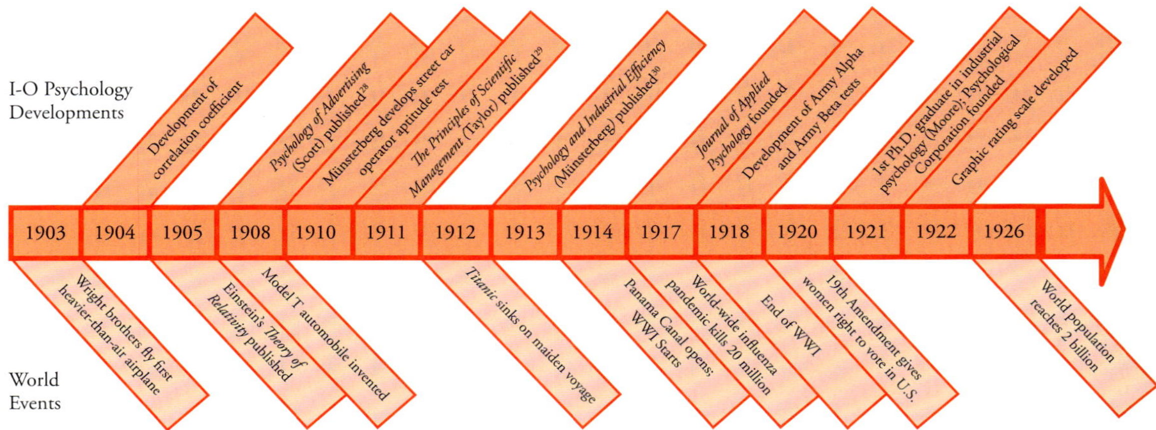

Figure 1-1 *Timeline of major I-O psychology developments and world events*

Although psychology's impact on the war effort was not substantial, the very process of giving psychologists so much recognition and authority was a great impetus to the profession. Psychologists were regarded as capable of making valuable contributions to society and of adding to a company's (and in war, a nation's) prosperity. Also in 1917, the oldest and most representative journal in the field of I-O psychology—the *Journal of Applied Psychology*—began publication.

After the war, there was a boom in the number of psychological consulting firms and research bureaus. The birth of these agencies ushered in the next era in I-O psychology.

Consider This...

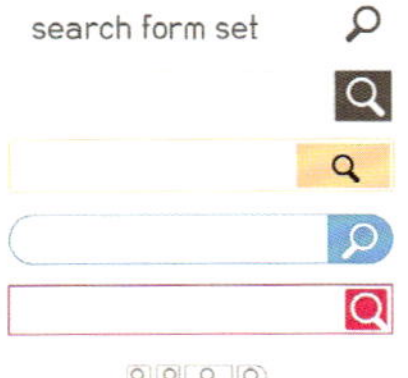

You can often get a feel for what is (or was) important at a certain time by looking at the topics under investigation by researchers. Consider the titles of some of the articles in the first volume of the *Journal of Applied Psychology*: "Practical Relations between Psychology and the War," "Mentality Testing of College Students," and "The Moron as a War Problem." Fast forward to 2021, and you will find such titles as "Exploring Public Sentiment on Enforced Remote Work during COVID-19," "The Effects of Blue-Light Filtration on Sleep and Work Outcomes," and "Words that Hurt: Leaders' Anti-Asian Communication and Employee Outcomes." What do you think will be the focus for researchers in I-O psychology this year? How about in a decade from now?

Between the Wars (1919–1940)

Applied psychology emerged from World War I as a recognized discipline. Society was beginning to realize that industrial psychology could solve practical problems. Following the war, several psychological research bureaus came into full bloom. The Bureau of Salesmanship Research was developed by Walter Van Dyke Bingham at the Carnegie Institute of Technology. There was little precedent for this kind of cooperation

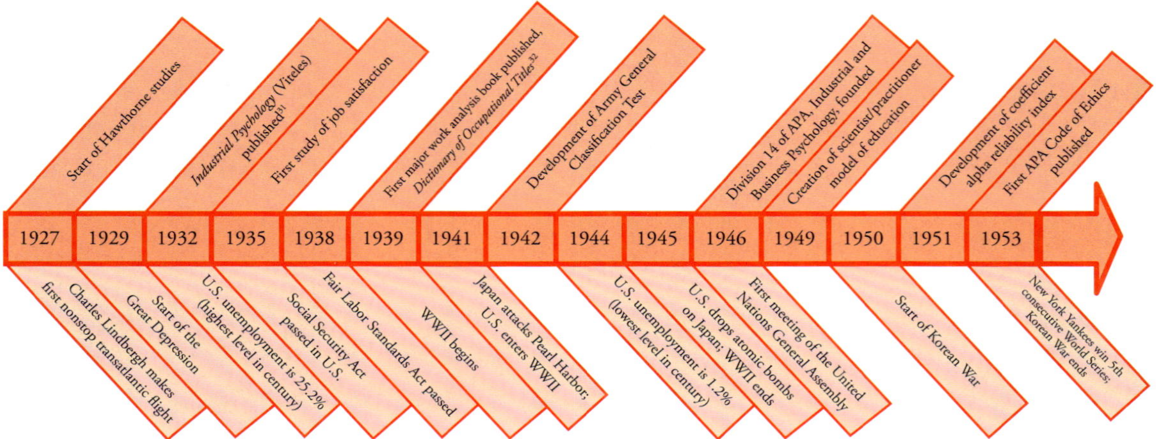

Walter Van Dyke Bingham

between college and industry. The bureau intended to use psychological research techniques to solve problems that had never been examined scientifically. Twenty-seven companies cooperated with Bingham, each contributing $500 annually to finance applied psychological research. One of the early products of the bureau was the book *Aids in Selecting Salesmen*. For several years, the bureau concentrated on the selection, classification, and development of clerical and executive personnel as well as salespeople.

Another influential organization during the period was the Psychological Corporation, founded by James Cattell in 1921. Cattell formed it as a business corporation and asked psychologists to buy stock in it. The purpose of the Psychological Corporation was to advance psychology and promote its usefulness to industry. The corporation also served as a clearinghouse for information. To protect against quacks and charlatans, who were becoming increasingly prevalent, it provided companies with reference checks on prospective psychologists. Unlike many agencies that began at the time, the Psychological Corporation has remained in business. Over the years it has changed its early mission, and today it is one of the country's largest publishers of psychological tests.

Hawthorne studies
A series of research studies that began in the late 1920s at the Western Electric Company and ultimately refocused the interests of I-O psychologists on how work behavior manifests itself in an organizational context.

In 1924, a series of experiments began at the Hawthorne Works of the Western Electric Company. Although initially they seemed to be of minor scientific significance, they became classics in industrial psychology. The **Hawthorne studies** were a joint venture between Western Electric and several researchers from Harvard University (none of whom were industrial psychologists by training). The original study attempted to find the relationship between lighting and efficiency. The researchers installed various sets of lights in workrooms where electrical equipment was being produced. In some cases, the light was intense; in other cases, it was reduced to the equivalent of moonlight. To the researchers' surprise, productivity seemed to have no relationship to the level of illumination. The workers' productivity increased whether the illumination was decreased, increased, or held constant. The results of the study were so bizarre, the researchers hypothesized that some other factors must be responsible for the increased productivity.

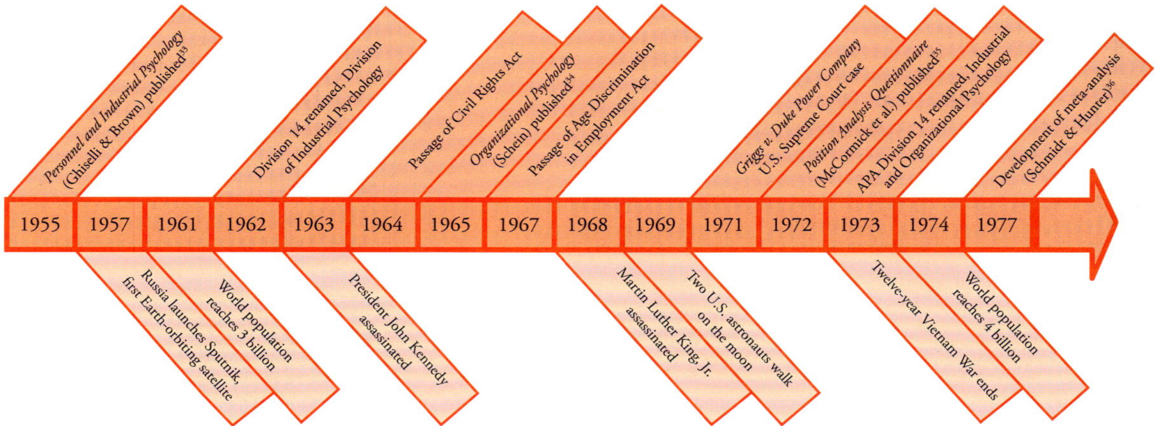

The precise reason for the change in behavior (for example, the novelty of the situation, special attention, or prestige from being selected for study) was not clear. Sometimes behavior change is due to just a change in the environment (for example, the presence of the researchers) and not to the effect of some experimentally-manipulated variable (for example, the amount of illumination). This finding is so important to researchers that it is known within the field of psychology as the *Hawthorne effect*.

The Hawthorne studies also revealed the existence of informal employee work groups and their controls on production. They also learned the importance of employee attitudes, the value of having a sympathetic and understanding supervisor, and the need to treat workers as people instead of merely human capital. Their revelation of the complexity of human behavior opened new vistas for industrial psychology, which for nearly 40 years had been dominated by the goal of improving company efficiency. Today, the Hawthorne studies, though regarded by some psychologists as having been based on flawed research methods and elitist biases,[37] are considered by some to be the single most influential event in the formation of industrial psychology. They also showed that researchers sometimes obtain totally unexpected results. Because the investigators were not tied to any one explanation, their studies took them into areas never before studied by industrial psychology and raised questions that otherwise might never have been asked. Industrial psychology was never the same again.

Morris Viteles

In 1932, Morris Viteles wrote a classic textbook that advanced the field of industrial psychology beyond personnel selection to also include motivation, job satisfaction, and leadership.[38] His book had a profound influence on educational programs in industrial psychology. Viteles worked both as a professor and in industry, and was an exemplar of the scientist-practitioner.[39]

This era in industrial psychology ended with the coincidental conclusion of the Hawthorne studies and the outbreak of World War II. Industrial psychologists were now faced with an immense task: helping to mobilize a nation for another global war.

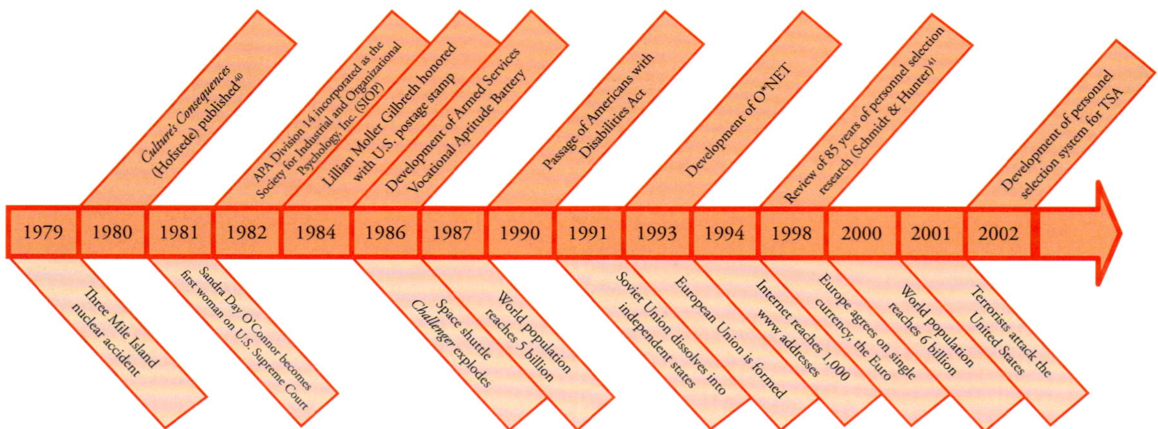

World War II (1941–1945)

When the United States entered World War II, industrial psychologists were more prepared for their role in the war effort than they had been in 1917. By this time, psychologists had studied the problems of employee selection and placement, and had refined their techniques considerably.

Walter Van Dyke Bingham chaired the advisory committee on classification of military personnel that had been formed in response to the army's need for classification and training. Unlike in World War I, this time the army approached the psychologists first. One of the committee's earliest assignments was to develop a test that could sort new recruits into five categories based on their ability to learn the duties and responsibilities of a soldier. The test that was finally developed was the **Army General Classification Test (AGCT)**, a benchmark in the history of group testing. Twelve million soldiers were classified into military jobs on the basis of the test.[42] The committee also worked on other projects, such as methods of selecting people for officer training, trade proficiency tests, and supplemental aptitude tests.

Army General Classification Test (AGCT)
A test developed during World War II by I-O psychologists for the selection and placement of military personnel.

Psychologists also advanced the development and use of situational stress tests, a project undertaken by the U.S. Office of Strategic Services (OSS).[43] The purpose of this testing program was to assess candidates for assignment to military intelligence units. During a three-day session of extremely intensive testing and observation, the candidates lived together in small groups under almost continuous observation by the assessment staff. Specially-constructed situational tests, many modeled after techniques developed in the German and British armies, were used to assess candidates in nontraditional ways. One test, for example, involved constructing a 5-foot cube from a collection of wooden poles, pegs, and blocks. It was impossible for one person to assemble the cube in the allotted time, so two "helpers" were provided. These were actually psychologists who played prearranged roles. One helper acted very passively and contributed little; the other obstructed work by making impractical suggestions and ridiculing and criticizing the candidate. Of course, no candidate could complete the project with this kind of "help." The real purpose of the test was not to see whether the candidates could construct the cube, but to assess their emotional and interpersonal reactions to stress and frustration.

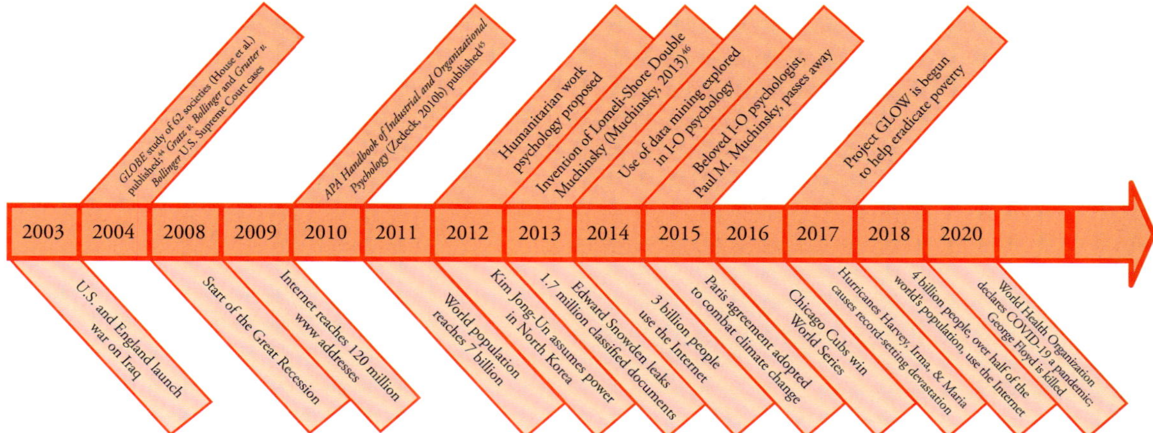

Throughout the war, industrial psychology was also being used in civilian life. The use of employment tests in industry increased greatly. Because the nation needed a productive workforce, psychologists were called on to help reduce employee absenteeism. Industry discovered that many of the techniques of industrial psychologists were useful, especially in the areas of selection, training, and machine design, and industrial leaders were particularly interested in the applications of social psychology. New methods of measuring soldier attitude and morale could also be used in industry. In short, the techniques developed during the war could be applied to business and industry in peacetime. World War II was a springboard for refining industrial psychological techniques and honing the skills of applied psychologists.

Each of the two world wars had a major effect on industrial psychology but in a somewhat different way. World War I helped form the profession and give it social acceptance. World War II helped develop and refine it. The next era in the history of I-O psychology saw the discipline evolve into subspecialties and attain higher levels of academic and scientific rigor.

Elton Mayo

Toward Specialization (1946–1963)

In this era, industrial psychology evolved into a legitimate field of scientific inquiry, having already been accepted as a professional practice. More colleges and universities began to offer courses in "industrial psychology," and graduate degrees (both M.S. and Ph.D.) were soon given. Division 14 of APA, Industrial and Business Psychology was created in 1946.

As in any evolving discipline, subspecialties of interest began to crystallize and industrial psychology became splintered. That part of industrial psychology specializing in personnel selection, classification, and training became identified as "personnel psychology." Sometime in the 1950s, interest grew in the study of organizations. Long the province of sociologists, this area caught the interest of psychologists. Elton Mayo was a founder of what became known as the human relations movement. Drawing upon the findings from the Hawthorne studies, it emphasized individual needs, informal groups, and social relationships as the primary bases for behavior within organizations. In the 1960s, industrial psychology research took on a stronger organizational flavor. Investigators gave more attention to social influences that impinge on behavior in organizations. Terms such as *organizational change* and *organization development* appeared in the literature regularly. Industrial psychology began to address a broader range of topics (the field would officially change its name to "industrial-organizational" psychology in 1973). Classic textbooks of the 1950s, such as *Personnel and Industrial Psychology*,[47] gave way in title (as well as in substance) to books with more of an organizational thrust. Traditional academic boundaries between disciplines began to blur in this postwar period. This melding of disciplines was healthy because it decreased the use of narrow, parochial attempts to address complex areas of research.

Government Intervention (1964–1993)

Fun fact:
The longest single-person filibuster (extended speech) in U.S. Senate history was by U.S. Senator Strom Thurmond at 24 hours and 18 minutes. Although it was meant to stop the passage of the Civil Rights Act of 1957, the bill was passed within two hours of its conclusion.

In the late 1950s and early 1960s, the nation was swept up in what became known as the "civil rights movement." As a nation, the United States became more sensitized to the plight of minorities who had systematically been denied equal opportunities to various sectors of life, including housing, education, and employment. In 1964, Congress passed the Civil Rights Act, a far-reaching piece of legislation designed to reduce unfair discrimination against minorities. One component of the Civil Rights Act, Title VII, addressed the issue of discrimination in employment. The significance of the law to I-O psychologists is explained as follows: for years, I-O psychologists were given a relatively free rein to develop a wide variety of psychological assessment devices (that is, tests, interviews, and so on) to make employment decisions. The result of these employment decisions was the disproportionately-small representation of minorities (most notably Blacks and women) in the workplace, particularly in positions above lower-level jobs. Because historically these decisions seemed to result in discrimination against minorities, Title VII authorized the government to monitor and remedy discriminatory employment practices. (We cover the Civil Rights Act in greater detail in Chapter 3.)

By 1978, the government had drafted a uniform set of employment guidelines to which employers were bound. Companies were legally mandated to demonstrate that their employment tests did not uniformly discriminate against any minority group. In addition, the new government standards were not limited to just paper-and-pencil tests or the personnel function of selection; they addressed all devices (interviews, tests, application blanks) used to make all types of personnel decisions (selection, placement, promotion, discharge, and so on).

The discipline of I-O psychology now had to serve two ultimate authorities. The first authority is what all disciplines must serve—namely, to perform high-quality work, be it conducting scientific research or providing services to clients. The second authority added was government scrutiny and evaluation. I-O psychologists now had to accept the consequences of being legally accountable for their actions. As professionals, I-O psychologists would continue to evaluate themselves, but government policies and agencies would also judge their actions. In 1990, President George H. W. Bush signed into law the Americans with Disabilities Act and in 1991 an updated version of the Civil Rights Act. Both acts were designed to remedy further inequities in the workplace. In 1993, President Bill Clinton signed into law the Family and Medical

Leave Act, which grants workers up to 12 weeks of unpaid leave from work to attend to family and medical issues.

I-O psychology also made a major contribution to the military during this era. I-O psychologists made great efforts to develop a test for the selection and classification of military personnel.[48] This massive research project involved many psychologists and took twelve years to complete. Called "Project A," it involved developing the **Armed Services Vocational Aptitude Battery (ASVAB)**. Every year the ASVAB is administered to more than one million military applicants. Since its development, over 40 million people have taken the ASVAB. Once selected, personnel are assigned to the many military jobs within the various branches of the Armed Services. Project A represents one of the finest contributions of I-O psychology; it fulfilled a pressing practical need through the application of scientific knowledge.

Armed Services Vocational Aptitude Battery (ASVAB) A test developed in the 1970s and '80s by I-O psychologists for the selection and placement of military personnel.

The Information Age (1994–2018)

In the early 1980s, the personal computer provided individuals with access to a technology previously limited to large businesses. By the early 1990s, the Internet enabled individuals and businesses throughout the world to be connected electronically. Although several years might be identified as the start of the Information Age, we have selected 1994 in part because that is the year the total number of Internet sites first surpassed 1,000. In one decade, that number grew to exceed 45 million.[49] Ten years later, it was estimated that three billion people were using the Internet.[50] In general, a major shift occurred in the way society functioned, primarily revolving around the explosion in available information and how that information changes our lives. For example, if all the people who were on Facebook in 2010 were a nation, it would have been the third most populous nation in the world.[51] Social media sites such as Facebook, LinkedIn, TikTok, and Twitter revolutionized how members of society interacted with each other, and made information the primary medium of social exchange (see Social Media and I-O Psychology: *Web 2.0 and the World of Work*). Amazon, Google, eBay, and Alibaba are highly successful companies that were created due to their ability to harness information and use it to their advantage.

The critical theme of the Information Age was that dramatic change was upon us, and both organizations and employees needed to find ways to adapt to the rapidly-changing world. The turbulent changes faced by organizations (such as the need to change products or services frequently in response to changing market conditions) led to the need for frequent changes in workers' responsibilities, tasks, and work relationships.[52] Organizations that once held rigid specifications for what employees were supposed to do in their job found it difficult to compete in an environment that required responsiveness to change. Due to the need for adaptability in the workforce, organizations continue to be more likely to hire generalists (i.e., people who are intelligent, ambitious, and willing to adjust to the demands of change) rather than specialists (i.e., people hired to perform a single job with pre-established responsibilities). Additionally, electronic communication (like via the Internet) revolutionized business and customer-oriented service. The concept of "e-business" emerged, entailing networks of suppliers, distributors, and customers who make products and render services by exchanging information online.[53] Finally, organizations saw a greater urgency to deliver products and services to customers quickly. In decades past, the typical standards for

Social Media and I-O Psychology: *Web 2.0 and the World of Work*

For many readers of this book, it might be hard to imagine a world without the internet. In 1998, Ron Nief and Tom McBride created the Beloit College Mindset List, which pointed out interesting facts about incoming college freshmen at the time. The list was meant to prepare college professors for the incoming students and help them understand and better appreciate the students' world view. The list has become an annual tradition, and in 2011, the list noted that the incoming class that year (the class that would be graduating in 2015) had never known a world without the Internet. More specifically, it noted that for these individuals, most of them born in 1993, "there has always been an Internet ramp onto the information highway" (www.themindsetlist.com/lists/2015-list/).[54]

The Internet as we know it today has evolved considerably. In its original form, known as Web 1.0, the Internet was fairly static, with a small number of individuals posting information for others to view.[55] It has since evolved to Web 2.0, with a focus on social interaction and the ability for everybody not only to consume the information that is posted, but contribute to its manufacturing. This shift from Web 1.0 to 2.0 is reflected in the ever-growing popularity of social networking sites, blogs, and wikis.

With the advent of social media, the world of work as we know it has changed, and is continuing to change. Whereas in its early days, only a select few could access the Internet, it is now easily accessible and capable of leading to socially-organized behavior, facilitating employee-led discourses and knowledge sharing, and influencing union strategy. The line between one's work life and personal life has become increasingly blurred, creating unique boundary issues and raising potential legal and ethical concerns that were unimaginable in previous decades. While it is unclear what the future has in store, it appears that the level of connectedness of individuals will only increase. As such, organizations and employees alike must consider social media's immediate and long-term impact on them to facilitate positive, rather than negative, outcomes.

judging organizations were the quality and quantity of their products and services. In the Information Age, we added a new critical standard: speed of delivery.

The Information Age also brought with it a change in the very language of work. A "job" is the traditional unit around which work is organized and the means by which individuals are linked to organizations. As individuals, we desire a sense of social identity about the job we hold. With the aforementioned changes that accompanied the Information Age, tasks and duties required of jobs also changed, as did the skills needed to perform them. As such, a "job" as a useful and meaningful way to describe work performed began to erode. Consider the many variations of jobs in modern society in addition to full-time regular employees.[56] There are part-time workers (20 hours/week) and on-call workers (as needed). There are also temporary workers (hired by an employment agency who are assigned to a particular company) and independent contractors (individuals who are not employees and thus receive no benefits). Additionally, some employees rotate across different locations of the same company as needed (e.g., a teller working in multiple branches of a bank).

With the innovations of telecommuting (working from home and connecting electronically to the office), virtual work teams and offices, and wireless communications,

Pinboys

Fun fact:
Being a pinboy was not for the faint of heart. As one former pinboy said, "I had broken ribs from getting hit with pins, smashed fingers, and, of course, your shins were always banged up. You had to watch for the wise guys who threw the ball 100 miles an hour just to see if they could make the pins fly" (Manzione 2011).[57] That said, it paid well, and many enjoyed the work, so turnover was low!

work is also no longer a physical place. Furthermore, integrated work is now performed in different continents at the speed of electronic transmission. As has been said regarding the irrelevance of national boundaries to the conduct of work, "geography is history."

Information has played such a big role in the conduct of work that many organizations added entire units or departments devoted to "IT"—information technology. The head of that unit often holds the title of "CIO"—chief information officer. Certainly, there have always been jobs that become obsolete while others emerge, often as a function of technology. For example, "pinboys" were individuals (often young boys) who were employed to manually reset bowling pins prior to the invention of the mechanical pinsetter. Similarly, prior to the invention of a reliable alarm clock, there existed a profession known as a "knocker-upper," whose job was to wake people (often by knocking on their windows and doors) so they could get to work on time. (Do you think they just yelled, "10 more minutes!" if they wanted to snooze the alarm?)

By any reasonable standard, these two decades witnessed a dramatic shift in how work is performed and where it is performed, if not a change in the meaning of the concept of work. Among the leading skills workers must possess today to remain competitive in the workplace is the willingness and capacity to deal effectively with change. These changes continue to affect the very substance of I-O psychology.

The Experience Age (2019–Present)

It would be easy to say we are still in the Information Age, given the continued focus on and apparently limitless advancements in technology that occur on a regular basis. Indeed, many consider this to be the case. However, it has also been noted that a shift has occurred such that the availability of information is not as much the focus anymore. Instead, the current focus is on seeking new experiences and connecting with others.[58] Rather than passively watching a movie, individuals have the option of making choices for storylines in interactive content (such as *Black Mirror: Bandersnatch* and *Minecraft: Story Mode*, both on Netflix). Instead of reading a mystery, people can immerse themselves in an escape room. The growth in this experience mindset is evidenced by escape room participation alone. Although they first appeared around 2007, over 68% of respondents to a poll reported visiting an escape room at least once in 2019.[59] With this desire to be a part of the action and experience new things, it is not surprising that some expect the augmented reality and virtual reality market to be worth over $800 billion by 2025.[60]

The COVID-19 pandemic added to the desire to feel connected with others, particularly through virtual means. As individuals across the globe were encouraged to stay at least six feet (two meters) away from individuals outside of their own household,[61] many worried about becoming socially isolated. Even the World Health Organization encouraged the use of the term "physical distancing" rather than "social distancing" to describe the need to remain physically but not socially distant from others.[62] Businesses and schools closed their doors for extended periods of time, and individuals sought myriad ways to stay connected with others. Because those ways that were deemed safe were primarily virtual, individuals turned to video conference and online collaboration tools such as Zoom, WebEx, and Microsoft Teams to socialize safely with others.

Work life, and I-O psychology, has been forever changed from the COVID-19 pandemic. Although remote work existed long before the pandemic, its use skyrocketed, and many organizations and employees expressed a plan to continue working remotely after physical distancing restrictions were eliminated. Work travel was halted for many, and with such travel restrictions came advancements in videoconferencing for meetings, interviews, and social gatherings. What was once a strange way to conduct business became the new normal, with people adapting to the changes and finding ways to make the experience more bearable, if not enjoyable.

The importance of health and safety, both inside and outside of the workplace, has similarly increased due to the COVID-19 pandemic. As we'll discuss in Chapter 12, organizations have brought the well-being of their employees to the forefront of their attention in ways that have never before existed.

The need for individuals to feel connected to others and immersed in their daily activities, whether in person or virtually, will continue long after the COVID-19 pandemic. The world of work will continue to change and adapt to the needs of society, and with those changes, I-O psychology will also adapt. Now more than ever we must be flexible, open-minded, and thoughtful in our problem solving as well as in our implementation of solutions (see COVID-19 and I-O Psychology: *Rethinking Business as Usual*).

The Science and Practice of I-O Psychology Today

I-O psychologists work in a variety of employment settings, including universities and colleges, consulting firms, industry (both private sector and not-for-profit), and government agencies. Across these settings, I-O psychologists hold a wide variety of job titles. They are uniquely qualified to serve in academic and research positions, as well as serve as trainers, assessors, coaches, facilitators, and consultants. I-O psychologists hold positions at all levels within organizations, frequently progressing from individual contributors through management to executive levels.[63]

As of 2018, the annual median income for M.S. graduates in I-O psychology was approximately $88,900, whereas Ph.D. graduates in I-O psychology earned approximately $125,000.[64] Worthy of note is that these annual salaries vary by individual and location, and are heavily influenced by whether the I-O psychologist is employed primarily as an academic or a practitioner. Some members of our profession who work in consulting firms earn more than $1 million annually.

The Scientist-Practitioner Model

There are two sides of I-O psychology: science and practice. As in any area of science, I-O psychologists pose questions to guide their investigation and then use scientific methods to obtain answers. In this respect, I-O psychology is an academic discipline.

COVID-19 and I-O Psychology: *Rethinking Business as Usual*

I-O psychology has historically been largely focused on the efficiency of organizations and their employees. The COVID-19 pandemic brought to light the need to rethink this focus and consider larger issues. Rather than taking a narrow view of how I-O psychology can impact the workplace, scholars have urged I-O psychologists (and others) to leave the "business as usual" mentality behind and instead consider the needs of larger society.[65]

The pandemic unfortunately exposed systemic inequalities that exist in society. For example, not everybody had the same access to healthcare, or the "luxury" of working from home during a global health crisis. Furloughs, layoffs, and precarious employment highlighted the reality that many individuals faced, whereby a lost paycheck meant going without food and risking the loss of one's home.

These realizations led many scholars to recommend that I-O psychologists reflect on our role and purpose, both within organizations as well as in society at large. If I-O psychologists hope to make the world of work a better place, there needs to be a focus on making the world a better place.

How should we as I-O psychologists change? One suggestion is that, rather than focusing the majority of our attention on management and other white-collar employees, as has largely been the case, we need to pay additional attention to the more vulnerable members of our society, including gig workers (freelance workers who perform on-demand services), frontline staff, and the newly unemployed. In addition, rather than making assumptions about how work is done, we should be challenging those assumptions and seeking alternative solutions. For example, is there a way for companies to stay afloat without extensive layoffs or cutting wages? Can remote workers be trusted to work without technological monitoring? What are the intended and unintended consequences of our work? How is our work contributing to the greater good? If we do not consider the full impact of our work, we are going to run the risk of becoming largely irrelevant in a world that is demanding a greater focus on making society better.[66]

Scientist-practitioner model
A model or framework for education in an academic discipline based on understanding the scientific principles and findings evidenced in the discipline and how they provide the basis for professional practice.

The other side of I-O psychology—the professional side—is concerned with the application of knowledge to solve real problems in the world of work. I-O psychologists can use research findings to hire better employees, reduce absenteeism, improve communication, increase job satisfaction, and solve countless problems in the workplace.

Most I-O psychologists feel a sense of kinship with both sides: science and practice. Accordingly, the education of I-O psychologists is founded on the **scientist-practitioner model**, which trains them in both scientific inquiry and practical application. The idea of being a scientist-practitioner is so ingrained in the hearts of I-O psychologists that in 1994, Paul Sackett, the president of SIOP at the time, ended his presidential address to SIOP members by sitting down at a piano to play and sing a whimsical parody of Gilbert and Sullivan's "I Am the Very Model of a Modern Major General" entitled "I Am the Very Model of a Scientist-Practitioner."[67] Figure 1-2 shows the first stanza from his song.

Within some professions (such as medicine), there is a close relationship between those individuals who conduct scientific studies (i.e., medical researchers) and those individuals who are practitioners (e.g., physicians). The medical researchers may, for

I am the very model of a scientist-practitioner
I know the founders of the field from Wilhelm Wundt to Titchener
I balance meeting client needs with research opportunities
I'm comfortable in boardrooms and in major universities

I know that work behavior has a long list of determinants
From aptitude to attitudes to effort and to temperaments
I understand incentive systems and reward contingencies
Though Victor Vroom would label this a matter of expectancies

I emphasize participation when it comes to setting goals
I know how stressful it can be to balance work and family roles
As scholar, mentor, innovator, strategist, and manager
I am the very model of a scientist-practitioner

Figure 1-2 *First stanza of "I Am the Very Model of a Scientist-Practitioner"*
Courtesy of Paul R. Sackett and SIOP.

Scientist-practitioner gap
The difference between scientific research findings on organizations and their management versus how organizations are actually managed.

example, develop and test new pharmaceutical products. If the results of their research are positive, the new drug treatments will be manufactured by a pharmaceutical company. In turn, product representatives of the company will call upon physicians to inform them of the availability of the new drug treatment. Lastly, physicians can prescribe the new medications to patients for treating their illnesses. In short, medicine has an established and accepted procedure for advancing research products from "lab to life." There has been a 50% reduction in death rates from heart disease over the past several decades because physicians have implemented the findings from medical research.[68]

I-O psychologists who study work aspire to have their research findings used by managers in running organizations. However, unlike medicine, there is often not a strong connection between I-O psychological research findings and the management of organizations. The difference between scientific research findings on organizations and their management versus how organizations are actually managed is called the **scientist-practitioner gap**. The scientist-practitioner gap is regarded as evidence that either managers are unaware of I-O psychological research findings, or that academic researchers study topics with little relevance to day-to-day organizational issues.

"Practitioners should look to the scientific literature for guidance on setting up effective workplace systems, and scientists should take their cues from practitioners in identifying issues relevant to employee well-being and organizational effectiveness."[72]

—Rupp & Beal 2007, p. 36

Several reasons have been proposed to explain why the gap exists. One explanation that has been provided is that, unlike medicine, management is not a profession.[69] That is, managers are not licensed (like physicians) and they are not required to keep abreast of scientific advances in their field. Additionally, most scientific writing is very technical, typically written for an academic readership, not business managers. This is in part due to the challenge of "translating" complex research findings into actionable management policies.[70] There are also legitimate differences in the types of research findings that are of interest to scientists and practitioners. As some scholars have noted, science is heavily quantitative, while practitioners prefer verbal explanations for phenomena.[71]

Given all of this, it is no wonder that, despite an abundance of high-quality studies being conducted and published by I-O psychology researchers every year, many practitioners appear to be unaware of the findings.[73] Indeed, an examination of 45 years of published research in I-O psychology revealed that academic research has had only a modest effect on management practices.[74] It has been suggested that if I-O psychology academic scientists want their research findings put into practice by managers, the scientists must change their approach to research (i.e., what they study and how they study it). Of course, as the quote in the margin highlights, the impetus for change does not lie squarely on the scientists, as practitioners also have their part to play.

Despite the evidence of the gap between the science and practice of I-O psychology, we saw earlier in this chapter that our history is marked by a continuous interweaving of scientific and professional contributions. At certain points in our history, particularly during the wars, the practice of I-O psychology has been at the vanguard of our professional efforts. In addition, there have been efforts to close the scientist-practitioner gap. In 2014, the SIOP Education and Training Committee started an initiative to encourage its members to be "Bridge Builders" to make connections in their communities, introduce people to the field, and help translate research findings.[75] Finally, researchers and practitioners have begun to team up for some very impressive feats. For example, I-O psychologists have been working closely with NASA to examine the practical and scientific challenges associated with future space explorations, including the mission to Mars (see Chapter 10's Faces of I-O Psychology: *Suzanne T. Bell*).

Consider This...

As you read in this section, the science and practice of I-O psychology can never be too far apart. Indeed, Morris Viteles, described earlier in this chapter as an exemplar scientist-practitioner, aptly summarized the two domains of I-O psychology: "If it isn't scientific, it's not good practice, and if it isn't practical, it's not good science" (Katzell & Austin 1992, p. 826).[76] Likewise, the first president of the APA's Division 14, Bruce Moore, provided the following comment on the duality of the science and practice of I-O psychology: "The extreme applied practitioner is in danger of narrow, myopic thinking, but the extreme pure scientist is in danger of being isolated from facts" (Farr & Tesluk 1997, p. 484).[77] What are some suggestions you have for further bridging the scientist-practitioner gap? What are steps that both sides can take to ensure relevant research is being conducted and the findings are being used?

Professional Affiliations

Many psychologists are united professionally through membership in the APA, founded in 1892. As of 2021, the APA had more than 122,000 members. The broad diversity of interests among psychologists is reflected by the fact that the APA has 54 divisions representing special-interest subgroups. There are not really so many different specialty areas of psychology, just many fields in which the same basic psychological principles are applied. Although some APA members have no divisional affiliation, others belong to more than one. The APA publishes many journals—vehicles through which psychologists can communicate their research findings to other scholars. The APA also holds regional and national conventions, sets standards for graduate training in certain areas of psychology (that is, clinical, counseling, and school), develops and enforces a code of professional ethics, and helps psychologists find employment. In 1988, the Association for Psychological Science (APS) was founded in part because the membership and emphasis of the APA had shifted significantly toward the healthcare practice areas of psychology. The purpose of the APS is to advance the discipline of psychology primarily from a scientific perspective. Most of its members are academic psychologists.

Society for Industrial and Organizational Psychology (SIOP) The professional organization that represents I-O psychologists in the United States.

I-O psychology is still represented by Division 14 of the APA, now called the **Society for Industrial and Organizational Psychology**, or **SIOP**. In 2020, SIOP had about 10,000 professional members. SIOP is the primary professional organization for I-O psychologists in the United States. It is also becoming increasingly diverse in terms of geographic representation, with almost a quarter of all new members who joined in 2016 living outside of the United States.[78] Figure 1-3 shows the global professional membership distribution for SIOP. SIOP's website, *www.siop.org*, provides information about careers and graduate training in I-O psychology. In other countries, what we call *I-O psychology* has other names. In the United Kingdom it is often referred to as *occupational psychology*, in many European countries as *work and organizational psychology*, and in South Africa as *industrial psychology*. Professional organizations of I-O psychologists around the world include the *European Association of Work and Organizational Psychology*, the *Japanese Association of Industrial-Organizational Psychology*, and in Australia the *College of Organisational Psychology*. As society has witnessed the globalization of business, I-O psychology has also been recognized as a valuable resource throughout the world. Along these lines, SIOP has entered into an alliance with other international I-O organizations as a way to achieve a stronger voice on matters of mutual professional interest.[79]

Figure 1-3 *Global professional membership distribution for SIOP as of 2016*

Courtesy of Evan Sinar & SIOP

Licensing of I-O Psychologists

What makes a psychologist a psychologist? What prevents people with no psychological training from passing themselves off as psychologists? One way professions offer high-quality service to the public is by regulating their own membership. Selective admission into the profession helps protect the public against quacks and charlatans who can cause great damage not only to their clients, but also to the profession they allegedly represent.

The practice of professional psychology is regulated by law in every state. A law that regulates both the title and practice of psychology is called a *licensing law*. **Licensure** limits those qualified to practice psychology as defined by state law. Each state has its own standards for licensure, and these are governed by regulatory boards. The major functions of any professional board are to determine the standards for admission into the profession and to discipline its members when professional standards are violated. Typically, licensure involves education, experience, examination, and administrative requirements. A doctoral degree in psychology from an approved program is usually required, as well as one or two years of supervised experience. Applicants must also pass an objective, written examination covering many areas of psychology, although the majority of questions pertain to the healthcare (i.e., clinical and counseling) areas of psychology. Specialty examinations (for example, in I-O psychology) usually are not given. Currently, psychologists must pass a uniform national examination to obtain a license. Finally, the applicant must meet citizenship and residency requirements and be of good moral character.

Licensure
The process by which a professional practice is regulated by law to ensure quality standards are met to protect the public.

The licensure of I-O psychologists is somewhat controversial. The original purpose of licensure in psychology was to protect the public in the healthcare areas of psychology. Because I-O psychologists are not healthcare providers, the need for licensure to protect the public is not so pressing.[80] Also, some I-O psychologists object to the heavy emphasis placed on clinical and counseling psychology in the licensure process. Many states treat I-O psychologists as they treat other types of applied psychologists who offer services to the public, by requiring them to be licensed. Other states regard I-O psychologists as having a sufficiently different mandate to exempt them from requiring licensure. Not surprisingly given all of this, only 17% of I-O psychologists reported being licensed as of 2019.[81] I-O psychologists must be familiar with their individual state requirements to ensure compliance with licensing bodies.

The Mandate of I-O Psychology

I-O psychology is confronted with a daunting task—to increase the fit between the workforce and the workplace at a time when the composition of both is rapidly changing. Today's workforce is unlike any other in our history. More people are seeking employment than ever before, and they have higher levels of education. There are more women entering the workforce seeking full-time careers, more dual-income couples, and more individuals whose native language is not English. Likewise, the nature of work is changing. There are increasing numbers of remote jobs, and jobs that require computer literacy and proficiency with electronic communication. Societal changes also influence employment, as evidenced by the impact of the COVID-19 pandemic and the continuing problems of drug abuse and violence in the workplace.

As a profession, we find ourselves on the threshold of some areas where we have little prior experience. We find the mandate of I-O psychology to be very challenging, with the unending variety of issues we address being a great source of stimulation. Although some disciplines rarely change their content, I-O psychology most certainly is not the "same old stuff." We can think of few other fields of work that are as critical to human welfare as I-O psychology. We as humans spend more of our lifetimes engaged in working than in any other activity. Thus, I-O psychology is devoted to understanding our major mission in life. When you have finished reading this book, you should have a much better understanding of human behavior in the workplace. Perhaps some of you will be stimulated enough to continue your work in I-O psychology. It is a most challenging, rewarding, and useful profession.

Chapter Review

Key Terms

I-O psychology
Army Alpha
Army Beta
Hawthorne studies
Army General Classification Test (AGCT)
Armed Services Vocational Aptitude Battery (ASVAB)
Scientist-practitioner model
Scientist-practitioner gap
Society for Industrial and Organizational Psychology (SIOP)
Licensure

Questions for Review

1. What is I-O psychology? How does I-O psychology relate to the profession of psychology as a whole? In what ways is it similar to other areas of inquiry? In what ways is it different?
2. What role did Walter Dill Scott, Frederick W. Taylor, Lillian Moller Gilbreth, and Hugo Münsterberg play in the development of I-O psychology?
3. In what ways has I-O psychology been involved in war efforts?
4. What were the Hawthorne studies? What is the Hawthorne effect? Why are the studies considered so influential even though they are said to be based on flawed research?
5. How did the civil rights movement impact I-O psychology?
6. In what ways did the Information Age change the way work is conducted and viewed?
7. How did the COVID-19 pandemic change the world of work? In what ways has I-O psychology been impacted by the pandemic?
8. What is the scientist-practitioner model? Why is this considered important to I-O psychology? What is the scientist-practitioner gap? Why does the gap exist?
9. How and why are some psychologists licensed? Why is the licensure of I-O psychologists somewhat controversial?

CHAPTER 2

Research Methods in I-O Psychology

Chapter Outline

Statement of Research Problem

Design of Research Study

Social Media and I-O Psychology: *Getting Past the WEIRD Participants*

Primary Research Methods

True Experiment

Quasi-Experiment

Non-Experiment

Secondary Research Methods

Archival Research

Meta-Analysis

Data Mining

Faces of I-O Psychology: *Alexis A. Fink*

Qualitative Research

Methods/Sources of Data Collection

Organizational Records

Questionnaires

Observation

Interviews/Focus Groups

Organizational Neuroscience

Measurement and Analysis

Measurement of Variables

The Correlation Coefficient

Determining Causality

The Lighter Side of I-O Psychology: *Spurious Correlations*

Conclusions from Research

COVID-19 and I-O Psychology: *The Need for Holistic Research*

Ethical Issues in Research

Chapter Review

Learning Objectives

- Explain the empirical research cycle.
- Summarize the relative advantages and disadvantages of the laboratory experiment, quasi-experiment, questionnaire, and observation research methods.
- Describe archival research, meta-analysis, and data mining.
- Identify the purpose of organizational neuroscience.
- Describe the value of qualitative research.
- Summarize the concept of correlation and its interpretation.
- Explain the limitations of assessing causality.
- Outline the ethical issues associated with I-O psychological research.

We all have hunches or beliefs about the nature of human behavior. Some of us believe that happy people work harder than sad people, dynamic leaders are big and tall, blue-collar workers prefer beer to wine, the only reason people work is to make money, and so forth. The list is endless. Which of these beliefs are true? The only way to find out is to conduct **research**, the systematic study of phenomena according to scientific principles. Much of this chapter is devoted to a discussion of research methods used in I-O psychology. Understanding the research process helps people solve practical problems, apply the results of studies reported by others, and assess the accuracy of claims made about new practices, equipment, and so on.

Research
A formal process by which knowledge is produced and understood.

I-O psychologists are continually faced with a host of practical problems. Knowledge of research methods makes us better able to find useful solutions to problems rather than merely stumble across them by chance. An understanding of research methods also helps us apply the results of studies reported by others. Some factors promote the generalizability of research findings; others impede it. **Generalizability** is defined as the degree to which the conclusions based on one research sample are applicable to another, often larger, population. People often assert the superiority of some new technique or method; a knowledge of research methods helps us determine which ones are truly valuable. It has been suggested that science has three goals:

Generalizability
The extent to which conclusions drawn from one research study spread or apply to a larger population.

1. **Description**
2. **Prediction**
3. **Explanation**

The descriptive function is like taking a photograph—a picture of a state of events. Researchers may describe levels of productivity, numbers of employees who quit during the year, average levels of job satisfaction, and so on. The second function is prediction. Researchers try to predict which employees will be productive, which ones are likely to quit, and which ones will be dissatisfied. This information is then used to select applicants who will be better employees. The explanatory function is the most difficult to unravel; it is a statement of *why* events occur as they do. It tries to find causes: why production is at a certain level, why employees quit, why they are dissatisfied, and so forth.

This chapter will give you some insight into the research process in I-O psychology. The process begins with a statement of the problem and ends with the conclusions drawn from the research. This chapter should help you become a knowledgeable consumer of I-O psychological research.

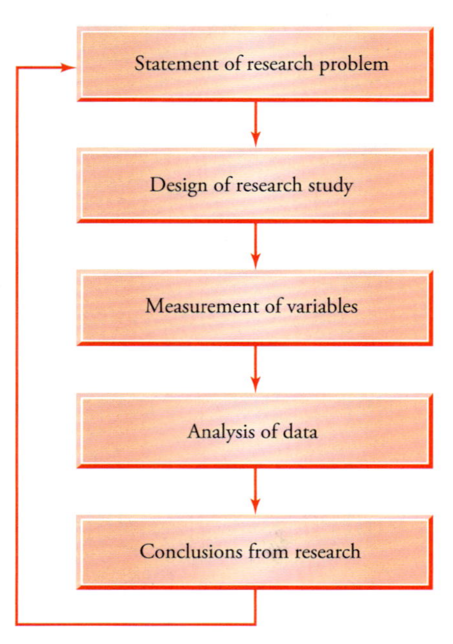

Figure 2-1 *The empirical research cycle*

Figure 2-1 shows the steps that scientists take in conducting empirical research. The research process is basically a five-step procedure with an important feedback factor; that is, the results of the fifth step influence the first step in future research studies. First, the research process begins with a statement of the problem: what question or problem needs to be answered? Second, how do you design a study to answer the question? Third, how do you measure the variables and collect the necessary data? Fourth, how do you apply statistical procedures to analyze the data? (In other words, how do you make some sense out of all the information collected?) Finally, how do you draw conclusions from analyzing the data? Let's look at each of these steps in more detail.

Statement of Research Problem

Theory
A statement that proposes to explain relationships among phenomena of interest.

Inductive method
A research process in which conclusions are drawn about a about a *general* class of objects or people based on knowledge of a *specific* member of the class under investigation.

Deductive method
A research process in which conclusions are drawn about a *specific* member of a class of objects or people based on knowledge of the *general* class under investigation.

Questions that initiate research don't arise out of thin air. They are based on existing knowledge—your own and others' experiences with the problem, personal intuition or insight, or a theory. A **theory** is a statement that proposes to explain relationships among phenomena—for example, a theory of why individuals are attracted to each other. As researchers conduct their studies, they become more familiar with the problem and may expand the scope of their questions. One person's research may stimulate similar research by someone else; thus, researchers often benefit from their colleagues' studies. After conducting much research on a topic, researchers may propose a theory about why the behavior occurs. The sequence that starts with data and culminates in theory is the **inductive method** of science. The opposite sequence is the **deductive method**, in which a researcher first forms a theory (perhaps by intuition or by studying previous research) and then tests the theory by collecting data. If the theory is accurate, the data will support it; if it is inaccurate, they will not.

The value of theory in science is that it integrates and summarizes large amounts of information and provides a framework for the research. Theories should aid in developing better research questions, allow us to interpret our findings in useful ways, and guide us in where we focus our research efforts.[1] As a scientific discipline, psychology is much more difficult to investigate than physics or chemistry.[2] People are far too variable, both across individuals and from day to day within one person, to be defined by a single formula or equation. For example, unlike many other sciences, psychology has no equivalent of universal natural laws, such as Newton's three laws of motion or the law of thermodynamics.

Theorizing, or theory development, is an ongoing process. A theory is proposed, then tested with empirical data, which in turn may result in the theory being fine-tuned or sharpened in focus. Theories are not "born" fully intact with unquestioned adherence, but are the objects of scientific scrutiny and evaluation. Within psychology, we typically speak of finding (or not finding) support for a theory rather than "proving" (or "disproving") the theory. With this in mind, some theories may receive extensive empirical support, while others may repeatedly be disconfirmed and ultimately dismissed by scientists.

A theory is an important way to specify research questions, but it is only one way to formulate a research problem. Other methods can also result in high-quality research. This is especially true in a pragmatic area like I-O psychology, where some research problems come from everyday work experiences. If 50% of a company's workforce quit every year, one doesn't need a theory to realize that this could be a serious problem. However, a theory can help explain why people are quitting and aid in identifying possible strategies for addressing the problem.

Design of the Research Study

Research design
A plan for conducting scientific research for the purpose of learning about a phenomenon of interest.

A **research design** is a plan for conducting a study. A researcher can use many strategies; the choice of method depends on the nature of the problem being studied as well as on cost and feasibility. Research strategies may be compared along several dimensions, but two are most important: (1) the naturalness of the research setting and (2) the investigator's degree of control over the study.

Naturalness of the Research Setting. In some research strategies, the problem can be studied in the environment in which it naturally occurs. This is desirable because we don't want the research strategy to destroy or distort the phenomenon under investigation. For example, the Hawthorne studies were conducted in the plant with actual employees performing their normal jobs. However, sometimes studies are conducted in laboratories with the hope that the findings will generalize to a real-world situation. Studies examining the effects of alcohol consumption on driving behaviors, for instance, cannot ethically be conducted on actual roadways. Instead, such research would occur in an artificial setting, with the intent of generalizing the findings to actual driving situations. Unfortunately, these research strategies may appear phony because they study the problem in unnatural ways. Some studies do not need to be conducted in a natural environment, however, because the behavior under investigation is assumed to be independent of the setting. A study to test whether people react faster to red or green lights could be conducted as appropriately in a laboratory as in a natural field setting. For the most part, the greater the realism of the research setting, the more generalizable the results. Simulations that have a great deal of realism are said to have *high fidelity*, while those that are more artificial are *low fidelity*.

Internal validity
The degree to which the relationships evidenced among variables in a particular research study are accurate or true.

External validity
The degree to which the relationships evidenced among variables in a particular research study are generalizable or accurate in other contexts.

Degree of Control. In some research strategies, the researcher has a high degree of control over the conduct of the study. In others, very little control is possible. In the Hawthorne studies, the researchers could control the exact amount of lighting in the work area by installing (or removing) lights, although it turned out that factors other than lighting affected the workers' performance. Suppose you want to study the relationship between people's ages and their attitudes toward I-O psychology. You are particularly interested in comparing the attitudes of people age 40 and over with those under 40. You develop a questionnaire that asks their opinions about I-O psychology (is it interesting, difficult to understand, and so on) and distribute it to your classmates. It turns out that every person in the class is under 40. Now you have no information on the over-40 group, so you can't answer your research question. This is an example of a low degree of control (you cannot control the age of the people in your class). Low control is particularly endemic to the questionnaire research method (discussed later in this chapter).

No one research strategy is best under all conditions; there are always trade-offs. In the I-O psychology attitude questionnaire scenario, the naturalness of the setting and the degree of control affect the internal and external validity of the research. **Internal validity** is the degree to which the relationships evidenced among variables in a particular research study are accurate or true. **External validity** is the extent to which findings from a research study are relevant to individuals and settings beyond those specifically examined in the study. External validity is synonymous with generalizability, and is a function not only of the realism of the research design, but also the types of people used as participants (see Social Media and I-O Psychology: *Getting Past the WEIRD Participants*). In general, the greater the control in a study, the more internal validity it will have and the greater the realism of the study, the greater the external validity. If a study lacks internal validity, it can have no external validity.

Social Media and I-O Psychology: *Getting Past the WEIRD Participants*

As a specialization, I-O psychology is subject to many of the same criticisms of the broader profession of psychology. One such criticism involves the samples of participants that have typically been used to answer empirical questions. Most behavioral scientists, including psychologists, have relied to a large extent on what they call "WEIRD" people. WEIRD stands for Western, Educated, Industrialized, Rich, and Democratic, and reflects the societies from which participants are usually drawn.[3] They argue that researchers often mistakenly believe that the results from their studies that use these participants will generalize to individuals in other societies. Unfortunately, WEIRD participants are often the exception to the rule, and quite different from the rest of the world. As a result, it would appear that more diverse samples are needed to obtain a better understanding of various phenomena.

Research within I-O psychology is equally guilty in many ways of limiting the types of people who have been studied. Until recently, it has been difficult to obtain data from diverse (i.e., non-WEIRD) samples, particularly when the researchers themselves may be WEIRD. Social media offer a new avenue for conducting research, revealing opportunities to broaden participant pools and create more heterogeneous samples. Social network sites such as Facebook allow researchers to gain access to people who were previously hard to access, as well as to recruit larger samples of participants.[4] Similarly, Facebook allows researchers to reach more people in a shorter amount of time than they would otherwise. The average Facebook user is connected to people with whom they have strong friendships, as well as individuals with whom they are weakly tied, including acquaintances and even strangers. These weak ties serve as bridges between people in a way that creates a diverse and elaborate web of social connections.[5] By recruiting participants through Facebook, by posting recruitment messages on group pages, and by encouraging snowball sampling (in which a request to participate is sent to one person, who forwards it to a second person, who then forwards it to a third person, and so forth), researchers are better able to ensure a more diverse, potentially non-WEIRD sample.

Other tools that have become increasingly popular for data collection are Prolific, Centiment, and Amazon's Mechanical Turk (MTurk). These are just a sampling of online services that allow researchers to recruit people from a large, global, diverse pool of individuals and provide compensation to them for their participation in an online study. The individuals who participate in the studies on these sites appear to be more demographically diverse than standard internet samples and far more diverse than typical college student samples that have been the convenient sample of choice for psychologists for decades.[6] In short, limiting ourselves to WEIRD samples that are not as reflective of the world's population as we might think is problematic for the science and practice of psychology as a whole, I-O psychology included. The use of social media to reach and recruit more diverse samples may be the key to obtaining a better understanding of workplace issues.

Primary Research Methods

Primary research methods
A class of research methods that generates new information on a particular research question.

This section is a discussion of three primary research methods used in I-O psychology. A **primary research method** provides an original or principal source of data that bears on a particular research question. No one method is perfect; that is, none offers a high degree of both naturalism and control. However, they each are important means of obtaining information within I-O psychology.

True Experiment

True experiment
A type of research method in which the investigator manipulates independent variables and randomly assigns subjects to experimental and control conditions.

Randomization
The assignment of participants to different experimental conditions on the basis of chance.

True experiments are conducted in contrived settings as opposed to naturally occurring organizational settings. True experiments are also called "laboratory experiments," given they are often conducted within researchers' lab spaces. In fact, some scholars have referred to a laboratory as a "special purpose setting" because the laboratory was created for the explicit purpose of conducting research.[7] However, true experiments can also exist outside of the laboratory, such as in the field or in natural environments. In a true experiment, the researcher has a high degree of control over the conduct of the study, especially over those conditions associated with the observations of behavior. The experimenter designs the study to test how certain aspects of an actual environment affect behavior. When a laboratory setting is used, it must mirror certain dimensions of the natural environment where the behavior normally occurs. A well-designed laboratory experiment will have some of the conditions found in the natural environment, but will omit those that would never be present. Furthermore, in a laboratory experiment, the researcher randomly assigns the study participants to the various treatment conditions, which enhances control and facilitates drawing causal inferences (saying that one thing caused another). While it may seem that laboratory experiments are superior to field experiments in terms of control, field experiments can be just as rigorous as laboratory experiments and offer the same levels of control.[8] The key is **randomization**, or the assignment of participants to different experimental conditions on the basis of chance. Regardless of setting, if the researcher can create pre-experimental equivalence between the groups that are being compared, then the necessary level of control has been achieved.

> **"True experimentation does not require a control freak, but it helps if one is a randomization freak."[9]**
>
> —Eden 2017, p. 96

Have you ever noticed that many people seem to engage in rituals prior to stressful events, such as eating the same meal or doing a series of orchestrated stretches prior to job interviews or athletic competitions? One group of researchers did, and an example of a true experiment can be found in their fun study that explored the effects of such rituals on performance and performance anxiety.[10] As part of their study, they told a sample of university students they would be singing the song "Don't Stop Believin'" by Journey in front of an experimenter, and that they would be paid money based on their singing accuracy score. The participants were randomly assigned to one of two conditions. In one condition, participants were asked to engage in a ritual. Specifically, participants were given the following instructions. "Please do the following ritual: Draw a picture of how you are feeling right now. Sprinkle salt on your drawing. Count up to five out loud. Crinkle up your paper. Throw your paper in the trash" (Brooks et al. 2016, p. 76).[11]

The participants were given one minute to complete the ritual. In the other condition, participants were simply asked to sit quietly for one minute prior to singing. After the minute was up, participants in both conditions sang their song into a karaoke machine that used its software program to assess accuracy based on the singer's volume, pitch, and note duration. After they finished singing, the participants completed measures on a computer that assessed how anxious they felt during their performance. The results showed that individuals who had completed the ritual sang more accurately than those who had not done the ritual. In addition, participants who had to sit quietly reported feeling significantly more anxious during their performance than did participants who had completed the ritual.

This study illustrates the defining characteristics of a true experiment. By randomly assigning people to conditions, they ensured that one group wasn't likely to have all of the "good" singers in it or all of the people who regularly conduct rituals. In addition, they ensured that participants were treated alike other than either engaging in the very specific ritual or not engaging in it. Besides that, they were treated identically, from performing the same exact task to answering the same questions afterwards. Thus, the degree of control was high, and helped to ensure that there were no other reasons for differences in the reported levels of performance anxiety. By ensuring this, the researchers were able to determine the causal link between engaging in a ritual and performance anxiety on a singing task. However, the realism of the setting was somewhat lacking, which raises the question of whether the results would generalize to other situations. That is, is singing into a karaoke machine in front of one person as part of a research study comparable to singing on stage to a large audience? Will engaging in a ritual meaningfully reduce performance anxiety or increase

Consider This...

Let's revisit the importance of randomization in a true experiment. Say you're interested in finding out if the presence of tattoos impacts interview ratings. You plan to show participants a video of an interview with either an applicant who has visible tattoos or an applicant without any tattoos, and have participants rate the applicant. Participants get the same instructions, the applicant is the same person with the same answers—the only difference is the presence or absence of tattoos. This is great for control purposes. However, let's pretend you failed to randomly assign participants and instead decided to simply have all of the participants sitting on the left side of the room view the tattooed applicant and the participants on the right side of the room view the non-tattooed applicant. This seems innocent enough, but consider the fact that people often sit with others who are like them, or with their friends. What if the left side of the room, by chance, had way more tattooed individuals compared to the right side of the room? Your results can't be trusted now, because you essentially have people with tattoos judging tattooed applicants and people without tattoos judging non-tattooed applicants (and that's not really what you are interested in). So consider this: what are some ways you could randomly assign participants to conditions? Would using the first three digits of people's social security number work? How about eye color? Why or why not?

performance in real-world situations? Clearly, there is a trade-off between control and realism for true experiments. Nevertheless, the true experiment is a classic research method for addressing highly-specific research questions, and the results from such experiments can often be interpreted with a high degree of clarity.

Quasi-Experiment

Quasi-experiment A type of research method for conducting studies that does not involve random assignment.

Quasi is defined as "seemingly but not actually;" therefore, a **quasi-experiment** resembles an experiment but actually provides less control over the variables under investigation. While a true experiment is the gold standard due to the high level of control, the quasi-experiment is the silver.[12] A quasi-experiment is a research strategy in which there is no random assignment, often because the study is occurring in a situation that does not allow researchers to assign people to conditions. For example, individuals are rarely assigned to work units randomly. Thus, any study in which comparisons are made between two already-established departments would constitute a quasi-experiment. As in a true experiment, the researcher tests the effects of a few variables on the subjects' behavior. However, because there is no random assignment of study participants, the conclusions by the researcher are less generalizable.[13]

An example of a quasi-experiment was an interesting study in which researchers assigned three sites within a healthcare system to participate in an intervention aimed at having participants create self-reflective job titles.[14] In the intervention, participants created job titles that they felt reflected the unique value they brought to their jobs. For example, a nurse who gives allergy shots to children may have a self-reflective title of "quick shot" or a doctor who handles infectious diseases may opt for the title of "germ slayer." Then, at two other sites, participants were provided an alternative intervention that was equivalent in duration to the job title intervention, but was focused on negotiation tactics. By giving a separate intervention focused on negotiation (rather than doing nothing at all), the experimenters could be certain that any changes that occurred in the self-reflective job title group were not due to having attention given to them by management and the research team. Finally, four sites were chosen to act as a pure control group and were not provided with any intervention. The experimenters sent surveys to all participants prior to the interventions and five weeks after the interventions. Their results revealed that employees who had completed the self-reflective titles intervention had significantly lower emotional exhaustion, felt that others understood them better, and felt safer in expressing themselves at work compared to those in the control group or the alternative intervention group.

The major strength of this study in terms of demonstrating the quasi-experiment method is that the context was real and random assignment did not occur. Actual workers were used in the context of their everyday jobs. Although the sites within the healthcare system were randomly assigned to the interventions, the employees were not randomly assigned to those sites. Thus, there could have been pre-existing differences between the sites at the start of the study. Nevertheless, although the study's design was not complex enough to rule out competing explanations for the observed behavior, it did allow the researchers to conclude that the use of self-reflective job titles probably caused the observed changes.

Non-Experiment

Non-experiment
A type of research method for conducting studies that does not involve the manipulation of variables or assignment of participants.

The final primary research method is that of the **non-experiment**, the most frequently used research method in I-O psychology.[15] Considering that a true experiment is one in which an investigator manipulates independent variables and randomly assigns participants to conditions, it should not come as a surprise that a non-experiment does none of these things. Rather, with a non-experiment, data are collected and analyzed without manipulation of variables or assignment of participants to conditions. All participants would receive the same questions, and any differences that may exist among survey respondents that could unduly influence the relationships being studied would be handled through statistical means.

An example of a non-experiment is a study in which the researchers were interested in exploring the ways individuals build and maintain their web of business connections, both within and outside their employing organization.[16] They surveyed participants to ascertain how internal (within the organization) and external (outside the organization) networking behaviors were related to decisions to voluntarily leave one's job. The researchers sent links to online surveys to 2,936 professional members of SIOP. In this initial survey, questions assessed the frequency with which individuals engaged in various networking behaviors, along with information regarding demographics, attitudes, and perceptions regarding employment opportunities, job search behaviors, and job offers. A total of 540 members completed the survey. Because job attitudes can change during the early stages of employment, the researchers selected only those respondents who reported being with their organizations for at least two years. This resulted in 371 respondents to the first survey. Two years later, these respondents were sent a second online survey that assessed whether they had voluntarily left their jobs during the two intervening years. The results indicated that external networking was related to higher incidence of voluntarily leaving one's organization (i.e., higher voluntary turnover), whereas internal networking appeared to be more beneficial for the employing organization (higher attitudes toward one's job and lower likelihood of turnover). The researchers concluded that organizations should invest in resources to enhance and encourage internal networking opportunities. Doing so would not only aid in employee retention, but could improve employees' attitudes toward work.

Consider This...

Reading about the findings from the study above probably wasn't the first time you've heard that networking—internal or external—is important. It's often said that it's not what you know, it's who you know. Although in actuality it's both what and who you know, the importance of networking can't be understated. Some research has shown that when we first start building our networks, we tend to limit our connections to those similar to us (the self-similarity principle) and those near us with whom we spend a lot of time (the proximity principle), such as coworkers in our departments.[17] It's important, however, to go beyond these and connect with others who are different than us and in different areas, as they can likely lead to more and better information and opportunities over time. With this in mind, what are some strategies you might use to build your own professional network? How can you make connections with people dissimilar to yourself?

An important note is that it is not the use of a survey or questionnaire that makes a study a non-experiment. Questionnaires and surveys can be used for experimental research as well, as they are simply the data collection method. They are discussed later in this chapter. The defining features that distinguish true experiments from quasi-experiments and non-experiments are the manipulation of variables and the (random vs. not random) assignment to conditions.

Secondary Research Methods

Secondary research methods
A class of research methods that examines existing information from research studies that used primary methods.

While a primary research method gathers or generates new information on a particular research question, a **secondary research method** looks at existing information, whether obtained from organizational records or from prior studies that used primary methods. In this section, we discuss archival research, meta-analysis, and data mining.

Archival Research

Archival research
A secondary research method that involves the extraction of information from existing records.

Perhaps the most basic of the secondary research methods is that of archival research. **Archival research** involves the extraction of information from existing records. These archival sources can include personnel records, customer databases, or any other existing available resource. Two national databases that are of particular interest to I-O psychologists include those maintained by the U.S. Department of Labor and the Bureau of Labor Statistics. In addition, many organizations provide archival data available for researchers upon request.

As an example of archival research, a team of researchers utilized two sources of archival data to explore the relationship between weather conditions and employee productivity.[18] They used precipitation levels in Tokyo for each day over a 2.5-year time period, as recorded by the National Climactic Data Center of the U.S. Department of Commerce, to reflect weather conditions. For employee productivity, they used existing data on loan application transactions completed by employees at a Japanese bank. They discovered that bad weather was indeed related to better employee productivity, with a one-inch increase in rain being related to 1.3% faster completion times for tasks.

Archival research has some advantages and disadvantages. A clear benefit for many researchers is that lengthy data collection can be avoided when existing data are available that can address the research questions. In addition, some research questions are best addressed with objective records. For example, a researcher interested in investigating the relationship between the number and type of accidents and injuries for men versus women can easily access workman's compensation claims and examine the various incidents by sex. Of course, disadvantages exist for archival research as well. Researchers relying on archival data are at the mercy of the data. That is, the researcher has to use what is available, which may not directly align with the preferred ways to define or measure variables. Missing data are also common, and many databases are cumbersome to navigate without considerable training.[19]

Archival research remains relatively underused by I-O psychologists.[20] For example, fewer than 10% of articles on leadership that were published in high-quality journals utilized archival data.[21] Similarly, only 12% of all articles published in the past decade in the *Journal of Applied Psychology* (one of the top journals in the field) utilized archival data.[22] Nevertheless, archival research remains a fruitful research method within the field.

Consider This...

What do you think about the finding that bad weather was predictive of employee productivity? Perhaps you dismissed the finding, given the small percent change in task completion time. Is 1.3% *that* big of a deal? Well, consider the point that if bad weather is related to faster completion times, good weather would be related to slower times. With this, the authors note that, given the number of workers in the organization, the amount of money each worker is paid, and the amount of rain that is typical in Tokyo, this is equal to around $937,500 of potential loss for the company in a single year! Now what do you think? What would you suggest based on these findings?

Meta-Analysis

Meta-analysis A quantitative secondary research method for summarizing and integrating the findings from original empirical research studies.

When 30 studies have been conducted on a topic, and 20 say one thing and 10 say another, how are we to determine what is the truth? The answer is meta-analysis. **Meta-analysis** is a statistical procedure designed to combine the results of many individual, independently-conducted empirical studies into a single result or outcome.[23] The logic behind meta-analysis is that we can arrive at a more accurate conclusion regarding a particular research topic if we combine or aggregate the results of many studies that address the topic, instead of relying on the findings of a single study. The result of a meta-analysis is often referred to as an "estimate of the true relationship" among the variables examined, because we believe such a result is a better approximation of the "truth" than would be found in any one study. A typical meta-analysis might combine the results from perhaps 25 or more individual empirical studies. As such, a meta-analysis is sometimes referred to as "a study of studies." This means we don't have to describe 30 different studies on a topic (you're welcome) because that's what the meta-analysis already did. In short, meta-analyses are magical in that, in a single study, we can synthesize a large number of studies and help advance the field.

Although the statistical equations performed in meta-analysis are beyond the scope of this book, they often entail adjusting for characteristics of a research study (for example, the quality of the measurements used in the study and the sample size) that are known to influence the study's results. By reducing errors of measurement, a meta-analysis increases the likelihood of achieving more accurate conclusions than could be reached in an individual study.[24]

As an illustration of a meta-analysis, a group of researchers explored the relationship between sleep and employee performance, safety, health, and attitudes.[25] Using data from 152 separate studies of sleep and work, they found that individuals who had better quality sleep exhibited higher performance on tasks, fewer thoughts about quitting their jobs, and lower levels of depression. The results of this meta-analysis can be of considerable practical value in assisting organizations, especially those that employ individuals who must work irregular schedules or night shifts.

Despite the apparent objectivity of this method, the researcher must make a number of subjective decisions in conducting a meta-analysis. For example, one decision involves determining which empirical studies to include. Every known study ever conducted on the topic could be included, or only those studies that meet some criteria of empirical quality or rigor could be included. The latter approach can be justified on the grounds that the results of a meta-analysis are only as good as the quality of the original studies used. The indiscriminate inclusion of low-quality empirical studies lowers the quality of the conclusion reached. The findings derived from poorly conducted primary research studies cannot be elevated in quality by conducting a meta-analysis. If researchers use faulty research methodology, utilize poor measures, or let their biases influence the study, a meta-analysis using the results from those researchers' studies will be similarly flawed. This is known colloquially as "garbage in, garbage out."

Another issue is referred to as the "file drawer effect." Research studies that yield negative or non-supportive results are not published as often as studies that have supportive findings, and therefore are not made widely available to other researchers. The unpublished studies are "filed away" by researchers, resulting in published studies being biased in the direction of positive outcomes. Thus, a meta-analysis of published studies could lead to a distorted conclusion because of the relative absence of (unpublished) studies reporting negative results. Evidence of the file drawer effect has been found among meta-analyses published by professional test vendors.[26] By selectively excluding those studies that reported negative results for their tests, the findings are inevitably biased in an upward direction. It's unclear how problematic the file drawer effect may be for any given meta-analysis.[27] As such, it is advisable to seek both published and unpublished research when conducting one.

Level of analysis
The unit or level (individuals, teams, organizations, nations, etc.) that is the object of the researchers' interest and about which conclusions are drawn from the research.

Original research studies on a similar topic sometimes differ in the **level of analysis** used by the researchers.[28] For example, one original study may have examined the individual attitudes of employees in a work team, whereas another original study may have examined the attitudes of different teams working with each other. It would not be appropriate to meta-analyze the findings from these two studies, because the level (or unit) of analysis in the first study was the individual, but in the second study it was the work team. Researchers must be careful meta-analyzing findings from original studies that focused on different levels.

Despite the difficulty in making some of these decisions, meta-analysis is a popular research procedure in I-O psychology. Continued refinements and theoretical extensions in meta-analytic techniques attest to the sustained interest in this method across the areas of psychology.

Data Mining

Data mining
A secondary research method that looks for patterns of association among the measured items in very large data sets.

Data mining (also known as *big data*) has been used to study consumer shopping decisions. Every time a supermarket scanner beeps, a new piece of information enters a database about shopping patterns. A single supermarket in just one day may sell 250,000 items. Data mining might reveal consistent patterns in items purchased both across and within shoppers. For example, laundry products are purchased by a broad spectrum of shoppers, while bottled water may more likely be purchased by people who also buy fresh vegetables. Other sources of big data are the various branches of the

U.S. government that record data on employment, crime, education, and so on. The value of data mining is not the number of individuals in a data set but the amount of information per individual that can be analyzed.[29]

I-O psychologists have embraced big data, utilizing it within organizations to make considerable improvements (see Faces of I-O Psychology: *Alexis A. Fink*). Some estimates suggest that integrating big data into healthcare could save up to $300 billion a year, while increasing data accessibility by a mere 10% would provide an additional $65 million net income for a typical Fortune 1000 company.[30] Given these estimates, it is not surprising that a great deal of emphasis has been placed on improving data mining capabilities within organizations.

Big data is more complex than simply having a large data set. Indeed, there are three defining characteristics of big data.[31]

1. **Volume**—there are a lot of cases and many variables per case.
2. **Velocity**—data collection occurs at a rapid and continuously increasing pace.
3. **Variety**—data come in many forms, both inside and outside of an organization by both active and passive means.

Fun fact:
With an estimated 33 zettabytes of data and an average download speed of 46 Mbps, it would take approximately 181.3 million years to download all of the data from the Internet!

As an example of data mining in practice, the U.S. Department of Labor conducted a survey on 98,000 employed adults that assessed how people spend their time performing work, commuting, childcare activities, etc.[32] The goal of the research was to ascertain what demographic and background variables accounted for the relative time spent in work versus nonwork activities. First, the data had to be prepared for analysis. In this study, 38,000 individuals were deleted from the analysis because of excessive missing data on key variables and other statistical issues. Next, the data set was made more manageable by reducing the original survey items from 134 to 39, focusing on the variables of greatest interest to the researcher. Third, the data were analyzed using statistical software programs that use mathematical algorithms, or rules, for determining patterns of associations among the variables. Finally, the data were interpreted to answer the questions posed by the researcher. In this study, the results revealed there were six distinctive profiles of time use in work and nonwork activities evidenced among the 60,000 people included in the study.

There are three research issues about data mining that are unique compared to other research methods in I-O psychology. First, most concepts examined in I-O psychology cover a wide range of possible scale values, from high to low, as a person's level of job performance or verbal ability. In data mining, the variables are simply recorded as yes or no, such as whether a particular product was purchased, or whether a person was over age 40. In the study by the U.S. Department of Labor, there were originally 139 variables, each measured either yes or no. A typical I-O psychological research study measures far fewer variables, but with most variables assuming a range of scale values.

Second, the traditional statistical index used in I-O psychological research is the correlation coefficient (described later in this chapter). Data mining also uses the correlation coefficient, but can involve other statistical indices not traditionally used in I-O psychology. One such example is an *affinity index*, a statistic that is based on the probability of two (or more) items being paired together. For example, consumer research reveals that people who purchase beer are also likely to purchase pretzels. This type of research finding (while informative) is not conventional in I-O psychology.

Faces of I-O Psychology: *Alexis A. Fink*

Alexis A. Fink

Ph.D. Old Dominion University

Led talent analytics teams at Facebook, Microsoft and Intel; led talent research projects at GE, NASA, BASF, and others.

Expertise areas: Talent analytics, talent management, large-scale organizational change, process optimization, assessment, leadership development, culture, diversity, data science, strategic workforce planning

The combination of a deep understanding of people at work and expertise with a variety of research approaches for understanding people at work make a background in I-O psychology widely applicable. Across my career, I've had opportunities to use techniques from interviews to advanced mathematical models to help organizations and the people in them be more effective and efficient—producing better business results as well as better lives and careers.

Working within an organization provides the opportunity to explore many different topics for insight and improvement. I've been able to apply research methods and analytical techniques to improve outcomes through work across areas like designing work processes for whole organizations, validating and implementing selection systems, growing leaders, and forecasting internal and external labor markets to inform strategic workforce plans.

Current talent analytics practice in organizations creates opportunities to use advanced mathematical and computer science methodologies, like machine learning, computational linguistics and optimization models. Increased availability of data, cheaper and more available computer power, and an explosion in analytical tools have created tremendous new opportunities to find patterns and implement programs and actions to support individual and organizational performance.

Many large organizations are complex enough to allow experimental or quasi-experimental designs as part of talent analytics research. The simple reality of rolling programs out to tens of thousands or hundreds of thousands of employees around the globe often requires phased implementations, which can provide insight into the impact of specific interventions. Implementation can be planned to create analytic opportunities using split plot designs, time series studies or full experimental manipulations, allowing true causal inference to inform investment decisions.

Advanced methods get a lot of attention, but through my career, I've discovered that often the most useful conversation comes from sharing simple descriptive information or qualitative methods such as interviews, focus groups or written comments. Advances in data visualization have made data storytelling much simpler, and applying good data visualization techniques can help convey key messages about patterns effectively and intuitively. Skill in gathering and analyzing qualitative information can help both inform quantitative study design and help leaders and decision makers understand the importance of trends in a way that a "percent favorable rating" can't.

Working inside organizations has allowed me to move from factory floors to Fortune 50 CEOs, solving organizational problems with advanced math, with informative visualizations for how many and where, and with compelling qualitative perspective on impacts and risks. My colleagues and I have been able to influence the lives of hundreds of thousands of individuals around the globe by influencing things like the effectiveness of their leaders and managers, their professional growth and their experiences with organizational processes like job hunting and performance management.

Lastly, it is currently fashionable in I-O psychological research to test theories. In the U.S. Department of Labor study, no theory was tested. Consistent with conventional practice, the data were "sifted through," looking for meaningful patterns. Future data mining research may involve testing theory, but at this point, its conduct is decidedly exploratory in nature.

As a final issue, it should be noted that in the survey by the U.S. Department of Labor, none of the participants were identified by name. The same is true of purchases at a supermarket. However, when personally identifiable information (PII) like the person's name, birth date, address, etc., are included in a data set, there are strict privacy regulations that must be followed by researchers. The liability for handling PII and its security rests with the organization storing the data.[33] The U.S. Department of Commerce, European Commission, and Swiss Administration identified seven principles and 16 supplemental principles to provide a "privacy shield" for personal information, including access, security, and enforcement.[34] Over 3,000 organizations abide by these principles. With the advent of data mining, ethical issues for conducting data analyses are of paramount importance in psychological research.[35]

Qualitative Research

Qualitative research
A class of research methods that involves collecting and analyzing data that are non-numerical in nature.

In recent years, there has been an increase in interest among some disciplines in what is called qualitative research. **Qualitative research** involves collecting and analyzing data that are not quantitative, or numerical, in nature. This can include investigating such things as text, voice or video recordings, or photographs. Qualitative research is often far more exploratory in nature than other research methods, and is used to generate theories and further research ideas. The essence of qualitative research is to recognize the number of different ways we can reach an understanding of a phenomenon. We can learn through watching, listening, and in some cases participating in the phenomena we seek to understand.

Data for qualitative research can be gathered in a variety of ways, including interviews and focus groups (described later in this chapter), diaries, case studies, and audio or visual recordings and documents. The data are analyzed in one of several ways. One way is through thematic analysis, which involves identifying patterns, or themes, that may exist within data. There are typically six steps involved in thematic analysis.[36] First, researchers must become familiar with the data, immersing themselves in the data to ensure a full understanding of what is being said (or written). Second, the data are coded in a systematic way. Third, the researchers search for potential themes and gather examples of data that fit into those themes. Fourth, the themes and data are reviewed to determine if any additional themes or examples exist. Fifth, the finalized themes are named and clear definitions for the themes are created. Lastly, a report is produced that links the themes and examples back to the research question and previous literature.

As an example of qualitative research that used thematic analysis, a group of researchers interviewed individuals who had decided to return to work less than a year after retiring.[37] Through their interviews, they identified several themes that explained why individuals typically sought "rehirement." Specifically, they became employed again because they were concerned and curious about work, felt in control of opportunities available to them, and felt confident they could make a contribution.

Given the interpretive nature of qualitative research, investigators often become more personally immersed in the entire research process, as opposed to being detached, objective investigators. For example, the authors of a study of U.S. military officers in combat in Iraq presented the following account:

> In one particular case, I interviewed a lieutenant that I got to know very well. And 10 days after I interviewed him, he was killed in an ambush. And I have the last recording of this young officer's voice. I was in Afghanistan when I was told he was killed, and I downloaded the recording, put it on a thumb drive, wrote a letter to his mother, and sent it to her. Nothing you learn in graduate school prepares you for a situation like that (Harms & Lester 2012, p.18).[38]

Another example of a qualitative study that demonstrates the intensive nature of this research method involves the long-term impact of unemployment.[39] The sample consisted of 72 men who had successful careers in such areas as finance, marketing, operations, and sales. They held professional positions, and their average last salary was $136,000 per year. They lost their jobs during the Great Recession and were seeking new employment. The authors developed a set of questions that became the basis of a lengthy telephone interview. Each interview was tape-recorded and transcribed, with each interview averaging 10 single-spaced pages in length. The authors spent many hours analyzing the transcriptions. Here are two verbatim comments from the interviews:

> Networking has pretty well gone down the tubes because it seems like everyone is in the same boat right now, among my colleagues, everyone. The companies we all work for, there are no openings. They're all just hanging on by their fingernails just trying to survive (Wanberg et al. 2012, p. 890).[40]

> It's hard. (Laughs.) It's really, really hard. It's so hard that some days you think you want to die . . . People who you never think would contemplate suicide are contemplating suicide because they feel like they're in a vortex of a black hole where the option is going and working at Whole Foods or moving back in with their families and feeling like they're a failure (p. 903).[41]

Through an analysis of the comments, the researchers identified more specific knowledge on the psychological effects of long-term unemployment. They learned about how repeated rejection leads to a sense of depersonalization and has a negative impact on families. The value of qualitative research was clearly evidenced through the powerful evocative words of the individuals in the study.

Ethnography
A research method that utilizes field observations to study a society's culture.

Another qualitative research approach is **ethnography**, which has been portrayed as the art and science of describing a group or culture.[42] The description may be of any group, such as a work group or an organization. An ethnographer details the routine daily lives of people in the group, focusing on the more predictable patterns of

Emic
An approach to researching phenomena that emphasizes knowledge derived from the participants' awareness and understanding of their own culture. Often contrasted with etic.

Etic
An approach to researching phenomena that emphasizes knowledge derived from the perspective of a detached objective investigator in understanding a culture. Often contrasted with emic.

behavior. Ethnographers try to keep an open mind about the group they are studying. Preconceived notions about how members of the group behave and what they think can severely bias the research findings.

It is difficult, if not impossible, however, for a researcher to enter into a line of inquiry without having some existing problem or theory in mind. Ethnographers believe that both the group member's perspective and the external researcher's perspective of what is happening can be melded to yield an insightful portrayal of the group. The insider's view is called the **emic** perspective, whereas the external view is the **etic** perspective. Because a group has multiple members, there are multiple emic views of how group insiders think and behave in the different ways they do. Most ethnographers begin their research process from the emic perspective and then try to understand their data from the external or etic perspective. High-quality ethnographic research requires both perspectives: an insightful and sensitive interpretation of group processes combined with data collection techniques.

While qualitative research has gained popularity and is looked upon more favorably within psychology and organizational behavior as a whole, it is still seen to a lesser extent in top I-O psychology journals in comparison to the more traditional quantitative research.[43] Nevertheless, there are efforts to integrate qualitative research more fully into graduate coursework[44] and into professional journal guidelines.[45] Regardless, there is no need to make an exclusive choice between qualitative and traditional research methods; rather, both approaches can help us understand topics of interest.

Methods/Sources of Data Collection

There are numerous means of collecting data that researchers can use when conducting research. These methods of data collection are described below, and include organizational records, questionnaires, observation, and interviews or focus groups. Researchers need to identify the knowledge they seek to gain and then determine if a particular method will be useful in doing so.[46] A well-trained I-O psychologist knows the advantages and disadvantages of each method.

Organizational Records

Organizational Records
A source of data consisting of information collected and maintained by an organization for reasons other than research.

Organizations collect a large amount of data, much of which can be useful for research purposes. These records could include information collected during the hiring process, such as employment applications or résumés, or information from current employees, such as supervisor ratings of performance, objective measures of sales or productivity, or data on absenteeism, accidents, and injuries.

Information from **organizational records** is frequently used in archival research, such as a series of studies that utilized existing company databases on various assessment tools (such as cognitive ability tests, physical ability tests, and assessment center data) and compared the data with other published data and national databases to evaluate issues of generalizability.[47] Organizational records can also be useful for other research methods. For example, researchers interested in examining the effects of a safety intervention may examine organizational records involving accidents and injuries prior to and after the intervention rather than collecting their own outcome data. In addition, because random assignment may not be possible, it may be ideal to control for differences in groups using statistical techniques. Thus, it could be possible to use past ratings of performance to statistically control for performance levels between groups of employees.

The quality of organizational records will vary by organization. In addition, some organizations keep records longer than others, though the ability to maintain electronic records has decreased the need for physical space and allowed for records to be maintained for longer periods of time. It is important to keep issues of privacy and confidentiality in mind with regard to organizational records. These topics are discussed at the end of this chapter with other ethical issues in research.

Questionnaires

Questionnaires A source of data in which subjects respond to written questions posed by the investigator.

Questionnaires (or surveys) rely on individuals' self-reports as the basis for obtaining information. They can be constructed to match the reading ability level of the individuals being surveyed. **Questionnaires** are a means of maintaining the anonymity of respondents if the subject matter being covered is sensitive.

Despite the popularity of the use of questionnaires in I-O psychology, it suffers from several practical limitations. First, some people are not willing to complete a questionnaire and return it to the researcher. Response rates are often low even with incentives for participation. Low response rate unfortunately raises the question of how representative or unbiased the responses are for the group as a whole. For example, one study revealed that nonrespondents to an organizational survey exhibited more negative attitudes about various aspects of their work than did respondents to the survey.[48] The researchers were able to ascertain the attitudes of both groups by means of interviews. Their findings cast doubt on the generalizability of the answers from respondents of some surveys to the larger population in question. More positively, responses to an online survey have been found to contain fewer incomplete or missing answers than responses to the same survey administered via the mail.[49] In addition, there appear to be very small differences in the quality of data collected by various survey methods (e.g., paper-and-pencil vs. online) and as such researchers should choose the method based on ease of administration.[50]

Another issue is the truthfulness of the responses given by respondents to questions asked. Research indicates questions that are perceived to be sensitive or threatening are more likely to produce distorted responses than benign questions. For example, one study revealed that as many as 70% of the people who tested positive for drug use in a urine analysis denied on a questionnaire having recently taken any illicit drugs.[51]

Despite their limitations, questionnaires are used extensively in I-O psychology to address a broad range of research questions. An example of a study that relied on questionnaire data was provided earlier in the discussion of non-experiments (the examination of the relationship between internal and external networking behaviors and employees' decisions to voluntarily leave their jobs).

Consider This...

The phrase "a penny for your thoughts" is an idiomatic way of requesting to know what is on someone's mind. Within the research context, it could be seen as an incentive for sharing one's view. That is, if you tell me what you're thinking, I'll give you a monetary incentive. Do you think that's necessary? Consider this: chances are likely that you have been asked to complete a survey at some point in your life, perhaps even recently. Maybe it was for a research study, or to provide input to an organization about a product it sells, or to give a rating regarding the service you received at a restaurant. Did you complete the survey? Were you offered an incentive for completing the survey? Would it have mattered? Some researchers found that offering prepaid monetary incentives significantly improved response rates. That might not be too surprising to you, but the researchers also found that the novelty of the incentive and the size of the incentive didn't seem to make a difference.[52] Why do you think that is? What impacts your own willingness to complete a survey?

Observation

Observation A data collection method in which the investigator monitors employees for the purpose of understanding their behavior and culture.

Observation is a method that can be used when the researcher is examining overt behaviors. In natural field settings, behavior may be observed over extended periods of time and then recorded and categorized. As an example of this data collection method in practice, one group of researchers sought to better understand how team members in high-performing and low-performing teams differ with regards to how they monitor one another and "talk to the room," or share relevant information to a room at large rather than to a specific person.[53] The researchers observed video recordings of anesthesia teams performing general anesthesia inductions, the first step in all operations that require general anesthesia. Participants consisted of nurses, resident physicians, and attending physicians at a teaching hospital who were organized into teams as the hospital needs and schedules dictated. Using a detailed coding scheme, the researchers coded each behavior of all team members, along with its time (beginning, end, and duration). Every time one team member was observing the actions of other teammates, the behavior was coded as "monitoring" and every time a team member gave task-relevant communication directed toward the room as a whole it was coded as "talking to the room." Team performance was determined by an experienced staff anesthesiologist who evaluated the teams using a checklist of behaviors based on guidelines established by the hospital and the medical community. The authors found that members of high-performing teams were more likely than those in other teams to provide assistance after monitoring a team member's actions. They also found that high-performing teams used talking to the room as a way to prevent breakdowns in communication and keep the team actively participating in coordination efforts. While these researchers utilized video-recordings for their observations, it is possible to observe "on the fly," though such direct observation runs the risk of being intrusive, which could inadvertently influence behavior. In addition, direct observations may not

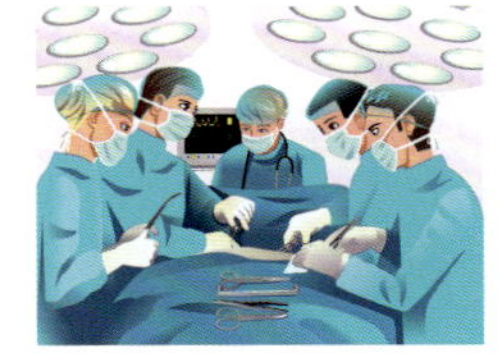

be as accurate or thorough as observations from videos, given limits in human attention and an inability to check coding accuracy.

Observation is often a useful method for generating ideas to test further with other research methods. The observation method is rich in providing data from environments where the behavior in question occurs. But how successful can observers be in acting like "flies on the wall," observing behavior but not influencing it? In the described study, the anesthesia team was aware that they were being recorded. Given this, to what degree did the nurses and physicians modify their conduct to project socially-desirable behaviors (e.g., monitoring of their team members)? Perhaps effective team members are more sensitive to social cues than ineffective team members and thus are better able to be perceived in a positive fashion. Note that we are dealing with interpretations of the behavior (the "why"), not merely the behavior itself (the "what"). It has been suggested that acceptance and trust of the observers by the study participants are critical to the success of this research method. With that in mind, the internet may be a fruitful mechanism for conducting observational research through the use of webcams and smartcards.[54]

Interviews/Focus Groups

Focus group
A small but diverse group of people who participate in a facilitated discussion to elicit responses to questions related to predetermined topics of interest.

Researchers also collect data through interviews and focus groups. Interviews occur when researchers pose questions to participants either individually or as groups (panel interviews) and record the responses. **Focus groups** also consist of questions posed by a researcher to a group of respondents, but participants are often asked to respond to the question through a discussion in which they build on each other's answers. The discussion is facilitated in such a way as to ensure sufficient detail in responses is given, and that the topic remains focused. In both interviews and focus groups, the researcher uses the responses to provide insight into the research question. For example, during the COVID-19 pandemic, the United States Forest Service conducted focus groups comprised of wildland fire personnel to learn about the conditions faced by field personnel, as well as to identify intended and unintended impacts of changing protocol.[55] The researchers asked the focus groups targeted questions, and generated new questions for future focus groups on the basis of the answers they received. In this way, they were able to craft additional questions while gaining insight into COVID-19 mitigation and wildland fire management.

Interviews and focus groups are frequently used within qualitative research. The questions that are posed can range from being highly structured and defined to less structured and dependent on previous answers. Depending on the research, it is typically advisable to have participants be diverse from one another so that the many perspectives that exist are considered. The qualitative study on unemployment described earlier utilized interviews as the means of data collection.

Organizational Neuroscience

Neuroscience is the scientific study of the body's nervous systems and their impact on behavior. Over the past 25 years, research in various scientific disciplines has examined neural activity associated with decision making and attitude formation in various areas of life. Within the context of the workplace and I-O psychology, this focused area of study is called **organizational neuroscience**.

Organizational neuroscience The scientific study of neural activity as evidenced in organizational attitudes and behavior.

The field of neuroscience is devoted to studying human behavior at its most fundamental basis—the physiological level. In less than a century, a wide variety of techniques have emerged for studying brain functions, including the following:[56]

- Structural magnetic resonance imaging (MRI) for identifying the structure of the brain
- Functional magnetic resonance imaging (fMRI) and functional near-infrared spectroscopy (fNIRS) for gauging oxygenation of brain regions to identify the process of brain activity
- Electroencephalography (EEG) and magnetoencephalography (MEG) for recording the brain's electrical output
- Heart rate variability (HRV), blood pressure variation, and galvanic skin response for measurements of the autonomic nervous system (the involuntary part of the nervous system)
- Lesion studies and transcranial magnetic stimulation (TMS) for determining the impact of neural function intervention

Each technique is used for a different purpose. Researchers interested in studying creativity, for example, have used MRI to reveal that different parts of the brain are activated in performing novel tasks versus routine tasks. EEG assessments are useful in measuring reaction time to stimuli. We have a faster reaction time to the color red than any other color, which is the basis for why stop lights and warning lights are red. It is hypothesized that differences in leadership may be attributable to varying patterns of neural activity, as might personality differences.

The most common methods used in organizational neuroscience currently are EEGs and fMRIs.[57] As an example of a study using fMRI methodology, a group of researchers was interested in demonstrating the distinctness between procedural justice and distributive justice.[58] As we will discuss in Chapter 11, justice is another word for fairness, and distributive justice refers to the fairness of outcomes, while procedural justice refers to the fairness of the processes used to determine those outcomes. The researchers examined whether being exposed to unfair procedures activated different parts of the brain than did being exposed to unfair outcomes. In fact, they found that unfair procedures activated parts of the brain that are related to social cognition while unfair outcomes activated parts of the brain that are associated with emotions. These findings demonstrated that the concepts are indeed distinct, providing justification for measuring the justice dimensions separately.

Advancements in the various techniques have created unique ways to approach research questions. In addition, while the cost of neuroscience instruments was once prohibitive, especially compared to more traditional I-O psychological research methods, they are becoming much cheaper and easier to use, and easier to interpret the output. Given this, perhaps it is only a matter of time before neurological assessments become part of a personnel selection system for high level jobs. Their greatest value may be in eliminating candidates for employment who, if hired, would produce grave harm to people.

Measurement and Analysis

Variable
An object of study whose measurement can take on two or more values.

Quantitative variables
Objects of study that inherently have numerical values associated with them, such as weight.

Categorical variables
Objects of study that do not inherently have numerical values associated with them, such as gender. Often contrasted with quantitative variables.

Independent variable
A variable that can be manipulated to influence the values of the dependent variable.

Dependent variable
A variable whose values are influenced by the independent variable.

Measurement of Variables

After developing a study design, the researcher must carry it out and measure the variables of interest. A **variable** is represented by a symbol that can assume a range of numerical values. **Quantitative variables** (age, time) are those that are inherently numerical (21 years or 16 minutes). **Categorical variables** (employment status, race) are not inherently numerical, but they can be "coded" to have numerical meaning: unemployed = 0, employed = 1; or White = 0, Black = 1, Hispanic = 2, Asian = 3, and so forth. For research purposes, it doesn't matter what numerical values are assigned to the categorical variables because they merely identify these variables for measurement purposes.

Variables Used in I-O Psychological Research. The term *variable* is often used in conjunction with other terms in I-O psychological research. Four such terms that will be used throughout this book are *independent, dependent, predictor,* and *criterion.* Independent and dependent variables are associated in particular with experimental research strategies. **Independent variables** are those that are manipulated or controlled by the researcher. They are chosen by the experimenter, set or manipulated to occur at a certain level, and then examined to assess their effect on some other variable. In the sample experiment described earlier on ritual engagement, the independent variable was ritual engagement (ritual vs. no ritual). In the quasi-experiment on self-reflective titles described earlier, the independent variable was the intervention (self-reflective job titles vs. negotiation intervention vs. no intervention).

Experiments assess the effects of independent variables on the dependent variable. The **dependent variable** is most often the object of the researcher's interest. It is usually some aspect of behavior (or, in some cases, attitudes). In the ritual engagement study, the dependent variables were the subjects' performance on a singing task and their performance anxiety. In the self-reflective job titles study, the dependent variables were the emotional exhaustion, self-verification, and psychological safety of the participants.

Consider This...

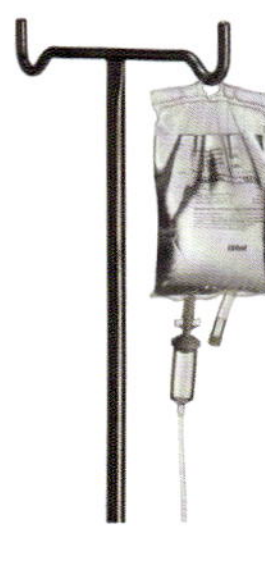

If you struggle with remembering the difference between independent and dependent variables, know that you are not alone, especially if this is the first time you have heard of these concepts. Like many new concepts, it is helpful to come up with a "trick" to help make sense of the material. One way that may be helpful to remember that the independent variable is the variable that is manipulated by the researcher and that the dependent variable is what is influenced by the independent variable is to think of an intravenous line, more commonly known as an IV. An IV is a soft, flexible tube that is used to administer medicine or fluids to a patient through the vein. What is put into the IV, and the amount, will differ and is determined by the physician with the hope that whatever is given to the patient will have the desired effect. Thus, the IV is manipulated (perhaps medicine vs. saline solution) and therefore represents the independent variable (which fortunately can also be abbreviated with IV). The dependent variable *depends on* the IV. For example, the health of the patient could be a dependent variable. Whether the patient gets better may *depend on* what is in the IV. Those who get the medicine may get better while those who don't get medicine may not see the same health benefits. Does this help? What other "tricks" might you use to help remember the concepts within this chapter—and others?

Predictor variable A variable used to predict or forecast a criterion variable.

Criterion variable A variable that is a primary object of a research study; it is forecasted by a predictor variable.

Predictor and criterion variables are often used in I-O psychology. When scores on one variable are used to predict scores on a second, the variables are called **predictor variables** and **criterion variables**, respectively. For example, a student's high school grade point average might be used to predict their college grade point average. Thus, high school grades are the predictor variable; college grades are the criterion variable. As a rule, criterion variables are the focal point of a study. Predictor variables may or may not be successful in predicting what we want to know (the criterion). Predictor variables are similar to independent variables; criterion variables are similar to dependent variables. The distinction between the two is a function of the research strategy. Independent and dependent variables are used in the context of experimentation. Predictor and criterion variables are used in any research where the goal is to determine the status of subjects on one variable (the criterion) as a function of their status on another variable (the predictor). Independent variables are associated with making causal inferences; predictor variables are not.

The Correlation Coefficient

Correlation coefficient A statistical index that reflects the degree of relationship between two variables.

I-O psychological research often deals with the relationship between two (or more) variables. In particular, we are usually interested in the extent that we can understand one variable (the criterion variable) on the basis of our knowledge about another (the predictor variable). A statistical procedure useful in determining this relationship is called the correlation coefficient. A **correlation coefficient** reflects the degree of linear relationship between two variables, which we shall refer to as X and Y. The symbol for a correlation coefficient is r, and its range is from –1.00 to 1.00. A correlation coefficient tells two things about the relationship between two variables: the direction of the relationship and its magnitude.

The direction of a relationship is either positive or negative. A positive relationship means that there is a direct relationship between the two variables. That is, as one variable increases, so does the other. An example of a positive correlation is the relationship between height and weight. As a rule, the taller a person is, the greater the weight; increasing height is associated with increasing weight. A negative relationship means that there is an inverse relationship between the two variables. That is, as one variable increases, the other decreases. An example of a negative correlation is between an accountant's skill level and the number of errors made. The more skilled the accountants are, the fewer errors that are made. Conversely, the less skilled the accountants are, the more errors there are.

The magnitude of the correlation is an index of the strength of the relationship. Large correlations indicate greater strength than small correlations. A correlation of .80 indicates a very strong relationship between the variables, whereas a correlation of .10 indicates a very weak relationship. Magnitude and direction are independent; a correlation of –.80 is just as strong as one of .80.

Correlations are depicted visually with *scatterplots*. A scatterplot is a plot of the values for a pair of variables. For example, a group of researchers were interested in the relationship between news consumption about COVID-19 and perceptions of uncertainty.[59] They predicted a positive relationship such that the more that individuals obtained and consumed news about the COVID-19 pandemic, the more uncertainty they would feel. For each participant in their sample, they gathered information about how much news they consumed in a given day as well as how uncertain they felt on that day. To create a scatterplot of this relationship, each participant's scores on these two variables would be plotted so that a visual depiction of the relationship could be seen. The stronger the relationship between the two variables, the tighter the spread of data points that runs through the scatterplot will be. The weaker the relationship, the more the data points will be spread out. (The researchers, by the way, found support for their prediction. The more people read and watched the news related to the COVID-19 pandemic, the more uncertainty they reported feeling.)

Figure 2-2 summarizes the concepts related to the correlation coefficient. Two scatterplots are shown at the top of the figure, one reflecting a negative correlation and the other reflecting a positive correlation. The stronger the correlation between two variables (either positive or negative), the more accurately we can predict one variable from the other. The only way to derive the exact numerical value of a correlation is to apply the statistical formula (which we do not provide in this book, but which is readily available in any statistics book). Although the eyeball-inspection method of looking at a scatterplot gives you some idea of what the correlation is, research has shown that people are generally not very good at inferring the magnitude of correlations by using this method.

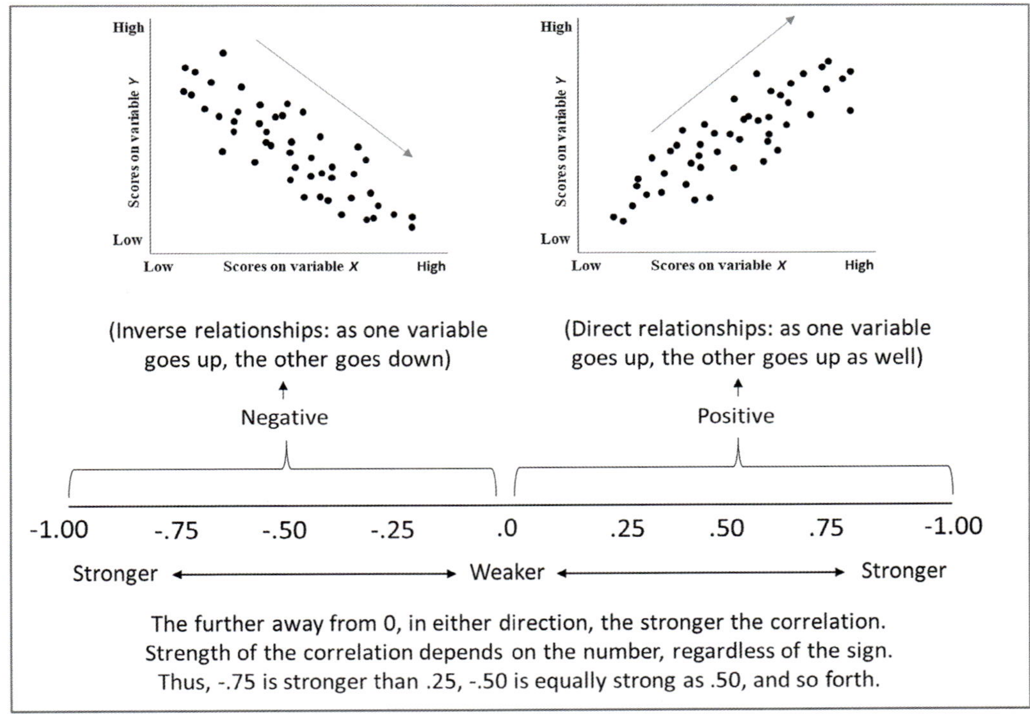

Figure 2-2 *Summary of key concepts for the correlation coefficient*

Determining Causality

Perhaps the most laudable goal of any field of scientific inquiry is the determination of causality. A complete understanding of any phenomenon is based upon knowing causal determinants. Unfortunately, rarely in the behavioral sciences do we achieve this result. In a notable case, many years of extensive research led to the conclusion that cigarette smoking causes cancer. That research finding became the basis of powerfully-worded warnings placed on packs of cigarettes. While cigarette smoking is the leading cause of lung cancer, the relationship between the two is not immutable. That is, there are some people who smoke but who do not develop lung cancer. There are also some people who develop lung cancer but never smoked. However, this causal relationship is a basis for laws and organizational policies. For example, cigarettes are heavily taxed, smoking is prohibited in many public places, and smokers can be denied insurance.

> **"Lacking evidence for causality leaves major unfinished business. Practical application of results without evidence of causality borders on malpractice."[60]**
>
> —Eden 2017, p. 94

What do we know about causal relationships in I-O psychology? By its very nature, I-O psychology is concerned about understanding behavior in a context (the workplace) where many factors are simultaneously exerting influence on individuals. They include transient moods, personality attributes, tolerance for stress, family issues, economic conditions, and many more. In short, our work lives exist in a complex and ever-changing context. Indeed, there are so many "moving parts" operating at one time it is extraordinarily difficult to disentangle "what causes what" to occur.[61] Causality can be determined in a laboratory experiment where a single variable can be isolated, and other possible determinants of behavior are removed in the experiment. In such a controlled environment, and only in such an environment, can causality be determined. Unfortunately for I-O psychology, the very behavior we wish to understand invariably cannot be removed from the uncontrolled context in which it occurs.

The inability to understand causal relationships contributes to the public perception that psychology is not as valuable to society as chemistry or physics.[62] Our inability to make precise predictions about a particular individual's behavior can be the source of public frustration. For example, when an individual commits a violent crime, it is common to have some people ask, "Why couldn't we have predicted (and prevented) this behavior?"

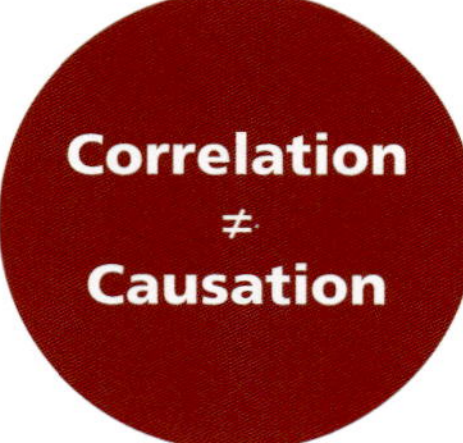

I-O psychological research is heavily based on the concept of correlation. While some I-O psychological research is based on the experimental method, most is based on the correlational method. A correlation coefficient does not permit any inferences to be made about causality—that is, whether one variable *caused* the other to occur. Even though a causal relationship may exist between two variables, just computing a correlation will not reveal this fact. Correlations reveal statistical associations among variables; correlations do not reveal causal relationships.

Suppose you wish to compute the correlation between the amount of alcohol consumed in a town and the number of people who attend church there. You collect data on each of these variables in many towns in your area. The correlation coefficient turns out to be .85. On the basis of this strong positive correlation, you conclude that because people drink all week, they go to church to repent (alcohol consumption causes church attendance). Your friends take the opposite point of view. They say that because people have to sit cramped together on hard wooden pews, after church they "unwind" by drinking (church attendance causes alcohol consumption). Who is correct? On the basis of the existing data, no one is correct because causality cannot be inferred from a single correlation coefficient. Proof of causality must await experimental research. In fact, the causal basis of this correlation is undoubtedly neither of the opinions offered. The various towns in the study have different populations, which produces a systematic relationship between these two variables, along with many others, such as the number of people who eat out in restaurants or attend movies. Computation of a correlation in this example does not even determine whether the churchgoers are the drinkers. The effect of a third variable on the two variables being correlated can cloud our ability to understand the relationship between the variables in purely correlational research (see The Lighter Side of I-O Psychology: *Spurious Correlations*).

Determining causality in I-O psychological research has been referenced as the "Holy Grail."[63] Our capacity to only understand the (statistical) association among factors, but not their causal relationship, impedes our ability to implement policies in the workplace that are "proven" to determine behavior.[64] Most of the research findings discussed in this book are based on correlational analyses.

The Lighter Side of I-O Psychology: *Spurious Correlations*

The example of a correlation between church attendance and amount of alcohol consumed may seem silly or unlikely, but there are actually a lot of things that are correlated that you would never expect to be. Tyler Vigen is an individual who has discovered some of these strange spurious correlations.[65] For example, using data from the U.S. Department of Agriculture and Centers for Disease Control and Prevention, he discovered that there is a very strong correlation (.94) between per capita cheese consumption and the number of people who died by becoming tangled in their bedsheets! It's doubtful there is a causal link there! As another example, the relationship between divorce rates in Maine and the per capita consumption of margarine is .99! Based on these results, you would think that it would be best if you consumed less cheese and less margarine if you value your life and/or your marriage. While that might indeed be the case, there are many possible reasons for these findings, though we're hesitant to guess.

We'll leave you with this: Although not as strong of a relationship, Vigen also found that there is a strong correlation (.66) between the number of people who drowned in a pool and the number of films that Nicolas Cage starred in between 1999 and 2009. Anyone up for a movie night?

Conclusions from Research

After analyzing the data, the researcher draws conclusions. A conclusion may be that alcohol intoxication impairs certain skills more than others, or jobs that require skills that are more adversely impaired by alcohol consumption warrant more restrictive standards than other jobs. The study described earlier as an example of a quasi-experiment concluded that emotional exhaustion decreased as a result of incorporating self-reflective job titles. A company might decide based on these conclusions to implement the use of such titles throughout the organization. Worthy of note, however, is that we typically prefer to know the results from several studies before implementing any major changes in an organization. We want to be as certain as possible that any organizational changes are grounded in repeatable, generalizable results.

Sometimes the conclusions drawn from a study modify beliefs about a problem. Note in Figure 2-1 that a feedback loop extends from "Conclusions from research" to "Statement of research problem." Theories may be altered if empirical research fails to confirm some of the hypotheses put forth. One of the most critical issues in conducting research is the quality of the generalizations that can be drawn from the conclusions. A number of factors determine the boundary conditions for generalizing the conclusions from a research study to a broader population or setting. One factor is the representativeness of individuals who serve as the research subjects. Much research is conducted in university settings, and university students often serve as subjects in research studies because they are an available sample. It has been a matter of great debate within the entire field of psychology whether the conclusions reached from studying college students generalize to a larger and more diverse population. There is no simple answer to this question: it depends greatly on the research topic under consideration. Asking typical college students to describe their vocational aspirations is highly appropriate. Asking typical college students to describe how they will spend their retirement years, 50 years from now, would have limited scientific value. Because I-O psychology is concerned with the world of work, and thus the population of concern to us is the adult working population, we are generally cautious in attempting to generalize findings based on studies of college students. In addition, it has been argued that researchers should take a more integrative holistic approach to research that considers many different stakeholders, topics, and processes simultaneously in order to obtain a complete understanding of a topic (see COVID-19 and I-O Psychology: *The Need for Holistic Research*).

COVID-19 and I-O Psychology: *The Need for Holistic Research*

Researchers across the globe united together to combat the COVID-19 crisis. Some researchers focused on treatment, others focused on developing a vaccine, and others focused on finding solutions to social problems that accompanied the virus. I-O psychology researchers tackled such issues as figuring out how to manage the increased stress that workers were experiencing, how to lessen the heightened conflicts between work and family that employees were facing, and helping employees navigate new challenges that were arising.

Researchers collaborated across countries and disciplines. By working together, they were able to gain unique perspectives and tackle problems using a variety of approaches. Vaccines were developed and information shared in less time than it normally takes, as individuals and organizations pivoted to meet the needs of society.

The COVID-19 pandemic proved to be a multifaceted phenomenon that impacted many people from all walks of life, on numerous fronts, including physical and mental well-being, both at work and at home. To address this multifaceted phenomenon, research also needed to be multifaceted.[66] Specifically, scholars argued that research needed to take a *multiphenomenon* approach, in which the interrelatedness of different topics is acknowledged. For example, with so many employees working remotely, could you truly tackle a topic such as work motivation without considering circumstances within one's home life? Similarly, researchers needed to take a *multistakeholder* perspective, in which they considered different stakeholders for any given problem in a systematic and exhaustive fashion. A case in point: employees may have had children who needed to be home-schooled during the pandemic. Only considering that employee as an employee, and not as a parent, would likely lead to an incomplete understanding and faulty conclusions about the employee. Finally, research required a *multimethod* approach, whereby mixed method designs—those that combine quantitative and qualitative research methods—were necessary to capture the unique situations and dynamic aspects that abounded.

Researchers must consider the context in which they are working. Research is not an isolated event. Rather, we must integrate various perspectives and be holistic in our approach. If we do not consider the circumstances that impact our results, our conclusions will not be of much value. Considering the need for I-O psychology research to benefit both science and practice, this is of utmost importance and an area that I-O psychologists became acutely aware of during the pandemic.

Research is a cumulative process. Researchers build on one another's work in formulating new research questions. They communicate their results by publishing articles in journals. Competent researchers must keep up to date in their areas of expertise. The conclusions drawn from research can affect many aspects of our lives. Research is a vital part of industry; it is the basis for changes in products and services. Research can be a truly exciting activity, although it may seem tedious if you approach it from the perspective of only testing stuffy theories, using sterile statistics, and inevitably reaching dry conclusions. Research is a craft, and a researcher, like an artist or craftsperson, has to pull together a wide variety of human experiences to produce a superior product.[67] Being a researcher is more like unraveling a mystery than following a cookbook. However, research is not flash-in-the-pan thrill seeking; it involves perseverance, mental discipline, and patience. There is no substitute for hard work. We can recall many times when we anxiously anticipated seeing statistical analyses that would foretell the results of a lengthy research study. This sense of anticipation is the fun of doing research—and research is a craft we try to pass on to our students.

Consider This...

Researchers from all scientific disciplines, though differing in the methods used in their respective disciplines, are all basically problem solvers.[68] They invoke research methods to solve problems and answer questions of interest to them. Along these lines, academics are sometimes accused of conducting "mesearch research," or using their own personal experiences when tackling research questions.[69] The criticism is often used when referring to researchers who engage in autoethnography, or a qualitative research method in which individuals use self-reflection of their own experiences to draw more general conclusions to others. However, many scholars joke that their research is "mesearch research" when it is something with which they have direct exposure or experience in general. For example, stress researchers may joke that their research is "mesearch research" when they are going through a particularly stressful time, even if their research does not involve them as participants in any of their studies. Not surprisingly, many scholars choose their areas of research based on personal experiences.

Ethical Issues in Research

The American Psychological Association has a code of ethics that must be honored by all APA members who conduct research.[70] The code of ethics was created to protect the rights of research participants and to avoid the possibility of unqualified people conducting research. It is the responsibility of the researcher to balance ethical accountability and the technical demands of scientific research practices. It is not at all unusual for psychologists to face ethical conflicts in the conduct of their work, including research.

Participants in psychological research are granted five rights that are specified in the code of ethics:[71]

1. **Right to informed consent**. Participants have the right to know the purpose of the research, the right to decline or withdraw participation at any time without negative consequences, and the right to be informed of any risks associated with their participation in the research. This right is perhaps the most fundamental because most research aims to meet the needs of the researcher, not the participants.

2. **Right to privacy**. Researchers must respect the participants' right to limit the amount of information they reveal about themselves. How much information participants might be required to reveal and the sensitivity of this information may offset their willingness to participate.

3. **Right to confidentiality**. Confidentiality involves decisions about who will have access to research data, how records will be maintained, and whether participants will be anonymous. Participants should have the right to decide to whom they will reveal personal information. By guaranteeing participants' confidentiality, researchers may be able to obtain more honest responses.

4. **Right to protection from deception**. Deception refers to a researcher intentionally misleading a participant about the real purpose of the research. Examples are withholding information and producing fake beliefs and assumptions. Deception is sometimes used by researchers in the belief that it is critical to understanding the phenomenon of interest. Researchers who wish to use deception must demonstrate to an institutional review board that the value of the research outweighs the harm imposed on participants and that the phenomenon cannot be studied in any other way. It has been argued that deception does not respect participants' rights, dignity, and freedom to decline participation, and may result in participants being suspicious of psychological research. In short, deception can be used in research, but participants are assured that it is used only as a last resort.

5. **Right to debriefing**. After the study is completed, debriefing must take place to answer participants' questions about the research, to remove any harmful effects brought on by the study, and to leave participants with a sense of dignity. Debriefing should include information about how the current study adds to knowledge of the topic, how the results of the study might be applied, and the importance of this type of research.

Researchers who violate these rights, particularly in studies that involve physical or psychological risks, are subject to professional censure and possible litigation. Many countries have developed codes of ethics regarding research. Although nations differ in the breadth of research issues covered, they typically emphasize the well-being and dignity of research participants in their ethics code by addressing informed consent, deception, protection from harm, and confidentiality.

The researcher is faced with additional problems when the participants are employees of companies. Even when managers authorize research, it can cause problems in an organizational context. Employees who are naïve about the purpose of research are often suspicious when asked to participate. They wonder how they were "picked" for inclusion in the study and whether they will be asked difficult questions. Research projects that arouse emotional responses may place managers in an uncomfortable interpersonal situation.

HARKing
Hypothesizing after results are known—a questionable practice of presenting a research finding after-the-fact as if it were a predicted finding.

Researchers must also abide by ethical principles in the presentation of their results. One problem that has garnered considerable attention is that of **HARKing**—hypothesizing after results are known.[72] Earlier, in our discussion of meta-analyses, we discussed the file drawer effect, which occurs when negative or non-supportive results don't get published. Unfortunately, some researchers may attempt to "find" effects by exploring their data for significant findings, and then creating hypotheses that "predict" (after-the-fact) those findings. This HARKing is problematic because the results may be an anomaly of the sample or the data rather than a finding truly supportive of theory. While exploratory research is necessary for helping to identify unanticipated discoveries, researchers must state this was their approach.[73] Otherwise, it is assumed that the study was confirmatory and it is in these cases that HARKing is a problem.

Study preregistration
The practice of specifying the intended hypotheses, methodology, and analyses for a study prior to data collection.

Due to problems with HARKing and the file drawer effect, several steps have been taken to address them. First, journal editors have become increasingly open to publishing unexpected or null findings. In addition, there has been a greater push for replication of findings to help ensure results are not anomalies. Lastly, **study preregistration** has become a popular practice for promoting transparency and openness in study hypotheses, methodology, and analysis prior to actual data collection.[74]

Ethical issues in psychology are not limited to the conduct of research. Adherence to the code of ethics also applies to such issues as conflict of interest, plagiarizing, and the treatment of clients. Following the terrorist attacks of 9/11, the APA began to examine the ethical implications of psychologists' roles in interrogating suspected terrorists.[75] For applied psychologists, there can be conflict between national security-related needs and the ethical obligations to all individuals, including suspected terrorists, not to inflict harm. I-O psychology is sometimes portrayed (incorrectly) as being a value-free science.[76] In addition, it is often the case that we become aware of the importance of ethics through the actions that violate them.[77] It is unethical behavior that gets reported, not ethical behavior. Indeed, differences have been identified among people regarding ethical sensitivity; individuals must be sensitive to ethical issues before they can behave ethically. The ethical conduct of psychologists is critical for maintaining the integrity of our profession.

Chapter Review

Key Terms

Research
Generalizability
Theory
Inductive method
Deductive method
Research design
Internal validity
External validity
Primary research methods
True experiment
Randomization
Quasi-experiment
Non-experiment
Secondary research methods
Archival research
Meta-analysis
Level of analysis
Data mining
Qualitative research
Ethnography
Emic
Etic
Organizational records
Questionnaires
Observation
Focus group
Organizational neuroscience
Variable
Quantitative variables
Categorical variables
Independent variable
Dependent variable
Predictor variable
Criterion variable
Correlation coefficient
HARKing
Study preregistration

Questions for Review

1. What are the three goals of science?
2. What are the steps that scientists take in conducting empirical research?
3. What is a theory? How do the inductive and deductive methods relate to theory development?
4. How does the naturalness of the research setting and the degree of control impact our conclusions about our research findings? How do these elements relate to internal validity and external validity?
5. What are the three primary research methods used in I-O psychology? How do they differ from one another?
6. Why is randomization important for a true experiment?
7. What are three secondary research methods used in I-O psychology? What do each of these methods entail?
8. What are three defining characteristics of big data?
9. How is data mining distinctive compared to other research methods in I-O psychology?
10. How does qualitative research differ from other research methods used in I-O psychology?
11. What is ethnography? What is the difference between the emic perspective and the etic perspective?

12. What are four ways that data are collected in I-O psychology? What are some advantages and disadvantages associated with each of these methods?
13. What are some common techniques used to study the body's nervous systems? How have using these techniques led to a better understanding of behavior?
14. What is the difference between quantitative variables and qualitative variables? How are independent and dependent variables distinguished? How do independent and dependent variables relate to predictor and criterion variables?
15. What is the correlation coefficient used for in research? What are examples of positive and negative correlations? What is a scatterplot and how is one created?
16. Why is the topic of causality important for researchers? How is it determined?
17. What are five rights that research participants are granted?
18. What is HARKing and why is it a problem?
19. What is study preregistration? What is the purpose of this practice?

CHAPTER 3

Chapter Outline

The Structural Context

The Social Context

Humanitarian Work Psychology

Diversity, Equity, and Inclusion

Social Media and I-O Psychology: *Slacktivism or Activism?*

The Environmental Context

Cross-Cultural Considerations

Sustainability Concerns

The Legal Context

Workplace Discrimination

The Lighter Side of I-O Psychology: *Plans for Breeding*

Faces of I-O Psychology: *Eric M. Dunleavy*

Workplace Health and Safety

Family and Medical Leave

COVID-19 and I-O Psychology: *Families First Coronavirus Response Act*

Child Labor

Chapter Review

Learning Objectives

- Explain the six structural contexts of work.
- Describe work's social contexts and how I-O psychology contributes to them.
- Differentiate among diversity, equity, and inclusion.
- Discuss the environmental context of work and I-O psychology's contribution to it.
- Describe the legal context of work and I-O psychology's involvement.
- Explain unfair discrimination and its repercussions to organizations and people.
- Summarize the Civil Rights Act of 1964 and Title VII, and describe their impact on work in the U.S.

Context refers to the setting or circumstances surrounding a word, idea, statement, or event that helps to provide meaning and understanding. When you are reading and encounter a word you don't know, you likely infer the meaning of that word from the rest of the sentence or passage in which the word is set. Similarly, full statements require the context of a conversation to understand their meaning and intent. When statements are taken out of context, they are often misconstrued and can lead to confusion and/or conflict.

The topic of context extends beyond our words, to all aspects of life. The American painter Kenneth Noland once remarked, "For me context is key—from that comes the understand of everything." This point is true for our understanding of employees within organizations. Without having a good grasp of the various elements surrounding workers and workplaces, we cannot fully understand work itself and the influences of employee behavior. Thus, this chapter is about exploring the structural, social, environmental, and legal contexts surrounding work. By examining the broader contexts in which work exists, we gain an appreciation of where we focus our attention and why, and create a knowledge base that allows us to make sense of the findings we encounter.

The Structural Context

The way an organization is structured has a great deal of influence on how employees behave and how work is conducted. There are six elements of organizational structure, each one contributing to the organization's effectiveness.

Departmentalization An element of organizational structure that concerns how organizations are divided into units based on the functions they perform, the customers they serve, the geographic areas they oversee, or the products they manage.

Departmentalization. The first element of organizational structure is based on the concept of division of labor. **Departmentalization** refers to how organizations are divided into units that perform similar functions. Similar work activities are often organized into departments, which enhances coordination of activities and permits more effective supervision and a more rational flow of work. Departments are often grouped according to functional area such as by production, sales, engineering, finance, and so on. Departments can also be grouped in other ways, however, such as by geographic location (e.g., Midwest, Mexico, Europe), product lines (e.g., MS Office, Windows, and Xbox within Microsoft), or by customer type (e.g., wholesale, retail, government).

Specialization An element of organizational structure that concerns how work is broken down into smaller routinized tasks.

Specialization. The second element of organizational structure is also based on division of labor, but is characterized by the degree to which work is broken down into smaller pieces to provide clear areas of **specialization**, which in turn improves the organization's overall performance. Assembly line work is an example of highly specialized work: there are very specific tasks required of individuals in those roles. Highly routinized work such as this is beneficial from an efficiency stance but problematic from the perspective of employee boredom.

Chain of command An element of organizational structure that concerns an organization's reporting structure.

Chain of Command. The third element of structure is **chain of command**, which deals with the organization's vertical growth and reporting structure. Each level within an organization has its own degree of authority and responsibility for meeting organizational goals, with higher levels having more responsibility. Each subordinate should be accountable to only one superior, a tenet referred to as the **unity of command**. Classical theorists thought the best way to overcome organizational fragmentation caused by division of labor was through a well-designed chain of command. Coordination among factions is achieved by people occupying positions of command in a hierarchy.

Unity of command The concept that each subordinate should be accountable to only one supervisor.

Centralization. The fourth element of organizational structure is **centralization**, or the extent to which decisions are determined by executives at higher levels in the organization and carried out by managers at lower levels. This approach is contrasted with granting the authority to make decisions (versus simply executing on them) to those managers at lower levels in the organization (i.e., a decentralized approach).

Centralization An element of organizational structure that concerns how decisions are carried out in an organization.

Span of Control. **Span of control** refers to the number of subordinates a manager is responsible for supervising. Large (or wide) spans of control produce flat organizations (that is, few levels between the top and bottom of the organization); small (or narrow) spans of control produce tall organizations (that is, many levels).

Span of control An element of organizational structure that concerns the number of subordinates a manager is responsible for supervising.

Formalization. The final element of organizational structure is **formalization**, or the extent to which there are very clear rules, procedures, and policies within an organization that dictate what is and is not allowable. Highly formalized organizations specify to a large degree what they expect of employee behaviors. Organizations with less formalization have looser rules and expectations of their employees.

Formalization An element of organizational structure that concerns the extent to which there are clear rules, procedures, and policies within an organization that dictate what is and is not allowable.

The six elements can combine in myriad ways to create various types of structure, and an organization continuously seeks to find a structure that is an optimal match to its environment. That is, the structure of an organization is an adaptive mechanism that permits the organization to function in its surroundings. Organizations that have maladaptive structures will ultimately cease to exist. Because individuals assume roles within organizations, employees feel the brunt of change caused by the continuing evolution of an organization's structure. It is in this regard that I-O psychology is involved in matters of organizational structure.

Consider This...

As with most things in life, there are pros and cons regarding the various elements of organizational structure. As noted above, for example, high levels of specialization are great from an efficiency standpoint but tend to cause boredom in employees that could result in high turnover. Similarly, highly centralized organizations tend to have lower costs and are better equipped to implement common policies and practices across the organization. On the downside, however, managers at lower levels may feel frustrated with their lack of decision-making power and the delays that come with having to wait for others to make decisions on matters they may be in a better position to address. Consider the advantages and disadvantages for each of the structural elements. For each of the elements, what would you prefer to have in an organization you work in? Why? What difference would it make to you depending on your level within the organization?

The Social Context

Organizations operate within the social context in which they are embedded. These larger-scale forces have a direct bearing on the workplace. Within this section, we will discuss the work that I-O psychologists are performing in the areas of humanitarian efforts as well as efforts to enhance diversity, equity, and inclusion at work.

Humanitarian Work Psychology

Since its inception over a century ago, I-O psychology has been regarded as an agent for helping organizations to be more effective. Indeed, I-O psychologists who work as practitioners are hired by organizations to achieve that very result. An examination of the organizations that are staffed with I-O psychologists reveals that these organizations are often large, in the private sector (i.e., non-government), and measure their effectiveness by such financial indices as sales volume, profit level, and market share. While this generalization does not extend to all I-O psychology practitioners, there is a plausible basis for how our profession is perceived.

Recently, there has been a call for I-O psychology to become more heavily involved in activities that benefit others and/or society as a whole. A focus on pro-social I-O psychology work has become of particular interest to some I-O psychologists. Pro-social I-O psychology work involves any work that utilizes I-O psychology research, practice, and expertise to help others, whether through unpaid volunteer efforts or paid activities that benefit more than the individual doing the work. Most corporate volunteer programs involve companies sponsoring paid release time from work for interested employees to assist nonprofit organizations, such as the Red Cross and the United Way.[1] Over 90% of Fortune 500 companies run employee volunteering programs, encouraging employees to perform community service while being compensated on company time.[2] Many programs require sustained participation, not a one-time contribution. Over the past 25 years, employees of Disney have given more than five million hours to help nonprofit organizations.

I-O psychologists interested in pro-social efforts assist in such endeavors as the Veteran Transition Project, which helps military service members transition into civilian life, and Project INCUBATE, which serves as a means to help eradicate poverty. Many I-O psychologists also serve as pro-bono consultants through such organizations as the Taproot Foundation, a nonprofit organization that pairs other nonprofits with volunteer business professionals who donate their expertise.

In addition, a call has emerged from within the discipline for I-O psychology to expand its focus to help the world become a better place by using the knowledge and skills we have developed. The name for this new direction for I-O psychology is **humanitarian work psychology**.[3] When we read or hear the word "humanitarian," it is often followed by the word "aid" or "relief." It typically refers to the giving of resources (e.g., food, clothing, shelter) to people who have an urgent need for them, such as following an earthquake or flood. In the case of humanitarian work psychology, it is directing the resources of I-O psychology (what we know and can do) to relieving global poverty, promoting social justice in organizations, protecting the rights of workers, and so on.[4] The push for humanitarian work psychology is the recognition of the long-standing ills afflicting the global population. It is consistent with

Humanitarian work psychology
The practice of I-O psychology directed to the societal goal of improving employment for all mankind.

the Ethical Principles of Psychologists and Code of Conduct: to promote good for mankind.[5]

The decision by I-O psychology to adopt a comprehensive perspective of organizational actions also aligns with the United Nations Global Compact.[6] The UN Global Compact is a set of policies and recommended actions for organizations to follow in the conduct of their business. The UN Global Compact is presented in Table 3-1. The intent of the Global Compact is to promote good by following principles pertaining to human rights, labor, environment, and anti-corruption. The UN has no authority to enforce organizational policies and actions. But the Global Compact does provide a specific set of initiatives for responsible organizations to follow, and as of 2021 it was endorsed by 14,670 organizations (including SIOP), representing 162 nations. All this is evidence of a growing recognition of the need for organizations to conduct themselves in responsible ways for the betterment of mankind. I-O psychology has joined other scientific disciplines in recognizing our inherent global interdependence, and the need to pursue goals that historically were not part of our legacy.

Table 3-1 *United Nations Global Compact: The Ten Principles*

From United Nations Global Compact: The Ten Principles, ©2008, United Nations. Reprinted with the permission of the United Nations.

The Global Compact asks companies to embrace, support and enact, within their sphere of influence, a set of core values in the areas of human rights, labour, the environment, and anti-corruption:

Human Rights

Principle 1: Businesses should support and respect the protection of internationally proclaimed human rights; and

Principle 2: make sure that they are not complicit in human rights abuses.

Labour

Principle 3: Businesses should uphold the freedom of association and the effective recognition of the right to collective bargaining;

Principle 4: the elimination of all forms of forced and compulsory labour;

Principle 5: the effective abolition of child labour; and

Principle 6: the elimination of discrimination in respect of employment and occupation.

Environment

Principle 7: Businesses should support a precautionary approach to environmental challenges;

Principle 8: undertake initiatives to promote greater environmental responsibility; and

Principle 9: encourage the development and diffusion of environmentally friendly technologies.

Anti-Corruption

Principle 10: Businesses should work against corruption in all its forms, including extortion and bribery.

Diversity, Equity, and Inclusion

Diversity
The practice or state of having broad representation of people with different personal characteristics, including backgrounds, demographics, and viewpoints.

The word **diversity** is frequently cited in both popular and scientific literatures, and is derived from "diverse," meaning *different*. Diversity within the workplace can promote hard work, improve creativity, lead to more open-mindedness, and enhance overall performance.[7] The right to be judged fairly (i.e., without regard to one's demographic membership) is established by law (as discussed later in this chapter). Thus, from a legal view, diversity, and the management of diversity, is a means to address discrimination in employment.[8] Therefore, to the extent that job candidates from various demographic groups are qualified, there should be proportional representation of them in the workforce. An organization that is staffed by a diverse range of employees is mirroring the society of which it is a part.

The focus on "visible" or mostly "demographic" characteristics as reflecting diversity has its critics, however, with some scholars noting that categorical and dichotomous views of diversity are overly simplistic.[9] In addition, views toward diversity and what it entails appear to be shifting with time. For example, a Deloitte study found that millenials are "more likely to define diversity as pertaining to the individual mix of unique experiences, identities, ideas, and opinions. Older participants, on the other hand, frame diversity in terms of demographics, equal opportunity, and representation of identifiable demographic characteristics" (Smith & Turner 2015, p. 8).[10] With the growth of millennials in the workplace, it may be tempting to believe that things will "work themselves out" since this group is well-versed in the central frames of the contemporary racial ideology.[11] Unfortunately, this is not likely to be the case.

In addition to the increased attention on diversity, there is a similarly strong focus on ensuring equity within the workforce. It is important to distinguish between the concepts of equity and equality. In 2012, business professor Craig Froehle created a cartoon that is now frequently reproduced as a means to visually depict the distinction (such as the image shown to the right). In it, three individuals of varying heights are seen trying to watch a baseball game from outside a fence. Equality is depicted with all three individuals standing on crates, and the tallest and the next tallest can see over while the shortest, despite the crate, cannot see over. Equity, conversely, shows that the crate previously given to the tallest person has instead been used to raise up the shortest person so that now all three individuals are able to see over the fence equally well. In this depiction, equality is portrayed as sameness, and fairness only exists if all individuals are treated the same. **Equity**, however, takes into account that individuals have differences and barriers that require unique solutions in order to achieve fairness.

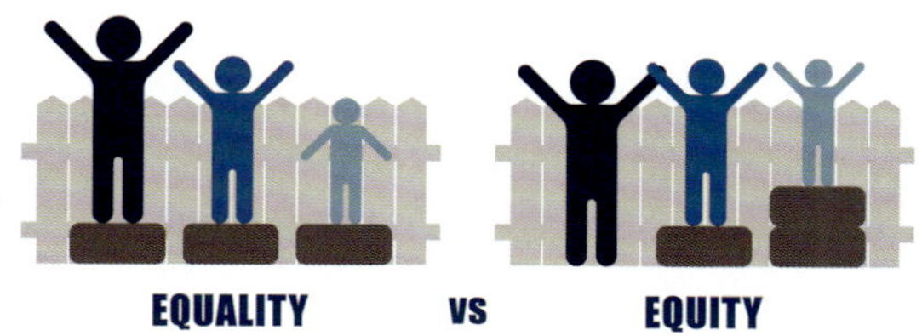

Equity
Fairness or justice without bias or favoritism, with adjustments made to rectify imbalances and ensure all individuals have access to the same opportunities.

Inclusion
The involvement and integration of people from all groups into organizational systems and processes while allowing each to retain their own identity.

Compared to diversity and equity, inclusion has received relatively less attention, though more so in recent years. **Inclusion** involves people from all groups feeling they contribute to the whole organization while still retaining their own identities. Inclusion emphasizes encouraging employee involvement and integrating diversity into organizational systems and processes.[12] By analogy, each of the 50 states has its own name and identity, but each is included in a national identity, the United States.

Inclusion generates a feeling of being an authentic insider who is both trusted and respected for contributions made. Inclusion advances the concept of diversity by going beyond nominal representation to feelings of self-worth. While the goals of inclusion are most laudable, they are not always easy to achieve in practice.[13]

Consider This...

The terms "diversity," "equity," and "inclusion" are often used interchangeably, yet they are separate constructs that should be treated as such. Failing to recognize and appreciate the differences among these constructs can make them more difficult to attend to separately and holistically. An apt metaphor that demonstrates their distinction is that diversity is ensuring many different people are invited to a party (representation), inclusion is asking those different people to dance (involvement), and equity is providing transportation to the party for those who do not have a ride (justice).[14] Although they have similar goals, the strategies used to achieve them are different, and not delineating them appropriately makes them harder to address. What are the implications for addressing only diversity, with no consideration for equity or inclusion? Is it possible to have equity and/or inclusion without diversity? Which do you think is easiest to address? Why? Which one is hardest? Why?

Organizations are keenly aware that diversity is an index of being a socially responsible employer. They differ in the extent to which they successfully pursue diversity initiatives, and they differ in the extent to which they make public statements about their efforts. Figure 3-1 shows a taxonomy that summarizes these differences across organizations.[15] "Reality" is whether organizations achieve a diverse workforce, and "Rhetoric" is whether they talk actively about their efforts.

The upper left quadrant ("Walk the talk") represents organizations that achieve diversity in reality in addition to verbally promoting their efforts in doing so. The lower right quadrant ("Low priority") represents organizations that neither achieve nor talk about their diversity efforts. The upper right quadrant ("Empty rhetoric") reflects organizations that talk about their diversity efforts, but in reality their workforce is not diverse. The lower left quadrant ("Just do it") refers to organizations that do not publicly discuss or promote their diversity achievements, but in reality have created a diverse workforce. Ideally, there should be alignment or consistency between what an organization does and what it says. If diversity is not an enacted value of the company,

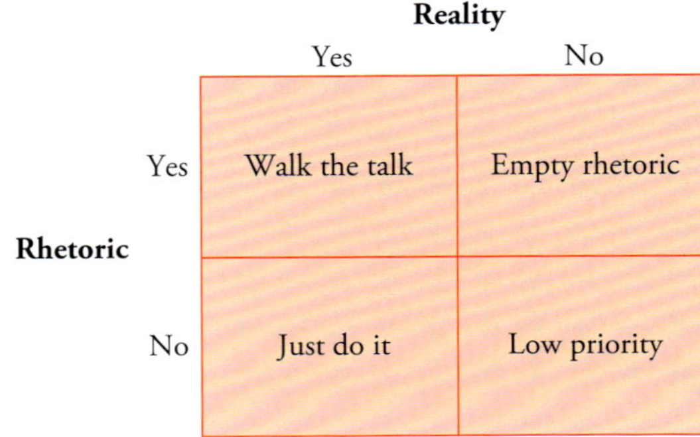

Figure 3-1 *Typology of organizational diversity initiatives*

Adapted from "Models of Global Diversity Management," by K. Jonsen and M. Özbilgin, in *Diversity at work: The practice of inclusion* (2014) by B. Ferdman (Ed.). Reprinted with permission of Wiley via Copyright Clearance Center.

it should not be proclaimed as one. However, if diversity is central to the company's identity, it is appropriate to communicate that.

Despite the increased attention on diversity, equity, and inclusion in the workplace, it is clear that much remains to be accomplished. An examination of three decades of research in more than 800 organizations concluded that most diversity programs have failed to increase diversity.[16] In addition, much to our dismay, many workplaces have remained largely unwelcoming for many individuals, whether it be based on race, color, sexual orientation, religion, physical attractiveness, disability status or any number of personal characteristics. Black, Indigenous, and People of Color (BIPOC) as well as Lesbian, Gay, Bisexual, Transgender, Queer and/or Questioning, Intersex, Asexual, Two-Spirit, and numerous additional ways in which people self-identify (LGBTQIA2S+) routinely experience harassment and discrimination both in and outside of work, from microaggressions to physical violence (see Social Media and I-O Psychology: *Slacktivism or Activism?*). It is estimated that by 2060, more than half of all Americans will belong to what is currently considered a minority group.[17] Additionally, one in five is expected to be foreign-born. Thus, the workforce is only going to become more diverse. It is imperative that our research and practices take advantage of this diversity and create a more equitable and inclusive workforce.

Social Media and I-O Psychology: *Slacktivism or Activism?*

Social media has played a role in many forms of activism over the years. From #MeToo, #BlackLivesMatter, and #BringBackOurGirls, these so-called hashtag activism campaigns have helped spread the word about various social issues and bring attention to the masses. Activism via social media has existed since social media first began, and it has received both accolades and criticisms. Critics have argued that online activism is useless, as clicking "like" on a post or changing one's status amounts to very little. Using the pejorative terms "slacktivism" or "clicktivism," critics note that social media activism is the laziest form of activism and could actually hurt "real world" activism because people may be lulled into thinking they have done something meaningful already. As one individual noted over a decade ago, "clicktivism is to activism as McDonalds is to a slow-cooked meal. It may look like food, but the life-giving nutrients are long gone" (White 2010).[18]

Proponents of social media activism, on the other hand, contend that online efforts are effective since they help spread ideas that aren't mainstream and offer alternative means of getting information to the public. In addition, research has demonstrated that, contrary to some beliefs, social media activism does not detract from activism that is offline.[19] Further, one need only look at examples of successful social media campaigns to see there can be an impact. For example, the #BlackLivesMatter movement has relied heavily on its extensive social media presence to organize countless rallies and events, often with large turnouts.

With any cause, there will be those who do more and those who do less, regardless of whether the cause has been promoted on social media. Perhaps more "slacktivists" are generated via social media than would otherwise exist, but there is also the possibility that additional passionate activists will become engaged because the cause came to their attention via social media. And there's no doubt that social media activism will continue.

The Environmental Context

For our purposes, the environmental context refers to an organization's physical surroundings and how that environment and the organization influence one another. With this in mind, we are focused on cross-cultural considerations as well as sustainability concerns.

Cross-Cultural Considerations

There is greater cultural diversity in the workforce, more U.S. companies doing business overseas, an increased number of partnerships or joint ventures between companies from different countries, and myriad electronic means of communication that render geographic boundaries between nations meaningless. With these changes comes a need to understand how the work context may differ for individuals around the globe. For example, the amount of time individuals spent at work in 2020 varied greatly across countries. Workers in Mexico averaged more hours at work (~2,124) than did employees in the United States (~1,767), Japan (~1,598), and Germany (~1,332).[20] In addition, most countries have government-mandated vacation time, with all members of the European Union having at least 20 days of mandated leave for employees and many countries in Africa having up to 30 days of required vacation time. The United States, however, does not have government-mandated vacation time, leaving that up to individual employers to determine. Does this mean that workers in countries that work less than Americans are "lazy?" Absolutely not, just as it is not correct to describe American workers as "compulsive." Rather, these differences in how much individuals work are merely a reflection of the values different cultures have for the role that work plays in life.

There are also cultural differences in what makes for a desirable employee. Many Western cultures consider the hiring of family members of employees to be undesirable. The term **nepotism** refers to showing favoritism in the hiring of family members.[21] In the United States, nepotism is usually viewed negatively because it results in unequal opportunity among job applicants, which is counter to our cultural values. In some non-Western cultures, however, nepotism in hiring is viewed positively. The logic is that a family member is a known commodity who can be trusted to be loyal, unlike an anonymous applicant. Why not give preferential treatment to candidates who are associated by birth or marriage with members of the hiring organization? Decisions and actions within the workplace are always embedded in a larger organizational and social context. They do not "stand apart" in a vacuum unrelated to the larger social system.

Nepotism
An approach to personnel staffing whereby family members receive preferential treatment because of birth or marriage.

Many differences must be addressed in the melding of workers and work-related practices across different nations. Not surprisingly, the full range of topics that I-O psychologists address is influenced by cross-cultural differences. Topics include preferences for how to select employees, the degree to which workers compete versus cooperate with each other, and preferred styles of leadership, among many others. We will revisit many of these points throughout the upcoming chapters as we cover these specific topics. In addition, we will cover broader cultural differences and their impact on employee behavior in greater detail in Chapter 9.

Consider This...

"I got this job based on my tremendous knowledge and work skills. At least that's what my Dad said when he hired me."

How common is nepotism? One estimate is that by the age of 30, approximately 22% of sons and 13% of daughters will work for the same employer at the same time as their father.[22] Consider how this compares with countries around the world. A ranking of countries on a scale of 1 (nepotism has enormous influence) to 7 (nepotism has no influence), the United States received a score of 4.2.[23] Conversely, countries where nepotism had a greater influence included Zambia (2.7), Venezuela (3.0), and Nepal (3.4). Countries where nepotism had less influence included Finland (6.4), Singapore (5.9), and Japan (5.8). How do you feel about nepotism? Nepotism in and of itself is not illegal. Do you think it should be? Why or why not? What policies would you want to see within an organization with regard to nepotism? Would you modify the policy depending on the location? How so?

Sustainability Concerns

The environment and the need for its protection has gained considerable attention in recent years. As the quote in the margin exemplifies, without a consideration for the protection of our environment, many I-O psychologists realize that organizational efforts will not matter. As a result, organizations have begun to implement programs aimed at environmental sustainability. For example, McDonald's UK created a program called "Planet Champion" in which employees came up with ideas to support sustainability. Among them were placing all grills and toasters on stand-by when not in use. By doing this, they were able to reduce carbon dioxide emissions by 20,000 tons per year and save 30% of its energy costs per year.[25]

"If humanity does not survive in the face of resource shortages (for example, clean water and food supplies for nine billion individuals by 2050) and environmental calamities (such as climate change and destruction of the ecosystems), no organizations will remain."[24]
—Ones & Dilchert 2012, p. 89

As the importance of the need for environmental sustainability has become clearer, it has been suggested that organizations should include ecological impact criteria in making business decisions.[26] Of course, in order to have a true impact, leaders of organizations must make sustainability a top priority, repeating the message in both words and actions.[27] Without both financial and human resources devoted to enacting sustainable behaviors, organizations will "look green" (to impress others) but not "be green."[28] It is a matter of debate whether the government should provide financial incentives for organizations going green, or impose formal penalties for not going green.

I-O psychology can facilitate organizational sustainability efforts. For example, I-O psychologists provide their expertise in the recruitment and hiring of employees who can contribute to an organization's "eco-friendly" business practices.[29] In addition, employees can be educated on how they can influence waste reduction and save energy and resources, such as by recycling, turning lights off, and fully shutting down computers. I-O psychologists' research on training and development, motivation, and many other areas are key in these efforts (and topics covered in later chapters). Not surprisingly, some scholars have noted that I-O psychology and environmental sustainability in organizations are a natural partnership.[30]

Corporate social responsibility The obligation of organizations to take an active part in improving society.

The term for this area of inquiry is **corporate social responsibility**, a topic that has been previously examined in other disciplines, but is a relatively newer area for I-O psychology. Sustainability is the intersection of economic ("profit"), social ("people"), and environmental ("planet") goals, as shown in Figure 3-2.[31] I-O psychologists must find a way to strike a critical and delicate balance among the three.[32] The involvement of I-O psychology in corporate social responsibility is consistent with the Code of Ethics of psychologists—to promote human welfare. It is also consistent with the principles of humanitarian work psychology discussed above.

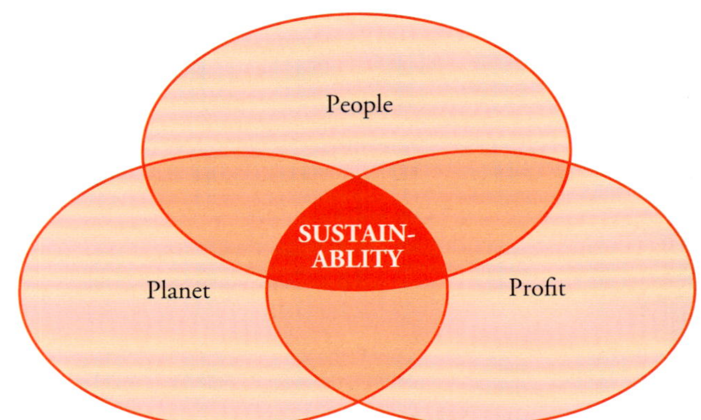

Figure 3-2 *The triple bottom line (profit, planet, and people) needed for environmental sustainability*

Adapted from *The triple bottom line*, by A. W. Savitz and K. Weber (2006). Reproduced with permission of Jossey-Bass via Copyright Clearance Center.

The Legal Context

The final work context that we will discuss is the legal context. There was a time when employees were at the mercy of their employers. Employers could hire, fire, and everything in between as they saw fit. As the country has evolved, so too have the laws that govern us. Within the realm of work, employment laws primarily exist to protect workers from wrongdoing by their employers.

In this section, we discuss the legal context for personnel decisions, with a focus on federal laws impacting work and workplaces in the United States. There are two caveats that must be noted before we begin this discussion. First, the employment law arena is vast and complex. A complete coverage of this area is far beyond the scope of this chapter (or book). Our focus is on a few select areas that we deem most important for students of I-O psychology. By necessity, there will be important legislation omitted from our coverage. The second caveat is that it is important to note that laws are constantly changing and are often quite complicated and vary by jurisdiction. Thus, the information provided herein should be considered a very basic primer of the legislation as of 2021, with an understanding that legal counsel should be consulted as needed for any employment law issue.

Workplace Discrimination

Civil Rights Act of 1964. For the first 60 years or so of I-O psychology, there was virtually no connection between psychologists and the legal community. Psychological tests were developed, administered, and interpreted by psychologists, and as a profession, psychologists governed themselves. However, during the late 1950s and early 1960s, the United States was swept up in the civil rights movement. At that time, civil rights concerned primarily the conditions under which Blacks lived and worked in this country. Blacks were denied access to colleges, restaurants, and jobs—in short, their civil rights were denied. Under the administration of President John F. Kennedy and President Lyndon Johnson, steps were taken to improve this aspect of American society. In 1964, the Civil Rights Act, a major piece of federal legislation aimed at reducing discrimination in all walks of life, was passed. The section of the law most relevant to I-O psychology is Title VII, which pertains to employment discrimination. In essence, this was the message: Blacks were grossly underemployed throughout the country in both private- and public-sector jobs, particularly in jobs above the lower levels of organizations.

To reduce discrimination in employment (one of the mandates of the Civil Rights Act), the federal government began to intervene in employment decisions; in essence, it would monitor the entire procedure to ensure fairness within the workplace. Thus, personnel decisions became deeply embedded within a legal context in the 1960s. Previously, the federal government had regulated *things* (e.g., food and drugs), but with this Act it regulated *behavior*.[33] The Civil Rights Act was expanded to cover other groups of people as well. In fact, five characteristics were identified for protection: race, sex, religion, color, and national origin.* People of all races, sexes, religions, etc., are afforded equal protection. They are referred to as **protected classes**, also called protected groups. The Pregnancy Discrimination Act of 1978 amended Title VII to provide further protection for women from discrimination on the basis of pregnancy. The Civil Rights Act pertains to all personnel functions, including selection, training, promotion, retention, and performance appraisal. Furthermore, any methods (tests, interviews, assessment centers, etc.) used for making personnel decisions are subject to the same legal standards (see The Lighter Side of I-O Psychology: *Plans for Breeding*). As part of the Civil Rights Act, the Equal Employment Opportunity Commission (EEOC) was established to investigate charges of prohibited employment practices.

Protected class
A designation for members of society who are granted legal status by virtue of a demographic characteristic, such as race, sex, national origin, color, religion, age, and disability.

Title VII specifies several unlawful employment practices, including the following:

- Employers may not fail or refuse to hire, or discharge, anyone based on their status in one of the protected classes.
- Employers may not separate or classify employees or applicants so as to deprive anyone of employment opportunities on the basis of any of the protected classes.
- Employment advertising or training opportunities may not indicate preferences for any group, as witnessed, for example, in separate classified advertisements for "Help Wanted—Men" and "Help Wanted—Women."

---

*Some scholars believe adding "sex" to the list of legally protected groups was a tactical gambit meant to decrease the likelihood that the Civil Rights Act would be voted into law. Other scholars believe its inclusion was sincere in addressing the legal rights of women. The interested reader is encouraged to examine both sides of this issue.[34]

Title VII covers all employers in the public and private sectors with at least 15 employees, including government agencies, the federal government, and labor unions. Americans working abroad for American companies are also covered. Exempt from Title VII requirements include Indian tribes, individuals denied employment due to national security reasons, publicly elected officials and their personal staff, and bona fide tax-exempt private clubs.

Bona fide occupational qualification (BFOQ) An exception to Title VII that allows in very rare circumstances for organizations to make decisions on the basis of sex, religion, or national origin due to business necessity.

A special caveat to Title VII is a defense known as a **bona fide occupational qualification**, or **BFOQ**. In some cases, an organization may be able make decisions on the basis of protected group status when such a designation is "reasonably necessary to the operation of that particular business or enterprise." For example, the Catholic Church may wish to hire Catholics, and not members of other religions. A court may find this acceptable for a priest, but not for a custodian. That is, the Catholic Church could argue that only a Catholic could effectively practice and preach Catholicism, but it would have a difficult time arguing that only a Catholic custodian could effectively clean the church. It is important to note that under Title VII, race and color can never be BFOQs. In addition, a BFOQ defense due to customer or client preference

The Lighter Side of I-O Psychology: *Plans for Breeding?*

The legal protections that are afforded to employees is no laughing matter. We have these protections in place in an effort to rectify historic problems and ensure everybody has a fair chance at everything life has to offer. With this in mind, there are some questions that shouldn't be asked in the employment process, because the answers may reveal that the individual is a member of a protected class, and that information may be used against them. As such, it is recommended that organizations avoid questions such as, "When did you graduate from high school?", "What is your native language?", and "What church do you attend?" as those potentially innocent questions could lead to discrimination based on age, national origin, and religion, respectively. Even questions that are meant to be "humorous" could get you in trouble. For example, one of the textbook authors was a part of a selection process in which a female applicant was asked, "What are your plans for breeding?" Life tip: You should never ask a woman this question—and especially not ask it as part of a selection process. And yet, it happened. The applicant was dumbfounded by the question, considering she didn't raise Golden Retrievers and the job was for a faculty position at a university.

Not all weird questions are legally problematic, however, and instead are meant to be ice-breakers, indicators of creativity, demonstrations of problem solving abilities, or some other key attribute deemed important by the organization. With that, we present you some silly interview questions that real organizations have asked.[35]

"What do you think of garden gnomes?" (asked by Trader Joe's)

"Why are manholes round?" (asked by UBS)

"If you were a tree, what kind of tree would you be, and why?" (asked by Walgreens)

"How many square feet of pizza are eaten in the U.S. each year?" (asked by Goldman Sachs)

"You've been given an elephant. You can't give it away or sell it. What would you do with the elephant?" (asked by ConnectWise)

Just remember—if you're going to ask a weird or funny question as part of a selection process, make sure you're not being inappropriate—legally or otherwise!

of a certain protected class is unlikely to be successful. Just because customers might expect their massage therapist to be female or expect their salesperson to be male, employers are generally not permitted to rely solely on such stereotypical assumptions when making employment decisions. Thus, it should be clear that while courts allow BFOQs as exceptions to Title VII, they define BFOQs narrowly and allow their usage as a defense only for very good reasons.

Consider This...

In 2016, the producers of the hit Broadway rap musical *Hamilton* placed ads in theater industry publications that called for "NON-WHITE men and women, ages 20s to 30s."[36] The rationale was that the musical is an artistic reimagining of history in which central historical figures (including Alexander Hamilton and Aaron Burr) were minorities. If race can never be a BFOQ, how do casting directors for actors and actresses get away with specifying these attributes? The short answer is they don't. As noted in the findings of one court case, "A film director casting a movie about African-American slaves may not exclude Caucasians from the auditions, but the director may limit certain roles to persons having the physical characteristics of African-Americans" (Ferrill v. Parker Group, Inc., 1999).[37] Following from this, the producers of *Hamilton* amended their ads to be in line with other ads vetted through Actors Equity, the actors' union, which include the qualifier, "Performers of all ethnic and racial backgrounds are encouraged to attend (the auditions)." With this modification, the issue was dropped. Nevertheless, some scholars note that this is a tricky area, particularly for creative works, as the First Amendment (which includes the right to free speech) may override Title VII in artistic works where race is integral to the story or artistic purpose.[38] What do you think? Which should prevail in such cases—the First Amendment or Title VII of the Civil Rights Act. Why?

Sexual harassment Unwelcome sexual advances, requests for sexual favors, and other verbal or physical conduct of a sexual nature that creates an intimidating, hostile, or offensive work environment.

***Quid pro quo* harassment** A legal classification of sexual harassment in which specified organizational rewards are offered in exchange for sexual favors.

The Civil Rights Act provides additional safeguards for individuals with regard to how they are treated. Title VII protects individuals from harassment at work. While all protected classes are sheltered from harassment, the form that has received the greatest attention is that of sexual harassment. The EEOC defines **sexual harassment** as:

> unwelcome sexual advances, requests for sexual favors, and other verbal or physical conduct of a sexual nature when submission to or rejection of this conduct explicitly or implicitly affects an individual's employment, unreasonably interferes with an individual's work performance, or creates an intimidating, hostile, or offensive work environment.

In this definition are the two kinds of sexual harassment actionable under federal law: *quid pro quo* harassment and hostile-environment harassment. ***Quid pro quo* harassment** occurs when sexual compliance is made mandatory for promotion, favors, or retaining one's job. **Hostile-environment harassment** is less blatant than *quid pro quo* and refers to conditions in the workplace that are regarded as offensive, such as unwanted touching and off-color jokes. More than 6,500 sexual harassment complaints were filed with the EEOC in 2020; $65.3 million dollars was paid in settlements.[39] Although most cases of sexual harassment involve women charging complaints against men, the reverse does occur (16.8% of the complaints filed in 2020

Hostile-environment harassment
A legal classification of sexual harassment in which individuals regard conditions in the workplace (such as unwanted touching or off-color jokes) as offensive.

were from men). In addition, in 1998 the U.S. Supreme Court upheld same-sex sexual harassment.

The EEOC treats situations slightly differently depending on who is doing the harassment. If the harasser is a supervisor, the employer would be liable unless it can prove it had an effective policy against harassment and the employee being harassed failed to use its complaint procedures. If the harasser is a coworker or non-employee over whom the employer has control (such as a client), the employer is only liable for sexual harassment if the employer knew or should have known of the harassment and failed to respond appropriately. Not surprisingly, the EEOC advises that organizations provide sexual harassment training to educate their employees on what sexual harassment entails and clearly communicate that such harassment will not be tolerated.

Age Discrimination in Employment Act. In 1967, the Age Discrimination in Employment Act (ADEA) was passed, which extends the protections guaranteed by the Civil Rights Act to people aged 40 and over. As such, age (40 years and over) is considered a protected class alongside race, sex, religion, national origin, color, and pregnancy.

The ADEA applies to employers with 20 or more employees. Independent contractors, elected officials and their appointees, and U.S. citizens employed abroad with foreign corporations are not covered under the ADEA. In addition, active duty and reserve members of the armed forces are not covered by ADEA, but civilians working within military departments are protected. Because of the ADEA, companies are not allowed to enforce mandatory retirement ages for all employees. Mandatory retirement ages can be enforced, however, in some circumstances. For example, retirement ages may be imposed when there are bona fide reasons for retirement (such as public safety concerns). Furthermore, mandatory retirement may be enforced when the individuals being asked to retire are "bona fide executives" or "high policymakers," in which case an employer can impose a compulsory retirement age of 65 as long as the executive has

Consider This...

A common question is whether the ADEA might protect younger workers from "reverse discrimination." The answer is no. The ADEA does not protect relatively young workers, who are under 40 years of age, from discrimination based on an employer's preference of older workers. The reason that older workers are protected is because of the potential for ageism, or discrimation based on one's age. And it does appear to be needed. A survey of 3,900 people over the age of 45 found that two-thirds of respondents have seen or experienced age discrimination on the job.[40] Yet some scholars argue that ageism is actually a bigger issue for younger workers, a concept referred to as "youngism."[41] A series of studies revealed that young adults were described more harshly than older adults, and more harshly than how those older adults were perceived at the same age. While young adults were praised as being tech-savvy, ambitious, and intelligent, they were also repeatedly criticized as being entitled, coddled, and disrespectful. Do you believe the ADEA should be revised? Why or why not? If you believe a revision is needed, what would you recommend?

been in their position for at least two years prior to the retirement date and receives annual retirement benefits of $44,000 or more.

To seek legal remedy for age discrimination or retaliation that violates the ADEA, an individual must file a charge with the EEOC within 180 days from the date of the alleged violation. The EEOC will investigate the charge of discrimination or retaliation, and if it determines there is merit to the charge, it will attempt to foster conciliation between the employee and the employer. Regardless of the EEOC's determination, after 60 days have passed, the employee may bring a civil action in court.

Americans with Disabilities Act. In 1990, the Americans with Disabilities Act (ADA) was signed into law by President George H. W. Bush. It was followed by its successor, the ADA Amendments Act in 2008. The ADA is the most important piece of legislation ever enacted for persons with disabilities, with disability becoming another protected group.[42] A *disability* is defined by the ADA as a physical or mental impairment that an individual has (or is regarded as having) that:

- substantially limits one or more major life activities including but not limited to: seeing, hearing, eating, standing, walking, sleeping, reading, thinking, learning, speaking, breathing, bending, lifting, caring for oneself, concentrating, communicating, working, and performing manual tasks; or
- substantially limits one or more major bodily functions, including but not limited to: normal cell growth, functions of the immune system, digestive, endocrine, bowel, bladder, neurological, brain, respiratory, circulatory, and reproductive functions.

The ADA extends to employees with invisible disabilities, such as Attention Deficit Hyperactivity Disorder (ADHD) and psychological disorders, such as Post-Traumatic Stress Disorder (PTSD).[43] Impairments that are episodic or in remission are also considered to be disabilities under the ADA if they limit one or more major life activities when the impairments are active. In addition, employees with temporary disabilities are covered, which could include pregnancy- and childbirth-related medical conditions and restrictions (though pregnancy itself is not an impairment within the meaning of the ADA and therefore is never on its own a disability). The challenge to employers under the ADA is that they must choose solutions that accommodate an applicant's disability yet still permit a valid assessment of that applicant's qualifications for the job.

An employment test that screens out an individual with a disability must be job-related and consistent with business necessity. The law states that employers must provide persons with disabilities *reasonable accommodation* in being evaluated for employment and in the conduct of their jobs. Employers are required to modify or accommodate their business practices in a reasonable fashion to meet the needs of persons with disabilities. This can include providing elevators or ramps for access to buildings for those who cannot walk or providing readers for those who have dyslexia or are blind. The fundamental premise of the law is that individuals with disabilities can effectively contribute to the workforce, and they cannot be discriminated against in employment decisions because of their disabilities.

Coverage for the ADA mirrors that of Title VII (e.g., employers with at least 15 employees). Worthy of note is that while rehabilitated drug users are covered, individuals currently engaging in the use of illegal drugs are not covered. This issue becomes

Consider This...

In 2001, the U.S. Supreme Court ruled on the case of *Martin v. PGA Tour.* Martin was a professional golfer who suffered from a physical disability in his right leg that restricted his ability to walk a golf course. He asked the PGA of America for permission to ride a golf cart during tour competition. The PGA refused on the grounds that riding in a cart would give Martin an unfair advantage over other golfers who are compelled by PGA rules to walk the course. Martin sued the PGA for the right to use a golf cart under the ADA, claiming that his riding in a cart was a reasonable accommodation the PGA could make in his pursuit of earning a living as a golfer. Furthermore, Martin contended it would not be an "undue burden" (or hardship) on the PGA to allow Martin to ride. The U.S. Supreme Court ruled in favor of Martin, saying that making shots was an essential job function but walking between shots was not. What reactions do you think the PGA may have received from other golfers? How would you recommend the PGA handle potential concerns from other golfers, keeping privacy concerns in mind?

tricky in situations where drug use may be legal in some locations but not in others (e.g., the use of marijuana is legal in some states but not nationally). Regardless, impairment is key, and the ADA makes it clear that both drugs and alcohol can be prohibited within the workplace at the organization's discretion, and that usage of such substances can result in disciplinary actions. Thus, while organizations cannot discriminate against an individual suffering from alcoholism, they can require that individuals do not consume alcohol at work or arrive at work intoxicated. Such behaviors can legally constitute grounds for dismissal, despite the nature of alcoholism as a disease.

An individual who has experienced a violation of the ADA must generally file a charge with the EEOC prior to filing a lawsuit in federal court. Certain filing deadlines, generally ranging from 180 days to 300 days depending on the location and circumstances, apply to the filing of an EEOC charge. In addition, limitations on compensatory and punitive damages may exist depending on the size and nature of the employer.

Adverse impact A type of unfair discrimination in which the result of using a particular personnel selection method has a negative effect on protected group members compared with majority group members. Often contrasted with disparate treatment.

Determining Unfair Discrimination. Through the Civil Rights Act, unfair discrimination may be charged under two legal theories. One is **adverse impact** (also called *disparate impact*), in which discrimination affects various groups (vis-à-vis the protected groups) differently.* This form of discrimination is typically viewed as unintentional and occurs when practices or policies within an organization that were thought to be unbiased result in a disproportionate negative impact on a certain group. Evidence that one group (e.g., women) are less likely to be hired compared to members of another group (e.g., men) is evidence of discrimination against those

*The word "discriminate" is neutral in meaning. It means to differentiate. The purpose of administering employment tests is to discriminate (differentiate) candidates who are more likely to perform well on the job from those who are less likely to do so. Employment laws were enacted to prohibit unfair discrimination—rejecting candidates on the basis of a protected group membership (e.g., race, sex, age, etc.). Over the years of using the word in an employment context, society has gotten linguistically lazy, usually dropping the word "unfair" from the term "unfair discrimination." In contemporary language, "discrimination" has become verbal shorthand for "unfair discrimination." Being consistent with common usage, the term "discrimination" is used in this book to mean "unfair discrimination."

Disparate treatment A type of unfair discrimination in which protected group members are afforded differential employment procedures compared to members of other groups. Often contrasted with adverse impact.

group members. The second theory is **disparate treatment**, which refers to intentional discrimination. Here, there would be evidence that a member of a protected class is treated differently from other members of the protected class (e.g., in the employment process). For example, a certain job might require a moderate amount of physical effort. Because men (on average) have greater physical strength and endurance than women (on average), the employer may assume men are more suitable for this job than women. The employer decides to not take a risk with female applicants and makes them, but not male applicants, complete a test of physical strength as part of the assessment process. Such an assessment process would be deemed a clear case of disparate treatment, as the female and male applicants for the same job are treated differently. Singling out some applicants or employees for different employment procedures constitutes disparate treatment.

Of the two legal bases of discrimination, adverse impact has garnered greater attention among I-O psychologists (see Faces of I-O Psychology: *Eric M. Dunleavy*). As noted, adverse impact exists when employment procedures result in a differential effect between protected minority and majority group members. In *Griggs v. Duke Power Company (1971)*, the U.S. Supreme Court ruled that individuals who bring suit against a company do not have to prove that the company's employment test is unfair; rather, the company has to prove that it is fair. How do organizations do this? A simple rule of thumb was created to operationalize the concept of adverse impact: the "80%" (or "4/5ths") rule. The rule states that adverse impact occurs if the selection ratio (that is, the number of people hired divided by the number of people who apply) for any group of applicants is less than 80% of the selection ratio for another group. Suppose 100 Whites apply for a job and 20 are selected. The selection ratio is thus 20/100, or .20. By multiplying .20 by 80%, we get .16. If fewer than 16% of Black applicants (for example) are hired, the selection test is deemed to produce adverse impact. So if 50 Blacks apply for the job and if at least 8 (50 × .16) Blacks are selected, then the organization has demonstrated that its employment test is fair; if at least 8 Blacks are not selected, however, then the test is deemed unfair because it has been shown to produce adverse impact.

If adverse impact is found to exist, the organization faces two alternatives. One is to demonstrate that the test is a valid (i.e., accurate) predictor of job performance. The second alternative is to use a different test that has no adverse impact (but may also be less valid than a test that does manifest adverse impact). Using less valid measures to reduce adverse impact violates no laws, but as we'll discuss in Chapter 6, doing so comes at the cost of not having the organization be staffed with the most qualified applicants.[44] If adverse impact does not result from using the selection method, then the organization is not required to demonstrate its validity. Obviously, however, it is a sound business decision to make sure a selection method predicts future job performance. A company would always want to know whether its selection method is identifying the best candidates for hire. There are other methods of assessing adverse impact in addition to the 80% rule. What they all have in common, however, is their intent of determining whether a disproportionately large percentage of one group of applicants is rejected for employment compared with another group.

Typically, when the EEOC investigates charges of prohibited employment practices, conciliation and persuasion will be used to eliminate prohibited practices. When there is a conclusion of "just cause" to believe charges of employment discrimination

Faces of I-O Psychology: *Eric M. Dunleavy*

Eric M. Dunleavy

Ph.D. University of Houston

Director, Personnel Selection and Litigation Support Services, DCI Consulting Group

Research interests: Adverse impact measurement, selection procedure development, and validation

Thought leader in personnel selection and equal employment opportunity (EEO) implications; conducts research and testifies in employment discrimination matters

The legal context around making employment decisions in the United States is complex and constantly changing. Organizations on the wrong end of an EEO-related ruling may pay significant damages to victims of discrimination, see lower employee morale, attract fewer qualified applicants, and suffer negative perceptions of organizational image in the court of public opinion. While the use of standardized selection procedures typically decreases the likelihood of intentional discrimination from occurring, there may be risk under a disparate impact theory of discrimination. Under this theory, any facially-neutral procedure can be evaluated to determine whether outcomes meaningfully disadvantage members of a protected group. If there are meaningful differences, the employer must usually demonstrate that the procedure is job-related, often through a validation study, to justify the impact. Even when an employer shows job-relatedness, the plaintiff or EEO agency may be able to show that an equally job-related and less adverse alternative was available and should have been used instead.

This chronology of disparate impact phases can involve important research conducted by I-O psychologists. Examples include statistical analysis of employment outcomes related to adverse impact, various forms of validation and other psychometric research to evaluate job relatedness, reviews of the research literature, report writing, and summarizing research results via testimony. At DCI Consulting Group, I lead a division of I-O psychologists that work on a wide variety of applied research projects for employers across a wide range of industries. We provide our objective expert opinions and let the chips fall where they may.

Being a practitioner in the personnel selection/EEO space is rewarding. I have had the opportunity to conduct research on a wide range of jobs, develop and validate procedures that impact organizations, and help clients understand the strengths and weaknesses of their procedures. I have worked with some of the best and brightest. Like any consulting job, work can also be stressful, especially given the changing nature of EEO. New laws are written, old laws are expanded to protect new classes, and enforcement priorities may change with political administrations. At the core of the EEO context is the basic notion that employers should not make employment decisions based on protected group status or in ways that disadvantage protected group members for no reason. Fortunately for I-O psychologists, selection procedures that are developed and validated using contemporary I-O psychology science and practice are often both valuable to organizations and legally defensible.

are true, the EEOC can file suit in court. If the organization cannot be persuaded to change its employment practices, then the issue is brought before the court for adjudication. Organizations that lose such cases are obligated to pay financial damages to the victims of their employment practices. The financial awards in these cases can be class-action settlements (the individual who is suing represents a class of similar people), back-pay settlements (the organization has to pay a portion of what victims would have earned had they been hired), or both. The courts have granted multi-million-dollar awards in single cases. However, not everyone who fails an employment test automatically gets their day in court. A lawsuit must be predicated on just cause, and the two parties can reach an agreement without resorting to litigation.

Table 3-2 shows 2020 statistics from the EEOC on the number of employment discrimination cases filed in the United States against members of protected classes (race, sex, religion, national origin, color, pregnancy, age, and disability). As can be seen in the table, the three protected groups with the greatest number of cases are disability, race, and sex, respectively. The number of cases that are filed with the EEOC attests that in the 50 years following passage of the Civil Rights Act, we have not eliminated employment discrimination, intentional or otherwise.[45] Additional information about the EEOC can be found at *www.eeoc.gov.*

In 1978, the EEOC published the *Uniform Guidelines on Employee Selection Procedures* for organizations to follow in making employment decisions. The *Guidelines* reflected the prevailing state of scientific knowledge at that time about test validation. Now over 40 years old, it has been argued they are outdated and should either be abolished or revised, because they are based upon scientific knowledge about validity that has since been refuted.[46] Some scholars have asserted the *Guidelines* are now actually a detriment to attaining the employment outcomes they were intended to achieve.[47] It has been argued that the *Guidelines* are not a scientific document.[48] Therefore, it is questionable whether new research advances in the science of validation will inspire a revision of them. The *Guidelines* are a tool of political advocacy; that is, a document designed to effectuate the intent of the Civil Rights Act. At the core of the issue is whether as a nation we desire equal opportunity (i.e., members of every protected group will receive equal consideration to enter all jobs) or equal employment (i.e.,

Table 3-2 *EEOC statistics on employment discrimination (2020)*

Protected Group	Law	# Cases	Monetary Benefits (Millions)
Race	CRA	22,064	$74.8
Sex	CRA	21,398	$153.2
National Origin	CRA	6,377	$26.3
Religion	CRA	2,404	$6.1
Color	CRA	3,562	$8.4
Pregnancy	CRA/PDA	2,698	$15.3
Age	ADEA	14,183	$76.3
Disability	ADA	24,324	$116.0

CRA = Civil Rights Act (1964); ADEA = Age Discrimination in Employment Act; ADA = Americans with Disabilities Act; PDA = Pregnancy Discrimination Act members of every protected group will be represented in all jobs). This distinction is based on values and cannot be resolved by scientific evidence.

In conclusion, issues of employment discrimination are complex. There are no simple answers or easy solutions to resolving these problems. I-O psychologists are not members of the legal community, and thus we are not positioned to solve legal problems.[49] However, I-O psychologists can help the legal system understand how psychological issues (such as test reliability, validity, passing scores, etc.) associated with selection tests can influence employment discrimination.

Affirmative Action. Although not a requirement under the Civil Rights Act, an important concept that is included in the EEOC *Guidelines* is that of affirmative action. **Affirmative action** is a social policy aimed at reducing the effects of prior discrimination. Originally, affirmative action was aimed primarily at the recruitment of new employees—namely, that organizations would take positive (or affirmative) action to bring members of minority groups that had previously been excluded into the workforce.

Affirmative action
A social policy that advocates members of protected groups will be actively recruited and considered for selection in employment.

There are four goals of affirmative action:[50]

1. **Correct present inequities**. If one group has "more than its fair share" of jobs or educational opportunities because of current discriminatory practices, then the goal is to remedy the inequity and eliminate the discriminating practices.
2. **Compensate past inequities**. Even if current practices are not discriminatory, a long history of past discrimination may put members of a minority group at a disadvantage.
3. **Provide role models**. Increasing the frequency of minority group members acting as role models could potentially change the career expectations, educational planning, and job-seeking behavior of younger minority group members.
4. **Promote diversity**. Increasing the minority representation in a student body or workforce may increase the range of ideas, skills, and/or values that can be brought to bear on organizational problems and goals.

As straightforward as these goals may appear, there is great variability in the operational procedures used to pursue the goals. The most passive interpretation is to follow procedures that strictly pertain to recruitment, such as extensive advertising in sources most likely to reach minority group members. A stronger interpretation of the goals is *preferential selection*: organizations will select minority group members from the applicant pool if they are judged to have substantially equal qualifications with nonminority applicants. The most extreme interpretation is to set aside a specific number of job openings or promotions for members of specific protected groups. This is referred to as the *quota interpretation* of affirmative action: organizations will staff themselves with explicit percentages of employees representing the various protected groups, based on local or national norms, within a specific time frame. Quotas are legally imposed on organizations as a severe corrective measure for prolonged inequities in the composition of the workforce. Quotas are not the typical interpretation of affirmative action. There is a common belief that affirmative action involves the abandonment of merit as an employment principle. Rather than presuming that affirmative action compels organizations to hire employees with less merit, affirmative action programs should be regarded as an attempt to get qualified employees who are representative of their proportion in the relevant labor market. In a landmark case involving such an issue, *Bakke v. University of California (1978)*, a White applicant sued a medical school after being denied admission through a process that had racial quotas. The public university argued that diversity was a legitimate objective and that legal protections based on race were designed to protect "minorities who have been historically excluded from the full benefits of American life." The U.S. Supreme Court rejected a quota system in university admissions but allowed the consideration of race as a factor in its admissions policy.

Affirmative action has been hotly debated by proponents and critics. In particular, over the past 30 years, the subject of affirmative action has been a major political issue.[51] Criticism of the quota interpretation in particular has been strident, claiming the strategy ignores merit or ability. Under a quota strategy, it is alleged that the goal is merely "to get the numbers right." Proponents of affirmative action believe it is needed to offset the effects of years of past discrimination against specific protected groups. Several states have reversed their commitment to affirmative action in the admission of students into their universities. Such admissions policies could result in less representation of some minority groups in the student population.

Has affirmative action been effective in meeting national goals of prosperity in employment for all people? Some experts questioned its overall effectiveness, asserting that unemployment rates are much higher and average incomes much lower now for some groups (particularly Blacks) than they were at the inception of affirmative action more than 40 years ago.[52] Although there appears to be consensus that affirmative action has not produced its intended goals,[53] there is considerable reluctance to discard it altogether. President Bill Clinton stated the nation should "amend it, not end it." It is feared that its absence may produce outcomes more socially undesirable than have occurred with its presence, however flawed it might be. Affirmative action policies are beneficial in that they emphasize outcomes rather than intentions, and they establish monitoring systems that ensure accountability.[54]

Several studies have shown that individuals viewed as having been hired because of affirmative action were not believed to have had their qualifications given much weight in the hiring process.[55] The stigma of incompetence was found to be fairly robust, and it is unclear whether the stigma would dissipate in the face of disconfirming information about the individuals' presumed incompetence. Subtle differences in the way jobs are advertised reflect a company's commitment to affirmative action and influence the attitudes of Black applicants to pursue employment with a company.[56] Thus, it appears that minority applicants are sensitive to the manner in which a company projects its stance on minority recruitment and selection. Researchers have also shown there are differences within minority group populations with regard to their support for affirmative action.[57] Blacks were found to support affirmative action more strongly than Hispanics. A thorough explanation of the benefits of affirmative action by organizations can be effective in creating positive attitudes, as opposed to relying on passive acceptance of the supposed need for affirmative action.[58]

In June 2003, the U.S. Supreme Court ruled on two major cases involving affirmative action. Both involved the admission of students into the University of Michigan. The first case, *Gratz v. Bollinger*, challenged the process used by the University of

Consider This...

Wardell Connerly

Wardell Connerly, founder and chairman of the American Civil Rights Institute, is an outspoken critic of racial and gender preferences in selection decisions. He contends that affirmative action creates the stigma of incompetence among beneficiaries of its practices. Connerly offered the following opinion on the perception of affirmative action by the general public: "Every day that I walk into class I have this feeling that people are wondering whether I'm there because I got in through affirmative action. The reality is the stigma exists. It exists, and they know it exists" (Evans 2003, p. 121).[59] Do you think that Connerly's views reflect those of a lot of other individuals? To what extent do you think the views are justified, if at all? What do you think could help alleviate Connerly's worries?

Michigan in admitting students into the undergraduate program. As an attempt to comply with the intent of affirmative action (increase minority representation), the University of Michigan assigned points to all the variables examined in the student's application, such as points for SAT scores, high school grade point average, extracurricular activities, and so on. For admission, 100 points were needed (out of 150 possible points). The university automatically assigned 20 points (or one-fifth of the total needed for admission) if a candidate was an "under-represented minority race." The Supreme Court ruled against the university, deciding that giving points for membership in certain races was unconstitutional. The second case, *Grutter v. Bollinger*, challenged the process used by the University of Michigan in admitting students into the law school. The law school did consider race in making selection decisions but did not use any point system to evaluate candidates for admission. Race could be considered a "plus" in each candidate's file, yet the entire selection system was flexible enough to consider the particular qualifications of each candidate. The Supreme Court ruled in favor of the University of Michigan's law school admissions system. If we consider both cases in their totality, it appears the Supreme Court recognized the legitimate need to have a broad representation of all groups in those candidates selected for admission, but it opposed the general practice that creates two groups of candidates based exclusively on group membership (in the *Gratz* case, those candidates who did and did not get points on the basis of their race).

The two opposing rulings by the Supreme Court illustrate the complexity of the issues raised by affirmative action. On the one hand, we recognize that society will be better served by having all segments of our population enjoying the benefits of admission into school or employment. On the other hand, it is not fair or lawful to explicitly reward some applicants (and in effect, punish others) for their particular group membership. Perhaps more than any other country, the United States is populated by an amalgam of citizens who (with the exception of Native Americans) originally came to this country from someplace else. Given the extreme diversity of people from various racial, cultural, and religious backgrounds, conflicts over who gets to participate in social benefits (education and employment) are perhaps inevitable. Affirmative action is an attempt to recognize the paramount need for all segments of society to be fairly represented in receiving these benefits. Nevertheless, there is ambiguity and disagreement over how best to achieve these goals. It is plausible for a law school with 4,000 applicants to scrutinize all or most of the applicants. It is implausible for an undergraduate program with 50,000 applicants to do likewise.[60]

Workplace Health and Safety

The need to be concerned about workplace health is evidenced by sobering statistics about work-related deaths, accidents, and diseases. As of 2017, it was estimated that 2.78 million workers worldwide die annually (corresponding to 7,500 deaths per day!) from workplace injuries and illnesses.[61] In addition, they estimate that 317 million work-related accidents occur on the job annually (153 every 15 seconds!). The decade of the 1970s witnessed the passage of laws in the U.S. designed to reduce the frequency and severity of workplace accidents and illnesses by creating enforceable health and safety standards.[62] Most notably, the Occupational Safety and Health Act of 1970 established guidelines to ensure employers provide their employees a workplace that is free from recognized hazards to health and safety, such as exposure to toxic chemicals or infectious materials, unsanitary conditions, excessive noise levels, extreme temperatures, or mechanical dangers.

To establish clear standards for workplace health and safety, the Occupational Safety and Health Act also created the National Institute for Occupational Safety and Health (NIOSH) as the research institution for the Occupational Safety and Health Administration (OSHA). OSHA is a division of the U.S. Department of Labor that oversees the administration of the Act and enforces standards in all 50 states. Example OSHA standards include requirements to provide protection from falls (such as through a safety harness or lifeline), provide safety equipment (usually free of charge), and train workers about the hazards they may encounter and how to protect themselves. OSHA may initiate workplace investigations without advance notice to ensure worker safety. Such investigations may also be triggered by worker complaints regarding health and/or safety issues. In such cases, workers are safeguarded by **whistleblower laws** stipulating that employers may not retaliate against employees for exercising their rights and filing a complaint (i.e., "blowing the whistle").

Whistleblower laws Anti-retaliation stipulations that employers are prohibited from taking any adverse action against employees for filing complaints or raising awareness of dangerous or illegal activities.

The Occupational Safety and Health Act applies to most private sector employers and federal agencies. The Act does not apply to individuals who are self-employed, immediate family members of farm employers, or workplace hazards that are regulated by another federal agency (such as the Mine Safety and Health Administration or the Department of Energy).

Family and Medical Leave

In 1993, President Bill Clinton signed the Family and Medical Leave Act (FMLA) into law. As a result, eligible employees are afforded up to 12 weeks of unpaid leave during any 12-month period for childbirth, adoption, foster care placement, or care for oneself or an immediate family member (child, spouse, parent) for a serious health condition. To receive FMLA benefits, one must have been with their company for at least 12 months and worked at least 1,250 hours during the past year. The law only applies to businesses that employ at least 50 employees within a 75-mile radius.

Many I-O psychologists have voiced strong criticism about how far behind the

United States is compared to other industrialized nations regarding laws surrounding family leave. For example, critics have noted that, whereas all other industrialized nations have some sort of mandated paid leave for the birth or adoption of a child, the United States has no such law.[63] Other nations provide new parents with paid leaves for up to 14 weeks (and in some cases, longer). Indeed, in Europe and Japan, maternity leave is state-supported until children reach school age. The lack of laws providing for paid leave is particularly problematic given FMLA's strict eligibility requirements, and the simple fact that frequently, employees are not financially secure enough to go unpaid for an extended period of time.[64] Time will tell whether the United States catches up with other parts of the world on these matters (see COVID-19 and I-O Psychology: *Families First Coronavirus Response Act*).

COVID-19 and I-O Psychology: *Families First Coronavirus Response Act*

On March 18, 2020, the Families First Coronavirus Response Act (FFCRA) was signed into law. FFCRA created the Emergency Paid Sick Leave Act and the Emergency Family and Medical Leave Expansion Act to help protect families and workers during the COVID-19 outbreak. Specifically, the Emergency Paid Sick Leave Act mandated that private employers with fewer than 500 employees and some public employers had to pay sick leave of up to 80 hours, or approximately 10 days, to employees who needed to take leave for certain reasons related to COVID-19. The Emergency Family and Medical Leave Expansion Act gave employees (those eligible under FMLA) an additional 12 weeks of family leave (10 weeks paid at two-thirds of their regular wages) to care for a child whose school was closed or whose childcare provider was unavailable due to COVID-19.

The benefits provided by FFRCA ended on December 31, 2020. As it was clear that the pandemic was not over, the American Rescue Plan Act (ARPA) went into effect April 1, 2021, and extended tax credits created by the FFCRA through September 30, 2021. The ARPA also expanded the qualifying reasons to use emergency paid sick leave and emergency family and medical leave (e.g., to include paid leave to get the COVID-19 vaccine or recover from side effects associated with the vaccine).

The FFCRA and ARPA were enacted to ensure that employees could take the time they needed to protect their own health and the health of their families and community members, while preventing their loss of employment and income for doing so. However, critics pointed out that excluding businesses with more than 500 employees from any of the paid leave provisions meant that many of the most vulnerable workers (such as grocery store chain employees and employees of hospitals) were not covered, despite being considered essential workers and being at risk of contagion every time they went to work.[65] In addition, employers were allowed to exempt additional employees from the paid leave, including health care providers and emergency responders, both of which were defined so broadly that many workers were at risk of being excluded.

The COVID-19 pandemic demonstrated that there are times when the government may need to intervene on behalf of its citizens. However, the need for such policies likely exists outside of the pandemic, and is the main reason that many I-O psychologists advocate for federally-mandated paid leave programs[66]—ideally ones that don't have expirations dates like FFCRA and ARPA did.

Child Labor

The International Labour Organization (ILO), an agency of the United Nations established in 1919 as part of the Treaty of Versailles, was created because of a desire to create better working conditions and stop exploitation of workers globally. As part of their mission of advancing social justice, the ILO created recommendations for governments with regard to children in the workplace. The ILO reported in 2017 that there were 168 million children worldwide engaged in child labor, many in hazardous jobs. Child labor refers to exploitative economic activities carried out by persons under 15 years of age. As part of their efforts to abolish forced or compulsory work, particularly for children, the ILO has recommended that governments prohibit children from engaging in hazardous work, including work that: exposes them to physical, psychological, or sexual abuse; is underground, under water, at dangerous heights, or in confined spaces; involves dangerous machinery, equipment, and tools; and/or is in unhealthy environments or exceptionally difficult conditions.[67]

Child labor The pattern of compelling children under the age of 15 to perform labor that is harmful to their overall health and/or psychological well-being.

Within the United States, the Fair Labor Standards Act (FLSA) of 1938 authorized federal **child labor** provisions to ensure that young workers do not engage in work that may endanger their health, well-being, or education. For example, the FLSA bars individuals under the age of 18 from working in hazardous occupations such as coal mining, demolition and excavation operations, and jobs that may lead to exposure to radioactive substances. The FLSA places additional restrictions for youth under the age of 16, such as restrictions in work hours (e.g., they may work no more than three hours on a school day and no more than eight hours on a non-school day), though there are exceptions. For example, if an individual has graduated from high school or has been permanently expelled from school, then these work hour restrictions don't apply, since the purpose of the law is to protect youths' educational opportunities. In addition, FLSA restrictions do not apply to adolescents employed by their parents in non-hazardous jobs, employed as performers (such as theater performers), employed in newspaper delivery, or engaged in their own business undertakings (e.g., mowing lawns or babysitting on a casual basis).

Consider This...

Despite criminal and civil penalties for organizations that willfully violate the FLSA, violations are not uncommon. For example, it has only been since 1998 that the FLSA has allowed 17-year-olds to drive, with restrictions, as part of their job. Despite the fact that the FLSA had banned driving for young workers, between 1980 and 1989, 33% of vehicle deaths at work occurred while a youth under age 17 was driving.[68] Similarly, a survey of adolescent workers in North Carolina found a considerable number of FLSA work hour violations, including two-thirds of adolescents under 16 working more than the allowable three hours on a school day and over half working after 7pm on a school night.[69] Why do you think these violations occur? Do you think most employers are willfully violating these restrictions? Or do you think that the employers are ignorant of the law? Do you think most adolescents are willfully violating the laws or are they ignorant of them? Who is to blame for violations—the employers or the employees? Why?

While child labor is relatively rare (and illegal in most circumstances) in the United States, it is not illegal in many other countries, and some U.S. companies utilize child labor to make their products in developing countries. Child workers typically are found in agriculture, working long hours, sometimes under inhumane and hazardous conditions for little or no pay. In its most extreme form, the exploitation of working children takes the form of slavery or forced labor. Children's work may be pledged by parents for payment of a debt, the children may be kidnapped and imprisoned in brothels or sweatshops, or they may be given away or sold by families. Indeed, in 2016 the ILO estimated that 11.5 million children worldwide were forced to work in slave-like conditions as domestic servants in private homes.[70] It is estimated that the working and living conditions are particularly bad for child domestic workers, with children working 10–12 hours a day for 6–7 days a week, with short breaks, meager pay, and a lack of proper nutrition and access to education. Furthermore, the child workers, who are employed in homes where having servants is a sign of social status, are sometimes sexually or physically abused.

While the ILO has made headway in abolishing child labor, and the FLSA has provided protections within the United States, much remains to be done to curtail the problem of the exploitation of child workers worldwide. It is unlikely that the subject of child labor will become a dominant issue among I-O psychologists, in part because of its inherent social repulsiveness. However, it underscores one of the major reasons we work: our services have economic and instrumental value. As adults we have the free will to decide how and where we will offer our services to enhance our economic standing in life. Children, on the other hand, do not possess this free will. They are compelled to work to enhance the economic standing of others.

Chapter Review

Key Terms

Departmentalization
Specialization
Chain of command
Unity of command
Centralization
Span of control
Formalization
Humanitarian work psychology
Diversity
Equity
Inclusion
Nepotism
Corporate social responsibility
Protected class
Bona fide occupational qualification (BFOQ)
Sexual harassment
***Quid pro quo* harassment**
Hostile-environment harassment
Adverse impact
Disparate treatment
Affirmative action
Whistleblower laws
Child labor

Questions for Review

1. How does an organization's structural context impact how employees behave? What are the six contexts discussed and how does each influence work? Why does organizational structure matter to employees?
2. What are the two social contexts for work?
3. Why are I-O psychologists involved in humanitarian work psychology?
4. What are diversity, inclusion, and equity? How do they differ from one another? Why are they each important in work?
5. What are the environmental contexts of work?
6. Why is it important to understand culture with regard to the environmental context?
7. How can I-O psychologists influence sustainability efforts?
8. What are the legal contexts of work? How do laws impact how work is done? What organizations (governmental and non-governmental) have been involved in work legislation?
9. What is the difference between "discrimination" and "unfair discrimination?"
10. Why were the Civil Rights Act of 1964 and Title VII so pivotal to work in the U.S.?
11. What are the protected classes?
12. By EEOC definition, what is sexual harassment? What are the steps necessary to file a harassment claim?
13. What is ageism? What Act made age discrimination illegal? What reasons would an organization have for discriminating against older workers?
14. What is the Americans with Disabilities Act? Why was this act important?
15. How does the EEOC determine if "unfair discrimination" has occurred?
16. What is affirmative action? Why do supporters like it? Why do detractors dislike it?
17. How is workplace health and safety in the U.S. enforced?
18. What is FMLA? Who qualifies for FMLA under current law? How were benefits enhanced during the COVID-19 pandemic for employees needing to take time off from their work?
19. What is the status of child labor laws in the U.S.? How do they vary? How are the laws violated? What is the status of child labor laws outside of the U.S.?

CHAPTER 4

Criteria: Standards for Decision Making

Chapter Outline

Social Media and I-O Psychology: *Criteria for "5 Star" Organizations*

Conceptual Versus Actual Criteria

Criterion Deficiency, Relevance, and Contamination

Work Analysis

Sources of Work Information

The Lighter Side of I-O Psychology: *Don't Be a Sucker*

Work Analytic Procedures

How to Collect Work Analytic Information

Managerial Work Analysis

Uses of Work Analytic Information

Evaluating Work Analytic Methods

Competency Modeling

Performance Criteria

Major Performance Criteria

COVID-19 and I-O Psychology: *Working While Sick*

Faces of I-O Psychology: *Lawrence Houston III*

Dynamic Performance Criteria

Chapter Review

Learning Objectives

- Describe the distinction between conceptual and actual criteria.
- Discuss the meaning of criterion deficiency, relevance, and contamination.
- Summarize the purpose of work analysis and the various methods of conducting one.
- Explain the major criteria of job performance examined by I-O psychologists.
- Discuss the concept of dynamic criteria.

How do you decide which class to take? Do you decide based on whether it fulfills a requirement for your degree? Do you decide based on who teaches the course? Does it matter what time the class is taught? How do you decide which restaurant to eat at if you go out, or which hotel to stay in when you go on a vacation? What helps you determine which books you check out from the library or which jobs you apply to for employment? How do you judge one class or restaurant or book or job as "good," versus another one as "bad"? We make judgments all the time in our lives. When making those judgments, we use specific criteria of interest to us.

Criteria
Standards used to help make evaluative judgments.

Criteria (the plural of *criterion*) are best defined as evaluative standards; they are used as reference points in making judgments. We may not be consciously aware of the criteria that affect our judgments, but they do exist. We use different criteria to evaluate different kinds of objects or people; that is, we use different standards to determine what makes a good (or bad) movie, dinner, ball game, friend, spouse, or teacher. In the context of I-O psychology, criteria are most important for defining the "goodness" of employees, programs, and units in the organization as well as the organization itself. When you and some of your associates disagree in your evaluations of something, what is the cause? Chances are good the disagreement is caused by one of two types of criterion-related problems. For example, take the case of rating Professor Jones as a teacher. One student thinks he is a good teacher; another disagrees. The first student defines "goodness in teaching" as (1) preparedness, (2) course relevance, and (3) clarity of instruction. In the eyes of the first student, Professor Jones scores very high on these criteria and receives a positive evaluation. The second student defines "goodness" as (1) enthusiasm, (2) capacity to inspire students, and (3) ability to relate to students on a personal basis. This student scores Professor Jones low on these criteria and thus gives him a negative evaluation. Why the disagreement? Because the two students have different criteria for defining goodness in teaching.

Disagreements over the proper criteria to use in decision making are common. Values and tastes also dictate people's choice of criteria. For someone with limited funds, a good car may be one that gets high gas mileage. But for a wealthy person, the main criterion may be physical comfort. Not all disagreements are caused by using different criteria, however. Suppose that both students in our teaching example define goodness in teaching as preparedness, course relevance, and clarity of instruction. The first student thinks Professor Jones is well-prepared, teaches a relevant course, and gives clear instruction. But the second student thinks he is ill-prepared, teaches an irrelevant course, and gives unclear instruction. Both students are using the same evaluative standards, but they do not reach the same judgment. The difference of opinion in this case is due to discrepancies in the meanings attached to Professor Jones's behavior. These discrepancies may result from perceptual biases, different expectations, or varying operational definitions associated with criteria. Thus, even people who use the same standards in making judgments do not always reach the same conclusion (see Social Media and I-O Psychology: *Criteria for "5 Star" Organizations*).

Social Media and I-O Psychology: *Criteria for "5 Star" Organizations*

A defining feature of social media is that individuals are able to create and share information, ideas, and opinions with others. We use social media sites as platforms to express ourselves, obtain information on a variety of topics, and to solicit feedback from others on a multitude of matters. When seeking advice from others on social media, however, it is important to remember that individuals have different conceptualizations of what is important. Searching for a lunch box for my son, for example, I found one on Amazon.com that had customer reviews ranging from 1 star to 5 stars. Digging into the content of the reviews, I discovered that many of the 5-star reviewers commented on how "cute" and durable the lunch box was. The 1 star reviewers were commenting on the lack of insulation (food apparently didn't stay cold long) and the size (hard to fit a juice box in with a sandwich without squishing the sandwich). Clearly the reviewers had different ideas of what constitutes a "good" lunch box.

Individuals are not just seeking information about products. They are also using input from others to make decisions regarding their employment. Glassdoor.com, for example, is a site where current and former employees can anonymously post reviews about an organization's compensation and benefits, culture and values, and career opportunities that others (such as prospective employees) can use when making employment decisions (such as whether to apply for or accept a job with a certain company). Glassdoor verifies that the reviews come from actual employees but keeps the authors of posts anonymous. In addition, they do not edit or alter content within reviews that are posted. In this way, it is believed that the reviews can be trusted as being the reviewers' true feelings, not being overly positive out of fear of repercussions from management. Looking at reviews, however, it is again clear that people have different criteria they use to form opinions about an organization. The pros and cons for organizations vary considerably depending on the reviewer. One reviewer may give a 5-star rating based on benefits and salary while another does so based on leadership and office culture. The usefulness of any rating depends upon our knowledge of the criteria used by the reviewer in making the rating.

Conceptual Versus Actual Criteria

Criteria are of prime importance. We must carefully consider what is meant by a "successful" worker, student, parent, and so forth. We cannot plunge headlong into measuring success, goodness, or quality until we have a fairly good idea of what (in theory, at least) we are looking for.

Conceptual criteria The theoretical standards that researchers seek to understand.

A good beginning point is the notion of conceptual criteria. **Conceptual criteria** are theoretical constructs, abstract ideas that can never actually be measured. They are ideal sets of factors that constitute a successful person (or object or collectivity) as conceived in the psychologist's mind. Let's say we want to define a successful college student. We might start off with intellectual growth; that is, capable students should experience more intellectual growth than less capable students. Another dimension might be emotional growth. A college education should help students clarify their own values and beliefs, and this should add to their emotional development and stability.

Finally, we might say that good college students should want to have some voice in civic activities, be a "good citizen," and contribute to the well-being of their community. As an educated person, good college students will assume active roles in helping to make society a better place in which to live. We might call this dimension a citizenship factor.

Thus, these three factors become the conceptual criteria for defining a "good college student." We could apply this same process to defining a "good worker," "good parent," or "good organization." However, because conceptual criteria are theoretical abstractions, we have to find some way to turn them into measurable, real factors. That is, we have to obtain **actual criteria** to serve as measures of the conceptual criteria that we would prefer to (but cannot) assess. The decision is then which variables to select as the actual criteria.

Actual criteria
The operational or actual standards that researchers measure or assess. Often contrasted with conceptual criteria.

A psychologist might choose grade point average as a measure of intellectual growth. Of course, a high grade point average is not equivalent to intellectual growth, but it probably reflects some degree of growth. To measure emotional growth, a psychologist might ask a student's advisor to judge how much the student has matured since first starting college. Again, maturation is not the same as emotional growth, but it is probably an easier concept to grasp and evaluate than the more abstract notion of emotional growth. Finally, as a measure of citizenship, a psychologist might count the number of volunteer organizations (student government, charitable clubs, and so on) the student has joined while in college. It could be argued that the sheer number (quantity) of joined organizations does not reflect the quality of participation in these activities, and that "good citizenship" is more appropriately defined by quality rather than quantity of participation. Nevertheless, because of the difficulties inherent in measuring quality of participation, plus the fact that one cannot speak of quality unless there is some quantity, the psychologist decides to use this measure. Table 4-1 shows the conceptual criteria and the actual criteria of success for a college student.

Thus, we are answering two questions with our conceptual and actual criteria. First, how do we define a "good" college student in theory? With the conceptual criteria as the evaluative standards, we are saying that a good college student should display a high degree of intellectual and emotional growth and should be a responsible citizen in the community. Second, how do we operationalize a good college student in practice? Using the actual criteria as the evaluative standards, we are saying a good college student is one who has earned high grades, is judged by an academic advisor to be emotionally more mature, and has joined many volunteer organizations throughout college. In a review of the relationship between the two sets of criteria (conceptual and actual), remember that the goal is to obtain a reasonable estimate of the conceptual criterion by selecting one or more actual criteria that we think are appropriate.

Table 4-1 *Conceptual and actual criteria for a successful college student*

Conceptual Criteria	Actual Criteria
Intellectual growth	Grade point average
Emotional growth	Adviser rating of emotional maturity growth
Citizenship	Number of volunteer organizations joined in college

Criterion Deficiency, Relevance, and Contamination

We can express the relationship between conceptual and actual criteria in terms of three concepts: deficiency, relevance, and contamination. Figure 4-1 shows the overlap between conceptual and actual criteria. The circles represent the contents of each type of criterion. Because the conceptual criterion is a theoretical abstraction, we can never know exactly how much overlap occurs. The actual criteria selected are never totally equivalent to the conceptual criteria we have in mind, so there is always a certain amount (though unspecified) of deficiency, relevance, and contamination.

Criterion deficiency The part of the conceptual criterion that is not measured by the actual criterion.

Criterion relevance The degree of overlap or similarity between the actual criterion and the conceptual criterion.

Criterion contamination The part of the actual criterion that is unrelated to the conceptual criterion.

Criterion deficiency is the degree to which the actual criteria fail to overlap the conceptual criteria; that is, how lacking the actual criteria are in representing the conceptual ones. There is always some degree of deficiency in the actual criteria. By careful selection of the actual criteria, we can reduce (but never eliminate) criterion deficiency. Conversely, criteria that are selected because they are simply expedient, without much thought given to their match to conceptual criteria, are grossly deficient. **Criterion relevance** is the degree to which the actual criteria and the conceptual criteria coincide. It's the overlap between the two, and we want this to be as large as possible. The greater the match between the conceptual and the actual criteria, the greater the criterion relevance. Again, because the conceptual criteria are theoretical abstractions, we cannot know the exact amount of relevance.

Criterion contamination is that part of the actual criteria that is unrelated to the conceptual criteria. It is the extent to which the actual criteria measure something other than the conceptual criteria. Contamination consists of two parts.

1. **Bias**—the extent to which the actual criteria systematically or consistently measure something other than the conceptual criteria
2. **Error**—the extent to which the actual criteria are not related to anything at all. This part of contamination is thought to be random

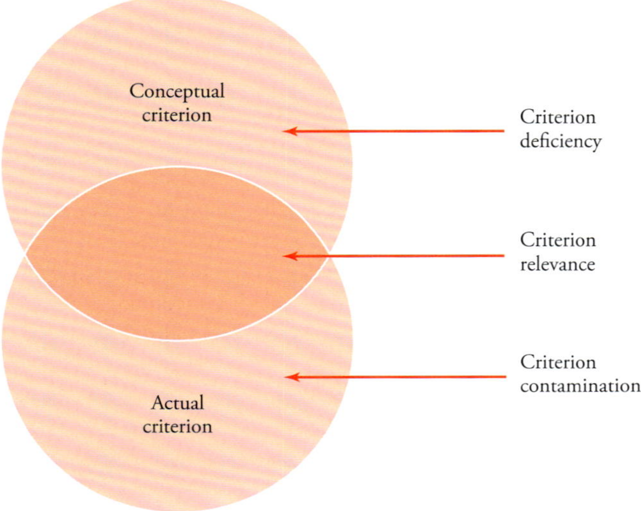

Figure 4-1 *Criterion deficiency, relevance, and contamination*

Both contamination and deficiency are undesirable in the actual criterion, and together they distort the conceptual criterion. Criterion contamination distorts the actual criterion because certain factors are included that don't belong (that is, they are not present in the conceptual criterion). Criterion deficiency distorts the actual criterion because certain important dimensions of the conceptual criterion are not included in the actual criterion.

Let us consider criterion deficiency and contamination in the example of setting criteria for a good college student. How might the actual criteria we chose be *deficient* in representing the conceptual criteria? Students typically begin a class with differing amounts of prior knowledge of the subject matter. One student may know nothing of the material, while another student may be very familiar with it. At the end of the term, the former student might have grown more intellectually than the latter student, but the latter student might get a higher grade in the course. By using the grade point average as our criterion, we would (falsely) conclude that the latter student grew more intellectually. So the relationship between good grades and intellectual growth is not perfect (that is, it is deficient). A rating of emotional maturity by an academic advisor might be deficient because the advisor is not an ideal judge. The advisor might have only a limited perspective of the student. Finally, it is not enough just to count how many volunteer groups to which a student belongs. Quality of participation is as important as (if not more important than) quantity.

How might these actual criteria be *contaminated*? If some academic majors are more difficult than others, then grades are a contaminated measure of intellectual growth; students in "easy" majors will be judged to have experienced more intellectual growth than students in difficult majors. This is a bias between earned grade point averages and the difficulty of the student's academic major. The source of the bias affects the actual criterion (grades) but not the conceptual criterion (intellectual growth). A rating of emotional maturity by the student's advisor could be contaminated by the student's grades. The advisor might believe that students with high grades have greater emotional maturity than students with low grades. Thus, the grade point average might bias an advisor's rating even though it probably has no relationship to the conceptual criterion of emotional growth. Finally, counting the number of organizations a student joins might be contaminated by the student's popularity. Students who join many organizations may simply be more popular rather than better citizens (which is what we are trying to measure).

If we know that these criterion measures are contaminated, why would we use them? In fact, when a researcher identifies a certain form of contamination, its influence can be controlled through experimental or statistical procedures. The real problem is anticipating the presence of contaminating factors. A problem with some criteria is that they are not under the direct control of the person being evaluated.[1] For example, police officers are typically expected to prevent crime and safeguard people's property and rights, and therefore may be evaluated on the number of arrests they make. However, many factors that contribute to crime rates, such as the socioeconomic status of individuals in the officers' beats and the population density of their cities, are outside of their control. Thus, two police officers may differ in the number of arrests they make for reasons other than one being a better officer than the other.

Psychologists have spent a great deal of time trying to discover new and better ways to measure actual criteria. They have used various analytical and computational procedures to get more precise assessments. However, as one scholar noted, "If we are measuring the wrong thing, it will not help us to measure it better" (Wherry 1957, p. 5).[2] Along these lines, some have argued that rather than dwelling on finding new ways to measure actual criteria, psychologists should spend more time choosing actual criteria that will be adequate measures of the conceptual criteria they really seek to understand.[3] Of course, the adequacy of the actual criterion as a measure of the conceptual criterion is always a matter of professional judgment—no equation or formula will determine it.

Work Analysis

Work analysis
A formal procedure by which the content of work is defined in terms of activities performed and attributes needed to perform the work.

The topic of work in society—what work is required and who should do it—can be traced back to Socrates in the 5th century BC.[4] However, the formal analysis of work began at the start of the 20th century. Two of the founding figures of I-O psychology were instrumental in developing the concept of work analysis as a means to increase industrial efficiency. Frederick Taylor advocated **work analysis** as a cornerstone of the principles of scientific management. Lillian Moller Gilbreth and her husband used time-and-motion studies to identify units or segments of work in performing a job, which they called a "Therblig" ("Therblig" is "Gilbreth" spelled backwards, almost). For many years, I-O psychology referred to work analysis as "job analysis." Only recently has the field of I-O psychology preferred to use the term "work analysis."[5] While jobs are often at the heart of work analysis, the psychological meaning of a job (i.e., a standardized set of tasks requiring specific skills for their conduct) is eroding because of the continuously changing nature of the modern work world. Thus, static "jobs" are in some ways a relic of the past, while the concept of work persists. Moreover, the study of work and its processes is the foundation of any human resource system, and will be for the foreseeable future.[6]

Consider This...

When we say that work analysis is the foundation of any human resource system, we mean it. In many ways, work analysis is the building block for practically everything that occurs at work. We use work analyses to determine what potential employees need to be able to do, whether certain tasks should be required versus preferred, how much employees should earn, and what things should be included in training efforts (among other things). Having a work analysis can also keep us from getting into legal trouble. We discuss the uses of work analytic information later in this chapter and highlight its importance. Do you have any experience with work analysis? It is often the case that people not directly involved in human resources are unaware of work analysis. Why do you think this is the case, given its importance? Knowing its importance, will you approach this material differently than you would if you didn't know how important it is?

I-O psychologists must often identify the criteria of effective work performance. These criteria then become the basis for hiring people (choosing them according to their ability to meet performance criteria), training them (to perform work tasks that are important), and paying them (high levels of performance warrant higher pay). Work analysis is a useful procedure in identifying the criteria or performance dimensions of a job; it is conducted by a work analyst. Work analysis has been defined as "any systematic process for gathering, documenting, and analyzing information about:

a. the content of the work performed by people in organizations (e.g., tasks, responsibilities, or work outputs),

b. the worker attributes related to its performance (often referred to as knowledge, skills, abilities, and other personal characteristics ("KSAOs"), or

c. the context in which work is performed (including physical and psychological conditions in the immediate work environment and the broader organizational and external environment" (Pearlman & Sanchez 2010, p. 73).[7]

Sources of Work Information

Subject matter expert (SME)
A person knowledgeable about a topic who can serve as a qualified information source.

The most critical issue in work analysis is the accuracy and completeness of the information. There are three major sources of work information, and each source is a **subject matter expert (SME)**. The qualifications for being an SME are not precise, but a minimum condition is that the person has direct, up-to-date experience with the work for a long enough time to be familiar with all of its tasks. It is also desirable if SMEs have strong verbal ability, a good memory, and are cooperative.

The most common source of information is a *job incumbent*—that is, the holder of a job. The use of job incumbents as SMEs is predicated upon their implicit understanding of their own jobs. The sampling method used to select SMEs is very important.[8] Experienced job incumbents provide the most valuable job information. It is also important that SMEs are not suspicious of the motives behind a work analysis. If they are, they may be inclined to magnify the importance of their abilities or the difficulty of their tasks as a self-protective tactic. In addition, it is important to treat SMEs with respect to ensure employees are willing to provide accurate and balanced information (see The Lighter Side of I-O Psychology: *Don't Be a Sucker*). Of course, new jobs, jobs that don't currently exist in an organization and for which there are no incumbents, also must be analyzed. Statistical methods may be used to forecast employee characteristics needed in the future as technology shifts the way work is conducted.

A second source of information is the *supervisor* of the job incumbent. Supervisors play a major role in determining what job incumbents do on their jobs, and thus they are a credible source of information. In addition, supervisors tend to provide ratings that are less inflated than are incumbent ratings.[9] The third source of job information is a trained *work analyst*. Work analysts are used as SMEs when comparisons are needed across many jobs. Because of their familiarity with work analytic methods, analysts often provide the most consistent across-job ratings. Work analyst expertise lies not in the subject matter of various jobs per se, but in their ability to understand similarities and differences across jobs in terms of work activities performed and human attributes needed.

In general, incumbents and supervisors are the best sources of descriptive job information, whereas work analysts are best qualified to comprehend the relationships

The Lighter Side of I-O Psychology: *Don't Be a Sucker*

It is important to remember that SME stands for subject matter expert, and that the SME's expertise deserves your respect, regardless of how you may view the job. Paul shared the following example of a time when he was reminded of this very thing. Here is the story, in his words.

> I was collecting work analysis data from employees in a book printing company. I was interviewing operators who ran large printing machines. Each machine performed a different function in the process of printing books. Few of the operators had a high school diploma, as the jobs were very simple. Basically each operator had to load thousands of sheets of paper in one end of the machine and then unload the sheets at the other end of the machine. It seemed like truly mindless work. Many of the employees I spoke with used the word "sucker." The expressions were like, "that sucker was running hot," or "those suckers were really moving," or "I hate it when that sucker jams." It was very warm in the room and my brain had started to fry from the heat and the tedium of work analysis. So I'm in the middle of my final interview of the day and I decide to speak the language of the locals, just for a change of pace. This particular worker ran a slicing machine that trimmed and squared the pages before they were bound. I forget my exact wording, but I asked a question like, "So, how do you load that sucker?" The employee's face went blank, and then I was dutifully (but politely) informed, "There are no suckers on my machine." It was only then I cleverly deduced a "sucker" was not a generic slang term, but referred to a small rubber suction (like the rubber tip on the end of a child's arrow) that descends on a piece of paper, lifts it (through suction), and enters it into a slot whereupon print is applied to it. This being a page trimming machine, no suckers were utilized. I was ashamed at my haughtiness, assuming these uneducated workers were merely filling my ears with local vernacular. I felt foolish for being such a sucker to my own hubris.

among a set of jobs. Most incumbents do not think of how they perform their jobs in the way work analysts think about work.[10] Incumbents more typically describe their jobs in terms of activities or tasks performed, not the KSAOs needed to perform the work. The link between KSAOs and task activities can be particularly difficult for incumbents to rate when the work allows for stylistic differences in behavior, thus leading to subjectivity in judgment. The most desirable strategy in understanding a job is to collect information from as many qualified sources as possible, as opposed to relying exclusively on one source.

Work Analytic Procedures

Task
The lowest level of analysis in the study of work; a basic component of work (such as typing for a secretary).

Position
A set of tasks performed by a single employee. For example, the position of a secretary is often represented by the tasks of typing, filing, and scheduling.

Job
A set of similar positions in an organization.

Job family
A grouping of similar jobs in an organization.

Task-oriented procedure
A procedure or set of operations in work analysis designed to identify important or frequently performed tasks as a means of understanding the work performed.

Functional Job Analysis (FJA)
A method of work analysis that describes the content of jobs in terms of People, Data, and Things.

Recall from Chapter 3 that it is incredibly important that all employment tests be job-related. It's impossible to create predictors of job performance without understanding what is required of the job. This is where work analysis comes in. The purpose of work analysis is to explain the activities that are performed on the job and the human attributes needed to perform the job. A clear understanding of work analysis requires knowledge of four work-related concepts, as shown in Figure 4-2. At the lowest level of aggregation are tasks. **Tasks** are the basic units of work that are directed toward meeting specific work objectives. A **position** is a set of tasks performed by a single employee. There are usually as many positions in an organization as there are employees. However, many positions may be similar to one another. In such a case, similar positions are grouped or aggregated to form a **job**. An example is the job of secretary; another job is that of receptionist. Similar jobs may be further aggregated based on general similarity of content to form a **job family**—in this case, the clerical job family.

It is possible to understand work from either a task-oriented or a worker-oriented perspective. Both procedures are used in conducting work analyses.

Task-Oriented Procedures. A **task-oriented procedure** seeks to understand work by examining the tasks performed, usually in terms of *what* is accomplished. Task-oriented procedures focus on *activities* involved in performing work. The procedure begins with a consideration of the tasks, responsibilities, or functions an incumbent performs to accomplish a job objective.[11] Tasks thus become the basic unit of analysis for understanding work using task-oriented procedures. The work analyst develops a series of *task statements*, which are concise expressions of tasks performed. Examples are "splice high-voltage cables," "order materials and supplies," and "grade tests." Task statements should not be written in too general terminology, nor should they be written in very detailed language. They should reflect a discrete unit of work with appropriate specificity. The number of tasks required to describe most jobs typically is between 300 and 500.[12]

Following the development of task statements, SMEs (most often incumbents) are asked to rate the task statements on a series of scales. The scales reflect important dimensions that facilitate understanding the job. Among the common scales used to rate task statements are frequency, importance, difficulty, and consequences of error. For example, the frequency scale would indicate whether a particular task was performed *rarely* (as infrequently as once or twice per year) to *very often* (several times per day). Based on an analysis of the ratings, we acquire an understanding of a job in terms of the rated frequency, importance, difficulty, and other dimensions of the tasks that make up the job.

A classic example of a task-oriented method of work analysis is **Functional Job Analysis (FJA)**.[13] FJA obtains two types of task information: (1) what a worker does—the procedures and processes engaged in by a worker as a task is performed, and (2) how a task is performed—the physical, mental, and interpersonal involvement of the worker with the task. These types of information are used to identify what a worker does and the results of those job behaviors. Perhaps the most notable characteristic of FJA is that tasks are rated along three dimensions: People, Data, and Things. When a task requires involvement with People, the worker needs interpersonal resources

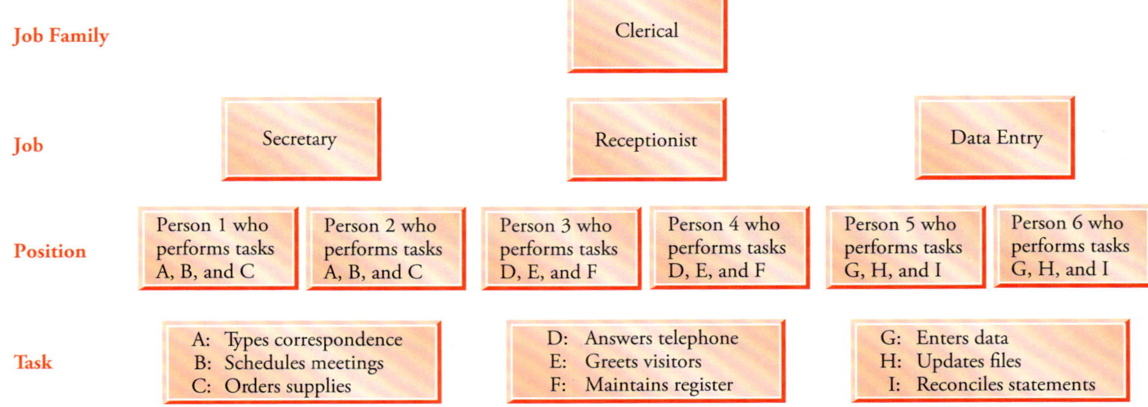

Figure 4-2 *Relationships among tasks, positions, jobs, and job families*

Consider This...

Why is it necessary to know about a task's frequency, importance, or difficulty? One reason is to determine the job requirements and to help decide which requirements are essential functions that are needed upon entry to the job, versus things that could potentially be taught after being hired (so maybe preferred but not required qualifications). To determine this, the work analyst might develop a scoring system in which a certain score indicates it is an essential function and everything below that is not essential. For example, consider only the two factors of frequency and importance. Perhaps the following (abbreviated) scale is used:

Frequency: never (0), rarely (1), occasionally (2), often (3), very often (4)

Importance: unimportant (0), slightly (1), important (2), very (3), critical (4)

Technically, there shouldn't be any tasks that never occur or are completely unimportant, but that can happen and sometimes does. However, those tasks would likely not be considered essential functions. For example, somebody may oversee making coffee for the office staff. Some may argue that it's critical, but is it really? More essential tasks would be those that are performed regularly with some degree of importance, or those that are critical even if only performed rarely. Can you think of examples of such tasks? Can you think of a situation in which a task could be considered essential even though it is rarely performed? How about a situation in which a task is essential even if it is only slightly important?

(sensitivity, compassion, etc.). When a task requires involvement with Data, the worker needs mental resources (knowledge, reasoning, etc.). When a task is defined primarily in relation to Things, the worker needs physical resources (strength, coordination, etc.). Each of these three dimensions (People, Data, Things) is presented in a hierarchy ranging from high to low. Thus, for example, a given job may be defined as requiring a medium level of People, a high level of Data, and a low level of Things. FJA has been used to analyze jobs in many sectors of society, but most frequently in the federal government. The method is regarded as one of the major systematic approaches to the study of work.

Worker-oriented procedure
A procedure or set of operations in work analysis designed to identify important or frequently utilized human attributes as a means of understanding the work performed.

Worker-Oriented Procedures. A **worker-oriented procedure** seeks to understand work by examining the human *attributes* needed to perform it successfully. The human attributes are classified into four categories: knowledge (K), skills (S), abilities (A), and other (O) characteristics. *Knowledge* is specific types of information people need to perform a job. Some knowledge is required of workers before they can be hired to perform a job, whereas other knowledge may be acquired on the job. *Skills* are defined as the proficiencies needed to perform a task. Skills are usually enhanced through practice—for example, skill at typing and skill at driving an automobile. *Abilities* are defined as relatively enduring attributes that generally are stable over time. Examples are cognitive ability, physical ability, and spatial ability. However, when considered over a lifetime, some abilities (e.g., physical stamina) decline at a faster rate than others (e.g., verbal ability). Skills and abilities are confused often and easily, and the distinction is not always clear. It is useful to think of skills as cultivations of innate abilities. Generally speaking, high levels of (innate) ability can be cultivated into high skill levels. For example, a person with high musical ability could become highly proficient in playing a musical instrument. Low levels of (innate) ability preclude the development of high skill levels. *Other* characteristics are all other personal attributes, most often personality factors (e.g., remaining calm in emergency situations) or capacities (e.g., withstanding extreme temperatures). Because personality measures are being increasingly used for personnel selection in a wide range of jobs (especially customer-service jobs), more emphasis may need to be placed on requisite personality attributes in work analysis.[14] Collectively, these four types of attributes, referred to as **KSAOs**, reflect an approach to understanding work by analyzing the human attributes needed to perform it.

KSAOs
An abbreviation for "knowledge, skills, abilities, and other" characteristics. Often used in the context of work analysis.

Like task statements, KSAO statements are written to serve as a means of understanding the human attributes needed to perform a job. They are written in standard format, using the wording "Knowledge of," "Skill in," or "Ability to." Examples are "Knowledge of city building codes," "Skill in operating a pneumatic drill," and "Ability to lift a 50-pound object over your head." The KSAO statements are also rated by SMEs, reflecting whether they are of *little importance* on the job, up to being *critically important.* Similar to analyzing the ratings of task statements, the ratings of KSAO statements are analyzed to provide an understanding of a job based on the human attributes needed to successfully perform the job.

Linkage analysis
A technique in work analysis that establishes the connection between the tasks performed and the human attributes needed to perform them.

Other analytic procedures can be followed to gain greater understanding of a job. A **linkage analysis** unites the two basic types of work analytic information: task-oriented (i.e., work activities) and worker-oriented (i.e., human attributes). A linkage analysis examines the relationship between KSAOs and tasks performed. The results of this analysis reveal which KSAOs are linked to the performance of many important and frequently performed tasks. Those KSAOs that are linked to the performance of tasks critical to the job become the basis of the employee selection test. A linkage analysis is also useful in establishing the relationship between each item on an employment test and the KSAOs needed for successful job performance.[15] Thus, if a high degree of mechanical ability is needed to perform a job, the linkage of test items that assess mechanical ability and job performance is strong and direct.

While incumbents are typically regarded as the most credible source for information about the jobs they perform, the linkage analysis that ties KSAOs to tasks performed has been found more reliable when provided by work analysts than incumbents.[16] One possible explanation for this finding involves an "inferential leap" in making the attribute-to-activity link. Suppose a task activity is typing and the human attribute under consideration by raters is finger dexterity. The link between finger dexterity and typing is direct, thus the inferential leap in judgment is small. However, consider the task activity of calling people on the telephone to sell a product (i.e., the job of a telemarketer) and the attribute under consideration is the personality dimension of sociability. In this case, the inferential leap (i.e., you have to be highly sociable to speak with people on the telephone to convince them to buy something) is large. Telemarketers perform their job by reading scripts on a computer screen. The script tells them what to say, and in most cases, how to respond to hesitation or reluctance by the prospective customer. Having a sociable personality probably wouldn't lower job performance, but sociability might not be the only reason for successful performance as a telemarketer. Telemarketer success could be the result of a highly sociable personality, or being very determined, or being verbally persuasive to overcome customer resistance. Some jobs can be structured so as to allow for idiosyncratic styles in behavior, and thus there can be different reasons for successful job performance. In one study, the highest incumbent agreement was for jobs involving use of equipment.[17] The implication is that there are not different ways one can successfully operate equipment. Jobs that permit wide variation in how they are performed make it more difficult to reach consensus in identifying which critical KSAOs are needed to be successful.

How to Collect Work Analytic Information

Some written material, such as task summaries and training manuals, may exist for a particular job. A work analyst should read this written material as a logical first step in conducting a formal work analysis. Then the work analyst is prepared to collect more extensive information about the job to be analyzed.

Procedures for Collecting Information. Three procedures are typically followed: the interview, direct observation, and a questionnaire. In the first procedure, the *interview*, the work analyst asks SMEs questions about the nature of their work. SMEs may be interviewed individually, in small groups, or through a series of panel discussions. The work analyst tries to gain an understanding of the tasks performed on the job and the KSAOs needed to perform them.

The second method is called *direct observation*: employees are observed as they perform their jobs. Observers try to be unobtrusive, observing the jobs but not getting in the workers' way. Observers generally do not talk to the employees because it interferes with the conduct of work. They sometimes take photos or videos to facilitate the observation. Direct observation is an excellent method for appreciating and understanding the adverse conditions (such as noise or heat) under which some jobs are performed; however, it is a poor method for understanding why certain behaviors occur on the job.

Taxonomy
A classification of objects designed to enhance understanding of the objects being classified.

The third procedure for collecting work information is a structured *questionnaire* or inventory. The analyst uses a commercially available questionnaire that organizes existing knowledge about work information into a taxonomy. A **taxonomy** is a classification scheme useful in organizing information—in this case, information about jobs. The information collected about a particular job is compared with an existing database of job information derived from other jobs previously analyzed with the questionnaire. This procedure is *deductive* because the work analyst can deduce an understanding of a job from a pre-existing framework for analyzing jobs.[18] Alternatively, the interview and direct observation procedures are *inductive* because the work analyst must rely on newly-created information about the job being analyzed. Because work analysts are often interested in understanding more than one job, the structured inventory is a very useful way to examine the relationships among a set of jobs.

Position Analysis Questionnaire (PAQ)
A method of work analysis that assesses the content of jobs on the basis of approximately 200 items in the questionnaire.

Taxonomic Information. There are several sources of taxonomic information for work analysis. One is the **Position Analysis Questionnaire (PAQ)**, which consists of 195 statements used to describe the human attributes needed to perform a job.[19] The statements are organized into six major categories: information input, mental processes, work output, relationships with other persons, job context, and other requirements. Some sample statements from the "relationships with other persons" category are shown in Figure 4-3. From a database of thousands of similar positions that have been previously analyzed with the PAQ, the work analyst can come to understand the focal job.

A second source of taxonomic information is research that resulted in an established taxonomy of human abilities needed to perform tasks.[20] The "Taxonomies of Human Performance" has 52 abilities required in the conduct of a broad spectrum of tasks. Examples of these abilities are oral expression, arm–hand steadiness, multi-limb coordination, reaction time, selective attention, and night vision. The amount of each ability that is needed to perform tasks is provided. For example, with a scale of 1 (low) to 7 (high), the following amounts of *arm-hand steadiness* are needed to perform these tasks:

Cut facets in diamonds	**6.32**
Thread a needle	**4.14**
Light a cigarette	**1.71**

This taxonomy permits jobs to be described in terms of required abilities and levels of those abilities needed to perform tasks.

Occupational Information Network (O*NET)
An online computer-based source of information about jobs.

The third source of taxonomic information available for work analysis is the U.S. Department of Labor. The **Occupational Information Network (O*NET)** is a national database of worker attributes and job characteristics. Based on analyses of thousands of jobs, massive compilations of information provide users with broad job and occupational assessments. It contains information about KSAOs, interests, general work activities, and work contexts.

I-O psychology has played a critical role in both the content and organization of O*NET. Figure 4-4 shows the conceptual model upon which O*NET is based. There are six domains of descriptive information: three worker-oriented and three work-oriented. As the figure shows, the *worker-oriented domains* include information about

Figure 4-3 *Sample items from the PAQ*

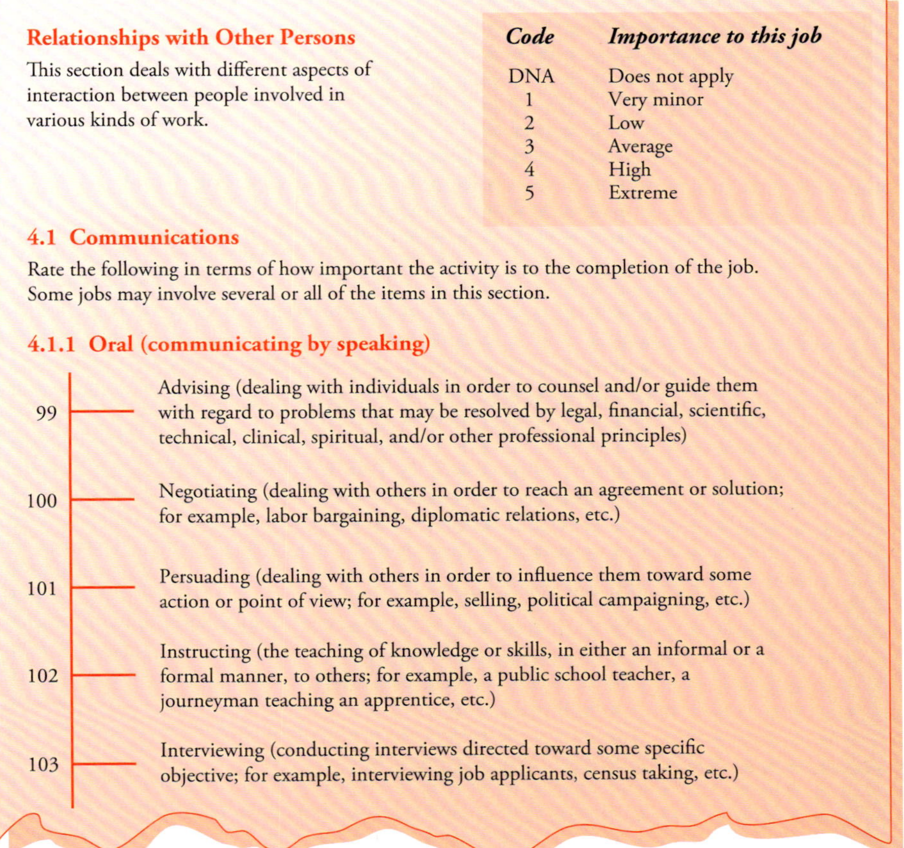

Relationships with Other Persons

This section deals with different aspects of interaction between people involved in various kinds of work.

Code	*Importance to this job*
DNA	Does not apply
1	Very minor
2	Low
3	Average
4	High
5	Extreme

4.1 Communications

Rate the following in terms of how important the activity is to the completion of the job. Some jobs may involve several or all of the items in this section.

4.1.1 Oral (communicating by speaking)

99 Advising (dealing with individuals in order to counsel and/or guide them with regard to problems that may be resolved by legal, financial, scientific, technical, clinical, spiritual, and/or other professional principles)

100 Negotiating (dealing with others in order to reach an agreement or solution; for example, labor bargaining, diplomatic relations, etc.)

101 Persuading (dealing with others in order to influence them toward some action or point of view; for example, selling, political campaigning, etc.)

102 Instructing (the teaching of knowledge or skills, in either an informal or a formal manner, to others; for example, a public school teacher, a journeyman teaching an apprentice, etc.)

103 Interviewing (conducting interviews directed toward some specific objective; for example, interviewing job applicants, census taking, etc.)

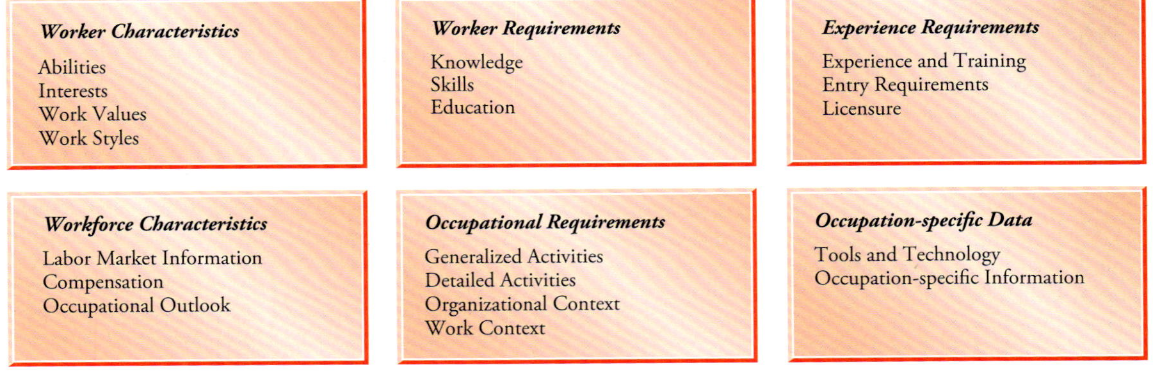

Figure 4-4 *Content model for the Occupational Information Network (O*NET)*

worker characteristics, worker requirements, and experience requirements. The *work-oriented domains* include information about workforce characteristics, occupational requirements, and occupation-specific data. This content model of O*NET reflects a thorough means of conceptualizing all work-related data of interest to individuals and organizations.[21] O*NET can be used as a starting point for work analysis, as it provides a broad-based assessment of approximately 900 occupations. Depending upon the specific need for more customized work analytic information, organization-specific data can then be collected to augment O*NET results.

O*NET can be used for a variety of purposes. The database provides the essential foundation for facilitating career counseling, education, employment, and training activities. Online recruitment companies have found the O*NET system of classifying jobs to be useful in matching people with work.[22] For example, Monster.com uses the O*NET system to organize more than 60 million résumés of people seeking employment or re-employment. Another application of O*NET is to assist individuals who lost their jobs to become re-employed.[23] The process involves several phases. Individuals take online assessments, which, based on their self-reported interests, identify possible job fits. Three types of fits are identified: good fits, potential fits and other best relative matches to the individual's values, interests, abilities and skills.

Additional information about O*NET can be found at *www.onetcenter.org*. A related database exists in Europe (The International Standard of Occupational Classifications and EurOccupations). O*NET is continuously being revised in response to the ongoing changes in the work world. O*NET is held in very high professional esteem and has been considered by some to be one of I-O psychology's most significant achievements.[24]

Consider This...

It is estimated that more than half of military veterans struggle to find work after leaving the military. There are many possible reasons for this, including that many veterans find it challenging to acclimate to civilian work cultures, that employers may hold negative stereotypes of military personnel being overly rigid or having anger management issues, and/or that the skills that are needed in the military don't translate to the civilian workforce.[25] One way that O*NET has attempted to help veterans in their post-military job pursuits is through the development of a partner site, *My Next Move for Veterans* (mynextmove.org/vets/). This interactive site helps veterans by highlighting civilian careers that are similar to jobs in the military, providing personalized career suggestions based on the veteran's interests and experience, and showing what is needed to be successful in a chosen field. Veterans who liked what they did in the military can find options in the civilian sector that mirror their military jobs. On the other hand, the estimated 55% of veterans who want to do something completely different than what they did in the military[26] can find jobs that match their interests and discover ways to translate their skills into terms that don't include military jargon. Go to the O*NET site (onetonline.org) and look around. What else could O*NET be used for? What else might you recommend be included in the information about jobs?

Managerial Work Analysis

With an emphasis on work activities that are performed on the job, traditional work analytic methods are typically well-suited to blue-collar and clerical jobs. In such jobs, the work performed is evidenced by overt behaviors, such as hammering, welding, splicing wires, typing, and filing. These behaviors are observable, and the product of the work (e.g., a typed letter) flows directly from the skill (e.g., typing). In managerial-level jobs, the link between the KSAOs and the work output is not nearly so direct. Managerial work involves such factors as planning, decision making, and forecasting, mainly cognitive skills, which are not so readily observable. As such, it is often more difficult to conduct an accurate work analysis for managerial-level jobs because of the greater inferential leap between the work performed and the KSAOs.

Several work analytic methods have been developed to assist in the understanding of managerial jobs. For example, the *Professional and Managerial Position Questionnaire* examines work along the dimensions of complexity, organizational impact, and level of responsibility.[27] Similarly, the *Personality-Related Position Requirements Form* analyzes work on the basis of the personality factors needed to perform them, including interest in negotiation, sensitivity to others, attention to details, and desire to generate ideas.[28] These personality dimensions are based on previous research that links them to managerial-level work activities. As a rule, however, the level of precision and accuracy of managerial work analyses are not as high as those for non-managerial jobs because the attributes measured are more abstract.

Uses of Work Analytic Information

Work analytic information produces the criteria needed for a wide range of applications in I-O psychology, as the ensuing chapters will show. It is instructive to consider its uses.

First, an analysis of KSAOs reveals those attributes that are needed for successful job performance, including those needed upon entry into the job. The identification of these attributes provides an empirical basis to determine what personnel selection tests should assess. Thus, rather than selection tests being based on hunches or assumptions, work analytic information offers a rational approach to test selection. This topic will be described in Chapter 5. Second, work analytic information provides a basis to organize different positions into a job and different jobs into a job family. Such groupings provide a basis for determining levels of compensation, because one basis of compensation is the value of the attributes needed to perform the work. Third, work analytic information helps determine the content of training needed to perform the job. The tasks identified as most frequently performed or most important become the primary content of training. This topic will be discussed in Chapter 7. Finally, work analytic information provides one basis to conduct performance evaluations. A work analysis reveals the tasks most critical to job success, so the performance evaluation is directed at assessing how well the employee performs those tasks. This topic will be discussed in Chapter 8. In addition to these uses of work analytic information, the information can be used in vocational counseling, offering insight into the KSAOs needed to perform successfully in various occupations.

Work analysis offers additional value to organizations. Recall that the Americans with Disabilities Act requires employers to make adjustments for accommodating people with disabilities. Work analysis can help ascertain what is a "reasonable accommodation" versus an "undue hardship" for an employer.[29] Although what is "reasonable" is a matter of opinion, employers may be able at the minimum to provide flexible work schedules and wheelchair ramps for workers with disabilities to facilitate the conduct of their jobs.

Evaluating Work Analytic Methods

Research comparing various methods of work analysis has revealed the methods are differentially effective and practical depending on the purposes for which they may be used. No one method was consistently best across the board. There are a series of potential inaccuracies in work analytic information caused by such factors as biases in how work analysts process information about the jobs they are analyzing, and loss of motivation among SMEs who are less than enthusiastic about participating in work analyses.[30] The chances for inaccuracies are considerably lower in task-oriented work analysis. That is, the ratings of observable and discrete tasks are less subject to error than the ratings of some abstract KSAOs. In addition, a well-trained work analyst can draw accurate inferences and conclusions using any one of several questionnaire methods. The converse is also true. No method can ensure accurate results when used by someone who is inexperienced with work analysis. The prevailing professional status of work analysis is that work analysis can yield reliable and useful information if sound professional decisions are made.[31]

Competency Modeling

Competency modeling
A process for determining the human characteristics (i.e., competencies) needed to perform successfully within an organization.

One way to establish the desired attributes of employees is called **competency modeling**. A *competency* is a characteristic or quality of people that a company wants its employees to manifest. In traditional work analytic terms, a competency is a critical KSAO. *Modeling* refers to identifying the array or profile of competencies that an organization desires in its employees. Experts agree that work analysis and competency modeling share some similarities in their approaches. Work analysis examines both the work that gets performed and the human attributes needed to perform the work, whereas competency modeling does not consider the work performed. The two approaches differ in the level of generalizability of the information across jobs within an organization, the method by which the attributes are derived, and the degree of acceptance within the organization for the identified attributes. First, work analysis tends to identify specific and different KSAOs that distinguish jobs within an organization. For example, one set of KSAOs would be identified for a paralegal, while another set of KSAOs would be identified for an attorney. In contrast, competencies are generally identified to apply to employees in all jobs within an organization or perhaps a few special differentiations among groups of jobs, such as for senior executives. These competencies tend to be far more universal and abstract than KSAOs, and as such are often called the "core competencies" of an organization. Here are some examples of competencies for employees:

- Exhibiting the highest level of professional integrity at all times
- Being sensitive and respectful of the dignity of all employees
- Staying current with the latest technological advances within your area
- Placing the success of the organization above your personal individual success

As can be inferred from this profile or "model," such competencies are applicable to a broad range of jobs and are specifically designed to be as inclusive as possible. KSAOs are designed to be more exclusive, differentiating one job from another.

Second, KSAOs are identified by work analysts using technical methods designed to elicit specific job information. As such, the entire work analysis project is often perceived by employees to be arcane. In contrast, competency modeling is likely to include review sessions and group meetings of many employees to ensure that the competencies capture the language and spirit that are important to the organization. As a result, employees readily identify with and relate to the resulting competencies, an outcome rarely achieved in work analysis.

Third, competency modeling tries to link personal qualities of employees to the larger overall mission of the organization. The goal is to identify those characteristics that tap into an employee's willingness to perform certain activities or to "fit in" with the work culture of the organization.[32] We will discuss the important topic of an organization's culture in Chapter 9. Work analysis, on the other hand, does not try to capture or include organizational-level issues of vision and values. Traditional work analysis does not have the "populist appeal" of competency modeling by members of the organization.

Performance Criteria

Objective performance criteria A set of factors used to assess job performance that are (relatively) factual in character.

Subjective performance criteria A set of factors used to assess job performance that are the product of someone's (e.g., supervisor, peer, customer) judgment of these factors.

It is important to first understand criteria before we undertake the development of psychological assessments designed to predict the criteria. So what criteria are used to evaluate job performance? No single universal criterion is applicable across all jobs. The criteria for success in a certain job depend on how that job contributes to the overall success of the organization. Nevertheless, there is enough commonality across jobs that some typical criteria have been identified. You may think of these criteria as the conventional standards by which employees are judged on the job. However, successful performance may be defined by additional criteria as well. The criteria we study and seek to understand are an implied statement of what we think is important.

Performance criteria may be objective or subjective. **Objective performance criteria** are taken from organizational records and supposedly do not involve any subjective evaluation. **Subjective performance criteria** are judgmental evaluations of a person's performance (such as a supervisor might render). Although objective criteria may involve no subjective judgment, some degree of assessment must be applied to give them meaning. Just knowing that an employee produced 18 units a day is not informative; this output must be compared with what other workers produce. If the average is 10 units a day, 18 units clearly represent "good" performance. If the average is 25 units a day, 18 units is not good. Objective and subjective performance criteria are not interchangeable and therefore one should not be used as a proxy for the other.[33] For example, if sales performance is the desired outcome, employees should not be rewarded based on supervisor ratings of overall performance. Conversely, if broadly defined performance is what is important, it would be inappropriate to reward employees purely on gross sales.

Major Performance Criteria

Production. Using units of production as a criterion is most common in manufacturing jobs. If an organization has only one type of job, then setting production criteria is easy. But most companies have many types of production jobs, so productivity must be compared fairly. That is, if average productivity in one job is 6 units a day and in another job it is 300 units a day, then productivities must be equated to adjust for these differences. Statistical procedures are usually used for this. Other factors can diminish the value of production as a criterion of performance. In an assembly-line job, the speed of the line determines how many units are produced per day. Increasing the speed of the line increases production. Furthermore, everyone working on the line has the same level of production. In a case like this, units of production are determined by factors outside the control of the individual worker, so errors that are under the worker's control may be the criterion of job performance. Errors are not fair criteria if they are more likely in some jobs than others. Due to automation and work simplification, some jobs are almost "goof-proof." Then error-free work has nothing to do with the human factor.

Maximum performance The level of performance that individuals can do during short, evaluative circumstances.

Typical performance The level of performance that individuals will do on a day-to-day, non-evaluated basis.

Another distinction that is of particular relevance with production criteria is that of typical versus maximum performance.[34] What individuals "can do" is often described as **maximum performance** and what they "will do" is described as **typical performance**.[35] In general, individuals will tend to work at a predictable, typical pace on a daily basis. When needed, however, they may increase their effort or pace for short bursts. For example, when employees are aware of being evaluated, they will typically work harder to avoid inviting disciplinary action.[36]

Sales. Sales volume is a common performance criterion for wholesale and retail sales jobs. People working in sales jobs are often paid on a commission basis; that is, a percentage of the total sales figure. For example, a real estate salesperson may receive 8% commission on the sale of a house. If a house sells for $200,000, a $16,000 commission is paid.

Sales volume is a highly objective criterion, but it can be contaminated by factors other than the performance of the salesperson. Salespeople are typically assigned to territories or geographic locations. These territories can differ in market potential (e.g., population, socioeconomic status), prevailing economic conditions, and company infrastructure (i.e., if the company services what it sells).[37] There can also be differences among salespeople regarding travel time in between accounts, and the proclivity to sell to existing customers versus generating new sales business. If there are these types of differences across salespeople, there are statistical adjustments that can be made to more fairly compare sales volume as a criterion of job performance.[38] Ideally, any differences in sales performance are then due to the ability of the salespeople.

Tenure or Turnover. Length of service (or tenure) is a very popular criterion in I-O psychological research. Turnover is typically calculated on an annual basis as a percentage of the company's workforce. For example, if a company has 200 employees and an annual turnover rate of 4%, eight employees leave the company per year. Turnover not only has a theoretical appeal but also is a practical concern. Most employers want to hire people who will stay with the company. Employees stay with an employer for many reasons, including the enjoyment and meaning they derive from their work, the lack of other employment opportunities, and to accommodate a spouse and/or children.[39] For obvious practical reasons, employers often don't want to hire chronic job-hoppers. The costs of recruiting, selecting, and training new hires can be extremely high. However, some industries (such as fast food) have extraordinarily high turnover rates, in the range of 200%–300% per year. While such massive turnover rates would cripple most industries, the cost associated with hiring and training workers for fast food jobs is minimal. Nevertheless, turnover can be disruptive in other ways. For example, research has demonstrated that high turnover in fast-food restaurants results in lower store sales, due to worse customer service in the form of longer customer wait times.[40] In addition, turnover may sever coworkers' relationships and disrupt communication between work units. These detrimental relationship effects were observed when comparing low turnover retail stores to high turnover retail stores.[41] Many factors should be considered in the measurement of turnover.[42] One is *voluntariness* (whether the employee was fired, quit to take another job with better promotional opportunities, or quit because of some source of dissatisfaction). Another factor is *functionality* (whether the employee was performing the job effectively or ineffectively). A meta-analysis that examined the relationship between turnover and performance found that poor performers were more likely to voluntarily quit their jobs than were good performers.[43] In this case, turnover may be seen as a good thing, in that poor performers have opted to leave the organization on their own volition, making room for more effective employees to be hired.

Absenteeism. Absence from work, like turnover, is an index of employee stability. Although some employee turnover is good for organizations, unexcused employee absenteeism invariably has bad consequences. Absenteeism is a pervasive problem in industry; it costs employers billions of dollars a year in decreased efficiency and increased benefit payments (for example, sick leave) and payroll costs. Absenteeism has social, individual, and organizational causes, and it affects individuals, companies, and even entire industrial societies. Absence appears to be the product of many factors, including family conflicts, job dissatisfaction, alcohol and drug abuse, and personality.[44] Employees are also more likely to be absent from work when their coworkers are also frequently absent, demonstrating that there are norms within workplaces that also impact absenteeism.[45] Excused absenteeism (e.g., personal vacation time) is generally not a problem because it is sanctioned and must be approved by the organization.

Presenteeism. Absenteeism, as noted above, is costly to organizations due to lost productivity. In addition, absences often place a burden on other employees who may be asked to take on additional work to cover for the absent employee. Missing work may also be a problem for employees who may not feel financially stable enough to miss a day's wages or may feel guilty for creating additional work for their coworkers. These issues may lead to what is known as presenteeism. Presenteeism refers to employees attending work despite having an illness or health problem for which it would be advisable not to go to work.[46] Of course, being present when sick also has problems, including potentially getting others sick if they are contagious, and reduced levels of productivity and work quality from not being fully healthy. It is estimated that presenteeism costs are even more costly than those of absenteeism.[47] Meta-analytic findings have revealed that a lack of job and personal resources as well as increased job demands are positively related to presenteeism.[48] The importance of presenteeism may be seen as individuals focus more attention on health issues in the workplace (see COVID-19 and I-O Psychology: *Working While Sick*).

COVID-19 and I-O Psychology: *Working While Sick*

There are many reasons that people decide to work when sick. To understand this, it is helpful to remember why people work at all. In addition to financial reasons for working, employment serves many other purposes, including providing structure and activity in one's day, enabling opportunities for social engagement and support, and building one's status and self-esteem.[49] Thus, it is not surprising that individuals may choose to work while sick.

Unfortunately, research shows that people frequently continue to work while experiencing infectious diseases.[50] Even those who should "know better" than to show up to work when they are ill have been known to do so. For example, prior to the pandemic it is estimated that presenteeism among physicians was as high as 90%![51] Presenteeism among health care workers may be just as high (if not higher), given their strong sense of duty and desire to help others, which may be intensified during a public health emergency.[52]

The causes of presenteeism are also likely heightened during a pandemic. Namely, the potential for layoffs and fears of financial insecurity may create pressure for individuals to work while sick to avoid job loss. Employees may also feel intensified guilt as their workplaces experience staff shortages, and therefore avoid calling in sick and placing a burden on their coworkers. The consequences of such presenteeism during a global health crisis can be monumental. Even digital presenteeism—working remotely while sick—can be devastating from a productivity standpoint, even if there is no increase in disease transmission.

To combat presenteeism, organizations should create flexible workplaces and allow for boundary setting. In addition, they should create a climate in which safety of employees is highlighted. Indeed, developing policies that were supportive of CDC COVID-19 prevention guidelines improved employee attitudes about the guidelines and minimized presenteeism both at work and within the nonwork community.[53]

Accidents. Research suggests that 80% of accidents are a result of human error.[54] Accidents are sometimes used as a criterion of job performance, although this measure has a number of limitations. First, accidents are used as a criterion mainly for blue-collar jobs. (Although white-collar workers can be injured at work, the frequency of such accidents is low.) Thus, accidents are a measure of job performance for only a limited sample of employees. Second, accidents are difficult to predict, and there is little stability or consistency across individuals in their occurrence.[55] Third, accidents can be measured in many ways: number of accidents per hours worked, miles driven, trips taken, and so on. Different conclusions can be drawn depending on how accident statistics are calculated. Fourth, accidents are not synonymous with injuries. Accidents can result in property damage ranging from minor to catastrophic with no personal injury. Personal injuries ranging from minor to fatal can result from accidents. Employers do not want to hire people who will have job-related accidents. But in the total picture of job performance, accidents are not used as a criterion as often as production, turnover, or absence.

Theft. Employee theft is a major problem for organizations. In a study of hundreds of U.S. companies, 54% said they expected their own employees to steal company funds, equipment, or merchandise over the next year.[56] Estimates of the annual cost of employee theft are highly variable, ranging from $50 billion to $200 billion per year. Losses from employee theft per year tend to exceed losses from customer shoplifting.[57] From an I-O psychologist's perspective, the goal is to hire people who are unlikely to steal from the company, just as it is desirable to hire people who have a low probability of incurring accidents. Some employees resort to theft as a means of off-setting perceived unfairness in how their employer treats them.[58]

Consider This...

Many organizations experience problems of theft by employees. Thefts include office supplies used in work, such as staplers and tape dispensers, as well as items that are intended for sale to customers. Sometimes cash is stolen. What all these items have in common is that they are assets or resources of the company. Now consider a situation where the biggest concern is not the theft of resources, but the theft of waste! For example, consider a company that prints U.S. postage stamps. The worth of each stamp is the value printed on the stamp—usually the cost of mailing one ounce of first-class mail—58¢ in 2021. Although there may be some concern that employees might steal the postage stamps for their personal use, the bigger concern would be the theft of misprints or errors. Printing errors occur when a stamp is printed off-center or, in extreme cases, when the printing on the stamp is correct but the image is inverted. One 58¢ stamp printed with an inverted image may be worth thousands of dollars to philatelists (stamp collectors). In the printing of postage stamps, errors occur as they do in all other types of printing. In this case, however, the errors have very high market value. To reduce the possibility of theft of misprints that were scheduled to be destroyed, the company would likely have extensive sets of search and security procedures for anyone leaving the company. What other forms of theft might an organization be concerned about?

A drawback in using theft as a job performance criterion is that only a small percentage of employees are ever caught stealing. The occurrence of theft often has to be deduced on the basis of shortages calculated from company inventories of supplies and products. In addition, many companies will not divulge any information about theft to outside individuals. Although companies often share information on such criteria as absenteeism and turnover, theft records are too sensitive to reveal. Despite these limitations, I-O psychologists regard theft as an index of employment suitability, and we will probably see much more research on theft in the years ahead.

Counterproductive work behavior
A broad range of employee behaviors that are harmful to other employees or the organization.

Counterproductive Work Behavior. **Counterproductive work behavior** (also called deviant work behavior) includes a broad range of intentional employee actions that are harmful for the organization and people associated with the organization (e.g., employees, customers).[59] Theft is an example of counterproductive behavior, but it was discussed as a separate criterion because of its extreme criticality for many organizations. Deviance can be classified as being either interpersonal or organizational.[60] Interpersonal counterproductive work behavior is targeted toward other individuals, and is represented by gossip, bullying, threats of violence, and theft from coworkers. Organizational counterproductive work behavior is targeted against the organization as a whole, and includes intentionally working slowly, damaging company property, and disclosing confidential information. A common thread running through all of these counterproductive behaviors is intentionality; that is, the employee deliberately engages in them. Some scholars have proposed that counterproductive work behaviors are committed by individuals who have aberrant personalities.[61] Several personality assessments have been specifically designed to identify such people (the topic of integrity testing is discussed in Chapter 5). For example, researchers have found that individuals with high (vs. low) levels of integrity (as measured by an integrity test) are less (vs. more) likely to engage in counterproductive work behaviors when they are passed over for promotions.[62] Thus, from a personnel selection standpoint, the goal of the organization is to screen out applicants who are predicted to engage in these behaviors. In contrast to attributes that are used to "select in" applicants because they reflect positive or desirable work behaviors, counterproductive work behaviors reflect criteria used to "screen out" applicants who are predicted to exhibit them on the job. Counterproductive work behavior is discussed in greater detail in Chapter 11.

Emotional labor
The requirement in some jobs that employees express emotions that are associated with enhanced performance in the job.

Emotional Labor. It is common for individuals to be expected to express certain emotions as part of their job. For example, a server may be expected to smile while greeting customers to demonstrate warmth and happiness. This expectation is referred to as **emotional labor**, a term selected deliberately to connote toil, or a sense of onerous duty on the part of the employee whose job requires it. Employees who exhibit particular emotions are engaging in *display rules*. Display rules are specific behavioral acts that reflect the underlying emotions customers expect. Examples include smiling, voice inflection, and emotion-consistent expressions. These display rules and corresponding emotions are typically found in the service industry, and are generally referenced as "service with a smile."[63] These positive emotional displays result in satisfied customers becoming repeat customers, and who in turn recommend the experience to others.[64] That said, research has revealed customers can "decode" displays of emotions by employees.[65] Customers prefer authentic emotional displays, not phoniness (i.e., those that appear contrived for the purpose of manipulation; see Faces of I-O

Psychology: *Lawrence Houston III*). An example would be employees who always smile irrespective of the nature of the customer/employee interaction.

Even call center employees who neither give nor receive face-to-face emotional displays with customers must be adept at handling customer complaints over the phone. Some call centers use computerized emotion detector systems to analyze emotions based on voice pitch, tone, cadence, and word usage. The intent of the system is to alert supervisors to highly disgruntled customers that drain the emotional capacity of employees in dealing with such extreme cases. The supervisors can intervene in the call, sparing the employee, and being more responsive to the irate customer.[66]

Faces of I-O Psychology: *Lawrence Houston III*

Lawrence Houston III

Ph.D. Pennsylvania State University

Research interests: Interpersonal relations in the workplace, including leadership, diversity management, employee onboarding, and impression management.

According to the Bureau of Labor Statistics, service jobs account for more than 80% of U.S. employment and about 73% of all new businesses in the private sector. In other words, the service sector is "where the action is." As an owner and manager of a recording studio that provided services to local musicians, I experienced first-hand the challenges of satisfying a diverse customer base and, ultimately, outperforming my competitors. While pursuing my doctorate degree in I-O psychology, I therefore became particularly passionate about understanding the process whereby employees regulate their behavior when interacting with customers (or coworkers) to meet or exceed expectations, and how these processes unfold across subgroups. In one study, my colleagues and I found that White customers expected to receive "service with a smile," and therefore were less likely to return to a store if an employee "faked it" as opposed to expressing genuine positive emotions.[67] Blacks, on the other hand, anchored their service expectations at a comparatively lower level than Whites did because of their prior experiences in the United States. Blacks tended to remain loyal customers if greeted with a friendly smile, even if that smile was not always genuinely felt. In another study, we found that the Black-White racial disparity in service performance evaluations occurred because customers and supervisors tended to hold negative, stereotypical expectations about Blacks' interpersonal warmth and, thus, viewed them as less fit for customer service jobs than Whites. Black employees, therefore, had to put in extra effort to amplify their positive expressions and appear more interpersonally warm than expected in order to be evaluated comparably to White employees. These findings highlight the importance for service managers to fully understand employees' and customers' diverse experiences and expectations. Companies can also help to manage their customers' expectations and ensure that service employees are fully recognized for their hard work. My colleagues and I have found that when employees managed their impressions on a daily basis, they became depleted; as a result, they were less likely to regulate their behavior to comply with organizational norms and refrain from counterproductive behaviors. Given that jobs in the service sector are collectively the largest contributor to the U.S. economy, I strongly believe that managers and researchers should continue to investigate ways to avoid potential inconsistencies in performance standards that can be attributed to the employee's and/or customer's race.

Not all required emotions need be positive. For jobs such as security personnel and bill collectors, the desired emotions would include aggressiveness, suspicion, and skepticism. The corresponding display rules would include a stern tone of voice, facial scowling, and arms crossed against the chest to indicate a defensive posture.[68] A third type of emotional display is that of being neither positive nor negative, but instead appearing unemotional.[69] The need for this type of emotional display is found in law enforcement, where keeping calm and not showing emotions can mean the difference between life and death.

Display rules can be differentiated between *surface acting* and *deep acting*. In surface acting, individuals regulate their emotional expressions by faking the necessary emotions. In deep acting, individuals attempt to change their cognitive processes to actually feel the required emotions.[70] Another difference between surface and deep acting is the length of time the "actor" (the employee) must engage in the behavior. A food server at a restaurant, for example, may only have to exhibit a warm, cheerful, and attentive demeanor for a few minutes at a time while taking orders and delivering the food to the table. These short bursts are examples of surface acting. Conversely, a funeral director would be required to exhibit the emotions of shared grief, compassion, and empathy for several hours in succession with the relatives of the deceased. Funeral directors most likely must regulate their internal emotions and are therefore engaging in deep acting. Surface acting exhibited by the food server may be more stressful because of the intermittent chronicity associated with having to exhibit the display rules (e.g., alternating "on/off" interactions of short duration with many customers).[71] In line with this, researchers have found that increased surface acting at work relates to emotional exhaustion at home in the evening and with insomnia at night.[72] Conversely, the duration of the funeral director's interactions (several hours per funeral) may require deeper immersion in the emotion to sustain the requisite behaviors. As such, deep acting may induce less stress in employees because the emotions are internalized by the employee, which is not required in surface acting. In summary, employees who must project certain emotions through display rules as part of their jobs may not allow their own personal emotional states to interfere with the emotional front they must exhibit for their customers.

Adaptive and Citizenship Behavior. This final criterion is somewhat contrary to the theme of this section—criteria of *job* performance—because its focus can extend beyond the job. Adaptive and citizenship behaviors reflect the importance of employees contributing to the welfare of the organization in ways that transcend their specific jobs.

The emergence of adaptive behavior as being important derived from the continuous pressures placed on organizations over the past 50 years (as discussed in Chapter 1), and the need for employees to adapt their own behavior to these changing work duties. With the constantly changing nature of work brought on in part from increased technology and globalization, there is considerable demand for employees who demonstrate high levels of versatility, flexibility, and adaptability.[73]

Adaptive behavior
A range of behaviors that enable employees to increase their capacity to cope with organizational change.

The essence of **adaptive behavior** is for people to be aware of changing conditions in their work environment, and to adjust their own behavior in a manner to become more effective. Examples include changing work conditions due to new customer

Consider This...

The research on emotional labor may have you thinking that surface acting is always bad, while deep acting is always good. This is not necessarily the case. For example, studies have shown that extraverts (vs. introverts) can engage in surface acting without the negative repercussions, especially when the service interactions are more autonomous. In addition, it appears that surface acting is less unpleasant—and actually satisfying—when it is rewarded, such as with tips or raises. This is good news, since deep acting is not always possible, given the time and attention it takes to step back and actually change one's feelings. Nevertheless, when it's possible, deep acting is probably the way to go, given the consistently-better outcomes associated with this approach versus just "faking it" with surface acting. It has been suggested that employees take recovery breaks to reduce the strain of emotional labor. In addition, mindfulness training has been shown to provide some assistance in managing the stress associated with emotional labor. Another suggestion is allowing employees to "be real" with regard to their emotions rather than requiring certain emotional displays. What do you think about these suggestions? In particular, what concerns might there be with letting employees "be real" at work? Do the benefits outweigh the problems, or vice versa?

demands and new technology systems to which employees must be responsive. Furthermore, the employees must accept the need to continuously adapt their behavior without displays of resistance or complaint. A meta-analysis on personality factors associated with adaptive work behavior found emotional stability and ambition to be most strongly predictive of it.[74]

Citizenship behavior Employee behavior that transcends job performance and is directed to the overall welfare of the organization.

In addition to employees being holders of a job, they can also be regarded as "citizens" of the organization. **Citizenship behavior** refers to those aspects of employee performance that transcend performing tasks on a job. They address contributions made by the employee for the betterment of the organization. As such, employees who make these behavioral contributions are regarded as "good citizens" of the organization. Citizenship behaviors are represented in two broad dimensions: personal support and organizational support. Personal support involves doing little things that help other employees perform their jobs more effectively. Examples include helping others by offering ideas and suggestions about their work, and being courteous and considerate in relations with coworkers. Organizational support refers to exhibiting loyalty to the organization through publically endorsing its mission and goals, and being a good "ambassador" of the organization by promoting its achievements. Employees who exhibit citizenship behavior are typically regarded favorably by organizations. A survey of human resource managers revealed that the degree to which a candidate was judged to be a "good fit" with the organization (not just the job) was increasingly important in making personnel selection decisions.[75] In fact, positive citizenship behaviors can carry more weight than successful task performance in supervisory assessments of overall work performance. The topic of citizenship behaviors is discussed in greater detail in Chapter 11.

Consider This...

By definition, citizenship behavior is behavior that transcends job performance. This is an important point, as this means that it is neither required nor expected. Indeed, as will be discussed in Chapter 11, these behaviors are also called "extra-role behaviors" because they go beyond the required role that an individual fills. Nevertheless, because citizenship behaviors are beneficial to the organization, they are desirable and may become expected by some, as well as expected for some individuals. For example, research suggests that unmarried employees may be expected by organizations to engage in more citizenship behaviors, under the assumption they have more time to devote to non-job activities compared to their married colleagues.[76] Some scholars have argued that requiring such behaviors, particularly for some employees and not others, is unfair and could be problematic for the organization.[77] What do you think? Should citizenship behavior be required of employees? Should it be given more, the same as, or less weight than task performance? Should some people, such as unmarried employees, be more responsible for citizenship behaviors, as research suggests is the case? Why or why not?

Summary of Job Performance Criteria. A consideration of the major performance criteria reveals marked differences not only in what they measure but also in how they are measured. They differ along an objective/subjective continuum. Some criteria are highly objective, meaning they can be measured with a high degree of accuracy. Examples are units of production, days absent, and dollar sales volume. There are few disagreements about the final tally because the units, days, or dollars are merely counted. Nevertheless, there could be disagreements about the interpretation or meaning of these objectively-counted numbers. Other criteria are less objective. Theft, for example, is not the same as being caught stealing. Based on company records of merchandise, an organization might know that employee theft has occurred but not know who did it. As was noted, although employee theft is a major problem, relatively few employees are ever caught stealing. The broader criterion of counterproductive work behavior includes dimensions that are particularly subjective. For example, we all probably waste some time on the job, but only at some point is it considered "deviant." Likewise, there is probably a fine line between being "outspoken" (it is good to express your feelings and opinions) and "argumentative" (it is bad to be negative and resist progress). Customer service behavior is a highly-subjective criterion. An employee's customer service performance is strictly a product of other people's perceptions, and there may be as many judgments of that behavior as there are customers. Likewise, how adaptive we are at work and the degree to which we are regarded as good organizational citizens are judgments typically made by others. How we perceive ourselves and how others perceive us within an organizational context can be quite different. Chapter 8 will examine sources of agreement and disagreement in assessing job performance.

From this discussion, it is clear that no single measure of job performance is totally adequate. Each criterion may have merit, but each can also suffer from weakness along other dimensions. For instance, few people would say that an employee's absence has no bearing on overall job performance, but no one would say that absence is a complete measure of job performance. Absence, like production, is only one piece of the broader picture. Don't be discouraged that no one criterion meets all our standards. It is precisely because job performance is multidimensional (and each single dimension is a fallible index of overall performance) that we are compelled to include many relevant aspects of work in establishing criteria. Furthermore, every job performance criterion suffers from some degree of deficiency and contamination.

Dynamic Performance Criteria

Dynamic performance criteria Aspects of job performance that change (increase or decrease) over time.

The concept of **dynamic performance criteria** applies to job performance criteria that change over time. It is significant because job performance is sometimes not stable or consistent over time, and this dynamic quality of criteria adds to the complexity of making personnel decisions. There are three potential reasons for systematic changes in job performance over time.[78] First, employees might change the way they perform tasks as a result of repeatedly completing them. Second, the knowledge and ability requirements needed to perform the task might change because of changing work technologies. Third, the knowledge and skills of the employees might change as a result of additional training.

Consider Figure 4-5, which shows the levels of three job performance criteria—productivity, absence, and accidents—over an eight-year period. The time period represents a person's eight-year performance record on a job. Notice that the pattern of behavior for the three criteria differ over time. The individual's level of accidents is stable over time, so accidents are a stable (not dynamic) performance criterion. A very different pattern emerges for the other two criteria. The individual's level of productivity increases over the years, more gradually in the early years and then more dramatically in the later years. Absence, on the other hand, follows the opposite pattern. The employee's absence was greatest in the first year of employment and

Figure 4-5 *Performance variations in three criteria over an eight-year period*

progressively declined over time. Absence and productivity are dynamic performance criteria. When a job applicant is considered for employment, the organization attempts to predict how well that person will perform on the job. A hire/no hire decision is then made on the basis of this prediction. If job performance criteria are static (like accidents in Figure 4-5), the prediction is more accurate because of the stability of the behavior. If job performance criteria are dynamic, however, a critical new element is added to the decision, *time*. It may be that initially, productivity would not be very impressive, but over time, the employee's performance would rise to and then surpass a satisfactory level. Dynamic performance criteria are equivalent to "hitting a moving target," as the level of the behavior being predicted is continuously changing. Furthermore, the pattern of change may be different across individuals. That is, for some people, productivity may start off low and then get progressively higher, whereas for others, the pattern may be the reverse.

Dynamic performance criteria can be explained by a learning curve.[79] Work productivity improves based on the accumulation of experience, and employees exhibit different rates of learning-by-doing. Conversely, individuals with a relatively flat learning curve will be much slower, in comparison, to exhibit performance improvements in their jobs. Learning curves can be thought of as "performance trajectories" that can elevate due to knowledge acquisition or skill development, or decline due to fatigue or stress.[80] From an empirical perspective, our ability to understand and predict learning curves can only be achieved by studying employee behavior over an extended time period. In practice, however, most research on employee behavior has tended to be cross-sectional (i.e., at one point in time).

Chapter Review

Key Terms

Criteria
Conceptual criteria
Actual criteria
Criterion deficiency
Criterion relevance
Criterion contamination
Work analysis
Subject matter expert (SME)
Task
Position
Job
Job family
Task-oriented procedure
Functional Job Analysis (FJA)
Worker-oriented procedure
KSAOs
Linkage analysis
Taxonomy
Position Analysis Questionnaire (PAQ)
Occupational Information Network (O*NET)
Competency modeling
Objective performance criteria
Subjective performance criteria
Maximum performance
Typical performance
Counterproductive work behavior
Emotional labor
Adaptive behavior
Citizenship behavior
Dynamic performance criteria

Questions for Review

1. What are criteria? What are conceptual criteria, and what are actual criteria? In what situations is it important to be aligned on both? How do values and experiences factor in to evaluating "good" and "bad" criteria?
2. What are criterion deficiency, relevance and contamination?
3. What is work analysis? What is an SME? What three types of people are usually sources for work analysis, and what are the advantages and disadvantages of using each type?
4. What are tasks, positions, jobs, and job families? How are they related?
5. What is a work analytic procedure?
6. What is a task-oriented procedure? What is a Functional Job Analysis and when is it typically used?
7. What are worker-oriented procedures? What does "KSAO" stand for? Why are KSAOs important in work analyses?
8. Why are linkage analyses important in work analyses?
9. What is a taxonomy?
10. What is a Position Analysis Questionnaire (PAQ) and how is a PAQ used in work analysis?
11. What is the Taxonomy of Human Performance and how is it used in work analysis?
12. What is O*NET and how is it used in work analysis?
13. How do traditional (blue-collar) work analyses differ from managerial work analyses?
14. How can work analyses be used?
15. What is competency modeling? How do organizations use it to select and evaluate personnel?
16. What are the two types of job performance criteria?
17. What types of behavior are frequently evaluated? What are the "positive" behaviors? What are their "negative" counterparts?
18. What are dynamic performance criteria? How can differences in a person's performance over time be explained?

CHAPTER 5

Predictors: Psychological Assessments

Chapter Outline

Assessing the Quality of Predictors
- Reliability
- Validity
- The Interplay Between Reliability and Validity

Predictor Development
- The Lighter Side of I-O Psychology: *The Poetry of Prediction*

Ability Tests
- Cognitive Ability
- Physical Ability
- Psychomotor Ability
- Sensory/Perceptual Ability

Personality Inventories
- Faking in Personality Assessment
- Social Media and I-O Psychology: *Assessing Personality via Facebook*
- Integrity Tests

Situational Judgment Tests

Biodata Inventories

Drug Testing

Computerized Adaptive Testing

Online Testing
- Faces of I-O Psychology: *John C. Scott*

Interviews
- Degree of Structure
- Interview Formats

Work Samples and Situational Exercises
- Work Samples
- Situational Exercises

Assessment Centers

Letters of Recommendation

Overview and Evaluation of Predictors
- COVID-19 and I-O Psychology: *Unanswered Questions*

Chapter Review

Learning Objectives

- Describe the major types of reliability and what they measure.
- Describe the major manifestations of validity and what they measure.
- Summarize the interplay between reliability and validity.
- Assess the role of various predictors in making assessments of people, including ethical issues and predictive accuracy.
- Explain how computerized adaptive testing works.
- Identify issues related with online testing.
- Compare and contrast the predictors in terms of their validity, fairness, applicability, and cost.

A predictor is any variable used to forecast a criterion. In weather prediction, barometric pressure is used to forecast rainfall. In medical prediction, body temperature is used to predict (or diagnose) illness. When hiring individuals for a job, we seek predictors of how well that person will perform on the job. How do we predict the best performer for a particular job? Let's work through some possibilities:

Idea #1: We could look at who has had the job before and select the person among them who did the best. But if somebody has to do the job well in the past to get the job in the *future*, how does one ever get that first job? It's the problem that many college students lament: This job needs experience, but you need experience to get the job in the first place. What do you do?

Idea #2: We could simply ask them how good they are at the job. This one is flawed by its simplicity, in that people may lie or not use the same standard as you do. Does "proficient in Excel" mean that you know *everything* there is to know with Excel, or that you have *opened* it before—or somewhere in between?

Idea #3: We could have them perform the job for a trial period and see how they do. What if you're hiring for a surgeon or a pilot? Do you really plan to have somebody operate on people for a week or fly an expensive plane with passengers and just see how they do?

Idea #4: We could ask people who know them whether they would be good at the job. But again, how do we know those people are being truthful or using the same standard as we are using?

Idea #5: We could flip a coin—if it's heads, we hire them; if it's tails, we don't hire them. This approach may be fine if we don't actually care who we hire or if anybody could do the job. It's not a great strategy if we're not okay with letting our decisions be made by chance.

Clearly, predicting job performance isn't as simple as it might seem on the surface. There are many things we must consider. While many of the ideas above are ones we actually do, and will discuss in this chapter, not all of them are appropriate for all jobs. For example, in some jobs it is appropriate to have applicants complete a work sample, in which they demonstrate their ability to perform an actual job. This may not work as well with surgeons—at least not with real patients. Instead, we may want them to demonstrate their skills in a simulation and/or show they have completed the necessary training to be a surgeon. In addition, not all predictors are created equally. In some cases, it makes sense to ask applicants questions about their knowledge, skills, abilities, and experiences. We do this in employment interviews and find they can be excellent predictors of performance. However, not all interviews are the same, nor should they be. A "good" interview will have questions that reflect elements important for the job in question (among other characteristics we'll discuss later in this chapter).

Fortunately, I-O psychologists have explored a multitude of devices as potential predictors of job performance criteria. This chapter will review the predictors traditionally used, examine their success, and discuss some problems inherent in their use. Before jumping into the specific predictors, we will begin with a discussion of how to determine whether a predictor is "good" or not by assessing the quality of predictors.

Assessing the Quality of Predictors

Psychometric
Literally, the measurement ("metric") of properties of the mind (from the Greek word "psyche"). The standards used to measure the quality of psychological assessments.

Reliability
A standard for evaluating tests that refers to the consistency, stability, or equivalence of test scores. Often contrasted with validity.

Test–retest reliability
A type of reliability that reveals the stability of test scores upon repeated applications of the test.

Equivalent-form reliability
A type of reliability that reveals the equivalence of test scores between two versions or forms of the test.

All predictor variables, like other measuring devices, can be assessed in terms of their quality or goodness. We can think of several features of a good measuring device. We would like it to be consistent and accurate; that is, it should repeatedly yield precise measurements. In psychology, we judge the goodness of our measuring devices by two **psychometric** criteria: reliability and validity. If a predictor is not both reliable and valid, it is useless.

Reliability

Reliability refers to the consistency, stability, or equivalence of a measure. A measure should yield the same estimate on repeated uses if the measured trait has not changed. Even though that estimate may be inaccurate, a reliable measure will always be consistent. For example, if you weighed yourself on a reliable scale three times back-to-back, you should get the same weight each time. The scale may be "off" and saying you are three pounds more than you truly are each time, but it's still giving you a consistent (i.e., reliable) reading. We will now discuss four types of reliability often used in I-O psychology.

Test–Retest Reliability. **Test–retest reliability** is perhaps the simplest assessment of a measuring device's reliability. We measure something at two different times and compare the scores. We can give a personality inventory to the same group of people at two different times and then correlate the two sets of scores. This correlation is called a *coefficient of stability* because it reflects the stability of the test over time. If the test is reliable, those who scored high the first time will also score high the second time, and those who scored low on the first will also score low on the second. If the test is unreliable, the scores will "bounce around" in such a way that there is no similarity in individuals' scores between the two trials.

When we say a test (or any measure) is reliable, how high should the coefficient of stability be? The answer is "the higher the better." A test cannot be too reliable. As a rule, reliability coefficients around .70 are professionally acceptable (although .80 and above are better). Furthermore, the length of time between administrations of the test must be considered in the interpretation of a test's test–retest reliability. Generally, the test–retest reliability coefficient will be higher when the time interval between administrations is shorter (e.g., one week vs. six months).

Equivalent-Form Reliability. A second type of reliability is parallel or **equivalent-form reliability**. Here, a test-developer creates two forms of a test to measure the same attribute and gives both forms to the same group of people. The two scores for each person are then correlated. The resulting correlation, called a *coefficient of equivalence*, reflects the extent to which the two forms are sufficiently comparable measures of the same concept. Of the three major types of reliability, this type is the least popular because it is usually challenging to come up with one good test, let alone two. Many tests do not have a "parallel form." It is not easy to construct two tests whose scores have similar meanings and statistical properties such that they are truly parallel or equivalent measures.[1] Nevertheless, in intelligence and achievement testing (to be discussed shortly), equivalent forms of the same test are sometimes available. If the resulting coefficient of equivalence is high, the tests are sufficiently comparable and are viewed as reliable measures of the same concept. If it is low, they are not. Like test-retest reliability, the general rule for equivalent-form reliability is that coefficients around .70 are acceptable (although, again, higher coefficients are even better).

Internal-consistency reliability
A type of reliability that reveals the homogeneity of the items comprising a test.

Internal-Consistency Reliability. The third major assessment is the **internal-consistency reliability** of the test—the extent to which it has homogeneous content. Two types of internal-consistency reliability are typically computed. One is called split-half reliability. Here, a test is given to a group of people, and when it is time to score the test, the researcher divides the items in half. While it is possible to divide the test literally in half and compare the first half of the questions with the second half, researchers typically opt to divide the test into odd- and even-numbered items. The rationale is that fatigue issues that may occur when taking a long test would be accounted for evenly, as opposed to comparing the first half (when people are just beginning a test and are fresh) with the second half (when they may be tired). Each person thus gets two sets of scores (one for each half), which are correlated. If the test has internal-consistency reliability, there will be a high degree of similarity between the responses to the items from the two halves. All other things being equal, the longer a test, the greater its reliability.

A second technique for assessing internal-consistency reliability is to compute one of two coefficients: Cronbach's alpha coefficient or Kuder-Richardson 20 (KR20). Both procedures are similar though not statistically identical, with KR20 reserved for tests with dichotomous responses (e.g., right vs. wrong, true vs. false). Conceptually, each test item is treated as a mini-test. Thus a 100-item test consists of 100 mini-tests. The response to each item is correlated with the response to every other item. The average of those inter-item correlations is related to the homogeneity of the test. If the test is homogeneous (the item content is similar), it will have a high internal-consistency reliability coefficient. If the test is heterogeneous (the items cover a wide variety of concepts), it is not internally consistent, and the resulting coefficient will be low. Internal-consistency reliability is frequently used to assess a test's homogeneity of content in I-O psychology with an acceptable coefficient lying in the .70-.80 range, with higher coefficients being better (more reliable).

Inter-rater reliability
A type of reliability that reveals the degree of agreement among the assessments provided by two or more raters.

Inter-Rater Reliability. When assessments are made based on raters' judgments, it is possible for the raters to disagree in their evaluations. Two different raters may observe the same behavior yet evaluate it differently. The degree of correspondence between judgments or scores assigned by different raters is most commonly referred to as **inter-rater reliability**, although it has also been called *inter-judge, inter-observer,* or *conspect reliability.* In some situations, raters must exercise judgment in arriving at a score. Two examples are multiple raters analyzing a job and multiple interviewers evaluating job candidates. The score or rating depends not only on the job or candidate but also on the persons doing the rating. The raters' characteristics may lead to distortions or errors in their judgments. Estimation of inter-rater reliability is usually expressed as a correlation and reflects the degree of agreement among the ratings. Evidence of high inter-rater reliability establishes a basis to conclude that the behavior was reliably observed, and in turn we conclude that such observations are accurate. Inter-rater reliability is frequently assessed to judge the degree of agreement across a variety of individuals and situations, including subject matter experts in work analysis, interviewers assessing the same candidates, evaluators in assessment center contexts (discussed later in this chapter), and coders conducting meta-analytic or qualitative studies.

Validity

Validity
A standard for evaluating tests that refers to the accuracy or appropriateness of drawing inferences from test scores. Often contrasted with reliability.

Reliability refers to consistency and stability of measurement; validity refers to accuracy. Validity concerns whether a test is correctly measuring what we intend to measure (i.e., what it was designed to measure). **Validity** is the accuracy or appropriateness for predicting or drawing inferences from test scores. In addition, whereas reliability is inherent in a measuring device, validity depends on the use of a test. Scores from a given test may be highly valid for predicting employee productivity but completely invalid for predicting employee absenteeism. In other words, it would be appropriate to draw inferences about employee productivity from the test scores but inappropriate to draw inferences about absenteeism.

There are several manifestations of validity, and they all involve determining the appropriateness of a measure (test) for drawing inferences. The word *validity* is often associated with two other words: *validation* and *validate*. Validation is the empirical process of determining the degree to which test scores are statistically related to criterion scores. To "validate a test" means to establish the degree to which it predicts one or more criteria. The results of a validation process may be to conclude a test is unrelated to a criterion of interest. The process of validating a test does not assure or guarantee any particular empirical outcome.

The word "valid" has a different meaning in everyday life compared to its use in psychology. We can speak of having a "valid" driver's license—either the driver's license is valid or not. This "either/or" thinking does not apply to the scientific meaning of the word "valid." Rather than either/or, the accuracy of a psychological test's scores to predict a criterion lies on a continuum, ranging from "not valid" to "highly valid." Arrayed along a continuum of validity, psychologists must decide if a test manifests enough validity to warrant its use. However, it is overly simplistic to think of tests as either being valid or not.

Validity has been a controversial topic within the field of psychology.[2] For many years, psychologists believed there were "types" of validity, just as there are types of reliability (test–retest, internal consistency, etc.). Now we believe there is but a single or unitary conception of validity. Rather than having types of validity, we have sources of evidence that we use to support our interpretations or inferences about whatever it is we're measuring.

Construct
Theoretical concept to explain aspects of behavior.

Operationalization
The process of determining how a construct will be assessed.

Psychologists are involved in the formulation, measurement, and interpretation of constructs. A **construct** is a theoretical concept we propose to explain aspects of behavior. Examples of constructs in I-O psychology are intelligence, motivation, work ethic, and leadership. Because constructs are abstractions (ideas), we must have real, tangible ways to assess them; that is, we need an actual measure of the proposed construct. The process of spelling out exactly how a construct will be measured is called **operationalization**. For example, a paper-and-pencil test of intelligence is one way to measure the psychological construct of intelligence. Another operationalization of intelligence might be ratings assigned by experts who have interacted with an individual. The degree to which an actual measure (i.e., a test of intelligence) is an accurate and faithful representation of its underlying construct (i.e., the construct of intelligence) is **construct validity**.

Construct validity
The degree to which a test is an accurate and faithful measure of the construct it purports to measure.

Construct Validity. In studying construct validity, psychologists seek to ascertain the linkage between what the test measures and the theoretical construct. Let us assume we wish to understand the construct of intelligence, and to do so we develop a paper-and-pencil test that we believe assesses that construct. To establish the construct validity of our test, we want to compare scores on our test with known measures of intelligence, such as verbal, numerical, and problem-solving ability. If our test is a faithful assessment of intelligence, then the scores on our test should converge with these other known measures of intelligence. More technically, there should be a high correlation between the scores from our new test of intelligence and the existing measures of intelligence. These correlation coefficients are referred to as *convergent validity coefficients* because they reflect the degree to which these scores converge (or come together) in assessing a common concept, intelligence.

Likewise, scores on our test should not be related to concepts that we know are *not* related to intelligence, such as physical strength, eye color, and gender. More technically, there should be very low correlations between the scores from our new test of intelligence and these concepts. These correlation coefficients are referred to as *divergent validity coefficients* because they reflect the degree to which these scores diverge (or are separate) from each other in assessing unrelated concepts. They are also known as discriminant validity coefficients because the concepts are distinguishable from other concepts. If, after collecting and evaluating information about the test, we accumulate a body of evidence supporting the notion that the test measures a psychological construct, then we say that the test manifests a high degree of construct validity.

Construct validation is a process of demonstrating evidence for five linkages or inferences, as illustrated in Figure 5-1.[3] Figure 5-1 shows two empirical measures and two constructs. X is a measure of construct 1, such as a test of intelligence that purports to measure the psychological construct of intelligence. Y is a measure of construct 2, such as a supervisor's assessment of an employee's performance that purports to measure the construct of job performance. Linkage 1 is the only one that can be tested directly because it is the only inference involving two variables that are directly measured (X and Y). In assessing the construct validity of X and Y, one would be most interested in assessing linkages 2 and 4, respectively. That is, we would want to know that the empirical measures of X and Y are faithful and accurate assessments of the constructs (1 and 2) they purport to measure. Because our empirical measures are never perfect indicators of the constructs we seek to understand, it has been suggested that researchers should devote more attention to assessing linkages 2 and 4.[4] For the purpose of constructing theories of job performance, one would be interested in linkage 3, the relationship between the two constructs. Finally, in personnel selection, we are interested in linkage 5; that is, the inference between an employment test score and the domain of performance on the job. Thus, the process of construct validation involves examining the linkages among multiple concepts of interest to us. We

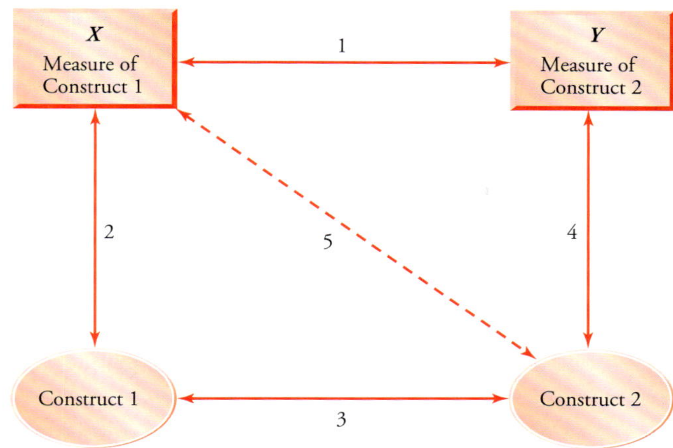

Figure 5-1
Inferential linkages in construct validation

Adapted from "Validity of Personnel Decisions: A Conceptual Analysis of the Inferential and Evidential Bases," by J. F. Binning and G. V. Barrett, *Journal of Applied Psychology, 74*, p. 480.

Consider This...

Construct validity and the five linkages that describe construct validation are often difficult concepts for students to grasp at first. Let's walk through another example to provide more context. Say we're interested in hiring realtors. We believe that extraverted people (individuals who tend to be outgoing and sociable) would likely make better realtors. Our two constructs would be (1) extraversion and (2) realtor job performance. We then need to operationalize both of those constructs. We decide to use an established personality measure to assess extraversion. (We could have used peer ratings of extraversion, number of minutes talked during the day, or something else to reflect this construct—our choice was just one of many possible ones.) We decide to use real estate sales figures as our measure of realtor job performance. (We could also have used client ratings of their realtor's job performance, number of open houses held in a month, or any one of many possibilities. Again, our operationalization is just one choice of many possible ones.) So, X is the extraversion measure and Y is the sales figures. Linkage 1 is the correlation between X and Y. We can get a real value for this since we have actual scores from the extraversion test and actual sales figures from our records. This is the only "real" value we'll be able to derive. All of the other linkages are formed through inferences. Does the extraversion measure truly get at extraversion? That's Link 2. Do sales figures really reflect sales performance? That's Link 4. If we can establish those three links, we can infer that Link 3 must exist. That is, if we are accurately measuring our constructs, and those measures are related, it should be the case that the constructs themselves are related. We don't *know* this; we are simply *inferring* it based on what we've already established. Lastly, with all of those points determined, we can say that our measure of extraversion must be predictive of the realtor job performance domain. This is key for personnel selection and will impact our use of the extraversion measure going forward as a predictor of realtors. We've given you two examples. Now create your own example to ensure full understanding. Suppose you're interested in hiring a chef. What constructs would you use? How would you operationalize them? Would you be able to draw inferences for Links 3 and 5 with your chosen constructs and measures?

always operate at the empirical level (X and Y), yet we wish to draw inferences at the conceptual level (constructs 1 and 2). Construct validation is the continuous process of verifying the accuracy of an inference among concepts for the purpose of furthering our ability to understand those concepts, and the confidence we have in the inferences made is directly related to the strength of the evidence collected.[5]

Criterion-related validity
The degree to which a test forecasts or is statistically related to a criterion.

Criterion-Related Validity. One manifestation of construct validity is the criterion-related validity of a test. As its name suggests, **criterion-related validity** refers to how much a predictor relates to a criterion. The two major variations of criterion-related validity are *concurrent* and *predictive*. Concurrent validity is used to diagnose the existing status of some criterion, whereas predictive validity is used to forecast future status. The primary distinction is the time interval between collecting the predictor and criterion data.

In measuring concurrent criterion-related validity, we are concerned with how well a predictor can predict a criterion at the same time, or concurrently. Examples abound. We may wish to predict a student's grade point average based on a test score, so we collect data on the grade point averages of many students, and then we administer a predictor test. If the predictor test is a valid measure of grades, there will be a high correlation between test scores and grades. We can use the same method in a work setting. We can predict a worker's level of productivity (the criterion) based on a test (the predictor). We collect productivity data on a current group of workers, administer a test, and then correlate their test scores with their productivity records. If the test is of value, then we can draw an inference about a worker's productivity based on the test score. In measurements of concurrent validity, there is no time interval between collecting the predictor and criterion data. The two variables are assessed concurrently, which is how the method gets its name. Thus, the purpose of assessing concurrent criterion-related validity is so the test can be used with the knowledge that it is predictive of the criterion.

In measuring predictive criterion-related validity, we collect predictor information and use it to forecast future criterion performance. A college might use a student's high school class rank to predict the criterion of overall college grade point average four years later. A company could use a test to predict whether job applicants will complete a six-month training program. Figure 5-2 graphically illustrates concurrent and predictive criterion-related validity.

Validity coefficient
A statistical index (expressed as a correlation coefficient) that reveals the degree of association between two variables.

The logic of criterion-related validity is straightforward. We determine whether there is a relationship between predictor scores and criterion scores based on a sample of employees for whom we have both sets of scores. If there is a relationship, we use scores on those predictor variables to select applicants on whom there are no criterion scores. Then we can predict the applicant's future (and thus unknown) criterion performance from their known test scores based on the relationship established through criterion-related validity. When predictor scores are correlated with criterion data, the resulting correlation is called a **validity coefficient**. Whereas an acceptable reliability coefficient is in the .70–.80 range, the desired range for a validity coefficient is .30–.40. Validity coefficients less than .30 are not uncommon, but those greater than .50 are rare. Just as a predictor cannot be too reliable, it also cannot be too valid. The greater the correlation between the predictor and the criterion, the more we know about the criterion based on the predictor.

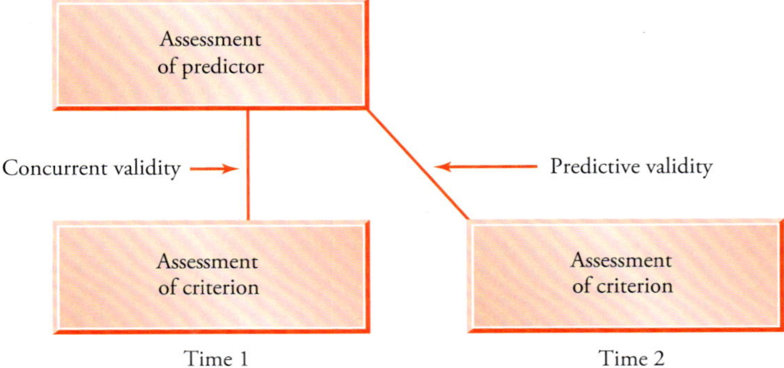

Figure 5-2 *Portrayal of concurrent and predictive criterion-related validity*

By squaring the correlation coefficient (*r*), we can calculate how much variance in the criterion we can account for by using the predictor. For example, if a predictor correlates .40 with a criterion, we can explain 16% (r^2) of the variance in the criterion by knowing the predictor. This particular level of predictability (16%) would be considered satisfactory by most psychologists, given all the possible causes of performance variation. A correlation of 1.0 indicates perfect prediction (and complete knowledge). However, tests with moderate validity coefficients are not necessarily flawed or inadequate. The results attest to the complexity of human behavior. Our behavior is influenced by factors not measured by tests, such as motivation and luck. We should thus have realistic expectations regarding the validity of our tests.

Some criteria are difficult to predict no matter what predictors are used; other criteria are fairly predictable. Similarly, some predictors are consistently valid and are thus used often. Other predictors do not seem to be of much predictive value no matter what the criteria are, and thus they fall out of use. Usually, however, certain predictors are valid for predicting only certain criteria. Later in this chapter there will be a review of the predictors typically used in I-O psychology and an examination of how accurate they are in predicting criteria.

Content validity
The degree to which subject matter experts agree that the items in a test are a representative sample of the domain of knowledge the test purports to measure.

Content Validity. Another manifestation of construct validity is content validity. **Content validity** is the degree to which a predictor covers a representative sample of the behavior being assessed. It is limited mainly to psychological tests but may also extend to interviews or other predictors. Historically, content validity was most relevant in achievement testing. Achievement tests are designed to indicate how well a person has mastered a specific area of knowledge. To be "content valid," an achievement test on Civil War history, for example, must contain a representative sample or mix of test items covering the domain of Civil War history, such as battles, military and political figures, and so on. A test with only questions about the dates of famous battles would not be a balanced representation of the content of Civil War history. If a person scores high on a content-valid test of Civil War history, we can infer that the individual is very knowledgeable about the Civil War.

How do we assess content validity? Unlike criterion-related validity, we do not compute a correlation coefficient. Content validity is assessed by subject matter experts in the field the test covers. Civil War historians would first define the domain of the Civil War and then write test questions about it. These experts would then decide how content valid the test is. Their judgments could range from "not at all" to "highly valid." Presumably, the test would be revised until it showed a high degree of content validity.

Face validity
The appearance that items in a test are appropriate for the intended use of the test by the individuals who take the test.

A similar type of validity based on people's judgments is called **face validity**. This is concerned with the appearance of the test items: do they look appropriate for such a test? Estimates of content validity are made by test developers; estimates of face validity are made by test takers. It is possible for a test to be content valid but not face valid, and vice versa. In such a case, the test developers and test takers would disagree over the relevance or appropriateness of the items for the domain being assessed. Within the field of psychology, content validity is thought to be of greater importance than face validity. However, the face validity of a test can greatly affect how individuals perceive the test as an appropriate, legitimate means of assessing them for some important decision (such as a job offer). Individuals are more likely to bring legal challenges against companies for using tests that they do not see as face valid. Thus, issues of content validity are generally more relevant for the science of I-O psychology, whereas issues of face validity are generally more relevant for the practice of I-O psychology.

Once used mainly for academic achievement testing, it is also relevant for employment testing. There is a strong and obvious link between the process of work analysis (discussed in Chapter 4) and the concept of content validation. The logic of content validity is that (a) if a test measures knowledge associated with a particular job and (b) the content of that test is related to the content of that job, then (c) the test is a useful predictor of job performance in that particular job. The problem with this logic is that, with content validity, there is no demonstrated empirical link between test performance and job performance (i.e., there is no evidence of the former predicting the latter). Establishing such a link is the result of assessing the criterion-related validity of a test. In fact, content-matched tests do not result in higher criterion-related validity coefficients than do tests that do not match the content of the job.[6] It is even possible for a test to have a high degree of content match with a job but manifest no criterion-related validity.

There is certainly no harm in having employment tests where the content of the test corresponds to the job. But the mere similarity of content between the two offers

Consider This...

Let's walk through the (flawed) logic of content validity. Consider a test that measures knowledge of street locations for the job of taxi driver. We can assume that knowledge of street locations is indeed relevant for taxi drivers, and our test does indeed measure that knowledge. However, this does not mean that the test is a useful predictor of job performance for a taxi driver. Why is that? Well, one reason could be that many taxi drivers use GPS to find streets. As such, knowledge of street locations may have a high degree of content match for the job, but in terms of actual job performance for a taxi driver, such knowledge may be useless given modern technology. What other examples can you think of in which a test might have the right content for the job but not actually relate to job performance? How about a situation in which a test has high face validity but isn't predictive of job performance?

no insights about the likely job performance of the selected candidates, which is the fundamental rationale of why assessments of job candidates are made. Indeed, the word "validity" has special significance for psychologists, as it addresses the meaning and accuracy of the inferences we make about people. As such, when the content of an employment test corresponds to the content of a job, most I-O psychologists would prefer to describe the "content representativeness" of the test rather than its "content validity." The distinction may be subtle but its importance is substantial.

The Interplay Between Reliability and Validity

As noted, reliability refers to the consistency and stability of measurement, whereas validity refers to the accuracy or appropriateness of inferences drawn from test scores. These two concepts are necessarily inter-related. Their relationship can be characterized by two important points. First, a test can be reliable but not valid. However, a test can never be valid without being reliable. A good metaphor for this is the game of darts, as shown in Figure 5-3. With a traditional game of darts, you have three darts that you throw separately within a single turn. Assume you are aiming for the inner bullseye, the red circle in the center of the dartboard, which is worth 50 points. If you hit the inner bullseye all three times, you could earn up to 150 points in your single turn. If this happened, we would say your aim is both accurate (valid) and reliable. If, however, you throw your three darts and they scatter all over the board, you have neither a reliable nor an accurate aim. It is possible to have a reliable throw that is not accurate. In this case, all of the darts may cluster around the upper left on the board. You are consistently throwing in the same spot, but it is not accurate (i.e., it is reliable but not valid). It is not possible to have an accurate shot that is not reliable. If one of the three darts happens to hit the bullseye, it does not mean your aim is accurate. Much like a game of darts, we don't always hit our target with regard to predicting job performance. We strive for reliability and validity in our measures, and are thankful when we achieve them.

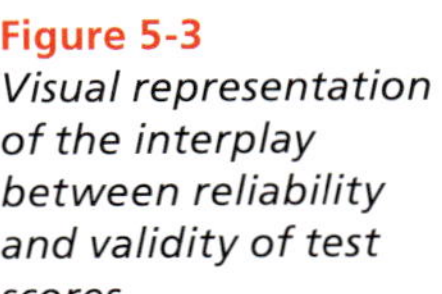

Figure 5-3
Visual representation of the interplay between reliability and validity of test scores

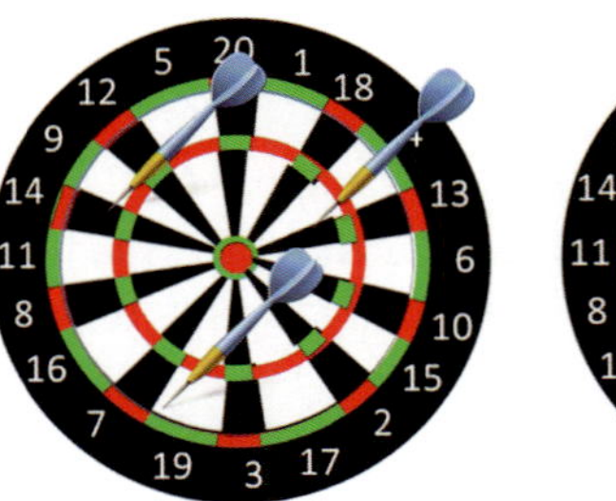

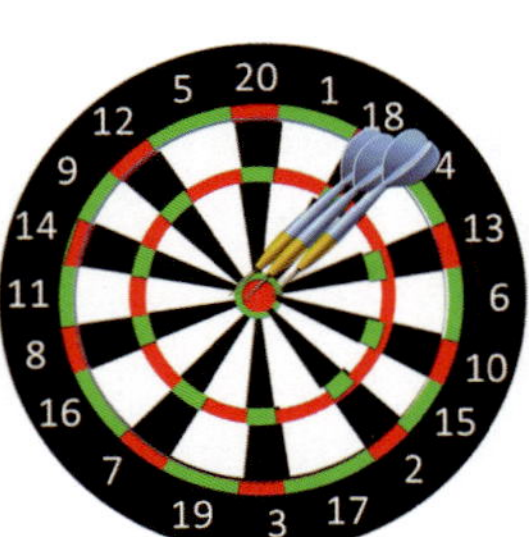

The second point regarding the relationship between reliability and validity is that reliability sets the upper limits. More specifically, the square root of a test's reliability sets the upper limit for its potential validity for any use. For example, if a test has a reliability of .70, the highest the validity coefficient can ever be expected to reach is .84 (the square root of .70). If a test has a reliability of .50, the validity coefficient will not be higher than .71. Clearly, the reliability of a test is important given this ceiling effect that occurs with regard to validity.

Predictor Development

The goal of psychological assessment is to know something about the individual being assessed for the purpose of making an inference about that person. In I-O psychology, the inference to be made often pertains to whether the individual is likely to perform well in a job. What the "something" is that we seek to know is a construct we believe is important to success on the job. That "something" could be the individual's intelligence, ambition, interpersonal skills, ability to cope with frustration, willingness to learn new concepts or procedures, and so on. How do we assess these characteristics of individuals? I-O psychologists have developed a broad array of predictor measures designed to help us make decisions (e.g., hire vs. not hire) about individuals (see The Lighter Side of I-O Psychology: *The Poetry of Prediction*). A discussion of these predictor measures is presented in the rest of this chapter. For the most part, these predictor measures can be classified along two dimensions.

Construct vs. Behavioral Sampling. The first dimension is whether the predictor seeks to measure directly the underlying psychological construct in question (e.g., mechanical comprehension), or whether it seeks to measure a sample of the same behavior to be exhibited on the job. For example, let us assume we want to assess individuals to determine whether they are suitable for the job of a mechanic. Based on a work analysis, we know the job of mechanic requires the individual to be proficient with tools and equipment, and with diagnosing mechanical problems. We could elect to assess mechanical ability with a paper-and-pencil test of mechanical comprehension. Such a test would reveal to what degree the individual possesses mechanical knowledge, but it would not assess proficiency in the use of tools (because it is a paper-and-pencil test). Alternatively, we could present the individual with a mechanical object in a state of disrepair and say, "This appears to be broken. Figure out what is wrong with it and then fix it." The individual's behavior in diagnosing and repairing the object would be observed and rated by knowledgeable individuals (i.e., subject matter experts). This latter type of assessment is called "behavioral sampling" because it samples the types of behavior exhibited on the job (in this case, diagnosing and repairing mechanical objects). This assessment would measure the individual's proficiency with tools used in diagnosis and repair; however, it is limited to only one particular malfunctioning mechanical object. The assessment lacks the breadth of coverage of a paper-and-pencil test. Furthermore, the behavioral sampling method of assessment measures whether individuals can perform the diagnosis and repair at this time, but not whether they could learn to do so with proper training. These types of issues and others will be presented in the discussion of predictor methods.

Past vs. Present Characteristics. A second distinction among predictors is whether they seek to measure something about the individual currently or something about the individual in the past. A job interview is a current measure of a person's characteristics because the interviewer assesses voice quality, interpersonal demeanor, and poise. An assessment of these factors would be used to predict whether the individual will succeed in a job. Alternatively, a predictor measure could assess whether the individual exhibited these behaviors in the past, not currently. An example would be a letter of recommendation solicited from a former employer who supervised the indi-

The Lighter Side of I-O Psychology: *The Poetry of Prediction*

In Chapter 1, we shared with you the first stanza from the song "I Am the Very Model of a Scientist-Practitioner," so it should come as no surprise that some I-O psychologists are well-versed (pun intended) in undertakings beyond "pure" I-O psychology. In addition to songwriting, we have other talents worthy of sharing. With that, we now present the opening of a poem written by Steven A. Meyer and Dale O. Jorgenson titled, "The Song of a Consultant."[7]

From the towers made of ivory
to the land of troubled business
came the well-equipped consultant
with a multitude of methods
based on elegant statistics
(to the layman all-confusing)
to explore the workers' problems
and the cause of low production.

Talks with management revealed that
most employees were unable
to produce the output needed
for the company's survival.
This presented quite a problem
for our dust-bowl Don Quixote:
should he focus on the skills that
lead to high performance? Or,
should he mess with "satisfaction,"
sating discontented workers
in the hope that such a tack would
make them glad to up production?

Then he read an old *Psych Bull* which
indicated no relation;
swore he "(Blank) the murky models
linking work to satisfaction!"

So concerned with high production,
choosing men of high potential
was the course he chose to take, of
using tests of such precision
no false pluses would they make. "I'll
analyze the jobs in question,
find the basic skills involved,
then use tests that somehow measure
aptitudes that make a difference—
lead to good work on the job."

With his Strong empiric background
he assembled inventories,
batteries of tests constructed,
separating hits from misses,
standardized with loving care, in
hopes that validity soon would be there.

Want to know what happens in the consultant's quest to help the organization predict employee performance and ultimately aid them in turning things around? Read the full poem in *Personnel Psychology* (one of our leading journals) to find out. Who knew I-O psychologists were so creative, talented, and fun? (Answer: We did.)

vidual in a previous job. Here, the intent is to make a prediction about future behavior (in the new job) on the basis of past behavior (in the old job). Thus, predictor measures are used to make inferences about future behavior based on current or past behavior. Some predictor measures can be developed that measure both past and current behaviors. The job interview is one example. The interviewer can assess the individual's behavior in the interview as it is happening and can also ask questions about the individual's previous work history.

Not all predictor measures fall neatly into either the construct/behavioral sampling categories or the assessment of past/present characteristics of individuals. However, this classification approach is a reasonable way to understand the varieties of predictor measures and their respective intents. In all cases, predictor measures are designed to forecast future behavior. They differ in the approaches they take in making these predictions. The degree to which these approaches differ in reliability, validity, fairness, social acceptability, legal defensibility, time, and cost has been the subject of extensive research in I-O psychology.

Ability Tests

Organizations must determine whether applicants will be able to successfully perform the requirements of the job (as determined by the work analysis). Some jobs may have a large physical component, such as a construction worker or firefighter. Other jobs may require fine motor skills, such as a jeweler or dental hygienist. Yet others will require tremendous cognitive ability, such as a nuclear physicist or a surgeon. For each of these jobs, applicants may be required to demonstrate their ability to do the job. Ability tests can be broken into four broad categories: cognitive ability, physical ability, psychomotor ability, and sensory/perceptual ability. We will discuss each of these in turn.

Cognitive Ability

Cognitive ability is the most heavily researched construct in psychology. Interest in the assessment of cognitive ability, or intelligence, began more than 100 years ago. Despite the length of time this construct has been assessed, however, there remains no singular or standard means to assess it. Furthermore, recent research suggests cognitive ability is even more complex than we have believed.

Intelligence traditionally has been conceptualized as having a singular, primary basis. This concept is known as *general mental ability* or *cognitive ability* and is symbolized by ***g***. By assessing *g*, we gain an understanding of a person's general level of intellectual capability. Tests that measure *g* have been found to be predictive of performance across a wide range of situations.[8] The criterion-related validity of *g* is impressive, often in the range of .40–.50. Many researchers believe cognitive ability is the single best predictor of future job performance. Simply put, if we could know only one attribute of a job candidate upon which to base a prediction, we would want an assessment of cognitive ability.

g
The symbol for "general mental ability," which has been found to be predictive of success in most jobs.

"*g* is to psychology what carbon is to chemistry."[9]

—Brand 1987, p. 257

Our method of assessing cognitive ability (i.e., a test) is heavily guided by how we view what we are trying to assess.[10] *Academic intelligence* represents what intelligence tests typically measure, such as fluency with words and numbers. Table 5-1 shows two sample test questions from a typical intelligence test. *Practical intelligence* is needed to be competent in the everyday world and is not highly

Table 5-1 *Sample test questions from a typical intelligence test*

1. What number is missing in this series?
   3–8–14–21–29–(?)
2. SHOVEL is to DITCHDIGGER as SCALPEL is to:
   (a) knife (b) sharp (c) butcher (d) surgeon (e) cut

related to academic intelligence. This is often what we think of as "street smarts" or common sense. *Creative intelligence* pertains to the ability to produce work that is both novel (i.e., original or unexpected) and appropriate (i.e., useful). A view of intelligence dominated by academic intelligence will lead us to assess that particular kind to the relative exclusion of practical and creative intelligence. The contemporary world of business seeks employees who are adaptable to highly changing conditions.[11] Real-life problems tend to be ill-defined, ambiguous, and dynamic, and such problems do not match the types of problems on which intelligence traditionally has been assessed. Thus, the concept of practical intelligence is intended to complement, rather than to contradict, the narrower views of *g*-based theories of intelligence.

Although research clearly supports the validity of general cognitive ability as a predictor, the use of cognitive ability is not without controversy. Some researchers believe that conceptualizing intelligence merely as *g* encourages oversimplification of the inherent complexity of intelligence. The idea is that intelligence is not a unitary phenomenon, and other dimensions of intelligence are also worthy of our consideration.[12] That said, meta-analytic data have found that *g* accounts for approximately 80% of the variability in criterion-related validity estimates while the remaining 20% of the variability is accounted for by other mental abilities.[13] From an I-O psychology perspective, therefore, the controversy regarding the assessment of cognitive ability rests primarily on the adequacy of measuring general mental ability (*g*) only or assessing multiple cognitive abilities in forecasting job behavior. The current body of research seems to indicate that, in most cases, measuring the *g* factor of intelligence offers superior predictive accuracy in forecasting success in most jobs.

Critics of cognitive ability tests also point to biases that exist for certain demographic groups. A great deal of research has revealed that members of some minority groups have lower average scores on general mental ability tests compared to majority group members.[14] Thus, if organizations select applicants based solely on their cognitive ability test scores, this could result in adverse impact, in that minority group members may be selected at much lower rates. Nevertheless, I-O psychologists argue that these findings should not result in cognitive ability tests being thrown out entirely. Indeed, some research has demonstrated that general mental ability tests are not predictively biased, in that minority and majority applicants who score the same tend to have practically the same level of later job performance,[15] with some possible small exceptions.[16] In addition, eliminating cognitive ability tests does not eliminate the chance for adverse impact, as other predictors (e.g., interviews, to be discussed later in this chapter) may assess cognitive ability and related constructs.[17] So, what are we to do then? The most frequent solution is to supplement the use of cognitive ability tests with other non-cognitive predictors (e.g., personality inventories, discussed shortly), which will help increase diversity and reduce adverse impact.[18] While it is possible to adjust scores based on group membership (e.g., giving bonus points to members of certain groups or setting different cutoff scores), this is not advisable from a legal perspective. Specifically, Section 106 of the Civil Rights Act states that it is unlawful for employers in connection with the selection or referral of "applicants or candidates for employment or promotion to adjust the scores of, use different cutoffs for, or otherwise alter the results of employment related tests on the basis of race, color, religion, sex, or national origin." Many I-O psychologists believe this prohibition by the Civil Rights Act is unwarranted. Namely, within-group norming, a practice in which individual scores are converted to standard scores or percentile scores within one's group, has been advocated as the most scientific solution to the issue of adverse impact for cognitive ability tests, yet it has been deemed unlawful for non-scientific reasons.[19] Although this may change, for now such score adjustments are not permitted.

Physical Ability

Researchers have examined the assessment of physical abilities, and in particular how these physical abilities relate to performance in some jobs.[20] Increases in productivity and reductions in lost work time and injuries can be achieved through physical ability testing in jobs that are physically demanding.[21] There are four critical physical abilities relevant to work performance (Fleishman & Quaintance 1984, pp. 463-4):[22]

- **Static strength**—"the ability to use muscle force to lift, push, pull, or carry objects"
- **Explosive strength**—"the ability to use short bursts of muscle force to propel oneself or an object"
- **Gross body coordination**—"the ability to coordinate the movement of the arms, legs, and torso in activities where the whole body is in motion"
- **Stamina**—"the ability of the lungs and circulatory (blood) systems of the body to perform efficiently over time"

A common research finding is that men exhibit greater static and explosive strength than women.[23] A physical ability test may be one component of an assessment process that includes other attributes, such as cognitive ability. The results of a work analysis should determine how much importance the physical ability test has in the overall assessment of candidates. If a job permits employees to perform a wide variety of tasks, it may be possible to assign women to those tasks that involve less static and explosive strength.[24] This may help avert potential problems with adverse impact (as discussed in Chapter 3) that could result if women were simply not selected for the job. Furthermore, physical ability tests are used to determine who *enters* a job, not necessarily who can *keep* it. With the advent of new technologies in law enforcement, for example, tasers make physical strength less important in subduing a criminal suspect.

In general, the research on physical abilities reveals they are related to successful job performance in physically demanding jobs, such as firefighters, police officers, and construction workers. However, physical ability testing represents an unusual challenge from an assessment perspective. Imagine, for example, a manual labor job that requires repeatedly lifting a 25-pound object (e.g., a bag of cement), and carrying it a distance of 40 feet every two minutes. The primary physical demand of the job is neither the weight (25 lbs.) nor the distance (40 feet), but the endurance required to do so 30 times per hour, 240 times per day. If the selection tests consisted of lifting a 25-pound object and carrying it a distance of 40 feet, not only could the vast majority of people do so (one time), such a test would fail to assess the critical physical ability, endurance (reflecting performance over time). One of the requisite characteristics of an effective selection test is its reasonableness in terms of time, especially for the job in question. The job of manual laborer would not warrant extensive assessment time. The assessment challenge with some physical abilities is to make accurate predictions about the sustained job behavior from a relatively brief sample of similar behavior exhibited in the selection test.

Psychomotor Ability

Psychomotor ability involves motor skills related to flexibility, balance, and coordination. Psychomotor ability is often distinguished between gross motor skills and fine motor skills. Gross motor skills are defined as those that involve larger groups of muscles (for example, arms or legs) and are akin to gross body coordination as discussed under physical ability. Fine motor skills are those that involve smaller groups of muscles such as those found in fingers. Within these two broader categories of psychomotor skills, there are innumerable context- and job-specific skills that may be needed within one's workplace, such as assembling parts, operating controls, putting in an IV, using a scalpel, typing, reaching, lifting, and walking. Common psychomotor tests assess finger dexterity, multi-limb coordination, rate control, and control precision.

Psychomotor tests have been used frequently for a variety of jobs, including aviation, automobile mechanics, sewing machine operators, craft workers, police, and firefighters. In an examination of psychomotor tracking abilities for predicting U.S. Air Force pilot training performance, researchers found that general psychomotor ability predicted how well pilots did on their flying work sample (criterion-related validity coefficient of .28).[25] Much research suggests that the predictive validity of psychomotor tests is due to its association with *g* and general psychomotor ability, with little predictive power of specific psychomotor abilities. In addition, the incremental validity of psychomotor ability over and above *g* is small. As such, the value of assessing psychomotor abilities is limited, as such assessments may not provide much predictive power beyond what we get by measuring cognitive ability.[26] Nevertheless, applicant reactions may be more favorable, given that the face validity of such measures may be higher for psychomotor tasks. Thus, including such tests may be a matter of gaining applicant approval rather than adding to our ability to predict training or job performance.

Sensory/Perceptual Ability

Some jobs require employees to be able to detect and recognize stimuli within their environment. This ability is known as sensory/perceptual ability. These tests would include such abilities as depth perception, peripheral vision, auditory attention, visual color discrimination, and sound localization, to name a few. Sensory/perceptual abilities have been found to be relevant for a number of jobs, including nuclear power plant control room operators,[27] pilots, air traffic controllers, and casino dealers. In addition, perceptual speed and accuracy have been shown to be better predictors than general intelligence in predicting task performance for warehouse workers.[28] For jobs in which sensory/perceptual ability is critical for safety reasons, such as for air traffic controllers or pilots, such tests can be a matter of life and death. It is a fact of life that as we age, our ability to interpret visual and auditory stimuli that we receive decreases, which in turn impairs our ability to accurately perceive our environment.[29] Thus, although the Age Discrimination in Employment Act generally prohibits mandatory retirement ages in the U.S. (as discussed in Chapter 3), there are some exceptions, most notably for pilots, federal law enforcement officers, and air traffic controllers.

Personality Inventories

Personality refers to the individual differences that people have that influence how they think, feel, and behave in the world. An individual's personality reflects a pattern of proclivities for interacting with one's environment. Even if we know someone's personality, we won't always know what they will do in any particular situation because personality doesn't dictate or determine what we will do. We will, however, be able to predict what they will likely do because personality reflects our "comfort zone" and preferences for certain thoughts, feelings, and behaviors. For example, if an individual is outgoing and talkative by nature, we might predict that they would interact with more people at a party than somebody who is reserved and quiet by nature. Of course, we won't always be correct, since an outgoing person may choose to keep to themselves, and a reserved person may purposefully choose to put themselves "out there" to meet others and network. If these individuals opt to go counter to their personalities, however, they may tire more easily or be uncomfortable, as they are going against their natural proclivities. As such, our predictions for their behavior based on their personalities were appropriate, since people will tend to do what makes them most comfortable.

Knowing that we can generally predict how people will behave if we know their personalities, it should not be surprising that personality assessment is frequently used to predict how individuals will behave on the job. Unlike cognitive ability tests, which have objective answers, personality inventories do not have right or wrong answers. Test takers answer how much they agree with certain statements (e.g., "People who work hard get ahead"). In personality inventories, similar types of questions typically comprise a scale, which reflects a person's introversion, dominance, confidence, and so on. Items are scored according to a predetermined key such that responding one way or another to an item results in a higher or lower score on a particular scale. Although there are no right/wrong answers to personality questions, employers have preferences for candidates who have high scores on selected personality scales. The basic rationale is that successful employees possess a particular personality structure, and scales reflective of that structure become the basis for selecting new employees.

There are as many personalities as there are people on the planet. We are all unique in our individual make-up. It would be impossible to capture every essence of every individual to predict their behaviors. Instead, we typically measure a set few that have been shown to have clear relationships with outcomes of interest. The five-factor model of personality has received the most empirical support. Often referred to as the **Big 5 personality theory**, it is comprised of five personality factors:[30]

Big 5 personality theory
A theory that defines personality in terms of five major factors: openness to experience, conscientiousness, extraversion, agreeableness, and emotional stability. Also called the "Five Factor" theory of personality.

- **Openness to experience**—the disposition to be curious, imaginative, and unconventional. Individuals high on openness to experience tend to be creative and interested in trying new things. Individuals low on this dimension tend to prefer their routines, aren't as open to new ideas or ways of doing things, and don't seek out variety.
- **Conscientiousness**—the disposition to be purposeful, determined, organized, and dependable. Individuals high on conscientiousness tend to be punctual, achievement-oriented, and have a high attention to detail. Those who are low on conscientiousness may be sloppy, disorganized, and have less focus on or need for perfection.

- **Extraversion**—the tendency to be sociable, assertive, active, talkative, energetic, and outgoing. Individuals high on extraversion (called "extraverts") tend to derive their energy from being around others and will gravitate towards social situations. Individuals low on extraversion (called "introverts," as the opposite end of extraversion is introversion) will tend to find their energy from within themselves and will prefer quieter, calmer, and more reserved situations.
- **Agreeableness**—the disposition to be cooperative, helpful, and easy to get along with others. Individuals high on agreeableness tend to be good natured and have a desire to cooperate with others. As such, they may be seen as warm and conflict-avoidant by others. Individuals low on agreeableness tend to be critical and suspicious of others and may be seen as cold or selfish.
- **Emotional stability**—the tendency to be calm, even-tempered, and emotionally balanced. Individuals high on emotional stability tend to have predictable and consistent reactions to moods. Individuals who are low on emotional stability (those high on neuroticism, the opposite end of emotional stability) tend to be worried, anxious, and react extremely to stressful events.

Consider This...

A great way to remember what each of the five factors reflects is to think of exemplars that would likely score high and low for each of the Big 5 factors. Consider famous characters from books, TV shows, or movies with which you're familiar. James Bond, for example, is a well-known fictional character who serves as a British secret agent. It doesn't matter what happens to him, he always stays calm under pressure and typifies a "cool and collected" persona. We would say Bond is likely high on emotional stability. And how about Curious George, the beloved monkey who seems to always run into trouble as he attempts to explore the world around him? True to his name, he is curious and always wanting to try new things. We would say Curious George is likely high on openness to experience. How about somebody we might consider low on agreeableness—who might we use as an exemplar? Perhaps we would choose Walt Kowalski, the irritable old man played by Clint Eastwood in *Gran Torino* who yells at kids to get off his lawn. What exemplars of high and low scorers would you choose for each of the Big 5? How do you think you would score on each of the Big 5? Take an online Big 5 test (many free ones are available, including one located at https://bigfive-test.com/). How do your predicted scores align with how you scored on the test?

A tremendous amount of research has been conducted on the Big 5 factors. Some of the key findings related to each of the factors is as follows:

- **Openness to experience**—Openness to experience is positively related to training performance[31] and speed of adjustment in a new job.[32]
- **Conscientiousness**—Of all of the Big 5 factors, conscientiousness consistently shows the highest correlations with job performance criteria for all occupations.[33] In addition, conscientiousness is positively related to one's salary,[34] motivation,[35] and safety performance at work[36] and is negatively related to turnover[37] and absenteeism.[38]

- **Extraversion**—Extraversion is positively related to sales performance,[39] salary,[40] and job satisfaction.[41]
- **Agreeableness**—Agreeableness is positively related to engagement in citizenship behaviors[42] and negatively related to retaliatory behaviors following mistreatment by others.[43] Agreeableness is also negatively related to salary.[44]
- **Emotional stability**—Emotional stability is positively related to salary[45] as well as to job satisfaction.[46]

The five personality factors are considered a durable framework for understanding personality structure among people of many nations, and have prompted some scholars to refer to their pattern of inter-relationships as a "human universal."[47] Nevertheless, some authors have cautioned the use of self-report personality tests in selection settings due to low predictive validity for overall job performance.[48] Instead, it may be better to use observer ratings of personality (e.g., from peers, friends, roommates, family members), as there is evidence they result in superior validity coefficients.[49]

On a conceptual level, intelligence and personality have typically been viewed as separate constructs. In support of this, correlations between personality and cognitive ability are generally low.[50] Intelligence traditionally has reflected the "can do" dimension of an individual; namely, the person "can do" the work because they are judged to possess an adequate level of cognitive ability. Personality traditionally has reflected the "will do" dimension of an individual; namely, the person "will do" the work because they are judged to possess the demeanor to do so. Thus, cognitive ability and personality are both predictive of job performance, each in its own way.[51] Namely, individuals hired based on their personality may be good performers due to their dependability, attentiveness, persistence, and similar attributes. Individuals hired based on cognitive ability may be good performers due to their ability to solve problems quickly and accurately.

Dark triad
A cluster of three dysfunctional personality types associated with counterproductive work behavior: Machiavellianism, narcissism, and psychopathy.

Another area of personality that has received considerable attention in recent years is the **dark triad**. The dark triad consists of three dysfunctional personality types that have been linked to increased counterproductive work behavior. These characteristics are Machiavellianism, narcissism, and psychopathy.[52] These personality types have traditionally been examined as personality disorders within the domain of clinical psychology. However, within I-O psychology, they are typically examined as extreme personalities rather than as disorders that may require treatment.

The first of the dark triad, *Machiavellianism*, is named after an Italian nobleman from the Renaissance, Niccolò Machiavelli. The focus of his most famous work, *The Prince*, is about acquiring and using political power. The foundation of Machiavellianism is having a dark and cynical interpretation of human nature. The goal in life is to get your way by manipulating other people. No actions or tactics are deemed inappropriate if they lead to obtaining what you want. Thus, the phrase, "the end justifies the means" is often associated with Machiavellianism.

The second is *narcissism*. It is named after a mythical Greek figure, Narcissus, who was infatuated with his own physical attractiveness. People with high levels of narcissism (i.e., "narcissists") exhibit a high degree of self-importance. They simultaneously desire to be in control of other people and be admired by them. Relentlessly self-promoting and unaffected by criticism, they exude subtle arrogance. They tend to be dismissive of advice, primarily because they don't view others as competent compared to themselves.[53]

The third member of the dark triad is *psychopathy*. Derived from Ancient Greek terms, *pathos* is suffering, and *psycho* refers to properties of the mind. Individuals high on psychopathy (i.e., "psychopaths") are sometimes portrayed in the popular media as being deranged killers. However, psychopaths are not inherently violent. They are characterized by lacking any concern for others. They may come across as glib, but they are emotionally shallow. Frequently exhibiting a sense of charisma, others may be drawn to them without being aware of the basis of attraction.

Only in recent years have I-O psychologists examined the dark triad in the workplace. Scores on assessments of the dark triad have been found predictive of counterproductive work behavior.[54] The majority of research on the dark triad within I-O psychology has focused on narcissism. One study found a link between narcissism and the hindsight bias (i.e., the tendency to claim one could have predicted an event after it has occurred).[55] Researchers found that when narcissists make a decision that turns out to be a good one, they assert that they knew it all along—no doubt in their minds. When they make a decision that turns out to be a bad one, however, they claim that nobody could have made the right choice. So, getting something right is obviously because they are good decision makers, and getting something wrong is because nobody would have done it right; it's not their fault. In addition, the researchers found that individuals higher on narcissism are less likely to think they should have done something differently, or question what they should change going forward. Instead, they blindly feel like winners after success, and therefore aren't learning from their previous (potentially faulty) decisions.

Paradoxically, some organizations may initially reward employees who exhibit dark triad behaviors because of their relentless pursuit of self-advancement. In such cases, organizations place more emphasis on the employees having reached certain performance criteria (e.g., sales volume), while being less concerned about the harm inflicted on others in the process. What may at first be seen as positive behaviors—such as assertiveness, confidence, and persuasion—may be as-yet-unidentified problematic behaviors such as domination, coercion, and manipulation. Indeed, psychopaths have been described as "snakes in suits," because they can work their way into leadership roles and are positioned to cause immeasurable harm within the organization due to their destructive personalities.[56]

People with dark triad personality traits can be easily confused with others who have healthy personalities. The dark triad attributes are subtle and only manifest themselves to others over time. The goal of personality assessment for these types of people is to screen them out of any future consideration for employment.[57] Nevertheless, individuals exhibiting dark triad attributes are also skilled at their concealment, even in times of formal scrutiny. As such, it is important to identify ways to manage such personalities in the workforce rather than focus solely on finding ways to keep them from entering it.

Faking in Personality Assessment

Faking
The behavior of job applicants to falsify or fake their responses to items on personality inventories to create a favorable impression.

A long-standing concern with using personality inventories for personnel selection is that job applicants might not give truthful responses. Rather, applicants may fake their answers to give what they believe are socially desirable responses. There are three important questions with regard to **faking** (or response distortion) on personality inventories. First, how common is faking? Second, is faking problematic for organizations? And third, how can faking be addressed?

Regarding the first question — How common is faking? — it is clear that individuals can and do engage in faking when taking personality inventories. Indeed, some scholars have noted that faking should be expected and is probably unavoidable because it is natural for job candidates to try to project highly positive images of themselves to hiring organizations.[58] The capacity and desire of people to present themselves in a positive way when relating to others is called "impression management." The distinction between subtle impression management and blatant response distortion is the fine line that differentiates describing oneself in a positive manner versus faking. Research has shown that response distortion is higher when competition is high, and when the purpose of the test is relatively transparent (or when applicants are told what the test measures).[59] In addition, the structure of personality inventory questions may paradoxically encourage or lead to answers that mimic faking.[60] Personality inventories do not permit candidates to qualify or explain their answers. A question such as, "I typically work hard at everything I do," requires a singular answer in a personality inventory. There is no opportunity, for example, for candidates to explain that they work hard on the job but not in recreational activities. To avoid the impression that they do not work hard on the job, their answer (e.g., "true" or "strongly agree") implies they work hard at everything in life, a most dubious response, likely to be interpreted as faking.

The second question — Is faking problematic for organizations? — may be a tad surprising to you. We know that faking "works" for applicants, in that they are able to successfully change their scores on personality inventories. For example, researchers have demonstrated that the differences in scores when individuals are told to provide honest versus when they are instructed to give fake answers can vary considerably.[61] Similarly, when comparing personality inventories from applicants versus non-applicants, with the assumption that non-applicants would have less reason to fake their responses, applicants tended to score higher on each of the Big 5 dimensions.[62] But what are the implications for organizations when applicants fake? Meta-analytic results suggest that faking does not substantially reduce the criterion-related validity for personality inventories.[63] One reason that faking does not reduce the predictive validity of personality inventories may be because faking, or the ability to fake, may itself be job-related and/or socially adaptive.[64] That is, when individuals choose to portray themselves as more conscientious than they are, they are demonstrating that they understand the importance of being conscientious within the workplace. As such, they may "bring it" and engage in more conscientious behaviors when at work than they would normally do. Recall that we are able to behave counter to our personalities when we need to. Thus, faking might simply be demonstrating that individuals understand when it may be appropriate to alter their tendencies and in what direction.

Despite evidence that faking may not be problematic for organizations, there remains a desire for many to halt it. As such, this leads to our third and final question—How can faking be addressed? There is no professionally-accepted remedy to faking.[65] However, assuming faking is something that is seen as problematic and to be avoided, five options for addressing it have been proposed:

1. Eliminate from further employment consideration those candidates who give faked responses, as determined through specific questions that reveal response distortion. Of practical concern with this option is the degree to which faking would result in elimination of candidates (i.e., a few or many).
2. Use statistical corrections on the test scores, essentially re-scoring the test. Of practical concern with this option is the magnitude of the re-scoring for candidates with faked responses. How much should their test scores be lowered because of detected faking?
3. Compare response times to questions with one another for each candidate separately. The rationale for this suggestion is based on findings that candidates take longer to respond dishonestly than to respond honestly to items.[66] Of practical concern with this option is that not all test items are easily timed, and there are many reasons beyond faking that could lead to longer response times on some items (e.g., item reading difficulty, distractions).
4. Use a different source of personality assessment, such as ratings from colleagues, former supervisors, family members, or even from information gleaned from how people present themselves online (see Social Media and I-O Psychology: *Assessing Personality via Facebook*). However, as empirically appealing as observer ratings may be, there could be logistical issues associated with obtaining them for making personnel selection decisions in an employment context.
5. Warn candidates against giving fake responses. This could occur prior to testing or even during the testing. For example, applicants could be warned during an online personality assessment that their responses are exhibiting a pattern similar to people who fake their responses. Warning candidates not to fake is the preferred method, because it lowers the mean response and increases the variability in the responses of the motivated-to-fake individuals, thus making their responses more like those of non-fakers.[67] Of practical concern with this option is candidates may perceive few negative consequences for faking versus the potential benefit of being hired.[68]

The decision to make a job offer is often the product of multiple assessments, some of which cannot be faked (e.g., ability tests and verification of educational attainment) and some that can be faked (e.g., personality inventories and interviews). With regard to personality inventories, faking may not be problematic. Nevertheless, there are options for addressing it if indeed that is the goal.

Social Media and I-O Psychology: *Assessing Personality via Facebook*

What can you tell about someone from their Facebook page? Some people are quite open about themselves online, sharing their political views, their opinions on recent news topics, details about their family events, and even what they may have eaten for dinner. Others are more private, perhaps using Facebook as a means to know what is going on with others rather than post anything about themselves. From status updates, somebody may appear easily riled, whereas another person may seem to be consistently positive about the world and its events. It would seem that you may be able to discover one's personality from how they present themselves on Facebook.

This is indeed what researchers have discovered. Researchers have found that the number of friends people have, how often they post, and what they post about are related to their self-reported personality. For example, various studies have shown that the number of friends and how frequently they post status updates is positively related to extraversion. Further evidence has suggested that individuals high on narcissism and psychopathy tend to post updates that are more negative (vs. positive) in nature. Furthermore, individuals who are higher on openness to experience tend to have more friends of the opposite sex. Researchers have even discovered some differences between individuals who use Facebook versus those who choose not to use Facebook.

It would seem that individuals can portray themselves in any way they wish online. The ability to invent and reinvent one's own image online is extraordinarily easy. Individuals can describe themselves in flattering terms on dating sites, highlight certain skills (whether true or not) on LinkedIn for employers to see, or portray their lives as more exciting on Facebook. Nevertheless, it may be that regardless of how you think you're presenting yourself, the number of posts and content of them may limit your ability to fake your personality. Some of the research in this area, for example, has looked beyond the specific things said in status updates, and instead looked at the structure of sentences to reveal differences in personality.

Thus, there are some clear issues that must be considered when using information obtained from social media sites when hiring employees (such as invasion of privacy issues, which may impact how applicants view an organization). Nevertheless, there is reason to believe that Facebook and other social networking sites may be one avenue for obtaining indirect information on an individual's personality.

Integrity Tests

Integrity test
A type of test that purports to assess a candidate's honesty or character.

The prevalence of personality assessment in personnel selection is also demonstrated by the development and use of honesty or integrity tests. **Integrity tests** are designed to identify job applicants who will not engage in deviant behavior on the job. These tests generally fall into one of two types.[69] In the first type, an *overt integrity test*, the job applicant clearly understands that the intent of the test is to assess integrity. The test typically has two sections: one deals with attitudes toward theft and other forms of dishonesty (namely, beliefs about the frequency and extent of employee theft, punitiveness toward theft, perceived ease of theft, and endorsement of common rationalizations about theft), and a second section deals with admissions of theft and other illegal activities (such as dollar amounts stolen in the past year, drug use, and gambling). The second type of test, called a *personality-based integrity test*, makes no reference to theft. These tests contain conventional personality assessment items that have been found to be predictive of theft.

Some scholars have argued that integrity tests are important predictors of counterproductive work behaviors.[70] Others have noted that integrity tests are "second only to cognitive ability tests" in predicting job performance.[71] However, there are others still who maintain that such a conclusion is premature and that more research is needed.[72] There has been some clear support, however, for their usage. For example, one study examined incarcerated offenders convicted of white-collar crimes, such as embezzlement and fraud.[73] Compared with a control sample of employees in upper-level positions of authority, offenders had greater tendencies toward irresponsibility, lack of dependability, and disregard of rules and social norms. This finding is supportive of why integrity testing was developed.

Despite their demonstrated effectiveness, concerns exist for integrity testing. First, like personality measures, respondents appear able to fake their answers to integrity tests when instructed to do so.[74] Second, there are concerns that integrity tests are biased, with one study's reported estimate of 40-60% of applicants failing such tests.[75] It is likely not surprising that applicant reaction is a third concern with integrity testing. Applicants consider integrity testing more invasive than other selection procedures and tend to dislike them because of their potential to erroneously discredit them.[76] This concern is likely to be minimized for personality-based measures. That is, because this type of test does not contain obvious references to theft, it is less likely to offend job applicants.

Polygraph
An instrument that assesses responses of an individual's central nervous system (heart rate, breathing, perspiration, etc.) that supposedly indicate giving false responses to questions.

Because we are discussing the concept of integrity, it is worthwhile to discuss another method that is occasionally used to establish truthfulness—the polygraph. A **polygraph** is an instrument that measures responses of the autonomic nervous system—physiological reactions of the body such as heart rate and perspiration. In theory, these autonomic responses will "give you away" when you are telling a lie. The polygraph is attached to the body with sensors for detecting the physiological reactions. Polygraphs are used more to evaluate people charged with criminal activity in a *post hoc* fashion (such as after a theft has occurred) than to select people for a job, although it has been used in the latter capacity as well.

The use of polygraphs is controversial. People can appear innocent of any wrongdoing according to the polygraph but in fact be guilty of misconduct, and vice versa. Research by the Federal Bureau of Investigation based on a crime simulation reported that the polygraph correctly identified 84.7% of the guilty group and 94.7% of the innocent group.[77] It is unknown how effective countermeasures (attempts to distort or defeat a polygraph examination) are because funding for research on countermeasures is limited to the Department of Defense Polygraph Institute and all findings from such research are classified.[78] In 1988, President Ronald Reagan signed into law a bill banning the widespread use of polygraphs for pre-employment screening by private-sector employers. However, polygraphs continue to be used in the hiring process of government agencies involved in national security as well as in law enforcement.

Situational Judgment Tests

Situational judgment test
A type of test that describes a problem to the test taker and requires the test taker to rate various possible solutions in terms of their feasibility or applicability.

Traditional multiple-choice test questions have one correct answer. Given this characteristic, test questions must be written such that there is indeed a correct answer to the question, and only one correct answer. In real life, however, many problems and questions don't have a single correct answer. Rather, an array of answers is possible, some more plausible or appropriate than others. There is a growing interest in designing tests that require the test taker to rate a series of answers (all correct to some degree) in terms of their overall suitability for resolving a problem. One name given to this type of assessment is **situational judgment test**.[79] An example of a situational judgment test (SJT) question is presented in Table 5-2. Research on this type of test reveals that it measures a construct similar to intelligence, but not the same as the traditional conception of *g*. SJTs reflect the theoretical rationale of practical intelligence discussed earlier in the chapter.

The preferred rank ordering of possible responses to a situation is determined by incumbents who serve as subject matter experts in the design of the SJTs. Furthermore, the situation-based questions are often derived from the incumbents' work experiences. SJTs could serve to reinforce the status quo within an organization, because the highest scoring job applicants would be those whose values and perceptions regarding how to respond to problem situations were most similar to those of incumbents.[80]

SJTs are a valuable means of assessing personnel because they provide incremental validity beyond cognitive ability and personality measures combined.[81] SJTs can be presented in paper-and-pencil and video-based formats, and both provide useful assessments of candidates.[82] Consider a video SJT administered to first-year medical students that depicted vignettes showing interactions between physicians and patients. The medical students had to rate the appropriateness of four responses to handling the interactions. The scores predicted performance as a medical intern seven years later and job performance as a physician nine years later.[83]

SJTs represent a type of assessment that is designed to measure an attribute other than cognitive ability. Personality inventories would represent another example. The fact that these types of assessments have been found to add to the prediction of job performance criteria above and beyond cognitive ability does not mean they are unrelated to *g*. It is clear that *g* is indirectly measured in both personality inventories and

Table 5-2 *Sample question from a situational judgment test*

You are a leader of a manufacturing team that works with heavy machinery. One of your production operators tells you that one machine in the work area is suddenly malfunctioning and may endanger the welfare of your work team. Rank order the following possible courses of action to effectively address this problem, from most desirable to least desirable.

1. Call a meeting of your team members to discuss the problem.
2. Report the problem to the Director of Safety.
3. Shut off the machine immediately.
4. Individually ask other production operators about problems with their machines.
5. Evacuate your team from the production facility.

SJTs.[84] That is, it takes cognitive ability to read and interpret multiple choice questions on a personality inventory. Likewise, it is difficult to believe that exercising good judgment (the "J" in SJT) is not cognitively based. In short, not only is cognitive ability ubiquitous in life's activities, it is a component of assessments expressly designed to measure attributes other than *g*.

Biodata Inventories

Biodata inventory A method of assessing individuals in which biographical information pertaining to past activities, interests, and behaviors in their lives is considered.

Biodata refers to biographical information. The theory of using biographical information as a method of personnel selection is based on our development as individuals. Our lives represent a series of experiences, events, and choices that define our development. Past and current events shape our behavior patterns, attitudes, and values. Because there is consistency in our behaviors, attitudes, and values, an assessment of these factors from our past experiences should be predictive of such experiences in the future. As such, **biodata inventories** consist of questions that ask applicants about their life history (i.e., past events) as opposed to questions about behavioral intentions or presumed behavior in a hypothetical situation.[85] These questions are meant to assess a wide variety of constructs that are assumed to be predictive of future job performance. Table 5-3 lists 16 dimensions of biographical information and an example item for each dimension.[86]

Table 5-3 *Sixteen biographical information dimensions*

Dimension	Example Item
Dealing with people	
1. Sociability	Volunteer with service groups
2. Agreeableness/cooperation	Argue a lot compared with others
3. Tolerant	Response to people breaking rules
4. Good impression	What a person wears is important
Outlook	
5. Calmness	Often in a hurry
6. Resistance to stress	Time to recover from disappointments
7. Optimism	Think there is some good in everyone
Responsibility/dependability	
8. Responsibility	Supervision in previous jobs
9. Concentration	Importance of quiet surroundings at work
10. Work ethic	Percent of spending money earned in high school
Other	
11. Satisfaction with life	How happy in general
12. Need for achievement	Ranking in previous job
13. Parental influence	Mother worked outside home when young
14. Educational history	Grades in math
15. Job history	Likes/dislikes in previous job
16. Demographic	Number in family

Adapted with permission from "From Dustbowl Empiricism to Rational Constructs in Biographical Data," by L. F. Schoenfeldt *Human Resource Management Review*, *9*, pp. 147–167. Copyright © 1999. Reproduced with permission of Pergamon via Copyright Clearance Center.

Biographical information is frequently recorded on an application blank. The application blank, in turn, can be used as a selection device based on the information presented. Scoring of biodata generally occurs in one of the following ways:

1. **Rational keying**—giving more points to response options that most reflect the constructs they are intended to reflect, as determined by expert judgments
2. **Empirical keying**—giving more points to options that are most predictive of the criterion of interest, such as job performance or turnover
3. **Hybrid keying**—a combination of rational and empirical keying such that points are given to options that are most predictive of the desirable criteria, but only if they also make conceptual sense

A meta-analytic review of biodata inventories revealed that the predictive validity for overall job performance is .37, with markedly higher predictive validity for those with empirical keying versus those with rational keying (.44 vs. .24, respectively).[87] The authors recommend using hybrid scoring to capture the predictive advantages of empirical keying while capitalizing on the interpretability of rational keying. In addition, they found that biodata inventories appear to have moderate-to-high overlap with the Big 5 personality dimensions, but only modest overlap with cognitive ability, suggesting they may add incremental validity when used in combination with other selection assessments.

Biographical questions should not be invasive. Invasiveness addresses whether the respondent will consider the item content to be an invasion of privacy. Asking questions about certain types of life experiences that are generally regarded as private matters (e.g., religious beliefs) is off limits for assessment.[88] There are two types of biodata questions that are regarded as intrusive: a question that refers to an event that could have been explained away if the applicant had the chance to do so, and a question with a response that does not reflect the type of person the respondent has since become.[89] Questions that are perceived to invade privacy invite litigation against the hiring organization by job applicants.

To what extent do individuals distort their responses to create a more socially desirable impression? Not surprisingly, faking does occur in responses to certain types of questions.[90] The questions most likely to be faked in a socially desirable direction are those that are difficult to verify for accuracy and have the appearance of being highly relevant to the job. When given the chance to elaborate on their answers to biodata items, candidates appear to give more elaboration to non-verifiable items than verifiable items.[91] As such, requiring elaboration may decrease the likelihood of faking.

Using biographical information is a logically defensible strategy in personnel selection. Biographical information has been portrayed as revealing consistent patterns of behavior that are interwoven throughout our lives.[92] By assessing what applicants have done, we can gain considerable insight into what they will do.

Consider This...

Biodata items sometimes lack content validity and face validity for the job in question even though they manifest empirical criterion-related validity, which can be a concern in personnel selection. Consider a case in point. A city had developed a biodata inventory to be used alongside some psychological tests to evaluate police officers for promotion to detectives. All questions were predictive of job performance as a detective, as determined by a criterion-related validity study. One of the questions was, "Did you have sexual intercourse for the first time before the age of 16?" Some officers who took the promotional exam and failed it sued the city for asking such a question in an employment test. The officers said the question had no relevance to the conduct of a detective's job and was an invasion of their privacy. They wanted the test results thrown out. The case was heard at the district court, where the judge ruled in favor of the officers and said they should be reconsidered for promotion. The city appealed the verdict to the state supreme court, which reversed the lower court ruling and allowed the test results to stand. The state supreme court based its decision on the grounds that the answer to that question did correlate with job performance as a detective. From a practical and legal standpoint, it is advisable to avoid asking such invasive questions in the first place, even though in this case a lengthy legal battle ultimately resulted in a decision favorable to the city. How would you feel if you were one of the police officers in this case? What construct do you think was being assessed by the question that made it predictive of detective job performance? Should the city continue using the test with this question? Why or why not?

Drug Testing

Drug testing
A method of assessment typically based on an analysis of urine that is used to detect illicit drug use by the candidate.

Drug testing is the popular term for efforts to detect substance abuse, the use of illegal drugs and the improper and illegal use of prescription and over-the-counter medications, alcohol, and other chemical compounds. Substance abuse is a major global problem that has far-reaching societal, moral, and economic consequences. The role that I-O psychology plays in this vast and complex picture is to detect substance abuse in the workplace. Employees who engage in substance abuse jeopardize not only their own welfare but also potentially the welfare of fellow employees and other individuals. I-O psychologists are involved in screening out substance abusers among both job applicants and current employees.

Unlike other forms of assessment used by I-O psychologists that involve estimates of cognitive or motor abilities, drug testing embraces chemical assessments. The method of assessment is typically a urine sample (hair or blood samples can also be used). There are two basic types of assessments. A screening test assesses the potential presence of a wide variety of chemicals. A confirmation test on the same sample identifies the presence of chemicals suggested by the initial screening test. I-O psychologists are not directly involved with these tests because they are performed in chemical laboratories by individuals with special technical training. Although the analysis of urine is beyond the purview of I-O psychology, making decisions about an applicant's suitability for employment is not.

In a classic yet particularly noteworthy study, researchers examined the effects of drug testing and reported sobering results.[93] A total of 5,465 job applicants were tested for the use of illicit drugs. After 1.3 years of employment, employees who tested positive for illicit drugs had an absenteeism rate 59.3% higher than employees who tested negative. The involuntary turnover rate (namely, employees who were fired) was 47% higher among drug users than nonusers. The estimated cost savings of screening out drug users in reducing absenteeism and turnover for one cohort of new employees was $52,750,000. This figure does not reflect the compounded savings derived by cohorts of new employees added each year the drug-testing program is in existence.

Despite the clear benefits of drug testing, it is not without its problems. Manufacturing positions are going unfilled due to a large percentage of applicants—nearly half in some cases—failing their drug tests.[94] This issue is further complicated by the fact that some states have decriminalized recreational marijuana use or allowed its usage for medicinal purposes. Despite its legality in some locations, organizations are not inclined to allow marijuana usage, legal or otherwise, by its employees due to insurance and liability reasons.

Computerized Adaptive Testing

Computerized adaptive testing (CAT)
A form of assessment using a computer in which the questions have been precalibrated in terms of difficulty, and the examinee's response (right or wrong) to one question determines the selection of the next question.

One of the major advances in psychological testing is called **computerized adaptive testing (CAT)**, or "tailored testing."[95] Here is how it works: CAT is an automated test administration system that uses a computer. The test items appear on the video display screen, and the examinee answers using the keyboard. Each test question presented is prompted by the response to the preceding question. The first question given to the examinee is of medium difficulty. If the answer given is correct, the second question selected from the precalibrated bank of questions will be slightly more difficult. If the answer given to that question is wrong, the third question selected by the computer is somewhat easier. And so on.

The purpose of CAT is to get as close a match as possible between the question difficulty level and the examinee's demonstrated ability level. In fact, by the careful calibration of question difficulty, one can infer ability level on the basis of the difficulty level of the questions answered correctly. CAT systems are based on complex mathematical models. Proponents believe that tests can be shorter (because of higher precision of measurement), less expensive and have greater security than traditional paper-and-pencil tests. The military is the largest user of CAT systems, testing thousands of examinees monthly. It has been estimated that approximately two-thirds of all military recruits are assessed via a CAT version of the ASVAB.[96] In an example of CAT used in the private sector, researchers found their CAT system achieved greater test security than traditional paper-and-pencil tests.[97] Additionally, traditional academic tests like the Scholastic Aptitude Test (SAT), the Graduate Record Exam (GRE), and the Graduate Management Admission Test (GMAT) are available for applicants using an online CAT system. An added benefit is that the results of the test are available to the applicant immediately upon completion of the test.

Consider This...

Consider the case of a track and field coach who wants to determine how high the new athletes on the team can jump. The coach would likely start with the bar at a moderate height with the assumption that it can be raised or lowered from that point depending on whether the jumpers clear it or not. So, assume the coach sets the bar at 5 feet. If the jumpers clear it, the bar may be raised to 6 feet. If that's cleared, it could be raised to 7 feet. If, at 7 feet, a jumper failed to clear it, it wouldn't make sense to lower it back down to 6 feet because that was already jumped successfully. Instead, the coach may lower it to 6 feet 6 inches. If it's cleared, the bar may be raised to 6 feet 9 inches. If it's not cleared at 6 feet 6 inches, it may be lowered to 6 feet 3 inches. Thus, the changes in height start out with large adjustments and then become increasingly smaller until the final height is determined. Ideally, the final score will be a height where if the bar were raised any higher the jumper would fail every time and if the bar were any lower the jumper would clear it every time. This is how CAT works. The questions at the start of the test will be "worth" more in that larger score gains (or losses) will result from getting the question correct (or incorrect). Later questions will result in smaller changes in one's score as the finer adjustments are made. What does this suggest in terms of how you should approach such tests? Should you spend more time on the questions at the start of the test or those at the end of the test? If questions at the end of the exam were remarkably easy compared to ones at the start of the test, would you predict the test taker did well or performed poorly on the test? Why?

Online Testing

In recent years, the biggest change in psychological testing is in the way tests are administered and scored. Psychological assessment is moving inexorably from paper-and-pencil testing to online/web-based testing (see Faces of I-O Psychology: *John C. Scott*). One of the goals of online testing is to reduce the time between candidate assessment and the personnel selection decision.[98] The movement "from paper to pixels" is affecting all phases of assessment.[99] As a society, we are growing more comfortable with computer-based services in life and that includes psychological assessment. The internet offers a faster and cheaper means of testing.[100] Test publishers can download new tests to secure testing sites in a matter of moments. Updating a test is also much easier because there is no need to print new tests, answer keys, or manuals.

There are some considerations that must be made as organizations move from in-person to online testing. One pertains to proctoring. With unproctored web-based testing, the applicant completes the test from any location with online access and without direct supervision of a test administrator. With proctored web-based testing, the applicant must complete the test in the presence of a test administrator, usually at a company-sponsored location. Many organizations will accept the results from only proctored web-based testing because unproctored web-based testing raises concerns including whether the candidate had others assist in answering the questions.[101] Indeed, it has been recommended that because of potential security issues, unproctored online testing should not be used for high-stakes situations.[102]

Faces of I-O Psychology: *John C. Scott*

John C. Scott

Ph.D. Illinois Institute of Technology

Chief Operating Officer and Co-Founder, APT*Metrics*, Inc.

Practice Focus: Talent Management and Leadership Assessment

As we confront the 21st century workplace and the speed of organizational change, organizations around the world have recognized the importance of ensuring a robust leadership pipeline for the future. The selection, development and retention of high-potential leaders have become critical strategic objectives for ensuring sustainable, competitive organizations. Fortunately, sophisticated leadership assessment programs that weren't possible even a few years ago can now be assembled and launched on a global scale to measure leadership potential with greater realism, efficiency and precision than ever before. This transformation has been largely precipitated by the explosive growth and stability of the Internet. By leveraging available technology, APT*Metrics* has developed leadership assessment programs in the form of virtual simulations that immerse candidates into real-life work scenarios to measure an exhaustive array of leadership characteristics that are required of 21st century leaders.

Typically, our simulations will include three to four interwoven story or plot lines that present business challenges drawn from the critical leadership experiences within the organization. These challenges may be tied to current issues being confronted by the organization and also those anticipated in the future. We are able to evaluate leadership candidates based upon how well they handle these challenges. This is accomplished through both open-ended and multiple-choice questions that are presented at various points throughout the simulation.

In order to create the most realistic and engaging simulations possible, our production approach borrows heavily from the television and film industry. For example, we incorporate music and sound design to reflect emotional sentiment and support the actors in their performance. We also leverage special effects like green screens, current technology (mobile phone-based stimulus, tablet use, etc.), engaging locations and the creative use of "cliff hangers" to help encourage participants to remain engaged with the story. The immersive quality of the multimedia simulation creates a sense of urgency and psychological involvement in the assessment. We design the story to drive the simulation and to elicit the candidate's best performance in the context of job-relevant business challenges. The wide range of relevant and realistic stimuli challenges leaders' capabilities and ensures that candidates are stretched to their highest potential.

Some advocates for web-based testing suggest that such assessments may reduce the extent of socially desirable responding (a form of faking), since there is more privacy when responding to questions. This does not appear to be true. According to the results of a meta-analysis, there is no difference between the amount of socially desirable responding that occurs between paper-and-pencil tests and computerized tests.[103] In addition, the presence of a proctor does not appear to increase the extent of socially desirable responding. As such, unproctored, web-based surveys are not advantageous over proctored, in-person surveys if the reason is to minimize social desirability in responses.

Interviews

The employment interview is the most commonly used method of personnel selection. It is universally used across different jobs, organizations, and cultures. In fact, in some cultures, it is used almost exclusively. Researchers have offered the following observation regarding our reliance on the interview in making selection decisions:

> As a practical matter, the interview is not needed because critical KSAOs usually can be assessed by other means and often done so more accurately. It would appear that there is a basic human need to want personal contact with others before placing them in a position of importance even if they have a proven track record, a tendency from which personnel managers and others involved in organizational selection do not appear to be exempt. It is almost as if a part of the human make up does not trust objective information completely, even if it is accurate: mere facts do not supersede an underlying desire for personal verification (Huffcutt & Culbertson 2011, p. 185).[104]

The employment interview is an interactive communication event between the interviewer and applicant, in which both parties engage in mutual listening, processing, and formulating of responses.[105] Both the interviewer and the applicant have an agenda in the interview.[106] The interviewer's objective is to judge the candidate's qualifications for the job. The applicant's main goal is to get the job. As such, various social factors can influence the outcome of the interview, quite apart from the objective qualifications of the candidate. Examples include the degree of similarity between the interviewer and candidate (in terms of gender, race, and attitudes), nonverbal behavior (smiling, head nodding, hand gestures), and verbal cues (pitch, speech rate, pauses, and amplitude variability). Because of these additional sources of variance in the outcome of the interview (hire or reject), interviews are a more dynamic means of assessment than traditional testing (e.g., a test of cognitive ability). Because interviews are used so often in employment decisions, they have attracted considerable research interest among I-O psychologists.

Candidates can be successfully coached to perform well in an employment interview.[107] Impression management is the process of creating a desired impression or effect on individuals we are trying to influence. In social interactions (such as an interview), we try to craft a positive image of ourselves (i.e., what we think others are looking for in us) for the purpose of increasing the likelihood that we will get what we want.[108] Astute job candidates often rehearse specific tactics of impression management in preparation for the interview. The outcome of the interview often tilts the final selection decision among otherwise equally qualified finalists in favor of one candidate (who performed well in the interview), or against another candidate (who performed poorly in the interview).

In an interview, the formal questions are typically preceded by informal rapport-building comments, where the goal of the interviewer is to put the candidate at ease by engaging in "small talk." During this brief exchange, interviewers develop perceptions of candidates through such factors as smiling, manner of dress, manner of speech, and firmness of handshake. This small talk phase may be limited to only the first two-three minutes of the interview. Although very brief in duration, how candidates come across to the interviewer have been found to be predictive of internship offers and performance on the formal questions in the interview.[109] Candidates can be trained in how to manage interviewer impressions of them from the moment the two parties meet. However, impression management may backfire if it is too forced or if the candidate's self-promotion is viewed as arrogance.[110] As such, candidates should be careful when attempting to manage the impressions of the interviewer.

Degree of Structure

Unstructured interview
A format for the job interview in which the questions are different across all candidates. Often contrasted with the structured interview.

Structured interview
A format for the job interview in which the questions are consistent across all candidates. Often contrasted with the unstructured interview.

Interviews can be classified along a continuum of structure, where structure refers to the amount of procedural variability. The degree of structure in an interview is determined by the degree of standardization in questions as well as the degree of standardization in the scoring of responses. In a highly **unstructured interview**, the interviewer may ask each candidate different questions. For example, one candidate may be asked to describe previous jobs held and duties performed, whereas another applicant may be asked to describe career goals and interests. In addition, the scoring of responses for an unstructured interview are largely unspecified ahead of time. Conversely, in a highly **structured interview**, the interviewer asks standard questions of all job candidates.[111] In general, information derived from a work analysis should be the primary basis for the questions posed in an interview. Regardless, whatever the focus of the questions (e.g., past work experiences or future career goals), they are posed to all candidates in a similar fashion. Furthermore, the interviewer would use a standardized rating scale to assess the answers given by each candidate. In reality, however, interviewer ratings of a candidate's responses to questions always involve some degree of subjectivity. Thus, no matter how structured the interview, the interviewer does exert some influence on the judgment of the candidate. Most employment interviews fall somewhere along the continuum between highly unstructured and highly structured.

For the most part, structured interviews are far superior to unstructured interviews in terms of their inter-rater reliability[112] and validity.[113] The predictor constructs most often assessed by interviewers of candidates are personality factors (conscientiousness, agreeableness, etc.) and applied social skills (interpersonal relations, team focus, etc.).[114] However, highly unstructured and highly structured interviews do not tend to measure the same constructs. In particular, highly unstructured interviews often focus more on constructs such as general intelligence, education, work experience, and interests, whereas highly structured interviews often focus more on constructs such as job knowledge, interpersonal and social skills, and problem solving.

Interview Formats

Employment interviews can be comprised of a wide variety of questions. The questions that are asked are designed to assess a specific construct of interest or explicitly address job requirements. Some interviews will include questions that directly address minimum qualifications. For example, if a job requires that an individual has certain knowledge or background, this information can be verified verbally through the interview. Interviews are also a common time to expound on or clarify areas of confusion with other selection instruments. For instance, interviewers may use the time during an interview to inquire about specific experiences listed on one's résumé, or to ask about gaps in employment that appear on a job application.

Consider This...

We know that the predictive validity of unstructured interviews is low, but there is evidence that they not only fail to *help* personnel selection decisions, but can actually hurt them. In a series of studies, a research team found that decision makers presented with the results of (valid) test scores and (invalid) unstructured interviews were overly confident about their hiring decisions compared to decision makers presented with test scores only.[115] Why does it matter that they exhibited overconfidence? Well, research shows that when individuals are overconfident (i.e., they are more confident than their accuracy/ability warrants), they think they know something better than they actually do, and therefore lack an awareness of how correct or incorrect their decisions are. Because of this, they are likely to take more risks. In addition, if they are (over)confident in their hiring decisions, they may think they have found the "right" candidate and stop the hiring process prematurely, or extend better job offers than they should. Thus, unstructured interviews don't help us predict better performers, but they make us *think* we can, so using unstructured interviews can be detrimental to our hiring process. What are some other problems with using unstructured interviews? In what ways might they create unfair advantages or disadvantages for candidates? Why do you think they continue to be used despite the issues they have?

Situational interview A type of job interview in which candidates are presented with a hypothetical problem and asked how they would respond to it.

Given the superiority of structured interviews, it is preferable to identify the questions that will be asked within an interview ahead of time and ask them of every applicant. There are two primary interview formats that guide the development of such questions. The first format is the **situational interview**, which presents a situation and asks for a description of the actions the applicant would take in that situation. Situational interviews focus on hypothetical, future-oriented contexts in which the applicants are asked how they would respond if they were confronted with these problems.[116] The rationale behind situational interviews is that intentions are predictive of actual behavior. A sample situational interview question might be:

> "Suppose you were working with an employee who you knew greatly disliked performing a particular job task. You were in a situation where you needed this task completed, and this employee was the only one available to assist you. What would you do to motivate the employee to perform the task? (Pulakos & Schmitt 1995, p. 292).[117]

A candidate's response to such a question is typically scored on the type of scale shown in Figure 5-4. Interviewers must use their best judgment to evaluate the candidate's response because the question clearly has no one correct answer. Thus, the situational judgment interview is the oral counterpart of the written situational judgment test. Each candidate responds to several such situational questions, and the answers to each question might be evaluated on different dimensions, such as "Taking Initiative" and "Problem Diagnosis." The criterion-related validity of the situational interview to predict job performance is estimated to be .39.[118] This level of predictive accuracy is less than that for tests of general mental ability.

Low	*Medium*	*High*
Responses showed limited awareness of possible problem issues likely to be confronted Responses were relatively simplistic, without much apparent thought given to the situation.	Responses suggested considerable awareness of possible issues likely to be confronted. Responses were based on a reasonable consideration of the issues present in the situation.	Responses indicated a high level of awareness of possible issues likely to be confronted Responses were based on extensive and thoughtful consideration of the issues present in the situation.
1	2 3 4	5

Figure 5-4 *Example of rating scale for scoring a situational interview*

Behavior description interview
A type of job interview in which candidates are asked to provide specific examples from their past to illustrate attributes important for the position.

The second format for guiding the development of structured interview questions is the **behavior description interview**, which asks applicants to provide specific examples of instances from their past that reflect important attributes for the position. Behavior description interviews are based on the premise that past behavior is the best predictor of future behavior.[119] A behavior description interview question that would correspond to the situational interview question provided above might be:

> Tell me about a time when you had to motivate an individual to do something they did not enjoy doing. Describe the situation, your actions in the situation, and the outcome.

A meta-analytic examination of situational and behavior description interviews found that even when they are written to assess the same constructs, the two interview types are only moderately correlated (.40-.47).[120] In addition, behavior description interviews are more strongly correlated with cognitive ability measures than are situational interviews, whereas situational interviews are stronger predictors of job performance than are behavior description interviews. Situational and behavior description interview questions should therefore not be assumed to be interchangeable, and the two interview types might be used in combination to achieve incremental validity.

Work Samples and Situational Exercises

Work Samples

Work samples
A type of personnel selection test in which the candidate demonstrates proficiency on a task representative of the work performed in the job.

Work samples are "high-fidelity simulations," where *fidelity* refers to the level of realism in the assessment.[121] A literal description of a work sample is that the candidate is asked to perform a representative sample of the work done on the job, such as using a word processor, driving a forklift, or drafting a blueprint.

A classic example of a work sample involves a predictor of job success for mechanics created in the early 1970s.[122] Using work analytic techniques, the mechanic's job was defined by success in the use of tools, accuracy of work, and overall mechanical ability. Tasks were designed that would show an applicant's performance in these three areas. Through the cooperation of job incumbents, a work sample was created that involved such typical tasks as installing pulleys and repairing gearboxes. The steps necessary to perform these tasks correctly were identified and given numerical values

Consider This...

The employment interview can cause a lot of anxiety for individuals, which is normal, especially when it is for a job that you desperately want or need. The key to reducing that anxiety and ultimately being successful is to be prepared for it. One of the key ways to be prepared is to practice how you might answer questions that you may be asked. When responding to behavior description questions, there is a recommended framework for applicants to use. This framework is called the STAR framework, which stands for Situation, Task, Action, and Results. First, you will want to describe the situation—Is this example from a previous job, a volunteer experience, or somewhere else? Who was the person assigning the task? When did this occur? You will then want to describe the task—What exactly were you asked to do? Was there a timeline given for accomplishing the task? What were the requirements or expectations for the task? Then you'll want to tell what action you did—What did you do? Did you involve others? When did you do it? How long did it take? Finally, you want to describe the results—What happened? Was it a success? What impact did your actions have on the final outcome? In short, you want to paint a picture that is detailed enough for the interviewer to know what you did, why you did it, and how you made a positive impact. It is not enough to describe what you did if you don't tell why it mattered. It doesn't matter what the impact was if it isn't clear what your role was in creating that impact. If you follow this formula to create your detailed responses, which takes practice and a willingness to toot your own horn, you will be better able to conquer behavior description interviews. Now, you try. Using the STAR framework, answer the following questions: (1) Give an example of when you had to work with somebody who was being difficult. What did you do? (2) Tell me about a time you were asked to do something that you didn't know how to do.

according to their appropriateness (for example, 10 points for aligning a motor with a dial indicator, 1 point for aligning it by feeling the motor, 0 points for just looking at the motor). Using a concurrent criterion-related validity design, each mechanic in the shop took the work sample. Their scores were correlated with the criterion of supervisor ratings of their job performance. The validity of the work sample was excellent: it had a coefficient of .66 with use of tools, .42 with accuracy of work, and .46 with overall mechanical ability. These finding showed that there was a substantial relationship between how well mechanics performed on the work sample and how well they performed on the job. In general, work samples are among the most valid means of personnel selection.

But work samples do have limitations.[123] First, they are effective primarily in jobs that involve either the mechanical trades (for example, mechanics, carpenters, and electricians) or the manipulation of objects. They are not very effective when the job involves working with people rather than things. Second, work samples assess what a person can currently do; they don't assess potential. They seem best suited to evaluating experienced workers rather than trainees. Finally, work samples are time-consuming and costly to administer. Because they are individual tests, they require extensive supervision and monitoring. Few work samples are designed to be completed in less than one hour. If there are 100 applicants to fill 5 jobs, it would not be worthwhile to give a work sample to all applicants. Despite their limitations, work samples are useful in personnel selection.

Situational Exercises

Situational exercise
A method of assessment in which examinees are presented with a problem and asked how they would respond to it.

Situational exercises are roughly the counterpart of work samples; that is, they are used mainly to select people for managerial and professional jobs. Unlike work samples, which are designed to be replicas of the job, situational exercises mirror only part of the job. Situational exercises involve a family of tests that assess problem-solving ability. Two examples are the *inbox assessment* (also called an in-basket or mailbox test) and the leaderless group discussion. The inbox assessment has applicants sort through a full mailbox (digital such as an email inbox or analog such as an in-basket) of things to do. The contents include carefully crafted correspondence that requires the applicant's immediate attention and response. The applicant takes the appropriate action to solve the problems presented, such as scheduling a meeting, delegating a task to a subordinate, or asking questions to better understand an issue. Oftentimes, there is not enough time for applicants to fully address all issues in the assessment. This is intentional, as it forces the applicant to prioritize information and determine which matters are urgent and which ones can wait. Raters score the applicant on such factors as productivity (how much work got done) and problem-solving effectiveness (versatility in resolving problems). The inbox test is predictive of the job performance of managers and executives, a traditionally difficult group of employees to select. But a major problem with the test is that, like a work sample, it is an individual test. Thus, if there are many applicants, too much time may be needed to score the test. The typical validity coefficient of the inbox test for predicting job performance is approximately .42.[124]

In a *leaderless group discussion* (LGD), a group of applicants (normally, two to eight) engage in a job-related discussion in which no spokesperson or group leader has been named. Raters observe and assess each applicant on such factors as individual prominence, group goal facilitation, and sociability. Scores on these factors are then used as the basis for hiring. The reliability of the LGD increases with the number of people in the group. The typical validity coefficient is in the .15–.35 range.

Although the LGD does not have the validity of a typical work sample, remember that the criteria of success for a manager are usually more difficult to define. The lower validities that occasionally occur in the selection of managerial personnel are as attributable to problems with the criterion and its proper articulation as anything else. Although high-fidelity simulations (like work samples) are often highly valid, they are also time-consuming to administer and costly to develop.[125] However, the converse is also undesirable—a selection method that is inexpensive but also has little predictive accuracy. Low-fidelity simulations may be a reasonable compromise between the twin goals of high validity and low cost.

Assessment Centers

Assessment center
A technique for assessing job candidates using a series of structured, group-oriented exercises that are evaluated by raters.

Assessment centers involve evaluating job candidates, typically for managerial-level jobs, using several methods and raters. The use of assessment centers could be traced back about 100 years to the testing of German and British military officers in WWI.[126] However, their use as an accepted means of assessing candidates in business and industry began in the 1960s by researchers at AT&T, who were interested in studying the lives of managers over the full span of their careers. **Assessment centers** are not places, but rather are compilations of group-oriented, standardized activities (that may be conducted in one setting but need not be). There is also the possibility that virtual assessment centers can be created. In lieu of face-to-face interactions between assessors and assessees, the assessees could be situated in different locations and would participate through webcams. Assessment centers provide a basis for judgments or predictions of human behaviors believed or known to be relevant to work performed in an organizational setting. Because assessment centers are expensive, they have been used mainly by large organizations; however, consulting firms also offer assessment centers for smaller companies. Here are five characteristics of the assessment center approach:

1. Those individuals selected to complete assessments as part of an assessment center (the assessees) are usually management-level personnel that a company wants to evaluate for possible selection, promotion, or training. Thus, assessment centers can be used to assess both job applicants for hire and current employees for development and/or possible advancement.
2. Assessees can be evaluated individually or in groups of up to 20.
3. Several raters (the assessors) do the evaluation. They work in teams and collectively or individually make recommendations (for example, hire vs. not hire, suggest areas in need of development). Assessors may be psychologists, but may be company employees unfamiliar with the assessees. They are often trained in how to appraise performance. The assessors' training may last from several hours to a few days.
4. Assessors evaluate the assessees on a number of performance dimensions judged relevant for managerial jobs. These dimensions typically include leadership, decision making, practical judgment, and interpersonal relations skills.
5. A wide variety of assessment methods or exercises are used. Many involve group exercises—for example, leaderless group discussions. Other methods include oral presentations, written case studies, role plays, inbox exercises, and interviews. Typically, each exercise is used to provide an evaluation of multiple performance dimensions, but it is rare to use each exercise to evaluate every performance dimension.[127] The assessment typically takes one to several days.

Assessment centers provide a complex evaluation of job candidates. While the major source of variance in ratings is ideally due to differences among the candidates (or assessees), research has shown that variance in assessment center ratings is also attributable to assessors, the exercises (e.g., leaderless group discussion, interview) used in the evaluations, and the dimensions of behavior (e.g., motivation, problem-solving ability) being rated. It is also a matter of theoretical debate whether there should be high agreement across different exercises designed to measure the same dimension of behavior. The lack of agreement can be reflective of the psychological complexity of the behavior being assessed.

Letters of Recommendation

One of the most commonly used and least valid of all predictors is the letter of recommendation. Letters of recommendation and reference checks are as widespread in personnel selection as the interview and the application blank. Unfortunately, they often lack comparable validity. Letters of recommendation are usually written on behalf of an applicant by a current employer, professional associate, or personal friend. The respondent rates the applicant on such dimensions as leadership ability and communication skills. The responses are then used as a basis for hiring. The typical validity coefficient for letters of recommendation is estimated to be somewhere between .18 and .29.[128]

Letters of recommendation are one of the least accurate forecasters of job performance. One of the biggest problems with letters of recommendation is their restricted range. As you might expect, almost all letters of recommendation are positive. Most often, the applicants themselves choose who will write the letters, so it isn't surprising that they pick people who will make them look good. Because of this restriction (that is, almost all applicants are described positively), the lack of predictive ability of the letter of recommendation is not unexpected. And because most letters of recommendation have a uniform tone, recipients of the letters can become highly sensitized to "reading between the lines" in forming evaluations of the candidates. The recipients not only form opinions of candidates about what is contained in the letters, but also what is not discussed or mentioned by the letter writer.

Consider This...

Despite their ineffectiveness, letters of recommendation continue to be used. As such, it may be in your best interest to consider who you would ask to write one for you. When looking for people to provide those letters, you may want to consider the disposition of your potential letter writers. Researchers have found that individuals with positive dispositions write lengthier and more favorable letters compared to individuals with negative dispositions.[129] So, when choosing whom to ask to write a letter on your behalf, consider their dispositions. Whom would *you* ask? Create a list of potential letter writers. You never know when you might need one.

Overview and Evaluation of Predictors

Personnel selection methods can be evaluated by many standards. We have identified four major standards that are useful in organizing all the information we have gathered about predictors.

1. *Validity* refers to the ability of the predictor to forecast criterion performance accurately. Many authorities argue that validity is the predominant evaluative standard in judging selection methods; however, the relevance of the other three standards is also substantial.
2. *Fairness* refers to the ability of the predictor to render unbiased predictions of job success across applicants in various subgroups of gender, race, age, and so on.

3. *Applicability* refers to whether the selection method can be applied across the full range of jobs. Some predictors have wide applicability in that they appear well suited for a diverse range of jobs; other methods have particular limitations that affect their applicability.
4. *Cost* of implementation of the method is the final standard. The various personnel selection methods differ markedly in their cost, which has a direct bearing on their overall value.

Table 5-4 presents 14 personnel selection methods appraised on each of the four evaluative standards. Each standard is partitioned into three levels: low, moderate, and high. This classification scheme is admittedly oversimplified, and in some cases the evaluation of a selection method did not readily lend itself to a uniform rating. Nevertheless, this system is useful in providing a broad-brush view of many personnel selection methods. Average validity coefficients in the .00–.20, .21–.40, and over .40 ranges were labeled low, moderate, and high, respectively. Selection methods that have many, some, and few problems of fairness were labeled low, moderate, and high, respectively. The applicability standard, the most difficult one to appraise on a single dimension, was classified according to the ease of using the method in terms of feasibility and generalizability across jobs. Finally, direct cost estimates were made for each selection method. Methods estimated as costing less than $50 per applicant were labeled low; $51–$100, moderate; and more than $100, high.

The ideal personnel selection method would be high in validity, fairness, and applicability, and low in cost. Inspection of Table 5-4 reveals that no method has an ideal profile. The 14 methods produce a series of tradeoffs among validity, fairness, applicability, and cost. This shouldn't be surprising; if there were one uniformly ideal personnel selection method, there probably would be little need to consider 13 others.

In terms of validity, the best methods are intelligence tests, work samples, assessment centers, and physical abilities tests. However, each of these methods is limited by

Table 5-4 *Assessment of 14 personnel selection methods along four evaluative standards*

	Evaluative Standards			
Selection Method	**Validity**	**Fairness**	**Applicability**	**Cost**
Cognitive ability tests	High	Moderate	High	Low
Physical ability tests	High	Moderate	Low	Low
Psychomotor ability tests	Moderate	Moderate	Low	Low
Sensory/perceptual tests	Moderate	Moderate	Low	Low
Personality inventories	Low	High	Moderate	Moderate
Integrity tests	High	Moderate	Low	Low
Situational judgment tests	Moderate	Moderate	High	Low
Biodata inventories	Moderate	Moderate	High	Low
Drug tests	Moderate	High	Moderate	Moderate
Interviews	Moderate	Moderate	High	Moderate
Work samples	High	High	Low	High
Situational exercises	Moderate	(Unknown)	Low	Moderate
Assessment centers	High	High	Low	High
Letters of recommendation	Low	(Unknown)	High	Low

problems with fairness, applicability, or cost. Ironically, the worst selection method in terms of validity, letters of recommendation, is one of the most frequently used. This method is characterized by high applicability and low cost, which no doubt accounts for its popularity. What we have learned about predictors is that some are useful in forecasting job success and others are not. Single validity coefficients greater than .50 are as unusual today as they were in the early years of testing. Because each single method of assessment has limited predictive capacity, it is common practice to use multiple methods in making predictions. The logic of using multiple methods to predict criteria is that each method offers incremental predictive accuracy of the criterion we seek to understand.[130] Although test validity coefficients are not as high as we would like, it is unfair to condemn them as useless. Also, keep in mind that validity coefficients are a function of both the predictor and the criterion. A poorly defined and deficient criterion will produce low validity coefficients no matter what the predictor is like.

Fairness refers to the likelihood that the method will have differential predictive accuracy according to membership in any group, such as sex or race. Although the issue of fairness has generated a great deal of controversy, no method is classified in Table 5-4 as having low fairness. Insufficient information is available on two of the methods (situational exercises and letters of recommendation) to render an evaluation of their fairness, but it seems unlikely they would be judged as grossly unfair. Although several methods have exhibited some fairness problems (thus warranting caution in their use), the problems are not so severe as to reject any method as a biased means of selecting personnel.

The applicability dimension was the most difficult to assess, and evaluation of this dimension is most subject to qualification. For example, work samples are characterized by low applicability because they are limited to only certain types of jobs (that is, jobs that involve the mechanical manipulation of objects). However, this limitation appears to be more than offset by the method's high validity and fairness. Simply put, the problem with this method is its feasibility for only a selected range of jobs. In contrast, other methods have high applicability (such as the interview) and qualify as an almost universal means of selection.

The cost dimension is perhaps the most arbitrary. Selection methods may have indirect or hidden costs—costs that were not included in their evaluation but perhaps could have been. The break points in the classification scheme are also subjective. For example, we considered a $60-per-applicant cost to be moderate; others might say it is low or high. These issues notwithstanding, one can see cost evaluations for each of the methods in Table 5-4. Some methods do not cost much (for example, letters of recommendation), but they do not appear to be worth much either.

Another issue with regard to the evaluation of predictors is the extent to which applicants can cheat on them. We did not include this among the criteria because this is relatively unknown. Getting a job offer in a highly competitive market can be dependent on the results of a predictor. As such, there are inducements to cheat on employment tests. There are different forms of cheating including crib sheets, fake IDs, gaining access to interview questions ahead of time, swapping out urine samples in drug tests, and bribing test proctors, to name a few.[131] It seems it is not a matter of if applicants will cheat, it is a matter of who will cheat and when. Organizations must consider test security for all predictors and take steps to ensure their selection system is not compromised.

This chapter has examined the major types of predictors used in personnel selection. These predictors have been validated against a number of different criteria for a variety of occupational groups. Some predictors have been used more extensively than others. Furthermore, certain predictors have historically shown more validity than others. The ideal predictor would be an accurate forecaster of the criterion, equally applicable across different groups of people, and not too lengthy or costly to administer. But predictors rarely meet all these standards in practice, and situations change, resulting in a need for new predictors (see COVID-19 and I-O Psychology: *Unanswered Questions*). Nevertheless, the need for effective predictors remains, as there is still a need for all organizations to make good personnel decisions. This process is the subject of the next chapter.

COVID-19 and I-O Psychology: *Unanswered Questions*

To say that the way work is being done has changed due to the COVID-19 pandemic is an understatement. With these changes came questions, and for many organizations these questions were directed at how the predictors that we have used for so long would need to change alongside the work itself. For example, although digital interviewing has occurred for years, its use increased sharply during the pandemic. The use of digital interviewing raised questions that had not been considered by many. Is it appropriate for organizations to allow some candidates to interview in person while others interviewed virtually? Are the two forms of interviews "comparable enough" that applicants can be evaluated fairly against one another? How do organizations ensure that candidates who may not have access to technology or be as technologically savvy are given a fair shake? We know that interview modality can unduly influence ratings and drop-out rates. So how do we ensure this doesn't happen?

Questions have also arisen regarding whether we need to consider new predictors. For example, it is unclear whether the same things that predict job performance in a traditional work setting will predict job performance in a remote setting. Do we need specific predictors of success for people working remotely? Are predictors of health and safety behaviors something we should be incorporating into all selection processes?

Organizations also saw drastic changes in terms of availability of candidates. Unemployment skyrocketed and yet, despite millions of jobs being available, organizations faced a shortage of workers. As such, it became important to consider how hiring practices might need to change when candidates were scarce, and employees were stretched thin. What parts of the process could be automated? Could artificial intelligence be used to score responses to ease pressures on current staff? Should applicant reactions to predictors be given greater emphasis to prevent candidates from exiting the process prematurely?

There is a clear opportunity for I-O psychologists to play a large role in shaping the ways organizations address these challenges. Thus, while many of these questions remain unanswered, they won't remain unanswered for long. Our knowledge of how best to predict outcomes of interest is constantly growing, and because of that, we can design research to address whatever these new challenges present.

Chapter Review

Key Terms

Psychometric
Reliability
Test-retest reliability
Equivalent-form reliability
Internal consistency reliability
Inter-rater reliability
Validity
Construct
Operationalization
Construct validity
Criterion-related validity
Validity coefficient
Content validity
Face validity
g
Big 5 personality theory
Dark triad
Faking
Integrity test
Polygraph
Situational judgment test
Biodata inventory
Drug testing
Computerized adaptive testing (CAT)
Unstructured interview
Structured interview
Situational interview
Behavior description interview
Work samples
Situational exercise
Assessment center

Questions for Review

1. What is a predictor? Why are predictors important and what purpose do they serve? What kinds of predictors are I-O psychologists interested in and why?
2. What is reliability? What are the four types of reliability and when would each be used?
3. What is validity? What are the four sources of evidence for validity?
4. What is a construct? What is operationalization? How are they related?
5. How are reliability and validity inter-related? Why can one not have validity without reliability?
6. What is construct sampling? What is behavior sampling? In what situations would each be valuable?
7. What is an example of a past characteristic? Of a present characteristic? In what situations would each be valuable?
8. What is cognitive ability (*g*)? What is special about *g*? How is it measured? What are drawbacks to measuring cognitive ability with tests?
9. What are the dimensions of physical ability? How is physical ability measured and how can tests be used incorrectly?
10. What are psychomotor and sensory/perceptual ability? How are they measured? For what kinds of jobs are these abilities imperative?
11. Why are personality inventories administered? How good are these inventories at predicting job success?

12. What are the Big 5 personality factors? What role does each play in helping to predict the success of a job candidate?
13. Which personality traits are part of the dark triad? What are the short-term impacts of these personality types on organizations? What are the long-term impacts?
14. What is "faking," and is it problematic for organizations? How can faking be reduced? Can it be eliminated?
15. What are types of integrity tests? How can they be used? What are the drawbacks to using them?
16. Why are situational judgment tests (SJTs) valuable?
17. What are biodata inventories and when do they increase the validity of the predictor?
18. Why do I-O psychologists have an interest in drug testing?
19. What is computerized adaptive testing (CAT)? What additional benefits does CAT provide in assessment?
20. How has online testing been integrated recently? What are its advantages and its drawbacks?
21. What is an interview? What are the types of interviews that can be conducted? What are their inherent drawbacks? Why are they widely used? Why are unstructured interviews so problematic?
22. What are work samples and situational exercises, and how are they similar? What degree of validity do they have? What are their drawbacks?
23. What are assessment centers? What role can they play in predicting employee success?
24. Why are recommendation letters used? When are they useful?
25. Which of the selection methods is best? What are the tradeoffs of using different methods? What are the methods with the highest validity? With the greatest applicability? When is cost less of a consideration?

CHAPTER 6

Organizational Strategy and Staffing

Chapter Outline

Recruitment

Social Media and I-O Psychology: *Social Recruitment*

The Lighter Side of I-O Psychology: *Responses to Rejection Letters*

Personnel Selection

Selection Decisions

Personnel Selection from a Human Perspective

COVID-19 and I-O Psychology: *College Admissions Amid COVID-19*

Validity Generalization

Determination of the Cutoff Score

Test Utility and Organizational Efficiency

Faces of I-O Psychology: *Joshua Brenner*

Placement and Classification

Chapter Review

Learning Objectives

- Explain the social and legal context for personnel decisions.
- Describe the process of personnel recruitment.
- Summarize how organizational strategy influences personnel decisions.
- Explain the concept and significance of validity generalization.
- Discuss the selection of employees and the process of assessing job applicants.
- Identify issues pertaining to the determination of the cutoff score.
- Explain the concept and significance of test utility related to organizational efficiency.
- Differentiate the personnel functions of placement and classification.

An organization's strategy refers to how it seeks to accomplish its goals. It is a topic that has been heavily researched in business, but it has only been addressed within I-O psychology in the past decade or so.

Just as individuals have financial budgets, so too do organizations. For most individuals, housing is the single largest expense item in their budget. Organizations, depending upon their strategy, differ in how much they spend on their human resources. For some organizations, human resources are the largest single expense item in their budget. For other organizations, the cost of human resources is not their leading expenditure. The organization's strategy is the basis for how much it spends on its human resources.

In the fast food industry, for example, customers desire to purchase inexpensive food served quickly. There is a highly routinized system for customers to order their food, pay for it, and have it served. The human component of the system (i.e., the people who perform these tasks) are but a relatively minor component in meeting the customer's needs. Jobs in this industry, particularly entry-level ones, require low levels of KSAOs. The tasks are highly structured and require little training time. Such jobs typically pay minimum wage. Fast-food employees frequently only work for brief periods of time, such as after school, over the summer, or until they can find better jobs. There is a large supply of people who can perform the relatively simple tasks in these jobs. It is rare to find a person who works in this industry as a career (with the possible exception of those individuals who work their way up into management positions). Turnover is very high, about 300% per year, meaning the average employee works only about four months before leaving. The turnover rate is not a problem, given the volume of people in the workforce who can replace departed workers. Accordingly, the recruitment process for these entry-level employees is not formalized and the selection process is cursory. The fast-food industry uses this approach to recruitment and selection because it fits its strategy. Customers are attracted by inexpensive food served quickly, not who takes their orders or serves them. By keeping their human resource costs to a minimum (albeit still a large percent of their expenses overall), owners can keep the cost of their food low, a critical component of their strategy.

A very different organizational strategy is evidenced in the medical field. Medicine is devoted to preventing illnesses and the treatment of the people who become ill or injured. The organizational strategy in the field of medicine is the opposite of the fast-food industry with regard to human resources. Rather than a cost to be minimized, the medical field regards human resources as an investment. It is precisely because of the high KSAOs needed to enter the field of medicine that qualified people are in low supply and high demand. The quality of human resources in the medical field is critical to achieving its goals. The amount of education and training required to be a physician is measured in years, not weeks or days. Once an individual enters the medical field, it typically becomes a lifetime career. Given the cost of recruitment, selection, and training, the medical field tries to minimize turnover. While a 300% annual turnover rate in the fast-food industry is typically deemed acceptable (albeit high), a 10% turnover rate in the medical field is typically deemed unacceptably high. As a result, many individuals in the medical field are well-compensated. Aside from physicians, people trained in diagnostics and specialized care, for example, command high salaries. In short, human resources in the medical field (and other industries that depend upon highly skilled individuals) are regarded as an investment, not a cost to be minimized. If an organization's strategy is built upon the value of its human resources, the organization must invest heavily in the recruitment, selection, training, compensation, and management of its employees. As such, the quality of the employees become an asset of the organization,[1] and the cost of their human resources is often the largest item in its budget.

Fast food and medicine represent industries where organizations within them have monumentally-different human resources strategies. Many industries fall somewhere between these two extremes. In many instances, there is also differential importance placed on jobs within an organization. The banking industry would be a case in point. Customer service jobs, such as tellers, require fewer KSAOs than financial analysts. Accordingly, a bank would not invest heavily in the recruitment, selection, and training of people who hold the job of teller, as compared with people who are responsible for making major investment decisions.

Organizational strategies that depend heavily on the quality of their employees for success have given birth to additional terms in the practice of I-O psychology. They were created to reflect the growing recognition of just how important people are for achieving an organization's goals, depending on its strategy. While "KSAO" is a conventional term used in I-O psychology to reflect human attributes, another term used is "talent." The processes of recruitment and selection result in the "acquisition" of new employees. Thus, "talent acquisition" is a common term used in organizations. Once a candidate becomes a new employee, "onboarding" begins (onboarding will be discussed further in Chapter 7). Onboarding (also known as organizational socialization) is the process that tries to ensure that new hires feel welcome in the organization and are prepared to fill their new position. Successful onboarding gives new employees the confidence and resources to make an impact more quickly in the organization. Onboarding helps bridge the gap between being hired and becoming a high-performing employee. These concepts are differentially relevant to organizations based on their position on the continuum between regarding employees as a cost to be minimized versus an investment to be carefully developed. Having high-quality employees is desirable for all organizations, but far more critical for the success of some than others.

To improve overall organizational performance, should companies attract, retain, and develop their human resources? In a meta-analysis of studies that examined the relationship between the quality of employees and the performance of the organization, the researchers concluded that it is essential that organizations hire, develop, and retain the best talent available to ensure high performance.[2] Thus, when the quality of employees is critical to the success of the organization, the employees should be carefully recruited and selected with equal effort applied to their retention.

Recruitment

Recruitment
The process by which individuals are solicited to apply for jobs.

The personnel function of **recruitment** is the process of attracting people to apply for a job. Organizations can select only from those candidates who apply. Attracting and keeping competent employees is critical to the success of most organizations. How organizations recruit new employees depends upon many factors. Among the factors are the skills required, how wide of a geographic area must be searched to find the needed personnel, the methods used by organizations to announce job vacancies, the messages organizations convey in their recruitment efforts to indicate they are an attractive employer, and the amount of money organizations are willing to commit to their recruitment budget. Over a century ago, many companies could recruit needed personnel by simply hanging a hand-written notice in a storefront window, "Help Wanted." Individuals passing on the sidewalk who saw the sign, and were looking for work, became job candidates. Some small stores may still use this recruitment method, but today such an approach simply won't attract the caliber of talent that most organizations need for staffing (see Social Media and I-O Psychology: *Social Recruitment*). As the need for a potential applicant pool expands from passersby on a sidewalk to a

Social Media and I-O Psychology: *Social Recruitment*

The number of people who use social media sites daily is staggering. As such, it is only natural that when organizations have something that they want a lot of people to see, they're going to use social media to disseminate it. Job announcements are no different. According to a survey conducted in 2012 by Jobvite, the most common social media outlet for recruitment is LinkedIn, with 93% of companies using it for such activities. Organizations are also relying on word of mouth through Facebook to reach future employees. Capitalizing on the notion that employee referrals may lead to high-quality hires, roughly two-thirds of all recruiters are using the social media powerhouse to reach individuals who they may not reach otherwise. In fact, to encourage employees to help in this effort, many organizations are offering referral bonuses to employees who help secure a viable applicant. Twitter has also become a popular tool for organizations to use in their recruiting efforts, with 54% of recruiters using it to help in the search for talent. For example, Citigroup, Garmin, Warner Brothers, Starbucks, FedEx, and Hallmark are just a few of the companies that have tweeted about current and upcoming job openings, using the power of social media to connect with potential applicants.

Of course, the use of social media for recruiting purposes is not only beneficial for organizations. Applicants benefit too. For example, by following the right companies on Twitter, job seekers can get information about job openings as soon they become available, if not before. In addition, Jobvite's survey revealed that it took less overall time to hire when social media were utilized in recruitment efforts as compared to when social media were not used to recruit. Not only is this advantageous for organizations, but applicants also benefit, as it means a person in need of a job may have a better chance of more quickly beginning work. In short, it would seem that updating that LinkedIn profile (and keeping it professional) may be a good first step in obtaining that dream job.

city, state, or nation, there are corresponding changes in not only where organizations look for talent but how they look. And as noted previously, the state of the economy will have a strong effect on how many people express interest in becoming employees.

Different recruiting approaches are used depending upon the job level in question and may include paper media, radio and television, job fairs, and online. Companies called "search firms" and individuals called "head hunters" specialize in matching people with jobs, but typically only serve clientele at the higher job levels. The fee charged by the search firm for a successful match might be 50% of the individual's annual salary. The importance of recruiting for organizations varies in direct proportion to the criticality of having talented employees for the organization's success.

When recruiting applicants, it is important to have a sizeable and suitable pool of talent. Otherwise, even the best selection process will be of little or no use.[3] However, larger applicant pools do not necessarily result in the selection of higher quality personnel.[4] Increasing the number of unqualified applicants in the pool does not enhance the quality of those selected. Increasing the applicant pool with more qualified applicants permits the employer to be extremely selective, with the result being the selected candidates have a high probability of being successful on the job. In addition, recruitment efforts should ensure applicants reflect the diversity of the population. Thus, the focus on recruitment should be on obtaining a large pool of qualified, diverse applicants.

How organizations recruit employees can be regarded from one of three conceptual positions. In times of high unemployment, organizations seek new talent the way that miners prospect for gold nuggets. The organizations sift through candidates looking for a proverbial gold nugget, and if found, the nugget is selected. In times of low unemployment, the process works in reverse. Now candidates sift through organizations, looking for their own proverbial gold nugget—the ideal employer. However, these "prospecting" theories of recruiting are extreme positions. More often, recruiting is a middling position more aptly regarded as "mating," where both the organization and the individual try to ascertain whether they are a good match with each other. The mating approach to recruiting is a most reasonable way to understand the process of meeting the needs of both parties.

Just as in any mating process, both parties share information with each other, but with the intent of increasing their perceived attractiveness to each other. Candidates engage in impression management, offering information about themselves they think recruiters want to hear. For example, they may highlight particularly successful experiences or exaggerate their accomplishments. Similarly, in attempts to impress candidates, recruiters may accentuate the organization's accomplishments in socially desirable activities such as diversity and environmental responsibility.[5] Organizations manage the image of the company on a continuous basis as a means of attracting potential employees.[6] Sponsoring college events, getting cited as a good place to work, and offering scholarships are indirect means of recruitment. Such activities serve as a signal to applicants that the culture and focus of the organization is positive. This can make organizations the "employers of choice" for potential employees, demonstrating the benefit of laying the groundwork for organizational attraction.

Despite advances in the more sophisticated electronic-based approaches to recruiting, the old-fashioned word-of-mouth source of candidates is still in force. Positive information through word-of-mouth channels (i.e., friends, relatives, neighbors) is associated with perceptions of organizational attractiveness and behavioral outcomes (e.g., applying for a job).[7] Onsite visits by candidates to the organization (as opposed to just a telephone contact, for example) signal to the candidates that the organization is serious about them and regards them to be important.[8] The site visit not only provides information for both parties about each other, but also serves to affirm the value each holds for the other. However, success in getting candidates interested in joining an organization (the purpose of recruiting) is not the same as actually getting new employees to join the organization (i.e., staffing the organization).[9] Some organizations have a difficult time filling key jobs even in times of high unemployment and with the most serious recruiting efforts.

Consider This...

What do you do when there is a labor shortage and you can't get applicants for your jobs? In 2021, the United States saw an unprecedented labor shortage in the hospitality industry. In response to this shortage, many businesses raised their wages to entice applicants, sometimes engaging in 'bidding wars' or attempting to poach employees from nearby competitors.[10] By raising wages to $15/hour (up from an average of $12/hour offered in the area at similar establishments), one coffee shop owner in Iowa received more applications in two weeks than he had in the previous nine years combined. Clearly, money is a motivator for enticing applicants to apply for jobs. What else do you think would motivate people to apply for jobs when there is a labor shortage? Do you think it is okay to poach employees from competitors? Why or why not?

Candidates form opinions of the fairness of methods used to evaluate them for selection into an organization.[11] The quality of a selection process that is acceptable to job candidates is "social validity,"[12] an extension of face validity (discussed in Chapter 5). Selection methods that produced the highest ratings of fairness have these characteristics: (1) are job-related (seemingly relevant to the work performed in the job), (2) provide candidates with an opportunity to demonstrate their ability to perform the job, and (3) provide prompt feedback on their performance. There is a positive correlation between candidates' performance on a selection test and their opinion of its fairness.[13] Researchers have found that job applicants hold negative views of an organization for using what they consider unfair selection procedures, even when the applicants are offered jobs.[14]

No one likes to be rejected, but organizations can provide thoughtful and considerate explanations as to why candidates were not accepted for hire.[15] Applicant reactions to assessment procedures are often vividly personal and highly emotional (see The Lighter Side of I-O Psychology: *Responses to Rejection Letters*). When candidates receive timely, customized, and informal notification of their rejection, they tend to have greater fairness perceptions and intentions to re-apply in the future.[16] It might be a wiser investment for organizations to explain to rejected candidates why they were denied employment in a way that reduces negative feelings and damage to self-esteem than to gird for potential litigation.[17]

The Lighter Side of I-O Psychology: *Responses to Rejection Letters*

Getting rejected isn't easy. Whether it's a love interest, a potential employer, college admission, or something else, being turned down for something you really want is a painful experience. For some, getting rejected will result in tears of sadness. For others, it might lead to anger and frustration. Yet for others, the reaction may be to respond to the rejection letter. Three prominent examples of this technique have been used.

One approach was to offer advice to the sender of the rejection letter. Chuck Davidow received not one, but two rejection letters from the same law firm on back-to-back days to inform he was not going to get the job for which he had applied.[18] He decided to send a letter to the interviewer in which he expressed his dismay at receiving two rejection letters and humorously asked if it was meant to express how badly they wanted to reject him. In his words, "Was this merely the second step of a 'No, no, a thousand times no' sort of response?" He recommended that it might be better to send a "single good, nasty, insulting letter" rather than multiple "we-appreciate-your-interest letters." He further suggested that another alternative to sending two form letters to reject him would be to send "a returnable postcard with boxes to check, marked 'YES, I am now thoroughly convinced that you have rejected me' and 'NO, I am not yet persuaded; better try again." Or, the organization could hire a firm to call him every morning to remind him that he was still rejected. Or, the organization could have other offices within the same firm send him rejection letters, including those in international offices, so he could at least receive the letters in another language.

Another response to a rejection letter was to reject the rejection. Jessica Irving received a rejection letter after she applied for a retail assistant position at a local Aldi supermarket.[19] She responded by noting that her skills were "on par with your store, with the ability to be exceptionally fast paced to scan items like every ALDI team member does." She described herself as "very persuasive." Indeed, she wrote that she was so persuasive she had decided to reject the rejection and closed her response by noting, "See you on Monday for my 9–5 shift :)."

A final response worth noting was one from a candidate for a head chef position. His response? A simple "F*** you" (with, of course, the expletive not disguised with asterisks!).[20]

Which was the right response? It's hard to say. Mr. Davidow's advice led to a job offer (which he declined but he remained in touch with the interviewer and they developed a longstanding friendship). Ms. Irving's response led to the organization advancing her to the next step in the selection process, offering her the chance to interview with the store. And the head chef? His response did not lead to a job offer or chance to proceed in the selection process. It did, however, lead the sender of the rejection letter to modify her template to include an invitation for rejected candidates to ask for specific feedback regarding their applications. So, despite their absurdity (or inappropriateness), each of the responses led to a favorable outcome of sorts. Nevertheless, these options may be best thought of as "do not try this at home" examples!

Personnel Selection

Personnel selection The process of determining those applicants who are selected for hire versus those who are rejected.

Personnel selection is the process of identifying from the pool of recruited applicants those to whom a job will be offered. As long as there are fewer job openings than applicants, some applicants will be hired and some won't. Selection is the process of separating the accepted from the rejected applicants. Ideally, the selected employees will be successful on the job and contribute to the welfare of the organization. Three major factors influence the quality of our personnel selection decisions: the validity of the predictor, the selection ratio, and the base rate.

Predictor cutoff A score on a test that differentiates those who passed the test from those who failed; often equated with the passing score on a test.

Predictor Validity. Figure 6-1 shows a predictor–criterion correlation of .80, which is reflected in the oval shape of the plot of the predictor and criterion scores.* Along the predictor axis is a vertical line—the **predictor cutoff**—that separates accepted from rejected applicants. We can think of the predictor cutoff score as the passing score. People above the cutoff (or cutscore) are accepted for hire; those below it are rejected. Also, observe the three horizontal lines. The solid line, representing the criterion performance of the entire group, cuts the entire distribution of scores in half. The dotted line, representing the criterion performance of the rejected group, is below the performance of the total group. Finally, the dashed line, which is the average criterion performance of the accepted group, is above the performance of the total group. In a simple and straightforward sense, that is what a valid predictor does in personnel selection: it identifies the more capable people from the total pool.

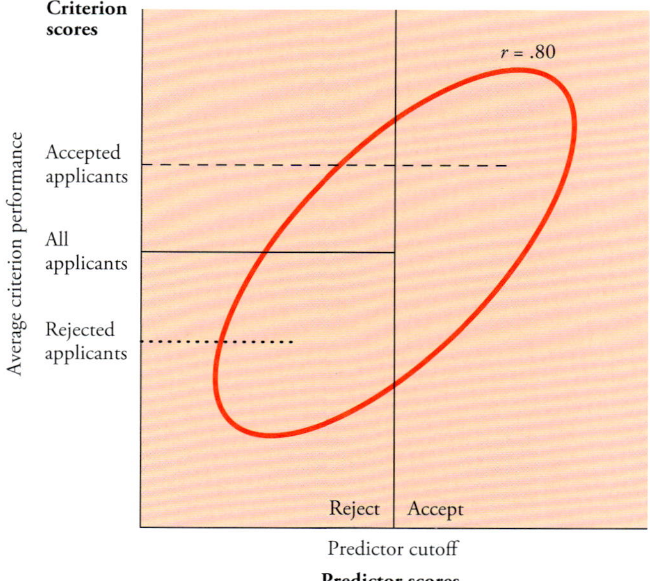

Figure 6-1 *Effect of a predictor with a high validity (r = .80) on test value*

*Note that an oval shape is used in lieu of each individual score (the plot based on predictor and criterion scores) that would typically be found in a scatterplot. The oval shape shown therefore reflects the shape of all the individual scores such that no scores fall outside of the oval. The stronger the correlation, the thinner the oval will be. The weaker the correlation, the more round the oval will become.

A different picture emerges for a predictor that has no correlation with the criterion, as shown in Figure 6-2. Again, the predictor cutoff separates those accepted from those rejected. This time, however, the three horizontal lines are all superimposed; that is, the criterion performance of the accepted group is no better than that of the rejected group, and both are the same as the performance of the total group. The value of the predictor is measured by the difference between the average performance of the accepted group and the average performance of the total group. As can be seen, these two values are the same, so their difference equals zero. In other words, predictors that have no validity also have no value.

Based on this example, we see a direct relationship between a predictor's value and its predictive validity: the greater the criterion-related validity of the predictor, the greater its value as measured by the increase in average criterion performance for the accepted group over that for the total group.

Selection ratio
A numeric index ranging between 0 and 1.00 that reflects the selectivity of the hiring organization in filling jobs; the number of job openings divided by the number of job applicants.

Selection Ratio. A second factor that determines the value of a predictor is the selection ratio (SR). The **selection ratio** is defined as the number of job openings (n) divided by the number of job applicants (N):

$$SR = \frac{n}{N} \quad \text{[Formula 6-1]}$$

When the SR is equal to 1.00 (there are as many openings as there are applicants) or greater (there are more openings than applicants), the use of any selection device has little meaning. The company can use any applicant who walks through the door. But most often, there are more applicants than openings (the SR is somewhere between 0 and 1.00) and the SR is meaningful for personnel selection.

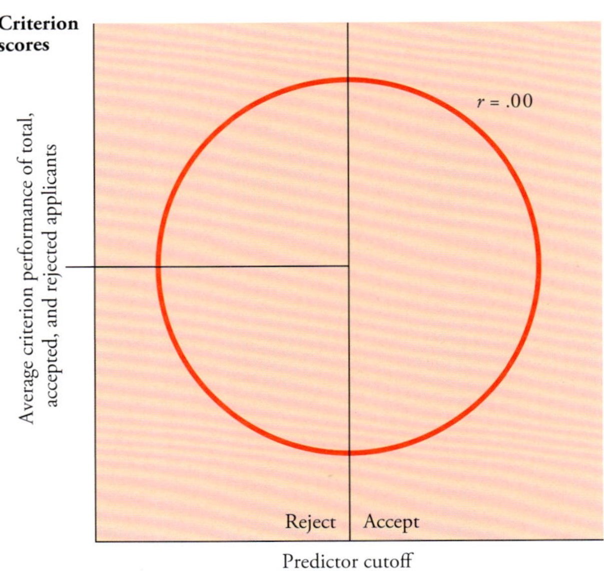

Figure 6-2 *Effect of a predictor test with no validity (r = .00) on test value*

The effect of the SR on a predictor's value can be seen in Figures 6-3 and 6-4. Let us assume we have a validity coefficient of .80 and the selection ratio is .75, meaning we will hire three out of every four applicants. Figure 6-3 shows the predictor–criterion relationship, the predictor cutoff that results in accepting the top 75% of all applicants, and the respective average criterion performances of the total group and the accepted group. If a company hires the top 75%, the average criterion performance of that group is greater than that of the total group (which is weighted down by the bottom 25% of the applicants). Again, value is measured by this difference between average criterion scores.

In Figure 6-4 we have the same validity coefficient (r = .80), but this time the SR is .25; that is, out of every four applicants, we will hire only one. The figure shows the location of the predictor cutoff that results in hiring only the top 25% of all applicants and the average criterion performances of the total and accepted groups. The average criterion performance of the accepted group is not only above that of the total group as before, but the difference is also much greater. In other words, when only the top 25% are hired, their average criterion performance is greater than the performance of the top 75% of the applicants, and both of these values are greater than the average performance of the total group.

The relationship between the SR and the predictor's value should be clear: the smaller the SR, the greater the predictor's value. This should also make sense intuitively. The fussier we are in hiring people (that is, the smaller the selection ratio), the more likely it is that the people hired will have the quality we desire.

Base rate
The percentage of employees who would be successful if individuals are randomly hired.

Base Rate. A third factor that affects the value of a predictor in improving the quality of the workforce is called the **base rate**, defined as the percentage of employees who would perform successfully if they were randomly hired. If a company has a base rate of 99% (that is, 99 out of every 100 randomly-hired employees would perform their jobs successfully), it is unlikely that any new selection method can improve upon this already near-ideal condition. If a company has a base rate of 100%, obviously no new selection system can improve upon a totally satisfactory workforce. The only "improvement" that might be attained with a new test is one that takes less time to administer or one that costs less (but still achieves the same degree of predictive accuracy). On the other hand, if the base rate were 0, that means that no randomly-hired employee would be able to perform the job satisfactorily (yikes!). In this case, it is unlikely that the issue is one that will be fixed by a new predictor. The job is either impossibly hard, the criteria for what is "successful" is too stringent, or the pool of applicants is inappropriate and underqualified. Thus, for base rates, the ideal situation for increasing the value of a predictor is when the base rate is at .50. That is, under random selection conditions, half of those hired would be successful and half would be unsuccessful.

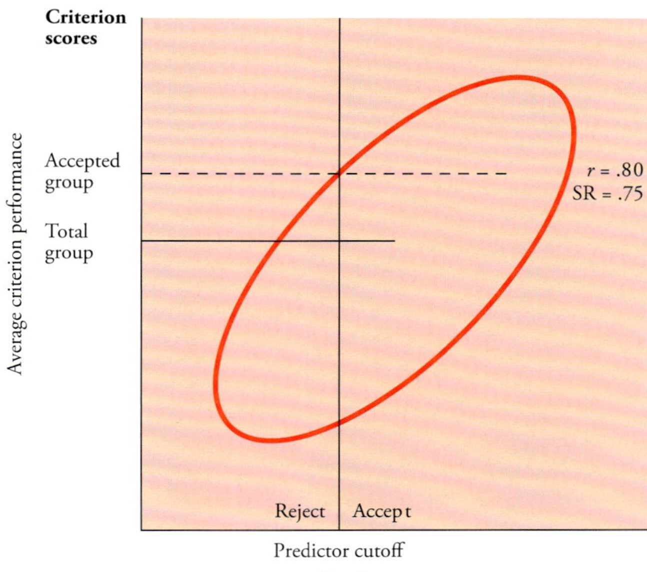

Figure 6-3 *Effect of a large selection ratio (SR = .75) on test value*

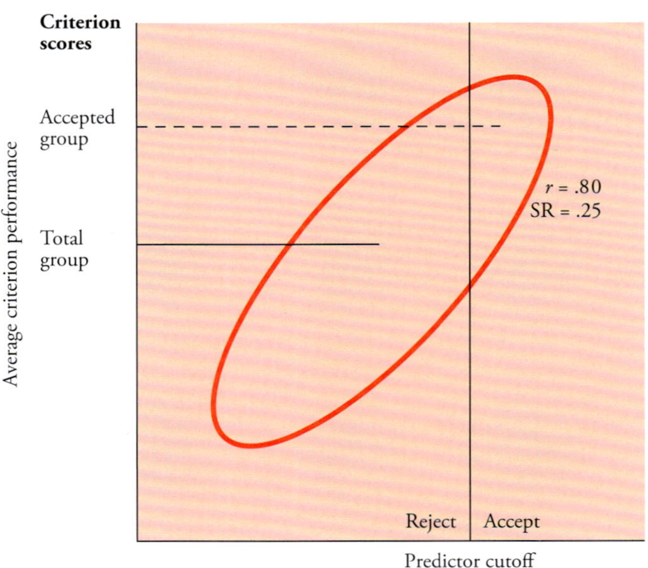

Figure 6-4 *Effect of a small selection ratio (SR = .25) on test value*

Consider This...

You've just read that the value of a predictor in personnel selection is determined by three things: (1) the criterion-related validity of the predictor, (2) the selection ratio, and (3) the base rate. These three things are much like the Bears' preferences in the *Goldilocks and the Three Bears* story. Recall that Goldilocks enters the Bears' home and tastes their porridge, sits in their chairs, and lies in their beds. For each, she finds one is too much of something (Papa Bear's porridge is too hot), one is too much in the opposite direction (Mama Bear's porridge is too cold), and one is "just right" (Baby Bear's is the perfect temperature, presumably in the middle of the temperature range). You can think of our three determinants of a predictor's value as being like the Bears' preferences. We want the criterion-related validity to be as high as possible, we want the selection ratio to be as low as possible, and we want the base rate to be "just right"—in the middle. Consider why this is the case. What is it that makes a predictor useless when its criterion-related validity is really small? What is the problem with having too high of a selection ratio? Why do we want the base rate to be "just right"? Do you think one of these three is more important than another? Why or why not?

Selection Decisions

The first documented personnel selection test in recorded history is reported in the Bible (Judges 12:4-6 King James Version). Two warring tribes differed in their ability to pronounce a word—"shibboleth." The members of one tribe could not utter the "sh" sound, and pronounced the word as "sibboleth." The inability to pronounce the word indicated the person was a member of the opposing tribe. Today, one meaning of shibboleth is a test that is used to make a major personnel decision (those tribesmen who could not pronounce the word were executed).

Unfortunately, the science of personnel selection is sometimes dismissed because it does not reflect the way hiring occurs "in the real world." Organizational decision makers frequently rely on their intuition as opposed to validated, empirically-derived predictors.[21] Despite the demonstrated empirical validity of psychological tests, some managers are reluctant to use them in making personnel selection decisions.[22] Instead, they rely on their own hunches or intuition in deciding who to hire. Improvements in selection decisions are not achieved by replacing scientific evidence with hunches. This chapter will discuss the science and practice of making personnel decisions, with the full realization that many organizations' practices are only loosely linked to science.

As long as the predictor used for selection has less than perfect validity (r = 1.00), we will always make some errors in personnel selection. The object is, of course, to make as few mistakes as possible. With the aid of the scatterplot, we can examine where the mistakes occur in making scientifcally-based selection decisions.

Criterion cutoff
A standard that separates successful from unsuccessful job performance.

Part (a) of Figure 6-5 shows a predictor–criterion relationship of about .80, where the criterion scores have been separated by a **criterion cutoff**. The criterion cutoff is the point that separates successful (above) from unsuccessful (below) employees. Management decides what constitutes successful and unsuccessful performance. Part (b) shows the same predictor–criterion relationship, except this time the predictor scores have been separated by a predictor cutoff. The predictor cutoff is the point that separates accepted (right) from rejected (left) applicants. The score that constitutes passing the predictor test is determined by the selection ratio, cost factors, or occasionally law (for example, in some public-sector organizations such state governments, it is usually set at 70% correct). Part (c) shows the predictor–criterion relationship intersected by both cutoffs. Each of the resulting four sections of the scatterplot is identified by a letter representing a different group of people:

True positives
A term to describe individuals who were correctly selected for hire because they became successful employees.

True negatives
A term to describe individuals who were correctly rejected for employment as they would have been unsuccessful employees.

Section A: Applicants who are above the predictor cutoff and above the criterion cutoff are called **true positives**. These are the people we predict will succeed on the job because they passed the selection test, and who in fact turn out to be successful employees. This group represents a correct decision: we correctly decided to hire them.

Section B: The people in this group are those we predicted would not succeed on the job because they failed the selection test and who, if hired anyway, would have performed unsatisfactorily. This group represents a correct decision: we correctly predicted they would not succeed on the job. These people are **true negatives**.

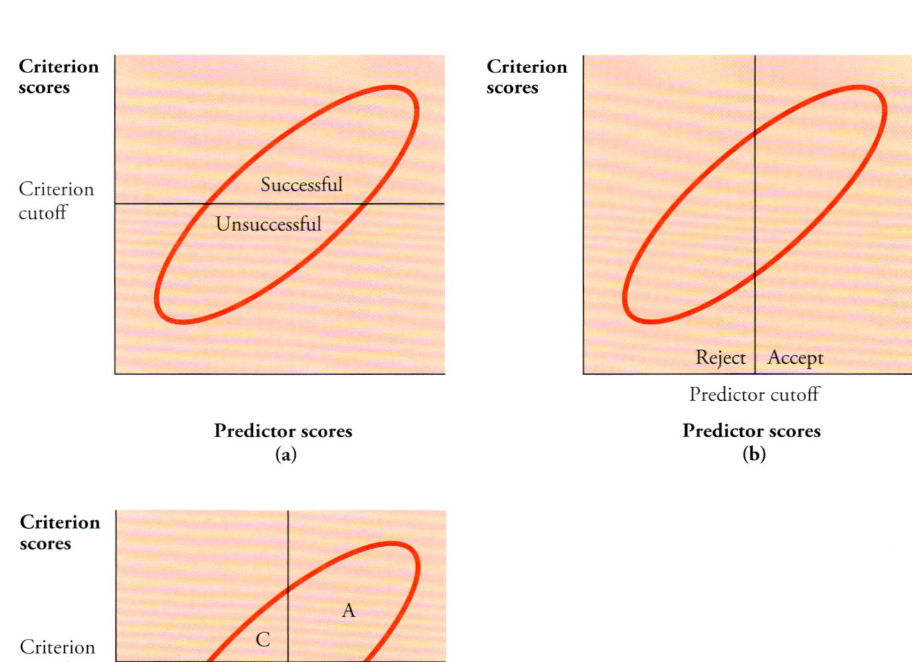

Figure 6-5 *Effect of establishing (a) criterion cutoff, (b) predictor cutoff, and (c) both cutoffs on a predictor–criterion scatterplot*

False negatives
A term to describe individuals who were incorrectly rejected for employment as they would have been successful employees.

False positives
A term to describe individuals who were incorrectly accepted for employment as they became unsuccessful employees.

Section C: People who failed the selection test but who would have succeeded had they been given the chance (and yet we predicted would not succeed on the job) are called **false negatives**. We have made a mistake in our decision-making process with these people. We falsely said they would fail but they would have succeeded. These are "the good ones we let get away."

Section D: The people who passed the selection test (and are thus predicted to succeed on the job) but perform unsatisfactorily after being hired are called **false positives**. We have also erred with these people. They are really ineffective employees who should not have been hired, but we mistakenly thought they would succeed. They are "the bad ones we let in."

Positive/negative refers to the result of passing/failing the selection test; true/false refers to the quality (good/bad) of our decision to hire the candidate. In personnel selection, we want to minimize the false positives and false negatives.

If there is no difference between making false positive and false negative decisions (that is, letting a bad worker in is no worse than letting a good one get away), it does no good to "juggle" the predictor cutoff scores. By lowering the predictor cutoff in Figure 6-5 (moving the line to the left), we decrease the size of section C, the false negatives. But by reducing the number of false negatives, we increase the space in section D, the false positives. The converse holds for raising the predictor cutoff (moving the line to the right). Furthermore, classification errors (false positives and false negatives) are also influenced by extreme base rates. For example, when the behavior being predicted occurs very rarely (such as employees who will commit violent acts in the workplace), the differential likelihood of one type of error over the other is great.[23] However, cutoff scores cannot be established solely for the purpose of minimizing false

Consider This...

The above discussion is all about setting the predictor cutoff such that individuals above that score are hired and those below it are rejected. What about setting a *maximum* cutoff score such that individuals below that score are hired and those above it are rejected? Of course, this occurs if you are dealing with something you don't want a lot of, such as errors on a test. You could easily reverse it so that you are interpreting it as accuracy and it's the same thing we've been talking about (where those more accurate are hired and those less accurate—with more errors—are rejected). But what about rejecting individuals who score *too high*? Would this ever be a good idea? Those who advocate for maximum cutoff scores often cite the reason being that individuals who score too high may be overqualified for a position and/or get bored with certain jobs. So, if a job required very little cognitive ability, for example, you may want to avoid hiring someone who scores exceptionally high on an aptitude test. If you do hire them, they may become bored and quit. What do you think of this? Can you think of other reasons to consider a maximum cutoff score? What are some reasons not to use such scores? How would you feel if you applied for a job and were rejected because you did too well on one of the assessments?

positives or false negatives. For example, if the base rate of employees committing violence in the workplace is 1%, by selecting all candidates, we would be correct 99% of the time. When violence occurs in the workplace, we derive no comfort from the fact that "only one" employee out of many was a perpetrator. There must be some rational relationship between the cutoff score and the purpose of the test.[24]

Multiple correlation
A statistical index used to indicate the degree of predictability (ranging from 0 to 1.00) in forecasting the criterion on the basis of two or more other variables.

Better personnel decisions are made based on more than one piece of information. Not surprisingly, combining two or more predictors often improves the predictability of the criterion. The combined relationship between two or more predictors and the criterion is referred to as a **multiple correlation**, symbolized as R. The only conceptual difference between r and R is that the range of R is from 0 to 1.00, whereas r ranges from –1.00 to 1.00. When R is squared, the resulting R^2 value represents the total amount of variance in the criterion that can be explained by two or more predictors. The increase in predictive accuracy resulting from using two or more predictors results in fewer selection mistakes (i.e., false negatives and false positives). That is why multiple predictors are used in making personnel selection decisions.

For many years, employers were not indifferent between making false positive and false negative mistakes. Most employers preferred to let a good employee get away (in the belief that someone else who is good could be hired) rather than hire a bad worker. The cost of training, reduced efficiency, turnover, and so on made the false positive highly undesirable. Although most employers still want to avoid false positives, false negatives are also important. If an applicant who fails the predictor test sues the employer on the grounds that the test was unfair, it may be very expensive for the company. If people do fail an employment test, employers want to be as sure as possible that they were not rejected because of unfair and discriminatory practices. Denying employment to a qualified applicant is unfortunate; denying employment to a qualified minority applicant can be both unfortunate and expensive. An organization can reduce both types of selection errors by increasing the validity of the predictor tests. The greater the validity of the predictors, the smaller the chance that people will be mistakenly classified. Additionally, economic factors can influence the amount of time and money that organizations are willing to invest in making personnel selection decisions.

Personnel Selection from a Human Perspective

Amid all the statistical terms and graphs, it may be tempting to forget that personnel selection is, first and foremost, about people; real people with real lives, who apply for selection into real organizations. The word "personnel" means "people." In an attempt to humanize the statistical approach to personnel selection, consider Figure 6-6.

Figure 6-6 is similar to Figure 6-5, except it will be explained by reference to four individual people. The organization in question is a college. The criterion of successful performance in college is the student's final college grade point average. The criterion cutoff is 2.00 (a C average) with a maximum of 4.00. The predictor is a standardized test of verbal ability. The college has set the predictor cutoff at a score of 500 on the verbal ability test. Applicants who score 500 and above are admitted, and applicants who score below 500 are rejected. Figure 6-6 shows four data points. These "data points" are people, four high school students among the many who applied for college admission.

Two of the applicants have the same test score, a score of 400. We will call these two students "Rowan" and "Jim." Because both Rowan and Jim scored below the predictor cutoff of 500, both were denied admission into the college. However, if the college had admitted them anyway, without regard to their test score, two very different outcomes regarding their performance in college would have occurred. Jim's college grade point average would have been below the criterion cutoff, approximately 1.50. As such, the college would have made the correct decision to reject Jim for admission, because he would not have earned a sufficiently high grade point average to receive his degree. Using the terminology of personnel selection, Jim is a true negative. Conversely, Rowan, who also scored 400 on the test, would in fact have succeeded in college. Rowan's college grade point average would have been approximately 2.50, well above the criterion cutoff of 2.00 needed to receive a degree. The college made a mistake in rejecting Rowan. Rowan would be termed a false negative. Why didn't the college "know" that Rowan would have been successful in college, while Jim would have been unsuccessful? It wouldn't, and it couldn't. Based on an inspection of Figure 6-6, it is evident that far more applicants who scored 400 on the test would have been true negatives than false negatives. The college made the best use of the information available to it in attempting to make correct personnel selection decisions on Rowan and Jim. In hindsight, the decision to reject Jim was correct, but the decision to reject Rowan was incorrect.

We now examine two other applicants who scored above the predictor cutoff, and accordingly, both were admitted into the college. Both of these applicants scored 600 on the test. These two "data points" are also people, who we will call "Dakota" and "Jordan." Despite having identical test scores, two very different outcomes occurred

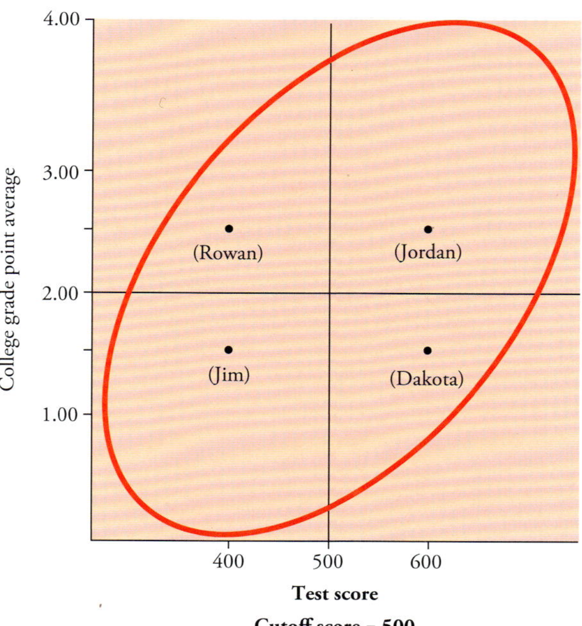

Figure 6-6 *Graphic depiction of four high school students' performance on an admission test and subsequent performance in college*

for them in college. Jordan earned a college grade point average of approximately 2.50, which was well above the criterion cutoff, and thus received a degree from the college. As such, Jordan would be termed a true positive, and the college made a correct decision. Dakota, however, never earned a college grade point average needed to receive a degree. Dakota's college grade point average (approximately 1.50) was below the criterion cutoff. The college made a mistake in admitting Dakota. Dakota would be termed a false positive. Why didn't the college "know" Jordan would be successful and Dakota would be unsuccessful? It wouldn't, and it couldn't. The logic for their selection is the same as the logic for Rowan and Jim. More applicants who scored 600 on the test are true positives than false positives.

Four high school students applied to college. The college admitted two and rejected two. Of the two that were admitted, one (Jordan) went on to get a degree. Of the two that were rejected, one (Rowan) would have graduated if given the chance. The lives of Jim, Rowan, Dakota, and Jordan were all affected by the high-stakes selection decisions made by the college. Across all applicants (not just the four discussed here), as evidenced in Figure 6-6, the college made more correct decisions (true positives and true negatives) than incorrect decisions (false positives and false negatives). Two of the incorrect decisions (Rowan and Dakota) were caused by the imperfect validity of the predictor test upon which selection decisions are made. Selection mistakes will always occur when predictor tests have imperfect validity, and no test has perfect validity. Thus personnel selection "errors," "mistakes," or "incorrect decisions," always occur. However, the number of incorrect decisions the college made is exceeded by the number of correct decisions that were made. As the validity of the selection process increases, the number of incorrect decisions is further reduced.

Because every predictor test has imperfect validity, the use of any single selection test will yield imperfect results. However, the validity of a personnel selection process can be increased by using multiple selection tests, with each one contributing to increased predictive accuracy. Just how good are we in predicting the criteria of interest to us? There is no one answer to this question, as it all depends upon the particular criterion in question. Consider Figure 6-7. The circle represents the variance in the criterion we are trying to predict. Assume the criterion is again success in earning a college degree. Five assessments have been found valid in predicting this criterion and are indicated by the shaded area of the circle. Each of the five predictors accounts for a "slice" or portion of the criterion variance. The five predictors are: (1) a standardized test of verbal ability, (2) a standardized test of numeric ability, (3) the student's high school grade point average, (4) a personal statement written by the student, and (5) letters of recommendation submitted on behalf of the student. The degree to which each assessment predicts academic success in college is shown by each of the respective slices of the circle. Assume the combined predictive capability of all five predictors results in a multiple correlation (R) of .70. The squared multiple correlation (R^2) would thus be .49. The unshaded portion of the circle is the amount of criterion variance that cannot be predicted. A question mark has been placed in this unshaded area to indicate it is that portion of the criterion variance that is unknown. The statistical term for the squared multiple correlation is the **coefficient of determination**, so named because it reflects the amount of criterion variance that can be determined from using the predictors. In this case, the coefficient of determination is .49, which can be interpreted as

Coefficient of determination The amount of criterion variance that can be predicted or explained from using predictors, computed as the squared multiple correlation.

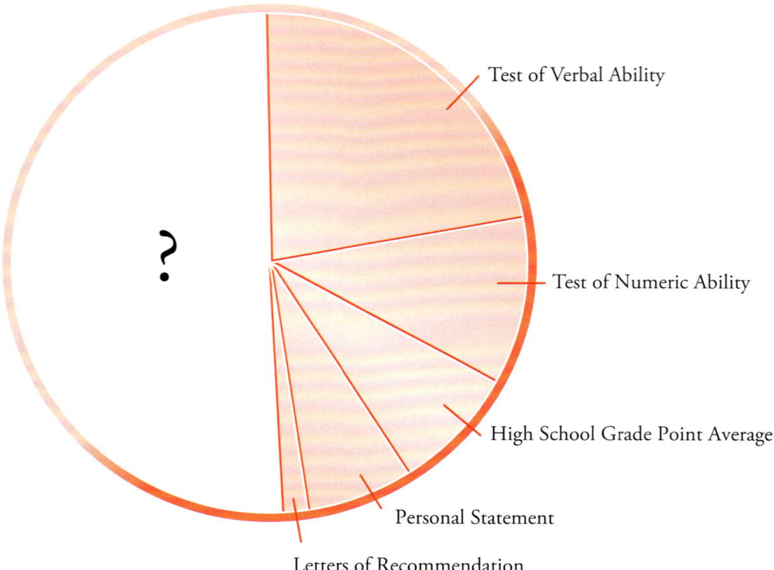

Figure 6-7 *Graphic depiction of the predictability of college grade point average using five assessment methods*

Coefficient of non-determination The amount of criterion variance that cannot be predicted or explained from using predictors, computed by subtracting the coefficient of determination from 1.00.

49% of the criterion variance that can be predicted or explained. The statistical term for that portion of the criterion variance that cannot be predicted or explained is the **coefficient of non-determination**. It is computed by simply subtracting the coefficient of determination from 1.00. In this case,

$$1.00 - .49 = .51$$

which again is interpreted as a percentage, or 51%. We thus can predict 49% of what we want to know, and cannot predict 51% of what we want to know.

A literal interpretation of Figure 6-7 is that there is slightly more (51%) that we can't predict than what we can predict (49%) about success in college. What is the reason for the unexplained variance? This has been the subject of debate since psychological assessments were invented over 100 years ago. There is no one reason for the unexplained variance. Human behavior is very complex, and thus difficult to predict. However, we know that success in any life activity is a function of the mix of the "can do" and "will do" factors. In this example, the best predictors are ability (verbal and numeric) tests, classic "can do" factors. The absence of highly valid "will do" tests has been the bane of predicting human behavior. "Will do" tests would assess a personality factor such as ambition, and test questions that seek to measure ambition are prone to faking by applicants. The "will do" factor is a major determinant of successful performance; the problem is our limited capacity to measure it and understand it. Thus, some students might have the ability to succeed in college, but they lack the ambition necessary to achieve it. Some students do not earn the needed grade point average to graduate (they "flunk out"), while others lose their ambition for college before graduating (they "drop out"). Success in college can also be a function of a good match between the student's interests and abilities, and having the resources (typically time and money) needed to complete the degree requirements. In short, there are multiple reasons for the unexplained variance in the criterion of academic success in college.

In an employment context, the overall level of predictability is often considerably less ($R^2 = .25$ would be more typical) than in an academic context. Vocational interests have been found to be related to work criteria, contributing an additional 4%-8% in predicted criterion variance beyond cognitive and personality measures.[25] However, like the assessment of personality, the assessment of vocational interests can be faked by job candidates trying to enhance their perceived fit with a job or organization.

Consider This...

People unfamiliar with the science of personnel selection may make statements like, "I could flip a coin and have a 50% chance of making a correct personnel decision." However, a coin, used as a method of personnel selection, has no validity. That is, 0% of the criterion variance is predicted by whether the coin turns up heads or tails. The probability (p) of getting a head or tail on a coin flip must not be confused with the coefficient of determination (R^2). A probability of .50 associated with a coin flip is not indicative of a slightly more accurate personnel selection method than evidenced by a selection method that produces a coefficient of determination of .49. Personnel selection by coin flipping would produce random hiring decisions, the "worst case scenario" in staffing. The reason I-O psychologists have spent over 100 years developing valid personnel selection tests is to improve upon random hiring decisions. The more strongly performance on a selection test is associated with performance on the job, the more correct selection decisions will be made. Flipping coins produces as many incorrect selection decisions as correct ones. The history of personnel selection in I-O psychology has been directed at making more correct selection decisions than incorrect ones. Even with our best tests, incorrect personnel decisions are still made. But their frequency is far less than what would result from random selection. With this in mind, how good would you feel about achieving a coefficient of determination of .49? When might you consider flipping a coin to determine which applicant should be hired? Why?

We conclude with a final consideration of Jim, Rowan, Dakota, and Jordan. Jordan was admitted to the college and went on to earn a degree. Jim was denied admission, and would not have graduated even if he had been admitted. Rowan would have graduated if given the opportunity. What Rowan lacked in the "can do" factors may have been offset by their level of ambition (the "will do" factor). Dakota had sufficient ability (according to our predictor) to earn a college degree, but may have lacked the necessary ambition or resources to succeed. Should colleges dismiss test scores in favor of alternative selection criteria (see COVID-19 and I-O Psychology: *College Admissions Amid COVID-19*)? From an organizational perspective, applicants with lower ability are less likely to be selected, despite an organization's awareness that high ambition can overcome lesser ability. As such, organizations give more weight to ability measures than may be warranted, but they have no better way to make personnel selection decisions in a practical and efficient manner.

COVID-19 and I-O Psychology: *College Admissions Amid COVID-19*

What does I-O psychology have to do with college admissions? More than you might think. ACT, the College Board, and Educational Testing Service (ETS)—the entities responsible for many standardized tests used for college admissions, including the ACT, the SAT, the GRE, and the TOEFL—employ many I-O psychologists. Graduate education in I-O psychology often includes considerable training in statistics, test development, and psychological measurement techniques. As such, I-O psychologists are quite at home in these organizations.

The role of standardized testing for admittance into college may be changing due to COVID-19 and the social justice movement from the recent past. In particular, many individuals found it difficult to take the necessary standardized tests during the pandemic. Furthermore, the disruptions occurring worldwide called into question whether the test scores would be as representative of applicants' abilities as they were intended to be. Moreover, evidence of historic social inequity that the standardized tests may have been contributing to (due to such things as adverse impact from questions and lack of access due to testing costs) was raising concerns over their use in college admissions.

As a result of the concerns being raised, a national movement ensued such that over two-thirds of public, four-year institutions of higher education declared themselves as test-optional, test-flexible, or test-blind.[26] Test-optional means applicants have the choice of whether they include their scores as part of their application. Test-flexible means students can substitute other exam results in place of the standardized testing scores. Test-blind means that even if students submit their scores, they won't be used to determine admittance.

These issues of adverse impact and social inequity are the same ones facing organizations. While standardized tests such as the ACT or SAT are rarely used within organizations, other predictors that are routinely used suffer some of the same disadvantages (e.g., cognitive ability tests). Thus, organizational leaders are faced with the same question of whether such options should be afforded to their job candidates. It's difficult to know whether organizations will follow higher education's lead.

Validity Generalization

Validity generalization A concept that reflects the degree to which a predictive relationship empirically established in one context spreads to other populations or contexts.

Certain events in history have had an impact on personnel selection and conceptions of validity.[27] The concept of validity generalization was developed shortly after the passage of federal legislation, which began to alter how I-O psychologists regarded validity evidence in support of personnel selection. The concept of **validity generalization** refers to a predictor's validity spreading or generalizing to other jobs or contexts beyond the one in which it was validated. For example, let us say that a test is found to be valid for hiring administrative assistants in a company. If that same test is found useful for hiring administrative assistants in another company, we say its validity has generalized. That same test could also be useful in selecting people for a different job, such as data entry. This is another case of the test's validity generalizing. The domains across which validity can generalize are shown in Figure 6-8.[28]

Validity generalization has long been a goal of I-O psychologists because its implication would certainly make our jobs easier. Unfortunately, when we examined whether a test's validity would generalize across either companies or jobs, we often found that it did not; that is, the test's validity was specific to the situation in which it was originally validated. The implication, of course, was that we had to validate every test in every situation in which it was used. We could not assume that its validity would generalize.

The failure to demonstrate validity generalization may not be due to validity truly not generalizing.[29] Rather, it appears the average sample size in typical criterion-related validity studies is too small to produce stable, generalizable conclusions, resulting in the (erroneous) conclusion that test validity is situation-specific.[30] Indeed, when tests are validated in large samples, the results appear to generalize (not be situation-specific). For example, researchers examined the validities of ten predictors that were used to forecast success in 35 jobs in the army. Using a sample of more than 10,000 individuals, results indicated highly similar validity coefficients across different jobs, meaning that differences among jobs did not change the predictor–criterion relationships.[31] Thus, the effects of situational moderators appear to disappear with appropriately large sample sizes.

One psychological construct that is supposedly common for success in all jobs (and which accounts for validity generalizing or spreading) is general mental ability (*g*) and, in particular, the dimension of *g* relating to information processing. Meta-analyses of the relationship between tests of cognitive ability and job performance have

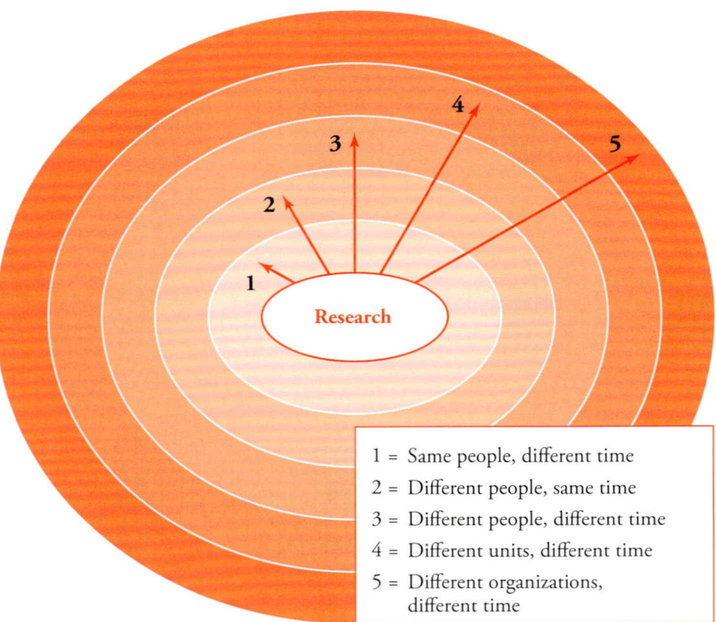

Figure 6-8 *The domains across which validity can generalize*

Source: From *Personnel selection in organizations*, by N. Schmitt and F. J. Landy. Copyright © 1993 John Wiley & Sons, Inc. Reprinted with permission of John Wiley & Sons, Inc. via Copyright Clearance Center.

consistently yielded evidence that the validity of intelligence does indeed generalize across a wide variety of occupations. Even in lower-level jobs, cognitive ability still exhibits respectable levels of predictive validity. However, the validity generalization conclusion about cognitive ability does not indicate that all cognitive tests are *equally* valid predictors across all jobs, all criteria, or all circumstances.[32]

As with any statistical method, validity generalization can be misused and abused.[33] It is perhaps due to its abuse that the reaction of the legal community to validity generalization has not been positive. Employers who are legally challenged to demonstrate the validity of their selection methods have not found the courts to be receptive to the theory of validity generalization.[34] As such, the legal defensibility of validity generalization is far more tenuous than its degree of scientific support. A potential legally-defensible solution takes the results from both local validation studies and validity generalization, and uses them to establish the validity of personnel selection systems.[35]

When research is designed improperly, the conclusions will most likely be erroneous. The paradoxical verdict on the validity generalization of *g* is based on the science versus practice of I-O psychology. At a scientific level, validity generalization has received much empirical support. At a practical level, validity generalization has *not* been deemed by the courts as an acceptable method of defending an organization against allegations of using discriminatory personnel selection procedures. Time will tell whether the I-O psychology scientific community can change the view of validity generalization for those outside of the field.

Determination of the Cutoff Score

Have you ever wondered how certain cutoff scores came to be? Why is 70% correct associated with passing a test (such as a driving test)? In educational institutions, why are the cutoffs of 90%, 80%, and 70% usually associated with the grades of A, B, and C, respectively? It has been reported that several thousand years ago, a Chinese emperor decreed that 70% correct was needed to successfully pass a test. That 70% correct figure, or a relatively close approximation, has been used throughout history in a wide range of assessment contexts as a standard to guide pass/fail decisions. Although I-O psychologists are primarily limited to assessment decisions in employment contexts, we too have had to wrestle with issues pertaining to where to set the cutoff score and how to interpret differences in test scores.[36]

There are legal, psychometric, and professional issues associated with setting cutoff scores.[37] Furthermore, the standards used in evaluating the suitability of established cutoff scores vary widely. In general, a cutoff score should be set to be reasonable and consistent with the expectations of acceptable job proficiency in the workplace. If a cutoff score is set too low, applicants who deserve to fail will pass. If it is set too high, then those who deserve to pass will fail. Thus, when determining the cutoff score, it is important to decide which is worse—having more false positives or more false negatives.[38]

Consider This...

Which is worse—having more false positives or more false negatives? If you were hiring surgeons at a hospital, would you want to hire people who should have been rejected, or reject people who should have been hired? If you were hiring for a cashier, which would you want? Does the job matter? If so, what is it about the job that impacts whether false positives or false negatives are acceptable? When would it be better to have more false positives than false negatives? How about a situation where it would be better to have more false negatives? Some people may be tempted to say that it's always okay to have a false negative (reject somebody who may have been successful) but not a false positive (hire somebody who turns out to be a failure), but this may not be a good strategy. Why? What are the implications of deciding you are only willing to have false negatives and few or no false positives?

There is no such thing as a single, uniform, correct cutoff score. Nor is there a single best method of setting cutoff scores for all situations.[39] Three suggestions regarding the setting of cutoff scores are provided here:[40]

- The process of setting a cutoff score should begin with a work analysis that identifies relative levels of proficiency on critical knowledge, skills, and abilities (KSAs).
- When possible, data on the actual relationship of test scores to criterion measures of job performance should be considered carefully.
- Cutoff scores should be set high enough to ensure that minimum standards of job performance are met.

Banding
A method of interpreting test scores such that scores of different magnitude in a numeric range or band (e.g., 90–95) are regarded as being equivalent.

Banding is an alternative method to top-down selection.[41] The traditional approach to personnel selection is to rank applicants based on their test scores and select the applicants with the highest scores. In test score banding, some differences in test scores are ignored, and individuals whose scores fall within the same band are selected on some basis other than the test score (such as sex or race), thereby eliminating or greatly reducing adverse impact. The width of the band is a function of the reliability of the test. Highly reliable tests produce relatively narrow bands, whereas less reliable tests produce wider test score bands. Thus, a one-point difference in test scores (e.g., a score of 90 vs. 89) is not judged to be of sufficient magnitude to reflect a meaningful difference in the applicants' respective abilities. One then extends this logic to a two-point difference in test scores, a three-point difference, and so on. Eventually, a certain magnitude of difference in test scores is determined to reflect a meaningful difference in ability. It is at this point where this band ends, and other bands may be formed from the distribution of test scores.

The use of banding for personnel selection is controversial. Some scholars have argued that banding violates scientific and intellectual values and should therefore be rejected as a method of selecting candidates.[42] A review of court cases that involved banding within personnel selection and promotion situations revealed that there is insufficient legal evidence to support the use of banding within personnel selection.[43] Nevertheless, banding remains a strategy in selection decision making and underscores the point that there is no one professionally agreed-upon method to determine passing scores on tests.

Test Utility and Organizational Efficiency

Utility
A concept reflecting the economic value (expressed in monetary terms) of making personnel decisions.

Many resources contribute to the success of an organization; employees are just one of them. Each resource must contribute to the organization's overall success. A basic question is how much the improved personnel selection techniques contribute to the overall profitability or efficiency. The **utility** of a test is literally its value—where "value" is measured in monetary or economic terms. Several studies have shown just how much utility a valid testing program can provide.

In a study that compared the job performance of bank tellers who scored at the 80th percentile on a selection test versus those who scored at the 20th percentile, those tellers that scored at the 80th percentile on average served 1,791 customers per month.[44] Conversely, those who scored at the 20th percentile served 945 customers per month. Quite clearly, better job performance followed from better test performance. However, measuring gains in job performance using valid employment tests is not the same as measuring the monetary value that accrues to the organization from greater job performance. In the case of the bank tellers, the question is how much value does the bank accrue from having the tellers serve 846 (1,791 - 945) more customers per month?

I-O psychologists have long struggled with finding ways to demonstrate to organizational leaders the utility of hiring high quality workers (as identified through testing) in a manner that is understandable and credible.[45] Complex statistical analyses have estimated the utility of using valid selection methods to identify high-performing employees. The benefits can be millions of dollars per year, depending upon the number of employees hired and the value of the job to the organization. However, we have more confidence in estimating the utility gains for certain types of jobs than others. For example, we have more confidence in estimating the utility of hiring good production workers in a factory than good counselors in a social services agency.[46] Furthermore, many business leaders find it difficult to accept and understand the results from complex statistical analyses. In short, I-O psychologists have had more success in demonstrating the gains in job performance from using valid selection methods than in translating gains in job performance into credible monetary indices.

Benchmarking
The process of comparing a company's products or procedures with those of the leading companies in an industry.

One method that is highly accepted among managers in getting organizations to adopt testing procedures is called benchmarking. **Benchmarking** is the process of comparing leading organizations in terms of their professional practices. By comparing their practices with those of other organizations, executives are able to see how they are doing relative to the competition. In addition, rather than trying something new without an understanding of whether it may work, decision makers can get real-world examples of interventions that have proven effective in practice.[47] In short, business leaders are often skeptical of the ability to assess the exact dollar value of using selection tests. However, if other leading companies in an industry are using tests, it becomes prudent to follow their practices (see Faces of I-O Psychology: *Joshua Brenner*).

Faces of I-O Psychology: *Joshua Brenner*

Joshua Brenner

Ph.D. Hofstra University

Global Talent Management, PepsiCo

Practice Focus: Talent Management and Employee Listening

As organizations adapt to the ever-changing marketplace and take action for both their customers and their employees, it is critical that any decision taken is informed by data and creates a positive competitive advantage. Benchmarking can help provide organizations with vital insight by comparing current thinking and internal metrics with how other organizations are thinking and their metrics. Through these comparisons, companies can:

- Identify gaps in internal strategy by comparing/contrasting external market practices to one's own practices
- Create a sense of urgency for change, if needed, when your company is scoring lower on given metrics as compared to your peers
- Set future priorities for your business by learning about external best practices that can be applied to your own organization

Throughout my career, benchmarks have served as an invaluable resource for informing my work and business strategy. One key area that benchmarks have been applied is to our global employee engagement surveys. After employees respond to our global surveys, we report out on their sentiment around key organizational factors to managers and leadership so that these leaders can take action to improve employee engagement and commitment to our business. While managers strive make their workplace a better one for their team, they may struggle to understand where they should focus their attention. Benchmarks created by The Mayflower Group, a consortium of top-tier global companies dedicated to innovative research and employee surveys, allows managers to compare themselves to others and show where they can improve relative to the external market. Additionally, these engagement survey benchmarks have been leveraged to inform our own survey strategy by reviewing "Best In Class" practices around (a) survey content and what organizations find meaningful for their employees, (b) survey administration practices and how to drive high survey response rates, and (c) survey reporting practices and how to best support action planning.

Outside of employee engagement surveys, benchmarks have helped us better understand how the external market is adapting to how COVID-19 is impacting the future of work. By establishing benchmarks with Fortune 500 companies, we've seen that there is a growing need to invest more resources into devising more effective virtual teamwork, addressing telecommuting needs as well as addressing work-family issues through more flexible work arrangements. These insights will help inform our business strategy in order to better attract and retain employees for the War For Talent.

I highly encourage I-O psychologists to consider leveraging benchmark publications, in addition to research publications and articles, when determining your HR strategies.

Placement and Classification

The vast majority of research in I-O psychology is on selection, the process by which applicants are hired. Another personnel function (albeit less common) involves deciding which jobs people should be assigned to *after* they have been hired. This personnel function is called either placement or classification, depending on the basis for the assignment. In many cases, selection and placement are not separate procedures. Usually, people apply for particular jobs. If they are hired, they fill the jobs they were applying for. In some organizations (and at certain times in our nation's history), however, decisions about selection and placement must be made separately.

Placement
The process of assigning individuals to jobs based on one test score.

Classification
The process of assigning individuals to jobs based on two or more test scores.

Placement differs from classification on the basis of the number of predictors used to make the job assignment. **Placement** is allocating people to two or more groups (or jobs) on the basis of a single predictor score. Many middle school students are placed into math classes based on a math aptitude test. **Classification** is allocating people to jobs on the basis of two or more valid predictor factors. For this reason, classification is more complex; however, it results in a better assignment of people to jobs than placement. Classification uses smaller selection ratios than placement, which accounts for its greater utility. The reason classification is not always used instead of placement is that it is often difficult to find two or more valid predictors to use in assigning people to jobs. The military has been the object of most classification research. Military recruits take a battery of different tests (including the ASVAB) covering such areas as intelligence, ability, and aptitude. On the basis of these scores, recruits are assigned to jobs in the infantry, medical corps, military intelligence, and so on. Other organizations that have to assign large numbers of employees to large numbers of jobs also use this procedure. Given this constraint, relatively few companies need to use classification procedures.

The problems and issues associated with staffing the military are even more complicated than in the civilian sector. Staffing the military is guided not only by the need for meeting job requirements and diversity representation (by race and sex), but also with thought given to deployment schedules and placement considerations including candidates' vocational interests.[48] As of 2021, the U.S. military had approximately 1.37 million active duty and 845,000 reserve personnel; 40% were racial minorities and 16% were female. Given the volume of candidates assessed annually and the growing complexity of technical advances in weaponry, the military is highly dependent on sophisticated classification methods to meet its staffing needs.[49] Furthermore, unlike the civilian sector of employment, the military does not hire people from outside the military (e.g., the civilian workforce) to fill middle- or higher-level jobs. Jobs in the military must be filled by current military personnel, adding greatly to the critical need of assigning people to jobs for which they are highly suited.

Chapter Review

Key Terms

Recruitment
Personnel selection
Predictor cutoff
Selection ratio
Base rate
Criterion cutoff
True positives
True negatives
False negatives
False positives
Multiple correlation
Coefficient of determination
Coefficient of non-determination
Validity generalization
Banding
Utility
Benchmarking
Placement
Classification

Questions for Review

1. Why would an employer exert effort in employee selection? In what kinds of situations would exerting effort be a waste of resources?
2. What is recruitment and how has it changed? What types of recruitment are most effective—and what factors indicate which types should be used?
3. What is personnel selection?
4. How are predictor cutoffs, selection ratios, and base rates related to one another?
5. What are the reasons for selecting a criterion cutoff? What are the repercussions of selecting a cutoff incorrectly?
6. What are true positives, true negatives, false positives, and false negatives? What are the issues associated with false positive and false negative selection decisions?
7. What is multiple correlation? How does it potentially improve selection decisions?
8. What are coefficients of determination and coefficients of non-determination? How is a coefficient of determination of .49 different from a coin flip?
9. What is validity generalization? How successful has it been in legal situations? How is it seen by I-O psychology practitioners? By I-O psychology researchers?
10. What is banding, and what are its advantages and drawbacks?
11. What is benchmarking and why has it gained traction with organizations?
12. What is the difference between placement and classification?

CHAPTER 7

Organizational Learning

Chapter Outline

Formal Versus Informal Organizational Learning

Learning and Task Performance

Assessing Training Needs

Methods and Techniques of Training

- Computer-Based Training
- COVID-19 and I-O Psychology: *Returning to "Normal" or Not?*
- Non–Computer-Based Training

Active Learning Approaches

- Error-Management Training
- Self-Regulatory Training

Special Training Topics

- Diversity Training
- Expatriate Training
- Sexual Harassment Training

Management Development Issues

- Social Media and I-O Psychology: *Workplace Romances, Social Media, and Sexual Harassment Concerns*
- Mentoring
- Faces of I-O Psychology: *Sandra L. Lee*
- Executive Coaching
- The Lighter Side of I-O Psychology: *We Need Coaching Too!*

Transfer of Training

Evaluation Criteria of Training Programs

Chapter Review

Learning Objectives

- Describe the roles of on-the-job training and onboarding within organizations.
- Discuss the relationship between learning and task performance.
- Outline the steps to assess training needs within an organization.
- Summarize the major methods of computer-based and non–computer-based training and their associated strengths and weaknesses.
- Identify training approaches and benefits of active learning approaches.
- Justify the importance of diversity training, expatriate training, and sexual harassment training in the workplace.
- Describe the role of mentoring and executive coaching in management development.
- Explain how knowledge and skills from training are transferred back to the job.
- Explain the evaluation of training and development programs.

The U.S. Department of Labor estimated that today, on average, 50% of an employee's knowledge and skills become outdated every 30–60 *months*, compared with an estimated 12–15 *years* in the 1970s. It is no wonder that employers worldwide spent, on average, a hefty $1,308 per employee in 2019 on training and development initiatives.[1] Although not all work is changing as rapidly as work that is information-intensive, we have reached a point where the skills we bring to a job are dwarfed in comparison to the new skills we must acquire as part of "learning a living." Prior to the advancement of the Internet, careers were chosen early in one's life by learning the knowledge required to gain admission into that career. In the post-Internet knowledge-based world, learning must occur continuously because individuals will likely have multiple careers over their years in the workforce.[2]

The economic and social pressures brought to bear on organizations affect the conduct of work and make it necessary for employees to serve larger strategic business needs. One implication of this changing nature of work is that greater relative importance is placed on skill *enhancement*. Organizations need to hire intelligent workers who are willing to learn new skills, often determined by external demands. For example, jobs may require increased technological sophistication, a greater emphasis on teamwork, the ability to deal with a diverse customer base, or any other issue related to the success of the organization. Simply put, organizations (and their employees) must continually learn new skills to adapt to a rapidly changing business world.

Training
The process through which the knowledge and skills of employees are enhanced for an immediate job or role.

Development
The process through which the knowledge and skills of employees are enhanced but for which there is no immediate use.

The title of this chapter is "Organizational Learning," which encompasses issues associated with the training and development of the workforce. Roughly speaking, **training** and **development** are both aimed at enhancing the KSAOs of employees, and differ only in their immediacy of use. That is, training is targeted at enhancing KSAOs needed for an immediate job or role, whereas development refers to enhancing KSAOs for which there may not be an immediate purpose.

The importance of organizational learning is escalating at a dizzying pace. The job title of the person in the organization responsible for these activities is evolving from "Director of Training and Development" to "Chief Learning Officer".[3] Thus "learning"

Consider This...

It has long been said that if you have a choice between putting a greater emphasis on selection or training, you should choose selection. The idea is that if you hire the right people, you may not need to train them, and if you do need to train them, at least you hired people who may be more able to be successful during and post-training. That said, one pair of scholars noted that, "Today's progressive corporations have moved from treating learning as an obligatory cost factor to regarding it as a weapon in the battle for competitive advantage" (Danielson & Wiggenhorn 2003, p. 17).[4] Given the speed at which knowledge and skills become obsolete, do you think the logic of choosing selection over training remains true in today's environment? Are there some jobs or industries where this may be the case, and others where it may be wiser to make a bigger investment in training? Should it be the responsibility of organizations or employees to ensure their knowledge and skills are kept up to date? Does your answer change how you think about the selection versus training decision?

has ascended to the same level previously reserved for finance (Chief Financial Officer) and operations (Chief Operating Officer). In an examination of over 12 years of data from 359 firms during pre- and post-recession time periods, researchers found that training contributed to firm profit growth prior to the recession, and aided those firms in developing surplus resources that helped them to recover from the subsequent economic downturn.[5]

Formal Versus Informal Organizational Learning

There is an important difference between learning through formalized organization-based training and informal or unintentional learning. Informal or unintentional learning is the knowledge we acquire and use to better our lives simply by paying attention to our environment and adapting to it. Informal learning is described as self-guided and learner-directed (i.e., we desire to learn and choose to do so). In the 1980s, a group of researchers from the Center for Creative Leadership created what is known as the 70:20:10 Model for Learning and Development. The numbers refer to a formula that describes how successful employees within organizations learn. It states that 70% of successful employees' knowledge comes from informal job-related experiences, 20% comes from interactions with others, and only 10% comes from formal organizational training and development efforts. Some estimates have the role of informal learning even higher, accounting for three-quarters of learning within organizations.[6] It is clear that in a world where it has become vital for people in organizations to continuously learn and develop, the responsibility falls far more on the capacity and willingness of those people to do so.

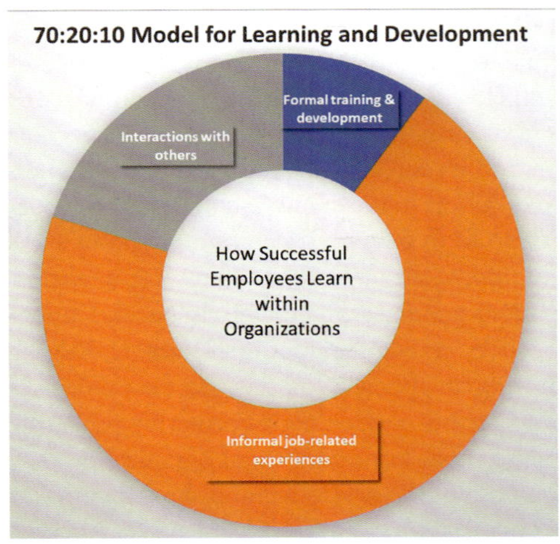

As important and valuable as formal training programs may be, they are limited in their power to effectuate the developmental growth needed in the contemporary work world. This may be even more the case for the development of leaders. It has been argued that one of the main sources of learning to lead is through experience.[7] For example, researchers have found that leaders who have global work experiences are stronger strategic thinkers than leaders without such experiences.[8] Thus, a great deal of learning within organizations occurs beyond the boundaries of formal training.

On-the-job training Instruction of employees while in the actual work environment. Typically informal, but occasionally supplemented by formal training.

Perhaps the most common means of informal training is **on-the-job training**, which occurs when an employee learns some aspect of the job by actually doing the work, oftentimes supervised or guided by a manager or experienced coworker. This informal training may be supplemented by formal training, depending on the activities being taught. For example, Uber drivers receive little formal training from Uber, relying more heavily on their own experiences on the road and advice from fellow drivers.[9]

Whether the 70:20:10 formula is accurate or not, the fact remains that informal training and development is prevalent in organizations. For many jobs, it is simply easier to have employees learn what to do while actually doing the work. When questions arise, relying on a nearby coworker for an answer may be easier than having to complete an entire training program. However, informal training and development efforts are limited in that organizations have very little control over them. An employee charged with assisting a fellow coworker to learn the ropes may teach inappropriate behaviors (such as how to cut corners) or take advantage of the newcomer (by giving the employee an unfair proportion of the work). In addition, some information is best conveyed uniformly, from a representative of the organization. For example, information on organizational policies (such as how to take vacation time or manage sick leave) is better handled through formal means.

Organizational socialization
The process of newcomers acquiring the social knowledge and skills needed to be successful in their workplace.

Onboarding
Formal or informal practices, policies, and programs that facilitate newcomer socialization to an organization.

The process of acquiring the social knowledge and skills to be successful within an organization and in one's role is known as **organizational socialization**.[10] It is essentially how employees "learn the ropes" and figure out how to become a contributing member of the organization. Socialization is largely informal, occurring through observation and informal interactions with colleagues.[11] In fact, socialization occurs more quickly and effectively when newcomers establish a wide range of relationships with their peers and managers[12] and are proactive in seeking out information.[13]

Not all socialization efforts are informal, however. One common way that organizations orient employees to their new workplace is through onboarding. **Onboarding** includes any organizational practices, programs, or policies that help newcomers become socialized, or adjusted, to the organization and its ways.[14] This means that newcomers learn knowledge that is specific to the organization, understand its culture, and recognize unique characteristics that will help them fit in better. Orientation programs serve three primary purposes.[15] First, they help to inform the newcomer about what it takes to be successful by providing relevant information, resources, and materials. Second, orientation programs serve to welcome newcomers by providing emotional support, helping newcomers meet other employees, and showing an appreciation that the newcomer has joined the organization. Third, orientation programs guide the newcomer by providing direct assistance in navigating the new organization. For example, an organization may assign a seasoned employee to act as a champion for the newcomer and show them what it takes to be an effective member of the organization. While onboarding may be formal or informal, onboarding practices that are required and offered formally are seen by employees as more helpful and result in greater socialization.[16]

Typically, onboarding efforts will occur at the start of employment, often on the first day of work. Employee socialization does not stop with onboarding, however. There are many tactics that are used to socialize employees. Socialization tactics can be grouped into three dimensions: (a) content, those in which there is an explicit sequence of learning events to socialize employees; (b) social, activities in which role models and feedback are available; and (c) context, learning that occurs collectively and formally.[17] High levels of socialization tactics during the first six months of employment can help newcomers remain satisfied with their new jobs, and extremely high levels of these tactics can reduce the likelihood that newcomers will quit.[18] Socialization can occur virtually via computer-based programs, a process known as *e-socialization*.[19] E-socialization appears to be less effective than traditional in-person socialization efforts, however, with one study showing that newcomers socialized virtually were less satisfied, less committed,

Consider This...

Many organizations employ individuals who work entirely remotely. During the COVID-19 pandemic, organizations that typically had onsite employees were forced to hire and onboard employees virtually. Indeed, it was not uncommon as employees returned to their physical workplaces to meet colleagues for the first time in person after they had been with the company for a year already. Knowing the challenges associated with e-socialization, what would you recommend to employers faced with similar circumstances? What would you recommend to employees, both newcomers as well as more seasoned employees?

and had less knowledge of social aspects of the organization than did newcomers who were socialized in person.[20]

The focus of the remainder of this chapter is on formal training and development that occurs beyond initial onboarding and socialization efforts. Whereas the focus on onboarding and socialization efforts is on the adjustment of newcomers to a new workplace, other training and development within organizations tend to focus on learning and skill acquisition that will directly impact one's task performance.

Learning and Task Performance

Learning
The process by which change in knowledge or skills is acquired through education or experience.

Declarative knowledge
A body of knowledge about facts and things.

Knowledge compilation
The body of knowledge acquired as a result of learning.

Learning is the process of encoding, retaining, and using information. The specific procedures by which we process information for both short-term and long-term use has been the subject of extensive research in cognitive psychology.[21] This section will examine some useful findings from this body of research that facilitate our understanding of how learning affects the training and development process.

Skill acquisition can be segmented into three phases:[22]

1. **Declarative knowledge** is knowledge about facts and things. The declarative knowledge of skill acquisition involves memorizing and reasoning processes that allow individuals to attain a basic understanding of a task. During this phase, individuals may observe demonstrations of the task and learn task-sequencing rules. Individuals must devote nearly all their attention to understanding and performing the task. Performance in the declarative knowledge stage is slow and prone to error. Only after people have acquired an adequate understanding of the task can they proceed to the second phase.
2. **Knowledge compilation** is the second stage of skill acquisition, whereby individuals integrate the sequences of cognitive and motor processes required to perform the task. Various methods for simplifying or streamlining the task are tried and evaluated. Performance then becomes faster and more accurate than in the declarative knowledge phase. Attentional demands are reduced as task objectives and procedures are moved from short-term to long-term memory.

Procedural knowledge
A body of knowledge about how to use information to address issues and solve problems.

3. **Procedural knowledge** is knowledge about how to perform various cognitive activities. This final phase of skill acquisition is reached when individuals have essentially automatized the skill and can perform the task efficiently with little attention.[23] After considerable practice, the person can successfully perform the task while simultaneously devoting attention to other tasks. This procedural knowledge becomes second nature to expert performers, so that they report difficulty in describing what they know that others do not know.[24]

Three major classes of abilities are critically important for performance in these three phases of skill acquisition.[25] *General mental ability (g)* is posited to be the most important factor in acquiring declarative knowledge. When individuals first confront a novel task, the attentional demands are high. As they begin to understand the demands of the task and develop a performance strategy, the attentional demands decrease and the importance of intellectual ability for task performance is lessened.

As individuals move along the skill acquisition curve, *perceptual speed abilities* become important. Individuals develop a basic understanding of how to perform the task, but seek a more efficient method for accomplishing the task with minimal attentional effort. Perceptual speed abilities appear to be most critical for processing information faster or more efficiently during skill acquisition.

Finally, *psychomotor abilities* (such as coordination) determine the final level of task performance in the procedural knowledge phase. Thus, it would appear that how well individuals perform various skills is determined by different abilities than those that impact initial task performance or the speed at which skills are acquired.[26]

It should be evident that there are complex relationships between individual abilities and phases of task performance. These findings explain why some individuals may be quick to acquire minimal competency in a task but do not subsequently develop a high degree of task proficiency. Alternatively, other individuals may initially learn a task slowly, but gradually develop a high level of task proficiency. These findings bear not only on why certain individuals learn at different rates of speed, but also on how training and development processes have to be targeted to enhance selected individual abilities.

When considering learning and task performance, a natural consideration is how one moves from being a novice to being an expert on a topic. There are three distinguishing characteristics of people who are regarded as experts on a topic versus novices.[27] The first is proceduralization and automaticity. *Proceduralization* refers to a set of conditional action rules: if Condition A exists, then Action B is needed. *Automaticity* refers to a state of rapid performance that requires little cognitive effort. Automaticity enables a person to accomplish a task without conscious monitoring, and thus allows concurrent performance of additional tasks. Experts not only "know" things but also know when that knowledge is applicable and when it should not be used. Novices may be equally competent at recalling specific information, but experts are much better at relating that information in cause-and-effect sequences. The second distinguishing characteristic between experts and novices is *mental models*, which is the way knowledge is organized. The mental models of experts are qualitatively better because they contain more diagnostic cues for detecting meaningful patterns in learning. Experts have more complex knowledge structures, resulting in faster solution times. The third and final characteristic is *meta-cognition*. Meta-cognition refers to individuals' knowledge of and control over

Consider This...

There is a well-established finding within the social psychology literature that sometimes people experience an increased level of performance when in the presence of others (social facilitation), while at other times they experience a decreased level of performance when others are around (social inhibition). In general, research has shown that social facilitation occurs for easy or well-learned tasks, and inhibition occurs for difficult or novel tasks. Based on these findings, what would you expect to happen to the performance of experts versus novices in the presence of others? What relevance might this have for organizations? Sometimes certain assignments are given to the newcomer of an organization, while others are given to the more seasoned employees who presumably may have greater expertise. Can you think of examples in which this could be problematic? How so?

their cognitions. Experts have a greater understanding of the demands of a task and their own capabilities. They are more likely to discontinue a strategy that would ultimately prove to be unsuccessful.

Expertise is developed through deliberate practice over an extended period of time.[28] One way of getting employees the knowledge and skills they need to gain expertise is through training programs and development opportunities within the workplace. The remainder of this chapter is related to these opportunities.

Assessing Training Needs

Training needs assessment
A systematic process of identifying and specifying training requirements. Consists of organizational, task, and person analyses.

Organizational analysis
Part of the training needs assessment in which the organization's strategic objectives and the availability of resources and support are identified.

It is important to understand what deficiencies exist in individual, team, and organizational performance prior to developing a training program. A **training needs assessment** is a systematic process that helps identify and specify training requirements to determine specific learning objectives, and to ascertain what training methods and techniques will be the most appropriate for reducing or eliminating any performance deficiencies.[29] In short, a training needs assessment helps figure out whether, and to what extent, training is needed.

There are three stages to a training needs assessment. The first stage consists of **organizational analysis**. The goals in this stage are to identify the organization's primary strategic objectives, determine whether there are resources available to develop and conduct training, and ascertain whether management and employees will support its implementation. Many training efforts fail due to barriers and constraints.[30] An organizational analysis helps identify those barriers and reduce them prior to training. Without proper resources for a training program, there is little reason to expect it will be successful. On the other hand, organizations that demonstrate a willingness to invest in training programs can reap great rewards, both within and outside of the training programs. In one case, research found that organizations that invest in internal training programs have significant increases in organizational innovation over the following two years.[31]

Task analysis
Part of the training needs assessment in which the tasks that require training are identified.

The second stage is **task analysis**. This stage seeks to identify whether some tasks are consistently performed poorly and/or whether there are deficient KSAOs across the workforce. Task analysis identifies what individuals must know to perform their jobs effectively.[32] In line with this, task analysis is used to develop clear and comprehensive training objectives.[33] Information from a work analysis (as discussed in Chapter 4) is highly relevant here. The tasks and KSAOs identified from the work analysis help determine training objectives, particularly when there is evidence that performance is subpar. Such evidence can come from performance appraisals that indicate substandard performance, or specific workplace incidents suggesting the need for training (such as accidents or noncompliance citations from external auditors). As an example, receiving a low grade from a health inspector may suggest the need for training on the policies and procedures for restaurant staff.

Person analysis
Part of the training needs assessment in which the people who need training are identified.

The final stage is **person analysis**, which has the goal of identifying which workers should be trained. It may be the case that not all employees are performing poorly or have deficient KSAOs. In addition, not all training will be beneficial to all people within an organization. For example, a task analysis may reveal that the workforce is deficient in terms of its selling skills. However, not all employees need to be skilled at making sales. Thus, this stage seeks to identify which workers should be trained rather than wasting resources by including people in training that have no need for it.

Not all performance deficiencies can be addressed through learning. Indeed, employees may know what they are supposed to do but lack the ability or motivation to do it—or do it properly. A training program on dunking a basketball would be a complete waste of time and money for the authors of this textbook, for example, as we readily admit our physical limitations in this regard. Thus, person analysis also addresses aspects of learners that can impact the training design and delivery, such as how motivated learners are or how much aptitude they have.[34]

Despite the advantages for conducting training needs assessments in terms of facilitating trainee motivation and ensuring efficient use of resources, it appears that in practice, few training needs assessments are conducted prior to the design and delivery of training programs. Sometimes it is obvious what the training requirements are, in which case needs assessments may be abbreviated or foregone entirely.[35] Another reason that training may be done without a needs assessment is that the training is done to meet a legal or certification requirement. For example, the Equal Employment Opportunity Commission (EEOC) has noted that the best tactic for eliminating sexual harassment in the workplace is through prevention, and has advised organizations to clearly communicate that such harassment will not be tolerated. They further note that providing sexual harassment training (to be described later in this chapter) is one way of doing this. As such, many organizations require all employees to complete sexual harassment training regardless of their current understanding of the law or motivation to learn about it. Finally, organizations no longer have the luxury of taking their time to conduct a detailed needs analysis.[36] That is, the failure to conduct training needs assessments is also a function of the changing nature of work and the need for organizations to be more agile.

Methods and Techniques of Training

As theories of learning evolved over time, so did training methods proposed by I-O psychologists.[37] Training methods used in the past tended to assume there was a certain amount or type of knowledge that employees needed to perform their jobs. The question became how best to impart that knowledge to the employee. Upon sufficient acquisition of this knowledge, the employee was deemed qualified to perform the job. However, a contemporary view of learning is that it is not simply a case of knowledge acquisition (as achieved through having taken a course or attended a workshop). In most jobs, there are multiple behavioral styles that can lead to successful job performance. In short, there is often more than one way to perform a job. What matters is whether the performance objectives of the job are fulfilled, with less emphasis placed on how the objectives were fulfilled. In this conception of learning, the role of training should be to encourage learning the various ways the performance objectives can be attained.

A wide array of formal training methods exists, including some that will not be covered here. They differ in the breadth of skills they seek to enhance. As we will describe below, for example, some methods (such as behavioral modeling) have a narrow focus, whereas others (such as business games) have a broader focus. The methods also differ in the types of skills they seek to enhance. Some (such as role playing) are designed primarily to improve social interpersonal skills, whereas others (such as intelligent tutoring systems) tend to focus on cognitive skills. The biggest trend in training methods over the past decade has been the shift toward computer-based training, which we will explain first (see COVID-19 and I-O Psychology: *Returning to "Normal" or Not?*). We will then provide an overview of various non-computer-based training methods.

Computer-Based Training

Just as computers and the Internet have altered how work is performed, so too have they offered revolutionary ways of enhancing organizational learning. The power of modern communication technology is so great, it has induced psychologists to advance new theories of how learning occurs, as well as how knowledge influences behavior. This approach to learning is called *e-learning*.[38] There is nothing particularly instructive about the computer, per se, as a medium for learning that makes it superior to reading a book. For example, the educational value of a book is not enhanced simply because it can be read on a computer screen. The conversion from paper to pixels does not enhance learning. Rather, what makes the computer such a powerful medium is its capacity to facilitate learning in ways that other media (such as a book) cannot do. The use of technology for delivering and facilitating training has become increasingly popular due to the expensive nature of face-to-face methods, as well as the need to bring training to employees that are separated geographically.[39]

Computer-based training
A method of training that utilizes computer technology to enhance the acquisition of knowledge and skills.

Computer-based training is well-suited for the view that training should encourage learning the various ways that performance objectives can be attained. Learning can occur through multiple channels, such as audio and visual conferencing,

COVID-19 and I-O Psychology: *Returning to "Normal" or Not?*

The COVID-19 pandemic created the need for organizations and trainers to change the ways they provided training to their employees. In order to determine exactly what those changes were, researchers surveyed over 1,500 training professionals.[40]

The biggest finding from the survey was that, not surprisingly, the use of virtual training efforts increased. Prior to the pandemic, trainers reported that approximately 41% of their training content was delivered in-person via instructor-led training. Virtual instructor-led training and e-learning (computer-based training not reliant on an instructor) comprised approximately 50% of their training efforts. After the onset of COVID-19, however, delivery of in-person training dropped to 22% and delivery of virtual/e-learning training jumped to 73%.

More surprising was that many of the organizations surveyed reported that they would not be returning to "normal" after the pandemic. Instead, because of the large investment of time and resources they had made in putting their training content in a virtual format, many were opting to stick with that delivery method even after a return to in-person training would be possible. The researchers reported that, anecdotally, trainers were reporting cost savings and increased efficiency through the use of virtual training.

There are different skills required for delivering training content virtually versus in person. As such, the researchers noted that trainers post-pandemic have the following KSAs:

- The ability to use learning and videoconferencing technologies
- An understanding of the challenges of engaging virtual learners—and the strategies to do so effectively
- The ability to multitask (for example, simultaneously managing the platform, monitoring the chat and learners' facial reactions in the video, and teaching the material)

Of course, not all organizations will stick with virtual training, and new training efforts may not be created with a virtual delivery option. As such, while these KSAs are important, a well-versed trainer should also be able to present material in a face-to-face context.

threaded discussions, chat rooms, and file sharing. The versatility of web-based training is congruent with the versatility in behavioral styles that are exhibited in successful job performance. Instead of learning the "one way" to perform a job, computer-based learning can help individuals discover "which way" works best for them. Computer-based training is highly interactive, and the learner becomes an active contributor to what is learned.

In addition to benefits for the learner, computer-based training has clear advantages for organizations. Although the costs associated with e-learning are great initially, cost savings may result, since learners may access the content from anywhere. Thus, organizations are saving on travel and lodging costs, as well as on recurring instructional costs associated with face-to-face training.

Programmed instruction
The most basic computer-based training that provides for self-paced learning.

Programmed Instruction. **Programmed instruction** is regarded as the basis from which all other computer-based training methods have been derived. It was developed as a manual training system long before the advent of the computer. It is a method of self-paced learning managed by both the trainee and the computer system. The basic framework of programmed instruction is as follows: information is presented to the trainee, a question is posed regarding the information, and depending on the trainee's response to the question, the program proceeds to the next question. If the trainee provides a correct answer, the trainee moves on to new information. If the answer is incorrect, the trainee is taken back to review the relevant information. This format allows trainees to move through the material at their own pace. Trainees who answer more questions correctly move rapidly through the material. It has been estimated that 80% of leading companies use programmed instruction in some form.[41]

There are many advantages of programmed instruction. For starters, it is standardized yet flexible, in that it allows individuals to repeat material for additional practice as needed. The consistency of the training is an advantage for ensuring learners receive the same content. In addition, the computer-based element allows for a variety of engaging features, from animation to graphics and special effects. In terms of its effectiveness, a study within an educational setting revealed that individuals presented information through programmed instruction learned more and demonstrated a higher quality of learning compared to individuals provided the same course content through lecturing.[42] Despite these advantages, programmed instruction can cause frustration and lower motivation for people who aren't comfortable with technology, and it requires greater self-discipline than some other methods, as people may be able to easily cheat or skip parts of the training without others knowing.[43]

Intelligent tutoring systems
A sophisticated type of computer-based training that uses artificial intelligence to customize learning to the individual.

Intelligent Tutoring Systems. **Intelligent tutoring systems** are more sophisticated than programmed instruction and use the concept of artificial intelligence to guide the instructional process. Based on the trainee's responses to questions posed, the system continuously modifies the level of instruction presented to the trainee. When the learner answers correctly, the system moves forward. When the learner responds incorrectly, the system either provides additional information to help the individual gain the necessary knowledge or guides the learner toward the correct answer.[44] Thus, the system is serving as a "tutor" to the learner, facilitating knowledge acquisition. Intelligent tutoring systems are also capable of varying the order and difficulty of the questions presented. The method differentiates itself from programmed instruction by its level of sophistication in tailoring the learning process to the pattern of trainee responses.

Interactive multimedia training
A type of computer-based training that combines visual and auditory information to create a realistic but non-threatening environment.

Interactive Multimedia Training. **Interactive multimedia training** is a more technologically-sophisticated system than intelligent tutoring. As the term *multimedia* suggests, the training combines text, photos, graphics, videos, animation, and sound to achieve a rich simulation of a real-life situation. These synthetic learning environments are interactive, in that they allow trainees to make decisions and then receive immediate feedback on the quality of the decisions.[45] Interactive multimedia training provides an opportunity to learn skills in a nonthreatening environment, where the consequences of errors are not as serious as in a real-life setting. For example, consider the following application of multimedia training in teaching medical students:

> This training, all computer-based, allows a medical student to take a medical history of a (hypothetical) patient, conduct an examination, and run lab tests. As part of the examination the medical student may choose to examine the patient's chest. The student checks the "examine chest" button and is then asked to choose a type of examination to conduct (visual inspection, palpitation, and auscultation). Imagine you are the student and you click on auscultation (listen to the sounds made by the lungs). You would hear the chest sounds that would be made by the particular patient. Based on your interpretation of the sounds, you would make a diagnosis and click the button that represented your diagnosis. You would then be informed of the accuracy of your diagnosis. If your diagnosis were incorrect you would be given an explanation and moved to supplementary materials designed to provide you with the knowledge needed to make a correct diagnosis (Blanchard & Thacker 2004, p. 248).[46]

Virtual reality training
A type of computer-based training that uses three-dimensional computer-generated imagery.

Virtual Reality Training. For simulations to be effective and increase the likelihood of transfer of learning, trainees must be provided with immediate feedback and the simulations must be realistic.[47] **Virtual reality training** accomplishes this by simulating a work environment in an artificial three-dimensional context. Virtual (meaning "almost") reality training permits trainees to learn skills that, if developed in an actual work environment, could result in harm to the trainee or damage to the environment. For example, virtual reality training has been used to train mining operators to drill in underground mines,[48] train police officers in how to safely stop a speeding car,[49] and train surgical trainees to perform laparoscopic surgery.[50] The method is effective because the trainee experiences a sense of "telepresence" in the environment. Virtual reality training requires a trainee to wear devices designed to produce sensory effects, such as a headset (for visual and auditory information), gloves (for tactile information), and possibly a treadmill (to create the sense of movement). By looking up, down, left, or right, a trainee experiences different visual images. How the trainee is responding to this virtual reality is monitored by sensory devices. Immersive simulations such as virtual reality training allow learners to become deeply engrossed in the situation, experiencing emotions and physiological reactions in a realistic, fun, meaningful, and safe environment.[51] Because of these points, as technology continues to advance and becomes less cost-prohibitive, we may find virtual reality training become even more prevalent within the workplace.

Non–Computer-Based Training

Although the preponderance of recent advances in training methods have involved computers, other training methods are available as well.

Business games
A method of training that simulates a business environment with specific objectives to achieve and rules for trainees to follow.

Business Games. **Business games** model the conduct of a company. They typically involve a hypothetical company, a stated business objective (e.g., to reach a certain level of profitability), and a set of rules and procedures for trainees to follow. The participants are presented with information regarding a business context or situation and, within the rules of the game, must make decisions about what to do. The game progresses until a certain objective has been met, such as a predetermined level of profitability. Some business games present trainees with an opportunity to reach certain desired objectives but at the cost of engaging in unethical or questionable behavior. The trainees are thus faced with conflicting objectives, and as part of the game must defend the choices they made. It is also possible to design business games that reward competition or cooperation among the participants, depending on the objective of the game. Indeed, the competitive and applied nature of business games can be very motivating for some individuals.[52] Well-crafted games contain surprises, interdependent outcomes, and twists and turns that engage participants.

Role playing
A training method directed primarily at enhancing interpersonal skills in which training participants adopt various roles in a group exercise.

Role Playing. **Role playing** is a training method often aimed at enhancing either human relations skills or sales techniques. The method originated in clinical psychology; problems involving human interaction, real or imaginary, are presented and then spontaneously acted out. The enactment is sometimes followed by a discussion to determine what happened and why. Participants suggest how the problem could be handled more effectively in the future.

Role playing is less tightly structured than acting, where performers have to say set lines on cue. Instead, with role playing, participants are assigned roles in the scenario to be enacted. For example, role plays may include unruly employees, disagreeable teammates, or clueless peers. Some role plays may be conducted in person, whereas others may be conducted virtually. Sometimes role plays involve multiple trainees. For example, the scenario may be a retail store. One person takes the role of an irate customer who is dissatisfied with a recent purchase. A second person is assigned the role of the clerk who must attend to the customer's complaint. Aside from observing some general guidelines about the process, the participants are free to act out their roles however they wish. Their performance is typically judged by people who do not have an active part in the role playing. In an educational setting, the observers may be other students in the class; in a business setting, they might be supervisors or peers.

Alternatively, sometimes role plays will be more structured in order to train individuals on reacting to specific situations. For example, rather than having two trainees role play the scenario with the irate customer, the customer may be played by a trainer so that a certain level of intensity is guaranteed or so that certain issues are raised that may not emerge by chance between two trainees. In these cases, while there still may not be specific scripts, the issues raised and responses to trainee statements are typically pre-established to provide some continuity across different training sessions.

Many variations of role playing are possible. In some exercises, participants repeat the enactment several times but switch roles. In other cases, participants reverse the role they play in real life; for example, the supervisor plays a union representative. The role forces the participant to adopt the other side's position and then defend it. Reactions to role playing vary, but many participants express apprehension about engaging in such activities. Once individuals relax and get into the role play, their true colors often emerge. People who are pushy at work tend to be pushy during role plays. Those who are passive when interacting with peers tend to be similarly passive during role plays. Thus, we can see true behavior in an artificial setting. This means that we can not only offer valuable feedback, but do so in a relatively safe environment where their workplace identity is not threatened. When executed properly, role plays can be particularly effective at enhancing organizational learning.

Consider This...

It is not just the trainees who may be apprehensive about engaging in role plays. A training program that requires trainers to lead or participate in role plays may leave newer trainers feeling intimidated at the thought of having to pretend to be someone they aren't, doing what may be thought of as closer to improvisational acting than to training and development. Despite their initial discomfort, however, trainers responsible for engaging in role plays will often become more comfortable and less incredulous as they see the positive impact that role plays can have on learning. How incredulous are you regarding role plays? Does the thought of doing them—as a trainer and/or a trainee—cause you any discomfort? Why? What do you think it would take for most people to become "believers" in the utility of role plays as a training tool?

Behavior modeling A method of training that makes use of imitative learning and reinforcement to modify human behavior.

Behavior Modeling. **Behavior modeling** is based on the technique of imitating or modeling the actions of another person whose performance on some task is highly regarded. An expert is used as a model for the behavior. The method provides opportunities for the trainer and other trainees to give reinforcement for appropriate imitation of the expert's behavior. The method typically has a narrow focus, with the intent of developing specific behavior skills. Behavior modeling is used for training in interpersonal skills, sales, industrial safety, employment interviews, and so on. One variation of the method involves recording the trainee's performance and comparing it with the expert's behavior. With the use of split-screen technology, the expert and the trainees can be shown side-by-side, and trainees can see where their behavior needs to be improved. Behavior modeling is predicated upon a set of behaviors (e.g., a salesperson handling an irate customer) that can be successfully imitated irrespective of the personal attributes (such as age or gender) of the trainee in question. A meta-analysis of behavioral modeling training concluded that skill development was greatest when learning points were presented with specific behavioral-based guidelines, as opposed to general descriptions.[53] For example, training is more effective when trainees are taught to "listen and respond with empathy to reduce defensiveness" rather than "listen carefully."

Active Learning Approaches

Learning can be approached passively or actively. Training programs that take an active learning approach encourage trainees to ask questions, explore material on their own, seek feedback, and reflect on their results. Because of the level of engagement, active learning propels trainees in their own development.[54] Active learning approaches differ from more traditional, passive approaches (such as lectures or videos) in two key ways.[55] First, active approaches put the trainees in control of their own learning, whereas passive approaches make the trainees a mere recipient of information. With active approaches, individuals must take more responsibility for their learning, making such decisions as where to focus their attention, how to monitor their progress, and how to judge the effectiveness of their efforts. The second distinction between active and passive learning approaches is that active approaches are based on the assumption that learning occurs inductively. Individuals manipulate their environment and arrive at conclusions on their own. Passive approaches, on the other hand, are based on the assumption that learning is deductive in nature, and that individuals obtain knowledge by having it provided to them by some external agent (such as a trainer or computer program). Individuals are better able to encode and retain information when they are active (vs. passive) learners.[56] By actively engaging with the material, individuals will have a richer understanding of the important concepts and be able to transfer them more readily to the workplace, even to situations that they didn't encounter during training. Two specific active learning approaches will be discussed: error-management training and self-regulatory training.

Consider This...

Have you ever asked a teacher a question and had the response come in the form of a question posed back to you? Or been asked, "Well, what do you think?" Chances are, your teacher may have been using the Socratic Method, a technique that involves getting students to come up with answers to questions themselves. This is a form of active learning in which the teacher engages in dialogue that directs the conversation to key points without explicitly answering the question. Learners' questions are reframed into new questions to guide them to the correct or optimal answer. So, rather than simply answering questions, the teacher aids students in finding solutions themselves. For many students, this can be a frustrating experience. This approach, however, like all active learning approaches, has real benefits and can truly enhance learning. Have you ever had a teacher use the Socratic Method? What classes would you think are better suited for this approach? Are there times it might be an inappropriate method to use? Why or why not?

Error-Management Training

One of life's great truths is that we learn from experience. Making mistakes, and learning from those mistakes, is a very powerful form of learning. Yet, there is a seeming paradox to making errors: while we learn from them, we are often punished for committing them. In school, low grades are assigned to students who make errors. In the workplace, employees can be disciplined, even fired, for making an error. As such, we learn to avoid making errors to prevent being punished. However, from a psychological perspective, errors enhance learning and could be a strategic component of training. This principle has led to **error-management training**, a concept where participants are explicitly encouraged to make errors and learn from them. An extensive review of the literature on the role of errors in learning concluded that people learn from their mistakes and perform better in the future, provided there is a careful review and explanation of what specific actions of the individual led to the mistake.[57]

Error-management training
A system of training in which employees are encouraged to make errors, and then learn from their mistakes.

Error-management training has the potential to be a very useful approach to learning. However, two issues must be squarely addressed in its consideration. First, it represents an inversion of conventional thinking about what contributes to our perception of a top performer within a company. Instead of employees who are highly regarded because "they rarely (if ever) make a mistake," the emphasis would switch to employees who "make mistakes, and have learned from their errors." The second issue is the practical reality that whatever mistakes are made must not inflict harm to the organization. As such, the "best" mistakes would be those that produce few or no negative consequences to the organization, their learning value to the individual is high, they are generalizable across other situations, and they are acceptable to all parties with vested interests in the outcome. Accordingly, perhaps such errors would be more acceptable in training environments such as simulations and trial runs, where the potential negative consequences to the organization are artificially constrained.

The fundamental premise of error-management training is sound: we learn from our mistakes. Errors enhance later recall of correct responses, facilitate active learning, direct the learner's attention to appropriate information, and help trainers know where to focus their efforts.[58] However, despite the learning potential to the individual of making mistakes, such employees may acquire the stigma of being "error-prone," while the error-avoidant employee may be regarded more favorably for assignments where the negative consequences of errors are potentially high. Having an organizational culture that does not take a punitive approach to errors is important in combatting these views. Creating such a culture requires open communication about errors, as well as early detection and recovery from errors.[59] Furthermore, some employees are likely to respond better to error-management training. For example, researchers have found that individuals who are highly conscientious and/or extraverted tend to perform better in error-management training programs than do individuals low on conscientiousness and/or extraversion.[60] Thus, the active learning approach of error-management training may be beneficial, but may not be as appropriate or effective for all individuals or organizations.

Self-Regulatory Training

Self-regulation refers to processes that allow individuals to monitor their thoughts, moods, and behaviors over time and adjust them accordingly to meet task requirements. Prompting people to self-regulate their actions and reactions during training can make them more likely to stay on task and find solutions for themselves, which aids in transferring knowledge and skills to unique situations outside of the training. **Self-regulatory training** has three general parts, as shown in Figure 7-1.[61] The first involves *practice behaviors* during training, which occurs when trainees actively engage in tasks to focus on skill improvement. The second part involves *self-monitoring*, or focusing their attention on how much progress they are making toward the training objectives. This part of the training is the cognitive component, requiring trainees to actively think about how they are doing and what they can do to improve their efforts. The third part is *self-evaluation reaction*, which involves the emotional responses that individuals may have for their progress.

Self-regulatory training
A system of training in which employees are prompted to monitor and adjust their actions and reactions during training.

Self-efficacy
The belief in one's capabilities and capacity to perform successfully.

For self-regulatory training to be most effective, individuals should have high levels of confidence in their abilities to successfully complete the tasks (called **self-efficacy**), and they should make appropriate attributions for the cause of their performance. That is, if individuals attribute the reason for their success to luck or the

Figure 7-1 *Components of self-regulatory training*

reason for their failure to an unfriendly trainer, the likelihood of their self-regulatory processes being engaged and maintained over time will be lessened. This is because they are making external attributions for their successes and failures. Rather than credit or blame external factors for their performance, trainees should form causal attributions that make it clear that good performance was due to their diligence and poor performance was a result of inappropriate effort or task strategies.

The effects of self-regulatory training interventions have been promising. One study found that individuals who engaged in self-regulation during training had higher declarative and procedural knowledge compared to those who were not prompted to self-regulate their thoughts and behaviors during training.[62] Another study found that prompting trainees to engage in self-regulation during training led to more time spent on the task, which then led to the trainees learning more.[63] We will revisit the topic of self-efficacy and self-regulation in Chapter 13 when we discuss goal-setting and self-regulation theories of motivation.

Special Training Topics

Training topics can vary widely within organizations and are largely determined by the needs of the organization and its employees. Training can focus on anything from specific knowledge that needs to be transmitted, to various skills that must be learned. There are three topics that are widely covered through training within organizations. These include training on diversity, training to prepare individuals for overseas assignments, and training to prevent and deter sexual harassment.

Diversity Training

The workforce has become increasingly diverse. With advances in technology and increased globalization comes an era where the people with whom we interact, whether as colleagues, clients, or employers, are often not the same as us. Diversity involves both *surface-level* characteristics, such as demographic differences that are easily seen with the naked eye, and *deep-level* characteristics, such as personality and values that are unknown at first glance. Rather than passively react to increases in diversity, organizations are advised to proactively manage it.

Diversity training
A method of training directed at improving interpersonal sensitivity and awareness of differences among employees.

The goal of **diversity training** is to increase knowledge about diversity, improve trainees' attitudes regarding diversity, and help them develop skills addressing diversity.[64] As one scholar summarized, diversity training involves "head (knowledge); hand (behaviors and skills); and heart (feelings and attitudes)" (Hayles 1996, p. 106).[65]

To accomplish these objectives, diversity training programs typically focus on diversity awareness (making participants more aware of various cultural assumptions, values, and biases), skill-building (monitoring one's own behaviors and responding appropriately to different situations), or a combination of diversity awareness and skill-building. Not surprisingly, a meta-analysis examining over 40 years of diversity research found that diversity programs were more successful when they went beyond merely increasing awareness.[66] Nevertheless, diversity awareness is an important component of most diversity programs. Increasing awareness involves three primary goals.[67] The first is to increase trainee knowledge about issues. This could include providing information about the organization's stance on diversity, dispelling myths about various groups, providing facts about the changing demographics in society, and helping people understand how stereotypes and biases are formed. These discussions can be emotionally charged and trigger reactance and defensiveness.[68] As such, it is recommended that traditional classroom methods be used by experienced trainers.

The second goal of diversity awareness is to encourage trainees to consider how they categorize people and find common ground between themselves and others. The focus here is on weakening beliefs that some people are in an "in-group," whereas others are in an "out-group." Instead, trainees are encouraged to find similarities and focus on individual identities rather than group characteristics. A common exercise used to make individuals rethink how they categorize others is the "Who am I?" exercise. In this activity, participants list and discuss how they view themselves. The idea is that participants may discover that their own self-identities are actually quite similar to how other seemingly-different people view themselves. Having participants consider others' perspectives and how their experiences may differ from their own may lead to more lasting positive effects for diversity programs in general.[69]

Lastly, diversity awareness seeks to challenge individuals' knowledge about themselves and their own belief systems. The intent is to get people to understand their own attitudes and behaviors, and to make people mindful of how they view and treat others. Training methods that are meant to increase participants' self-knowledge are often confrontational in nature. For example, one exercise on social privilege has participants line up on one side of a room and respond to a number of statements (e.g., "I attended a private school") by taking a pace forward if the statement reflects an advantage that they had, or move backward if the statement reflects a disadvantage that they have experienced.[70] Typically, participants from the dominant racial group take many more paces forward than participants representing other ethnic or racial groups, thereby demonstrating what occurs within society in a very "in-your-face" way. This exercise can also include privilege based on sex, sexual orientation, socioeconomic status, and other characteristics that are related to having a social advantage over others. Table 7-1 shows sample items from such an activity.

In general, diversity programs are largely successful at increasing knowledge for participants, both in the short-term and the long-term.[71] However, whereas the training effects on cognitive learning persist over time, participants' reactions to diversity training and any attitudinal changes that occurred tend to decay over time. Even in the short-term, changes in attitudes from diversity programs are not uniform. For example, diversity programs appear to be successful at changing general attitudes toward diversity, but less effective in changing attitudes toward specific groups of people.[72]

Of course, not all diversity programs result in positive outcomes. There is evidence that diversity programs sometimes lead to defensiveness and an increase in negative behaviors.[73] In addition, when some individuals are represented in small numbers within an organization (e.g., there are only a few people of a certain race or religion), then diversity efforts that are intended to bring awareness to those groups may make those individuals feel overly scrutinized or stereotyped. These individuals

Table 7-1 *Sample items in a privilege walk exercise designed to increase diversity awareness*

Privilege Statements
1. If your family had health insurance, take one step forward.
2. If you have visible or invisible disabilities, take one step backward.
3. If you completed high school, take one step forward.
4. If you have ever felt unsafe walking alone at night, take one step backward.
5. If you were raised in a home that had libraries of both children's and adults' books, take one step forward.
6. If you took out loans for your education, take one step backward.
7. If you commonly see people of your race or ethnicity as heroes or heroines on television programs or in movies, take one step forward.
8. If you ever got a good paying job because of a friend or family member, take one step forward.
9. If you have been divorced or impacted by divorce, take one step backward.
10. If your parents completed college, take one step forward.

may also fear that any positive outcomes they receive (e.g., promotions, awards) will be attributed to their membership in that group rather than due to their competence or qualifications. This may lead to the unintended consequences of disengagement and underperformance. Thus, organizations may want to consider which groups their diversity training efforts are targeting and what the representation is of those highlighted in such efforts.[74] Nevertheless, even if there is little that an organization can do to compel changes in how people feel about each other over the long term, organizations should adopt a zero-tolerance policy for discrimination and harassment practices.

Expatriate Training

Expatriate
A person native to one country who serves a period of employment in another country.

The term **expatriate** refers to an employee who serves on an overseas assignment (typically for a defined time period, such as 2–5 years). The need for expatriate training has grown for two reasons. The first is the increase in the number of individuals so assigned, and the second is the relatively high failure rate of employees in such assignments. For example, about one-third of expatriate managers terminate their international assignments prematurely.[75] Even if the managers complete their assignments, their performance in that role may not be regarded as successful. Determining annual costs for expatriate failures is difficult, but it was estimated in 1996 for U.S. companies to be approximately $2 billion.[76] We can only imagine what that cost is today.

It is not unusual for global organizations to desire their employees to sequentially assume multiple international assignments, resulting in a group of people who continuously move from one locale to another. Regardless of the time spent travelling or number of assignments an individual is given, however, training may be needed to enhance an expatriate's chances for success. A study examining German expatriates on assignment in either Japan or the United States found that individuals who felt uncomfortable interacting with members of the host nation tended to withdraw into an enclave of fellow German expatriates.[77] Fortunately, training can help expatriates feel more comfortable interacting with members of the host country, thereby helping with adjustment issues.

There is a difference between serving in an international assignment versus developing cross-cultural competence.[78] Thus, not surprisingly, a key aspect of expatriate training is a focus on cross-cultural issues. Many programs serve as a means of educating individuals about what differences to expect in their target destination and how to cope with these differences. Individuals receive information on such topics as business customs, etiquette, and potential barriers to communication. By making people aware of such things as differences between expressions and gestures across cultures, the fear of the unknown is lessened and potential mishaps may be avoided. Figure 7-2 shows various meanings of common hand gestures worldwide, which puts into context how simple gestures can create confusion or conflict depending on where they are used. Worthy of note, the comprehensiveness of the training is more important than the length of the training.[79]

In addition, it appears that *when* training occurs and *who* is involved with the training makes a difference on expatriate adjustment and performance. For example, research conducted on a sample of 206 expatriates found that individuals who received cross-cultural training after arriving to their destination performed better on their assignments than individuals who received no such training or only received training prior to their departure.[80] Regarding the importance of who is involved in training, the adjustment of one's family members is a major factor in an expatriate's success.[81] As such, including the expatriate's spouse and other family members in cross-cultural training and, if feasible, sending them overseas to preview their new environment is advisable.[82]

Finally, it is important to consider the full life-cycle of the international assignment when considering expatriate training. It is crucial that organizational decision makers consider training expatriates on their reentry to their home countries following their international assignments, as there have been well-established emotional, cognitive, and behavioral problems associated with returning to one's home country.[83] Given the havoc these problems can wreak on the returning employee's performance, well-being, intentions to quit, and their overall career development, training expatriates to deal with common issues that arise upon their return is clearly an important consideration.

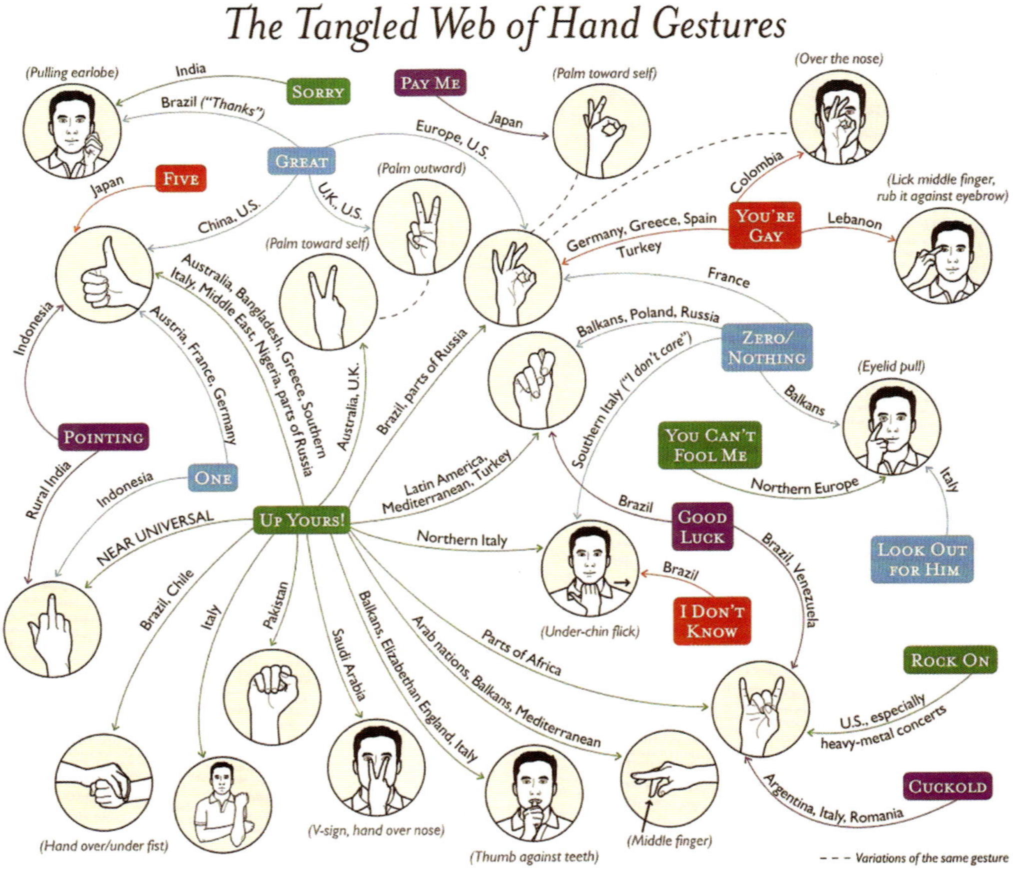

Figure 7-2 *Various meanings of common hand gestures worldwide*

Source: From "Etiquette 101: Hand Gestures," in *Condé Nast Traveler*, 2008, *43*(4), p. 114. Reprinted with permission. © Boris Kachka/Conde Nast Traveler/Conde Nast.

Consider This...

At Disney World, all employees (i.e., "cast members") must point with two fingers (e.g., when giving directions to a park attendee) because pointing with one finger is considered rude in some cultures. Thus, the "Disney Point" is used to avoid inadvertently offending a guest. Hand gestures are ubiquitous, however, and often used as a means of connecting with others and signaling a common bond. For example, many college students use hand gestures that have symbolic meaning at their universities. At Texas A&M University, it is common to see students give a thumbs-up gesture along with the phrase "Gig 'em," particularly during sporting events, as it "signals optimism, determination, loyalty, and the Aggie Spirit" (Texas A&M University 2021).[84] Similarly, students at the University of Texas will create "horns" using their fingers to represent their mascot, a Texas Longhorn. These gestures are ingrained in the histories of the schools and continue to be passed on to new generations of students. Look at the images in Figure 7-2, however, and you'll see that in some countries, these gestures are offensive. Do you think the universities should do anything to stop the use of these gestures? Do you think continuing their use is disrespectful to students who may be from these countries? Should the universities take the approach that Disney has taken, and create "replacement" gestures that are not offensive to others? Why or why not?

Sexual Harassment Training

In Chapter 3, we discussed the topic of sexual harassment, including *quid pro quo* harassment (occurring when specified organizational rewards are offered in exchange for sexual favors) and hostile-environment harassment (occurring when there is a pattern of unwelcome activities that individuals regard as offensive). Recall that the EEOC advises that organizations provide sexual harassment training to educate their employees on what sexual harassment entails and clearly communicate that such harassment will not be tolerated. It should therefore not be surprising that organizations devote considerable training resources to deter the likelihood of sexual harassment in the workplace. Indeed, it is estimated that sexual harassment at work costs an average of $2.6 billion annually in lost productivity—approximately $1,053 per victim.[85] So, in addition to the EEOC recommendation, there is a financial incentive for such training as well.

"The average person will spend about 90,000 hours at work throughout their lifetime. With this in mind, workplace romances are bound to happen. However, HR professionals have a responsibility to protect employees from favoritism, retaliation and incidents of sexual harassment."[87]

—Alex Alonso, Ph.D., Chief Knowledge Officer for the Society for Human Resource Management

Sexual behavior at work is largely depicted as something harmful and offensive, a manifestation of human behavior that "has no place" in the workplace.[86] At some point "sexual behavior" blurs into "sexual harassment," and furthermore, what is regarded as sexual harassment isn't always sexual in nature. Additionally, what can be alleged as sexual harassment isn't always offensive, being neither sexual nor harassing to some people. Not all sexual behavior at work is offensive (such as jokes or sexual bantering), and flirtation can lead to love and romance. There are non-sexual forms of harassment, such as bullying, threatening, and social undermining. These harassing behaviors can acquire a "sexual" dimension, but the behavior in question is offensive independent of gender.

The inherent complexity of "sexual harassment" as a manifestation of human behavior in the workplace leads to uncertainty as to what exactly organizations should do in their training initiatives designed to decrease the frequency of its occurrence. Sexual harassment training frequently consists of teaching sensitivity to other people's values and preferences. It should not be assumed, for example, that people prefer to be touched (such as on the hand or arm) when engaged in conversation. There are also broad cultural differences in the degree to which physical contact between people is regarded as acceptable. People differ in the degree to which verbal statements, including profanity, are considered offensive or inappropriate. Most sexual harassment training programs are designed to be fundamentally educational in nature. Participants are taught to recognize the manifestations of harassment and understand why victims are likely to find it offensive. However, some people engage in purposeful and intentional forms of sexual harassment. In these cases, knowledge-based sexual harassment training will be ineffectual in decreasing its occurrence, and in its place the organization must seek to control its occurrence through sanctions (e.g., suspensions and terminations).

Recent research on sexual harassment has been extended to include the organizational context in which it occurs. For example, as we move to a more service-oriented economy, organizations place strong emphasis on employees being highly attentive to customer needs. However, employees in service jobs can also be targeted for sexual harassment by clients and customers—the people that the organization relies on for business.[88] Thus, the potential for sexual harassment for employees can transcend the traditional boundaries of an organization to include other individuals not directly under the organization's control. Furthermore, boundaries between work and nonwork have become blurred as employees engage in workplace romances and technology cuts across areas. As such, sexual harassment issues are becoming more complex for organizations (see Social Media and I-O Psychology: *Workplace Romances, Social Media, and Sexual Harassment Concerns*).

Management Development Issues

Management development
The process by which individuals serving in management or leadership positions enhance their talents to better perform the job.

Management development is the process by which individuals learn to perform effectively in managerial roles. Management development is distinct from typical training programs in that the learning objectives are typically aimed at the acquisition of knowledge, skills, and competencies beneficial for future (usually higher-level) positions in the organization, rather than on those important for one's current position. Organizations are interested in management development in large part because they recognize its value as a strategy to improve organizational performance. Without sufficient development, however, many managers will fail in their roles. For example, a summary of the existing literature on managerial failure revealed that approximately 50% of managers will fail, and half of those will be fired.[89] The financial burden of managers failing is extraordinarily high due to costs associated with the failed manager's replacement and missed business objectives. Furthermore, managers can wreak havoc on their employees, causing a great deal of stress and animosity. Indeed, approximately 75% of employees consider their immediate boss to be the most stressful aspect of their jobs.[90]

Social Media and I-O Psychology: *Workplace Romances, Social Media, and Sexual Harassment Concerns*

Given the amount of time that people spend at work, it is not surprising that friendships are frequently formed between coworkers. These colleagues may decide to connect on LinkedIn, friend each other on Facebook, and follow each other on Instagram. Occasionally, these friendships develop into something more romantic in nature. In a 2021 survey of 1,000 employed Americans reflecting the entire U.S. adult population, it was revealed that 34% of people have been involved in a workplace romance. Of these, nearly 70% dated a coworker, 21% dated a subordinate, and 18% dated someone higher up in the organizational ranks.[91]

However, not all relationships last. What happens when members of failed romances stay connected through social media? A flirtatious post on a coworker's Facebook wall may have been welcomed during the relationship, but afterwards may be grounds for a sexual harassment claim if posted during work hours or from a work computer. Furthermore, even if the posts occur outside of business hours, they may be problematic. Those connections through social media that individuals share may create hostile environments outside the office that impact employees inside the office.[92]

Given the potential for harassment claims, what is an organization to do? A survey conducted by the Society for Human Resource Management (SHRM) reported that 42% of organizations have a written or verbal policy addressing workplace romance.[93] However, even if a policy does exist, 75% of romantically-involved coworkers do not let their organizations know about the romance.[94] The idea of having policies regarding workplace romances is nothing new. Some have even proposed "love contracts" that members of a romantic relationship sign that affirms the relationship is consensual and won't affect their work. However, few human resource practitioners in the SHRM survey report using these, and most deem them to be ineffectual. What is new is the intersection between workplace romances and social media use. Some scholars have argued that because some romances may sour and morph into harassment, "corporations must update their sexual harassment policies to include all social media applications, regardless of who owns the device and whether or not such contacts take place inside or outside office boundaries" (Mainiero & Jones 2013, p. 192).[95]

Clearly, social media have blurred the lines between personal and professional lives, as have workplace romances. A lot remains to be seen regarding what will and won't work as deterrents to sexual harassment complaints that are borne out of failed romances and social media gaffes. Until then, individuals embarking on relationships with colleagues would be wise to keep things professional, even when they get personal.

The literature on management development tends to focus on major issues or processes managers address as part of their professional maturation. In contrast, the literature on personnel training tends to be more concerned with specific methods or techniques of training. However, the larger systemic issues of needs assessment, skill enhancement, and transfer are equally applicable to both training and development.

There are four broad categories of behaviors related to managerial effectiveness.[96] The first category is intrapersonal skills, which includes self-awareness and self-control, emotional maturity, and integrity. Self-awareness is particularly key to managerial development.[97] Managers must be aware of how others perceive them and of their own flawed interpersonal tendencies to be successful. The second category of managerial behaviors is interpersonal skills, which includes social skills, empathy, and relationship development. The third category is business skills, which includes planning, organization, and monitoring skills. Finally, the fourth category of behaviors related to managerial effectiveness is leadership skills, which includes leading through others and the ability to build and maintain a team. When multiple categories of behaviors can be targeted, the impact on the manager's subsequent performance will be strengthened, as will the effectiveness of that manager's team of employees (see Faces of I-O Psychology: *Sandra L. Lee*).

Underutilization of managerial skills and practices contribute to derailment.[98] Derailment occurs when a manager who has been judged to have the ability to go higher fails to live up to their full potential and is fired, demoted, or plateaued below the expected level of achievement. It has been suggested that managerial derailment is almost always linked to relationship problems.[99] When relationships are healthy and strong, mistakes are forgiven. When they erode, however, tolerance for mistakes dissipates and mistakes lead to managerial derailment.

Managerial skills are often difficult to train in traditional formats. As such, two special forms of training and development that are particularly salient for managerial development deserve discussion: mentoring and executive coaching.

Mentor
Typically a more senior or experienced person who helps to professionally develop a less experienced person (the protégé).

Protégé
Typically a more junior and less experienced person who is provided career guidance by a more experienced person (the mentor).

Mentoring

Mentoring became an established means of developing managers starting around 1980. Mentoring can be regarded as one process that facilitates the transition between phases or stages of our lives, and mentoring can be provided by parents, teachers, or other people serving as role models who are sources of positive influence. Mentoring in an employment context is merely an extension of that concept.[100]

Mentors are more senior or experienced individuals who advise and shepherd new people (**protégés**) in the formative years of their careers. Mentors are typically at a higher position in an organization than their protégés.[101] Nevertheless, peer mentoring, in which a more experienced employee serves as a mentor to a less-seasoned colleague, is common as well. Mentoring can be informal, where the relationship between mentor and protégé forms spontaneously and is based on mutual attraction and shared interests, or it can be formal, in which the relationship is formed and dictated by the organization.

Faces of I-O Psychology: *Sandra L. Lee*

Sandra L. Lee

Ph.D. Colorado State University

Vice President, Human Resources and Organization Effectiveness, Natera

Currently supporting a post-IPO biotech company in managing their scale and growth through a broad range of human resources initiatives with a focus on culture and talent development.

Before joining Natera, Dr. Lee spent nearly twenty years in progressively larger leadership roles focused on talent management, organizational culture, organizational change, selection and assessment, and leadership development at various companies, including McKesson, Life Technologies (now Thermo Fisher), The Home Depot, and Motorola.

Like many practitioners, I've spent the last 20 years building systems and processes to drive business outcomes. Every business has a strategy, and aligning the people, processes, and culture to cultivate the desired results has been the aim of my work. Often this has manifested in building (a) succession planning systems identifying, developing, and cultivating talent with the right skills for the future needs of the business; (b) development programs building out skills for the future, or (c) performance management programs to align individual goals with company direction and goals.

The processes and systems I've implemented as a practitioner are fairly well-covered, well-documented, and based on solid research. However, some of the greatest impact I've made has been through the one-on-one conversations I've had with leaders. I've been honored to work with brilliant scientists, electrical engineers, and savvy sales executives. Each of these groups of individuals has been brilliant in their own right, and all in need of someone who can translate complex I-O psychology concepts into a simple, practical conversation.

While at a biotech company, I had a conversation with a scientific leader whose team was struggling with personality differences among team members. He shared an example of how one person said something and another took it negatively. The employee complained about it to him later. He wanted help in figuring out how to manage to keep this relationship from going sideways. Knowing this was a group of scientists, I suggested we look at the scientific method. In all science, we collect multiple data points before drawing conclusions. Why wouldn't this extend to how we make judgments about people and what their behavior says about them? Pausing before drawing conclusions allows new information to be collected and considered. This was a different application of what the microbiologist did daily with genetic data. He lit up, as the metaphor had resonated with him. He liked it and agreed to use it as a coaching model with his team.

The point of this story isn't as much about how fabulous the scientific method is (and it is) nor how as I-O psychologists we should be so proud (but we should, too). Rather, I've found the key to making impacts with my brilliant leaders is to meet them in their context and speak a language they already understand. The burden is on us to understand their world and find what is relatable.

Mentoring relationships typically progress through four phases.[102] As depicted in Figure 7-3, the first phase is *relationship initiation*, which occurs as the two individuals are connected, whether formally or informally, and determine whether a mentoring relationship will be valuable. This has been referred to as the "make or break" part of the mentoring relationship, in that some relationships never move beyond superficial interpersonal interactions.[103] The second phase is *cultivation*, which is when the heart of mentoring occurs. At this stage, the mentor provides instruction, support, and advice to the protégé and, in return, the protégé demonstrates commitment and engagement to the process and admiration for the mentor. The mentor and protégé are seen as being in a mutually-beneficial partnership at this point. The third phase is *separation*, when the protégé has essentially "outgrown" the relationship and no longer needs the ongoing support of the mentor. With successful completion of the mentoring arrangement, both parties typically have a sense of satisfaction. Alternatively, separation may occur prematurely (e.g., if the mentor–protégé relationship has not been successful or a breach in trust has occurred). In this case, there may be feelings of resentment or anger from one or both parties. The final phase of the mentoring relationship is *redefinition*. This phase typically occurs after each party has adjusted to their new roles and there is mutual recognition that the prior mentoring relationship is over. At this point, the mentor and the protégé decide what the future of their relationship holds. If the partnership was a success, they may continue their bond at a lower intensity or have more of a peer-like friendship. If the partnership ended on bad terms, however, hostility and resentment may dictate that all ties are cut between the two parties.

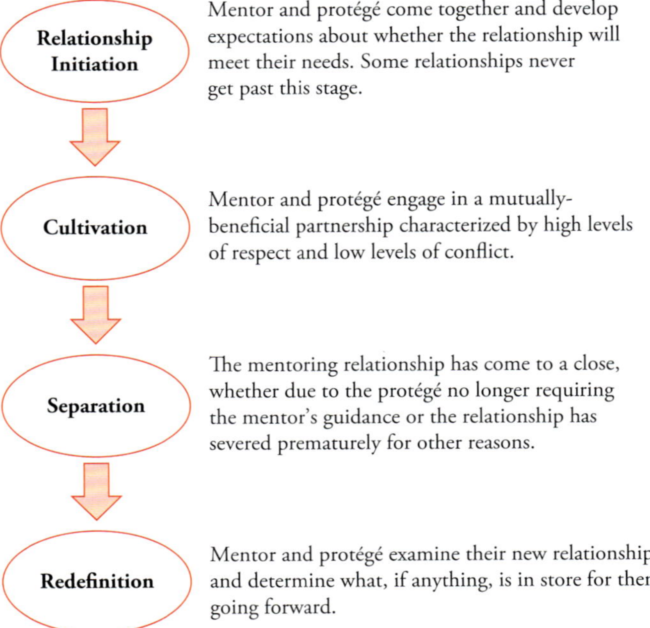

Figure 7-3 *The four phases of mentoring relationships*

There are three key factors to consider in mentoring relationships.[104] First is the frequency of meetings between mentor and protégé, which influences the amount of time mentors and protégés spend together. The second factor of importance is the scope, or breadth, of mentoring functions received by the protégé in tandem with the breadth of subjects addressed during the mentoring relationship. Mentoring functions include the general areas in which mentors can provide guidance, including task-related and/or psychosocial areas.[105] Mentoring behaviors such as sponsorships, exposure, visibility, and coaching are more directly related to enhancing task-related aspects of work that facilitate objective career success. Lastly, it is important to consider the degree to which the protégé is influenced by the mentor. Behaviors associated with psychosocial mentoring, such as role modeling, acceptance and confirmation, counseling, and friendship, are more highly related to satisfaction with the mentor than with career success. Lastly, it is important to consider the degree to which the protégé is influenced by the mentor. Some mentors provide tremendous influence, whereas others offer only superficial ideas and suggestions to protégés.

As in most relationships, there are benefits and drawbacks for both protégés and mentors. The benefits for protégés are much clearer than are those for mentors. The nature of the relationship is based on the premise that the mentor can help the protégé in some way. Mentors provide career-related support, such as increased visibility, protection from organizational politics, and career coaching. Psychosocial support from mentors can increase the protégé's self-esteem and self-efficacy. The amount of support may vary, however, by the sex of the mentor. A meta-analytic study revealed that protégés with female mentors received more psychosocial support than protégés with

Consider This...

Mentoring is not viewed as an acceptable activity in some countries. Consider the issue of power distance. We will discuss "power distance" more in Chapter 9, but the crux of the power distance concept is the degree to which differences in power are accepted and expected in a society. Power differentials are highly evident and formalized in boss-subordinate relationships. Part of the effectiveness of mentoring is that individuals with more power, status, and expertise can use their resources to develop a protégé. Furthermore, the mentor is willing (if not desirous) to do so. In cultures low on the dimension of power distance, mentoring is a more common means of professional development. Although the mentor has more formal power at work than does the protégé, the power is not used to distance the two parties from each other. In cultures that are high on power distance, the degree of inequality between the boss and subordinate is a defining characteristic of their relationship. For a boss to mentor a subordinate would, in effect, lessen the distance between them. Thus, a large power distance is not compatible with mentoring, particularly the psychosocial dimensions. Serving as a counselor, confidant, and friend lessens the inequality between the two parties. In low power distance cultures, mentoring is a manifestation of power (i.e., choosing to help someone when it is possible to do so). In high power distance cultures, *not* mentoring is a manifestation of power (i.e., asserting the inequality between the two parties). What implications does this have for organizations with offices around the world? How about for the mentoring of expatriates?

male mentors.[106] In addition, protégés have faster rates of promotion, higher motivation, and more positive interpersonal relations than peers who are not in mentoring relationships.[107] For mentors, however, the benefits are primarily limited to greater personal satisfaction in their work lives. While there may be organizational recognition for mentoring efforts, this is not the norm, particularly for informal mentoring relationships. The drawbacks for protégés can include being paired with a mentor who does not know how to be a good mentor, despite both parties desiring the mentor to have such skills. Mentors and protégés can have mismatched values, personalities, and work styles, and the negative consequences of the mismatch fall more heavily on the protégé. The drawbacks for mentors include protégés who are unwilling to learn, engage in breaches of trust, are jealous, and highly competitive (the mentor may be the immediate boss of the protégé, and the protégé may be well-positioned to assume the mentor's job). Although there are substantial drawbacks for both protégés and mentors from a failed relationship, both parties can reap great rewards when the relationship is seen as a mutually-beneficial partnership.

Executive Coaching

Executive coaching An individualized developmental process for business leaders provided by a trained professional (the coach).

Another means of developing managers is through **executive coaching**. Executive coaching is an individually-customized type of training that is typically directed toward top-level employees of an organization.[108] Two parties are involved: the coach and the person being coached. Unlike mentors, coaches don't need to be experts in the area in which their coachee works, as coaches tend to focus on developing broader skills, such as those related to leadership, communication, interpersonal relations, and managing conflict (see The Lighter Side of I-O Psychology: *We Need Coaching, Too!*).[109] Coaches listen carefully, provide a supportive environment, and then take an active and direct role in preparing solutions and developing plans of action for the coachee to follow.

It has been estimated that 93% of U.S.-based global companies use coaching.[110] Executive coaches can be used to help individuals learn a new skill (skill coaching), to perform better in their present job (performance coaching), or prepare them for a future leadership role (development coaching).[111] Thus, a fundamental tenet of coaching is learning.

Part of the value of coaching is that it is specifically geared to the person's problems and needs. As a one-on-one activity, coaching has no general curriculum designed to appeal to a wide audience. Coaching can be conducted in person, online, or over the phone. There are no formal standards or requirements to be a coach—it is an unlicensed and unregulated activity. Coaches can be members of the International Coach Federation, which has developed its own certification mechanism and code of ethics. However, in practice, a coach needs only to be professionally credible to others. Of course, given the wide range of needs that require coaching, including interpersonal problems, I-O psychologists are well-equipped to serve as executive coaches.

Much of what is known about coaching is primarily from the perspective of the coach and the process of coaching. For example, a review of the coaching research concluded that successful coaching requires a long-term focus, a focus on continuous learning, a focus on setting clear goals or outcomes to be achieved, and regular communication between the coach and the coachee.[112] Recently, attention has also been

The Lighter Side of I-O Psychology: *We Need Coaching, Too!*

It's a good thing that coaches don't have to know the jobs of the individuals they coach! If they did, it might be pretty hard to find a coach for some occupations. Coburg Banks, a recruiting firm, has seen a lot of résumés from a lot of different people. And some of the job titles have been downright weird. They compiled a list of the 100 oddest titles they have ever come across on actual résumés.[113] While some of them are clearly efforts to make a job seem more glamorous or impressive than perhaps it really is, others leave one wondering what the job could possibly entail. Here is a sampling of those odd job titles:

Hair Boiler	Bride Kidnapping Expert	Teen Exorcist
Slaughterer	Professional Sleeper	Crayon Evangelist
Wet Leisure Attendant	Dream Alchemist	Sales Ninja
Twisted Brother	Marker of the Swans	Pet Food Taster
Chief Everything Officer	Hyphenated-Specialist	Face Feeler
Zombie	Beverage Dissemination Officer	Marketing Rock Star
Happiness Advocate	Chief Troublemaker	Water Slide Tester

It's unclear what level these jobs are, or if they rise to the level that would be appropriate for executive coaching. But that's not the point. The point is that clearly there are myriad jobs in the world, and many ways to describe them. If coaches had to know the specifics of each of these professions, nobody would get coaching. That sound you just heard? That was the sound of the collective sigh of relief from coaches around the world.

given to the individuals being coached. Participants can be classified according to their level of coachability.[114] At the lowest level, the participant is regarded as uncoachable; at the highest level, the participant is committed to inner-directed lifelong learning. Participants low in coachability will probably not benefit from coaching in any form through any means. Participants high in coachability will continue to grow and develop throughout their lifetime, and a particular coach is but one source of growth in their lifelong development.

Executive coaches typically charge between $200 and $3,000 per hour, with an average cost of $350 an hour.[115] Given its high costs, it is logical to question whether the expense is worth it. Fortunately, there appears to be evidence that coaching is effective. A meta-analysis found that coaching resulted in substantial improvements in performance.[116] In addition, coaching was related to greater well-being, greater ability to cope with present and future job demands, and more positive attitudes about work. Lastly, coaching was related to the setting and attainment of goals. A separate meta-analysis found that the positive effects associated with coaching were stronger when coaches were internal (vs. external) to the organization and when feedback from multiple sources was excluded from the coaching process.[117] Moreover, the duration of the coaching and the coaching format (face-to-face vs. e-coaching) did little to impact the effectiveness of the coaching.

Transfer of Training

Transfer of training The application back to the job of knowledge and skills learned in training.

A successful training program doesn't end when the training program ceases. Instead, the hope is that individuals will transfer what they have learned within training back to the job itself. This **transfer of training** is greatly facilitated by the individual's motivation to sustain the new behaviors.[118] Motivation is enhanced when the organization has a culture that supports continuous learning, and there are organizational consequences associated with having succeeded or failed in training. Some employees leave training with new skills and with strong intentions to apply those skills to their job, but limitations in the post-training environment interfere with the actual transfer of training. If training does not transfer back to the job, employees will likely think the training was a waste of their time and employers will question their investment in the training itself.[119]

Consider This...

Many on-the-job accidents occur in coal mines. Consider what occurred in the development of a safety training program to reduce accidents. Coal miners were observed and interviewed about their work. Observations revealed that the miners engaged in dangerous behaviors, such as not wearing their hard hats, leaving off their masks (which filtered out coal dust), and smoking in the mine (where an open flame could trigger an explosion). In addition to being unsafe, some of these behaviors were blatant violations of safety rules. After the miners finished their work shifts, they were interviewed about their jobs, including why they didn't wear safety equipment at times. Many said they believed there was no relationship between what they did in the mine and what happened to them. They felt their lives were in the hands of luck, fate, or God, and it did not matter how they conducted themselves. They all seemed to have personal anecdotes about other miners who were extremely safety conscious (that is, always wore all the safety equipment and were exceedingly cautious people in general), yet who serious injuries or death in accidents through no fault of their own, such as a cave-in. Thus, the miners seemed to believe that if "your number was up," you would get hurt or killed, and there was nothing you could do about it. Although a hard hat was a fine thing to wear, it would not do much good if five tons of rock fell on you. Therefore, many miners were not interested in engaging in safe behavior because their behavior did not matter one way or another. This example suggests that if people are not motivated to be trained or to learn some new behaviors, it is pointless to try to train them. Do you agree with this sentiment? How would you encourage the miners to be safer in their workplace? If the miners aren't going to transfer training back to the job, is it even worth trying? Why or why not?

Behavioral change occurs over time, and sometimes the change takes longer than expected. Transfer of training as a transitioning process passes through three phases.[120] The first is letting go of old behaviors that are to be replaced with something new, and the second is the in-between time, when the old ones are gone but the new ones are not yet consistently used. The third and final phase is when the new behaviors make sense and the individual uses them in a productive manner. It is at the end of this third phase when the transfer of training is complete.

One important distinction is between *generalization*, the extent to which trained skills and behaviors are exhibited in the transfer setting, and *maintenance*, the length of time that trained skills and behaviors continue to be used on the job.[121] Supervisory support is a major environmental factor that can affect the transfer process. In the post-training environment, supervisor support includes reinforcement, modeling of trained behaviors, and goal-setting activities. A meta-analysis revealed that transfer of training was greater for individuals who were higher on cognitive ability, conscientiousness, and motivation.[122] In addition, transfer was most enhanced when there was a supportive work environment. Along these lines, post-training knowledge and behavior are more likely to perseverate in organizations that have strong social support systems.[123] Specifically, transfer of training is enhanced in organizations that have a culture that recognizes the importance of continuous learning.

One element of training design that can facilitate learning and transfer are after-action reviews (AARs), which consist of a systematic replay and discussion regarding one's performance on recently completed tasks. AARs have traditionally been a standard element in military training, but have become increasingly popular in organizational training and development realms as well. In one study, researchers found that AARs increased leadership behavior following a leadership development program.[124] This was especially true for learners who were high in conscientiousness, openness to experience, and emotional stability, and those who had a strong base of developmental experiences from which to draw. Similarly, research has found that teams who used AARs exhibited greater performance, cohesion, and open communication than teams that did not use AARs.[125]

Evaluation Criteria of Training Programs

As is the case with any assessment or evaluation, some measure of performance must be obtained. Measures of performance refer to criteria, and the criteria used to evaluate training are just as important as those used in personnel selection. Relevance, reliability, and freedom from bias are all key considerations.

Reaction criteria
A standard for judging the effectiveness of training that refers to the reactions or feelings of individuals about the training they received.

The most common means of evaluating training is a classic typology that reflects four levels of training criteria that increase in complexity: reaction, learning, behavior, and results.[126] **Reaction criteria** refer primarily to the participants' reaction to the training program. These criteria measure impressions and opinions about the training; for example, did they believe it was useful or added to their knowledge? Reaction criteria are treated as a measure of the face validity of the training program. Most reactions to training depend on the instructional content, but reactions are also based on the level of anxiety associated with training and pre-training motivation.[127] Although most evaluations assess trainee reactions, complete evaluation must go beyond these reactionary assessments.[128]

Learning criteria
A standard for judging the effectiveness of training that refers to the amount of new knowledge and skills acquired through training.

Learning criteria refer to what knowledge has been acquired, skills improved, or attitudes changed as a result of training. Three measures can be taken. The first is immediate knowledge learned or skills acquired, which is often assessed at the conclusion of the training. The second is knowledge retention, where evaluators assess at a later time (as through a test) what has been learned. The third measure is a behavioral/skill demonstration. This measure is more than a score on a knowledge test, involving perhaps a demonstration in a role-playing exercise or a simulation that is a behavioral manifestation of the knowledge, attitudes, or skills obtained or changed in training. Collectively, reaction and learning criteria are called *internal criteria*; that is, they refer to assessments internal to the training program itself.

Behavioral criteria
A standard for judging the effectiveness of training that refers to changes in performance that are exhibited on the job as a result of training.

Behavioral criteria refer to actual changes in performance once the employee is back on the job. These criteria are most clearly reflected in the concept of transfer of training. These criteria address to what extent the desired changes in the job behaviors of the trainee are realized by the training program. If the goal of the training program is to increase production, then the behavioral criterion assesses output before and after training. Other behavioral criteria are absenteeism, scrap rate, accidents, and grievances. All of these are objective criteria; they can be measured easily and have relatively clear meaning, as discussed in Chapter 4. But if the goal of the training program is to increase managers' sensitivity toward people with disabilities, then "increased sensitivity" has to be translated into some objective behavioral criteria. Note that scores on learning criteria and on behavioral criteria do not always correspond to a high degree. Some people who perform well in training do not transfer their new knowledge or skills back to the job. This is particularly true for training programs aimed at changing attitudes or feelings.

Results criteria
A standard for judging the effectiveness of training that refers to the economic value that accrues to the organization as a function of the new behaviors exhibited on the job.

Results criteria relate to the economic value of the training program to the company. It is usually neither easy nor obvious to demonstrate the degree to which training enhances the overall goals of the organization. Unfortunately, the data needed to demonstrate the value of training can be time-consuming to collect. Even then, such data may be insufficient in convincing others that the training was worthwhile.[129] Furthermore, there can be hidden costs to even the most successful training programs.

Collectively, behavioral and results criteria are called *external criteria*; they are evaluations external to the training program itself. Consideration of these four criteria sometimes produces different conclusions about the effectiveness of training than a judgment reached by just one or two criteria. For example, reaction criteria appear to be more strongly related to learning criteria than to subsequent job behavior criteria.[130]

In a major meta-analytic review of the effectiveness of training in organizations, researchers concluded that organizational training exerted a moderate effect on reaction, learning, behavior, and results criteria.[131] Although there were differences in various types of training, on the whole, organizational training is moderately effective in enhancing performance outcomes. Training programs that produce a large effect are relatively scarce.

The success of any training and development system is intimately tied to the culture of the organization. The organization sets the tone for the relative importance and need placed on enhancing the skills of its employees. Training and development activities are a mirror of the organization's deeper values. As such, it is important to have alignment between the organization's culture and training initiatives.[132] For example, a traditional authoritarian organization may not be supportive of individuals who attempt to take risks and try out new strategies. Mistakes and errors may be viewed as actions to be avoided rather than as opportunities from which to learn and develop. It is also important to link training objectives to training evaluation criteria.[133] Given the subtleties of how we learn, what we learn, and the duration of our learning, methods of assessing learning must be appropriately refined. Learning is the foundation of training and development, and organizational learning is the foundation for organizational growth.

Chapter Review

Key Terms

- Training
- Development
- On-the-job training
- Organizational socialization
- Onboarding
- Learning
- Declarative knowledge
- Knowledge compilation
- Procedural knowledge
- Training needs assessment
- Organizational analysis
- Task analysis
- Person analysis
- Computer-based training
- Programmed instruction
- Intelligent tutoring systems
- Interactive multimedia training
- Virtual reality training
- Business games
- Role playing
- Behavior modeling
- Error-management training
- Self-regulatory training
- Self-efficacy
- Diversity training
- Expatriate
- Management development
- Mentor
- Protégé
- Executive coaching
- Transfer of training
- Reaction criteria
- Learning criteria
- Behavioral criteria
- Results criteria

Questions for Review

1. What is the difference between "training" and "development?" How are they similar?
2. Who is typically responsible for on-the-job training?
3. What is organizational socialization? What are aspects of informal organizational socialization? What are aspects of formal organizational socialization?
4. What is learning? What are its three components and how do they relate to one another?
5. What is a training needs assessment? Why should a training needs assessment be completed? What are the three steps to complete one?
6. For each of the computer-based training models (programmed instruction, intelligent tutoring systems, interactive multimedia, virtual reality, and business games), for what kinds of training situations is each best? What are the drawbacks to each of them?
7. How can role-play and behavior modeling contribute to learning? What are the drawbacks of each?
8. What are error-management training and self-regulatory training? How does company culture impact the use of these types of active learning approaches?

9. What are the three types of special training discussed? Why do organizations conduct these trainings, and how effective are they in achieving organizational objectives?
10. How does management development differ from training? What are two types of development currently being used? How is mentorship different from coaching? How does the length of the relationship impact the success of the development effort?
11. What is transfer of training? Which of the criteria are internal to the training program and which are external?
12. Can organizational training programs be categorized as "effective" overall? Why or why not?

CHAPTER 8

Performance Management

Chapter Outline

The Performance Management Process

COVID-19 and I-O Psychology: *Performance Management Challenges*

Purposes of Performance Management Systems

Faces of I-O Psychology: *Steven T. Hunt*

Performance Appraisal and the Law

Performance Rating Scales

Rating Errors and Biases

Rater Training

Rater Motivation

Peer and Self-Assessments

Peer Assessments

Self-Assessments

360° Feedback

Feedback in Performance Management Contexts

Giving Feedback

Seeking Feedback

Reactions to Feedback

The Lighter Side of I-O Psychology: *You Rock!*

Reactions to Performance Appraisals

Future of Performance Management

Social Media and I-O Psychology: *The Crowdsourced Performance Review*

Chapter Review

Learning Objectives

- Discuss the concept of performance management.
- Describe the performance management process.
- Describe the six purposes of performance management systems.
- Outline the attributes of a legally-defensible performance appraisal system.
- Summarize the major rating errors and biases.
- Discuss the various types of performance rating systems.
- Explain the purpose and types of rater training.
- Discuss the bases of rater motivation.
- Describe peer assessment, self-assessment, and 360° feedback.
- Describe the role of feedback giving, seeking, and reactions within performance management.
- Explain the rationale behind various reactions to performance management systems.
- Describe the debate regarding abandoning performance ratings and suggestions for alternatives to performance reviews within organizations.

Mary Kay Ash

If you want your organization to succeed, you need to focus on the performance of the individuals within it. Mary Kay Ash, founder of Mary Kay Cosmetics, once said, "People are definitely a company's greatest asset. It doesn't make any difference whether the product is cars or cosmetics. A company is only as good as the company it keeps." Indeed, it is the reason that companies compete for top talent so vigorously. High-performing employees can greatly contribute to organizational performance. Indra Nooyi, former chairperson and CEO of PepsiCo, noted, "If you want to improve the organization, you have to improve yourself and the organization gets pulled up with you." As such, individual performance is considered to be a *driver* of organizational performance. Accordingly, organizations are concerned about how well their employees are performing. How can organizational decision makers know how well their employees are performing? And if employees aren't performing well, what can (or should) they do about it? The answers to these questions lie in the concept of performance management.

Indra Nooyi

Performance management
The process of how an organization manages and aligns all of its resources to achieve high performance.

Performance appraisal
The documentation and assessment of an employee's performance.

Performance management is a continuous process of assessing and developing the performance of individuals and teams and aligning that performance with the organization's goals.[1] Within this definition, there are two key elements. First, there is the notion that performance management is a continuous process. The idea is that managing the performance of individuals and teams is not a one-time event. Rather, it is an ongoing process that involves establishing goals, observing and evaluating performance, and providing feedback and coaching to continuously develop individuals. Of particular relevance is the distinction between performance management and **performance appraisal**. While the terms are often used interchangeably in practice, there is a clear distinction between the two, with performance appraisal subsumed within the bigger concept of performance management. Generally speaking, performance appraisals are the evaluations of an individual's performance that occur periodically within organizations. They identify the person's strengths and weaknesses, and, in doing so, suggest areas that are in need of development. This evaluation usually results in a score or formal rating being assigned, which would then be shared with the employee.[2] Performance management, on the other hand, is an ongoing activity that seeks to integrate goal setting with ways in which the employee can be developed going forward.[3] Thus, performance appraisal, while an important part of performance management, is only one piece of the performance management puzzle.[4]

The second key part of the definition of performance management concerns alignment. Performance management is a shared vision within the organization, with all employees understanding how their individual performance contributes to organizational performance.[5] Implicit in this view is the idea of multiple goals, in particular, the overall goals of the organization and the specific goals of each of its employees. When the goals of the organization and the goals of employees are *aligned*, or directly related and connected to one another, individual performance contributes to organizational performance.[6]

The concept of alignment is difficult to measure, but organizations seem to be aware when there is little connection between individual performance (of its employees) and overall organizational performance. In a survey of organizational leaders, only about 12% of organizations believed there was a successful alignment between the two.[7] Some of the symptoms of misalignment include employees being caught up in many urgent but not important activities, a sense of burnout from working hard but accomplishing little, and high conflict among units within the organization.[8]

The issue of alignment is also important from a broader organizational perspective. For performance management to be effective, it must be aligned with organizational values, culture, priorities, and business needs.[9] Similarly, an organization's performance management practices should be bundled with its other human resource activities, and that bundle should be aligned with the organization's strategic goals.[10] For example, performance management should be tied to an organization's staffing plan, as well as its training and development activities. If it is clear from a job analysis what knowledge and skills are necessary to perform well in a particular job, individuals should be initially selected based on those skills, and later assessed and developed on those skills. To assume that performance management can operate distinctly from other human resources functions is grossly naïve.

The Performance Management Process

The process of performance management entails defining, evaluating, and reviewing performance, as well as providing consequences for performance.[11] As shown in Figure 8-1, the performance management process begins with the setting of goals and communication of performance expectations. Here, managers identify what they want employees to achieve, and they communicate these expectations to employees. These criteria for successful job performance are ideally established through a careful job analysis. Recall that job analysis and job performance criteria were discussed in Chapter 3.

The second step in the performance management process is the evaluation of work contributions. This evaluation occurs through careful monitoring of an employee's performance, combined with an assessment of the employee's strengths and weaknesses, whether in terms of the established performance standards or in comparison to other employees. These issues are a large focus of the current chapter and will be discussed in greater detail shortly.

Once performance is evaluated, the third step in the performance management process is to provide feedback to the employee. Both superior and subordinate are usually very uneasy about this step. Employees often get defensive about negative performance aspects. Superiors are often nervous about having to confront employees face-to-face with negative evaluations. If feedback is not given, however, or not given well, employee performance may actually decline rather than improve. We discuss feedback of appraisal information in greater detail later in this chapter. In addition, it is during this third stage that employees are provided coaching and other developmental opportunities to ensure future success. These developmental activities were described in Chapter 7.

The last step in the performance management process involves providing rewards to reinforce employee behaviors. Providing rewards helps emphasize what is valued

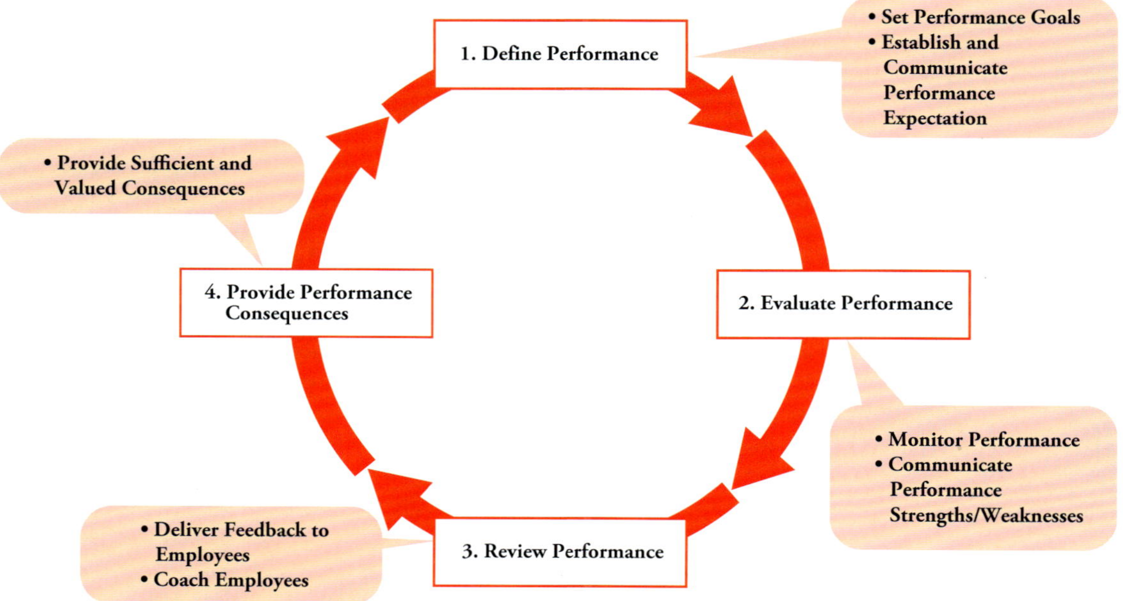

Figure 8-1 *Integrated performance management process*

Adapted from "Development and Validation of the Performance Management Behavior Questionnaire," by A. J. Kinicki, K. J. Jacobson, S. J. Peterson, and G. E. Prussia, in *Personnel Psychology* (2013) by Blackwell Publishing, Inc. Reprinted with permission of Blackwell Publishing, Inc. via Copyright Clearance Center.

by an organization, while also encouraging employees to continue to exert effort on the appropriate tasks. Rewarding individuals for good performance, as well as not rewarding them for poor performance, is a key part of what is known as transactional leadership. Providing consequences that are contingent on the employee's performance are "crucial transactions" between managers and employees.[12] You'll read more about transactional leadership in Chapter 14.

Once consequences are given, new goals are set and the revised expectations are communicated to employees. Performance is then evaluated based on those revised goals and expectations, feedback and coaching is provided, and new consequences are established. In this manner, the performance management process continues in a recurring cycle that integrates numerous topics discussed throughout this book. This process of performance management is influenced by events that occur both within and outside of the organization. While the process itself will remain intact, the decisions within the steps will be influenced, and managers will need to adapt accordingly (see COVID-19 and I-O Psychology: *Performance Management Challenges*).

COVID-19 and I-O Psychology: *Performance Management Challenges*

The COVID-19 pandemic created numerous challenges within performance management. While the performance management process itself remained in place, each of the steps was impacted by the pandemic.

The first step of defining performance was challenged by the changing performance context and need for organizations and their employees to pivot and learn how to do things differently. Many cities had at least temporary lockdowns in place, and physical distancing requirements were established that led to a substantial number of people working remotely. This simultaneously led to the need for employees to adapt to new technologies and adjust to different communication and work protocols. To what extent should this ability to adapt and adjust be incorporated into performance expectations? In addition, employees who were deemed essential workers were in precarious positions, in which they were exposed to health hazards and long working hours. To what extent should those changed circumstances factor into performance goals?

Monitoring and evaluating performance became similarly challenging. With more people working remotely, managers became less able to see their employees' work. Unfortunately, there is evidence that such inability to monitor work leads to more severe appraisals.[13] In addition, the inability to view individuals made it difficult (if not impossible) to comprehend external barriers to performance, such as distractions from children who were also stuck at home. Unless employees voiced their struggles, managers were unaware of the situational constraints, and ratings may have suffered accordingly. Although there are digital means of monitoring performance, such surveillance risked damaging trust between managers and employees.[14] For this reason, many organizations opted to forego formal evaluations during the pandemic, acknowledging that evaluations would likely be lower given the turmoil employees were experiencing.

Delivering feedback to employees became challenging as well, as managers could no longer do so in a face-to-face setting. The pandemic highlighted the need for managers to exhibit people skills—demonstrating compassion, empathy, resilience, and hope—to their employees.[15]

Lastly, performance consequences became tricky during the pandemic. With some industries hemorrhaging money and business struggling to stay afloat, pay increases and other bonuses became virtually impossible to provide for some. As such, organizations had to become more creative with valued consequences for rewarding performance and loyalty.

In short, the need to manage performance remained just as important during the COVID-19 pandemic as it was before. The challenge was figuring out how to do so in a largely remote and incredibly tumultuous time. Organizations and employees alike needed to learn how to adapt to the changing conditions and continue to develop during the crisis in order to survive and thrive in the "new normal."

Purposes of Performance Management Systems

There are six purposes of performance management systems, as follows:[16]

Strategic. The purpose of the human resources function in an organization is to maximize the contributions of employees to the goals of the organization, and assessments of employee job performance can play a major role in accomplishing that function. The issue of alignment that was discussed previously is critical. When individual and organizational goals are aligned, the performance management system communicates and reinforces what is most important for individuals to address. When individuals make improvements in these areas, both the individuals and the organization as a whole benefit (see Faces of I-O Psychology: *Steven T. Hunt*).

Administrative. Performance management systems are a key source of information for such things as making salary adjustments, deciding who should be promoted or recognized for exceptional performance, and identifying individuals whose employment should be terminated. Appraisals identify the better-performing employees, and employees who cannot perform well in their current jobs will not be considered for positive organizational outcomes, such as advancements in pay or promotions. For example, an employee who is judged to be performing in the top 10% of the workforce might get a 12% raise or a promotion. An employee who performs in the bottom 10% might get only a 2% raise, or may be one of the first to be laid off if there are reductions in force.

Communication. Performance management systems are clear sources of information for employees. They tell employees what is expected of them, how well they are performing, and where they should focus their attention. Through formal and informal discussions, supervisors are able to communicate which activities are of critical importance and which activities require less attention.

Developmental. It can be argued that the ultimate goal of performance management is performance improvement.[17] As part of this, a key element of successful performance management systems is that employees are provided with feedback that highlights their job-related strengths and weaknesses. Deficiencies or weaknesses then become the targets for coaching or training. Training should involve only those areas where poor performance can be attributed to the individual and not to aspects of the work environment. Also included here is the role of performance management systems in promoting employee engagement (to be discussed in Chapter 11). Scholars have suggested that designing performance management systems to focus on employee engagement will lead to higher levels of performance.[18]

Succession planning
The process involving long-term projections about the future staffing needs of an organization in order to ensure key roles are filled as needed.

Organizational Maintenance. Performance management systems are often used for workforce planning efforts, including succession planning. **Succession planning** is a concept in which fairly long-term projections (typically three to five years) about future staffing needs in an entire company are based on the anticipated promotion of current employees. It is possible to use information from performance management systems to determine how well employees within an organization are doing overall,

Faces of I-O Psychology: *Steven T. Hunt*

Steven T. Hunt

Ph.D. The Ohio State University

Chief Expert, Work & Technology, SAP

Research interests: Using technology to increase workforce productivity and adaptability; understanding relationships among employee attributes, company culture, technological innovations, socioeconomic changes and business performance

Author of hundreds of articles and several chapters and books on human resources (HR) methods and the changing nature of work including: *Commonsense talent management: using strategic human resources to increase company performance* (Wiley Press, 2014) and *Hiring success: the art and science of staffing assessment and employee selection* (Wiley Press, 2007). Currently working on a new book, *Talent Tectonics: managing employee experience for a changing world* (Wiley Press, planned release in 2022).

My career is driven by a belief that applying evidence-based psychological theories to workforce management can greatly improve the world. The opening statement from my book *Commonsense Talent Management* largely sums up why I became an I-O psychologist: "Fewer things are more important to happiness than having meaningful and fulfilling work… Despite the value of high-quality work environments, our society is plagued by examples of poorly run companies. [This] is tragic because we have the knowledge to avoid most of these problems, but many organizations do not use this knowledge" (Hunt, 2014, p. xvii).[19]

Most of my work focuses on development and use of technology-enabled systems to support workforce staffing, management, and development. I have helped create HR technology systems used by thousands of organizations around the globe, including many of the largest employers in the world. These systems have collectively influenced the careers of millions of employees. My work involves helping companies reimagine ways to design organizations and manage workforces for a changing world, by taking advantage of technological innovations and capabilities. This includes making companies aware of psychological theories that are relevant to the challenges they are addressing and the technology solutions they are using. This work often requires integrating research from diverse areas of psychology to inform the design and use of new technology-enabled processes that have never been studied by psychologists, because they never existed before the technology was invented. It has also led to writing several books that explain the relevance of I-O psychology knowledge for a business and technology audience that often has little interest in the actual field of I-O psychology.

Being at the intersection of I-O psychology and technology has placed me in a world of constant innovation and learning, where every challenge creates a new opportunity and every opportunity creates a new challenge. It provides me with a sense of gratitude to know that my work applying psychological principles to technology design and use has positively impacted the careers of millions of employees. It is a blessing to have a career where one can improve the world, advance science, help colleagues, provide for family, and have fun all at the same time.

and identify possible training needs for individuals and workgroups that will enable them to be ready for promotion at a later date. In addition, performance management systems help in the evaluation of various interventions. For example, if an organization invests in a training program for its salespeople, it is possible to see whether their performance improved following the program. If sales increased, the training program may be deemed a success. If performance remained the same or decreased, it provides some evidence that the training program may not be working as intended.

Documentation. In many criterion-related validity studies, assessments of the criterion are derived from performance appraisals. Recall that the criterion is a measure of job performance, and that is what performance appraisals are supposed to measure. When I-O psychologists want to validate a new predictor test, they correlate test scores with criterion measures, which are often exhumed from a company's performance appraisal files. Thus, performance management systems help document the validity of predictor measures used for selection of applicants. In addition, formal performance appraisals provide a legally-defensible basis for personnel decisions. As discussed in Chapter 6, personnel decisions must be based on reason, not caprice. There must be a defensible explanation for why some employees are promoted or discharged or receive differential pay raises compared with others. As will be discussed shortly, personnel decisions based on performance appraisals are subject to the same legal standards as tests. Both tests and performance evaluations are used as techniques for improving human resources. Although performance appraisals may trigger discordant reactions from some employees, the alternative of making personnel decisions with no rational basis is simply unacceptable.

It is important to note that performance management systems often serve multiple purposes concurrently. For example, information from appraisals may be used to provide developmental feedback *and* be used as a basis for salary decisions, rather than simply for developmental purposes. Unfortunately, the "personnel development" and "salary administration" aspects of appraisal are often uncomfortable partners. Many employees attach far more meaning to pay raises, because they are more immediate and instrumental than revelations about weaknesses on the job. If the two functions are combined in the same appraisal, employees can become defensive. When admitting weaknesses means getting a smaller raise, personnel development may take a backseat.

Supervisors must often assume "split roles" when conducting appraisals.[20] One role is a counselor or coach in discussing employee development or performance improvement. The other is a judge in making salary decisions. Unfortunately, evidence shows that most supervisors cannot play both roles simultaneously. The problem may be addressed by having two appraisals—for example, one in January for employee development and the other in June for salary. Or the supervisor may handle development, while the human resources department handles salary. Although both functions are important, it is customary practice that they not be conducted at the same time by the same person.

Performance Appraisal and the Law

Federal law on fair employment practices also pertains to performance appraisal. A review of court cases involving alleged discrimination revealed that charges of discrimination frequently relate to the assessment of an employee's job performance.[21] Charges of discrimination may be brought under the laws discussed in Chapter 3, including Title VII of the Civil Rights Acts of 1964 and 1991, the Age Discrimination in Employment Act, and the Americans with Disabilities Act. In addition, there are charges that can result in litigation that are more closely tied to performance appraisals.

Negligence. Employers may be charged with negligence if they fail to conduct timely appraisals according to company policy. For example, a company policy may be that employee appraisals will occur every year on the employee's anniversary date. If a manager waits too long to give employees their appraisal (and perhaps the pay raise that might accompany it), the employer may be found to be guilty of a breach of duty to conduct appraisals with due care.

Defamation. The disclosure of untrue unfavorable performance information that damages the reputation of the employee can be grounds for litigation. Given that not all appraisals will be positive, it is important that great care is taken to ensure the accuracy of appraisals. For the most part, while performance appraisals will often be considered statements of opinion rather than fact (and therefore not subject to charges of defamation),[22] appraisals are often used as the basis for providing references for future employment. If statements made result in the person not being hired, it could lead to charges of defamation.

Misrepresentation. Employers may be charged with misrepresentation if they disclose untrue favorable performance information that results in a risk of harm to prospective employers or third parties. For example, employers will often refuse to provide negative performance information to a prospective employer to avoid charges of defamation. If this failure to share information results in the person being hired and that person causes harm, the former employer could be held liable due to their misrepresentation of the facts.

Tables 8-1 and 8-2 show recommendations for legally-sound performance appraisals. In terms of the criteria assessed in the appraisal, it is particularly important that employees are evaluated on job-related factors, ideally derived from a job analysis.[23] Procedurally, it is crucial to document performance and let employees know about areas in which they are deficient. The importance of this can be seen in a 2013 court case, *Chlystek v. Donovan*, in which the court sided with an employee who claimed he had been discriminated against because of his age when a younger, less-qualified employee received a promotion instead of him. The employer attempted to defend itself by claiming that the younger employee was promoted because there were performance issues with the older employee. However, the court determined that the older employee had received "glowing reviews" for 16 years, and as such, the employer's claims that the older employee was a poor performer were questionable. Thus, when it comes to performance evaluations, it is important to be fair, yet honest. As this court case showed, it is a mistake to ignore performance problems or sugarcoat them.[24]

As our economy continues to emphasize service and information, there will be the tendency to use subjective performance criteria, particularly at the professional and managerial levels. Also, more organizations are increasingly relying on multiple sources of evaluation (customers, subordinates, and peers). Using both subjective criteria and untrained raters can lead to discrimination claims that are difficult to defend. When such criteria and raters are used, they should be used in conjunction with objective criteria and trained raters whose input is given greater weight.

Table 8-1 *Content recommendations for legally-sound performance appraisals*

Appraisal Criteria
■ Should be objective rather than subjective ■ Should be job-related or based on job (work) analysis ■ Should be based on behaviors rather than traits ■ Should be within the control of the ratee ■ Should relate to specific functions, not global assessments

Source: From "Current Legal Issues in Performance Appraisal," by S. B. Malos, in J. W. Smither (Ed.), *Performance appraisal* (p. 80). Copyright © 1998. Reprinted with permission of John Wiley & Sons, Inc. via Copyright Clearance Center.

Table 8-2 *Procedural recommendations for legally-sound performance appraisals*

Appraisal Procedures
■ Should be standardized and uniform for all employees within a job group ■ Should be formally communicated to employees ■ Should provide notice of performance deficiencies and of opportunities to correct them ■ Should provide access for employees to review appraisal results ■ Should provide formal appeal mechanisms that allow for employee input ■ Should use multiple, diverse, and unbiased raters ■ Should provide written instructions for training raters ■ Should require thorough and consistent documentation across raters that includes specific examples of performance based on personal knowledge ■ Should establish a system to detect potentially discriminatory effects or abuses of the system overall

Source: From "Current Legal Issues in Performance Appraisal," by S. B. Malos, in J. W. Smither (Ed.), *Performance appraisal* (p. 83). Copyright © 1998. Reprinted with permission of John Wiley & Sons, Inc. via Copyright Clearance Center.

Performance Rating Scales

A wide variety of rating scales have been developed, all intended to provide accurate assessments of how people are performing.[25] There are three major types of rating scales used in performance assessment:

1. Graphic rating scales
2. Employee-comparison methods
   a. Rank order
   b. Paired comparison
   c. Forced distribution
3. Behavioral checklists and scales
   a. Critical incidents
   b. Behaviorally anchored rating scales (BARS)

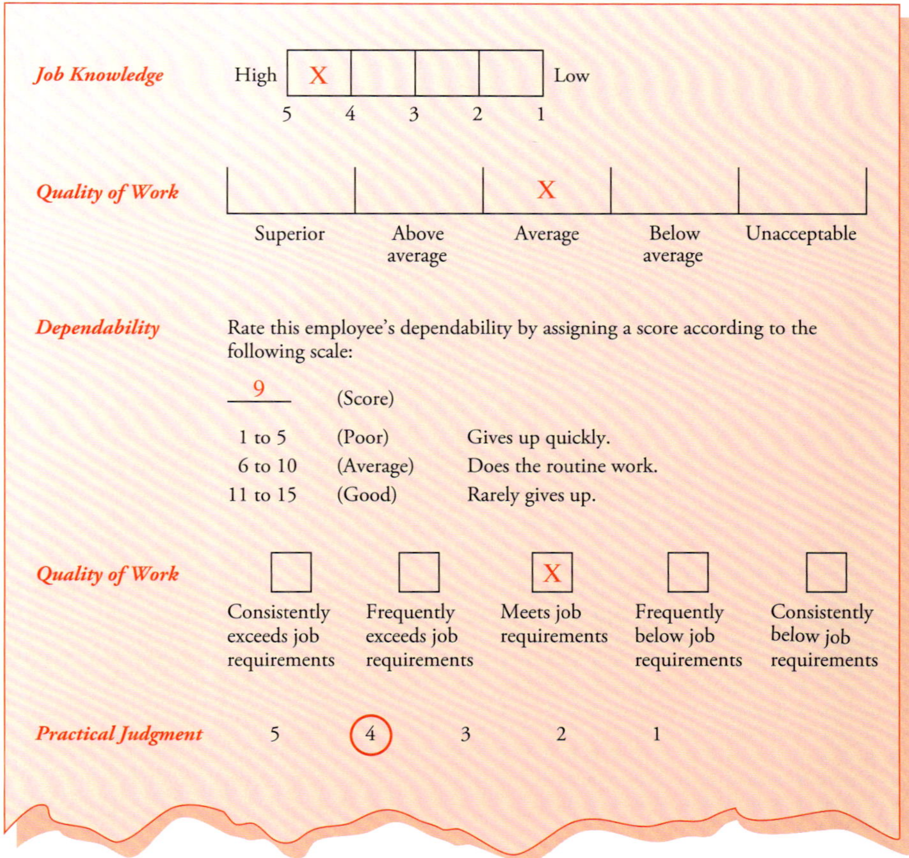

Figure 8-2 *Examples of graphic rating scales for various performance dimensions*

Graphic rating scales are the most commonly used method in performance appraisal. Individuals are rated on a number of traits or factors. The rater judges "how much" of each factor the individual has. Usually, performance is judged on a 5- or 7-point scale, and the number of factors ranges between 5 and 20. The more common dimensions rated are quantity of work, quality of work, practical judgment, job knowledge, cooperation, and motivation. Examples of typical graphic rating scales are shown in Figure 8-2. Graphic rating scales are particularly susceptible to rating errors (discussed in the next section). As such, other methods of performance appraisal have been developed.

Employee-comparison methods involve individuals being compared with one another, not against some defined standard. As a result, not all employees can be rated as equally high (or low), since they are in reference to one another. Raters are compelled to differentiate among the people being rated. The three major employee-comparison methods are rank order, paired comparison, and forced distribution.

With the *rank-order method*, the rater ranks employees from high to low on a given performance dimension. The person ranked first is regarded as the "best" and the person ranked last as the "worst." However, we do not know how good the "best" is or how bad the "worst" is. We do not know the level of performance. For example, the Nobel Prize winners in a given year could be ranked in terms of their overall contributions to science. But we would be hard pressed to conclude that the Nobel laureate ranked last made the worst contribution to science. Rank-order data are all relative to some standard—in this case, excellence in scientific research. Another problem is that it becomes quite tedious and perhaps somewhat meaningless to rank order large numbers of people. What usually happens is that the rater can sort out the people at the top and bottom of the pile. For those with undifferentiated performance, however, the rankings may be somewhat arbitrary.

With the *paired-comparison method*, each employee is compared with every other employee in the group being evaluated. The rater's task is to select which of the two is better on the dimension being rated. The method is typically used to evaluate employees on a single dimension: overall ability to perform the job. The number of evaluation pairs is computed by the formula $n(n - 1)/2$, where n is the number of people to be evaluated. For example, if there are 10 people in a group, the number of paired comparisons is $10(9)/2 = 45$. At the conclusion of the evaluation, the number of times each person was selected as the better of the two is tallied. The people are then ranked by the number of tallies they receive.

A major limitation is that the number of comparisons made mushrooms dramatically with large numbers of employees. If 50 people are to be appraised, the number of comparisons is 1,225; this obviously takes too much time. The paired-comparison method is best for relatively small samples.

The *forced-distribution method* is most useful when the other employee-comparison methods are most limited—that is, when the sample is large. Forced distribution is typically used when the rater must evaluate employees on a single dimension, but it can also be used with multiple dimensions. The procedure is based on the normal distribution and assumes that employee performance is normally distributed, with most employees being average performers, fewer being good or bad performers, and even fewer being exceptionally good or exceptionally bad performers. With this in mind,

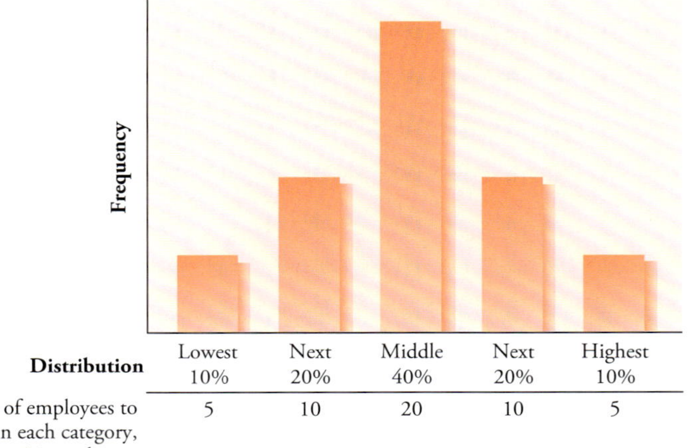

Figure 8-3 *The forced-distribution method of performance appraisal*

the distribution is divided into five to seven categories. Using predetermined percentages (based on the normal distribution), the rater evaluates employees by placing each employee into one of the categories. This method "forces" the rater to distribute the employees across all categories (which is how the method gets its name). Thus, it is impossible for all employees to be rated excellent, average, or poor. An example of the procedure for a sample of 50 employees is illustrated in Figure 8-3.

Some raters react negatively to the forced-distribution method, saying that the procedure creates artificial distinctions among employees. This is partly because the raters think that performance is not normally distributed, but rather negatively skewed; that is, most of their employees are performing very well. The dissatisfaction can be partially allayed by noting that the lowest 10% are not necessarily performing poorly, just not as well as the others. The problem (as with all comparison methods) is that performance is not compared with a defined standard. The meaning of the differences among employees must be supplied from some other source. That said, some individuals are attracted to organizations that use forced distributions. For example, one study showed that individuals who were higher on cognitive ability and believed the forced distribution system was fair were more likely to be attracted to an organization that used such techniques.[26]

Top-grading
A method of performance whereby employees are graded on their overall contribution to the organization, and each year the bottom 10% of the employees are dismissed.

One method of performance appraisal based on the forced distribution method is **top-grading**.[27] This method involves identifying the bottom 10% of a company's workforce (as shown in Figure 8-3) and eliminating their positions. The loss of the bottom 10% of the workforce not only removes the lowest performing employees, but also serves to induce even higher performance in the remaining 90% of the workforce. This is repeated year after year, with the result that the workforce gets progressively better, as well as progressively smaller. It is for this reason that top-grading is also known as a "vitality curve" and "rank and yank." The results of one study supported such a strategy for improving workforce quality, but its effectiveness diminished substantially beyond its initial years of implementation.[28] In addition, "rank and yank" may result in increased adverse impact (as described in Chapter 3) when used for purposes of layoffs. Adverse impact is likely the greatest in the first year following layoffs, and progressively worse over time, especially if those who were "yanked" are replaced.[29] The method also lends itself to internal political maneuvering by managers that has little to do with performance.[30] For example, managers may retain poor performing employees throughout the year just to have someone to rank at the bottom, sparing other employees from being "yanked." It is a statistical fact that no matter how well employees are performing, every year 10% of the workforce must be ranked in the bottom 10%. After repeated "yankings," the bottom 10% may actually be performing their jobs successfully, and it is a matter of debate how much more work the surviving employees can absorb due to the annual departure of 10% of the workforce. Given the ruthless nature of top-grading, it has fallen out of favor as a means of assessing performance, with such companies as Microsoft, Accenture, and Amazon all having used it in the past but abandoning it in recent years.[31]

Behavioral checklists and scales represent some of the most concrete methods of assessing performance. The key term is *behavior*. Rather than focusing on subjective traits (such as "ambition" and "cooperativeness"), employees are assessed on the basis of behaviors that are identified either directly or indirectly via the critical-incidents method. **Critical incidents** are behaviors that result in exceptionally good or poor job performance. Critical incidents are usually grouped by aspects of performance: job knowledge, decision-making ability, leadership, and so on. The end product is a list of behaviors (good and bad) that constitute effective and ineffective job performance.

Critical incidents
Specific behaviors indicative of exceptionally good or bad job performance.

The idea behind critical incidents is that each employee's performance can be described in terms of the occurrence of these critical behaviors. For example, a negative critical incident for a machine operator might be "leaves machine running while unattended." A positive one might be "always wears safety goggles on the job." Discussing performance in such clear terms is more understandable than using such vague statements as "poor attitude" or "careless work habits."

As a rating scale, these behaviors are formed into a checklist that raters use when observing performance. If written well, it should be easy to determine if employees engage in the behaviors. Additionally, feedback can be very specific regarding what was and was not done correctly, thereby leading to more immediate changes in performance.

Behaviorally anchored rating scales (BARS)
A type of performance appraisal rating scale in which the scale points are descriptions of behavior.

Behaviorally anchored rating scales (BARS) are a combination of the critical-incidents and rating-scale methods. Performance is rated on a scale, but the scale points are anchored with behavioral incidents. The development of BARS is time-consuming, especially in reaching agreement on the job behaviors.

Some of the advantages of BARS are that the method has face validity for both the rater and ratee, and also appears useful for training raters. However, one disadvantage is that BARS are job specific; that is, a different behaviorally anchored rating scale must be developed for every job. Furthermore, it is possible for employees to exhibit

Consider This...

Are some behaviors too "obvious" to include in a checklist? Consider this: It is common for hospital patients in intensive care to receive catheters—flexible tubes inserted into the body to remove fluid—during treatment. Unfortunately, many patients who receive catheters experience complications, including pain, infections, and even death.[32] To combat this, Johns Hopkins medical center instituted a 5-step behavioral checklist for medical personnel to follow when inserting catheters: (1) wash hands with soap, (2) clean the patient's skin with antiseptic, (3) cover the entire patient with sterile drapes, (4) wear a sterile mask, hat, gown, and gloves, and (5) put a sterile dressing over the insertion site. Some of these steps may seem obvious—*of course they should wash their hands with soap!*—yet, it was believed that one-third of the time, doctors were skipping one of these critical steps, and approximately one in nine catheters were leading to infection. Therefore, nurses were instructed to evaluate doctors according to all five steps and intervene if any were skipped. Within one year of using the checklist, the infection rate from central line catheters dropped from 11% to 0%. Two years after its use, it was estimated that the checklist had prevented 43 infections, avoided 8 deaths, and saved the hospital approximately $2 million! What are some other jobs that might benefit from checklists that include seemingly "obvious" behaviors?

different behaviors (on a single performance dimension) depending on situational factors such as the degree of urgency.

The accuracy of judgmental evaluations in performance appraisal refers to the extent to which the ratings are valid measures of the "true" variable being measured. The "true" variable can refer to a global construct, such as overall job performance, or a dimension of job performance, such as interpersonal relations ability. One method of assessing the accuracy of judgmental data is to correlate them with performance appraisals from another method, such as objective production data. In studies that have conducted this type of analysis, the resulting correlations have been only moderate. Although these results may be interpreted to mean that judgmental data exhibit only moderate validity, the key question is whether the objective production data can be assumed to represent "true" performance. Objective production data might be incomplete or marginally relevant. Because we never obtain measures of the conceptual criterion (that is, "true" performance), we are forced to deal with imperfect measures that, not surprisingly, yield imperfect results. Indeed, rater disagreement and halo error exist even among such expert raters as Olympic judges, who are intensely trained to make accurate evaluations.[33] Instructing raters to keep a structured diary for continuous record keeping of performance (rather than using memory recall) also appears to produce more accurate assessments of the employees.[34]

After many years of research on various types of performance appraisal rating scales, I-O psychologists have concluded that the variance in rated performance due to the rating scale format is slight, typically less than 5%. Other sources of variance in rated performance are more substantial. These topics are examined next.

Rating Errors and Biases

As discussed, the most common means of appraising performance is through judgmental ratings. Because errors occur in making ratings, it is important to understand the major types of rating errors and biases that impact evaluations. Biases occur when raters evaluate ratees higher or lower for a reason other than the criteria of interest. For example, raters may give higher ratings to individuals whom they perceive as being similar to them, a bias known as the *similar-to-me effect*. Personality characteristics of the rater can also impact their judgments, creating biased assessments. For instance, rater agreeableness, extraversion, and emotional stability are all significantly positively related to their ratings.[35] Similarly, introverted employees appear to rate their extraverted and disagreeable peers lower than their other peers.[36] Thus, raters' personality traits influence performance ratings. Factors about the ratee can also lead to biased ratings. For example, men who cry in response to negative feedback appear to be more likely to receive biased evaluations from raters, given such behavior is seen as atypical in the workplace.[37]

Serial position error
A rating error in which the rater has better recall of information presented at the beginning or end of a sequence, and worse recall of information in the middle of the sequence.

Contrast error
A rating error in which the rater assesses ratees as performing better (or worse) than they actually performed due to comparisons with other ratees who performed particularly poorly (or well).

Halo error
A rating error in which the rater assesses the ratee as performing well on a variety of dimensions, despite having credible knowledge of only a limited number of performance dimensions.

In addition, when making appraisals, the rater may unknowingly commit relatively common errors in judgment. Serial position errors occur as a function of the sequence in which information is received. Contrast errors are a result of a faulty comparison of two (or more) individuals. Others, such as halo errors, leniency errors, and central-tendency errors, occur in part as a function of the rating scales used. Each of these errors (discussed next) stem from rater bias and misperception.

Serial position errors reflect the tendency for individuals to remember information when it is presented at a certain place within a sequence (or its serial position: e.g., first, second, last). Research has demonstrated that people are better at recalling information presented first (the *primacy effect*) or last (the *recency effect*) in a sequence. This means that raters will be more likely to recall information about individuals they observe first or last. Similarly, they will be better able to recall information early in one's relationship (e.g., first impressions) or information from events that just recently occurred. Thus, if evaluations are only occurring once every six months, the most recent behavior may be given more weight than behavior exhibited at other times.

Contrast error occurs when raters compare (or contrast) one individual with another when making evaluations. This would only be an error if individuals are supposed to be compared against a set standard rather than against one another. Managers are likely to have contrast effects when they rate numerous people within a short time period. If a manager evaluates a particularly strong employee, the employee that is rated afterwards may seem worse by comparison. If the manager rates the second employee lower than what they might have if the strong employee had not been rated previously, then a contrast error has occurred. The same issue arises when employees are rated higher than they should be simply because they are being compared to a weak employee.

Halo errors are evaluations based on the rater's general opinions about an employee. Halo errors occur when the rater generally has a *favorable* attitude toward the employee that permeates all evaluations of this person. When a rater has a generally *unfavorable* attitude about an employee that permeates evaluations, it is referred to as

Consider This...

While the term "contrast error" may be new to you, the concept is likely one you've encountered many times, and might even have used to your benefit. Consider a situation in which a classmate gives an amazing presentation. Are you more or less likely to volunteer to go next? If you are like a lot of students, you are less likely to raise your hand and you may even try to avoid eye contact with the instructor. On the other hand, you might be more willing to volunteer if the person who just went did a terrible job. You're essentially capitalizing on the contrast effect, by avoiding looking worse by comparison to the stellar presenter and attempting to look better by comparison to the poor presenter. What are some other examples in which you may have used the contrast error to help you? Can you think of times the contrast error may have led to worse ratings for you? How did it make you feel? How might the situation have been prevented?

a *horn* error. Typically, the rater has strong feelings about at least one important aspect of the employee's performance. The feelings are then generalized to other performance factors, and the employee is judged (across many factors) as uniformly good or bad. Whereas an employee truly may be good or bad across many areas, it is when these evaluations are based on insufficient information that it is considered an error. For example, a rater who is impressed by an employee's particularly good idea might allow those feelings to carry over to the evaluation of leadership, cooperation, motivation, and so on. This occurs even though the "good idea" is not related to these other factors. Some consider halo errors to be the most serious and pervasive of all rating errors.[38]

Leniency error
A rating error in which the rater assesses a disproportionately large number of ratees as performing well (positive leniency) or poorly (negative leniency) in contrast to their true levels of performance.

Leniency errors are yet another type of rating error that impacts evaluations. Just as some teachers are "hard graders" and others "easy graders," raters can be characterized by the leniency of their appraisals. Harsh raters give evaluations that are lower than the "true" level of ability (if it can be ascertained); this is called *severity* or *negative leniency*. Easy raters give evaluations that are higher than the "true" level; this is called *positive leniency*. These errors usually occur because raters apply personal standards derived from their own values or previous experience. It appears that the tendency to make leniency errors is stable with individuals; that is, people tend to be consistently lenient or harsh in their ratings.[39] In addition, research suggests that the most lenient raters are those high in agreeableness and low in assertiveness and performance management competence.[40]

Central-tendency error
A rating error in which the rater assesses a disproportionately large number of ratees as performing in the middle or central part of a distribution of rated performance in contrast to their true levels of performance.

Central-tendency error refers to the rater's unwillingness to assign extreme—high or low—ratings. In contrast to leniency and severity errors, where individuals' ratings are unjustifiably high or low, everyone is "average," and only the middle (central) part of the scale is used with central-tendency errors. This may happen when raters are asked to evaluate unfamiliar aspects of performance. Rather than not respond, they play it safe and say the person is average in this "unknown" ability.

Worthy of note is the point that the absence of rating errors does not necessarily indicate *accuracy* in the ratings. The presence of the rating errors leads to inaccurate ratings, but accuracy involves other issues besides the removal of these error types. I-O psychologists are seeking to develop statistical indicators of rating accuracy, some based on classical issues in measurement.

Consider This...

The rating errors and biases noted above are the most frequently studied, but not the only ones that exist. For example, there is evidence that women receive less frequent feedback than men,[41] and that the feedback they receive is less honest.[42] In addition, there appears to be a backlash against women who violate gender-role norms, such that women who embody agentic traits (those pertaining to assertiveness, independence, and competence) are viewed more negatively than those who embody communal traits (those pertaining to interpersonal sensitivity and a concern for others). This is because there is a stereotype that men are more agentic and women are more communal, and therefore a woman who exhibits agentic traits is seen as violating gender norms. These women are viewed as less likeable, less hireable, and less worthy of promotions and salary increases.[43] Within performance reviews, they also receive more negatively-phrased agentic terms, and positive feedback related to gender role-aligned behaviors, showing that the bias is indeed based on a violation of norms.[44] Do these findings concern you? What other biases would you guess exist within the performance management realm? What would you suggest to managers and employees for combatting these rating errors and biases?

Rater Training

Rater error training The process of educating raters about the various rating errors that exist and how to minimize their frequency of occurrence.

Frame-of-reference training The process of providing a common perspective and set of standards to all raters to increase the accuracy of their evaluations.

Raters can be trained to make fewer rating errors. Three of the most common types of rater training include rater error training, frame-of-reference training, and behavioral observation training. **Rater error training** is a formal process in which appraisers are taught about the typical errors that exist when rating others, with the idea being that having an awareness of the errors and what causes them will lead to a reduction in their occurrence.

One concern raised with rater error training is that the reduction of errors does not necessarily increase accuracy in ratings, which presumably is the ultimate goal of training raters. For example, certain types of rater training reduce classic rating errors such as halo and leniency but do not increase rating accuracy.[45] By increasing rater awareness of these effects, raters may actually over-correct their behaviors (such as becoming more severe to combat leniency). In addition, sometimes raters give uniformly high ratings to an employee that are in fact justified. That is, the employee truly performs well across many dimensions. Raters who are taught about halo effect, however, may "correct" themselves and provide more variation in their ratings, thereby resulting in decreased rather than increased accuracy. The relationship between rating errors and accuracy is uncertain because of our inability to know what "truth" is.[46]

The problems described above have led to a greater focus in rater training on increasing accuracy rather than on the reduction of errors.[47] A particularly promising approach to this is **frame-of-reference training**, which involves providing raters with common reference standards (i.e., frames) by which to evaluate performance.[48] Raters are shown vignettes of good, poor, and average performances and are given feedback on the accuracy of their ratings of the vignettes. The objective of frame-of-reference training is to provide raters a uniform standard (or a frame of reference) for making performance evaluations.[49] That is, the dimensions are explained, and examples are given, to demonstrate what various levels of execution look like for each dimension. The logic is that individuals can be trained to utilize the same standards of judgments as possessed by highly knowledgeable experts in rendering evaluations. In this way, raters can be "calibrated" so that they agree on what constitutes varying levels of performance effectiveness for each performance dimension.[50] Frame-of-reference training is helpful in teaching raters to pay more attention to certain dimensions of job behavior (e.g., oral communication) compared to an ideal standard.[51] A meta-analytic review of frame-of-reference training found that frame-of-reference training is an effective rater training method that does appear to improve rating accuracy.[52]

Behavioral observation training
The process of teaching raters what to observe and how best to record, recall, and use their observations for performance ratings.

The third type of rater training is **behavioral observation training**, which seeks to make raters better at observing, recalling, and using observation for their performance assessments. In a typical behavioral observation training program, raters are provided with critical incidents to watch for when rating others. They are also taught how to use such tools as diaries to aid in the recording of observations to be used at a later date. The diary not only serves as a record-keeping tool, but also as a memory aid, so that biases such as recency effect or halo error are less likely to appear in ratings.

Rater Motivation

While distortions in ratings may certainly be unintentional, such as those that occur due to the biases and errors described above, there are also intentional distortions that are common. These intentional distortions have been described as being "games raters play" and are in some ways adaptive and necessary.[53] For example, if there is a sense that most other raters are inflating their ratings of their subordinates, then good raters have to play politics to protect and enhance the careers of their own subordinates. To the extent that a rating inflation strategy actually enhances the prospects of the better subordinates, it may be interpreted as being in the best interests of the organization to do so. Indeed, if it is the norm within the organization to distort ratings, not doing so can be viewed as problematic.

Rater motivation
A concept that refers to organizationally-induced pressures that compel raters to distort their evaluations.

Rater motivation, also referred to as *conscious rating*, refers to the deliberate distortion of ratings.[54] These distortions occur when raters purposefully give ratees scores that are higher or lower than they actually deserve. These distortions typically occur to achieve some particular result. Intentional rating distortion is more likely to be a result of the rater's *unwillingness* to provide accurate ratings than of their *capacity* to rate accurately. If the situation is examined from the rater's perspective, there are many reasons to provide inaccurate ratings.

Managers tend to have one of four intentions when rating their employees.[55] First, they may intend to *be accurate*, or rate objectively and impartially. However, there are typically no rewards from the organization for accurate appraisals and few, if any, sanctions for inaccurate appraisals. Official company policies often emphasize the value of accurate performance appraisals, but organizations typically take no specific steps to reward this supposedly valued activity. Thus, even if the intention is to be accurate, this may not be the final result.

Managers may also intend to *avoid conflict* or appease their employees. Negative evaluations typically result in defensive reactions from subordinates, which can be stressful for raters. The simplest way to avoid unpleasant or defensive reactions in appraisal interviews is to give uniformly positive feedback (i.e., inflated ratings). Giving everyone high ratings may be seen by raters as a way to keep morale high and interpersonal relationships good.[56] For example, raters sometimes have the goal of increasing group harmony.[57] When this is their goal, they tend to provide more uniformly inflated ratings across employees.

The third intention is *benevolence*. In this case, managers hope to provide the employee with a considerate or helpful rating. For example, it may be that high ratings are needed to guarantee promotions, salary increases, and other valued rewards. Low ratings, on the other hand, result in these rewards being withheld from subordinates. Managers may be motivated to obtain valued rewards for their employees. Related to the notion of benevolence is liking, or the interpersonal attraction a rater may have for the person being rated. Research shows that the extent to which a rater likes the ratee is strongly positively related to the ratings they assign.[58] However, ratings aren't as distorted for ratings of organizational citizenship, or for when ratings are made for the purpose of development, or for when ratings are made by peers. It is important to note that these findings are based on correlations, which means causality is unclear. It could be that raters inflate ratings because they like the employee. Conversely, it could also be that raters tend to like employees who are better performers. Nevertheless, it is clear that benevolence and liking are clear reasons that rating distortion occasionally occurs.

Finally, managers may rate with the intention of *impression management*, or making themselves appear in a better light. For example, one of the duties of managers is to develop their subordinates. If managers consistently rate their subordinates as less than good performers, it can appear that the managers are not doing their jobs. Thus, high ratings make the rater look good and low ratings make the rater look bad. Whatever intentions managers have for employees will determine how they rate the employees.

The above examples all depict rating inflation. However, raters may also intentionally provide employees with deflated ratings, or ratings lower than their performance might suggest they deserve. Raters may artificially lower their ratings of employees to shock employees and alert them that there is a problem that needs to be addressed.[59] In addition, raters may deflate their ratings to teach an employee a lesson, or send a signal that the employee may want to consider looking elsewhere for employment. Finally, raters might give harsher ratings to provide compelling documentation in the event that the employee is terminated in the near future. The raters may be attempting to create a "paper trail" to justify their future actions by providing ratings that indicate performance is below standards. In this way, they may be trying to avoid potential legal recourse resulting from a termination without cause (terminations that are unrelated to misconduct).

These examples demonstrate that raters can easily distort their ratings to achieve desired goals. Furthermore, managers tend to vary their rating distortions by employee to achieve their goals. For example, one study found that raters lowered the performance ratings of high performers to achieve greater fairness (i.e., fewer differences among those being rated), and elevated the ratings of low performers to motivate them.[60] Additionally, rater motivation is influenced by the purpose of the rating. Research has revealed that ratings for administrative purposes tend to be more lenient than those made for developmental purposes.[61]

There is no simple way to counteract a rater's motivation to distort ratings. The problem will not be solved by just increasing the capability of raters. In addition, the environment must be modified in such a way that raters are motivated to provide accurate ratings. Accurate ratings are most likely to occur in environments where the following conditions exist:[62]

- Good and poor performance are clearly defined.
- Distinguishing among workers in terms of their levels of performance is widely accepted.
- There is a high degree of trust in the system.
- Low ratings do not automatically result in the loss of valued rewards.
- Valued rewards are clearly linked to accuracy in performance appraisal.

The importance of the context in which ratings are made is further demonstrated by meta-analytic findings that being held accountable by the ratee results in consistently higher ratings, whereas being held accountable by a superior results in no discernable distortion.[63] Thus, it seems that the problem of rating inflation will more likely be solved by changing the context in which ratings are made, not by changing the rater or the rating scale.

Peer and Self-Assessments

Most research on judgmental performance appraisal deals with evaluations made by a superior (supervisor, manager). However, valuable information about job performance can also be provided by colleagues or peers. Self-evaluations will also be discussed. Our knowledge is somewhat limited, but these methods do offer added understanding of performance.

Peer Assessments

Peer assessment
A technique of performance appraisal in which individuals assess the behavior of their peers or coworkers. Peer assessments include nominations, ratings, and rankings.

In **peer assessment**, members of a group appraise the performance of their fellow peers. Three techniques are commonly used. One is **peer nomination**, in which each person names a specified number of coworkers as being highest on the particular dimension of performance. This is a common approach used when a limited number of employees must be identified for a promotion, award, training program, or the like. The second is **peer ratings**, in which each group member appraises the others on a set of performance dimensions, using one of several kinds of rating scales. The third technique is **peer ranking**, where each member places all others in order from best to worst on one or more performance dimensions.

Peer nomination
A technique of appraising the performance of coworkers by identifying a specified number of coworkers who are the best on a particular performance dimension.

Peer ratings
A technique of appraising the performance of coworkers by evaluating them on a dimension of their job behavior.

Peer ranking
A technique of appraising the performance of coworkers by placing them in order from best to worst on a dimension of their job behavior.

The reliability of peer assessments is determined by the degree of inter-rater agreement. Most studies report high reliability coefficients (in the .80s and .90s), indicating that peers agree about the job performance of group members. The validity of peer assessments is determined by correlating them with criterion measures usually made later, such as who successfully completed a training program, who got promoted first, the size of raises, and so on. What is uncanny is that group members who have known one another a relatively short time (two to three weeks) can be quite accurate in their long-term predictions about one another. Validity coefficients are impressive, commonly in the .40–.50 range. That said, researchers have found that peer ratings vary depending on how connected they are to the person being evaluated. Peers who are well-connected to another peer are considered to be in the peer's core network, whereas those with fewer direct connections are in their peripheral network. Core peer ratings are more valid predictors of job performance than peripheral peer ratings, perhaps because they are based on firsthand (vs. secondhand) performance information.[64]

The peer nomination technique appears best in identifying people who have extreme levels of attributes as compared with other members of the group. Peer nominations are limited in that they fail to capture the complexities of social interactions.[65] Individuals may be nominated for reasons having little to do with the attribute under consideration. For example, individuals may be nominated as a repayment for a past social debt (e.g., "I owe you"), out of reciprocity (e.g., "I'll nominate you if you nominate me"), or to create a future social debt (e.g., "I nominated you and now you owe me"). Peer ratings are used most often, but have only marginal empirical support. It has been suggested that their use be limited to giving feedback to employees on how others perceive them. Relatively little research is available on the value of peer rankings.

There is some evidence that peer assessments are biased by friendship (that is, employees evaluate their friends most favorably), but friendships may be formed on the basis of performance. Also, many work group members do not like to evaluate one another, so part of the method's success hinges on convincing participants of its value. Indeed, lack of user acceptance may be a serious obstacle to this otherwise-promising method.

Consider This...

Over four decades ago, a sample of college professors reported that peer assessments were heavily biased by friendship, with peers likely rating and being rated by their friends more favorably than would be justified.[66] Problems with knowing the people to be rated and fostering a "mutual admiration society" caused the professors to question the value of peer assessment. Do you think this is still the case? In what situations might peer assessments be less likely to suffer from a friendship bias? How might you design a study to test your assertion?

Although peers may have the same or similar job titles, there can be contextual differences in their jobs that serve to diminish their equivalence as peers (or equals).[67] For example, the manager of human resources, the manager of sales, and the manager of finance are all managers. However, despite being at the same organizational level (manager), they may have considerably different responsibilities and perspectives, thereby weakening their degree of comparability. Despite reluctance to use peer assessments for administrative decisions, research continues to support their predictive accuracy. Indeed, peer assessments appear to be superior to self-assessments in predicting advancement.[68]

Self-Assessments

Self-assessment
A technique of performance appraisal in which individuals assess their own behavior.

With **self-assessment**, as the term suggests, employees appraise their own performance. Self-assessments are used to help individuals make decisions regarding where to focus their attention and how much effort to exert.[69] As would be expected, individuals are likely to devote attention to areas where they see deficits and ignore areas that they don't see as requiring any improvements. Unfortunately, individuals don't appear to have a good understanding of their strengths and weaknesses. Self-assessments of job performance are higher than assessments from others.[70] For example, a survey of 393 Canadian police officers and found that close to 80% of the officers believed they were in the top 10-20% performers.[71] Statistically, this is quite a trick! This underscores the biggest problem with self-assessment: positive leniency. Most people have higher opinions of their own performance than others do. If they believe they are more skilled than they actually are, they are unlikely to devote the necessary attention to improving in those areas.

Dunning-Kruger effect
A cognitive bias in which individuals overestimate their knowledge or skills, especially individuals with low knowledge or ability.

This tendency for people to believe they are smarter and more capable than they are in reality is quite common, and is termed the **Dunning-Kruger effect**. This effect is especially pronounced for individuals of lower ability, suggesting that low performers fail to recognize what it takes to perform well. That is, the very knowledge and skills that are needed to be good at a task are the same ones that a person needs in order to know if they are good (or bad) at it. If a person lacks those skills or abilities, they will not only perform poorly but will also be ignorant of their poor performance.[72] In line with this, one study revealed that self-ratings of job performance were *negatively* correlated with the personnel selection test scores used to hire the employees into their jobs.[73]

One clever study demonstrated just how prevalent and pervasive inflation bias is in self-assessments of ability.[74] Applicants were asked to rate their own abilities in real clerical tasks as well as in bogus tasks that sounded real but were nonsense. Three of the bogus tasks were "operating a matriculation machine," "typing from audio-fortran reports," and "circumscribing general meeting registers." The clerical applicants rated themselves high on the real tasks (where their ability was not verified) and also on the tasks that did not even exist. Another study found that managers evaluated themselves more leniently compared with both how they evaluated their supervisors and how their supervisors evaluated them.[75] The reason for this may pertain to perceptions of factors beyond the control of the individual.[76] When we rate ourselves, we tend not to lower our own evaluations if we perceive that any shortcomings in our performance were beyond our control. When other people rate us, however, they tend to perceive us as being responsible for our performance. Thus, it may be that self-assessments are of higher quality when used for developmental purposes rather than for administrative purposes.[77]

360° Feedback

360° feedback
A process of evaluating employees from multiple rating sources, usually including supervisor, peer, subordinate, and self. Also called multisource feedback.

The technique of **360° (360-degree) feedback**, also called *multisource feedback* (MSF), is the practice of using multiple raters from different perspectives in the assessment of individuals. The term "360° feedback" derives from the geometric rationale for multiple-rater assessment, as shown in Figure 8-4. The target employee is evaluated by other individuals, who interact in a social network. For example, feedback about a target employee may be solicited from the individual's coworkers, subordinates, customers, and superiors. The employee also provides self-assessments. The multiple raters make their assessments of the employee, and then the assessments are compared. The original purpose for MSF was to enhance individuals' awareness of their strengths and weaknesses to guide developmental planning. It now serves a multitude of purposes for organizations, including performance management, staffing, and the identification of high-potential employees, to name a few.[78]

360° feedback programs are seen as effective if they lead to sustained behavior change.[79] In terms of ensuring effectiveness, raters should be held accountable for providing accurate and useful feedback, ratees should be held accountable to use the feedback they receive, and organizations as a whole should be held accountable for providing resources for employees to improve based on the feedback.[80] In addition, 360° feedback program participants should have an accountability partner and at-work learning partner who help identify strengths and developmental needs, aid in establishing goals, and help participants practice new behaviors and discover strategies for improvement.[81]

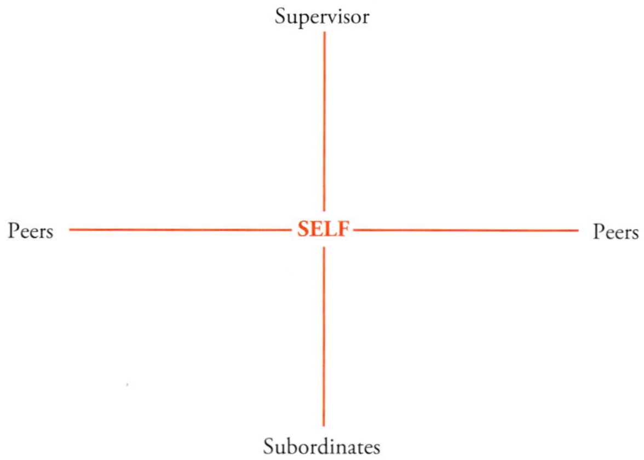

Figure 8-4 *360° feedback relationships*

Beyond accountability, ratees should share the results of their 360° assessments with their raters.[82] Similar to telling friends and loved ones about New Year's resolutions, sharing their MSF results is a way to publicly acknowledge their commitment to their developmental efforts. Moreover, without some follow-up between the ratee and the raters, raters may feel nothing is being done with their feedback, and negative attitudes toward the ratee and the process may develop.[83]

MSF assessment activities are usually based on two key assumptions: (1) awareness of any discrepancies between how we see ourselves and how others see us enhances self-awareness, and (2) enhanced self-awareness is a key to maximum performance as a manager, and thus becomes a foundation for management and leadership development programs.[84] Self-awareness involves an understanding of how people see themselves (and how they make those assessments) and an understanding of how others perceive them.[85] This latter component is particularly important, and people should be asked not only to assess themselves, but also to predict how others will assess them. Indeed, asking people to predict how others will rate them may result in lower defensiveness and subsequently greater openness to the feedback received.[86]

Consider This...

It is particularly instructive to understand how *disagreement* among raters in 360° feedback is interpreted. The classic measurement perspective treats disagreement among raters as error variance—that is, something undesirable that reduces inter-rater reliability. With 360° feedback, however, differences in rater perspectives are regarded as potentially valuable and useful, and are not treated as errors per se. For example, when your self-ratings differ substantially from those of a boss or peer group, it may be indicative of a "blind spot" that can be clarified through discussions. Such differences provide an opportunity for professional development and personal learning, to understand why you are perceived as you are by others. Sometimes the problem is simply that you haven't demonstrated your abilities to some people. Sometimes it's a matter of different skillsets that are valued, so you're good at what one group values, but another group values something else. With this in mind, if you received feedback from your peers that said you were a good performer, but your boss thought you were a poor performer, what would you do? Is it important to you that people view you in the same way across perspectives? Why or why not?

A disturbing finding regarding the accuracy of MSF is that performance ratings appear to be more strongly influenced by idiosyncratic rating tendencies of individuals and the source of the ratings (peers, subordinates, supervisor) than the specific dimensions of behavior (e.g., leadership, interpersonal skills, etc.) being rated.[87] Along these lines, subordinates appear to be more lenient and fall prey to halo errors more so than peers and superiors.[88] In fact, some researchers have concluded that MSF given to managers on the basis of traditional behavioral dimensions (e.g., leadership, sociability, etc.) is not helpful in enhancing job performance.[89] That is, managers could use the feedback to improve *themselves* along these dimensions (e.g., they could become more sociable), but such improvements will not necessarily translate into improved *job performance*. The rationale for the development purpose of MSF is that behavioral change will result in improved job performance. It may be that feedback of a different type might be more effective at increasing job performance.

I-O psychologists are divided in their opinions about the use of 360° feedback for both developmental and administrative purposes. The term *feedback* suggests that the method is best suited for its original intent, providing developmental feedback to employees. However, in recent years, some organizations have shifted to use 360° feedback for both developmental *and* administrative purposes. There are various issues associated with using 360° feedback for dual purposes, as shown in Table 8-3.[90] The major practical differences between the two purposes include source anonymity (i.e., the actual identity of the peers and subordinates), the implications of negative feedback, and adherence to legal guidelines. In short, both the employer's responsibilities and the employee's adaptive behavior differ as a function of how MSF is used by the organization.

It is important to carefully determine the purpose of a 360° feedback system and then clearly communicate and monitor the system in accordance with the stated purpose. Simply put, an organization should not state that MSF is used for only

Table 8-3 *The effects of purpose on MSF systems*

Decision Points	Developmental Purposes	Administrative Purposes
1. Content of instrument	Tied to employee short- and long-term developmental needs	Tied to job description or established performance goals
2. Frequency of use	As needed	Consistent with performance review timetable
3. Source anonymity	Of less importance	Of critical importance
4. Threat/implications of negative feedback	Low (limited consequences)	High (potentially serious consequences)
5. Data ownership	Individual receiving feedback	Organization
6. Adherence to legal guidelines	Of less importance	Of great importance

Source: From Balzer, W. K., Greguras, G. J., and Raymark, P. H., "Multisource Feedback," in J. C. Thomas (Ed.), *Comprehensive handbook of psychological assessment*, Vol. 4. Copyright © 2003, by M. Hersen. Reprinted with permission of John C. Wiley & Sons, Inc., via Copyright Clearance Center.

developmental purposes and then discharge an employee due to low evaluations (such as from peers). Some experts think that it may be possible to gradually shift from development-only MSF to a system that also is used for administrative decision making. Others are far less confident.

Feedback in Performance Management Contexts

As noted earlier, providing feedback is the third step in the performance management process. Without feedback, employee performance may actually decline rather than improve. Feedback on job performance has two properties: information and motivation. Feedback can tell the employee how to perform better as well as increase the desire to perform well. In this section, we discuss research related to giving and seeking feedback as well as typical reactions to feedback.

"We all need people who will give us feedback. That's how we improve."
—Bill Gates

Giving Feedback

The process of giving feedback is an essential part of the performance management process. It is also one of the most difficult and most dreaded activities, by both supervisors and employees, mainly because not all feedback is likely to be positive in nature. Despite negative feedback's role in increasing substandard performance and guiding subsequent employee development, supervisors tend to dislike giving it. The reluctance or failure of individuals to communicate bad news is known as the "mum effect" and is a pervasive and problematic phenomenon.[91] Individuals often avoid giving negative feedback in an effort to protect themselves and abide by organizational norms.[92] This tendency to delay giving negative feedback is likely to backfire, with many managers not giving feedback until problems are severe and their annoyance with the problems is at extremely high levels. At this point, emotions are elevated and the feedback provided may be overly harsh.[93] The destructive nature of the feedback detracts from the purpose of the message and all but ensures its rejection.

A large-scale meta-analysis on the effects of feedback on performance found that, although feedback generally improves performance, roughly one-third of feedback interventions actually result in decreased, rather than increased, performance.[94] They found that when feedback is directed at the self rather than at the task, the effectiveness of the feedback decreases. Thus, to be successful and result in performance improvement, feedback should be focused on behaviors and tasks, and not on the feedback recipient's traits or personal characteristics. In addition, individuals have to be careful when giving negative feedback, as it may be perceived as a personal attack, particularly for highly-competitive individuals.[95] As such, it is advisable to train everyone within organizations on how to deliver feedback in considerate and nonthreatening ways.

Seeking Feedback

In addition to passively receiving feedback, employees can also actively seek feedback. With an increasing number of individuals working virtually and having less direct contact with their supervisors and peers, the only way that many people have of knowing how well they are doing is to proactively seek input from others. There are three motives people have for seeking feedback from others.[96] These motives influence whether individuals will seek, and how they will seek, information from other people.

1. **Instrumental Motive:** Individuals may seek feedback from others to improve their performance. By finding out how others view their performance, employees have a better understanding of where they should focus their attention. Along these lines, organizational newcomers seek feedback relatively frequently at first, and then less so as they "learn the ropes."[97] In addition, people are more likely to seek feedback from sources they see as being credible, in part because they see the value of the feedback as being higher.[98]

"If you want to improve, you must be content to be thought foolish and stupid."

—Epictetus

2. **Ego-based Motive:** Individuals may also seek feedback to defend or enhance their views of themselves. Feedback can be very intimidating for people. To the extent it is negative, it has the potential to hurt one's self-image. As a result, it isn't surprising that many people avoid feedback altogether. Alternatively, employees may distort feedback or discount it if it fails to conform to their positive, ego-protective views of themselves. In general, individuals who are more confident in themselves and who think more highly of themselves are more likely to seek feedback.[99]

3. **Image-based Motive:** Individuals may be motivated to seek feedback to make themselves look better to other people. For example, people might seek feedback from others when they are in a good mood, or from people with whom they are friends, to obtain positive feedback that makes them look good. Along these lines, individuals may be less likely to seek feedback if they believe the feedback will make them look bad.

Whether individuals will seek feedback is influenced by their self-efficacy and whether they can and do consider others' perspectives. Specifically, a series of studies revealed that when individuals feel capable of being successful (they have high self-efficacy), they are less likely to seek feedback if they don't consider others' viewpoints.

However, they are more likely to seek feedback if they put themselves in others' shoes and imagine things from that other person's perspective.[100] The organizational environment is also important in determining the extent to which individuals will seek feedback. For example, individuals appear to be more likely to seek feedback in a supportive feedback environment.[101] A supportive feedback environment is one in which the quality of feedback is high, sources are credible and available, people are considerate when delivering feedback, and feedback seeking is encouraged. Along these lines, employees are more likely to seek feedback from their colleagues and their supervisor when they believe that mistakes and problems that may be brought up won't be held against them.[102] The organizational culture can also impact how feedback seeking is viewed. Some cultures may create the sense that feedback seeking is a sign of insecurity.[103] Nevertheless, unless they are poor performers already, individuals tend to be viewed more positively rather than negatively for seeking feedback from others.[104]

Consider This...

Elon Musk, entrepreneur and business magnate, once said, "Really pay attention to negative feedback and solicit it, particularly from friends. Hardly anyone does that, and it's incredibly helpful." He has certainly shown his willingness to do this himself, as his tweet from February, 2020 demonstrates, in which he solicited critical feedback from the public. Some might consider it scary to seek feedback like this in such a public forum, where the whole world will know whether or not you actually listened to and responded to the feedback. It can also be humbling if you received a lot of negative feedback and very little positive feedback. Would you be willing to seek feedback in this way? What influences the ways you seek feedback and from whom you seek it?

Please let us know what improvements we can make to any aspect of Tesla SolarGlass roof! Critical feedback is much appreciated.

11:25 AM · Feb 10, 2020 · Twitter for iPhone

Reactions to Feedback

Reactions to feedback are among some of the most important issues in the workplace.[105] In particular, reactions to feedback are an important predictor of performance.[106] Initial negative feedback leads to increased effort, but repeated negative feedback may result in decreased effort, lowered goals, rejection of the feedback, or withdrawal from the task. In addition, if somebody attributes negative feedback to something that is within their control, they are likely to exert more effort to remedy the issue.[107] If, however, they believe that the feedback is about something that they can't influence, there is little reason to believe they will try to change their behaviors, and as such, performance is not likely to improve.

Reactions are in part dependent on the feedback provider as well as the feedback itself. For example, it is unlikely that employees will accept or choose to respond to feedback provided from an invalid or inaccurate rating system.[108] Reactions also depend in part on the recipient's understanding of the feedback (see The Lighter Side of I-O Psychology: *You Rock!*). In line with the Dunning-Kruger effect discussed earlier, the acceptance of feedback and desire to seek self-improvement are also impacted by one's competence. A series of studies revealed that the least-skilled individuals were the most oblivious to their performance deficits, believing their performance to be better than it really was. When provided with explicit feedback about their deficiencies, these low-skilled individuals were likely to disparage and discount, or ignore, the feedback and make fewer plans for self-improvements.[109]

The Lighter Side of I-O Psychology: *You Rock!*

For feedback to be effective, it must be understood. This means that the feedback provider must be clear, and the feedback recipient must be paying attention and capable of comprehending the feedback. Nevertheless, misunderstandings are bound to occur. Thankfully, such misunderstandings are often easily remedied and occasionally funny. For example, when Tori was in graduate school, she and her friend Jaime (who teaches at Eastern Kentucky University) had to give a class presentation together. Although they had thoroughly prepared and knew their material, they were still very nervous. They took deep breaths and gave their presentation. After class, their professor gave them feedback. She looked at Tori and Jaime and said, "Well, you rocked." Jaime and Tori turned to each other, high-fived, and began congratulating themselves. Their professor interrupted them by saying, "No... you rocked... as in you swayed back and forth." This funny, albeit humbling, moment was very impactful. Jaime and Tori are more cognizant of their movements when presenting to avoid being distracting. They are also not as quick to congratulate themselves. Most importantly, they make sure they understand the feedback they are receiving so that they don't misinterpret information.

Consider This...

There is an adage that says, "feedback is a gift." The idea is that feedback recipients should be thankful for the feedback and make an effort to use it, since somebody took the time to give it to them. Instead of viewing feedback as a gift, however, some have suggested it would be better to say, "feedback is an investment," in that feedback will impact the development of the recipient, which in turn will provide a return on the investment by ultimately benefitting the feedback provider, the team, and the organization.[110] By viewing feedback in this manner, feedback providers will see the need to provide accurate and relevant feedback, as well as to remain involved in the feedback recipient's development over time. Does viewing feedback as a gift or investment change the way you might give, seek, and/or receive it? Is there a metaphor you think is more appropriate?

Reactions to Performance Appraisals

In addition to reactions to feedback in general, researchers have also examined reactions to performance appraisals more specifically. These reactions include:

- the perceived accuracy or agreement with the evaluation
- employee motivation following the appraisal
- fairness perceptions regarding the appraisal
- satisfaction with the appraisal
- the perceived utility (or usefulness) of the appraisal

Reaction criteria are almost always relevant, and an unfavorable reaction may doom the most carefully constructed performance management system.[111] Related to this, employees often fail to see the value of performance management systems, with less than a third of workers believing their organization's system actually helps them improve their performance.[112] Fortunately, there are several things that managers can do to positively influence these reactions. For example, three factors consistently contribute to effective performance appraisal interviews: the supervisor's knowledge of the subordinate's job and performance in it, the supervisor's support of the subordinate, and a welcoming of the subordinate's participation.[113] In particular, employee participation for the sake of having one's "voice" heard appears to be more important to the employee than participation for the purpose of influencing the end result.[114]

There are seven characteristics that contribute to employees' accepting their evaluations and feeling they are fair:[115]

1. Solicitation of employee input prior to the evaluation and use of it
2. Two-way communication during the appraisal interview
3. The opportunity to challenge/rebut the evaluation
4. The rater's degree of familiarity with the ratee's work
5. The consistent application of performance standards
6. Basing of ratings on actual performance achieved
7. Basing of recommendations for salary/promotions on the ratings

Furthermore, performance management systems are more likely to be seen as fair to the extent that supervisors are seen as being neutral, employees are involved in the setting of objectives, and the system is clear and easily understood.[116] Likewise, the most important determinant of employee attitudes about performance appraisal is the supervisor.[117] When the supervisor is perceived as trustworthy and supportive, then attitudes about performance appraisal are favorable. Of course, employee reactions are not the only thing that matters, as it is important to understand supervisor reactions as well. Along these lines, managers' reactions to performance management systems are affected by their overall satisfaction with them (that is, their attitude toward the systems' ability to document the performance of their subordinates) and the appraisal's improvement value.[118]

Future of Performance Management

Performance appraisals have been described as "the organizational practice that managers and employees love to hate" (Culbertson et al. 2013, p. 35).[119] Indeed, the dislike for them is so intense that people have called for their elimination within organizations[120] or drastic transformation (see Social Media and I-O Psychology: *The Crowdsourced Performance Review*). In recent years, I-O psychologists have debated the merits of performance ratings, with two separate sides emerging.[121] Critics of performance ratings argue, among other things, that ratings inconsistently lead to improved performance, the relationship between performance and ratings is weak, and conflicting purposes of ratings within organizations is problematic. On the other side, advocates for retaining ratings within organizations argue that performance will always be evaluated (so if not ratings, what then?), alternatives to ratings may be worse, and "it's too hard" is no reason to abandon ratings.

"Done effectively, performance management communicates what is important to the organization, drives employees to achieve results, and implements the organization's strategy. Done poorly, performance management not only fails to achieve these benefits but can also undermine employee confidence and damage relationships."[122]

—Pulakos & O'Leary 2011, p. 147

Given the widespread dissatisfaction with appraisals, many companies, including Accenture, Deloitte, and Microsoft, have eliminated or limited their use of formal performance reviews. Despite the push for other organizations to join these companies, it is tricky, given that there are estimates that 89% of companies link their compensation to performance ratings.[123] Nevertheless, organizations have begun to experiment with various alternatives to performance ratings. One alternative that has been suggested is calibration meetings, which consist of meetings among managers to compare and justify ratings and ensure comparability across organizational units.[124] Another alternative is the "feedforward interview," in which employees engage in a self-evaluation during an interview, designed to determine the employee's strengths and conditions that help facilitate the expression of those strengths.[125]

Performance management practices may be conventional, transitional, or cutting-edge.[126] Conventional practices have been prominent since 1950, and are directed towards individuals, conducted annually, and consist of complex ratings primarily provided by supervisors with little or no input from peers or other individuals. Transitional practices gained prominence in the mid-1990s, and are directed mostly toward individuals, but also toward some teams. Transitional practices, unlike conventional practices, utilize more simplified ratings and allow input from peers and others through 360° feedback systems. In addition, rather than relying on annual evaluations, midyear reviews also occur as needed. Finally, cutting-edge performance management practices, prominent beginning in 2010, utilize crowdsourced feedback to provide input from peers and others. These systems focus on both individuals and teams, and are conducted far more frequently, typically monthly or quarterly. The biggest distinction for these practices, however, is that they are predominantly ratingless.

Overall, there is nothing to be gained by conducting performance appraisals merely for the sake of doing so. At times, however, there can be the perception that more effort is placed into conducting performance appraisals than in making use of the information they provide. There will be greater acceptability of the performance management system throughout the organization if tighter linkages can be made between individual and organizational performance. Doing so will achieve the alignment that is fundamental to the concept of performance management.[127]

Social Media and I-O Psychology: *The Crowdsourced Performance Review*

Crowdsourcing is a term that combines the word "crowd" with "outsourcing," and refers to the act of gathering input and help from a large group of people to accomplish a goal. With an entire online community at our fingertips, we see people solicit opinions to influence what products they should purchase, where they should eat dinner, and what hotel they should stay in while on vacation. As Eric Mosley, CEO of Globoforce, noted, "It's everywhere, from 'star rankings' on Amazon.com's product pages to services like Angie's List, Zagat.com, and TripAdvisor. Now, people make decisions based on feedback from dozens, hundreds, or tens of thousands of other people" (Mosley 2013, p. 4).[128]

Mosley has argued that using the "wisdom of crowds" can generate more influential performance reviews for employees. He notes that, given the widespread use of crowdsourcing for all kinds of information, combined with the seemingly universal adoption of social media, it is a natural fit to incorporate both into the workplace. He suggests that rather than rely on one-time evaluations of performance by a manager, performance reviews should be "informed by a yearlong narrative of [one's] accomplishments, skills, and behavior" (p. 3).[129] These accolades can come from peers, customers, managers in other departments, direct reports, and so forth, and are simply meant to be an ongoing record of things an employee has done well. He refers to these various accolades as "social recognition" and suggests that by incorporating such recognition into a performance management system, a culture of collaboration can be created. He further notes that using this crowdsourced means of gathering performance data should be more accurate and meaningful than traditional approaches that rely on a manager only valuing performance data. He notes that, "Social recognition aggregates the opinions and thoughts of many individuals to arrive at a richer, more accurate conclusion than one person alone could attain" (p. 51).[130]

Mosley notes that when applying a crowdsourced approach to performance management, the input should remain positive instead of negative. He notes that while negative feedback must be given at times, it is not something that should be made public and would create a negative, rather than positive, culture if implemented. He notes that managers should "praise in public, criticize in private" or else risk introducing "a toxic element to a culture you're trying to nurture" (pp. 165–6).[131] The closest relative to the crowdsourced review is 360° feedback, with the biggest difference being that, rather than just having many people rate one person, the crowdsourced approach has many people rating many other people, including one another. In addition, 360° feedback is not typically focused only on positive recognition and is rarely made public (unless a person chooses to share their feedback). Thus, the notion of a crowdsourced performance review can be seen as a drastic departure from traditional performance reviews. Perhaps this approach will gain momentum within the workplace.

Chapter Review

Key Terms

Performance management
Performance appraisal
Succession planning
Top-grading
Critical incidents
Behaviorally anchored rating scales (BARS)
Serial position error
Contrast error
Halo error
Leniency error
Central-tendency error
Rater error training
Frame-of-reference training
Behavioral observation training
Rater motivation
Peer assessment
Peer nomination
Peer ratings
Peer ranking
Self-assessment
Dunning-Kruger effect
360° feedback

Questions for Review

1. What is the performance management process? How does performance appraisal relate to the performance management process?
2. What are the six purposes of performance management systems? How does succession planning fit into these purposes?
3. What are the concepts of negligence, defamation, and misrepresentation within the context of performance management? What are some ways to make performance appraisal content and procedures be legally sound?
4. What are the defining features of graphic rating scales, employee-comparison methods, and behavioral checklists and scales? What are advantages and disadvantages of the different types of performance rating scales?
5. What are some of the common errors of judgment that can plague performance ratings?
6. What are three types of rater training? What do they entail?
7. Why do some raters intentionally distort their ratings? What can be done to make raters more motivated to provide accurate ratings?
8. What are three techniques of peer assessments? What are advantages and disadvantages to using peer assessments?
9. What are advantages and disadvantages to self-assessments? What is the Dunning-Kruger effect?
10. What are two key assumptions of 360° assessments? How are disagreements between perspectives interpreted?
11. Why does feedback not always result in performance improvement?
12. Why do people seek feedback?
13. What are typical reactions to feedback and what influences those reactions? What contributes to employee acceptance of performance evaluations?

CHAPTER 9

Culture and Organizational Change and Development

Chapter Outline

Culture

National Culture
Organizational Climate and Culture
Social Media and I-O Psychology: *The New Water Cooler*

Perceptions of Fit

COVID-19 and I-O Psychology: *Fit Disruption or Fit Enhancement?*

Organizational Change

Faces of I-O Psychology: *Mark G. Ehrhart*
Downsizing, Outsourcing, and Offshoring
The Lighter Side of I-O Psychology: *The Man Who Outsourced His Job*
Mergers and Acquisitions

Organization Development

Leadership Development as OD
Team Building as OD
Survey Feedback as OD

Chapter Review

Learning Objectives

- Describe the various ways nations can differ with regard to their culture and how they impact individuals and organizations.
- Discuss the concept of fit and its importance for individuals and organizations.
- Differentiate between organizational climate and culture, and explain how both are important for individuals and organizations.
- Discuss the rationale for and models of organizational change.
- Explain downsizing, outsourcing, offshoring, and mergers and acquisitions.
- Describe the practice of organization development.

One of the most influential organizational scholars of all time is Peter Drucker. As a business consultant, educator, and author, he contributed largely to modern business. He has been touted as having an innate ability to adapt and to embrace change. As some have noted, there isn't any Nobel Prize for management thinking, but it's probably just as well, as it would have been won every year by the same man—Peter Drucker.[1]

With accolades like that, it's hard to not take notice of things Drucker has said. One quote in particular that has been attributed to Drucker and repeated by managers and consultants for decades is, "Culture eats strategy for breakfast." But what does this mean? Mark Fields, former CEO of Ford Motor Company, explained it as this: "You can have the best plan in the world, and if the culture isn't going to let it happen, it's going to die on the vine" (Durbin 2006).[2] Said differently, it means that while strategy—an organization's plan of action to achieve its goals—is certainly important, it is the organization's culture that will make the biggest difference in whether the strategy can be successfully implemented.

Peter Drucker

This chapter deals with the ever-important topic of culture and organizational change and development. We begin with a broad discussion of culture, to include national culture and its influences on the workplace, as well as organizational culture and climate. In general, culture reflects the learned social behaviors that govern how individuals will behave in different contexts. Thus, understanding national and organizational culture is important for predicting how people will act and what they may prioritize when executing plans. We also discuss the larger topic of organizational change and development. To execute change of any kind, it is important to understand the context in which the change will occur. In some cases, it may be necessary to change the culture prior to enacting change. The need for change management is paramount to creating and sustaining a competitive advantage. Change is inevitable and occurring at a rapid rate; organizations must be ready and able to adapt in response to changing conditions. As one business leader noted, "The rate of change internally has to be greater than the rate of change externally or else you're pedaling backward" (Martins 2011, p. 691).[3]

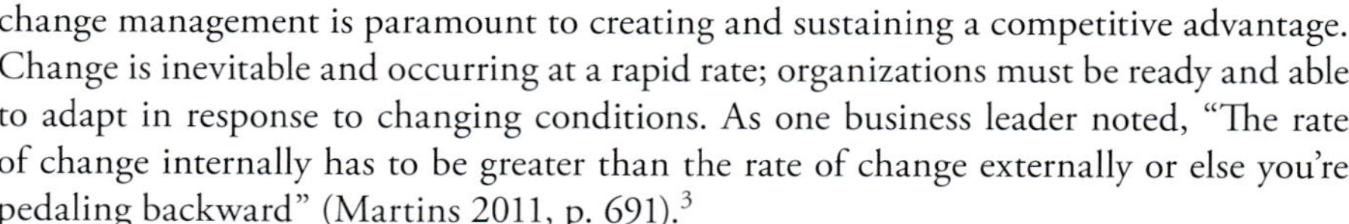

Culture

Individuals differ in myriad ways. Each individual is unique due to their different backgrounds, experiences, values, preferences, knowledge, and so forth. This makes it incredibly difficult to predict how people will behave in various situations. One factor that can help in our ability to predict what individuals will do is the culture within which they reside.

National Culture

Nations have identifiable cultures that are reflected in all aspects of life, including the conduct of business. These cultural dimensions reveal the values, preferences, and emphases individuals within the society place on various aspects. There are six major dimensions that are useful in understanding cross-cultural differences.[4]

1. **Power distance.** *Power distance* refers to the extent to which less powerful members of a society expect and accept that power is distributed unequally. Individuals in high power distance cultures acknowledge that hierarchies exist, and inequalities are natural and should therefore be expected. Individuals in low power distance cultures, however, require justifications for power imbalances and seek to create greater equities among people. Within organizations, power distance may be manifested in numerous ways. Organizations in high power distance cultures may tend to be more hierarchical, such that authority is clearly granted to those higher in the company. In addition, decision making will likely be more centralized, and orders may be followed without question. In fact, employees will likely expect clear direction from their managers, and may become uncomfortable if asked for their input. Conversely, organizations in low power distance cultures may tend to be flatter, with authority distributed more equally among its members. Decision making may be more decentralized, and employees may feel comfortable in questioning their superiors and/or offering input into decisions that are being made.
2. **Individualism–collectivism.** *Individualism* refers to the belief that people in a society primarily look after themselves and their immediate family members. *Collectivism* is the belief that people in a society are integrated into strong, cohesive in-groups, which throughout their lifetime protect them in exchange for unquestioning loyalty. People in collectivistic societies are likely to view their families in a broader sense, moving beyond their immediate families to include distant relatives and even neighbors in their community. This aspect of culture can be seen in many management practices. For example, within an individualistic culture, rewarding employees based on their individual merit will be more positively received than rewarding based on group output, whereas in collectivist cultures the opposite would be truer. Group harmony, cooperation, and acceptance by others is very important in collectivistic cultures, and self-reliance, competition, and personal freedom without regard for others' opinions are of greater value to people in individualistic cultures.
3. **Masculinity–femininity.** *Masculinity* stands for a society in which traditional male roles, such as assertiveness, achievement orientation, competitiveness, and a focus on material resources, are emphasized. *Femininity*-centered cultures stress values such as modesty, compassion, concern for the weak, and a focus on quality of life. Masculine countries tend to have distinct roles for men and women, whereas feminine cultures tend to see an overlap in gender roles. Within organizations, this cultural distinction is often thought of as "tough vs. tender" management. Workers in masculine cultures will likely value work and extrinsic rewards over leisure time and intrinsic rewards; the opposite is expected of workers in feminine cultures.
4. **Uncertainty avoidance.** *Uncertainty avoidance* is the extent to which members of a culture feel threatened by uncertain or unknown situations. People in high uncertainty avoidance cultures are uneasy with ambiguity and prefer to have structure and rigidity in their lives so they know what to expect. People in low uncertainty avoidance cultures, however, are more relaxed and able to "go with the flow." They do not require as much structure and are more comfortable with change and risk. Organizations in high uncertainty avoidance cultures are likely to have formal rules and regulations, with strict standardization in place. They will also be more likely

to have clear systems and plans in place to minimize risk and ensure safety of its members. Conversely, organizations in low uncertainty avoidance cultures will be less rigid and have fewer formal regulations in place. They will be more open to change, and employees will be more encouraged to take risks.

5. **Long-term–short-term orientation.** The extent to which a society prioritizes time-honored traditions and norms versus a future-oriented perspective reflects its *short-term orientation* or *long-term orientation*, respectively. In short-term orientation cultures, there is a strong focus on the past and present, with an emphasis on obtaining immediate gratification. Conversely, long-term orientation cultures focus on persistence and perseverance, with a willingness to delay short-term gratification to gain long-term success and fulfillment. Organizations in long-term orientation cultures may prefer candidates who demonstrate potential for high levels of future performance and may accordingly make large investments in their employees' development. They will also place more emphasis on rewards that will pay off over time, such as retirement benefits. Organizations in short-term orientation cultures, however, may prefer candidates who have already proven themselves as good workers and reward them in more immediate ways, such as with cash bonuses.
6. **Indulgence–restraint.** *Indulgence* reflects a society that values the satisfaction of natural human needs and desires related to having fun and enjoying life. *Restraint* reflects a society that values suppressing one's desires and abiding by social norms that place lower emphasis on leisure, freedom, and expressions of happiness. Organizations in indulgent cultures will place a greater emphasis on high levels of job satisfaction within the workplace and encourage a collegial workplace in which employees have fun with one another. In restrained cultures, the focus will be more on work with an assumption that friendships and fun are reserved for when individuals are off duty.

A major meta-analysis based on over 600 individual studies found the concept of cultural tightness/looseness—the strength of social norms and the degree of sanctioning behavior within societies—influenced the impact of the cultural dimensions.[5] The cultural factors appear to exert stronger influence over behavior in nations with tight cultures. In culturally-tight societies, cultural norms and sanctions dictate behavior more than individual preferences and styles. In loose cultures, however, there is more variability in how people behave, indicative of less-imposing cultural prescriptions.

It is important to note that culture can vary along more than the six dimensions presented here. Indeed, one criticism is that these dimensions, and the notion of cross-cultural differences in general, is biased in favor of a Western value system for comparing and contrasting cultures.[6] That is, the cultural dimensions presented here are supposedly purely descriptive, not implicitly evaluative. However, if avoiding uncertainty is not only different from accepting the ambiguous or unpredictable, but also worse, then cultures that are comfortable with the uncertain are "better" than those that are not. Critics contend that Western nations seem to fare better than Eastern nations on these cultural dimensions and that Eastern nations would emerge more favorably if a different set of cultural values were used to differentiate nations.

The diversity and differentiation created by multicultural employees can cause organizational tension that, if left unattended, can quickly lead to conflict in a global company.[7] The key challenge is to build an organization in which there are core values

Consider This...

In Chapter 7, we discussed the importance of expatriate training for individuals and their families before going abroad on an assignment. Consider a situation in which an organization, headquartered in the United States, has operations in China, Greece, and Sweden. These four countries have cultures that look approximately as follows:[8]

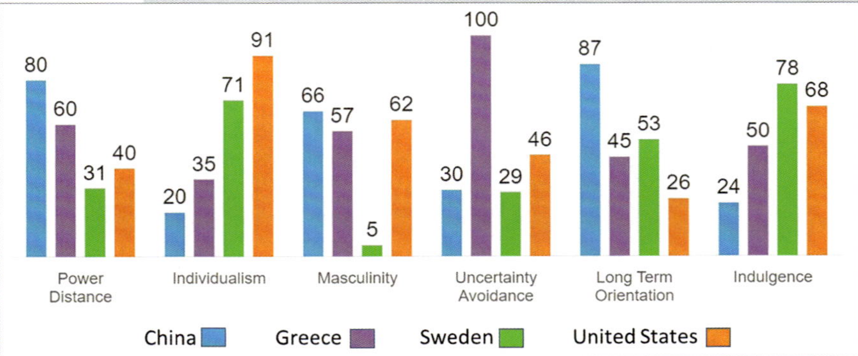

Three employees from the United States are being given 2-year managerial assignments at the company's other sites. Chad Stevens is going to China, Graeme Reid is going to Greece, and Swanand Patel is going to Sweden. Based on the cultural differences between the countries, we might expect that Chad will need to go by "Mr. Stevens" rather than "Chad." He will be expected to make decisions without much input from his subordinates, as asking for their advice may make them uncomfortable given the greater power distance of China compared to the United States. Similarly, due to the difference in masculinity–femininity between Sweden and the United States, Swanand may find that his team in Sweden expects him to be more modest and compassionate than his team in the United States expected, and he may find them put off if he is too aggressive or competitive in the workplace. What other difficulties might you expect Chad, Graeme, and Swanand to experience in their transition? What difficulties might their families have if they aren't prepared properly?

that transcend specific cultures, uniform policies that are regarded as fair and reasonable, and consistent business practices that can be implemented globally but are respectful of local cultural customs.

The culture people grow up in causes them to see the world differently. We tend to believe that our view of the world is correct, which in turn leads us to think and act in certain ways. We can come to believe that other ways of thinking and acting are strange, bizarre, or unintelligible. For example, Europeans typically receive 30–40 paid vacation days per year. U.S. workers typically have fewer paid vacation days and many managerial-level employees do not use their full allotment of vacation time. It is not uncommon for managerial-level U.S. employees to work while on vacation through the use of modern electronic technology. This practice has long been what appears to be primarily an American custom.[9] To most members of other cultures, the practice of "working while on vacation" is a contradiction in terms. Western (the United States,

Canada, northern Europe, Australia, and New Zealand) and non-Western (the rest of the world) cultures reflect different sets of values that guide thinking and behavior. Table 9-1 lists some of these value differences.

Table 9-1 *Examples of Western and Non-Western values*

Western Values	Non-Western Values
Individualism	Collectivism, group
Achievement	Modesty
Equality, egalitarian	Hierarchy
Winning	Collaboration, harmony
Pride	Saving face
Respect for results	Respect for status, ascription
Respect for competence	Respect for elders
Time is money	Time is life
Action, doing	Being, acceptance
Systematic, mechanistic	Humanistic
Tasks	Relationships, loyalty
Informal	Formal
Directness, assertiveness	Indirectness
Future, change	Past, tradition
Control	Fate
Specific, linear	Holistic
Verbal	Nonverbal

Source: From Marquardt, M., "Around the World: Organization Development in the International Context," in J. Waclawski and A. H. Church (Eds.), *Organization development: A data-driven approach to organizational change* (2002). Reprinted with permission of John Wiley & Sons, Inc. via Copyright Clearance Center.

These differences in values can be reduced to four key dimensions that most affect global organizations:[10]

1. **Leadership roles and expectations.** The democratic style of leadership is the hallmark of Western managers. Employees are encouraged and expected to voice their opinions to better serve the operation of the organization. Disagreements with managers are not uncommon, and employees are encouraged to challenge and question orders. In non-Western cultures, managers are expected to make decisions rather than solicit opinions from employees. There are status differentials based on title, and lower-level employees who speak out may be considered disrespectful. Managers must act in a certain formal style or they may lose credibility.
2. **Individualism and groups.** As extensive research has indicated, the United States is the most individualistic culture in the world. As a culture, Americans greatly value independence, and successful task completion (or "getting the job done") is more important than relationships. The social interaction of different ages, genders, and races is consistent with Western values of equality and informality. Indeed, the U.S. employment laws (Civil Rights Act, Age Discrimination in Employment Act, Americans with Disabilities Act, etc.) are designed to achieve this very outcome. Non-Western cultures tend to be more group-oriented or collectivistic. Group members support each other in exchange for loyalty and acceptance in the group. Individuals identify on a personal level with the social network to which they be-

long. The social interaction of people of differing status may be seen as a means of subverting authority and power in the workplace and may cause embarrassment and loss of status.

3. **Communication.** Latin American, Middle Eastern, and southern European cultures value expressive communication styles. The passion with which they communicate is designed to establish and maintain social relations. Voices are raised to reflect emotions such as joy, anger, and excitement, and hugging and touching often accompany conversation. The Western style of communication places more emphasis on the factual accuracy of what is said. The primary goal is to reach an objective, unemotional conclusion that leads to actions being taken by the listener. Displays of emotion are thought to indicate a lack of professionalism and rationality. There can be extreme variability in communication styles across cultures in trying to make a point, ranging from intentional exaggeration of desire or intent in the Middle East to prolonged silence and pauses in Asian cultures. In short, there is ample opportunity for people of different cultures to misunderstand each other based on their communication styles.
4. **Decision making and handling conflict.** Western cultures are highly action-oriented. They like to get work done, not waste time, and derive pleasure from achievement. Western cultures prefer frankness and candor in dealing with conflict. They accept and expect conflict and use power to resolve differences. Non-Western cultures are much more indirect in conveying disagreement or criticism. Greater emphasis is placed on avoiding conflict than on finding ways to resolve it. Circuitous, indirect communication is used in the desire to protect honor and avoid shame. The desire to avoid conflict is rooted in courtesy and respect. Age is often the deciding factor in determining the most important member in a group.

A broad-based view of culture in global organizations would be as follows. At one extreme, if everyone behaved the same, the world would operate under a single powerful culture. At the other extreme, if everyone behaved differently, our behavior would not be influenced by cultural values. Reality lies somewhere in the middle. As the world becomes increasing connected, what were once highly disparate cultures are producing some common ground, as required to successfully run a business populated with employees from many nations. Individuals who are members of global organizations must adopt the values of the particular company to be accepted as contributing organizational members. However, as individuals (in non-business roles), we do not surrender our own cultural identities that were shaped long before becoming socialized to a corporate culture.

Organizational Climate and Culture

Organizational climate
The shared meaning of what and how things are done within an organization.

Organizational climate refers to the shared meaning organizational members have for what is rewarded, supported, and expected regarding what and how things are done within the organization.[11] It is often described as the shared meaning associated with specific factors of importance to organizations. For example, safety climate reflects such things as the importance placed on safety training programs, the presence of and status of a safety officer or safety committee within the workplace, and the influence of safe behaviors on promotions. Other types of climate include service climate, justice climate, and diversity climate. Climates are stronger within work units that are smaller, cohesive, have high levels of interaction, and receive high levels of information and consistent behaviors from their leaders.[12]

Norms
A set of shared group expectations about appropriate behavior.

An important concept when considering organizational climate is that of norms. **Norms** are shared group expectations about appropriate behavior. They establish the behavior expected of everyone in the group, such as when employees take coffee breaks, how much they produce, when they stop for the day, and what they wear. Norms are unwritten rules that govern behavior. They can be either descriptive or injunctive. *Descriptive norms* develop through a process of observation. As a group behaves in certain ways, members will see such behavior as appropriate. For example, if members of a group consistently leave for lunch ten minutes early, over time such behavior will begin to be viewed as acceptable. *Injunctive norms*, on the other hand, develop through a process of conforming to gain social approval. If members of a group receive praise from their peers for behaving in a certain way, such behavior will be repeated. However, if such behavior is criticized, the behavior would not be repeated.

Norms are not always contrary to formal organizational rules or independent of them. Sometimes norms can greatly promote organizational goals. For example, there may be a norm against leaving for home before a certain amount of work has been done. Although quitting time is 5:00 p.m., the group may expect employees to stay until 5:15 or 5:30 to finish a certain task. In this case, the deviant is the one who conforms to the formal rule (that is, leaving at 5:00 p.m.) instead of the group norm. Similarly, norms can exist for the engagement of organizational citizenship behaviors (introduced in Chapter 4 and described in greater detail in Chapter 11).[13] Thus, norms that emphasize that employees help one another and engage in above-and-beyond activities can be developed and maintained within work settings. When group norms and organizational goals are complementary, high degrees of effectiveness can result.

Organizational culture
The language, values, attitudes, beliefs, and customs of an organization.

Related to organizational climate is organizational culture. **Organizational culture** refers to the language, values, attitudes, beliefs, and customs of an organization.[14]

Consider This...

Just because norms exist doesn't mean they are followed by everybody. Noncompliant members are called *deviants*. Group members will often try to convince deviants to change their behavior and abide by the norms through positive reinforcement or punishment. Positive reinforcement can be praise or inclusion in group activities. Punishment can be a dirty look, a snide remark, exclusion from group activities, or actual physical abuse. The clearer and more important the norm and the more cohesive the group, the greater the pressure. Eventually, a deviant either changes or is rejected. If rejected, the deviant becomes an *isolate*, and the pressure to conform stops. Because the group may need the isolate to perform work tasks, they usually reach a truce; the isolate is tolerated at work but excluded from group activities and relationships. Have you ever experienced a situation in which your saw (or were) a deviant or isolate in a group due to noncompliance of group norms? Do you think a deviant would ever be successful in refusing norms yet still not be considered an isolate? If so, when? If not, why not?

It represents a complex pattern of variables that, when taken collectively, gives each organization its unique "flavor." Whereas organizational climate explains *what* and *how* things are done in an organization, organizational culture explains *why* such things are done. In this manner, organizational culture is a driving force behind organizational climate. In addition, organizational culture is longer lasting that climate, which can more easily fluctuate over time. The culture of an organization has three layers:[15]

1. **Observable artifacts.** Artifacts are the surface-level actions that can be observed. It is from these observations that individuals may derive some deeper meaning or interpretation about the organization. There are four major categories of cultural artifacts: *symbols* (e.g., physical objects or locations); *language* (e.g., jargon, slang, gestures, humor, gossip, and rumors); *narratives* (e.g., stories, legends, and myths about the organization); and *practices* (e.g., rituals, taboos, and ceremonies).[16] Although these artifacts are easy to observe, they are not necessarily easy to interpret or understand.
2. **Espoused values.** Espoused values are those beliefs or concepts that are specifically endorsed by management or the organization at large. Organizations per se do not possess values, but rather key individual leaders within the organization espouse these values. Two examples are "Safety is our top priority" and "We respect the opinions of all our employees." *Enacted* values are those that are converted into employee behavior. A perceived difference between espoused and enacted values can be a source of cynicism among employees. For example, despite the espoused values, actual safety efforts may be haphazard, or employees may be criticized for speaking out.
3. **Basic assumptions.** Basic assumptions are unobservable and are at the core of the organization. They help define what employees should pay attention to, how they should react, and what actions they should take in various circumstances. They frequently start out as values but over time become so deeply ingrained that they are taken for granted. Basic assumptions are rarely confronted or debated and are extremely difficult to change. Indeed, challenging assumptions (such as questioning a university's view on the value of education in society) may produce anxiety or lead to defensiveness of organizational members.[17]

These three layers of organizational culture are often likened to parts of an iceberg, as shown in Figure 9-1, such that artifacts are on the surface and easily observable to others. Values lie just beneath the surface and are "seen" in the actions and beliefs of managers and employees. Assumptions are much deeper and are largely unobservable. They are there, but are often taken for granted as they are so deeply embedded in the organization and its people.

Culture exists beyond any one individual, and is transmitted to others through stories, rituals, and experiences of newcomers.[18] Culture may also be communicated through other channels, such as a company's intranet, official policies, mission statement, and any other means of value expression (see Social Media and I-O Psychology: *The New Water Cooler*).

Understanding the culture of an organization is critical to making sense of the behavior observed in the organization.[19] A narrow description of behavior, divorced from the cultural context in which it occurs, is of limited value for understanding the

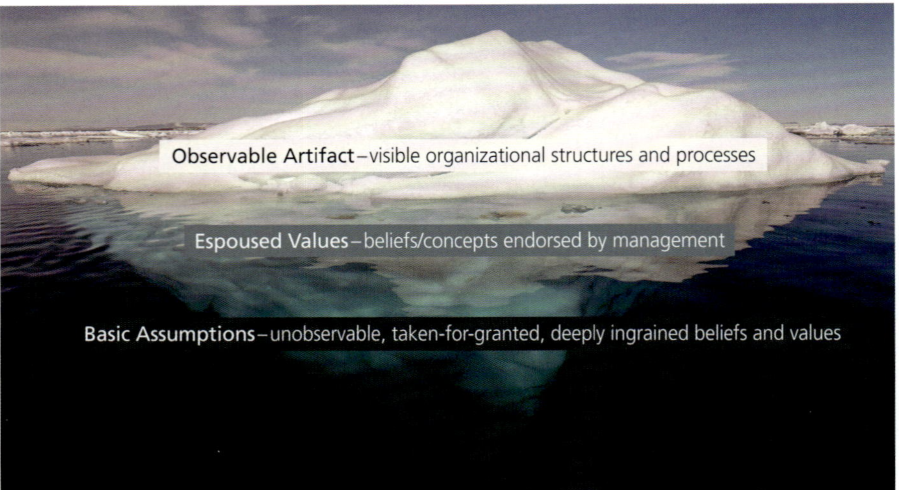

Figure 9-1 *Three layers of organizational culture*

organization. For example, researchers examined the types of clothes worn by members of a hospital staff to understand how the hospital views itself.[20] They found that the manner of dress among the staff was symbolic of their sense of organizational identity. Furthermore, differing views among staff members about dress were deeply felt. The authors offered the following two quotes from nurses working in the hospital:

> *Head nurse of a rehabilitation unit:* "Patients who wear pajamas and see hospital garb around them think of themselves as sick. If *they and their caretakers wear street clothes*, patients will think of themselves as moving out of the sick role and into rehabilitation. They will be ready for life outside the hospital. This is the rehab philosophy, and this is what makes this unit unique." [emphasis added]

> *Nurse on the evening shift of the same unit:* "We are medical and health professionals. We do professional work. We take care of sick patients, we deal with their bodily fluids and get their slime all over us. So we should all look like medical professionals; *we should be dressed in scrubs*." [emphasis added] (Pratt & Rafaeli 1997, p. 862).[21]

An organization's culture can be revealed in very subtle ways. Territoriality in organizations can occur through the use of nameplates on doors and family photos on desks.[22] These artifacts serve to establish a sense of an individual belonging to that organization by the implicit marking of "turf."

Another example is seen in a ritual among businesspeople from different organizations who meet for the first time: the exchange of business cards.[23] Along with the individual's name on the card is often found the organization's logo, a visual symbol of its identity. The selection of a company's logo sends a message, coded as a symbol. The message may seek to express such values as excellence, elitism, and innovation.

The culture of an organization is critically related to its effectiveness. It serves to shape how the organization does what it does, and in so doing becomes a determinant of its success. The Competing Values Framework describes four types of organizations

Social Media and I-O Psychology: *The New Water Cooler*

Once upon a time, people would gather around the office water cooler to discuss the previous evening's television shows and exchange details regarding the latest office gossip. The topics discussed and the fervor with which they captured individuals' attention was one way to gauge a company's culture. Were the conversations light-hearted and supportive or competitive and sprinkled with animosity? Did the discussions only occur when the boss was gone, or was the boss actively involved in the discourse?

Of course, the water cooler was and continues to simply be a metaphor for a gathering place in which people can chat about hot topics. Although individuals rarely stand around an actual water cooler anymore, the notion of a metaphoric water cooler still exists, whether it be the office coffee maker, the photocopier, or a particularly outgoing receptionist's desk. Increasingly, the office water cooler is online, on various social media platforms. In addition, these virtual water coolers allow for the culture of an organization to be identified as employees communicate about their unique experiences and perceptions of the workplace. Many organizations have begun to realize the role that social media can play in monitoring employees' views about the organization's culture. For example, using internal platforms such as SharePoint, an application used by over three-quarters of Fortune 500 companies, companies can solicit input from employees and gauge the level of engagement and satisfaction within the workforce. In addition, organizations can utilize data mining of sites like Glassdoor.com to ascertain what topics are most discussed and how a company is viewed by its current and former employees. Thus, by keeping an eye on the new (virtual) water cooler, organizations can determine whether the culture they are striving for is the culture that is being realized in practice.

Consider This...

It has been proposed that the cartoons employees tape on their office doors not only reflect the organization's culture but are also a product of it.[24] The simple act of posting cartoons on doors is a message to the observer that such behavior (the individual expression of the message of the comic) is acceptable to the organization. The cartoons posted by individuals are statements of their own values, as the cartoons often portray cynicism and sarcasm presented as satire. These cartoons are artifacts of the organization's culture, and they offer insight into how individuals view the organization's values. Such artifacts are not easy to decipher and can convey different meaning to the sender and receiver of the message. Despite their subtlety, they are valuable expressions and have purpose. Look around at the office doors of your organization, or in the buildings on your campus. What do you see? Are there cartoons or messages posted? What do they convey? Do you notice any differences across departments or hierarchical levels? How does this reflect the culture of the organization?

determined by different (or competing) values.[25] These are considered "competing values" because the core values that guide the cultures are at opposite ends of a continuum. The first continuum is flexibility and discretion versus stability and control. The second continuum is an internal focus and integration versus external focus and differentiation. These values in turn determine the indicators of effectiveness that the organization uses to judge itself, and in large part govern what is considered to be good and appropriate for the organization. When the values on the continua are combined, four types of organizations result, which define effectiveness in different ways, prefer different types of leaders, are guided by different values, and yield different cultures (see Figure 9-2).

The first type of culture is the *collaborative culture*, which is also known as a clan culture. This culture has an internal focus combined with an emphasis on flexibility and discretion. In this culture, there is an assumption that the business environment can best be managed through teamwork and by regarding customers as partners. Their leaders tend to be facilitative and emphasize developing relationships. Effectiveness in a collaborative culture is achieved through loyalty and internal cohesiveness. Companies with this culture can feel very family-like, with a focus on people and a mentality that "we're in this together." An example of a collaborative culture is Tom's of Maine. The husband-and-wife founders, Tom and Kate Chappell, started their all-natural personal products business with a desire to care for their children's health. They grew their company with clear respect for relationships with coworkers, customers, owners, agents, suppliers, and their greater community. In addition, their stated mission highlights their belief in the importance of full and honest dialogue, meaningful and safe work, and an acknowledgement of the value of each person's contribution to their goals. This emphasis on togetherness and teamwork embodies the clan culture.

The second type of culture in the Competing Values Framework is the *creative culture*, also known as an adhocracy. Like the collaborative culture, there is a focus on flexibility and discretion, but rather than having an internal focus, the adhocracy has an external focus with an emphasis on differentiation. This culture assumes that its business environment is turbulent and dynamic. Leaders in a creative culture tend to

Figure 9-2 *The Competing Values Framework*

be visionary and emphasize innovation and the "entrepreneurial spirit." Effectiveness is achieved by challenging assumptions, taking risks, and remaining nimble. Indeed, the mentality of "risk it to get the biscuit" exemplifies the creative culture such that achievement and success require taking chances and moving beyond the status quo. An example of a creative culture is Tesla, the electric-automobile manufacturer. They have made headlines for their innovative approach to their business model, organizational structure and internal communication, customer focus, and their product designs. Their decision in 2014 to make many of their patents open-source was risky but in line with their external orientation, making them the epitome of an adhocracy.

The third culture is the *competition culture*, also known as a market culture. Companies with this culture are highly results-oriented and focused on reaching their goals and meeting quotas. Leaders in such cultures are tough and demanding, and prioritize profitability and enhancing productivity. The mentality of "we're in it to win it" reflects this culture, as the goal is to make as much profit and capture as much market share as possible, beating out others to be the leader of the pack. An example of a competition culture is Amazon. A notoriously competitive—if not combative—environment that demands results,[26] Amazon embodies the notion of a market culture. They are hard-hitting and push their employees to work hard. As one employee noted, "Amazon is where overachievers go to feel bad about themselves" (Kantor & Streitfeld 2015).[27]

The final type of culture is the *controlling culture*, also known as a hierarchy. This culture prioritizes processes and procedures, with the goal of minimizing mistakes and ensuring things are done correctly. In line with the mentality of "my way or

Consider This...

There is no one "correct" culture. Each of the four types of cultures from the Competing Values Framework has pros and cons. Whereas collaborative cultures are cooperative, inclusive, and people-oriented, the familial nature of this culture may blur the boundaries between personal and professional relationships and lead to "overstepping" in some cases. As Henry Ford, who once required factory workers to ask permission from their supervisor to buy a car—and only if they were married with children[28]—remarked in his memoir, "Paternalism has no place in the industry. Welfare work that consists of prying into employees' private concerns is out of date" (Ford 1922, p. 130).[29] Similarly, creative cultures, while innovative and adaptable, may take excessive risk at times and suffer the repercussions that come with that added risk taking. Competitive cultures often achieve high revenue and profit, but the work environments may become hyper-competitive and unpleasant. Lastly, controlling cultures, although predictable, reliable, and efficient, may be overly rigid and find it difficult to react swiftly to changes in the environment. In addition, the authoritarian nature of the culture may lead to the creation of rules or policies that some may view as going too far. For example, in 2006, Ford's Dearborn Truck Plant in Dearborn, Michigan instituted a policy in which only Ford vehicles could be parked in its lot; any other vehicles would have to be parked across the street.[30] While some employees approved of the rule, others felt it infringed on their rights outside of the company. What are some other advantages and disadvantages for the four types of cultures? What are some other examples of situations in which a culture could go "too far" and become problematic?

the highway," there is often a very clear chain of command and leaders emphasize the following of company policies and procedures. Effectiveness is typically achieved by standardization and control. The Ford Motor Company is an example of a controlling culture. Ford has a clear organizational structure in place, with a traditional corporate hierarchy. Specific and rigid processes exist to ensure high efficiencies, keep costs low, and maintain direction and control of its global enterprise.

There is nothing inherently superior about one value or organizational type versus another. The values simply undergird how the organization tries to be effective. Furthermore, one can readily imagine how certain leader types, such as the hard-charging competing type (for example), may not be a good match with a collaborative culture. The Competing Values Framework illustrates how the culture of an organization, based upon its values, is integrally related to not only the effectiveness of the organization, but also how effectiveness is defined.

Perceptions of Fit

Person-organization fit
The match between one's values and goals with those of an organization.

Person-vocation fit
The match between one's interests and aptitude with the requirements of a particular occupation.

Person-environment fit
The match between one's values and preferences with the work environment.

Person-job fit
The match between one's knowledge, skills, and abilities with the requirements of a particular job.

As the research on organizational culture attests, organizations develop values that strongly influence employee behavior. When recruiting and selecting new employees, organizations consider (implicitly or explicitly) the likelihood an individual will be a good fit or match with the organization. The name for the match between an individual and the organization is **person-organization fit**. Another form of fit is **person-vocation fit**. This form of fit has to do with whether one's interests and aptitude align with the overall requirements of a particular field of study or area of work. Vocational inventories, such as those completed in order to help individuals determine what they want to do with their lives, are key to determining whether an individual will enjoy a certain career path. Yet another form of fit is **person-environment fit**. Person-environment fit refers to the level of compatibility between an individual and the environment in which they work (see COVID-19 and I-O Psychology: *Fit Disruption or Fit Enhancement?*). Some individuals may be quite comfortable working in dangerous situations, as the environment may align with their adventurous attitude. Others may prefer an environment that is quiet or one that is free from risk. These preferences reflect a consideration of person-environment fit. A final form of fit is **person-job fit**. In earlier chapters, we spent a good amount of time discussing the need for job applicants to be selected based on their knowledge, skills, and abilities. When assessing whether candidates "have what it takes" to perform the job duties, we are assessing person-job fit. It is only when there is person-job fit that person-organization fit should be considered for employment. Whereas person-job fit and person-organization fit are important for selection and retention purposes, person-vocation fit is central to whether an individual is likely to pursue work in a certain area or remain happy in it over time.

While all forms of fit are important, the remainder of this section will focus on person-organization fit. Person-job fit was covered in earlier chapters (though the term wasn't used). Person-vocation fit is a topic best left for career counselors and vocational psychologists. Lastly, person-environment fit, while relevant to I-O psychology, has received considerably less attention to date.

COVID-19 and I-O Psychology: *Fit Disruption or Fit Enhancement?*

The COVID-19 pandemic had a considerable impact on many industries, from shifts in the way business in the hospitality was conducted to changes in how educational institutions delivered content to students. Of all the industries to be impacted, health care was arguably one of the most directly influenced areas. One way in which healthcare was impacted is in the disruption—or possible enhancement—the pandemic had on the person-environment fit for healthcare workers.[31]

Regarding the environment for healthcare workers, the COVID-19 pandemic created an increase in demands without a simultaneous increase in resources. While other businesses were facing work stoppages and slowdowns, healthcare facilities experienced a surge in business, with an overwhelming rise in demands and responsibilities.

Although healthcare providers are regularly around sick patients, the lack of knowledge regarding the COVID-19 virus, especially at the start of the pandemic, created increased tension for workers in terms of their health as well as the health of their loved ones to whom they returned home after work. The pressures to keep up with the demands of the increased workload while maintaining the safety of their families likely disrupted the perceived fit between the healthcare employees and their work environments.

On the other hand, the COVID-19 pandemic may have enhanced the person-environment fit for some healthcare workers. For example, prior to the pandemic, many nurses reported feeling burned out due to a lack of meaningful work, respect, and ability to provide input at their work. These issues may have disappeared during the pandemic, as the increased demands combined with inadequate human resources may have created opportunities in which nurses had broader decision-making authority and could make more meaningful contributions. In addition, the appreciation and respect for individuals in healthcare became greater and more vocal during the pandemic.

Despite the possibility that the COVID-19 pandemic may have improved person-environment fit perceptions, it is likely that many workers would prefer things to return to the pre-pandemic ways, at least with regard to pressures, stress, and fear of virus exposure. The healthcare environment has changed—and may be changed for some time—and the impact of these changes may be extensive. The views of the working environment may impact career choices for would-be healthcare providers, with some opting to turn away from the profession due to the changes and others opting to pursue it as a "call to action" in the crisis. Similarly, decisions for those already in healthcare about remaining in the field will likely be impacted. What is clear is that the environment and the changes within it are far-reaching.

The process of gauging the degree of person-organization fit between the two parties is mutual. From the organization's perspective, it seeks to understand the candidate's values, skills, goals, and personality in attempting to predict the likely behavior of the candidate if hired. The degree of fit is ascertained by comparing the assessment of the candidate against the organization's values, expectations, and culture.

If a strong match is perceived, the organization would extend a job offer to the candidate. The candidate also gauges the degree of fit, but from the perspective of whether this particular organization is likely to deliver on the employment opportunities that the candidate seeks. If the candidate perceives a strong match, the job offer will be accepted. If not, the candidate will seek employment elsewhere, or enter into employment knowing it will be but for a short time.[32]

There is a strong link between organizational culture and person-organization fit. It is the people populating the organization who most define its culture.[33] That is, people (e.g., employees) are not actors who fill predetermined roles in an established culture, but rather it is the personalities, values, and interests of these people over time that make the organization what it is. The attraction–selection–attrition (ASA) cycle proposes that people with similar personalities and values are drawn to (attraction) certain organizations and hired into these organizations (selection), and people who don't fit into the pattern of shared values eventually leave the organization (attrition).[34] This process occurs over time, however, not immediately.

There are dimensions of culture that run deep throughout the organization. Some dimensions may be specific to certain departments or levels of the organization, and other dimensions of culture might be weakly held.[35] There would be low perceived person-organization fit if the candidate expressed values that are contrary to those deeply held within the organization. It is possible that a candidate might be regarded as a better fit with one department or branch of the organization compared to others. Time is a critical issue to understanding person-organization fit.[36] There is no consensus as to how long it takes for a new employee to fit into a larger group, and how long a new employee will tolerate feeling like a misfit before action is taken (e.g., appealing to the organization for guidance or quitting). It will be recalled from earlier chapters that onboarding is the process organizations use to shorten the time new employees need to feel that they fit. Achieving fit accelerates the adjustment process, facilitating increased job performance and reduced turnover.

The concept of person-organization fit is used by recruiters in gauging the match between candidates for specific jobs within the company and the organization as a whole.[37] An important note when using this construct as a predictor is that person-organization fit appears to be more predictive of turnover than of job performance.[38]

Organizational Change

The remainder of this chapter will deal with an ever-widening area of I-O psychology—the process of effecting change in and systemically developing organizations. Organizations are created to fulfill some purpose or objective. As we discussed in Chapter 3, organizations exist in a larger environment that encompasses economic, legal, and social factors. Thus, there must be a sense of fit between the organization and the environment in which it exists. For the past half-century, changes in the business world have accelerated to rates unparalleled in history. As the external world rapidly changes, so too must organizations.

Organizational change
The methods by which organizations evolve to become more adaptive to pressing economic and social conditions.

The process of altering organizations to be more adaptive and congruent with their business environments is called **organizational change**. For reasons discussed in Chapter 1, the business world began to change in the 1980s. Among the forces responsible for the change were the adoption and diffusion of computers into work life, the evolving diversity of the workforce, the emergence of advanced communication technologies, the globalization of business, and redistributions of economic power. There has always been a need for most organizations to change in response to environmental pressures, and recent years especially have witnessed an ever-growing need for all organizations to respond to the pressures placed on them by transforming environmental conditions. What is different now than in prior years is: (1) the greater strength of environmental pressures prompting change, (2) the speed at which change must occur, (3) the acceptance that responsiveness to change is a continuous organizational process, and (4) the pervasiveness of organizations caught up and affected by changing environmental conditions. While there is resounding recognition of the need for change, it is not at all easy or clear how to enact it.

A vivid example of needed organizational change can be seen in the textile industry. For more than 100 years, the textile industry in the United States enjoyed economic prosperity. In the beginning, there was a strong reliance on cotton to produce textiles. However, consumer demands for new types of yarn created from a blend of cotton and synthetic fibers forced the textile industry to design a new line of manufacturing technology to produce these blended synthetic fibers. In addition, global competition, primarily from China, threatened the U.S. textile industry. The industry sought political solutions to some of its problems; it lobbied the U.S. government to impose quotas and tariffs on goods made in China to give the Chinese less of a competitive edge. The U.S. government did impose quotas and tariffs on Chinese textile products, but only for a limited time. The industry needed drastic changes to remain afloat. It began making textiles and yarns that had little to no competition from overseas markets. Although the cut-and sew functions of the textile industry are now performed almost exclusively outside of the U.S., by federal law, the U.S. military must purchase U.S.-made textile products (uniforms, tents, etc.). There has been a massive loss of jobs in the U.S. textile industry, estimated to be in excess of 500,000. The remaining U.S. textile companies have been compelled to invent new products (e.g., sweat-resistant fibers), use the latest and most efficient computer-based manufacturing techniques, and select and train a workforce that is vastly superior to its predecessors a mere generation ago.

Organizational change can occur with and without planning. However, I-O psychologists are most interested in intentional, planned change efforts. Within organizations, those individuals who are responsible for managing change efforts are known as *change agents*. Unfortunately, many change agents fail due to resistance of organizational members toward change. People may be resistant to change for many reasons, including a fear of the unknown, a difficulty in breaking old habits, or an unwillingness to go against group norms that may exist in terms of how things are and have always been done. Research has revealed that overcoming resistance to change involves educating and communicating the rationale behind the need for change efforts,[39] emphasizing employee commitment to the organization,[40] facilitating positive relationships between managers and employees,[41] and ensuring employees view the change as fair.[42] In addition, and related to these points, fostering a climate that is supportive of implementation efforts is crucial to gaining buy-in for organizational change interventions (see Faces of I-O Psychology: *Mark G. Ehrhart*).

There are two well-known models for how systematic change occurs in organizations. The first model, proposed by Kurt Lewin in 1951, suggests that there are three steps to enacting deliberate change within organizations.[43] The first step involves *unfreezing* the status quo. With this step, it is important to communicate the need for change and make employees understand how the change will affect them. In addition

Faces of I-O Psychology: *Mark G. Ehrhart*

Mark G. Ehrhart

Ph.D. University of Maryland, College Park

Professor, Department of Psychology, University of Central Florida

Research interests: Organizational climate, organizational citizenship behavior, leadership, implementation, and the integration of these topics across levels of analysis and in customer service and healthcare/social service settings.

Most of my early work on organizational climate was in customer service settings, but in recent years I have had an opportunity to shift my focus to healthcare and social service settings, such as mental health, child welfare, substance abuse treatment, and nursing. One specific issue that I have been addressing in my research is the implementation of evidence-based practice. An evidence-based practice, broadly speaking, is an intervention or approach that has strong research evidence to support that it actually "works." The challenge is that even though evidence may support the use of such practices, employees may resist making changes to how they are doing their jobs, whether it be counselors providing therapy or nurses taking care of patients. Although there are numerous ways to enhance implementation effectiveness, one of the most important factors identified in the research literature is the organizational context, and that is where I-O psychology comes into play. The goal for the I-O psychologist is to create an organizational context that influences people to overcome their resistance to change, to effectively implement new innovations into their daily routines, and to use such practices in the way they were originally intended to maximize their effectiveness. With this in mind, Dr. Gregory Aarons and I created an intervention called Leadership and Organizational Change for Implementation (LOCI). Using a mix of didactic training, one-on-one coaching, multisource survey feedback, and organizational strategy meetings, this intervention helps leaders to create an organizational climate that supports implementation efforts. The primary idea of this training is that leaders need to send a consistent message across a variety of mechanisms (including their communications, role modeling, reward systems, policies, procedures, etc.) that implementing evidence-based practice is a core value of the organization and a priority for leadership. So, for example, when workers see that leaders are always mentioning evidence-based practice in team meetings, are measuring the extent to which such practices are being used effectively, are including experience with evidence-based practices as a criterion in hiring systems, and are regularly providing training opportunities for evidence-based practices, workers will have a clear understanding that implementation is a priority for the organization and will be more motivated to support the organization's implementation efforts. One of the core values of the field of I-O psychology is that our practice should be founded in scientific evidence, so this line of research aligns with that core value by supporting the implementation of practices that have the strongest scientific evidence. In addition, it adds meaning to my work knowing that the research I am doing has the potential to improve the lives of patients and clients in healthcare and social service settings.

to creating awareness, rationale for change should be provided to decrease resistance and gain support for the change. The next step is the *change*, or movement to the desired end state. At this step, the actual changes occur. Whether this is implementing new procedures, installing new equipment, or enacting new policies, this is the step where the actual change takes place. The final step is *refreezing*, which entails making the change the new norm. If the change involved new ways of doing things, the refreezing step would involve making those new behaviors the preferred behaviors, resistant to change and ingrained as the new status quo.

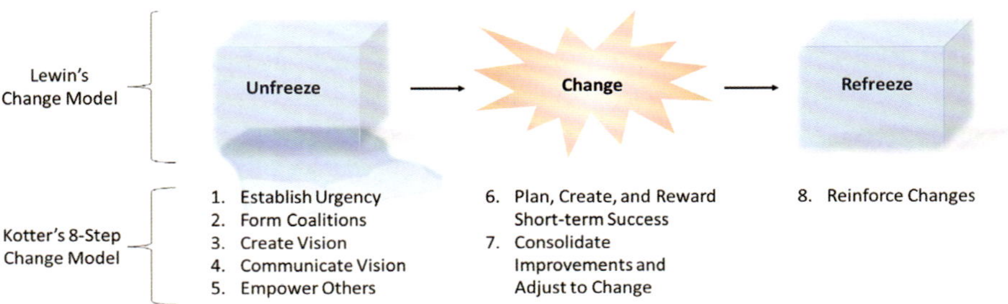

Figure 9-3 *A comparison of the Lewin and Kotter change models*

The second model of enacting systematic change in organizations was proposed by John Kotter, who built on Lewin's earlier work.[44] He proposed an eight-stage model that essentially broke down Lewin's three steps into sub-components based on common mistakes he saw organizations make when trying to implement change (see Figure 9-3). For example, Kotter's first five steps entail establishing urgency for the need to change, forming coalitions to lead the change, creating a vision to direct the change, communicating that vision throughout the organization, and empowering others to act on the vision. Indeed, this is the essence of Lewin's unfreezing stage, as these steps are meant to shift employees away from the status quo and toward the proposed change. Kotter's next two steps involve actual change, including the planning, creating, and rewarding of short-term successes and the consolidation of improvements and adjustments to the new activities. Finally, Lewin's third stage, refreezing, is embodied in Kotter's final step, which involves reinforcing the changes by showing clear links between new behaviors and organizational success.

The process of implementing organizational change is far from clean. Oftentimes, plans don't proceed as desired. People may opt to do things in their own way rather than following the organization's plan. Employees may not behave as you would expect them to, with some that you would predict to be supportive of the change efforts actually being resistant and those who you might expect to have difficulties with the change being more ready to adapt. In short, the process of implementing change can be very messy in practice.[45]

One striking example of how organizational change actually occurs, including unanticipated outcomes that derived from unintended processes, can be seen with the case of a church.[46] The desire for change began with some parishioners who were bored with the Sunday morning service. So instead of attending a traditional religious service, they decided to offer a free Sunday breakfast to homeless people. After five weeks of serving food, a physician in the group decided to also offer the homeless people free medical advice. This grew into the offering of vision, dental, and medical services. Within a few years, the church had created a separate social service organization. This organization obtained city funds to run a day care center for the homeless, serve approximately 200,000 meals per year, offer job training, and provide legal assistance. The homeless people sang in the church choir and served as ushers at the Sunday morning church service. This entire series of events started with a simple act of generosity.

This case is not atypical in organizational change. The magnitude of the proposed intended change was small: to offer a free breakfast to some homeless people on Sunday mornings. Because there were no objections or resistance to the breakfast, the concept of accepting change got a toehold. Had the free breakfast idea been poorly received, none of the subsequent changes would have resulted. The success of the small, intended change amplified the possibility for more radical changes. The entire process snowballed, sustaining itself into continuous radical change. The sheer magnitude of the radical changes produced resistance and displeasure from other organizations. Some local businesses situated near the church objected to the amount of disruption the church's activities created in the neighborhood. However, the resistance came primarily after the new activities were fully operational.

The case provides insights into when resistance to change can best be overcome. Had the resistance emerged initially, the attempt at change may well have failed before it could even begin. After the change process produced momentum, further changes emerged, and the resistance was "too little, too late" to stop it. In sum, both the process and the outcomes of organizational change could not have been envisioned at the outset, and the timing of events in the change process can be just as important as the nature of the events themselves.

Downsizing, Outsourcing, and Offshoring

Downsizing
The process by which an organization reduces its number of employees to achieve greater overall efficiency.

One of the most radical and tumultuous ways an organization can change in response to pressures is called **downsizing**. An organization may believe it has too many employees to be responsive to its environment. The most common reason for the decision to cut jobs is the organization's conclusion that it can "do more with less" (i.e., have greater efficiency with fewer employees). For most organizations, the single largest expense is the wages and salaries paid to their employees. By eliminating jobs, they reduce costs. Therefore, some organizations have been compelled to cut jobs to help ensure their economic survival. The work that was done by the departed employees will have to be performed by the remaining employees or through technical changes in work processes (e.g., automation). Another term given to this process of cutting jobs is *reduction-in-force*. It is not unheard-of for large organizations to reduce their size by several thousand employees at one time.

Where do the eliminated jobs come from within an organization? Within the structure of an organization, job cuts can occur *horizontally* or *vertically*. A horizontal cut involves the loss of jobs within a department, but the department remains within the organization. For example, if there are 50 employees who work in the accounting department, the department might be slashed in half: 25 employees lose their jobs and 25 remain. A vertical cut involves the elimination of all jobs in the department. In this example, 50 employees have their jobs eliminated. The organization still needs

Outsourcing
The process of eliminating jobs by having work contracted to other organizations.

the accounting function performed, but instead of having it performed by its own employees, the accounting function is outsourced to a professional accounting firm. **Outsourcing** the services performed by these individuals is less costly to the organization than hiring its own employees to perform these services (see The Lighter Side of I-O Psychology: *The Man Who Outsourced His Job*).

The Lighter Side of I-O Psychology: *The Man Who Outsourced His Job*

Outsourcing is a common means for organizations to save money and not have to do the work themselves. So imagine the surprise when one company was willing to have its own employees do a job, and pay them well for it, only to discover that the work was—you guessed it—being outsourced. Such is the case of a software engineer who decided he would rather surf the web, watch cat videos, and bid for items on eBay than actually do his work himself.[47]

According to a spokesperson for a firm hired to complete a security check for the organization, the man was earning a six-figure salary, and spent roughly one-fifth of it to pay a company in China to do his work. Their investigation also revealed that the employee was pulling the same scam at other organizations, pretending to work for them (remotely) for a large salary while outsourcing his work for a much smaller fee. In total, it is estimated he was earning several hundred thousand dollars a year while he paid the Chinese company approximately $50,000 a year to perform his work.

We don't know the legal ramifications of his actions, but what he did was clearly unethical and did result in the man losing his job(s). While unethical behavior is certainly not something we condone, and isn't a laughing matter, the absurdity of his actions and the belief that he wouldn't get caught is comical. The lesson is clear: do your own work and watch those cat videos on your own time!

Offshoring
The process of eliminating jobs by having work performed in cheaper labor markets.

Yet another source of job loss is **offshoring**. The work performed domestically (often jobs in the operating core) is exported to cheaper labor markets in other countries. For example, the average wage rate for U.S. production workers in 2011 was $24 per hour, compared to 67¢ per hour for Chinese production workers.[48] While the actual costs have changed, the discrepancy remains, with even cheaper labor markets found in Vietnam, Laos, and Cambodia.

So what do organizational structures look like after such workforce reductions? It is common for decision making to become more decentralized following a downsizing. Figure 9-4 shows the top part of an organizational chart for a manufacturing company before downsizing. The company is structured by both function (production and sales) and location (California and Texas). There are small spans of control. Each person below the president has two subordinates. A total of 15 people are needed to staff this part of the organization with such a configuration. Figure 9-5 shows the same company following reorganization—in this case, downsizing. A total of eight positions have been eliminated by this reorganization. The sales function has been consolidated into one job. The plant managers from the four locations now report directly to the vice president. Each plant manager now also provides information directly to the sales

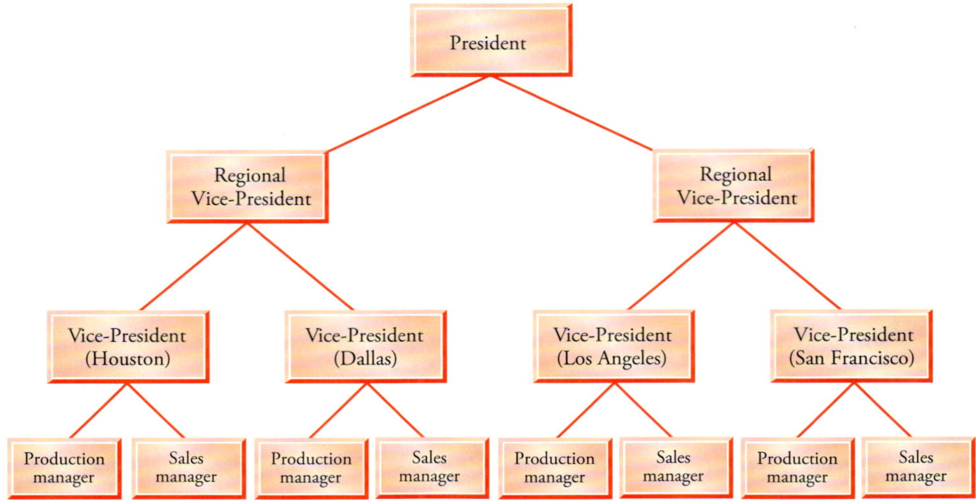

Figure 9-4 *Top part of an organizational chart before downsizing*

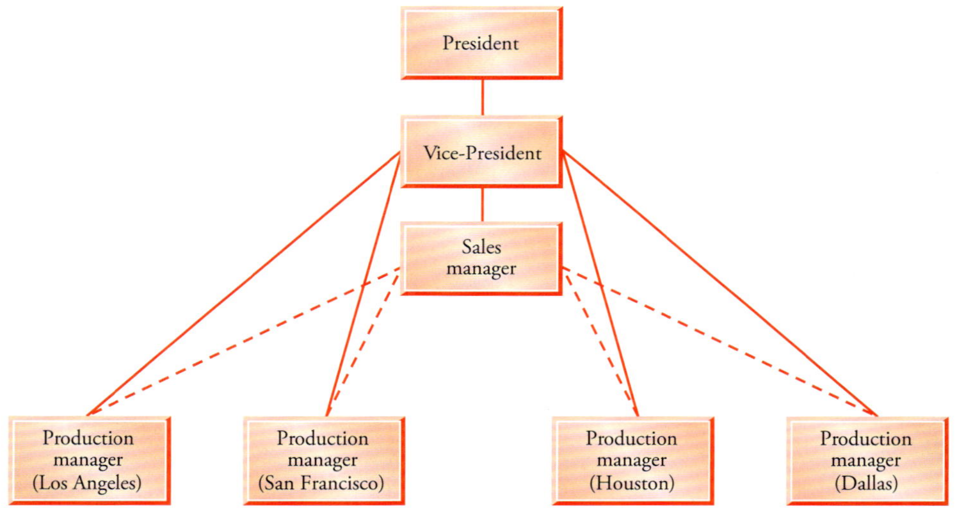

Figure 9-5 *Top part of an organizational chart after downsizing*

manager (as indicated by the dotted lines), but administratively the plant managers report to the vice president. The vice president now has a span of control of five. The positions lost in this reorganization are one vice president, three sales managers, and the entire layer of (middle) managers.

What consequences might we expect from this reorganization? There would be less administrative control from the loss of managerial jobs. There would be greater

Consider This...

How would you feel if you lost your job because you were fired? Probably not pleased, but in all likelihood you received some signals along the way that you were not performing satisfactorily. In turn, you probably had some control over whether you would change your job behavior. How would you feel if you lost your job because it was eliminated? You were not released; rather, the job you were filling was eliminated to make the organization more efficient. You could have been an exemplary employee, but you lost your job through no fault of your own. Which do you think would be more emotionally painful? Why?

pressure on the organization's locations to coordinate with each other because of the loss of direct supervision. There would probably be more stress placed on the surviving employees to work harder and find new ways to do the work of the employees whose jobs were eliminated. The organization would have fewer salary expenditures associated with the elimination of eight positions. Eight people would be out of work.

When downsizing occurs, it is easy to focus attention only on those employees who have lost their jobs. It is important, however, for organizations to also consider the survivors of layoffs. It is not uncommon for individuals who were fortunate to keep their jobs during massive layoffs to experience "survivor guilt," in which they feel uncertain, anxious, and remorseful about keeping their jobs.[49] It is important for management to provide surviving employees with reassurance regarding their future with the organization. Although they can't (and shouldn't) make any promises, it would be in their best interest to ensure the most valued employees know they are seen as important to the organization's future. Indeed, it has been suggested that this may be even more effective in retaining those employees than monetary bonuses or the like.[50]

When organizations are contracting in size, the overall social order of employment is altered. If, as a rule, organizations reduce the number of middle managers needed to run the business, then these displaced middle managers will not simply find new jobs as middle managers in some other companies. Rather the *job* of middle manager is being reduced in frequency, requiring holders of middle-management jobs to enter new jobs, not new positions in the same job family. This may necessitate professional retraining, learning new skills to fill jobs that continue to exist. Thus, issues of organizational structure affect not only I-O psychology but also the sociology of employment and the economics of across-occupational mobility.

Severe job cuts do achieve short-term reductions in costs, but they do not achieve long-term profitability.[51] Organizations typically grow in size because there is a demand for the products they make or services they perform. When the demand shrinks, it becomes necessary to eliminate jobs. However, there are less traumatic ways to achieve it than mass layoffs. One example is for the organization to offer an incentive for early retirement, such as one month of severance pay for every year of employment with the company. Another possibility is that when natural attrition occurs (e.g., an employee leaves to take a job elsewhere), the company does not hire a replacement. Massive job cuts serve to reduce a company's costs, but they also produce massive disruptions to the larger social order.

Mergers and Acquisitions

One strategy organizations can use in response to environmental pressures is to become smaller—that is, to downsize. Another strategy is to become larger. But rather than just becoming a larger version of what the organization already is, organizations can choose to "marry" another organization as a way of increasing their size. The logic behind an organizational marriage is similar to that of the marriage of individuals; that is, the overall quality of life for both parties will be enhanced.

Organizational merger
The joining or combining of two organizations of approximately equal status and power.

Acquisition
The process by which one organization acquires or subsumes the resources of a second organization.

Organizational marriages encompass both mergers and acquisitions. The technical distinction between a merger and an acquisition is slim. An **organizational merger** is the marriage or joining of two organizations of equal status and power. Their union is mutually decided. Both organizations think they will be more prosperous by their formal association with the other. An **acquisition** is the procurement of property (in this case, an organization) by another organization. The purchasing organization is in the dominant or more powerful position. Unlike a marriage of individuals, an acquisition can be a union between two organizations where only one party agrees to the new relationship. The dominant organization thus acquires an unwilling partner to enhance its financial status in what is called a *hostile takeover*. Other acquisitions are characterized by more friendly relations between the two organizations, but nevertheless the more powerful organization acquires the less powerful organization. The acquiring organization is referred to as the *parent*, and the organization being acquired is the *target*. For this discussion, mergers and acquisitions will be portrayed as the combining of two companies, regardless of the difference in power between the two. There is relatively little research on this topic. What we do know applies mainly to the characteristics of the two organizations as they affect the quality of their marriage and the individual responses of employees to their organization being united with another.

There are three phases in the merger process: precombination, combination, and postcombination.[52] Most of the emphasis in the precombination phase is on financial issues, such as what a target company is worth, tax implications, and expected returns on the investment. Little thought or concern is directed to psychological or cultural issues. In the combination phase, individuals jockey for power and cultures clash as people focus on differences between the partners and which side won which battles. It is in the postcombination phase that the importance of integrating the two cultures becomes acute. Declines in employee morale and customer satisfaction indicate there are other criteria of a successful merger besides initial financial appeal. The postcombination phase is steeped in concerns about implementation, and there is no predetermined date when the merger is declared to be "finalized." All parties involved in the merger must continue to understand and adapt to the new culture (and new company) that was birthed.

The International Labour Organization estimated that in the decade of the 1990s, over 10 million workers lost their jobs due to mergers and acquisitions.[53] This figure does not include job loss associated with small companies that were driven out of business because they could not compete with the new "super organizations" (such as large retail stores). Chronic fear of job loss alters the expressed values of employees.[54] Some employees pretend to support organizational policies or otherwise act in an inauthentic manner to increase the perceived likelihood that they will not be targeted for job loss. The employees feign conformance to perceived organizational values so as not to stand out as being different, yet many organizations claim they value diversity of opinion.

Consider This...

Consider the topics of organizational culture from earlier in this chapter. What happens when the cultures of the two organizations in a merger or acquisition clash? It can be quite devastating. Consider the challenges that Amazon faced in its acquisition of Whole Foods.[55] Amazon, as noted earlier, is a competitive organization that pushes hard and demands results. Whole Foods, on the other hand, had a focus on personal touch, close relationships, and empowering its workers. The acquisition led to Whole Foods' customers and employees expressing anger and frustration, and the company dropping from Fortune's list of best companies to work for—for the first time in two decades. How do you think Amazon could have ensured a smoother acquisition for its target? Which culture types according to the Competing Values Framework do you think would have an easier time merging? Which would have a more difficult time? Why?

"A handshake and a high five - I can't see this merger working."

Organization Development

Organization development
A field of study involving organization-wide, data-driven efforts to systematically increase organization effectiveness and well-being.

In Chapter 1, we noted that there is clear overlap between I-O psychology and the field of **organization development** (OD). It is not surprising, then, that many I-O psychologists conduct work in the area of OD.

OD has been defined as "an effort (1) planned, (2) organization-wide, and (3) managed from the top, to (4) increase organization effectiveness and health through (5) planned interventions in the organization's 'processes,' using behavioral science knowledge" (Beckhard 1969, p. 9).[56] There are several key elements of this definition. First, OD interventions are planned ahead of time. Organizational change efforts can be evolutionary or revolutionary.[57] Revolutionary change involves change that occurs rapidly in giant, radical spurts. Evolutionary change, on the other hand, occurs gradually over time, with incremental attempts to improve an organization. Most change within organizations is evolutionary, with continuous fixing of problems or attempts to improve the ways things are done. Regardless of the timing and extent of change, OD efforts are carefully planned with the purpose of aiding the survival and development of the organization.

Additional key elements of OD efforts are that they are organization-wide and focus on increased organization effectiveness and health. Rather than focusing on individual employees or work groups within an organization, OD interventions are system-wide. Furthermore, the focus is not only on improving the effectiveness of the organization, but also improving employee well-being. OD efforts involve links between leadership practices, employee results, customer results, and business performance.[58] With these links, the overall effectiveness of an organization, as well as the well-being of the individual employees within the organization, are attended to. Leadership practices such as an emphasis on quality, training, and involvement lead to engaged and productive employees. These employees communicate with each other and participate in meaningful teamwork activities, all related to their well-being. These characteristics of the workforce, in turn, lead to more satisfied and loyal customers, which ultimately results in a productive and profitable organization. Thus, OD interventions meaningfully impact an organization's overall health through its members.

Finally, fundamental to OD efforts is that they rely on behavioral science knowledge. This means that interventions must be based on data rather than intuition. It is important to gather information from interviews, focus groups, and organizational surveys when engaging in OD interventions. Of particular importance are surveys in OD work. Survey results help the OD consultant see the larger system, help track progress, and provide an internal benchmark for comparisons over time. They also assist in focusing attention on and providing direction for next steps in development efforts.[59]

OD interventions can take many forms. The most common involve leadership development, team building, and survey feedback. Each of these techniques, discussed below, are meant to advance the overall effectiveness of an organization.

Leadership Development as OD

One area within OD that has garnered considerable attention from I-O psychologists is that of leadership development. Developing leaders is a critical concern for organizations. Thus, it is no wonder that organizations spend billions of dollars on leadership development every year.[60] Leadership development efforts are aimed at expanding the capacity of individuals to perform well in leadership roles within organizations. For leaders to be effective, they must be intuitive, dynamic, and collaborative.[61] We discuss leadership in greater detail in Chapter 14.

Team Building as OD

In Chapter 10, we will discuss teams and the essential role they play within organizations. Given the increasing importance of teams within workplaces, OD efforts are often targeted at team building. Team-building strategies focus on improving trust, openness, and coordination among team members, with the ultimate goal of enhancing the performance of the team.[62] Common elements of team-building interventions include helping teams learn to set goals and priorities, determine how to allocate work and define roles for team members, and examine processes important for efficient and effective teamwork. As such, team building is a continuous process rather than a one-time event.

Survey Feedback as OD

As noted earlier, surveys are of paramount importance within OD. As part of an organization-wide improvement process, surveys are a powerful tool. There are several benefits of utilizing surveys within the context of OD efforts.[63] First, the questions themselves can serve as a way to draw attention to the organization's goals with regard to the intervention, as well as the behaviors that will be expected of employees going forward. Similarly, the results of surveys help to focus attention and energy on the areas that need the most consideration during the intervention. Finally, surveys are essential as a way of tracking progress over time.

Survey results are important for linkage research, an approach that links employee and customer data to measures of business performance.[64] Linkage research pinpoints aspects identified by employees of the work environment that correlate (or link) to important organizational outcomes, such as firm performance, productivity, and/or customer satisfaction. Linkage research helps produce higher levels of organizational performance by informing and driving OD efforts. One example in which survey results and linkage research helped inform OD efforts was for a large automotive credit branch system in North America.[65] Employees completed a survey assessing their evaluation of a recent customer service initiative. Customers also completed surveys to assess their satisfaction with the quality service initiative. Business performance metrics were also collected, including retail market share, loss-to-liquidation ratios, and productivity metrics. Looking at how individual items on the employee survey related to the customer satisfaction survey and business performance metrics provided a clearer understanding of how the organization was performing. For example, among other findings, work units that achieved higher levels of customer satisfaction were those whose employees believed they received sufficient training to improve their job performance and be effective team members. These findings demonstrated the links between the quality of business decisions and customer satisfaction with employee opinions regarding their work environment. Moreover, those branches in which customers were more satisfied reported better business results. Thus, the importance of gaining a better of understanding of an organization's workforce through surveys is essential to the OD goals of increasing organization effectiveness and health.

Chapter Review

Key Terms

Organizational climate
Norms
Organizational culture
Person-organization fit
Person-vocation fit
Person-environment fit
Person-job fit
Organizational change
Downsizing
Outsourcing
Offshoring
Organizational merger
Acquisition
Organization development

Questions for Review

1. What is culture? To what levels can culture be ascribed? Why is culture an important aspect of I-O psychology?
2. What are the six dimensions of culture? How does the combination of the dimensions impact the prevailing culture?
3. How does culture affect one's worldview? What major outlook differences exist between Western and non-Western cultures? How can these differences cause friction in the work environment?

4. What four differences in values most impact global organizations?
5. What is the difference between organizational climate and organizational culture?
6. What are norms? How does rejection of norms impact groups? How does that rejection impact individuals?
7. What are the three levels of organizational culture? Which is least likely to change, and why? How does culture relate to organizational effectiveness?
8. What is the Competing Values Framework and what are its dimensions? What aspects become visible to those outside the company? How can one infer an organization's culture and values when one is unaffiliated with it?
9. What are the two most important types of "fit" for I-O psychology? Why is person-organization fit important?
10. What is the attraction-selection-attrition (ASA) cycle?
11. What is organizational change? Why is it important to manage change, and what makes change so difficult to enact? What factors influence the rate of organizational change?
12. Who and what are involved in intentional, planned change efforts?
13. What two models of systematic change were described? How are they similar, and how are they different? What are the three essential steps, per Lewin's model?
14. What do downsizing, outsourcing, and offshoring have in common when discussing organizational change? What are their differences? How do these types of organizational changes impact employees?
15. What impact does a significant staff reduction have on an organization's reporting structure? On workers who remain employed? What strategies can organizations employ to strengthen their relationships with these employees?
16. What is the difference between a merger and an acquisition? What issues are possible with the combination of organizations? How can such issues be overcome, or even avoided?
17. What are organization development's (OD's) five definitional elements? Why is organization development important for organizations?
18. What is leadership OD?
19. Why is there a focus on team-building OD?
20. How can survey feedback OD contribute to improved organization performance?

CHAPTER 10

Teams and Teamwork

Chapter Outline

Level of Analysis

Defining Characteristics of Work Teams

Types of Teams

- Social Media and I-O Psychology: *Social Media Teams*
- COVID-19 and I-O Psychology: *Virtually All Virtual*

Team Life Cycle

Team Structure and Composition

- Faces of I-O Psychology: *Suzanne T. Bell*

Team Processes

- Transition Processes
- Action Processes
- Interpersonal Processes

Team Cognition

- Shared Mental Models
- Decision Making in Teams

Personnel Selection for Teams

- The Lighter Side of I-O Psychology: *Collective Nouns*

Training for Teams

Performance Appraisal in Teams

Concluding Comments

Chapter Review

Learning Objectives

- Explain what is meant by level of analysis.
- Explain the concept of teamwork.
- Describe the various types of teams.
- Describe how teams and team members develop over time.
- Describe the structure, composition, and processes of teams.
- Explain how teams make decisions and share mental models.
- Explain how personnel selection, training, and performance appraisal apply to teams.

The concept of teamwork dates to antiquity.[1] Nevertheless, early I-O psychologists tended to make individuals, rather than teams, the object of their attention. That is, we have long been concerned with finding the right person for the job, training the individual, and subsequently monitoring that individual's performance on the job. Numerous historic events transpired, however, that created a clear interest in team research, including tragic Persian Gulf military events that initiated funding to explore team decision making in the United States.[2] Since the 1980s, there has been a tremendous upsurge of interest in using work groups, not just individuals, as the organizing principle through which work is accomplished. Indeed, a 2019 survey on global workplace trends revealed that almost a third of businesses reported that most or almost all of their work is done in teams. In addition, a little over half of team-based organizations experienced a significant improvement in performance following their transition to being team-based.[3]

"Teams of people working together for a common purpose have been a centerpiece of human social organization ever since our ancient ancestors first banded together to hunt game, raise families, and defend their communities. Human history is largely a story of people working together to explore, achieve, and conquer."[4]

—Kozlowski & Ilgen 2006, p. 77

The evolution of teams and teamwork has compelled I-O psychology to address a host of new issues. Some have lamented that teams have become so commonplace that employees and managers just assume they will be effective.[5] However, teams are not universally superior to individuals for conducting work across all relevant performance indices. For example, teams do not necessarily produce better quality decisions than do individuals. It is a myth that companies that use teams are more effective than those that do not.[6] Teams are not a panacea for all work-related ills. A "team halo effect" can exist in the work world. When people seek to understand team performance, they tend to give teams credit for their success. However, individuals (as opposed to the collective group) tend to receive the blame for poor team performance.

Some of what we have learned about individuals in the workplace generalizes to teams, but other issues are more specific to teams. There is nothing magical about transforming individuals into work teams. Teams are merely one means of performing work. In this chapter, we will examine teams as a means of accomplishing work, including the factors that lead to successful team performance.

Level of Analysis

A shift in the focus from individuals to teams as a means of conducting work also requires a shift in the conduct of I-O psychological research. Researchers can and do examine different entities as the object of their investigations. Historically, I-O psychology focused on the individual with regard to such factors as desired knowledge, skills, abilities, and other personal characteristics (KSAOs) for employment, needed training, and standards of job performance. In such cases, the **level of analysis** is the individual; that is, the conclusions drawn from the research are about individuals. However, research questions can also be posed at the team level of analysis and at the organizational level of analysis. Consider an organization that has 100 employees. A researcher may be interested in assessing the relationship between the degree to which employees feel a sense of organizational identification with the company and job performance. At the *individual* level of analysis, the researcher would have a sample size of 100 individuals, obtain measures of organizational identification and job performance, correlate the

Level of analysis
The unit or level (individuals, teams, organizations, nations, etc.) that is the object of the researchers' interest and about which conclusions are drawn from the research.

two variables, and arrive at a conclusion regarding the relationship between them. However, the 100 employees could also be organized into 25 four-person work teams. In this case, the researcher would have a sample size of 25 (i.e., the 25 teams). Each team would be represented by a score reflecting its sense of organizational identification (as a team) and their work performance (as a team). The researcher would correlate these two variables and, based on a sample size of 25, arrive at a conclusion about the relationship between the two variables at the *team* level of analysis. It is also possible to study the relationship between organizational identification and performance at the *organizational* level of analysis. In this case, the 100-employee company would be a sample size of 1. There would be one measure of organizational identification (for the entire company) and one measure of performance (for the entire company). The researcher would then have to collect data from additional organizations. The researcher would correlate these two variables, based on a sample size of however many organizations were in the study, and arrive at a conclusion about the relationship between the two variables at the *organizational* level of analysis. Figure 10-1 is a diagram showing these levels of analysis.

What *is* the relationship between organizational identification and performance? The answer depends on the level of analysis under consideration. It is possible to arrive at three different conclusions, depending on whether the level of analysis is the individual, team, or organization. Furthermore, some constructs do not exist at particular levels of analysis. Size is one example. Teams and organizations can differ in their size (i.e., number of members), but individuals are always one. For the most part, I-O psychologists have not focused their research interests on the organizational level of analysis. Studying complete organizations and their relationships with other organizations is more traditionally the province of sociology. There is often a link between a

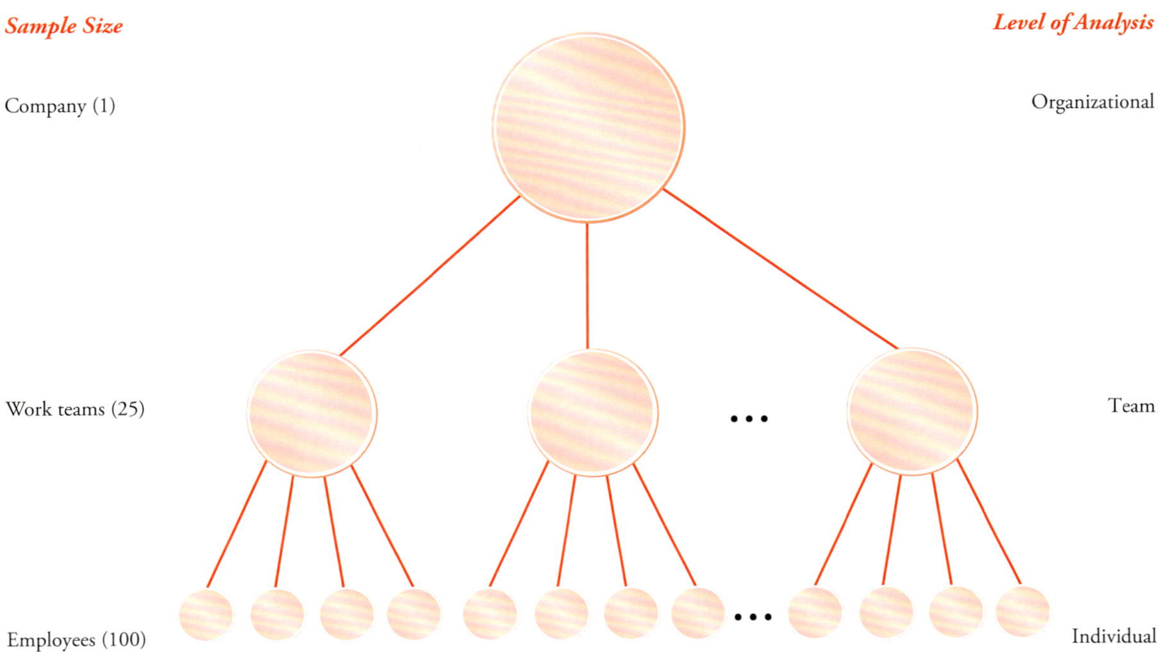

Figure 10-1 *Three levels of analysis*

particular scientific discipline and the level of analysis of its research. The field of economics examines variables at the industry (petroleum, agriculture, manufacturing, etc.) level of analysis, and the field of political science frequently examines variables at the national level of analysis.

The term *micro* is often used to describe research at the individual level of analysis, while *macro* is used to describe research at the organizational level of analysis. Research at the team level is positioned somewhere between the micro and the macro, bridging the gap between the individual and the organizational system.[7] This research that occurs in an organizational context where processes at two levels are examined simultaneously is termed *meso* (meaning "in between," as in the word *mezzanine*) research.[8] Thus, I-O psychology researchers who study relationships between variables at both the individual and team levels of analysis are engaging in meso research. The area of multilevel research and theory addresses a fundamental dilemma in understanding human behavior in organizations; namely, we as individuals obtain employment in a larger social collectivity (an organization) and are often members of some smaller level of aggregation (such as a team, department, unit, or shift).[9] The dilemma is to disentangle the sources of influence on our behavior from the perspectives of individuals, teams, and organizations.

We can now move onto a discussion of teams and teamwork within organizations. The first question that we'll address is, "What is a team?"

Defining Characteristics of Work Teams

When discussing teams, one of the first things to consider is how they are different from groups, if at all. Although people often use the terms "groups" and "teams" interchangeably, there are clear characteristics of teams that make them unique and distinct from groups. Inappropriately calling a group a team may hurt the ability to empower teams and may set members up for disappointment.[10] In this section, we discuss the defining characteristics that make teams unique and distinct from groups.

Team
A social aggregation in which a limited number of individuals interact on a regular basis to accomplish a set of shared objectives for which they have mutual responsibility.

Teams are bounded social units that work within a larger social system—the organization. A work team has identifiable memberships (that is, members and nonmembers alike clearly know who is a member and who is not) and an identifiable task or set of tasks to perform. Tasks may include monitoring, producing, serving, generating ideas, and doing other activities. The team's work requires that members interact by exchanging information, sharing resources, and coordinating with and reacting to one another in accomplishing the team's task. Furthermore, there is always some degree of interdependence within the members of a team, which is not always the case with mere groups of people. By combining different perspectives and capitalizing on the strengths of the individual members, they are able to achieve results that exceed the pooled or combined results of all their members. As such, the whole is greater than the sum of the parts.

Another point worthy of mention is how many people it takes to form a team. While many scholars will consider a team to be two or more individuals working together, others believe a team must consist of at least three members and treat dyads (two-person units) separate from teams. Regardless, the issues discussed throughout this chapter apply to both dyads and teams of three or more individuals.

Consider This...

A common debate for sports fans is whether a particular sport is a team sport or an individual sport. Two sports that have been argued on both sides are baseball and soccer (called football in most countries outside of the U.S.).[11] Although baseball has many individualized aspects (such as the pitcher vs. the batter), Babe Ruth, considered by many to be the greatest baseball player of all time, once stated, "The way a team plays as a whole determines its success. You may have the greatest bunch of individual stars in the world, but if they don't play together, the club won't be worth a dime." Similarly, soccer has been argued as being individualistic, in that a prolific scorer or adept goalie can carry a team. Yet, Mia Hamm, two-time Olympic gold medalist and two-time FIFA Women's World Cup soccer champion once said, "I am a member of a team, and I rely on the team, I defer to it and sacrifice for it, because the team, not the individual, is the ultimate champion." What do you think? Based on the defining characteristics of teams (vs. groups) described here, would these sports be team sports or individual sports in your opinion? How so?

Babe Ruth

Mia Hamm

Types of Teams

The term *team* has been used in many contexts to describe types of work operations, such as project teams, sales teams, new product teams, process improvement teams, cost-reduction teams, and so on (see Social Media and I-O Psychology: *Social Media Teams*). One way to differentiate teams is by their objectives. It is also possible to differentiate teams by other variables, such as the nature of their interactions (e.g., face-to-face vs. virtual). We present five basic types of teams (problem-resolution, creative, tactical, *ad hoc*, and virtual), as well as the concept of multiteam systems (or "team of teams").

Problem-resolution team
A type of team created for the purpose of focusing on solving ongoing problems or issues.

Problem-resolution teams are created for the purpose of focusing on solving ongoing problems or issues. Such teams require each member of the team to be truthful and embody a high degree of integrity. Each member must believe that the team will be consistent and mature in its approach to dealing with problems. The members must have an elevated degree of trust in a process of problem resolution that focuses on issues, rather than on predetermined positions or conclusions. Diagnostic teams at the Centers for Disease Control and Prevention are an exemplar of this type.

Creative team
A type of team created for the purpose of developing innovative possibilities or solutions.

Creative teams are responsible for exploring possibilities and alternatives, with the broad objective of developing a new product or service. A necessary feature of the team's structure is autonomy. For a creative team to function, it needs to have autonomy from systems and procedures as well as an atmosphere in which ideas are not prematurely quashed. Creative teams need to be insulated within the organizational structure to remain focused on the result to be achieved, rather than on organizational processes. The IBM PC was developed by a creative team that endured many failures before arriving at a successful product. The design team needed protection from typical organizational pressures that reflect impatience with failure. The "incubation period" for the PC was many years and could not have been shortened by performance expectations imposed by others.

Social Media and I-O Psychology: *Social Media Teams*

Social media have become crucial for organizations, particularly with regard to their marketing and public relations. Organizations must have a clear and strong online presence to compete effectively in the digital world. While some organizations rely on individuals to maintain their online presence (often on top of other job responsibilities), many are turning to specialized teams of individuals who share the responsibility of managing the organization's Facebook and Twitter accounts, posting videos, photos, and promotional materials to YouTube, Instagram, and Pinterest, and writing blog posts, among other things. In short, these social media teams act as the digital face and voice of an organization.

Although many organizations use social media regularly, there are certainly some dominant players in the social media realm. Taco Bell's social media team, for example, is extremely active online. Their presence has a passionate following, in part based on the team's ability to think creatively and engage customers in humorous yet constructive dialogue. They have even made waves (and attracted even more followers) by interacting with other notable brands. For example, in 2012, Old Spice's social media team tweeted "Why is it that 'fire sauce' isn't made with any real fire? Seems like false advertising." Taco Bell's social media team didn't miss a beat, tweeting, "@OldSpice is your deodorant made with really old spices?" To this, Old Spice's team quipped back, "@TacoBell Depends. Do you consider volcanos, tanks and freedom to be spices?" Similarly, Chipotle turned to TikTok in 2020 to bring audiences the #ChipotleLidFlip and #GuacDance challenges, generating hundreds of millions of views in a matter of days for each.

While much of social media teams' work is focused on marketing, they have also used social media as a platform to highlight workers, such as Dove's 2020 Instagram campaign honoring healthcare workers during the COVID-19 pandemic. Go Teams!

Tactical team
A type of team created for the purpose of executing a well-defined plan or objective.

Tactical teams are responsible for executing a well-defined plan. To do, so there must be high task clarity and unambiguous role definition. The success of tactical teams depends on a high degree of responsiveness from team members, a clear understanding of who does what, and a clear set of performance standards. An example of a tactical team is a police SWAT team or a cardiac surgical team. Each operational procedure must be well defined, and each task must be highly focused and specific. Furthermore, the standards of excellence must be clear to everyone, and ways of measuring success or failure must be understood by the entire team.

***Ad hoc* team**
A type of team created for a limited duration that is designed to address one particular problem.

The fourth type of team is defined primarily by its limited life span. It is sometimes called an *ad hoc* (Latin for "to this") team and is basically a cross between a problem-resolution and a tactical team. An ***ad hoc* team** is created for a specific purpose, addressing itself "to this" particular problem. The team members are selected from existing employees in an organization, and after the team has completed its work, the team disbands. Thus, membership in the team (and indeed the life span of the team itself) is finite. *Ad hoc* teams are used in organizations that encounter unusual or atypical problems that require an atypical response (the creation of the *ad hoc* team). If the problem tends to recur, there may be pressure to establish the team on a longer-term basis, as a more formalized and permanent unit.

Virtual team
A type of team in which the members, often geographically dispersed, interact through electronic communication and may never meet face-to-face.

Lastly, a fifth type of team that has emerged is the **virtual team**, or those teams whose members work together through electronic media to accomplish their goals.[12] Virtual teams have several defining characteristics.[13] First, communication among team members primarily takes place electronically. The electronic communication processes use multiple communication channels, which may include text, graphic, audio, and video communication. Second, the team members are usually dispersed geographically. They may be in different cities, nations, or even continents. It is not unusual for the members of a virtual team to never meet face-to-face, which for some people may be a difficult obstacle to overcome. Third, virtual team members may interact synchronously or asynchronously. Synchronous interaction occurs when team members communicate at the same time, as in chat sessions or video conferencing. Asynchronous interaction occurs when team members communicate at different times, as through email or electronic bulletin boards. In 2014, a sample of published field studies found that most virtual teams relied on email to communicate, while the least frequently used means of communication was videoconferencing due to the expensive and cumbersome nature of the technology.[14] These circumstances have changed, however, because of ever-increasing technological advancements in part catapulted forward by the COVID-19 pandemic. The pandemic necessitated the ability for teams to work remotely for an extended period of time (see COVID-19 and I-O Psychology: *Virtually All Virtual*).

Multiteam systems
Teams of teams that function interdependently to achieve overarching system-level goals.

Our lives are influenced by the interplay among various sets of teams operating in sequences.[15] They are called **multiteam systems**, and they have become so ingrained in our society that we might not think of them as functioning in such a manner. Imagine there is a severe automobile accident where a life is in peril. Here is a likely sequence of actions by multiple teams: an emergency phone call reporting the accident is made to the police. The police department contacts the dispatch center of the fire department to send a crew to the scene. The police arrive at the scene to control the flow of traffic around the accident. The firefighters have the responsibility to extinguish any vehicle fire that may have started, reduce the likelihood of a fire starting, and use extrication tools and equipment. Emergency Medical Technicians (EMTs), another team, work to stabilize the victim for transportation, sometimes while firefighters work to free the victim. The victim is placed in an ambulance and rushed to the nearest hospital. At the hospital another team is standing by—the surgical team needed to perform a lifesaving operation. The surgical team might consist of nurses, anesthesiologists, medical technicians, and physicians. Following the surgery, the patient is admitted into the intensive care unit of the hospital and attended to by a recovery team of doctors and nurses.

Multiteam systems are characterized by the interdependency among teams that not only have their own team-level goals, but also have overarching system-level goals.[16] Note the interconnectedness of the five teams that respond to this automobile accident—police, fire, EMT, surgical, and recovery. Each team has a specific goal and follows a process that has beginning and ending points. Each team is specially trained to perform its tasks with great efficiency and under severe time pressure. Furthermore, one team cannot do its work without coordinating appropriately with the other teams.

Multiteam systems benefit greatly from having members with broad functional experiences. As such, it may be important to either select such team members, or

COVID-19 and I-O Psychology: *Virtually All Virtual*

Virtual teams have been around for a long time, though not all teams took advantage of this modality. With the COVID-19 pandemic, however, many teams became virtual out of necessity. This included teams and individuals who had never before needed to utilize this format, and as a result there were some challenges.

Research has shown that virtual teams tend to communicate more frequently, but that the efficiency decreases.[17] In addition, as teams get accustomed to working virtually, they may err on the side of over-sharing, as they may not grasp what information is relevant and must be shared, versus irrelevant and doesn't need to be shared.

In addition to potential information overload and decreased efficiency, teams also tend to engage in fewer casual conversations and have delayed response times when communicating. These factors may lead to lower trust and cohesion among members as well as problems with getting on the same page and acting as a single unit.[18]

There are numerous things that teams can do to become more effective and avoid some of the pitfalls if they must become virtual.[19] First, they should choose the appropriate way to communicate. If a quick response is needed without a lot of detail, instant messaging may be most appropriate. If greater collaboration is needed, video-based communication may be ideal. Second, it is important to be concise and clear when communicating with team members, to avoid confusion and limit the amount of unnecessary information that is shared. Third, only necessary people should be included in meetings, and the roles of all meeting attendees should be clarified.

Setting rules and establishing norms related to virtual interactions are also important, such as indicating when and how people should speak, when informal dialogue is acceptable, and so forth. Team leaders may also consider using breakout groups or polling members anonymously to encourage participation and ensure all voices are heard. Along these lines, another idea to implement is when brainstorming ideas, it may be best to silently think of ideas before sharing them with the group. Lastly, sending a recording or notes of the meeting to team members who may have been absent is a good way to foster inclusion, help build trust, and ensure clarity among team members.

Virtual teams face many challenges, but with proper planning and thoughtful attention, many of the obstacles can be overcome. It is likely that the number of teams that are virtual will continue to rise, and it is therefore important that managers and team members carefully consider how best to work virtually.

train them across different areas, since broad functional knowledge bases help provide a common framework that minimizes language and goal differences that could be harmful if left unaddressed.[20] These teams must coordinate and communicate effectively to achieve the systems-level goal (i.e., to save a life, in the case of the automobile accident), despite having different cultures, norms, goals, and processes within each individual team.[21] This "team of teams" concept involving coordination and communication among multiple teams is fertile for advancing our understanding from both scientific and practical perspectives.[22]

Team Life Cycle

The ways in which individuals come together to form a team, and the stages they go through as the team develops, is known as the team life cycle. The process of becoming a team is more complicated than simply putting individuals together into a group. It takes time for individuals to begin seeing themselves as a cohesive, functioning unit.

Five stage model of group development A framework that proposes groups proceed through a sequence of five stages: forming, storming, norming, performing, and adjourning.

One of the best-known models of team development is the **five stage model of group development**.[23] This model suggests that groups proceed through a predictable sequence of five stages. The first stage is the *forming* stage. In this stage, individuals come together, but still act more as individuals than as a cohesive unit. At this point, individuals are getting to know one another and do things to avoid conflict. There is a lot of uncertainty at this time, with individuals not knowing each other or what is expected of them. The forming stage is followed by the *storming* stage. In this stage, there is a great deal of interpersonal conflict and jockeying for position and status within the group. Next is the *norming* stage. This stage occurs once the team members understand their roles and have an agreed-upon goal and plan for accomplishing the goal. Members now understand their roles in the group and accept their positions. The fourth stage is the *performing* stage. This is when the team members coordinate their actions and behave as a cohesive, fully-functioning unit. Their actions are smooth and

Consider This...

Have you ever noticed that movies that focus on sports teams, military combat units, space exploration teams, and superhero groups are extraordinarily common, and Hollywood has done a fantastic job of depicting the five-stage model of group development, whether intentionally or unintentionally? The plotline for the movies is eerily identical, in that we are typically introduced to a group of individuals first. These are the primary characters whose individual personalities, abilities, and other defining characteristics are explored. The individual characters are not yet an identifiable unit at this stage, but are being brought together to become a group. This is clearly the forming stage. Then, like clockwork, the members of the group begin disagreeing and engaging in conflict. There are alpha personalities who are battling for a position of authority, somebody who can't seem to buy into the concept of teamwork, and other common disputes. Obviously, this is the storming stage of group development. Eventually, tempers cool and the group members see that they're going to have to set some ground rules in order to get along and be successful. Here they are figuring out their roles, or engaging in the norming stage. Finally, there is the pivotal scene (or scenes) in which the members of the group work seamlessly together to beat the enemy (or opposing team, or whatever the group is up against). Movies will then often have the teams disband (mission accomplished—adjourning stage in effect). Occasionally such adjournment does not occur, as the team will be remaining intact (sequel possibility!). Does this plotline sound familiar? In what movies can you see the five-stage model of group development depicted? By working through your own example and applying this model, you'll be better able to remember it and you'll start to notice it more and more going forward.

coordinated, and performance is optimal. The final stage is the *adjourning* stage. This stage occurs when the team is disbanding. At this point, the team has completed its task and members engage in reflection.

The five-stage model of group development is intuitively appealing. It is easy for individuals to think of teams they have been members of and identify these various stages as having occurred. However, the model doesn't hold true for all teams, and teams may progress through the model at different rates. For example, some teams may have a very short forming stage, moving quickly into the storming stage of conflict. In addition, the final two stages in the model may not occur for all teams. Some teams may never become fully functioning and cohesive. Others may be permanent teams that never disband.

Socialization
The process of mutual adjustment between the team and its members, especially new members.

Life cycles within teams can also be examined for individuals within a team and how their adjustment impacts, and is impacted by, the team itself. **Socialization** is the process of mutual adjustment that produces changes over time in the relationship between a person and a team. We discussed organizational socialization in Chapter 7, and while team socialization is similar, it differs somewhat. In the case of teams, socialization is the process a person goes through in joining a team, being on a team, and eventually leaving a team. Likewise, the team itself is affected by the arrival, presence, and departure of a team member. The socialization process can range from a formal orientation session to the team to informal one-on-one feedback between a senior team member and the newcomer. The relationship between a senior team member and a newcomer can take on many of the properties of the mentor–protégé relationship discussed in Chapter 7. New team members can be apprised of the ways of the team by subtle observation of an older team member or by seeking feedback from the team (e.g. "What does it take to be successful on the team?" and "Am I fitting in?").

The way in which socialization occurs is based on three psychological concepts: evaluation, commitment, and role transition.[24] *Evaluation* involves attempts by the team and the individual to assess and maximize each other's value. This includes the team identifying the goals to which individuals can contribute, and individuals evaluating how participation on the team can satisfy their personal needs. Thus, the evaluation process is mutual. Research has shown that when new members join a team, the existing members treat the newcomer differently depending on their physical attractiveness and sex.[25] In general, team members mimic attractive newcomers, ingratiate themselves to attractive male newcomers who are committed to the task, and challenge attractive female newcomers who are committed to the task. Thus, socialization is dependent in part on the evaluation existing members have made with regard to the new members' physical characteristics.

The second socialization concept is *commitment*, which is the sense of loyalty, union, and connection between the individual and the team. When individuals are committed to the team, they are likely to accept the team's goals, work hard to achieve them, and feel warmly toward the team. When a team is strongly committed to an individual, it is likely to accept that person's needs, work hard to satisfy them, and feel warmly toward the person. Changes in commitment transform the relationship between a team and an individual. These transformations are governed by specific levels of commitment that mark the boundaries between different membership roles the person could play in the team. Both the team and the individual try to initiate a *role transition* when commitment reaches a certain level.

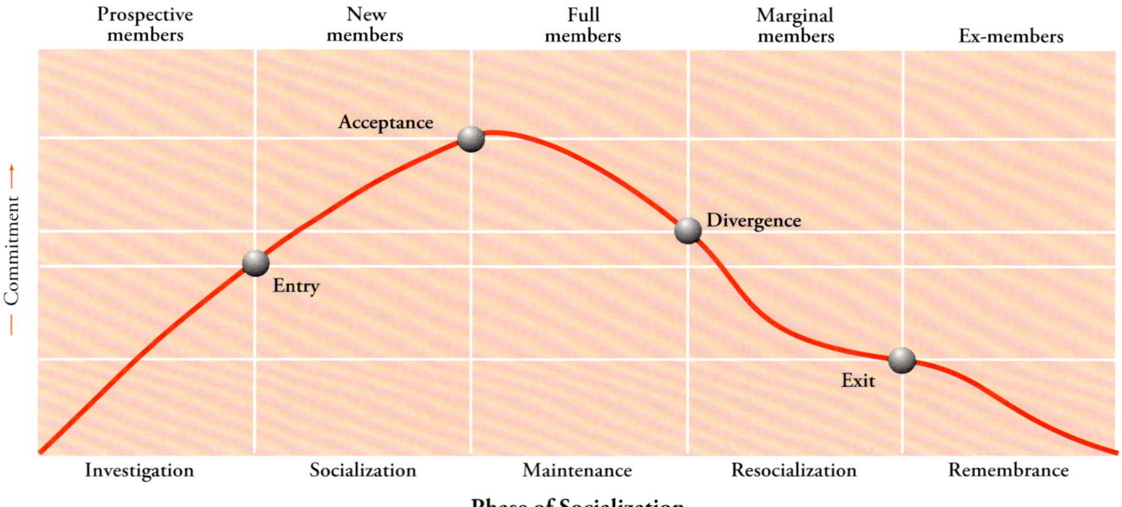

Figure 10-2 *The socialization process for team members*

Source: Adapted from "Socialization in Organizations and Work Groups," by R. L. Moreland and J. M. Levine, in M. E. Turner (Ed.), *Groups at work*, pp. 69-112 (2001). Reprinted with permission of Lawrence Erlbaum Associates via Copyright Clearance Center.

Figure 10-2 shows the team commitment over time as an individual passes through five phases of team membership: investigation, socialization, maintenance, resocialization, and remembrance.

During the *investigation* phase, the team searches for individuals who can contribute to the achievement of team goals. Likewise, the individual, as a prospective member of the team, searches for a team that will be satisfying. If both parties achieve an initial sense of commitment, the investigation phase ends and the *socialization* phase begins. In this phase, the individual assimilates into the team and the team accommodates itself to the individual. If both parties accept each other, the individual becomes a full member of the team. This acceptance marks the end of the socialization phase and the beginning of *maintenance*. Now both parties try to maximize their respective needs—the achievement of the team and the satisfaction of the individual. This phase lasts as long as both parties meet their needs. However, as commitment weakens between the team and individual, another role transition based on the divergence of commitment occurs, resulting in *resocialization*. During resocialization, the team and the individual try again to influence each other so that the team's needs are more likely to be satisfied. If the resocialization process is not successful, team membership ends with a period of *remembrance*. The team recalls the individual's contributions to the achievement of its goals, and the individual recalls experiences with the team. Over time, feelings of commitment between the team and the individual often stabilize, usually at a low level.

This socialization process reveals the subtleties and phases of group dynamics. Both the individual and the team are mutually trying to influence each other to achieve the same purpose: assimilating the individual into the team. The socialization process occurs over time, although the length of the time period varies across individuals and teams. Teams have "lives" based on the state of socialization of their members, and this socialization process is constantly evolving.

Team Structure and Composition

Teams are, by definition, comprised of individuals who are working together to achieve a common goal. Teams can be structured in a variety of ways to achieve their goals. Team structure involves the way in which teams break complex tasks into smaller parts.[26] How the tasks are deconstructed will create a situation in which different team members are responsible for different tasks, and the members' efforts combine to achieve a single goal.

Team structure has three separate dimensions:[27]

1. **Skill differentiation**—dictates who will perform various tasks. When teams have high skill differentiation, members have highly-specialized knowledge or capabilities that make it more difficult to substitute one member for another. Low skill differentiation, on the other hand, would enable team members to be readily substitutable for one another to execute tasks.
2. **Authority differentiation**—dictates who has the power to make decisions. High authority differentiation occurs when decision-making authority is assigned to a single member, whereas low authority differentiation occurs when the collective team has the authority to make decisions.
3. **Temporal stability**—refers to whether the team members are together for a short or long duration. Teams with high temporal stability have worked together in the past and/or will work together for quite a while going forward. Teams that are created for "one-shot" efforts or short-term projects have lower temporal stability.

"Alone we can do so little; together we can do so much."
—Helen Keller

When accomplishing a team's goal, team members may take on one or more roles within the team. Recall from Chapter 9 that roles are sets of expectations about appropriate behavior in a position. They are essentially the different "hats" that people wear. Figure 10-3 shows a three-dimensional model of role behavior in groups called the TRIAD (Tracking Roles In And Across Domains).[28] This model suggests there are 13 different role clusters:

1. Team leader	5. Attention seeker	10. Teamwork support
2. Task motivator	6. Negative	11. Evaluator
3. Power seeker	7. Social	12. Problem solver
4. Critic	8. Coordinator	13. Task completer
	9. Follower	

In order to determine the role that a person would likely have in a team, the TRIAD assesses where an individual falls on three dimensions:

1. **Dominance** (how dominant, active, and control-seeking an individual is)
2. **Sociability** (how sociable, friendly, and agreeable a person is)
3. **Task Orientation** (how focused a person is on solving a task)

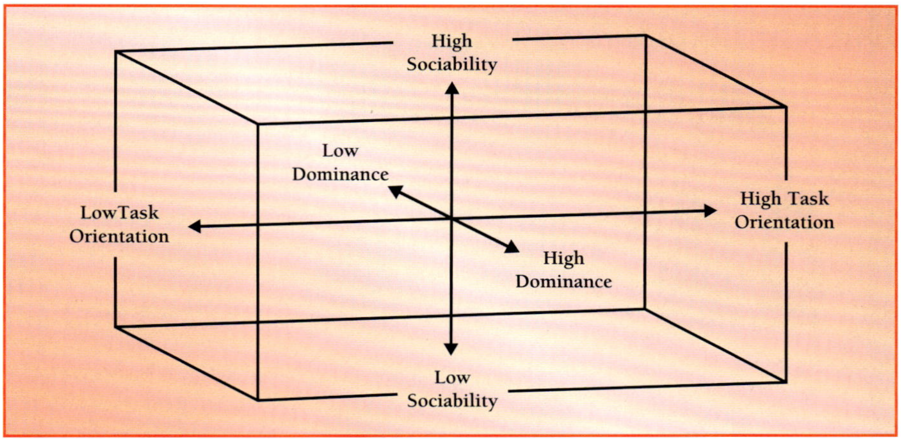

Figure 10-3 *The TRIAD model*

Note: TRIAD = Tracking Roles In and Across Domains

Source: Adapted from "Team Roles: A Review and Integration," by T. Driskell, J. E. Driskell, C. S. Burke, and E. Salas (2017). *Small Group Research*. Reprinted with permission of Sage Publications, Ltd. via Copyright Clearance Center.

Individuals can fall anywhere from high to low on any of these three dimensions, and where they fall on those dimensions in the three-dimensional space shown in Figure 10-3 determines which role they likely have in the team. For example, individuals who have high task orientation, average sociability, and high dominance characterize team leaders. These individuals help drive the team forward by facilitating activities, structuring tasks, and coordinating and commanding efforts. An individual with average task orientation, low sociability, and high dominance, however, would be classified as a power seeker who may be overly domineering and have negative consequences for the team. Knowing what roles are filled by various team members will help determine who should be removed, what training may be needed, and which specific roles should be replaced, either by incumbents or newcomers, if turnover or attrition occurs.[29]

When discussing team structure, it is only natural to talk about team composition, which refers to the characteristics of team members and how they relate to team processes and outcomes (see Faces of I-O Psychology: *Suzanne T. Bell*). Research on team composition has focused on which characteristics are most important for team effectiveness, as well as how those characteristics should be distributed within a team. Research has found that the effectiveness of teams within lab settings is influenced by the team's minimum and maximum general mental ability level (*g*).[30] Thus, the team's strongest and weakest link in terms of cognitive ability can impact the team's overall performance. In field settings, the team's minimum agreeableness was related to lower team performance. In addition, as the average level of conscientiousness, openness to experience, and preference for teamwork increased, so too did team performance.

Team composition also concerns how diverse a team is or should be. A meta-analysis on the influence of job-related diversity and demographic diversity on team performance found that when objective measures of performance are used, job-related diversity results in enhanced performance, and no negative issues result from

Faces of I-O Psychology: *Suzanne T. Bell*

Suzanne T. Bell

Ph.D. Texas A&M University

Professor, Industrial and Organizational Psychology, DePaul University

Research interests: Strategic staffing of organizations, organizational training, team effectiveness.

Thought leader in team composition. Research funded by National Aeronautics and Space Administration (NASA).

NASA and its international partners are focused on developing the capabilities to send humans to Mars in the 2030s. The mission to Mars will challenge the frontiers of human collaboration as the small team of astronauts live and work in an extreme environment. The crew is expected to be confined to a space the size of a small studio apartment for 2½ years. As the crew travels further into deep space, the extreme distance will result in significant communication delays with Earth, adding to their isolation. Complex feats such as space walks, landing, and launch from Mars will be executed by the small crew with unparalleled levels of autonomy from mission control. It's estimated that once the crew reaches Mars, mission control back on Earth will receive updates, error notifications, and information about emergencies with a 22-minute delay.

The small astronaut teams will be composed of members diverse in professional background, national background, and other attributes, who need to work together as a team. They'll need to rely on one another for social support, keep interpersonal conflicts manageable, coordinate seamlessly to execute complex tasks, and adapt to whatever comes their way. I-O psychologists are involved in research focused on optimizing the performance of future space teams. My collaborators and I are creating predictive models of how team composition influences the performance and well-being of future long-distance space exploration teams.

There is a large body of research that suggests that team composition, or the configuration of team member attributes, can have a profound influence on teamwork and effectiveness. Beyond the knowledge and skills of team members, personality, values, and demographics can shape the way team members think, feel and behave toward one another, ultimately influencing the team's ability to work together. We use this extensive team composition literature as a foundation for our NASA-funded research. We also recognize and integrate the extreme circumstances future space teams will encounter, and collect data at Johnson Space Center in the Human Exploration Research Analog (HERA). Teams of four people are confined to this small habitat for up to 45 days, mostly isolated from the rest of the world. We collect data on a number of variables, including team member attributes, team members' relationships with one another, and how well the teams perform on specially-designed tasks. We combine these data and data from other analog environments with what we already know about team composition to create our models. We use innovative methodologies and analytics to test our predictions. Our research can inform how to best staff astronaut teams, and also how to most effectively manage a team with a given composition over the course of a mission. We help NASA push the boundaries of future human space exploration, by pushing the boundaries of team science.

demographic diversity. However, when subjective measures are used, demographic diversity in a team appears to result in biased downward ratings of performance.[31] The authors of the meta-analysis concluded that demographic diversity is not necessarily problematic for teams, but that diverse teams may be better assessed with objective performance indicators to avoid potential rater biases.

Team Processes

Team processes
The operations within a team that permit it to function smoothly and efficiently.

As important as the structure of a team is to its functioning, the majority of research on teams has been directed to the processes that guide how teams function. The very nature of teamwork implies that individuals must coordinate their activities and manage interpersonal interactions to be successful. These operations within a team that permit it to function smoothly and efficiently are generally termed **team processes**. Team processes include *transition processes* (behaviors and actions that focus on planning and evaluation), *action processes* (behaviors and actions that facilitate goal accomplishment), and *interpersonal processes* (behaviors and actions that concern managing team member affect/emotions).[32] Although other models of team processes exist, researchers have found this particular model to be a better depiction of team processes compared to competing models.[33] We will now discuss each of these three factors and the behaviors that comprise them.

Transition Processes

Transition processes include behaviors and actions that focus on planning and evaluation. These occur during time that is specifically set aside for such activities, such as staff meetings or retreats. That is, they occur when a team is transitioning from one project or way of doing things to another. These behaviors include mission analysis, goal specification, and strategy formulation and planning.

Mission analysis When a team is given a task, team members must take the time to understand their charge and identify the resources and constraints that exist for the task. When considering these factors, the team is engaging in a mission analysis. As part of this analysis, the team members must look at their past performance to determine what worked and didn't work. In addition, they must look forward to see if there might be anything that could impede their progress if they don't account for it. Mission analysis is a critical process for all teams. Without engaging in these activities, the team runs the risk of focusing their attention and efforts on the wrong things, potentially to the point where it becomes too late for the team to recover.

Goal specification. Along with the mission analysis, teams must set timelines and prioritize goals. Teams must be flexible, however, with timelines and priorities, as situations may change and obstacles may appear. As such, teams may need to redefine their goals periodically to continue making progress. In general, goals will be more effective for teams to the extent they are specific, attainable, and valued by team members. The issue of goal setting is discussed more in Chapter 13.

Strategy formulation and planning. Teams must also be strategic in terms of their planning. They must create contingency plans in the event that their original plans don't work out as intended. To the extent that team members take the time to anticipate potential problems and actions they will take if those problems occur, they will be better equipped to deal more swiftly with the issues. Of course, in addition to creating a "Plan B" ahead of time, effective teams must be able to adapt in the moment to changing circumstances. Planning efforts can be distinguished between taskwork and teamwork planning.[34] Taskwork planning involves preparations related to task completion, whereas teamwork planning involves more interpersonal requirements, such as identifying team member capabilities or specifying team roles. Both forms of planning are important, and one should not be given primary emphasis at the expense of the other.

Consider This...

Colin Powell

Within the domain of warfare and competition, there is an adage that states that no plan survives contact with the enemy. The idea behind the sentiment is that once you've confronted your adversary, you will likely need to adjust your plan to account for their response to your encounter. As Colin Powell, retired four-star general and former Secretary of State, once said, "there's always somebody on the other side that's just as smart as you and is trying to outthink you. So, leaders must always be thinking about contingency plans and examining 'what-if' scenarios."[35] Do you think having a "Plan B" is more or less important for some teams than others? Who should be responsible for coming up with the contingency plan?

Action Processes

Action processes include behaviors and actions that facilitate goal accomplishment. These include activities that keep things running smoothly and efficiently. Coordination, monitoring, and backup behaviors are in this category.

Coordination behaviors. Coordination behaviors involve the sharing of information to accomplish tasks. Key to coordination is communication. Interpersonal communication in successful work teams is characterized by a consistent pattern.[36] It is often described as open, frequent, and candid. Formal, regularly-scheduled meetings are held to discuss team progress. More informal communication occurs on a daily basis as team members discuss specific work issues. In high-performing groups, team members communicate problems they are having and freely solicit advice. They are not reluctant to discuss problems and concerns that might otherwise be artfully avoided. Continuous communication is regarded as not only acceptable but also desirable, because it helps the team achieve results it might not attain otherwise. Nevertheless, there can be too much of a good thing. While too little communication may keep important information from being shared, communicating too much may lead to work overload and ultimately hurt performance.[37]

Monitoring behaviors. For a team to reach its goals, the members need to know how they are progressing toward the goals. Monitoring behaviors help accomplish this. These behaviors include tracking and interpreting information to see how well a team is doing in terms of using its resources and reaching its objectives, and then sharing that information with all team members.[38] To the extent that team members know what is expected of them and have an idea of how well they are doing, they can more easily and effectively achieve their directives.

Backup behaviors. Backup behaviors are those actions that are supportive in nature. For example, helping a teammate complete a task, coaching a teammate to do the task, or actually doing the task for a teammate are all backup behaviors. Such behaviors are critically important for teams, as it makes the team truly behave as a single unit, greater than simply the sum of its parts.[39] Nevertheless, there are downsides to such behaviors within teams. For example, teams can incur costs associated with backing up teammates, called "harmful help."[40] Team members may neglect their own work to assist a chronically under-performing teammate. In addition, team members who know they will be assisted by others may decrease their level of effort in subsequent tasks. Thus, team members can acquire a sense of "learned helplessness" in the conduct of their work roles, secure in knowing other members will cover for them. In addition, giving help to teammates appears to be related to lower creativity for those giving assistance.[41] Therefore, it is important to consider the costs of backup behaviors, and only engage in them when the potential negative effects can be mitigated.

Interpersonal Processes

Interpersonal processes include behaviors and actions that concern managing team member affect/emotions. These include conflict management, motivation and confidence building, and mood and emotion management.

Conflict management. Conflict among members is unavoidable in any team. Conflict management behaviors include those behaviors that prevent conflict from occurring as well as those that help members deal with conflict once it does occur. It is important to note that not all conflict is bad. There are two distinct types of conflict: beneficial and competitive.[42] At the root of *beneficial conflict* is the desire of two or more members with differing ideas and interests to understand the views of the other. The team members try to understand each other's perspective and seek to fashion a mutually-satisfactory decision. Such experiences tend to strengthen relationships, as members become more confident that future conflicts can also be resolved. In contrast, the basis of *competitive conflict* is the desire to win, to be judged "right" in a contest of opinions and values. The individuals in conflict regard the competition as a test of their status, power, and credibility within the organization. High-performing work teams seek to diminish the manifestations of competitive conflict.

Conflict can also be categorized as *task conflict* (focused on work activities), *process conflict* (focused on how work activities are accomplished), and *relationship conflict* (focused on interpersonal dynamics). In a meta-analysis of the relationship between team member conflict and group performance, task conflict was actually related to *higher* performance, especially when the team wasn't also experiencing relationship conflict.[43] That is, task conflict can actually help a team perform better, particularly with regard to financial performance and the quality of its decisions. It is conflict that is focused on interpersonal relationships among team members that appears to be dysfunctional. Even so, not all task conflict is good either. Research has found that task conflict resulted in higher performance when teams were comprised of members who had high levels of openness to experience and emotional stability.[44] When team members were low on these two personality characteristics, however, task conflict had a negative impact on group performance.

Consider This...

Why do you think openness to experience and emotional stability make a difference in the relationship between task conflict and group performance? Recall that individuals who are high on openness to experience tend to be curious, creative, and willing to try new things. Individuals who are high on emotional stability tend to be calm, confident, and emotionally resilient. Why do you suppose that having team members with these traits leads to better (or improved) performance when task conflicts arise? What would you suggest teams who do *not* have individuals with these traits do if they are likely to experience task conflict?

Faultlines Imaginary dividing lines that separate a group into two or more subgroups.

Related to the concept of conflict is that of "faultlines" within a team.[45] **Faultlines** refer to subgroups emerging within the team. Subgroups may form on the basis of shared attributes (such as race or gender), job duties, or past work experiences. For example, a team of medical personnel may have a faultline based on rank, such that a subgroup of nurses and a subgroup of physicians emerge. The critical question is the extent to which faultlines disrupt information sharing and interfere with team functioning. If it's the case that a nurse is hesitant to speak up in front of a physician, this faultline is disrupting communication and could cause problems. Stronger faultlines lead to greater conflict, lower team cohesion, and reduced team performance and satisfaction.[46] Some teams may rise above the presence of subgroups, while others may allow the subgroups to produce conflict within the team. Informational faultlines, or subgroups that emerge based on knowledge, skill, and expertise, appear to be related to performance problems.[47] To minimize the potential problems of faultlines, teams should establish shared goals, leaders of the teams should focus on relationships, and neutral parties should be identified who can serve as "connectors" between the subgroups to help convey information and translate potentially contradictory or sensitive perspectives.[48]

Motivation and confidence building. The second category of interpersonal processes is aimed at creating a sense of collective confidence and motivation among the team members. These efforts would include such things as encouraging each other and creating a feeling of safety among members. It is important that members cultivate a sense of psychological safety within the team.[49] The team becomes a "safe harbor" for the expression of ideas and opinions that will not be treated with rebuke. Such a norm allows members to engage in interpersonal risk-taking that may advance the welfare of the team, as opposed to members being reluctant to speak up about issues. These efforts, if successful, result in heightened **collective efficacy**, or a shared belief that the team can be successful. Teams with a strong sense of collective efficacy tend to set more challenging goals and, when confronted with difficulties, keep on trying rather than giving up.[50] In short, they are more likely to succeed. However, there does appear to be a caveat to this statement. Namely, it may be detrimental to teams if they experience collective efficacy too early in their life cycle, because excessive confidence in the early phases of a group project may cause teams to be narrow minded and not consider alternative views when determining long-term strategies or procedures for approaching complex tasks.[51] As such, although collective efficacy is valuable for teams, it appears to be something that is better developed after team members have a chance to engage in a little conflict regarding processes and strategies.

Collective efficacy
A group's shared belief in their ability to work together to be successful as a unit.

Mood and emotion management. The final category of interpersonal processes deals with regulating team member emotions, including anger and frustration. These include behaviors directed at calming members who may be stressed and helping increase morale and cohesion. Related to this is **team cohesion**, or the extent to which team members feel attached to their team and have a desire to remain a part of it. The attachment is posited to manifest itself in how the team performs its tasks, particularly as it relates to the accepted interdependence among team members. Team-oriented cohesion provides a safe environment for members to express their opinions. Although at times some opinions may be regarded as dissenting, they are not viewed as threatening the cohesiveness of the team itself. There is research that suggests greater team cohesion may follow from successful team performance, as opposed to causing the performance to occur.[52] Rewards that focus on team achievements are likely to enhance cohesion, whereas individual rewards encourage competition among team members, which weakens cohesion. Other teams and individuals within an organization often take notice of cohesive teams and sometimes express the desire to be members of a cohesive unit themselves. Cohesive teams have also been found to exert more influence than less cohesive teams in the running of the organization. Still, cohesion is not critical for success in all team tasks; it appears to be most crucial in tasks that require highly efficient and synchronized member interactions.

Team cohesion
A measure of how attached to and willing to remain in a team that team members feel.

Related to the issue of managing emotions and building cohesion is the concept of trust. Trust is defined as the belief that even though you have no control over another person's behavior toward you, that person will behave in a way that benefits you. There are several components to trust. Namely, trust develops over time, it is not necessarily mutual or reciprocal between parties, and it entails a willingness to be vulnerable to actions taken by the trusted party that may be harmful.[53] There is an important distinction among trust, trust propensity, and trustworthiness.[54] *Trust* is the intention to accept vulnerability based on positive expectations of the party being trusted. Trust is earned, and people differ in their threshold to be trusting. *Trust propensity* is a personality characteristic, a willingness to rely on others, and thus be vulnerable. *Trustworthiness* is the quality of a party to be trusted.

Research suggests that trust is influenced by the individual's perceived ability, benevolence, and integrity.[55] In short, we are more likely to trust somebody who (a) is honest (vs. somebody who lies to us), (b) is kind (vs. somebody who is mean), and (c) is capable (vs. somebody who doesn't know what they're doing). In addition, in the early phases of teamwork, perceptions of integrity have the largest impact on trust and the perceptions of benevolence have the least impact. Perceptions of ability becomes less predictive of trust over time.[56]

In general, trust develops slowly within a team, even among teams with stable memberships. It is also the most fragile of the interpersonal processes. Once betrayed, it is very difficult to restore. Despite that, distrust can occasionally be a good thing.[57] For example, if a key member is seen as being untrustworthy, distrust by other members of that one member may actually help the rest of the team band together and overcome obstacles that may result from the untrustworthy member. Remaining blindly devoted to members and giving them the "benefit of the doubt" may result in more harm. Alternatives to trust are close supervision and the continual monitoring of behavior.

Team Cognition

As we've just described, teams must plan, make decisions, solve problems, and generally think as a collective unit. How individuals think is reflected in their behavior, and the term given to the thinking process is *cognition*. A team is a social aggregation in which a limited number of individuals interact on a regular basis to accomplish a set of shared objectives for which they have mutual responsibility. The fusion of cognition (as a psychological process) and a team (as an interacting collectivity) produces the concept of **team cognition**, which reflects how the team acquires, stores, and uses information.[58] In the following sections we discuss two avenues of research related to team cognition that have received considerable attention: shared mental models and team decision making.

Team cognition The way in which a team acquires, stores, and uses information.

Shared Mental Models

The concept of a **shared mental model** refers to team members having some degree of similarity in how they approach problems and evaluate potential solutions. They reflect the idea of being "on the same page" in terms of knowing what tasks to do and how to do them.[59] Shared mental models are posited to influence the behavior of the group. For example, a group of researchers found that when teams have these shared mental models, the team members are more likely to anticipate each other's actions and proactively share the workload and help one another. In turn, this implicit coordination is related to heightened team performance.[60]

Shared mental model The cognitive processes held in common by members of a team regarding how they acquire information, analyze it, and respond to it.

As shown in Figure 10-4, four broad categories reflect what is actually shared among team members in their mental models: task-specific information, task-related knowledge, knowledge of teammates, and shared attitudes and beliefs.[61] Each type of knowledge has increasingly broader generalizability across differing tasks. *Task-specific information* is shared information among team members that allows them to act without the need to discuss it. Task-specific information involves the particular procedures, sequences, actions, and strategies necessary to perform a task. It can be generalized

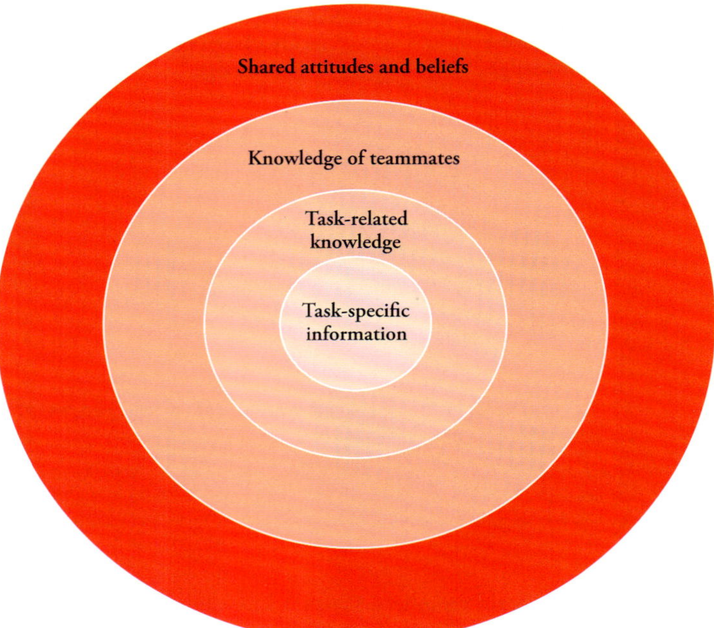

Figure 10-4 *Generalizability of four types of shared knowledge in mental models*

only to other instances of similar tasks. *Task-related knowledge* refers to common knowledge about task-related processes, but it is not limited to a single task. It is more generalizable because it is knowledge of processes that applies to many specific tasks. *Knowledge of teammates* refers to how well the members understand each other, including their performance, strengths, weaknesses, and tendencies. Thus, team members must learn how the collective expertise of the team is distributed across the members. This type of shared knowledge helps teammates compensate for one another, predict each other's actions, and allocate resources according to member expertise. The final category of *shared attitudes and beliefs* permits team members to arrive at comparable interpretations of the problems they face. It enhances team cohesion, motivation, and consensus. Shared mental models do not refer to a unitary concept. It appears that all the types of knowledge in these four categories need to be shared in effective teams.

Figure 10-5 shows a graphic depiction of types of shared knowledge within a team.[62] Knowledge can be common among members (i.e., everyone knows the same thing), as depicted in (a). Alternatively, knowledge can be distributed across team members according to expertise or role, as depicted in (c). In reality, knowledge is most likely not completely common nor distributed, but rather shared across members with some portions that are common and some distributed, as depicted in (b). There is also not a singular way that knowledge can be "shared" among team members.[63] Some common knowledge must be held by all members of a team, particularly as it relates to the specific task. Other types of knowledge are shared by being distributed or apportioned

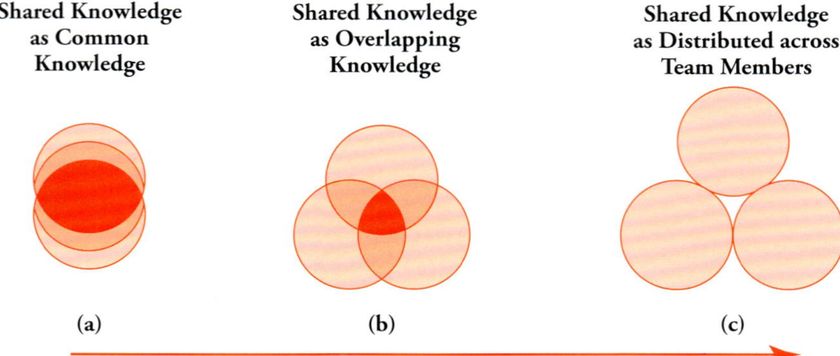

Figure 10-5 *Varieties of shared knowledge (circles represent knowledge held by individual team members)*

Source: Adapted from N. J. Cooke, J. C. Gorman, & L. J. Rowe (2009). An ecological perspective on team cognition (pp. 157–182). In E. Salas, G. F. Goodwin, & C. S. Burke (Eds.), *Team effectiveness in complex organizations*. Psychology Press. Reprinted with permission of Taylor and Francis via Copyright Clearance Center.

across the team members. Certain knowledge is complex or specialized, and it is unrealistic to expect all members of a team to possess this level of knowledge equally. Thus, what is important is that the knowledge resides within the team as a team, not held by each team member. Shared knowledge is common in military combat teams and surgical teams. Cross-training (where team members learn to perform the tasks of others) has been found to enhance shared mental models.[64]

Groupthink
A phenomenon associated with team decision making in which members feel threatened by forces external to the team, resulting in deterioration in the cognitive processing of information.

As compelling as the evidence is for shared mental models for effective team performance, there is a potential dark side to team members "thinking alike." The phenomenon is called **groupthink**. Noted problems in history that arose from groupthink are the Bay of Pigs invasion of Cuba in 1961 and the explosion of the space shuttle *Challenger* in 1986. Groupthink refers to a deterioration in cognitive processing caused by team members feeling threatened by external forces. The defects in decision making include incomplete consideration of options and alternatives, poor information search, and selective information processing. Groupthink is a model of thinking in which team members consider consensus to be more important than rational, independent thinking. Not all aspects of groupthink are bad though. For example, although some dimensions of the groupthink phenomenon (such as suppressing dissenting opinions) appear to be related to negative team performance, some other dimensions (such as a strong sense of group identity) are related to positive team performance.[65] Groupthink is more likely found in teams that have a strong sense of social identity.[66] In such cases, team members often feel compelled to maintain and enhance their evaluation of the team and to protect the image of the team. When the image is questioned by a collective threat, the response among members is to seek concurrence about the threat and, by virtue of that, attain greater acceptance as *bona fide* team members. A threat to an individual member of a team is not as likely to engender groupthink as is a threat to the team itself. In short, effective team performance requires members to operate on similar or complementary knowledge bases, but under conditions of perceived threat to the team, groupthink often produces the opposite effect and can drive the team to undesirable behavior.

The amount of research on shared mental models is growing, but we still have much to learn about the process of forming a "team mentality" and how the performance of a team is affected by it. Shared mental models provide teams with a common framework from which to perceive, interpret, and respond to novel environments.[67] It has been estimated that team cognition contributes more to team effectiveness than do motivation and cohesion.[68] Successful teams develop a system for sharing information among the members, and the absence of team cognition cannot be compensated for by other important variables associated with teamwork.

Decision Making in Teams

Decision making in teams is different from individual decision making.[69] In teams, information is often distributed unequally among members and must be integrated. Choosing among alternatives is made more complicated by having to integrate the often-differing perspectives and opinions of team members. The integration process usually includes dealing with uncertainty, with the effects of status differences among members, and with the failure of some members to appreciate the significance of the information they hold. Ambiguity, time pressures, heavy workloads, and other factors may become sources of stress that affect the group's ability to perform its task.

Effective team decision making is related to characteristics of the individuals who make up the team, pairs of people within the team, and how the team functions as a team.[70] There are three key concepts with relation to team decision making:

1. **Team informity**—Teams can be well informed on some issues but poorly informed on others. Team informity is the degree to which team members are adequately informed about the issue they are evaluating.
2. **Staff validity**—Teams are composed of individuals who differ in their ability to make accurate decisions. Some individuals make poor decisions, while others typically make very accurate decisions. Staff validity is the average of the individual team members' abilities to make accurate decisions.
3. **Dyadic sensitivity**—A team leader must often listen to the differing opinions or recommendations of team members. The relationship between the leader and each team member is a dyad. Dyadic sensitivity is the leader's consideration of each team member's recommendation in reaching an overall decision. Thus, an effective decision-making team leader knows which member's opinion should be given more weight than others'.

In short, getting accurate information, making accurate recommendations, and ensuring that these recommendations are incorporated into the team's overall decision are the core requirements for effective decision making in teams.

Personnel Selection for Teams

Selecting the right team members is a key determinant of team effectiveness.[71] Some of what I-O psychologists have learned about the selection of individuals into organizations, however, is not wholly transferable to the selection of teams. Traditional work analytic methods identify the knowledge, skills, abilities, and other characteristics (KSAOs) needed for individual job performance, yet these methods tend to be insensitive to the social context in which work occurs. Teams, by definition, are social entities that interact in a larger social context. Choosing team members on the basis of individual-task KSAOs alone is not enough to ensure optimal team effectiveness.[72] Successful team members need two general types of skills.[73] *Taskwork skills* are those needed by team members to perform the actual task. These skills serve as the foundation for the operational side of performance. Because team members must coordinate their actions and work independently, they must also possess *teamwork skills*. These are behavioral, cognitive, and attitudinal skills. These skills are necessary for ensuring the members of the team are able to synchronize, integrate, and interact effectively.

Successful selection of team members requires identifying the best mix of personnel for effective team performance. Thus, the selection requirements for particular individuals may involve complementing the abilities that other individuals will bring to the task. Creating the right mix can also mean considering those factors that account for interpersonal compatibility. Establishing team requirements involves identifying and assessing the congruence among members with regard to personality and values. Five social skills are particularly critical for individuals to enhance the performance of the group:[74]

1. Gain group acceptance
2. Increase group solidarity
3. Be aware of the group consciousness
4. Share the group identification
5. Manage others' impressions of them

We are also learning about the relationship between personality variables and team effectiveness. Research has shown that extraverts are perceived by other team members as having greater effect than introverts on group outcomes.[75]

Thus, individuals with more reserved personalities may be less successful in getting the team to accept their ideas and suggestions. A related (and not too surprising) finding is that especially-talented team members are likely to feel frustrated when they must work with lower-ability individuals on interdependent tasks.[76] This may be particularly important given that performance in organizations (and therefore teams) is not likely evenly distributed.[77] Instead, there may be a few star performers who do a disproportionate amount of the work. These individuals may become particularly frustrated with their teammates.

Consider This...

Star performers are talented, hardworking, and very effective in their roles. These top employees are highly valuable, and their efforts can take a team—and an organization—to the next level. Indeed, because of their effectiveness, they are also often difficult to find, hire, and retain in organizations. With this, you would expect that they would be treated very well, in an effort to keep them happy. Unfortunately, research finds that this is not always the case. Not only is there the potential that they do more work than others and become frustrated, as noted above, but they also appear to suffer a "social penalty" from their colleagues. One study revealed that peers were more likely to belittle, insult, and undermine higher performers than they were low performers.[78] This was even more the case when the team was more collaborative in nature! In addition, it appears that resource availability impacts how star performers are treated. Namely, if resources are limited then peers will likely feel threatened and lash out at the star performers. If resources are shared, however, the star performer is seen as an asset that is supported. Thus, it seems that individuals penalize star performers when it is not in their own interest to support them. Knowing this, what would you recommend to managers of high performers? How would you recommend resources be allocated for teams to reduce the likelihood of peers lashing out at the top performer? If you were the star performer on a team, what would you do?

In general, research results suggest that individuals with outgoing and somewhat dominant personalities strongly influence the functioning of teams, yet a team composed of only those personality types may be thwarted by its own internal dynamics. Although this stream of research suggests that the "will do" factors of personality are critical for team success, the "can do" factors of ability cannot be dismissed or minimized. Cognitive and technical skills are also needed. As one leading business executive said, "A collaboration of incompetents, no matter how diligent or well-meaning, cannot be successful" (Locke et al. 2001, p. 503) (see The Lighter Side of I-O Psychology: *Collective Nouns*).[79]

Research on teams has revealed other aspects of team performance that highlight the need for selected interpersonal skills. Teams often face situations that are not what they had anticipated, at which point their success depends on their ability to adapt to these changing contexts.[80] The most adaptable team members have the same profile of attributes identified in Chapter 5 as high individual performers.[81] These team members were characterized by high cognitive ability, strong need for achievement, and an openness to new experiences. Similarly, as noted earlier, backup behaviors are unique supportive behaviors that are essential within teams. Team members should be willing to provide help to others when their own tasks demand less than their full attention and resources. The legitimacy of the need to back up team members often derives from an uneven workload distribution—some tasks in a team context are more demanding than others.[82] Three personality factors predicted willingness to back up teammates: conscientiousness, emotional stability, and extraversion. Thus, within the context of team selection, these personality characteristics may become particularly relevant.

The Lighter Side of I-O Psychology: *Collective Nouns*

You may be aware that, when describing a group of mammals, there is often a collective noun associated with the group. For example, bees form a swarm, dogs are a pack, puppies are a litter, geese are in a gaggle, fish comprise a school, and a group of crows is called a murder. But did you know that there are also collective nouns for other things, like a soufflé of clouds, a wealth of information, and even a thicket of idiots! In addition, there are also collective nouns for various occupations. Some of the names are from a long time ago, which may explain the strange and somewhat comical nature of them. With that, we present a sampling of collective nouns of occupations and professions.[83]

Academics = Faculty	Cooks = Hastiness	Magicians = Illusion
Bakers = Tabernacle	Dentists = Brace	Mechanics = Clutch
Barbers = Babble	Dermatologists = Rash	Midwives = Expectation
Barmen = Promise	Geneticists = Helix	Monks = Abominable Sight
Brewers = Feast	Golfers = Lie	Philosophers = Ponder
Bureaucrats = Shuffle	Gynecologists = Smear	Plumbers = Flood
Butchers = Goring	Interpreters = Tongue	Professors = Pomposity
Butlers = Sneer	Journalists = Scoop	Waiters = Order
Carpenters = Pound	Librarians = Catalogue	Webmasters = Linkage

Training for Teams

Cross-training
Educating employees on how to perform tasks that are outside their typical roles and responsibilities.

Much of what we know about team training has come, directly or indirectly, from military applications. The military has been primarily responsible for advanced training technologies (such as intelligent tutoring systems) as well as strategies in team training, such as **cross-training**. Training team members on other team members' roles assumes that exposure to and practice on other teammates' tasks should result in better team member knowledge about task responsibilities and coordination requirements. With this added knowledge, team members gain an understanding of what other team members require to be effective and an awareness of how and why mishaps may occur. In addition, cross-training increases an organization's flexibility, since employees can assist others as needed, such as when there are absences or issues arise that create backlogs in work.

The logic of team training is the same as the logic of individual training, although the mechanisms are somewhat different. The process begins with a work analysis, but one aimed at the functioning of teams. A team task analysis is an extension of the traditional task analysis to those tasks that require coordination.[84] Subject matter experts are asked to provide information (e.g., ratings of difficulty, importance) on each task in

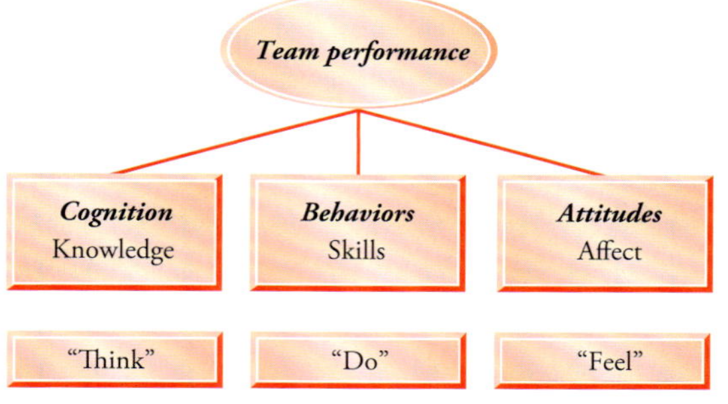

Figure 10-6 *The structure of team training*

From "Methods, Tools, and Strategies for Team Training," by E. Salas and J. A. Cannon-Bowers, 1997, in M. A. Quiñones and A. Ehrenstein (Eds.), *Training for a rapidly changing workplace* (pp. 249-280). Washington, DC: American Psychological Association.

which there is interdependency. The information obtained is then used to specify team training objectives and to develop realistic scenarios for practice.

The results of a team task analysis provide information about the knowledge, skills, and attitudes the team members must possess to be successful. These three are referred to as the *thinking*, *doing*, and *feeling* needed for the structure of team training, as shown in Figure 10-6. Identifying the criteria for team effectiveness serves to guide instructional activities in team training. The instructional activities focus on providing team members with shared mental models and knowledge structures. These activities are designed to foster common ways for team members to analyze information and make decisions. Moreover, training for teams can help with the processes discussed earlier, including how and when to engage in mission analyses, monitoring and coordination, and backup behaviors. For example, research has shown that training team leaders on how to facilitate effective teamwork leads to higher-quality team transition processes, which in turn lead to higher-quality action and interpersonal processes.[85]

Performance Appraisal in Teams

Chapter 8 addressed the topic of performance management, primarily as it applies to individual employees. Performance management practices have evolved over time to include a greater focus on teams, in addition to individuals.[86] Although all of the issues identified for individual performance appraisals apply to teams, there are some additional considerations for teams that do not apply to individuals.

Team members differ in their responses to the "weakest link" in their team.[87] Team members tend to feel high levels of sympathy for a member who exhibits low performance for reasons that are beyond their control. Likewise, members feel low levels of sympathy for a team member who performs poorly because of factors under their control. If the group feels sympathy, they are more willing to train the poor performer or assist the individual by doing a portion of their tasks. But if the group feels little sympathy, they may attempt to motivate the low performer (perhaps with veiled threats) or to simply reject the individual.

Consider This...

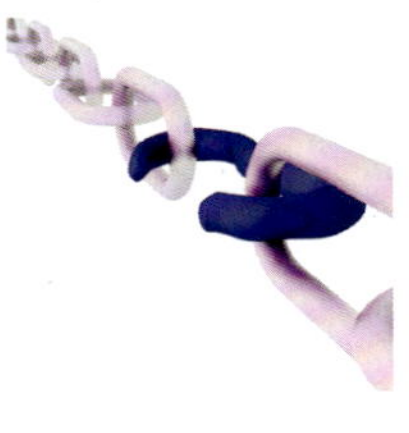

There is an old saying that a team is only as good as its weakest link. Do you believe this? Sheldon Patinkin, a former artistic consultant for The Second City (an improvisational comedy group) and Steppenwolf Theatre, was known to provide a variation of this quote, saying that a team was only as good as its ability to compensate for its weakest link. The idea was that anybody can have a bad day, and that for a team to be successful, its members needed to be able to overcome those bad days as a group. If you're the person having the bad day, would you want to be called out for it, or helped in such a way that outsiders were unable to realize you, as an individual, were having a bad day? The likely response is that you'd want to be helped, and likewise it would be expected that you would help other members of your team. As such, it's the team's ability and willingness (or inability and unwillingness) to step up and compensate for a "weak link" that matters. How do you feel about this analogy? Patinkin was referring to theatre ensembles when he said this. Do you think it applies to other settings, such as the workplace or school? Why or why not?

A major issue in team performance appraisal is the extent to which individuals slacken their performance within the team. A team member may assume that individual slacking will not be noticed within the larger social context of a team, or that other members will elevate their performance within the team to achieve a satisfactory team level of performance. The term given to this phenomenon of slacking is **social loafing**, and it refers to the demotivating effect on individuals of working in a group or team context. When team outcomes are emphasized, individuals see less connection between their own contributions (time, effort, and skills) and the recognition and rewards they receive.[88] Individual team members feel they have less incentive to work hard. There are three ways in which a lack of individual incentives can contribute to social loafing.[89]

Social loafing
A phenomenon identified in teams in which certain individuals withhold effort or contributions to the collective outcome.

- **Free riding.** In some situations, social loafing derives from a desire to benefit from (or free ride on) the efforts of others. When a team task makes individual contributions anonymous and rewards are shared equally, team members can reduce their own individual effort but still enjoy an equal share of the results. Thus, social loafing is more likely to occur when team members believe their own contributions cannot be identified.
- **The "sucker" effect.** When conditions allow team members to take a free ride, some team members may assume that other group members will do so. Rather than be a "sucker" who contributes more than others, people reduce their effort to match the low level they expect from others.
- **Felt dispensability.** In some cases, social loafing results from the feeling of being dispensable. Team members may feel dispensable when more able team members are available to accomplish the task or when they believe their efforts are redundant because they duplicate the contributions of others. When team members feel dispensable, they often reduce their effort.

These three forms of social loafing share the following characteristics: (1) individual team members are concerned with the impact of their personal contributions on team performance, (2) team members expect some return on their effort, and (3) teamwork can weaken the links among individual effort, contributions to team success, and individual outcomes. Therefore, although effective team processes (e.g., interaction, trust, cohesion) are important to achieve team success, it is individuals who make up teams, and many organizational rewards (such as salary and career progression) are administered at the individual level.

Not all the research on team performance appraisal is limited to social loafing. Peer appraisals have been found to be effective at the individual level, and they also appear to have a positive influence at the team level. Research has found that developmental peer appraisals in work teams has a positive impact on team communication, task focus, and member relationships.[90] As the volume of research on team performance appraisal grows, we will have additional data with which to assess the generalizability of findings previously established in appraising individuals.

The issue of performance management for teams is certainly a tricky one. It will be recalled from Chapter 8 that one purpose of performance management is to identify performance differences across individuals and to reward them differentially. If we strive for teamwork and a sense of unity across team members, we should not differentially reward the "best" individual team members. We will have to develop appraisal and reward processes that treat all members of a group as a single entity, not as individuals. Organizations get what they reward. If they choose to appraise and reward individual job performance, then they should not decry a lack of teamwork and cooperation among their employees.[91] With this in mind, organizations that rely on teams should plan to manage the performance of both the teams *and* the individuals within those teams. By measuring both, individuals can be held accountable for their individual contributions while also being motivated to support the collective mission of the team.[92] In addition, individuals often belong to multiple teams simultaneously.[93] As a result, it is important to consider how individuals should be evaluated and rewarded on the basis of their multiple team memberships and expectations.

Concluding Comments

As the world becomes increasingly complex, organizations must find new ways to adapt to this complexity. Teams are viewed as one means of doing so. Indeed, the growing use of teams to conduct work is an organizational response to a changing world.[94] The past 30 years provided the strongest catalyst for I-O psychologists to understand teams and how teamwork functions. However, the actual use of teams as a means of accomplishing work has been with us since long before the birth of I-O psychology. What is new about teams is our growing reliance on them to accomplish work that was once performed by individuals.

"It seems clear that after we compile all the lessons we have learned over the last century, one message is clear: industries, governments, and organizations count on teams . . . Teams have proven to be beneficial and will continue to proliferate as the complexity of our world increases. Teams always have and always will exist."[95]

—Salas et al. 2007, p. 432

Organizations will be better able to adapt to chaotic business environments to the extent that employees are able to engage in spontaneous "teaming," assembling and disassembling as teams "on the fly" as needs arise.[96] The conversion from an individual to a team perspective of work requires that we re-examine our knowledge about many facets of I-O psychology. Furthermore, although some of our concepts might generalize directly from individuals to teams, some procedures might be incompatible.[97] We believe I-O psychology should gird itself for the journey of understanding how work performed by teams requires insight into new psychological concepts and existing concepts with unknown validity when generalized to teams.

Chapter Review

Key Terms

Level of analysis
Team
Problem-resolution team
Creative team
Tactical team
***Ad hoc* team**
Virtual team
Multiteam systems
Five stage model of group development
Socialization
Team processes
Faultlines
Collective efficacy
Team cohesion
Team cognition
Shared mental model
Groupthink
Cross-training
Social loafing

Questions for Review

1. What is meant by "level of analysis?" What are levels of interest to I-O psychologists? What is the distinction between micro, macro, and meso research?
2. What are the defining characteristics of work teams? What are the different types of teams and how are they distinguished from one another?
3. What are the five stages of group development? What do each of the stages entail?
4. What is socialization? What do the concepts of evaluation, commitment, and role transition mean in the context of socialization? What are the five phases of socialization? What do these phases entail?
5. What do skill differentiation, authority differentiation, and temporal stability refer to in the context of team structure?
6. How does the TRIAD model identify roles that individual team members may hold within a team?
7. What are team processes? What do transition processes, action processes, and interpersonal processes entail? Why is mission analysis a critical process for teams? When can backup behaviors be harmful?
8. How can conflict be categorized? Is all conflict bad? When is conflict functional versus dysfunctional?

9. What are faultlines within teams?
10. What is collective efficacy? When might collective efficacy be detrimental to teams?
11. What is team cohesion? How do trust, trust propensity, and trustworthiness differ? What are some influencers of trust?
12. What is team cognition? What sorts of information comprise a team's shared mental models? How do the levels of shared knowledge differ among team members?
13. What is groupthink? Why does it occur?
14. What leads to effective team decision making?
15. How do taskwork skills differ from teamwork skills? What are five social skills that are critical for team performance?
16. What is cross-training? What are some examples of cross-training?
17. What is social loafing? How does a lack of individual incentives contribute to social loafing?

CHAPTER 11

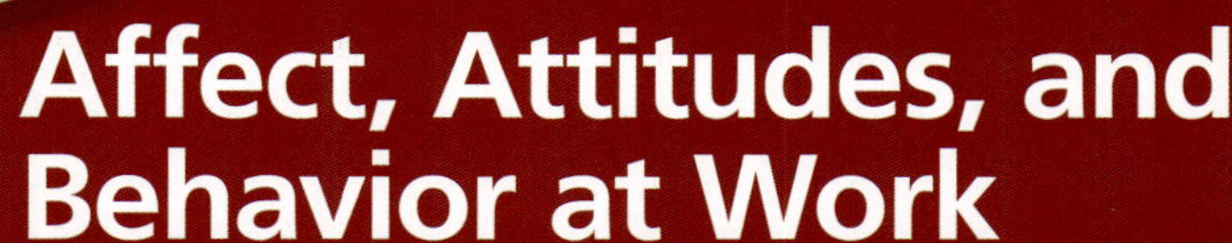

Affect, Attitudes, and Behavior at Work

Chapter Outline

Affect, Moods, and Emotions
- Broaden-and-Build Theory of Positive Emotions
- The Lighter Side of I-O Psychology: *Working From Home*

Job Attitudes
- Job Satisfaction
- Work Commitment
- Employee Engagement
- Faces of I-O Psychology: *John C. Howes*

Organizational Justice

Behaviors
- Organizational Citizenship Behavior
- Counterproductive Work Behavior

Organizational Politics
- Social Media and I-O Psychology: *The Cyberbully's Blog*

The Psychological Contract
- COVID-19 and I-O Psychology: *Health and Safety Psychological Contracts*
- Violations of the Psychological Contract

Chapter Review

Learning Objectives

- Explain the role of affect, moods, and emotions in the workplace.
- Explain the organizational attitudes of job satisfaction, work commitment, employee engagement, and organizational justice.
- Discuss the concepts of organizational citizenship behavior and counterproductive work behavior, and their relationships to other concepts.
- Describe the concept of organizational politics.
- Describe the concept of the psychological contract in employment and its changing nature.

Since the dawn of time and throughout the world, a recurring theme in mythology, religion, and literature is the dichotomy of good versus bad. The archetype of the hero is often juxtaposed with that of the villain in a battle of some sort. We see this with popular movies and books through such characters as Luke Skywalker and Darth Vader, Harry Potter and Lord Voldemort, and Frodo and Sauron. In some cases, a single person faces an internal battle in which they must make a choice between an action that is honorable and virtuous versus one that is perhaps immoral or unethical. We see this depicted, for example, in Shakespeare's *Othello* and *Macbeth*. While the stories are entertaining, they are also educational. Since 1946, nestled within the pages of *Highlights for Children*, Goofus and Gallant have epitomized good versus bad, with Gallant demonstrating how to behave properly and Goofus showing what *not* to do in various situations. For example, in the cartoon shown above, we see ill-mannered Goofus dangerously running with scissors while well-behaved Gallant safely walks with his scissors.

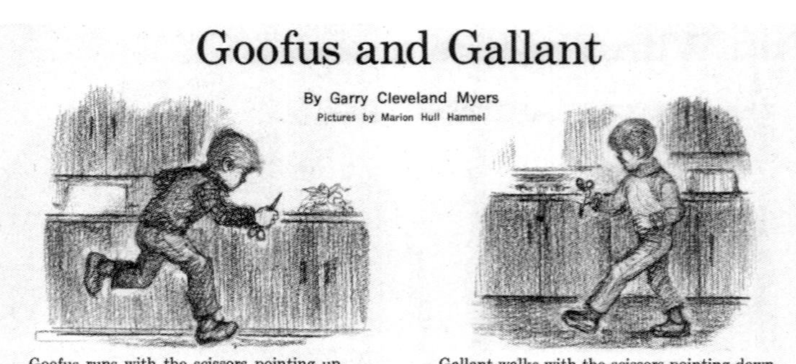

Why is this archetype of good versus bad so pervasive and universal? The answer lies in the question itself: we experience this dichotomy on a continuous basis in all aspects of our lives. We have good days and bad days. We make good decisions and bad decisions. And so forth. The list is endless.

This chapter reflects the timeless elements of good versus bad. We begin our discussion with a focus on affect, moods, and emotions. We certainly have good moods and bad moods, and experience emotions that may be viewed as good (such as happiness and pride) or bad (such as anger and sadness). We explore how the workplace is impacted by our feelings and our expressions of those feelings. We then discuss work attitudes, or evaluations we have about our work, and how these attitudes can be strengthened (to be good), what may lead them to be weak or low (i.e., bad), and how they are related to important work outcomes. Third, we discuss behaviors individuals may exhibit while at work. On the good side, we have citizenship behaviors, and on the bad side, we have counterproductive work behaviors, both first introduced in Chapter 4. We also discuss organizational politics, a topic that was long considered to be a divisive behavior in the workplace, yet has become less negative in its connotations. Lastly, we examine psychological contracts and the impact that violations of such contracts have on employees and organizations.

Affect, Moods, and Emotions

For the most part, I-O psychology has not addressed the emotional dimensions of work life; historically, it has been more interested in cognitive issues (as witnessed by the amount of research on *g*). However, moods and emotions play an undeniable role in how we feel about life, including work. By studying workplace emotions, we may be better able to understand why people behave the way they do within organizations.[1]

Affect
A broad range of feelings that encompass moods and emotions, typically described along a positive-negative continuum.

Moods and emotions fall under the broader term **affect**. The concept of affect refers to a broad range of feelings that are typically described along a positive–negative continuum. Affect can be conceptualized as either being a trait or a transient state. As a trait, it refers to a fundamental difference in how people view life, their general disposition, and attitude. People who are high on trait positive affect tend to be active, alert, enthusiastic, inspired, and interested. People who are high on trait negative affect, on the other hand, are pessimistic about life and "see the glass as half-empty rather than half-full." They tend to feel anxious and fearful, as opposed to calm and composed.

Moods
General and long-lasting feelings not directed at a particular target.

Affect can also be described as a momentary experience or transient state. In these cases, the terms that are typically used are moods and emotions. **Moods** refer to feelings that are general in nature and relatively long lasting. They are not necessarily directed at a particular object, but rather may exist without a person knowing their specific cause.[2] Given their somewhat vague and diffuse causes, moods may not be directly controllable. Nevertheless, organizations may be successful in elevating employees' moods.[3] For example, organizations could concentrate on providing a work environment free of minor irritations and hassles that produce frequent, if mild, feelings of frustration and annoyance.

"Work . . . is a place where all our basic processes, including emotional processes, play out daily. People feel guilty at work, they feel angry, they feel happy, they feel anxious, often all in the same day. Events at work have real emotional impact on participants."[4]

—Weiss 2002, p. 1

Emotions
Discrete, target-specific feelings that are of relatively short duration.

Emotions are feelings that are more discrete and of shorter duration than moods. While moods are typically either positive or negative, one can simultaneously experience multiple emotions of varying intensity and direction. In addition, unlike moods, emotions are typically directed at a particular target. As one scholar noted, "emotional events are elicited *by* something, are reactions *to* something, and are generally *about* something" (Ekkekakis 2012, p. 322).[5]

Emotions have received considerable attention in the literature. Emotions impact how we appraise situations (who we blame vs. assign credit when bad and good events occur), influence how confident we are with our decisions, and color how we view risks.[6] Emotions also affect which memories we recall and how much we are willing to process information.[7] Emotions are complex. So-called negative emotions do not always result in outcomes that are bad for organizations. Feelings of guilt and shame are related to lower well-being, lower job satisfaction and increased likelihood of burnout.[8] Yet, guilt and shame—and the likelihood of experiencing those emotions—also have benefits in the workplace, as they are deterrents of unethical behaviors[9] and are related to decreased absenteeism.[10] One study found that individuals who were made to feel guilty about engaging in counterproductive behaviors subsequently engaged in behaviors that benefitted the organization, in an apparent attempt to make up for the undesirable behaviors and alleviate their guilt.[11] Similarly, sadness, although an unpleasant emotion that has been linked to lower job performance,[12] has been shown to inspire greater task perseverance.[13] Even envy has a positive side. Although it can lead to the undermining of the target of their envy, research also shows that enviers may seek advice from their target, and when they do, they tend to perform better.[14]

Anger is another emotion that has mixed results in the workplace. On the downside, anger has been found to be associated with greater counterproductive behaviors at work.[15] However, anger's effects on others may vary by the intensity with which it is expressed. For example, in an examination of locker room speeches during halftime at high school and college basketball games, researchers found that moderate levels of unpleasant affective displays (like anger) from their coaches were related to high effort levels when the team returned to the second half of their game.[16] Effort tended to decrease, however, following low and high levels of unpleasant affective displays. Thus, it appears that while it may not be surprising that too much anger can be problematic, too little (from coaches, at least) can also fail to have the desired effect. Anger's complexity is also clear within negotiations. Specifically, negotiators facing an angry partner are more likely to seek out diagnostic information about their partner's preferences and priorities, allowing them to reach higher joint gains.[17] However, expressions of anger have also been shown to cause deadlocks in negotiations.[18]

Dual threshold model of workplace anger A framework for how anger is realized at work, depending on whether the anger is expressed and/or inappropriate.

Adding to the complexity, researchers have suggested that anger may not be equally problematic in all organizations. According to the **dual threshold model of workplace anger**, when individuals feel angry, it can generate one of three forms of anger within the workplace: suppressed, expressed, or deviant.[19] These three forms are differentiated by two thresholds—expression and impropriety. As shown in Figure 11-1, if individuals feel angry but fail to express that anger, it is said to be suppressed. This suppression can be either silent or muted. Silent suppression is when the anger is

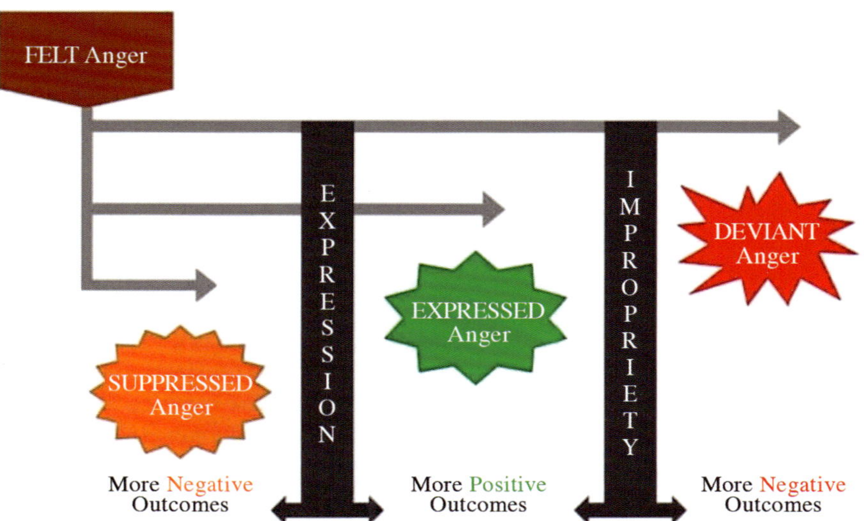

Figure 11-1 *Dual Threshold Model of Workplace Anger*

Adapted from "Crossing the line(s): A dual threshold model of anger in organizations, Essential Features of the Dual Threshold Model (Figure 2)" by D. Geddes & R.R. Callister in *Academy of Management Review32*(3), Copyright © 2007. Reproduced with permission of Academy of Management Review via Copyright Clearance Center..

intentionally concealed from all others, whereas with muted suppression, individuals conceal their anger from the individuals causing the anger, but share their concerns with uninvolved parties (such as trusted colleagues). If the anger that an individual feels is expressed, however, the next threshold that matters is impropriety. If anger is expressed but is not seen as being deviant or inappropriate, then it falls in the expressed anger range. If, however, the expressed anger is deemed inappropriate (i.e., it crosses the threshold of impropriety), then it is considered deviant.

Expressed anger that does not pass the threshold of impropriety is likely to be related to the most positive outcomes. The logic is that anger can alert employees and managers to violations of norms and help air problems as they arise. Without voicing concerns, problems are likely to continue, and improvements won't result. Thus, suppressing emotions is not ideal. On the other hand, expressing emotions in ways that are deemed inappropriate or will result in punishment is not ideal either. Rather, it is when anger is suitably expressed that positive outcomes will be possible.

The key for organizations with regard to the dual threshold model is their impact on the two thresholds. Individuals can be encouraged to voice concerns and be given a safe space to air grievances. Doing so may result in more felt anger being expressed rather than suppressed. In addition, the line of impropriety can be moved. In some organizations, simply raising one's voice in anger can be considered an act of impropriety, whereas in other organizations it would take far more to result in a punishable offense. To the extent that individuals can be granted some leniency for emotional displays, deviant anger can be reduced. As such, moving either or both of these thresholds can lessen the likelihood of negative outcomes and increase the likelihood of positive outcomes.

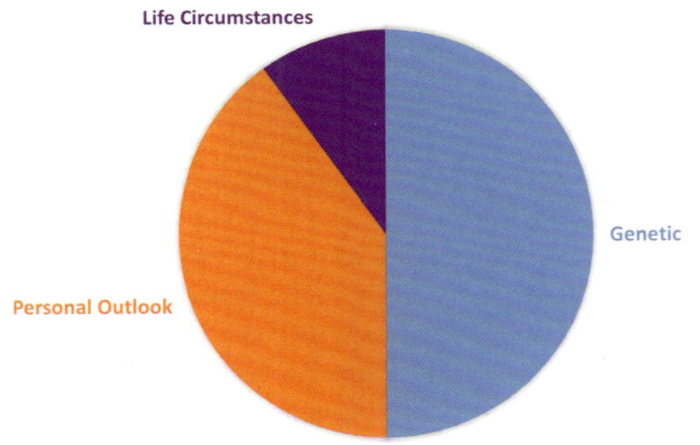

The final emotion that we'll discuss here is happiness. It turns out that happiness does more than just make us feel good. In one lab study, researchers found that being happy made people approximately 12% more productive.[20] At work, researchers found that happiness was negatively related to turnover intentions in a Taiwanese sample.[21] Another study found that employee happiness was related to greater organizational commitment, higher task performance, stronger citizenship performance, lower turnover intentions, and fewer counterproductive work behaviors.[22] In addition, it appears that happier workers have fewer absences, are more cooperative and friendly,[23] and are more willing to help others.[24] So, what is the downside to happiness? It may lie in our ability to influence it within the workplace. It has been suggested that 50% of happiness is genetically predetermined, 40% is the result of one's personal outlook, and 10% is due to life circumstances.[25] This suggestion is supported by research that has shown that employees' happiness demonstrated consistency over time.[26] Thus, it appears that individuals have a set point from which they fluctuate depending on events in their environment. So, can managers influence their employees' happiness? Probably in the short-term (e.g., through bonuses, promotions, or some other outcomes of value to the employees), but any long-term changes to happiness will require substantial effort on the part of the employees themselves.[27]

Emotional labor The requirement in some jobs that employees express emotions to customers or clients that are associated with enhanced performance in the job.

Emotion regulation The attempts to control one's emotions or mood.

Emotional intelligence A construct that reflects a person's capacity to understand and manage emotions of themselves and others.

Emotional contagion The tendency for individuals to synchronize their emotions with others in their environment, experiencing and expressing another's emotions whether consciously or unconsciously.

In Chapter 4, we noted that organizations frequently require employees to engage in **emotional labor** by displaying certain emotions while at work. In our previous discussion, we noted that individuals may engage in surface acting, during which they alter their outward emotional expression without changing how they truly feel. Alternatively, they may engage in deep acting, in which they try to change their internal emotions to correspond to what is required of them. When individuals attempt to modify their emotions, they are engaging in **emotion regulation**. Meta-analytic research has revealed that surface acting is particularly harmful to one's well-being, attitudes toward work, and job performance, whereas deep acting does not appear to have the same negative consequences.[28] In addition, there is evidence that when employees have particularly difficult emotional interactions at work and engage in surface acting, they tend to have increased alcohol consumption after work. Engaging in deep acting, however, reduced the desire to detach from work and was related to lower-than-normal alcohol consumption after work.[29]

A related concept to emotion regulation that we first discussed in Chapter 4 is **emotional intelligence**, which reflects the ability to recognize emotions in oneself and in others and to control one's emotions in socially-acceptable ways. Emotional intelligence is positively related to job performance and organizational citizenship behaviors and negatively related to counterproductive work behaviors.[30] In addition, emotional intelligence can predict job performance above and beyond cognitive ability and the Big 5 personality dimensions.[31] Given its focus on managing emotional responses, it may come as no surprise that emotional intelligence appears to be most predictive of performance in jobs that require emotional labor.[32] The value of emotional intelligence in the workplace can be seen in research that found that emotional intelligence assessed during college was significantly positively related to salary levels over a decade later. This relationship was explained by the tendency for individuals higher on emotional intelligence to enter into and/or maintain valuable mentoring relationships that help them succeed in their careers.[33]

Emotions that are experienced by one person can spread to others, an effect known as **emotional contagion**. Individuals have an automatic tendency to mimic others with whom they interact, including their facial expressions and mannerisms. As such, when somebody is angry or sad, people nearby may also become angry or sad without realizing it. This emotional convergence between individuals happens for both positive and negative emotions, and has very real consequences for the workplace. For example, a study of Israeli soldiers, in which trainers interviewed confederates pretending to be either a happy soldier or a distressed soldier, revealed that trainers reported emotions in line with the soldiers they interviewed.[34] Those interviewers who saw the happy soldier reported more positive emotions in themselves, whereas those who saw the distressed soldier reported more negative emotions. The researchers found that the effects for the positive crossover from soldier to interviewer were stronger than the effects for the negative crossover, suggesting that positive emotions may be more contagious than negative emotions.

Consider This...

Saturday Night Live has been a staple in the late-night live television scene since its debut in 1975. Each week, the show parodies various aspects of contemporary society. Being live, the show has experienced some controversial moments, including intentional sabotage from performers and guests. However, the live aspect also has created some magnificent examples of emotional contagion. One example was a sketch featuring the fictional character Debbie Downer, played by Rachel Dratch. Debbie Downer is based on the slang term of the same name, which refers to an individual who perpetually brings up bad news or disappointing information in a social setting, causing people in the group to experience negative shifts in their moods. In the first-ever sketch featuring Debbie Downer, the cast and celebrity guest (Lindsay Lohan) are eating breakfast at Walt Disney World. Everybody is having fun and smiling, until Debbie Downer begins lamenting about mad cow disease, feline AIDS, and a train explosion, among other topics. Her bad mood is contagious, impacting the others. The truly fun part of this sketch is the actual emotional contagion the cast members experienced while performing the sketch. As one character would start to smile, others would follow suit. Soon, the cast was stifling giggles as they tried to complete the sketch. Have you ever experienced emotional contagion? What was the circumstance? Are there situations where you seem to be more susceptible to others' emotions? Do you think positive emotions or negative emotions are more contagious? Why?

Broaden-and-Build Theory of Positive Emotions

Broaden-and-build theory of positive emotions
A theory that positive emotions prompt individuals to expand their thinking and action repertoires in ways that result in increased resources and enhanced functioning.

There has been an increased focus on the positive side of psychology, with a realization that, historically, much of the focus was on the dysfunctional, pathological side of psychology. The increased focus on positive constructs can be seen within the area of emotions by looking at the **broaden-and-build theory of positive emotions**.[35] This theory challenges the traditional assumptions that only negative emotions hold value for people. Certainly, there is an advantage to experiencing fear or anger, as they would initiate the fight-or-flight mechanism necessary for survival. But what about positive emotions such as joy and gratitude? The broaden-and-build theory of positive emotions suggests that they, too, are evolutionarily advantageous and increase the likelihood of survival.

According to the broaden-and-build theory, positive emotions *broaden* individuals' attention and awareness and prompt them to think and act in more diverse ways than they might otherwise. Whereas negative emotions narrow one's thinking and actions to lead to a specific outcome (the fight-or-flight response), positive emotions expand one's views. When individuals experience positive emotions, they are exposed to and subsequently *build* a wide range of resources.[36] These resources can be cognitive (increased intellectual complexity), social (more high-quality friendships), psychological (greater resilience), or physical (heightened functioning of the immune system). These resources enable individuals to subsequently function more effectively.

The broaden-and-build theory of positive emotions does not differentiate between the types of positive emotions experienced, nor does it speculate whether the reasons for the positive emotions matter. Rather, the focus is that the experience of positive emotions broadens our thinking and action repertoires in ways that result in increased resources and enhanced functioning. Many individuals appear to realize this, as humor, a key means of eliciting positive emotions, is common during times of stress—and effective in mitigating distress and the harmful effects that may result (see The Lighter Side of I-O Psychology: *Working From Home*).[37]

The Lighter Side of I-O Psychology: *Working From Home*

The thought of working from home is an appealing one for many individuals. For others, however, it is just short of a nightmare situation. One reason is that some people prefer to keep their work and home lives separate, whereas others have a greater preference for integrating the two domains. Not surprisingly, these individuals are known in the literature as "segmenters" and "integrators," respectively.[38] So, when individuals were compelled to work remotely during the COVID-19 pandemic, some individuals were begrudgingly forced to merge their work and family domains. In addition, many families also faced the stress of having school-age children at home for their studies. For segmenters, this was the opposite of their ideal work situation! Thankfully, many individuals were able to take the changes in stride, demonstrating resilience and adaptability in the face of challenging times. And, fortunately for individuals in need of help generating positive emotions, the internet did not disappoint, as people across the globe turned to social media to share the humorous side to their struggles. Individuals challenged others to refer to their children as "coworkers" and post what they did during the day, resulting in such comments as, "My coworker asked for yogurt and is now crying because I gave her yogurt" and "My coworker yelled 'WATCH ME WIGGLE MY BUTT!' repeatedly during my last conference call." Others posted photos with humorous captions, such as a photo of a cat on an office chair with the caption, "Trouble with working from home: office bullying."

The lesson here? When things get tough, humor may help. And if you post it online, it can help us, too!

As individuals experience positive emotions, and good things result, they will experience even more positive emotions that will lead to even better results in an ongoing upward spiral (as depicted in Figure 11-2).[39] For example, experiencing positive emotions leads people to perceive more positive meaning in their life's events.[40] This positive meaning in return leads to positive emotions. As such, a positive cycle is created that leads continuously upward. This theory has received considerable empirical support, demonstrating the importance of positive emotions within our work lives, and lives in general.[41]

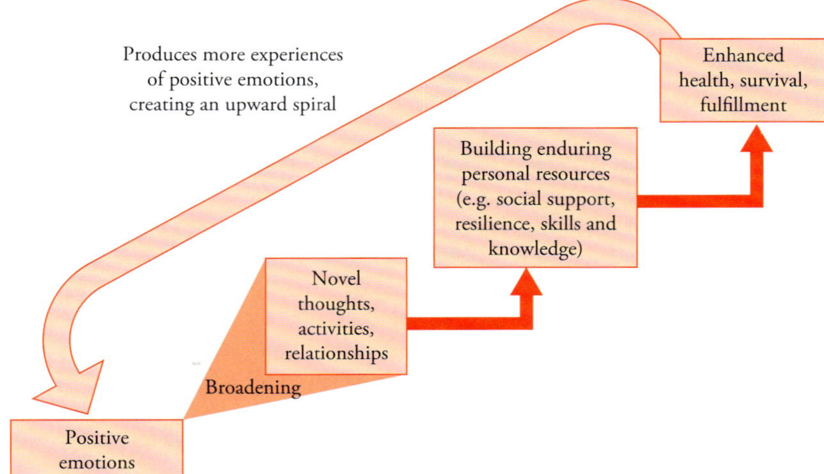

Figure 11-2 *Broaden-and-build theory of positive emotions*

Adapted from "Positive Emotions," by B. L. Fredrickson and M. A. Cohn, in M. Lewis, J. M. Haviland-Jones, and L. Feldman Barrett (Eds.), *Handbook of emotions* (3rd ed., pp. 777–796) (2008). Reprinted with permission of Guilford Press via Copyright Clearance Center.

Job Attitudes

Work-related attitudes are relatively enduring evaluations that individuals have of various aspects of employment, including their employer, their boss, and the job they hold.[42] Job attitudes have cognitive and affective components.[43] They reflect internal evaluations or beliefs about something in the work domain (the cognitive component). In addition, they are emotionally charged, reflecting one's feelings about the object (the affective component). Attitudes can vary in both intensity and favorability, and they influence individual behavior.

This section presents an examination of four important attitudes employees hold about their work: how satisfied, committed, and engaged they are with their work, and how fair they view their work. Job satisfaction is the most frequently researched job attitude. Work commitment has also received a great deal of attention, but has been plagued to some extent by definitional confusion, being viewed as everything from an attitude to an indicator of motivation to a feeling of congruence or identification.[44] Similarly, employee engagement can be viewed as an attitude or a form of motivation. Lastly, although some authors view fairness perceptions as attitudes,[45] others view them as antecedents to attitudes rather than attitudes in their own right.[46] We treat these concepts as attitudes, but encourage consideration of how they may be viewed differently depending on the questions being asked and the measures being used.

Job Satisfaction

Job satisfaction The degree of pleasure employees derive from their jobs.

Job satisfaction is an internal evaluation of the favorability of one's job.[47] In short, it reflects the degree of pleasure that employees derive from their jobs. Because work is one of our major life activities, I-O psychologists have had a long-standing interest in job satisfaction. One hundred years ago, employment conditions were, by today's standards, unacceptable. Work was often performed under unsafe conditions, work hours were very long, offices were not air-conditioned, and benefits we often take for granted today, such as paid vacations, medical insurance, and retirement contributions, did not exist. You might think that the employees of today, who enjoy more favorable working conditions, would be highly satisfied with their jobs; however, that is not the case. Although some employees derive great pleasure and meaning from their work, many others regard work as drudgery.

Why is this so? The answer lies in individual differences in expectations and, in particular, the degree to which a job meets one's expectations. An employee's affective reaction to a job is based on a comparison of the actual outcomes derived from the job with those outcomes that are expected.[48] Of course, feelings of job satisfaction can change with time and circumstances.[49] In addition, people differ in what is important to them, and this may also change for the same person. There are broad differences in what people expect from their jobs and thus broad reactions to them. What is stressful and overwhelming to one person may be a welcome challenge to another. What one person finds boring, another may find relaxing. Why people differ in their preferences for job outcomes is posited to be related to their developmental experiences and levels of aspiration. Said differently, it seems that your satisfaction with a job is impacted by what you want to get out of the job.[50]

Research has revealed that people develop overall feelings about their jobs as well as about selected dimensions or facets of their jobs, such as their supervisor, coworkers, promotional opportunities, pay, and so on. I-O psychologists differentiate these two levels of feelings as *global job satisfaction* and *job facet satisfaction*, respectively. Considerable research has been devoted to the measurement of job satisfaction. The Job Descriptive Index[51] has been used to measure job satisfaction for more than 50 years, and it is regarded with professional esteem within I-O psychology.[52] Likewise, the Minnesota Satisfaction Questionnaire[53] is highly regarded within the profession. A version of the Minnesota Satisfaction Questionnaire is shown in Figure 11-3.

The extent to which individuals feel satisfied about their jobs is a function of affect as well as objective job conditions (e.g., level of pay, hours of work, and physical working conditions). One model of job satisfaction (depicted in Figure 11-4) is based on these two components.[54] These aspects lead to an assessment or interpretation of the job circumstances. The interpretation is based on many considerations, including the perceived adequacy of the pay for the work performed, the level of stress on the job, and the match of the job to the person's skills and abilities.

Researchers have confirmed the validity of affect, and have established a linkage between personality and job satisfaction.[55] Job satisfaction was found to correlate –.29 with neuroticism, .25 with extraversion, .02 with openness to experience, .17 with agreeableness, and .26 with conscientiousness. As a set, these Big 5 personality dimensions had a multiple correlation coefficient of .41 with job satisfaction. Similarly, it appears that feelings of job satisfaction are inheritable, based on a study of identical twins reared apart.[56] In short, feelings of job satisfaction are related both to the objective conditions of work (that are under the control of the organization) and to the personality of the worker.

Honeymoon-hangover effect
The tendency for employees to initially have heightened levels of job satisfaction in new jobs, followed by a drop in satisfaction levels similar to what they had in their previous jobs.

There is evidence for a "**honeymoon-hangover effect**" with regard to job satisfaction.[57] Specifically, individuals appear to report their highest levels of job satisfaction after being on their jobs for about three months. This period of heightened job satisfaction is known as the "honeymoon period." However, job satisfaction levels tend to decrease in the months thereafter, to a level similar to what the individuals reported

Ask yourself: How satisfied am I with this aspect of my job?

Very Sat. means I am very satisfied with this aspect of my job.

Sat. means I am satisfied with this aspect of my job.

N means I can't decide whether I am satisfied or not with this aspect of my job.

Dissat. means I am dissatisfied with this aspect of my job.

Very Dissat. means I am very dissatisfied with this aspect of my job.

On my present job, this is how I feel about . . .	*Very Dissat.*	*Dissat.*	*N*	*Sat.*	*Very Sat.*
1. Being able to keep busy all the time	☐	☐	☐	☐	☐
2. The chance to work alone on the job	☐	☐	☐	☐	☐
3. The chance to do different things from time to time	☐	☐	☐	☐	☐
4. The chance to be "somebody" in the community	☐	☐	☐	☐	☐
5. The way my boss handles subordinates	☐	☐	☐	☐	☐
6. The competence of my supervisor in making decisions	☐	☐	☐	☐	☐
7. Being able to do things that don't go against my conscience	☐	☐	☐	☐	☐
8. The way my job provides for steady employment	☐	☐	☐	☐	☐
9. The chance to do things for other people	☐	☐	☐	☐	☐
10. The chance to tell people what to do	☐	☐	☐	☐	☐
11. The chance to do something that makes use of my abilities	☐	☐	☐	☐	☐
12. The way company policies are put into practice	☐	☐	☐	☐	☐
13. My pay and the amount of work I do	☐	☐	☐	☐	☐
14. The chances for advancement on this job	☐	☐	☐	☐	☐
15. The freedom to use my own judgment	☐	☐	☐	☐	☐
16. The chance to try my own methods of doing the job	☐	☐	☐	☐	☐
17. The working conditions	☐	☐	☐	☐	☐
18. The way my coworkers get along with each other	☐	☐	☐	☐	☐
19. The praise I get for doing a good job	☐	☐	☐	☐	☐
20. The feeling of accomplishment I get from the job	☐	☐	☐	☐	☐

Figure 11-3 *Minnesota Satisfaction Questionnaire (short form)*

Source: From *Manual for the Minnesota Satisfaction Questionnaire*, by D. J. Weiss, R. V. Dawis, G. W. England, and L. H. Lofquist, © 1967. Minneapolis: Industrial Relations Center, University of Minnesota. Reproduced with permission of Vocational Psychology Research, University of Minnesota. http://www.psych.umn.edu/psylabs/vpr

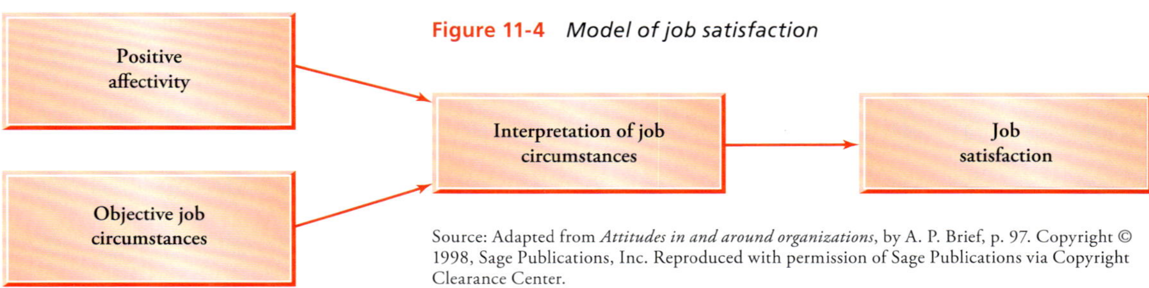

Figure 11-4 *Model of job satisfaction*

Source: Adapted from *Attitudes in and around organizations*, by A. P. Brief, p. 97. Copyright © 1998, Sage Publications, Inc. Reproduced with permission of Sage Publications via Copyright Clearance Center.

for their previous job. This drop in job satisfaction following the honeymoon period is known as the "hangover." Individuals who report lower job satisfaction with their previous jobs appear to be more likely to experience this pattern than are individuals who report greater satisfaction in their previous jobs.

Consider This...

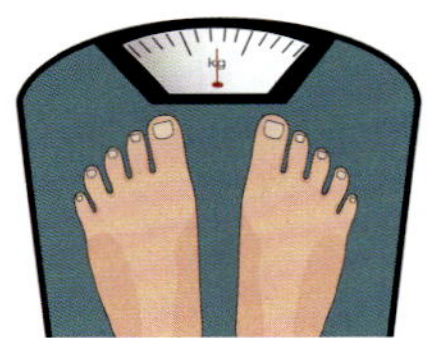

Within the human body, there is a biological control that regulates one's weight towards a predetermined level. This explains why individuals who gain or lose considerable weight often return to their pre-change weight, and often more quickly than would be expected simply from an increase in caloric intake or expenditure of effort. The honeymoon-hangover effect suggests a similar "set point" for job satisfaction, whereby employees will ultimately revert to a certain level of job satisfaction, regardless of the job or situation. As such, organizational efforts to improve long-term job satisfaction in employees may be futile. As discussed with happiness earlier, improvements in job satisfaction are possible, but their effects may be short-lived. What implications does this have for the workplace? Should managers devote time, attention, and other resources to making their employees more satisfied with their jobs? Why or why not?

The relationship between job satisfaction and important job-related criteria has been examined extensively. Three criteria will be presented: performance, turnover, and absence. The relationship between job satisfaction and job performance has been researched for more than 50 years. The reason is obvious—ideally, we would like to be both productive and happy in our work. However, the relationship between satisfaction and performance is not as strong as we might imagine, with one meta-analysis reporting the best estimate of their correlation to be .30.[58]

In order to more fully understand the relationship between job satisfaction and performance, researchers have meta-analytically examined the effect of situational strength on the relationship.[59] Situational strength refers to the notion that some situations are "strong" and contain cues that make it obvious about how an individual should behave. Other situations are "weak" and provide few if any cues about how one should behave. The researchers found that the relationship between job satisfaction and job performance is weaker for "strong" occupations (e.g., first-line supervisors of production workers) and is stronger for "weak" occupations (e.g., door-to-door salespeople). They argue that the reason for this finding is that the stronger the situation, the more behavior is constrained, leaving less freedom for the individual to choose how to behave and respond. Additionally, in terms of the direction of the relationship, job satisfaction is more likely to lead to job performance than job performance leading to job satisfaction.[60]

Turnover and absence are often referred to as *withdrawal behavior* because they reflect the employee withdrawing from a noxious employment condition, either temporarily (absence) or permanently (turnover). The relationship between how much you like your job and whether you withdraw from it has attracted considerable interest among I-O psychologists. In general, the more people dislike their job, the more likely they are to quit. The magnitude of the satisfaction–turnover correlation, on average, is about –.40. However, this relationship is influenced by several factors, including the availability of other work. People would rather endure a dissatisfying job than be unemployed.[61] Conversely, when alternative employment is readily available, workers are more likely to leave dissatisfying jobs.[62]

The correlation between job satisfaction and absence is considerably smaller, approximately –.25.[63] Absence from work can be caused by many factors that have nothing to do with how much you like your job, including transportation problems and family responsibilities. However, when researchers control for methodological issues in the design of research addressing this relationship (including whether the absence from work is paid or unpaid, and whether organizational sanctions are imposed on absent workers), a mild but consistent negative relationship emerges between the two. A practical implication of the finding is that if you like your job, you are more likely to make the extra effort needed to get to work (such as when you have a flat tire) than if you are dissatisfied with your job.

Some scholars argue that job satisfaction is a critical attitude to measure even without having to make a clear "business case" for it.[64] Because jobs are important aspects of our lives, having a better understanding of our evaluations of them is reason enough to study job satisfaction. In addition, job satisfaction plays a role in obtaining overall life satisfaction. Thus, regardless of whether individuals view their jobs as laborious, frustrating, tedious, fulfilling, or something else, it appears job satisfaction is an essential attitude for individuals. However, given the relatively meager relationship between job satisfaction and job outcomes, other attitudes are clearly worthy of attention.

Work Commitment

Work commitment The extent to which employees feel a sense of allegiance to their work.

Work commitment is the extent to which an employee feels a sense of allegiance and loyalty to one or more targets within the sphere of employment. The targets can include one's occupation or profession, the employing organization, a work team, or a particular component of one's job (e.g., being a good leader). Commitment is just one of several types of bonds that may exist between a person and a target. Indeed, there are four types of bonds, which are summarized in Table 11-1.[65]

First, there are *acquiescence bonds*, which are characterized by a perceived lack of alternatives. Employees who don't believe there are other jobs available for their skill sets may feel "stuck" with their organizations. Their bonds are more about compliance

Table 11-1 *A continuum of bond types*

	Acquiescence	Instrumental	Commitment	Identification
Defining feature	Perceived absence of alternatives	High cost or loss at stake	Volition, dedication, and responsibility	Merging of oneself with the target
How the bond is experienced	Resignation to the reality of the bond	Calculated acceptance of the bond	Embracement of the bond	Self-defined in terms of the bond

Adapted from "Reconceptualizing Workplace Commitment to Redress a Stretched Construct: Revisiting Assumptions and Removing Confounds," by H. J. Klein, J. C. Molloy, and C. T. Brinsfield, in *Academy of Management Review* (2012). Reprinted with permission from the Academy of Management via Copyright Clearance Center.

and resignation than volitional commitments to their organizations. Next, there are *instrumental bonds*. These bonds are primarily transactional in nature, with a focus on what might be lost if the target weren't in the picture. Employees who opt to remain in an occupation due to time, energy, money, etc. associated with education would be characterized as having instrumental bonds. They are accepting that a bond exists based on a calculated examination of the costs and benefits of remaining versus leaving their particular occupations. *Commitment bonds* are next on the continuum, and reflect a choice to be dedicated to and responsible for a particular target. Employees who make the conscious decision to be loyal to their supervisors are indicating a commitment to that individual. Choice is key here, and as such the employees will readily embrace the bond. Finally, *identification bonds* reflect a merging of an individual with a target. The bond is defined by the individual. Employees who consider the organization's values to be the same as theirs may identify with the organization, creating a bond that reflects a psychological merging of the employee and organization.

One of the most popular ways to conceptualize commitment separates commitment into three components:[66]

1. The *affective* component refers to the employee's emotional attachment to, and identification with, one's work. Affective commitment reflects allegiance based on liking (of work and/or a job).
2. The *continuance* component refers to commitment based on the costs that the employee associates with leaving one's work. Continuance commitment reflects allegiance because of a lack of viable alternatives.
3. The *normative* component refers to the employee's feelings of obligation to remain with one's work. Normative commitment reflects allegiance to work/a job out of a sense of loyalty.

For many years, most research on work commitment was directed to the organization as a target of one's allegiance. However, more recent research has been directed toward other targets of commitment.[67] The loss of job security in the contemporary workplace brings into question why employees would commit to their organization. Because of downsizing, outsourcing, offshoring, etc., employees can lose their jobs through no fault of their own (i.e., they are not fired), thereby weakening the basis of being in a committed relationship. Organizational changes resulting in job loss can undermine employee commitment, yet commitment is essential for any reconfigured organization (e.g., after downsizing) to succeed.[68] The dilemma of how to inspire employee commitment in a work world of instability is captured in the following statement issued by Apple Computers regarding why individuals should select that organization as their employer:

> Here's the deal Apple will give you: Here's what we want from you. We're going to give you a really neat trip while you're here. We're going to teach you stuff you couldn't learn anywhere else. In return we expect you to work like hell, buy the vision as long as you're here. We're not interested in employing you for a lifetime, because that's not the way we are thinking about this. It's a good opportunity for both of us that's probably finite" (Meyer 2009, pp. 37–8).[69]

To the extent this philosophy is embodied implicitly (if not explicitly) in the contemporary values of organizations, individuals will not exhibit commitment to organizations in exchange for long-term employment. The basis of commitment must be targeted to something else of value to the individual. In the case of Apple Computers, employee commitment should be offered ("buy the vision") in exchange for skill and knowledge acquisition that can generalize to other employment opportunities ("We're going to teach you stuff you couldn't learn anywhere else"). The concept of commitment has not been rendered obsolete by the contemporary work world, but rather organizational commitment has been supplanted by commitment to other aspects or targets associated with employment.[70]

Organizational commitment reflects employees' relationships with their organization, which has implications for their decisions to continue membership in the organization and showing up for work when scheduled.[71] Committed employees are more likely to remain in the organization and choose to attend work when scheduled than are uncommitted employees. However, the construct of commitment does not necessarily explain *why* employees remain with their employer.[72] Some behavior is habituated (i.e., we are in the habit of getting up, getting dressed, and going to work), which has nothing to do with commitment. Sample items from a questionnaire measuring organizational commitment are listed in Figure 11-5.[73]

Meta-analytic data indicate the average correlations between organizational commitment and other work-related constructs are as follows:

Overall job satisfaction[74] = .53
Turnover[75] = –.28
Job performance[76] = .20.

The general pattern of results suggests that organizational attitudes tend to be substantially intercorrelated. Performance is determined by ability, motivation, and situational constraints, whereas turnover is determined in part by external variables (e.g., economic circumstances). The linkage between organizational attitudes and behavior is thus moderated by factors beyond the control of the individual.

I really feel as if this organization's problems are my own.

This organization has a great deal of personal meaning for me.

Too much in my life would be disrupted if I decided I wanted to leave my organization now.

One of the major reasons I continue to work for this organization is that leaving would require considerable sacrifice; another organization may not match the overall benefits I have here.

I think that people these days move from company to company too often.

I was taught to believe in the value of remaining loyal to one organization.

Figure 11-5 *Sample items from an organizational commitment questionnaire*

Source: From "Organizational Commitment: The Utility of an Integrated Definition," by R. B. Dunham, J. A. Grube, and M. B. Castaneda, 1994, *Journal of Applied Psychology, 79*, pp. 370-380.

Employee Engagement

Employee engagement The degree to which individuals feel invigorated, dedicated, and absorbed in their work.

Employee engagement is a concept that reflects the extent to which individuals have very high levels of energy for and a strong sense of identity and attachment to their work. Engaged employees are passionate and enthusiastic about their work and focus their attention on efforts that will have a positive impact on organizational outcomes.[77]

Employee engagement has three dimensions:[78]

1. **Vigor**—a sense of personal energy for work. Energy exists along a continuum, with vigor on one end and emotional exhaustion on the other. Of the three dimensions, vigor is the most predictive of job performance.[79]
2. **Dedication**—a sense of pride in one's work. This dimension captures the idea that engaged individuals are highly involved in their work and experience a feeling of challenge from it.
3. **Absorption**—the capacity to be engrossed in work and experience a sense of being "in the zone" while working. When absorbed in their work, engaged employees have high levels of concentration and enjoyment of their tasks.

Some have regarded employee engagement as lying on a continuum where the opposite end is *burnout*, which is characterized by emotional exhaustion, cynicism, and feelings of reduced personal accomplishment. These scholars suggest that engagement's focus on energy, involvement, and a sense of efficacy, are the positive counterparts to these burnout dimensions.[80] From this perspective, if you're high on engagement you would necessarily be low on burnout, and vice versa. Others suggest, however, that engagement is not the opposite of burnout, and that instead it is more cognitive than emotional in nature.[81] That is, the focus on concentration and engrossment in a task may be more a function of one's outlook and mindset than their emotional state. From this perspective, it would be possible to be simultaneously high (or low) on engagement and burnout if an individual is cognitively engaged and emotionally burned out (or cognitively disengaged yet flourishing emotionally).

Consider This...

An important element of employee engagement is that the intense work involvement combines both high effort and positive affect. That is, people are working hard because they enjoy it, not because they feel a compulsion to do so. In fact, when individuals feel negative affect rather than positive affect and they feel an uncontrollable need to work, they are likely experiencing workaholism rather than engagement.[82] Although on the surface they may look the same, with employees devoting long hours and attention to work activities, the consequences of employee engagement and workaholism differ in important ways. Whereas engagement is associated with positive outcomes such as higher job satisfaction and increased citizenship behavior,[83] workaholism has been linked to negative outcomes such as heightened conflicts between one's work and family lives[84] and lower well-being.[85] Do you think that managers would be able tell if their employees were engaged versus suffering from workaholism? Who do you think is responsible for ensuring employees are engaged in their work? Who do you think is responsible for ensuring employees are not suffering from workaholism?

Employee engagement is premised on the belief that individuals have the capacity to contribute far more to being productive than organizations typically allow them to be. It is important to create a work environment that is supportive of work engagement by providing the necessary physical, political, financial, and social resources for employees to feel dedicated to their work.[86] Examples include allowing employees to take some risks in the conduct of their work, and not rebuke or censure them if their risk-taking leads to unsuccessful outcomes. Thus, employee engagement can be thought of as an interaction of individuals and work (see Faces of I-O Psychology: *John C. Howes*). Engagement can occur when both facilitate each other, and engagement will not occur when either (or both) thwart(s) each other. For example, employee engagement will not manifest itself if the employee just wants a paycheck and/or a job allows no discretion in individual decision making and behavior.

Meta-analytic evidence has revealed that employee engagement predicts employee effectiveness beyond what is predicted by job satisfaction, organizational commitment, and job involvement.[87] Thus, it makes an incremental contribution over-and-above what other attitudinal measures offer. In a contemporary work world characterized by high employment instability, individuals may be grateful for any work, let alone engaged work. However, employee engagement is not proposed as a solution for job loss or unemployment. It represents a prescription for both employees and employers to derive the most value from each other during the duration of their relationship.

Organizational Justice

Organizational justice The theoretical concept pertaining to the fair treatment of people in organizations. The three types of organizational justice are distributive, procedural, and interactional.

Organizational justice is concerned with the fair treatment of people in organizations. Organizational justice has been among the most frequently researched topics in I-O psychology in the last two decades.[88] The attention to this construct appears warranted, considering organizational justice has been found to be associated with many important workplace topics, including performance, turnover, absenteeism, job satisfaction, and organizational commitment.

Various configurations or typologies of organizational justice have been proposed over the years. However, the most current research and thinking on the topic have yielded the typology shown in Figure 11-6, consisting of distributive, procedural, and interactional justice (which is further divided into interpersonal and informational

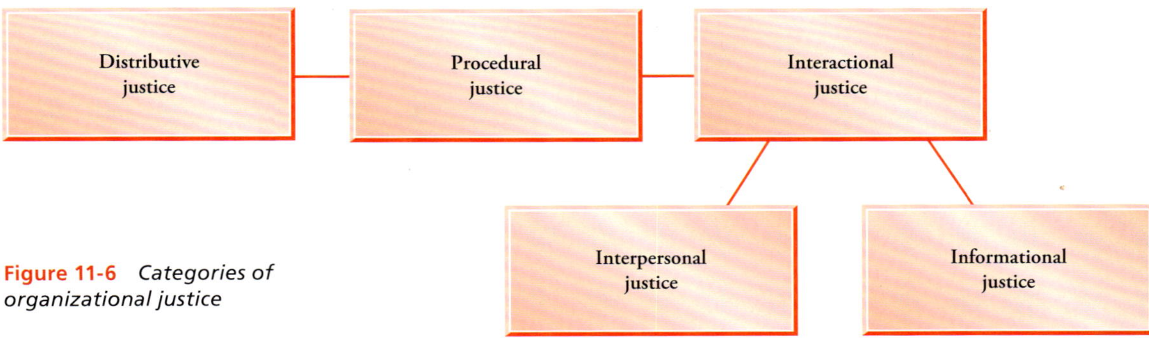

Figure 11-6 *Categories of organizational justice*

Faces of I-O Psychology: *John C. Howes*

John C. Howes

Ph.D. Colorado State University

Co-Founder and Chief Experience Management Officer: qChange

Dr. Howes spent nearly 25 years in progressively-larger leadership roles at various companies, including IBM, Nike, St. Charles Health System, Scottish Power/PacifiCorp, Honeywell, AlliedSignal, and Sprint. Following this, John made the leap to the world of entrepreneurship and co-founded qChange. qChange provides real-time feedback to grow leaders, build better teams, and improve business performance. Within qChange, John practices I-O psychology through consulting, thought leadership, business growth, customer experience, and data science/AI.

Individuals spend a massive amount of their lives at work, and the concept of work is changing. One of the reasons I decided to go into the field of Industrial and Organizational Psychology is because of the impact we can have on individuals, teams, departments, whole organizations, and even communities, by creating more engaging workplaces and providing workers with better employee experiences.

Within qChange, we focus on concepts such as pride, satisfaction, advocacy, and loyalty to measure engagement. When employees are more engaged, they show greater commitment to the organization and deliver increased discretionary effort towards organizational goals. Decades of our research have shown that engaged employees work harder, stay longer, care more about their job, and find more gratification in helping their company succeed. But engagement isn't always enough. In addition, we help organizations understand whether they are creating an enabling work environment. When that happens, employees are better able to perform quality work and provide the best products and services to their customers. Measuring and improving on this concept of performance enablement helps organizations and teams maximize performance by focusing employee passion and energy. Finally, when we work with organizations on creating the best employee experience, we're helping them understand what matters most to their employees. Do they feel a sense of belonging, of purpose, of achievement? Are they happy and do they bring a level of vigor to their work?

I've been fortunate to work with fantastic organizations that take real action to improve their workplaces. As I-O psychologists, we conduct statistical linkage research that repeatedly demonstrates our impact on the bottom line for organizations. I've been involved in studies that have shown our work improves sales, workplace safety, absenteeism and turnover, stress levels, and many other financial performance measures. The really great part of this type of I-O psychology work, however, is that by focusing on engagement, enablement, and a positive employee experience, we're able to have an impact on hundreds of thousands of employees. Again, if most adults spend an extremely large percentage of their waking hours working, to make this a better experience for them is very rewarding.

Distributive justice The fairness with which the outcomes or results are distributed among members of an organization.

Procedural justice The fairness of the means used to achieve results in an organization.

Interactional justice The fairness with how people are treated within an organization and the timeliness, completeness, and accuracy of the information received in an organization.

justices).[89] **Distributive justice** refers to the fairness of the outcomes, results, or ends achieved. **Procedural justice** is the fairness of the means used to achieve the results. As the name suggests, it deals with the perceived fairness of the policies and procedures used to make decisions. In essence, the distinction between distributive and procedural justice is the difference between content and process that is basic to many philosophical approaches to the study of justice.

There are three dimensions to conceptualizing procedural justice.[90] The first dimension emphasizes the desire for *advance notice* regarding decisions. Having some warning ahead of time regarding decisions that impact them is a key factor influencing whether individuals will view the decision-making process as fair. Part of the issue here is that procedures are perceived to be fairer when affected individuals have an opportunity to either influence the decision process or offer input. Indeed, researchers have found that higher levels of participation in decision making by employees are associated with higher levels of perceived procedural fairness.[91] The second dimension of procedural justice involves the *right to appeal decisions*. In general, individuals view procedures that allow them to address decisions that impact them and dispute perceived discrepancies as being fairer. Along these lines, giving workers the opportunity to respond to their own performance evaluations, including the possibility of modifying them, is one of the most influential factors in their acceptability.[92] The final dimension of procedural justice concerns the *adequacy with which decisions are explained*. In short, individuals assess the fairness of policies and procedures by the extent to which they have received sufficient explanation regarding them.

In applying the concept of procedural justice to a personnel selection system, one could posit several components of what constitutes a "fair" selection process.[93] Ideally, the selection test should be job-related (or more precisely from the applicant's view, face valid), allow candidates to demonstrate their proficiency, and be scored consistently across applicants. Furthermore, candidates should receive timely feedback on their application for employment, be told the truth, and be treated respectfully in the assessment process. Note that these procedural justice issues pertain to the selection *process*, not the outcome of whether the applicant is accepted or rejected (which is a matter of distributive justice). There are six criteria by which procedures can be judged as fair: (1) consistent, (2) bias-free, (3) accurate, (4) correctable in case of an error, (5) representative of all concerned, and (6) based on prevailing ethical standards.[94]

A third major type of organizational justice is **interactional justice**, which has two components: interpersonal and informational. *Interpersonal justice* is manifested by showing concern for individuals and respecting them as people who have dignity. Ostensible displays of politeness and respect for citizens' rights enhance perceptions of fair treatment by authorities, such as the police and the courts. Politeness within the workplace is critical and costs little to give, but can cost dearly if absent. The lack of politeness, sensitivity, and caring for the emotional pain inflicted by organizations on employees only adds insult to injury.[95]

Informational justice is manifested by providing knowledge about procedures that demonstrates regard for people's concerns. This form of interactional justice involves openly sharing information and giving adequate accounts and explanations of the procedures used to determine the outcomes. For explanations to be perceived as fair, they

Consider This...

We mentioned the two young boys, Goofus and Gallant, from the *Highlights for Children* magazine at the start of this chapter. Since the 1940s, they have been demonstrating for young children what is proper and polite (shown by Gallant) versus improper and impolite (shown by Goofus). It's important to note, however, that while the concept of politeness is universal, how it is expressed may differ by culture.[96] What is considered rude in one culture may be considered polite in another. For example, while burping and slurping during meals is considered inappropriate in many cultures, it is a way of showing appreciation for a good meal in some parts of China and Taiwan.[97] Similarly, while you might never consider spitting on another person to be polite, the Maasai tribe in Kenya consider it to be a compliment and spit at one another in much the same way other cultures shake hands.[98] What other differences in politeness exist between cultures? Knowing there are differences in how politeness is expressed, how do you think it might impact interactional justice? What recommendations would you make to people working with individuals from other cultures regarding interpersonal justice issues?

must also be recognized as genuine in intent (without ulterior motives) and based on sound reasoning.

A classic study illustrates interpersonal and informational justice.[99] In the study, two announcements of a worksite smoking ban were made to employees of a large company. The announcements differed in the amount of information they gave about the need for the ban and the degree of interpersonal sensitivity shown for the personal impact of the ban. Some employees received a great deal of information about the reason for the smoking ban, while others received only the most cursory information.

Furthermore, some employees received a personally-sensitive message ("We realize that this new policy will be very hard on those of you who smoke. Smoking is an addiction, and it's very tough to stop. We are quite aware of this, and we do not want you to suffer."), while other employees received a message showing less personal concern ("I realize that it's tough to stop smoking, but it's in the best interest of our business to implement the smoking ban. And, of course, business must come first."). Immediately after the announcement, employees completed surveys on their acceptance of the ban. Although heavy smokers were least accepting of the ban, they showed the greatest incremental gain in acceptance after they received thorough information presented in a highly-sensitive manner. Regardless of how much they smoked, all smokers were aware of the procedural justice that resulted from the organization providing detailed information in a socially-sensitive way. By contrast, the way in which the smoking ban was presented had no influence on any of the nonsmokers' acceptance of the ban.

A major meta-analytic review of 25 years of organizational justice research concluded that distributive justice, procedural justice, and the two types of interactional justice (interpersonal and informational) each contribute incremental variance to perceptions of fairness in the workplace.[100] Although the different justice dimensions are not totally distinct, each reflects a facet of "what is fair." It is often difficult to arrive at consensus on fairness, and there can be far-reaching implications for organizations when there are differing views on what constitutes fairness in their practices. Much of what is known about organizational justice has been discovered from its violation; that is, organizational injustice.[101] Because justice is expected as the norm, it is more informative to examine deviations from the norm (i.e., injustice) than behavior consistent with the norm (i.e., justice). The fair treatment of employees by organizations has important effects on individual employee attitudes, such as satisfaction and commitment, and on individual behaviors, such as absenteeism and citizenship behavior.[102] Of the three major types of justice, procedural justice appears to be most closely related to organizational attitudes and behaviors.[103]

Behaviors

Individuals can engage in a variety of behaviors while at work. Though the vast majority of attention has been devoted to behaviors related to task performance, I-O psychologists have also examined "extra" behaviors that individuals engage in within organizations. Some of these behaviors can be beneficial to organizations, while others can cause harm to the organization and its constituents. Below, we examine organizational citizenship behavior, counterproductive work behavior, and political behavior, and the implications of each for individuals and organizations.

Organizational Citizenship Behavior

The classic approach to thinking about a job is in terms of the tasks that comprise it. In fact, one purpose of work analysis (as described in Chapter 4) is to identify these tasks. In turn, performance appraisal (as discussed in Chapter 8) is concerned with assessing how well employees perform the tasks that comprise their jobs. However, organizational researchers have discovered that some employees contribute to the welfare or effectiveness of their organization by going beyond the duties prescribed in their jobs. That is, they make extra discretionary contributions that are neither required nor expected.

Organizational citizenship behavior Employee behavior that transcends job performance and is directed to the overall welfare of the organization.

The most frequently-used term for this phenomenon is **organizational citizenship behavior**. It is also referred to as *pro-social behavior*, *extra-role behavior*, and *contextual behavior*. We first mentioned citizenship behavior in Chapter 4 on criteria and again in Chapter 6 on personnel decisions. Recall that organizational citizenship behavior can be directed at individuals or organizations.

There are five dimensions of citizenship behavior:[104]

1. **Altruism** (also called *helping behavior*) reflects willfully helping specific people with an organizationally-relevant task or problem.
2. **Conscientiousness** refers to being punctual, having attendance better than the group norm, and judiciously following company rules, regulations, and procedures.
3. **Courtesy** is being mindful and respectful of other people's rights.

4. **Sportsmanship** refers to avoiding complaints, petty grievances, gossiping, and falsely magnifying problems.
5. **Civic virtue** is responsible participation in the political life of the organization. Civic virtue reflects keeping abreast of current organizational issues as well as more mundane issues, such as attending meetings, attending to in-house communications, and speaking up on issues. It has been suggested that civic virtue is the most admirable manifestation of organizational citizenship behavior because it often entails some sacrifice of individual productive efficiency.

Employees who exhibit pro-social behavior are highly valued by their managers. Indeed, they should be, because they contribute above and beyond the normal requirements and expectations of the job. A meta-analysis of the individual and organizational consequences of employees who engage in organizational citizenship behavior found that employees who were perceived as exhibiting citizenship behaviors received higher performance evaluations and pay raises, and had lower rates of absence, compared to employees who exhibited less citizenship behavior.[105] Across different organizational units, organizational citizenship behavior correlated .41 with unit productivity (objectively measured, not rated) and .42 with cost reduction.

Why do employees engage in citizenship behaviors? Scholars have suggested there are two motives for doing so.[106] One is to "do good" (citizenship) and the other is to "look good" (impression management). To do good is founded on the pro-social motive of contributing to the welfare of the organization beyond one's job duties, to be a "good soldier."[107] To look good is to influence how others perceive you for self-serving reasons, to be a "good actor." Employees can be both good soldiers and good actors at the same time, but an individual is typically more driven by one motive over the other.

Research suggests that some people, given selected aspects of their personality, are more likely to engage in organizational citizenship behaviors than are others. Notably, agreeableness (one's level of good-naturedness) and conscientiousness (one's level of reliability and discipline) appear relevant to organizational citizenship behavior.[108] Thus, organizations can use personality to select employees who have a propensity to engage in these behaviors.[109]

There also appear to be situational antecedents that influence whether individuals engage in organizational citizenship behavior. For example, research has found that individuals are less likely to engage in organizational citizenship behaviors when they are experiencing role conflict or role ambiguity.[110] In addition, when organizations are viewed positively, employees will be more likely to engage in citizenship behaviors. For example, employees are likely to define their relationship with the organization as a social exchange. In exchange for being treated fairly, employees would engage in discretionary gestures of organizational citizenship behavior. However, to the degree the organization is perceived as lacking fairness, employees will only do what is obligated of them.[111] There do appear to be some gender differences in this, however. Specifically, women tend to feel obligated to engage in citizenship behavior even when they perceive relatively low organizational support, whereas men tend to perform citizenship behaviors only when they perceive relatively high levels of organizational support.[112]

Despite the positive benefits for organizational citizenship behavior, some cautionary statements are needed. First, individuals who feel pressured to engage in citizenship behaviors may perform more pro-social behaviors but are also more likely to experience role overload.[113] In addition, organizational citizenship behavior may become dysfunctional if it interferes with the person's individual task performance.[114] This is problematic not only for an organization, but for the employee as well, considering research has found that spending time on actual task performance is more related to career outcomes (promotions, salary increases, and speed of advancement) than is spending time on citizenship behaviors.[115] It is important to note that time management skills may play a role here. Researchers have found that individuals who are skilled at time management are able to reap the benefits of engaging in helping behaviors, but those who aren't skilled at managing their time feel the negative impact on their task performance.[116]

By definition, citizenship behaviors transcend job performance and are discretionary. This means that unlike task performance, such behaviors are not explicitly required of employees. However, there may be more of an expectation for some people to engage in citizenship behaviors. For example, one study found that men who engaged in the altruism dimension of organizational citizenship behavior on the job received higher evaluations than men who did not engage in altruistic behavior. Conversely, women who did not engage in altruistic behavior had lower evaluations than did men who did not engage in altruistic behavior.[117] The authors concluded that assisting others with tasks and going the "extra mile" (i.e., being a helper) is central to a female gender stereotype perception. Men who engage in helping others exceed the male gender stereotype perception, while women who help others are simply demonstrating "typical" female behavior. In turn, these gender-based stereotypes influence the evaluations received by men and women on the job. Similarly, researchers have found cultural differences between how organizational citizenship behavior is viewed. For example, employees in Hong Kong and Japan were more likely to regard some facets of organizational citizenship behavior as an expected or defined part of the job than were employees in the United States and Australia.[118] Thus, it appears that what employees in some cultures consider extra-role (discretionary) behavior, employees in other cultures consider in-role (expected) behavior.

Counterproductive Work Behavior

Counterproductive work behavior
A broad range of employee behaviors that are harmful to other employees or the organization.

Counterproductive work behavior refers to a broad range of employee behaviors that negatively impact the organization and its constituents. They are volitional in nature, meaning they are intended to cause harm.[119] The phenomenon has also been called *workplace incivility*, *organizational deviance*, and *insidious workplace behavior*.[120] Deviant behaviors can be directed at harming either the organization or individuals, including oneself.[121] Counterproductive work behaviors can be grouped into several categories.

- *Verbal* behaviors are rudeness, ostracism, spreading rumors, and sarcasm.
- *Physical* behaviors include bullying and overt violence such as kicking, beating, or spitting upon others.
- *Sabotage* includes damage to a company's property, products, or reputation.

- *Work-directed* behaviors include lateness, excessive absence, theft, and working slowly.
- *Workplace* (or *occupational*) *homicide* is the most extreme form of organizational deviance.

Counterproductive work behaviors can result from a number of factors. Abusive supervisors who engage in the undermining and belittling of employees prompt organizational deviance.[122] Organizational deviance may be used to retaliate against somebody. For example, employees are likely to ignore and exclude other employees whom they feel have been rude or demeaning in some way.[123] Retaliatory acts are often rooted in feeling powerless to alter one's work environment. One form of retaliation—sabotage—can be classified according to *severity* (minor/major), *recurrence* (one time/ongoing), and *visibility* (overt/covert).[124] If an employee intentionally directs customer service calls to the wrong party, this insidious sabotage would be described as minor, ongoing, and covert.

Consider This...

As the economy becomes increasingly service oriented, more acts of workplace incivility are directed toward customers. For example, consider this exchange at an airport ticket counter, as originally reported in *Sweet Revenge: The Wicked Delights of Getting Even*:

> His last words were, "If everybody working for this organization is as incompetent as you, no wonder your airline loses money." He then stormed off. I wished him a good flight as if nothing happened.
>
> The little old lady behind him in line had heard everything, of course, as she sweetly asked how I managed to stay so polite and cheerful in the face of his behavior. I told her the truth. "He's going to Kansas City," I explained, "and his bags are going to Tokyo." She laughed and told me that I'd done the right thing (Barreca 1997, p. 133).[125]

Do you think the employee was justified in what they did? How would you rate the severity of this action? What, if any, consequences do you think there should be for the employee? How about for the angry customer? How common do you think behaviors like this are?

Thermodynamics of revenge
A framework that describes revenge within organizations as consisting of a period of heating up due to a sparking event, followed by one of four forms of cooling down.

One interesting framework for explaining revenge within organizations is known as the "**thermodynamics of revenge**."[126] According to this framework, revenge thoughts and actions follow a pattern of "heating up" and "cooling down."

Heating up: In terms of heating up, there is typically a sparking event of one of two types. One is a violation of rules, norms, or promises by the organization. An organizational agent changes the rules or criteria of decision making after the fact to justify a self-serving judgment. The second is status or power derogation, such as destructive criticism or public ridicule intended to embarrass the employee. Because of this event, the employee "heats up" and experiences anger and bitterness, often feeling a need to satisfy a burning desire for revenge.

Cooling down: After heating up, the individual enters a "cooling down" phase, which can take one of four forms.

1. *Venting*–the employee talks heatedly and animatedly to friends, "blows off steam," and has little or no intention of acting on their feelings.
2. *Dissipation*–the employee gives the harm-doer the benefit of the doubt and searches for plausible explanations for the harm-doer's behavior.
3. *Fatigue*–the employee maintains their negative feelings for long periods of time. They do not forgive, forget, and let go. They often obsessively ruminate and express regret about not getting even with the harm-doer.
4. *Explosion*–this can manifest itself in the employee working harder to prove the critic wrong, mobilizing opposition to the harm-doer, or engaging in confrontations such as physical violence.

Workplace bullying has gained considerable attention within I-O psychology. Bullying can involve a single bully targeting others or involve multiple bullies ganging up on one or more individuals. Reasons for bullying are numerous, and can include hidden agendas or old scores that individuals believe must be settled.[127] Both high and low performers can be the targets of workplace aggression, but the type of aggression appears to differ for each.[128] Namely, aggression aimed at low performers appears to be more direct, whereas aggression aimed at high performers is more subtle and indirect. For example, yelling, profanity use, and direct threats are more common means of bullying low performers, and sabotage, withholding information or resources, and avoidance are more common forms of bullying directed at high performers.

Occasionally, an organization's practices and policies may constitute bullying. For example, a practice of requiring employees to indefinitely work beyond their assigned shifts when workflow is heavy, without concern for employees' needs, can be considered organizational bullying. In addition, the culture of the organization may create situations that allow greater incivility. Employees who believe their organization has treated them deliberately and unnecessarily in a harmful manner will perceive the organization as being cruel.[129] This perceived organizational cruelty is likely to lead to health and well-being problems for the employee as well as potential retaliatory behaviors.

It is the traditional perspective of I-O psychology to focus on individuals. Within the topic of organizational deviance, the conventional focus would be to assume individuals who engage in retaliatory acts are the "bad apples" in the barrel, who should be disciplined for the incivility. However, an alternative perspective is that organizations may embody a culture of "everyone for themselves" which, in turn, produces a very broad range of behaviors.[130] Among them are counterproductive work behaviors. Organizational incivility can be the product of "bad barrels" that permit such behavior to occur in addition to "bad apples" within "good barrels." Along these lines, bullying may be either stifled or encouraged through the rules that teams set and how strongly members identify with their team.[131] When team members identify strongly with a team that values respect and pro-social interactions, bullying won't be tolerated. If the team values aggression and disrespect, however, a team member who feels strongly connected to that team will be more likely to engage in interpersonally-deviant behaviors.

Workplace incivility Low-intensity deviant behavior with ambiguous intent to harm the target individual, in violation of workplace norms for mutual respect.

Scholars have proposed a spiraling effect of incivility in the workplace.[132] **Workplace incivility** is low-intensity deviant behavior with ambiguous intent to harm the target individual, in violation of workplace norms for mutual respect. Uncivil behaviors are characteristically rude and discourteous, displaying a lack of regard for others. The spiraling effect refers to the prospects that incivility can escalate into intense aggressive behavior. The spiral of incivility often begins with a thoughtless act or a rude comment. This can be followed by a maligning insult, which prompts a counter-insult. If the spiral of escalation continues, threats of physical attack can follow, ultimately leading to violence. There is a "tipping point" in the spiral where the accumulation of minor affronts escalates into coercive action.

Even mild acts of aggression can have a tremendous impact when they are experienced over extended periods of time. Microaggressions are brief yet commonly-occurring verbal, behavioral, or situational slights targeted against certain individuals.[133] The daily, ongoing impact of microaggressions can create considerable distress for the targets, resulting in a hostile work environment and feelings of oppression.[134] A meta-analysis of workplace aggression found that coworkers are more likely than supervisors to be targets of workplace aggression.[135] This finding may be attributable to coworkers having less retaliatory power than supervisors, as well as their greater representation within an organization.

Cyberaggression Hostile or aggressive behavior at the workplace that occurs through electronic media.

The widespread use of computers in the workplace has led to another form of aggression—cyberaggression.[136] **Cyberaggression**, also referred to as *cyberbullying*, involves inflicting intentional harm to others through electronic media. A common form of cyberaggression is flaming, or the intentional use of insulting language through electronic means (email, blogs) designed to inflict harm. With the pervasiveness of social media, cyberbullying has become a real threat for organizations (see Social Media and I-O Psychology: *The Cyberbully's Blog*). Cyberaggression is a form of cyberdeviancy, which involves the misuse of technology to cause harm to the organization or its stakeholders.[137] Cyberdeviancy also includes cyberloafing, or the wasting of time by sending personal email and shopping online during company time.

Organizational Politics

Organizational politics Behavior exhibited within organizations by employees meant to influence decisions; the behavior is driven by the employee's self-interest.

The concept of **organizational politics** seeks to explain behavior within organizations that accounts for (among other things) how and why decisions get made. An idealistic view of organizations is that they are guided by rational and reasoned individuals who make decisions that solely enhance the welfare of the organization. That is, employees sublimate or negate their personal interests in favor of doing what is in the best interest of the organization. In reality, organizations are not populated with selfless individuals. Organizations are arenas for individual behavior to manifest itself, and people are motivated by many factors, including self-interest. Concerns about career progression and potential job loss are such examples. The concept of organizational politics examines how individuals use their organizational membership to influence decisions that enhance their self-interest.

Social Media and I-O Psychology: *The Cyberbully's Blog*

Bullies have been around since the dawn of time, inflicting pain and suffering on their victims. Even the sweet Peanuts character, Charlie Brown, suffers the wrath of Lucy, the bully who has tormented him on the comic book pages for over 50 years, most notably by constantly moving a football just as he goes to kick it. Bullies are not limited to playgrounds and comic strips, however. They now exist in the workplace, from the front lines to the boardrooms. Moreover, they exist online, in a world where they are shielded by a sense of anonymity combined with the possibility of widespread and instantaneous impact. As such, harassment by cyberbullies, although not face-to-face, has the potential to be just as damaging, if not more so, to their victims.

Social media blur the lines between work and nonwork in many ways. Blogs are one way in which boundaries are obscured. Blogs (or web logs) emerged in the late 1990s, allowing people to provide commentary on a particular subject. Frequently interactive, they typically allow individuals to comment on the content, thereby establishing a social connection with others. Bloggers post seemingly anything they want, whenever they want, and as such the blog is fertile ground for cyberbullies—and for blurring the lines between work and nonwork. The cyberbully should beware, however, as what is written outside of work could get them in trouble on the job. Furthermore, it could get the organization in trouble.

Take, for example, the unfortunate experience of a California probations employee who reported his coworker's misconduct on the job.[138] A separate coworker created a blog away from work, using his personal computer. In this blog, employees started to post derogatory comments about the whistle-blowing employee, who happened to have a disability: he was born with a disfigured right hand that he usually attempted to keep hidden in his pocket. His coworkers referred to him as "the Rat" and his hand, as "the claw" in their blog posts. The posts become increasingly vulgar and more inappropriate, and the employee filed a complaint. It was found that although the blog was created outside of work, it was clear that people were accessing the blog while on the job and that the employer was aware of this. In the end, the employer was found liable for having knowledge of the harassment and not taking sufficient steps to stop it. A jury ordered the company to pay the employee over $800,000. Clearly, employers should beware of cyberbullying, as what happens outside of work may not stay outside of work.

Organizational politics is the capacity and willingness of individuals within organizations to impact decision making for the purpose of furthering their own interests.[139] This can include withholding information, forming coalitions to gain support for their positions, spreading rumors, complimenting and volunteering to help individuals in charge, and other acts that will gain individuals more power and influence. Self-serving behavior that may coincidentally enhance the welfare of other employees is the cornerstone of organizational politics. Fundamentally, organizational politics addresses the question of "who gets what, when, and how."[140]

Consider This...

Organizational politics has traditionally been viewed as representing the dark side of behavior in organizations, involving exclusively self-serving tactics such as manipulation, coercion, deceit, and subversion.[141] Scholars have noted that the contemporary stance, however, is to view organizational politics as neutral or even positive, with a focus on how decisions get made in organizations.[142] The logic is that it is natural to be focused on one's own needs, and that not all self-serving behaviors are deceitful or destructive. In addition, some innocent behaviors may be unjustly viewed as politicking. For example, some individuals may view complimenting a manager or offering to help on a project as politicking, when perhaps it was simply a kind gesture or an act of citizenship behavior. When do you think nice gestures become evidence of politicking? Have you ever engaged in politics? How would you feel if you learned your coworker had an influence on a decision that benefited your colleague but hurt you? What if your coworker's politicking helped you, too? Would you feel differently?

"When you mix people and power, you get politics."
—Sir Winston Churchill

The use of political tactics in organizations is widespread, and is often regarded as a fact of organizational life. One study found that 90% of managers believe that it was necessary to engage at least occasionally in organizational politics to be successful.[143] Nevertheless, organizations differ with regard to the frequency, intensity, and nature of its use.

Three aspects of organizational politics are noteworthy. One is the various forms of its occurrence. Tactics can include such things as bypassing the chain of command to gain approval for a particular decision and creating norms of obligations and reciprocity (i.e., "you owe me").[144] There are many political games played in organizations.[145] Many of the games played do not seek to subvert the larger goals of the organization, but all games are designed to enhance the self-interests of those who play them. For example, the *budgeting game* is the awarding of a valued resource (money) to a department or unit in exchange for support or compliance. Implicit is the understanding that the following year's budget can be reduced if the support that was anticipated is not perceived to have materialized. People who play the budgeting game often espouse the business version of the "Golden Rule"—"Those who control the gold, rule." The *expertise game* is the flaunting or feigning of technical knowledge, emphasizing such knowledge is critical and irreplaceable, for the purpose of influencing decision outcomes favorable to the individual. The basis of the expertise game is "knowledge is power," and the particular knowledge is hoarded by those who possess it. The *rival camps game* is typically played between two groups within an organization, such as production and sales. Individuals external to these two camps will form temporary alliances with one group in exchange for something of value to them. However, in the next political battle between the two camps, external individuals may "switch sides" in their support. The two rival camps are played off against each other by non-members, with the recipient of their support being the one who offers more in return than the other.

A second area is devoted to understanding "political skill"—what attributes do people have that enable them to successfully engage in organizational politics? There are four components of political skill.[146] The first is *social astuteness*. Politically-skilled people have a well-crafted ability to observe social cues and to intuit the motives and values of other individuals. *Interpersonal influence*, the second component, is the capacity to take control of social encounters and do so with considerable ease. The third component, *building networks and forming coalitions*, is fundamental to organizational politics. A politically-skilled individual is not a renegade or rogue member of the organization, but someone who knows how to cultivate interpersonal resources to achieve desired outcomes. The final component is *projected virtue*. Politically-skilled individuals can disguise their true intentions, and project themselves to others as being virtuous in their motives. They may make emotional appeals to others for what is ostensibly the good of the organization, but such displays are disingenuous. Research has revealed that political skill is predictive of job performance above and beyond personality and cognitive ability.[147] In addition, politically-skilled individuals are better able to adapt to their environments.[148] Given the relationships between political skill and job performance and adaptability, measures of political skill may be viable selection instruments.

The third area is how others respond to the tactics of organizational politics. There are parallels between organizational politics and stress.[149] They both are characterized by ambiguity, unpredictability, and an overall sense of uneasiness. Organizational politics can undermine the principles of organizational justice and a sense of fair play. When used routinely throughout the organization, it can produce feelings of cynicism and apathy among employees. An organizational culture heavily steeped in organizational politics can evoke perceptions that few things are as they appear, backroom deals are how decisions get made, and people are foolish to believe what is publicly espoused. Individuals who are recognized as political game-players are treated with suspicion, even on those occasions when their actions may not be self-serving. Such individuals may be recognized for their acumen in getting what they want, but their tactics create ill will among other employees. Given these findings, it is not too surprising that research shows that perceived organizational politics in one's workplace is positively correlated with the desire to leave the organization (.43) and negatively correlated with job satisfaction (–.57) and affective commitment (–.54).[150] This pattern of results is highly similar in direction and magnitude to how perceived violations of organizational justice influence employee attitudes and behavior.

The Psychological Contract

Psychological contract
The implied exchange relationship that exists between an employee and the organization.

The **psychological contract** is the exchange relationship between an individual employee and the organization.[151] It is not a formal written contract between the two parties, but rather an implied relationship based on mutual contributions.[152] Employees have beliefs about the organization's obligations to them as well as their obligations to the organization. These perceptions of employer obligations may be in direct contrast to what employment laws stipulate about treatment of workers by organizations.[153] For example, employees may believe the organization has agreed to provide job security and promotional opportunities (not legally required) in exchange for hard work and loyalty by the employee. Thus, the contract is composed of a belief that some form of a promise has been made and that the terms and conditions of the contract have been accepted by both parties.

The psychological contract is founded on two principles: *mutuality* (the extent to which workers and employers share beliefs about specific terms of the exchange) and *reciprocity* (their commitments to each).[154] The psychological contract is made not once, but is revised throughout the employee's tenure in the organization. The longer the relationship endures and the two parties interact, the broader the array of contributions that might be included in the contract. Psychological contracts change over time, with employees' perceived obligations and contributions adjusting to reflect the ever-changing employment relationship (see COVID-19 and I-O Psychology: *Health and Safety Psychological Contracts*).[155]

COVID-19 and I-O Psychology: *Health and Safety Psychological Contracts*

Psychological contracts are in the "eye of the beholder," such that the employees are the ones who determine whether or not a contract exists and what the contract is based on. It is likely that the COVID-19 pandemic changed many employees' views of what their organizations owed to them, as well as what they owed to their organizations. In particular, the issue that was top-of-mind for employees around the world was that of health and safety. While health and safety are likely in some employees' psychological contracts regardless of a pandemic (e.g., police officers, hospital workers, construction workers), the issue became much more important for employees who may have considered safety issues of little concern to them at work.

Psychological contracts regarding safety typically involve perceptions that an employer is obligated to provide employees a safe workplace, provide proper equipment, and keep the safety of employees as a top priority. In return for providing these, employees would reciprocate by following safety rules and reporting concerns and hazards as they encounter them.[156]

Many organizations struggled to find a balance between staying in business and providing a healthy workplace for their employees. A lot of them were forced, out of a business necessity, to ask their employees to return to work sites earlier than employees may have felt comfortable doing. Some organizations that required customers to wear masks to help protect their employees were faced with angry customers. Because of customers' actions, many employees felt it necessary to scale back or quit. This raised a question previously unexamined: To what extent did employees consider the financial impact of safety decisions in their contract formation?

Numerous other questions emerged during the pandemic. Are some employees' health and safety psychological contracts more relevant than others' contracts (e.g., are hospital workers' views more or less important than non-medical office staff?). Are health/safety-related psychological contracts more important than those same employees' non-health/safety-related contracts? Should organizations consider the psychological contracts of their customers? How might those contracts impact the contracts of employees?

As employees face new challenges, their psychological contracts will continue to evolve. The pandemic demonstrated this, and brought considerable research topics to light. Which topics might you tackle?

Psychological contracts lie along a continuum from the transactional to the relational.[157] *Transactional contracts* are characterized by short time frames and specific obligations. Financial resources are the primary vehicle of exchange. *Relational contracts* are characterized by lengthy, ongoing relationships with diffuse obligations. Transactional contracts are predicated on total self-interest, whereas relational contracts implicitly acknowledge the value of the relationship itself, in which one party may put the immediate interests of the other party ahead of their own. At the relational end of the continuum, obligations are ambiguous and constantly evolving. These contracts are long term, and exchange not only financial resources, but also socioemotional resources such as loyalty and affiliation. In general, relational obligations are associated with more positive outcomes, whereas transactional obligations are associated with negative ones. As shown in Figure 11-7, relational contracts are linked to pro-social behaviors and organizational commitment, while transactional contracts are more related to antisocial behaviors and alienation from the organization.[158]

There is an element of power in all contracts. Power can be distributed either equally (i.e., symmetrically) between the two parties or unequally (i.e., asymmetrically). Asymmetrical power is most common in employment relationships. Power asymmetries affect the perceived voluntariness of the exchange relationship, dividing the two parties into contract makers (relatively powerful) and contract takers (relatively powerless). As contract takers, employees cannot easily influence the employment relationship. This may result in a perceived loss of control in the relationship, which is likely to intensify feelings of mistreatment and injustice when violations are felt. As the more powerful party, the employer can dictate terms of the contract to the less powerful employee, who must either accept them or exit the relationship.

Figure 11-7 *Relationship between the psychological contract and the range of social behaviors*

Source: Adapted from "'Till death do us part . . .': Changing work relationships in the 1990s," by J. McClean Parks and D. L. Kidder, 1994, in C. L. Cooper and D. M. Rousseau (Eds.), *Trends in organizational behavior*, (p. 120). Reproduced with permission of Wiley via Copyright Clearance Center.

Violations of the Psychological Contract

The psychological contract is violated (that is, breached) when one party in a relationship perceives that another has failed to fulfill their obligations. Table 11-2 lists typical organizational violations of the psychological contract and related example quotes from employees.[159] The failure of one party to meet its obligations to another can be expected to erode both the relationship and the affected party's belief in the reciprocal obligations of the two parties. Violations by an employer may affect not only what employees feel they are owed by the employer, but also what they feel obligated to offer in return. Violation of a psychological contract undermines the very factors (e.g., trust) that led to the emergence of a relationship. If the employer reneges on an implied promise, the employer's integrity is questioned. Employee perception of a contract breach is not a function of a broken promise by the organization, but rather whether the organization fulfills the employee's expectations.[160] Expectations are derived from past work experiences, norms, and comparisons made to other employers. A violation signals that the employer's original motives to build and maintain a mutually-beneficial relationship have changed or were false from the beginning. The psychological contract binds the employee and employer—a form of guarantee that if each does their part, then the relationship will be mutually beneficial. Thus, violations weaken the bond.

What is the typical employee response to violations of the psychological contract? Not surprisingly, they appear to negatively influence employees' intent to remain with the employer and job satisfaction.[161] It appears that psychological contracts become less relational and more transactional following violations.[162] Employees turn away from the socioemotional aspects of work and focus on the monetary benefits of the relationship. This has the effect of increasing the psychological distance between the employee and the employer, making the contract more transactional. A sequential pattern of five employee responses to violations has been identified. The first is *voice*: employees voice their concerns over the violations and seek to reinstate the contract. Employees are somewhat reluctant to use formal mechanisms of voice because they fear subsequent reprisal by management.[163] People who use formal voice mechanisms (grievance or appeal systems) are often labeled as organizational dissenters and experience retaliation. Instead, employees are more likely to use subtle influence tactics to affect procedural justice. If unsuccessful, voice is followed by *silence*. Silence connotes compliance with the organization, but a loss of commitment. Silence is followed by *retreat*, as indicated by passivity, negligence, and shirking of responsibility. *Destruction* may then occur, whereby employees retaliate against the employer through theft, threats, sabotage, and in extreme cases, homicide. Finally, in the *exit* stage, employees quit the organization or provoke the organization to dismiss them.

A meta-analysis of employee perceptions regarding the extent to which an organization has failed to fulfill its obligations revealed that breaches of the psychological contract were associated with higher mistrust, lower job satisfaction, lower organizational commitment, lower pro-social behavior, and lower job performance compared with the perceptions by employees that their psychological contract was not breached.[164] In addition, researchers have found a cascading effect, such that the negative effects of psychological contract breaches strengthen over time.[165] Actions from

Table 11-2 *Types of violation of the psychological contract*

Violation Type	Definition	Examples
Training/development	Absence of training or training experience not as promised	"Sales training was promised as an integral part of marketing training. It never materialized."
Compensation	Discrepancies in promised and realized pay, benefits, and bonuses	"Specific compensation benefits were promised. Either they were not given to me, or I had to fight for them."
Promotion	Promotion or advancement schedule not as promised	"I perceived a promise that I had a good chance of promotion to manager in one year. While I received excellent performance ratings, I was not promoted in my first year."
Job security	Promises not met regarding the degree of job security one could expect	"The company promised that no one would be fired out of the training program, that all of us were safe until placement. In return for this security we accepted lower pay. The company subsequently fired four people from the training program."
Feedback	Feedback and reviews inadequate compared with what was promised	"I did not receive performance reviews as promised."
People	Employer perceived as having misrepresented the type of people at the firm, in terms of things such as their expertise, work style, or reputation	"It was promised as dynamic and as having a challenging environment . . . rubbing elbows with some of the brightest people in the business . . . a lie. The true picture started to come out after the initial hype of working at one of the best 100 companies in the country had worn off."

Source: Adapted from "Violating the Psychological Contract: Not the Exception but the Norm." by S. L. Robinson and D. M. Rousseau, 1994. *Journal of Organizational Behavior*, 15, pp. 245–259. Reproduced with permission of John Wiley & Sons, Ltd. via Copyright Clearance Center.

both the individual and the organization (in terms of responsiveness and restitution) will impact how the employee ultimately views a psychological contract violation.[166] Depending on how the employee and organization respond to a breach, the employee may opt to reinstate the previous contract, or enact one that is more or less favorable to the employee than was the original contract. In some cases, if the breach was severe enough without adequate response from the organization, the employee may fail to form a functional psychological contract, and instead disengage from the work.

Based on a multinational analysis, researchers concluded that the psychological contract as a promise-based exchange is widely generalizable to a variety of societies.[167] Given the rise of global business, cultural differences in the psychological contract will most likely continue to evolve. For example, traditionally, Asians prefer to first establish a relationship between parties and then carry out business transactions, whereas Westerners prefer to create a relationship through repeated business transactions. In the future, it is likely that both styles will manifest themselves in new and varied forms.

Chapter Review

Key Terms

Affect

Moods

Emotions

Dual threshold model of workplace anger

Emotional labor

Emotion regulation

Emotional intelligence

Emotional contagion

Broaden-and-build theory of positive emotions

Job satisfaction

Honeymoon-hangover effect

Work commitment

Employee engagement

Organizational justice

Distributive justice

Procedural justice

Interactional justice

Organizational citizenship behavior

Counterproductive work behavior

Thermodynamics of revenge

Workplace incivility

Cyberaggression

Organizational politics

Psychological contract

Questions for Review

1. What are affect, mood, and emotions? How do they impact the work environment?
2. What is the dual threshold model of workplace anger and when can workplace anger improve organizational outcomes?
3. What factors have been shown to impact happiness? How are employers able to influence the happiness of employees?
4. What is emotional labor? How do surface and deep acting affect employees?
5. What is emotional intelligence and how does using it impact the various measures of job performance?
6. What is emotional contagion?

7. What are "broadened" and "built" in the broaden-and-build theory of positive emotions?
8. How is job satisfaction defined? What role do expectations play in job satisfaction?
9. What is the honeymoon-hangover effect?
10. What is work commitment? What are its components? How are work commitment and job satisfaction correlated?
11. What is employee engagement and what are its three dimensions?
12. What are the components (and sub-components) of organizational justice? Why is perceived organizational justice important to job satisfaction?
13. What is organizational citizenship behavior? Who is most likely to participate in it? What role does gender play in expectations of it and in participation in it?
14. What are counterproductive work behaviors and what are their categories?
15. What is the concept behind the thermodynamics of revenge? What are the various potential reactions to a "sparking incident?"
16. How does bullying in the workplace manifest itself? Where else, besides in the workplace, can workplace bullying occur? How are workplace incivility and cyber-aggression related to bullying?
17. What are organizational politics? When are they considered positive? When are they considered negative?
18. Who participates in a psychological contract? From whose perspective is it usually considered, and what attitudes and actions do breaches of a psychological contract lead to?

CHAPTER 12

Workplace Health and Well-Being

Chapter Outline

Physical Stressors

Task-Related Stressors

Role Stressors

Social Stressors

Social Media and I-O Psychology: *The Stress Potential of Social Media at Work*

Work Schedule-Related Stressors

Shift Work

Flexible Work Arrangements

Career-Related Stressors

Traumatic Events

Stressful Change Processes

Stress-Management Interventions and Wellness Programs

Balancing Work and Nonwork

Faces of I-O Psychology: *YoungAh Park*

Work-Family Conflict

Work-Family Enrichment

The Lighter Side of I-O Psychology: *Mesearch Research*

Work-Family Interventions

The Stigma of Dirty Work

COVID-19 and I-O Psychology: *Pandemic Taint*

Alcohol and Drug Abuse in the Workplace

Chapter Review

Learning Objectives

- Explain the different types of work stressors and their impact on employees.
- Summarize the psychological effects of unemployment.
- Describe the basis for and findings regarding stress-management interventions and wellness programs.
- Explain the basis of work-family conflict and work-family enrichment.
- Discuss how work schedules affect workplace psychological health.
- Describe the stigmatizing effect of dirty work on employees.
- Outline how drug and alcohol abuse affect the workforce.

Every year, the American Psychological Association surveys individuals across the United States about their stress levels. They obtain information on the primary causes of stress and how individuals are responding to the stress, both physically and mentally. In 2020, their findings caused them to sound an alarm. They warned that America was facing a mental health crisis, with the levels of stress facing its citizens being at an all-time high. Not surprisingly, the COVID-19 pandemic was a large factor in the problem. As they noted:

> Behind this devastating loss of life is immense stress and trauma for friends and families of those who died; for those infected; for those who face long recoveries; and for all Americans whose lives have been thrown into chaos in countless ways, including job loss, financial distress, and uncertain futures for themselves and their nation (APA 2020, Forward).[1]

A year later, survey findings revealed that the crisis they had predicted had become a reality.[2] They found that the extreme stress levels, combined with an apparent inability for many to cope, had already started to reveal serious mental and physical problems, including troubling changes in weight, sleep, and alcohol use. In addition, 47% of the respondents reported canceling or delaying health care services and 53% reported that they were engaging in less physical activity since the start of the pandemic.

The focus on stress management due to the negative impact of the pandemic on health and well-being has not gone unnoticed within the workplace. A survey of over 1,000 full-time employees and 300 human resources and benefits leaders at companies across the United States revealed that 58% of employers were prioritizing mental health benefits in 2021 over all other possible benefits. And for good reason, considering over half of the respondents reported experiencing stress, a third experiencing burnout, and a quarter experiencing loneliness and/or depression.[3]

Workplace health and well-being
A broad-based concept that refers to the mental, emotional, and physical well-being of employees in relation to the conduct of their work.

The topic of this chapter is on **workplace health and well-being** (also known as *occupational health*), a broad area that has become of utmost importance in recent years. Much of the focus in this area is on stress, a pervasive phenomenon, not only for one's work life but for life in general. It is also the biggest challenge to achieving psychological health. When individuals feel "stressed," they are not experiencing high levels of affective well-being. In general, job stress is related to low organizational commitment, higher turnover rates, and an increase in counterproductive work behaviors.[4]

Stressor
Anything that evokes a stress reaction.

There are many things that can evoke stress reactions in the workplace. These **stressors** can be one-time events, such as getting fired or losing a large client, or they can be ongoing problems such as daily hassles or constantly having to deal with a rude colleague. They can be caused by people, technology, or any number of things. Work stressors can be grouped into the following eight categories.[5]

1. **Physical stressors:** Stressful aspects of the environment, such as aversive working conditions.
2. **Task-related stressors:** Aspects of one's task that create stress, such as interruptions, monotony, or feeling like there is too much to do in too little time.
3. **Role stressors:** Stressful aspects associated with one's role, including role conflict, role ambiguity, and role overload, as discussed later in this chapter.
4. **Social stressors:** Interpersonal aspects that cause stress, such as conflicts, bullying, and/or sexual harassment from a supervisor, coworker, or customer.

5. **Work schedule-related stressors:** Aspects about one's work time arrangement that creates stress, such as shift work and overtime.
6. **Career-related stressors:** Stress-inducing aspects related to one's livelihood, including layoffs, unemployment, and a lack of career opportunities.
7. **Traumatic events:** Major incidents that cause stress, such as exposure to danger, natural disasters, and workplace homicide.
8. **Stressful change processes:** Stressors resulting from huge changes, such as mergers and acquisitions or the widespread implementation of new technology.

We present additional detail on each of these stressors next.

Physical Stressors

The physical environment of one's work can be the cause of stress at times. It is easy to imagine the stressful nature of dangerous jobs, such as logging (the profession with the dubious honor of being the most dangerous job in 2018 based on its fatal work injury rate).[6] But even "safe" workplaces pose a threat to our psychological and physical health. Excessive noise, extreme temperatures, and potential exposure to toxic chemicals can make workplaces uncomfortable, if not dangerous. Indeed, in 2019, there were 5,133 workplace fatalities in the United States, equivalent to a worker dying every 99 minutes.[7] In addition, there were 2.8 million workplace injuries recorded.[8] These fatal and nonfatal work injuries have been estimated to have cost the U.S. economy approximately $171 billion.[9] Given these figures, it is no surprise that workplace safety is of utmost concern for organizations.

Workplace safety refers to the decreased likelihood of physical harm or danger while performing one's job.[10] Safety is influenced by actions of both the organization as well as its employees. In terms of steps that organizations can take to minimize harm, The National Institute for Occupational Safety and Health (NIOSH) created a Hierarchy of Controls model to highlight practices organizations can implement to control high risk occupational hazards. As shown in Figure 12-1, the most effective and broadest strategies are to *eliminate the hazard* or *substitute the hazard.*

If it is not possible to physically remove or replace the hazard, then *engineering*

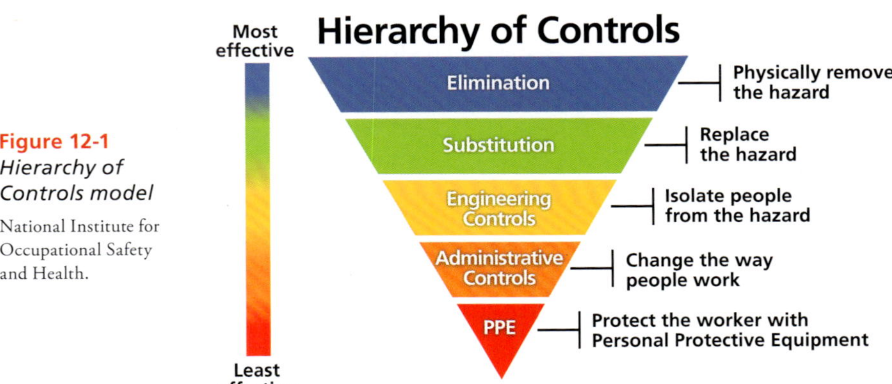

Figure 12-1 *Hierarchy of Controls model*

National Institute for Occupational Safety and Health.

controls are recommended to separate people from the hazard. For example, crystalline silica is a common mineral that often appears in materials used to make glass, pottery, and bricks. Unfortunately, inhaling crystalline silica dust may result in silicosis, a potentially fatal respiratory disease with no effective treatment. Exposure to such dust is a potential hazard in many occupations, including construction, and elimination of the hazard may not be possible. As such, engineering controls, such as water sprays to prevent the dust from becoming airborne, may be used to essentially remove the hazard at the source so it does not reach the worker and cause harm. If elimination, substitution, and engineering controls are not available or feasible, NIOSH recommends *administrative controls*, or changing the way individuals work. Examples include conducting the work when there are fewer people present (such as doing road construction at night instead of the daytime) or initiating safety training to provide education on strategies for staying safe. Finally, the least effective in terms of controlling the risk of occupational hazards is the use of *personal protective equipment (PPE).* Both administrative controls and the use of PPE are usually used when the hazards are more difficult to control (i.e., the other strategies are not possible).

In addition to the practices noted by NIOSH, scholars have noted the importance of communicating health and safety information to employees.[11] This transfer of information can be in any form, from written to verbal communication, as long as the key information is understandable to the intended audience.

Of course, simply because there are policies and procedures in place and information is communicated to employees does not mean that those policies and procedures will be followed. There are four key ways that organizational safety is within the control of the employee:[12]

1. **Use of personal protective equipment:** The effective and correct use of all PPE, such as helmets, goggles, masks, or any other paraphernalia that protects against workplace hazards.
2. **Engaging in work practices to reduce risk:** The proper use of any safety procedure, including making appropriate decisions, using the equipment properly, practicing procedures, and any other actions that decrease the likelihood of unsafe outcomes.
3. **Exercising employee rights and responsibilities:** Following procedures as deemed by the organization or the larger regulatory organization.
4. **Personal resources:** The intangible aspects of the worker (such as empowerment, engagement, and physical capacity) that influence their safety performance.

Safety compliance Obeying formal safety rules and engaging in required safety activities.

Safety participation Voluntary behaviors that impact workplace safety.

Researchers have found that safety behaviors are related to decreased occupational accidents and injuries.[13] Yet employees differ with regard to how eagerly they adhere to safety performance measures. This eagerness can be distinguished between safety compliance and safety participation.[14] **Safety compliance** involves obeying formal safety rules and engaging in mandated activities directed at workplace safety. This would include such actions as following prescribed safety procedures and wearing protective equipment. **Safety participation** involves the voluntary engagement of behaviors that impact workplace safety. These could include attending optional safety meetings or following suggested, though not required, safety behaviors (such as bending at the knees rather than waist when lifting heavy objects). It has been proposed that safety knowledge, skill, and motivation are direct determinants of safety performance.[15] Regarding safety knowledge and skill, understanding how to perform one's job safely and possessing the ability to do so are prerequisites to engaging in safety behaviors. Safety motivation refers to a desire to perform safety-related activities and procedures. Researchers have found support for positive relationships between both safety knowledge and motivation with safety compliance and participation.[16]

Consider This...

When considering the stressful nature of the physical environment, it is important to note that not everybody will react the same way to the environment. Some individuals may be more bothered by temperatures, sounds, odors, and other aspects of the environment than will others. Even when aspects of the environment are not hazardous or do not impact the majority of individuals, these aspects may still need to be accommodated. Consider, for example, that many individuals on the autism spectrum and non-autistic individuals with sensory processing disorders are hypersensitive to some sensory stimuli. Fluorescent lights may be considered too bright, a coworker's perfume may be too strong, and sounds that many employees are able to tune out may be unbearable for these employees.[17] Recall that the Americans with Disabilities Act requires employers to make reasonable accommodations for individuals with disabilities (as discussed in Chapter 3). How might organizations offer accommodations for sensory issues such as the examples provided here? Should employers be allowed to prevent their workers from wearing perfumes or colognes? To what extent do you believe the employee should have a say in what the accommodation is (vs. the organization determining it)?

Task-Related Stressors

Recall from Chapter 4 that tasks are the basic components of one's work that are directed toward meeting specific work objectives. Tasks that individuals must perform can be the cause of stress for some. For example, individuals may feel they have too many tasks to perform with not enough time to perform them, and subsequently feel overwhelmed. In addition, the nature of the tasks may produce boredom or frustration, and lead to feelings of monotony if there is not enough variety in them. Interruptions that prevent or delay tasks from being completed can also be stressful for the individual trying to finish them.

Challenge stressors Job demands or characteristics that create positive feelings of achievement or fulfillment.

Not all task-related stressors impact people in the same way. Some stressors may actually result in increased performance, but others might result in performance deficits. Job stressors can be separated into two broad categories: challenge stressors and hindrance stressors.[18] **Challenge stressors** include job demands or characteristics that produce positive feelings, such as feelings of achievement or fulfillment. These would include such things as job overload, time pressures, or high levels of responsibility.

Hindrance stressors Job demands or characteristics that are demotivating and hinder the ability to achieve one's goals.

Hindrance stressors, on the other hand, are demands or characteristics that are demotivating and problematic, in that they hinder individuals' abilities to achieve their goals. These would include such things as concerns about job insecurity and organizational politics. Challenge stressors positively impact performance while hindrance stressors negatively impact performance.[19] Similarly, hindrance stressors are negatively related to job satisfaction and organizational commitment and positively related to turnover, whereas challenge stressors yielded opposite relationships with those same outcome variables.[20] It may be helpful to expand the challenge-hindrance framework to include a third stressor, threats, because threats capture the potential for personal harm or loss. Indeed, by using survey data along with results from a separate diary study, researchers found that threat stressors are distinct from challenge and hindrance stressors, and are related to increased psychological distress, emotional exhaustion, and anxiety.[21]

Job demands-resources model An explanatory model describing the ways in which resources can buffer the negative psychological and physical effects of job demands.

Burnout The exhaustion and diminished interest in work that individuals feel after prolonged exposure to occupational stress.

The impact of stressors on individuals can be lessened by the presence of resources the individuals have available to them. A model that helps explain how resources can provide a buffer against the stressors that individuals face is the **job demands-resources model**.[22] Individuals are faced with numerous demands throughout their day. With these demands come certain physiological and psychological costs. For example, as individuals are given more duties to perform, they may become physically tired and emotionally drained. Over time, these demands and the physical and emotional toll that accompanies them may lead individuals to experience burnout. **Burnout** refers to the exhaustion and diminished interest in work that individuals feel after prolonged exposure to occupational stress. Resources can help to buffer the impact of stressors and minimize the negative effects on one's health and motivation, and include anything that helps individuals achieve their goals, reduces the costs associated with job demands, and helps individuals grow and develop. This can include supervisor support, rewards, and feedback. Meta-analytic findings indicate that job demands such as risks and hazards are related to burnout, whereas resources such as a supportive environment are related to engagement.[23]

Role Stressors

Role A set of expectations about appropriate behavior in a position.

When an employee enters an organization, there is much for that person to learn: expected performance levels, recognition of superiors, dress codes, and time demands. Roles ease the learning process. **Roles** are usually defined as the expectations of others about appropriate behavior in a specific position. Each of us plays several roles simultaneously (parent, employee, club member, and so on), but the focus here will be on job-related roles.

There are five important aspects of roles. First, they are impersonal; the position itself determines the expectations, not the individual. Second, roles are related to task behavior. An organizational role is the expected behaviors for a particular job. Third, roles can be difficult to pin down. The problem is defining who determines what is expected. Because other people define our roles, opinions differ over what our role should be. How we see our role, how others see our role, and what we actually do may differ. Fourth, roles are learned quickly and can produce major behavior changes. Fifth, roles and jobs are not the same; a person in one job might have several roles.

Role conflict
Tension created due to incompatible demands from within one role (intra-role conflict) or between two different roles (inter-role conflict).

Roles can occasionally create stress. **Role conflict** occurs when an individual is faced with incompatible or competing demands. Individuals experiencing role conflict feel like they are being pulled in different directions and unable to reasonably meet all the demands placed on them. For example, employees who are asked by a supervisor to arrive at work early may experience role conflict if they also must drop children off at school at the same time. In this example, the roles of employee and parent are conflicting. This would be considered *inter-role conflict* because the tension is between two separate roles (i.e., role of employee and role of parent). Considerable research has been directed towards understanding and ameliorating work-family conflict (the inter-role conflict between one's work and nonwork roles), and will be presented in greater detail later in this chapter. Conflict can also be within a single role, which is called *intra-role conflict*. An example would be if an employee is asked by two separate supervisors to complete a task by the end of the day and there may only be enough time to complete one of the tasks. This incompatibility is existing within the one role—that of employee.

Role ambiguity
Uncertainty about the behaviors to be exhibited in a role, or the boundaries that define a role.

Role ambiguity refers to uncertainty about the behaviors to be exhibited in a role, or the boundaries that define a role. First-time parents often feel apprehensive about their performance in a role they have never previously fulfilled. The same can be said for an employee who is asked to represent many other employees who hold a wide range of opinions or attitudes. A comprehensive meta-analysis found that role ambiguity is strongly negatively correlated with job performance.[24] Reducing role ambiguity for employees could result in meaningful improvements in job performance.

Role overload
The feeling of being overwhelmed from having too many roles or too many responsibilities within a single role.

Finally, **role overload** occurs when an individual feels overwhelmed from having too many responsibilities. This sense of overload can occur from having too many demands within one particular role or from having too many roles in one's life. First-time parents, in addition to frequently experiencing role ambiguity, often feel overwhelmed, in part because they now have a whole new role with demands and responsibilities that must be merged with their existing roles. This additional role may make them feel overly burdened by the total number of responsibilities placed on them. Role differentiation, the extent to which different roles are performed by employees in the same subgroup, is another aspect of role overload. One person's job might be to maintain good group relations, such as a work-unit coordinator. This person's role might thus require providing emotional or interpersonal support to others. Another's role might be to set schedules, agendas, and meet deadlines; such a person is usually an administrator. When all the roles in a work group fit together like the pieces of a puzzle, the result is a smoothly running, effective group. However, all the pieces may not fit together.

Fun Fact
The word role has its origins in the French word "rôle," which referred to the rolls of paper that held actors' lines. Over time, it came to refer to the specific part played by an actor.

Social Stressors

Aristotle, the Greek philosopher, once said, "Man is by nature a social animal." For many people, there is a strong reliance on others and a genuine desire to be around others. While interpersonal relationships can bring us comfort, social interactions can also cause stress. Within the workplace, social stressors include anything interpersonal that creates tension or causes distress. This could include conflict with or harassment and bullying from colleagues, customers, supervisors, or anybody else within one's work environment (see Social Media and I-O Psychology: *The Stress Potential of Social Media at Work*).

In Chapter 11, we discussed bullying within the context of counterproductive work behaviors. Recall that victims of bullying can experience problems with their health and well-being. This is particularly troubling, considering a survey of over 2,000 people in the U.S. found that 31% of individuals reported being bullied as an adult.[25] The survey further revealed that, of those who had been bullied:

- 71% suffered from stress
- 70% experienced anxiety/depression
- 55% reported a loss of confidence
- 39% suffered from sleep loss
- 26% had headaches
- 22% experienced muscle tension or pain
- 17% noted an inability to function day-to-day

Fortunately, the above findings mean that not everybody is the victim of bullying. Nevertheless, bullying is just one of many possible interpersonal situations that can cause stress. As long as employees have interactions with others, there will continue to be the opportunity for uncomfortable, tense, and anxiety-provoking situations. Thankfully, personal characteristics can serve as resources for managing stressful events. Not all individuals are impacted by stressors in the same ways or to the same extent. Some people are more resilient to their effects, while others succumb to their negative effects more easily. Stress reactions differ for individuals depending on their levels of resilience, tolerance for ambiguity, and perceptions of control.[26] In general, those individuals who are higher on each of those characteristics tend to have fewer negative reactions to stressors.

Psychological capital A personal resource consisting of hope, optimism, self-efficacy, and resilience that impacts one's psychological health and helps combat occupational stress.

Another personal resource available to individuals is their psychological capital. **Psychological capital** reflects a composite of self-efficacy, optimism, hope, and resilience.[27] As such, an individual with high levels of psychological capital is confident, has a positive view of their future, is perseverant, and is able to bounce back in the face of adversity. Psychological capital is related to heightened psychological well-being, job satisfaction, organizational commitment, organizational citizenship behaviors, and job performance as well as lower anxiety and job stress.[28] Thus, individuals with greater psychological capital are likely to demonstrate lower stress and heightened psychological health, while individuals who lack hope, are unsure of themselves, are pessimistic about the future, and are unable to recover from problems are likely to have more stress and lower psychological health. Scholars have also begun to examine psychological capital at the team[29] and organizational[30] levels, extending the promising findings beyond the individual.

Social Media and I-O Psychology: *The Stress Potential of Social Media at Work*

Everywhere you turn, there are references to social media. One need not be online to be reminded of the social world that awaits them there. News anchors invite you to follow them on Twitter, companies request that you like them on Facebook, and restaurants invite you to leave favorable reviews for them on Yelp. It seems that social media are inescapable, and when it comes to employees, social media can be potentially overwhelming.

Social media can be stressful for employees due to potential information overload, invasiveness, and uncertainty.[31] Individuals are constantly being inundated with information from a variety of social media outlets. As such, they may feel overwhelmed by the sheer amount of information they encounter. Second, individuals may feel like the constant exposure to social media, particularly as it pertains to work, may interfere with their non-work lives.

Considering the conversation on social media never stops and workers can be connected to it 24 hours a day, they may feel as if work is invading their private lives. Lastly, because there are so many different social media outlets, all possibly conveying different—and perhaps competing—messages, it may be difficult for people to keep track of what is important and urgent. Thus, social media may create uncertainty, which can be stressful for employees as they try to navigate the workplace.

Currently, little research exists regarding how to manage social media to reduce its capacity to induce stress. Nevertheless, given the potential stress that social media can cause, individuals may want to consider how they can best manage their social media usage. Researchers have suggested we should learn how to limit the effects of social media that produce information overload (such as knowing how to turn off notification alerts).[32] In short, despite its advantages and appeal, it may be healthy to disconnect from social media every now and then.

Work Schedule-Related Stressors

Not all employees work from 8:00 a.m. to 5:00 p.m., Monday through Friday. Individuals frequently work evenings, weekends, and holidays, depending on the nature of their job. Similarly, there is no set number of hours that people work. Some individuals may be asked to routinely work overtime. These schedule-related elements can cause stress and physical harm to employees.

Shift work
A non-traditional work pattern in which an operation functions 24 hours per day. Typical work shifts are 7:00 a.m. to 3:00 p.m., 3:00 p.m. to 11:00 p.m., and 11:00 p.m. to 7:00 a.m.

Shift Work

The nature of the services performed may necessitate "non-traditional" schedules. Police officers, firefighters, and healthcare providers must supply 24-hour-a-day service. In industrial manufacturing, some technology requires constant monitoring and operation. It isn't practical to shut off furnaces, boilers, and chemical process operations at 5:00 p.m. just because workers go home. In those cases, it is advantageous to have different shifts work around the clock. Psychologists have become interested in how different hours (or **shift work**) affect occupational health.

There are no uniform shift-work hours; companies use different shifts (see Figure 12-2). Usually a 24-hour day is divided into three 8-hour work shifts, like 7:00 a.m.–3:00 p.m. (day shift), 3:00 p.m.–11:00 p.m. (swing shift), and 11:00 p.m.–7:00 a.m. (night shift). Some companies have employees work just one shift, but workers generally don't like the swing and night shifts, so many firms rotate the shifts. Employees may work two weeks on the day shift, two weeks on the swing shift, and then two weeks on the night shift. A shift workweek need not be Monday through Friday. Also, there may be an uneven number of days off between shifts, such as two days off after the swing shift and three after the night shift.

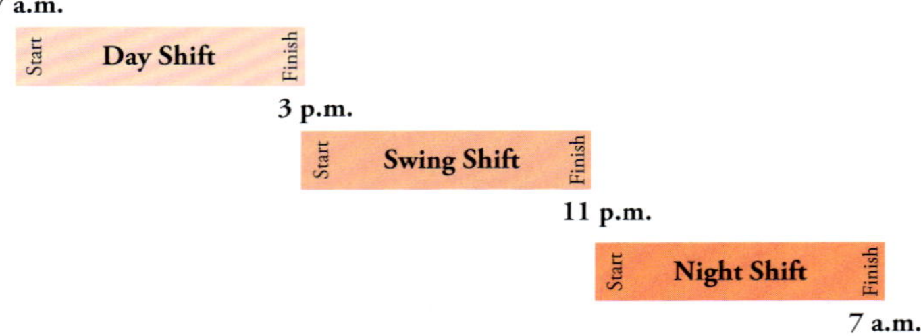

Figure 12-2 *Sample shift work schedule*

At least one major source of physiological difficulty is the rotation of workers across shifts. If workers were assigned to a fixed shift (day, swing, or night), their behavior would be consistent, which would help them adjust their circadian rhythms. Some people prefer to work afternoons or nights, so part of the solution may be personnel selection. Workers could choose a shift; if enough workers of the appropriate skill level were placed in the shift of their choice, that would meet both individual and organizational needs. Rotating shift work produces many adjustment problems. There is also evidence that backward rotation (from day to night to swing shifts) is more difficult to adjust to than forward rotation (from day to swing to night),[33] but when the backward rotation occurs slowly (vs. abruptly), the effects are not as problematic and may even be better than a fast forward-rotating schedule.[34] One interesting study examined a naturally occurring "shift" in work hours: the conversion to daylight saving time, which affects most workers (some geographic areas don't alter time).[35] In daylight saving time, the clock is advanced forward, typically resulting in one less hour of sleep. In a 24-year study of coal miners, the first Monday following the time switch, there were more workplace injuries and injuries of greater magnitude compared to other workdays. Conversely, on the Monday following the switch back to standard time (when an hour of sleep can be gained), there were no changes in injury quantity or severity compared to other workdays.

Shift workers experience many problems in physiological and social adjustment. Most physiological problems are associated with interruptions of the circadian rhythm. Our bodies respond to light and dark cycles through production of melatonin, a hormone that regulates sleep cycles and bolsters the immune system. Artificial light cannot make up for the qualities of natural light, nor can sleeping during the day make up for the darkness of nighttime sleep. The findings attest to the costs of fatigue and adjustment associated with nocturnal work routines. In addition, because most people work during the day and sleep at night, shift workers also have social problems. They often experience difficulties with children, marital relationships, and recreation. For example, one study found that divorces and separations were 50% more frequent in night-shift workers than in any other group of workers.[36]

Health issues are also a concern. The World Health Organization's International Agency for Research on Cancer (IARC) concluded in 2007 that working the night shift is related to a higher incidence of cancer.[37] Shift work has been found to be associated with digestive problems, cardiovascular disease, and weight gain.[38] It has been estimated that 20% of workers will have to leave shift work in a short time because of serious disturbances.[39] And it has been reported that shift workers experience less need fulfillment, are more likely to quit their jobs, and participate in fewer voluntary organizations.[40]

Consider This...

過労死

In 1969, a 29-year-old worker in a Japanese company died from a stroke, and became the first reported case of *karoshi*, a term that literally translates to "death from overwork."[41] The medical causes of karoshi are typically heart attacks and strokes. This sudden mortality is often attributed to excessive work hours, such as the cases of a 34-year-old who suffered a fatal heart attack after working 110 hours per week and a 22-year-old nurse who similarly died of a heart attack after working for 34 straight hours five times in a single month.[42] Research by the World Health Organization has concluded that working 55 or more hours per week is a serious health hazard, associated with a 35% greater risk of stroke and 17% greater risk of heart disease compared to working 35–40 hours per week.[43] They argue that governments and organizations should enforce bans on mandatory overtime and ensure maximum limits on the number of hours one can work in a week. Do you agree that such bans are needed? Who should be responsible for creating and enforcing them: the government, organizations, or another entity? What other steps do you think should be taken to help prevent ailments related to overwork?

Flexible Work Arrangements

Not all non-traditional schedules will create stress, however. In fact, some arrangements are enacted with the goal of reducing stress and creating flexibility for workers. The concept of flexible work arrangements allows individuals more discretionary control regarding when and where work is performed. Flexible work arrangements offer temporal flexibility (when work is done) and spatial flexibility (where work is done). More specifically, flexible work allows employees to determine where they work, when they start and stop work, which days or shifts they work, and how many hours they work. Employees are more motivated to use flexible work arrangements to avoid distractions and be more efficient in their work than to use such arrangements to manage competing work and family obligations.[44] Regardless of why it is chosen, flexible work does provide employees more discretion in how they manage work-family conflict.

High-skill workers are more likely to choose flexible work arrangements for themselves, whereas low-skill workers are often obligated to use such alternate arrangements due to needs of the organization.[45]

Teleworker
A person who works outside of a traditional physical location using electronic technology.

Flexplace
Any location outside of the traditional workplace where work can be performed.

One of the earliest adoptions of flexible work occurred in 1930 during the Great Depression. The Kellogg Company, the largest maker of cereal, wanted to reduce growing unemployment by converting from three 8-hour shifts to four 6-hour shifts. It was reported that employee morale increased, there were fewer industrial accidents, and work productivity increased.[46] Many years later, there are numerous other ways to facilitate flexible work arrangements. The use of laptop computers, tablets, and cell phones allows work to be conducted independent of any physical location. New words have entered our language reflective of the contemporary work world, such as **teleworker** (a person who works outside of a traditional physical location using electronic technology) and **flexplace** (any location outside of the traditional workplace, such as one's home, a café, or even a vacation resort, where work can be performed). The meaning of "flexible work" may shift over time as it becomes increasingly more common. While flexible work can offer greater personal control over people's lives, it is not without limitations. For example, although telecommuting can lead to positive benefits such as greater job satisfaction, an increased sense of autonomy, and a surge in productivity for some individuals, it can also lead to longer workdays, a reduction in knowledge sharing with colleagues, and a blurring of boundaries between work and home.[47] Furthermore, teleworking can produce social isolation from other employees and supervisors.[48] One of the benefits of traditional employment is it provides face-to-face contact with coworkers, which allows people to become members of a social network. Such opportunities are not as readily available to employees who work from home.

Flextime
A schedule of work hours that permits employees flexibility in when they arrive at and leave work.

Flextime. One variation in flexible work schedules is flexible working hours, popularly known as **flextime**. The main objective of flextime is to create an alternative to the traditional fixed working schedule by giving workers some choice in arrival and departure times. The system is usually arranged so that everyone must be present during certain designated hours ("coretime"), but there is latitude in other hours ("flexband"). For example, coretime may be 9:00 a.m. to 3:00 p.m. and flexband may be 6:00 a.m. to 6:00 p.m. Some employees may start working at 9:00 a.m. and work until 6:00 p.m.; some may end at 3:00 p.m. by starting at 6:00 a.m.; others work any combination in between (see Figure 12-3). Flexible working hours may alleviate problems with family commitments, recreation, second jobs, commuting, and stress.

An examination of the impact of flextime at two organizational levels—lower-level and professional employees—concluded that flextime primarily benefited lower-level employees by giving them more flexibility in their schedules. For professional employees, the flextime system merely formalized the already-existing informal system they had with the company.[49] A six-year study of flextime reported large reductions in employee absenteeism compared with a control group that had regular work hours.[50] However, the rates of turnover in the two groups were the same.

Meta-analytic evidence has found that the availability of flextime policies is related to reduced work-family conflict, whereas the actual use of such policies is unrelated to work-family conflict.[51] The authors surmised that the reason for this finding is that having flextime policies in place may provide employees with a sense of control regarding whether they use the policies or not. This would presumably impact the extent to which they see their work as interfering with their family lives. Actually using the policies, however, may increase *or* decrease control because some employees may be using flextime by choice, whereas others may be forced to use it (e.g., being told they have to arrive early or leave late to accommodate a coworker's needs).

A two-week study of flextime usage and its impact found that flextime use varied considerably from one day to the next.[52] When flextime was used, people had stronger boundaries between their work and nonwork domains, because the flextime allowed them to complete goals in one domain (e.g., work) before leaving for the other domain (e.g., home). Further, with the greater boundaries, individuals also reported greater well-being on flextime days. Despite the ample evidence that flextime benefits individuals, it is likely to be detrimental to the functioning of teams. If employees must work as a team, the individualized schedules that flextime permits may limit the continuity of the team. However, additional research is needed to investigate this issue.

Flexible Start Time		Core Time		Flexible Stop Time
6 a.m.	9 a.m.	12 p.m.	3 p.m.	6 p.m.

Figure 12-3 *Example of flexible work hours schedule*

Compressed workweek
A schedule of work hours that typically involves more hours per day and fewer days per week.

Compressed Workweek. Employees traditionally have worked 8 hours a day, 5 days a week, for a 40-hour workweek. Some employees work 10 hours a day for 4 days, popularly known as the "4/40." These **compressed workweeks** are often found in law enforcement and healthcare occupations.

There are several obvious advantages to a compressed workweek for both the individual and the organization. Individuals have a three-day weekend, which gives them more recreation time, the chance to work a second job if needed or wanted, more time for family life, and so on. However, the possible drawbacks include worker fatigue, fewer productive hours, and more accidents. Indeed, research has found that compressed workweeks seem to increase job satisfaction, but do not lead to improvements in productivity.[53] In addition, satisfaction with compressed workweeks appears to be related to lower emotional exhaustion, which can lead to better physical health, and consequently to lower absenteeism.[54]

A major review of the 4/40 concluded that the work schedule had a positive effect on home and family life as well as on leisure and recreation.[55] There appeared to be no change in employee job performance, however, and worker fatigue definitely increased. A few studies have been reported on reactions to a 12-hour shift, typically noon to midnight and then midnight to noon. The results are mixed. One study found that nurses on 12-hour shifts experienced substantial fatigue associated with the longer hours that could pose risks for both the nurses and their patients.[56] Conversely, another study revealed significant improvements in attitudes toward the work schedule, general affect, and fatigue in a sample of police officers who switched from a rotating 8-hour-shift work schedule to a fixed 12-hour schedule.[57] Similarly, an examination of underground miners who switched from an 8-hour to a 12-hour schedule revealed that the miners reported improved sleep quality with the new schedule, but fatigue had either no change or only slight improvement.[58] The findings from such studies may be influenced by the variety of jobs examined in the research.

Career-Related Stressors

Career-related stressors include those that are related to one's livelihood, including layoffs, unemployment, and a lack of career opportunities. Being employed has both intended and unintended consequences for the individual.[59] Earning a living is the most obvious intended consequence of employment, but the primary psychological meaning of work derives from the unintended or latent consequences. The five important latent consequences of employment are: (1) imposition of a time structure on the waking day, (2) regular shared experiences and contacts with people outside the nuclear family, (3) the linking of individuals to goals and purposes, (4) the definition of aspects of personal status and identity, and (5) the enforcement of activity. It is believed that these unintended consequences of employment reflect enduring human needs. Accordingly, when individuals are unemployed and/or are deprived of these functions, their needs are unsatisfied.

Fun Fact
The slang term, "funemployment", originated between 2007–2009 during the Great Recession, when millions lost their jobs. It refers to a period of time when individuals who lost their jobs chose to pursue leisure activities and take advantage of their "time off."

The possibility of job loss is a major concern for the contemporary worker. Millions of employees have lost their jobs through downsizing, outsourcing, offshoring, and mergers and acquisitions. Perilous economic conditions have resulted in large-scale job loss, both domestically and globally. Given this, the primary focus in this section is on what we have learned about the meaning of work to individuals as a result of involuntary unemployment.

Research provides support for the notion that individuals who are able to maintain some time structure while unemployed are more likely to experience greater well-being.[60] There is evidence that unemployment negatively impacts psychological and physical health, and is related to heightened suicide and mortality.[61] For example, a meta-analysis of psychological and physical well-being during unemployment concluded that when measured at a single point in time, unemployed individuals had lower well-being than employed individuals. However, when measured over time, it appeared that well-being declined as individuals move from employment to unemployment, but improved as they transitioned from unemployment to re-employment.[62] In a separate meta-analysis comparing unemployed individuals with employed individuals, the researchers similarly found that unemployed individuals had significantly lower levels of psychological health than did their employed counterparts.[63] Furthermore, a greater proportion of the people in the unemployed sample could be deemed clinically depressed. Unemployment is psychologically devastating because it creates feelings of uncertainty and loss of control in one's life.[64]

Unemployment is disruptive in other ways as well. For example, the loss of a job appears to be related to decreases in life satisfaction for both individuals and their partners, particularly when the couples had children.[65] In addition, unemployment early in life can cause a significant wage penalty later in life, especially if there are repeated instances of unemployment.[66] There is even an indication that unemployment can result in changes to one's personality. Specifically, individuals who experience unemployment have been shown to have clear changes to their levels of agreeableness, conscientiousness, and openness to experience compared to individuals who have maintained continuous employment.[67] These changes appear to be less extreme for those individuals who become re-employed following the period of unemployment.

Clearly, it seems that job loss and unemployment produce a cascade of worry, uncertainty, and financial restrictions, as well as family difficulties. For this reason, researchers have also examined ways to assist unemployed individuals to cope during these difficult times. Unemployment requires considerable self-regulation of effort and emotion. Individuals must sustain effort for long periods of time, despite rejections and the tedium of the job search process. Furthermore, they must regulate their emotions. Job search involves putting oneself on the line and dealing with feelings about being judged harshly, evaluated critically, and ultimately rejected. In a study that examined unemployed people over a 20-week period, researchers found that individuals who were able to limit the extent to which they engaged in negative self-talk (beating themselves up over their situation) and those who had strategies for staying on course with their job search (such as setting goals) had better mental health and a higher job search intensity than those who were self-defeating or lacked motivational control.[68] Individuals who can manage the negative emotions associated with job loss may appear to be stable and confident in interviews and thus improve their chances of receiving job offers.[69] The best intervention programs for unemployed individuals incorporate exercises that promote feelings of self-esteem, optimism, and control as well as job-seeking skills.[70]

Consider This...

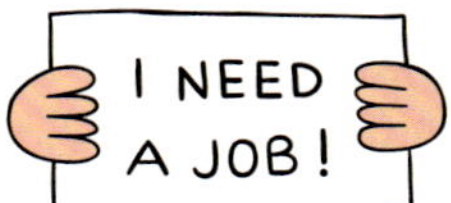

A group of I-O psychologists developed a measure for unemployed job seekers to aid them in their job searches.[71] The measure, called "Getting Ready for Your Next Job," helps job seekers gain insight into their job search intensity and clarity, their level of confidence and stress regarding the job search, barriers and support that exist for them as they search for a job, and how the search is going. Interested individuals can view the measure at *www.ynj.csom.umn.edu*. A unique element of the inventory is that it serves both a diagnostic and informational/support function. For example, questions ask about the extent to which the individuals have engaged in a variety of job search behaviors, such as talking to friends, relatives, or past employers for advice or possible job leads, or talking to a temporary agency or search firm. It notes that each of the methods asked about are important and that using a variety of methods is a good idea. In addition, the inventory provides instruction to the inventory-taker to engage in activities to increase their likelihood of success, such as having the person list additional people they could contact and contact each of them within the next week. By receiving specific instructions, the individual has a clear direction for going forward. Would you consider using such an inventory to aid in a job search? Do you think individuals receiving unemployment benefits should be required to use such a form to receive the benefits? Why or why not?

Traumatic Events

There are times when unexpected, traumatic events occur at work. Some may be natural disasters, such as devastation that may be caused by hurricanes, tornadoes, earthquakes, wildfires, and floods. Others might involve mass violence at work, such as the trauma caused when, in 1986, a United States Postal Service worker, Patrick Henry Sherrill, shot 20 coworkers (killing 14 of them) before killing himself. This event is where the term "going postal" originated and remains one of the deadliest examples of workplace violence to date. Other traumatic events may occur due to problems within the workplace. For example, in 1984, there was a major gas leak at Union Carbide India, a pesticide plant located in Bhopal, India. While the company disputes the causes of the disaster, which claimed upwards of 16,000 lives, it has been suggested that the leak occurred due to poor maintenance and poor management. As another example, in 2013, the Rana Plaza building in Bangladesh, an eight-story commercial building being used as a garment factory, collapsed and left 1,134 workers dead and approximately 2,500 more injured. The causes for the collapse were many, most notably a blatant disregard for worker safety despite clear structural concerns.

Major incidents such as these can cause a tremendous amount of stress, not only during the events but in their aftermath as well. Research has demonstrated that traumatic events at work, such as police officers being exposed to the gruesome death of others, are related to increased fears, flashbacks, and depression.[72] There is some evidence to suggest that trauma need not be experienced firsthand to cause problems. For example, a study of child welfare workers found that vicarious events (those witnessed or experienced secondhand) caused greater distress than trauma experienced firsthand.[73] Such secondary trauma is fairly prevalent among members of helping professions, including health workers,[74] social workers,[75] members of the military,[76] law enforcement professionals,[77] and therapists.[78]

Following many crises that impact entire workplaces, such as natural disasters, pandemics, or mass shootings, it is common for organizations to have to shift the ways in which work is conducted or where work is conducted. Ideally, these shifts are seamless and allow for minimal interruptions in workflow, yet it is often the case that organizations have not planned for disruptions. Such business continuity planning has been a relatively unexplored area for I-O psychologists, but the COVID-19 pandemic and scrambling of businesses to stay afloat led some I-O psychologists to call for more work in this area.[79]

It is possible to experience positive outcomes following a traumatic event, however. When this occurs, it is referred to as post-traumatic growth.[80] One meta-analysis found that approximately half of individuals who have experienced a traumatic event (not necessarily at work) display some degree of post-traumatic growth.[81] Although post-traumatic growth has primarily been examined in clinical settings, it has been suggested that I-O psychologists should partner with our clinical colleagues to explore it from an organizational lens. For example, while the COVID-19 pandemic has been examined primarily from a stress-inducing perspective, it could lead to post-traumatic growth for individuals, such as increases in technological competence due to having to navigate working remotely.[82] This area of inquiry will be an interesting one to monitor for years to come.

Stressful Change Processes

Heraclitus of Ephesus is believed to have coined the adage that "change is the only constant in life." Unfortunately, huge changes are often the cause of stress, and within the workplace, this can include many situations, from the implementation of new technology to changes in processes and reporting structures, such as due to the result of a merger or acquisition.

In Chapter 9, we discussed the process of mergers and acquisitions and noted that, in some situations, the cultures between the two companies may clash. When this occurs, individuals jockey for power as they focus on differences between the companies and attempt to determine which side won which battles. Conflict can erupt over even minor issues. Consider the following account:

> In one health care merger, the two sides could not even agree on starting times for meetings. One organization's managers began 9:00 A.M. meetings promptly whereas the other's managers only left their offices at the top of the hour, collected their papers, chatted with their assistants, and grabbed a cup of coffee before arriving at the conference room around 9:15. In the pre-merger culture this was no problem, because everyone knew that 9:00 A.M. meetings actually began at 9:15. But it infuriated counterparts from the partner organization, who described the tardiness as "disrespectful" and "undisciplined." Of course, the latecomers regarded their new partners as "uptight" and having "misplaced priorities" (Marks 2002, p. 46).[83]

If the two cultures are not adequately integrated and conflicts continue, employee morale is likely to decrease and stress levels will rise. Fears of losing one's job amid a merger or acquisition are common, and therefore all of the problems related to career-related stressors become relevant.

Even changes that are positive in nature can bring stress. A promotion, for example, would be something that most people might find to be a positive change that reflects an advancement in status and possibly a greater salary. However, the promotion may also come with additional responsibilities, longer hours, and increased role ambiguity. Thus, the change, albeit a good one, may create stress. It is therefore important to be aware of one's physical and psychological well-being during times of change, regardless of whether the outcome of the change would be considered good or bad.

Consider This...

H.P. Lovecraft wrote, "The oldest and strongest emotion of mankind is fear, and the oldest and strongest kind of fear is fear of the unknown."[84] Yet, there are many things that we don't know, and a lot of change is unpredictable. Unfortunately, much of the focus on managing change within the workplace has focused on intentional, deliberate change.[85] In what ways is unexpected change different from anticipated change? How can organizations help employees handle change that is sudden and unexpected? Research has shown that leaders can increase their followers' commitment to change, openness to change, and readiness to change, as well as reducing their followers' negative reactions of resistance to change and cynicism about change.[86] What do you think they do that is so effective? What could a leader do to help you manage changes at work?

Stress-Management Interventions and Wellness Programs

By the end of the 20th century, I-O psychology recognized the need to expand its focus from reducing accidents and illnesses to promoting workplace psychological health. Workplace psychological health embraces the concept that organizations should actively create work environments that facilitate personal well-being. Being in a state of well-being has been referred to as "flourishing" in life, indexed by being inspired to learn, being reasonably independent, and possessing self-confidence.[87] Scholars have suggested that organizations should include measures of workplace psychological health as criteria for judging their own success.[88]

To help employees combat stress, many organizations offer *stress-management interventions*, which are aimed at helping employees restore resources that have been diminished by their work environment. For example, as part of a workshop aimed at increasing job control and feedback for employees in a call center, employees identified obstacles that prevented them from working effectively. In addition, employees were given more discretion in their day-to-day activities, including handling complaints and scheduling meetings. This intervention led to an increase in employee well-being as well as heightened job performance.[89]

As noted in the previous section, there are numerous stressors that can evoke stress within the workplace. The purpose of stress-management interventions is ultimately to help employees manage that stress and determine strategies to alleviate the psychological and physical ailments that accompany the stress. For example, many employees are preoccupied with work and feel the urge to respond immediately to work-related emails and texts that they receive, even if they are received after the traditional workday is over.[90] They referred to this as "workplace telepressure" and found such behaviors to be associated with reduced psychological and physical health. With this in mind, a stress-reduction intervention aimed at reducing workplace telepressure may focus on time management techniques and other boundary-management strategies to reduce the pressure and therefore alleviate the negative effects.

In addition to stress-management interventions, organizations have also begun to offer *wellness programs*. Wellness programs are similar to stress-management programs in that they address employee health and well-being. However, they are different in that they are more future focused. Rather than being directed at restoring resources that have been depleted, they aim to be preventive, focused on proactively enhancing resources before problems emerge.[91] Healthcare is typically among the largest costs of all industrialized nations. It is simply cheaper to promote health than to pay the costs of poor health. Thus, it is advantageous to have both employers and employees contribute to fostering workplace psychological health.

Wellness programs within organizations may include traditional occupational safety and health aspects (such as strategies to avoid injuries and chronic diseases that could be caused from work) as well as elements of stress management and general health promotion strategies.[92] A meta-analysis on the effectiveness of stress management interventions found that interventions designed to increase employees' personal resources (and therefore had a wellness component) yielded large effects, meaning they were particularly effective.[93]

A large-scale survey of 1,997 private and non-federal government employers found that 49% of small firms and 81% of large firms offer wellness programs, such as those to help employees stop smoking, lose weight, or engage in other lifestyle or behavioral coaching.[94] Furthermore, many firms offer incentives for participation in programs, or impose hefty penalties on individuals who do not participate in such programs.

There are many benefits of participating in organizational health and wellness programs. A meta-analysis on wellness programs found that participation led to lower absenteeism and increased job satisfaction.[95] Indeed, continuous participation in a wellness initiative at PepsiCo resulted in a decrease in absenteeism and up to $136 saved in healthcare costs per month for each participant.[96]

Balancing Work and Nonwork

Sigmund Freud was once asked what he thought a "normal" person should be able to do well. He is reported to have said "Lieben und Arbeiten" ("to love and to work") (Erickson 1963, p. 265).[97] Freud believed that it is through one's family that love-related needs are gratified, and that work has a more powerful effect than any other aspect of human life in binding a person to reality. Therefore, Freud's call for a normal person to love and to work can be interpreted as an emphasis on both work and family for healthy psychological functioning.[98]

Fun Fact
It has been suggested that the split in a person's work and home identities dates to the Industrial Revolution of the mid-19th century. It was then that it became necessary for a person to leave the home and "go to work."

Interest in family-related issues by I-O psychologists has manifested itself primarily in the past 30 years. For many years, we tended to limit our focus to work-related issues (e.g., tasks, jobs, occupations, organizations) and left the subject of domestic matters (e.g., family) to other areas of professional study. However, I-O psychologists began to see legitimate linkages or connections between the two spheres of work and family, and thus have expanded the field's areas of inquiry (see Faces of I-O Psychology: *YoungAh Park*).

Work-family balance reflects an overall assessment of compatibility between work and family roles.[99] This construct has received increased attention in recent years, but is limited in that it does not state how one role may impact the other role. Whether the responsibilities and obligations of work and family interfere with one another or benefit one another has been a topic of great interest to work-family researchers. On the one hand, one's work and family roles can interfere with one another and cause problems. The feeling of having too little time or energy to complete all tasks in both life domains can feel overwhelming and wreak havoc on an individual. On the other hand, the money earned from work can certainly help make home life easier. Furthermore, having a job can make you a more interesting person at home, giving you things to talk about with your loved ones. Thus, the interactions between work and family can result in either *negative spillover*, in which one domain hinders the other, or *positive spillover*, in which one domain benefits the other. These two forms of spillover result in work-family conflict and work-family enrichment, respectively. Much of the research to date has focused on work-family conflict and work-family enrichment (as opposed to the more general work-family balance). As such, we focus on these two constructs in greater detail in the following sections.

Faces of I-O Psychology: *YoungAh Park*

YoungAh Park

Ph.D. Bowling Green State University

Associate Professor, School of Labor and Employment Relations, University of Illinois at Urbana-Champaign

Research interests: Work-family issues, work stress, recovery from stress

Before my academic career, I worked for multinational companies. My motivation to move to my last corporate job was to increase my salary, but it did not take long to learn that money is not everything, and there are other important aspects. Back then, I struggled as a working mom to balance my work and family lives. I had also witnessed many employees' stress. It is no wonder, then, that I quickly gravitated toward occupational stress and health research in my graduate program, and since then, much of my research has focused on employee work stress spilling over to the family domain and even crossing over to one's partner. In one study, my collaborators and I found that on days when office workers received frequent rude and inconsiderate work emails, so-called "email incivility," they were likely to experience affective and physical distress, which extended into the next morning. In a follow-up study, I showed that employees who received uncivil email at work were likely to bring their stress home, affecting their partners at home negatively on the weekend. As a result, those partners withdrew more from their tasks as a stress reaction once returning to their own workplace the next week. This employee-to-partner crossover was more pronounced when the employees ruminated about negative aspects of their work on the weekend. Along these lines, I have recently investigated elementary school teachers' job stress involving information and communication technology (ICT; e.g., text messages, emails), given that many parents easily communicate to their child's teachers through ICT anytime and anywhere (I did it too!). The issue is that the work-related ICT use can be stressful for teachers, but our preliminary findings also suggest that when teachers received support from their principal for work-family balance, they perceived greater control over work-family boundary management, and subsequently the work-related ICT communication demands were less associated with their weekly strain. My hope with this research is to bring more organizational and managerial attention to work stress involving ICT and possible interventions to minimize the negative effects of stress on working individuals.

Work-Family Conflict

Work-family conflict The result of conflicting demands between work and family, making it difficult to effectively participate in both domains.

Work-family conflict is the result of having conflicting demands of work and family responsibilities. Work-family conflict has its theoretical basis in the scarcity hypothesis, which states that individuals have a finite amount of resources (time, energy, attention).[100] When too much of one resource is allocated to a particular domain, the others suffer. For every hour that an employee spends working, there is one less hour the person can devote to their family life. Similarly, when people experience a great deal of stress at home, they may not have the energy to perform as effectively at work. The result of these situations is work-family conflict. This conflict can be viewed as bi-directional, with both work and family interfering with one another, or can be described directionally, with work interfering with family or family interfering with work.

Researchers have also demonstrated that work-family conflict can have a considerable negative impact on one's psychological and physical health. Work-family conflict is related to poor eating habits, weight gain, lower sleep quality and quantity, and increased alcohol abuse.[101] A broad national survey of employees revealed that employees experiencing work-family conflict were up to 30 times more likely to experience a clinically significant psychological health problem than were employees who reported no work-family conflict.[102] Researchers used meta-analytic data to determine whether work-family conflict causes strain or strain causes work-family conflict.[103] They found that work-family conflict and strain have reciprocal effects. Thus, work-family conflict is both a result of increased strain and a cause of it.

Work-family conflict results in negative outcomes for both work and family domains. Where conflict is seen as originating (from work-to-family or family-to-work) is important when predicting outcomes.[104] Work-to-family conflict is more strongly associated with work-related outcomes such as lower job satisfaction, organizational commitment, and performance as well as increased tardiness, absenteeism, and turnover.[105] Family-to-work conflict is more strongly associated with family-related outcomes, including lower satisfaction with one's marriage and family. The reason the origin of the conflict seems to matter is because that is where the blame for the conflict is attributed. So, when individuals see work as causing the conflict, their satisfaction and commitment with their work suffers. This explains to some extent why I-O psychologists have focused more attention on work interfering with family rather than family interfering with work.

Of course, the negative outcomes of work-family conflict are not solely for the employee and the organization. There is evidence of crossover effects such that employee work-to-family conflict can impact others' (such as spouses, roommates, children) family satisfaction and stress levels.[106] Within the workplace, researchers have shown that supervisor work-family conflict impacts how employees' view the workplace climate for family sacrifice (a climate that supports putting the demands of work before the demands of family), which in turn relates to employee work-family conflict.[107] Specifically, if the supervisor is experiencing work-family conflict and employees are aware of this (whether from being told so by the supervisor or by inferring it from the supervisor's behaviors), they may not view the work climate as being amenable to family sacrifices, because if this were the case, the supervisor might not be experiencing the conflict. This realization or interpretation of the climate, in turn, is related to the employees' work-family conflict. Thus, while work-family conflict is a stressor experienced within a single individual, the effects of the conflict are much broader.

Given the negative consequences of work-family conflict, researchers have devoted considerable attention to understanding who is most likely to experience conflict, and under what circumstances it is likely to occur. In line with the notion that people "blame" the domain seen as causing the conflict, meta-analytic evidence has revealed that work demands are related to work-to-family conflict, whereas family demands are related to family-to-work conflict.[108] Furthermore, the number of children at home is a strong predictor of both directions of work-family conflict. In addition, single parents report more conflict than do married parents. Lastly, while it is often believed that women experience more work-family conflict than men, it appears that men and women actually report very similar levels of conflict.

One consequence of work-family conflict may be guilt.[109] Flexible work hours and increased vacation time are appealing because they have the potential to reduce feelings of guilt among people incurring work-family conflict. In addition, although work-family conflict can lead to decreases in well-being in the short term, over time it may be related to increased well-being.[110] Indeed, individuals may adapt to the conflict and become more resilient over time as a result.

Most of our knowledge about work-family conflict is based upon the traditional concept of a family, and employees working in managerial and professional jobs.[111] We know far less about single-parent families and members of other types of occupations. Researchers have found greater conflict in occupations that require substantial interactions between people to accomplish work.[112] Jobs such as police detectives, firefighters, and medical practitioners appear to produce higher work-family conflict than taxi drivers, insurance examiners, and bank tellers. Jobs that induce low work-family conflict offer an opportunity for individuals to leave their work at the office.

Consider This...

Researchers have found that cultural values influence the relationship between work-family conflict and important outcomes.[113] For example, work-to-family and family-to-work conflict are less related to job, family, and life satisfaction for individuals in more collectivistic cultures (vs. for individuals in less collectivistic ones). Recall from Chapter 9 that collectivism reflects an emphasis on the needs of groups (collectives) over those of individuals. Why do you think the prioritization of groups over individuals would matter for the relationship between work-family conflict and one's satisfaction? Specifically, why do people with greater collectivistic values seem to be less negatively impacted by conflict (in terms of their satisfaction levels) than are individuals with a more individualistic perspective? The researchers did not find that power distance or uncertainty avoidance impacted the relationship. Does the lack of impact for these two cultural values surprise you? Why or why not?

Work-Family Enrichment

Work-family enrichment The extent to which work and family roles enhance and facilitate one another's functioning.

In line with the push toward positive psychology, work-family researchers have focused their attention on the benefits of individuals participating in multiple roles. Many concepts have emerged to describe the positive relationship between one's work and personal life, with the fundamental idea being that the positive spillover between work and family can enrich, enhance, and facilitate one another (see The Lighter Side of I-O Psychology: *Mesearch Research*).[114] **Work-family enrichment** is the extent to which one's work and family roles and the experiences in those roles enhance and facilitate functioning in the other role. This positive impact of one role by the other occurs through the transfer of resources or positive affect.[115] Individuals acquire a variety of resources from different role experiences.[116] For example, in addition to material resources like money, work also helps individuals gain skills and broaden their perspectives, develop their social network, and generate greater psychological resources such

The Lighter Side of I-O Psychology: *Mesearch Research*

As was first noted in Chapter 2, academics sometimes gravitate to studying the topics they know best. This tendency is known as 'mesearch research' when a researcher chooses subject matter with which they have personal experience.[117]

As a case in point, Tori (one of the authors of this textbook) is married to John (Howes, featured as a Faces of I-O Psychology in Chapter 11) and they have four children—Rook, Audrey, Matthew, and Ryan. They also have two dogs—Obi and Izzy—and one cat—Cat. On her university profile page, it notes that, "in her spare time, she enjoys running, golfing, playing board games and traveling with her family, and learning new things, which currently include picking locks and crocheting. Along with her husband, John, she moonlights as a chauffeur, maid, personal chef, life coach, tutor, and counselor to their four kids, as a caretaker to their two dogs, and as a servant to their cat." Shockingly, one of her main areas of research is on work-family interactions. Note: I said interactions. Not conflict. Because there is *never* any conflict in the family. Only enrichment. Lots and lots of enrichment. And if you believe that, you should most definitely do your own mesearch research on the topic of gullibility.

as self-efficacy. With these additional resources, individuals are better able to manage the interactions between their multiple roles. Work and family are also likely enriched by each other through an affective pathway. Positive affect that is generated in one domain, such as work, can spill over to the other domain. Employees who receive accolades from their boss may develop a good mood at work that transfers over to their home life, thereby enriching interactions with their families.

Work-family enrichment is impacted by work-related variables (such as family-supportive supervisors and job resources) and nonwork-related variables (such as spousal support and community involvement).[118] A meta-analysis on the relationship between Big 5 personality dimensions and work-family enrichment found that extraversion, agreeableness, conscientiousness, and openness to experience are related to higher levels of enrichment.[119]

Similar to the notion that individuals appear to "blame" a particular domain for causing conflict, people will credit their enhanced performance in one role to the resources generated in the other.[120] Thus, whereas negative outcomes were associated with the originating domain with work-family conflict, positive benefits would be associated for work-family enrichment. In line with this, studies have shown that enrichment originating in the family (vs. work) is positively related to family satisfaction, while enrichment originating at work (vs. family) is positively related to lower turnover intentions.[121] However, both directions of enrichment appear to be related to job satisfaction, organizational commitment, and increased physical and mental health.[122]

By simply sharing the positive events that occur at work with loved ones at home, individuals are able to highlight their resources and affirm their self-worth.[123] In addition, by capitalizing on and sharing their experiences, individuals can relive and savor the positive experience, thereby enhancing their mood. This good mood can be contagious to their partner, ultimately facilitating positive work-family interactions. Along these lines, the more people talk with their partner about the good things that happen at work, the more their work engagement facilitates their work-family interactions.[124] Similarly, sharing positive events from work with one's spouse is related to better mood and increased life satisfaction.[125] Thus, it appears that when people capitalize on their work experiences by sharing them with their loved ones, they feel better, and feel like their work is better able to help them function more effectively at home.

Work-Family Interventions

Recall from Chapter 3 that the United States lags behind other industrialized nations with regard to laws surrounding family leave. Namely, whereas most other countries have some form of federally-mandated paid leave for such events as the birth or adoption of a child, the United States has no such paid leave, instead only requiring *unpaid* leave for up to 12 weeks (per the Family and Medical Leave Act). In addition, this requirement only covers employees who have worked at least 1,250 hours during the past year for a company that employs at least 50 workers. Thus, interventions to address work-family struggles are largely left to the discretion of individuals and their employers.

Idiosyncratic deals
Special arrangements made between an employee and employer to help the employee meet personal needs and preferences.

At an individual level, some employees create what are known as **idiosyncratic deals** with their employers: special arrangements meant to help them meet their personal needs and preferences.[126] For example, an employee may ask to start and end the workday earlier to allow them to pick up a child from school. Alternatively, employees may negotiate with their managers for training opportunities that may not be available to others (such as a special workshop). When organizational policy and support are lacking, idiosyncratic deals become important coping strategies for individuals.[127]

Boundary theory
A conception that individuals differ along a continuum with regard to how much they prefer to segment versus integrate their work and nonwork lives.

Individuals also must consider how they manage their boundaries between their work lives and their home lives. According to **boundary theory**, individuals differ along a continuum with regard to how much they prefer to segment versus integrate their work and home lives. On the one end, individuals preferring *segmentation* strive to have very clear demarcations between their work and home lives. These individuals erect "mental fences" and wish to keep work at work and home at home. On the other end of the continuum, individuals preferring *integration* are comfortable and welcoming of the merging of the two domains, having a much looser, and sometimes nonexistent, boundary between work and home.[128] Occasionally, these preferences are violated, such as when individuals preferring segmentation were forced to work from home during the COVID-19 pandemic alongside other family members, thereby having more integration than they would have liked. When these boundaries are violated, individuals are more likely to experience greater work-family conflict.[129] Thus, individuals should attempt to manage their boundaries depending on their personal preferences. That said, the impact of boundary interruptions (such as a call from a spouse during work hours) will depend on whether an employee's goals are seen as being obstructed or facilitated. If the call is seen as helpful, the employee is likely to feel good and be satisfied, regardless of boundary management preference. Conversely, if the interruption is seen as obstructing a goal, then the employee will feel bad and be less satisfied.[130]

When considering work-family interventions, the importance of a supportive supervisor cannot be overstated. For example, researchers measured blood pressure and heart rate with wrist monitors and utilized daily diaries to assess work-family conflict.[131] They found that episodes of work-family conflict were related to increased blood pressure when individuals perceived their supervisors as being unsupportive relative to those who reported having family-supportive supervisors. Thus, supervisor support is important not only for creating idiosyncratic deals, but also appears to have a positive impact on employee health.

Organizations can also be impactful in helping employees effectively integrate their work and family roles. Flexible work hours, shorter workweeks, working from home, and leaves of absence are examples of organizational initiatives to reduce work-family conflict.[132] In addition, onsite or near-site childcare centers have been developed to reduce work-family conflict. Organizations benefit from employer-provided childcare support through increased employee commitment and reduced employee stress.[133] Moreover, simply having formal work-family benefits in place helps retain employees and increases their commitment and satisfaction, even when employees don't use the benefits themselves.[134] Finally, organizations have successfully been able to help employees increase the positive synergy between their work and nonwork roles by helping the employees learn how to transfer their resources from work, such as their knowledge, skills, and positive affect, to their nonwork lives.[135]

Consider This...

Flexible working hours and organization-based childcare were created with the hopes of lowering work-family conflict. However, it has been suggested that these interventions were based upon the needs of employees in predominately Western cultures. In Asian, Eastern European, and Latin American countries, parents of employees often live close to their children and grandchildren.[136] This older generation is a resource not as readily available to employees in Western cultures. Accordingly, there may be less need for organizations to provide means of reducing work-family conflict in other parts of the world. Do you think that organizations should be responsible for providing work-family interventions? Should this be influenced by the extent to which employees have family nearby? Why or why not?

The Stigma of Dirty Work

Dirty work describes work that most people would rather not perform due to some aspect of the job that society finds repulsive, distasteful, or degrading.[137] When individuals engage in dirty work, they are seen as being tainted. Taint can take several forms:[138]

1. **Physical taint:** having direct contact with dirty or deadly environments. For example, garbage collectors or custodians may be seen as tainted because they come into contact with unsanitary items on a regular basis.
2. **Social taint:** having contact with stigmatized individuals. For example, a manager at a homeless shelter, while an honorable profession, may be seen as tainted because they regularly encounter stigmatized individuals (in this case, the homeless).

3. **Moral taint:** engaging in activities seen as deviant or immoral. For instance, individuals employed as exotic dancers may be viewed as tainted due to the nature of their work.
4. **Emotional taint:** engaging in uncomfortable, burdensome, or inappropriate emotions. For example, Border Patrol agents are trained to act in a very stoic, unemotional manner with the general public, which may facilitate the public's negative views toward them.[139]

Stigma
A characteristic or mark that is devalued in some way such that individuals possessing that characteristic or mark are devalued as well.

Stigmas are characteristics that are devalued in some way such that individuals possessing that characteristic are therefore devalued as well. Each type of taint that is associated with dirty work is theorized to leave stigmatizing marks on individuals, which can stick to them even after they no longer perform the dirty work.[140] This "stickiness" is the result of other individuals attributing the marks' cause to inherent characteristics of the marked individual. Whereas other sources of stigma (e.g., age, disability) may be perceived to be beyond one's control, occupations are perceived as choices rather than results of circumstances.[141] As such, the decision to engage oneself in a tainted job is often seen as a direct reflection of the person, and therefore the stigma is difficult to remove even long after the person has left the job.

It has been suggested that morally-tainted dirty work will have more stickiness than other kinds of dirty work because immoral acts are seen as illustrative of the individual's true character.[142] Physical and social taint will have less stickiness because of the tainted individual's willingness to do what others are not willing to do but should (or must) be done, thus making the person appear somewhat altruistic. In addition, social taint should have even less stigmatization because the morality of helping others further offsets the stickiness.

Even jobs that are not normally seen as dirty can take on dirty characteristics depending on the tasks involved (see COVID-19 and I-O Psychology: *Pandemic Taint*). Consider a study that examined 499 employees working at animal shelters, jobs that are not necessarily dirty, but do involve one particularly dirty task for some—animal euthanasia.[143] The researchers found that employees who were responsible for conducting animal euthanasia had greater stress reactions than did employees who were not responsible for such tasks. They were also more reluctant to discuss their work than were their counterparts. However, these same employees reported more psychological investment in their work, suggesting that engaging in the stigmatized task was a form of identification—a way to unite themselves to others within the profession and separate themselves from those not in the profession. Another examination of animal shelter employees who were responsible for euthanizing animals found that those who were given more access to information about the nature of the job prior to being hired were less likely to leave the job prematurely.[144] In addition, those who believed in the value of the job were less likely to exit the job.

There are many ways in which individuals attempt to deal with the stress that results from the stigma associated with dirty work. For example, a qualitative study involving legal brothel workers in Nevada found that workers will attempt to manage the stress associated with dirty work by establishing clear boundaries and distance

Consider This...

Would you consider "manager" to be a dirty job? You might say it depends on where they work, which is a fair answer given the above discussion about different occupations exhibiting more or less taint. So how about the fictional manager from the TV series, *The Office*—Michael Scott. He works at Dunder Mifflin, a paper company. One might say he isn't in a dirty job, as there is no reason to think that in his cozy, laid-back office setting there is any physical, social, moral, or emotional taint. However, there may indeed be some stigma associated with his role. In particular, there were many instances on the show where he terminated the employment of a member of the staff. Terminating workers' employment could be viewed as having considerable social and moral taint.[145] Thus, Michael's job may have taken on characteristics of dirty work and been subject to stigmatization. Can you think of other jobs that would, on the surface, appear free from taint, but could be considered stigmatized due to certain tasks? Do you think that tasks such as terminating employees are ones that would have long-lasting, or "sticky" taint? Why or why not?

between their work and personal lives.[146] Similarly, interviews of domestic workers, whose job involves cleaning (and is therefore "dirty" due to their physical environment), found that these workers would engage in a variety of adaptive and maladaptive coping strategies that contributed to a more positive or negative view of themselves.[147] There are also activities that managers can do to help their employees adjust to and cope with their dirty work. Interviews with managers across a variety of dirty work occupations found that, when hiring employees, managers tend to select individuals with an affinity for the work and provide the employees with a realistic preview of the stigma associated with the work. Once hired, they help socialize the workers by aiding them in managing their relationships with those outside of the work and desensitizing the employee to the particularly dirty aspects of the job. Finally, they help the workers by providing ongoing support and protecting the employee from hazards associated with their dirty work.[148]

Views toward stigmatized jobs and industries can change over time. For example, the cosmetic surgery and tattoo industries have gone from being seen as deviant to having relative mainstream acceptance in society. Whereas cosmetic surgeons were often described as "beauty doctors" and seen as disreputable, plastic surgeons have become more acceptable in the eyes of society, seen now as respectable medical professionals.[149] Similarly, whereas tattoos were once associated with marginal groups and sideshow spectacles, they have gained more widespread acceptance, being sported by members of all classes. Nevertheless, tattoos have not gained total acceptance, as evidenced by the findings that not all tattoos are deemed suitable for the workplace.[150] Thus, a stigma may remain within the workplace for those with tattoos, if not for the artists themselves.

COVID-19 and I-O Psychology: *Pandemic Taint*

It has been suggested that the COVID-19 pandemic created, altered, and highlighted the ways in which occupations were seen as tainted.[151] In some cases, employees in occupations that were once revered were experiencing taint for the first time. For example, doctors who were regularly exposed to COVID-19 patients—or seen as being at risk of such exposure—were experiencing the effects of physical taint. While they had always had exposure to illnesses as a natural part of their jobs, COVID-19 and the uncertainty surrounding the virus created new apprehension that made such medical providers particularly tainted.

In much the same way that doctors and other medical professionals may have experienced heightened taint, employees in other occupations may have been similarly impacted. For example, door-to-door salespeople, once considered a normal part of business development for some organizations, may have been seen as endangering individuals in their homes by soliciting their goods. As such, although they may not have been morally tainted prior to the COVID-19 pandemic, the face-to-face nature of their business that defied physical distancing recommendations may have led them to be seen as deviant or of dubious virtue.

Of additional interest during the pandemic was that some occupations experienced simultaneous reverence and stigma. For example, the same medical workers that became tainted due to their constant exposure to COVID-19 patients were hailed as "frontline heroes" by many. How do individuals navigate a world in which they are simultaneously celebrated as heroes and ostracized as spreaders of disease?

The indefinite duration of the COVID-19 pandemic raised the question of how long a newly "dirty" job may be considered dirty. Will the taint that arose due to the pandemic be "sticky" like it is for some other occupations, or will those jobs that were once admired become, once again, regarded with honor rather than stigma? Will the workers within those jobs endure lasting effects of the stigma, regardless of the pandemic's duration?

These questions and others remain unknown. Yet I-O psychologists are working to better understand these issues. Perhaps you will be the one to investigate these questions and provide potential solutions to problems that have been created due to the COVID-19 pandemic.

For as long as taint is a potential issue for workers who previously did not experience the stain, managers will need to provide the aforementioned support and guidance to help their employees work through the possible impacts the taint could have on their health and well-being.

Alcohol and Drug Abuse in the Workplace

"Alcohol and work. This has always been an uneasy relationship. Genius may be fired by wine. More commonplace talent is often fired because of it."[152]

—Moore 1994, p. 75

Substance abuse The ingestion of a broad array of substances (such as alcohol, drugs, and tobacco) at levels deemed to be harmful to the user or others around them.

Alcoholism and drug abuse are global problems affecting all arenas of life. It is estimated that close to half of all Americans are suffering from a substance abuse problem, and that the lost productivity and healthcare costs from employees with addictions are costing employers upwards of $740 billion annually.[153] Safety is also an issue, as an estimated 21% of American workers report being in danger, injured, or needing to redo a project or work late due to a colleague's alcohol use.[154]

The term **substance abuse** covers the ingestion of a broad array of substances, including alcohol, prescription drugs, and illegal drugs, at levels deemed harmful to the user or others around them. Some people include tobacco (both smoking and chewing), but most of our knowledge is limited to alcohol and illegal drugs. It is important to distinguish between *workforce* substance use and impairment and *workplace* substance use and impairment. Workforce substance use and impairment concerns alcohol and drug use away from work by members of the working population. In general, I-O psychologists are interested in what happens during work and/or what impacts workplace behavior. As such, we are more interested in workplace substance use and impairment, or the consumption of alcohol or drugs immediately prior to coming to work or during work, such that one's work is negatively impacted. We are also interested in situations in which the use of alcohol or drugs results in hangover effects that impair employee functioning while on the job.

The prevalence of workplace substance use and abuse is difficult to determine. Individuals are not apt to be forthcoming with such information for obvious reasons. However, some surveys have estimated that up to a third of Americans have admitted to drinking alcohol during working hours when working from home.[155] It is unclear what percent drink while in the workplace, though even small percentages of the workforce can be reflective of large numbers. For example, although only 8% of the workforce in 2013 reported alcohol use before or during work, that constituted a little over 10.3 million workers![156] Similarly, 3% of the workforce reported using illicit drugs before or during work, which constituted close to 4 million workers. Whereas the Americans with Disabilities Act regards former drug use as a disability and thus provides legal protection to former drug users, current drug users are not covered by the law.

Certain segments of the U.S. workforce have much higher usage rates than the national average. For example, substance use and abuse are more common among men than women, and both workforce and workplace alcohol and drug use tend to decrease with age. In addition, employees within arts, entertainment, sports, and media tend to engage in more alcohol and drug use than individuals in other broad occupational categories.[157]

Although I-O psychologists may approach the topic of substance abuse from several perspectives, a primary area of concern is performance impairment—that is, the extent to which substance abuse contributes to lower job performance. We do know that cognitive skills such as vigilance, monitoring, reaction time, and decision making are adversely affected by many kinds of drugs. We do not know, however, whether these drugs simply lengthen the amount of time needed to perform these cognitive functions, or whether they cause attention to be focused on irrelevant or competing stimuli. In addition, very little is known regarding the influence of hangovers on cognitive and psychomotor functioning. Jobs that involve the use of these skills in areas like the transportation industry (for example, pilots and railroad engineers) have regrettably contributed to our knowledge through tragic accidents. Some drugs (such as anabolic steroids) have been found to enhance aspects of physical performance (most notably, strength and speed), but their long-term effects can be very harmful to the user.

Substance abuse has long-term negative relationships to work adjustment, both as a cause and as an effect. A longitudinal study of polydrug use (alcohol, marijuana, and cocaine) found that polydrug use predicted lower job satisfaction four years later and that job instability (i.e., being fired or laid off) predicted subsequent substance abuse.[158] Although low to moderate doses of alcohol and drugs typically cause positive emotional experiences (which is the reason their use is often repeated later), high levels of consumption often lead to negative emotional experiences, particularly for naïve users. In addition, there is evidence that substance abuse is tied to important organizational outcomes. For example, prescription drug abuse has been tied to increased absenteeism.[159]

Given the negative effects associated with workplace substance use, there is an interest in identifying ways to minimize such usage. These efforts to manage drug and alcohol use at work can be quite successful. An examination of over 13,000 individuals in Australia revealed that workplace policies on alcohol and drug use were associated with a reduction in employee substance use.[160] However, alcohol and drug testing alone without other policies in place was unrelated to reduced substance use or abuse.

In trying to minimize workplace substance abuse, it is also important to understand what influences such usage. Problem drinking has been linked to a permissive norm that may exist as part of a workplace culture.[161] That is, individuals who want to be accepted by coworkers may match or exceed the drinking level of the referent group. One study examined the relationship between job insecurity (i.e., feelings of possible impending loss of employment) and substance abuse.[162] The researcher found that job insecurity was substantially related to both the frequency and quantity of alcohol use during the workday, but only to the frequency of illicit drug use.

Organizations typically address the problem of drug use at work in two ways.[163] The first is drug testing, designed to exclude drug users from the workplace. A large proportion of U.S. organizations test employees for alcohol and illicit drugs, but that number is on the decline, in part because tests as typically administered cannot determine use or impairment during the workday.[164] Instead, they simply reveal that a substance has been used at some point in the recent past, which could have been while not at work. The second means of addressing the problem of drug use by employees is through **employee assistance programs** (EAPs). EAPs started mostly after World War II to rehabilitate veterans who came home with alcohol abuse problems. Drug abuse treatment was added to the EAPs mainly after the Vietnam War for veterans returning with drug problems. Currently EAPs address all kinds of adjustment, stress, and family problems faced by workers. Such programs are mandated by the federal government for all employers who receive more than a specified amount of federal funding. Researchers have found that organizations in geographic areas with high unemployment rates are more likely to use pre-employment drug testing, whereas worksites with low turnover more often provide an EAP.[165]

Employee assistance programs
Voluntary work-sponsored programs that provide free and confidential help with personal and work-related problems, including substance abuse and mental health problems.

It is difficult for I-O psychologists to conduct high-quality research on substance abuse. Given ethical concerns, alcohol or drugs can be administered in an experimental setting only under the most restrictive conditions. Reliance on self-report measures is problematic, given the factors of social desirability and accuracy. Civil and legal issues are also associated with drug testing, both in this country and internationally, particularly pertaining to the constitutional rights of individuals to refuse to submit to drug testing. As with most complex social problems, researchers and scholars from many professions (such as pharmacology, toxicology, law, and genetics) must take an interdisciplinary approach to addressing these issues. Although I-O psychologists will contribute only a small piece of the total picture, we envision our efforts as concentrated in two traditional areas: individual assessment and performance measurement. Perhaps in 20 years, an evaluation of working conditions may also include the propensity of certain jobs to induce substance abuse and the likelihood your coworker is under the influence of drugs or alcohol. Whether we are ready for it or not, we believe society will expect I-O psychologists to provide information on problems our predecessors could scarcely have imagined.

Chapter Review

Key Terms

Workplace health and well-being
Stressor
Safety compliance
Safety participation
Challenge stressors
Hindrance stressors
Job demands-resources model
Burnout
Role
Role conflict
Role ambiguity
Role overload
Psychological capital
Shift work
Teleworker
Flexplace
Flextime
Compressed workweek
Work-family conflict
Work-family enrichment
Idiosyncratic deals
Boundary theory
Stigma
Substance abuse
Employee assistance programs

Questions for Review

1. What defines workplace health and well-being? Why has recent research been focused on it?
2. What is a stressor? What are the categories of stressors? Which are commonly addressed by organizations? Which by workers?
3. What is the difference between safety compliance and safety participation? Why does it matter whether an employee engages in one versus the other?
4. What kinds of task stressors can enhance performance? Which decrease performance?
5. How do resources counteract task stressors?
6. What is burnout? How can it be avoided?

7. What are the three types of role stressors? How can the impact of these stressors be reduced?
8. What are social stressors?
9. What are work schedule-related stressors? What has research shown regarding their effects on workers? What are possible remedies for these stressors?
10. How does unemployment impact workers?
11. What are the negative and possible positive outcomes of traumatic events?
12. How does uncertainty about work-related change affect employees?
13. For all types of stressors, what kinds of resources can organizations provide? What kinds of resources can workers bring and/or develop?
14. How have organizations responded to stress in the workplace? What are aspects of wellness programs that contribute to improved worker health?
15. What have studies shown about work-life balance? How does work-to-family conflict manifest itself? How does family-to-work conflict affect both family and work?
16. How can work-family enrichment facilitate improved worker health?
17. What are idiosyncratic deals? Why are they needed, and what could make their use unnecessary?
18. What is boundary theory? How does a lack of boundaries between work and family roles contribute to decreased well-being?
19. What are the types of dirty work taints? Why might the taints persist long after the employee discontinues the work? How has the definition of which jobs are "dirty work" changed over time?
20. What impact do alcohol and drug use have on workplaces? How are organizations attempting to manage it? What are the difficulties in researching it?

CHAPTER 13

Work Motivation

Chapter Outline

Work Motivation Theories

- Biological-Based Theory
- Maslow's Hierarchy of Needs
- Two-Factor Theory
- Flow Theory
- Self-Determination Theory
- Equity Theory
- Expectancy Theory
- Goal-Setting Theory

Job Characteristics Model

Synthesis and Application of Work Motivation Theories

- The Lighter Side of I-O Psychology: *Dear Desperate*

The Impact of Time on Work Motivation

- Social Media and I-O Psychology: *Cyberloafing*

Overqualification and Work Motivation

- COVID-19 and I-O Psychology: *A Blessing for the Overqualified?*

Fun and Games of Work Motivation

- Faces of I-O Psychology: *David R. Earnest*

Chapter Review

Learning Objectives

- Summarize the conceptual basis and degree of empirical support for these work motivation theories: biological-based, Maslow's hierarchy, two-factor, flow, self-determination, equity, expectancy, goal-setting, and the job characteristics model.
- Provide an overview and synthesis of the work motivation theories.
- Describe the points of convergence among the work motivation theories.
- Discuss practical examples of applying motivational strategies.
- Explain the impact of time and overqualification on work motivation.
- Explain the role of fun and games for work motivation.

Michael Jordan

"I can accept failure, everyone fails at something. But I can't accept not trying."
—Michael Jordan

If you were to do a search for the greatest professional basketball players of all time, you would likely find that the top choice on almost all of the lists is either Michael Jordan or LeBron James. Not surprisingly, they have many similar accomplishments, including being named the National Basketball Association's Most Valuable Player numerous times, leading their teams to several championships, and playing on teams that won Olympic gold medals. Undoubtedly, they have incredible knowledge, skills, and abilities when it comes to playing basketball. Nevertheless, having knowledge, skills, and abilities does not guarantee good performance. You also need motivation.

LeBron James

"Every night on the court I give my all, and if I'm not giving 100 percent, I criticize myself."
—LeBron James

The capacity and willingness to expend effort is the motivational or "will do" component of behavior. One's knowledge, skills, and abilities are the "can do" elements. Without that drive or willingness to focus one's attention, expend the necessary effort, and work hard enough to achieve an objective, the "can do" will never result in anything more than potential.

Motivation is the process that is concerned with the direction, intensity, and persistence of our behavior over time. There are three noteworthy components to this definition. First, *direction* addresses the choice of activities we make in expending effort. If given a choice, what will you focus your efforts on? Consider a situation in which your friends invite you to go to a movie the evening before a calculus exam that you are unprepared to take. If you're motivated to do well in the class, you would likely direct your attention to studying for the exam, whereas if you're not motivated you might choose to attend the movie. Second, *intensity* refers to how hard we choose to work, or how much effort we choose to expend. If you are motivated to do well in your calculus class, you would be willing to try hard to understand the material. Rather than only practicing the easier problems, you may be more willing to put forth the effort to understand even the harder problems. Third, *persistence* reflects behavior and effort over time, as opposed to a one-time choice between courses of action (direction) or high levels of effort aimed at a single task (intensity). The idea is that it might not be enough to read the book and try hard on one exam to do well in your calculus class.

Consider This...

Jack Ma

Jack Ma, co-founder and former executive chairman of Alibaba Group and one of the wealthiest people in the world, knows something about the importance of motivation. He failed his university entrance exam three times. He was rejected from all 30 jobs he initially applied for after college, including being the only one of 25 applicants who was rejected by KFC and the only one of five applicants rejected for a position as a police officer. He applied to Harvard ten times and was rejected all ten times. Despite these rejections, Ma maintained his focus, continued to work hard, and persisted until he achieved success! How will *you* handle future rejections? What will it take for you to stay motivated in the face of failure?

You will likely have to keep on trying during the entire course. In addition, you would be willing to persist with your efforts even if you experienced an earlier setback. So, if you're really motivated to do well in the class, you would be more willing to spend several evenings a week studying for the class, and to continue to try regardless of how well you performed on earlier exams.

As a general rule, motivation is thought of as being intrinsically or extrinsically driven. *Intrinsic motivation* is the drive to do things simply for the sake of doing them. Here, the reasons for engaging in an activity are internally derived. *Extrinsic motivation*, on the other hand, is dictated by the prospect of some instrumental outcome and is externally derived. For example, the motivation that people have to read books or run may be intrinsic or extrinsic. Some people are intrinsically motivated, wanting to read or go for a jog simply because they enjoy such activities. Others, however, may only read or run when there is something of value to gain or lose. For instance, some people only read when they are assigned to do so for a class and their grade depends on it. Similarly, some people may only run when someone (or something) is chasing them or to pass a required fitness test.

Sample Intrinsic Motivators

- Enjoyment
- Self-expression
- Curiosity
- Growth
- Passion
- Purpose
- Interest

Sample Extrinsic Motivators

- Pay raises
- Promotions
- Awards
- Bonuses
- Prizes
- Benefits
- Grades

Recall from Chapter 4 that there is distinction between the upper limit of what people *can do* (maximum performance) versus what they *will do* (typical performance). One conception of motivation is that it accounts for the difference between typical and maximum performance. Individuals with high ability may be able to sustain an acceptable level of typical performance, but they would be capable of much greater (i.e., maximum) performance if they were sufficiently motivated to perform at this higher level. They stand in sharp contrast with individuals who have to work very hard to be successful because they lack high ability. Of course, individuals with high ability can also seek out jobs that don't require high effort if they are averse to working hard.

Consider This...

The degree to which greater effort can compensate for lesser ability in attaining satisfactory performance varies across jobs. In *Star Wars Episode V: The Empire Strikes Back*, Yoda, the Jedi Master, is teaching Luke Skywalker how to use the Force. Luke is being told to lift his X-wing fighter out of the swamp. For those of you who aren't *Star Wars* fans, Luke is essentially having to lift an aircraft off the ground—using his mind. Luke conveys his skepticism about his being able to do it, but says he will give it a try. At this point, Yoda says one of his most famous lines: "Do... or do not. There is no try." Apparently, being a Jedi and using the Force require abilities (that Luke has) and not motivation. What other jobs can you think of where motivation cannot compensate for one's abilities? Which jobs can?

It should be clear at this point that poor performance may or may not be a function of low levels of motivation. Poor performance could also result from deficient knowledge, skills, abilities, or resources and support. Determining the cause of poor performance is difficult, as is knowing the remedy for it. It is often the case that a mix of factors is at play. Thus, a careful diagnosis is needed to determine whether performance problems are best addressed with training (as covered in Chapter 7) or motivational interventions (as described in this chapter).

Work Motivation Theories

Over the past 50 years, there has been a profusion of work motivation theories. Only in the past couple of decades, however, have attempts been made to identify consistency in the psychological constructs that underlie the theories. As will be witnessed, certain psychological constructs coalesce more readily across theories than others.

Whereas there are dozens of theories of motivation, only a few theories of work motivation will be presented here. They differ markedly in the psychological constructs that are hypothesized to account for motivation. Each theory will be presented along with a summary of some of the supporting empirical research. At the conclusion of this presentation, there will be a discussion of points of convergence among the theories and the fundamental perspectives that have been taken in addressing work motivation.

Biological-Based Theory

In Chapter 2, we noted that I-O psychologists have begun to explore the brain with a focus on organizational neuroscience. Researchers have now examined the physiological bases of many organizational phenomena, including motivation. The **biological-based theory of motivation** examines the role of physiological responses (such as activity in the brain's neurons) and inherited traits (such as personality) in the determination of motivation. There is certainly reason to believe that motivation may have a physiological element, determined by factors outside of our control. Researchers have found, for example, that when individuals make mistakes, there is a unique response within the brain's neurons that occurs approximately 50 milliseconds after the mistake is made, even when people are unaware of making the error.[1] In addition to changes in basic neural responses, errors lead to an engagement of the sympathetic nervous systems, such that one's heart rate briefly slows immediately following a mistake.[2] From an evolutionary perspective, the idea is that we are physiologically motivated to avoid errors because their occurrence can jeopardize our safety.

Biological-based theory of motivation A theory that presumes motivation is genetically predisposed, determined by one's physiology and traits.

As further evidence of the biological basis of motivation, consider the role of dopamine within the body. Dopamine is a neurotransmitter (an organic chemical produced by the body) that is involved in reward, motivation, and attention (among other things). When released, dopamine creates feelings of pleasure and reward, which motivates us to repeat the behavior that led to its release.[3] In contrast, when dopamine levels are low, we feel apathetic and have diminished motivation.[4] Furthermore, researchers have identified a gene (*D4DR*) that determines how receptive neurons are to dopamine.[5] Thus, there is reason to believe that some individuals are genetically predisposed to be more (or less) motivated compared to others.

Within the realm of I-O psychology specifically, researchers have provided evidence to support the proposition that genetic factors influence work motivation.[6] Recall from Chapter 5 that a contemporary interpretation of personality is represented in the Big 5 theory. One personality factor of considerable relevance for motivation is conscientiousness, which can also be thought of as the "will to achieve."[7] Highly conscientious individuals are attentive to detail, rule abiding, and honest as well as exhibit high ambition. Researchers have found that conscientiousness of individuals when they are age 16 or 17 is predictive of unemployment later in life.[8] Specifically, teens who had lower conscientiousness were twice as likely to have periods of unemployment in subsequent decades compared to their counterparts with high levels of conscientiousness. This suggests that our willingness to expend effort is a defining component of our personality.

Applying the biological-based theory of motivation to the workplace is tricky. We can certainly assess traits (e.g., conscientiousness) during the personnel selection process in an effort to hire individuals who may be more predisposed to working hard. However, we cannot use our knowledge of the genetic role of dopamine receptivity in the selection process, as the **Genetic Information Nondiscrimination Act of 2008 (GINA)** prohibits employers from using genetic information when making employment decisions, including hiring, firing, promotion, and job placement decisions.[9] Given that some organizations and healthcare providers may be tempted to use such information to save on health coverage costs, this is an important piece of legislation that combats potential discrimination based on genetic information.

Genetic Information Nondiscrimination Act of 2008 (GINA)
An act that prohibits discrimination on the basis of genetic information with respect to employment and health insurance.

Of course, there are ways that organizations could use knowledge of biological-based motivation to their advantage. For example, the findings regarding the body's natural tendency to react to errors gives additional credence to the power of error-management training, discussed in Chapter 7. In addition, there are many ways that organizations can help increase their employees' levels of dopamine naturally. For instance, research has shown that dopamine levels can be heightened through exercise,[10] meditation,[11] exposure to safe levels of sunlight,[12] getting enough high-quality sleep,[13] and listening to music.[14] Organizations can use this knowledge by creating space for meditation, providing access to fitness centers, designing workspaces with natural lighting, discouraging "all-nighters," and allowing employees to listen to music at work. By doing these things, organizations can potentially enhance employee motivation as well as their well-being[15] and overall performance.[16]

Maslow's Hierarchy of Needs

It is hard to imagine a discussion of motivation without talking about **Maslow's hierarchy of needs**. This is one of the most well-known theories of motivation, and is based on the assumption that humans are motivated to satisfy certain needs. These needs are prioritized and typically presented as a pyramid, with the needs at the base of the pyramid given more immediate attention than those above them. The needs

Maslow's hierarchy of needs
A theory of motivation that suggests that motivation is based on the satisfaction of a prioritized sequence of needs.

at the base of the pyramid are physiological needs, including air, food, and water. Once our physiological needs are sufficiently met,* we then focus our attention on our need for safety and security. This includes physical, psychological, and employment security. Together, our physiological needs and our need for safety and security represent our most basic needs. Next, Maslow suggests we will focus on psychological needs, the first of which is our need for love and belonging. The second need is esteem, whereby we are motivated to gain respect, feel appreciated, and feel valued by our peers. Lastly, we strive for self-actualization. Here, we focus on self-fulfillment and attempt to realize our full potential through personal and creative self-growth. In a way, to be self-actualized you essentially seek to do what the old U.S. Army slogan said—"Be All You Can Be."

Maslow's hierarchy has received considerable criticism over the years, most notably due to the lack of empirical support for the theory. Namely, there appears to be little evidence that individuals give more weight to the fulfillment of needs at the bottom of the pyramid. Indeed, in a study across 123 countries, researchers found that higher-level needs such as social support and feeling respected were important despite lower-level needs not being fulfilled.[17] Of course, these findings wouldn't surprise Maslow, who noted that the order of the hierarchy isn't as rigid as it is sometimes depicted and was fascinated with the people who appeared to focus on self-actualization to the point where lower-level needs were ignored. For example, he noted there were musicians or artists who would become so entranced with their work that they would disregard the need for food or sleep, seemingly becoming the metaphorical "starving artists." Figure 13-1 shows the hierarchy with questions employees might ask themselves at each level.

Consider This...

Why would we present a theory that has little empirical support? One reason is that there is large intuitive appeal for the theory. Can you imagine caring about whether somebody liked you if you were literally dying of thirst in the middle of the desert? More importantly, however, is that despite its lack of support, Maslow's hierarchy continues to be referenced in workplaces, and it would be a shame to not have an awareness of it. Chip Conley, founder of the California boutique hotel chain Joie de Vivre Hospitality and strategist who helped Airbnb become the global hospitality giant that it is today, used Maslow's hierarchy as inspiration for creating his business model![18] How might you apply Maslow's hierarchy to your employees' and your own motivation in the workplace?

*Maslow's hierarchy is often depicted as lower needs having to be fully met before higher needs emerge. This is not actually how Maslow envisioned his hierarchy. Rather, he did not see the needs as all-or-none, and instead said that most members of society have all needs partially satisfied and partially unsatisfied, with those at the bottom of the hierarchy typically being satisfied to a greater extent than those at or near the top of the hierarchy.[19]

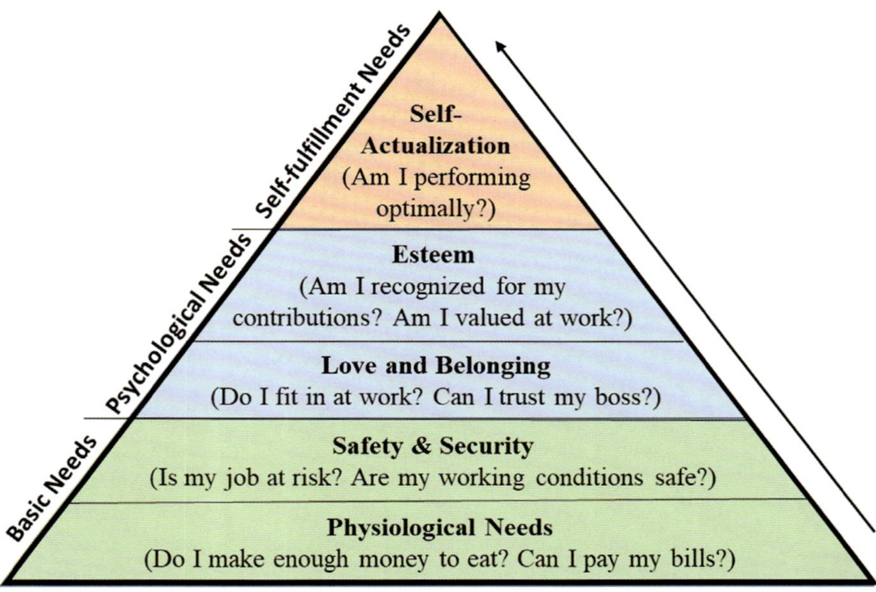

Figure 13-1 *Maslow's Hierarchy and corresponding questions*

Two-Factor Theory

Two-factor theory A theory of motivation that suggests that people are motivated by intrinsic factors, whereas extrinsic factors will ensure people are not dissatisfied but will not increase motivation.

Another early theory of motivation is the **two-factor theory** (also called the motivator-hygiene theory), which says that the things that motivate employees are distinct from the things that will cause dissatisfaction if they are not present.[20] Specifically, there are two factors—those that are more intrinsic in nature (such as recognition, growth, advancement) and those that are more extrinsic in nature (such as pay, work conditions, supervision). The intrinsic factors are motivator factors whereas the extrinsic ones are hygiene factors.

This theory suggests that focusing on improving hygiene factors will only ensure that employees are not dissatisfied, but will not necessarily motivate them. Thus, increasing pay, improving work conditions, and establishing a better relationship with one's supervisor may alleviate or remove dissatisfaction and prevent an employee from quitting, but they won't make the employee more motivated to work harder. Rather, to motivate employees, the focus needs to be on the intrinsic elements. Recognizing hard work and providing opportunities for growth and advancement will motivate an employee to work harder. It is important, however, that the extrinsic factors be acceptable in order for the intrinsic factors to take effect. It won't matter how much recognition somebody gets; if they don't have a reasonable salary, they will not likely remain with an organization or be motivated to perform well.

Similar to Maslow's hierarchy, the two-factor theory has received relatively little empirical support and has garnered its share of criticism. In particular, critics have argued that some elements of jobs could be both hygiene factors and motivator factors, such as pay.[21] While one's salary is certainly extrinsically derived, people place differing symbolic meaning on money, and some see money as a sign of achievement, status, and freedom.[22] As such, money is more motivating for some people than this theory would suggest. Nevertheless, much like Maslow's hierarchy, having an understanding of this theory is important, given its seemingly ubiquitous presence in the minds of managers.

Flow Theory

Flow theory
A theory of motivation that suggests that individuals will experience an intense level of enjoyment, concentration, and lack of self-awareness when actively engaged in pursuits that have clear goals, unambiguous feedback, and a match between one's skills and the challenge of the task.

Thinking back to Maslow's recognition of the "starving artist," have you ever felt so deeply engaged in an activity that you seemingly forgot about everything but the activity itself? Perhaps you've found yourself still engrossed in a book at 3:00 a.m., unaware that the night had turned to morning. This is actually the premise behind **flow theory**. The expression "time flies when you're having fun" is certainly relevant to this theory, as is the feeling of being "in the zone."

Flow is a mental and emotional state of optimal sensation, characterized by focused attention, a clear mind, distortion of time, a loss of self-consciousness, and intense intrinsic enjoyment.[23] In many ways, flow can be thought of metaphorically as "intrinsic motivation on steroids." When in a state of flow, a person becomes fully immersed in what they are doing. They feel in complete control, with their actions seeming almost spontaneous and automatic.

To experience flow, there are three necessary preconditions that must be in place.[24] First, there must be a balance between the challenge of the task and the skills of the person performing the task. If the task requirements exceed skill levels, frustration and anxiety are likely to ensue. If skills exceed the task requirements, then boredom or apathy is likely. It is only when both the needs of the task and the abilities of the individual are high that flow will occur. Figure 13-2 depicts the ways in which challenge and skill level combinations are related, with sample activities that fall into each category.

A second precondition for flow to occur is the need for there to be clear goals. Individuals must understand what is required of them for the activity at hand. If it isn't clear what must be done, feelings of uncertainty and self-consciousness will result, making it unlikely that flow is experienced. Lastly, there must be clear and immediate feedback that is inherent in the task itself for flow to be possible. The presence of unambiguous feedback reaffirms one's actions and reduces uncertainty, allowing an individual to let go and become fully immersed in an activity.

Some people are more apt to experience flow than are other individuals. A group of researchers examined flow proneness (or the tendency to experience flow) in 444 pairs of adult twins and found evidence for a genetic basis for flow experiences.[25] Flow proneness has also been shown to be related to the personality characteristics of emotional stability and conscientiousness, such that individuals who are emotionally unstable are less likely to experience flow, whereas individuals who are high on conscientiousness are more prone to experience flow.[26]

There has been a good deal of support for the beneficial aspects of being in flow at work. For example, work-related flow is related to heightened self-efficacy[27] and higher quality customer service performance.[28] In addition, there is evidence that as feelings of flow increase, performance anxiety decreases.[29] However, the relationship between flow and performance appears to be dependent on whether an individual

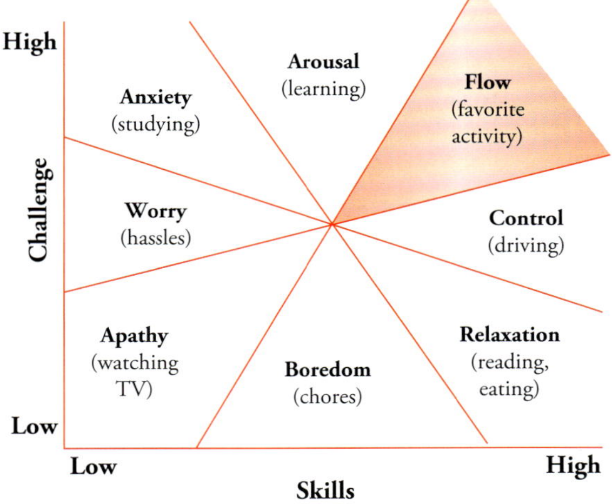

Figure 13-2 *Challenge and skill combinations, according to flow theory*

Adapted from *Finding flow: The psychology of engagement with everyday life*, by M. Csikszentmihalyi (1997). Reproduced with permission of Basic Books via Copyright Clearance Center.

is conscientious or not. Specifically, some research found that flow was related to heightened task and citizenship performance for employees who were high in conscientiousness, but unrelated when employees were low in conscientiousness.[30] There is also evidence that flow is beneficial for work-family interactions. For example, a study of 83 people over a period of four consecutive days found that when individuals experienced flow at work and then went home and were psychologically detached from work, they were more invigorated and less exhausted at home compared to people who experienced lower levels of flow during the workday.[31]

Self-Determination Theory

As noted earlier, motivation can generally be intrinsic or extrinsic in nature. A long-held belief and heavily researched concept is the *undermining effect*, which is the finding that adding external incentives to a task that was initially enjoyable could actually *decrease* intrinsic motivation. Take, for example, a student who gains a great deal of enjoyment from reading. Yet, when an instructor assigns a certain book to be read as part of a course requirement, the student feels less than enthused. The extrinsic requirement to read has diminished the student's intrinsic motivation for reading. Why might this be? **Self-determination** theory is a theory of motivation that helps to explain why sometimes extrinsic motivators (rewards and incentives) result in positive versus negative outcomes. The theory proposes that individuals have three basic needs that result in intrinsic motivation if they are fulfilled. These needs are:[32]

Self-determination theory
A theory of motivation based on the fulfillment of basic needs to experience intrinsic motivation.

1. **Autonomy:** People want to feel like they have a say in what it is they do. When they feel like they have the discretion to make their own choices, they are more likely to derive enjoyment from a task.
2. **Competence:** As a general rule, people prefer to feel capable of doing things. When they feel like they are able to perform successfully and experience mastery over a task, they are more likely to gain a sense of enjoyment in doing it.
3. **Relatedness:** People have a desire for interaction and belongingness. When they feel connected to others, they are more likely to experience intrinsic motivation.

When these needs are met, intrinsic motivation flourishes and the direction, intensity, and persistence of effort is heightened. However, when extrinsic rewards undermine these basic needs, intrinsic motivation will be lessened.[33] Consider the example of the student whose intrinsic motivation for reading diminished after being assigned a book to read for class. According to self-determination theory, one possible explanation is that the student doesn't have as much autonomy as usual. In addition to not getting to choose the book, the teacher likely imposed a deadline for having the book read. Another possibility is that perhaps the student doesn't feel capable of doing well, given the deadline or content of the book. Lastly, if they feel alone in their dislike for the book or in their ability, they may feel disconnected from others and like they don't fit in. In short, these factors have undermined the student's intrinsic motivation by negatively impacting the student's basic self-determination needs.

I wouldn't have chosen *this* book. (Low autonomy)
This book is *too hard* to read. (Low competence)
I'm the only one who doesn't like this book. *I don't fit in.* (Low relatedness)

Extrinsic motivators can vary considerably in terms of how *controlled* versus *autonomous* they are. On the one end, rewards may be very externally regulated, based on outside rewards and punishments. For example, a soldier who typically enjoys running may be forced to run as part of a physical training requirement for the military. Failure to do the run will result in a negative evaluation. Motivators such as these would be the most likely to hinder intrinsic motivation, as feelings of autonomy are drastically reduced. That is, the individual is not in control of when runs occur or why they are running. On the other end of the continuum, extrinsic motivators can be integrated into the person's own value system, and therefore be less likely to detract from feelings of autonomy. For example, an individual may run in part because of the health benefits associated with the activity. If the person values good health, the extrinsic driver of getting in shape won't be as detrimental to the enjoyment of the activity due to the ties to their personally-prescribed values. In this case, the extrinsic motivator of running is self-directed or autonomous. Rather than running because they should or must do the run, they actually *want* to do it. The importance of tying extrinsic motivations to values can be seen with research that has shown firefighters and fundraisers perform better and are more productive and persistent with their efforts when they are driven by a synergistic combination of intrinsic motivation and pro-social values.[34] Intrinsic motivation appears to matter more for the quality of one's performance, or how well somebody does something, whereas extrinsic motivation appears to be a better predictor of quantity of performance, or how much somebody gets accomplished.[35] Furthermore, when incentives are directly linked to performance (such as sales commissions and performance bonuses), intrinsic motivation is less related to performance than when the incentives are indirectly linked (such as with base salaries, which aren't directly related to actual performance levels). This is in line with the undermining effect, given that the direct link makes it clearer that the reason for hard work is to earn the incentive.

A tremendous amount of research has supported the basic assumptions of self-determination theory. By allowing employees to initiate their own behaviors, feel confident, and feel connected to others, supervisors can facilitate autonomous motivation. When workplace policies or practices thwart any of these three basic needs, controlled motivation will likely ensue and quality of performance will suffer.[36]

Consider This...

Some ways in which actual leaders have supported their followers' needs for autonomy, competence, and relatedness within their organizations include:[37]

Autonomy: encourage innovation; consult with individuals impacted by decisions; be less prescriptive when assigning tasks; allow followers to express ideas; provide rationale for decisions

Competence: provide opportunities for development; provide regular feedback; allow followers to learn at their own pace; help build follower self-esteem and confidence; provide mentoring

Relatedness: utilize team-building activities; learn about followers' lives outside of work; respect followers' backgrounds and experiences

Knowing the importance of autonomy, competence, and relatedness—and what leaders have done within their organizations—what would you suggest to your professors when assigning students work? Do you consider each of these needs to be equal in terms of importance for you?

Equity Theory

Equity theory
A theory of motivation based on the comparison of one's inputs to outcomes with those of another person to determine if a situation is fair. These determinations of equity dictate subsequent actions taken.

Equity theory suggests that motivation exists in a social context, and is based on how fair individuals see situations and interactions.[38] This theory states that employees intuitively make comparisons between themselves and others to determine how hard to work. The comparisons involve *inputs*, or contributions they make to a situation (like their level of effort, knowledge, or specific skill set), and the *outcomes* they receive (like pay, recognition, or other benefits). In general, there should be a match between their inputs and outcomes such that increases in one should lead to increases in the other. In short, individuals would compare their ratio of inputs to outcomes with the ratio of inputs and outcomes of another person, such as a coworker. If they perceive the ratios are equal, they see the situation as equitable, or fair. If, however, they feel there is a mismatch between the ratios of inputs and outcomes, they will feel distress and will be motivated to reduce the inequity.

Assume you have a job in which you earn $15 an hour. You are talking with your coworker and discover that you both make the same amount of money for doing the same job. Your inputs and outcomes are the same as your coworker's inputs and outcomes; therefore you would likely see that as being fair. In equity theory's terms, you perceive that there is *equity*. Imagine you compare your inputs and outcomes with another more experienced coworker who makes $20 an hour. Although this coworker makes more than you do (greater outcomes), you note that this person also has more experience than you do (greater inputs). Thus, you would still perceive that there is equity. What if, however, you discovered that your first coworker (who has the same experience as you) makes $2 more per hour than you for doing the same amount of work? Frustrating, right? In this case, the ratios of inputs to outcomes don't match because your coworker is getting more than you (more outcomes) despite having the same level of inputs (as far as you can tell). In this situation, you perceive that there is *inequity*, or unfairness. It is important to note that ratios are compared, not just inputs or outcomes. That is, you might perceive equity if your coworker makes more money than you, but also has more experience. Figure 13-3 shows how comparing ratios of inputs to outcomes is much like placing the ratios on a scale. When the scale tips to one side (because one person's ratio is higher than the other's), there is inequity. When the ratios are the same, the scale is even and equity is perceived.

According to equity theory, feelings of *inequity* motivate individuals to take action to make things fair. If you feel like you are under-rewarded (or your ratio is less than that of your coworker), you may try to restore equity by (1) reducing your inputs (slacking off) or (2) increasing your outcomes (whether by asking for a raise or doing something unethical like stealing from the organization). You could also reduce the feelings of inequity by (3) distorting your perceptions of the situation. For example, if you modify your thinking so that you now believe your coworker is actually doing more than you originally believed (such as performing tasks that nobody likes to do), you may come to think that the pay difference is fair. Alternatively, your coworker might make more money than you, but you get other benefits that your coworker doesn't get (such as preferred hours, a parking space, and greater recognition for your work). By changing how you think about the comparison, you fashion the ratio of your coworker's inputs to outcomes to match the ratio of your inputs to outcomes. Of course, you could also make yourself feel better by (4) changing the person with whom you compare yourself, or (5) leaving the situation (by quitting).

Much of the support for equity theory comes from it being the basis for organizational justice perceptions (described in Chapter 11). Recall that justice perceptions refer to how people perceive the fairness of outcomes (distributive justice), the fairness in how decisions regarding outcomes are reached (procedural justice), and the fairness with how people are treated (interactional justice).

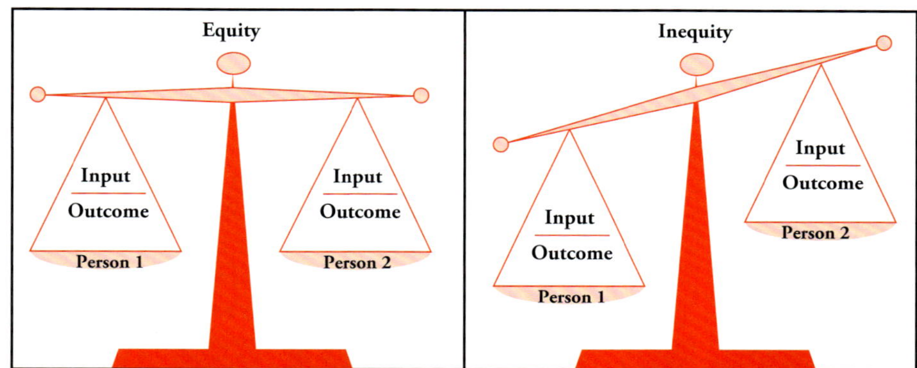

Figure 13-3
Comparison of input to outcome ratios to determine equity and inequity, according to equity theory

What should be clear at this point is that a large part of whether an individual views a situation as being equitable or not depends on the person with whom they are making their comparisons. When making comparisons, employees could choose to look at others (such as coworkers) or themselves (perhaps comparing what they now earn vs. what they earned in a previous job). They could also choose to look internally (maybe at coworkers in their current organization) or look externally (to colleagues at different organizations). Comparisons don't even have to be made with actual people for feelings of inequity to result. Thoughts of "what might have been" can serve as the basis for comparison.[39] If employees *imagine* that an outcome could have been much better than it actually was given their level of input, they will likely feel inequity in the form of resentment. The most important consideration is that the comparison be realistic. It would be unrealistic, for example, for an entry-level employee to use the CEO of the organization or fanciful imagined outcomes for the basis of comparisons.

In the examples thus far, inequity has been framed as under-reward, without much thought given to over-reward. The reason for this is simple. Although equity theory suggests that *any* inequity—whether due to under-reward or over-reward—should result in motivation to restore equity, there is simply less empirical support for the notion that inequity in one's favor leads to such action. It would seem that people are more likely to act to restore equity when they are the ones at a *disadvantage*. Individuals differ, however, in their preference for equity (or tolerance for inequity).[40] This **equity sensitivity** predicts the extent to which individuals will be likely to take action when faced with inequity. On one end of the continuum are *benevolents*, or those individuals with a greater tolerance for under-reward. It's not that they prefer to be treated unfairly. Rather, they have more tolerance for it than do others. On the other end are *entitleds*, or those that have a greater preference for being over-rewarded (or higher outcome/input ratio compared to others). In the middle are *equity sensitives*, or those individuals who prefer to have equal ratios. According to this view, benevolent and equity sensitive employees would be likely to take action to reduce inequity that was due to perceived over-reward, whereas entitled employees would be content with such inequity. These individual differences in equity preferences can have huge implications in the workplace. For example, recent research on entitlement highlights the dysfunctional nature of believing that one deserves more of the proverbial pie than others, regardless of one's contribution or performance. In particular, research has demonstrated that entitled individuals engage in greater instances of organizational deviance,[41] more coworker abuse[42] and fewer extra-role behaviors[43] compared to others. Given that millennials have been branded as being more entitled than past generations,[44] more research on this may be worthwhile.

Equity sensitivity
The individual differences that people have regarding their preference for equity (or tolerance for inequity).

Expectancy Theory

Expectancy theory is a cognitive theory of motivation that suggests that employees are rational decision makers who will expend effort on activities that lead to desired rewards.[45] At its simplest level, expectancy theory suggests that effort is a function of the employee's beliefs that (1) effort will lead to performance, (2) performance will lead to an outcome, and (3) the outcome is valued. To the extent that employees hold these beliefs, they should be motivated to exert effort.

Expectancy theory
A theory of motivation based on the perceived degree of relationship between how much effort a person expends and the performance that results from that effort.

Expectancy Within expectancy theory, the belief that effort leads to performance.

The first belief, that effort leads to performance, is termed **expectancy**, and answers the question, "How likely is it that my effort will lead to performance?" In some jobs, there may seem to be no relationship between how hard you try and how well you do. In others, there may be a very clear relationship: the harder you try, the better you do. In general, expectancy theory proposes that people must see a relationship (an expectancy) between how hard they try and how well they perform. Expectancies can range from 0 (no chance that trying harder will improve performance) to 1 (trying harder will definitely improve performance). If expectancy is low, it will make very little difference to them whether they work hard because effort and performance seem unrelated. In other words, effort will seem futile. If somebody is physically short and lacks the ability to jump very high, no amount of practice or effort will result in the person being able to dunk a basketball in a regulation hoop. Putting energy towards trying to do so is a waste of time and effort. As another example, on assembly lines, the group performance level is determined by the speed of the line. No matter how hard employees work, they cannot produce any more until the next object moves down the line. Employees soon learn they need only keep pace with the line. Thus, there is no relationship between individual effort and performance, and subsequently very little motivation to expend extra effort. Alternatively, sales jobs are characterized by high expectancy. Salespeople who are paid on commission realize that the harder they try (the more sales calls they make), the better their performance (sales volume).

Instrumentality Within expectancy theory, the belief that performance will lead to an outcome.

The expectancy theory belief that performance will lead to an outcome is termed **instrumentality**. Instrumentality is defined as the perceived degree of relationship between performance and outcome attainment. It answers the question, "How likely is it that performance will lead to certain job outcomes?" Similar to expectancies, instrumentalities can range from 0 (no chance performance will lead to an outcome) to 1 (performance will definitely lead to an outcome). Instrumentality exists in the employee's mind. Thus, whether or not performance will *actually* lead to certain outcomes is not the point. What matters is whether the employee *believes* that the connection or relationship is real. If a person thinks that pay increases are highly conditional on performance, then the instrumentality associated with that outcome (a pay raise) is very high. If an employee thinks that pay raises are given based on favoritism and are unrelated to job performance, then the instrumentality associated with that outcome is zero. Not surprisingly, for motivation to occur, a person must believe that there is some relationship between job performance and attainment of outcomes (instrumentalities must be high). If a person does not see performance as a means of obtaining a valued outcome, increased effort simply won't seem worth it. Reward practices and the supervisor are crucial in establishing high instrumentalities. If a supervisor says, "Your performance has been very good lately; therefore, I will reward you with a raise (or promotion)," the individual will see that the attainment of a pay raise or a promotion is conditional on (instrumental to) good performance. Conversely, if a supervisor says, "We don't give pay raises or promotions on the basis of performance; we grant them only on the basis of seniority," the individual will not be motivated to perform well as a means to get the outcomes. Perhaps the only motivation is to work hard enough not to be fired, so these outcomes would eventually result from longer service with the organization. When outcomes are made contingent on performance and the individual understands this relationship, expectancy theory predicts that job performance will be enhanced.

Consider This...

Although expectancy theory suggests that having a clear relationship between performance and outcomes is essential for motivation, strong expectancies can be problematic if not managed well. For example, in 2016, Wells Fargo revealed that its employees had fraudulently opened millions of fake accounts in order to meet sales goals.[46] Essentially, sales incentives were in place that encouraged opening as many accounts as possible through cross-selling (selling additional products or services to existing customers). Employees knew that opening more accounts would lead to sales bonuses (i.e., there was a high instrumentality), and therefore they were motivated to do so. Unfortunately, some employees did so illegally, without the consent of the account owners. Another potential issue of having a clear instrumentality is that it can create feelings of work intensification (needing to do more work in less time). For example, if an employee earns $1.50 for every toy they assemble, and they know they need to earn $750 per week before taxes to afford their expenses, they know they will need to assemble 500 toys (500 toys x $1.50). They may experience heightened stress as they feel this sense of work intensification.[47] With these points in mind, what would you recommend to a manager when implementing a reward system for performance? How would you keep employees from engaging in unethical behaviors and minimize the stress that could be caused from the high instrumentality that you are creating to improve motivation?

Valence
Within expectancy theory, the extent to which outcomes are valued.

Finally, the third belief that is essential for effort to be exerted, that the outcomes are valued, is known as **valence**.[48] Valences are the employee's feelings about the outcomes and are usually defined in terms of attractiveness or anticipated satisfaction. They answer the question, "How valuable or attractive are the job outcomes to me?" If the outcomes are seen as attractive, the employee assigns a positive valence to them. If they are seen as negative, they are given negative valences, and if the employee feels indifferent about an outcome, that outcome would have a valence of zero. Whether an outcome is seen as positive or negative (or neutral) depends on the person and situation. For example, a manager may try to incentivize employees by offering a certain parking spot to whomever is deemed "employee of the month." For some people, this might be seen as a valuable outcome, particularly if there is limited nearby parking available. Others may not find such an outcome very valuable. For example, if they use public transportation to get to work or could have an even better spot on their own, such an enticement may have little value, or even be seen as a worse option. Thus, valences will vary by person, situation, and outcome. Figure 13-4 shows the questions people might ask to determine if they are motivated to try harder per expectancy theory.

The last key aspect of expectancy theory is how motivational force, or the overall motivation of an individual, is predicted. According to expectancy theory, motivational force is determined with the following equation:

Motivational Force = Expectancy × Sum of all Instrumentalities x Valence combinations

Based on this equation, we can see that expectancies are crucial for overall motivation, since motivational force will be nonexistent if expectancies are 0 (the individual believes there is no chance that trying harder will improve performance). In addition, this equation demonstrates that one's overall motivation can be strengthened by additional valued outcomes, since instrumentalities are weighted by the valence of the outcome and then added. Thus, having one valued outcome is good, but having multiple valued outcomes that are contingent on performance is even more motivating. Of course, if there are no valued outcomes expected, then expectancies won't matter. Therefore, each is important to overall motivation.

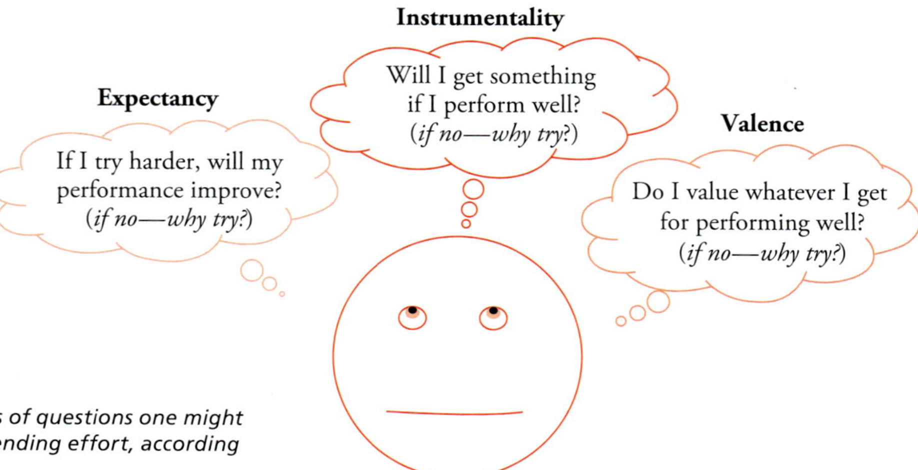

Figure 13-4 *The types of questions one might ask oneself about expending effort, according to expectancy theory*

Goal-Setting Theory

Goal-setting theory A theory of motivation based on directing one's effort toward the attainment of specific goals that have been set or established.

Goal-setting theory is based on directing one's effort toward the attainment of specific goals that have been set or established. Its basic premise is that setting clear, specific, and challenging goals leads to enhanced task performance by way of increased performance motivation. Goals are what the individual is consciously trying to attain, particularly as they relate to future objectives. Goals influence all indicators of motivation, including direction, intensity, and persistence of effort.[49] They indicate where a person should direct efforts, how much effort is needed, and for how long. In addition, they encourage the development of novel task strategies to accomplish goals.

Goal-setting theory is one of the most widely studied theories of motivation. As such, much is known regarding what makes goals effective versus ineffective. For example, it has become fairly well-established that specific (vs. vague) goals lead to higher performance.[50] In general, goals direct attention and action, and identify the target of intended behavior. Thus, when they are stated specifically, the focus of the person's effort becomes well defined.

It has also been well-documented that difficult (vs. easy) and attainable (vs. unattainable) goals lead to greater performance levels. For example, there is a significant, positive relationship between goal difficulty and motivation, which remains positive up to the point at which either one's skill level is no longer sufficient to attain the goal (i.e., it becomes unattainable), or the individual becomes uncommitted to its achievement.[51] Furthermore, specifying challenging goals leads to greater levels of motivation than does a simple "do your best" instruction. The reason difficulty seems to matter is because if a goal is difficult, it normally requires more effort, over a longer period of time, to be attained. Thus, the difficulty of a goal can be expected to impact an individual's intensity and persistence of effort. In addition, goal setting requires the development of a task-related strategy. When people contemplate a goal, they must also consider the means for its attainment, especially when the goal is seen as difficult. It may be that harder tasks are more likely to stimulate more strategy development than are easy tasks.

Self-efficacy
The belief in one's capabilities and capacity to perform successfully.

The importance of goal attainability can be further seen in research on self-efficacy. **Self-efficacy** is the belief in one's capabilities and capacity to perform successfully. When individuals have high self-efficacy, they feel they are capable of performing successfully, whereas if they have low self-efficacy, they will not think they are able to be successful.[52] When individuals feel they can be successful, they are more likely to focus their attention, exert extra effort, and persist in the face of initial failure in order to achieve their goal. If they think there is little chance of success, however, such as when a goal is overly difficult and viewed as unattainable, they are not likely to try hard or persevere when faced with an obstacle. Instead, they will see any impediments and initial failures as reflecting their views regarding their unlikelihood for success and simply quit. Given the importance of self-efficacy, much research has been conducted on ways to increase self-efficacy in individuals. Four ways to increase self-efficacy include:[53]

1. **Performance accomplishments**—Simply stated, when an individual successfully performs a task, confidence in performing that task again in the future will increase. This is also known as *enactive mastery*. This is a common technique in training whereby simple tasks are attempted and practiced before harder ones. The idea is that once individuals feel capable of being successful, the difficulty of a task (or goal) can be raised (within reason) without negatively impacting self-efficacy.
2. **Vicarious experience**—When others who are similar to you are able to successfully perform a task, it is easier for you to believe that you are also able to be successful. This is the notion of vicarious experience. In a training context, this often is reflected with the behavioral modeling technique. In order to show that employees can be successful, they are shown others doing the task to demonstrate that it can be done.
3. **Persuasion**—Individuals are more likely to feel confident in their abilities when they receive coaching and encouragement. Essentially, convincing people that they have the necessary KSAOs to be successful can increase their self-efficacy.
4. **Arousal**—Being energized and "amped up" can help people feel like they can be successful. This is often seen prior to sporting events when a team jumps around and shouts. This triggers their collective arousal as a means of building their confidence levels.

In addition to goals varying in terms of specificity and difficulty, goals can also differ in terms of their content. For example, goals can be categorized as learning goals (those aimed at increasing development) or performance goals (those aimed at demonstrating competence). Both learning and performance goals are important. Employees

Goal orientation The way in which individuals approach or avoid goals in achievement situations.

must be able to pursue the appropriate goals at the right time in order to be most effective.[54] Indeed, individuals appear to have a tendency to approach tasks with certain goals in mind. This tendency is a trait known as **goal orientation**. There are two general goal orientations that people have. The first is *learning goal orientation*, which is a tendency to approach tasks with the objective of learning for its own sake. The second is *performance goal orientation*, which involves approaching or avoiding tasks with the goal of gaining favorable judgments or avoiding negative judgments from others. One meta-analysis showed that individuals with high levels of learning goal orientation (vs. those with low levels) tend to perform better on tasks. On the other hand, individuals who tend to approach tasks with the goal of avoiding negative judgments from others are more likely to perform poorly compared to those who don't approach tasks with this mindset.[55]

Consider This...

When you take a class, do you tend to approach it with the goal of learning as much as you can, regardless of the grade you earn? Do you approach the class with the goal of getting a high grade to demonstrate your competence and prove to others (e.g., the professor, classmates) how much you know? Do you approach the class with the goal of getting a high grade to keep from looking like a failure and having people think you are incompetent? Perhaps you do more than one of these—you aim to try to learn a lot *and* get a high grade to look good to others. Based on the research findings described above, how well you perform in the class is related to these goals you set regarding the class. As such, you could benefit from adjusting how you approach classes and other tasks. Why do you think the goal of avoiding negative judgments is related to lower performance, while the goal of learning for its own sake is related to higher performance? What do you think people with those goals might do differently that could be tied to higher or lower performance?

The relationship between goals and performance is also impacted by how committed individuals are to the goals. In general, when individuals are more committed to goals, they are likely to exert more effort and persevere over time. Goal commitment is enhanced when individuals believe they can attain the goal and when such goal attainment is seen as important.[56] In addition, individuals are typically more committed to self-set or participatively-set (vs. assigned) and publicly declared (vs. those kept private) goals. It seems that having a voice in setting the goal and/or announcing a goal to others creates a sense of importance for individuals that isn't there otherwise. Also, when progress toward a goal is impeded by factors outside of one's control, individuals experience decreased enthusiasm and increased frustration, which negatively impacts their goal commitment (as well as their effort and task performance).[57]

Finally, the impact of goals on performance is also influenced by the nature of the task as well as feedback regarding progress toward one's goals. Regarding the nature of the task, research has revealed that goals are more effective for simple (vs. complex) tasks and tasks that are independent (vs. interdependent). As for feedback, research has consistently demonstrated that people who receive feedback on how well they are doing are more likely to accomplish their goals. Feedback is important because it helps individuals know if they need to adjust the level or direction of effort or utilize different strategies to reach their goals.[58] In short, feedback tells us whether our efforts are "on target."

The importance of feedback is not necessarily in the receipt of it, but with what is done with it. Along these lines, researchers have extended goal-setting theory to include the concept of self-regulation. There is not a single theory of self-regulation. Rather, a family of theories share some basic commonalities. **Self-regulation** involves self-monitoring (paying attention to one's goal and its related feedback), self-evaluation (appraising one's goal progress), and self-reactions (responses to the discrepancies between actual and desired goal states).[59] Thus, **self-regulation theories** assert that individuals play an active role in monitoring their own behavior, seeking feedback, responding to the feedback, and forming opinions regarding their likelihood of success in future endeavors. In essence, feedback can provide an "error message" that the individual is off-track in pursuit of their goal. It is at this point that the individual responds to the information provided by the feedback. For example, individuals might alter their behavior to reduce the discrepancy between the current progress toward attaining the goal and the needed progress toward goal attainment. Alternatively, they may alter their goal by making it easier if negative feedback is received or harder if positive feedback is received.[60]

Self-regulation
The process of monitoring goals, evaluating progress, and responding to discrepancies between actual and desired goal states.

Self-regulation theories
Theories of motivation based on the setting of goals and the receipt of accurate feedback that is self-monitored to enhance the likelihood of goal attainment.

There is also evidence that goal setting is effective for groups.[61] Group goals can be more difficult to attain, however, because in many cases, the success of the overall group depends on more than just the success of individual members. A basketball team may set a goal of winning a certain number of games in a season, but its success is determined by more than just the number of points each player scores. Player coordination and integration must also be considered. One player might help the team by passing, another by rebounding, and the others by shooting.

The principles of goal-setting theory generalize widely.[62] Overall, results from an impressive number of studies have demonstrated that setting specific, difficult goals leads to increased performance on a wide range of variables, including quantity, quality, and time spent. The effects of goal setting are long-lasting, and the theory is applicable to individuals, groups, and entire organizations. Nevertheless, it is important to note that goal setting is not without criticism. For example, some have suggested that goal setting can have harmful effects.[63] If a goal is too challenging, it may hurt one's self-efficacy and decrease the individual's motivation. In addition, goal setting may harm cooperation, lead to tunnel vision, and increase risk taking and competition. Along these lines, research has found that increased time pressure from goals made people take more risks, which is potentially disastrous depending on the situation.[64] Furthermore, and in part related to the argument that goals may unduly increase competition, goal setting may lead to unethical behavior. Participants in a laboratory study who were given goals were more likely to distort how productive they were than were participants who were simply asked to do their best, particularly if they just barely missed reaching those goals.[65] Thus, despite its advantages for motivation, goal setting has some potentially deleterious effects.

Job Characteristics Model

Job characteristics model
A model that specifies that a job can be made more or less motivating depending on the levels of five core job dimensions.

Job enrichment
The process of designing work so as to enhance individual motivation to perform the work.

The **job characteristics model** is a framework that suggests that the way in which a job is designed can impact the people within those jobs' motivation levels.[66] Thus, given the proper design of jobs, work can facilitate motivation in individuals. According to this view, there are characteristics or attributes of jobs that are more (or less) motivating than others. The number of these attributes and their identification have been the subject of extensive research. The process of designing jobs to possess those attributes that are motivating is called **job enrichment**.

The job characteristics model is credited with advancing the concept that work itself can be designed to have motivating properties, and that the motivation of individuals is not independent of a work context. Along these lines, the job characteristics model specifies the particular job characteristics (also called *core job dimensions*) that induce motivation:[67]

1. **Skill variety**—the extent to which a job requires a number of different activities, skills, and talents
2. **Task identity**—the degree to which a job requires completion of a whole, identifiable piece of work—that is, doing a job from beginning to end, with visible results
3. **Task significance**—the job's impact on the lives or work of other people, whether within or outside the organization
4. **Autonomy**—the degree of freedom, independence, and discretion in scheduling work and determining procedures that the job provides
5. **Task feedback**—the degree to which carrying out the activities required results in direct and clear information about the effectiveness of performance

The job characteristics model suggests that it is properties of the job or the workplace that foster motivation in people. In short, motivation is not a durable personal attribute or a trait that some people possess more of than others, but rather a variable attribute that can be enhanced if properly and intentionally designed within a work environment. Thus, whereas managers do not always have immediate control over things like culture, technology, or the people within a job, they often do have control over how the job is designed.[68] As such, it is a concrete way in which managers can improve motivation within the workplace.

The value of the core job attributes is embodied in the concept of job crafting. Many jobs permit some degree of latitude on the part of employees as to how the job is performed. The employer is concerned with the outcome of the job (i.e., whether the work gets accomplished), and is less concerned about how the employee structures the process of work. **Job crafting** is the process of allowing employees to make subtle modifications in the boundaries of their tasks and interpersonal relationships to provide more autonomy and feedback. That is, how work is performed reflects an interactionistic perspective between the psychological needs or preferences of individuals and the required output of the job. In essence, job crafting permits some psychological flexibility in how work is performed, and in so doing, can lead to greater psychological

Job crafting
The process of allowing employees to customize their tasks and interpersonal interactions.

Consider This…

The job characteristics model helps explain why many people find assembly line work to be unmotivating. Often, the number of skills needed are minimal and may be purely physical (put two pieces together and send down the line). In addition, it may be unclear to workers how their two pieces that go together are connected to the final product. In some cases, they may not even know what they are making. Is it part of a car? If so, which part? Can you tell from the final product what my contribution was? In addition, does what the person is doing impact other people's lives? They may feel their work doesn't matter, especially if they can't tell what it is they're working on. Typically, assembly line workers don't have a say in how they assemble the pieces on the line and they don't control the speed. Lastly, they may not be able to tell if they have made any mistakes when assembling the pieces, as quality control may happen further down the line. Combined, these examples show that assembly line work is often low on all five core job dimensions. How could you modify the design of an assembly line worker's job to make these job dimensions all high?

health.[69] In short, with job crafting, employees become active architects of their jobs rather than passive incumbents.[70]

Support for the value of the core job dimensions to enhance motivation has been evidenced in many empirical studies. For example, in a meta-analysis of research that examined the five core job dimensions, the researchers found the five motivational characteristics of work explained 25% of the variance in job performance, 34% in job satisfaction, and 24% in organizational commitment.[71] They concluded that the motivating properties of work (and thus how work can be designed to increase motivation) have meaningful implications for important constructs in I-O psychology. Organizations, as a result, need not be passive in their desire to identify motivated employees. By the way they design work, organizations can help achieve the very outcomes they strive to attain.

Worthy of note is that while some jobs can be redesigned to enhance worker motivation to perform them, other jobs cannot be altered in any meaningful way. The motivational characteristics of work reflect the underlying mental demands of work.[72] For example, the job of parking lot attendant is monotonous because it involves little information processing. As such, this job would best be staffed with employees who are content with the lack of stimulation inherent in the highly repetitive nature of the tasks performed. Other jobs, such as air traffic controller, already have a very high level of information processing, and adding to it would only increase stress. There is also the issue of matching abilities and pay to the job characteristics. Jobs characterized by higher scores on the core job dimensions are associated with higher aptitudes and higher pay.[73] Thus, when organizations want to make jobs more motivating, it should be realized that they will need people with more ability, and should be prepared to pay them accordingly.

Synthesis and Application of Work Motivation Theories

It may be overwhelming at this point to consider the number of theories of work motivation that have been presented. It is almost inevitable to ask which theory has the greatest practical value or, perhaps more to the point, which theory will "work" for you (see The Lighter Side of I-O Psychology: *Dear Desperate*). There is no simple answer to this question, but some practical guidelines are available to assist in the decision. In essence, it is a matter of "matching" motivational strategies with varying organizational contexts.[74]

It is important to begin with a general assessment of the situation we face and then systematically narrow our focus. There are three major determinants to human behavior: ability, motivation, and situational factors (including constraints). The most obvious beginning point for our assessment is constraints. Constraints are obstacles or impediments that limit the range of our behavior. It would be our initial goal to remove the constraints, or at the least reduce their limiting effect on our behavior. The lack of a needed piece of equipment (e.g., a computer) is an example of a situational constraint. Gaining access to a computer might readily improve your behavior in a way that "trying harder" might not.

The Lighter Side of I-O Psychology: *Dear Desperate*

Years ago, Paul envisioned an advice column akin to the syndicated "Dear Abby" column that appears in newspapers.[75] He speculated that I-O psychologists could send their burning questions to a columnist who would provide advice. Of course, Paul took a more satirical approach and gave the following example from a "guest advice columnist" to a query.

Dear I-O, I work for a large corporation as an internal change agent. Last week the CEO pulled me aside and said I was to find a way to motivate the entire workforce. Furthermore, I was told my results must be immediately effective. I panicked. I went through every motivation book I could get my hands on, and now I am more confused than ever. Is motivation a trait I should look for in people, should I make people feel inequity to get them to work harder, do I impose a variable schedule of paychecks, do I determine valences, instrumentalities, and expectancies, or what?

Desperate

Dear Desperate, None of the above. Given the urgency of your problem and its magnitude there is only one solution that is viable. The solution has an anatomical origin. Unbeknownst to the medical profession, there is a nerve that runs directly from the buttocks to the brain. A swift kick applied to the buttocks by a supervisor at the start of each workday will most likely achieve the results your CEO desires.

So, there you have it. Perhaps this particular guest advice columnist should pursue endeavors other than providing advice!

If your behavior is not constrained or limited, the next step is to examine whether you have sufficient skills and abilities to engage in the desired behavior. Perhaps you have a computer, but you don't have the knowledge, ability, or sufficient training to use it. If lack of ability does not appear to be a major issue, the problem may have a large motivational component. In short, there is nothing preventing you from engaging in the behavior and you have the ability to engage in the behavior, but you are unwilling or uninterested in doing so.

Once you've determined that the issue is motivational in nature, it is important to consider what the motivational issue may be. If you feel bored or indifferent, the motivational issue is one of arousal. If you are interested and try to succeed but your efforts result in failure, perhaps your energies are being channeled in the wrong direction. If you are going in the wrong direction to achieve your goal, trying harder will not result in success. Alternatively, some successful behaviors require a high intensity of motivation. In this context, "trying harder" would be an appropriate strategy because moderate levels of effort may not be adequate to attain the desired outcome. Finally, there is the persistence dimension to motivation. Some outcomes can be achieved by engaging in short but intense bursts of energy (e.g., getting a good grade by "cramming" the night before the exam). Other outcomes can be achieved only by persistence and dedicated effort over the long haul, not by a sudden burst of effort. Becoming physically fit through proper exercise and diet is an example of an outcome that can be achieved only through persistence.

The motivational theories presented in this chapter do not compete with one another. In addition, one is not necessarily better or worse than another. Rather, they work in combination with each other and are useful in different ways and at various times. For example, if a manager has an unmotivated employee, several of the theories may be used to diagnose the employee's lack of motivation. Equity theory would suggest the issue may be due to perceptions of unfairness. Expectancy theory would suggest the lack of motivation may be a result of not understanding or seeing a connection between one's effort, performance, and/or outcomes, or not valuing the outcomes that are currently in place. Goal-setting theory would suggest the absence of goals, or the presence of goals that are overly easy, vague, unattainable, or to which employees are not committed. Self-determination theory would suggest the issue may lie in the employee not feeling autonomous, competent, or connected to others. The job characteristics model might suggest the job itself has attributes that are demotivating that should be redesigned.

Furthermore, after studying these various theories, one can reasonably ask whether any unifying themes run through them. The biggest unifying theme that cuts across each of the theories is the capacity of the different perspectives to account for the key components of motivation. Each theory provides an understanding of how the direction, intensity, and persistence of behavior is impacted by various factors, whether internal or external to the individual.

In addition, the theories of work motivation that have been presented here can be synthesized in terms of their conceptual proximity to action.[76] Theories of motivation can be examined along a continuum ranging from distal (i.e., distant) to proximal (i.e., near) in terms of the constructs examined. *Distal* constructs such as personality exert indirect effects on behavior. *Proximal* constructs begin with the individual's

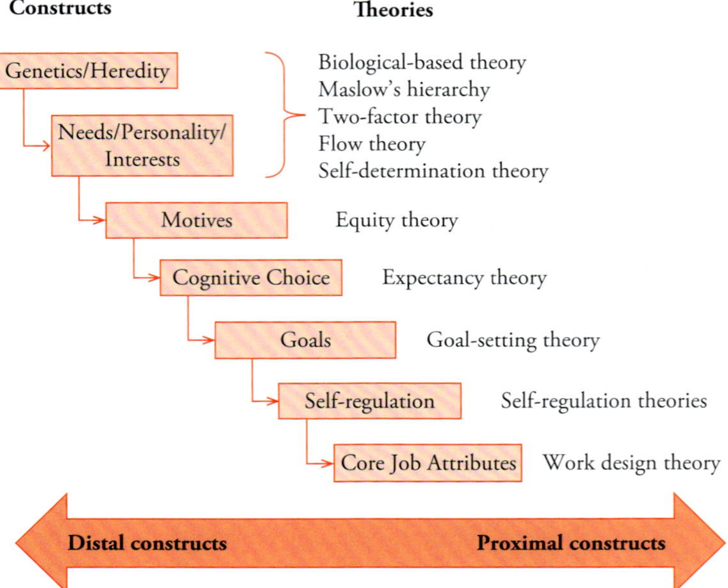

Figure 13-5 *A framework of motivation constructs and theories*

Adapted from "Work Motivation: New Directions in Theory and Research," by R. Kanfer, 1992, in C. L. Cooper and I. T. Robertson (Eds.), *International review of industrial and organizational psychology*, Vol. 7, p. 4. Reproduced with permission of John Wiley & Sons, Inc. via Copyright Clearance Center.

goals and characteristics of the workplace that directly influence behavior. Figure 13-5 portrays the motivation constructs and associated theories arrayed along the distal/ proximal continuum.

As illustrated by the arrangement of the motivational theories, the array of explanations for motivation range from genetic predisposition to the characteristics of jobs. At the extreme distal end is the construct of genetics/heredity. As noted earlier, this view takes the approach that motivation is determined by factors inherent in each of us, and largely outside of our control. Also on the more distal end are Maslow's hierarchy, flow theory, and self-determination theory. Given that Maslow's hierarchy focuses on individuals' inherent needs, it is more distal. Two-factor theory focuses on intrinsic motivation, and because individuals differ in their propensity to experience flow, we put these on the more distal side of the continuum. Self-determination theory is also placed here, given its view that motivation can be influenced by our own intrinsic interests (which is based on whether basic needs are met) in an activity as well as through extrinsic means.

As we progress along the continuum toward proximal constructs, there is increasing reliance on the assumption that people have clear motives for their behaviors and make conscious, deliberate, controllable choices about how much effort they opt to expend. This is the antithesis of a genetic/dispositional orientation toward motivation.

Proximal theories are heavily predicated upon a cognitive explanation for motivation. Equity theory proposes that individuals are rational decision makers who calculate fairness beliefs on the basis of how they see themselves and others treated. Their motivation is a direct result of these cognitive assessments.

Expectancy theory and goal-setting theory are other examples of this orientation. Like equity theory, expectancy theory postulates that individuals are consciously aware of the results or outcomes they wish to attain, perceive relationships between their behavior and attaining those outcomes, and also perceive a relationship between their effort and their behavior. The theory elevates motivation to a conscious choice made by the individual. Furthermore, goal-setting theory offers motivation as an opportunity to engage in self-control or self-regulation. Goal-setting theory proposes that one way we can take some control over our lives is to decide how hard we are willing to work.

As noted earlier, self-regulation theories of motivation are extensions and modifications of goal-setting theory. Self-regulation theories also involve consciously setting goals. Feedback is sought on the degree to which the individual is on target in pursuit of the goal. That feedback is used to modify or maintain the chosen paths of action to goal attainment. The process of self-monitoring or self-evaluation clearly is predicated upon a conscious, rational, deliberate strategy of using information to guide behavior.

Finally, the job characteristics model specifies there are dimensions or components of the job itself that induce motivation. Although there are individual differences with regard to how people will respond to these job characteristics, it is the properties of the work environment that facilitate energized behavior. The job characteristics model contains the most proximal constructs, constructs that in fact can be designed or structured by the organization to induce motivation.

You can think of the more distal theories as those that are more difficult for organizations to influence and the proximal as ones that can be impacted by managers. While this is somewhat true, organizations can in fact influence motivation via the more distal theories. For example, while there is a natural propensity to experience flow, which makes this a more distal theory in the framework, managers can make flow more likely by ensuring there is a balance between the challenge of the task and the skill of the individual, setting clear goals, and providing unambiguous and immediate feedback. Likewise, self-determination theory notes the importance of autonomy, competence, and relatedness. While these three needs tie into intrinsic motivation and are inherent in everybody, they are certainly able to be impacted by organizations (as we considered earlier). Lastly, the more distal theories are likely to influence motivation in part through their impact on the concepts embedded in the more proximal theories. Thus, impacting the distal theories can impact the later theories. For example, ensuring a challenge/skill balance per flow theory will likely result in employees feeling competent (per self-determination theory), which will in turn possibly lead to employees feeling like their effort will result in increased performance (the first link in expectancy theory) and make them more willing to set difficult goals (key according to goal-setting theory). A general summary of the major theories of work motivation discussed in this chapter is presented in Table 13-1.

The Impact of Time on Work Motivation

As can be seen from the various theories, motivation is not a static concept. Instead of existing in a single, unchanging state, it is impacted by the individual, the situation, and an interaction of the two. It is reasonable, then, that time would be a mitigating factor on motivation. For example, motivation is impacted when the time to complete a task is restricted through deadlines. Goals often include deadlines. Short deadlines are typically more difficult to meet than longer deadlines and create a sense of urgency, which can

Table 13-1 *Summary and organizational applicability of work motivation theories*

Theory	Source of Motivation	Organizational Applicability
Biological-based theory	Physiological factors and inherited traits	Limited: Traits that are related to higher motivation can be assessed for personnel selection.
Maslow's hierarchy	Drive to satisfy a prioritized sequence of needs	Limited: Though needs can be assessed and addressed, has limited empirical support.
Two-factor theory	Satisfaction of intrinsic factors within the workplace	Limited: Demonstrates limits of extrinsic rewards, but they remain necessary to avoid dissatisfaction.
Flow theory	Enjoyment of a task that has clear goals, unambiguous feedback, and a match between the challenge of the task and a person's skill level	Moderate: Whereas goals can be clarified and feedback provided, not all tasks can be matched to one's skill level, therefore limiting the extent to which flow can be facilitated.
Self-determination theory	Desire to fulfill the basic needs of autonomy, competence, and relatedness	Strong: Theory provides input into how and when incentives can lead to positive rather than negative effects at work.
Equity theory	Drive to reduce feelings of tension caused by perceived inequity	Moderate-strong: Fairly strong links to organizational justice, but feelings of inequity can be reduced without changes in behavior.
Expectancy theory	Relationship among effort-performance links, performance-reward links, and desired outcomes	Strong: Theory provides a rational basis for why people expend effort, although not all behavior is consciously determined as postulated.
Goal-setting theory	Intention to direct behavior in pursuit of acceptable goals	Strong: Ability to set goals is not restricted to certain types of people or jobs.
Self-regulation theories	Self-monitoring of feedback designed to enhance goal attainment	Strong: Organizations can provide directive feedback to individuals to facilitate goal attainment.
Job characteristics model	Attributes of jobs that can facilitate motivation	Moderate: Not all jobs can be designed to be stimulating or motivating.

increase the commitment that people have toward their goals.[77] Deadlines can also be problematic, however, as they can impair creativity.[78] In addition, people take longer to complete a task when they miss a deadline compared to those who do not set a deadline at all.[79] Lastly, as noted earlier, time pressures may increase risk taking.[80]

Related to the topic of deadlines is the concept of procrastination. Procrastination occurs when people purposefully delay their progress on an activity or project despite knowing they may be worse off by delaying.[81] Rather than focus on a particular task, they opt to focus on other activities (see Social Media and I-O Psychology: *Cyberloafing*). Procrastination has been described as the "quintessential self-regulatory failure" (Steel 2007, p. 65).[82] Outcomes that occur in the distal future are likely to be discounted relative to outcomes occurring more immediately.[83] As such, activities for which an outcome won't occur for a while will likely be put off until later. One meta-analysis found that individuals who had high levels of conscientiousness and self-efficacy were less likely to procrastinate compared to individuals low on conscientiousness and self-efficacy.[84] In addition, research has shown that individuals are more likely to procrastinate when their workloads are heavy, in part because the excessive amounts of work make them fatigued and psychologically detached from their work.[85] A study of over 22,000 people found that procrastination was related to lower salaries, shorter durations of employment, and a greater likelihood of being unemployed.[86]

Social Media and I-O Psychology: *Cyberloafing*

A startling infographic was released in 2012 by Learn Stuff that suggests 6 out of 10 people visit social media sites while at work, and are interrupted on average every 10.5 minutes by instant messages, tweets, and Facebook messages.[87] Moreover, they report it then takes those interrupted employees 23 minutes to get back on task. Furthermore, they estimate that on average each social media user costs their employer $4,452 a year in lost productivity! While having information at our fingertips and access to a massive social network has its advantages, it can clearly also wreak havoc on employee motivation. This act of wasting time at work on the Internet is known as *cyberloafing*.

Cyberloafing can be thought of as an indicator of low work motivation. If individuals are directing their efforts on activities that are unrelated to their work, they are clearly not motivated. Moreover, this appears to be even more the case when people haven't slept well or have had less sleep than usual.[88] Indeed, they found an increased level of cyberloafing on the Monday following daylight saving time. Apparently, having one less hour of sleep than normal was related to more cyberloafing at a national level!

So, besides hoping their employees are well-rested, what can organizations do to decrease cyberloafing and redirect employee motivation back to work activities? One study found that simply having policies in place to deter social media use will likely be ineffective. Instead, individuals will only be persuaded to cease their social media usage when policies are coupled with a belief that they are likely to be caught and they are aware that severe punishments have actually been enforced in the past.[89] However, threatening employees with a severe punishment (e.g., they could be fired) can run the risk of being seen as overly harsh and decreasing morale.

However, making people feel busier without making them feel overwhelmed or overloaded, such as by having them break larger tasks into subtasks, can actually minimize chronic procrastination and enhance productivity.[90]

Planning fallacy The tendency to underestimate how long it will take to complete a task.

Unfortunately, people often underestimate how long it will take for them to complete a task, a phenomenon known as the **planning fallacy**. The estimate that people have for how long an activity will take is more related to when they start the activity than when they finish.[91] So, if they don't think a task will take very long to finish, individuals will delay starting it. In a way, then, predicting that a task will be completed in a shorter period of time can reduce the time it takes to finish a task, simply because less time is allocated for the task.

One strategy found to reduce the planning fallacy is to "unpack" tasks into subtasks.[92] By identifying the various components that comprise the larger task, individuals are much better at accurately predicting how long a task will take. In addition, the planning fallacy appears to be reduced when people take a third-person perspective when imagining a task rather than a first-person view.[93] Taking this third-person perspective makes individuals less likely to be overly optimistic in their plans and forces them to consider potential obstacles that they might not otherwise consider.

Consider This...

Individuals are faced with an onslaught of interruptions throughout the day, from colleagues soliciting input, family members making impromptu visits, or supervisors requesting urgent tasks that divert attention from in-progress work activities. In fact, a study that included all types of interruptions—colleagues, family, social media, etc.—estimated that the typical office worker is interrupted every three minutes and five seconds during the workday.[94] Unfortunately, time is a finite resource, and the impact of lost minutes in a workday when there isn't a lot of free time can be quite detrimental to productivity. It is no wonder, then, that a quick Google search of "work interruptions" yields page after page of websites offering tips on how to minimize, defeat, and avoid them. It seems the common view toward interruptions is that they be avoided at all costs. This is likely an overly simplistic perspective, however, as distractions at work may be a welcomed break from an arduous task, and some interruptions may in fact be warranted and appreciated. Indeed, the fact that individuals often allow themselves to be distracted (e.g., by leaving their personal cell phones on during work hours) and purposefully take breaks from their work (i.e., intentional interruptions/distractions) demonstrates that there are perceived benefits to work reprieves. It would seem, then, that balancing the "good" interruptions with the "bad" ones is key to maintaining productivity. What interruptions do you find good versus bad? What strategies can you use to minimize the bad interruptions?

In addition to unpacking tasks, pacing and spacing are key in the allocation of time and effort to accomplish goals that have deadlines.[95] *Pacing* pertains to how we regulate ourselves in pursuit of a single goal, and *spacing* is how we allocate our time and effort in pursuing multiple goals. It is suggested that individuals create a plan that identifies tasks that are particularly difficult and important, with deadlines to create a sense of accountability and urgency. This strategy fosters sensitivity to the discrepancy between tasks completed and their projected dates of completion, thereby informing us as to whether we are ahead of or behind schedule.

Overqualification and Work Motivation

In 1996, the city of New London, Connecticut declined to interview Robert Jordan, an applicant for the position of police officer. Fearing that the city was discriminating against him on the basis of his age, Jordan filed a complaint. It was then revealed that the decision to exclude him from the hiring process was due to his test scores on a written examination that had been completed earlier in the application process. While this occurs all the time, this situation was unique in that his test scores were deemed too *high* rather than too low. The city claimed this decision was made to prevent likely dissatisfaction and turnover that would result from Jordan being overqualified for the position.[96] The court upheld the decision, noting that although it may have been an "unwise" decision, it was not illegal.

Overqualification occurs when an employee has more knowledge, skills, abilities, education, experience, or other qualifications than are required by (or used on) the job.[97] Whether someone is overqualified can be objectively determined (by comparing their qualifications with the job requirements) or subjectively determined (indicated by their beliefs regarding the match or mismatch of qualifications and requirements). Recall in Chapter 9 that we discussed the topic of person-job fit. An individual who perceives they are overqualified for a job will feel there is a person-job misfit.

Labor market trends may contribute to overqualification of applicants.[98] For example, there is evidence that college graduates who accept jobs that are beneath them in terms of their qualifications may be setting themselves up for a lifetime of lower wages compared to graduates who obtain employment that is aligned with their qualifications.

"The best way to appreciate your job is to imagine yourself without one."

—Oscar Wilde

The issue of overqualification has direct relevance for work motivation. Per equity theory, perceived overqualification implies inequity, in that an individual has assigned more inputs than outcomes to themselves compared to some other referent (whether other employees or set standards). Similarly, overqualification implies that the work and goals related to it will be easy. Given what we know about the importance of challenging goals for motivation, it would be assumed that motivation for such work would be low. This same rationale applies to the importance of the balance between one's skill level and the level of challenge in the task that is described by flow theory. Thus, given these points, overqualification would be expected to lead to lower work motivation and subsequent related outcomes. Research has supported this prediction, demonstrating that perceived overqualification is related to unfavorable job attitudes, greater intentions to quit, a greater likelihood to engage in counterproductive work behaviors, and lower job performance.[99] However, researchers have found that overqualified employees who feel empowered are no more likely to leave than are employees with appropriate qualifications.[100] In addition, overqualified employees may be able to change their appraisal of their person-job mismatch under some circumstances, and subsequently experience fewer negative consequences (see COVID-19 and I-O Psychology: *A Blessing for the Overqualified?*).

COVID-19 and I-O Psychology: *A Blessing for the Overqualified?*

Overqualification can be a frustrating experience for many individuals; they may view their career prospects within their organizations as poor, given they feel their job is inadequate compared to their KSAOs.[101] As noted, this mismatch between their qualifications and their job—whether real or imagined—can lead to many negative outcomes for both them and the organizations in which they are employed.

The COVID-19 pandemic has been considered by some to be a potential blessing in disguise for overqualified employees.[102] This is because of two possibilities for overqualified individuals that could occur with the uncertainties in the economy that accompanied the pandemic.

The first possibility is that the overqualified employees are able to keep their jobs while others lose theirs. At this point, the overqualified person may reassess their person-job misfit and/or take on responsibilities that were previously assigned to someone who is now gone.

Regarding reassessment, the overqualified employee who was spared a layoff may now perceive that what they saw as a person-job mismatch is now more of a fit because, during the crisis, having any job—even one that was "beneath" them—is better than having no job. And, in the evaluation of which employees should stay and which should be let go, the additional KSAOs the overqualified person brought may have become the new "right" qualifications. At this point, the previously-overqualified worker may take on additional tasks and responsibilities that help them realize they are now simply "qualified."

The second possibility during the pandemic is that overqualified employees do, indeed, lose their jobs. At this point, the pandemic may be a blessing in disguise, in that the employees can frame their losses as opportunities to find jobs that fit their KSAOs. Thus, the frustrations that they had regarding the mismatch between their qualifications and their job can be removed and their career prospects made even better following the pandemic than they were before.

These possibilities demonstrate the importance of how we approach situations and cognitively appraise our circumstances. In addition, they show that this particular group may be able to find the silver lining in suboptimal employment situations and economic downturns.

Fun and Games of Work Motivation

Thomas Edison was once quoted as saying, "I never did a day's work in my life. It was all fun." The Wizard of Menlo Park, as one reporter referred to him, was not saying he didn't actually work. One of the most prolific inventors in history, with 1,093 U.S. patents in his name, Edison was most certainly a hard worker. In fact, another one of his famous quotes was, "The reason a lot of people do not recognize opportunity is because it goes around wearing overalls and it looks like hard work." Edison was making the point that so many of us realize, and that is that having fun at work is not only possible, but perhaps necessary for some.

Fun Fact:
January 28th is Fun at Work Day.

What is fun? And how important is fun at work? The extent to which fun is important to people varies by individual.[103] For individuals who deem it important to have fun at work, having fun appears to be related to higher job satisfaction[104] and productivity.[105] Even "goofing off" (when the fun is unrelated to actual work) has been shown to be beneficial, as it allows a break to refresh and re-energize oneself.[106]

Several of the motivational theories we covered help explain why and how having fun can help increase motivation. Enjoyment of one's work is a clear example of an intrinsic motivator, and therefore making work fun would help motivate employees according to the two-factor theory. To the extent that workplace fun involves peers and generates camaraderie with coworkers, employees may have their needs for love and belongingness (per Maslow's hierarchy) and relatedness (per self-determination theory) met. In addition, enjoyment of one's task is a defining characteristic of flow theory.

Gamification
The incorporation of game techniques and mechanics in nongame contexts as a means of enhancing motivation.

Another practical means of enhancing motivation within the workplace that has garnered a lot of attention in recent years is gamification. **Gamification** refers to the use of game techniques and mechanics in nongame contexts. For example, gaming elements such as progress bars, leader boards, badges, levels, points, and virtual goods are layered over existing content in order to engage and motivate individuals within that context.[107] Within training contexts, such elements have been used to increase motivation by making learning fun.[108] Similarly, organizations have applied gamification to their employee referral systems in order to enhance their selection processes.[109] Within the educational realm, researchers have shown that incorporating meaningful gamification into the design and delivery of courses can lead to increased perceptions of learning, engagement, and motivation.[110] In addition, gamification applications and elements, such as allowing employees to customize their avatars and providing interactive feedback, have been shown to satisfy autonomy and competence needs, ultimately increasing intrinsic motivation.[111] In short, integrating various gaming elements into existing content provides feedback, recognition, and the potential for competition, all things that can increase motivation for individuals (see Faces of I-O Psychology: *David R. Earnest*).[112]

Faces of I-O Psychology: *David R. Earnest*

David R. Earnest

Ph.D. The University of Memphis

Visiting Assistant Professor, Austin Peay State University

Research interests: Recruitment, intercultural competencies, and teaching of psychology

Though not directly observable, motivation is the driving force behind our thoughts, actions, and feelings. Whether in the workplace or in the classroom, motivation influences our attention, attendance, performance, and organizational attitudes. As such, motivation, in its many forms, is a fundamental process we must understand to achieve desired results. Historically, motivators used in the workplace have included both extrinsic (e.g., bonuses, promotion, titles, and the corner office) and intrinsic (e.g., accolades, competence, and self-esteem) rewards. The use of extrinsic and intrinsic rewards as motivators is a common practice in the classroom as well. Professors routinely use extra credit, positive feedback, research opportunities, and other methods to engage students and foster academic and professional growth.

Gamification—specifically, meaningful gamification—is a relatively new approach to motivating students through the integration of play into classroom instruction. Play can take on many forms, including providing narrative, role-play, creation, and exploration. Meaningful gamification, in particular, strives to motivate students through play and intrinsic means. As we have all experienced, play is fun, engaging, and motivating. In our study, Dr. Stansbury and I found that by incorporating meaningful gamification (role-play, experience points for completing assignments, and extra credit earned through pro-social organizational behaviors) into an I-O psychology course, students reported greater perceptions of learning, engagement, and motivation than students enrolled in a traditional non-gamification course (Stansbury & Earnest 2017).[113] In our gamification course, students role-played as various parts of an organization (operating core, strategic apex, technostructure, etc.) while working to tackle common organizational problems through a semester-long team project. Student grades and feedback were provided in the form of experience points earned through the mastery of KSAOs and content. Additionally, students were rewarded with extra credit for displaying pro-social organizational citizenship behaviors that facilitated individual, team, and/or classroom performance. This model allowed for the inclusion of the critical meaningful gamification elements of play, exposition, narrative, feedback, autonomy, and social relatedness.

Findings from our research support claims that meaningful gamification can enhance the learning process. Despite similar student grades across meaningfully gamified and traditional courses, students in the meaningful gamification courses rated their learning process more positively and believed that they learned more than traditional course students. In addition, students in the meaningful gamification courses reported developing collaborative, teamwork, problem-solving, and critical thinking skills that are associated with traditional game play. Beyond the classroom, these same playful elements could be included into workplace environments to enhance employee perceptions and skill development. Meaningful gamification provides an avenue for merging the worlds of work and play.

Chapter Review

Key Terms

Biological-based theory of motivation

Genetic Information Nondiscrimination Act of 2008 (GINA)

Maslow's hierarchy of needs

Two-factor theory

Flow theory

Self-determination theory

Equity theory

Equity sensitivity

Expectancy theory

Expectancy

Instrumentality

Valence

Goal-setting theory

Self-efficacy

Goal orientation

Self-regulation

Self-regulation theories

Job characteristics model

Job enrichment

Job crafting

Planning fallacy

Gamification

Questions for Review

1. To what do direction, intensity, and persistence refer regarding motivation?
2. How are intrinsic and extrinsic motivation distinguished?
3. What is the biological-based theory and what findings are in support of it?
4. What is the Genetic Information Nondiscrimination Act of 2008?
5. What is the conceptual basis for Maslow's hierarchy of needs? How might you improve motivation for employees using this theory?
6. What is the rationale behind the two-factor theory? How might you improve motivation for employees using this theory?
7. What is flow? What are the three preconditions for flow?
8. What is the conceptual basis for self-determination theory? What actions can managers take to ensure their employees have the three basic needs of autonomy, competence, and relatedness met?
9. How is equity determined according to equity theory? If employees feel under-rewarded, what are five ways in which they might restore equity? What is equity sensitivity and how does it relate to equity theory?
10. What determines motivation according to expectancy theory?
11. What types of goals are most likely to lead to higher performance?
12. What is self-efficacy? What are four ways to increase one's self-efficacy?
13. What is goal orientation? How are different orientations related to performance?
14. What impacts how committed individuals are to their goals?
15. What is self-regulation? Why and how is feedback important for goal setting and goal attainment?

16. What are the five core job dimensions in the job characteristics model? How can a job be redesigned to increase employee motivation?
17. What is job enrichment? Can jobs be enriched?
18. What is job crafting? Why would an individual want to engage in job crafting?
19. What are the three determinants to human behavior? What should an organization do in response to each of these?
20. What is procrastination? What has been shown to predict procrastination?
21. What is the planning fallacy? What can be done to counteract the planning fallacy?
22. What is overqualification? What is its relevance to work motivation?
23. How is having fun at work supported by motivational theories?
24. What is gamification? How is gamification used in organizations?

CHAPTER 14

Leadership

Chapter Outline

Theoretical Approaches to Leadership
- The Trait Approach
- Faces of I-O Psychology: *Melissa Wolfe*
- The Behavioral Approach
- Social Media and I-O Psychology: *Follow the Leader (on Twitter)*
- The Power and Influence Approach
- The Contingency Approach
- COVID-19 and I-O Psychology: *Leading in a Pandemic*
- Leader-Member Exchange Theory
- Full-Range Leadership Theory
- Authentic Leadership
- Servant Leadership
- The Lighter Side of I-O Psychology: *An Authentic Political Leader?*
- Strategic Leadership
- Implicit Leadership Theory
- Substitutes for Leadership

Points of Convergence Among Approaches

Dark Side of Leadership

Leadership in Teams

Cross-Cultural Issues in Leadership

Diversity Issues in Leadership

Entrepreneurship

Concluding Comments

Chapter Review

Learning Objectives

- Describe the major theoretical approaches to the study of leadership: trait, behavioral, power and influence, contingency, full-range leadership model, authentic leadership, servant leadership, strategic leadership, implicit leadership, and substitutes for leadership.
- Outline the points of convergence among the leadership approaches.
- Describe the dark side of leadership.
- Explain how leadership is evidenced in teams.
- Summarize cross-cultural issues in leadership.
- Discuss diversity issues in leadership.
- Describe the concept of entrepreneurship.

Abraham Lincoln

When you think of leadership, many ideas might come to mind. Your thoughts might relate to power, authority, and influence. Maybe you think of actual people, such as Abraham Lincoln, Barack Obama, Malala Yousafzai, or Mahatma Gandhi. Or perhaps you think of behaviors engaged in by effective leaders, such as giving orders or supporting followers. Maybe you consider whether you are a leader, or will become a leader someday. But what exactly is leadership? And what does it take to be an effective leader? This isn't an easy answer. Yet, as one leadership scholar noted, "Even if we can't precisely define or articulate its substance, we know that 'leadership' is a real, if rare phenomenon. We sense it when it is present, and when it is missing its absence is palpable" (Birnbaum 2013, p. 261).[1]

Malala Yousafzai

The concept of leadership is a fascinating one, and has generated a lot of attention since the dawn of time. With this focus on leadership, there is much known. However, leadership is also a controversial area in which much remains to be learned.[2] This chapter will examine how I-O psychologists have tried to grapple with the multifaceted concept of leadership, particularly as it relates to behavior in the world of work.

Researchers have approached the concept of leadership from many different perspectives. Some researchers have examined what strong leaders are like as people by looking at demographic variables, personality traits, skills, and so on. Without followers, there can be no leaders; accordingly, some researchers have examined leader-follower relationships. Presumably "strong" leaders accomplish things that "weak" leaders do not; thus, other researchers have focused on the effects of leadership. An interesting question addresses contextual effects in leadership—for example, is leadership of a prison more demanding than leadership of a business organization? The situation in which leadership occurs has attracted much attention. Although the diversity of interests in the domain of leadership research expands our basis of understanding, it also creates ambiguity as to exactly what leadership is all about.

It is also a matter of scientific debate whether "leadership" is different from "management" or "administration." Historically and practically, these terms have been used interchangeably. For example, one might readily encounter this sentence: "The leaders of the company manage its resources and are responsible for its administration." A slight variation would be: "The management of the company administers its operations by providing leadership." Are these terms really synonymous? Some researchers think not, believing that management requires administrative oversight but not necessarily the manifestation of leadership. Leadership implies providing a vision of the future and inspiring others to make that vision a reality. As such, a large component of leadership is implicitly future-oriented. In contrast, management and administration refer more to present-oriented activities. According to some scholars, leadership has a heroic, larger-than-life quality that differentiates it from related concepts. Some people believe that individuals can be trained to be managers, but leaders possess unique qualities that cannot be developed in everyone. This debate of whether leaders are born or made is evidenced in some of the theories presented here.

Leadership researchers have also given considerable attention to the question of how important leaders are to leadership. Often the focus is on the traits and behaviors of leaders and how they impact leader emergence and effectiveness. Recent theorists, however, have also questioned the extent to which followers matter, as well as the degree to which the situation the leaders are in matters. Within this area, scholars are seeking to answer the questions of why some leaders seem to be able to effectively lead some people but not others, and why some leaders are effective in some situations but not others. Some scholars, for instance, have described leadership as a process that is inextricably linked to the needs and goals of followers.[3] Casual observation suggests that some people are easier for leaders to work with than others.

In general, leadership is of interest to the I-O psychologist practitioner as well as to the scientist. In fact, leadership is one of the richer areas of interplay between the two; it has had a healthy influx of ideas from both camps. Identifying and developing leaders are major concerns of organizations today. Companies often train their higher-level personnel in skill areas (interpersonal relations, decision making, planning, etc.) that directly affect their performance as leaders. A number of consulting firms exist whose purpose is to enhance the leadership skills of key business personnel. Not surprisingly, the military is also greatly concerned with leadership (see Faces of I-O Psychology: *Melissa Wolfe*). It sponsors a wide variety of research projects that have the potential for enhancing our understanding of this subject. The balance between the theory and practice of leadership is fairly even as a result of this dual infusion of interest.

Theoretical Approaches to Leadership

Numerous theoretical approaches have been developed to explain leadership. In fact, more theories of leadership exist than there is room in this book to present. We focus on the approaches that have been the most dominant historically and currently.

The Trait Approach

Trait approach
A conception that leadership is best understood in terms of traits or dispositions held by an individual that are accountable for the observed leadership.

The **trait approach** is the oldest conception of leadership. Traits are relatively stable characteristics that individuals possess, determined in part by their genetics and/or the interaction between their genetics and the environment. Thus, the trait approach to leadership maintains that individuals' traits or dispositions—such as personality, temperament, and cognitive abilities—are responsible for their leadership performance across situations.[4] These traits do not "cause" behavior, but are labels or terms used to make sense of behaviors.[5] In this view of leadership, effective leaders are described as possessing characteristics (traits) that are associated with leadership talents. The list of such traits is extensive and often includes personality characteristics such as being decisive, dynamic, outgoing, assertive, strong, bold, and persuasive. Various other traits have also been proposed as related to the acceptance of a leader, including being tall, good-looking, poised, articulate, confident, and authoritative. The constellation of traits in a person can prompt others to regard the person as "born to lead" or a "natural leader." Research has revealed that although the presence of such traits is associated with people in leadership positions, their presence does not guarantee success.[6]

Faces of I-O Psychology: *Melissa Wolfe*

Melissa Wolfe

Ph.D. Central Michigan University

Applied Research Psychologist, Center for Army Profession & Leadership, U.S. Army

Research interests: Leadership, counterproductive leadership, leader development, behavioral assessment, culture, diversity, talent management.

Research on command responsibilities and counterproductive leader behaviors has been leveraged in Army regulations, doctrine, and leader development assessment programs to ensure a high standard of leadership within the Army.

The U.S. Army relies on a relatively small number of psychologists to apply knowledge of human behavior to manning, training, equipping, and leadership. I am located with the Center for Army Profession & Leadership (CAPL) and work with a team of ten psychologists with diverse specialties, including I-O, social, human factors, and legal psychology, all serving in a practitioner-scientist mode.

Our team of psychologists is invaluable to the core mission of CAPL, which as an organization is responsible for leadership and leader development doctrine, studies, products, and programs within the Army. We take a scientific approach to leadership and leader development, conducting applied research to identify and develop the most cutting edge and optimal practices to help soldiers increase their effectiveness and succeed in their missions. As applied psychologists, we leverage our research as well as knowledge of other research in the creation and validation of leader development and leadership products, programs, or policies. Our work spans a broad range of projects related to leadership, leader development and assessment, which keeps us energized and helps us keep current on latest trends and research.

I lead our research and assessment division, responsible for leader development and talent management efforts for the Army. Our team of research psychologists manages and monitors the Army's developmental and talent management assessment programs to ensure they function appropriately and achieve their purpose. This includes conducting program evaluations that capture user feedback on their experience as well as analyzing psychometric data from the instruments, to ensure they have sufficient reliability and validity. We also develop, validate, and implement new assessment measures of leadership and leader development techniques to enhance leader self-awareness. We serve as subject matter experts for the Army and frequently evaluate new leadership concepts and leader development tools to ensure their validity, usefulness, and alignment with Army leadership doctrine and regulations. Our efforts help improve the quality of leadership in the Army, resulting in a better-led force and leaders who are effective in the full range of military operations. My work in the Army is incredibly inspiring and fulfilling. CAPL's mission has a very large scope, which means that our work has a direct impact on hundreds of thousands of Soldiers and Army Civilians, helping them to become better leaders and achieve their missions.

An extension of the trait approach to leadership is that certain traits are more (or less) critical for success because of their influence on behaviors of importance to leaders. Classic research identified three motives or needs that drive the behavior of leaders.[7] They are the *need for power*, the *need for achievement*, and the *need for affiliation*. In this sense, requisite leadership traits are represented not as attributes that people possess, but as the underlying basis for why they behave as they do. The need for power is reflected in the desire to influence other people, to control events, and to function in a position of formal authority. The need for achievement is evidenced in the desire to solve problems, attain results, and accomplish objectives. The need for affiliation is manifested in the desire to associate or affiliate with other people in a social context, to provide guidance and support for them, and to derive gratification from helping others to succeed. These three needs are staples in the field of personality, where one's personality is defined from the perspective of the dominant needs that drive leader behavior.

Other research on personality as a basis for explaining leadership has also been conducted. One study revealed that traits such as self-confidence, dominance, and achievement orientation are able to differentiate effective leaders from ineffective ones.[8] In the same study, the researchers found that individual differences such as interpersonal skills, oral and written communication, and decision making similarly predicted leader effectiveness. Other researchers have found that individuals who are high on conscientiousness and extraversion are more likely to be seen as effective leaders, and individuals high in conscientiousness and agreeableness are more likely to improve the performance of groups working under them.[9] These findings together suggest that leaders are both born *and* made.

Consider This...

As we've just established, it seems that leaders are both born and made. This should be a comfort to anybody who desires to be in a position of leadership. The belief that leaders are born (what was called the Great Man Theory) has fallen by the wayside as we continue to find evidence that individuals who were once ineffective leaders have become effective over time through development of their skills and modifications of their behaviors. Indeed, the idea that leaders can be developed forms the entire basis for the leadership consulting profession! If leaders were only born, there would be no use for coaching, since nothing could be done to make an individual a more competent leader. What traits do you have that might make you a good leader? What characteristics do you have that you might be able to develop to be more effective as a leader? Do you think there are any traits that simply cannot be developed and whose lack might hinder one's ability to be an effective leader? Which ones, and why?

In general, the trait approach was dominant in the early days of leadership research, then fell out of favor for a long time, and has again resumed a position at the forefront of leadership research.[10] Traits offer the potential to explain why people seek leadership positions and why they act the way they do when they occupy these positions. It is now evident that some traits and skills increase the likelihood of leadership emergence, even though they do not ensure leadership success. Despite this progress, the utility of the trait approach for understanding leadership is limited by the elusive nature of traits. Traits interact with situational demands and constraints to influence a leader's behavior, and this behavior interacts with other situational variables to influence group process variables, which in turn affect group performance. It is therefore difficult to understand how leader traits can affect subordinate motivation or group performance unless we examine how traits are expressed in the actual behavior of leaders. Emphasis on leadership behavior ushers in the next era of research on leadership.

The Behavioral Approach

Behavioral approach A conception that leadership is best understood in terms of the actions taken by an individual in the conduct of leading a group.

The **behavioral approach** to leadership shifts the focus from traits that leaders possess to specific behaviors or actions in which leaders engage. Whereas the trait approach addresses the extent to which leaders are born, the behavioral approach addresses the extent to which leaders are made.

A major contribution to the behavioral approach to leadership was made in the 1950s by researchers at The Ohio State University. Their research is regarded as classic among efforts to understand the phenomenon of leadership. The researchers asked workers to describe the actions of their supervisors in leadership situations. Based on the results, two critical leadership factors were identified. One relates to how the leader gets work accomplished. This factor was named *initiating structure* and addresses how leaders provide direction or structure to get workers to accomplish tasks. The second factor addresses how the leader interacts on a personal level with workers. This factor was named *consideration* and concerns the people-oriented aspects of leadership (i.e., being considerate of others). Many decades after its original development, researchers are still reporting evidence of its value. For instance, one meta-analysis revealed that initiating structure was highly correlated with leader effectiveness, while consideration was predictive of workers being satisfied with their leader.[11]

Over the years, the behavioral approach was expanded to include other dimensions of leadership besides those originally identified in the Ohio State studies. Research from the behavioral approach has identified specific leader behaviors that are associated with effective leadership. Two such behaviors are *monitoring* the employees' work and *providing clarification* on ambiguous issues. Researchers discovered that although monitoring is an important leadership behavior, it alone does not account for effective leadership. Monitoring an employee's work may identify a problem, but it is also necessary to find a solution to the problem. Likewise, clarifying a work problem by delegating assignments to different employees will be effective only if the employees accept their assignments and have the skills needed to perform them. It became evident that the behavioral approach (i.e., the identification of specific leader behaviors) interacted in complex ways with other factors, such as the skill level of the employees. So, although the behavioral approach identified critical leader behaviors, being an effective leader was more complicated than simply eliciting those behaviors. It was concluded that how a leader exercises power and influence with subordinates is particularly important to understand. This realization led to the next phase of leadership research [see Social Media and I-O Psychology: *Follow the Leader (on Twitter)*].

Social Media and I-O Psychology: *Follow the Leader (on Twitter)*

There is a famous proverb that states, "He who thinks he leads, but has no followers, is only taking a walk." It would seem that social media, and Twitter in particular, may be taking this proverb to a whole new level. Leaders from all over the world have found a powerful platform in Twitter as a way of speaking to, and engaging with, their followers. World leaders such as U.S. President Joe Biden (@JoeBiden) and India's Prime Minister Narendra Modi (@NarendraModi) have millions of followers each. The presidency of Mexico (@ PresidenciaMX) sends an average of 70 tweets a day. Pope Francis (@Pontifex) has thousands of retweets for every tweet he sends. In short, world leaders are active and influential, and sometimes controversial, on Twitter.

Organizational leaders have also begun to find a voice on Twitter. With over three million followers, Arianna Huffington (@ariannahuff), founder of The Huffington Post and founder and CEO of Thrive Global, uses her influence on Twitter to provide tips on enhancing one's well-being and productivity. With close to 2.4 million followers, Aaron Levie (@levie), CEO of file-storing and sharing service Box, tweets about technology, innovation, and his personal insights on current events. Then there's Elon Musk (@ElonMusk), co-founder of SpaceX, PayPal, SolarCity, and Tesla Motors, who reaches out to his 60+ million followers with tweets about the future of space and high-speed travel.

While followers on Twitter are certainly not necessary for a leader to be successful, it is another way in which leaders can broaden their impact and strengthen their influence. Furthermore, and perhaps more the case of how Twitter and leadership are related, the number of Twitter followers may be reflective of one's influence outside of social media. For example, Warren Buffett, Chairman and CEO of Berkshire Hathaway and one of the world's wealthiest people, had only tweeted nine times (with his first tweet being "Warren is in the house"), yet had amassed over 1.7 million followers!

The Power and Influence Approach

Power and influence approach
A conception that leadership is best understood by the use of the power and influence exercised by a person with a group.

The **power and influence approach** is yet another way of conceptualizing leadership. The trait approach focused on what attributes a leader possesses; the behavioral approach focuses on what a leader does. The power and influence approach asserts that leadership is an exercise of power by one person (the leader) over other people (the subordinates). Furthermore, how the leader exercises power is by influencing the subordinates to behave in certain ways. As such, this approach to leadership attempts to understand the meaning of power and the tactics of influence.

Power and Leader Effectiveness. Power manifests itself in many ways. A classic taxonomy proposes five bases of power: reward, coercive, legitimate, expert, and referent (see Figure 14-1).[12]

1. **Reward power.** This is the capacity to offer positive incentives for desirable behavior. To the extent that you can provide something of value to somebody, you have power over them. This could include promotions, raises, vacations, good work assignments, and so on. In general, power to reward an employee is defined by the formal authority inherent in a superior's role.

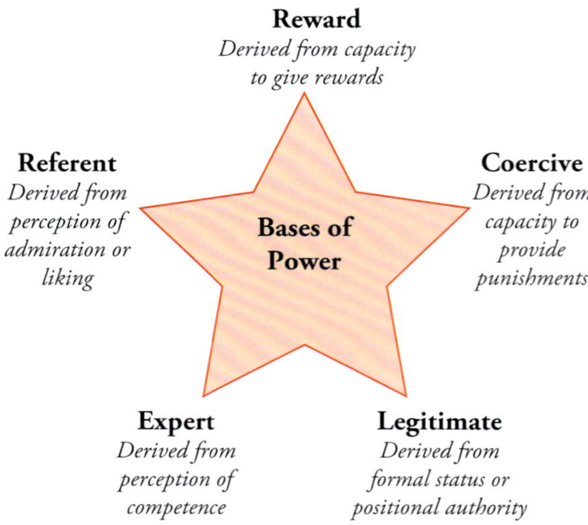

Figure 14-1 *Graphic illustration of five bases of power*

2. **Coercive power.** This is the capacity to punish undesirable behavior. Dismissal, docking of pay, reprimands, and unpleasant work assignments are examples. To the extent that you can sanction others in this way, you have power over them. Like reward power, this capacity to punish is also defined by formal authority and policies inherent in the organization.
3. **Legitimate power.** Sometimes referred to as *authority*, this means that the employee believes the organization's power is justified. Norms and expectations help define the degree of legitimate power. If a boss asks an individual to work overtime, this would likely be seen as legitimate, given the boss's authority. However, if a coworker makes the same request, it might be turned down. The coworker has no legitimate authority to make the request, although the individual might agree.
4. **Expert power.** This base of power relies on expertise that an individual has in a given area. If others rely on you for your knowledge and judgments, you have power. Consultants, for example, are called on to help handle problems because they are seen as experts in certain areas. The source of expert power is the perceived experience, knowledge, or ability of a person. It is not formally sanctioned in the organization.
5. **Referent power.** This is the most abstract type of power. One employee might admire another, want to be like that person, and want that person's approval. That person is a *referent*, someone the employee refers to. The source of referent power is the referent's personal qualities. Cultural factors may contribute to these qualities. Younger people will often defer to an older person partly because age, to some, is a personal quality that engenders deference. Norms can also generate referent power. An employee may wish to identify with a particular group and will bow to the group's expectations.

The second part of the power and influence approach is, of course, influence. The success of an influence attempt is a matter of degree.[13] It produces three qualitatively-distinct outcomes. *Commitment* occurs when an individual (the target) eagerly accepts a request from another individual (the agent) and takes great effort to carry out the request effectively. *Compliance* describes an outcome in which the target is willing to do what the agent asks, but is apathetic rather than passionate about it and makes only a minimal effort. *Resistance* exists when the target is opposed to the request, rather than merely indifferent about it, and actively tries to avoid carrying it out.

Some researchers have proposed that the way power is exercised largely determines whether it results in enthusiastic commitment, indifferent compliance, or stubborn resistance. Effective leaders use combinations of power in a subtle fashion

Consider This...

Margaret Thatcher

Margaret Thatcher, former Prime Minister of the United Kingdom, is quoted as saying, "Being powerful is like being a lady. If you have to tell people you are, you aren't." Considering the five bases of power, how would these apply to Thatcher's quote? Which bases of power are likely to be obvious and easily inferred without needing to be stated? Which ones might need to be voiced? Do you think Thatcher's point holds true when power is considered in this way? Why or why not?

that minimizes status differentials and avoids threats to the self-esteem of subordinates. In contrast, leaders who exercise power in an arrogant and manipulative manner are likely to engender resistance.

Individuals differ in the extent to which they use the various bases of power. Authoritarian managers rely on reward and coercive power. Managers with a participative style rely on expert and referent power. Members of the military frequently rely heavily on the legitimate power inherent in military rank. Leaders' use of expert, referent, and reward power has been shown to be related to higher levels of organizational citizenship behaviors among followers when the followers see the leader as being ethical. If followers perceive the leader as unethical, citizenship behaviors are reduced when referent power is used.[14]

The Contingency Approach

Contingency approach
A conception that leadership is best understood in terms of the actions taken by an individual in the conduct of leading a group.

Fiedler's contingency model
A contingency approach to leadership that suggests a leader's effectiveness will depend on the interaction between their leadership style and the favorability of the situation.

The **contingency approach** to leadership moves away from a focus on the leaders and their behaviors and influence to one that also includes a consideration of the situation in which leadership is occurring. Theories that fall under this approach assume that the leader's traits and behaviors that will be most effective will be contingent upon, or depend on, what is happening in the environment (see COVID-19 and I-O Psychology: *Leading in a Pandemic*). According to contingency theories, it is not enough to simply think about the leader in isolation. Instead, you must consider the leader, the followers, and the situation together.[15]

> **"Leaders constitute the spark, followers the flammable material, and the situation the oxygen—and without an appropriate mix of all three components, nothing of much significance will ever happen!"[16]**
>
> —Barling 2014, p. 292

The most comprehensive leadership theory that takes a contingency approach is **Fiedler's contingency model**.[17] Fiedler proposed that leaders have a relatively fixed leadership style based on their personality. He developed a personality scale that reveals the leader's orientation. The leader is classified as being task-oriented, relationship-oriented, or a mix of the two.

Once the leader's style is identified, it is important to determine the favorability of the situation, as this is what will determine whether the leader's style will be effective or ineffective. The favorability of the situation is determined by three factors:

leader-member relations, the degree of task structure, and the leader's position power. When all three of these are high—the followers respect and trust the leader, the task is clear and structured, and the leader's position grants them clear authority and power—the situation is said to be most favorable. When all three of these are low, the situation is most unfavorable. According to Fiedler's model, task-oriented leaders are more effective under these extreme conditions of favorability and unfavorability. Relationship-oriented leaders are more effective under the intermediate conditions (such as when task structure and position power are low but leader-member relations are high).

COVID-19 and I-O Psychology: *Leading in a Pandemic*

There is evidence that the work context impacts the relationship between leader personality and leader performance.[18] For example, a leader who is effective in an organization that is highly structured with formalized rules and procedures may be ineffective in a loosely-structured and more informal organization. Similarly, an organization with a culture that is risk-averse and demands perfection is quite different from an organization with a culture that encourages risk-taking and views mistakes as learning opportunities. The characteristics needed for a leader to be successful in each organization might be just as different as their cultures.

The COVID-19 pandemic brought challenges to the forefront that many leaders may not have faced before. For example, during the pandemic, there was a greater need to lead individuals who were geographically dispersed. The lockdowns that were in place globally required employees to work remotely. Just as this was a new situation for many employees, their leaders were forced to figure out how to navigate this new landscape. Another new challenge faced by many leaders was the need to focus on the safety and security of their employees. While the well-being of employees is often on the minds of managers, the pandemic raised new concerns related to the workplace environment, policies that were in place for mitigating risks, and strategies for moving forward in a time of uncertainty during the global health crisis. Similarly, many leaders faced resource constraints unlike anything they have previously encountered. As such, they needed to determine how to remain productive amidst disruptions in revenue and the size of their workforce. All of these challenges were in addition to simply managing the uncertainty that organizations worldwide were facing.

What leader characteristics are the most important during a pandemic? Some evidence suggests that a composite of the following characteristics is most predictive of heightened performance during a pandemic:[19]

- Caring, sympathetic, and considerate toward others
- Focuses on getting things finished
- Understands people and why they behave in certain ways
- Capable of persuading others to a point of view
- Involves others in decision making
- Trusts people
- Willing to work around standard procedures to get results when necessary
- Openly expresses feelings and emotions

Of course, these are admirable characteristics regardless of the context. Nevertheless, the data suggest that during a pandemic, they are most likely to produce success for leaders who embody them.

There are several other theories that take a contingency approach to leadership, including one that suggests the effectiveness of a leader depends on the level of confidence and ability of the followers (i.e., situational leadership theory).[20] Another theory suggests a leader should provide different leadership styles depending on the situation, with a goal of helping followers achieve their goals (i.e., path goal leadership theory).[21] The common theme that cuts across all contingency theories is the consideration of the situation when examining leader effectiveness.

The various theories within the contingency approach to leadership have received support over the years. The enthusiasm, however, has diminished and fewer researchers are focusing on this approach. In fact, trait, behavioral, and contingency theories have all received far less attention, making way for newer approaches to leadership.[22] Though these approaches to leadership have waned, the realization that the interaction among leaders, followers, and the situation is important has remained. A more recent approach to understanding situations is to consider the adaptive nature of the leader. Leaders must operate in contexts that are complex, constantly changing, and unpredictable. As such, the current emphasis is on a leader's ability to adapt to a wide variety of situations and circumstances. The idea is that a leader who is more adaptable will be more effective regardless of the context. Thus, it is not that the situation doesn't matter. On the contrary, the point is that the situation *does* matter, but because the situation is continuously changing, the leader needs to be ready and able to adapt as the need arises.

Leader-Member Exchange Theory

Leader–member exchange theory A theory of leadership based on the nature of the relationship between a leader and members of the group being led.

Another approach to leadership is one that considers the relationships between leaders and their followers. According to **leader–member exchange theory** (LMX), leaders differentiate their followers in terms of (1) their competence and skill, (2) the extent to which they can be trusted (especially when not being watched by the leader), and (3) their motivation to assume greater responsibility within the unit.[23] Followers (termed "members" in this theory) with these attributes develop high-quality relationships with the leader and become part of the *in-group*. In-group members go beyond their formal job duties and take responsibility for completing tasks that are most critical to the success of the work group. In return, they receive more attention, support, and sensitivity from their leaders. Members who do not have these attributes are in the *out-group*; they do the more routine, mundane tasks and have a more formal relationship with the leader. Leaders influence out-group members by using formal authority, but this is not necessary with in-group members. Thus, leaders use different types and degrees of influence depending on whether the follower is in the in-group or out-group.

Regarding the antecedents of LMX relationship quality, relationship quality is higher when there is perceived and/or actual similarity between the leader and follower, when leaders are seen as being fair, and when members perform well and are competent.[24] Each of these factors aids in the development of trust, which is key for high-quality relationships.

Research has also revealed how LMX theory is useful in explaining dimensions of organizational behavior. One meta-analysis showed that strong, high-quality LMX relationships are related to higher job satisfaction, organizational commitment, and task and citizenship performance, and to lower intentions to leave the organization.[25] Researchers have also found that when there is a strong LMX relationship, employees trust their manager and offer less resistance to organizational change.[26] Similarly, the stronger the LMX relationship, the greater the employee's commitment to the psychological contract that bonds the individual to the organization.[27] In-group members even appear to get more leniency from leaders when they misbehave, with leaders viewing rude in-group members as less deviant compared to when outgroup members are rude.[28]

It is important to consider how other people in the organization play a role in the exchange relationships between leaders and members. Each exchange relationship is a bi-directional lens through which both parties see each other in the work context.[29] Because employees are situated within an organizational hierarchy (with others above and below them), each relationship is its own lens. Thus, an individual within an organization views others through multiple lenses, like a kaleidoscope. Along these lines, researchers have found that individuals compare their LMX relationship with the relationships that the leader has with other individuals. When people feel they have a better relationship with their leader than their teammates have with the leader, they are more confident in their ability to perform their job, which leads to better job performance, more citizenship behaviors, and higher job satisfaction.[30] In addition to teammates' LMX relationships having an impact, the presence of multiple leaders is also an important consideration. When an employee has two leaders, each exchange relationship exists with the other in mind.[31] When the exchange relationships are aligned with one another, the member is more satisfied and less likely to leave the organization. When they are misaligned, however, the member is less satisfied and more likely to quit.

More than any other theory of leadership, LMX emphasizes the importance of the relationship between each leader and each follower. Scholars have also begun to examine the relationships between leaders and their bosses, and the impact that those relationships have on the leaders' followers. The relationship between the leader and that leader's boss is termed the leader-leader exchange (LLX). Studies have shown that when LLX relationships are of high quality, leaders are more empowering with their followers[32] and are better able to develop high quality LMX relationships with followers.[33] Lastly, strategic alliances are formed by leaders with individuals within and outside of the organization that are mutually beneficial to fulfillment of the leader's and the organization's goals.[34] Thus, exchange relationships exist beyond just the leader and followers, to include the leader and that leader's peers, supervisors, and other internal and external constituents.

Full-range leadership theory
A perspective that identifies the full spectrum of behaviors that comprise leadership, including transformational, transactional, and non-leadership behaviors.

Transformational leadership
A conception that leadership is the process of inspiring a group to pursue goals and attain results.

Full-Range Leadership Theory

The next leadership theory addresses the distinction between a manager and a leader perhaps better than any other leadership theory. The **full-range leadership theory** consists of three separate groups of behaviors that form the full spectrum of leadership.[35] At the highest end of the spectrum is **transformational leadership**, which is a view of leadership that involves influence by a leader over subordinates, but the effect of the influence is to empower subordinates, who then also become leaders in the process of transforming the organization. According to this perspective, a successful leader transforms the members into believing in themselves, generating confidence in their respective abilities, and elevating their self-expectations. In short, a transformational leader's success is indexed by the group's capacity to function at a much higher level of performance than previously evidenced. A transformational leader unleashes the power and harnesses the talent within a group to help it be successful. Understanding this conversion process is the object of research on transformational leadership.

Transformational leaders make followers feel more aware of their own importance and value to the success of the group.[36] Followers are expected to sublimate their self-interests for the overall benefit of the group. The desire to be trusted and respected by the leader prompts the group to respond with greater effort and commitment to achieve a common goal.

Transformational leaders behave in ways to achieve superior results by using one or more of the five components of transformational leadership:[37]

- **Attributed charisma.** The term charisma comes from the Greek word *kharisma*, meaning "gift of grace" and implies that a charismatic leader possesses a divinely inspired gift. Followers see leaders as powerful and charming, able to inspire devotion. There is a clear emotional element inherent in charisma. Effective charismatic leaders can manipulate and use their environments in ways that generate an emotional reaction in their followers.[38] For example, a leader may stage a presentation by giving a speech in front of a building that has symbolic significance for the followers. Thus, whether a leader is charismatic or not is more determined through gut feelings

Consider This...

Kenny Nguyen

The use of props and "staging" of activities by leaders has been around for ages. When Richard Nixon was Vice President of the United States, he was accused of inappropriately accepting gifts from people who wanted Nixon to use his influence on their behalf. In his defense, Nixon appeared on television and explained that he returned all the gifts he had received, except one—a black and white cocker spaniel puppy that his six-year-old daughter had named "Checkers," and that his family had come to love as their family pet. The talk by Nixon became long remembered as "Nixon's Checkers speech." As another example, Kenny Nguyen, CEO of ThreeSixtyEight, gave a TEDx Talk in which he spoke about the art of saying no. In his talk, he refers to the "sword of yes" and the "shield of no" and picks up a sword and a shield, thereby bringing his points to life. Earl Butz, Secretary of Agriculture under President Nixon, appeared before a congressional committee to explain the financial budget of the Department of Agriculture. While seated before the committee, Butz pulled a loaf of sliced bread out of a paper bag. He proceeded to stack the slices in various sized piles, demonstrating symbolically how the Department of Agriculture budget was allocated to various directives. In these examples, leaders used a dog, sword and shield, and loaf of bread to explain issues of importance. The props were remembered long after people had forgotten the content of the speeches. What important events do you recall where props and staging were used? What makes these events memorable?

and emotional ties than through logical decisions and systematic thought processes. Worthy of note is that there is a separate theory of leadership entirely surrounding charismatic leadership that states that followers impart charisma onto the leaders, at times even romanticizing the leader.[39] Given the theoretical linkages of charismatic leadership and transformational leadership,[40] we do not cover charismatic leadership separately in our discussion of approaches to leadership.

- **Idealized influence**. Transformational leaders behave in ways that make them role models for their followers. Unlike charisma, their influence is driven by how followers attribute their beliefs and values rather than by their charm and personal appeal. While attributed charisma refers to followers' perceptions of the leader as being larger than life, idealized influence refers to the behaviors leaders engage in that reflect confidence and allow them to be admired, respected, and trusted. In essence, this involves "walking the talk," or backing up one's values and beliefs with actions that accurately reflect them.
- **Inspirational motivation**. Transformational leaders behave in ways that motivate and inspire those around them by providing meaning and challenge to their followers' work. Leaders get followers involved in envisioning attractive future states; they create clearly communicated expectations that followers want to meet.
- **Intellectual stimulation**. Transformational leaders stimulate their followers' efforts to be innovative and creative by questioning assumptions, reframing problems, and approaching old situations in new ways. These leaders encourage their followers to question the status quo and challenge their own assumptions. New ideas and creative problem solutions are solicited from followers, who are included in the process of addressing problems and finding solutions.
- **Individualized consideration**. Transformational leaders pay special attention to each individual follower's needs for advancement and growth by acting as a coach or mentor. Followers and colleagues are developed to successively higher levels of potential. Individual differences in needs and desires are recognized, and the leader's own behavior demonstrates acceptance of these differences.

Transactional leadership
A conception that leadership involves providing rewards and punishments in exchange for certain behaviors of followers.

The next set of leadership behaviors in the full-range leadership theory include transactional behaviors. **Transactional leadership** consists of managerial and supervisory behaviors that focus on providing rewards and punishments to enact change in followers. There are clearly-defined expectations for both leaders and followers, with associated consequences. Three components comprise transactional leadership:[41]

- **Contingent reward**. Transactional leaders engage in exchange relationships with their followers. When employing contingent reward behaviors, they provide rewards if followers perform in ways that are desired. The rewards can be economic (e.g., bonuses), emotional (e.g., praise), or tangible (e.g., a certificate). Although this form of leadership is fairly effective, it is considered less effective than transformational leadership.
- **Active management-by-exception**. The exchange relationships that transactional leaders use can also be based on punishments, as in the case of active management-

by-exception. When engaging in these behaviors, leaders actively search for mistakes and deviations from the rules, and take corrective action in the form of punishments as they find the problems.

- **Passive management-by-exception**. This is the lowest form of transactional leadership. Similar to active management-by-exception, leaders provide punishment for undesirable behaviors. These leaders are passive, however, rather than active in their pursuit of problems. They wait for issues to arise before intervening.

In essence, transactional leadership is a "carrot and stick" approach, such that contingent reward is the "carrot" used for reinforcing desirable behaviors and management-by-exception is the "stick" that punishes deviations. These behaviors are derived from one's formal position and as such are perhaps best thought of as management, not leadership per se.[42]

Laissez-faire leadership
A form of non-leadership in which managers deflect all responsibility and leave followers on their own.

This brings us to the lowest end of the full-range leadership spectrum, **laissez-faire leadership**, which is essentially the absence of leadership. The term "laissez faire" literally means "allow to do." Laissez-faire leaders are hands-off with their followers, allowing others to make decisions and abdicating their own authority. While laissez-faire leaders are not micro-managers and can't be accused of being overly involved, employees are not always fond of them. Not surprisingly, employees tend to be less satisfied with their supervisors when they fail to reward good performance or fail to punish poor performance.[43] Furthermore, such passive leadership is related to lower employee mental health and overall work attitude, in part because employees experience greater ambiguity and conflict about what they are supposed to do, as well as heightened psychological work fatigue.[44]

Consider This...

Warren Buffett

Laissez-faire leadership is the most inactive form of leadership, often considered to be non-leadership. Indeed, a failure to provide direction to followers and the avoidance of responsibility could be poor management. Yet, this is a leadership style that has been used by some arguably-effective leaders.[45] For example, Martin Van Buren and Herbert Hoover, former U.S. Presidents, were known to be hands off in their approaches, trusting the talents, skills, and experience levels of the people who surrounded them. Similarly, Queen Victoria ruled the United Kingdom during a time when the idea that "heaven helps those who help themselves" was popular, and along these lines she tended to step in only when necessary. Some successful business leaders have also been more hands off. Warren Buffett, American business magnate, for example, often only intervened to fix problems, and even then, he was fine with letting mistakes occur so his people could learn from them. Why do you think some individuals are able to be successful using this style of "non-leadership" while others are deemed ineffective? How would you feel about having a laissez-faire leader? How comfortable would you be as a leader just sitting back and trusting your team to work without your guidance?

In a summary of the literature on the full-range leadership theory (see Figure 14-2), researchers cited a considerable number of studies demonstrating that transformational leadership is consistently related to employee satisfaction and performance across a variety of situations and cultures.[46] Moreover, one study showed that transformational leadership behaviors had a much stronger effect on performance and citizenship behaviors of agents in an insurance company than did transactional leadership behaviors.[47] Not surprisingly, the three lowest forms of leadership according to the full-range leadership theory—active and passive management-by-exception and laissez-faire leadership—are largely ineffective.

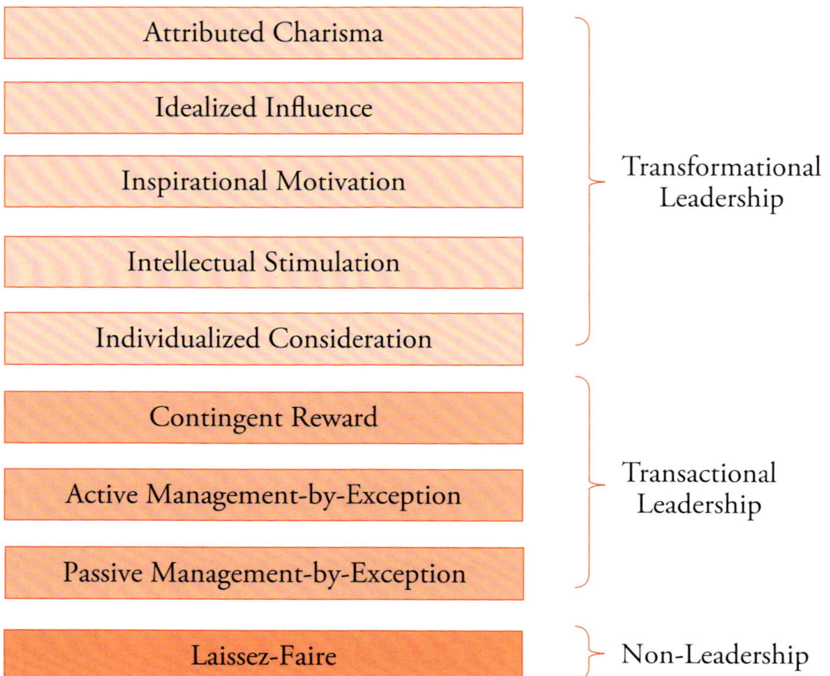

Figure 14-2
Full-range leadership theory

Considering the amount of research in support of transformational leadership, three points should be made. First, transformational leadership builds on transactional leadership.[48] As such, leaders who engage in both types of behaviors are typically more effective than those who only engage in only one set of behaviors. Second, leaders don't have to engage in all forms of transformational behaviors at *all* times. Rather, to be outstanding, they must ensure they do so at the *right* time. Third, as is often the case, there are some potential downsides for leaders who engage in transformational leadership behaviors. Specifically, there is evidence that transformational leadership behaviors can lead to increased emotional exhaustion and turnover intentions for leaders, particularly when those behaviors are directed at followers who are lower on conscientiousness and/or competence.[49] These detrimental consequences appear to outweigh the benefits that followers and the leader receive. As such, caution is needed when choosing when and whether to engage in transformational leadership behaviors.

Authentic Leadership

Authentic leadership
A conception that leaders who are self-aware, transparent in their relationships with others, unbiased in their decision making, and internally moral will be more trusted, and therefore more effective.

A newer leadership perspective that has its roots in transformational leadership, positive psychology, and ethics is that of **authentic leadership**. This theory focuses on leaders being genuine in their thoughts and actions. Authentic leadership has four main components:[49]

1. **Self-awareness:** Leaders must be aware of their own strengths and weaknesses and how their views of themselves compare to views others have of them. Without self-awareness, a leader can't be "true to oneself," which is key to being authentic.[51]
2. **Relational transparency:** Authentic leaders present themselves to others as they truly are, rather than as fake portrayals of themselves. This means that they don't try to appear better than they really are, but instead share their doubts, insecurities, and vulnerabilities alongside their strengths and accomplishments. In short, they are open and honest with their followers.
3. **Balanced processing:** Authentic leaders analyze information and come to decisions in very unbiased ways. To obtain a balanced view of issues, they solicit information from others, even if it is unlikely to go in their favor. In doing so, they can maintain high levels of integrity in their decision making.
4. **Internalized moral perspective:** A strong internal moral compass is a key aspect of authentic leaders. They think and behave in accordance with a value system that is guided by internal standards. Because of their highly-developed value structures, authentic leaders are ethical, even in the most ethically-challenging situations.[52]

Leaders vary in terms of their level of authenticity, with some being very authentic and others being very inauthentic. Fortunately, leaders can be developed to become more authentic.[53] By engaging in such activities as self-reflection and discussion about case studies involving moral dilemmas, leaders can become more sensitive to the consequences of their decisions and more confident in their ability to make moral decisions. Such training would help prepare leaders to proactively handle ethical crises within their organizations.[54] It may not matter for future generations though. Some scholars have proposed that because millennials tend to focus on extrinsic rewards, they may be less interested in the intrinsic outcomes that are offered by authentic leaders.[55] Thus, it may be that authentic leadership will be less effective for future generations of workers. It is also unclear whether authentic leadership is ideal for all occupations (see The Lighter Side of I-O Psychology: *An Authentic Political Leader?*).

Servant Leadership

Servant leadership
A conception that leadership involves putting the needs of followers ahead of one's own needs.

Another approach to leadership that has overlap with transformational, authentic, and LMX leadership theories is **servant leadership** theory.[56] Servant leaders place a strong emphasis on ethics and relationships between themselves and their followers. They put the interests of followers ahead of their own and strive to develop employees, not simply to help the organization but to truly help the employees.

Servant leaders focus on empowering followers and helping them grow and succeed.[57] In addition, they care about the communities in which they reside, not just their own organization and its employees.

The Lighter Side of I-O Psychology: *An Authentic Political Leader?*

An important aspect of being an authentic leader is being honest, both to oneself and to one's followers. Is it possible to be honest and effective in all situations? Maybe not. The American humorist Mark Twain once quipped, "An honest politician is an oxymoron." Research shows that individuals who are more willing to engage in "cheap talk" and renege on their campaign promises are more likely to be elected. In 2014, a grassroots coalition, RepresentUs, ran a satirical political campaign to raise awareness of corruption in the political system. The campaign put forward Gil Fulbright, a fake contender in the Kentucky Senate race, the most expensive Senate race at the time, costing over $100 million. Campaign ads showed Fulbright being exceptionally honest, with such statements as, "People of Kentucky, you deserve complete honesty, so here it is. I don't care about you. Unless you are a donor, a lobbyist who can write a big fat check, the result that you get from voting for me is negligible."[58] Fulbright even went so far as to say he'd be willing to change his name for the right price, offering several possibilities including "Phillip Mamouf-Wifarts." Yikes! Maybe honesty isn't always the best policy?

Servant leaders' selfless focus on their followers appears to result in positive outcomes. For example, an examination of 815 employees and 123 supervisors revealed that servant leadership was related to employees: (a) having more commitment to the supervisor, (b) feeling more confident in their abilities to perform well, (c) having higher justice perceptions, and (d) believing there was a greater focus on customer service within the organization. In turn, these perceptions and beliefs were related to more organizational citizenship behaviors.[59] Thus, it appears that servant leaders entice their followers to go above and beyond normal task requirements by influencing employees' attitudes and beliefs.

The reason servant leadership positively influences organizational outcomes is because servant leaders focus on the employee's development.[60] This emphasis on the employee helps fulfill the employee's need for autonomy, relatedness, and competence. With these needs fulfilled, employees have heightened task performance as well as organizational citizenship behaviors.

Servant leadership also appears to influence teams and organizations as a whole in addition to individuals. For example, research has found that servant leadership is related to groups believing they are highly capable, which in turn is related to higher levels of group performance.[61] In addition, in an examination of servant leadership behaviors of chief executive officers (CEOs), researchers found that CEO servant leadership predicted firm performance. That is, CEOs who focused their attention on the long-term prosperity of their firms and the development of their employees achieved superior financial results.[62] It seems that servant leaders, by showing that they care more about the organization's success than their own personal success and demonstrate that they value honesty more than profits, promote a benevolent climate that generates employee commitment and makes employees want to perform better.

Strategic Leadership

Strategic leadership
An approach to leadership that focuses on leaders in the upper echelon of organizations; aimed at flexible, adaptable, forward thinking that creates and furthers organizational goals.

Thus far, the approaches to leadership have dealt with leadership *within* organizations. Another approach to leadership, termed **strategic leadership**, is one that focuses on leadership *of* organizations.[63]

Strategic leadership is a leader's ability to anticipate and visualize future needs, remain flexible amidst changing circumstances, think strategically, and collaborate with others to initiate changes.[64] There are five fundamental ways in which strategic leaders, or those in the upper echelon of the organization such as the CEO and top management teams, are different from leadership at lower levels of the organization:[65]

1. They set the strategy for the organization.
2. They engage in more boundary-spanning activities. Boundary-spanning activities are any communication and coordination activities that connect typically disconnected groups, such as forming a connection between a finance team and a marketing team that do not normally interact.
3. They create organizational structures and policies (vs. merely work within those structures).
4. They indirectly affect lower-level leaders through hiring practices, performance appraisals, and so forth.
5. They serve a symbolic role, especially in large organizations.

Research on strategic leadership is somewhat more integrative than other approaches to leadership. Namely, rather than rely on a separate theory, researchers in this area tend to integrate principles from transformational, transactional, charismatic, situational, and leader-member exchange theories. For example, transformational leadership has an implicit focus on leading change efforts. Strategic leadership also focuses on change, but with a greater emphasis placed on the need to think and act strategically, with a tactical view that considers environmental trends and alignment between the organization and its surroundings.

As an example of research on strategic leadership, using meta-analytic data combined with sophisticated modeling techniques, researchers found that there are several paths to heightened performance. Specifically, shorter CEO tenure combined with top management teams with longer tenure, greater diversity, and larger numbers are related to larger boards of directors, which is subsequently related to higher firm performance.[66]

Implicit Leadership Theory

Implicit leadership theory
A conception that leadership is a perceived phenomenon as attributed to an individual by others.

A radically different view of leadership than what has been presented thus far is that leadership exists only in the mind of the beholder, usually the follower. It may be that "leadership" is nothing more than a label we attach to a set of outcomes; that is, we observe a set of conditions and events and make the attribution that leadership has occurred or exists. Unlike the previous theories presented, **implicit leadership theory** regards leadership as a subjectively-perceived construct rather than an objective entity. Implicit leadership theory is also referred to as the *attribution theory of leadership* or *social information processing theory*.

Individuals hold conceptions of prototypical leaders (that is, what they think leaders are like) and then evaluate actual leaders according to their conceptions.[67] People judged as "good" leaders are likely to be those whose actions and demeanors conform to the conception we hold. Thus "effectiveness" in leadership is determined not objectively, but through the confirmation of expectations. In one study, supervisor weight was negatively related to the subordinate's perception of the leader's competence, suggesting weight plays a role in people's perception of what constitutes a good leader.[68] Some scholars have concluded that leadership has assumed a heroic, larger-than-life quality in people's minds—a kind of "romance of leadership." Along these lines, leadership may serve a symbolic role, causing people to feel assured and confident that the fate and fortune of an organization are in good hands.[69] Thus, leadership may not account for as much of an organization's success as we believe, but "leadership" has a symbolic value in producing subordinate support, which may then paradoxically produce organizational effectiveness.

Leadership may be best understood from the perspective of followers.[70] Leadership is viewed as a process through which one person, the leader, changes the way followers envision themselves. A follower-centered perspective of leadership is deemed most insightful because it is through followers' reactions and behaviors that leadership attempts succeed or fail. It is proposed that followers regulate their own behavior because of the meaning derived from leadership acts. Thus, a useful way to gauge the effectiveness of leaders is through the self-identity of followers. Followers tend to regard effective leaders as sensitive, intelligent, dedicated, and dynamic (and not manipulative, domineering, or pushy).[71] It may be beneficial to train leaders to present themselves as followers want to see them.

Implicit leadership theories held by leaders and followers can influence the quality of their leader-member exchange relationship.[72] Specifically, when leaders and followers hold similar views regarding what constitutes leadership, they view each other more positively, which leads to a higher-quality exchange relationship.

Substitutes for Leadership

Employees seek both guidance and good feelings from their work settings.[73] Guidance usually comes from role or task structuring; good feelings may stem from any type of recognition. Although these factors must be present, they do not necessarily have to come from a superior. Other sources may provide guidance and recognition as well. In these cases, the need for formal leadership is lessened. This premise is the basis for **substitutes for leadership** and highlights the point that a leader is merely one vehicle for providing guidance and good feelings. Indeed, some organizations have abandoned formal supervisory positions as increasingly more work is performed by employees organized into teams (as was discussed in Chapter 10). Leaders and substitutes for leadership can simultaneously affect work groups.[74] For example, leaders can create less need for formal supervision by carefully selecting employees who can function relatively independently. Such substitutes have very important effects on the work group, but they do not diminish the role of the leader. In fact, numerous researchers have reached similar conclusions—that substitutes for leadership cannot fully replace the role of the leader.[75]

Substitutes for leadership
The conception that there are sources of influence in an environment that can serve to act in place of, or be substitutes for, formal leadership.

There has been a good deal of support for the substitutes for leadership theory. In an early study, researchers examined four environmental sources from which employees get structure and direction in how to perform their work: the job itself, technology, the work unit, and the leader.[76] The authors found that only when the first three sources of structure were weak did the influence of the leader strongly affect employees. It seems that employees can derive typical leader qualities (that is, structure and direction) from inanimate sources in their environments, and that leadership functions need not be associated with someone in authority. Heightened mindfulness, or being more attentive and aware of one's surroundings, can substitute for low levels of transformational leadership in fostering intrinsic motivation and performance.[77] Similarly, high levels of learning goal orientation (discussed in Chapter 13) can serve as a substitute for transformational leadership in promoting organizational citizenship behaviors.[78] There is also evidence that some individuals can direct themselves, a concept called *self-leadership*. When individuals have a low need for leadership, they appear to be more engaged and receive higher performance ratings when they engage in self-leadership. Conversely, when employees have a high need for leadership, transformational leadership from one's leader appears to be more strongly related to employee engagement and performance.[79] In summary, the research on substitutes for leadership suggests that leadership can be thought of as a series of processes or functions that facilitate organizational and personal effectiveness. These processes or functions need not necessarily emanate from a person in a formal leadership role, but may be derived from characteristics of the work being performed by the group members.

Points of Convergence Among Approaches

Despite the profusion of leadership approaches and related empirical findings, there is some convergence in the findings from different lines of leadership research. There appear to be three consistent themes.[80]

Importance of Influencing and Motivating. Influence is the essence of leadership. Leaders are heavily involved in influencing the attitudes and behaviors of people, including subordinates, peers, and outsiders. The array of influence tactics available to a leader are all designed to induce followers to pursue selected goals and objectives. Leaders' own personal needs and how they use power affect the type of influence attempts they make. Skillful leaders provide an appealing vision for the future and inspire people to pursue it.

Importance of Maintaining Effective Relationships. Leaders recognize the importance of cooperative relationships among people and are skillful in facilitating successful ones. Organizations operate more effectively when employees work within an environment of trust, loyalty, and mutual respect. Employees are more satisfied with leaders who demonstrate concern for their needs and values. Alternatively, leaders who regard organizations as simply arenas for their own self-enhancement are likely to alienate the very people who can make the organization be successful.

Importance of Making Decisions. Decisions are made in the present, but their consequences occur in the future. A leader who makes good decisions is skillful in shaping the future. Such talent is the hallmark of a good leader. Several of the traits and skills that predict leadership effectiveness are relevant for decision making. Leaders with extensive technical knowledge and cognitive skills are more likely to make high-quality decisions. These skills are important for analyzing problems, identifying causal patterns and trends, and forecasting likely outcomes of different strategies for attaining objectives. It is typically impossible for one leader to possess all the information needed to make an informed decision. Consequently, the ability to obtain relevant information, the skill to know the differential importance of the information as it relates to a given decision, and the capacity to weigh various decision options are all critical leadership skills. Self-confidence and tolerance for ambiguity and stress help leaders cope with the responsibility for making major decisions based on incomplete information.

Dark Side of Leadership

Leadership theories have traditionally examined factors that enhance leadership through their presence, such as certain traits, behaviors, or relationships with followers. These views have been considered the "bright side" approach to leadership. A starkly different view that has been steadily gaining momentum by leadership scholars is the "dark side" approach, which examines factors that can make leaders more effective through their *absence*. It is not simply the lack of "bright side" features (e.g., charisma, monitoring behaviors) that can make a leader destructive. Instead, the dark side of leadership involves the presence of factors that actively compromise and chip away leadership, making it undesirable.

In Chapter 5 (in the discussion of the dark triad), we noted that some leaders may be "snakes in suits," or exhibit high levels of psychopathy.[81] Similar to this, there is evidence that narcissists tend to rise within organizations, given their confidence levels and willingness to step on others to get ahead. Given the negative effects of these dark personality traits (even if the effects are small in some cases[82]), it should be easy to see that not all leaders may act in the best interests of their followers. Indeed, there can be a "dark side" to transformational leaders.[83] Because they have excellent social skills, at times to the point of being charming, they are readily liked by their followers. But sometimes lurking behind the mask of likability is a person with pronounced adjustment problems, such as psychopaths and narcissists. Only after these people fail in their leadership roles do we ever learn of their maladjustment, which was cleverly concealed by their ability to manipulate people to like them.

Whether it is because of some personality trait or maladjustment, one thing is clear: some leaders are toxic, creating stress and wreaking havoc on those who refuse to follow their directives. In Chapter 11, we discussed workplace bullying and noted that the bully can be one's leader. The issue of abusive supervision (ongoing hostile verbal and nonverbal behaviors) has attracted much interest among researchers in recent years.[84] One reason for this increased focus is because of the level of devastation that such leaders can cause.[85] For example, one meta-analysis found that employees exposed to abusive supervision were less satisfied with and committed to their jobs, and had greater work-family conflict and depression.[86] Similarly, employees with abusive supervisors appear to have low emotional attachment with their organization and tend to engage in few organizational citizenship behaviors.[87]

Unruly, abusive, and unethical leaders can also be detrimental to the leaders themselves, as well as result in potential legal troubles for the organization. One study showed that abusive leaders tend to experience diminished self-worth and poorer performance outcomes.[88] As for organizations, consider a case from 2011, in which a full-time cashier who worked for the convenience store QC Mart in Iowa quit her job after her employer issued a memo (see Figure 14-3) regarding a "new contest." The contest: "guess the next cashier who will be fired!" This supervisor was clearly being abusive in his use of power. The case led to litigation and bad press for the convenience store — two things no organization ever wants.

NEW CONTEST – GUESS THE NEXT CASHIER WHO WILL BE FIRED!!! To win our game, write on a piece of paper the name of the next cashier you believe will be fired. Write their name (the person who will be fired), today's date, today's time, and your name. Seal it in an envelope and give it to the manager to put in my envelope. Here's how the game will work. We are doubling our secret shopper efforts, and your store will be visited during the day **AND** at night several times a week. Secret shoppers will be looking for cashiers wearing a hat, talking on a cell phone, not wearing a QC Mart shirt, having someone hanging around/behind the counter, and/or no car personal car parked by the pumps after 7:00 pm, among other things. If the name in your envelope has the right answer, you will win **$10.00 CASH**. Only one winner per firing unless there are multiple right answers with the exact same name, date, and time. Once we fire the person, we will open all the envelopes, award the prize, and start the contest again. **AND NO FAIR PICKING MIKE MILLER FROM ROCKINGHAM. HE WAS FIRED AROUND 11:30 AM TODAY FOR WEARING A HAD AND TALKING ON HIS CELL PHONE. GOOD LUCK!!!!!!**

Figure 14-3 *Memo issued by convenience store manager exhibiting abusive supervision* (linguistic errors in original)

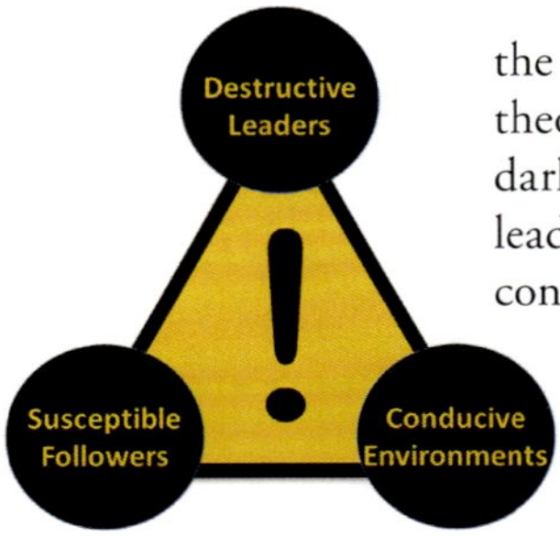

Finally, when discussing the dark side of leadership, it is important to consider the role of followers and the environment. In much the same way that the bright side theorists have argued for the importance of followers and the situation, so too have the dark side scholars. It has been suggested that there is a "toxic triangle of destructive leadership," whereby a devious, toxic leader needs to have susceptible followers and conducive environments to accomplish their (destructive) goals.[89] Susceptible followers can be conformers or colluders.[90] *Conformers* are those followers who tend to be obedient, and therefore don't engage in destructive behavior by themselves. *Colluders*, on the other hand, contribute to the leader's toxicity, actively advancing the leader's mission. One way to reduce the impact of destructive leadership is to hire and promote confident, capable followers who will challenge leaders when necessary, helping to foster a healthy workplace. Research has also shown that conscientious individuals and individuals who are apt to engage in avoidant coping (such as skipping work or daydreaming) appear to be less likely to be negatively impacted by abusive supervisors.[91] Of course, it would be advantageous to select for conscientious individuals regardless of the leader, but selecting for or encouraging avoidant coping is not recommended.

Consider This...

Maya Angelou

It's often said that people don't quit a job, they quit a boss. This isn't 100% true, as people leave when (among other things), they don't enjoy their job, their strengths aren't being utilized, and they feel stagnant in their careers. However, it is often the boss who has the most control over these things, providing growth opportunities, protection from toxicity, and an enjoyable workplace experience.[92] Unfortunately, many leaders not only don't protect their followers from toxicity, but they also bring it themselves in the form of undue pressure, suspicion, and hostility. Maya Angelou, American poet and civil rights activist, once said, "I've learned that people will forget what you said, people will forget what you did, but people will never forget how you made them feel." This is a blessing for leaders who treat their followers well, but a curse for those who are toxic. Have you had any experiences with toxic leaders? How can you ensure you are not engaging in destructive leadership activities? How would you react if you found out you were the cause of employees wanting to leave your organization?

Leadership in Teams

Leadership research has long focused on the ways that individuals are led, and what leaders can do to best meet their needs. With the ever-increasing use of teams within organizations, however, there has been a similarly-growing interest in leading teams. In Chapter 10, we noted that some of what we know about individuals in the workplace generalizes to teams, while some does not. The topic of leadership is one of those areas in which we see some stark differences between individuals and teams.

Shared leadership Leadership within a team whereby team members distribute leadership roles among the different members of the team rather than relying on a single individual to serve as the sole leader.

Within a team setting, the leader cannot simply focus only on the individuals that comprise the team. Instead, the leader must focus on the functioning of the team as a whole. Leading teams requires adaptability.[93] Leadership must evolve as the team evolves and develop along with the team. Whether a team is in its planning phases or is actively performing, the leader must be able to make accommodations and address the team's needs accordingly.[94]

One concept that has received considerable attention is that of **shared leadership**. Here, the focus is less on specific leaders, and more on leadership in general.[95] The "shared" element of shared leadership reflects the point that, with a team, there may be more than one person who takes on a leadership role. Who the leader is may depend on what the team is experiencing at the moment. Leadership could be evenly dispersed among all members of the team. Alternatively, the team members could take turns being the leader as needed. Teams that engage in shared leadership appear to be more satisfied and committed to their teams and engage in more cooperation and helping behaviors. Moreover, although the effects don't appear to be as strong, shared leadership is related to both subjective and objective performance measures. These effects seem to be particularly true when the work is complex.[96]

The importance of team leadership appears also to be a function of the environment. Team leadership may be less important when the team is in a calm environment. When the team is in danger of clear physical or psychological harm, however, team leadership becomes essential.[97] For example, a team of firefighters may be more likely to rely on outside administration as the point of authority when they are not actively involved in fighting fires. When they are in harm's way, however, and are risking their lives for the lives of others, the leadership from within the team is more likely to be of utmost importance.

In Chapter 10, we also discussed multiteam systems, or multiple teams that interact with one another to accomplish higher-level goals. Leaders of these "team of teams" must not only be concerned with the functioning of each team, including how individual members coordinate and cooperate with one another, but they must also manage the interactions between each of the separate teams.[98] Furthermore, and along these lines, it is important for leaders to consider how they treat each team for which they are responsible. For example, when leaders of multiple teams pay more attention to certain teams, those teams tend to feel more empowered and subsequently perform better.[99] Thus, leaders of multiteam systems must care about and respond to the needs of each individual team as well as all of the teams (i.e., the system). If leaders have too small of a focus, or don't consider the needs of all individuals and teams, they will likely be ineffective in coordinating activities and will be limited in terms of effectiveness.[100]

Cross-Cultural Issues in Leadership

For many years, most of what we knew about cross-cultural leadership issues derived from international business. For example, one company might conduct business in two countries (such as the United States and Japan). Research findings indicated which leadership practices would and would not generalize across the two nations. However, we are now in the era of global business, where commerce is conducted on a worldwide basis. A major study was completed on leadership and culture. It is called GLOBE, an acronym for *Global Leadership and Organizational Behavior Effectiveness*. The goal of the massive research project was to address how culture is related to societal, organizational, and leadership effectiveness. The researchers measured the practices and values of managers in different industries (financial services, food processing, telecommunications, etc.) and organizations (951 of them) within 62 societies representing 59 nations (alphabetically from Albania to Zimbabwe). The initial product of their work was a book that represents our best understanding of cross-cultural issues in leadership.[101]

The GLOBE researchers drew upon prior cultural research (including that discussed in Chapter 3) in establishing major cultural dimensions (such as power distance, individualism–collectivism, and uncertainty avoidance), as well as proposing some additional dimensions. Understandably, the results of the research are complex and multifaceted; however, here are some of the major findings:

- In some cultures, the concept of leadership is denigrated. Members of the culture are highly suspicious of individuals who are in positions of authority, for fear they will acquire and abuse power. In these cultures, substantial constraints are placed on what individuals in positions of authority can and cannot do. Alternatively, in some cultures, the concept of leadership is romanticized; leaders are given exceptional privileges and status and are held in great esteem.
- Twenty-two leadership traits were identified as being universally desirable. Two examples are decisiveness and foresight.
- Eight leadership traits were identified as being universally undesirable. Two examples are irritability and ruthlessness.
- Many leadership traits were culturally contingent, being desirable in some cultures and undesirable in others. Two examples are ambition and elitism.
- Members of different cultures share common observations and values about what constitutes effective and ineffective leadership. Six styles of leadership were identified: charismatic, team-oriented, participative, autonomous, humane-oriented, and self-protective. Although all cultures recognized these six leadership styles, they were seen as differentially contributing to outstanding leadership. Anglo and Nordic European cultures, for example, tend to see charismatic and participative leadership styles as being particularly effective. Asian and Sub-Saharan African cultures are more favorably disposed to humane-oriented and self-protective leadership styles. Middle Eastern cultures do not place great value on team-oriented and participative styles for achieving success.

The researchers found clear cultural underpinnings to the way societies generate and distribute wealth and take care of their people. The findings indicate that decisions designed to change the way governments operate or the way societies allocate their resources must take into consideration cultural issues. Certain leadership traits (such as integrity) appear to be universally endorsed, though it is unclear whether the leader behaviors associated with these traits would be common across cultures.[102] For example, in one culture, a leader with high integrity might be regarded as someone who gives great thought and consideration to an issue before making a decision. In another culture, high integrity by a leader might be manifested by soliciting a wide range of opinions from others before making a decision. There is a major difference in leadership values between Western and Middle Eastern cultures. In the Middle East, interpersonal relationships (especially among those in positions of power) are based upon establishing and maintaining a strong sense of honor between the parties. Both parties engage in practices of giving and preserving a sense of shared honor that is the basis for their extended relationship. In Western cultures, relationships are founded more on the perceived instrumental value of the relationship (i.e., what is to be gained from the relationship). There is a strong recognition that the relationship will endure only to the extent both parties have something to gain from the exchange, which may be for a limited period of time.[103]

The manifestation of specific behaviors from culturally-endorsed traits awaits further research in the GLOBE project. The myriad findings from the GLOBE study will provide us with a much better understanding of how cultural issues influence a wide range of human behavior. Most leadership research has had a technological, modern, and U.S. bias.[104] The GLOBE project will help us understand leadership from other perspectives from around the world.

Diversity Issues in Leadership

There have been substantial economic, political, and social changes within the United States since the passage of the Civil Rights Act in 1964. In addition to prohibiting some forms of discrimination in the workplace, the U.S. labor market has evolved and the nature of leadership has changed. For example, the national economy experienced a shift from manufacturing to service jobs.[105] There have also been changes to the demographic makeup, such as that the ratio of women to men in the workforce is nearly 1:1. The labor market for skilled workers has tightened, and there will be increased competition for talented personnel. As noted in Chapter 9, as organizations shrink, fewer middle managers will be needed and the responsibilities of first-line managers will expand.

As the labor market has shifted, barriers for members of certain groups have become apparent. There is evidence, for example, that women are under-represented in managerial positions and, in particular, the chief executive positions within organizations.[106] The issue, however, isn't limited to managerial ranks. The metaphor "glass labyrinth" is used to describe the hurdles that women face at all levels of organizations. This is as opposed to the misnomer of a "glass ceiling," which implies that women progress evenly and then suddenly and unexpectedly encounter resistance to advancement.[107] Along these lines, one study found that both male and female managers viewed female subordinates as having lower career motivation than their male counterparts, seemingly supporting the "think leader, think male" view—the unfounded view that men are more suited for leadership positions.[108]

One explanation for gender differences in leadership is cultural. This view holds that because of the historic role of women as family caretakers, they are socialized to be sensitive, nurturing, and caring. When they carry that socialization over into organizational roles, women are likely to be warm, considerate, and democratic leaders.[109] In addition, gender roles influence perceptions of leadership styles.[110] The *agentic*, or male gender role, is to be competent, aggressive, independent, decisive, and forceful. The *communal*, or female gender role, is to be kind, concerned, and sympathetic to the needs of others. The concept of leadership has typically been defined in terms of masculine characteristics. Along these lines, there can be a backlash against women leaders who exhibit more agentic characteristics. As such, there can be a double standard in leadership: men don't have to be communal, but women have to be both. That said, there is a growing recognition of the importance of communal skills among leaders.[111] While Western leadership styles emphasize achievement, the Eastern leadership style more heavily values the importance of relationships. The era of global business has made us more aware of the criticality of organizational success being dependent on collaboration with others and building strong relationships. As such, it is proposed the "female role" may be more suited to leadership than in the past.

One explanation often put forth as to why there are relatively few women in top-level managerial jobs is "lack of fit." As mentioned, men are stereotypically viewed as forceful, achievement-oriented, and tough. Women are stereotypically viewed as caring, relationship-oriented, and kind. Accordingly, men are often perceived as a better fit. When researchers compared performance evaluations and promotions for men and women, women who were promoted had higher performance ratings than men, suggesting stricter standards for promotion were applied to women.[112] There appears to be no empirical basis for the disproportionately-small representation of women in top leadership jobs in the United States. In fact, meta-analytic research has found only small male–female differences in leadership styles.[113] Various reasons have been tied to why women and racial minorities experience difficulties with participating in leadership development activities, including being slotted into jobs that don't facilitate advancement, having problems obtaining influential mentors or sponsors, and being excluded from informal networks where critical information and career opportunities are shared.[114]

Consider This...

In 2002, I-O psychologist Karen Lyness lamented, "I have been struck by how much more we seem to know about barriers for women and people of color than about how best to overcome the barriers" (Lyness 2002, p. 265).[115] Two decades later, the barriers still exist, and it's unclear how to fix the problem. For example, top management positions and opportunities for greater influence appear to remain largely out of reach for many members of the Black community, with only 8% of managers and 4.3% of chief executives in 2020 classifying themselves as Black.[116] While the numbers are slightly better for women (40% in management positions and 29% in chief executive positions), they remain far from equal to their male counterparts. Why do you think this is? What ideas do you have for addressing the situation? What role does I-O psychology play in finding a solution?

The topic of diversity in leadership is not limited to the heterogeneity within leadership positions. Rather, it also concerns the ways in which leaders must manage diversity within their organizations. A review of the team diversity and leadership literatures led a group of scholars to develop the Leading Diversity model (LeaD) to explain the requirements for the effective leadership of diverse teams.[117] The LeaD model suggests that leaders must have a good understanding of the ways diversity can lead to favorable and unfavorable situations. In addition, leaders have to be both proactive and reactive when attending to a diverse team to predict and/or diagnose the team's needs. Leaders must also be able to engage in both task- and person-focused leadership behaviors to fully meet the needs of a diverse team.

Entrepreneurship

Entrepreneurship
The process by which individuals pursue opportunities and organize resources that can lead to new job creation and business growth.

All business organizations were created by individuals who at some point in time thought they had a "good idea." Such individuals who started these businesses are called *entrepreneurs*, and *entrepreneurship* is the underlying concept of business creation. Although **entrepreneurship** has been addressed for over 100 years, there has been renewed interest in the topic, particularly when society has been confronted with massive job loss.[118] It is believed that a greater understanding of how businesses are created will lead to the development of new organizations (often called "start-up" companies) that will grow and prosper. Such organizations would not only add value to society by the products and services they offer, but also as a source of employment. However, not all entrepreneurial activities enhance social welfare. Interestingly, organized crime, across many different cultures, follows the same basic principles of entrepreneurship found in successful legal businesses. The only differentiating characteristic is the readiness of criminal entrepreneurs to use physical violence to attain their goals.[119] The similarities between legal and illegal enterprises also extend to how they are structured to be effective. In fact, a member of a London street gang called the Black Disciples that sold crack cocaine within a twelve-square-block area was quoted as saying the following:

> So how *did* the gang work? An awful lot like most American businesses, actually, though perhaps none more so than McDonald's. In fact, if you were to hold a McDonald's organizational chart and a Black Disciples org chart side by side, you could hardly tell the difference (Leavitt & Dubner 2005, p. 99).[120]

I-O psychologists have recently become drawn into the study of entrepreneurship because of its growing emergence in society, and because I-O psychology has much to offer in understanding entrepreneurship. Successful entrepreneurs have much in common with successful leaders, although they are not identical. At the heart of entrepreneurship is innovation: thinking of new ways or methods to extract value out of an opportunity that presents itself. A six-step process that is the basis for entrepreneurship is as follows:[121]

1. **Existence of opportunity**. There must be an opportunity to provide a new product or service that is desired, or to improve upon an existing one.
2. **Discovery of opportunity**. A person must perceive this opportunity to exist. Not perceived, the opportunity is "missed." When a person perceives an opportunity when in fact there is none, the perception is an "illusion."
3. **Decision to pursue the opportunity**. A person must decide whether the opportunity is of sufficient magnitude to warrant the expenditure of time, money, and skill needed to pursue it.
4. **Resource acquisition**. Once the decision is made to pursue the opportunity, a person has to marshal the resources needed for its pursuit.
5. **Entrepreneurial strategy**. Strategy is the process by which a person can convert or transform the opportunity, upon application of the resources, into a product or service valued by others.

6. **Organizing process**. The organizing process is the means by which the entrepreneurial strategy is enacted. It may involve the founding of a new organization, or some other process of pursuing the opportunity that previously did not exist.

Apart from the existence of an objective opportunity (which naturally occurs in the environment), the remaining five steps all involve a human component. That is, each requires a person who: sees the opportunity, decides to act upon it, obtains the needed resources, develops a strategy, and develops an organizing process to create the new product or service. It is this strong human component to entrepreneurship that interests I-O psychologists. Entrepreneurship is highly interdisciplinary. Reliance on one scientific discipline to understand a topic that cuts across disciplines is rarely effective. For example, the fourth step (resource acquisition) entails the procurement of money needed to pursue the opportunity. This step is typically the domain of investment management. There are individuals who will provide the needed money for some entrepreneurial activity. Such people are called "venture capitalists," and it is their goal to identify a potentially-lucrative opportunity, invest their money (capital) in it, and share in the success of the venture. Research that focuses only on the financial dimension of entrepreneurship fails to understand the importance of the individual entrepreneur whose idea is being supported. Likewise, an examination of the psychological profile (e.g., intelligence, personality, values, etc.) of successful entrepreneurs fails to understand the situations in which they operate.

There is disagreement within I-O psychology about whether entrepreneurship is truly different from leadership.[122] Some scholars believe that entrepreneurship is nothing more than leadership embedded within an entrepreneurial organization.[123] However, there is evidence that highly creative individuals who inspire innovation are not necessarily skilled in other leadership dimensions, such as interpersonal skills. In addition, a meta-analysis revealed that entrepreneurs are more conscientious and open to new experiences than their managerial counterparts.[124]

A compelling finding from the study of entrepreneurs is their high rate of failure. Nearly 90% of all startups fail. Approximately 21.5% of startups fail in the first year, 30% in the second year, 50% in the fifth year, and 70% in their 10th year.[125] The goal of all businesses is to grow and prosper. However, the initial goal is just to survive, and research indicates organizational survival is more the exception than the rule. The reasons for failure rest in each of the six steps. The goal of I-O psychology isn't to contribute to understanding entrepreneurship from a financial perspective. Rather, the goal is to contribute from a human perspective. A blending of knowledge from different fields is necessary to understand entrepreneurship.[126]

Concluding Comments

As was discussed earlier, sometimes research investigations meld major topics of interest to I-O psychologists. A notable example combined motivation and leadership in a study that addressed the motivation to lead.[127] The researchers proposed the existence of a personality construct that explains why some people seek leadership positions. Using sophisticated analytic methods, the researchers identified three types of people who desire to lead others. The first type sees themselves as having leadership qualities:

social scientists in general. A list of the major reasons unions distrust I-O psychologists is presented in Table 15-1.[9]

In the state of New York, psychologists became unionized. People questioned why these highly-trained, licensed, well-paid professionals who clearly had earned the right to work in their chosen fields would choose to unionize.[10] The answer was that the 3,200 members of the New York State Psychological Association were frustrated by their lack of power in dealing with managed healthcare. The psychologists became members of a powerful labor union, the American Federation of Teachers, which at the time had more than 400,000 members. As members of a large union, they now have a stronger voice in negotiating issues regarding their employment, one of the classic reasons workers join unions. Some psychologists had stereotypical concerns about becoming unionized. They worried that joining the union resulted in a loss of status, because union membership was viewed as something for individuals "who work with their hands not their heads for a living" (Verdi 2000, p. 32).[11] Yet, even professions that historically have not been aligned with unions turn to them for help with employment-related matters.

Table 15-1
Reasons unions distrust I-O psychologists

I-O psychologists are associated with management.
I-O psychologists are associated with F. W. Taylor's scientific management (i.e., emphasis on efficiency, time and motion studies).
I-O psychologists are associated with job enrichment techniques that interfere with job classification and standards systems.
I-O psychologists are moralistic intellectuals who want social reform.
Their methods (e.g., attitude surveys) have been used to avoid or beat union organizing attempts or to lower pay demands.
Unions are ignored in textbooks and journals of I-O psychology.
Methods of psychological testing emphasize differentiation among workers (hence, anti-solidarity and anti-seniority systems).
Many psychologists have not had work experiences similar to union members, which causes suspicion and communication barriers.

Source: From "The Relationship Between Psychology and Organized Labor: Past Present, and Future," by G. E. Huszczo, J. G. Wiggins, and J. S. Currie, 1984, American Psychologist, 39, pp. 432–440.

What Is a Union?

Union
A labor organization with defined members whose purpose is to enhance the welfare of its members in their employment relationship with the company.

Unions are organizations designed to promote and enhance the social and economic welfare of their members. Basically, unions were created to protect workers from exploitation. Unions originally sprang from the abysmal working conditions in this country more than 100 years ago. Workers got little pay, had almost no job security, had no benefits, and, perhaps most important, worked in degrading and unsafe conditions. Unions gave unity and power to employees. This power forced employers to deal with workers as a group. Certain federal laws compelled employers to stop certain activities (such as employing children) and engage in others (such as making Social Security contributions). Collectively, labor unions and labor laws brought about many changes in the workplace. For example, the length of the average workweek in the United Kingdom over the past century was heavily influenced by the power

Consider This...

Rightly or wrongly, unions have had the image of representing the "common man" in labor over the "privileged intellectuals." Some union leaders become suspicious and skeptical of the motives of formally-educated people, feeling they are more likely to share values held by management. Unfortunately, this sentiment that some unions hold is hurting them. Unions rarely hire outside professionals; they generally promote from within their own ranks. Furthermore, unions are currently experiencing a decline in membership, an unprecedented number of unions are being decertified, and unions are losing their effectiveness in negotiating for desired employment conditions. In short, unions could benefit from fresh ideas and from organizational change interventions. But unless they are willing to look beyond their own ranks for expertise, it is unlikely that they (like any organization) will have sufficient internal strength to pull themselves up by the bootstraps. The paradoxical split between I-O psychology (the study of people at work) and labor unions (which represent a significant portion of workers) has been detrimental to both parties. Given all of this, what do you think could be done to ease the tensions between unions and management (and I-O psychologists)? In what ways could I-O psychology help unions in today's world?

of labor unions.[12] At the start of the 20th century, the standard workweek was 54 hours. This was followed later by the 48-hour and 44-hour workweeks, and by the 1960s the 40-hour workweek was standard. By 2004, the average workweek was 37.2 hours, with considerably greater hours being evidenced in managerial and professional occupations. In many ways, the problems facing the North American worker today are not as severe as they were 75 to 100 years ago. At the start of the 20th century, issues of employee welfare were primarily directed to such factors as hours of work, pay, and methods of dispute resolution.[13] However, in the 21st century, the concept of worker welfare has expanded to include smoking bans at the worksite, healthy eating at work, and provisions for gyms and health checks. As such, unions continue to give a sense of security and increased welfare to their members.

Why do workers join unions? What can unions accomplish? Unions have consistently contributed to the attainment of certain outcomes. Based upon labor research, unions have made these contributions to worker welfare:

- They have increased wages; in turn, employers have raised the wages of some non-union workers.
- They have bargained for and gotten benefits such as pensions, insurance, vacations, and rest periods.
- They have provided formal rules and procedures for discipline, promotion, wage differentials, and other important job-related factors. This has led to less arbitrary treatment of employees.

Other reasons people join unions include that unions can provide better communication with management, better working conditions, increased employee unity, and

Figure 15-1
Badge worn by unionized workers advocating equality of treatment for all employees

higher morale. There are also social reasons, like belonging to a group with whom workers can share common experiences and fellowship. In addition, unions make social justice issues, such as bargaining for better childcare, primary negotiating concerns.[14] Unions that pursued social justice issues attracted more members than unions that bargained over traditional economic issues. Matters of social justice have an appeal to a wide constituency, which is the base from which unions derive power. Thus, there are both economic and personal reasons for joining unions.

Figure 15-1 shows a badge worn by unionized employees. It identifies three employment issues desired by union members: a full pension after 30 years of service to the company; that workers receive pay on days when they are sick and cannot attend work, and the use of personal time away from work that is not counted as vacation time. But note the one word on the badge that is in the largest font—"equal." The foundation of labor unions is equal treatment across all workers. That is, it would be unacceptable to the union if some workers got sick pay and others didn't, some got personal time and others didn't, and so forth. Equality of treatment is the basis of *solidarity* (i.e., a feeling of unity that binds members of the labor union together).

Unions as Organizations

The percentage of unionized employees in the U.S. workforce has been steadily declining over the past 75 years. It is now 10.8%, about 14.3 million workers.[15] The reasons for the decline will be discussed later in the chapter. The largest labor union is the National Education Association (2.3 million members). Other large unions are the International Brotherhood of Teamsters and the United Steelworkers. Historically, unions were strongest among blue-collar employees, but now white-collar workers (particularly government employees and teachers) are the dominant union base.

Fun fact:
As of 2018, a whopping 90.4% of Iceland's workforce belonged to a union!

Each union has a headquarters, but its strength is its many locals. A local may represent members in a geographic area (for example, all tollbooth collectors in Philadelphia) or a particular plant (for example, Amalgamated Beef Packers at Armour's Dubuque, Iowa, slaughterhouse). The local elects officials. If it is large enough, it affords some officials full-time jobs. Other officials are full-time company employees who may get time off for union activities. The shop (or union) steward has a union position equivalent to that of a company supervisor. Stewards represent the union on the job site; they handle grievances and discipline. Usually, the steward is elected by union members for a one-year term.

A union represents an organization (a group of workers) within another organization (the company). The local depends on the company for its existence. Large companies often have a multiunion labor force and thus multiple organizations within themselves. In this case, the employer must deal with several collectively-organized groups—for example, production workers, clerical workers, and truck drivers. Each union negotiates separately, trying to improve the welfare of its members. A large, multiunion employer is a good example of how organizations are composed of interdependent parts. Each union has a certain degree of power, which can influence the behavior of the total organization.

Union members pay dues, which are the union's chief resource. The union can also collect money for a strike fund, a pool that members can draw from if they are on strike and do not get paid. (Strikes will be discussed in more detail shortly.) Unions use their funds to offer members such things as special group automobile insurance rates or union-owned vacation facilities. Unions are highly dependent on their members. Increased membership gives a union more bargaining clout, generates more revenue, and provides a greater range of services for members. Without members, a union cannot exist; indeed, declining membership can threaten its very survival.

Union shop
A provision of employment stipulating that new employees must join the union that represents employees following a probationary period.

Open shop
A company that may have a union, but does not require union membership for continued employment.

In a union company, the labor contract may stipulate that those hired for jobs represented by the union must join the union after a probationary period. This is a **union shop**; the employee has no choice about joining. Requiring union membership as a precondition to employment (as opposed to joining after the probationary period) is known as a *closed shop*, and was deemed illegal in the United States under the Taft-Hartley Act of 1947. Despite this, requirements to join unions pre-employment continue to exist in practice but are not written into contracts. In addition, as of 2021, 27 states have "right-to-work" laws prohibiting compulsory union membership as a condition of continued employment (see Figure 15-2). Unionized companies in which the employee has the choice of joining the union are called **open shops**. However, considerable pressure can be put on an employee by the union to join.

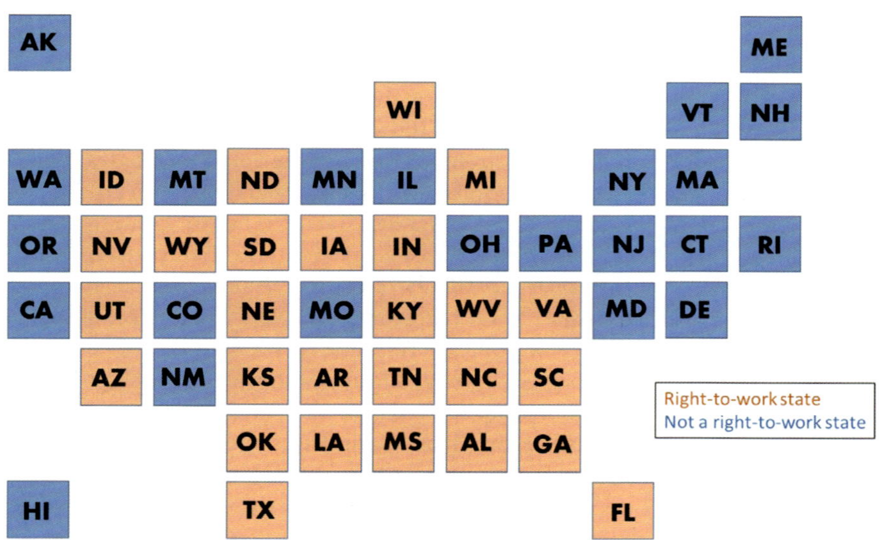

Figure 15-2 *Right-to-work states as of 2021*

Consider This...

Right-to-work laws can be somewhat contentious. Those in favor of such laws argue that requiring union membership violates the First Amendment because (a) the right to association also includes the right not to associate, and (b) oftentimes union dues are used for political purposes rather than union purposes, and therefore forced membership violates First Amendment freedoms. Opponents of right-to-work laws argue that such laws are "anti-union," in that they weaken the union by depriving them of revenue and membership numbers, thereby reducing their bargaining power and limiting their ability to be proactive about workers' rights issues. Both sides are able to cite statistics that support their positions, whether the focus is on how such states fare in terms of worker salaries, unemployment rates, and income growth. What do you think? Are right-to-work laws anti-union? Do you think employees who are in an open shop but who choose to not pay dues or be members should benefit from the work of the union? Would you want to live in a right-to-work state? Why or why not?

The Formation of a Union

National Labor Relations Act (NLRA) The most influential federal law influencing union/management relations in collective bargaining.

National Labor Relations Board (NLRB) An agency of the federal government that has oversight responsibility for enforcing laws pertaining to union/management relations.

Authorization card A card employees sign authorizing an election to determine whether a union will represent employees in the collective bargaining process.

The formation of labor unions is governed by laws across different nations; there is no universal procedure. In the United States, the most influential federal law pertaining to labor unions is the **National Labor Relations Act** (NLRA) that was enacted by Congress in 1935. The NLRA established the rights of employers and employees engaged in collective bargaining. When employees in the United States want to consider being represented by a labor union, they follow a standard procedure. First, they invite representatives to solicit union membership. Federal law allows organizers to solicit membership as long as this does not endanger employees' safety or performance. Solicitations usually occur over lunch or at break time. It is illegal for employers to threaten physically, interfere with, or harass organizers. It is also illegal to fire employees for pro-union sentiments.

Both the union and the company typically mount campaigns on behalf of their positions. The union emphasizes how it can improve the workers' lot. The company's countercampaign stresses how well off the employees already are, the costs of union membership, and the loss of freedom. Then a federal agency, the **National Labor Relations Board** (NLRB), becomes involved. The NLRB sends a hearing officer to oversee the union campaign and monitor developments.

There is a two-step process that certifies a labor union to represent employees in their relationship with the company. First, employees are asked to sign cards authorizing a union election. If fewer than 30% sign the **authorization cards**, the process ends. If 30% or more sign, the second step begins. An election is held to determine whether a union will represent the employees. The NLRB officer must determine which employees are eligible to be in the union and thus eligible to vote. Management personnel (supervisors, superintendents, and managers) are excluded. The hearing officer schedules the election, provides secret ballots and ballot boxes, counts the votes,

Certification election An election in which employees vote to determine whether a union will represent them in the collective bargaining process.

and certifies the election. This expression of voter preference is termed a **certification election**. If more than 50% of the voters approve, the union is voted in. If the union loses the election, it can repeat the entire process at a later date. A union that loses a close election will probably do so. In one study, researchers reported that employees who abstained from voting in a union certification election possessed less extreme work and union attitudes and believed less in the ability of their vote to affect the election outcome, compared with employees who did vote in the election.[16] Carefully note who determines the outcome of a certification election: the employees who vote. If 100 employees are declared eligible to vote, 30 employees vote in favor of the union, 20 employees vote against the union, and 50 employees do not vote, the union becomes certified to represent all 100 employees.

So, why do workers join unions? As shown in Figure 15-3, the process begins by workers regarding a labor union as being instrumental in helping them to attain the results or outcomes they desire. If such union instrumentality is accepted, a labor union will be supported. To the extent that the labor union continues to remain instrumental in attaining the desired outcomes, workers will exhibit loyalty to the union. Within this framework, the concept of organizational citizenship behaviors (as discussed in Chapter 11) is extended to become "union citizenship behaviors."[17] The two constructs are composed of similar dimensions, including active participation, exerting a voice, and demonstrating civic virtue. The difference is that the behaviors are directed to the union as a means of contributing to its effectiveness. The workers view the union as being essential to their well-being, and thus they contribute to the maintenance of the social exchange relationship with management. Union citizenship behaviors have clear implications for work. For example, research has found that union citizenship behavior that is directed at helping fellow employees deal with workplace grievances is related to lower absenteeism.[18]

Union formation is primarily determined by three factors: (1) dissatisfaction with one's job, (2) general attitudes towards unions, and (3) union instrumentality.[19] However, if workers do not support the concept of third-party representation (i.e., a labor union), they will more readily endure dissatisfying jobs than pursue an alternative deemed unacceptable.

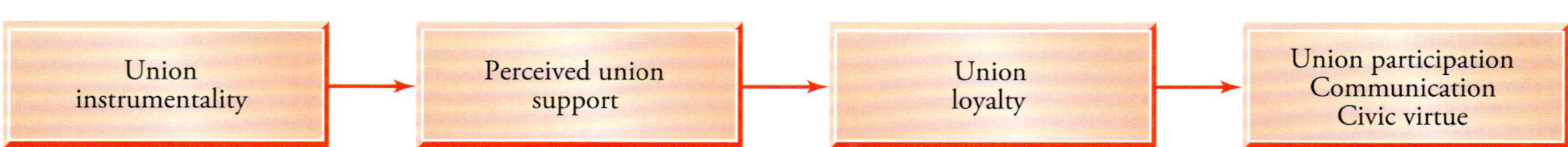

Figure 15-3 *A model of union participation*

Source: From L. E. Tetrick, L. M. Shore, L. N. McClurg, and R. J. Vandenberg, 2007. "A Model of Union Participation: The Impact of Perceived Union Support, Union Instrumentality, and Union Loyalty," *Journal of Applied Psychology, 92*, 820–828.

The Labor Contract

Labor contract
A formal agreement between labor and management that specifies the terms and conditions of employment.

Once a union is recognized, its officials are authorized to negotiate a **labor contract**. This is a formal agreement between union and management that specifies the conditions of employment over a set period.

Both sides prepare a preliminary list of what they want included; the union presents its *demands* and the employer its *offers*. The union tends to ask for more than it knows it can get; management tends to offer less. While both sides seek a satisfactory agreement, they often resort to bombast, which is a hallmark of such negotiations.

Union officials may allege that management is making huge profits and taking advantage of workers. Management may allege that malicious union leaders have duped the good workers and that their policies may force the company into bankruptcy. Over time, both sides usually come to an agreement; the union often gets less than it wanted and management gives more. When agreement is not reached (an **impasse**), other steps are taken, as will be discussed.

Impasse
A point in the collective bargaining process at which both the union and management conclude they are unable to reach an agreement in the formation of a labor contract.

Contract negotiations take place between two teams of negotiators. The union side typically consists of local union officials, shop stewards, and perhaps a representative of the national union. Management usually fields a team of a few human resource and production managers, who follow preset guidelines. The contract contains many articles; there are also many issues to bargain over. The issues can generally be classified into five categories: compensation and working conditions, employee security, union security, management rights, and contract duration. Table 15-2 gives examples of these issues and the positions typically taken by each side.

In the process, each bargaining team checks with its members to see whether they will compromise on the initial positions. Social media is one way through which union members can communicate with each other during contract negotiations (see Social Media and I-O Psychology: *Members Unite... Online*). Each side may be willing

Table 15-2 *Typical bargaining issues and positions taken by union and management*

Issue	Union's Position	Management's Position
Compensation	Higher pay, more benefits, cost-of-living adjustments	Lower company expenditures, not yielding to all union demands
Employee security	Seniority is the basis for promotions, layoffs, and recall decisions	Merit or job performance is the basis for these decisions
Union security	A union shop in which employees must join the union when hired	An open shop in which employees can choose to join the union
Management rights	Union wants more voice in setting policies and making decisions that affect employees	Management feels certain decisions are its inherent right and does not want to share them with the union
Contract duration	Shorter contracts	Longer contracts

to yield on some points but not others. Eventually, they reach a tentative agreement. Union members then vote on the contract. If they approve it, the contract is *ratified* and remains in effect for the agreed-on time (typically two to three years). If members reject the contract, further negotiation is necessary.

Both sides will use whatever external factors are available to influence the contract in their favor. If there is high unemployment and the company can easily replace workers who go on strike, management has an advantage. If the company does much of its business around Christmas, the union may choose that time to negotiate a contract, knowing the company can ill afford a strike then. Each side looks for factors that will bolster its position.

Social Media and I-O Psychology: *Members Unite... Online*

There is evidence that members of trade unions are more intense users of the internet than their non-unionized counterparts. And for good reason. Social media allow unions to make information readily available to members and activists. Social media sites also help in recruiting and mobilizing union memberships. In addition, through social media, union members can move beyond traditional trade union discourses and practices to more novel and impactful means of negotiations that allow for new and unique forms of power and representation.

Take, for example, the power of social media for organizing protests and campaigns. Information can spread rapidly through various social media channels, and a flash mob (a group of people who assemble suddenly in a public place) can be summoned to support employees who are on strike. Moreover, demonstrations can be organized to a far larger scale than what was possible a mere decade ago. For example, in May of 2014, fast food workers in 150 U.S. cities and 33 countries staged various flash mobs, protests, and walkouts in an effort to rally for higher wages.

Demonstrations can even be made virtually, as has been the case for protestors on Second Life, an online 3D virtual world in which individuals can interact. Protestors have staged strikes within Second Life, having their avatars (their virtual representations of themselves) meet at a specified rally location to carry out online what they may not have been able to do in the real world. Famous movements like Occupy Wall Street have taken to Second Life to protest in a virtual space. At one point there was even a special "Union Island" created to allow trade unionists from around the globe a place to meet and access resources about labor unions in general. Indeed, it is clear that technological advances and the advent of social media have altered the landscape of union and management relations.

Collective Bargaining and Impasse Resolution

Collective bargaining The process by which labor and management negotiate a labor contract.

Whether the **collective bargaining** process runs smoothly often depends on the parties' approaches. The parties may utilize distributive or integrative bargaining postures.[20] Distributive bargaining is predominant in the United States. This assumes a win/lose relationship; whatever the employer gives the union, the employer loses, and vice versa. Because both sides are trying to minimize losses, movement toward a compromise is often painful and slow. The alternative is integrative bargaining. Both sides work to improve the relationship while the present contract is in effect. Contract renewal is not seen as the time and place for confrontation. Instead, both parties seek to identify common problems and propose acceptable solutions that can be adopted when the contract expires. Labor and management collaboratively seek "win-win" resolutions to the issues they face. Although it is not always a strict either/or decision, distributive bargaining is far more characteristic of union/management relations than is integrative bargaining.

Consider This...

You'll notice in the paragraph above that distributive bargaining was noted as being a painful and slow process toward a compromise. In addition, you just read that integrative bargaining will ideally produce a win-win for both parties. A key point here is that a compromise is not a win-win, even though many people may think of it in that way at first. A compromise is reached when each side makes a concession so that an agreement can be made. Technically speaking, then, if both sides had to give up something, it would best be considered a "lose-lose" for the parties. It is only by working collaboratively to ensure that issues are addressed for both sides that a win-win can result. What steps could labor and management take to ensure they are bargaining integratively rather than distributively? Do you think some issues are easier to bargain integratively than others? Which ones and why?

What happens if the two parties cannot reach an agreement? In some cases, the labor contract may stipulate what will be done if an impasse is reached. In other cases, union and management must jointly determine how to break the impasse. In either case, there are three options, all involving third parties: mediation, fact-finding, and arbitration.

Mediation
A method of dispute settlement in which a neutral third party offers advice to the union and management to help them agree on a labor contract.

Mediation. **Mediation** is the most frequently used and informal third-party option. A neutral third party (a mediator) assists union and management in reaching voluntary agreement. Mediators have no power to impose a settlement; rather, they facilitate bringing both parties together. A mediator functions like a marriage counselor in trying to resolve conflict between the parties.

Where do mediators come from? The Federal Mediation and Conciliation Service (FMCS) has a staff of qualified mediators. An organization may contact FMCS for the services of such a person. The mediator need not be affiliated with FMCS; any third party acceptable to labor and management may serve. Generally, however, both parties prefer someone who has training and experience in labor disputes, so FMCS is often used.

How a mediator intervenes is not clear-cut. Mediation is voluntary; thus, no mediator can function without the trust, cooperation, and acceptance of both parties. Acceptance is important because an effective mediator obtains confidential information that the parties have withheld from each other. If the information is used indiscriminately, the parties' bargaining strategy and leverage could be weakened. The mediator tries to reduce the number of disputed issues; ideally, they reach a point where there are no disputes at all. Mediators can be thwarted in bringing both parties to agreement if there is a *fixed-pie* perception.[21] A fixed-pie perception is the belief that one party's gain will be achieved only if the other party loses. A mediator can possibly offset this perception by offering ideas where both sides can gain, or by proposing the two parties trade off issues (i.e., give and get) in multi-issue cases. The mediator encourages information sharing to break the deadlock. Without a mediator, it is often difficult for parties to "open up" after assuming adversarial roles. The mediator facilitates the flow of information and progress toward compromise. If the mediator is unsuccessful, both parties may engage in the next phase: fact-finding.

Fact-finding
A method of dispute settlement in which a neutral third party makes public the respective positions of labor and management with the intention that the public will influence the two sides to resolve their disputes in establishing a labor contract.

Arbitration
A method of dispute settlement in which a neutral third party resolves the dispute between labor and management by using a decision that is typically final and binding on both parties.

Interest arbitration
A type of arbitration used to resolve disputes between labor and management in the formation of a labor contract.

Conventional arbitration
A form of arbitration in which the arbitrator is free to fashion whatever decision is deemed most fair in resolving a dispute.

Final-offer arbitration
A form of arbitration in which the arbitrator is obligated to accept the final offer of either the union or management in their dispute.

Fact-finding. **Fact-finding** is more formal than mediation. A qualified mediator may also serve as a fact-finder, but the role is different. In fact-finding, the third party reviews the facts, makes a formal recommendation to resolve the dispute, and makes the recommendation public. It is presumed that if the recommendation is public, the parties will be pressured to accept it or use it for a negotiated settlement.

However, fact-finding has typically not produced the desired pressure. Public interest is aroused only when a strike threatens or actually imposes direct hardship on the public. Fact-finding may be most useful when one party faces internal differences and needs recommendations from an expert to overcome opposition to a settlement. There appears to be a difference in the effectiveness of fact-finding between private- and public-sector employers. In the public sector, fact-finding has met with limited success. Parties learn that rejecting a fact-finding recommendation is not politically or economically costly, so they are unlikely to value the opinion of the fact-finder. In the private sector, fact-finding can be helpful primarily because the final technique of settlement (arbitration) is strongly opposed by unions and management. However, fact-finding is not used very often in the private sector.

Arbitration. **Arbitration** is the final and most formal settlement technique. Both parties must abide by the decision of the neutral third party. "Final and binding" is usually associated with arbitration. The use of arbitration may be stipulated in the labor contract; it may also be agreed on informally. This is called **interest arbitration** because it involves the interests of both parties in negotiating a new contract.

Arbitrators must have extensive experience in labor relations. The American Arbitration Association (AAA) maintains the standards and keeps a list of qualified arbitrators. Arbitrators listed by AAA can also serve as mediators listed by FMCS. Effective mediators, fact-finders, and arbitrators all need the same skills. What distinguishes the services is the clout of the third party.

There are many forms of interest arbitration. With voluntary arbitration, the parties agree to the process. It is most common in the private sector to settle disputes that arise while a contract is still in effect. Compulsory arbitration is legally required. It is most common in the public sector.

There are other types of arbitration. With **conventional arbitration**, arbitrators create the settlement they deem appropriate. In **final-offer arbitration**, the arbitrator must select the proposal of either union or management; no compromise is possible. For example, suppose the union demands $12 per hour and the company offers $10. In conventional arbitration, the arbitrator could decide on any wage, but would possibly split the difference and decide on $11. In final-offer arbitration, the arbitrator must choose the $10 or the $12. An additional variation also holds for final-offer arbitration. The arbitrator may make the decision with **total-package arbitration**: the arbitrator chooses the complete proposal of either the company or the union on all issues. The decision may also be made with **issue-by-issue arbitration**: the arbitrator might choose the company wage offer, but select the union demand on vacation days. Decisions on voluntary versus compulsory arbitration, conventional versus final-offer arbitration, and total-package versus issue-by-issue arbitration are determined by law for public-sector employers and by mutual agreement in the private sector.

Total-package arbitration A form of final-offer arbitration in which the arbitrator is obligated to accept either the union's position or management's position on every issue in dispute between the parties.

Issue-by-issue arbitration A form of final-offer arbitration in which the arbitrator is obligated to accept either the union's position or management's position on an issue-by-issue basis in disputes between the parties.

Interest arbitration is more common in the public sector. Historically, the private sector has been opposed to outside interference in resolving labor problems that are "private" affairs. Thus, private-sector employers will readily seek the advice of a mediator but shun strategies that require certain courses of action. The public sector, however, is quite different. Bus drivers, for example, may be permitted to strike because the public can find other means of transportation. Alternatively, firefighters, for example, perform a service vital to the welfare of society. The cessation of their services due to a labor strike could have a devastating effect on the general public. As such, firefighters would be prohibited by law from using a labor strike as a bargaining tactic. Therefore, other means of reaching a settlement (e.g., fact-finding and arbitration) are made available to them.

Responses to Impasse

Consider the situation in which union and management cannot resolve their disputes. They may or may not have used a mediator. Assume the private sector is involved because mediation, fact-finding, and arbitration might be required in the public sector. What happens if the two parties cannot agree?

In collective bargaining, both sides can take actions if they are not pleased with the outcome. These actions are tactics designed to bring about favorable settlements. The union can call for a **labor strike**. Union members must vote for a strike. If members support a strike and no settlement is reached, they will stop work at a particular time. That point is typically the day after the current contract expires (literally, 12:01 a.m.). If employees go on strike without union approval, it is called a *wildcat strike* and can result in disciplinary actions against those employees who went on the unauthorized strike. Taking a strike vote during negotiations brings pressure on management to agree to union demands.

Labor strike A cessation of work activities by unionized employees as a means of influencing management to accept the union position in a dispute over the labor contract.

The NLRA protects the right to strike, but only for those workers covered by the law. The NLRA doesn't cover, for example, certain transportation workers, government employees, or public employees. In addition, not all strikes are protected. For example, sit-in strikes, those in which striking employees refuse to leave the workplace and prevent others from getting work done, are not protected.

The right to strike is a very powerful tactic. A company's losses from a long strike may be greater than the concessions made in a new contract. Also, unions are skilled in scheduling their strikes (or threatening to do so) when the company is particularly vulnerable (such as around Christmas for the airline industry). Management is not defenseless in the case of a strike, however. If it anticipates a strike, it might boost production beforehand to stockpile goods. Most public-sector employees, on the other hand, perform services, and services cannot be stockpiled. It is also possible to hire

Consider This...

You may be aware of teacher strikes in recent years. For example, in 2018, a series of teacher strikes now referred to as Red for Ed (in part a name given due to the red shirts donned by protesting educators) took place in West Virginia, Kentucky, Oklahoma, and Arizona. In 2019, teachers in Los Angeles and Chicago engaged in strikes that caused large-scale disruptions. In 2020 and 2021, teachers around the world engaged in strikes at varying times in response to premature school reopenings and inadequate protection amid the COVID-19 crisis. By and large, these strikes have been successful, as school districts and government officials have seen the repercussions of not having teachers in the classrooms. But wait. Public school teachers are considered state government employees, and the NLRA doesn't apply to government employees. How does this work? Well, some states, such as Illinois and California, allow most government employees to strike (except police and firefighters). However, most states do not have such allowances, including Kentucky, West Virginia, and Oklahoma. In those cases, the teachers who decided to go on strike did so at a great risk, as they could have been fired or put in jail. Fortunately for them, they got the pay raises they were seeking and were not punished. Would you have been willing to strike, knowing you could lose your job or go to jail? What situations would make you more or less willing to strike?

workers to replace those on strike. Given the time it takes to recruit, hire, and train new workers, replacements will not be hired unless a long strike is predicted.

Although a strike hurts management, it is frustrating for the workers as well. Because they are not working, they do not get paid. The employees may have contributed to a strike fund, but such funds usually pay only a fraction of regular wages. A strike is the price employees pay to get their demands met. It sometimes also limits their demands. By the time a union faces a strike, it is usually confronted with two unpalatable options. One is to accept a contract it does not like; the other is to strike. Employees may seek temporary employment while they are on strike, but such jobs are not always available. On the basis of labor economists' studies of the costs of strikes to both employees and employers, strikes rarely benefit either party. Sometimes the company suffers more; in other cases, the union does. There are rarely any consistent "winners" in a strike.

Fun fact: The term "strike" comes from a nautical term. In 1768, London sailors were upset with their pay and decided to do something about it. They took the action of "striking," or removing the topsails of their ships, to render the ships motionless until their demands were met. Word got out about the sailors "striking for better pay" and a new term for the labor tactic of work cessation was coined!

One study explored some of the dynamics associated with strikes. The researchers examined the attitudes of unionized automobile workers at several times, including when contracts were being negotiated, during an ensuing strike, and seven months after the strike ended.[22] They found that union members on strike (1) had a higher opinion of the union and its leadership than before the strike, (2) evaluated the benefit package more highly after the strike, (3) became more militant toward the employer during the strike, and (4) reported more willingness to engage in union activities. The results of this study support predictions based on theories of conflict and attitude formation.

Another study examined the attitudes of unionized professors in a North American university.[23] After being unable to reach an agreement with the university over such employment issues as pay equality and perceived university support of the faculty, the professors voted to go on strike. The researchers measured changes in attitudes of the professors during the labor dispute. The initial decision to go on strike was supported by 59% of the professors. The primary reason for going on strike was the rational desire to improve faculty employment conditions. Five weeks into the strike, another 20% (now 79% of the faculty) voted to continue the strike based on the emotional desire to punish the university for not agreeing to the union's original demands. After the union bargaining committee succeeded in fashioning a settlement favorable to the professors, 99% of the faculty voted to accept the negotiated settlement. The research results revealed that, over time, union members' resolve to prolong a labor strike became strengthened by emotional commitment to the process of collective bargaining.

Sometimes a strike uncovers information about the quality of the workforce. For example, when one company replaced strikers with temporary help, new production records were set. In this case, the strike revealed a weakness in the employees. Striking workers sometimes receive support from third parties, such as members of the community. Individuals may show support for striking workers by blowing their car horns as they drive by the picket line, wearing a lapel button supporting the strikers, or writing a letter to the editor of a newspaper supporting the strikers. In a study examining such third-party support, supportive individuals were found to be those who supported labor unions in general, or who felt management's offer to the workers was unfair.[24] The researchers suggested union leaders should work on projecting their image to the public, creating a reservoir of goodwill that might result in public support for a strike.

Work slowdown
A tactic used by some employees to influence the outcome of union/management negotiations in which the usual pace of work is intentionally reduced.

A strike is not the only option available to the union. **Work slowdowns** have also been used, wherein workers operate at lower levels of efficiency. They may simply put forth less effort and thus produce less, or they may be absent to reduce productivity. Because strikes are illegal in the police force, police officers who are dissatisfied with their contracts may call in sick *en masse* with what has become known as the "blue flu." Such tactics can exert pressure on management to yield to union demands. It should be noted that work slowdowns are not protected actions, and therefore employees who choose to engage in them could be fired or prosecuted.

Sabotage
A tactic used by some employees to influence the outcome of union/management negotiations in which company equipment is intentionally damaged to reduce work productivity.

Sabotage is another response to impasse in negotiations. A factory increased production from 2,000 to 3,000 units per day by modifying a drill press. Wages were not raised, however, and workers resented it. They found that bumping the sheet metal against the drill would eventually break the drill. Then the employee handling the drill would have to wait idly for a replacement. By some curious accident, average production continued at around 2,000 units per day. Management got the "message." Although sabotage is not a sanctioned union activity like a strike, it is a way of putting pressure on management to accept demands.

Lockout
Action taken by management against unionized employees to prevent them from entering their place of work as a means of influencing the union to accept the management position in a dispute over the labor contract.

Management also has a major tactic to get the union to acquiesce. It is called a **lockout** and is considered the employer's equivalent of a strike. The company threatens to close if the union does not accept its offer. Employees cannot work, and thus "pay" for rejecting the employer's offer. A threatened lockout may cause a majority of workers to pressure a minority holding out against a contract issue. Like strikes, lockouts are costly to both the company and the union, and they are not undertaken lightly. They are management's ultimate response to an impasse.

Before this section ends, note that strikes, slowdowns, sabotage, and lockouts represent failures in the collective bargaining process. These actions are taken because a settlement was *not* reached. Like most responses to frustration, they are rarely beneficial in the long run. Some unions may want to "teach the company a lesson;" some companies want to break a union. But the two parties have a symbiotic relationship. A company cannot exist without employees; without a company, employees have no jobs. Collective bargaining reflects the continual tussle for power, but neither side can afford to be totally victorious. If a union exacts so many concessions that the company goes bankrupt, it will have accomplished nothing. As one scholar put it, "Labor does not seek to kill the goose that lays the golden eggs; it wants it to lay more golden eggs, and wants more eggs for itself" (Estey 1981, p. 83).[25] If management drives employees away by not making enough concessions, it will not have a qualified workforce. Industrial peace is far more desirable for all parties than warfare. Conflict can provide opportunities for change and development; if conflict gets out of hand, it can be devastating.

Consider This...

The use of the terms "warfare" and "devastating" in the paragraph above may seem like hyperbole, but the unfortunate truth is that labor disputes can lead to truly devastating consequences that border on the brink of war. Take, for example, what is now known as the Ludlow Massacre, a 1914 event in which Colorado National Guard soldiers and private guards employed by the Colorado Fuel and Iron Company attacked a tent colony of coal workers and their families. The coal workers had been striking against unsafe working conditions and the attack was meant to end the strike. The attack resulted in the deaths of approximately 21 people, including the miners' wives and children. The miners retaliated, attacking many anti-union establishments before federal soldiers intervened. In total, between 69 and 199 people were killed during the strike, making it the deadliest in U.S. history. The strike was finally halted when the union ran out of money. The strikers' demands were not met, many workers were replaced, and hundreds of strikers were arrested and indicted for murder. Clearly, collective bargaining is a delicate process. Neither side should lose sight of the bigger picture, even though short-term, narrow issues are often at the heart of the dispute. With this in mind, at what point should strikes, slowdowns, and lockouts be stopped? What criteria would you use to make this decision?

WAR IN COLORADO! WOMEN AND BABIES SLAUGHTERED

VOLLEYS FIRED IN STREETS

PROPOSES GOVERNMENT OWNERSHIP OF ROCKEFELLER'S COLORADO MINES

THE COLORADO SITUATION

MEXICANS CHEER AS U.S. TROOPS ENTER HARBOR

Grievances

Collective bargaining is mainly directed toward resolving disputes over new labor contracts; however, disputes also occur over contracts that are in effect. No matter how clearly a labor contract is written, disagreements can arise over its meaning. Developing a clear and precise contract involves writing skills in their highest form. Despite the best intentions of those involved, events occur that are not covered clearly in a labor contract. For example, companies often include a contract clause stating that sleeping on the job is grounds for dismissal. A supervisor notices that an employee's head is resting on his arms and his eyes are closed. The supervisor infers the employee is asleep and fires him. The employee says he was not sleeping but felt dizzy and chose to rest for a moment rather than risk falling down. Who is right?

Grievance
A formal complaint made by an employee against management alleging a violation of the labor contract in effect.

If the supervisor dismissed the employee, the employee would probably file a **grievance**, or formal complaint. The firing decision can be appealed through a grievance procedure, which is usually a provision of a labor contract. First, the employee and supervisor try to reach an understanding. If they do not, the shop steward represents the employee in negotiating with the supervisor. This is often done whether or not the steward thinks the employee "has a case;" above all, the steward's job is to represent union members. If it is not resolved, the case may then be taken to the company's director of industrial relations, who hears testimony from both sides and issues a verdict. This may be a compromise—such as the employee keeps their job but is put on probation. The final step is to call in an arbitrator. The arbitrator examines the labor contract, hears testimony, and renders an opinion. This process is called rights or **grievance arbitration**; it involves the rights of the employee. The labor contract usually specifies that union and management share the cost of arbitration, which may be $2,000 per hearing. This is done to prevent all grievances from being routinely pushed to arbitration. Each side must believe it has a strong case before calling in an arbitrator.

Grievance arbitration
A type of arbitration used in resolving disputes between labor and management in interpretation of an existing labor contract. Also called rights arbitration.

The arbitrator must be acceptable to both sides; this means they must be seen as neither pro-union nor pro-management. The arbitrator may decide in favor of one side or issue a compromise decision. The decision is final and binding. If an arbitrator hears many cases in the same company and repeatedly decides in favor of one side, that arbitrator may become unacceptable to the side that always loses. Articles of the labor contract that are repeated subjects of grievance (due mainly to ambiguous language) become prime candidates for revision in the next contract.

Think of grievances as a somewhat contaminated criterion of the quality of union/management relations. In general, when the working relationship is good, there are fewer grievances. However, in some organizations, work problems are resolved informally between the conflicting parties and never develop into formal grievances. Although formal grievances are usually indicative of conflict, their absence does not always reflect a problem-free work environment. Also, the more ambiguous the labor contract, the more likely conflicts will ensue. A poorly written or inconsistently interpreted contract invites grievances. There can be much grievance activity in a recently-unionized organization; employees use grievances to "test" management's knowledge of the labor contract. Particularly in the public sector, where collective bargaining is more recent, employees are expected to act as "management" even though they may have little or no training in dealing with labor unions. This can contribute to errors in contract administration. Research suggests that employees are more likely to file a grievance when management actions against them are perceived as a threat and when the employees attribute the discipline to a manager's personal disposition (animus toward a worker).[26] Furthermore, employees appear to be less likely to file a grievance when they perceive managers as simply following rules that require punishment for the specific worker behavior.

Employee concern over capricious management decisions is one of the major reasons employees opt for union representation. The amount of procedural justice afforded by a grievance system is the strongest predictor of employee satisfaction with a union.[27] The assertion that grievances are best resolved at the lowest step of the grievance process was challenged by researchers who found that grievants who won their cases at higher levels of the grievance process showed greater faith in the fairness and perceived justice of the dispute resolution process.[28] Research has also found that at higher levels in the grievance process, managers were influenced by the grievant's work history as documented in performance appraisals, even when that history was not relevant to evaluating the merits of the grievance.[29] Consistent with procedural justice, employees with access to a grievance system are more willing to continue working for the organization.[30]

Over time, employment litigation has increased, with a corresponding increase in company costs and negative publicity.[31] With the increased number of lawsuits in the courts, there has been growing support for *alternative dispute resolution* procedures among employees, legislators, and the courts. Arbitration is being proposed as a means of resolving disputes between employees and employers. The arbitration process may be voluntary (i.e., the employee has the option to submit the dispute to an impartial arbitrator) or mandatory (i.e., the employee is required to submit any dispute to an impartial arbitrator as a condition of employment at the company). Likewise, the outcome of the arbitration process can be nonbinding (meaning if the arbitrator's judgment does not satisfy the employee, the employee can choose to pursue the dispute in court) or binding (meaning the outcome of the arbitration process is final and binding and may not be pursued in court). Such forced arbitration, while legal, has been called ethically questionable because it "denies employees access to the public, transparent court system" (Lefkowitz 2017, p. 385).[32] Not surprisingly, job applicants are more inclined to view an employer negatively if they use either mandatory or binding arbitration as a means of resolving disputes. The finding is interpreted as limiting avenues of procedural justice for employees.

In conclusion, although there is much publicity about strike-related issues, union members think the union's highest priority should be enhancing their welfare. Unions serve many purposes; however, the most pressing need they fill is to ensure fair treatment in employment. Of course, this is a primary reason that unions appeal to workers.

Influence of Unions on Non-Unionized Companies

Even if they do not have unionized employees, companies are still sensitive to union influence. Companies that are unresponsive to employees' needs invite unionization. A non-union company that wants to remain so must be receptive to its workers' ideas and complaints. If a company can satisfy its employees' needs, a union is unnecessary (i.e., if the company does voluntarily what a labor union would force it to do). A given community or industry often has a mix of union and non-union companies. If unionized employees get concessions from management on wages, benefits, hours, and so on, these become reference points for non-unionized employees. Thus, for example, a non-union company may feel compelled to raise wages to remain competitive. If a labor contract calls for formal grievance procedures, a non-union company may well follow suit. Workers are aware of employment conditions in other companies, which gives them a frame of reference for judging their own. If a company does not offer comparable conditions, employees may see a union as a means of improving their welfare. This is not to say that non-union companies must offer identical conditions. There are costs associated with a union (for example, dues); a non-union company might set

Union/non-union wage differential
The average difference in wages paid to union versus nonunion employees across an industry or geographic area for performing the same jobs.

wages slightly lower than those paid in a unionized company so the net effect (higher wages minus dues) is comparable. What economists call the **union/non-union wage differential** has been the subject of extensive research. The union/non-union wage differential varies with the national unemployment rate and ranges from 8.9% to 12.4%.[33] The higher wages for unionized employees get passed on to customers of the companies through the higher costs for goods produced or services supplied. It is argued that the higher cost of union labor is offset by higher work quality and efficiency.

Although a prudent non-union employer keeps abreast of employment conditions in the community and the industry, a company cannot act to keep a union out "at all costs." For example, an employer cannot fire workers without penalty just because they support a union. The history of labor relations is full of cases of worker harassment by unions or management to influence attitudes toward unionization. But both sides can suffer for breaking the law.

Behavioral Research on Union/Management Relations

Thus far, this chapter has examined the structure of unions, collective bargaining, and various issues in union/management relations. For the most part, psychological issues have not been discussed. With the exception of grievances, there is little behavioral research on union/management relations. However, over the past few decades, interest in this area has increased. We are beginning to see an interdisciplinary approach to topics that historically were treated with parochialism. This section will examine research on union/management relations with a strong behavioral thrust.

Employee Support for Unions

Numerous studies have examined why employees support a union, particularly with regard to personal needs and job satisfaction. One pair of researchers sampled the attitudes toward unionization of more than 400 college professors at a university experiencing many financial and resource cutbacks.[34] They measured satisfaction with areas like fairness of the university's personnel decisions, adequacy of financial support, representation of faculty interests in the state legislature, and salary. The professors were also asked to rate their inclination to accept a union. Professors who were dissatisfied with employment conditions were much more likely to support a union. Respondents also were consistent in their attitudes toward a union and their perceptions of its impact and effectiveness. Proponents of a union saw it as an effective way to protect employment interests and as having a positive impact. In general, results indicated that unionization is more attractive as employment conditions deteriorate.

Another study found that feelings of dissatisfaction correlated with acceptance of unionization. In particular, dissatisfaction with work, pay, and promotions each correlated .35 with attitude toward unionization. Additionally, unionization was more appealing to people who were less involved in their jobs.[35]

An examination of union activity in 250 units of a large organization revealed that in half the units, there had been some union activity; the other half had had no activity.[36] Using an immense sample of more than 80,000 employees, the researchers found that employee attitudes predicted the level of unionization activity. The strongest predictor was dissatisfaction with supervision. Another study found that pro-union voting in a certification election was positively correlated with dissatisfaction; also, dissatisfaction with economic issues was more predictive than dissatisfaction with non-economic factors.[37] Furthermore, research has shown the importance of two other factors in union support.[38] The first factor is attitude toward collective bargaining. The more acceptable unions in general are to a person, the more likely they will vote for unionization. The second factor is attitude toward unions as being instrumental in enhancing worker welfare. Employees may not be satisfied with their employment conditions, but they may feel that unions can do little to aid them.

Fun fact:
Though it would be inappropriate to say they were a union, the first recorded labor strike in history was in Ancient Egypt (~1170 BCE) in which laborers working for Pharaoh Ramesses III were upset about consistent and increasing delays in their rations. Their strike challenged the power dynamic at the time, and records indicate that the workers subsequently were paid on time.

These studies show that dissatisfaction with employment conditions is predictive of support for unionization. The more satisfied workers are, the less likely they are to think a union is necessary or that it can improve their welfare. These results are not surprising. They reveal the types of dissatisfaction associated with a disposition toward unions. Some authors tout the social benefits of unions (for example, association with similar people), but it is mainly the perceived economic advantages that give unions their appeal. Not all support for unions, however, is based on dissatisfaction with economic conditions. The faculty at one college, for example, wanted a union mainly because they distrusted administrative decision making and were dissatisfied with work content. Pro-union voting was motivated by the faculty's desire to have more power in dealing with the administration.[39] Not surprisingly, perceptions of union support appeared to be related to increased union participation, while perceptions of administrative support were related to decreased union participation.[40] The decision to support a union is grounded in theories of organizational justice. Perceived union support and union instrumentality are closely linked to workers' desire for procedural justice.[41] Similarly, unionization is supported on the basis of interactional justice—in this case, higher-quality interactions between employees and management.[42]

Union Influence

What influence do unions have on enhancing employee welfare? Various studies have produced different conclusions. In one study of 41 colleges, faculty were unionized in 18 colleges and non-unionized in 23. The researcher proposed nine criteria of effectiveness for a college, including student academic development, faculty and administrator satisfaction, and ability to acquire resources. Non-unionized colleges were significantly more effective on three of the nine criteria; unionized colleges were not significantly more effective on any. The researcher also collected attitude data from faculty members on four factors relating to their work. These results are presented in Figure 15-4. Faculty power and "red tape" were seen as increasing since unionization; collegiality was seen as decreasing.[43] The study revealed some major differences in the effectiveness of union and non-union colleges; however, the cause was not determined. Unionization may cause colleges to be less effective, which would be a strong argument against unions. However, less effective colleges may turn to unions for improvement, which is obviously an argument supporting unionization.

New organizational members may be socialized to consider joining a union. There are two types of socialization. The first is *institutional*, which refers to collective and formal practices used to provide newcomers with a common set of experiences and information to elicit standardized responses. In contrast, *individual* socialization

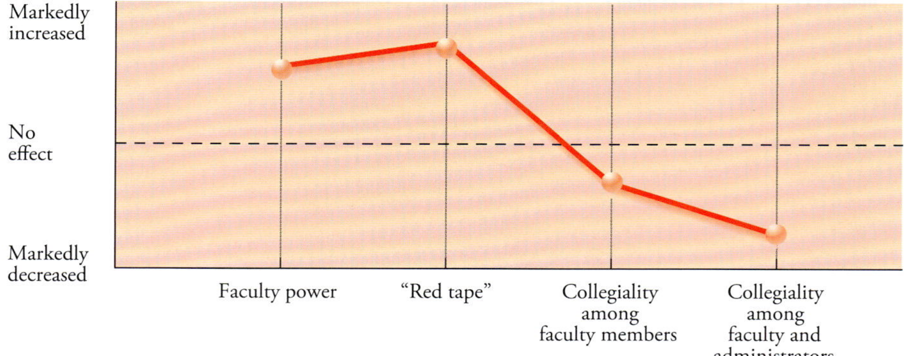

Figure 15-4 *Perceptions of the effects of faculty unionization*

From "The Relationship Between Faculty Unionism and Organizational Effectiveness," by K. Cameron, 1982, *Academy of Management Journal*, 25, p. 13. Reproduced with permission of Academy of Management via Copyright Clearance Center.

practices are idiosyncratic and informal. Individual socialization is informal, in that learning takes place on the job through interactions with other organizational members. In one study on the impact of socialization efforts and attitudes toward unions and later union involvement, researchers found that individual socialization practices positively impacted both affective and behavioral involvement in the union.[44] Institutional socialization practices were shown to be either ineffective or counterproductive. The practical implications are that important interactions occur between union officials and new members in developing new members' affective attachment to the union and later participation in union activities. Informal and individual socialization tactics may be undertaken by active or interested rank-and-file members and not necessarily by union stewards. Institutional socialization efforts (e.g., an orientation program to the union) seemingly are more effective in increasing awareness, whereas individual socialization efforts are more effective in producing involvement.[45]

Dispute Settlement

I-O psychologists have examined the process by which disputes are settled in both laboratory and field settings. As in some other areas of I-O psychology research, the generalizability of laboratory findings in this area is somewhat limited. The value of laboratory studies is to prepare people for undertaking actual collective bargaining in the future and to help develop questionnaires for later field use in dispute settlement. The limitations of laboratory and field research on dispute settlement are the classic ones discussed in Chapter 2. There is questionable generalizability from laboratory studies, and field studies fail to identify causal relationships.[46]

Several studies have looked at mediation and arbitration as means of settling disputes. One study determined that when the costs of arbitration are high, negotiators are more likely to reach a resolution on their own before they resort to arbitration. However, when cost is not much of an issue, they are more likely to accept arbitration.[47] Researchers have also found that when individuals anticipate they will be using final-offer arbitration, they get closer to agreement at the conclusion of their bargaining than individuals who anticipate using conventional arbitration.[48] Another study concluded that final-offer, conventional, total-package, and issue-by-issue arbitration all produced different bargaining outcomes even though they are all variations of the same resolution process (arbitration).[49] Even the words people use in online dispute resolution affect the likelihood of settlement. Looking at disputes between buyers and sellers on eBay (an online auction service), researchers found that settlement is more likely when parties engage in face-saving gestures, such as by providing a possible causal account for the misunderstanding between the two parties.[50] Conversely, settlement is less likely when parties feel attacked by verbal expressions of negative emotions or by making demands. These behavioral studies on dispute settlement have enhanced our understanding in ways that traditional labor economic research has been unable to do.

The criteria for dispute resolution include getting the two parties to resolve their own differences and having both parties feel some measure of satisfaction in the resulting outcome. Mediation is generally more effective as a means of dispute settlement when it is followed by binding arbitration (compared with mediation alone). That is, when both parties know (and have agreed in advance) that a settlement will be made for them by a third party (an arbitrator), they are more likely to reach a voluntary agreement on their own.[51] Thus, it may be best to utilize a hybrid means of dispute settlement where arbitration *precedes* (not follows) mediation. The three-phase process would work as follows. In phase one, the two parties present their cases to an arbitrator, who then makes a ruling. The ruling is sealed in an envelope and is not revealed to the two parties. In the second phase, the two parties engage in traditional mediation with no third party present. A precise time period is set for the two parties to reach an agreement. With a fixed time period set for the mediation phase, neither party can afford to engage in posturing or delays.[52] Any wasted time in the mediation phase increases the likelihood a settlement will not be reached, thereby placing control of the settlement in the hands of the arbitrator. If the two sides reach an agreement, the dispute is settled and the arbitrator's (unknown) ruling is rendered moot. However, if the two parties do not resolve their dispute in mediation, the third phase of the process is to make the arbitrator's ruling known to both parties, and they are both obligated to accept it. Researchers report that this hybrid method of "putting the cart before the horse" did result in successful voluntary agreements in the mediation phase, and is often used in highly contested disputes.

Commitment to the Union

The concept of employee commitment to a union addresses the notion of dual allegiance: can a person be loyal to both a labor union and the employing company? Researchers have examined the antecedents of both union and company commitment.

Union commitment The sense of identity and support unionized employees feel for their labor union.

Our understanding of **union commitment** was enhanced through a major study in which the researchers measured commitment of more than 1,800 union members.[53] Union commitment was found to be composed of four dimensions: loyalty, responsibility to the union, willingness to work for the union, and belief in unionism. The research revealed the importance of socialization to new union members. The researchers found that union commitment increases when both formal and informal efforts are made to involve a member in union activities soon after joining. Coworker attitudes and willingness to help are crucial to the socialization process. Improving the socialization of new members improves their commitment, which is one index of union strength.

In a study of membership decline in 20 unions, the unions with the greatest decline in membership showed the strongest commitment to the union by the surviving members.[54] Members in locals with more severe losses expressed a greater willingness to participate in future strikes. Another study reported that union loyalty was best predicted by union instrumentality, extrinsic job dissatisfaction, and early socialization experiences with unions.[55] The researchers proposed that greater union loyalty resulted in more formal participation in union activities. In a study of dual allegiance, satisfied workers felt allegiance to both the company and the union, whereas dissatisfied workers showed allegiance only to the union.[56]

Union commitment occurs in a context of organizational rights that are provided by the union, as well as organizational citizenship behaviors on the part of union members.[57] The degree of commitment to the union can be understood in terms of the psychological contract between the employee and the organization (as discussed in Chapter 11), and the role the union plays in maintaining this relationship. Two dimensions explain why employees are committed to a union.[58] The first is *instrumentality*, the perceived value or usefulness associated with union membership. The second is *ideology*, the individual's acceptance and support of the ideals or principles upon which labor unions are based.

A typology of union members' commitment to the union based on these two dimensions is shown in Figure 15-5.[59] Each dimension (instrumentality and ideology) is divided into two levels, high and low, resulting in a four-cell classification model. The *alienated member* is the noncommitted member who is likely to be nonparticipative and who might intend to withdraw membership. The *instrumental member* can be expected to retain membership and to support union activities directed at improving wages and working conditions. Members committed primarily because of their pro-union ideology (*ideological members*) support and take part in union activities, such as attending meetings. The *devoted member* category, representing members with high degrees of commitment on both dimensions, is postulated to contain the most active union members. Other forms of union participation activities include holding office, serving on union committees, and voting in elections.[60]

		Ideological commitment to the union	
		Low	High
Instrumental commitment to the union	High	Instrumental member	Devoted member
	Low	Alienated member	Ideological member

Figure 15-5 *Typology of union commitment*

Source: Adapted from "Union Membership Behavior: The Influence of Instrumental and Value-Based Commitment," by M. Sverke and A. Sjöberg, 1995, (pp. 229–254), in L. E. Tetrick and J. Barling (Eds.), *Changing employment relations.* Washington, DC: American Psychological Association.

Finally, researchers should be fully aware of the reasons that either the union or the company would encourage research on allegiance.[61] I-O psychologists should not allow themselves to be "used" by either side to further their own aims by conducting such research. A similar point, as noted earlier, was how I-O psychologists were involved in union-busting by using personality tests to detect "pro-union" job candidates.

I-O Psychology and Labor Relations

There are many areas where I-O psychology might contribute to the field of labor relations.[62] These include many of the issues already examined, including why workers join unions, dispute settlement, and dual commitment. Four traditional I-O psychology topics are examined from a labor union perspective: personnel selection, training, leadership development, and organizational change.

Personnel Selection and Promotion. In both union and non-union companies, management determines the knowledge, skills, and abilities needed to fill jobs. The human resources office usually determines fitness for employment in lower-level jobs. For higher-level jobs, responsibility is spread through various units of the company.

One of the classic differences between unions and management is their preference for determining how employees will be promoted or advanced to higher jobs. The clear preference of management is merit, as determined by an assessment of current job performance. Recall from Chapter 8 that performance appraisals are conducted for use in making promotion decisions. Unions, in contrast, prefer seniority as the basis for subsequent job moves, because it is objective and available to any employee as long as they remain in the organization long enough.[63]

A compromise position between merit and seniority is "qualified seniority." The employees must first meet some standard of proficiency (such as passing a job knowledge test), and among those who pass, the employee with the most seniority is promoted into the job. Union leaders have suggested using the ultimate measure of a person's suitability for employment, the job tryout, for all jobs. From the union perspective, this method affords equal opportunity for all members, with the final decision made based on documented performance in the tryout period. Job tryouts are usually too costly and impractical in terms of training, development, and performance management.[64] However, the logic of such a selection method is unassailable in theory: there is no need to predict (by use of a test, interview, work sample, etc.) behavior on the job when you can actually insert people into jobs and see how they perform. In practice, this idea ignores the problem of having multiple applicants for few openings as well as the consequences of issues or errors during the tryout period.

Apprentice training
A method of training in which the trainee learns to perform a job by serving under the supervision of an experienced worker who provides guidance, direction, and support.

Personnel Training. One area in which unions have significant influence is personnel training. One of the oldest forms is **apprentice training**, and unions have a long history of this kind of training, especially in trades and crafts. Apprenticeship is governed by law; at the national level, it is administered by the Department of Labor. The Office of Apprenticeship Training, Employer, and Labor Services (OATELS) works closely with unions, vocational schools, state agencies, and others. In 2020, there were more than 26,000 apprentice programs employing over 636,000 apprentices.[65] Apprentices go through a formal program of training and experience. They are supervised on the job and are given the facilities needed for instruction. There is a progressive wage schedule over the course of apprenticeship, and the individual becomes well versed in all aspects of the trade.

Most apprentice programs are in heavily-unionized occupations (such as construction, manufacturing, and transportation); thus, unions work closely with OATELS.

Fun fact:
Despite the 12% decline in the number of new apprentices in 2020 compared to 2019, the numbers were still the third-highest ever, with an overall 70% growth in new apprentices since 2011.

Figure 15-6 shows the cooperation among various organizations and agencies in the carpentry trade. Although not all unions are involved in apprentice programs, the linkage between unions and apprenticeship is one of the oldest in the history of American labor.

Leadership Development. Often employees elected to leadership roles within their unions (e.g., shop stewards) or within the organization (e.g., supervisors) have had little developmental instruction in how to behave in a position of leadership. Studies have shown it is possible to train individuals on important aspects of union leadership. For example, in one effort to teach supervisors to take effective disciplinary action with employees, the supervisors were placed into either a training group or a control group.[66] Following simulated role-playing exercises, both unionized employees and

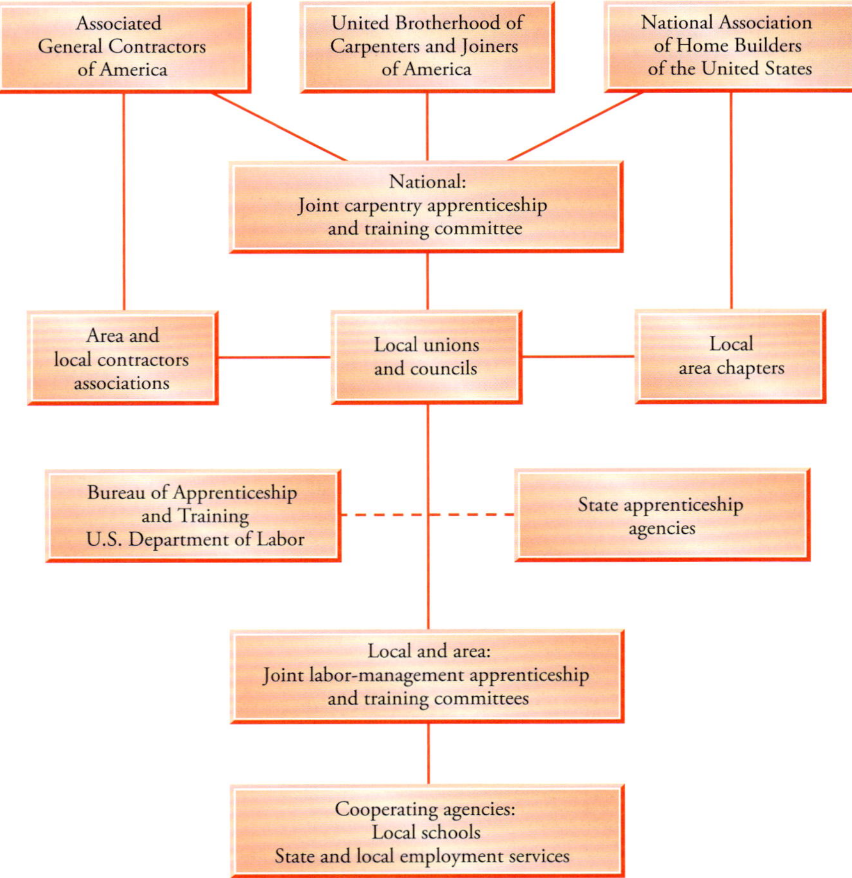

Figure 15-6 *Cooperation among unions, industry, and government in the apprenticeship system of the carpentry trade*

Source: From *Apprenticeship: Past and present* (p. 25) by U.S. Department of Labor, 1994. Washington, DC: U.S. Government Printing Office.

disciplinary subject matter experts (managers, union officials, and attorneys) rated the trained supervisors higher on disciplinary fairness than the supervisors in the control group. Another study examined whether training union officers in the skills necessary for implementing principles of organizational justice would increase citizenship behaviors on the part of members of a labor union.[67] The results showed that three months after training, the perceptions of union fairness among members whose leaders were in the training group were higher than among members whose leaders were in the control group. Lastly, another example involved teaching shop stewards methods of procedural justice using cases based on organizational incidents.[68] The training improved knowledge of what constitutes fairness and resulted in fewer grievances among employees regarding alleged unfairness in work. These examples illustrate how concepts such as procedural justice and organizational citizenship behavior can be used to improve the quality of leadership in organizations with labor unions.

After examining the relationship between union leadership and member attitudes, researchers concluded that union leaders should make sure their members see the connection between the actions union leadership is taking to achieve desired employment outcomes and the attainment of those outcomes.[69] Workers seek unions to represent them in employment relations because they perceive the union as being valuable in doing so. In turn, effective labor unions should send a "union utility" message back to their members. Namely, the union is delivering on what the members want, and without the union, the members would be receiving less.

Organizational Change. As was discussed in Chapter 9, it is difficult to bring about change in any organization. It is even more difficult to bring about change in an organization whose employees are represented by a labor union. The following is an assessment of the process of managing change in a unionized workplace:[69]

1. Labor/management relationships have evolved over time and fall somewhere on a continuum between open warfare and efforts to create labor/management partnerships. Even those relationships near the partnership end of the continuum, however, usually manifest some discord.

2. Management in a unionized workplace is governed by laws that do not apply in a non-union environment. These laws, particularly those relating to bargaining and labor contracts, are a major factor in the management of change.

3. Management faces more sources of resistance, more reasons for resistance, and a greater ability to resist in a unionized than a non-union workplace.

It is important for organizations to change in response to changing environmental conditions (international competition, increasing costs, etc.), a theme identified throughout this book. However, in a unionized company, change must take place at two levels. First, management must make all the business changes that are necessary to remain competitive in the rapidly changing world. Second, it needs to change its relationship with its union. A union is in a position to delay, prevent, or make such changes more difficult, and what it elects to do will be largely determined by its relationship with management. If that relationship is less than positive, management must improve it before the company can effectively make the many business changes that are required. Typically, business changes lead to fewer jobs, different roles and responsibilities for existing jobs, new or revised work rules, and changes in pay, benefits, and work hours. Employees will resist much of the change, both individually and through their elected union representatives. This resistance will confirm their union as a legitimate force in the change process and require management to work not only with employees, but also with the union that represents them.

A union may refuse to discuss a company proposal that affects an issue covered by a previously-negotiated labor contract, such as wages, hours, or conditions of work. In such a case, the matter is closed to discussion and the union could exercise its right to have a "deal be a deal" until the scheduled termination of the labor contract in effect, which might be several years in the future. When the contract expires, the company may, after appropriate bargaining, implement planned changes at the risk of other union resistance tactics. The psychology of union resistance to change is predicated, in part, upon the union not wanting to appear irrelevant in the relationship between employees and the company. Individuals are often reluctant to change because the change represents some loss (or perceived loss) of control over their lives.

The union, therefore, can become an instrument for increasing employee control, even to the possible long-term detriment of the employees. If the union shows little resistance to proposed management changes, the very viability of the union as an agent of the employees can be questioned. There remains a gap in our knowledge about organizational change in unionized companies. Consider Figure 15-7. It is a badge made by a labor union (the United Steelworkers) expressing protest against a safety program initiated by management. The name given to the program was "Behavioral Safety;" the program was designed to encourage workers to behave safely in steel factories. The union badge represents a defiant statement against the Behavioral Safety program ("No B.S."). While the labor union was in favor of reducing work-related injuries to their members, the union resented the assumption that the behavior of their members was responsible for the injuries ("Don't Blame Workers"). The union's explanation for the work-related injuries incurred by their members pertained to factors under the control of management ("Eliminate Hazards"). This badge is symbolic of unions offering resistance to proposed management changes (i.e., a safety program designed to reduce work-related injuries), even if the change was for the workers' benefit. If the union supported the safety program, the instrumental value of the union as an agent of the employees could be questioned.

Figure 15-7 *Badge worn by union members expressing contempt for a management program on behavioral safety*

What Is the Future of Labor Unions?

As mentioned previously, in the United States membership in labor unions has steadily declined over the past 75 years. The highwater mark for unionized employees was around 35% of the total workforce in 1945. It is only because 37% of government employees are unionized (compared to 7% of the private sector) that the total percentage of unionized employees in the workforce today is still in double digits (12%).[71]

There are several possible reasons for the decline in labor unions. First, the percentage of the workforce employed in manufacturing, a traditional labor stronghold, is declining. Companies that manufactured products are finding more favorable economic conditions in other countries (offshoring, discussed in Chapter 9). Most prominent is the cost of labor. Many countries do not have minimum wage laws. Immense cost savings to employers are achieved by exporting jobs to cheaper labor markets. Also, corporate tax rates differ markedly across nations. For example, when a large manufacturing company shifted its corporate headquarters from the U.S. to Bermuda, its annual corporate tax was reduced from $40 million owed to the United States government to $27,653 owed to Bermuda.[72]

Second, the sectors of the economy that are growing (e.g., customer service, healthcare) have shown little interest in having its employees be represented by labor unions. Employers in those sectors have become increasingly resistant to organizing attempts by voluntarily offering the types of employment conditions that unions achieve for their members. Employers like to tout their attractiveness through such reports as the "Best Places to Work."[73] The vast majority of these highly-rated companies are union-free; it is unclear whether a union presence could make major improvements in employment conditions (see COVID-19 and I-O Psychology: *Union Impact During the Pandemic*).

Third, proponents of organized labor claim the union/management playing field is far from even, with labor being greatly disadvantaged by current federal laws. For example, employers can require all workers to attend anti-union informational meetings on company time, but unions are not allowed to do the same. While laws prohibit employers from firing workers who express pro-union sentiments, the consequences for doing so are not severe.

Finally, the nature of employment has changed in the 21st century. Today, workers are less likely to devote their entire career to a single employer compared to decades ago. Also, the era of huge companies (employing thousands of workers each) has given way to relatively small employers. Approximately 52% of the U.S. workforce is employed by companies that have fewer than 500 employees. Furthermore, 75% of new job growth in the nation is with small employers.[74] Being smaller, there is more capacity for cooperation between workers and management, with a corresponding reduction in a "them vs. us" mentality. The very nature of work itself is characterized by a different structure than in the past. Work is now routinely conducted across nations. For example, a U.S. owned company could have a production plant in the Philippines using German-made equipment to process raw material from Argentina that is assembled in Vietnam and transported to worldwide markets by ships from South Korea. Information transmission is now continuous and immediate. Time, when we work and when we sleep, is irrelevant to global commerce. It is always "work

COVID-19 and I-O Psychology: *Union Impact During the Pandemic*

Like many organizations, unions were hit hard during the COVID-19 pandemic. For example, UNITE-HIRE—a union representing individuals in the hotel, food service, laundry, warehouse, and casino industries—was hit especially hard, as its members were among the most frequently laid off, and members consequently stopped paying dues.

Other unions, however, had sufficient resources to continue to advocate for their workers. In particular, and not surprisingly, many unions rallied on behalf of their members with regard to the health and safety of workers. The AFL-CIO, for example, sued OSHA to compel the agency to adopt an emergency protocol specifically related to the pandemic. Similarly, the United Auto Workers persuaded General Motors, Ford, and Fiat Chrysler to shut down for two weeks to slow the spread of the virus.[75]

Unions also advocated for their members regarding forced vaccination mandates. For example, the United Food and Commercial Workers (UFCW) International Union, the largest meatpacking union in the U.S., expressed concerns when a vaccination mandate was ordered before the U.S. Food and Drug Administration (FDA) had a fully approved a vaccine. Once the FDA granted full approval for a vaccine, the UFCW agreed to support the requirement that Tyson Foods had for its employees to be vaccinated against COVID-19. The union was also able to secure paid sick leave for meatpacking workers during the negotiations.[76]

Pay was also on union agendas, particularly for front-line workers. For example, the UFCW fought for and won temporary premium pay for thousands of workers at Safeway, Kroger, Giant, and Shoppers.[77] Similarly, the loss of pay due to layoffs was a possibility for many, and as such the Teamsters reached an agreement with DHL that would help minimize layoffs as a result of COVID-19.[78]

The importance and integral role of unions has been starkly clear during the COVID-19 pandemic. Unions successfully negotiated additional pay, health and safety measures, paid sick leave, and reduced layoffs. In addition, unionized workers have expressed great security in speaking up about workplace hazards.[79] Thus, despite the ongoing decline in union membership within the United States, unions have proven their worth on many fronts. Time will tell whether their impact during this global crisis will improve future membership numbers.

time" in some part of the world, a cornerstone of the new global economy. Labor unions in the United States have not evolved at the same rate of change as the world of business.

Do these changing global conditions render labor unions obsolete? Not at all. Labor unions will have to develop different strategies for attracting new members and appealing to the growing sectors of the national economy to once again serve a prominent role in the U.S. economy. Labor unions are but a means to an end. Organized labor has long advocated principles that would be the foundation of a better society for all. Work plays a central role, perhaps the defining role, in any healthy society. Most of us need jobs to thrive.[80] Unemployment, particularly long-term unemployment, has corrosive consequences for humanity. Many people desire meaningful work, jobs that utilize the full range of talent that they have to offer. Underemployment often leads to alienation and aversion to work. Lastly, we need to balance work and nonwork activities to sustain psychological health. None of these—unemployment, underemployment, or overemployment (working 60-80 hours per week)—lead to a fulfilling life. In sum, there is no shortage of problems in the contemporary work world. The pressing issue for labor unions is whether they can offer viable solutions to employment problems in the new global economy. While organized labor would be facilitated by new legislation favorable to their goals, ultimately, the value of labor unions will be what it has always been: offering workers a higher quality of life with their presence than their absence.

Labor union representation in other countries is typically much higher than in the United States. For example, it is almost 80% in Belgium, 60% in Denmark, and 30% in the U.K.[81] The average employee in Europe works 1,640 hours per year and gets five weeks of vacation; the average worker in the U.S. works 1,900 hours per year and gets two weeks of vacation.[82] It is a matter of debate whether labor unions in the U.S. will be able to muster the resources and appeal that they once held, especially in comparison to other developed nations in the world.

Labor unions were originally developed to decrease the disparity between two segments of society (management—the "haves," and the workers—the "have nots").[83] Labor unions bargained for outcomes (e.g., higher wages, better benefits) to reduce the inequality between the two. However, increased global commerce in the 21st century has produced a new form of the "haves" and the "have nots."

Growing global trade has been accompanied by widening inequality among countries. Work—or its absence—significantly shapes these inequalities, with many citizens unable to find work, or enough of it, when they want it. Unemployment is high in many countries, and as former UN Secretary General Kofi Annan stated, "The best anti-poverty program is employment. And the best road to economic empowerment and social well-being is decent work" (Pocock 2008, pp. 573-4).[84] It remains to be seen if, in the 21st century, emerging nations will turn to labor unions to improve their economic welfare, as happened with industrialized nations at the start of the 20th century.

Chapter Review

Key Terms

Union-busting
Union
Union shop
Open shop
National Labor Relations Act (NLRA)
National Labor Relations Board (NLRB)
Authorization card
Certification election
Labor contract
Impasse
Collective bargaining
Mediation
Fact-finding
Arbitration
Interest arbitration
Conventional arbitration
Final-offer arbitration
Total-package arbitration
Issue-by-issue arbitration
Labor strike
Work slowdown
Sabotage
Lockout
Grievance
Grievance arbitration
Union/non-union wage differential
Union commitment
Apprentice training

Questions for Review

1. How has the relationship between unions and I-O psychologists historically been characterized? Why?
2. What are unions? Why do workers typically join unions?
3. What are the distinctions between a union shop, a closed shop, and an open shop?
4. What are right-to-work laws?
5. What rights are afforded individuals with regard to unions?
6. How are unions formed?
7. What are typical bargaining issues and positions taken by union and management?
8. What is the distinction between distributive and integrative bargaining?
9. What are three options involving third parties for breaking an impasse? What do they involve?
10. What are potential responses to impasse that unions and employers may take?
11. What are grievances? How are they typically handled within a union setting?
12. How do unions impact non-unionized companies?
13. What factors influence commitment to a union?
14. What influence do unions have on enhancing employee welfare?
15. What does research show with regard to dispute settlement in unionized settings?
16. What are instrumentality and ideology with regard to union commitment? How do these dimensions combine to form four types of members?
17. How do unions impact personnel selection and promotion, personnel training, leadership development, and organizational change within an organization?
18. How would you summarize the future of labor unions?

Endnotes

Chapter 1

1. Zickar, M. J., & Gibby, R. E. (2007). Four persistent themes throughout the history of I-O psychology in the United States. In L. L. Koppes (Ed.), *Historical perspectives in industrial and organizational psychology* (pp. 61–80). Mahwah, NJ: Erlbaum.
2. Payne, S. C., & Pariyothorn, M. M. (2007). I-O psychology in introductory psychology textbooks: A survey of authors. *The Industrial-Organizational Psychologist, 44*(4), 37–42.
3. Culbertson, S. S. (2011). The academic's forum: I-O coverage in general psychology courses. *The Industrial-Organizational Psychologist, 49*(2), 62–65.
4. Vinchur, A. J., & Koppes, L. L. (2011). A historical survey of research and practice in industrial and organizational psychology. In S. Zedeck (Ed.), *APA handbook of industrial and organizational psychology* (Vol. 1, pp. 3–36). Washington, DC: APA.
5. Zickar, M. J., & Gibby, R. E. (2007)—see #1.
6. Campbell, J. P. (2007). Profiting from history. In L. L. Koppes (Ed.), *Historical perspectives in industrial and organizational psychology* (pp. 441–457). Mahwah, NJ: Erlbaum.
7. Muchinsky, P. M. (2002). The high society: What is your orientation: Are you an I or an O? *The Industrial-Organizational Psychologist, 40*(1), 57–60.
8. Cucina, J. M., & Jackson, F. (2016). Update of Landy's (1997) I-O psychology family trees. *The Industrial-Organizational Psychologist 54*(1). Retrieved October 15, 2021, from https://www.siop.org/Research-Publications/TIP/TIP-Back-Issues/2016/July/ArtMID/20282/ArticleID/872/An-Update-of-Landys-1997-Psychology-Family-Tree; and Culbertson, S. S. (2010). The academic's forum: Fun with family trees (Tracing your academic lineage). *The Industrial-Organizational Psychologist, 48*(1), 81–84.
9. Aamodt, M. G. (2010). Thomas Alva Edison: An I-O psychologist? *The Industrial-Organizational Psychologist, 48*(2), 47–53.
10. Bryan, W. L. (1904). Theory and practice. *Psychological Review, 11,* 71–82.
11. Bryan, W. L., & Harter, N. (1897). Studies in the physiology and psychology of the telegraphic language. *Psychological Review, 4,* 27–53.
12. Bryan, W. L. (1904)—see #10, p. 80.
13. Koppes, L. L. (2002). The rise of industrial-organizational psychology: A confluence of dynamic forces. In D. K. Freedheim (Ed.), *History of psychology* (pp. 367–389). New York: Wiley.
14. Koppes, L. L., & Pickren, W. (2007). Industrial and organizational psychology: An evolving science and practice. In L. L. Koppes (Ed.), *Historical perspectives in industrial and organizational psychology* (pp. 3–35). Mahwah, NJ: Erlbaum.
15. Landy, F. J. (1997). Early influences on the development of industrial and organizational psychology. *Journal of Applied Psychology, 82,* 467–477.
16. Van De Water, T. J. (1997). Psychology's entrepreneurs and the marketing of industrial psychology. *Journal of Applied Psychology, 82,* 486–499.
17. Wren, D. A. & Bedeian, A. G. (2004). The Taylorization of Lenin: Rhetoric or reality? *International Journal of Social Economics, 31,* 287–299.
18. Koppes, L. L. (1997). American female pioneers of industrial and organizational psychology during the early years. *Journal of Applied Psychology, 82,* 500–515.
19. Yost, E. (1943). *American women of science.* New York: Stokes.
20. Koppes, L. L. (1997)—see #18, p. 511
21. Lillian Moller Gilbreth: A profile. (1944, June). *California Magazine*, pp. 20–21+.
22. Koppes, L. L. (2010). Lillian Evelyn Moller Gilbreth (1878-1972): Biography of Lillian Evelyn Moller Gilbreth. *American Psychological Association, Division 35.* Retrieved October 15, 2021, from https://www.apadivisions.org/division-35/about/heritage/lillian-gilbreth-biography
23. Landy, F. J. (1992). Hugo Münsterberg: Victim or visionary? *Journal of Applied Psychology, 77,* 787–802.
24. Benjamin, L. T., Jr. (2006). Hugo Münsterberg's attack on the application of scientific psychology. *Journal of Applied Psychology, 91,* 414–425.

25. Landy, F. J. (1992)—see #23, p. 801.

26. Prieto, L.C. (2012). Women issues to Wonder Woman: Contributions made by the students of Hugo Münsterberg. *Journal of Management History, 18*, 166-177.

27. Salas, E., DeRouin, R. E., & Gade, P. A. (2007). The military's contribution to our science and practice: People, places, and findings. In L. L. Koppes (Ed.), *Historical perspectives in industrial and organizational psychology* (pp. 169–189). Mahwah, NJ: Erlbaum.

28. Scott, W. D. (1908). *The psychology of advertising*. New York: Arno Press.

29. Taylor, F. W. (1911). *The principles of scientific management*. New York: Harper.

30. Münsterberg, H. (1913). *Psychology and industrial efficiency*. Boston: Houghton Mifflin.

31. Viteles, M. S. (1932). *Industrial psychology*. New York: W. W. Norton

32. U. S. Employment Service, & U. S. Bureau of Manpower Utilization. (1939). *Dictionary of occupational titles*. Washington: U.S. Govt. Print. Off.

33. Ghiselli, E. E., & Brown, C. W. (1955). *Personnel and industrial psychology*. New York: McGraw-Hill.

34. Schein, E. H. (1965). *Organizational psychology*. Englewood Cliffs, NJ: Prentice-Hall.

35. McCormick, E. J., Jeanneret, P. R., & Mecham, R. C. (1972). A study of job characteristics and job dimensions as based on the Position Analysis Questionnaire (PAQ). *Journal of Applied Psychology, 56*, 347–368.

36. Schmidt, F. L., & Hunter, J. E. (1977). Development of a general solution to the problem of validity generalization. *Journal of Applied Psychology, 62*, 529–540.

37. Lefkowitz, J. (2017). *Ethics and values in industrial-organizational psychology* (2nd ed.). New York: Routledge.

38. Viteles, M. S. (1932) - see #31.

39. Mills, M. J. (2012). The beginnings of industrial psychology: The life and work of Morris Viteles. *The Industrial-Organizational Psychologist, 49*(3), 39–44.

40. Hofstede, G. (1980). *Culture's consequences: International differences in work-related values*. Beverly Hills, CA: Sage.

41. Schmidt, F. L., & Hunter, J. E. (1998). The validity and utility of selection methods in personnel psychology: Practical and theoretical implications of 85 years of research findings. *Psychological Bulletin, 124*(2), 262–274.

42. Harrell, T. W. (1992). Some history of the Army General Classification Test. *Journal of Applied Psychology, 77*, 875–878.

43. Murray, H. A., & MacKinnon, D. W. (1946). Assessment of OSS personnel. *Journal of Consulting Psychology, 10*, 76–80.

44. House, R. J., Hanges, P. J., Javidan, M., Dorman, P. W., & Gupta, V. (Eds.). (2004). *Culture, leadership, and organizations: The GLOBE study of 62 societies*. Thousand Oaks, CA: Sage.

45. Zedeck, S. (Ed.). (2010b). *APA handbook of industrial and organizational psychology*. Washington, DC: APA.

46. Muchinsky, P. M. (2013). Three bold ideas. *The Industrial-Organizational Psychologist, 51*(2), 152–157.

47. Ghiselli, E. E., & Brown, C. W. (1955) - see #33.

48. Campbell, J. P., & Knapp, D. J. (2010). Project A: 12 years of R & D. In J. L. Farr & N. T. Tippins (Eds.), *Handbook of employee selection* (pp. 865–886). New York: Routledge.

49. Zakon, R. H. (2021). *Hobbes' Internet Timeline 25*. Retrieved October 15, 2021, from https://www.zakon.org/robert/internet/timeline/

50. Internet Live Stats. (n.d.). *Internet Users*. Retrieved December 8, 2021, from https://www.internetlivestats.com/internet-users/

51. Kapp, K. M., & O'Driscoll, T. (2010). *Learning in 3D*. San Francisco: Pfeiffer.

52. Murphy, K. R. (1999). The challenge of staffing a post-industrial workplace. In D. R. Ilgen & E. D. Pulakos (Eds.), *The changing nature of performance* (pp. 295–324). San Francisco: Jossey-Bass.

53. Pearlman, K., & Barney, M. F. (2000). Selection for a changing workplace. In J. F. Kehoe (Ed.), *Managing selection in changing organizations* (pp. 3–72). San Francisco: Jossey-Bass.

54. McBride, T., Nief, R., and Westerberg, C. (2015). The Mindset List for the Class of 2015. *The Mindset Lists*. Retrieved October 15, 2021, from http://themindsetlist.com/lists/2015-list

55. Richards, J. (2012). What has the Internet ever done for employees? A review, map and research agenda. *Employee Relations, 34*, 22–43.

56. Cappelli, P., & Keller, J. (2013). Classifying work in the new economy. *Academy of Management Review, 38*, 575–596.

57. Manzione, G. (2011, March 14). Memory lane: A pinboy's tale. *United States Bowling Congress*. Retrieved December 2, 2021, from https://www.bowl.com/news/newsdetails.aspx?id=12884905118

58. Bennett, S. (2019, February 19). The Experience Age has arrived. *BATimes*. Retrieved October 15, 2021, from https://www.batimes.com/articles/the-experience-age-has-arrived/

59. Bachousi, J. (2020, August 19). Escape Rooms trends. *Institute of Entrepreneurship Development*. Retrieved October 15, 2021, from https://ied.eu/project-updates/escape-rooms-trends/

60. Zion Market Research. (2019, February 21). Global Augmented and Virtual Reality Market Will Reach USD 814.7 Billion by 2025. *Globe Newswire*. Retrieved October 15, 2021, from https://www.globenewswire.com/news-release/2019/02/21/1739121/0/en/Global-Augmented-and-Virtual-Reality-Market-Will-Reach-USD-814-7-Billion-By-2025-Zion-Market-Research.html

61. Wilder-Smith, A., & Freedman, D. O. (2020). Isolation, quarantine, social distancing and community containment: Pivotal role for old-style public health measures in the novel coronavirus (2019-nCoV) outbreak. *Journal of Travel Medicine, 27*, taaa020.

62. World Health Organization. (2021). *COVID-19 Physical Distancing*. Retrieved October 15, 2021, from https://www.who.int/westernpacific/emergencies/covid-19/information/physical-distancing

63. Zelin, A., Lider, M., & Doverspike, D. (2015, December). SIOP Career Study Executive Report. *SIOP.org*. Retrieved December 3, 2021, from https://www.siop.org/Portals/84/PDFs/Professionals/SIOP_Careers_Study_Executive_Report_FINAL-Revised_031116.pdf?ver=2019-06-26-075622-550

64. Society for Industrial and Organizational Psychology. (2020). *Income and Employment Report 2020*.

65. Bapuji, H., de Bakker, F., Brown, J., Higgins, C., Rehbein, K., & Spicer, A. (2020). Business and society research in times of the corona crisis. *Business & Society, 59*(6), 1067–1078; and Bapuji, H., Patel, C., Ertug, G., & Allen, D. G. (2021). COVID-19 is an opportunity to rethink I-O psychology, not for business as usual. *Industrial and Organizational Psychology, 14*(1–2), 50–54.

66. Brammer, S., Branicki, L., & Linnenluecke, M. (2020). COVID-19, societalization, and the future of business in society. *Academy of Management Perspectives, 34*(4), 493–507.

67. Sackett, P. R. (1994). "I am the very model of a scientist-practitioner". *The Industrial-Organizational Psychologist, 32*(1), 51–52.

68. Pfeffer, J. (2007). A modest proposal: How we might change the process and product of managerial research. *Academy of Management Journal, 50*, 1334–1345.

69. Cascio, W. F. (2007). Evidence-based management and the marketplace of ideas. *Academy of Management Journal, 50*, 1009–1012.

70. Brandon, S. E. (2011). Impacts of psychological science on national security agencies post-9/11. *American Psychologist, 66*, 495–506.

71. Rynes, S. L. (2012). The research practice gap in I/O psychology and related fields: Challenges and potential solutions. In S. W. J. Kozlowski (Ed.), *The Oxford handbook of organizational psychology* (Vol. 1, pp. 409–452). New York: Oxford University Press.

72. Rupp, D. E., & Beal, D. J. (2007). Checking in with the scientist–practitioner model: How are we doing? *The Industrial–Organizational Psychologist, 45*, 35–40

73. Rynes, S. L., Brown, K. G., & Colbert, A. E. (2002). Seven common misconceptions about human resource practices: Research findings versus practitioner beliefs. *Academy of Management Executive, 16*(3), 92–103; and Sanders, K., van Riemsdijk, M., & Groen, B. (2008). The gap between research and practice: A replication study on HR professionals' beliefs about effective human resource practices. *The International Journal of Human Resource Management, 19*, 1976–1988.

74. Cascio, W. F., & Aguinis, H. (2008). Research in industrial and organizational psychology from 1963 to 2007: Changes, choices, and trends. *Journal of Applied Psychology, 93*, 1062–1081.

75. Allen, J. A., Behrend, T. S., Bell, S. T., & Smoak, V. J. (2014). Suggested practices for making I-O connections: Let's build bridges and grow I-O! *The Industrial-Organizational Psychologist, 51*(4), 166–170.

76. Katzell, R. A., & Austin, J. T. (1992). From then to now: The development of industrial-organizational psychology in the United States. *Journal of Applied Psychology, 77*, p. 826.

77. Farr, J. L., & Tesluk, P. E. (1997). Bruce V. Moore: First president of Division 14. *Journal of Applied Psychology, 82*, 478-485.

78. Kraut, A. I. (2017). An old-timer's impressions of SIOP conference 2017. *The Industrial and Organizational Psychologist, 55*(1).

79. Griffith, R. L., & Wang, M. (2010). The internationalization of I-O psychology: We're not in Kansas anymore. *The Industrial-Organizational Psychologist, 48*(1), 41–45.

80. Howard, A., & Lowman, R. L. (1985). Should industrial/ organizational psychologists be licensed? *American Psychologist, 40*, 40–47.

81. Society for Industrial and Organizational Psychology. (2020)—see #64.

Chapter 2

1. Campbell, J. P. (1990). The role of theory in industrial and organizational psychology. In M. D. Dunnette & L. M. Hough (Eds.), *Handbook of industrial and organizational psychology* (2nd ed., Vol. 1, pp. 39–74). Palo Alto, CA: Consulting Psychologists Press.

2. Ibid.

3. Henrich, J., Heine, S. J., & Norenzayan, A. (2010). The weirdest people in the world? *Behavioral and Brain Sciences, 33*, 61–135.

4. Gregori, A., & Baltar, F. (2013). Ready to complete the survey on Facebook. Web 2.0 as a research tool in business studies. *International Journal of Marketing Research, 55*, 131–148.

5. Bhutta, C. B. (2012). Not by the book: Facebook as a sampling frame. *Sociological Methods & Research, 41*, 57–88.

6. Buhrmester, M., Kwang, T., & Gosling, S. D. (2011). Amazon's Mechanical Turk: A new source of inexpensive, yet high quality, data? *Perspectives on Psychological Science, 6*, 3–5.

7. Stone-Romero, E. F. (2011). Research strategies in industrial and organizational psychology: Nonexperimental, quasi-experimental, and randomized experimental research in special purpose and nonspecial purpose settings. In S. Zedeck (Ed.), *APA handbook of industrial and organizational psychology* (Vol. 1, pp. 37–72). Washington, DC: APA.

8. Eden, D. (2017). Field experiments in organizations. *Annual Review of Organizational Psychology and Organizational Behavior, 4*, 91–122.

9. Ibid., p. 96.

10. Brooks, A. W., Schroeder, J., Risen, J. L., Gino, F., Galinsky, A. D., Norton, M. I., & Schweitzer, M. E. (2016). Don't stop believing: Rituals improve performance by decreasing anxiety. *Organizational Behavior and Human Decision Processes, 137*, 71–85.

11. Ibid., p. 76.

12. Eden, D. (2017)—see #8.

13. Shadish, W. R. (2002). Revisiting field experimentation: Field notes for the future. *Psychological Methods, 7*, 3–18.

14. Grant, A. M., Berg, J. M., & Cable, D. M. (2014). Job titles as identity badges: How self-reflective titles can reduce emotional exhaustion. *Academy of Management Journal, 57*, 1201–1225.

15. Stone-Romero, E. F. (2011)—see #7.

16. Porter, C. M., Woo, S. E., & Campion, M. A. (2016). Internal and external networking differentially predict turn-over through job embeddedness and job offers. *Personnel Psychology, 69*, 635–672.

17. Uzzi, B., & Dunlap, S. (2005). How to build your network. *Harvard Business Review*, December. Retrieved October 16, 2021, from https://hbr.org/2005/12/how-to-build-your-network

18. Lee, J. J., Gino, F., & Staats, B. R. 2014. Rainmakers: Why bad weather means good productivity. *Journal of Applied Psychology, 99*: 504–513.

19. Shultz, K. S., Hoffman, C. C., & Reiter-Palmon, R. (2005). Using Archival Data for I-O Research: Advantages, Pitfalls, Sources, and Examples. *Psychology Faculty Publications, 5*, 31–37.

20. Antonakis, J., Bastardoz, N., Liu, Y., Schriesheim, C. A. (2014). What makes articles highly cited? *The Leadership Quarterly, 25*, 152–179; and Scandura, T. A., Williams, E. A. (2000). Research methodology in organizational studies: Current practices and implications for future research. *Academy of Management Journal, 43*, 1248–1264.

21. Ibid.

22. Barnes, C. M., Dang, C. T., Leavitt, K., Guarana, C. L., & Uhlmann, E. L. (2015). Archival data in micro-organizational research: A toolkit for moving to a broader set of topics. *Journal of Management, 44*(4), 1453–1478.

23. Hunter, J. E., & Schmidt, F. L. (1990). *Method of meta-analysis: Correcting error and bias in research findings.* Newbury Park, CA: Sage; Rosenthal, R. (1991). *Meta-analytic procedures for social research* (2nd ed.). Newbury Park, CA: Sage.
24. Cohn, L. D., & Becker, B. J. (2003). How meta-analysis increases statistical power. *Psychological Methods, 8*, 243–253."
25. Litwiller, B., Snyder, L. A., Taylor, W. D., & Steele, L. M. (2017). The relationship between sleep and work: A meta-analysis. *Journal of Applied Psychology, 102*, 682–699.
26. McDaniel, M. A., Rothstein, H. R., & Whetzel, D. L. (2006). Publication bias: A case study of four test vendors. *Personnel Psychology, 59,* 927–953.
27. Dalton, D. R., Aguinis, H., Dalton, C. M., Bosco, F. A., & Pierce, C. A. (2012). Revisiting the file drawer problem in meta-analysis: An assessment of published and non-published correlation matrices. *Personnel Psychology, 65*, 221–249; and Ferguson, C. J., & Brannick, M. T. (2012). Publication bias in psychological science: Prevalence, methods for identifying and controlling, and implications for the use of meta-analyses. *Psychological Methods, 17*, 120–128.
28. Ostroff, C., & Harrison, D. A. (1999). Meta-analysis, level of analysis, and best estimates of population correlations: Cautions for interpreting meta-analytic results in organizational behavior. *Journal of Applied Psychology, 84,* 260–270.
29. George, G., Haas, M., & Pentland, A. (2014). Big data and management. *Academy of Management Journal, 57*, 321–326.
30. Marr, B. (2015, September 30). Big data: 20 mind-boggling facts everyone must read. *Forbes*. Retrieved October 16, 2021, from https://www.forbes.com/sites/bernardmarr/2015/09/30/big-data-20-mind-boggling-facts-everyone-must-read/?sh=41a137f917b1
31. McAbee, S. T., Landis, R. S., & Burke, M. I. (2017). Inductive reasoning: The promise of big data. *Human Resource Management Review, 27*, 277–290.
32. Stanton, J. M. (2013). Data mining: A practical introduction for organizational researchers. In J. M. Cortina & R. S. Landis (Eds.), *Modern research methods for the study of behavior in organizations* (pp. 199–230). New York: Routledge.
33. Reynolds, D. (2010). A primer on privacy: What every psychologist needs to know about data protection. *The Industrial-Organizational Psychologist, 48*(2), 27–32.
34. International Trade Administration, U.S. Department of Commerce. (n.d.). *Privacy Shield Framework.* Retrieved December 2, 2021, from https://www.privacyshield.gov/Program-Overview
35. Wasserman, R. (2013). Ethical issues and guidelines for conducting data analysis in psychological research. *Ethics & Behavior, 23*, 3–15.
36. Braun, V., & Clarke, V. (2006). Using thematic analysis in psychology. *Qualitative Research in Psychology, 3*, 77–101.
37. Luke, J., McIlveen, P., & Perera, H. N. (2016). A thematic analysis of career adaptability in retirees who return to work. *Frontiers in Psychology, 7*, 193.
38. Harms, P. D., & Lester, P. B. (2012). Boots on the ground: A first-hand account of conducting psychological research in combat. *The Industrial-Organizational Psychologist, 49*(3), 15–21.
39. Wanberg, C. R., Basbug, G., Van Hooft, E. A., & Samtani, A. (2012). Navigating the black hole: Explicating layers of job search context and adaptational responses. *Personnel Psychology, 65*, 887–926.
40. Ibid., p. 890.
41. Ibid., p. 903.
42. Fetterman, D. M. (1998). Ethnography. In L. Bickman & D. J. Rog (Eds.), *Handbook of applied social research methods* (pp. 473–504). Thousand Oaks, CA: Sage.
43. Pratt, M. G., & Bonaccio, S. (2016). Qualitative research in I-O psychology: Maps, myths, and moving forward. *Industrial and Organizational Psychology, 9*, 693–715.
44. Bickmeier, R. M., Rogelberg, S. G., & Berka, G. C. (2016). Integrating qualitative and quantitative methods. In doctoral education: A case study. *Industrial and Organizational Psychology, 9*, 748–753.
45. Wilhelmy, A. (2016). Journal guidelines for qualitative research? A balancing act that might be worth it. *Industrial and Organizational Psychology, 9*, 726–732.
46. Dudley-Meislahn, N., Vaughn, E. D., Sydell, E. J., & Seeds, M. A. (2013). Advances in knowledge measurement. In J. M. Cortina & R. S. Landis (Eds.), *Modern research methods for the study of behavior in organizations* (pp. 443–481). New York: Routledge.

47. Hoffman, C. C. (1999). Generalizing physical ability test validity: A case study using transportability, validity generalization, and construct validity evidence. *Personnel Psychology*, 52, 1019–1041; Hoffman, C. C., Holden, L. M, & Gale, E. (2000). So many jobs, so little "n": Applying expanded validation models to support generalization of cognitive ability. *Personnel Psychology*, 53, 955–991; and Hoffman, C. C., & McPhail S. M. (1998). Exploring options for supporting test use in situations precluding local validation. *Personnel Psychology*, 51, 987–1003.

48. Rogelberg, S. G., Luong, A., Sederburg, M. E., & Cristol, D. S. (2000). Employee attitude surveys: Examining the attitudes of noncompliant employees. *Journal of Applied Psychology, 85*, 284–293.

49. Stanton, J. M. (1998). An empirical assessment of data collection using the Internet. *Personnel Psychology, 51,* 709–725.

50. Church, A. H. (2001). Is there a method to our madness? The impact of data collection methodology on organizational survey results. *Personnel Psychology, 54*, 937–969.

51. Tourangeau, R., & Yan, T. (2007). Sensitive questions in surveys. *Psychological Bulletin, 133*, 859–883.

52. Rose, D. S., Sidle, S. D., & Griffith, K. H. (2007). A penny for your thoughts: Monetary incentives improve response rates for company-sponsored employee surveys. *Organizational Research Methods, 10*(2), 225–240.

53. Kolbe, M., Grote, G., Waller, M. J., Wacker, J., Grande, B., Burtscher, M. J., & Spahn, D. R. (2014). Monitoring and talking to the room: Autochthonous coordination patterns in team interaction and performance. *Journal of Applied Psychology, 99*, 1254–1267.

54. Stanton, J. M., & Rogelberg, S. G. (2002). Beyond online surveys: Internet research opportunities for industrial-organizational psychology. In S. G. Rogelberg (Ed.), *Handbook of research methods in industrial and organizational psychology*, 275–294. Malden, MA: Blackwell.

55. Flores, D., Fox, R. L., Iverson, J. O., Venette, S., Conley, C., Jahn, J., Howes, S. S., & Haire, E. R. (2021). *Pivoting during the pandemic: How COVID-19 and the 2020 wildland fire year created a novel learning opportunity for U.S. Forest Service wildland fire management*. Gen. Tech. Rep. RMRS-GTR. Fort Collins, CO: U.S. Department of Agriculture, Forest Service, Rocky Mountain Research Station.

56. Massaro, S., & Pecchia, L. (2019). Heart Rate Variability (HRV) analysis: A methodology for organizational neuroscience. *Organizational Research Methods, 22*(1), 354–393; Murray, M. M., & Antonakis, J. (2019). An introductory guide to organizational neuroscience. *Organizational Research Methods, 22*(1), 6–16; and Adis, C. S., & Thompson, J. C. (2013). A brief primer on neuroimaging methods for industrial/organizational psychology. In J. M. Cortina & R. S. Landis (Eds.), *Modern research methods for the study of behavior in organizations* (pp. 405–442). New York: Routledge.

57. Jack, A. I., Rochford, K. C., Friedman, J. P., Passarelli, A. M., & Boyatzis, R. E. (2019). Pitfalls in organizational neuroscience: A critical review and suggestions for future research. *Organizational Research Methods, 22*(1), 421–458.

58. Dulebohn, J. H., Conlon, D. E., Sarinopoulos, I., Davison, R. B., & McNamara, G. (2009). The biological bases of unfairness: Neuroimaging evidence for the distinctiveness of procedural and distributive justice. *Organizational Behavior and Human Decision Processes, 110*, 140-151.

59. Yoon, S., McClean, S. T., Chawla, N., Kim, J. K., Koopman, J., Rosen, C. C., Trougakos, J. P. & McCarthy, J. M. (2021). Working through an "infodemic": The impact of COVID-19 news consumption on employee uncertainty and work behaviors. *Journal of Applied Psychology, 106*(4), 501–517.

60. Eden, D. (2017)—see #8, p. 94.

61. Hanges, P. J., & Wang, M. (2012). Seeking the holy grail in organizational science: Uncovering causality through research design. In S. W. J. Kozlowski (Ed.), *The Oxford handbook of organizational psychology* (Vol. 1, pp. 79–116). New York: Oxford University Press.

62. Lilienfeld, S. O. (2012). Public skepticism of psychology. *American Psychologist, 67*, 111–129.

63. Hanges, P. J., & Wang, M. (2012)—see #61.

64. Jaffe, S. R., Strait, L. B., & Odgers, C. L. (2012). From correlates to causes: Can quasi-experimental studies and statistical innovations bring us closer to identifying the causes of anti-social behavior? *Psychological Bulletin, 138*, 272–295.

65. Vigen, T. (n.d.). Spurious Correlations. *tylervigen.com*. Retrieved October 16, 2021, from https://www.tylervigen.com/spurious-correlations

66. Fleuren, B., Nübold, A., & Hülsheger, U. R. (2021). COVID-19 and the need for integrative holistic research. *Industrial and Organizational Psychology, 14*(1–2), 152–155.

67. Daft, R. L. (1983). Learning the craft of organizational research. *Academy of Management Review, 8,* 539–546.

68. Klahr, D., & Simon, H. A. (1999). Studies of scientific discovery: Complementary approaches and convergent findings. *Psychological Bulletin, 125,* 524–543.

69. Pickles, M. (2017, May 10). 'Mesearch'—when study really is all about me. *BBC.com*. Retrieved October 16, 2021, from https://www.bbc.com/news/business-39856894

70. American Psychological Association. (revised 2017, January 1). *Ethical Principles of Psychologists and Code of Conduct.* Retrieved October 16, 2021, from https://www.apa.org/ethics/code/

71. Aguinis, H., & Henle, C. A. (2002). Ethics in research. In S. G. Rogelberg (Ed.), *Handbook of research methods in industrial and organizational psychology* (pp. 34–56). Malden, MA: Blackwell.

72. Kerr, N. L. (1998). HARKing: Hypothesizing after the results are known. *Personality and Social Psychology Review, 2,* 196–217.

73. Hollenbeck, J. R., & Wright, P. M. (2016). Harking, sharking, and tharking: Making the case for post hoc analysis of scientific data. *Journal of Management, 43,* 5–18.

74. Toth, A. A., Banks, G. C., Mellor, D., O'Boyle, E. H., Jr., Dickson, A., Davis, D. J., DeHaven, A., Bochantin, J., & Borns, J. (2020). Study preregistration: An evaluation of a method for transparent reporting. *Journal of Business and Psychology*. Advance online publication. https://doi.org/10.1007/s10869-020-09695-3

75. Behnke, S. H., & Moorehead-Slaughter, O. (2012). Ethics, human rights, and interrogation. In J. H. Lawrence & M. D. Matthews (Eds.), *The Oxford handbook of military psychology* (pp. 50–62). New York: Oxford University Press.

76. Lefkowitz, J. (2017). *Ethics and values in industrial-organizational psychology* (2nd ed.). New York: Routledge.

77. Reynolds, S. J. (2008). Moral attentiveness: Who pays attention to the moral aspects of life? *Journal of Applied Psychology, 93,* 1027–1041.

Chapter 3

1. Caligiuri, P., Mencin, A., & Hang, K. (2013). Win-win-win: The influence of company-sponsored volunteerism programs on employees, NGOs, and business units. *Personnel Psychology, 66,* 825–860.

2. Grant, A. M. (2012). Giving time, time after time: Work design and sustained employee participation in corporate volunteering. *Academy of Management Review, 37,* 589–615.

3. Carr, S. C., MacLachlan, M., & Furnham, A. (Eds.) (2012). *Humanitarian work psychology.* New York: Palgrave Macmillan.

4. Reichman, W., & Berry, M. O. (2012). The evolution of industrial and organizational psychology. In S. C. Carr, M. MacLachlan, & A. Furnham (Eds.), *Humanitarian work psychology* (pp. 34–51). New York: Palgrave Macmillan.

5. American Psychological Association. Ethical Principles of Psychologists and Code of Conduct. *APA.org.* Retrieved November 8, 2021, from https://www.apa.org/ethics/code

6. United Nations. (n.d.). The Ten Principles of the UN Global Compact. *United Nations Global Compact.* Retrieved November 8, 2021, from https://www.unglobalcompact.org/what-is-gc/mission/principles

7. Phillips, K. W. (2014, October). How diversity makes us smarter. *Scientific American*. Retrieved November 8, 2021, from https://www.scientificamerican.com/article/how-diversity-makes-us-smarter/

8. Kalev, A., Dobbin, F., & Kelly, E. (2006). Best Practices or Best Guesses? Assessing the Efficacy of Corporate Affirmative Action and Diversity Policies. *American Sociological Review, 71*(4), 589–617.

9. Griffin, K. A., Cunningham, E. L., & George Mwangi, C. A. (2016). Defining diversity: Ethnic differences in Black students' perceptions of racial climate. *Journal of Diversity in Higher Education, 9*(1), 34–49.

10. Smith, C., & Turner, S. (2015). The Radical Transformation of Diversity and Inclusion: the Millennial Influence. *Deloitte University, the Leadership Center for Inclusion*. Retrieved November 8, 2021, from https://www2.deloitte.com/content/dam/Deloitte/us/Documents/about-deloitte/us-inclus-millennial-influence-120215.pdf
11. Williams, S. A. S., & Conyers, A. (2016). Race pedagogy: Faculty preparation matters. *Administrative Theory & Praxis, 38*: 234–250.
12. Roberson, Q. M. (2006). Disentangling the meanings of diversity and inclusion in organizations. *Group & Organization Management, 31*, 212–236.
13. Winters, M.-F. (2014). From diversity to inclusion: An inclusion equation. In B. M. Ferdman & B. R. Deane (Eds.), *Diversity at work: The practice of inclusion* (pp. 205–228). San Francisco: Jossey-Bass.
14. McCleary-Gaddy, A. (2019). Be explicit: Defining the difference between the Office of Diversity & Inclusion and the Office of Diversity & Equity. *Medical Teacher, 41*, 1443–1444.
15. Jonsen, K., & Özbilgin, M. (2014). Models of global diversity management. In B. M. Ferdman & B. R. Deane (Eds.), *Diversity at work: The practice of inclusion* (pp. 364–390). San Francisco: Jossey-Bass.
16. Dobbin, F., & Kalev, A. (2016). Why diversity programs fail. *Harvard Business Review Magazine, July-August 2016*. Retrieved November 8, 2021, from https://hbr.org/2016/07/why-diversity-programs-fail
17. Colby, S. L., & Ortman, J. M. (2014). *Projections of the size and composition of the U.S. population: 2014–2060 (Current Population Reports, P25–1143)*. Washington, DC: U.S. Census Bureau. Retrieved November 8, 2021, from https://www.census.gov/library/publications/2015/demo/p25-1143.html
18. White, M. (2010, August 12). Clicktivism is ruining leftist activism. *The Guardian*. Retrieved November 8, 2021, from https://www.theguardian.com/commentisfree/2010/aug/12/clicktivism-ruining-leftist-activism
19. Freelon, D., Marwick, A., & Kreiss, D. (2020). False equivalencies: Online activism from left to right. *Science, 369*, 1197–1201.
20. Organisation for Economic Co-operation and Development. (2020). Hours worked. *OECD Data*. Retrieved November 8, 2021, from https://data.oecd.org/emp/hours-worked.htm
21. Jones, R. G. (Ed.) (2012). *Nepotism in organizations*. New York: Routledge.
22. Chalabi, M. (2017, March 24). Measuring nepotism: Is it more prevalent in the US than in other countries? *The Guardian*. Retrieved November 8, 2021, from https://www.theguardian.com/us-news/2017/mar/24/nepotism-data-ivanka-trump
23. Schwab, K., & Porter, M. E. (2006). The Global Competitiveness Report 2006–2007. *World Economic Forum, Geneva, Switzerland*. Retrieved November 8, 2021, from https://www3.weforum.org/docs/WEF_GlobalCompetitivenessReport_2006-07.pdf
24. Ones, D. S., & Dilchert, S. (2012). Employee green behaviors. In S. E. Jackson, D. S. Ones, & S. Dilchert (Eds.), *Managing human resources for environmental sustainability* (p. 89). San Francisco: Jossey-Bass.
25. Haddock-Millar, J., Muller-Camen, M., & Miles, D. (2012). Human resource development initiatives for managing environmental concerns at McDonald's UK. In S. E. Jackson, D. S. Ones, & S. Dilchert (Eds.), *Managing human resources for environmental sustainability* (pp. 341–361). San Francisco: Jossey-Bass.
26. Stern, P. C. (2011). Contributions of psychology to limiting climate change. *American Psychologist, 66*, 303–314.
27. Sonenshein, S. (2012). Being a positive social change agent through issue selling. In K. Golden-Biddle & J. E. Dutton (Eds.), *Using a positive lens to explore social change and organizations* (pp. 49–69). New York: Routledge.
28. DuBois, C. L. Z., Astakhova, M. N., & DuBois, D. A. (2013). Motivating behavior change to support organizational environmental sustainability goals. In A. H. Huffman & S. R. Klein (Eds.), *Green organizations: Driving change with I-O psychology* (pp. 186–207). New York: Routledge.
29. Huffman, A. H., Watrous-Rodriguez, K. M., Henning, J. B., & Berry, J. (2009). "Working" through environmental issues: The role of I/O psychologists. *The Industrial-Organizational Psychologist, 47*(2), 27–36.
30. Klein, S. R., & Huffman, A. H. (2013). I-O psychology and environmental sustainability in organizations: A natural partnership. In A. H. Huffman & S. R. Klein (Eds.), *Green organizations: Driving change with I-O psychology* (pp. 3–16). New York: Routledge.

31. Savitz, A. W., & Weber, K. (2006). *The triple bottom line.* San Francisco: Jossey-Bass.
32. Lombardo, T., Schneider, S., & Bryan, L. K. (2013). Corporate leaders of sustainable organizations: Balancing profit, planet, and people. In J. Olson-Buchanon, L. K. Bryan, & L. F. Thompson (Eds.), *Using industrial-organizational psychology for the greater good: Helping those who help others* (pp. 75–109). New York: Routledge.
33. Guion, R. M. (1998). *Assessment, measurement, and prediction for personnel decisions.* Mahwah, NJ: Erlbaum.
34. Highhouse, S. (2011). Was the addition of sex to Title VII a joke? *The Industrial-Organizational Psychologist, 48*(3), 102–107.
35. Forsey, C. (2018, October 15). 15 fun, weird & unexpected interview questions (with sample answers). *Hubspot Blog.* Retrieved November 8, 2021, from https://blog.hubspot.com/marketing/funny-weird-interview-questions
36. Heywood, L. [@BroadwayGirlNYC]. (2016, March 29). *Don't throw away your shot. #Hamilton #Broadway #auditions #casting #opencall #singers #rappers #actorsofcolor* [Tweet]. Twitter. https://twitter.com/BroadwayGirlNYC/status/714900143997370368
37. Ferrill v. Parker Group, Inc. 168 F. 3d 468 – Court of Appeals, 11th Circuit 1999
38. Robinson, R. K. (2007). Casting and caste-ing: Reconciling artistic freedom and antidiscrimination norms. *Calif. L. Rev., 95,* 1.
39. U.S. Equal Employment Opportunity Commission. (2020). Charges alleging sex-based harassment (charges filed with EEOC) FY2010-FY2020. *EEOC.gov.* Retrieved November 8, 2021, from https://www.eeoc.gov/statistics/charges-alleging-sex-based-harassment-charges-filed-eeoc-fy-2010-fy-2020
40. American Association of Retired Persons. (2018, August 2). Age discrimination in the workplace common, survey says. *AARP.org.* Retrieved November 8, 2021, from https://www.aarp.org/work/working-at-50-plus/info-2018/age-discrimination-common-at-work.html
41. Francioli, S. P., & North, M. S. (2021). Youngism: The content, causes, and consequences of prejudices toward younger adults. *Journal of Experimental Psychology: General.* Advance online publication. https://doi.org/10.1037/xge0001064
42. O'Keeffe, J. (1994). Disability, discrimination, and the Americans with Disabilities Act. In S. M. Bruyere & J. O'Keeffe (Eds.), *Implications of the Americans with Disabilities Act for psychology* (pp. 1–14). New York: Springer.
43. Santuzzi, A. M., Waltz, P. R., Finkelstein, L. M., & Rupp, D. E. (2014). Invisible disabilities: Unique challenges for employees and organizations. *Industrial and Organizational Psychology, 7,* 204–219.
44. Pyburn, K. M., Ployhart, R. E., & Kravitz, D. A. (2008). The diversity-validity dilemma: Overview and legal content. *Personnel Psychology, 61,* 143–151.
45. Lindsey, A., King, E. B., McCausland, T., Jones, K. P., & Dunleavy, E. (2013). What we know and don't: Eradicating employment discrimination 50 years after the Civil Rights Act. *Industrial and Organizational Psychology, 6,* 391–413.
46. Banks, G. C., & McDaniel, M. A. (2012). Meta-analysis as a validity summary tool. In N. Schmitt (Ed.), *The Oxford handbook of personnel assessment and selection* (pp. 156– 175). New York: Oxford University Press.
47. McDaniel, M. A., Kepes, S., & Banks, G. C. (2011). The *Uniform Guidelines* are a detriment to the field of personnel selection. *Industrial and Organizational Psychology, 4,* 494–514.
48. Sharf, J. C. (2011). Equal employment versus equal opportunity: A naked political agenda covered by a scientific fig leaf. *Industrial and Organizational Psychology, 4,* 537–539.
49. Bobko, P., & Roth, P. L. (2010). An analysis of the methods for assessing and indexing adverse impact: A disconnect between academic literature and some practice. In J. L. Outtz (Ed.), *Adverse impact: Implications for organizational staffing and high stakes selection* (pp. 29–49). New York: Routledge.
50. Campbell, J. P. (1996). Group differences and personnel decisions: Validity, fairness, and affirmative action. *Journal of Vocational Behavior, 49,* 122–158.
51. Crosby, F. J., & VanDeVeer, C. (Eds.). (2000). *Sex, race, & merit.* Ann Arbor: University of Michigan Press.
52. Guion, R. M. (1998)—see #33; and Heilman, M. E. (1996). Affirmative actions' contradictory consequences. *Journal of Social Issues, 52*(4), 105–109.
53. Lindsey, A., King, E. B., McCausland, T., Jones, K. P., & Dunleavy, E. (2013)—see #45.

54. Dovidio, J. F., & Gaertner, S. L. (1996). Affirmative action, unintentional racial biases, and intergroup relations. *Journal of Social Issues, 52*, 51–75.

55. Heilman, M. E., Block, C. J., & Lucas, J. A. (1992). Presumed incompetent? Stigmatization and affirmative action efforts. *Journal of Applied Psychology, 77*, 536–544; and Heilman, M. E., & Alcott, V. B. (2001). What I think you think of me: Women's reactions to being viewed as beneficiaries of preferential selection. *Journal of Applied Psychology, 86*, 574–582.

56. Highhouse, S., Stierwalt, S., Bachiochi, P., Elder, A. E., & Fisher, G. (1999). Effects of advertised human resource management practices on attraction of African American applicants. *Personnel Psychology, 52*, 425–442.

57. Kravitz, D. A., & Klineberg, S. L. (2000). Reactions to two versions of affirmative action among Whites, Blacks, and Hispanics. *Journal of Applied Psychology, 85*, 597–611.

58. White, F. A., Charles, M. A., & Nelson, J. K. (2008). The role of persuasive arguments in changing affirmative action attitudes and expressed behavior in higher education. *Journal of Applied Psychology, 93*, 1271–1286.

59. Evans, D. C. (2003). A comparison of other-directed stigmatization produced by legal and illegal forms of affirmative action. *Journal of Applied Psychology, 88*, 121-130.

60. Gutman, A. (2003). The *Grutter, Gratz, & Costa* rulings. *The Industrial-Organizational Psychologist, 41(*2), 117–127.

61. International Labour Organization. (2017). World statistic: The enormous burden of poor working conditions. *ILO.org*. Retrieved November 18, 2021, from https://www.ilo.org/wcmsp5/groups/public/---dgreports/---dcomm/documents/publication/wcms_686645.pdf

62. Brotherton, C. (2003). The role of external policies in shaping organizational health and safety. In D. A. Hofmann & L. E. Tetrick (Eds.), *Health and safety in organizations* (pp. 372–396). San Francisco: Jossey-Bass.

63. Hammer, L. B., & Zimmerman, K. L. (2011). Quality of work life. In S. Zedeck (Ed.), *APA handbook of industrial and organizational psychology* (Vol. 3, pp. 399–431). Washington, DC: APA.

64. Mills, M. J., & Culbertson, S. S. (2017). The elephant in the family room: Work-family considerations as central to evolving HR and I-O. *Industrial and Organizational Psychology, 10*, 26–31.

65. Glynn, S. J. (2020, April 17). Coronavirus paid leave exemptions exclude millions of workers from coverage. *Center for American Progress*. Retrieved November 8, 2021, from https://www.americanprogress.org/article/coronavirus-paid-leave-exemptions-exclude-millions-workers-coverage/

66. Mills, M. J., & Culbertson, S. S. (2017)—see #64.

67. International Labour Organization. (1999). Recommendation 190: Recommendation concerning the prohibition and immediate action for the elimination of the worst forms of child labour. *ILO.org*. Retrieved November 8, 2021, from www.ilo.org/public/english/standards/relm/ilc/ilc87/com-chir.htm

68. Castillo, D. N., Landen, D. D., & Layne, L. A. (1994). Occupational injury deaths of 16 and 17 year olds in the United States. *American Journal of Public Health, 84*(4), 646–649.

69. Abboud Dal Santo, J., Bowling, J. M., & Harris, T. A. (2010). Effects of work permits on illegal employment among youth workers: Findings of a school-based survey on child labor violations. *American Journal of Public Health, 100*(4), 635–637.

70. International Labour Organization. (2017). Child labour and domestic work. *ILO.org*. Retrieved November 8, 2021, from https://www.ilo.org/ipec/areas/Childdomesticlabour/lang--en/index.html

Chapter 4

1. Pritchard, R. D., Culbertson, S. S., Malm, K., & Agrell, A. (2009). Improving performance in a Swedish police traffic unit: Results of an intervention. *Journal of Criminal Justice, 37*, 85–97.
2. Wherry, R. J. (1957). The past and future of criterion evaluation. *Personnel Psychology, 10,* 1–5.
3. Wallace, S. R. (1965). Criteria for what? *American Psychologist, 20,* 411–417.
4. Primoff, E. S., & Fine, S. A. (1988). A history of job analysis. In S. Gael (Ed.), *The job analysis handbook for business, industry, and government* (pp. 14–29). New York: Wiley.
5. Morgeson, F. P., & Dierdorff, E. C. (2011). Work analysis: From technique to theory. In S. Zedeck (Ed.), *APA handbook of industrial and organizational psychology* (Vol. 2, pp. 3–41). Washington, DC: APA; and Sanchez, J. I., & Levine, E. L. (2012). The rise and fall of job analysis and the future of work analysis. *Annual Review of Psychology, 63*, 397–425.
6. Sanchez, J. I., & Levine, E. L. (2001). The analysis of work in the 20th and 21st centuries. In N. Anderson, D. S. Ones, H. K. Sinangil, & C. Viswesvaran (Eds.), *Hand book of industrial, work, and organizational psychology* (Vol. 1, pp. 71–89). London: Sage.
7. Pearlman, K., & Sanchez, J. I. (2010). Work analysis. In J. L. Farr & N. T. Tippins (Eds.), *Handbook of employee selection* (pp. 73-98). New York: Routledge.
8. Landy, F. J., & Vasey, J. (1991). Job analysis: The composition of SME samples. *Personnel Psychology, 44,* 27–50.
9. DuVernet, A. M., Dierdorff, E. C., & Wilson, M. A. (2015). Exploring factors that influence work analysis data: A meta-analysis of design choices, purposes, and organizational context. *Journal of Applied Psychology, 100*, 1603–1631.
10. Dierdorff, E. C., & Morgeson, F. P. (2009). Effects of descriptor specificity and observability on incumbent work analysis ratings. *Personnel Psychology, 62*, 601–628.
11. Williams, K. M., & Crafts, J. L. (1997). Inductive job analysis. In D. L. Whetzel & G. R. Wheaton (Eds.), *Applied measurement methods in industrial psychology* (pp. 51–88). Palo Alto, CA: Consulting Psychologists Press.
12. Clifford, J. P. (1994). Job analysis: Why do it, and how should it be done? *Public Personnel Management, 23*, 321–338.
13. Fine, S. A., & Cronshaw, S. F. (1999). *Functional job analysis.* Mahwah, NJ: Erlbaum.
14. Foster, J., Gaddis, B., & Hogan, J. (2012). Personality-based job analysis. In M. A. Wilson, W. Bennett, S. G. Gibson, & G. M. Alliger (Eds.), *The handbook of work analysis* (pp. 247–264). New York: Routledge.
15. Doverspike, D., & Arthur, W. A., Jr. (2012). The role of job analysis in test selection and development. In M. A. Wilson, W. Bennett, S. G. Gibson, & G. M. Alliger (Eds.), *The handbook of work analysis* (pp. 381–399). New York: Routledge.
16. Baranowski, L. E., & Anderson, L. E. (2006). Examining rating source variation in work behavior and KSA linkages. *Personnel Psychology, 58*, 1041–1054.
17. Lievens, F., Sanchez, J. I., Bartram, D., & Brown, A. (2010). Lack of consensus among competence ratings of the same occupations: Noise or substance? *Journal of Applied Psychology, 95*, 562–571.
18. Peterson, N. G., & Jeanneret, P. R. (1997). Job analysis. In D. L. Whetzel & G. R. Wheaton (Eds.), *Applied measurement methods in industrial psychology* (pp. 13–50). Palo Alto, CA: Consulting Psychologists Press.
19. McCormick, E. J., & Jeanneret, P. R. (1988). Position Analysis Questionnaire (PAQ). In S. Gael (Ed.), *The job analysis handbook for business, industry, and government* (Vol. 2, pp. 825–842). New York: Wiley.
20. Fleishman, E. A., & Quaintance, M. K. (1984). *Taxonomies of human performance.* Orlando, FL: Academic Press.
21. Morgeson, F. P., & Dierdorff, E. C. (2011)—see #5.
22. Levine, J. D., & Oswald, F. L. (2012). O*NET: The Occupational Information Network. In M. A. Wilson, W. Bennett, S. G. Gibson, & G. M. Alliger (Eds.), *The handbook of work analysis* (pp. 281–301). New York: Routledge.

23. Jeanneret, P. R., D'Egidio, E. L., & Hanson, M. A. (2004). Assessment and development opportunities using the Occupational Information Network (O*NET). In J. C. Thomas (Ed.), *Comprehensive handbook of psychological assessment* (Vol. 4, pp. 192–202). Hoboken, NJ: Wiley.

24. Peterson, N. G., & Sager, C. E. (2010). The Dictionary of Occupational Titles and the Occupational Information Network. In J. L. Farr & N. T. Tippins (Eds.), *Handbook of employee selection* (pp. 887–908). New York: Routledge.

25. Nagorny, L., & Pick, D. (2021). 5 reasons why employers are not hiring vets. *Military.com*. Retrieved October 26, 2021, from https://www.military.com/hiring-veterans/resources/5-reasons-why-employers-are-not-hiring-vets.html

26. Steinhauer, J. (2020, March 16). Veterans are working but not in jobs that match their advanced training. *The New York Times*. Retrieved October 26, 2021, from https://www.nytimes.com/2020/03/07/us/politics/veterans-jobs-employment.html

27. Mitchell, J. L., & McCormick, E. J. (1990). *Professional and managerial position questionnaire.* Logan, UT: PAQ Services.

28. Raymark, P. H., Schmit, M. J., & Guion, R. M. (1997). Identifying potentially useful personality constructs for employee selection. *Personnel Psychology, 50,* 723–736.

29. Brannick, M. T., & Levine, E. L. (2002). *Job analysis.* Thousand Oaks, CA: Sage.

30. Morgeson, F. P., & Campion, M. A. (1997). Social and cognitive sources of potential inaccuracy in job analysis. *Journal of Applied Psychology, 82,* 627–655.

31. Sackett, P. R., & Laczo, R. M. (2003). Job and work analysis. In W. C. Borman, D. R. Ilgen, & R. J. Klimoski (Eds.), *Handbook of psychology: Industrial and organizational psychology* (Vol. 12, pp. 21–37). Hoboken, NJ: Wiley.

32. Schippmann, J. S., Ash, R. A., Battista, M., Carr, L., Eyde, L. D., Hesketh, B., Kehoe, J. F., Pearlman, K., Prien, E. P., & Sanchez, J. I. (2000). The practice of competency modeling. *Personnel Psychology, 53,* 703–740.

33. Bommer, W. H., Johnson, J. L., Rich, G. A., Podsakoff, P. M., & Mackenzie, S. B. (1995). On the interchangeability of objective and subjective measures of employee performance: A meta-analysis. *Personnel Psychology, 48*, 587–605.

34. Sackett, P. R., Zedeck, S., & Fogli, L. (1988). Relations between measures of typical and maximum job performance. *Journal of Applied Psychology, 73*, 482–486.

35. Klehe, U.-C., & Anderson, N. (2007). Working hard and working smart: Motivation and ability during typical and maximum performance. *Journal of Applied Psychology, 92*, 978–992.

36. DuBois, C. L. Z., Sackett, P. R., Zedeck, S., & Fogli, L. (1993). Further exploration of typical and maximum performance criteria: Definitional issues, prediction, and White-Black differences. *Journal of Applied Psychology, 78*, 205–211.

37. Hausknecht, J. P., & Langevin, A. M. (2010). Selection for service and sales jobs. In. J. L. Farr & N. T. Tippins (Eds.), *Handbook of employee selection* (pp. 765–780). New York: Routledge.

38. McManus, M. A., & Brown, S. H. (1995). Adjusting sales results measures for use as criteria. *Personnel Psychology, 48*, 391–400.

39. Hom, P. W., Mitchell, T. R., Lee, T. W., & Griffeth, R. W. (2012). Reviewing employee turnover: Focusing on proximal withdrawal states and an expanded criterion. *Psychological Bulletin, 138*, 831–858.

40. Kacmar, K. M., Andrews, M. C., Van Rooy, D. L., Steiberg, R. C., & Cerrone, S. (2006). Sure everyone can be replaced… but at what cost? Turnover as a predictor of unit level performance. *Academy of Management Journal, 49*, 133–144.

41. Call, M. L., Nyberg, A. J. A., Ployhart, R. E., & Weekley, J. A. (2015). The dynamic nature of collective turnover and unit performance: The impact of time, quality, and replacement. *Academy of Management Journal, 58*, 1208–1232.

42. Campion, M. A. (1991). Meaning and measurement of turn over: Comparison of alternative measures and recommendations for research. *Journal of Applied Psychology, 76*, 199–212. https://doi.org/10.1037/0021-9010.76.2.199

43. Williams, C. R., & Livingstone, L. P. (1994). Another look at the relationship between performance and voluntary turnover. *Academy of Management Journal, 37,* 269–298.

44. Rhodes, S. R., & Steers, R. M. (1990). *Managing employee absenteeism.* Reading, MA: Addison-Wesley; and Martocchio, J. J., & Harrison, D. A. (1993). To be there or not to be there: Questions, theories, and methods in absenteeism research. In G. R. Ferris (Ed.), *Research in personnel and human resources management* (Vol. 11, pp. 259–329). Greenwich, CT: JAI Press.

45. ten Brummelhuis, L. L., Johns, G., Lyons, B. J., & ter Hoeven, C. L. (2016). Why and when do employees imitate the absenteeism of coworkers? *Organizational Behavior and Human Decision Processes, 134*, 16–30.

46. Johns, G. (2010). Presenteeism in the workplace: A review and research agenda. *Journal of Organizational Behavior, 31*(4), 519–542.

47. Goetzel, R. Z., Long, S. R., Ozminkowski, R. J., Hawkins, K., Wang, S., & Lynch, W. (2004). Health, absence, disability, and presenteeism cost estimates of certain physical and mental health conditions affecting U.S. employers. *Journal of Occupational and Environmental Medicine, 46*(4), 398–412.

48. Miraglia, M., & Johns, G. (2016). Going to work ill: A meta-analysis of the correlates of presenteeism and a dual-path model. *Journal of Occupational Health Psychology, 21*, 261–283.

49. Jahoda, M. (1981). Work, employment, and unemployment: Values, theories and approaches in social research. *American Psychologist, 36,* 184–191.

50. Webster, R. K., Liu, R., Karimullina, K., Hall, I., Amlôt, R., & Rubin, G. J. (2019). A systematic review of infectious illness presenteeism: Prevalence, reasons and risk factors. *BMC Public Health, 19*(1), 1-13.

51. Bergström, G., Bodin, L., Hagberg, J., Aronsson, G., & Josephson, M. (2009). Sickness presenteeism today, sickness absenteeism tomorrow? A prospective study on sickness presenteeism and future sickness absenteeism. *Journal of Occupational and Environmental Medicine, 51*(6), 629-638.

52. Kinman, G., & Grant, C. (2021). Presenteeism during the COVID-19 pandemic: Risks and solutions. *Occupational medicine, 71*(6-7), 243-244.

53. Probst, T. M., Lee, H. J., Bazzoli, A. M., Jenkins, M. R., & Bettac, E. L. (2021). Work and non-work sickness presenteeism: The role of workplace COVID-19 climate. *Journal of Occupational and Environmental Science, 63*, 713–718.

54. Tetrick, L. E., Perrewé, P. L., & Griffin, M. A. (2010). Employee work-related health, stress, and safety. In J. L. Farr & N. T. Tippins (Eds.), *Handbook of employee selection* (pp. 531–550). New York: Routledge.

55. Senders, J. W., & Moray, N. P. (1991). *Human error: Cause, prediction, and reduction.* Hillsdale, NJ: Erlbaum.

56. Harris, W. G., Jones, J. W., Klion, R., Arnold, D. W., Camara, W., & Cunningham, M. R. (2012). Test publishers' perspective on "An updated meta-analysis:" Comment on Van Iddekinge, Roth, Raymark, and Odle-Dusseau (2012). *Journal of Applied Psychology, 97*, 531–536.

57. Avery, D. R., McKay, P. F., & Hunter, E. M. (2012). Demography and disappearing merchandise: How older workers influence retail shrinkage. *Journal of Organizational Behavior, 33*, 105–120.

58. Greenberg, J., & Scott, K. S. (1996). Why do workers bite the hands that feed them? Employee theft as a social exchange process. In B. M. Staw & L. L. Cummings (Eds.), *Research in organizational behavior* (Vol. 18, pp. 111–156). Greenwich, CT: JAI.

59. Rotundo, M., & Spector, P. E. (2010). Counterproductive work behavior and withdrawal. In. J. L. Farr & N. T. Tippins (Eds.), *Handbook of employee selection* (pp. 489–512). New York: Routledge.

60. Berry, C. M., Ones, D. S., & Sackett, P. R. (2007). Interpersonal deviance, organizational deviance, and their common correlates: A review and meta-analysis. *Journal of Applied Psychology, 92*, 410–424.

61. Wu, J., & LeBreton, J. M. (2011). Reconsidering the dispositional basis of counterproductive work behavior: The role of aberrant personality. *Personnel Psychology, 64*, 593–626.

62. Fine, S., Goldenberg, J., & Noam, Y. (2016). Beware of those left behind: Counterproductive work behaviors among nonpromoted employees and the moderating effect of integrity. *Journal of Applied Psychology, 101*, 1721–1729.

63. Grandey, A. A., Fisk, G. M., & Steiner, D. D. (2005). Must "service with a smile" be stressful? The moderating role of personal control for American and French employees. *Journal of Applied Psychology, 90*, 893–904.

64. Groth, M., Hennig-Thurau, T., & Wang, K. (2013). The customer experience of emotional labor. In A. A. Grandey, J. M. Diefendorff, & D. E. Rupp (Eds.), *Emotional labor in the 21st century* (pp. 127–152). New York: Routledge.

65. Groth, M., Hennig-Thurau, T., & Walsh, G. (2009). Customer reactions to emotional labor: The roles of employee acting strategies and customer detection accuracy. *Academy of Management Journal, 52*, 958–974.

66. van Jaarsveld, D., & Poster, W. R. (2013). Call centers: Emotional labor over the phone. In A. A. Grandey, J. M. Diefendorff, & D. E. Rupp (Eds.), *Emotional labor in the 21st century* (pp. 153–173). New York: Routledge.

67. Grandey, A. A., Houston, L., & Avery, D. R. (2019). Fake it to make it: Emotional labor reduces the racial disparity in service performance judgments. *Journal of Management, 45*(5), 2163–2192.

68. Beal, D. J., Trougakos, J. P., Weiss, H. M., & Green, S. G. (2006). Episodic processes in emotional labor: Perceptions of affective delivery and regulation strategies. *Journal of Applied Psychology, 91*, 1053–1065.

69. Trougakos, J. P., Jackson, C. L., & Beal, D. J. (2011). Service without a smile: Comparing the consequences of neutral and positive display rules. *Journal of Applied Psychology, 96*, 350–362.

70. Grandey, A. A. (2000). Emotion regulation in the workplace: A new way to conceptualize emotional labor. *Journal of Occupational Health Psychology, 5*, 95–110.

71. Rupp, D. E., & Spencer, S. (2006). When customers lash out: The effects of customer interactional justice on emotional labor and the mediating role of discrete emotions. *Journal of Applied Psychology, 91*, 971–978.

72. Wagner, D. T., Barnes, C. M., & Scott, B. A. (2014). Driving it home: How workplace emotional labor harms employee home life. *Personnel Psychology, 67*, 487–516.

73. Dorsey, D. W., Cortina, J. M., & Luchman, J. (2010). Adaptive and citizenship-related behaviors at work. In J. L. Farr & N. T. Tippins (Eds.), *Handbook of employee selection* (pp. 463–488). New York: Routledge; and Pulakos, E. D., Mueller-Hanson, R. A., & Nelson, J. K. (2012). Adaptive performance and trainability as criteria in selection research. In N. Schmitt (Ed.), *The Oxford handbook of personnel assessment and selection* (pp. 595–613). New York: Oxford University Press.

74. Huang, J. L., Ryan, A. M., Zabel, K. L., & Palmer, A. (2014). Personality and adaptive performance at work: A meta-analytic investigation. *Journal of Applied Psychology, 99*, 162–179.

75. Rynes, S. L., Brown, K. G., & Colbert, A. E. (2002). Seven common misconceptions about human resource practices: Research findings versus practitioner beliefs. *Academy of Management Executive, 16*(3), 92–103.

76. Bolino, M. C., Klotz, A. C., Turnley, W. H., & Harvey, J. (2013). Exploring the dark side of organizational citizenship behavior. *Journal of Organizational Behavior, 34*, 542–559.

77. Culbertson, S. S., & Mills, M. J. (2011). Negative implications for the inclusion of citizenship performance in ratings. *Human Resource Development International, 14*, 23–38.

78. Steele-Johnson, D., Osburn, H. G., & Pieper, K. F. (2000). A review and extension of current models of dynamic criteria. *International Journal of Selection and Assessment, 8*, 110–136.

79. Sturman, M. C. (2007). The past, present, and future of dynamic performance research. In J. J. Martocchio (Ed.), *Research in personnel and human resources management* (Vol. 26, pp. 49–110). Bingley, UK: Emerald Group Publishing, Ltd.

80. Sonnentag, S., & Frese, M. (2012). Dynamic performance. In S. W. J. Kozlowski (Ed.), *The Oxford handbook of organizational psychology* (Vol. 1, pp. 548–575). New York: Oxford University Press.

Chapter 5

1. Clause, C. S., Mullins, M. E., Nee, M. T., Pulakos, E. D., & Schmitt, N. (1998). Parallel test form development: A procedure for alternative predictors and an example. *Personnel Psychology, 51*, 193–208.
2. Newton, P. E., & Shaw, S. D. (2013). Standards for talking and thinking about validity. *Psychological Methods, 18*, 301–319.
3. Binning, J. F., & Barrett, G. V. (1989). Validity of personnel decisions: A conceptual analysis of the inferential and evidential bases. *Journal of Applied Psychology, 74*, 478–494.
4. Edwards, J. R., & Bagozzi, R. P. (2000). On the nature and direction of relationships between constructs and measure. *Psychological Methods, 5*, 155–174.
5. Schmitt, N., Arnold, J. D., & Neiminen, L. (2010). Validation strategies for primary studies. In J. L. Farr & N. T. Tippins (Eds.), *Handbook of employee selection* (pp. 51– 71). New York: Routledge.
6. Murphy, K. R., Dzieweczynski, J. L., & Zhang, Y. (2009). Positive manifold limits the relevance of content- matching strategies for validating selection test batteries. *Journal of Applied Psychology, 94*, 1018–1031.
7. Mayer, S., & Jorgenson, D. (1975). The Song of a Consultant. *Personnel Psychology, 28*(3).
8. Schmitt, N. (2014). Personality and cognitive ability as predictors of effective performance at work. *Annual Review of Organizational Psychology and Organizational Behavior, 1*, 45–65.
9. Brand, C. (1987). The importance of general intelligence. In S. Modgil & C. Modgil (Eds.), *Arthur Jensen: Consensus and controversy* (pp. 251-265). New York: Falmer.
10. Daniel, M. H. (1997). Intelligence testing. *American Psychologist, 52*, 1038–1045.
11. Hedlund, J., & Sternberg, R. J. (2000). Practical intelligence: Implications for human resources research. In G. R. Ferris (Ed.), *Research in personnel and human resources management* (Vol. 19, pp. 1–52). New York: Elsevier.
12. Murphy, K. R. (1996). Individual differences and behavior in organizations: Much more than *g*. In K. R. Murphy (Ed.), *Individual differences and behavior in organizations* (pp. 3–30). San Francisco: Jossey-Bass.
13. Lang, J. W. B., Kersting, M., Hülsheger, U. R., & Lang, J. (2010). General mental ability, narrower cognitive abilities, and job performance: The perspective of the nested-factors model of cognitive abilities. *Personnel Psychology, 63*, 595–640.
14. Roth, P. L., Le, H., Oh, I.-S., Van Iddekinge, C. H., Buster, M. A., Robbins, S. B., & Campion, M. A. (2014). Differential validity for cognitive ability tests in employment and educational settings: Not much more than range restriction? *Journal of Applied Psychology, 99*(1), 1–20.
15. Berry, C. M., & Zhao, P. (2015). Addressing criticisms of existing predictive bias research: cognitive ability test scores still overpredict African Americans' job performance. *Journal of Applied Psychology, 100*(1), 162–179.
16. Berry, C. M., Zhao, P., Batarse, J. C., & Reddock, C. (2020). Revisiting predictive bias of cognitive ability tests against Hispanic American job applicants. *Personnel Psychology, 73*(3), 517–542.
17. Oh, I.-S. (2013). Adverse impact is unlikely to be eliminated as long as cognitively loaded constructs are assessed. *Industrial and Organizational Psychology, 6*(4), 506–508.
18. Ployhart, R. E., & Holtz, B. C. (2008). The diversity–validity dilemma: Strategies for reducing racioethnic and sex subgroup differences and adverse impact in selection. *Personnel Psychology, 61*(1), 153–172.
19. Sackett, P. R., & Wilk, S. L. (1994). Within-group norming and other forms of score adjustment in preemployment testing. *American Psychologist, 49*(11), 929–954.
20. Fleishman, E. A., & Quaintance, M. K. (1984). *Taxonomies of human performance.* Orlando, FL: Academic Press.
21. Gebhardt, D. L., & Baker, T. A. (2010). Physical performance tests. In J. L. Farr & N. T. Tippins (Eds.), *Handbook of employee selection* (pp. 277–298). New York: Routledge.
22. Fleishman, E. A., & Quaintance, M. K. (1984)—see #20, pp. 463–4.

23. Courtright, S. H., McCormick, B. W., Postlethwaite, B. E., Reeves, C. J., & Mount, M. K. (2013). A meta-analysis of sex differences in physical ability: Revised estimates and strategies for reducing differences in selection contexts. *Journal of Applied Psychology, 98*, 623–641.

24. Baker, T. A., & Gebhardt, D. L. (2012). The assessment of physical capabilities in the workplace. In N. Schmitt (Ed.) *The Oxford handbook of personnel assessment and selection* (pp. 274–296). New York: Oxford University Press.

25. Wheeler, J. L. and Ree, M. J. (1997). The role of general and specific psychomotor tracking ability in validity. *International Journal of Selection and Assessment, 5*, 128–36.

26. Carretta, T. R., & Ree, M. J. (2000). General and specific cognitive and psychomotor abilities in personnel selection: The prediction of training and job performance. *International Journal of Selection and Assessment, 8*(4), 227–236.

27. Schumacher, S., Kleinmann, M., & Melchers, K. G. (2011). Job requirements for control room jobs in nuclear power plants. *Safety Science, 49*(3), 394–405.

28. Mount, M. K., Oh, I.-S., & Burns, M. (2008). Incremental validity of perceptual speed and accuracy over general mental ability. *Personnel Psychology, 61*, 113–139.

29. Boyce, P. (2003). *Human Factors in Lighting* (2nd edition). Taylor & Francis Group: London.

30. McCrae, R. R., & Costa, P. T. (1987). Validation of the five-factor model of personality across instruments and observers. *Journal of Personality & Social Psychology, 56*, 586–595.

31. Lievens, F., Harris, M. M., Van Keer, E., & Bisqueret, C. (2003). Predicting cross-cultural training performance: The validity of personality, cognitive ability, and dimensions measured by an assessment center and a behavior description interview. *Journal of Applied Psychology, 88*, 476–489.

32. Wanberg, C. R., & Kammeyer-Mueller, J. D. (2000). Predictors and outcomes of proactivity in the socialization process. *Journal of Applied Psychology, 85*, 373–385.

33. Barrick, M. R., & Mount, M. K. (1991). The big five personality dimensions and job performance: A meta-analysis. *Personnel Psychology, 44*, 1–26.

34. Spurk, D., & Abele, A. E. (2010). Who earns more and why? A multiple mediation model from personality to salary. *Journal of Business and Psychology, 26*, 87–103.

35. Judge, T. A., & Ilies, R. (2002). Relationship of personality to performance motivation: A meta-analytic review. *Journal of Applied Psychology, 87*, 797–807.

36. Wallace, C., & Chen, G. (2006). A multilevel integration of personality, climate, self-regulation, and performance. *Personnel Psychology, 59*, 529–557.

37. Zimmerman, R. D. (2008). Understanding the impact of personality traits on individuals' turnover decisions: A meta-analytic path model. *Personnel Psychology, 61*, 309–348.

38. Judge, T. A., Martocchio, J. J., & Thoresen, C. J. (1997). Five-factor model of personality and employee absence. *Journal of Applied Psychology, 82*, 745–755.

39. Vinchur, A. J., Schippmann, J. S., Switzer, F. S., III, & Roth, P. L. (1998). A meta-analytic review of predictors of job performance for salespeople. *Journal of Applied Psychology, 83*, 586–597

40. Spurk, D., & Abele, A. E. (2010) — see #34.

41. Judge, T. A. Heller, D., & Mount, M. K. (2002). Five-factor model of personality and job satisfaction: A meta-analysis. *Journal of Applied Psychology, 87*, 530–541.

42. Ilies, R., Scott, B. A., & Judge, T. A. (2006). The interactive effects of personal traits and experienced states on intraindividual patterns of citizenship behavior. *Academy of Management Journal, 49*, 561–575.

43. Skarlicki, D. P., Folger, R., & Tesluk, P. E. (1999). Personality as a moderator in the relationship between fairness and retaliation. *Academy of Management Journal, 42*, 100–108.

44. Spurk, D., & Abele, A. E. (2010) — see #34.

45. Ibid.

46. Judge, T. A. Heller, D., & Mount, M. K. (2002) — see #41.

47. McCrae, R. R., & Costa, P. T. (1997). Personality trait structure as a human universal. *American Psychologist, 52*, 509–516.

48. Morgeson, F. P., Campion, M. A., Dipboye, R. L., Hollenbeck, J. R., Murphy, K. R., & Schmitt, N. (2007). Reconsidering the use of personality tests in personnel selection contexts. *Personnel Psychology, 60*, 683–729.

49. Oh, I.-S., Wang, G., & Mount, M. K. (2011). Validity of observer ratings of the five-factor model of personality traits: A meta-analysis. *Journal of Applied Psychology, 96*, 762–773; and Connelly, B. S., & Ones, D. S. (2010). An other perspective on personality: Meta-analytic interpretation of observers' accuracy and predictive validity. *Psychological Bulletin, 136*, 1092–1122.

50. Judge, T. A., Jackson, C. L., Shaw, J. C., Scott, B. A., & Rich, B. L. (2007). Self-efficacy and work-related performance: The integral role of individual differences. *Journal of Applied Psychology, 2*, 107–127; and Roth, P. L., Switzer, F. S. III, Van Iddekinge, C. H., & Oh, I.-S. (2011). Toward better meta-analytic matrices: How input values can affect research conclusions in human resource management simulations. *Personnel Psychology, 64*, 899–936.

51. Kehoe, J. F. (2002). General mental ability and selection in private sector organizations. A commentary. *Human Performance, 15,* 96–106.

52. Muris, P., Merckelbach, H., Otgaar, H., & Meijer, E. (2017). The malevolent side of human nature: A meta- analysis and critical review of the literature on the dark triad (narcissism, Machiavellianism, and psychopathy). *Perspectives on Psychological Science, 12*, 183–204.

53. Kausel, E. E., Culbertson, S. S., Leiva, P. I., Slaughter, J. E., & Jackson, A. T. (2015). Too arrogant for their own good? Why and when narcissists dismiss advice. *Organizational Behavior and Human Decision Processes, 131*, 33–50.

54. O'Boyle, E. H., Jr., Forsyth, D. R., Banks, G. C., & McDaniel, M. A. (2012). A meta-analysis of the dark triad and work behavior: A social exchange perspective. *Journal of Applied Psychology, 97*, 557–579.

55. Howes, S. S., Kausel, E. E., Jackson, A. T., & Reb, J. (2020). When and why narcissists exhibit greater hindsight bias and less perceived learning. *Journal of Management, 46*(8), 1498–1528.

56. Babiak, P., & Hare, R. D. (2006). *Snakes in suits: When psychopaths go to work.* New York: Regan Books.

57. Guenole, N. (2014). Maladaptive personality at work: Exploring the darkness. *Industrial and Organizational Psychology, 7*, 85–97.

58. Morgeson, F. P., Campion, M. A., Dipboye, R. L., Hollenbeck, J. R., Murphy, K. R., & Schmitt, N. (2007)—see #48.

59. Berry, C. M., & Sackett, P. R. (2009). Faking in personnel selection: Tradeoffs in performance versus fairness resulting from two cut-score strategies. *Personnel Psychology, 62*, 835–863.

60. McFarland, L. A. (2013). Applicant reactions to personality tests: Why do applicants hate them? In N. D. Christiansen & R. P. Tett (Eds.), *Handbook of personality at work* (pp. 281–298). New York: Routledge.

61. Viswesvaran, C., & Ones, D. S. (1999). Meta-analyses of fakability estimates: Implications for personality measurement. *Educational and Psychological Measurement, 59*, 197–210.

62. Birkeland, S. A., Manson, T. M., Kisamore, J. L., Brannick, M. T., & Smith, M. A. (2006). A meta-analytic investigation of job applicant faking on personality measures. *International Journal of Selection and Assessment, 14*, 317–335.

63. Barrick, M. R., Mount, M. K., & Judge, T. A. (2001). Personality and performance at the beginning of the new millennium: What do we know and where do we go next? *International Journal of Selection and Assessment, 9*, 9–30; and Huber, C. R., Kuncel, N. R., Huber, K. B., & Boyce, A. S. (2021). Faking and the validity of personality tests: An experimental investigation using modern forced choice measures. *Personnel Assessment and Decisions,* Volume 7, Issue 1, Article 3.

64. Morgeson, F. P., Campion, M. A., Dipboye, R. L., Hollenbeck, J. R., Murphy, K. R., & Schmitt, N. (2007)—see #48.

65. Griffith, R. L., & Robie, C. (2013). Personality testing and the "F-word." In N. D. Christiansen & R. P. Tett (Eds.), *Handbook of personality at work* (pp. 253–280). New York: Routledge.

66. Fine, S., & Pirak, M. (2016). Faking fast and slow: Within-person response time latencies for measuring faking in personnel testing. *Journal of Business and Psychology, 31*, 51–64.

67. Salgado, J. F. (2016). A theoretical model of psychometric effects of faking on assessment procedures: Empirical findings and implications for personality at work. *International Journal of Selection and Assessment, 24*, 209–228.

68. Oswald, F. L., & Hough, L. M. (2011). Personality and its assessment in organizations. Theoretical and empirical assessments. In S. Zedeck (Ed.), *APA handbook of industrial and organizational psychology* (Vol. 2, pp. 153–184). Washington, DC: APA.

69. Sackett, P. R., & Wanek, J. E. (1996). New developments in the use of measures of honesty, integrity, conscientiousness, dependability, trustworthiness, and reliability for personnel selection. *Personnel Psychology, 49,* 787–829.

70. Harris, W. G., Jones, J. W., Klion, R., Arnold, D. W., Camara, W., & Cunningham, M. R. (2012). Test publishers' perspective on "An updated meta-analysis:" Comment on Van Iddekinge, Roth, Raymark, and Odle-Dusseau (2012). *Journal of Applied Psychology, 97,* 531–536.

71. Ones, D. S., Viswesvaran, C., & Schmidt, F. L. (2012). Integrity tests predict counterproductive work behaviors and job performance well: Comment on Van Iddekinge, Roth, Raymark, and Odle-Dusseau (2012). *Journal of Applied Psychology, 97*(3), p. 541.

72. Van Iddekinge, C. H., Roth, P. L., Raymark, P. H., & Odle-Dusseau, H. (2012). The critical role of the research question, inclusion criteria, and transparency in meta-analyses of integrity test research: A reply to Harris et al. (2012) and Ones, Viswesvaran, and Schmidt (2012). *Journal of Applied Psychology, 97*(3), 543–549.

73. Collins, J. M., & Schmidt, F. L. (1993). Personality, integrity, and white collar crime: A construct validity study. *Personnel Psychology, 46,* 295–311.

74. Berry, C. M., Sackett, P. R., & Wiemann, S. (2007). A review of recent developments in integrity test research. *Personnel Psychology, 60,* 271–301.

75. Alliger, G. M., & Dwight, S. A. (2001). Invade or evade? The trade-off between privacy invasion and item fakability. *Applied HRM Research, 6,* 95–104.

76. Stone-Romero, E. F., Stone, D. L., & Hyatt, D. (2003). Personnel selection procedures and invasion of privacy. *Journal of Social Issues, 59,* 343–368.

77. Podlesny, J. A., & Truslow, C. M. (1993). Validity of an expanded-issue (Modified General Question) polygraph technique in a simulated distributed-crime-roles context. *Journal of Applied Psychology, 78,* 788–797.

78. Honts, C. R., & Amato, S. L. (2002). Countermeasures. In M. Kleiner (Ed.), *Handbook of polygraph testing* (pp. 251– 264). San Diego: Academic Press.

79. McDaniel, M. A., Morgeson, F. P., Finnegan, E. B., Campion, M. A., & Brauerman, E. P. (2001). Use of situational judgment tests to predict job performance: A clarification of the literature. *Journal of Applied Psychology, 86,* 730–740.

80. Ployhart, R. E., & MacKenzie, W. I. (2011). Situational judgment tests: A critical review and agenda for the future. In S. Zedeck (Ed.), *APA handbook of industrial and organizational psychology* (Vol. 2, pp. 237–252). Washington, DC: APA.

81. McDaniel, M. A., Hartman, N. S., Whetzel, D. L., & Grubb, W. L., III. (2007). Situational judgment tests, response instructions, and validity: A meta-analysis. *Personnel Psychology, 60,* 63–91.

82. Christian, M. S., Edwards, B. D., & Bradley, J. C. (2010). Situational judgment tests: Constructs assessed and a meta-analysis of their criterion-related validities. *Personnel Psychology, 63,* 83–117.

83. Lievens, F., & Sackett, P. R. (2012). The validity of interpersonal skills assessment via situational judgment tests for predicting academic success and job performance. *Journal of Applied Psychology, 97,* 460–468.

84. Bobko, P., & Roth, P. L. (2012). Reviewing, categorizing, and analyzing the literature on black-white mean differences for predictors of job performance: Verifying some perceptions and updating/correcting others. *Personnel Psychology, 66,* 91–126.

85. Mael, F. A. (1991). A conceptual rationale for the domain and attributes of biodata items. *Personnel Psychology, 44,* 763–792.

86. Schoenfeldt, L. F. (1999). From dust bowl empiricism to rational constructs in biographical data. *Human Resource Management Review, 9*(2), 147–167.

87. Speer, A. B., Tenbrink, A. P., Wegmeyer, L. J., Sendra, C. C., Shihadeh, M., & Kaur, S. (2021, October 21). Meta-analysis of biodata in employment settings: Providing clarity to criterion and construct-related validity estimates. *Journal of Applied Psychology.* Advance online publication. http://dx.doi.org/10.1037/apl0000964

88. Nickels, B. J. (1994). The nature of biodata. In G. S. Stokes, M. D. Mumford, & W. A. Owens (Eds.), *Biodata handbook: Theory, research, and use of biographical information in selection and performance prediction* (pp. 1–16). Palo Alto, CA: Consulting Psychologists Press.
89. Mael, F. A., Connerly, M., & Morath, R. A. (1996). None of your business: Parameters of biodata invasiveness. *Personnel Psychology, 49,* 613–650.
90. Becker, T. E., & Colquitt, A. L. (1992). Potential versus actual faking of a biodata form: An analysis along several dimensions of item type. *Personnel Psychology, 45,* 389–406; and Kluger, A. N., Reilly, R. R., & Russell, C. J. (1991). Faking biodata tests: Are option-keyed instruments more resistant? *Journal of Applied Psychology, 76,* 889–896.
91. Levashina, J., Morgeson, F. P., & Campion, M. A. (2012). Tell me some more: Exploring how verbal ability and item verifiability influence responses to biodata questions in a high-stakes selection context. *Personnel Psychology, 65,* 359–383.
92. Mumford, M. D., & Stokes, G. S. (1992). Developmental determinants of individual action: Theory and practice in applying background measures. In M. D. Dunnette & L. M. Hough (Eds.), *Handbook of industrial and organizational psychology* (2nd ed., Vol. 3, pp. 61–138). Palo Alto, CA: Consulting Psychologists Press.
93. Normand, J., Salyards, S. D., & Mahoney, J. J. (1990). An evaluation of preemployment drug testing. *Journal of Applied Psychology, 75,* 629–639.
94. Schwartz, N. D. (2017, July 24). Economy needs workers, but drug tests take a toll. *The New York Times, 166*(57669), A1–A15.
95. Wainer, H. (2000). *Computerized adaptive testing* (2nd ed.). Mahwah, NJ: Erlbaum.
96. Tonidandel, S., Quiñones, M. A., & Adams, A. A. (2002). Computer-adaptive testing: The impact of test characteristics on perceived performance and test takers reactions. *Journal of Applied Psychology, 87,* 320–332.
97. Overton, R. C., Harms, H. J., Taylor, L. R., & Zickar, M. J. (1997). Adapting to adaptive testing. *Personnel Psychology, 50,* 171–185.
98. Tippins, N. T., Beaty, J., Drasgow, F., Gibson, W. M., Pearlman, K., Segall, D. O., & Shepard, W. (2006). Unproctored internet testing in employment settings. *Personnel Psychology, 59,* 189–225.
99. Thompson, L. F., Surface, E. A., Martin, D. L., & Sanders, M. G. (2003). From paper to pixels: Moving personnel surveys to the Web. *Personnel Psychology, 56,* 197–227.
100. Naglieri, J. A., Drasgow, F., Schmit, M. J., Handler, L., Prifitera, A., Margolis, A., & Velasquez, R. (2004). Psychological testing on the Internet: New problems, old issues. *American Psychologist, 59,* 150–162.
101. Ployhart, R. E., Weekley, J. A., Holtz, B. C., & Kemp, C. (2003). Web-based and pencil-and-paper testing of applicants in a proctored setting: Are personality, biodata, and situational judgment tests comparable? *Personnel Psychology, 56,* 733–752.
102. Scott, J. C., & Lezotte, D. V. (2012). Web-based assessments. In N. Schmitt (Ed.), *The Oxford handbook of personnel assessment and selection* (pp. 485–513). New York: Oxford University Press.
103. Gnambs, T., & Kaspar, K. (2017). Socially desirable responding in web-based questionnaires: A meta-analytic review of the candor hypothesis. *Assessment, 24,* 746–762.
104. Huffcutt, A. I., & Culbertson, S. S. (2011). Interviews. In S. Zedeck (Ed.), *APA handbook of industrial and organizational psychology* (Vol. 2, pp. 185-203). Washington, DC: APA.
105. Huffcutt, A. I., Culbertson, S. S., & Riforgiate, S. (2015). Functional forms of competence: Interviewing. In A. F. Hannawa & B. H. Spitzberg (Eds.), *The handbook of communication science* (Vol. 22, pp. 431–448). Berlin: Mouton de Gruyter.
106. Barrick, M. R., Swider, B. W., & Stewart, G. L. (2010). Initial evaluations in the interview: Relationships with subsequent interviewer evaluations and employment offers. *Journal of Applied Psychology, 95,* 1163–1172.
107. Maurer, T. J., & Solamon, J. M. (2006). The science and practice of a structured employment interview coaching program. *Personnel Psychology, 59,* 433–456.
108. Barrick, M. R., Shaffer, J. A., & DeGrassi, S. W. (2009). What you see may not be what you get: Relationships among self-presentation tactics and ratings of interview and job performance. *Journal of Applied Psychology, 94,* 1394–1411.
109. Barrick, M. R., Swider, B. W., & Stewart, G. L. (2010)—see #106.

110. Dipboye, R. L., Macan, T. H., & Shahani-Denning, C. (2012). The selection interview from the interviewer and applicant perspectives: Can't have one without the other. In N. Schmitt (Ed.), *The Oxford handbook of personnel assessment and selection* (pp. 323–352). New York: Oxford University Press.

111. Levashina, J., Hartwell, C. J., Morgeson, F. P., & Campion, M. A. (2014). The structured employment interview: Narrative and quantitative review of the research literature. *Personnel Psychology, 67*, 241–293.

112. Huffcutt, A. I., Culbertson, S. S., & Weyhrauch, W. S. (2013). Employment interview reliability: New meta-analytic estimates by structure and format. *International Journal of Selection and Assessment, 21*, 264–276.

113. Huffcutt, A. I., Culbertson, S. S., & Weyhrauch, W. S. (2014). Moving forward indirectly: Reanalyzing the validity of employment interviews with indirect range restriction methodology. *International Journal of Selection and Assessment, 22*, 297–309.

114. Huffcutt, A. I., Conway, J. M., Ruth, P. L., & Stone, N. J. (2001). Identification and meta-analytic assessment of psychological constructs measured in employment interviews. *Journal of Applied Psychology, 86*, 897–913.

115. Kausel, E. E., Culbertson, S. S., & Madrid, H. (2016). Overconfidence in personnel selection: When and why unstructured interview information can hurt hiring decisions. *Organizational Behavior and Human Decision Processes, 137*, 27–44.

116. Latham, G. P., Saari, L. M., Pursell, E. D., & Campion, M. A. (1980). The situational interview. *Journal of Applied Psychology, 65*, 422–427.

117. Pulakos, E. D., & Schmitt, N. (1995). Experience-based and structured interview questions: Studies of validity. *Personnel Psychology, 48,* p. 292.

118. McDaniel, M. A., Whetzel, D. L., Schmidt, F. L., & Maurer, S. D. (1994). The validity of employment interviews: A comprehensive review and meta-analysis. *Journal of Applied Psychology, 79,* 599–616.

119. Janz, T. (1989). The patterned behavior description interview: The best prophet of the future is the past. In R. W. Eder and G. R. Ferris (Eds.), *The employment interview: Theory, research, and practice* (pp. 158–168). Thousand Oaks, CA: Sage.

120. Culbertson, S. S., Weyhrauch, W. S., & Huffcutt, A. I. (2017). A tale of two formats: Direct comparison of matching situational and behavior description interview questions. *Human Resource Management Review, 27*, 167–177.

121. Motowidlo, S. J., Hanson, M. A., & Crafts, J. L. (1997). Low-fidelity simulations. In D. L. Whetzel & G. R. Wheaton (Eds.), *Applied measurement methods in industrial psychology* (pp. 241–260). Palo Alto, CA: Consulting Psychologists Press.

122. Campion, J. E. (1972). Work sampling for personnel selection. *Journal of Applied Psychology, 56*, 40–44.

123. Callinan, M., & Robertson, I. T. (2000). Work sample testing. *International Journal of Selection and Assessment, 8*, 248–260.

124. Whetzel, D. L., Rotenberry, P. F., & McDaniel, M. A. (2014). In-basket validity: A systematic review. *International Journal of Selection and Assessment, 22*, 62–79.

125. Lievens, F., & Patterson, F. (2011). The validity and incremental validity of knowledge tests, low-fidelity simulations, and high-fidelity simulations for predicting job performance in advanced-level high-stakes selection. *Journal of Applied Psychology, 96*, 927–940.

126. Highhouse, S., & Nolan, K. P. (2012). One history of the assessment center. In D. J. Jackson, C. E. Lance, & B. J. Hoffman (Eds.), *The psychology of assessment centers* (pp. 25–44). New York: Routledge.

127. Arthur, W. A., Jr., & Day, E. A. (2011). Assessment centers. In S. Zedeck (Ed.), *APA handbook of industrial and organizational psychology* (Vol. 2, pp. 205–235). Washington, DC: APA.

128. Aamodt, M. G., & Williams, F. (2005, April). *Reliability, validity, and adverse impact of references and letters of recommendation*. Paper presented at the 20th annual meeting of the Society for Industrial and Organizational Psychology, Los Angeles, CA.

129. Judge, T. A., & Higgins, C. A. (1998). Affective disposition and the letter of reference. *Organizational Behavior and Human Decision Processes, 75*, 207–221.

130. Arthur, W. A., Jr., & Villado, A. J. (2008). The importance of distinguishing between constructs and methods when comparing predictors in personnel selection research and practice. *Journal of Applied Psychology, 93*, 435–442.

131. Foster, D. (2013). Security issues in technology-based testing. In J. A. Wollack & J. J. Fremer (Eds.), *Handbook of test security* (pp. 39–83). New York: Routledge.

Chapter 6

1. Ployhart, R. E. (2012). Personnel selection: Ensuring sustainable organizational effectiveness through the acquisition of human capital. In S. W. J. Kozlowski (Ed.), *The Oxford handbook of organizational psychology* (Vol. 1, pp. 221–246). New York: Oxford University Press.

2. Crook, T. R., Todd, S. Y., Combs, J. G., & Woehr, D. J. (2011). Does human capital matter? A meta-analysis of the relationship between human capital and firm performance. *Journal of Applied Psychology, 96*, 443–456.

3. Osicki, M., & Kulkarni, M. (2010). Recruitment in a global workplace. In K. Lundby (Ed.), *Going global* (pp. 113–142). San Francisco: Jossey-Bass.

4. Breaugh, J. A. (2012). Employee recruitment: Current knowledge and suggestions for future research. In N. Schmitt (Ed.), *The Oxford handbook of personnel assessment and selection* (pp. 68–87). New York: Oxford University Press.

5. Jones, D. A., Willness, C. R., & Madey, S. (2014). Why are job seekers attracted by corporate social performance? Experimental and field tests of three signal-based mechanisms. *Academy of Management Journal, 57*, 383–404.

6. Griepentrog, B. K., Harold, C. M., Holtz, B. C., Klimoski, R. J., & Marsh, S. M. (2012). Interpreting social identity and the theory of planned behavior: Predicting withdrawal from an organizational recruitment process. *Personnel Psychology, 65*, 723–753.

7. Van Hoye, G., & Lievens, F. (2009). Tapping the grapevine: A closer look at word-of-mouth as a recruitment source. *Journal of Applied Psychology, 94*, 341–352.

8. Breaugh, J. A., Macan, T. H., & Grambow, D. M. (2008). Employee recruitment: Current knowledge and directions for future research. In G. P. Hodgkinson & J. L. Ford (Eds.), *International review of industrial and organizational psychology* (Vol. 23, pp. 45–82). Chichester, UK: Wiley-Blackwell.

9. Dineen, B. R., & Soltis, S. M. (2011). Recruitment: A review of research and emerging directions. In S. Zedeck (Ed.), *APA handbook of industrial and organizational psychology* (Vol. 2, pp. 43–66). Washington, DC: APA.

10. Kaplan, J. (2021, August 14). After a coffee shop owner in Iowa raised wages to $15, he got nearly 50 applications in 2 weeks. *Business Insider*. Retrieved September 29, 2021, from https://www.businessinsider.com/coffee-shop-owner-raised-wages-15-got-50-job-applications-2021-8; and Dean, G. (2021, August 21). The labor shortage has created a 'bidding war' for staff as restaurants tempt them to stay by hiking wages, says a burger chain owner. *Business Insider*. Retrieved September 29, 2021, from https://www.businessinsider.com/labor-shortage-restaurants-bidding-war-staff-workers-employment-farm-burger-2021-8

11. Truxillo, D. M., Bauer, T. N., & Garcia, A. M. (2017). Applicant reactions to hiring procedures. In H. W. Goldstein, E. D. Pulakos, J. Passmore, & C. Semedo (Eds.), *The Wiley Blackwell handbook of the psychology of recruitment, selection and employee retention* (pp. 53–70). Wiley Blackwell.

12. Schuler, H. (1993). Social validity of selection situations: A concept and some empirical results. In H. Schuler, J. L. Farr, & M. Smith (Eds.), *Personnel selection and assessment* (pp. 11–26). Hillsdale, NJ: Erlbaum.

13. McCarthy, J. M., Van Iddekinge, C. H., Lievens, F., Kung, M.-C., Sinar, E. F., & Campion, M. A. (2013). Do candidate reactions relate to job performance or affect criterion-related validity? A multi-study investigation of relations among reactions, selection, test scores, and job performance. *Journal of Applied Psychology, 98*, 701–719.

14. Ployhart, R. E., & Ryan, A. M. (1998). Applicants' reactions to the fairness of selection procedures: The effects of positive rule violations and time of measurement. *Journal of Applied Psychology, 83,* 3–16.

15. Eveleth, D. M., & Eveleth, H. (2021). Job-seeker reactions to rejection emails. *International Journal of Technology and Human Interaction, 17*, 1–15.

16. Cortini, M., Galanti, T., & Barattucci, M. (2019). The effect of different rejection letters on applicants' reactions. *Behavioral sciences (Basel, Switzerland), 9*(10), 102.

17. Harris, L. (2000). Procedural justice and perceptions of fairness in selection practice. *International Journal of Selection and Assessment, 8,* 148–157.

18. Rosen, K. R. (2016, November). This job candidate's response to a rejection letter was so brilliant, it got him hired. *New York Magazine: The Vindicated*. Retrieved September 29, 2021, from https://nymag.com/vindicated/2016/11/read-a-rejection-letter-reply-so-brilliant-it-got-him-hired.html

19. Ferri, L. (2019, September 9). Fed up teenager who won a job interview with Aldi by boldly 'rejecting her rejection' is a step closer to securing the role - and reveals how the first knock-back HELPED her this time. *Daily Mail.com*. Retrieved December 5, 2021, from https://www.dailymail.co.uk/news/article-7446009/Jessica-Irving-western-Sydney-one-step-closer-job-Aldi-rejecting-rejection.html

20. Davies, A. (2020, August 10). Woman is stunned when job candidate replies to her rejection letter with 'F**k you." *Tyla blog*. Retrieved September 29, 2021, from https://www.tyla.com/news/funny-sweary-reply-rejection-letter-candidate-head-chef-20200810

21. Slaughter, J. E., & Kausel, E. E. (2014). Employee selection decisions. In S. Highhouse, R. S. Dalal, & E. Salas (Eds.), *Judgment and decision making at work* (pp. 57–79). New York: Routledge.

22. Highhouse, S. (2008). Stubborn reliance on intuition and subjectivity in employee selection. *Industrial and Organizational Psychology, 1*, 333–342.

23. Martin, S. L., & Terris, W. (1991). Predicting infrequent behavior: Clarifying the impact on false-positive rates. *Journal of Applied Psychology, 76,* 484–487.

24. Cascio, W. F., Alexander, R. A., & Barrett, G. V. (1988). Setting cutoff scores: Legal, psychometric, and professional issues and guidelines. *Personnel Psychology, 41*, 1–24.

25. Van Iddekinge, C. H., Putka, D. J., & Campbell, J. P. (2011). Reconsidering vocational interests for personnel selection: The validity of an interest-based selection test in relation to job knowledge, job performance, and continuance intentions. *Journal of Applied Psychology, 96*, 13–33.

26. Moody, J. (2021, August 18). How recent events reshaped college admissions. *U.S. News and World Report*. Retrieved September 29, 2021, from https://www.usnews.com/education/best-colleges/articles/how-recent-events-reshaped-college-admissions

27. Outtz, J. L. (2011). The unique origins of advancements in selection and personnel psychology. In S. Zedeck (Ed.), *APA handbook of industrial and organizational psychology* (Vol. 2, pp. 445–465). Washington, DC: APA.

28. Schmitt, N., & Landy, F. J. (1993). The concept of validity. In N. Schmitt & W. C. Borman (Eds.), *Personnel selection in organizations* (pp. 275–309). San Francisco: Jossey-Bass.

29. Schmidt, F. L., & Hunter, J. E. (1980). The future of criterion-related validity. *Personnel Psychology, 33,* 41–60.

30. Salgado, J. F. (1998). Sample size in validity studies of personnel selection. *Journal of Occupational & Organizational Psychology, 71*, 161–164.

31. Schmidt, F. L., & Hunter, J. E. (1978). Moderator research and the law of small numbers. *Personnel Psychology, 31*, 215–232.

32. Guion, R. M. (1998). *Assessment, measurement, and prediction for personnel decisions.* Mahwah, NJ: Erlbaum.

33. Oh, I.-S., & Roth, P. L. (2017). On the mystery (or myth) of challenging principles and methods of validity generalization (VG) based on fragmentary knowledge and improper or outdated practices of VG. *Industrial and Organizational Psychology, 10*, 479–485.

34. Biddle, D. A. (2008). Are the Uniform Guidelines outdated? Federal guidelines, professional standards, and validity generalization (VG). *The Industrial-Organizational Psychologist, 45*(4), 17–23.

35. Newman, D. A., Jacobs, R. R., & Bartram, D. (2007). Choosing the best method for local validity estimation: Relative accuracy of meta-analysis versus a local study versus Bayes-analysis. *Journal of Applied Psychology, 92*, 1394–1413.

36. Strickler, L. J. (2000). Using just noticeable differences to interpret test scores. *Psychological Methods, 5,* 415–424.

37. Cascio, W. F., Alexander, R. A., & Barrett, G. V. (1988)—see #24.

38. Zieky, M. J. (2001). So much has changed: How the setting of cutscores has evolved since the 1980s. In G. J. Cizek (Ed.), *Setting performance standards: Concepts, methods, and perspectives* (pp. 19–52). Mahwah, NJ: Erlbaum.

39. Cascio, W. F., Alexander, R. A., & Barrett, G. V. (1988)—see #25.

40. Ibid.

41. Campion, M. A., Outtz, J. L., Zedeck, S., Schmidt, F. L., Kehoe, J. F., Murphy, K. R., & Guion, R. M. (2001). The controversy over score banding in personnel selection: Answers to 10 key questions. *Personnel Psychology, 54*, 149–185.

42. Schmidt, F. L., & Hunter, J. E. (2004). SED banding as a test of scientific values in I/O psychology. In H. Aguinis (Ed.), *Test-score banding in human resource selection: Technical, legal, and societal issues* (pp. 151–174). Westport, CT: Praeger.

43. Barrett, G. V., & Lueke, S. B. (2004). Legal and practical implications of banding for personnel selection. In H. Aguinis (Ed.), *Test-score banding in human resource selection: Technical, legal, and societal issues* (pp. 71–112). Westport, CT: Praeger.

44. Cascio, W. F., & Fogli, L. (2010). The business value of employee selection. In J. L. Farr & N. T. Tippins (Eds.), *Handbook of employee selection* (pp. 235–252). New York: Routledge.

45. Winkler, S., König, C. J., & Kleinmann, M. (2010). Single-attribute utility analysis may be futile, but this can't be the end of the story: Causal chain analysis as an alternative. *Personnel Psychology, 63*, 1041–1065.

46. Yoo, T. Y., & Muchinsky, P. M. (1998). Utility estimates of job performance as related to the Data, People, and Things parameters of work. *Journal of Organizational Behavior, 19,* 353–370.

47. Brenner, J., Jain, S., Leas, K., Samudio, D. C., & Amundson, M. (2021). Mayflower group benchmark on changes in work due to COVID-19: Now and in the future. *Industrial and Organizational Psychology, 14*, 139–143; and Jayne, M. E., & Rauschenberger, J. M. (2000). Demonstrating the value of selection in organizations. In J. F. Kehoe (Ed.), *Managing selection in changing organizations* (pp. 123–157). San Francisco: Jossey-Bass.

48. De Angelis, K., & Segal, D. R. (2012). Minorities in the military. In J. H. Laurence & M. D. Matthews (Eds.), *The Oxford handbook of military psychology* (pp. 325–343). New York: Oxford University Press.

49. Rumsey, M. G. (2012). Military selection and classification in the United States. In J. H. Laurence & M. D. Matthews (Eds.), *The Oxford handbook of military psychology* (pp. 129–147). New York: Oxford University Press.

Chapter 7

1. Statista.com. (2021). *Average spend on workplace training per employee worldwide from 2008-2019 (in U.S. dollars).* Retrieved October 18, 2021, from https://www.statista.com/statistics/738519/workplace-training-spending-per-employee/

2. Molloy, J. C., & Noe, R. A. (2010). "Learning" a living: Continuous learning for survival in today's talent market. In S. W. J. Kozlowski & E. Salas (Eds.), *Learning, training, and development in organizations* (pp. 333–362). New York: Routledge.

3. Danielson, C. C., & Wiggenhorn, W. (2003). The strategic challenge for transfer: Chief learning officers speak out. In E. F. Holton & T. T. Baldwin (Eds.), *Improving learning transfer in organizations* (pp. 16–38). San Francisco: Jossey-Bass.

4. Ibid., p. 17.

5. Kim, S. L., & Ployhart, R. E. (2014). The effects of staffing and training on firm productivity and profit growth before, during, and after the Great Recession. *Journal of Applied Psychology, 99*, 361–389.

6. Bear, D. J., Tompson, H. B., Morrison, C. L., Vickers, M., Paradise, A., Czarnowsky, M., Soyars, M., & King, K. (2008). *Tapping the potential of informal learning. An ASTD research study*. Alexandria, VA: American Society for Training and Development.

7. McCall, M. W. (2004). Leadership development through experience. *Academy of Management Executive, 18*, 127–130.

8. Dragoni, L., Oh, I.-S., Tesluk, P. E., Moore, O. A., VanKatwyk, P., & Hazucha, J. (2014). Developing leaders' strategic thinking through global work experience: The moderating role of cultural distance. *Journal of Applied Psychology, 99*, 867–882.

9. Huet, E. (2014, October 8). Uber skimps on driver training, then charges drivers $65 for basic driver skills course. *Forbes*. Retrieved October 18, 2021, from https://www.forbes.com/sites/ellenhuet/2014/10/08/uber-skimps-on-driver-training-then-charges-drivers-65-for-basic-driver-skills-course/?sh=48c5bda822b4

10. Van Maanen, J., & Schein, E. H. (1979). Toward a theory of organizational socialization. In B. M. Staw (Ed.), *Research in organizational behavior* (pp. 209–264. Greenwich, CT: JAI.

11. Feldman, D. C. (1989). Socialization, resocialization, and training: Reframing the research agenda. In I. L. Goldstein (Ed.), *Training and development in organizations* (pp. 376–416). Jossey-Bass.

12. Rollag, K., Parise, S., & Cross, R. (2005). Getting new hires up to speed quickly. *MIT Sloan Management Review, 46*, 35–41.

13. Cooper Thomas, H. D., Paterson, N. L., Stadler, M. J., & Saks, A. M. (2014). The relative importance of proactive behaviors and outcomes for predicting newcomer learning, well-being, and work engagement. *Journal of Vocational Behavior, 84*, 318–331.

14. Klein, H. J., & Polin, B. (2012). Are organizations onboard with best practice onboarding? In C. Wanberg (Ed.), *The Oxford handbook of socialization* (pp. 267–287). New York: Oxford University Press.

15. Klein, H. J., & Heuser, A. (2008). The learning of socialization content: A framework for researching orientating practices. *Research in Personnel and Human Resources Management, 27*, 278–336.

16. Klein, H. J., Polin, B., & Sutton, K. L. (2015). Specific onboarding practices for the socialization of new employees. *International Journal of Selection and Assessment, 23*, 263–283.

17. Van Maanen, J., & Schein, E. H. (1979)—see #10; and Jones, G. R. (1986). Socialization tactics, self-efficacy, and newcomers' adjustments to organizations. *Academy of Management Journal, 29*, 262–279.

18. Wang, D., Hom, P. W., & Allen, D. G. (2017). Coping with newcomer "Hangover": How socialization tactics affect declining job satisfaction during early employment. *Journal of Vocational Behavior, 100*, 196–210.

19. Gruman, J. A., & Saks, A. M. (2018). E-socialization: The problems and the promise of socializing newcomers in the digital age. In D. Stone & J. Dulebohn (Eds.), *The brave new world of eHRM 2.0* (pp. 111–139). Information Age Publishing.

20. Wesson, M. J., & Gogus, C. I. (2005). Shaking hands with a computer: An examination of two methods of organizational newcomer orientation. *Journal of Applied Psychology, 90*, 1018–1026.

21. Weiss, H. M. (1990). Learning theory and industrial and organizational psychology. In M. D. Dunnette & L. M. Hough (Eds.), *Handbook of industrial and organizational psychology* (2nd ed., Vol. 1, pp. 171–221). Palo Alto, CA: Consulting Psychologists Press.

22. Anderson, J. R. (1985). *Cognitive psychology and its implications* (2nd ed.). New York: Freeman.

23. Kanfer, R., & Ackerman, P. L. (1989). Motivation and cognitive abilities: An integrative/aptitude–treatment interaction approach to skill acquisition. *Journal of Applied Psychology, 74*, 657–690.

24. DuBois, D. A. (2002). Leveraging hidden expertise: Why, when, and how to use cognitive task analysis. In K. Kraiger (Ed.), *Creating, implementing, and managing effective training and development* (pp. 80–114). San Francisco: Jossey-Bass.

25. Ackerman, P. L. (1987). Individual differences in skill learning: An integration of psychometric and information processing perspectives. *Psychological Bulletin, 102*, 3–27; and Farrell, J. N., & McDaniel, M. A. (2001). The stability of validity coefficients over time: Ackerman's (1988) model and the general aptitude test battery. *Journal of Applied Psychology, 86*, 60–79.

26. Kanfer, R., & Ackerman, P. L. (1989)—see #23.

27. Ford, J. K., & Kraiger, K. (1995). The application of cognitive constructs and principles to the instructional systems model of training: Implications for needs assessment, design, and transfer. In C. L. Cooper & I. T. Robertson (Eds.), *International review of industrial and organizational psychology* (Vol. 10, pp. 1–48). New York: Wiley.

28. Salas, E., Weaver, S. J., & Shuffler, M. L. (2012). Learning, training, and development in organizations. In S. W. J. Kozlowski (Ed.), *The Oxford handbook of organizational psychology* (Vol. 1, pp. 330–372). New York: Oxford University Press.

29. Surface, E. A. (2012). Training needs assessment: Aligning learning and capability with performance requirements and organizational objectives. In M. A. Wilson, W. Bennett, S. Gibson, & G. M. Alliger (Eds.), *The handbook of work analysis: The methods, systems, applications and science of work measurement in organizations* (pp. 439–464). New York: Routledge.

30. Salas, E., Weaver, S. J., & Shuffler, M. L. (2012)—see #28.

31. Sung, S. Y., & Choi, J. N. (2014). Do organizations spend wisely on employees? Effects of training and development investments on learning and innovation in organizations. *Journal of Organizational Behavior, 35*, 393–412.

32. Arthur, W. A., Jr., Bennett, W., Edens, P. S., & Bell, S. T. (2003). Effectiveness of training in organizations: A meta-analysis of design and evaluation features. *Journal of Applied Psychology, 88*, 234–245.

33. Salas, E., Weaver, S. J., & Shuffler, M. L. (2012) — see #28.

34. Kraiger, K., & Culbertson, S. S. (2013). Understanding and facilitating learning: Advancements in training and development. In N. Schmitt, & S. Highhouse (Eds.), *Handbook of psychology: Industrial and organizational psychology* (Vol. 12, pp. 244–261). New York: John Wiley & Sons.

35. Surface, E. A. (2012) — see #29.

36. Bell, B. S., Tannenbaum, S. I., Ford, J. K., Noe, R. A., & Kraiger, K. (2017). 100 years of training and development research: What we know and where we should go. *Journal of Applied Psychology, 102*, 305–323.

37. Kraiger, K. (2008). Transforming our models of learning and development: Web-based instruction as enabler of third-generation instruction. *Industrial and Organizational Psychology, 1*, 454–467.

38. Clark, R. C., & Mayer, R. E. (2008). *e-Learning and the science of instruction* (2nd ed.). San Francisco: Pfeiffer.

39. Noe, R. A., Clarke, A. D. M., & Klein, H. J. (2014). Learning in the twenty-first century workplace. Annual *Review of Organizational Psychology and Organizational Behavior, 1*, 245–275.

40. Kaszycki, A., DeLong, T., Melzer, A., & DuVernet, A. M. (2021). The vital role of training in an organization's response to a pandemic. *Industrial and Organizational Psychology, 14*(1–2), 248–250.

41. Van Buren, M. (2001). *The 2001 ASTD state of the industry report.* Alexandria, VA: ASTD.

42. Stanisavljevic, J., & Djuric, D. (2013). The application of programmed instruction in fulfilling the physiology course requirements. *Journal of Biological Education, 47*, 29–38.

43. Martin, B. O., Kolomitro, K., & Lam, T. C. M. (2014). Training methods: A review and analysis. *Human Resource Development Review, 13*, 11–35.

44. Blanchard, P. M., & Thacker, J. W. (2004). *Effective training: Systems, strategies, and practices* (2nd ed.). Upper Saddle River, NJ: Prentice Hall.

45. Cannon-Bowers, J. A., & Bowers, C. (2010). Synthetic learning environments: On developing a science of simulation, games, and virtual worlds for training. In S. W. J. Kozlowski & E. Salas (Eds.), *Learning, training, and development in organizations* (pp. 229–262). New York: Routledge.

46. Blanchard, P. M., & Thacker, J. W. (2004) — see #44.

47. Noe, R. A. (2010). *Employee training and development* (5th ed.). Alexandria, VA: ASTD Press.

48. Zhang, H. (2017). Head-mounted display-based intuitive virtual reality training system for the mining industry. *International Journal of Mining Science and Technology, 27*, 717–722.

49. Blanchard, P. M., & Thacker, J. W. (2004) — see #44.

50. Portelli, M., Bianco, S. F., Bezzina, T., & Abela, J. E. (2020). Virtual reality training compared with apprenticeship training in laparoscopic surgery: A meta-analysis. *The Annals of The Royal College of Surgeons of England, 102*(9), 672–684.

51. Salas, E., & Kozlowski, S. W. J. (2010). Learning, training, and development in organizations: Much progress and a peek over the horizon. In S. W. J. Kozlowski & E. Salas (Eds.), *Learning, training, and development in organizations* (pp. 461–476). New York: Routledge.

52. Martin, B. O., Kolomitro, K., & Lam, T. C. M. (2014) — see #43.

53. Taylor, P. J., Russ-Eft, D. F., & Chen, D. W. (2005). A meta-analytic review of behavior modeling training. *Journal of Applied Psychology, 90*, 692–709.

54. Kraiger, K., & Culbertson, S. S. (2013) — see #34.

55. Bell, B. S., & Kozlowski, S. W. J. (2010). Toward a theory of learner-centered training design: An integrative framework of active learning. In S. W. J. Kozlowski & E. Salas (Eds.), *Learning, training, and development in organizations* (pp. 263–300). New York: Routledge.

56. Gureckis, T. M., & Markant, D. B. (2012). Self-directed learning: A cognitive and computational perspective. *Perspectives on Psychological Science, 7*, 464–481.

57. Metcalf, J. (2017). Learning from errors. *Annual Review of Psychology, 68*, 465–489.

58. Ibid.

59. van Dyck, C., Frese, M., Baer, M., & Sonnentag, S. (2005). Organizational error management culture and its impact on performance: A two-study replication. *Journal of Applied Psychology, 90*, 1228–1240.

60. Cullen, M. J., Muros, J. P., Rasch, R., & Sackett, P. R. (2013). Individual differences in the effectiveness of error management training for developing negotiation skills. *International Journal of Selection and Assessment, 21*, 1–21.

61. Bell, B. S., & Kozlowski, S. W. J. (2010)—see #55.

62. Sitzmann, T., Brown, K. G., Ely, K., Kraiger, K., & Wisher, R. A. (2009). A cyclical model of motivational constructs in Web-based courses. *Military Psychology, 21*, 534–551.

63. Sitzmann, T., & Ely, K. (2010). Sometimes you need a reminder: The effects of prompting self-regulation on regulatory processes, learning, and attrition. *Journal of Applied Psychology, 95*, 132–144.

64. Roberson, L., Kulik, C. T., & Tan, R. Y. (2012). Effective diversity training. In S. W. J. Kozlowski (Ed.), *The Oxford handbook of organizational psychology* (Vol. 1, pp. 341–365). New York: Oxford University Press.

65. Hayles, V. R. (1996). Diversity training and development. In R. L. Craig (Ed.), *The ASTD training and development handbook: A guide to human resource development* (3rd ed., p. 106). New York: McGraw-Hill.

66. Bezrukova, K., Spell, C. S., Perry, J. L., & Jehn, K. A. (2016). A meta-analytical integration of over 40 years of research on diversity training evaluation. *Psychological Bulletin, 142*, 1227–1274.

67. Roberson, L., Kulik, C. T., & Tan, R. Y. (2012)—see #64.

68. Chrobot-Mason, D., & Quiñones, M. A. (2002). Training for a diverse workplace. In K. Kraiger (Ed.), *Creating, implementing, and managing effective training and development* (pp. 117–159). San Francisco: Jossey-Bass.

69. Lindsey, A., King, E. B., Hebl, M. R., & Levine, N. (2015). The impact of method, motivation, and empathy on diversity training effectiveness. *Journal of Business and Psychology, 30*, 605–617.

70. Pendry, L. F., Driscoll, D. M., & Field, S. C. T. (2007). Diversity training: Putting theory into practice. *Journal of Occupational and Organizational Psychology, 80*, 27–50.

71. Bezrukova, K., Spell, C. S., Perry, J. L., & Jehn, K. A. (2016)—see #66.

72. Roberson, L., Kulik, C. T., & Tan, R. Y. (2012)—see #64.

73. Sanchez, J. I., & Medkik, N. (2004). The effects of diversity awareness training on differential treatment. *Group & Organization Management, 29*, 517–536.

74. Apfelbaum, E. P., Stephens, N. M., & Reagans, R. E. (2016). Beyond one-size-fits-all: Tailoring diversity approaches to the representation of social groups. *Journal of Personality and Social Psychology, 111*(4), 547–566.

75. Wildman, J. L., Xavier, L. F., Tindall, M., & Salas, E. (2010). Best practices for training intercultural competence in global organizations. In K. Lundby (Ed.), *Going global* (pp. 256–300). San Francisco: Jossey-Bass.

76. Punnett, B.J. (1997). Towards an effective management of expatriate spouses. *Journal of World Business, 3*, 243–58.

77. Stahl, G. K., & Caligiuri, P. (2005). The effectiveness of expatriate coping strategies: The moderating role of cultural distance, position level, and time on the international assignment. *Journal of Applied Psychology, 90*, 603–615.

78. Caligiuri, P., & Hippler, T. (2010). Maximizing the success and retention of international assignees. In K. Lundby (Ed.), *Going global* (pp. 333–376). San Francisco: Jossey- Bass.

79. Moon, H., Choi, B., & Jung, J. (2012). Previous international experience, cross-cultural training, and expatriates' cross-cultural adjustment: Effects of cultural intelligence and goal orientation. *Human Resource Development Quarterly, 23*, 285–330.

80. Wurtz, O. (2014). An empirical investigation of the effectiveness of pre-departure and in-country cross-cultural training. *International Journal of Human Resource Management, 25*, 2088–2101.

81. Nam, K. A., Cho, Y., & Lee, M. (2014). West meets East? Identifying the gap in current cross-cultural training research. *Human Resource Development Review, 13*, 36–57.

82. Arthur, W. A., Jr., & Bennett, W. (1995). The international assignee: The relative importance of factors perceived to contribute to success. *Personnel Psychology, 48*, 99–114.

83. Szkudlarek, B., & Sumpter, D. M. (2015). What, when, and with whom? Investigating expatriate reentry training with a proximal approach. *Human Resource Management, 54*, 1037–1057.

84. Texas A&M University. (2021). Aggie Terminology. *Tamu.edu*. Retrieved October 18, 2021, from https://www.tamu.edu/traditions/aggie-culture/aggie-terminology/index.html

85. Deloitte. (2019). The economic costs of sexual harassment in the workplace. *Deloitte Access Economics*. Retrieved October 18, 2021, from https://www2.deloitte.com/content/dam/Deloitte/au/Documents/Economics/deloitte-au-economic-costs-sexual-harassment-workplace-240320.pdf

86. Berdahl, J. L., & Aquino, K. (2009). Sexual behavior at work: Fun or folly? *Journal of Applied Psychology, 94*, 34–47.

87. Gurciek, K. (2011, February 11). Workplace romance report: Cupid's arrows are flying. *SHRM.org*. Retrieved December 5, 2021, from https://www.shrm.org/hr-today/news/hr-news/pages/workplace-romance-report-cupids-arrows-are-flying.aspx

88. Gettman, H. J., & Gelfand, M. J. (2007). When the customer shouldn't be king: Antecedents and consequences of sexual harassment by clients and customers. *Journal of Applied Psychology, 62*, 757–770.

89. Hogan, J., Hogan, R., & Kaiser, R. B. (2011). Management derailment. In S. Zedeck (Ed.), *APA handbook of industrial and organizational psychology* (Vol. 3, pp. 555–576). Washington, DC: APA.

90. Hogan, R. (2007). *Personality and the fate of organizations*. Hillsdale, NJ: Erlbaum.

91. Society for Human Resource Management (2021). SHRM Survey: Half of U.S. workers have a crush on a co-worker. Retrieved October 18, 2021, from https://shrm.org/about-shrm/press-room/press-releases/Pages/Half-of-US-Workers-Have-Crushed-on-a-Co-Worker.aspx?_ga=2.3708851.227158123.1634516297-147011337.1629302432

92. Mainiero, L. A., & Jones, K. J. (2013). Sexual harassment versus workplace romance: Social media spillover and textual harassment in the workplace. *Academy of Management Perspectives, 27*, 187–203.

93. Society for Human Resource Management (2021)—see #91.

94. Ibid.

95. Mainiero, L. A., & Jones, K. J. (2013)—see #92, p. 192.

96. Hogan, R., & Warrenfeltz, R. (2003). Educating the modern manager. *Academy of Management Learning and Education, 2*, 74–84.

97. Hogan, J., Hogan, R., & Kaiser, R. B. (2011)—see #89.

98. Lombardo, M. M., & McCauley, C. D. (1988). *The dynamics of management derailment* (Tech. Report No. 134). Greensboro, NC: Center for Creative Leadership.

99. Hogan, J., Hogan, R., & Kaiser, R. B. (2011)—see #89.

100. Eby, L. T. (2011). Mentoring. In S. Zedeck (Ed.), *APA hand book of industrial and organizational psychology* (Vol. 2, pp. 503–526). Washington, DC: APA.

101. Eby, L. T. (2012). Workplace mentoring: Past, present, and future perspectives. In S. W. J. Kozlowski (Ed.), *The Oxford handbook of organizational psychology* (Vol. 1, pp. 615–642). New York: Oxford University Press.

102. Kram, K. E. (1985). *Mentoring at work*. Glenview, IL: Scott Foresman.

103. Eby, L. T. (2012)—see #101.

104. Wanberg, C. R., Welsh, E. T., & Hezlett, S. A. (2003). Mentoring research: A review and dynamic process model. In J. J. Martocchio & G. R. Ferris (Eds.), *Research in personnel and human resources management* (Vol. 22, pp. 39–124). Kidlington, UK: Elsevier.

105. Allen, T. D., Eby, L. T., Poteet, M. L., Lentz, E., & Lima, L. (2004). Career benefits associated with mentoring for protégés: A meta-analysis. *Journal of Applied Psychology, 89*, 127–136; and Eby, L. T., Allen, T. D., Hoffman, B. J., Baranik, L. E., Sauer, J. B., Baldwin, S. P., Morrison, A., Kinkade, K. M., Maher, C. P., Curtis, S., & Evans, S. C. (2013). An interdisciplinary meta-analysis of the potential antecedents, correlates, and consequences of protégé perceptions of mentoring. *Psychological Bulletin, 139*, 441–476.

106. O'Brien, K. E., Biga, A., Kessler, S. R., & Allen, T. D. (2010). A meta-analytic investigation of gender differences in mentoring. *Journal of Management, 36*, 537–554.

107. Eby, L. T. (2011)—see #100.

108. Bono, J. E., Purvanova, R. K., Towler, A. J., & Peterson, D. B. (2009). A survey of executive coaching practices. *Personnel Psychology, 62*, 361–404.

109. Peterson, D. B. (2002). Management development: Coaching and mentoring programs. In K. Kraiger (Ed.), *Creating, implementing, and managing effective training and development* (pp. 160–191). San Francisco: Jossey-Bass; and Salas, E., Weaver, S. J., & Shuffler, M. L. (2012)—see #28.

110. Grant, A. M., Cavanagh, M. J., Parker, H. M., & Passmore, J. (2010). The state of play in coaching today: A comprehensive review of the field. In G. P. Hodgkinson & J. L. Ford (Eds.), *International review of industrial and organizational psychology* (Vol. 25, pp. 125–167). Chichester, UK: Wiley-Blackwell.

111. Sperry, L. (2013). Executive coaching and leadership assessment: Past, present, and future. *Consulting Psychology Journal: Practice and Research, 65*, 284–288.

112. Blackman, A., Moscardo, G., & Gray, D. E. (2016). Challenges for the theory and practice of business coaching: A systematic review of empirical evidence. *Human Resource Development Review, 15*, 459–486.

113. Wilkinson, M. (n.d.). The 100 oddest job titles. *Coburg Banks*. Retrieved October 19, 2021, from https://www.coburgbanks.co.uk/blog/friday-funnies/the-100-oddest-job-titles/

114. Peterson, D. B. (2011). Executive coaching: A critical review and recommendations for advancing practice. In S. Zedeck (Ed.), *APA handbook of industrial and organizational psychology* (Vol. 2, pp. 527–566). Washington, DC: APA.

115. Tyler, K. (2021, July 7). Executive coaches ease leadership transitions. *HR Magazine. 59*(9). Retrieved October 19, 2021, from https://www.shrm.org/hr-today/news/hr-magazine/pages/0914-executive-coaching.aspx

116. Theeboom, T., Beersma, B., & van Vianen, A. E. M. (2014). Does coaching work? A meta-analysis on the effects of coaching on individual level outcomes in an organizational context. *Journal of Positive Psychology, 9*, 1–18.

117. Jones, R. J., Woods, S. A., & Guillaume, Y. R. F. (2016). The effectiveness of workplace coaching: A meta-analysis of learning and performance outcomes from coaching. *Journal of Occupational and Organizational Psychology, 89*, 249–277.

118. Beier, M. E., & Kanfer, R. (2010). Motivation in training and development: A phase perspective. In S. W. J. Kozlowski & E. Salas (Eds.), *Learning, training, and development in organizations* (pp. 65–98). New York: Routledge.

119. Machin, M. A. (2002). Planning, managing, and optimizing transfer of training. In K. Kraiger (Ed.), *Creating, implementing, and managing effective training and development* (pp. 263–301). San Francisco: Jossey-Bass.

120. Baldwin, T. T., Ford, J. K., & Blume, B. D. (2009). Transfer of training 1998–2008: An updated review and agenda for future research. In G. P. Hodgkinson & J. L. Ford (Eds.), *International review of industrial and organizational psychology* (Vol. 24, pp. 41–70). Chichester, UK: Wiley-Blackwell.

121. Baldwin, T. T., & Ford, J. K. (1988). Transfer of training: A review and directions for future research. *Personnel Psychology, 41*, 63–105.

122. Blume, B. D., Ford, J. K., Baldwin, T. T., & Huang, J. L. (2010). Transfer of training: A meta-analytic review. *Journal of Management, 36*, 1065–1105.

123. Tracey, J. B., Tannenbaum, S. I., & Kavanagh, M. J. (1995). Applying trained skills on the job: The importance of the work environment. *Journal of Applied Psychology, 80*, 239–252.

124. DeRue, D. S., Nahrgang, J. D., Hollenbeck, J. R., & Workman, K. (2012). A quasi-experimental study of after-event reviews and leadership development. *Journal of Applied Psychology, 97*, 997–1015.

125. Villado, A. J., & Arthur, W., Jr. (2013). The comparative effect of subjective and objective after-action reviews on team performance on a complex task. *Journal of Applied Psychology, 98*, 514–528.

126. Kirkpatrick, D. L. (1976). Evaluation of training. In R. L. Craig (Ed.), *Training and development handbook: A guide to human resource development* (2nd ed., pp. 1–26). New York: McGraw Hill.

127. Sitzmann, T., Brown, K. G., Casper, W. I., Ely, K., & Zimmerman, R. D. (2008). A review and meta-analysis of the nomological network of trainee reactions. *Journal of Applied Psychology, 93*, 280–295.

128. Salas, E., Weaver, S. J., & Shuffler, M. L. (2012)—see #28.

129. Brown, K. G., & Sitzmann, T. (2011). Training and employee development for improved performance. In S. Zedeck (Ed.), *APA handbook of industrial and organizational psychology* (Vol. 2, pp. 469–504). Washington, DC: APA.

130. Warr, P. B., Allan, C., & Birdi, K. (1999). Predicting three levels of training outcome. *Journal of Occupational and Organizational Psychology, 72,* 351–375.

131. Arthur, W. A., Jr., Bennett, W., Edens, P. S., & Bell, S. T. (2003) — see #32.

132. Smith, E. M., Ford, J. K., & Kozlowski, S. W. J. (1997). Building adaptive expertise: Implications for training design strategies. In M. A. Quiñones & A. Ehrenstein (Eds.), *Training for a rapidly changing workplace* (pp. 89–118). Washington, DC: APA.

133. Kraiger, K., & Jung, K. M. (1997). Linking training objectives to evaluation criteria. In M. A. Quiñones & A. Ehrenstein (Eds.), *Training for a rapidly changing workplace* (pp. 151–176). Washington, DC: APA.

Chapter 8

1. Aguinis, H. (2019). *Performance management* (4th ed.). Upper Saddle River, NJ: Pearson.
2. DeNisi, A. S., & Murphy, K. R. (2017). Performance appraisal and performance management: 100 years of progress? *Journal of Applied Psychology, 102*, 421–433.
3. den Hartog, D. N., Boselie, P., & Paauwe, J. (2004). Performance management: A model and research agenda. *Applied Psychology: An International Review, 53*, 556–569.
4. Aguinis (2019) — see #1.
5. Fletcher, C. (2008). *Appraisal, feedback, and development* (4th ed.). New York: Routledge.
6. Andrews, R., Boyne, G. A., Meier, K. J., O'Toole, L. J., & Walker, R. M. (2012). Vertical strategic alignment and public service performance. *Public Administration, 90*, 77–98.
7. Aguinis, H. (2009). An expanded view of performance management. In J. W. Smither & M. London (Eds.), *Performance management* (pp. 1–44). San Francisco: Jossey-Bass.
8. Schiemann, W. A. (2009). Aligning performance management with organizational strategy, values, and goals. In J. W. Smither & M. London (Eds.), *Performance management* (pp. 45–88). San Francisco: Jossey-Bass.
9. Pulakos, E. D., Hanson, R. M., Arad, S., & Moye, N. (2015). Performance management can be fixed: An on-the-job experiential learning approach for complex behavior change. *Industrial and Organizational Psychology, 8*, 51–76.
10. DeNisi, A. S., & Smith, C. E. (2014). Performance appraisal, performance management, and firm-level performance: A review, a proposed model, and new directions for future research. *Academy of Management Annals, 8*, 127–179.
11. Kinicki, A. J., Jacobson, K. J. L., Peterson, S. J., & Prussia, G. E. (2013). Development and validation of the Performance Management Behavior Questionnaire. *Personnel Psychology, 66*, 1–45.
12. Barling, J. (2014). *The science of leadership: Lessons from research for organizational leaders.* New York: Oxford University Press.
13. Tziner, A., & Rabenu, E. (2018). *Improving performance appraisal at work: Evolution and change.* Edward Elgar Publishing.
14. Chernyak-Hai, L., & Rabenu, E. (2018). The new era workplace relationships: Is social exchange theory still relevant? *Industrial and Organizational Psychology, 11*(3), 456–481.
15. Tziner, A., & Rabenu, E. (2021). The COVID-19 pandemic: A challenge to performance appraisal. *Industrial and Organizational Psychology, 14*(1–2), 173–177.
16. Aguinis (2009) — see #7; and Cleveland, J. N., Murphy, K. R., & Williams, R. E. (1989). Multiple uses of performance appraisal: Prevalence and correlates. *Journal of Applied Psychology, 74*, 130–135.
17. DeNisi, A. S., & Pritchard, R. D. (2006). Performance appraisal, performance management and improving individual performance: A motivational framework. *Management and Organization Review, 2*, 253–277.

18. Gruman, J. A., & Saks, A. M. (2011). Performance management and employee engagement. *Human Resource Management Review, 21*, 123–136; and Mone, E. M., & London, M. (2010). *Employee engagement through effective performance management.* New York: Routledge.

19. Hunt, S. T. (2014). *Common sense talent management: Using strategic human resources to improve company performance.* San Francisco, CA: Wiley.

20. Meyer, H. H., Kay, E., & French, J. R. P., Jr. (1965). Split roles in performance appraisal. *Harvard Business Review, 43*, 123–129.

21. Malos, S. B. (1998). Current legal issues in performance appraisal. In J. W. Smither (Ed.), *Performance appraisal* (pp. 49–94). San Francisco: Jossey-Bass.

22. *Jensen v. Hewlett-Packard Co.* (1993) 14 Cal.App.4th 958, 965.

23. Werner, J. M., & Bolino, M. C. (1997). Explaining U.S. court of appeals decisions involving performance appraisal: Accuracy, fairness, and validation. *Personnel Psychology, 50*, 1–24.

24. Stoneburner, C. (2013, April 18). *Failure to document performance issues dooms employer's defense to age discrimination claim.* Retrieved September 27, 2021, from https://employmentdiscrimination.foxrothschild.com/2013/04/articles/employee-termination/failure-to-document-performance-issues-dooms-employers-defense-to-age-discrimination-claim/

25. Pulakos, E. D. (1997). Ratings of job performance. In D. L. Whetzel & G. R. Wheaton (Eds.), *Applied measurement methods in industrial psychology* (pp. 291–318). Palo Alto, CA: Consulting Psychologists Press.

26. Blume, B. D., Rubin, R. S., & Baldwin, T. T. (2013). Who is attracted to an organisation using a forced distribution performance management system? *Human Resource Management Journal, 23*, 360–378.

27. Smart, B. (2005). *Topgrading: How leading companies win by hiring, coaching, and keeping the best people.* New York: Penguin.

28. Scullen, S. E., Bergey, P. K., & Aiman-Smith, L. (2005). Forced distribution rating systems and the improvement of workplace potential: A baseline simulation. *Personnel Psychology, 58*, 1–32.

29. Giumetti, G. W., Schroeder, A. N., & Switzer, F. S. III. (2015). Forced distribution rating systems: When does "rank and yank" lead to adverse impact? *Journal of Applied Psychology, 100*, 180–193.

30. Dominick, P. G. (2009). Forced rankings: Pros, cons, and practices. In J. W. Smither & M. London (Eds.), *Performance management* (pp. 411–444). San Francisco: Jossey-Bass.

31. Farager, J. (2021, February 26). Performance: Why 'rank and yank' fell out of favour. *Personnel Today.* Retrieved September 27, 2021, from https://www.personneltoday.com/hr/why-rank-and-yank-fell-out-of-favour/

32. Gavin, K. (2018, July 10). More than half of catheterized hospital patients experience complications. *LabBlog at University of Michigan Health.* Retrieved September 27, 2021, from https://labblog.uofmhealth.org/rounds/more-than-half-of-catheterized-hospital-patients-experience-complications; and Marantz, Henig, R. (2009, December 23). A hospital how-to guide Mother would love. *The New York Times.* Retrieved September 27, 2021, from https://www.nytimes.com/2009/12/24/books/24book.html

33. Weekley, J. A., & Gier, J. A. (1989). Ceilings in the reliability and validity of performance ratings: The case of expert raters. *Academy of Management Journal, 32*, 213–222.

34. DeNisi, A. S., & Peters, L. H. (1996). Organization of information in memory and the performance appraisal process: Evidence from the field. *Journal of Applied Psychology, 81*, 717–737.

35. Harari, M. B., Rudolph, C. W., & Laginess, A. J. (2014). Does rater personality matter? A meta-analysis of rater Big-Five-performance rating relationships. *Journal of Occupational and Organizational Psychology, 88*, 387–414.

36. Erez, A., Schilpzand, P., Leavitt, K., Woolum, A. H., & Judge, T. A. (2015). Inherently relational: Interactions between peers' and individuals' personalities impact reward giving and appraisal of individual performance. *Academy of Management Journal, 58*, 1761–1784.

37. Motro, D., & Ellis, A. P. J. (2017). Boys, don't cry: Gender and reactions to negative performance feedback. *Journal of Applied Psychology, 102*, 227–235.

38. Cooper, W. H. (1981). Ubiquitous halo. *Psychological Bulletin, 90*, 218–244.

39. Kane, J. S., Bernardin, H. J., Villanova, P., & Peyrefitte, J. (1995). Stability of rater leniency: Three studies. *Academy of Management Journal, 38*, 1036–1051.

40. Bernardin, H. J., Thomason, S., Buckley, M. R., & Kane, J. S. (2016). Rater rating-level bias and accuracy in performance appraisals: The impact of rater personality, performance management competence, and rater accountability. *Human Resource Management, 55*, 321–340.

41. Thomas, R., Cooper, M., Konar, E., Rooney, M., Noble-Tolla, M., Boher, A., Lee, Y., Krivkovich, A., Starikova, I., Robinson, K., Nadeau, M-C and Robinson, N. (2018). Women in the workplace. *McKinsey and Company.* Retrieved September 27, 2021, from https://www.mckinsey.com/featured-insights/diversity-and-inclusion/women-in-the-workplace

42. Jampol, L., & Zayas, V. (2020). Gendered white lies: Performance feedback is upwardly distorted to women. *Personality and Social Psychology Bulletin, 47*, 57–69.

43. Roth, P. L., Purvis, K. L., & Bobko, P. (2012). A meta-analysis of gender group differences for measures of job performance in field studies. *Journal of Management, 38*(2), 719–739; Williams, M., & Tiedens, L. (2016). The subtle suspension of backlash: A meta-analysis of penalties for women's implicit and explicit dominance behavior. *Psychological Bulletin, 142*(2), 165–197; and Rudman, L. A. (1998). Self-promotion as a risk factor for women: The costs and benefits of counterstereotypical impression management. *Journal of Personality and Social Psychology, 74*(3), 629–645.

44. Ciancetta, L. M., & Roch, S. G. (2021). Backlash in performance feedback: Deepening the understanding of the role of gender in performance appraisal. *Human Resource Management, 60*(4), 641–657.

45. Hedge, J. W., & Kavanagh, M. J. (1988). Improving the accuracy of performance evaluations: Comparison of three methods of performance appraisal training. *Journal of Applied Psychology, 73*, 68–73.

46. Sulsky, L. M., & Balzer, W. K. (1988). Meaning and measurement of performance rating accuracy: Some methodological and theoretical concerns. *Journal of Applied Psychology, 73*, 497–506.

47. Smither, J. W. (2012). Performance management. In S. W. J. Kozlowski (Ed.), *The Oxford handbook of organizational psychology* (Vol. 1, pp. 285–329). New York: Oxford University Press.

48. Sulsky, L. M., & Day, D. V. (1992). Frame-of-reference training and cognitive categorization: An empirical investigation of rater memory issues. *Journal of Applied Psychology, 77*, 501–510.

49. Gorman, C. A., & Rentsch, J. R. (2009). Evaluating frame-of-reference rater training effectiveness using performance schema accuracy. *Journal of Applied Psychology, 94*, 1336–1344.

50. Gorman, C. A., & Rentsch, J. R. (2017). Retention of assessment center rater training: Improving performance schema accuracy using frame-of-reference training. *Journal of Personnel Psychology, 16*(1), 1–11.

51. Uggerslev, K. L., & Sulsky, L. M. (2008). Using frame-of-reference training to understand the implications of rater idiosyncrasy for rating accuracy. *Journal of Applied Psychology, 93*, 711–719.

52. Roch, S. G., Woehr, D. J., Mishra, V., & Kieszczynska, U. (2012). Rater training revisited: An updated meta-analytic review of frame-of-reference training. *Journal of Occupational and Organizational Psychology, 85*, 370–395.

53. Kozlowski, S. W. J., Chao, G. T., & Morrison, R. F. (1998). Games raters play: Politics, strategies, and impression management in performance appraisal. In J. W. Smither (Ed.), *Performance appraisal* (pp. 163–208). San Francisco: Jossey-Bass.

54. Spence, J. R., & Keeping, L. M. (2011). Conscious rating distortion in performance appraisal: A review, commentary, and proposed framework for research. *Human Resource Management Review, 21*, 85–95.

55. Spence, J. R., & Keeping, L. M. (2013). The road to performance ratings is paved with intentions: A framework for understanding managers' intentions when rating employee performance. *Organizational Psychology Review, 3*, 360–383.

56. Barnes-Farrell, J. L. (2001). Performance appraisal: Person perception processes and challenges. In M. London (Ed.), *How people evaluate others in organizations* (pp. 135–154). Mahwah, NJ: Erlbaum.

57. Wong, K. F. E., & Kwong, J. Y. Y. (2007). Effects of rater goals on rating patterns: Evidence from an experimental field study. *Journal of Applied Psychology, 92*, 577–585.

58. Sutton, A. W., Baldwin, S. P., Wood, L., & Hoffman, B. J. (2014). A meta-analysis of the relationship between rater liking and performance ratings. *Human Performance, 26*, 409–429.

59. Aguinis (2019)—see #1.

60. Wang, X. M. W., Wong, K. F. E., & Kwong, J. Y. Y. (2010). The roles of rater goals and rater performance levels in the distortion of performance ratings. *Journal of Applied Psychology, 95*, 546–561.

61. Greguras, G. J., Robie, C., Schleicher, D. J., & Goff, M. (2003). A field study of the effects of rating purpose on the quality of multisource ratings. *Personnel Psychology, 56*, 1–22; and Jawahar, I. M., & Williams, C. R. (1997). Where all the children are above average: The performance appraisal purpose effect. *Personnel Psychology, 50*, 905–925.

62. Murphy, K. R., & Cleveland, J. N. (1995). *Understanding performance appraisal: Social, organizational, and goal-based perspectives*. Thousand Oaks, CA: Sage.

63. Harari, M. B., & Rudolph, C. W. (2017). The effect of rater accountability on performance ratings: A meta-analytic review. *Human Resource Management Review, 27*, 121–133.

64. Zhao, H. H., Li, N., Harris, T. B., Rosen, C. C., & Zhang, X. (2021). Informational advantages in social networks: The core-periphery divide in peer performance ratings. *Journal of Applied Psychology, 106*(7), 1093–1102.

65. Luria, G., & Kalish, Y. (2013). A social network approach to peer assessment: Improving predictive validity. *Human Resource Management, 52,* 537–560.

66. Cederblom, D., & Lounsbury, J. W. (1980). An investigation of user acceptance of peer evaluations. *Personnel Psychology, 33*, 567–580.

67. Dierdorff, E. C., & Surface, E. A. (2007). Placing peer ratings in context: Systematic influences beyond ratee performance. *Personnel Psychology, 60*, 93–126.

68. Shore, T. H., Shore, L. M., & Thornton, G. C. (1992). Construct validity of self- and peer evaluations of performance dimensions in an assessment center. *Journal of Applied Psychology, 77*, 42–54.

69. Bell, B. S., & Federman, J. E. (2010). Self-assessments of knowledge: Where do we go from here? *Academy of Management Learning & Education, 9*, 342–347.

70. Heidemeier, H., & Moser, K. (2009). Self-other agreement in job performance ratings: A meta-analytic test of a process model. *Journal of Applied Psychology, 94*, 353–370.

71. Coutts, L. M., & Schneider, F. W. (2004). Police officer performance appraisal systems: How good are they? *Policing: An International Journal of Police Strategies & Management, 27*, 67–81.

72. Cherry, K. (2021, August 6). The Dunning-Kruger Effect. *VeryWellMind*. Retrieved September 27, 2021, from https://www.verywellmind.com/an-overview-of-the-dunning-kruger-effect-4160740

73. Beehr, T. A., Ivanitskaya, L., Hansen, C. P., Erofeev, D., & Gudanowski, D. M. (2001). Evaluation of 360degree feedback ratings: Relationships with each other and with performance and selection predictors. *Journal of Organizational Behavior, 22*, 775–788.

74. Anderson, C. D., Warner, J. L., & Spencer, C. C. (1984). Inflation bias in self-assessment examinations: Implications for valid employee selection. *Journal of Applied Psychology, 69*, 574–580.

75. Mount, M. K. (1984). Psychometric properties of subordinate ratings of managerial performance. *Personnel Psychology, 37*, 687–702.

76. Bernardin, H. J., Hagan, C. M., Kane, J. S., & Villanova, P. (1998). Effective performance management. In J. W. Smither (Ed.), *Performance appraisal* (pp. 3–48). San Francisco: Jossey-Bass.

77. Greguras, G. J., Robie, C., Schleicher, D. J., & Goff, M. (2003) — see #61.

78. Bracken, D. W., Rose, D. S., & Church, A. H. (2016). The evolution and devolution of 360° feedback. *Industrial and Organizational Psychology, 9*, 761–794.

79. Bracken, D. W., Timmreck, C. W., Fleenor, J. W., & Summers, L. (2001). 360 feedback from another angle. *Human Resource Management Journal, 40*, 3–20.

80. London, M., Smither, J. W., & Adsit, D. L. (1997). Accountability: The Achilles' heel of multisource feedback. *Group and Organization Management, 22*, 162–184; and Bracken, D. W., Rose, D. S., & Church, A. H. (2016) — see #78.

81. Young, S. F., Gentry, W. A., & Braddy, P. W. (2016). Holding leaders accountable during the 360° feedback process. *Industrial and Organizational Psychology, 9*, 811–813.

82. Bracken, D. W., Rose, D. S., & Church, A. H. (2016) — see #78.

83. Goldsmith, M., & Morgan, H. (2004). Leadership is a contact sport: The "follow-up" factor in management development. *Strategy + Business, 36*, 71–79.

84. Tornow, W. W. (1993). Perceptions or reality: Is multi-perspective measurement a means or an end? *Human Resource Management, 32*, 221–230.

85. Taylor, S. N. (2016). Don't give up on the self too quickly. *Industrial and Organizational Psychology, 9*, 795–813.

86. Taylor, S. N., & Bright, D. S. (2011). Exploring conditions for openness in multisource feedback assessment. *Journal of Applied Behavioral Science, 47*, 432–460.

87. Hoffman, B. J., Lance, C. E., Bynum, B., & Gentry, W. A. (2010). Rater source effects are alive and well after all. *Personnel Psychology, 63*, 119–151.

88. Ng, K. Y., Koh, C., Ang, S., Kennedy, J. C., & Chan, K. Y. (2011). Rating leniency and halo in multisource feed-back ratings: Testing cultural assumptions of power distance and individualism-collectivism. *Journal of Applied Psychology, 96*, 1033–1044.

89. Balzer, W. K., Greguras, G. J., & Raymark, P. H. (2003). Multisource feedback. In J. C. Thomas (Ed.), *Comprehensive handbook of psychological assessment* (Vol. 4, pp. 390–411). Hoboken, NJ: Wiley.

90. Hoffman, B. J., & Woehr, D. J. (2009). Disentangling the meaning of multisource performance rating source and dimension factors. *Personnel Psychology, 62*, 735–765.

91. Rosen, S., & Tesser, A. (1970). On reluctance to communicate undesirable information: The MUM effect. *Sociometry, 33*, 253–263.

92. Marler, L. E., McKee, D., Cox, S., Simmering, M., & Allen, D. G. (2012). Don't make me the bad guy: Self-monitoring, organizational norms, and the mum effect. *Journal of Managerial Issues, 24*, 97–116.

93. Baron, R. A. (1990). Countering the effects of destructive criticism: The relative efficacy of four interventions. *Journal of Applied Psychology, 75*, 235–245.

94. Kluger, A. N., & DeNisi, A. S. (1996). The effects of feedback interventions on performance: A historical review, a meta-analysis, and a preliminary feedback intervention theory. *Psychological Bulletin, 119*, 254–284.

95. Raver, J. L., Jensen, J. M., Lee, J., & O'Reilly, J. (2012). Destructive criticism revisited: Appraisals, task outcomes, and the moderating role of competitiveness. *Applied Psychology: An International Review, 61*, 177–203.

96. Ashford, S. J., Blatt, R., & VandeWalle, D. (2003). Reflections on the looking glass: A review of research on feedback-seeking behavior in organizations. *Journal of Management, 29*, 773–799.

97. Ashford, S. J., & Cummings, L. L. (1985). Proactive feedback seeking: The instrumental use of the information environment. *Journal of Occupational Psychology, 58*, 67–79.

98. Vancouver, J. B., & Morrison, E. W. (1995). Feedback inquiry: The effect of source attributes and individual differences. *Organizational Behavior and Human Decision Processes, 62*, 276–285.

99. Bernichon, T., Cook, K. E., & Brown, J. D. (2003). Seeking self-evaluative feedback: The interactive role of global self-esteem and specific self-views. *Journal of Personality and Social Psychology, 84*, 194–204.

100. Sherf, E. N., & Morrison, E. W. (2020). I do not need feedback! Or do I? Self-efficacy, perspective taking, and feedback seeking. *Journal of Applied Psychology, 105*(2), 146–165.

101. Steelman, L A., Levy, P. E., & Snell, A. F. (2004). The feedback environment scale (FES): Construct definition, measurement, and validation. *Education and Psychological Measurement, 64*, 165–184.

102. van der Rijt, J., van de Wiel, M. W. J., Van den Bossche, P., Segers, M. S. R., & Gijselaers, W. H. (2012). Contextual antecedents of informal feedback in the workplace. *Human Resource Development Quarterly, 23*, 233–257.

103. London, M., & Smither, J. W. (2002). Feedback orientation, feedback culture, and the longitudinal performance management process. *Human Resource Management Review, 12*, 81–100.

104. Ashford, S. J., & Northcraft, G. B. (1992). Conveying more (or less) than we realize: The role of impression-management in feedback seeking. *Organizational Behavior and Human Decision Processes, 53*, 310–334.

105. Anderson, L. J., & Jones, R. G. (2000). Affective, behavioral, and cognitive acceptance of feedback: Individual difference moderators. In N. M. Ashkanasy & C. E. Haertel (Eds.), *Emotions in the workplace: Research, theory, and practice* (pp. 130–140). Westport, CT: Quorum.

106. Nease, A. A., Mudgett, B. O., & Quiñones, M. A. (1999). Relationships among feedback sign, self-efficacy, and acceptance of performance feedback. *Journal of Applied Psychology, 84*, 806–814.

107. Ilgen, D. R., & Davis, C. A. (2000). Bearing bad news: Reactions to negative performance feedback. *Applied Psychology: An International Review, 49*, 550–565.

108. Kinicki, A. J., Prussia, G. E., Wu, B., & McKee-Ryan, F. M. (2004). A covariance structure analysis of employees' response to performance feedback. *Journal of Applied Psychology, 89*, 1057–1069.

109. Sheldon, O. J., Dunning, D., & Ames, D. R. (2014). Emotionally unskilled, unaware, and uninterested in learning more: Reactions to feedback about deficits in emotional intelligence. *Journal of Applied Psychology, 99*, 125–137.

110. Bracken, D. W., Rose, D. S., & Church, A. H. (2016)—see #78.

111. Keeping, L. M., & Levy, P. E. (2000). Performance appraisal reaction: Measurement, modeling, and method bias. *Journal of Applied Psychology, 85*, 708–723.

112. Pulakos, E. D. (2009). *Performance management: A new approach for driving business results*. West Sussex, UK: Wiley-Blackwell.

113. Cederblom, D. (1982). The performance appraisal interview: A review, implications and suggestions. *Academy of Management Review, 7*, 219–227.

114. Cawley, B. D., Keeping, L. M., & Levy, P. E. (1998). Participation in the performance appraisal process and employee reactions: A meta-analytic review of field investigations. *Journal of Applied Psychology, 83*, 615–633.

115. Greenberg, J. (1986). Determinants of perceived fairness of performance evaluations. *Journal of Applied Psychology, 71*, 340–342.

116. Kavanagh, P., Benson, J., & Brown, M. (2007). Understanding performance appraisal fairness. *Asia Pacific Journal of Human Resources, 45*(2), 132–150.

117. Dickinson, T. L. (1993). Attitudes about performance appraisal. In H. Schuler, J. L. Farr, & M. Smith (Eds.), *Personnel selection and assessment* (pp. 141–162). Hillsdale, NJ: Erlbaum.

118. Russell, J. S., & Goode, D. L. (1988). An analysis of managers' reactions to their own performance appraisal feedback. *Journal of Applied Psychology, 73*, 63–67.

119. Culbertson, S. S., Krome, L. R., McHenry, B. J., Stetzer, M. W., & van Ittersum, K. (2013). Performance appraisals: Mend them, don't end them. In M. Paludi (Ed.), *The psychology for business success* (Vol. 4, pp. 35–51). Westport, CT: Praeger Press.

120. Culbert, S. A., & Rout, L. (2010). *Get rid of the performance review! How companies can stop intimidating, start managing—and focus on what really matters*. New York: Business Plus.

121. Adler, S., Campion, M. A., Colquitt, A. L., Grubb, A., Murphy, K. R., Ollander-Krane, R., & Pulakos, E. D. (2016). Getting rid of performance reviews: Genius or folly? A debate. *Industrial and Organizational Psychology, 9*, 219–252

122. Pulakos, E. D., & O'Leary, R. S. (2011). Why is performance management broken? *Industrial and Organizational Psychology, 4*, 146–164.

123. Mercer (2013). *2013 Global performance management survey report executive summary*. Retrieved September 27, 2021, from https://www.mercer.com/content/dam/mercer/attachments/global/Talent/Assess-BrochurePerfMgmt.pdf

124. Catano, V. M., Darr, W., & Campbell, C. A. (2007). Performance appraisal of behavior-based competencies: A reliable and valid procedure. *Personnel Psychology, 60*, 201–230.

125. Kluger, A. N., & Nir, D. (2010). The feedforward interview. *Human Resource Management Review, 20*, 235–246.

126. Ledford, G. E., Jr., Benson, G., & Lawler, III, E. E., (2016). *Cutting-edge performance management: 244 organizations report on ongoing feedback, ratingless reviews and crowd-sourced feedback*. Scottsdale, AZ: WorldatWork.

127. Hauenstein, N. M. A. (1998). Training raters to increase the accuracy of appraisals and the usefulness of feedback. In J. W. Smither (Ed.), *Performance appraisal* (pp. 404–444). San Francisco: Jossey-Bass.

128. Mosley, E. (2013). *The crowdsourced performance review: How to use the power of social recognition to transform employee performance*. New York: McGraw-Hill, p. 4.

129. Ibid., p. 3.

130. Ibid., p. 51.

131. Ibid., pp. 165-6.

Chapter 9

1. Rao, M. S. (2019). Technology, humanity and prosperity: Why Peter Drucker is more relevant today than ever before. *The People Space*. Retrieved November 26, 2021, from https://www.thepeoplespace.com/ideas/articles/technology-humanity-and-prosperity-why-peter-drucker-more-relevant-today-ever; and Colvin, G. (2005, November 28). Peter Drucker: 1909-2005. *CNN Money*. Retrieved November 29, 2021, from https://money.cnn.com/magazines/fortune/fortune_archive/2005/11/28/8361937/index.htm
2. Durbin, D.-A. (2006, January 24). Ford takes close look at itself as job, factory cuts are set. *Arizona Daily Star*.
3. Martins, L. L. (2011). Organizational change and development. In S. Zedeck (Ed.), *APA handbook of industrial and organizational psychology* (Vol. 3, 691-728). Washington, DC: APA.
4. Hofstede, G. (1980). *Culture's consequences: International differences in work-related values*. Beverly Hills, CA: Sage; Hofstede, G. (2001). *Culture's consequences* (2nd ed.): *Comparing values, behaviors, institutions, and organizations across nations*. Thousand Oaks, CA: Sage; and Hofstede, G. J., & Minkov, M. (2010). *Cultures and Organizations: Software of the Mind* (3rd edition). USA: McGraw-Hill.
5. Taras, V., Kirkman, B. L., & Steele, P. (2010). Examining the impact of *Culture's Consequences*: A three-decade meta-analytic review of Hofstede's cultural value dimensions. *Journal of Applied Psychology, 95*, 405–439.
6. Ailon, G. (2008). Mirror, mirror on the wall: Culture's consequences in a value test of its own design. *Academy of Management Review, 33*, 885–904.
7. Marquardt, M. (2002). Around the world: Organization development in the international context. In J. Waclawski & A. H. Church (Eds.), *Organization development: A data-driven approach to organizational change* (pp. 266–285). San Francisco: Jossey-Bass.
8. Hofstede Insights. (n.d.). *Compare Countries*. Retrieved November 26, 2021, from https://www.hofstede-insights.com/product/compare-countries/
9. Battista, M., Pedigo, P., & Desrosiers, E. (2010). Navigating the complexities of a global organization. In K. Lundby (Ed.), *Going global* (pp. 1–21). San Francisco: Jossey-Bass.
10. Marquardt, M. (2002)—see #7.
11. Ehrhart, M. G., Schneider, B., & Macey, W. H. (2014). *Organizational climate and culture*. New York: Routledge.
12. Ibid.
13. Ehrhart, M. G., & Naumann, S. E. (2004). Organizational citizenship behavior in work groups: A group norms approach. *Journal of Applied Psychology, 89*, 960–974.
14. Schein, E. H. (1965). *Organizational psychology*. Englewood Cliffs, NJ: Prentice-Hall.
15. Ostroff, C., Kinicki, A. J., & Tamkins, M. M. (2003). Organizational culture and climate. In W. C. Borman, D. R. Ilgen, & R. J. Klimoski (Eds.), *Handbook of psychology: Industrial and organizational psychology* (Vol. 12, pp. 565–593). Hoboken, NJ: Wiley.
16. Trice, H. M., & Beyer, J. M. (1993). *The cultures of work organizations*. Upper Saddle River, NJ: Prentice-Hall.
17. Ostroff, C., Kinicki, A. J., & Tamkins, M. M. (2003)—see #15.
18. Ehrhart, M. G., Schneider, B., & Macey, W. H. (2014)—see #11.
19. Schein, E. H. (1996). Culture: The missing concept in organizational studies. *Administrative Science Quarterly, 41*, 229–240.
20. Pratt, M. G., & Rafaeli, A. (1997). Organizational dress as a symbol of multilayered social identities. *Academy of Management Journal, 40,* 862–898.
21. Ibid., p. 862.
22. Brown, G., Lawrence, T. B., & Robinson, S. L. (2005). Territoriality in organizations. *Academy of Management Review, 30*, 577–594.
23. Baruch, Y. (2006). On logos and business cards: The case of UK universities. In A. Rafaeli & M. G. Pratt (Eds.), *Artifacts and organizations* (pp. 181–198). Mahwah, NJ: Erlbaum.
24. Anand, N. (2006). Cartoon displays as autoproduction of organizational culture. In A. Rafaeli & M. G. Pratt (Eds.), *Artifacts and organizations* (pp. 85–100). Mahwah, NJ: Erlbaum.
25. Cameron, K. L., & Quinn, R. E. (2006). *Diagnosing and changing organizational cultures* (rev. ed.). San Francisco: Jossey-Bass.

26. Kantor, J., & Streitfeld, D. (2015, August 15). Inside Amazon: Wrestling big ideas in a bruising workplace. *NYT.com*. Retrieved November 26, 2021, from https://www.nytimes.com/2015/08/16/technology/inside-amazon-wrestling-big-ideas-in-a-bruising-workplace.html

27. Ibid.

28. Ballaban, M. (2014, March 23). When Henry Ford's benevolent secret police ruled his workers. *Jalopnik.com*. Retrieved November 26, 2021, from https://jalopnik.com/when-henry-fords-benevolent-secret-police-ruled-his-wo-1549625731

29. Ford, H. (1922). *My life and work*. Garden City Publishing: Garden City, NY.

30. Ellis, D. (2006, January 27). Ford bans competitors' vehicles from lot. *CNNMoney.com*. Retrieved November 26, 2021, from https://money.cnn.com/2006/01/27/news/companies/ford_parkinglot/

31. Jay, A., & LeNoble, C., A. (2021). Healthcare work in the wake of COVID-19: A focus on person-environment fit. *Industrial and Organizational Psychology, 14*, 94–97.

32. Kristof-Brown, A. L., & Billsberry J. (2013). Fit for the future. In A. L. Kristof-Brown & J. Billsberry (Eds.), *Organizational fit: Key issues and new directions* (pp. 1–18). Malden, MA: Wiley.

33. Schneider, B. (1996). When individual differences aren't. In K. R. Murphy (Ed.), *Individual differences and behaviors in organizations* (pp. 548–572). San Francisco: Jossey-Bass.

34. Schneider, B. (1987). The people make the place. *Personnel Psychology, 40*, 437–454.

35. Ehrhart, M. G., Schneider, B., & Macey, W. H. (2014) — see #11.

36. Jansen, K. J., & Shipp, A. J. (2013). A review and agenda for incorporating time in fit research. In A. L. Kristof-Brown & J. Billsberry (Eds.), *Organizational fit: Key issues and new directions* (pp. 195–221). Malden, MA: Wiley.

37. Ostroff, C., & Zhan, Y. (2012). Person-environment fit in the selection process. In N. Schmitt (Ed.), *The Oxford handbook of personnel assessment and selection* (pp. 252–273). New York: Oxford University Press.

38. Arthur, W. A., Jr., Bell, S. T., Villado, A. J., & Doverspike, D. (2006). The use of person-fit in employment decision making: An assessment of its criterion-related validity. *Journal of Applied Psychology, 91*, 786–801.

39. Fiss, P. C., & Zajac, E. J. (2006). The symbolic management of strategic change: Sensegiving via framing and decoupling. *Academy of Management Journal, 49*, 1173–1193.

40. Peccei, R., Giangreco, A., & Sebastiano, A. (2011). The role of organisational commitment in the analysis of resistance to change: Co-predictor and moderator effects. *Personnel Review, 40*, 185–204.

41. van Dam, K., Oreg, S., & Schyns, B. (2008). Daily work contexts and resistance to organisational change: The role of leader-member exchange, development climate, and change process characteristics. *Applied Psychology: An International Review, 57*, 313–334.

42. Foster, R. D. (2010). Resistance, justice, and commitment to change. *Human Resource Development Quarterly, 21*, 3–39.

43. Lewin, K. (1951). *Field theory in social science*. New York: Harper & Row.

44. Kotter, J. P. (1995). Leading changes: Why transformation efforts fail. *Harvard Business Review*, March–April, 59–67.

45. Burke, W. W. (2008). *Organizational change: Theory and practice* (2nd ed.). Thousand Oaks, CA: Sage.

46. Plowman, D. A., Baker, L. T., Beck, T. E., Kulkari, M., Solansky, S. T., & Travis, D. V. (2007). Radical change accidentally: The emergence and amplification of small change. *Academy of Management Journal, 50*, 515–543.

47. Semuels, A. (2013, January 17). Man reportedly outsources his own job to China, watches cat videos. *Los Angeles Times*. Retrieved December 14, 2021, from https://www.latimes.com/business/la-xpm-2013-jan-17-la-fi-mo-man-outsourced-job-to-china-20130117-story.html

48. DeMeuse, K. P., Marks, M. L., & Dai, G. (2011). Organizational downsizing, mergers and acquisitions, and strategic alliances: Using theory and research to enhance practice. In S. Zedeck (Ed.), *APA handbook of industrial and organizational psychology* (Vol. 3, pp. 729–768). Washington, DC: APA.

49. DuBois, S. (2011). *Survivor's guilt: Managing 30,000 layoffs at HSBC*. Retrieved November 26, 2021, from http://fortune.com/2011/08/02/ survivors-guilt-managing-30000-layoffs-at-hsbc

50. Wiley, J. W., Brooks, S. M., & Hause, E. L. (2003). The impact of corporate downsizing on employee fulfillment and organizational capability. In K. P. De Meuse & M. L. Marks (Eds.), *Resizing the organization: Managing layoffs, divestitures, and closings* (pp. 108–130). San Francisco: Jossey-Bass.

51. Feldman, D. C., & Ng, T. W. H. (2012). Selecting out: How firms choose workers to lay off. In N. Schmitt (Ed.), *The Oxford handbook of personnel assessment and selection* (pp. 849–864). New York: Oxford University Press.

52. Marks, M. L. (2002). Mergers and acquisitions. In J. W. Hedge & E. D. Pulakos (Eds.), *Implementing organizational interventions: Steps, processes, and best practices* (pp. 43–77). San Francisco: Jossey-Bass.

53. Sendanyoye, J. (2003). *The employment effects of mergers and acquisitions in commerce: report for discussion at the Tripartite Meeting on the Employment Effects of Mergers and Acquisitions in Commerce, Geneva, 2003*. ILO.

54. Hewlin, P. F. (2009). Wearing the cloak: Antecedents and consequences of creating facades of conformity. *Journal of Applied Psychology, 94*, 727–741.

55. Gelfand, M. J., Gordon, S., Li, C., Choi, V., & Prokopowicz, P. (2018, October 2). One reason mergers fail: The two cultures aren't compatible. *Harvard Business Review*. Retrieved November 26, 2021, from https://hbr.org/2018/10/one-reason-mergers-fail-the-two-cultures-arent-compatible

56. Beckhard, R. (1969). *Organization development: Strategies and models*. Reading, MA: Addison-Wesley.

57. Burke, W. W. (2008)—see #45.

58. Wiley, J. W. (1996). Linking survey results to customer satisfaction and business performance. In A. I. Kraut (Ed.), *Organizational surveys* (pp. 330–359). San Francisco: Jossey-Bass.

59. Burke, W. W. (2006). Organizational surveys as leverage for organization development and change. In A. Kraut (Ed.), *Getting action from organizational surveys: New concepts, technologies and applications* (pp. 131–149). San Francisco: Jossey-Bass.

60. Meinert, D. (2014). Leadership development spending is up. *SHRM HR Magazine*. Retrieved November 26, 2021, from https://www.shrm.org/hr-today/news/hr-magazine/pages/0814-execbrief.aspx

61. Rowland, D. (2016). *Why leadership development isn't developing leaders*. Retrieved November 26, 2021, from https://hbr.org/2016/10/why-leadership-development-isnt-developing-leaders?autocomplete=true

62. Dyer, W. W. G., Dyer, W. G., & Dyer, J. H. (2007). *Team building: Proven strategies for improving team performance*. Hoboken, NJ: Jossey-Bass.

63. Burke, W. W. (2006)—see #59.

64. Wiley, J. W. (1996)—see #58.

65. Wiley, J. W., & Campbell, B. H. (2006). Using linkage research to drive high performance: A case study In organization development. In A. Kraut (Ed.), *Getting action from organizational surveys: New concepts, technologies and applications* (pp. 150–180). San Francisco: Jossey-Bass.

Chapter 10

1. Kozlowski, S. W. J., & Ilgen, D. R. (2006). Enhancing the effectiveness of work groups and teams. *Psychological Science in the Public Interest, 7*, 77–124.

2. Mathieu, J. E., Hollenbeck, J. R., van Knippenberg, D., & Ilgen, D. R. (2017). A century of work teams in the Journal of Applied Psychology. *Journal of Applied Psychology, 102*, 452–467.

3. Volini, E., Roy, I., Schwartz, J., Hauptmann, M., & Van Durme, Y. (2019). Organizational performance: it's a team sport. *Deloitte Insights*. Retrieved September 28, 2021, from at https://www2.deloitte.com/us/en/insights/focus/human-capital-trends/2019/team-based-organization.html

4. Kozlowski, S. W. J., & Ilgen, D. R. (2006)—see #1, p. 77.

5. Tannenbaum, S. I., Mathieu, J. E., Salas, E., & Cohen, D. (2012). Teams are changing: Are research and practice evolving fast enough? *Industrial and Organizational Psychology, 5*, 2–24.

6. Naquin, C. E., & Tynan, R. O. (2003). The team halo effect: Why teams are not blamed for their failures. *Journal of Applied Psychology, 88*, 332–340.

7. Kozlowski, S. W. J., & Bell, B. S. (2003). Work groups and teams in organizations. In W. C. Borman, D. R. Ilgen, & R. J. Klimoski (Eds.), *Handbook of psychology: Industrial and organizational psychology* (Vol. 12, pp. 333–375).

8. Rousseau, D. M., & House, R. J. (1994). Meso organizational behavior: Avoiding three fundamental biases. In C. L. Cooper & D. M. Rousseau (Eds.), *Trends in organizational behavior* (Vol. 1, pp. 13–30). New York: Wiley.

9. Klein, K. J., & Kozlowski, S. W. J. (2000). *Multilevel theory, research, and methods in organizations.* San Francisco: Jossey-Bass.

10. West, M. A., & Lyubovnikova, J. (2012). Real teams or pseudo teams? The changing landscape needs a better map. *Industrial and Organizational Psychology, 5*, 25–28.

11. Christy, A. (2021, April 1). Why baseball is the best team sport. *Alex Christy blog.* Retrieved September 28, 2021, from https://alexchristy17.medium.com/why-baseball-is-the-best-team-sport-b605154f9bb2

12. Hoch, J. E., & Kozlowski, S. W. J. (2014). Leading virtual teams: Hierarchical leadership, structural supports, and shared team leadership. *Journal of Applied Psychology, 99*, 390–403.

13. Avolio, B. J., Kahai, S., Dumdum, R., & Sivasubramaniam, N. (2001). Virtual teams: Implications for e-leadership and team development. In M. London (Ed.), *How people evaluate others in organizations* (pp. 337–358). Mahwah, NJ: Erlbaum.

14. Purvanova, R. K. (2014). Face-to-face versus virtual teams: What have we really learned? *The Psychologist-Manager Journal, 17*, 2–29.

15. Mathieu, J. E., Marks, M. A., & Zaccaro, S. J. (2001). Multi-team systems. In N. Anderson, D. S. Ones, H. K. Sinangil, & C. Viswesvaran (Eds.), *Handbook of industrial, work, & organizational psychology* (Vol. 2, pp. 289–313). London: Sage.

16. Zaccaro, S. J., Marks, M. A., & DeChurch, L. A. (2012). Multiteam systems: An introduction. In S. J. Zaccaro,M. A. Marks, & L. A. DeChurch (Eds.), *Multiteam systems: An organizational form for dynamic and complex environments* (pp. 3–32). New York: Taylor & Francis.

17. DeSanctis, G., & Monge, P. (2006). Communication processes for virtual organizations. *Journal of Computer-Mediated Communication, 3*(4), Article JCMC347.

18. Marlow, S. L., Lacerenza, C. N., & Salas, E. (2017). Communication in virtual teams: A conceptual framework and research agenda. *Human Resource Management Review, 27*(4), 575–589.

19. Bilotta, I., Cheng, S. K., Ng, L. C., Corrington, A. R., Watson, I., Paoletti, J., Hebl, M. R., & King, E. B. (2021). Remote communication amid the coronavirus pandemic: Optimizing interpersonal dynamics and team performance. *Industrial and Organizational Psychology, 14*(1–2), 36–40.

20. De Vries, T. A., Hollenbeck, J. R., Davison, R. B., Walter, F., & Van Der Vegt, G. S. (2016). Managing coordination in multiteam systems: Integrating micro and macro perspectives. *Academy of Management Journal, 59*, 1823–1844.

21. Connaughton, S. L., Williams, E. A., & Shuffler, M. L. (2011). Social identity issues in multi-team systems: Considerations for future research. In S. J. Zaccaro, M. A. Marks, & L. A. DeChurch (Eds.), *Multiteam systems: An organizational form for dynamic and complex environments* (pp. 109–140). New York: Taylor & Francis.

22. Mathieu, J. E., Marks, M. A., & Zaccaro, S. J. (2001)—see #15.

23. Tuckman, B. W. (1965). Developmental sequences in small groups. *Psychological Bulletin, 63*, 384–399. Later revised by Tuckman, B. W., & Jensen, M. C. (1977). Stages of small-group development revisited. *Group and Organization Studies, 2*, 419–427.

24. Moreland, R. L., & Levine, J. M. (2001). Socialization in organizations and work groups. In M. E. Turner (Ed.), *Groups at work* (pp. 69–112). Mahwah, NJ: Erlbaum.

25. Min, S. W., Humphrey, S. E., Aime, F., Petrenko, O. V., Quade, M. J., & Fu, S. Q. (2021). Dealing with new members: Team members' reactions to newcomer's attractiveness and sex. *Journal of Applied Psychology.* Advance online publication. https://doi.org/10.1037/apl0000872

26. Mathieu, J. E., Hollenbeck, J. R., van Knippenberg, D., & Ilgen, D. R. (2017)—see #2.

27. Hollenbeck, J. R., Beersma, B., & Schouten, M. E. (2012). Beyond team types and taxonomies: A dimensional scaling conceptualization for team description. *Academy of Management Review, 37*, 82–106.

28. Driskell, T., Driskell, J. E., Burke, C. S., & Salas, E. (2017). Team roles: A review and integration. *Small Group Research, 48*, 482–511.

29. Ibid.

30. Bell, S. T. (2007). Deep-level composition variables as predictors of team performance: A meta-analysis. *Journal of Applied Psychology, 92*, 595–615.

31. van Dijk, H., van Engen, M. L., & van Knippenberg, D. (2012). Defying conventional wisdom: A meta-analytical examination of the differences between demographic and job-related diversity relationships with performance. *Organizational Behavior and Human Decision Processes, 119*, 38–53.

32. Marks, M. A., Mathieu, J. E., & Zaccaro, S. J. (2001). A temporally based framework and taxonomy of team processes. *Academy of Management Review, 26*, 356–376.

33. LePine, J. A., Piccolo, R. F., Jackson, C. L., Mathieu, J. E., & Saul, J. R. (2008). A meta-analysis of teamwork processes: Tests of a multidimensional model and relationships with team effectiveness criteria. *Personnel Psychology, 61*, 273–307.

34. Fisher, D. M. (2014). Distinguishing between taskwork and teamwork planning in teams: Relations with coordination and interpersonal processes. *Journal of Applied Psychology, 99*, 423–436.

35. Greengard, S. (2008). Lessons in leadership. *PM Network, 22*(8), 58–63.

36. Yeatts, D. E., & Hyten, C. (1998). *High-performing self-managed work teams.* Thousand Oaks, CA: Sage.

37. Cannon-Bowers, J. A., & Bowers, C. (2011). Team development and functioning. In S. Zedeck (Ed.), *APA handbook of industrial and organizational psychology* (Vol. 1, pp. 597–650). Washington, DC: APA.

38. Kolbe, M., Grote, G., Waller, M. J., Wacker, J., Grande, B., Burtscher, M. J., & Spahn, D. R. (2014). Monitoring and talking to the room: Autochthonous coordination patterns in team interaction and performance. *Journal of Applied Psychology, 99*, 1254–1267.

39. McIntyre, R. M., & Salas, E. (1995). Measuring and managing for team performance: Lessons from complex environments. In R. A. Guzzo & E. Salas (Eds.), *Team effectiveness and decision making in organizations* (pp. 9–45). San Francisco: Jossey-Bass.

40. Barnes, C. M., Hollenbeck, J. R., Wagner, D. T., DeRue, D. S., Nahrgang, J. D., & Schwind, K. M. (2008). Harmful help: The costs of backing-up behavior in teams. *Journal of Applied Psychology, 93*, 529–539.

41. Mueller, J. S., & Kamdar, D. (2011). Why seeking help from teammates is a blessing and a curse: A theory of help seeking and individual creativity in team contexts. *Journal of Applied Psychology, 96*, 263–276.

42. Yeatts, D. E., & Hyten, C. (1998)—see #36.

43. de Wit, F. R. C., Greer, L. L., & Jehn, K. A. (2012). The paradox of intragroup conflict: A meta-analysis. *Journal of Applied Psychology, 97*, 360–390.

44. Bradley, B. H., Klotz, A. C., Postlethwaite, B. E., & Brown, K. G. (2013). Ready to rumble: How team personality composition and task conflict interact to improve performance. *Journal of Applied Psychology, 98*, 385–392.

45. Jackson, S. E., & Joshi, A. (2011). Work team diversity. In S. Zedeck (Ed.), *APA handbook of industrial and organizational psychology* (Vol. 1, pp. 651–686). Washington, DC: APA.

46. Thatcher, S. M. B., & Patel, P. C. (2012). Group Faultlines: A Review, Integration, and Guide to Future Research. *Journal of Management, 38*(4), 969–1009.

47. Bezrukova, K., Thatcher, S. M. B., Jehn, K. A., & Spell, C. S. (2012). The effects of alignments: Examining group faultlines, organizational cultures, and performance. *Journal of Applied Psychology, 97*, 77–92.

48. Blindenbach-Driessen, F. (2020, March 26). Managing tensions between operations and innovations: 3 ways to prevent faultlines from breaking up in a time of crisis. *Organizing4Innovation.* Retrieved September 28, 2021, from https://www.organizing4innovation.com/3-ways-to-avoid-faultlines-to-crack-in-a-time-of-crisis/

49. Burke, C. S., Shuffler, M. L., Salas, E., & Gelfand, M. A. (2010). Multicultural teams: Critical team processes and guidelines. In K. Lundby (Ed.), *Going global* (pp. 46–82). San Francisco: Jossey-Bass.

50. Bandura, A. (2000). Exercise of human agency through collective efficacy. *Current Directions in Psychological Science, 9*, 75–78.

51. Goncalo, J. A., Polman, E., & Maslach, C. (2010). Can confidence come too soon? Collective efficacy, conflict and group performance over time. *Organizational Behavior and Human Decision Processes, 113*, 13–24.

52. Beal, D. J., Cohen, R. R., Burke, M. J., & McLendon, C. L. (2003). Cohesion and performance in groups: A meta-analytic clarification of construct relations. *Journal of Applied Psychology, 88*, 989–1004.

53. Schoorman, F. D., Mayer, R. C., & Davis, J. H. (2007). An integrative model of organizational trust: Past, present, and future. *Academy of Management Review, 35*, 344–354.

54. Colquitt, J. A., Scott, B. A., & LePine, J. A. (2007). Trust, trustworthiness, and trust propensity: A meta-analytic test of their unique relationships with risk taking and job performance. *Journal of Applied Psychology, 92*, 909–927.

55. Mayer, R. C., Davis, J. H., & Schoorman, F. D. (1995). An Integrative Model of Organizational Trust. *Academy of Management Review, 20*(3), 709–734; and Gill, H., Boies, K., Finegan, J. E., & McNally, J. (2005). Antecedents of trust: Establishing a boundary condition for the relation between propensity to trust and intention to trust. *Journal of Business and Psychology, 19*(3), 287–302.

56. Jarvenpaa, S., & Knoll, K., & Leidner, D. (1998). Is anybody out there? Antecedents of trust in global teams. *Journal of Management Information Systems, 14*. 29–64.

57. Priem, R. L., & Nystrom, P. C. (2014). Exploring the dynamics of workgroup fracture: Common ground, trust-with-trepidation, and warranted distrust. *Journal of Management, 40*, 764–795.

58. Gibson, C. B. (2001). From knowledge accumulation to accommodation: Cycles of collective cognition in work groups. *Journal of Organizational Behavior, 22*, 121–134.

59. Mohammed, S., Ferzandi, L., & Hamilton, K. (2010). Metaphor no more: A 15-year review of the team mental model construct. *Journal of Management, 36*, 876–910.

60. Fisher, D. M., Bell, S. T., Dierdorff, E. C., & Belohlav, J. A. (2012). Facet personality and surface-level diversity as team mental model antecedents: Implications for implicit coordination. *Journal of Applied Psychology, 97*, 825–841.

61. Cannon-Bowers, J. A., & Salas, E. (2001). Reflections on shared cognition. *Journal of Organizational Behavior, 22*, 195–202.

62. Cooke, N. J., Gorman, J. C., & Rowe, L. J. (2004). *An ecological perspective on team cognition.* Cognitive Engineering Research Inst. Mesa AZ.

63. Cannon-Bowers, J. A., & Salas, E. (2001) - see #61.

64. Marks, M. A., Sabella, M. J., Burke, C. S., & Zaccaro, S. J. (2002). The impact of cross-training on team effectiveness. *Journal of Applied Psychology, 87*, 3–13.

65. Choi, J. N., & Kim, M. U. (1999). The organizational applications of groupthink and its limitations in organizations. *Journal of Applied Psychology, 84*, 297–306.

66. Turner, M. E., & Horvitz, T. (2001). The dilemma of threat: Group effectiveness and ineffectiveness under adversity. In M. E. Turner (Ed.), *Groups at work* (pp. 445–470). Mahwah, NJ: Erlbaum.

67. Marks, M. A., Zaccaro, S. J., & Mathieu, J. E. (2000). Performance implications of leader briefings and team-interaction training for team adaptation to novel environments. *Journal of Applied Psychology, 85*, 971–986.

68. DeChurch, L. A., & Mesmer-Magnus, J. R. (2010). The cognitive underpinnings of effective teamwork: A meta-analysis. *Journal of Applied Psychology, 95*, 32–53.

69. Guzzo, R. A. (1995). Introduction: At the intersection of team effectiveness and decision making. In R. A. Guzzo & E. Salas (Eds.), *Team effectiveness and decision making in organizations* (pp. 1–8). San Francisco: Jossey-Bass.

70. Hollenbeck, J. R., LePine, J. A., & Ilgen, D. R. (1996). Adapting to roles in decision-making teams. In K. R. Murphy (Ed.), *Individual differences and behaviors in organizations* (pp. 300–333). San Francisco: Jossey-Bass.

71. Mohammed S., Cannon-Bowers J. A., & Foo, S. C. (2010). Selection for team membership: A contingency and multilevel perspective. In Farr J. L., Tippins N. T. (Eds.), *Handbook of employee selection* (pp. 801–822). New York: Routledge.

72. Klimoski, R. J., & Jones, R. G. (1995). Staffing for effective group decision making: Key issues in marketing people and teams. In R. A. Guzzo & E. Salas (Eds.), *Team effectiveness and decision making in organizations* (pp. 291– 332). San Francisco: Jossey-Bass.

73. Salas, E., Burke, C. S., & Cannon-Bowers, J. A. (2002). What we know about designing and delivering team training: Tips and guidelines. In K. Kraiger (Ed.), *Creating, implementing, and managing effective training and development* (pp. 234–259). San Francisco: Jossey-Bass.
74. Prieto, J. M. (1993). The team perspective in selection and assessment. In H. Schuler, J. L. Farr, & M. Smith (Eds.), *Personnel selection and assessment* (pp. 221–234). Hillsdale, NJ: Erlbaum.
75. Barry, B., & Stewart, G. L. (1997). Composition, process, and performance in self-managed groups: The role of personality. *Journal of Applied Psychology, 82,* 62–78.
76. Janz, B. D., Colquitt, J. A., & Noe, R. A. (1997). Knowledge worker team effectiveness: The role of autonomy, interdependence, team development, and contextual support variables. *Personnel Psychology, 50,* 877–904.
77. Aguinis, H., & O'Boyle, E., Jr. (2014). Star performers in twenty-first century organizations. *Personnel Psychology, 67,* 313–350.
78. Campbell, E. M., Liao, H., Chuang, A., Zhou, J., & Dong, Y. (2017). Hot shots and cool reception? An expanded view of social consequences for high performers. *Journal of Applied Psychology, 102*(5), 845–866.
79. Locke, E. A., Jirnauer, D., Roberson, Q. M., Goldman, B., Latham, M. E., & Weldon, E. (2001). The importance of the individual in an age of groupism. In M. E. Turner (Ed.), *Groups at work.* Mahwah, NJ: Erlbaum.
80. LePine, J. A., Colquitt, J. A., & Erez, A. (2000). Adaptability to changing task contexts: Effects of general cognitive ability, conscientiousness, and openness to experience. *Personnel Psychology, 53,* 563–593.
81. LePine, J. A. (2003). Team adaptation and postchange performance: Effects of team composition in terms of members' cognitive ability and personality. *Journal of Applied Psychology, 88,* 27–39.
82. Porter, C. O. L. H., Hollenbeck, J. R., Ilgen, D. R., Ellis, A. P. J., West, B. J., & Moon, H. (2003). Backing up behaviors in teams: The role of personality and legitimacy of need. *Journal of Applied Psychology, 88,* 391–403.
83. *Collective nouns: A guide to collective nouns.* (n.d.). Retrieved October 20, 2021, from http://www.collectivenouns.biz/list-of-collective-nouns/collective-nouns-people/
84. Salas, E., & Cannon-Bowers, J. A. (1997). Methods, tools, and strategies for team training. In M. A. Quiñones & A. Ehrenstein (Eds.), *Training for a rapidly changing workplace* (pp. 249–280). Washington, DC: APA.
85. Maynard, M. T., Mathieu, J. E., Rapp, T. L., Gilson, L. L., & Kleiner, C. (2021). Team leader coaching intervention: An investigation of the impact on team processes and performance within a surgical context. *Journal of Applied Psychology, 106*(7), 1080–1092.
86. Ledford, G. E., Jr., Benson, G., & Lawler, III, E. E., (2016). *Cutting-edge performance management: 244 organizations report on ongoing feedback, ratingless reviews and crowd-sourced feedback.* Scottsdale, AZ: WorldatWork.
87. Jackson, C. L., & LePine, J. A. (2003). Peer responses to a team's weakest link: A test and extension of LePine and Van Dyne's model. *Journal of Applied Psychology, 88,* 459–475.
88. Karau, S. J., & Williams, K. D. (2001). Understanding individual motivation in groups: The collective effort model. In M. E. Turner (Ed.), *Groups at work* (pp. 113–142). Mahwah, NJ: Erlbaum.
89. Locke, E. A., Jirnauer, D., Roberson, Q. M., Goldman, B., Latham, M. E., & Weldon, E. (2001)—see #79.
90. Druskat, V. A., & Wolff, S. B. (1999). Effects and timing of developmental peer appraisals in self-managing work groups. *Journal of Applied Psychology, 84*, 58–74.
91. Kerr, S. (1995). On the folly of rewarding A, while hoping for B. *Academy of Management Executive, 9,* 7–14.
92. Aguinis, H. (2019). *Performance management* (4th ed.). Upper Saddle River, NJ: Pearson.
93. O'Leary, M., Mortensen, M., & Woolley, A. (2011). Multiple team memberships: A theoretical model of its effects on productivity and learning for individuals and teams. *Academy of Management Review, 36,* 461–478.

94. Salas, E., Priest, H. A., Stagl, K. C., Sims, D. E., & Burke, C. S. (2007). Work teams in organizations: A historical reflection and lessons learned. In L. L. Koppes (Ed.), *Historical perspectives in industrial and organizational psychology* (pp. 407–438). Mahwah, NJ: Erlbaum.

95. Ibid., p. 432.

96. Edmondson, A. C. (2012). Teamwork on the fly: How to master the new art of teaming. *Harvard Business Review, 90*, 72–80.

97. Campion, M. A., Papper, E. M., & Medsker, G. J. (1996). Relations between work team characteristics and effectiveness: A replication and extension. *Personnel Psychology, 49*, 429–452.

Chapter 11

1. Fisher, C. D., & Ashkanasy, N. M. (2000). The emerging role of emotions in work life: An introduction. *Journal of Organizational Behavior, 21*, 123–129.

2. Frijda, N. H. (2009). Mood. In D. Sender & K. R. Scherer (Eds.), *The Oxford companion to emotion and the affective sciences* (pp. 258–259). New York: Oxford University Press.

3. Fisher, C. D. (2000). Mood and emotions while working: Missing pieces of job satisfaction? *Journal of Organizational Behavior, 21*, 185–202.

4. Weiss, H. M. (2002). Antecedents of emotional experiences at work. *Motivation and Emotion, 26*, 1–2.

5. Ekkekakis, P. (2012). Affect, mood, and emotion. In G. Tenenbaum, R. C. Eklund, & A. Kamata (Eds.), *Measurement in sport and exercise psychology*, p. 322. Champaign, IL: Human Kinetics.

6. Lerner, J. S., & Keltner, D. (2000). Beyond valence: Toward a model of emotion-specific influences on judgment and choice. *Cognition and Emotion, 14*, 473–493.

7. Reb, J., Greguras, G. J., Luan, S., & Daniels, M. A. (2014). Performance appraisals as heuristic judgments under uncertainty. In S. Highhouse, R. S. Dalal, & E. Salas (Eds.), *Judgment and decision making at work* (pp. 13–36). New York: Routledge.

8. Gil-Monte, P. R. (2012). The influence of guilt on the relationship between burnout and depression. *European Psychologist, 17*(3), 231–236; and Zhang, M., Zhao, K., & Korabik, K. (2019). Does work-to-family guilt mediate the relationship between work-to-family conflict and job satisfaction? Testing the moderating roles of segmentation preference and family collectivism orientation. *Journal of Vocational Behavior, 115*, Article 103321.

9. Feinberg, M., Ford, B. Q., & Flynn, F. J. (2020). Rethinking reappraisal: The double-edged sword of regulating negative emotions in the workplace. *Organizational Behavior and Human Decision Processes, 161*, 1–19.

10. Schaumberg, R. L., & Flynn, F. J. (2017). Clarifying the Link Between Job Satisfaction and Absenteeism: The Role of Guilt Proneness. *Journal of Applied Psychology, 102*, 982–992.

11. Ilies, R., Peng, A. C., Savani, K., & Dimotakis, N. (2013). Guilty and helpful: An emotion-based reparatory model of voluntary work behavior. *Journal of Applied Psychology, 98*, 1051–1059.

12. Shockley, K. M., Ispas, D., Rossi, M. E., & Levine, E. L. (2012). A meta-analytic investigation of the relationship between state affect, discrete emotions, and job performance. *Human Performance, 25*, 377–411.

13. Forgas, J. P. (2013). Don't worry, be sad! On the cognitive, motivational, and interpersonal benefits of negative mood. *Current Directions in Psychological Science, 22*, 225–232.

14. Lee, K., & Duffy, M. K. (2019). A functional model of workplace envy and job performance: When do employees capitalize on envy by learning from envied targets? *Academy of Management Journal, 62*(4), 1085–1110.

15. Rodell, J. B., & Judge, T. A. (2009). Can "good" stressors spark "bad" behaviors? The mediating role of emotions in links of challenge and hindrance stressors with citizenship and counterproductive behaviors. *Journal of Applied Psychology, 94*, 1438–1451.

16. Staw, B. M., DeCelles, K. A., & de Goey, P. (2019). Leadership in the locker room: How the intensity of leaders' unpleasant affective displays shapes team performance. *Journal of Applied Psychology, 104*(12), 1547–1557.

17. Rees, L., Chi, S.-C. S., Friedman, R., & Shih, H.-L. (2020). Anger as a trigger for information search in integrative negotiations. *Journal of Applied Psychology, 105*(7), 713–731.
18. Yip, J. A., & Schweinsberg, M. (2017). Infuriating impasses: Angry expressions increase exiting behavior in negotiations. *Social Psychological and Personality Science, 8*: 706–714.
19. Geddes, D., & Callister, R. R. (2007). Crossing the line(s): A dual threshold model of anger in organizations. *Academy of Management Review, 32*(3), 721–746.
20. Oswald, A. J., Proto, E., & Sgroi, D. (2015). Happiness and productivity. *Journal of Labor Economics, 33*(4), 789–822.
21. Wang, Y.-D., & Yang, C. (2016). How appealing are monetary rewards in the workplace? A study of ethical leadership, love of money, happiness, and turnover intention. *Social Indicators Research, 129*(3), 1277–1290.
22. Thompson, A., & Bruk-Lee, V. (2021). Employee happiness: Why we should care. *Applied Research in Quality of Life, 16*(4), 1419-1437.
23. Bateman, T., & Organ, D. W. (1983). Job satisfaction and the good soldier: The relation between affect and employee "citizenship." *Academy of Management Journal, 261*, 587–595; and Judge, T. A., Thoresen, C. J., Bono, J. E., & Patton, G. K. (2001). The job satisfaction–job performance relationship: A qualitative and quantitative review. *Psychological Bulletin, 127*, 376–407.
24. Spector, P. E. (1997). *Job satisfaction: Application, assessment, causes, and consequences* (Vol. 3). Beverly Hills: Sage.
25. Lyubomirsky, S. (2008). *The how of happiness: A scientific approach to getting the life you want.* New York: Penguin Press.
26. Thompson, A., & Bruk-Lee, V. (2021) — see #22.
27. Fujita, F., & Diener, E. (2005). Life satisfaction set point: stability and change. *Journal of Personality and Social Psychology, 88*(1), 158.
28. Hülsheger, U. R., & Schewe, A. F. (2011). On the costs and benefits of emotional labor: A meta-analysis spanning three decades of research. *Journal of Occupational Health Psychology, 16*, 361–389.
29. Sayre, G. M., Grandey, A. A., & Chi, N.-W. (2020). From cheery to "cheers"? Regulating emotions at work and alcohol consumption after work. *Journal of Applied Psychology, 105*(6), 597–618.
30. Miao, C., Humphrey, R. H., & Qian, S. (2017). Are the emotionally intelligent good citizens or counterproductive? A meta-analysis of emotional intelligence and its relationship with organizational citizenship behavior and counterproductive work behavior. *Personality & Individual Differences, 116*, 144–156.
31. O'Boyle, E. H., Jr., Humphrey, R. H., Pollack, J. M., Hawver, T. H., & Story, P. A. (2011). The relation between emotional intelligence and job performance: A meta-analysis. *Journal of Organizational Behavior, 32*, 788–818.
32. Joseph, D. L., & Newman, D. A. (2010). Emotional intelligence: An integrative meta-analysis and cascading model. *Journal of Applied Psychology, 95*, 54–78.
33. Rode, J. C., Arthaud-Day, M., Ramaswami, A., & Howes, S. S. (2017). A time-lagged study of emotional intelligence and salary. *Journal of Vocational Behavior, 101*, 77–89.
34. Westman, M., Shadach, E., & Keinan, G. (2013). The crossover of positive and negative emotions: The role of state empathy. *International Journal of Stress Management, 20*, 116–133.
35. Fredrickson, B. L. (2001). The role of positive emotions in positive psychology: The broaden-and-build theory. *American Psychologist, 56*, 218–226.
36. Vacharkulksemsuk, T., & Fredrickson, B. L. (2013). Looking back and glimpsing forward: The broaden-and-build theory of positive emotions as applied to organizations. In A. B. Bakker (Ed.), *Advances in positive organizational psychology* (Vol. 1, pp. 45–60). Bingley, UK: Emerald.
37. Fritz, H. L., Russek, L. N., & Dillon, M. M. (2017). Humor use moderates the relation of stressful life events with psychological distress. *Personality and Social Psychology Bulletin, 43*, 845–859.
38. Ashforth, B. E., Glen, E. K., & Fugate, M. (2000). All in a day's work: Boundaries and micro role transitions. *Academy of Management Review, 25*, 472–491.
39. Fredrickson, B. L., & Cohn, M. A. (2008). Positive emotions. In M. Lewis, J. M. Haviland-Jones, & L. F. Barrett (Eds.), *Handbook of emotions* (pp. 777–796). The Guilford Press.
40. Fredrickson, B. L. (2000). Cultivating positive emotions to optimize health and well-being. *Prevention & Treatment, 3*, 1–25.
41. Fredrickson, B. L. (2013). Updated thinking on positive ratios. *American Psychologist, 68*, 814–822.

42. Schleicher, D. J., Hansen, S. D., & Fox, K. E. (2011). Job attitudes and work values. In S. Zedeck (Ed.), *APA handbook of industrial and organizational psychology* (Vol. 3, pp. 137–190). Washington, DC: APA.

43. Judge, T. A., Hulin, C. L., & Dalal, R. S. (2012). Job satisfaction and job affect. In S. W. J. Kozlowski (Ed.), *The Oxford handbook of organizational psychology* (Vol. 1, pp. 496–525). New York: Oxford University Press.

44. Klein, H. J. (2014). Distinguishing commitment bonds from other attachments in a target-free manner. In J. K. Ford, J. R. Hollenbeck, & A. M. Ryan (Eds.), *The nature of work* (pp. 117–146). Washington, DC: APA.

45. Ng, T. W. H., & Feldman, D. C. (2010). The relationships of age with job attitudes: A meta-analysis. *Personnel Psychology, 63*, 677–718.

46. Judge, T. A., & Kammeyer-Mueller, J. D. (2012). Job attitudes. *Annual Review of Psychology, 63*, 341–367.

47. Judge, T. A., Hulin, C. L., & Dalal, R. S. (2012)—see #43.

48. Hulin, C. L., & Judge, T. A. (2003). Job attitudes. In W. C. Borman, D. R. Ilgen, & R. J. Klimoski (Eds.), *Handbook of psychology: Industrial and organizational psychology* (Vol. 12, pp. 255–276). Hoboken, NJ: Wiley.

49. Dawis, R. V. (2004). Job satisfaction. In J. C. Thomas (Ed.), *Comprehensive handbook of psychological assessment* (Vol. 4, pp. 470–481). Hoboken, NJ: Wiley.

50. Warr, P. B., & Clapperton, G. (2010). *The joy of work? Jobs, happiness, and you.* New York: Routledge.

51. Smith, P. C., Kendall, L., & Hulin, C. L. (1969). *The measurement of satisfaction in work and retirement.* Chicago: Rand McNally.

52. Kinicki, A. J., McKee-Ryan, F. M., Schriesheim, C. A., & Carson, K. P. (2002). Assessing the construct validity of the Job Descriptive Index: A review and meta-analysis. *Journal of Applied Psychology, 87,* 14–32.

53. Weiss, D. J., Dawis, R. V., England, G. W., & Lofquist, L. H. (1967). *Manual for the Minnesota Satisfaction Questionnaire.* Minneapolis: Industrial Relations Center, University of Minnesota.

54. Brief, A. P. (1998). *Attitudes in and around organizations.* Thousand Oaks, CA: Sage.

55. Judge, T. A., Heller, D., & Mount, M. K. (2002). Five-factor model of personality and job satisfaction: A meta-analysis. *Journal of Applied Psychology, 87,* 530–541.

56. Ilies, R., & Judge, T. A. (2003). On the heritability of job satisfaction: The mediating role of personality. *Journal of Applied Psychology, 88,* 750–759.

57. Boswell, W. R., Shipp, A. J., Payne, S. C., & Culbertson, S. S. (2009). Changes in newcomer job satisfaction over time: Examining the pattern of honeymoons and hangovers. *Journal of Applied Psychology, 94*, 844–858.

58. Judge, T. A., Thoresen, C. J., Bono, J. E., & Patton, G. K. (2001)—see #23.

59. Bowling, N. A., Khazon, S., Meyer, R., & Burrus, C. (2015). Situational strength as a moderator of the relationship between job satisfaction and job performance: A meta-analytic examination. *Journal of Business and Psychology, 30*, 89–104.

60. Riketta, M. (2008). The causal relation between job attitudes and performance: A meta-analysis of panel studies. *Journal of Applied Psychology, 93*, 472–481.

61. Hom, P. W., & Kinicki, A. J. (2001). Toward a greater understanding of how dissatisfaction drives employee turnover. *Academy of Management Journal, 44*, 975–987.

62. Carsten, J. M., & Spector, P. E. (1987). Unemployment, job satisfaction, and employee turnover: A meta-analytic test of the Muchinsky model. *Journal of Applied Psychology, 72*, 374–381.

63. Johns, G. (1997). Contemporary research on absence from work: Correlates, causes, and consequences. In C. L. Cooper & I. T. Robertson (Eds.), *International review of industrial and organizational psychology* (Vol. 12, pp. 115–173). Chichester: Wiley.

64. Judge, T. A., Thoresen, C. J., Bono, J. E., & Patton, G. K. (2001)—see #23.

65. Klein, H. J., Molloy, J. C., & Brinsfield, C. T. (2012). Reconceptualizing workplace commitment to redress a stretched construct: Revisiting assumptions and removing confounds. *The Academy of Management Review, 37*(1), 130–151.

66. Allen, N. J., & Meyer, J. P. (1990). The measurement and antecedents of affective, continuance, and normative commitment to the organization. *Journal of Occupational Psychology, 63*, 1–18.

67. Meyer, J. P. (2016). Employee commitment: An introduction and roadmap. In J. P. Meyer (Ed.), *Handbook of employee commitment* (pp. 3–12). Cheltenham, UK: Edward Elgar.

68. Meyer, J. P. (2009). Commitment in a changing world of work. In H. J. Klein, T. E. Becker, & J. P. Meyer (Eds.), *Commitment in organizations* (pp. 37–68). New York: Routledge.

69. Ibid., pp. 37–38.

70. Becker, T. E., Klein, H. J., & Meyer, J. P. (2009). Commitment in organizations: Accumulated wisdom and new directions. In H. J. Klein, T. E. Becker, & J. P. Meyer (Eds.), *Commitment in organizations* (pp. 419–452). New York: Taylor & Francis.

71. Gellatly, I. R., & Hedberg, L. M. (2016). Employee turnover and absenteeism. In J. P. Meyer (Ed.), *Handbook of employee commitment* (pp. 195–207). Cheltenham, UK: Edward Elgar.

72. Solinger, O. N., Van Olffen, W., & Roe, R. A. (2008). Beyond the three-component model of organizational commitment. *Journal of Applied Psychology, 93*, 70–83.

73. Dunham, R. B., Grube, J. A., & Castaneda, M. B. (1994). Organizational commitment: The utility of an integrated definition. *Journal of Applied Psychology, 79*, 370–380.

74. Brown, S. P. (1996). A meta-analysis and review of organizational research in job involvement. *Psychological Bulletin, 120*, 235–255.

75. Ibid.

76. Riketta, M. (2002). Attitudinal organizational commitment and job performance: A meta-analysis. *Journal of Organizational Behavior, 23,* 257–266.

77. Macey, W. H., & Schneider, B. (2008). The meaning of employee engagement. *Industrial and Organizational Psychology, 1*, 3–30.

78. Schaufeli, W. B., Salanova, M., Gonzalez-Romá, V., & Bakker, A. B. (2002). The measurement of engagement and burnout: A confirmative analytic approach. *Journal of Happiness Studies, 3*, 71–92.

79. Demerouti, E., & Cropanzano, R. (2010). From thought to action: Employee work engagement and job performance. In A. B. Bakker & M. P. Leiter (Eds.), *Work engagement: A handbook of essential theory and research* (pp. 147–163). New York: Psychology Press.

80. Maslach, C., Schaufeli, W. B., & Leiter, M. P. (2001). Job burnout. *Annual Review of Psychology, 52*, 397–422.

81. Mills, M. J., Culbertson, S. S., & Fullagar, C. J. (2012). Conceptualizing and measuring engagement: An analysis of the Utrecht Work Engagement Scale. *Journal of Happiness Studies, 13*, 519–545.

82. Gorgievski, M., Bakker, A. B., & Schaufeli, W. B. (2010). Work engagement and workaholism: comparing the self-employed and salaried employees. *Journal of Positive Psychology, 5*, 83–96.

83. Saks, A. M. (2006). Antecedents and consequences of employee engagement. *Journal of Managerial Psychology, 21*, 600–619.

84. Bakker, A. B., Shimazu, A., Demerouti, E., Shimada, K., & Kawakami, N. (2014). Work engagement versus workaholism: A test of the spillover-crossover model. *Journal of Managerial Psychology, 29*(1), 63–80.

85. ten Brummelhuis, L. L., Rothbard, N. P., & Uhrich, B. (2017). Beyond nine to five: Is working to excess bad for health? *Academy of Management Discoveries, 3*, 262–283.

86. Spreitzer, G. M., Lam, C. F., & Fritz, C. (2010). Engagement and human thriving: Complementary perspectives on energy and connections to work. In A. B. Bakker & M. P. Leiter (Eds.), *Work engagement: A handbook of essential theory and research* (pp. 132–146). New York: Psychology Press.

87. Mackay, M. M., Allen, J. A., & Landis, R. S. (2017). Investigating the incremental validity of employee engagement in the prediction of employee effectiveness: A meta-analytic path analysis. *Human Resource Management Review, 27*, 108–120.

88. Colquitt, J. A., Conlon, D. E., Wesson, M. J., Porter, C. O. L. H., & Ng, K. Y. (2001). Justice at the millennium: A meta-analytic review of 25 years of organizational justice research. *Journal of Applied Psychology, 86*, 425–445.

89. Colquitt, J. A. (2012). Organizational justice. In S. W. J. Kozlowski (Ed.), *The Oxford handbook of organizational psychology* (Vol. 1, pp. 526–547). New York: Oxford University Press.

90. Posthuma, R. A., & Campion, M. A. (2005). When do multiple dimensions of procedural justice predict agreement to publicly endorse your employer in recruitment advertisements? *Journal of Occupational and Organizational Psychology, 78*, 431–452.

91. Schminke, M., Ambrose, M. L., & Cropanzano, R. (2000). The effect of organizational structure on perceptions of procedural fairness. *Journal of Applied Psychology, 85*, 294–304.

92. Gilliland, S. W., & Chan, D. (2001). Justice in organizations: Theory, methods, and applications. In N. Anderson, D. S. Ones, H. K. Sinangil, & C. Viswesvaran (Eds.), *Handbook of industrial, work, and organizational psychology* (Vol. 2, pp. 143–165). London: Sage.

93. Gilliland, S. W. (1993). The perceived fairness of selection systems: An organizational justice perspective. *Academy of Management Review, 18*, 694–734.

94. Leventhal, G. S. (1980). What should be done with equity theory? New approaches to the study of fairness in social relationships. In K. Gergen, M. Greenberg, & R. Willis (Eds.), *Social exchange: Advances in theory and research* (pp. 27–55). New York: Plenum Press.

95. Folger, R., & Skarlicki, D. P. (2001). Fairness as a dependent variable: Why tough times can lead to bad management. In R. Cropanzano (Ed.), *Justice in the workplace* (Vol. 2, pp. 97–120). Mahwah, NJ: Erlbaum.

96. Moreira, M. (2019, October 29). Mind your manners: why politeness wins in the workplace. *Welcome to the Jungle*. Retrieved October 11, 2021, from https://www.welcometothejungle.com/en/articles/why-politeness-wins-in-the-workplace

97. Nelson, B. (2020, May 2). 10 rude manners that are actually polite in other countries. *Readers Digest*. Retrieved October 11, 2021, from https://www.rd.com/list/rude-american-manners/

98. Andersen, G. H. (2021, September 17). How to be polite in 15 different countries. *Readers Digest*. Retrieved October 12, 2021, from https://www.rd.com/list/be-polite-different-countries/

99. Greenberg, J. (1994). Using socially fair treatment to promote acceptance of a work site smoking ban. *Journal of Applied Psychology, 79*, 288–297.

100. Colquitt, J. A., Conlon, D. E., Wesson, M. J., Porter, C. O. L. H., & Ng, K. Y. (2001)—see #88.

101. Greenberg, J. (2007). Positive organizational justice: From fair to fairer—and beyond. In J. E. Dutton & B. R. Ragins (Eds.), *Exploring positive relationships at work* (pp. 159–178). Mahwah, NJ: Erlbaum.

102. Simons, T., & Roberson, Q. M. (2003). Why managers should care about fairness: The effects of aggregate justice perceptions on organizational outcomes. *Journal of Applied Psychology, 88*, 432–443.

103. Cohen-Charash, Y., & Spector, P. E. (2001). The role of justice in organizations: A meta-analysis. *Organizational Behavior and Human Decision Processes, 86*, 278–321.

104. LePine, J. A., Erez, A., & Johnson, D. E. (2002). The nature and dimensionality of organizational citizenship behavior: A critical review and meta-analysis. *Journal of Applied Psychology, 87*, 52–65.

105. Podsakoff, N. P., Whiting, S. W., Podsakoff, P. M., & Blume, B. D. (2009). Individual- and organizational-level consequences of organizational citizenship behaviors: A meta-analysis. *Journal of Applied Psychology, 94*, 122–141.

106. Grant, D. M., & Mayer, D. M. (2009). Good soldiers and good actors: Prosocial and impression management motives as interactive predictors of affiliative citizenship behavior. *Journal of Applied Psychology, 94*, 900–912.

107. Organ, D. W. (1994). Organizational citizenship behavior and the good soldier. In M. G. Rumsey, C. B. Walker, & J. H. Harris (Eds.), *Personnel selection and classification* (pp. 53–68). Hillsdale, NJ: Erlbaum.

108. Wang, Q., & Bowling, N. A. (2016). A comparison of general and work-specific personality measures as predictors of organizational citizenship behavior. *International Journal of Selection & Assessment, 24*, 172–188.

109. Organ, D. W., Podsakoff, P. M., & Podsakoff, N. P. (2011). Expanding the criterion domain to include organizational citizenship behavior: Implications for employee selection. In S. Zedeck (Ed.), *APA handbook of industrial and organizational psychology* (Vol. 2, pp. 281–323). Washington, DC: APA.

110. Eatough, E. M., Chang, C. H., Miloslavic, S. A., & Johnson, R. E. (2011). Relationship of role stressors with organizational citizenship behavior: A meta-analysis. *Journal of Applied Psychology, 96*, 619–632.

111. Organ, D. W. (1988). *Organizational citizenship behavior: The good soldier syndrome.* Lexington, MA: Lexington Books.

112. Thompson, P. S., Bergeron, D. M., & Bolino, M. C. (2020). No obligation? How gender influences the relationship between perceived organizational support and organizational citizenship behavior. *Journal of Applied Psychology, 105*(11), 1338–1350.

113. Bolino, M. C., Turnley, W. H., Gilstrap, J. B., & Suazo, M. M. (2010). Citizenship under pressure: What's a "good soldier" to do? *Journal of Organizational Behavior, 31*, 835–855.

114. Culbertson, S. S., & Mills, M. J. (2011). Negative implications for the inclusion of citizenship performance in ratings. *Human Resource Development International, 14*, 23–38; and Pierce, J. L., & Aguinis, H. (2013). The too-much-of-a-good-thing effect in management. *Journal of Management, 39*, 313–338.

115. Bergeron, D. M., Shipp, A. J., Rosen, B., & Furst, S. A. (2013). Organizational citizenship behavior and career outcomes: The cost of being a good citizen. *Journal of Management, 39*, 958–984.

116. Rapp, A. A., Bachrach, D. G., & Rapp, T. L. (2013). The influence of time management skill on the curvilinear relationship between organizational citizenship behavior and task performance. *Journal of Applied Psychology, 98*, 668–677.

117. Heilman, M. E., & Chen, J. J. (2005). Same behavior, different consequences: Reactions to men's and women's altruistic citizenship behavior. *Journal of Applied Psychology, 90*, 431–441.

118. Lam, S. S., Hui, C., & Law, K. S. (1999). Organizational citizenship behavior: Comparing perspectives of supervisors and subordinates across four international samples. *Journal of Applied Psychology, 84*, 594–601.

119. Spector, P. E., & Fox, S. (2005). The stressor-emotion model of counterproductive work behavior. In S. Fox & P. E. Spector (Eds.), *Counterproductive work behavior: Investigations of actors and targets* (pp. 151–174). Washington, DC: APA.

120. Edwards, M. S., & Greenberg, J. (2010). What is insidious workplace behavior? In J. Greenberg (Ed.), *Insidious workplace behavior* (pp. 3–28). New York: Routledge.

121. Campbell, J. P. (2012). Behavior, performance, and effectiveness in the twenty-first century. In S. W. J. Kozlowski (Ed.), *The Oxford handbook of organizational psychology* (Vol. 1, pp. 159–194). New York: Oxford University Press.

122. Tepper, B. J., Henle, C. A., Lambert, L. S., Giacalone, R. A., & Duffy, M. K. (2008). Abusive supervisors and subordinates' organization deviance. *Journal of Applied Psychology, 93*, 721–732.

123. Scott, K. L., Restubog, S. L. D., & Zagenczyk, T. J. (2013). A social exchange-based model of antecedents of workplace exclusion. *Journal of Applied Psychology, 98*, 37–48.

124. Seabright, M. A., Ambrose, M. L., & Schminke, M. (2010). Two images of workplace sabotage. In J. Greenberg (Ed.), *Insidious workplace behavior* (pp. 77–99). New York: Routledge.

125. Barreca, R. (1997). *Sweet revenge: The wicked delights of getting even*. New York: Berkley.

126. Bies, R. J., Tripp, T. M., & Kramer, R. M. (1997). At the breaking point. In R. A. Giacalone & J. Greenberg (Eds.), *Antisocial behavior in organizations* (pp. 18–36). Thousand Oaks, CA: Sage.

127. Tehrani, N. (2012). Introduction to workplace bullying. In N. Tehrani (Ed.), *Workplace bullying: Symptoms and solutions* (pp. 1–17). New York: Routledge.

128. Jensen, J. M., Patel, P. C., & Raver, J. L. (2014). Is it better to be average? High and low performance as predictors of employee victimization. *Journal of Applied Psychology, 99*, 296–309.

129. Shore, L. M., & Coyle-Shapiro, J. A. M. (2012). Perceived organizational cruelty: An expansion of the negative employee-organization relationship domain. In L. M. Shore, J. A-M. Coyle-Shapiro, & L. E. Tetrick (Eds.), *The employee-organization relationship* (pp. 139–168). New York: Routledge.

130. Kish-Gephart, J. J., Harrison, D. A., & Trevino, L. K. (2010). Bad apples, bad cases, and bad barrels: Meta-analytic evidence about sources of unethical decisions at work. *Journal of Applied Psychology, 95*, 1–31.

131. Ramsay, S., Troth, A., & Branch, S. (2011). Work-place bullying: A group processes framework. *Journal of Occupational and Organizational Psychology, 84*, 799–816.

132. Andersson, L. M., & Pearson, C. M. (1999). Tit for tat? The spiraling effect of incivility in the workplace. *Academy of Management Review, 24*, 452–471.

133. Sue, D. W. (2010). *Microaggressions in everyday life: Race, gender, and sexual orientation*. New Jersey: Wiley.

134. Glomb, T. M., Steele, P., & Arvey, R. D. (2002). Office sneers, snipes, and stab wounds: Antecedents, consequences, and implications of workplace violence and aggression. In R. G. Lord, R. J. Klimoski, & R. Kanfer (Eds.), *Emotions in the workplace* (pp. 227–259). San Francisco: Jossey-Bass.

135. Hershcovis, M. S., Turner, N., Barling, J., Arnold, K. A., Dupre, K. E., Inness, M., LeBlanc, M. M., & Sivanathan, N. (2007). Predicting workplace aggression: A meta-analysis. *Journal of Applied Psychology, 92*, 228–238.

136. Barclay, L. J., & Aquino, K. (2011). Workplace aggression and violence. In S. Zedeck (Ed.), *APA handbook of industrial and organizational psychology* (Vol. 3, pp. 615–640). Washington, DC: APA.

137. Weatherbee, T. G. (2010). Counterproductive use of technology at work: Information & communications technologies and cyberdeviancy. *Human Resource Management Review, 20*, 35–44.

138. Anderson, T. (2012, July 1). Legal Report July 2012. *Security Management*. Retrieved December 19, 2021, from https://www.asisonline.org/security-management-magazine/articles/2012/07/legal-report-july-2012/

139. Vigoda-Gadot, E., & Drory, A. (2006). Preface. In E. Vigoda-Gadot & A. Drory (Eds.), *Handbook of organizational politics* (pp. *ix–xx*). Cheltenham, UK: Edward Elgar.

140. Lasswell, H. (1936). *Politics: Who gets what, when, how?* New York: Whittlesey.

141. Hochwarter, W. A. (2012). The positive side of organizational politics. In G. R. Ferris & D. C. Treadway (Eds.), *Politics in organizations: Theory and research considerations* (pp. 27–65). New York: Routledge.

142. Ferris, G. R., & Treadway, D. C. (2012). Politics in organizations: History, construct specification, and research directions. In G. R. Ferris & D. C. Treadway (Eds.), *Politics in organizations: Theory and research considerations* (pp. 3–26). New York: Routledge.

143. Buchanan, D. (2008). You stab my back, I'll stab yours: Management experience and perceptions of organizational political behaviour. *British Journal of Management, 19*, 49–64.

144. Beugne, C. D., & Liverpool, P. R. (2006). Politics as determinants of fairness perceptions in organizations. In E. Vigoda-Gadot & A. Drory (Eds.), *Handbook of organizational politics* (pp. 122–135). Cheltenham, UK: Edward Elgar.

145. Mintzberg, H. (1989). *Mintzberg on management: Inside our strange world of organizations*. New York: Free Press.

146. Liu, Y., Ferris, G. R., Treadway, D. C., Prati, M. L., Perrewé, P. L., & Hochwarter, W. A. (2006). The emotion of politics and the politics of emotions. In E. Vigoda-Gadot & A. Drory (Eds.), *Handbook of organizational politics* (pp. 161–186). Cheltenham, UK: Edward Elgar.

147. Blickle, G., Kramer, J., Schneider, P. B., Meurs, J. A., Ferris, G. R., Mierke, J., Witzki, A. H., & Momm, T. D. (2011). Role of political skill in job performance prediction beyond general mental ability and personality in cross-sectional and predictive studies. *Journal of Applied Social Psychology, 41*, 488–514.

148. Ferris, G. R., Treadway, D. C., Brouer, R. L., & Munyon, T. P. (2012). Political skill in the organizational sciences. In G. R. Ferris & D. C. Treadway (Eds.), *Politics in organizations: Theory and research considerations* (pp. 487–528). New York: Routledge.

149. Cropanzano, R., & Li, A. (2006). Organizational politics and workplace stress. In E. Vigoda-Gadot & A. Drory (Eds.), *Handbook of organizational politics* (pp. 139–160). Cheltenham, UK: Edward Elgar.

150. Chang, C. H., Rosen, C. C., & Levy, P. E. (2009). The relationship between perceptions of organizational politics and employee attitudes, strain, and behavior: A meta-analytic examination. *Academy of Management Journal, 52*, 779–801.

151. Rousseau, D. M. (1995). *Psychological contracts in organizations: Understanding written and unwritten agreements*. Thousand Oaks, CA: Sage.

152. Coyle-Shapiro, J. A. M., Costa, S. P., Doden, W., & Chang, C. (2019). Psychological contracts: Past, present and future. *Annual Review of Organizational Psychology and Organizational Behavior, 6*, 145–169.

153. Rousseau, D. M. (2011). The individual-organizational relationship: The psychological contract. In S. Zedeck (Ed.), *APA handbook of industrial and organizational psychology* (Vol. 3, pp. 191–220). Washington, DC: APA.

154. Dabos, G. E., & Rousseau, D. M. (2004). Mutuality and reciprocity in the psychological contracts of employees and employers. *Journal of Applied Psychology, 89*, 52–72.

155. Payne, S. C., Culbertson, S. S., Lopez, Y. P., Boswell, W. R., & Barger, E. J. (2015). Contract breach as a trigger for adjustment to the psychological contract during the first year of employment. *Journal of Occupational and Organizational Psychology, 88*, 41–60.

156. Walker, A. (2010). The development and validation of a psychological contract of safety scale. *Journal of Safety Research, 41*, 315–321.

157. Rousseau, D. M. (2011)—see #153.

158. McClean Parks, J., & Kidder, D. L. (1994). Till death do us part...Changing work relationships in the 1990s. In C.L. Cooper and D.M. Rousseau (Eds.), *Trends in Organisational Behaviour*, 111-136.

159. Robinson, S. L., & Rousseau, D. M. (1994). Violating the psychological contract: Not the exception but the norm. *Journal of Organizational Behavior, 15*, 245–259.

160. Montes, S. D., & Zweig, D. (2009). Do promises matter? An exploration of the role of promises in psychological contract breach. *Journal of Applied Psychology, 94*, 1243–1260.

161. Turnley, W. H., & Feldman, D. C. (2000). Re-examining the effects of psychological contract violations: Unmet expectations and job dissatisfaction as mediators. *Journal of Applied Psychology, 84,* 594–601.

162. Robinson, S. L., Kraatz, M. S., & Rousseau, D. M. (1994). Changing obligations and the psychology contract: A longitudinal study. *Academy of Management Journal, 37*, 137–152.

163. Dulebohn, J. H. (1997). Social influences in justice evaluations of human resources systems. In G. R. Ferris (Ed.), *Research in personnel and human resources management* (Vol. 15, pp. 241–292). Greenwich, CT: JAI Press.

164. Zhao, H., Wayne, S. J., Glibkowski, B. C., & Bravo, J. (2007). The impact of psychological contract breach on work-related outcomes: A meta-analysis. *Personnel Psychology, 60*, 647–680.

165. Ng, T. W. H., Feldman, D. C., & Simon, S. K. (2010). Psychological contract breaches, organizational commitment, and innovation-related behaviors: A latent growth modeling approach. *Journal of Applied Psychology, 9*, 744–751.

166. Tomprou, M., Rousseau, D. M., & Hansen, S. D. (2015). The psychological contracts of violation victims: A post-violation model. *Journal of Organizational Behavior, 36*, 561–581.

167. Rousseau, D. M., & Schalk, R. (2000). Learning from cross-national perspectives on psychological contracts. In D. M. Rousseau & R. Schalk (Eds.), *Psychological contracts in employment: Cross-national perspectives* (pp. 283–304). Thousand Oaks, CA: Sage.

Chapter 12

1. American Psychological Association. (2020, October). *Stress in America® 2020: A national mental health crisis* [Press release]. Retrieved November 20, 2021, from https://www.apa.org/news/press/releases/stress/2020/report-october

2. American Psychological Association. (2021, March 11). *One year later, a new wave of pandemic health concerns* [Press release]. Retrieved November 20, 2021, from https://www.apa.org/news/press/releases/stress/2021/one-year-pandemic-stress

3. Lyra Health. *Workforce Health Survey: The state of mental health at work in 2021.* Retrieved November 20, 2021, from https://get.lyrahealth.com/state-of-mental-health-report.html

4. Sonnentag, S., & Frese, M. (2013). Stress in organizations. In N. Schmitt, & S. Highhouse (Eds.), *Handbook of psychology: Industrial and organizational psychology* (Vol. 12, pp. 560–592). New York: John Wiley & Sons.

5. Ibid.

6. NCW Risk Management. (2021, January 12). *Top 10 most dangerous jobs of 2020.* Retrieved November 20, 2021, from https://www.ncwriskmanagement.com/blog/2021/01/top-10-most-dangerous-jobs-of-2020

7. Bureau of Labor Statistics. (2020, December 16). *Census of Fatal Occupational Injuries Summary, 2019* [Press release]. Retrieved November 20, 2021, from https://www.bls.gov/news.release/cfoi.nr0.htm

8. Bureau of Labor Statistics. (2021, November 3). *Employer-related workplace injuries and illnesses, 2020* [Press release]. Retrieved November 20, 2021, from https://www.bls.gov/news.release/osh.nr0.htm

9. National Safety Council. (n.d.). *Work Injury Costs–2019.* Retrieved November 20, 2021, from https://injuryfacts.nsc.org/work/costs/work-injury-costs/

10. Beus, J. M., McCord, M. A., and Zohar, D. (2016). Workplace safety: A review and research synthesis. *Organizational Psychology Review, 6*(4), pp. 352–381.

11. Burke, M. J., Sarpy, S. A., Tesluk, P. E., & Smith-Crowe, K. (2002). General safety performance: A test of a grounded theoretical model. *Personnel Psychology, 55*(2), 429–457.

12. Ibid.; and Beus, J. M., McCord, M. A., & Zohar, D. (2016) — see #10.

13. Neal, A., Griffin, M. A., & Hart, P. M. (2000). The impact of organizational climate on safety climate and individual behavior. *Safety Science, 34*(1–3), 99–109; and Clarke, S. (2006). Safety climate in an automobile manufacturing plant: The effects of work environment, job communication and safety attitudes on accidents and unsafe behaviour. *Personnel Review, 35*(4), 413–430.

14. Griffin, M. A. & Neal, A. (2000). Perceptions of safety at work: A framework for linking safety climate to safety performance, knowledge, and motivation. *Journal of Occupational Health Psychology, 5*(3), 347–358.

15. Neal, A., Griffin, M. A., & Hart, P. M. (2000) — see #13.

16. Christian, M. S., Bradley, J. C., Wallace, J. C., & Burke, M. J. (2009). Workplace safety: a meta-analysis of the roles of person and situation factors. *Journal of Applied Psychology, 94*(5), 1103–1127.

17. de Vries, B. (2021). Autism and the right to a hypersensitivity-friendly workspace. *Public Health Ethics*, phab021.

18. Cavanaugh, M. A., Boswell, W. R., Roehling, M. V., & Boudreau, J. W. (2000). An empirical examination of self-reported work stress among U.S. managers. *Journal of Applied Psychology, 85*, 65–74.

19. LePine, J. A., Podsakoff, N. P., & LePine, M. A. (2005). A meta-analytic test of the challenge stressor-hindrance stressor framework: An explanation for inconsistent relationships among stressors and performance. *Academy of Management Journal, 48*, 764–775.

20. Podsakoff, N. P., LePine, J. A., & LePine, M. A. (2007). Differential challenge stressor-hindrance stressor relationships with job attitudes, turnover intention, turnover, and withdrawal behavior: A meta-analysis. *Journal of Applied Psychology, 92*, 438–454.

21. Tuckey, M. R., Searle, B. J., Boyd, C. M., Winefield, A. H., & Winefield, H. R. (2015). Hindrances are not threats: Advancing the multidimensionality of work stress. *Journal of Occupational Health Psychology, 20*, 131–147.

22. Demerouti, E., Bakker, A. B., Nachreiner, F., & Schaufeli, W. B. (2001). Job demands-resources model of burnout. *Journal of Applied Psychology, 86*, 499–512.

23. Nahrgang, J. D., Morgeson, F. P., & Hofmann, D. A. (2011). Safety at work: A meta-analytic investigation of the link between job demands, job resources, burnout, engagement, and safety outcomes. *Journal of Applied Psychology, 96*, 71–94.

24. Tubré, T.C. & Collins, J.M. (2000). Jackson and Schuler (1985) revisited: A meta-analysis of the relationships between role ambiguity, role conflict, and job performance. *Journal of Management, 26*, 155–169.

25. American Osteopathic Association. (n.d.). *Adult bullying: Survey finds 31% of Americans have been bullied as an adult.* Retrieved November 20, 2021, from https://findado.osteopathic.org/adult-bullying-survey-finds-31-americans-bullied-adult

26. Tetrick, L. E., & Peiró, J. M. (2012). Occupational safety and health. In S. W. J. Kozlowski (Ed.), *The Oxford handbook of organizational psychology* (Vol. 2, pp. 1228–1244). New York: Oxford University Press.

27. Luthans, F., Youssef-Morgan, C. M., & Avolio, B. J. (2015). *Psychological capital and beyond.* New York: Oxford University Press.

28. Avey, J. B., Reichard, R. J., Luthans, F., & Mhatre, K. H. (2011). Meta-analysis of the impact of positive psychological capital on employee attitudes, behaviors, and performance. *Human Resource Development Quarterly, 22*, 127–152.

29. Broad, J. D., & Luthans, F. (2017). Leading and developing health and safety through collective psychological capital. In E. K. Kelloway, K. Nielsen, & J. K. Dimoff (Eds.), *Leading to occupational health and safety: How leadership behaviours impact organizational safety and well-being* (pp. 255–280). Chichester, UK: Wiley-Blackwell.

30. Memili, E., Welsh, D.H.B., & Kaciak, E. (2014). Organizational psychological capital of family franchise firms through the lens of the leader–member exchange theory. *Journal of Leadership & Organizational Studies, 21*, 200–209.

31. Bucher, E., Fieseler, C., & Suphan, A. (2013). The stress potential of social media in the workplace. *Information, Communication & Society, 16*, 1639–1667.

32. Ibid.

33. van Amelsvoort, L. G. P. M., Jansen, N. W. H., Swaen, G. M. H., van den Brandt, P. A., & Kant, I. (2004). Direction of shift rotation among three-shift workers in relation to psychological health and work-family conflict. *Scandinavian Journal of Work, Environment & Health, 30*, 149–156.

34. Karlson, B., Eek, F., Ørbæk, P., & Österberg, K. (2009). Effects on sleep-related problems and self-reported health after a change of shift schedule. *Journal of Occupational Health Psychology, 14*(2), 97–109.

35. Barnes, C. M., & Wagner, D. T. (2009). Changing to daylight saving time cuts into sleep and increases workplace injuries. *Journal of Applied Psychology, 94*, 1305–1317.

36. Smith, C. S., Folkard, S., & Fuller, J. A. (2003). Shiftwork and working hours. In J. C. Quick & L. E. Tetrick (Eds.), *Handbook of organizational health psychology* (pp. 163–184). Washington, DC: APA.

37. International Agency for Research on Cancer. (2007). *Painting, firefighting and shiftwork: IARC monographs on the evaluations of carcinogen risks to humans* (Vol. 98). Retrieved November 20, 2021, from https://publications.iarc.fr/Book-And-Report-Series/Iarc-Monographs-On-The-Identification-Of-Carcinogenic-Hazards-To-Humans/Painting-Firefighting-And-Shiftwork-2010

38. Caruso, C. C., Hitchcock, E. M., Dick, R. B., Russo, J. M., & Schmit, J. M. (2004). *Overtime and extended work shifts: Recent findings on illnesses, injuries, and health behaviors.* Cincinnati, OH: U.S. Department of Health and Human Services, Centers for Disease Control and Prevention, National Institute for Occupational Safety and Health. DHHS (NIOSH) Publication No. 2004–143.

39. Costa, G. (1996). The impact of shift and night work on health. *Applied Ergonomics, 27*, 9–16.

40. Frost, P. J., & Jamal, M. (1979). Shift work, attitudes and reported behaviors: Some association between individual characteristics and hours of work and leisure. *Journal of Applied Psychology, 64*, 77–81.

41. Nishiyama, K., & Johnson, J. V. (1997). Karoshi-death from overwork: Occupational health consequences of the Japanese production management. *International Journal of Health Services, 27*, 625–641. Retrieved November 20, 2021, from http://dx.doi.org/10.2190/1JPC-679V-DYNT-HJ6G

42. International Labour Organization. (2013). *Case study: Karoshi: Death from overwork.* Retrieved November 20, 2021, from https://www.ilo.org/safework/info/publications/WCMS_211571/lang--en/index.htm

43. Pega, F., Náfrádi, B., Momen, N. C., Ujita, Y., Streicher, K. N., Prüss-Üstün, A. M., Descatha, A., Driscoll, T., Fischer, F. M., Godderis, L., Kiiver, H. M., Li, J., Magnusson Hanson, L. L., Rugulies, R., Sørensen, K., & Woodruff, T. J. (2021). Global, regional, and national burdens of ischemic heart disease and stroke attributable to exposure to long working hours for 194 countries, 2000–2016: a systematic analysis from the WHO/ILO Joint Estimates of the Work-related Burden of Disease and Injury. *Environment International, 154*, 106595.

44. Shockley, K. M., & Allen, T. D. (2012). Motives for flexible work arrangement use. *Community, Work & Family, 15*, 217–231.

45. Spreitzer, G. M., Cameron, L., & Garrett, L. (2017). Alternative work arrangements: Two images of the new world of work. *Annual Review of Organizational Psychology and Organizational Behavior, 4*, 473–499.

46. Kossek, F. R., & Michel, J. S. (2011). Flexible work schedules. In S. Zedeck (Ed.), *APA handbook of industrial and organizational psychology* (Vol. 1, pp. 535–572). Washington, DC: APA.

47. Allen, T. D., Golden, T. D., & Shockley, K. M. (2015). How effective is telecommuting? Assessing the status of our scientific findings. *Psychological Science in the Public Interest, 16*, 40–68.

48. Golden, T. D., Veiga, J. F., & Dino, R. N. (2008). The impact of professional isolation on teleworker job performance and turnover intentions: Does time spent teleworking, interacting face-to-face, or having access to communication-enhancing technology matter? *Journal of Applied Psychology, 93*, 1412–1421.

49. Narayanan, V. K., & Nath, R. (1982). Hierarchical level and the impact of flextime. *Industrial Relations, 21*, 216–230.

50. Dalton, D. R., & Mesch, D. J. (1990). The impact of flexible scheduling on employee attendance and turnover. *Administrative Science Quarterly, 35*, 370–387.

51. Allen, T. D., Johnson, R. C., Kiburz, K. M., & Shockley, K. M. (2013). Work-family conflict and flexible work arrangements: Deconstructing flexibility. *Personnel Psychology, 66*, 345–376.

52. Spieler, I., Scheibe, S., Stamov-Roßnagel, C., & Kappas, A. (2017). Help or hindrance? Day-level relationships between flextime use, work–nonwork boundaries, and affective well-being. *Journal of Applied Psychology, 102*(1), 67–87.

53. Baltes, B. B., Briggs, T. E., Huff, J. W., Wright, J. A., & Neuman, G. A. (1999). Flexible and compressed workweek schedules: A meta-analysis of their effects on work-related criteria. *Journal of Applied Psychology, 84*, 496–513.

54. Deery, S. J., Walsh, J., Zatzick, C. D., & Hayes, A. F. (2017). Exploring the relationship between compressed work hours satisfaction and absenteeism in front-line service work. *European Journal of Work and Organizational Psychology, 26*(1), 42–52.

55. Ronen, S., & Primps, S. B. (1981). The compressed work week as organizational change: Behavioral and attitudinal outcomes. *Academy of Management Review, 6*, 61–74.

56. Thompson, B. J., Stock, M. S., & Banuelas, V. K. (2017). Effects of accumulating work shifts on performance-based fatigue using multiple strength measurements in day and night shift nurses and aides. *Human Factors, 59*, 346–356.

57. Pierce, J. L., & Dunham, R. B. (1992). The 12-hour work day: A 48-hour, four-day week. *Academy of Management Journal, 35,* 1086–1098.

58. Duchon, J. C., Keran, C. M., & Smith, T. J. (1994). Extended workdays in an underground mine: A work performance analysis. *Human Factors, 36*, 258–268.

59. Jahoda, M. (1981). Work, employment, and unemployment: Values, theories and approaches in social research. *American Psychologist, 36,* 184–191.

60. Van Hoye, G., & Lootens, H. (2013). Coping with unemployment: Personality, role demands, and time structure. *Journal of Vocational Behavior, 82*, 85–95.

61. Wanberg, C. R. (2012). The individual experience of unemployment. *Annual Review of Psychology, 63*, 369–396.

62. McKee-Ryan, F. M., Song, Z., Wanberg, C. R., & Kinicki, A. J. (2005). Psychological and physical well-being during unemployment: A meta-analytic study. *Journal of Applied Psychology, 90*, 53–76.

63. Paul, K. I., & Moser, K. (2009). Unemployment impairs mental health: Meta-analyses. *Journal of Vocational Behavior, 74*, 264–282.

64. Fryer, D., & Payne, R. (1986). Being unemployed: A review of the literature on the psychological experience of un-employment. In C. L. Cooper & I. Robertson (Eds.), *International review of industrial and organizational psychology* (Vol. 1, pp. 235–278). London: Wiley.

65. Luhmann, M., Weiss, P., Hosoya, G., & Eid, M. (2014). Honey, I got fired! A longitudinal dyadic analysis of the effect of unemployment on life satisfaction in couples. *Journal of Personality and Social Psychology, 107*, 163–180.

66. Gregg, P., & Tominey, E. (2005). The wage scar from male youth unemployment. *Labour Economics, 12*, 487–509.

67. Boyce, C. J., Wood, A. M., Daly, M., & Sedikides, C. (2015). Personality change following unemployment. *Journal of Applied Psychology, 100*, 991–1011.

68. Wanberg, C. R., Zhu, J., Kanfer, R., & Zhang, Z. (2011). After the pink slip: Applying dynamic motivation frameworks to the job search experience. *Academy of Management Journal, 55*, 261–284.

69. Gowan, M. A., Riordan, C. M., & Gatewood, K. D. (1999). Test of a model of coping with involuntary job loss following a company closing. *Journal of Applied Psychology, 84*, 75–86.

70. Wanberg, C. R. (1997). Antecedents and outcomes of coping behaviors among unemployed and re-employed individuals. *Journal of Applied Psychology, 82,* 731–744.

71. Wanberg, C. R., Zhang, Z., & Diehn, E. W. (2010). Development of the Getting Ready for Your Next Job inventory for unemployed individuals. *Personnel Psychology, 63*, 439–478.

72. Greene, C. L. (2001). Human remains and psychological impact on police officers: Excerpts from psychiatric observations. *Australasian Journal of Disaster and Trauma Studies, 5*(2). Retrieved November 20, 2021, from https://www.massey.ac.nz/~trauma/issues/2001-2/greene.htm

73. Horwitz, M. J. (2006). Work-Related Trauma Effects in Child Protection Social Workers. *Journal of Social Service Research, 32*, 1–18.

74. Ogińska-Bulik, N., Gurowiec, P. J., Michalska, P., & Kędra, E. (2021). Prevalence and predictors of secondary traumatic stress symptoms in health care professionals working with trauma victims: A cross-sectional study. *PloS one,16*(2), e0247596.

75. Bride, B. E. (2007). Prevalence of secondary traumatic stress among social workers. *Social Work, 52*, 63–70.

76. Cieslak, R., Anderson, V., Bock, J., Moore, B. A., Peterson, A. L., & Benight, C. C. (2013). Secondary traumatic stress among mental health providers working with the military: prevalence and its work- and exposure-related correlates. *The Journal of Nervous and Mental Disease, 201*(11), 917–925.

77. Hawkins, H.C. (2001). Police officer burnout: A partial replication of Maslach's burnout inventory. *Police Quarterly, 4*(3), 343–360.

78. Lobel, J. A. (1997). *The vicarious effects of treating female rape survivors: The therapist's perspective* [Doctoral dissertation, University of Pennsylvania]. Penn Libraries, University of Pennsylvania, Scholarly Commons. Retrieved November 20, 2021, from https://repository.upenn.edu/dissertations/AAI9712968/

79. Payne, S. C., Thompson, R. J., & Greer, T. W. (2021). A call for I-O psychologists to contribute to business continuity planning and assessment. *Industrial and Organizational Psychology, 14*, 229–234.

80. Tedeschi, R. G., & Calhoun, L. G. (2004). Posttraumatic growth: Conceptual foundations and empirical evidence. *Psychological Inquiry, 15*, 1–18.

81. Wu, X., Kaminga, A. C., Dai, W., Deng, J., Wang, Z., Pan, X., & Liu, A. (2019). The prevalence of moderate-to-high posttraumatic growth: A systematic review and meta-analysis. *Journal of Affective Disorders, 243*, 408–415.

82. Bowling, N. A., & Schumm, J. A. (2021). The COVID-19 pandemic: A source of posttraumatic growth? *Industrial and Organizational Psychology, 14*, 184–188.

83. Marks, M. L. (2002). Mergers and acquisitions. In J. W. Hedge & E. D. Pulakos (Eds.), *Implementing organizational interventions: Steps, processes, and best practices* (pp. 43–77). San Francisco: Jossey-Bass.

84. Lovecraft, H. P. (1939). Supernatural Horror in Literature. *The Recluse*, Introduction. (Original work published in 1927).

85. Howes, S. S., Howes, J. C., & Huffcutt, A. I. (2021). Ch-ch-ch-changes, and I-O psychology's role in managing them. *Industrial and Organizational Psychology, 14*, 156–159.

86. Peng, J., Li, M., Wang, Z., & Lin, Y. (2021). Transformational leadership and employees' reactions to organizational change: Evidence from a meta-analysis. *The Journal of Applied Behavioral Science, 57*(3), 369–397.

87. Hofmann, D. A., & Tetrick, L. E. (2003). The etiology of the concept of health: Implications for "organizing" individuals and organizational health. In D. A. Hofmann & L. E. Tetrick (Eds.), *Health and safety in organizations* (pp. 1–26). San Francisco: Jossey-Bass.

88. Cleveland, J. N., & Colella, A. (2010). Criterion validity and criterion deficiency: What we measure well and what we ignore. In J. L. Farr & N. T. Tippins (Eds.), *Handbook of employee selection* (pp. 551–567). New York: Routledge.

89. Holman, D., & Axtell, C. (2016). Can job redesign interventions influence a broad range of employee outcomes by changing multiple job characteristics? A quasi-experimental study. *Journal of Occupational Health Psychology, 21*, 284–295.

90. Barber, L. K., & Santuzzi, A. M. (2015). Please respond ASAP: Workplace telepressure and employee recovery. *Journal of Occupational Health Psychology, 20*, 172–189.

91. Richardson, K. M. (2017). Managing employee stress and wellness in the new millennium. *Journal of Occupational Health Psychology, 22*, 423–428.

92. Anger, W. K., Elliot, D. L., Bodner, T., Olson, R., Rohlman, D. S., Truxillo, D. M., Kuehl, K. S., Hammer, L. B., & Montgomery, D. (2015). Effectiveness of total worker health interventions. *Journal of Occupational Health Psychology, 20*, 226–247.

93. Richardson, K. M., & Rothstein, H. R. (2008). Effects of occupational stress management intervention programs: A meta-analysis. *Journal of Occupational Health Psychology, 13*, 69–93.

94. Claxton, G., Rae, M., Panchal, N., Whitmore, H., Damico, A., Kenward, K., & Long, M. (2015). Health benefits in 2015: Stable trends in the employer market. *Health Affairs, 34*, 1779–1788.

95. Parks, K. M., & Steelman, L. A. (2008). Organizational wellness programs: A meta-analysis. *Journal of Occupational Health Psychology, 13*, 58–68.

96. Caloyeras, J. P., Liu, H., Exum, E., Broderick, M., & Mattke, S. (2014). Managing manifest diseases, but not health risks, saved PepsiCo money over seven years. *Health Affairs, 33*, 124–131.

97. Erickson, E. H. (1963). *Childhood and society* (2nd ed.). New York: Norton.

98. Quick, J. C., Murphy, L. R., Hurrell, J. J., & Orman, D. (1992). The value of work in the risk of distress and the power of prevention. In J. C. Quick, L. R. Murphy, & J. J. Hurrell (Eds.), *Stress and well-being at work* (pp. 3–13). Washington, DC: APA.

99. Wayne, J. H., Butts, M. M., Caper, W. J., & Allen, T. D. (2017). In search of balance: A conceptual and empirical integration of multiple meanings of work-family balance. *Personnel Psychology, 70*, 167–210

100. Allen, T. D. (2013). The work-family role interface: A synthesis of the research from industrial and organizational psychology. In N. Schmitt, & S. Highhouse (Eds.), *Handbook of psychology: Industrial and organizational psychology* (Vol. 12, pp. 698–718). New York: John Wiley & Sons.

101. Allen, T. D., & Armstrong, J. (2006). Further examination of the link between work-family conflict and physical health: The role of health-related behaviors. *American Behavioral Scientist, 49*, 1204–1221; and Wang, M., Liu, S., Zhan, Y., & Shi, J. (2010). Daily work-family conflict and alcohol use: Testing the cross-level moderation effects of peer drinking norms and social support. *Journal of Applied Psychology, 95*, 377–386.

102. Frone, M. R. (2000). Work-family conflict and employee psychiatric disorders: The national comorbidity survey. *Journal of Applied Psychology, 85*, 888–895.

103. Nohe, C., Meier, L. L., Sonntag, K., & Michel, A. (2015). The chicken or the egg? A meta-analysis of panel studies of the relationship between work-family conflict and strain. *Journal of Applied Psychology, 100*, 522–536.

104. Amstad, F. T., Meier, L. L., Fasel, U., Elfering, A., & Semmer, N. K. (2011). A meta-analysis of work-family conflict and various outcomes with a special emphasis on cross-domain versus matching-domain relations. *Journal of Occupational Health Psychology, 16*, 151–169.

105. Ibid.; and Baltes, B. B., & Heydens-Gahir, H. A. (2003). Reduction of work-family conflict through the use of selection, optimization, and compensation behaviors. *Journal of Applied Psychology, 88*, 1005–1018.

106. Li, A., Cropanzano, R., Butler, A., Shao, P., & Westman, M. (2021). Work–family crossover: A meta-analytic review. *International Journal of Stress Management, 28*(2), 89–104.

107. Wang, P., Wang, Z., & Luo, Z. (2020). From supervisors' work–family conflict to employees' work–family conflict: The moderating role of employees' organizational tenure. *International Journal of Stress Management, 27*(3), 273–280.

108. Byron, K. (2005). A meta-analytic review of work-family conflict and its antecedents. *Journal of Vocational Behavior, 62*, 169–198.

109. Livingston, B. A., & Judge, T. A. (2008). Emotional responses to work-family conflict: An examination of gender role orientation among working women. *Journal of Applied Psychology, 93*, 207–216.

110. Matthews, R. A., Wayne, J. H., & Ford, M. T. (2014). A work-family conflict/subjective well-being process model: A test of competing theories of longitudinal effects. *Journal of Applied Psychology, 99*, 1173–1187.

111. Casper, W. J., Eby, L. T., Bordeaux, C., Lockwood, A., & Lambert, D. (2007). A review of research methods in IO/OB work-family research. *Journal of Applied Psychology, 92*, 28–41.

112. Dierdorff, E. C., & Ellington, J. K. (2008). It's the nature of work: Examining behavior-based sources of work-family conflict across occupations. *Journal of Applied Psychology, 93*, 883–892.

113. Allen, T. D., French, K. A., Dumani, S., & Shockley, K. M. (2020). A cross-national meta-analytic examination of predictors and outcomes associated with work–family conflict. *Journal of Applied Psychology, 105*(6), 539–576.

114. Morganson, V. J., Culbertson, S. S., & Matthews, R. A. (2013). Individual strategies for navigating the work-life interface. In D. Major & R. Burke (Eds.), *Handbook of work-life integration among professionals: Challenges and opportunities* (pp. 205–224). Cheltenham, UK: Edward Elgar.

115. Crain, T. L., & Hammer, L. B. (2013). Work-family enrichment: A systematic review of antecedents, outcomes, and mechanisms. In A. B. Bakker (Ed.), *Advances in positive organizational psychology*, (Vol. 1, pp. 303–328). Bingley, UK: Emerald.

116. Greenhaus, J. H., & Powell, G. N. (2006). When work and family are allies: A theory of work-family enrichment. *Academy of Management Review, 31*, 72–92.

117. Pickles, M. (2017, May 10). 'Mesearch'—when study really is all about me. *BBC.com*. Retrieved from http://www.bbc.com/news/business-39856894.

118. Crain, T. L., & Hammer, L. B. (2013)—see #115.

119. Michel, J. S., Clark, M. A., & Jaramillo, D. (2011). The role of the Five Factor model of personality in the perceptions of negative and positive forms of work-nonwork spillover: A meta-analytic review. *Journal of Vocational Behavior, 79*, 191–203.

120. Voydanoff, P. (2005). Social integration, work-family conflict and facilitation, and job and marital quality. *Journal of Marriage and Family, 67*, 666–679.

121. Crain, T. L., & Hammer, L. B. (2013)—see #115.

122. McNall, L. A., Nicklin, J. M., & Masuda, A. D. (2010). A meta-analytic review of the consequences associated with work-family enrichment. *Journal of Business and Psychology, 25*, 381–396.

123. Ilies, R., Keeney, J., & Scott, B. A. (2011). Work-family interpersonal capitalization: Sharing positive work events at home. *Organizational Behavior and Human Decision Processes, 114*, 115–126.

124. Culbertson, S. S., Mills, M. J., & Fullagar, C. J. (2012). Work engagement and work-family facilitation: Making homes happier through positive affective spillover. *Human Relations, 65*, 1155–1177.

125. Ilies, R., Keeney, J., & Goh, Z. W. (2015). Capitalising on positive work events by sharing them at home. *Applied Psychology, 64*, 578–598.

126. Hornung, S., Rousseau, D. M., & Glaser, J. (2008). Creating flexible work arrangements through idiosyncratic deals. *Journal of Applied Psychology, 93*, 655–664.

127. Morganson, V. J., Culbertson, S. S., & Matthews, R. A. (2013)—see #114.

128. Ashforth, B. E., Kreiner, G. E., & Fugate, M. (2000). All in a day's work: Boundaries and micro role transitions. *Academy of Management Review, 25*, 472–491.

129. Yang, J., Zhang, Y., Shen, C., Liu, S., & Zhang, S. (2019). Work-family segmentation preferences and work-family conflict: Mediating effect of work-related ICT use at home and the multilevel moderating effect of group segmentation norms. *Frontiers in Psychology, 10*, Article 834.

130. Hunter, E. M., Clark, M. A., & Carlson, D. S. (2019). Violating work-family boundaries: Reactions to interruptions at work and home. *Journal of Management, 45*, 1284–1308.

131. Shockley, K. M., & Allen, T. D. (2013). Episodic work-family conflict, cardiovascular indicators, and social support: An experience sampling approach. *Journal of Occupational Health Psychology, 18*, 262–275.

132. Frone, M. R. (2003). Work-family balance. In J. C. Quick & L. E. Tetrick (Eds.), *Handbook of organizational health psychology* (pp. 143–162). Washington, DC: APA.

133. Hipp, L., Morrissey, T. W., & Warner, M. E. (2017). Who participates and who benefits from employer-provided child-care assistance? *Journal of Marriage and Family, 79*, 614–635.

134. Hammer, L. B., Van Dyck, S. E., & Ellis, A. M. (2013). Organizational policies supportive of work-life integration. In D. Major & R. Burke (Eds.), *Handbook of work-life integration among professionals: Challenges and opportunities* (pp. 288–309). Cheltenham, UK: Edward Elgar.

135. Heskiau, R., & McCarthy, J. M. (2021). A work-famiy enrichment intervention: Transferring resources across life domains. *Journal of Applied Psychology, 106*(10), 1573–1585.

136. Spector, P. E., Allen, T. D., Poelmans, S. A., Lapierre, L. M., Cooper, C. L., O'Driscoll, M., Sanchez, J. I., Abarca, N., Alexandrova, M., Beham, B., Brough, P., Ferreiro, P., Fraile, G., Lu, C. Q., Lu, L., Moreno-Velazquez, I., Pagon, M., Pitariu, H., Salamatov, V., Shima, S., Simoni, A. S., Siu, O. L., & Widerszal-Bazyl, M. (2007). Cross-national differences in relationships of work demands, job satisfaction, and turnover intentions with work-family conflict. *Personnel Psychology, 60*, 805–835.

137. Ashforth, B. E., & Kreiner, G. E. (1999). How do you do it? Dirty work and the challenge of constructing a positive identity. *Academy of Management Review, 24*, 413–434.

138. Ashforth, B. E., Kreiner, G. E., Clark, M. A., & Fugate, M. (2007). Normalizing dirty work: Managerial tactics for countering occupational taint. *Academy of Management Journal, 50*, 149–174.

139. Rivera, K. D. (2015). Emotional taint: Making sense of emotional dirty work at the U.S. Border Patrol. *Management Communication Quarterly, 29*(2), 198–228.

140. Bergman, M. E., & Chalkley, K. M. (2007). "Ex" marks a spot: The stickiness of dirty work and other removed stigmas. *Journal of Occupational Health Psychology, 12*, 251–265.

141. Kreiner, G. E., Ashforth, B. E., & Sluss, D. M. (2006). Identity dynamics in occupational dirty work: Integrating social identity and system justification perspectives. *Organization Science, 17*, 619–636.

142. Bergman, M. E., & Chalkley, K. M. (2007) — see #140.

143. Baran, B. E., Rogelberg, S. G., Lopina, E. C., Allen, J. A., Spitzmüller, C., & Bergman, M. E. (2012). Shouldering a silent burden: The toll of dirty tasks. *Human Relations, 65*, 597–626.

144. Lopina, E. C., Rogelberg, S. G., & Howell, B. (2012). Turnover in dirty work occupations: A focus on pre-entry individual characteristics. *Journal of Occupational and Organizational Psychology, 85*, 396–406.

145. Baran, B. E., Rogelberg, S. G., Lopina, E. C., Allen, J. A., Spitzmüller, C., & Bergman, M. E. (2012) — see #143.

146. Blithe, S. J., & Wolfe, A. W. (2017). Work-life management in legal prostitution: Stigma lockdown in Nevada's brothels. *Human Relations, 70*, 725–750.

147. Bosmans, K., Mousaid, S., De Cuyper, N., Hardonk, S., Louckx, F., & Vanroelen, C. (2016). Dirty work, dirty worker? Stigmatisation and coping strategies among domestic workers. *Journal of Vocational Behavior, 92*, 54– 67.

148. Ashforth, B. E., Kreiner, G. E., Clark, M. A., & Fugate, M. (2017). Congruence work in stigmatized occupations: A managerial lens on employee fit with dirty work. *Journal of Organizational Behavior, 38*, 1260–1279.

149. Adams, J. (2012). Cleaning up the dirty work: Professionalization and the management of stigma in the cosmetic surgery and tattoo industries. *Deviant Behavior, 33*, 149–167.

150. Burgess, M., & Clark, L. (2010). Do the "savage origins" of tattoos cast a prejudicial shadow on contemporary tattooed individuals? *Journal of Applied Social Psychology, 40*, 746–764.

151. Gerum, D. R. (2021). Tainted heroes: The emergence of dirty work during pandemics. *Industrial and Organizational Psychology, 14*, 41–44.

152. Moore, D. A. (1994). Company alcohol policies: Practicalities and problems. In C. L. Cooper & S. Williams (Eds.), *Creating healthy work organizations* (pp. 75–96). Chichester, England: Wiley.

153. Place, A. (2021, September 16). As addiction rates soar, employers can offer a lifeline. *Employee Benefit News*. Retrieved November 21, 2021, from https://www.benefitnews.com/news/how-to-help-employees-with-addiction?sf151995484=1

154. Galbicsek, C. (2021, October 14). Alcoholism among professionals. *Alcohol Rehab Guide*. Retrieved November 21, 2021, from https://www.alcoholrehabguide.org/resources/alcoholism-workplace/

155. American Addiction Centers. (n.d.). Drinking when working from home. *Alcohol.org*. Retrieved November 21, 2021, from https://www.alcohol.org/guides/work-from-home-drinking/

156. Frone, M. R. (2013). *Alcohol and illicit drug use in the work force and workplace*. Washington, DC: APA.

157. Ibid.

158. Galaif, E. R., Newcomb, M. D., & Carmona, J. V. (2001). Prospective relationships between drug problems and work adjustment in a community sample of adults. *Journal of Applied Psychology, 86*, 337–350.

159. Van Hasselt, M., Keyes, V., Bray, J., & Miller, T. (2015). Prescription drug abuse and workplace absenteeism: Evidence from the 2008–2012 National Survey on Drug Use and Health. *Journal of Workplace Behavioral Health, 30*, 379–392.

160. Pidd, K., Kostadinov, V., & Roche, A. (2016). Do workplace policies work? An examination of the relationship between alcohol and other drug policies and workers' substance use. *International Journal of Drug Policy, 28*, 48–54.

161. Bacharach, S. B., Bamberger, P. A., & Sonnenstuhl, W. J. (2002). Driven to drink: Managerial control, work-related risk factors, and employee problem drinking. *Academy of Management Journal, 45,* 637–658.

162. Frone, M. R. (2008). Employee substance use? The importance of temporal context in assessments of alcohol and illicit drug use. *Journal of Applied Psychology, 93,* 199–206.

163. Bennett, N., Blum, T. C., & Roman, P. M. (1994). Pressure of drug screening and employee assistance programs: Exclusive and inclusive human resource management practices. *Journal of Organizational Behavior, 15,* 549–560.

164. Frone, M. R. (2013)—see #156.

165. Bennett, N., Blum, T. C., & Roman, P. M. (1994)—see #163.

Chapter 13

1. Hajcak, G. (2012). What we've learned from mistakes: In sights from error-related brain activity. *Current Directions in Psychological Science, 21,* 101–106.

2. Hajcak, G., McDonald, N., & Simons, R. (2004). Error-related psychophysiology and negative affect. *Brain and Cognition, 56,* 189–197.

3. Volkow, N. D., Wise, R. A., & Baler, R. (2017). The dopamine motive system: implications for drug and food addiction. *Nature Reviews Neuroscience, 18*(12), 741–752.

4. Chong, T. T., & Husain, M. (2016). The role of dopamine in the pathophysiology and treatment of apathy. *Progress in brain research, 229,* 389–426.

5. Ridley, M. (1999). *Genome: The autobiography of a species in 23 chapters.* New York: Harper Collins.

6. Ilies, R., Arvey, R. D., & Bouchard, T. J. (2006). Darwinism, behavioral genetics, and organizational behavior: A review and agenda for future research. *Journal of Organizational Behavior, 27,* 121–141.

7. Digman, J. M., & Takemoto-Chock, N. K. (1981). Factors in the natural language of personality: Re-analysis and comparison of six major studies. *Multivariate Behavioral Research, 16,* 149–170.

8. Egan, M., Daly, M., Delaney, L., Boyce, C. J., & Wood, A. M. (2017). Adolescent conscientiousness predicts lower lifetime unemployment. *Journal of Applied Psychology, 102,* 700–709.

9. The Genetic Information Nondiscrimination Act of 2008 (GINA), 42 U.S.C. § 2000ff. (2008). Retrieved October 29, 2021, from https://www.dol.gov/agencies/oasam/centers-offices/civil-rights-center/statutes/genetic-information-nondiscrimination-act-of-2008/guidance

10. Pal, R., Singh, S. N., Chatterjee, A., & Saha, M. (2014). Age-related changes in cardiovascular system, autonomic functions, and levels of BDNF of healthy active males: role of yogic practice. *Age (Dordrecht, Netherlands), 36*(4), 9683.

11. Kjaer, T. W., Bertelsen, C., Piccini, P., Brooks, D., Alving, J., & Lou, H. C. (2002). Increased dopamine tone during meditation-induced change of consciousness. *Cognitive Brain Research, 13*(2), 255–259.

12. Tsai, H. Y., Chen, K. C., Yang, Y. K., Chen, P. S., Yeh, T. L., Chiu, N. T., & Lee, I. H. (2011). Sunshine-exposure variation of human striatal dopamine D(2)/D(3) receptor availability in healthy volunteers. *Progress in neuro-psychopharmacology & biological psychiatry, 35*(1), 107–110.

13. Korshunov, K. S., Blakemore, L. J., & Trombley, P. Q. (2017). Dopamine: A modulator of circadian rhythms in the central nervous system. *Frontiers in cellular neuroscience, 11,* 91; and Volkow, N. D., Tomasi, D., Wang, G. J., Telang, F., Fowler, J. S., Logan, J., Benveniste, H., Kim, R., Thanos, P. K., & Ferré, S. (2012). Evidence that sleep deprivation downregulates dopamine D2R in ventral striatum in the human brain. *The Journal of Neuroscience, 32*(19), 6711–6717.

14. Salimpoor, V. N., Benovoy, M., Larcher, K., Dagher, A., & Zatorre, R. J. (2011). Anatomically distinct dopamine release during anticipation and experience of peak emotion to music. *Nature neuroscience, 14* (2), 257–262; and Ferreri, L., Mas-Herrero, E., Zatorre, R. J., Ripollés, P., Gomez-Andres, A., Alicart, H., Olivé, G., Marco-Pallarés, J., Antonijoan, R. M., Valle, M., Riba, J., & Rodriguez-Fornells, A. (2019). Dopamine modulates the reward experiences elicited by music. *Proceedings of the National Academy of Sciences, 116*(9) 3793–3798.

15. Hilton, L. G., Marshall, N. J., Motala, A., Taylor, S. L., Miake-Lye, I. M., Baxi, S., Shanman, R. M., Solloway, M. R., Beroesand, J. M., & Hempel, S. (2019). Mindfulness meditation for workplace wellness: An evidence map. *Work (Reading, Mass.), 63*(2), 205–218; and Figueiro, M. G., Steverson, B., Heerwagen, J., Kampschroer, K., Hunter, C. M., Gonzales, K., Plitnick, B., & Rea, M. S. (2017). The impact of daytime light exposures on sleep and mood in office workers, *Sleep Health, 3*, 204–215.
16. Keeler, K., & Cortina, J. M. (2020, April 21). Working to the beat: A self-regulatory framework linking music characteristics to job performance. *Academy of Management, 45*(2); and Hafner, M., Stepanek, M., Taylor, J., Troxel, W. M., & van Stolk, C. (2017). Why sleep matters - the economic costs of insufficient sleep: A cross-country comparative analysis. *Rand Health Quarterly, 6*(4), 11.
17. Tay, L., & Diener, E. (2011). Needs and subjective well-being around the world. *Journal of Personality and Social Psychology, 101*, 354 –365.
18. Conley, C. (2007). *Peak: How great companies get their mojo from Maslow*. New York: John Wiley & Sons.
19. Maslow, A. H. (1943). A theory of human motivation. *Psychological Review, 50*, 370-396.
20. Herzberg, F. (1968). One More Time: How Do You Motivate Employees? *Harvard Business Review, 46*(1): 53–62.
21. Rynes, S. L., Gerhart, B., & Parks, L. (2005). Personnel psychology: Performance evaluation and pay for performance. *Annual Review of Psychology, 56*, 571–600.
22. Mickel, A. E., & Barron, L. A. (2008). Getting 'more bang for the buck': Symbolic value of monetary rewards in organizations. *Journal of Management Inquiry, 17*, 329–338.
23. Csikszentmihalyi, M. (1990). *Flow: The psychology of optimal experience*. New York: Harper and Row.
24. Nakamura, J., & Csikszentmihalyi, M. (2009). Flow theory and research. In S. J. Lopez & C. R. Snyder (Eds.), *The Oxford handbook of positive psychology* (2nd ed., pp. 195– 206). New York: Oxford University Press.
25. Mosing, M. A., Magnusson, P. K. E., Pedersen, N. L., Nakamura, J., Madison, G., & Ullén, F. (2012). Heritability of proneness for psychological flow experiences. *Personality and Individual Differences, 53*, 699–704.
26. Ullén, F., de Manzano, Ö., Almeida, R., Magnusson, P. K. E., Pedersen, N. L., Nakamura, J., Csikszentmihalyi, M., & Madison, G. (2012). Proneness for psychological flow in everyday life: Associations with personality and intelligence. *Personality and Individual Differences, 52*, 167–172.
27. Salanova, M., Bakker, A. B., & Llorens, S. (2006). Flow at work: Evidence for an upward spiral of personal and organizational resources. *Journal of Happiness Studies, 7*, 1–22.
28. Kuo, T. H., & Ho, L. A. (2010). Individual difference and job performance: The relationships among personal factors, job characteristics, flow experience, and service quality. *Social Behavior and Personality, 38*, 531–552.
29. Fullagar, C. J., Knight, P. A., & Sovern, H. S. (2013). Challenge/skill balance, flow, and performance anxiety. *Applied Psychology: An International Review, 62*, 236–259.
30. Demerouti, E. (2006). Job characteristics, flow, and performance: The moderating role of conscientiousness. *Journal of Occupational Health Psychology, 11*, 266–280.
31. Demerouti, E., Bakker, A. B., Sonnentag, S., & Fullagar, C. J. (2012). Work-related flow and energy at work and at home: A study on the role of daily recovery. *Journal of Organizational Behavior, 33*, 276–295.
32. Ryan, R. M., & Deci, E. L. (2000). Self-determination theory and the facilitation of intrinsic motivation, social development, and well-being. *American Psychologist, 55*, 68–78.
33. Ibid.
34. Grant, A. M. (2008). Does intrinsic motivation fuel the prosocial fire? Motivational synergy in predicting persistence, performance, and productivity. *Journal of Applied Psychology, 93*, 48–58.
35. Cerasoli, C. P., Nicklin, J. M., & Ford, M. T. (2014). Intrinsic motivation and extrinsic incentives jointly predict performance: A 40-year meta-analysis. *Psychological Bulletin, 140*, 980–1008.
36. Deci, E. L., Olafsen, A. H., & Ryan, R. M. (2017). Self-determination theory in work organizations: The state of a science. *Annual Review of Organizational Psychology and Organizational Behavior, 4*, 19-43.

37. Forner, V. W., Jones, M., Berry, Y., & Eidenfalk, J. (2020). Motivating workers: How leaders apply self-determination theory in organizations. *Organization Management Journal, 18*, 76–94.

38. Adams, J. S. (1963). Toward an understanding of inequity. *Journal of Abnormal and Social Psychology, 67*, 422–436; and Adams, J. S. (1965). Inequity in social exchange. In L. Berkowitz (Ed.), *Advances in experimental social psychology* (Vol. 2, pp. 267–299). New York: Academic Press.

39. Folger, R. (1986). Rethinking equity theory: A referent cognitions model. In H. W. Bierhoff, R. L. Cohen, & J. Greenberg (Eds.), *Justice in social relations* (pp. 145– 162). New York: Plenum Press.

40. Huseman, R. C., Hatfield, J. D., & Miles, E. W. (1987). A new perspective on equity theory: The equity sensitivity construct. *Academy of Management Review, 12*, 222–234; and King, W. C., Miles, E. W., & Day, D. D. (1993). A test and refinement of the equity sensitivity construct. *Journal of Organizational Behavior, 14*, 301–317.

41. Miller, B. K. (2015). Entitlement and conscientiousness in the prediction of organizational deviance. *Personality and Individual Differences, 82*, 114–119.

42. Harvey, P., & Harris, K. J. (2010). Frustration-based outcomes of entitlement and the influence of supervisor communication. *Human Relations, 63*, 1639–1660.

43. Blakely, G. L., Andrews, M. C., & Moorman, R. H. (2005). The moderating effects of equity sensitivity on the relationship between organizational justice and organizational citizenship behaviors. *Journal of Business and Psychology, 20*, 259–273.

44. Beaton, C. (2016). Millennials are entitled but are punished for being anything else. *Forbes.* Retrieved September 19, 2021, from https://www.forbes.com/sites/carolinebeaton/2016/09/30/millennials-are-entitled-but-punished-for-being-anything-else/?sh=1a92529d4680

45. Vroom, V. H. (1964). *Work and motivation.* New York: Wiley.

46. Rodriguez, B. (2018, December 28). Wells Fargo agrees to $575 million settlement affecting all 50 states in wake of fake accounts. *The Des Moines Register.* Retrieved September 20, 2021, from https://www.usatoday.com/story/money/business/2018/12/28/wells-fargo-fake-accounts-settlement/2432088002/

47. Ogbonnaya, C., Daniels, K., & Nielsen, K. (2017). Does contingent pay encourage positive employee attitudes and intensify work? *Human Resource Management Journal, 27*(1), 94–112.

48. Mayer, K. (2021, June 14). A $30K raise or remote work forever? Employees want remote. *Human Resources Executive.* Retrieved September 20, 2021, from https://hrexecutive.com/a-30k-raise-or-remote-work-forever-employees-want-remote/?eml=20210615&oly_enc_id=2359B6906323G4W

49. Locke, E. A., & Latham, G. P. (2002). Building a practically useful theory of goal setting and task motivation: A 35-year odyssey. *American Psychologist, 57*, 705–717.

50. Ibid.; and Mitchell, T. R. (1997). Matching motivational strategies with organizational contexts. In B. M. Staw & L. L. Cummings (Eds.), *Research in organizational behavior* (Vol. 19, pp. 57–149). Greenwich, CT: JAI Press.

51. Locke, E. A., & Latham, G. P. (1990). *A theory of goal setting and task performance.* Englewood Cliffs, NJ: Prentice Hall.

52. Bandura, A. (1977). Self-efficacy: Toward a unifying theory of behavioral change. *Psychological Review, 84* (2): 191–215.

53. Bandura A. (1997). *Self-efficacy: The exercise of control.* New York: W. H. Freeman and Company.

54. Schmidt, A. M., Beck, J. W., & Gillespie, J. Z. (2013). Motivation. In N. Schmitt, & S. Highhouse (Eds.), *Handbook of psychology: Industrial and organizational psychology* (Vol. 12, pp. 311–340). New York: John Wiley & Sons.

55. Payne, S. C., & Pariyothorn, M. M. (2007). I-O psychology in introductory psychology textbooks: A survey of authors. *The Industrial-Organizational Psychologist, 44*(4), 37–42.

56. Locke, E. A., & Latham, G. P. (2002)—see #49.

57. Beck, J. W., Scholer, A. A., & Hughes, J. (2017). Divergent effects of distance versus velocity disturbances on emotional experiences during goal pursuit. *Journal of Applied Psychology, 102*, 1109–1123.

58. Locke, E. A., & Latham, G. P. (2002)—see #49.

59. Kanfer, R., Frese, M., & Johnson, R. E. (2017). Motivation related to work: A century of progress. *Journal of Applied Psychology, 102*, 338–355.

60. Ilies, R., & Judge, T. A. (2005). Goal regulation across time: The effects of feedback and affect. *Journal of Applied Psychology, 90*, 453–467.

61. Pritchard, R. D., Jones, S. D., Roth, P. L., Stuebing, K. K., & Ekeberg, S. E. (1988). Effects of group feedback, goal setting, and incentives on organizational productivity. *Journal of Applied Psychology, 73*, 337–358.

62. Locke, E. A., & Latham, G. P. (2002)—see #49.

63. Ordóñez, L. D., Schweitzer, M. E., Galinsky, A. D., & Bazerman, M. H. (2009). Goals gone wild: The systematic side effects of overprescribing goal setting. *Academy of Management Perspectives, 23*, 6–16.

64. Van Mierlo, H., & Kleingeld, A. (2010). Goals, strategies, and group performance: Some limits of goal setting in groups. *Small Group Research, 41*, 524–555.

65. Schweitzer, M. E., Ordóñez, L. D., & Douma, B. (2004). The dark side of goal setting: The role of goals in motivating unethical behavior. *Academy of Management Journal, 47*, 422–432.

66. Hackman, J. R., & Oldham, G. R. (1976). Motivation through the design of work: Test of a theory. *Organizational Behavior and Human Performance, 16*, 250–279.

67. Ibid.

68. Grant, A. M., Fried, Y., & Juillerat, T. (2011). Work matters: Job design in classic and contemporary perspectives. In S. Zedeck (Ed.), *APA handbook of industrial and organizational psychology* (Vol. 1, pp. 417–454). Washington, DC: APA.

69. Bond, F. W., Flaxman, P. E., & Bunce, D. (2008). The influence of psychological flexibility on work redesign: Mediated moderation of a work reorganization intervention. *Journal of Applied Psychology, 93*, 645–654.

70. Grant, A. M., Fried, Y., & Juillerat, T. (2011)—see #68.

71. Humphrey, S. E., Nahrgang, J. D., & Morgeson, F. P. (2007). Integrating motivational, social, and contextual work design features: A meta-analytic summary of theoretical extensions of the work design literature. *Journal of Applied Psychology, 92*, 1332–1356.

72. Morgeson, F. P., & Humphrey, S. E. (2006). The work design questionnaire (WDQ): Developing and validating a comprehensive measure for assessing job design and the nature of work. *Journal of Applied Psychology, 91*, 1321–1339.

73. Campion, M. A., & Berger, C. J. (1990). Conceptual integration and empirical test of job design and compensation relationships. *Personnel Psychology, 43*, 525–554.

74. Mitchell, T. R. (1997)—see #50.

75. Muchinsky, P. M. (2005). Dear I-O. *The Industrial-Organizational Psychologist, 43*(1), 168–172.

76. Kanfer, R. (1992). Work motivation: New directions in theory and research. In C. L. Cooper & I. T. Robertson (Eds.), *International review of industrial and organizational psychology* (Vol. 7, pp. 1–53). London: Wiley.

77. Schmidt, A. M., Beck, J. W., & Gillespie, J. Z. (2013)—see #54.

78. Amabile, T., Hadley, C. N., & Kramer, S. J. (2002). Creativity under the gun. *Harvard Business Review, 80*, 52–61.

79. Soman, D., & Cheema, A. (2004). When goals are counterproductive: The effects of violation of a behavioral goal on subsequent performance. *Journal of Consumer Research, 31*, 52–62.

80. Van Mierlo, H., & Kleingeld, A. (2010)—see #64.

81. Steel, P. (2007). The nature of procrastination: A meta-analytic and theoretical review of quintessential self-regulatory failure. *Psychological Bulletin, 133*, 65–94.

82. Ibid., p. 65.

83. Steel, P., & König, C. J. (2006). Integrating theories of motivation. *Academy of Management Review, 31*, 889–913.

84. van Eerde, W. (2003). A meta-analytically derived nomological network of procrastination. *Personality and Individual Differences, 35*, 1410–1418.

85. DeArmond, S., Matthews, R. A., & Bunk, J. (2014). Workload and procrastination: The roles of psychological detachment and fatigue. *International Journal of Stress Management, 21*, 137–161.

86. Nguyen, B., Steel, P., & Ferrari, J. R. (2013). Procrastination's impact in the workplace and the workplace's impact on procrastination. *International Journal of Selection and Assessment, 21*, 388–399.

87. Jones, K. (2012, November 1). How social media is destroying productivity (Infographic). *Business2Community.com*. Retrieved December 13, 2021, from https://www.business2community.com/infographics/how-social-media-is-destroying-productivity-infographic-0321503

88. Wagner, D. T., Barnes, C. M., Lim, V. K. G., & Ferris, D. L. (2012). Lost sleep and cyberloafing: Evidence from the laboratory and a Daylight Saving Time quasi-experiment. *Journal of Applied Psychology, 97*, 1068–1076.

89. Ugrin, J. C., & Pearson, J. M. (2013). The effects of sanctions and stigmas on cyberloafing. *Computers in Human Behavior, 29*, 812–820.

90. Wilcox, K., Laran, J., Stephen, A. T., & Zubcsek, P. P. (2016). How being busy can increase motivation and reduce task completion time. *Journal of Personality and Social Psychology, 110*, 371–384.

91. Buehler, R., Peetz, J., & Griffin, D. (2010). Finishing on time: When do predictions influence completion times? *Organizational Behavior and Human Decision Processes, 111*, 23–32.

92. Kruger, J., & Evans, M. (2004). If you don't want to be late, enumerate: Unpacking reduces the planning fallacy. *Journal of Experimental Social Psychology, 40*, 586–598.

93. Buehler, R., Griffin, D., Lam, K. C. H., & Deslauriers, J. (2012). Perspective on prediction: Does third-person imagery improve task completion estimates? *Organizational Behavior and Human Decision Processes, 117*, 138–149.

94. Schulte, B. (2015). Work interruptions can cost you 6 hours a day. An efficiency expert explains how to avoid them. *The Washington Post*. Retrieved September 20, 2021, from http://www.washingtonpost.com/news/inspired-life/wp/2015/06/01/interruptions-at-work-can-cost-you-up-to-6-hours-a-day-heres-how-to-avoid-them/

95. Mitchell, T. R., Harman, W. S., Lee, T. W., & Lee, D.-Y. (2008). Self-regulation and multiple deadline goals. In R. Kanfer, G. Chen, & R. D. Pritchard (Eds.), *Work motivation: Past, present, and future* (pp. 197–231). New York: Routledge/Taylor Francis.

96. Demonte, E. K., & Arnold, D. W. (2000). Court upholds employer's non-linear application of test. *The Industrial-Organizational Psychologist, 37*(3), pp. 152–3. Retrieved September 19, 2021, from https://www.siop.org/Portals/84/TIP/Archives/373.pdf

97. Erdogan, B., Bauer, T. N., Peiró, J. M., & Truxillo, D. M. (2011). Overqualified employees: Making the best of a potentially bad situation for individuals and organizations. *Industrial and Organizational Psychology, 4*, 215–232.

98. Feldman, D. C., & Maynard, D. C. (2011). A labor economic perspective on overqualification. *Industrial and Organizational Psychology, 4*, 233–235.

99. Harari, M. B., Manapragada, A., & Viswesvaran, C. (2017). Employee overqualification and manager job insecurity: Implications for employee career outcomes. *Journal of Vocational Behavior, 102*, 28–47.

100. Erdogan, B., & Bauer, T. N. (2009). Perceived overqualification and its outcomes: The moderating role of empowerment. *Journal of Applied Psychology, 94*, 557–565.

101. Erdogan, B., Karakitapoglu-Aygun, Z., Caughlin, D. E., Bauer, T. N., & Gumusluoglu, L. (2020). Employee overqualification and manager job insecurity: Implications for employee career outcomes. *Human Resource Management, 59*, 555–567.

102. Howard, E., & Luksyte, A. (2021). Can the COVID-19 pandemic be good for overqualified employees' careers? *Industrial and Organizational Psychology, 14*, 277–279.

103. Lamm, E., & Meeks, M. D. (2009). Workplace fun: The moderating effects of generational differences. *Employee Relations, 31*(6), 613–631.

104. Karl, K. A., & Peluchette, J. V. (2006). How does workplace fun impact employee perceptions of customer service quality? *Journal of Leadership and Organizational Studies, 13*(2), 2–13.

105. Owler, K., Morrison, R., & Plester, B. (2010). Does fun work? The complexity of promoting fun at work. *Journal of Management & Organization, 16*(3), 338–352.

106. Block, W. (2001). Cyberslacking, business ethics and managerial economics. *Journal of Business Ethics, 33*(3), 225–231.

107. Kapp, K. M. (2012). *The gamification of learning and instruction: Game-based methods and strategies for training and education*. San Francisco: Pfeiffer.

108. Huckabee, I., & Bisette, T. (2014 Spring). Learning made fun. *Training Industry Magazine*, 32–35.

109. Ordioni, J. (2013, April 26). Game on for employee gamification. *ERE Daily*. Retrieved October 29, 2021, from https://www.ere.net/game-on-for-employee-gamification/

110. Stansbury, J. A., & Earnest, D. R. (2017). Meaningful gamification in an Industrial/Organizational psychology course. *Teaching of Psychology, 44*, 38–45.

111. Mitchell, R., Schuster, L., & Seung Jin, H. (2020). Gamification and the impact of extrinsic motivation on needs satisfaction. Making work fun? *Journal of Business Research, 106*, 323–330; and Peng, W., Lin, J. H., Pfeiffer, K. A., & Winn, B. (2012). Need satisfaction supportive game features as motivational determinants: An experimental study of a self-determination theory guided exergame. *Media Psychology, 15*(2), 175–196.

112. Muntean, C. I. (2011, June). *Raising engagement in e-learning through gamification*. Paper presented at the 6th annual International Conference on Virtual Learning, Kelowna, British Columbia, Canada.

113. Stansbury, J. A., & Earnest, D. R. (2017)—see #110.

Chapter 14

1. Birnbaum, R. (2013). Genes, memes, and the evolution of human leadership. In M. G. Rumsey (Ed.), *The Oxford handbook of leadership* (pp. 243–266). New York: Oxford University Press.

2. Barling, J., Christie, A., & Hoption, C. (2011). Leadership. In S. Zedeck (Ed.), *APA handbook of industrial and organizational psychology* (Vol. 1, pp. 183–240). Washington, DC: APA.

3. Hollander, E. P. (2009). *Inclusive leadership: The essential leader-follower relationship*. New York: Routledge.

4. Zaccaro, S. J., Kemp, C., & Bader, P. (2004). Leader traits and attributes. In J. Antonakis, R. Sternberg, & A. Ciancola (Eds.), *The nature of leadership* (pp. 101–124). Thousand Oaks, CA: Sage.

5. Day, D. V., & Zaccaro, S. J. (2007). Leadership: A critical historical analysis of the influence of leader traits. In L. L. Koppes (Ed.), *Historical perspectives in industrial and organizational psychology* (pp. 383–405). Mahwah, NJ: Erlbaum.

6. Kirkpatrick, S. A., & Locke, E. A. (1991). Leadership: Do traits matter? *Academy of Management Executive, 5*(2), 48–60.

7. McClelland, D. C., & Boyatzis, R. E. (1982). Leadership motive pattern and long-term success in management. *Journal of Applied Psychology, 67*, 737–743.

8. Hoffman, B. J., Woehr, D. J., Maldagen-Youngjohn, R., & Lyons, B. D. (2011). Great man or great myth? A quantitative review of the relationship between individual differences and leader effectiveness. *Journal of Occupational and Organizational Psychology, 84*, 347–381.

9. DeRue, D. S., Nahrgang, J. D., Wellman, N., & Humphrey, S. E. (2011). Trait and behavioral theories of leadership: An integration and meta-analytic test of their relative validity. *Personnel Psychology, 64*, 7–52.

10. Dinh, J. E., Lord, R. G., Gardner, W. L., Meuser, J. D., Liden, R. C., & Hu, J. (2014). Leadership theory and research in the new millennium: Current theoretical trends and changing perspectives. *The Leadership Quarterly, 25*, 36–62.

11. Judge, T. A., Piccolo, R. F., & Ilies, R. (2004). The forgotten ones? The validity of consideration and initiating structure in leadership research. *Journal of Applied Psychology, 89*, 36–51.

12. French, J. R. P., Jr., & Raven, B. (1960). The bases of social power. In D. Cartwright & A. F. Zander (Eds.), *Group dynamics* (2nd ed., pp. 607–623). Evanston, IL: Row Peterson.

13. Yukl, G. (1994). *Leadership in organizations* (3rd ed.). Engle wood Cliffs, NJ: Prentice Hall.

14. Reiley, P. J., & Jacobs, R. R. (2016). Ethics matter: Moderating leaders' power use and followers' citizenship behaviors. *Journal of Business Ethics, 134*, 69–81.

15. Barling, J. (2014). *The science of leadership: Lessons from research for organizational leaders*. New York: Oxford University Press.

16. Ibid., p. 292.

17. Fiedler, F. E. (1967). *A theory of leadership effectiveness*. New York: McGraw-Hill.

18. Judge, T. A., & Zapata, C. P. (2015). The person-situation debate revisited: Effect of situation strength and trait activation on the validity of the Big Five personality traits in predicting job performance. *Academy of Management Journal, 58*, 1149–1179.

19. Johnson, J. W. (2021). Identifying the best-fit leaders for the pandemic context. *Industrial and Organizational Psychology, 14*, 123–125.

20. Hersey, P. & Blanchard, K. H. (1969). Life cycle theory of leadership. *Training and Development Journal, 23*, 26–34.

21. House, R. J. (1971). A path-goal theory of leader effectiveness. *Administrative Science Quarterly, 16*, 321–339.

22. Rumsey, M. G. (2013). The elusive science of leadership. In M. G. Rumsey (Ed.), *The Oxford handbook of leadership* (pp. 455–466). New York: Oxford University Press.

23. Dansereau, F., Graen, G. B., & Haga, W. (1975). A vertical dyad linkage approach to leadership in formal organizations. *Organizational Behavior and Human Performance, 13*, 46–78.

24. Erdogan, B., & Bauer, T. N. (2015). Leader-member exchange theory. *International Encyclopedia of the Social & Behavioral Sciences, 13*, 641–647.

25. Dulebohn, J. H., Bommer, W. H., Liden, R. C., Brouer, R. L., & Ferris, G. R. (2012). A meta-analysis of antecedents and consequences of leader-member exchange: Integrating the past with an eye toward the future. *Journal of Management, 38*, 1715–1759.

26. Furst, S. A., & Cable, D. M. (2008). Employee resistance to organizational change: Managerial influence tactics and leader-member exchange. *Journal of Applied Psychology, 93*, 453–462.

27. Henderson, D. J., Wayne, S. J., Shore, L. M., Bommer, W. H., & Tetrick, L. E. (2008). Leader-member exchange, differentiation, and psychological contract fulfillment: A multi-level examination. *Journal of Applied Psychology, 93*, 1208–1219.

28. Kluemper, D. H., Taylor, S. G., Bowler, W. M., Bing, M. N., & Halbesleben, J. R. B. (2019). How leaders perceive employee deviance: Blaming victims while excusing favorites. *Journal of Applied Psychology, 104*(7), 946–964.

29. Martin, R., Epitropaki, O., Thomas, G., & Topakas, A. (2010). A review of leader-member exchange research: Future prospects and directions. In G. P. Hodgkinson & J. L. Ford (Eds.), *International review of industrial and organizational psychology* (Vol. 25, pp. 35–88). Chichester, UK: Wiley-Blackwell.

30. Hu, J., & Liden, R. C. (2013). Relative leader-member exchange within team contexts: How and when social comparison impacts individual effectiveness. *Personnel Psychology, 66*, 127–172.

31. Vidyarthi, P. R., Erdogan, B., Anand, S., Liden, R. C., & Chaudhry, A. (2014). One member, two leaders: Extending leader-member exchange theory to a dual leadership context. *Journal of Applied Psychology, 99*, 468–483.

32. Zhou, L., Wang, M., Chen, G., & Shi, J. (2012). Supervisors' upward exchange relationships and subordinate outcomes: Testing the multilevel mediation role of empowerment. *Journal of Applied Psychology, 97*, 668–680.

33. Venkataramani, V., Green, S. G., & Schleicher, D. J. (2010). Well-connected leaders: The impact of leaders' social network ties on LMX and members' work attitudes. *Journal of Applied Psychology, 95*, 1071–1084.

34. Graen, G. B. (2013). Overview of future research directions for team leadership. In M. G. Rumsey (Ed.), *The Oxford handbook of leadership* (pp. 167–183). New York: Oxford University Press.

35. Avolio, B. J. (2011). *Full range leadership development*. Los Angeles: Sage.

36. Bass, B. M. (1998). *Transformational leadership*. Mahwah, NJ: Erlbaum.

37. Avolio, B. J. (2011)—see #35.

38. Gardner, W. L., & Avolio, B. J. (1998). The charismatic relationship: A dramaturgical perspective. *Academy of Management Review, 23*, 32–58.

39. Meindl, J. R. (1990). On leadership: An alternative to the conventional wisdom. In B. M. Staw & L. L. Cummings (Eds.), *Research in organizational behavior* (Vol. 12, pp. 159-204). Greenwich, CT: JAI Press.

40. Meuser, J. D., Gardner, W. L., Dinh, J. E., Hu, J., Liden, R. C., & Lord, R. G. (2016). A network analysis of leadership theory: The infancy of integration. *Journal of Management, 42*, 1374–1403.

41. Avolio, B. J. (2011) - see #35.

42. Barling, J. (2014) — see #15.

43. Hinkin, T. R., & Schriesheim, C. A. (2008). An examination of "nonleadership:" From laissez-faire leadership to leader reward omission and punishment omission. *Journal of Applied Psychology, 93*, 1234–1248.

44. Barling, J., & Frone, M. R. (2017). If only my leader would do something! Passive leadership undermines employee well-being through role stressors and psychological resource depletion. *Stress and Health, 33*, 211–222.

45. Miller, K. (n.d.). 5 Famous Laissez Faire Leaders. *Future of Working: The Leadership and Career Blog*. Retrieved September 24, 2021, from https://futureofworking.com/5-famous-laissez-faire-leaders/

46. Walumbwa, F. O., & Wernsing, T. (2013). From transactional and transformational to authentic leadership. In M. G. Rumsey (Ed.), *The Oxford handbook of leadership* (pp. 392–400). New York: Oxford University Press.

47. MacKenzie, S. B., Podsakoff, P. M., & Rich, G. A. (2001). Transformational and transactional leadership and salesperson performance. *Journal of the Academy of Marketing Science, 29*, 115–134.

48. Bass, B. M. (1985). *Leadership and performance beyond expectations*. New York: Free Press.

49. Lin, S.-H. (J.), Scott, B. A., & Matta, F. K. (2019). The dark side of transformational leader behaviors for leaders themselves: A conservation of resources perspective. *Academy of Management Journal, 62*(5), 1556–1582.

50. Avolio, B. J., Gardner, W. L., & Walumbwa, F. O. (2007). *Authentic leadership scale* (ALQ version 1.0 self). Redwood City, CA: Mind Garden.

51. May, D. R., Chan, A. Y. L., Hodges, T. D., & Avolio, B. J. (2003). Developing the moral component of authentic leadership. *Organizational Dynamics, 32*, 247–260.

52. Walumbwa, F. O., & Wernsing, T. (2013) — see #45.

53. Nübold, A., Van Quaquebeke, N. & Hülsheger, U. R. (2020). Be(com)ing real: A multi-source and an intervention study on mindfulness and authentic leadership. *Journal of Business and Psychology, 35*, 469–488.

54. Wagner, S. H. (2013). Leadership and responses to organizational crises. *Industrial and Organizational Psychology, 6*, 140–144.

55. Anderson, H. J., Baur, J. E., Griffith, J. A., & Buckley, M. R. (2017). What works for you may not work for (Gen) Me: Limitations of present leadership theories for the new generation. *The Leadership Quarterly, 28*, 245–260.

56. Greenleaf, R. K. (1970). *The servant as leader*. Newton Centre, MA: The Robert K. Greenleaf Center.

57. Eva, N., Robin, M., Sendjaya, S., van Dierendonck, D., & Liden, R. C. (2019). Servant Leadership: A systematic review and call for future research. *The Leadership Quarterly, 30*, 111–132.

58. RepresentUs. (2014, July 9). *Honest Political Ads – Gil Fulbright for Senate* [Video]. YouTube. https://www.youtube.com/watch?v=wz_V4lRdtjo&t=62s

59. Walumbwa, F. O., Hartnell, C. A., & Oke, A. (2010). Servant leadership, procedural justice climate, service climate, employee attitudes, and organizational citizenship behavior: A cross-level investigation. *Journal of Applied Psychology, 95*, 517–529.

60. Chiniara, M., & Bentein, K. (2016). Linking servant leadership to individual performance: Differentiating the mediating role of autonomy, competence and relatedness need satisfaction. *Leadership Quarterly, 27*, 124–141.

61. Hu, J., & Liden, R. C. (2011). Antecedents of team potency and team effectiveness: An examination of goal and process clarity and servant leadership. *Journal of Applied Psychology, 96*, 851–862.

62. Peterson, S. J., Galvin, B. M., & Lange, D. (2012). CEO servant leadership: Exploring executive characteristics and firm performance. *Personnel Psychology, 65*, 565–596.

63. Boal, K. B., & Hooijberg, R. (2001). Strategic leadership research: Moving on. *The Leadership Quarterly, 11*, 515–549.

64. Ireland, R. D., & Hitt, M. A. (2005). Achieving and maintaining strategic competitiveness in the 21st century: The role of strategic leadership. *Academy of Management Perspectives, 19*, 63–77.

65. Meuser, J. D., Gardner, W. L., Dinh, J. E., Hu, J., Liden, R. C., & Lord, R. G. (2016)—see #40.

66. Bergh, D. D., Aguinis, H., Heavey, C., Ketchen, D. J., Boyd, B. K., Su, P., Lau, C. L. L., & Joo, H. (2016). Using meta-analytic structural equation modeling to advance strategic management research: Guidelines and an empirical illustration via the strategic leadership-performance relationship. *Strategic Management Journal, 37*, 477–497.

67. Lord, R. G., Foti, R. J., & Phillips, J. S. (1982). A theory of leadership categorization. In J. G. Hunt, U. Sekaran, & C. Schriesheim (Eds.), *Leadership: Beyond establishment views* (pp. 104–121). Carbondale, IL: Southern Illinois University Press.

68. Henderson, A. A., Matthews, R. A., McKersie, S. J., & Whitman, M. V. (2021). Leading when overweight: The influence of supervisor body weight on subordinates' perceptions and citizenship behaviors. *Journal of Business and Psychology*. https://doi.org/10.1007/s10869-021-09763-2

69. Meindl, J. R., & Ehrlich, S. B. (1987). The romance of leadership and the evaluation of organizational performance. *Academy of Management Journal, 30*, 91–109.

70. Lord, R. G., & Brown, D. L. (2004). *Leadership processes and follower self-identity*. Mahwah, NJ: Erlbaum.

71. Epitropaki, O., & Martin, R. (2004). Implicit leadership theories in applied settings: Factor structure, generalizability, and stability over time. *Journal of Applied Psychology, 89*, 293–310.

72. Riggs, B. S., & Porter, C. O. L. H. (2017). Are there advantages to seeing leadership the same? A test of the mediating effects of LMX on the relationship between ILT congruence and employees' development. *The Leadership Quarterly, 28*, 286–300.

73. Kerr, S., & Jermier, J. M. (1978). Substitutes for leadership: Their meaning and measurement. *Organizational Behavior and Human Performance, 22*, 375–403.

74. Podsakoff, P. M., MacKenzie, S. B., & Bommer, W. H. (1996). Meta-analysis of the relationship between Kerr and Jermier's substitutes for leadership and employee job attitudes, role perceptions, and performance. *Journal of Applied Psychology, 81*, 380–399.

75. Dionne, S. D., Yammarino, F. J., Atwater, L. E., & James, L. R. (2002). Neutralizing substitutes for leadership theory: Leadership effects and common-source bias. *Journal of Applied Psychology, 87*, 454–464; and Muchiri, M. K., & Cooksey, R. W. (2011). Examining the effects of substitutes for leadership on performance outcomes. *Leadership & Organization Development Journal, 32*, 817–836.

76. Pierce, J. L., Dunham, R. B., & Cummings, L. L. (1984). Sources of environmental structuring and participant responses. *Organizational Behavior and Human Performance, 33*, 214–242.

77. Kroon, B., van Woerkom, M., & Menting, C. (2017). Mindfulness as substitute for transformational leadership. *Journal of Managerial Psychology, 32*, 284–297.

78. Zacher, H., & Jimmieson, N. L. (2013). Leader-follower interactions: Relations with OCB and sales productivity. *Journal of Managerial Psychology, 28*, 92–106.

79. Breevaart, K., Bakker, A. B., Demerouti, E., & Derks, D. (2016). Who takes the lead? A multi-source diary study on leadership, work engagement, and job performance. *Journal of Organizational Behavior, 37*, 309–325.

80. Yukl, G. (1994)—see #13.

81. Babiak, P., & Hare, R. D. (2006). *Snakes in suits: When psychopaths go to work*. New York: ReganBooks.

82. Landay, K., Harms, P. D., & Credé, M. (2019). Shall we serve the dark lords? A meta-analytic review of psychopathy and leadership. *Journal of Applied Psychology, 104*(1), 183–196.

83. Itzkovich, Y., Heilbrunn, S. and Aleksic, A. (2020). Full range indeed? The forgotten dark side of leadership, *Journal of Management Development, 39*, 851–868.

84. Tepper, B. J. (2000). Consequences of abusive supervision. *Academy of Management Journal, 43*, 178–190.

85. Mackey, J. D., Ellen, B. P., III, McAllister, C. P., & Alexander, K. C. (2021). The dark side of leadership: A systematic literature review and meta-analysis of destructive leadership research. *Journal of Business Research, 132*, 705–718.

86. Mackey, J. D., Frieder, R. E., Brees, J. R., & Martinko, M. J. (2017). Abusive supervision: A meta-analysis and empirical review. *Journal of Management, 43*, 1940–1965.

87. Aryee, S., Chen, Z. X., Sun, L., & Debrah, Y. A. (2007). Antecedents and outcomes of abusive supervision: Test of a trickle-down model. *Journal of Applied Psychology, 92*, 191–201.

88. Priesemuth, M., & Bigelow, B. (2020). It hurts me too! (or not?): Exploring the negative implications for abusive bosses. *Journal of Applied Psychology, 105*(4), 410–421.

89. Padilla, A., Hogan, R., & Kaiser, R. B. (2007). The toxic triangle: Destructive leaders, susceptible followers, and conducive environments. *The Leadership Quarterly, 18*, 176–194.

90. Thoroughgood, C. N., Padilla, A., Hunter, S. T., & Tate, B. W. (2012). The susceptible circle: A taxonomy of followers associated with destructive leadership. *The Leadership Quarterly, 23*, 897–917.

91. Nandkeolyar, A. K., Shaffer, J. A., Li, A., Ekkirala, S., & Bagger, J. (2014). Surviving an abusive supervisor: The joint roles of conscientiousness and coping strategies. *Journal of Applied Psychology, 99*, 138–150.

92. Goler, L., Gale, J., Harrington, B., & Grant, A. M. (2018, January 11). Why people really quit their jobs. *Harvard Business Review*. Retrieved September 24, 2021, from https://hbr.org/2018/01/why-people-really-quit-their-jobs

93. Kozlowski, S. W. J., Watola, D. J., Jensen, J. M., Kim, B. H., & Botero, I. C. (2009). Developing adaptive teams: A theory of dynamic team leadership. In E. Salas, G. F. Goodwin, & C. S. Burke (Eds.), *Team effectiveness in complex organizations: Foundations, extensions, and new directions* (pp. 113–155). San Francisco: Jossey-Bass.

94. Morgeson, F. P., DeRue, D. S., & Karam, E. P. (2010). Leadership in teams: A functional approach to understanding leadership structures and processes. *Journal of Management, 36*, 5–39.

95. Shuffler, M. L., Burke, C. S., Kramer, W. S., & Salas, E. (2013). Leading teams: Past, present, and future perspec tives. In M. G. Rumsey (Ed.), *The Oxford handbook of leadership* (pp. 144–166). New York: Oxford University Press.

96. Wang, D., Waldman, D. A., & Zhang, Z. (2014). A meta-analysis of shared leadership and team effectiveness. *Journal of Applied Psychology, 99*, 181–198.

97. Graen, G. B. (2013)—see #34.

98. Zaccaro, S. J., Marks, M. A., & DeChurch, L. A. (2012). Multiteam systems: An introduction. In S. J. Zaccaro, M. A. Marks, & L. A. DeChurch (Eds.), *Multiteam systems: An organizational form for dynamic and complex environments* (pp. 3–32). New York: Taylor & Francis.

99. Luciano, M. M., Mathieu, J. E., & Ruddy, T. M. (2014). Leading multiple teams: Average and relative external leadership influences on team empowerment and effectiveness. *Journal of Applied Psychology, 99*, 322–331.

100. Mathieu, J. E., Marks, M. A., & Zaccaro, S. J. (2001). Multi-team systems. In N. Anderson, D. S. Ones, H. K. Sinangil, & C. Viswesvaran (Eds.), *Handbook of industrial, work, & organizational psychology* (Vol. 2, pp. 289–313). London: Sage.

101. House, R. J., Hanges, P. J., Javidan, M., Dorman, P. W., & Gupta, V. (Eds.). (2004). *Culture, leadership, and organizations: The GLOBE study of 62 societies.* Thousand Oaks, CA: Sage.

102. Ibid.

103. Weir, T. (2010). Developing leadership in global organizations. In K. Lundby (Ed.), *Going global* (pp. 203–230). San Francisco: Jossey-Bass.

104. Lowe, K. B., & Gardner, W. L. (2000). Ten years of *The Leadership Quarterly*: Contributions and challenges for the future. *The Leadership Quarterly, 11*, 459–514.

105. Offerman, L. R., & Gowing, M. K. (1990). Organizations of the future. *American Psychologist, 45*, 95–108.

106. O'Neil, D. A., Hopkins, M. M., & Bilimoria, D. (2008). Women's careers at the start of the 21st century: Patterns and paradoxes. *Journal of Business Ethics, 80*, 727–743.

107. Eagly, A. H., & Carli, L. L. (2007). *Through the labyrinth: The truth about how women become leaders.* Boston, MA: Harvard Business School Press.

108. Hoobler, J. M., Lemmon, G., & Wayne, S. J. (2014). Women's managerial aspirations: An organizational development perspective. *Journal of Management, 40*, 703–730.

109. Chemers, M. M., & Murphy, S. E. (1995). Leadership and diversity in groups and organizations. In M. M. Chemers, S. Oskamp, & M. A. Costanzo (Eds.), *Diversity in organizations: New perspectives for a changing workforce* (pp. 157–188). Thousand Oaks, CA: Sage.

110. Rosette, A. S., & Tost, L. P. (2010). Agentic women and communal leadership: How role prescriptions confer advantage to top women leaders. *Journal of Applied Psychology, 95*, 221–235.

111. Ayman, P., & Korabik, K. (2010). Leadership: Why gender and culture matter. *American Psychologist, 65*, 157–170.

112. Lyness, K. S., & Heilman, M. E. (2006). When fit is fundamental: Performance evaluations and promotions of upper-level female and male managers. *Journal of Applied Psychology, 91*, 777–785.

113. Eagly, A. H., Johannesen-Schmidt, M. C., & van Engen, M. L. (2003). Transformation, transactional, and laissez-faire leadership styles: A meta-analysis comparing women and men. *Psychological Bulletin, 129,* 569–591.

114. Lyness, K. S. (2002). Finding the key to the executive suite: Challenges for women and people of color. In R. Silzer (Ed.), *The 21*st *century executive* (pp. 229–273). San Francisco: Jossey-Bass.

115. Ibid., p. 265.

116. U. S. Department of Labor. (2021). 2020 Annual Averages – Employed persons by industry, sex, race, and occupation. *BLS.gov*. Retrieved November 3, 2021, from https://www.bls.gov/cps/cpsaat11.htm

117. Homan, A. C., Gündemir, S., Buengeler, C., & van Kleef, G. A. (2020). Leading diversity: Towards a theory of functional leadership in diverse teams. *Journal of Applied Psychology, 105*(10), 1101–1128.

118. Baron, R. A., & Henry, R. A. (2011). Entrepreneurship: The genesis of organizations. In S. Zedeck (Ed.), *APA handbook of industrial and organizational psychology* (Vol. 1, pp. 241–273). Washington, DC: APA.

119. Gottschalk, P. (2009). *Entrepreneurship and organised crime: Entrepreneurs in illegal business.* Cheltenham, UK: Edward Elgar.

120. Levitt, S. D., & Dubner, S. J. (2005). *Freakonomics: A rogue economist explores the hidden side of everything*. London: Allen Lane.

121. Shane, S. (2003). *A general theory of entrepreneurship*. Cheltenham, UK: Edward Elgar.

122. Antonakis, J., & Autio, E. (2007). Entrepreneurship and leadership. In J. R. Baum, M. Frese, & R. A. Baron (Eds.), *The psychology of entrepreneurship* (pp. 189–208). Mahwah, NJ: Erlbaum.

123. Vecchio, R. P. (2003). Entrepreneurship and leadership: Common trends and common threads. *Human Resources and Management Review, 13*, 303–327.

124. Zhao, H., & Seibert, S. E. (2006). The big five personality dimensions and entrepreneurial status: A meta-analytic review. *Journal of Applied Psychology, 91*, 259–271.

125. Camberato, J. (2020, January 24). 2019 Small Business Failure Rate: Startup Statistics by Industry. *National Business Capital and Services.* Retrieved September 24, 2021, from https://www.nationalbusinesscapital.com/2019-small-business-failure-rate-startup-statistics-industry/

126. Baron, R. A., Frese, M., & Baum, J. R. (2007). Research gains: Benefits of closer links between I/O psychology and entrepreneurship. In J. R. Baum, M. Frese, & R. A. Baron (Eds.), *The psychology of entrepreneurship* (pp. 347–373). Mahwah, NJ: Erlbaum.

127. Chan, K. Y., & Drasgow, F. (2001). Toward a theory of individual differences and leadership: Understanding the motivation to lead. *Journal of Applied Psychology, 86*, 481–498.

128. Hackman, J. R., & Wageman, R. (2007). Asking the right questions about leadership. *American Psychologist, 62*, 43–47.

129. Dirks, K. T., & Ferrin, D. L. (2002). Trust in leadership: Meta-analytic findings and implications for research and practice. *Journal of Applied Psychology, 87,* 611–628.

Chapter 15

1. Cascio, W. F., & Aguinis, H. (2008). Research in industrial and organizational psychology from 1963 to 2007: Changes, choices, and trends. *Journal of Applied Psychology, 93*, 1062–1081.
2. Lefkowitz, J. (2017). *Ethics and values in industrial-organizational psychology* (2nd ed.). New York: Routledge.
3. Ibid.
4. Scott, J. C., Aguinis, H., McWha, I., Rupp, D. E., & Thompson, L. F. (2013). News from the SIOP-United Nations team: SIOP has joined the UN Global Compact and so can you! *The Industrial-Organizational Psychologist, 50*(4). Retrieved October 21, 2021, from http://www.hermanaguinis.com/TIP2013.pdf
5. Shostak, A. B. (1964). Industrial psychology and the trade unions: A matter of mutual indifference. In G. Fisk (Ed.), *The frontiers of management psychology.* New York: Harper & Row.
6. Rosen, H., & Stagner, R. (1980). Industrial/organizational psychology and unions: A viable relationship? *Professional Psychology, 11*, 477–483.
7. Zickar, M. J., & Kostek, J. A. (2013). History of personality testing within organizations. In N. D. Christiansen & R. P. Tett (Eds.), *Handbook of personality at work* (pp. 173–190). New York: Routledge.
8. Zickar, M. J. (2001). Using personality inventories to identify thugs and agitators: Applied psychology's contribution to the war against labor. *Journal of Vocational Behavior, 59,* 149–164.
9. Huszczo, G. E., Wiggins, J. G., & Currie, J. S. (1984). The relationship between psychology and organized labor: Past, present, and future. *American Psychologist, 39*(4), 432–440.
10. Verdi, B. (2000). Psychologists seek protection under the union label. *The Industrial-Organizational Psychologist, 38*(1), 31–35.
11. Ibid., p. 32.
12. Blyton, P. (2008). Working time and work-life balance. In P. Blyton, N. Bacon, J. Fiorito, & E. Heery (Eds.), *Industrial relations* (pp. 513–528). Thousand Oaks, CA: Sage.
13. Guest, D. (2008). Worker well-being. In P. Blyton, N. Bacon, J. Fiorito, & E. Heery (Eds.), *Industrial relations* (pp. 529–547). Thousand Oaks, CA: Sage.
14. Schiavone, M. (2008). *Unions in crisis?* London: Praeger.
15. Bureau of Labor Statistics. (2021, January 22). Union affiliation of employed wage and salary workers by selected characteristics. *BLS.gov*. Retrieved October 21, 2021, from https://www.bls.gov/news.release/union2.t01.htm
16. Hepburn, C. G., & Barling, J. (2001). To vote or not to vote: Abstaining from voting in union representation elections. *Journal of Organizational Behavior, 22*, 569–591.
17. Tetrick, L. E., Shore, L. M., McClurg, L. N., & Vandenberg, R. J. (2007). A model of union participation: The impact of perceived union support, union instrumentality, and union loyalty. *Journal of Applied Psychology, 92*, 820–828.
18. Deery, S. J., Iverson, R. D., Buttigieg, D. M., & Zatzick, C. D. (2014). Can union voice make a difference? The effect on union citizenship behavior on employee absence. *Human Resource Management, 53*, 211–228.
19. Godard, J. (2008). Union formation. In P. Blyton, N. Bacon, J. Fiorito, & E. Heery (Eds.), *Industrial relations* (pp. 377–405). Thousand Oaks, CA: Sage.
20. Pruitt, D. G. (1993). *Negotiation in social conflict.* Pacific Grove, CA: Brooks/Cole.
21. Gelfand, M. J., Fulmer, C. A., & Severance, L. (2011). The psychology of negotiation and mediation. In S. Zedeck (Ed.), *APA handbook of industrial and organizational psychology* (Vol. 3, pp. 495–554). Washington, DC: APA.
22. Stagner, R., & Effal, B. (1982). Internal union dynamics during a strike: A quasi-experimental study. *Journal of Applied Psychology, 67,* 37–44.
23. Cloutier, J., Denis, P. L., & Bilodeau, H. (2013). The dynamics of strike votes: Perceived justice during collective bargaining. *Journal of Organizational Behavior, 34*, 1016–1038.
24. Kelloway, E. K., Francis, L., Catano, V. M., & Dupre, K. E. (2008). Third-party support for strike actions. *Journal of Applied Psychology, 93*, 806–817.
25. Estey, M. (1981). *The unions: Structure, development, and management* (3rd ed.). New York: Harcourt Brace Jovanovich.

26. Gordon, M. E., & Bowlby, R. L. (1989). Reactance and intentionality attributions as determinants of the intent to file a grievance. *Personnel Psychology, 42,* 309–330.

27. Fryxell, G. E., & Gordon, M. E. (1989). Workplace justice and job satisfaction as predictors of satisfaction with union and management. *Academy of Management Journal, 32,* 851–866.

28. Gordon, M. E., & Bowlby, R. L. (1988). Propositions about grievance settlements: Finally, consultation with grievants. *Personnel Psychology, 41,* 107–124.

29. Klaas, B. S. (1989). Managerial decision making about employee grievances: The impact of the grievant's work his tory. *Personnel Psychology, 42,* 53–68.

30. Olson-Buchanan, J. B. (1996). Voicing discontent: What happens to the grievance filer after the grievance? *Journal of Applied Psychology, 81,* 52–63.

31. Richey, B., Bernardin, H. J., Tyler, C. L., & McKinney, N. (2001). The effect of arbitration program characteristics on applicants' intentions toward potential employees. *Journal of Applied Psychology, 86,* 1006–1013.

32. Lefkowitz, J. (2017)—see #2, p. 385.

33. Jarrell, S. B., & Stanley, T. D. (1990). A meta-analysis of the union–nonunion wage gap. *Industrial and Labor Relations Review, 44,* 54–67.

34. Feuille, P., & Blandin, J. (1974). Faculty job satisfaction and bargaining sentiment: A case study. *Academy of Management Journal, 17,* 678–692.

35. Bigoness, W. J. (1978). Correlates of faculty attitudes toward collective bargaining. *Journal of Applied Psychology, 63,* 228–233.

36. Hamner, W. C., & Smith, F. J. (1978). Work attitudes as predictors of unionization activity. *Journal of Applied Psychology, 63,* 415–421.

37. Schriesheim, C. A. (1978). Job satisfaction, attitudes toward unions, and voting in a union representation election. *Journal of Applied Psychology, 63,* 548–552.

38. Youngblood, S. A., DeNisi, A. S., Molleston, J. L., & Mobley, W. H. (1984). The impact of work environment, instrumentality beliefs, perceived labor union image, and subjective norms on union voting intentions. *Academy of Management Journal, 17,* 576–590; and Zalesny, M. D. (1985). Comparison of economic and non-economic factors in predicting faculty vote preference in a union representation election. *Journal of Applied Psychology, 70,* 243–256.

39. Hammer, T. H., & Berman, M. (1981). The role of noneconomic factors in faculty union voting. *Journal of Applied Psychology, 66,* 415–421.

40. Goeddeke, F. X., Jr., & Kammeyer-Mueller, J. D. (2010). Perceived support in a dual organizational environment: Union participation in a university setting. *Journal of Organizational Behavior, 31,* 65–83.

41. Aryee, S., & Chay, Y. W. (2001). Workplace justice, citizenship behavior, and turnover intentions in a union context: Examining the mediating role of perceived union support and union instrumentality. *Journal of Applied Psychology, 86,* 154–160.

42. Fuller, J. B., Jr., & Hester, K. (2001). A closer look at the relationship between justice perceptions and union participation. *Journal of Applied Psychology, 86,* 1096–1106.

43. Cameron, K. L. (1982). The relationship between faculty unionism and organizational effectiveness. *Academy of Management Journal, 25,* 6–24.

44. Fullagar, C. J., Gallagher, D. G., Gordon, M. E., & Clark, P. F. (1995). Impact of early socialization on union commitment and participation: A longitudinal study. *Journal of Applied Psychology, 80,* 147–157.

45. Fullagar, C. J., Clark, P. F., Gallagher, D. G., & Gordon, M. E. (1994). A model of the antecedents of early union commitment: The role of socialization experiences and steward characteristics. *Journal of Organizational Behavior, 15,* 517–533.

46. Gordon, M. E., Schmitt, N., & Schneider, W. G. (1984). Laboratory research on bargaining and negotiations: An evaluation. *Industrial Relations, 23,* 218–233.

47. Neale, M. A. (1984). The effects of negotiation and arbitration cost salience on bargainer behavior: The role of the arbiter and constituency in negotiator judgment. *Organizational Behavior and Human Performance, 34,* 97–111.

48. Starke, F. A., & Notz, W. W. (1981). Pre- and post-intervention effects of conventional versus final offer arbitration. *Academy of Management Journal, 24,* 832–850.

49. Grigsby, D. M., & Bigoness, W. J. (1982). Effects of mediation and alternative forms of arbitration on bargaining behavior: A laboratory study. *Journal of Applied Psychology, 67,* 549–554.

50. Brett, J. M., Olekalns, M., Friedman, R., Goates, N., Anderson, C., & Lisco, C. C. (2007). Sticks and stones: Language, face, and online dispute resolution. *Academy of Management Journal, 50*, 85–99.

51. Conlon, D. E., Moon, H., & Ng, K. Y. (2002). Putting the cart before the horse: The benefits of arbitrating before mediating. *Journal of Applied Psychology, 87*, 978–984.

52. Conlon, D. E., Meyer, C. J., Lytle, A. L., & Willaby, H. W. (2007). Third party interventions across cultures: No "one best choice." In J. J. Martocchio (Ed.), *Research in personnel and human resources management (*pp. 309– 349). Oxford, UK: JAI.

53. Gordon, M. E., Philpot, J. W., Burt, R. E., Thompson, C. A., & Spiller, W. E. (1980). Commitment to the union: Development of a measure and an examination of its correlates. *Journal of Applied Psychology, 65*, 479–499.

54. Mellor, S. (1990). The relationship between membership de cline and union commitment: A field study of local unions in crisis. *Journal of Applied Psychology, 75,* 258–267.

55. Fullagar, C., & Barling, J. (1989). A longitudinal test of a model of the antecedents and consequences of union loyalty. *Journal of Applied Psychology, 74*, 213–227.

56. Margenau, J. M., Martin, J. E., & Peterson, M. M. (1988). Dual and unilateral commitment among stewards and rank-and-file union members. *Academy of Management Journal, 31,* 359–376.

57. Tetrick, L. E. (1995). Developing and maintaining union commitment: A theoretical framework. *Journal of Organizational Behavior, 16,* 583–595.

58. Sverke, M., & Kuruvilla, S. (1995). A new conceptualization of union commitment: Development and test of an integrated theory. *Journal of Organizational Behavior, 16,* 505–532.

59. Sverke, M., & Sjöberg, A. (1995). Union membership behavior: The influence of instrumental and value-based commitment. In L. E. Tetrick & J. Barling (Eds.), *Changing employment relations* (pp. 229–254). Washington, DC: APA.

60. Kelloway, E. K., Catano, V. M., & Carroll, A. E. (1995). The nature of member participation in local union activities. In L. E. Tetrick & J. Barling (Eds.), *Changing employment relations* (pp. 333–348). Washington, DC: APA.

61. Gordon, M. E., & Ladd, R. T. (1990). Dual allegiance: Renewal, reconsideration, and recantation. *Personnel Psychology, 43*, 37–69.

62. Hartley, J. F. (1992). The psychology of industrial relations. In C. L. Cooper & I. T. Robertson (Eds.), *International review of industrial and organizational psychology* (Vol. 7, pp. 201–243). London: Wiley.

63. Bownas, D. A. (2000). Selection programs in a union environment: A commentary. In J. F. Kehoe (Ed.), *Managing selection in changing organizations* (pp. 197–209). San Francisco: Jossey-Bass.

64. Ibid.

65. U.S. Department of Labor. (2020). Registered Apprenticeship National Results Fiscal Year 2020. *BLS.gov*. Retrieved October 21, 2021, from https://www.dol.gov/agencies/eta/apprenticeship/about/statistics/2020

66. Cole, N. D., & Latham, G. P. (1997). Effects of training in procedural justice on perceptions of disciplinary fairness by unionized employees and disciplinary subject matter experts. *Journal of Applied Psychology, 82*, 699–705.

67. Skarlicki, D. P., & Latham, G. P. (1996). Increasing citizenship behavior within a labor union: A test of organizational justice theory. *Journal of Applied Psychology, 81,* 161–169.

68. Skarlicki, D. P., & Latham, G. P. (1997). Leadership training in organizational justice to increase citizenship behavior within a labor union: A replication. *Personnel Psychology, 50,* 617–654.

69. Hammer, T. H., Bayazit, M., & Wazeter, D. L. (2009). Union leadership and member attitudes: A multi-level analysis. *Journal of Applied Psychology, 94*, 392–410.

70. Blackard, K. (2000). *Managing change in a unionized workplace.* Westport, CT: Quorum.

71. Sweet, S., & Meiksins, P. (2013). *Changing contours of work* (2nd ed.). Thousand Oaks, CA: Sage.

72. Johnston, D. C. (2004). *Perfectly legal: The covert campaign to rig our tax system to benefit the super rich—and cheat everybody else.* New York: Portfolio.

73. Glassdoor. (2021). 2021 Best Places to Work. *Glassdoor.com*. Retrieved October 21, 2021, from https://www.glassdoor.com/Award/Best-Places-to-Work-LST_KQ0,19.htm

74. Engdahl, L. (2020, March 31). Unions are giving workers a seat at the table when it comes to the coronavirus response. *Economic Policy Institute, Working Economics Blog*. Retrieved October 21, 2021, from https://www.epi.org/blog/unions-are-giving-workers-a-seat-at-the-table-when-it-comes-to-the-coronavirus-response/

75. Polansek, T. (2021, September 3). Tyson Foods, unions strike deal over COVID-19 vaccine mandate. *Reuters*. Retrieved October 21, 2021, from https://www.reuters.com/legal/government/tyson-foods-meatpacking-union-strike-deal-over-vaccine-mandate-2021-09-03/

76. United Food & Commercial Workers Local 400. (2020, March 23). Live updates: New policies in effect at Giant, Kroger, Safeway and Shoppers (multiple updates). *UFCW400.org*. Retrieved October 21, 2021, from https://www.ufcw400.org/2020/03/23/enhanced-policies-in-effect-at-giant-kroger-safeway-shoppers/

77. International Brotherhood of Teamsters. (2020, April 15). Teamsters, DHL reach agreement to help minimize layoffs. *Teamster.org*. Retrieved October 21, 2021, from https://teamster.org/2020/04/teamsters-dhl-reach-agreement-help-minimize-layoffs/

78. Jamieson, D. (2020, May 23). One way to protect workers in a pandemic: Make it harder to fire them. *Huffpost*. Retrieved October 21, 2021, from https://www.huffpost.com/entry/workers-unions-coronavirus-firing_n_5ec6d63dc5b6b9606d452ac6?ncid=engmodushpmg00000006

79. Conte, C., & Carr, A. R. (2012). *Outline of the U.S. economy*. Washington, DC: U.S. Department of State.

80. Yates, M. D. (2009). *Why unions matter* (2nd ed.). New York: Monthly Review Press.

81. Hayter, S., & Stoeveska, V. (2011). *Trade union density and collective bargaining coverage: International statistical inquiry 2008–09*. Geneva: International Labor Organization.

82. Lichtenstein, N. (2013). *State of the union: A century of American labor* (revised ed.). Princeton, NJ: Princeton University Press.

83. Pocock, B. (2008). Equality at work. In P. Blyton, N. Bacon, J. Fiorito, & E. Heery (Eds.), *Industrial relations* (pp. 572–587). Thousand Oaks, CA: Sage.

84 Ibid., pp. 573–4.

Image Credits

Chapter 1

Page 6:
Walter Dill Scott–Library of Congress/Science Source

Frederick W. Taylor–Frederick Winslow Taylor Collection (SCW.001)/Samuel C. Williams Library, Stevens Institute of Technology

Page 7:
Lillian Moller Gilbreth–Smithsonian Institute Libraries/Science Source

Hugo Münsterberg–Library of Congress/Science Source

Page 8: *Robert Yerkes*–National Library of Medicine/Science Source

Page 10: *Walter Van Dyke Bingham*–Courtesy of Carnegie Mellon University Archives

Page 11: *Morris Viteles*–University of Pennsylvania Archives

Page 13: *Elton Mayo*–Josef Breitenbach Collection/Center for Creative Photography, University of Arizona

Page 17: *Pinboys*–Lewis Hines/Library of Congress

Page 21: Illustration 23644773 © Masterofall686 | Dreamstime.com

Chapter 2

Page 32: Christos Georghiou/Shutterstock

Page 33:
Anna Semenchenko/iStock

edge69/iStock

Page 36: Fejas/Shutterstock

Page 43:
Florida Center for Instructional Technology *ClipartETC* (Tampa, FL: University of South Florida, 2009)

Artisticco/Shutterstock

Page 45: Graphic courtesy of Nicholas Lue and SITNBoston, licensed under CC BY-NC-SA 4.0.

Page 47: Stock Up/Shutterstock

Page 49: Janista/iStock

Page 53: V_ctoria /Shutterstock.com

Chapter 3

Page 64: iam2mai/Shutterstock

Page 65: Kharlamova/iStock

Page 68: Ken Benner/CartoonStock

Page 72: David A Litman/Shutterstock

Page 73: imlucky/123RF

Page 75: haizuladri/123RF

Page 81: *Wardell Connerly*–acri.org

Page 84: ID 102406850 © Lineartist | Dreamstime.com

Chapter 4

Page 93: DNY59/iStock

Page 113: MrAnnoying, CC BY-SA 4.0 *https://creativecommons.org/licenses/by-sa/4.0*, via Wikimedia Commons

Chapter 5

Page 125: Illustration 26319227 © Michael Bretherton | Dreamstime.com

Page 128: 168579445 © Chernetskaya | Dreamstime.com

Page 137: Spencer Platt/Getty Images

Page 147: iQoncept/Shutterstock

Page 149: Illustration 62969888 © Anton Kubalik | Dreamstime.com

Page 153: Illustration 17818768 © Iqoncept | Dreamstime.com

Page 158: illusart/iStock

Chapter 6

Page 166:
Juhele, CC0, via Wikimedia Commons

Illustration 180287403 © Sabelskaya | Dreamstime.com

Page 170: Illustration 85327782 © Adonis1969 | Dreamstime.com

Page 176: delcarmat/Shutterstock

Page 178: masterSergeant/iStock

Page 187: bearsky23/Shutterstock

Chapter 7

Page 194: studiolaut/Shutterstock

Page 197: ID 208679776 © Dinara Lesnikova | Dreamstime.com

Page 199: boygointer/123RF

Page 206: Illustration 16766038 © Lemony | Dreamstime.com

Page 207: {{PD-US}}

Page 214: Texas A&M University

Page 220: garagestock/Shutterstock

Page 223: patrimonio designs ltd/Shutterstock

Chapter 8

Page 230:
Mary Kay Ash–LizKoz, CC BY-SA 4.0 *https://creativecommons.org/licenses/by-sa/4.0*, via Wikimedia Commons

Indra Nooyi–Flickr/Courtesy of PepsiCo

Page 237: Feodora Chiosea/iStock

Page 242: Sara Sanders/SHS Design

Page 243: AbbythePup, CC BY-SA 4.0 *https://creativecommons.org/licenses/by-sa/4.0*, via Wikimedia Commons

Page 246: St. Petersburg College Library, Public domain, via Wikimedia Commons

Page 253: Christophe Boisson/Shutterstock

Page 256: Elon Musk [@Elon Musk]/Twitter

Chapter 9

Page 264: *Peter Drucker*–Jeff McNeill, CC BY-SA 2.0 *https://creativecommons.org/licenses/by-sa/2.0*, via Wikimedia Commons

Page 267: ID 8362554 © Yuliyan Velchev | Dreamstime.com

Page 270: eugenesergeev/123RF

Page 272: AWeith, CC BY-SA 4.0 *https://creativecommons.org/licenses/by-sa/4.0*, via Wikimedia Commons

Page 273: Jonny Hawkins/CartoonStock

Page 275: TennesseePhotographer/iStock

Page 285: karen roach/Shutterstock

Page 287: John Morris/CartoonStock

Chapter 10

Page 295:
Babe Ruth–Charles M. Conlon, Public domain, via Wikimedia Commons

Mia Hamm–Johnmaxmena (talk) John Mena, Public domain, via Wikimedia Commons

Page 306: *Colin Powell*–Department of State of the United States of America, Public domain, via Wikimedia Commons

Page 308: Illustration 162272159 © Mast3r | Dreamstime.com

Page 315: Illustration 112034333 © Zdenek Sasek | Dreamstime.com

Chapter 11

Page 324: Copyright © Highlights for Children, Inc., Columbus, Ohio. All rights reserved.

Page 329: NBCUniversal/Getty Images

Page 334: juliasart/123RF

Page 342:
Bakhtiar Zein/Shutterstock

Illustration 211013638 © Alexb09d4n | Dreamstime.com

Page 346: Illustration 14867583 © Roughcollie | Dreamstime.com

Page 346 / 347: jabkitticha/123RF

Page 348: Illustration 217994427 © Maria Argutinskaya | Dreamstime.com

Page 350: Illustration 113467045 © Olivier Le Moal | Dreamstime.com

Chapter 12

Page 360: kanvictory/123RF

Page 363: lightfieldstudios/123RF

Page 373: emrVectors/iStock

Page 375: benchart/123RF

Page 380: Jahn Henne., CC BY-SA 3.0 *https://creativecommons.org/licenses/by-sa/3.0*, via Wikimedia Commons

Page 383: rastudio/123RF

Page 385: NBCUniversal/Getty Images

Chapter 13

Page 392:
Michael Jordan–landmarkmedia/Shutterstock

LeBron James–Tinseltown/Shutterstock

Jack Ma–Photo 51426419 © Minipig5188 | Dreamstime.com

Page 393: Creative Commons Attribution-Share Alike 3.0

Page 396: sunnyws/Shutterstock

Page 400:

Aha-Soft/Shutterstock

Sportpoint/iStock

Page 401: GeorgeManga/iStock

Chapter 14

Page 426:
Abraham Lincoln–Alexander Gardner, Public domain, via Wikimedia Commons

Malala Yousafzai–DFID–UK Department for International Development, CC BY 2.0 *https://creativecommons.org/licenses/by/2.0*, via Wikimedia Commons

Page 429: photographer: Anderson / Alfred von Domaszewski, Public domain, via Wikimedia Commons

Page 433: *Margaret Thatcher*–Margaret Thatcher Foundation, CC BY-SA 3.0 *https://creativecommons.org/licenses/by-sa/3.0*, via Wikimedia Commons

Page 435: Lisa Dima, CC BY-SA 4.0 *https://creativecommons.org/licenses/by-sa/4.0*, via Wikimedia Commons

Page 437: *Kenny Nguyen*–Courtesy of Kenny Nguyen/TedX Talks

Page 439:
Christoph Roser at AllAboutLean.com under the free CC-BY-SA 4.0 license

Warren Buffett–Aaron Friedman, CC BY 2.0 *https://creativecommons.org/licenses/by/2.0*, via Wikimedia Commons

Page 442: Frank L. Ridley, CC BY-SA 4.0 *https://creativecommons.org/licenses/by-sa/4.0*, via Wikimedia Commons

Page 448:
Maya Angelou–Kingkongphoto & www.celebrity-photos.com from Laurel Maryland, USA, CC BY-SA 2.0 *https://creativecommons.org/licenses/by-sa/2.0*, via Wikimedia Commons

Illustration 26362794 © Jrcasas | Dreamstime.com

Page 452: Photo 227988754 © Elnur | Dreamstime.com

Chapter 15

Page 460: Illustration 205551495 © Koya79 | Dreamstime.com

Page 461: Courtesy of IUE-CWA Local 301

Page 467: michaeldb/123RF

Page 470: ©sheilaf2002/123RF.COM

Page 472: Photo of Seattle Star front page April 28, 1914

Page 483: Courtesy of United Steelworkers

Author Index

Aamodt, M. G., 489n9, 508n128
Abarca, N., 543n136
Abboud Dal Santo, J., 498n69
Abela, J. E., 513n50
Abele, A. E., 504n34, 504n40, 504nn44–45
Ackerman, P. L., 512n23, 512nn25–26
Adams, A. A., 507n96
Adams, J., 544n149
Adams, J. S., 547n38
Adis, C. S., 494n56
Adler, S., 522n121
Adsit, D. L., 520n80
Agrell, A., 499n1
Aguinis, H., 491n74, 493n27, 495n71, 517n1, 517n4, 517n7, 517n16, 519n59, 529n77, 529n92, 535n114, 553n66, 556n1, 556n4
Ailon, G., 523n6
Aiman-Smith, L., 518n28
Aime, F., 526n25
Alcott, V. B., 498n55
Aleksic, A., 553n83
Alexander, K. C., 553n85
Alexander, R. A., 510n24, 510n37, 510nn39, 511n40
Alexandrova, M., 543n136
Alicart, H., 545n14
Allan, C., 517n130
Allen, D. G., 491n65, 512n18, 521n92
Allen, J. A., 491n75, 533n87, 544n143, 544n145
Allen, N. J., 532n66
Allen, T. D., 515nn105–106, 539n44, 539n47, 539n51, 542nn99–101, 542n113, 543n131, 543n136
Alliger, G. M., 506n75
Almeida, R., 546n26
Alving, J., 545n11
Amabile, T., 548n78
Amato, S. L., 506n78
Ambrose, M. L., 533n91, 535n124
American Addiction Centers, 544n155
American Association of Retired Persons, 497n40
American Osteopathic Association, 538n25
American Psychological Association, 495n70, 495n5, 537nn1–2
Ames, D. R., 522n109
Amlôt, R., 501n50
Amstad, F. T., 542nn104–105
Amundson, M., 511n47
Anand, N., 523n24
Anand, S., 551n31
Andersen, G. H., 534n98
Anderson, C., 558n50
Anderson, C. D., 520n74
Anderson, H. J., 552n55
Anderson, J. R., 512n22
Anderson, L. E., 499n16
Anderson, L. J., 521n105
Anderson, N., 500n35
Anderson, T., 536n138
Anderson, V., 541n76
Andersson, L. M., 535n132
Andrews, M. C., 500n40, 547n43
Andrews, R., 517n6
Ang, S., 521n88
Anger, W. K., 541n92
Antonakis, J., 492nn20–21, 494n56, 555n122
Antonijoan, R. M., 545n14
Apfelbaum, E. P., 514n74
Aquino, K., 515n86, 536n136
Arad, S., 517n9
Armstrong, J., 542n101
Arnold, D. W., 501n56, 506n70, 549n96
Arnold, J. D., 503n5
Arnold, K. A., 535n135
Aronsson, G., 501n51
Arthaud-Day, M., 531n33
Arthur, W. A., Jr., 499n15, 508n127, 508n130, 513n32, 514n82, 516n125, 517n131, 524n38
Arvey, R. D., 535n134, 545n6
Aryee, S., 554n87, 557n41
Ash, R. A., 500n32
Ashford, S. J., 521nn96–97, 521n104
Ashforth, B. E., 531n38, 543n128, 543n137, 544n138, 544n141, 544n148
Ashkanasy, N. M., 530n1
Astakhova, M. N., 496n28
Atwater, L. E., 553n75
Austin, J. T., 491n76
Autio, E., 555n122
Avery, D. R., 501n57, 502n67
Avey, J. B., 538n28
Avolio, B. J., 526n13, 538n27, 551n35, 551nn37–38, 552n41, 552nn50-51
Axtell, C., 541n89
Ayman, P., 555n111

Babiak, P., 505n56, 553n81
Bacharach, S. B., 545n161
Bachiochi, P., 498n56
Bachousi, J., 491n59
Bachrach, D. G., 535n116
Bader, P., 550n4
Baer, M., 514n59
Bagger, J., 554n91
Bagozzi, R. P., 503n4
Baker, L. T., 524n46
Baker, T. A., 503n21, 504n24
Bakker, A. B., 533n78, 533n82, 533n84, 538n22, 546n27, 546n31, 553n79
Baldwin, S. P., 515n105, 519n58
Baldwin, T. T., 516nn120–122, 518n26
Baler, R., 545n3
Ballaban, M., 524n28
Baltar, F., 492n4
Baltes, B. B., 540n53, 542n105
Balzer, W. K., 519n46, 521n89
Bamberger, P. A., 545n161
Bandura, A., 527n50, 547nn52–53
Banks, G. C., 495n74, 497nn46–47, 505n54
Banuelas, V. K., 540n56
Bapuji, H., 491n65
Baran, B. E., 544n143, 544n145

Baranik, L. E., 515n105
Baranowski, L. E., 499n16
Barattucci, M., 509n16
Barber, L. K., 541n90
Barclay, L. J., 536n136
Barger, E. J., 536n155
Barling, J., 518n12, 535n135, 550n2, 551nn15–16, 552n42, 552n44, 556n16, 558n55
Barnes, C. M., 492n22, 502n72, 527n40, 539n35, 549n88
Barnes-Farrell, J. L., 519n56
Barney, M. F., 490n53
Baron, R. A., 521n93, 555n118, 555n126
Barreca, R., 535n125
Barrett, G. V., 503n3, 510n24, 510n37, 510nn39, 511n40, 511n43
Barrick, M. R., 504n33, 505n63, 507n106, 507nn108–109
Barron, L. A., 546n22
Barry, B., 529n75
Bartram, D., 499n17, 510n35
Baruch, Y., 523n23
Basbug, G., 493nn39–41
Bass, B. M., 551n36, 552n48
Bastardoz, N., 492nn20–21
Batarse, J. C., 503n16
Bateman, T., 531n23
Battista, M., 500n32, 523n9
Bauer, T. N., 509n11, 549n97, 549nn100–101, 551n24
Baum, J. R., 555n126
Baur, J. E., 552n55
Baxi, S., 546n15
Bayazit, M., 558n69
Bazerman, M. H., 548n63
Bazzoli, A. M., 501n53
Beal, D. J., 491n72, 502nn68–69, 528n52
Bear, D. J., 511n6
Beaton, C., 547n44
Beaty, J., 507n98
Beck, J. W., 547n54, 548n57, 548n77
Beck, T. E., 524n46
Becker, B. J., 493n24
Becker, T. E., 507n90, 533n70
Beckhard, R., 525n56
Bedeian, A. G., 489n17
Beehr, T. A., 520n73
Beersma, B., 516n116, 526n27
Beham, B., 543n136
Behnke, S. H., 495n75
Behrend, T. S., 491n75
Beier, M. E., 516n118
Bell, B. S., 513n36, 513n55, 514n61, 520n69, 525n7
Bell, S. T., 491n75, 513n32, 517n131, 524n38, 527n30, 528n60
Belohlav, J. A., 528n60
Benight, C. C., 541n76
Benjamin, L. T., Jr., 489n24
Bennett, N., 545n163, 546n165
Bennett, S., 491n58
Bennett, W., 513n32, 514n82, 517n131
Benovoy, M., 545n14
Benson, G., 522n126, 529n86
Benson, J., 522n116
Bentein, K., 552n60
Benveniste, H., 545n13
Berdahl, J. L., 515n86
Berg, J. M., 492n14
Berger, C. J., 548n73
Bergeron, D. M., 534n112, 535n115
Bergey, P. K., 518n28
Bergh, D. D., 553n66
Bergman, M. E., 544n140, 544nn142–143, 545n145
Bergström, G., 501n51
Berka, G. C., 493n44
Berman, M., 557n39
Bernardin, H. J., 518n39, 519n40, 520n76, 557n31
Bernichon, T., 521n99
Beroesand, J. M., 546n15
Berry, C. M., 501n60, 503nn15–16, 505n59, 506n74
Berry, J., 496n29
Berry, M. O., 495n4
Berry, Y., 547n37
Bertelsen, C., 545n11
Bettac, E. L., 501n53
Beugne, C. D., 536n144
Beus, J. M., 537n10, 538n12
Beyer, J. M., 523n16
Bezrukova, K., 514n66, 514n71, 527n47
Bezzina, T., 513n50
Bhutta, C. B., 492n5
Bianco, S. F., 513n50
Bickmeier, R. M., 493n44
Biddle, D. A., 510n34
Bies, R. J., 535n126
Biga, A., 515n106
Bigelow, B., 554n88
Bigoness, W. J., 557n35, 557n49
Bilimoria, D., 554n106
Billsberry J., 524n32
Bilodeau, H., 556n23
Bilotta, I., 526n19
Bing, M. N., 551n28
Binning, J. F., 503n3
Birdi, K., 517n130
Birkeland, S. A., 505n62
Birnbaum, R., 550n1
Bisette, T., 550n108
Bisqueret, C., 504n31
Blackard, K., 558n70
Blackman, A., 516n112
Blakely, G. L., 547n43
Blakemore, L. J., 545n13
Blanchard, K. H., 551n20
Blanchard, P. M., 513n44, 513n46, 513n49
Blandin, J., 557n34
Blatt, R., 521n96
Blickle, G., 536n147
Blindenbach-Driessen, F., 527n48
Blithe, S. J., 544n146
Block, C. J., 498n55
Block, W., 550n106
Blum, T. C., 545n163, 545n165
Blume, B. D., 516n120, 516n122, 518n26, 534n105
Blyton, P., 556n12
Boal, K. B., 552n63
Bobko, P., 497n49, 506n84, 519n43
Bochantin, J., 495n74
Bock, J., 541n76
Bodin, L., 501n51
Bodner, T., 541n92
Boher, A., 519n41
Boies, K., 528n55
Bolino, M. C., 502n76, 518n23, 534nn112–113
Bommer, W. H., 500n33, 551n25, 551n27, 553n74
Bonaccio, S., 493n43
Bond, F. W., 548n69
Bono, J. E., 516n108, 531n23, 532n58, 532n64

Bordeaux, C., 542n111
Borns, J., 495n74
Bosco, F. A., 493n27
Boselie, P., 517n3
Bosmans, K., 544n147
Boswell, W. R., 532n57, 536n155, 538n18
Botero, I. C., 554n93
Bouchard, T. J., 545n6
Boudreau, J. W., 538n18
Bowers, C., 513n45, 527n37
Bowlby, R. L., 557n26, 557n28
Bowler, W. M., 551n28
Bowling, J. M., 498n69
Bowling, N. A., 532n59, 534n108, 541n82
Bownas, D. A., 558nn63–64
Boyatzis, R. E., 494n57, 550n7
Boyce, A. S., 505n63
Boyce, C. J., 540n67, 545n8
Boyce, P., 504n29
Boyd, B. K., 553n66
Boyd, C. M., 538n21
Boyne, G. A., 517n6
Bracken, D. W., 520nn78–80, 520n82, 522n110
Braddy, P. W., 520n81
Bradley, B. H., 527n44
Bradley, J. C., 506n82, 538n16
Brammer, S., 491n66
Branch, S., 535n131
Brand, C., 503n9
Brandon, S. E., 491n70
Branicki, L., 491n66
Brannick, M. T., 493n27, 500n29, 505n62
Brauerman, E. P., 506n79
Braun, V., 493n36
Bravo, J., 537n164
Bray, J., 544n159
Breaugh, J. A., 509n4, 509n8
Brees, J. R., 553n86
Breevaart, K., 553n79
Brenner, J., 511n47
Brett, J. M., 558n50
Bride, B. E., 541n75
Brief, A. P., 532n54
Briggs, T. E., 540n53
Bright, D. S., 520n86
Brinsfield, C. T., 532n69
Broad, J. D., 538n29
Broderick, M., 542n96
Brooks, A. W., 492nn10–11
Brooks, D., 545n11
Brooks, S. M., 525n50
Brotherton, C., 498n62
Brouer, R. L., 536n148, 551n25
Brough, P., 543n136
Brown, A., 499n17
Brown, C. W., 490n33, 490n47
Brown, D. L., 553n70
Brown, G., 523n22
Brown, J., 491n65
Brown, J. D., 521n99
Brown, K. G., 491n73, 502n75, 514n62, 516n127, 517n129, 527n44
Brown, M., 522n116
Brown, S. H., 500n38
Brown, S. P., 533nn74–75
Bruk-Lee, V., 531n22, 531n26
Bryan, L. K., 497n32
Bryan, W. L., 489nn10–12
Buchanan, D., 536n143
Bucher, E., 538nn31–32
Buckley, M. R., 519n40, 552n55
Buehler, R., 549n91, 549n93
Buengeler, C., 555n117
Buhrmester, M., 492n6
Bunce, D., 548n69
Bunk, J., 549n85
Bureau of Labor Statistics, 537nn7-8, 556n15
Burgess, M., 544n150
Burke, C. S., 526nn28–29, 527n49, 528n64, 529n73, 530nn94–95, 554n95
Burke, M. I., 493n31
Burke, M. J., 528n52, 538nn11–12, 538n16
Burke, W. W., 524n45, 525n57, 525n59, 525n63
Burns, M., 504n28
Burrus, C., 532n59
Burt, R. E., 558n53
Burtscher, M. J., 494n53, 527n38
Buster, M. A., 503n14
Butler, A., 542n106
Buttigieg, D. M., 556n18
Butts, M. M., 542n99
Bynum, B., 521n87
Byron, K., 542n108
Cable, D. M., 492n14, 551n26
Calhoun, L. G., 541n80
California Magazine, 489n21
Caligiuri, P., 495n1, 514nn77–78
Call, M. L., 500n41
Callinan, M., 508n123
Callister, R. R., 531n19
Caloyeras, J. P., 542n96
Camara, W., 501n56, 506n70
Camberato, J., 555n125
Cameron, K. L., 523n25, 557n43
Cameron, L., 539n45
Campbell, B. H., 525n65
Campbell, C. A., 522n124
Campbell, E. M., 529n78
Campbell, J. P., 489n6, 490n48, 492nn1–2, 497n50, 510n25, 535n121
Campion, J. E., 508n122
Campion, M. A., 492n16, 500n30, 500n42, 503n14, 504n48, 505n58, 505n64, 506n79, 507n91, 508n111, 508n116, 509n13, 511n41, 522n121, 530n97, 533n90, 548n73
Cannon-Bowers, J. A., 513n45, 527n37, 528n61, 528n63, 528n71, 529n73, 529n84
Caper, W. J., 542n99
Cappelli, P., 491n56
Carli, L. L., 554n107
Carlson, D. S., 543n130
Carmona, J. V., 544n158
Carr, A. R., 559n79
Carr, L., 500n32
Carr, S. C., 495n3
Carretta, T. R., 504n26
Carroll, A. E., 558n60
Carson, K. P., 532n52
Carsten, J. M., 532n62
Caruso, C. C., 539n38
Cascio, W. F., 491n69, 491n74, 510n24, 510n37, 510n39, 511n40, 511n44, 556n1
Casper, W. I., 516n127
Casper, W. J., 542n111
Castaneda, M. B., 533n73
Castillo, D. N., 498n68
Catano, V. M., 522n124, 556n24, 558n60
Caughlin, D. E., 549n101

Cavanagh, M. J., 516n110
Cavanaugh, M. A., 538n18
Cawley, B. D., 522n114
Cederblom, D., 520n66, 522n113
Cerasoli, C. P., 546n35
Cerrone, S., 500n40
Chalabi, M., 496n22
Chalkley, K. M., 544n140, 544n142
Chan, A. Y. L., 552n51
Chan, D., 534n92
Chan, K. Y., 521n88, 555n127
Chang, C., 536n152
Chang, C. H., 534n110, 536n150
Chao, G. T., 519n53
Charles, M. A., 498n58
Chatterjee, A., 545n10
Chaudhry, A., 551n31
Chawla, N., 494n59
Chay, Y. W., 557n41
Cheema, A., 548n79
Chemers, M. M., 555n109
Chen, D. W., 513n53
Chen, G., 504n36, 551n32
Chen, J. J., 535n117
Chen, K. C., 545n12
Chen, P. S., 545n12
Chen, Z. X., 554n87
Cheng, S. K., 526n19
Chernyak-Hai, L., 517n14
Cherry, K., 520n72
Chi, N.-W., 531n29
Chi, S.-C. S., 531n17
Chiniara, M., 552n60
Chiu, N. T., 545n12
Cho, Y., 514n81
Choi, B., 514n79
Choi, J. N., 513n31, 528n65
Choi, V., 525n55
Chong, T. T., 545n4
Christian, M. S., 506n82, 538n16
Christie, A., 550n2
Christy, A., 526n11
Chrobot-Mason, D., 514n68
Chuang, A., 529n78
Church, A. H., 494n50, 520n78, 520n82, 520n80, 522n110
Ciancetta, L. M., 519n44
Cieslak, R., 541n76
Clapperton, G., 532n50
Clark, L., 544n150
Clark, M. A., 543n119, 543n130, 544n138, 544n148
Clark, P. F., 557nn44–45
Clark, R. C., 513n38
Clarke, A. D. M., 513n39
Clarke, S., 538n13
Clarke, V., 493n36
Clause, C. S., 503n1
Claxton, G., 541n94
Cleveland, J. N., 517n16, 520n62, 541n88
Clifford, J. P., 499n12
Cloutier, J., 556n23
Cohen, D., 525n5
Cohen, R. R., 528n52
Cohen-Charash, Y., 534n103
Cohn, L. D., 493n24
Cohn, M. A., 531n39
Colbert, A. E., 491n73, 502n75
Colby, S. L., 496n17
Cole, N. D., 558n66
Colella, A., 541n88
Collins, J. M., 506n73, 538n24
Colquitt, A. L., 507n90, 522n121
Colquitt, J. A., 528n54, 529n76, 529n80, 533nn88-89, 534n100
Colvin, G., 523n1
Combs, J. G., 509n2
Conley, C., 494n55, 546n18
Conlon, D. E., 494n58, 533n88, 534n100, 558nn51–52
Connaughton, S. L., 526n21
Connelly, B. S., 505n49
Connerly, M., 507n89
Conte, C., 559n79
Conway, J. M., 508n114
Conyers, A., 496n11
Cook, K. E., 521n99
Cooke, N. J., 528n62
Cooksey, R. W., 553n75
Cooper, C. L., 543n136
Cooper, M., 519n41
Cooper, W. H., 518n38
Cooper Thomas, H. D., 512n13
Corrington, A. R., 526n19
Cortina, J. M., 502n73, 546n16
Cortini, M., 509n16
Costa, G., 539n39
Costa, P. T., 504n30, 504n47
Costa, S. P., 536n152
Courtright, S. H., 504n23
Coutts, L. M., 520n71
Cox, S., 521n92
Coyle-Shapiro, J. A. M., 535n129, 536n152
Crafts, J. L., 499n11, 508n121
Crain, T. L., 543n115, 543n118, 543n121
Credé, M., 553n82
Cristol, D. S., 494n48
Cronshaw, S. F., 499n13
Crook, T. R., 509n2
Cropanzano, R., 533n79, 533n91, 536n149, 542n106
Crosby, F. J., 497n51
Cross, R., 512n12
Csikszentmihalyi, M., 546nn23–24, 546n26
Cucina, J. M., 489n8
Culbert, S. A., 522n120
Culbertson, S. S., 489n3, 489n8, 499n1, 498n64, 499n66, 502n77, 505n53, 507nn104–105, 508nn112–113, 508n115, 508n120, 513n34, 513n54, 522n119, 532n57, 533n81, 535n114, 536n155, 542n114, 543n124, 543n127
Cullen, M. J., 514n60
Cummings, L. L., 521n97, 553n76
Cunningham, E. L., 495n9
Cunningham, M. R., 501n56, 506n70
Currie, J. S., 556n9
Curtis, S., 515n105
Czarnowsky, M., 511n6

Dabos, G. E., 536n154
Daft, R. L., 495n67
Dagher, A., 545n14
Dai, G., 524n48
Dai, W., 541n81
Dalal, R. S., 532n43, 532n47
Dalton, C. M., 493n27
Dalton, D. R., 493n27, 539n50
Daly, M., 540n67, 545n8
Damico, A., 541n94
Dang, C. T., 492n22
Daniel, M. H., 503n10
Daniels, K., 547n47
Daniels, M. A., 530n7
Danielson, C. C., 511nn3–4
Dansereau, F., 551n23

Darr, W., 522n124
Davies, A., 510n20
Davis, C. A., 521n107
Davis, D. J., 495n74
Davis, J. H., 528n53, 528n55
Davison, R. B., 494n58, 526n20
Dawis, R. V., 532n49, 532n53
Day, D. D., 547n40
Day, D. V., 519n48, 550n5
Day, E. A., 508n127
Dean, G., 509n10
De Angelis, K., 512n48
DeArmond, S., 549n85
de Bakker, F., 491n65
Debrah, Y. A., 554n87
DeCelles, K. A., 530n16
DeChurch, L. A., 526n16, 528n68, 554n98
Deci, E. L., 546nn32–33, 546n36
De Cuyper, N., 544n147
Deery, S. J., 540n54, 556n18
D'Egidio, E. L., 500n23
de Goey, P., 530n16
DeGrassi, S. W., 507n108
DeHaven, A., 495n74
Delaney, L., 545n8
Deloitte, 515n85
DeLong, T., 513n40
de Manzano, Ö., 546n26
Demerouti, E., 533n79, 533n84, 538n22, 546nn30–31, 553n79
DeMeuse, K. P., 524n48
Demonte, E. K., 549n96
Deng, J., 541n81
den Hartog, D. N., 517n3
Denis, P. L., 556n23
DeNisi, A. S., 517n2, 517n10, 517n17, 518n34, 521n94, 557n38
Derks, D., 553n79
DeRouin, R. E., 490n27
DeRue, D. S., 516n124, 527n40, 550n9, 554n94
DeSanctis, G., 526n17
Descatha, A., 539n43
Deslauriers, J., 549n93
Desrosiers, E., 523n9
de Vries, B., 538n17
De Vries, T. A., 526n20
de Wit, F. R. C., 527n43
Dick, R. B., 539n38
Dickinson, T. L., 522n117
Dickson, A., 495n74
Diehn, E. W., 540n71
Diener, E., 531n27, 546n17
Dierdorff, E. C., 499n5, 499nn9–10, 499n21, 520n67, 528n60, 542n112
Digman, J. M., 545n7
Dilchert, S., 496n24
Dillon, M. M., 531n37
Dimotakis, N., 530n11
Dineen, B. R., 509n9
Dinh, J. E., 550n10, 552n40, 553n65
Dino, R. N., 539n48
Dionne, S. D., 553n75
Dipboye, R. L., 504n48, 505n58, 505n64, 508n110
Dirks, K. T., 555n129
Djuric, D., 513n42
Dobbin, F., 495n8, 496n16
Doden, W., 536n152
Dominick, P. G., 518n30
Dong, Y., 529n78
Dorman, P. W., 490n44, 554nn101–102
Dorsey, D. W., 502n73
Douma, B., 548n65
Doverspike, D., 491n63, 499n15, 524n38
Dovidio, J. F., 498n54
Dragoni, L., 511n8
Drasgow, F., 507n98, 507n100, 555n127
Driscoll, D. M., 514n70
Driscoll, T., 539n43
Driskell, J. E., 526nn28–29
Driskell, T., 526nn28–29
Drory, A., 536n139
Druskat, V. A., 529n90
Dubner, S. J., 555n120
DuBois, C. L. Z., 496n28, 500n36
DuBois, D. A., 496n28, 512n24
DuBois, S., 524n49
Duchon, J. C., 540n58
Dudley-Meislahn, N., 493n46
Duffy, M. K., 530n14, 535n122
Dulebohn, J. H., 494n58, 537n163, 551n25
Dumani, S., 542n113
Dumdum, R., 526n13
Dunham, R. B., 533n73, 540n57, 553n76
Dunlap, S., 492n17
Dunleavy, E., 497n45, 497n53
Dunning, D., 522n109
Dupre, K. E., 535n135, 556n24
Durbin, D.-A., 523n2
DuVernet, A. M., 499n9, 513n40
Dwight, S. A., 506n75
Dyer, J. H., 525n62
Dyer, W. G., 525n62
Dyer, W. W. G., 525n62
Dzieweczynski, J. L., 503n6

Eagly, A. H., 554n107, 555n113
Earnest, D. R., 550n110, 550n113
Eatough, E. M., 534n110
Eby, L. T., 515nn100–101, 515n103, 515n105, 515n107, 542n111
Eden, D., 492nn8–9, 492n12, 494n60
Edens, P. S., 513n32, 517n131
Edmondson, A. C., 530n96
Edwards, B. D., 506n82
Edwards, J. R., 503n4
Edwards, M. S., 535n120
Eek, F., 539n34
Effal, B., 556n22
Egan, M., 545n8
Ehrhart, M. G., 523nn11–13, 523n18, 524n35
Ehrlich, S. B., 553n69
Eid, M., 540n65
Eidenfalk, J., 547n37
Ekeberg, S. E., 548n61
Ekkekakis, P., 530n5
Ekkirala, S., 554n91
Elder, A. E., 498n56
Elfering, A., 542nn104–105
Ellen, B. P., III, 553n85
Ellington, J. K., 542n112
Elliot, D. L., 541n92
Ellis, A. M., 543n134
Ellis, A. P. J., 518n37, 529n82
Ellis, D., 524n30
Ely, K., 514nn62–63, 516n127
Engdahl, L., 559n74
England, G. W., 532n53
Epitropaki, O., 551n29, 553n71
Erdogan, B., 549n97, 549nn100–101, 551n24, 551n31
Erez, A., 518n36, 529n80, 534n104
Erickson, E. H., 542n97
Erofeev, D., 520n73

Ertug, G., 491n65
Estey, M., 556n25
Eva, N., 552n57
Evans, D. C., 498n59
Evans, M., 549n92
Evans, S. C., 515n105
Eveleth, D. M., 509n15
Eveleth, H., 509n15
Exum, E., 542n96
Eyde, L. D., 500n32

Farager, J., 518n31
Farr, J. L., 491n77
Farrell, J. N., 512n25
Fasel, U., 542nn104–105
Federman, J. E., 520n69
Feinberg, M., 530n9
Feldman, D. C., 512n11, 525n51, 532n45, 537n161, 537n162, 549n98
Ferguson, C. J., 493n27
Ferrari, J. R., 549n86
Ferré, S., 545n13
Ferreiro, P., 543n136
Ferreri, L., 545n14
Ferri, L., 510n19
Ferrin, D. L., 555n129
Ferris, D. L., 549n88
Ferris, G. R., 536n142, 536nn146–148, 551n25
Ferzandi, L., 528n59
Fetterman, D. M., 493n42
Feuille, P., 557n34
Fiedler, F. E., 551n17
Field, S. C. T., 514n70
Fieseler, C., 538nn31–32
Figueiro, M. G., 546n15
Fine, S., 501n62, 505n66
Fine, S. A., 499n4, 499n13
Finegan, J. E., 528n55
Finkelstein, L. M., 497n43
Finnegan, E. B., 506n79
Fischer, F. M., 539n43
Fisher, C. D., 530n1, 530n3
Fisher, D. M., 527n34, 528n60
Fisher, G., 498n56
Fisk, G. M., 501n63
Fiss, P. C., 524n39
Flaxman, P. E., 548n69
Fleenor, J. W., 520n79
Fleishman, E. A., 499n20, 503n20, 503n22
Fletcher, C., 517n5
Fleuren, B., 495n66
Flores, D., 494n55
Flynn, F. J., 530nn9–10
Fogli, L., 500n34, 500n36, 511n44
Folger, R., 504n43, 534n95, 547n39
Folkard, S., 539n36
Foo, S. C., 5328n71
Ford, B. Q., 530n9
Ford, H., 524n29
Ford, J. K., 512n27, 513n36, 516nn120–122, 517n132
Ford, M. T., 542n110, 546n35
Forgas, J. P., 530n13
Forner, V. W., 547n37
Forsey, C., 497n35
Forsyth, D. R., 505n54
Foster, D., 508n131
Foster, J., 499n14
Foster, R. D., 524n42
Foti, R. J., 553n67
Fowler, J. S., 545n13
Fox, K. E., 532n42
Fox, R. L., 494n55
Fox, S., 535n119
Fraile, G., 543n136
Francioli, S. P., 497n41
Francis, L., 556n24
Fredrickson, B. L., 531n35, 531n36, 531nn39–41
Freedman, D. O., 491n61
Freelon, D., 496n19
French, J. R. P., Jr., 518n20, 550n12
French, K. A., 542n113
Frese, M., 502n80, 514n59, 537nn4–5, 548n59, 555n126
Fried, Y., 548n68, 548n70
Frieder, R. E., 553n86
Friedman, J. P., 494n57
Friedman, R., 531n17, 558n50
Frijda, N. H., 530n2
Fritz, C., 533n86
Fritz, H. L., 531n37
Frone, M. R., 542n102, 543n132, 544nn156–157, 545n162, 545n164, 552n44
Frost, P. J., 539n40
Fryer, D., 540n64
Fryxell, G. E., 557n27
Fu, S. Q., 526n25
Fugate, M., 531n38, 543n128, 544n138, 544n148
Fujita, F., 531n27
Fullagar, C. J., 533n81, 543n124, 546n29, 546n31, 557nn44–45, 558n55
Fuller, J. A., 539n36
Fuller, J. B., Jr., 557n42
Fulmer, C. A., 556n21
Furnham, A., 495n3
Furst, S. A., 535n115, 551n26

Gaddis, B., 499n14
Gade, P. A., 490n27
Gaertner, S. L., 498n54
Galaif, E. R., 544n158
Galanti, T., 509n16
Galbicsek, C., 544n154
Gale, E., 494n47
Gale, J., 554n92
Galinsky, A. D., 492nn10–11, 548n63
Gallagher, D. G., 557nn44–45
Galvin, B. M., 552n62
Garcia, A. M., 509n11
Gardner, W. L., 550n10, 551n38, 552n40, 552n50, 553n65, 554n104
Garrett, L., 539n45
Gatewood, K. D., 540n69
Gavin, K., 518n32
Gebhardt, D. L., 503n21, 504n24
Geddes, D., 531n19
Gelfand, M. J., 515n88, 525n55, 527n49, 556n21
Gellatly, I. R., 533n71
Gentry, W. A., 520n81, 521n87
George, G., 493n29
George Mwangi, C. A., 495n9
Gerhart, B., 546n21
Gerum, D. R., 544n151
Gettman, H. J., 515n88
Ghiselli, E. E., 490n33, 490n47
Giacalone, R. A., 535n122
Giangreco, A., 524n40
Gibby, R. E., 489n1, 489n5
Gibson, C. B., 528n58
Gibson, W. M., 507n98
Gier, J. A., 518n33
Gijselaers, W. H., 521n102
Gill, H., 528n55

Gillespie, J. Z., 547n54, 548n77
Gilliland, S. W., 534nn92–93
Gil-Monte, P. R., 530n8
Gilson, L. L., 529n85
Gilstrap, J. B., 534n113
Gino, F., 492nn10–11, 492n18
Giumetti, G. W., 518n29
Glaser, J., 543n126
Glassdoor, 558n73
Glen, E. K., 531n38
Glibkowski, B. C., 537n164
Glomb, T. M., 535n134
Glynn, S. J., 498n65
Gnambs, T., 507n103
Goates, N., 558n50
Godard, J., 556n19
Godderis, L., 539n43
Goeddeke, F. X., Jr., 557n40
Goetzel, R. Z., 501n47
Goff, M., 520n61, 520n77
Gogus, C. I., 512n20
Goh, Z. W., 543n125
Golden, T. D., 539nn47–48
Goldenberg, J., 501n62
Goldman, B., 529n79, 529n89
Goldsmith, M., 520n83
Goler, L., 554n92
Gomez-Andres, A., 545n14
Goncalo, J. A., 528n51
Gonzales, K., 546n15
Gonzalez-Romá, V., 533n78
Goode, D. L., 522n118
Gordon, M. E., 557nn26–28, 557nn44–46, 558n53, 558n61
Gordon, S., 525n55
Gorgievski, M., 533n82
Gorman, C. A., 519nn49–50
Gorman, J. C., 528n62
Gosling, S. D., 492n6
Gottschalk, P., 555n119
Gowan, M. A., 540n69
Gowing, M. K., 554n105
Graen, G. B., 551n23, 551n34, 554n97
Grambow, D. M., 509n8
Grande, B., 494n53, 527n38
Grandey, A. A., 501n63, 502n67, 502n70, 531n29
Grant, A. M., 492n14, 495n2, 516n110, 546n34, 548n68, 548n70, 554n92
Grant, C., 501n52
Grant, D. M., 534n106
Gray, D. E., 516n112
Green, S. G., 502n68, 551n33
Greenberg, J., 501n58, 522n115, 534n99, 534n101, 535n120
Greene, C. L., 540n72
Greengard, S., 527n35
Greenhaus, J. H., 543n116
Greenleaf, R. K., 552n56
Greer, L. L., 527n43
Greer, T. W., 541n79
Gregg, P., 540n66
Gregori, A., 492n4
Greguras, G. J., 520n61, 520n77, 521n89, 530n7
Griepentrog, B. K., 509n6
Griffeth, R. W., 500n39
Griffin, D., 549n91, 549n93
Griffin, K. A., 495n9
Griffin, M. A., 501n54, 538nn13–15
Griffith, J. A., 552n55
Griffith, K. H., 494n52
Griffith, R. L., 492n79, 505n65
Grigsby, D. M., 557n49
Groen, B., 491n73
Grote, G., 494n53, 527n38
Groth, M., 502nn64–65
Grubb, A., 522n121
Grubb, W. L., III, 506n81
Grube, J. A., 533n73
Gruman, J. A., 512n19, 518n18
Guarana, C. L., 492n22
Gudanowski, D. M., 520n73
Guenole, N., 505n57
Guest, D., 556n13
Guillaume, Y. R. F., 516n117
Guion, R. M., 497n33, 497n52, 500n28, 510n32, 511n41
Gumusluoglu, L., 549n101
Gündemir, S., 555n117
Gupta, V., 490n44, 554nn101–102
Gurciek, K., 515n87
Gureckis, T. M., 513n56
Gurowiec, P. J., 540n74
Gutman, A., 498n60
Guzzo, R. A., 528n69

Haas, M., 493n29
Hackman, J. R., 548nn66–67, 555n128
Haddock-Millar, J., 496n25
Hadley, C. N., 548n78
Hafner, M., 546n16
Haga, W., 551n23
Hagan, C. M., 520n76
Hagberg, J., 501n51
Haire, E. R., 494n55
Hajcak, G., 545nn1–2
Halbesleben, J. R. B., 551n28
Hall, I., 501n50
Hamilton, K., 528n59
Hammer, L. B., 498n63, 541n92, 543n115, 543n118, 543n121, 543n134
Hammer, T. H., 557n39, 558n69
Hamner, W. C., 557n36
Handler, L., 507n100
Hang, K., 495n1
Hanges, P. J., 490n44, 494n61, 494n63, 554nn101–102
Hansen, C. P., 520n73
Hansen, S. D., 532n42, 537n166
Hanson, M. A., 500n23, 508n121
Hanson, R. M., 517n9
Harari, M. B., 518n35, 520n63, 549n99
Hardonk, S., 544n147
Hare, R. D., 505n56, 553n81
Harman, W. S., 549n95
Harms, H. J., 507n97
Harms, P. D., 493n38, 553n82
Harold, C. M., 509n6
Harrell, T. W., 490n42
Harrington, B., 554n92
Harris, K. J., 547n42
Harris, L., 509n17
Harris, M. M., 504n31
Harris, T. A., 498n69
Harris, T. B., 520n64
Harris, W. G., 501n56, 506n70
Harrison, D. A., 493n28, 501n44, 535n130
Hart, P. M., 538n13, 538n15
Harter, N., 489n11
Hartley, J. F., 558n62
Hartman, N. S., 506n81
Hartnell, C. A., 552n59
Hartwell, C. J., 508n111
Harvey, J., 502n76
Harvey, P., 547n42
Hatfield, J. D., 547n40

Hauenstein, N. M. A., 522n127
Hauptmann, M., 525n3
Hause, E. L., 525n50
Hausknecht, J. P., 500n37
Hawkins, H. C., 541n77
Hawkins, K., 501n47
Hawver, T. H., 531n31
Hayes, A. F., 540n54
Hayles, V. R., 514n65
Hayter, S., 559n81
Hazucha, J., 511n8
Heavey, C., 553n66
Hebl, M. R., 514n69, 526n19
Hedberg, L. M., 533n71
Hedge, J. W., 519n45
Hedlund, J., 503n11
Heerwagen, J., 546n15
Heidemeier, H., 520n70
Heilbrunn, S., 553n83
Heilman, M. E., 497n52, 498n55, 535n117, 555n112
Heine, S. J., 492n3
Heller, D., 504n41, 504n46, 532n55
Hempel, S., 546n15
Henderson, A. A., 553n68
Henderson, D. J., 551n27
Henle, C. A., 495n71, 535n122
Hennig-Thurau, T., 502nn64–65
Henning, J. B., 496n29
Henrich, J., 492n3
Henry, R. A., 555n118
Hepburn, C. G., 556n16
Hersey, P., 551n20
Hershcovis, M. S., 535n135
Herzberg, F., 546n20
Hesketh, B., 500n32
Heskiau, R., 543n135
Hester, K., 557n42
Heuser, A., 512n15
Hewlin, P. F., 525n54
Heydens-Gahir, H. A., 542n105
Heywood, L., 497n36
Hezlett, S. A., 515n104
Higgins, C., 491n65
Higgins, C. A., 508n129
Highhouse, S., 497n34, 498n56, 508n126, 510n22
Hilton, L. G., 546n15
Hinkin, T. R., 552n43
Hipp, L., 543n133
Hippler, T., 514n78
Hitchcock, E. M., 539n38
Hitt, M. A., 552n64
Ho, L. A., 546n28
Hoch, J. E., 526n12
Hochwarter, W. A., 536n141, 536n146
Hodges, T. D., 552n51
Hoffman, B. J., 515n105, 519n58, 521n87, 521n90, 550n8
Hoffman, C. C., 492n19, 494n47
Hofmann, D. A., 538n23, 541n87
Hofstede, G., 490n40, 523n4
Hofstede, G. J., 523n4
Hofstede Insights, 523n8
Hogan, J., 499n14, 515n89, 515n97, 515n99
Hogan, R., 515nn89–90, 515nn96–97, 515n99, 554n89
Holden, L. M, 494n47
Hollander, E. P., 550n3
Hollenbeck, J. R., 495n73, 504n48, 505n58, 505n64, 516n124, 525n2, 526n20, 526nn26-27, 527n40, 528n70, 529n82
Holman, D., 541n89
Holtz, B. C., 503n18, 507n101, 509n6
Hom, P. W., 500n39, 512n18, 532n61
Homan, A. C., 555n117
Honts, C. R., 506n78
Hoobler, J. M., 554n108
Hooijberg, R., 552n63
Hopkins, M. M., 554n106
Hoption, C., 550n2
Hornung, S., 543n126
Horvitz, T., 528n66
Horwitz, M. J., 540n73
Hosoya, G., 540n65
Hough, L. M., 506n68
House, R. J., 490n44, 526n8, 551n21, 554nn101–102
Houston, L., 502n67
Howard, A., 492n80
Howard, E., 549n102
Howell, B., 544n144
Howes, J. C., 541n85
Howes, S. S., 494n55, 505n55, 531n33, 541n85
Hu, J., 550n10, 551n30, 552n40, 552n61, 553n65
Huang, J. L., 502n74, 516n122
Huber, C. R., 505n63
Huber, K. B., 505n63
Huckabee, I., 550n108
Huet, E., 511n9
Huff, J. W., 540n53
Huffcutt, A. I., 507nn104–105, 508nn112–114, 508n120, 541n85
Huffman, A. H., 496n29, 496n30
Hughes, J., 548n57
Hui, C., 535n118
Hulin, C. L., 532n43, 533nn47–48, 532n51
Hülsheger, U. R., 495n66, 503n13, 531n28, 552n53
Humphrey, R. H., 531nn30-31
Humphrey, S. E., 526n25, 548nn71-72, 550n9
Hunt, S. T., 518n19
Hunter, C. M., 546n15
Hunter, E. M., 501n57, 543n130
Hunter, J. E., 490n36, 490n41, 493n23, 510n29, 510n31, 511n42
Hunter, S. T., 554n90
Hurrell, J. J., 542n98
Husain, M., 545n4
Huseman, R. C., 547n40
Huszczo, G. E., 556n9
Hyatt, D., 506n76
Hyten, C., 527n36, 527n42

Ilgen, D. R., 521n107, 525nn1–2, 525n4, 526n26, 528n70, 529n82
Ilies, R., 504n35, 504n42, 530n11, 532n56, 543n123, 543n125, 545n6, 548n60, 550n11
Inness, M., 535n135
International Agency for Research on Cancer, 539n37
International Brotherhood of Teamsters, 559n77
International Labour Organization, 498n61, 498n67, 498n70, 539n42
International Trade Administration, U.S. Department of Commerce, 493n34
Internet Live Stats, 490n50
Ireland, R. D., 552n64
Ispas, D., 530n12
Itzkovich, Y., 553n83
Ivanitskaya, L., 520n73
Iverson, J. O., 494n55

Iverson, R. D., 556n18

Jack, A. I., 494n57
Jackson, A. T., 505n53, 505n55
Jackson, C. L., 502n69, 505n50, 527n33, 529n87
Jackson, F., 489n8
Jackson, S. E., 527n45
Jacobs, R. R., 510n35, 551n14
Jacobson, K. J. L., 517n11
Jaffe, S. R., 494n64
Jahn, J., 494n55
Jahoda, M., 501n49, 540n59
Jain, S., 511n47
Jamal, M., 539n40
James, L. R., 553n75
Jamieson, D., 559n78
Jampol, L., 519n42
Jansen, K. J., 524n36
Jansen, N. W. H., 539n33
Janz, B. D., 529n76
Janz, T., 508n119
Jaramillo, D., 543n119
Jarrell, S. B., 557n33
Jarvenpaa, S., 528n56
Javidan, M., 490n44, 554nn101–102
Jawahar, I. M., 520n61
Jay, A., 524n31
Jayne, M. E., 511n47
Jeanneret, P. R., 490n35, 499nn18–19, 500n23
Jehn, K. A., 514n66, 514n71, 527n43, 527n47
Jenkins, M. R., 501n53
Jensen, J. M., 521n95, 535n128, 554n93
Jensen, M. C., 526n23
Jermier, J. M., 553n73
Jimmieson, N. L., 553n78
Jirnauer, D., 529n79, 529n89
Johannesen-Schmidt, M. C., 555n113
Johns, G., 501nn45-46, 501n48, 532n63
Johnson, D. E., 534n104
Johnson, J. L., 500n33
Johnson, J. V., 539n41
Johnson, J. W., 551n19
Johnson, R. C., 539n51
Johnson, R. E., 534n110, 548n59
Johnston, D. C., 558n72
Jones, D. A., 509n5
Jones, G. R., 512n17
Jones, J. W., 501n56, 506n70
Jones, K., 549n87
Jones, K. J., 515n92, 515n95
Jones, K. P., 497n45, 497n53
Jones, M., 547n37
Jones, R. G., 496n21, 521n105, 528n72
Jones, R. J., 516n117
Jones, S. D., 548n61
Jonsen, K., 496n15
Joo, H., 553n66
Jorgenson, D., 503n7
Joseph, D. L., 531n32
Josephson, M., 501n51
Joshi, A., 527n45
Judge, T. A., 504n35, 504n38, 504nn41–42, 504n46, 505n50, 505n63, 508n129, 518n36, 530n15, 531n23, 532n43, 532nn46–48, 532nn55–56, 532n58, 532n64, 542n109, 548n60, 550n11, 551n18
Juillerat, T., 548n68, 548n70
Jung, J., 514n79
Jung, K. M., 517n133

Kaciak, E., 538n30
Kacmar, K. M., 500n40
Kahai, S., 526n13
Kaiser, R. B., 515n89, 515n97, 515n99, 554n89
Kalev, A., 495n8, 496n16
Kalish, Y., 520n65
Kamdar, D., 527n41
Kaminga, A. C., 541n81
Kammeyer-Mueller, J. D., 504n32, 532n46, 557n40
Kampschroer, K., 546n15
Kane, J. S., 518n39, 519n40, 520n76
Kanfer, R., 512n23, 512n26, 516n118, 540n68, 548n59, 548n76
Kant, I., 539n33
Kantor, J., 524nn26–27
Kaplan, J., 509n10
Kapp, K. M., 490n51, 550n107
Kappas, A., 540n52
Karakitapoglu-Aygun, Z., 549n101
Karam, E. P., 554n94
Karau, S. J., 529n88
Karimullina, K., 501n50
Karl, K. A., 549n104
Karlson, B., 539n34
Kaspar, K., 507n103
Kaszycki, A., 513n40
Katzell, R. A., 491n76
Kaur, S., 506n87
Kausel, E. E., 505n53, 505n55, 508n115, 510n21
Kavanagh, M. J., 516n123, 519n45
Kavanagh, P., 522n116
Kawakami, N., 533n84
Kay, E., 518n20
Kędra, E., 540n74
Keeler, K., 546n16
Keeney, J., 543n123, 543n125
Keeping, L. M., 519nn54–55, 522n111, 522n114
Kehoe, J. F., 500n32, 505n51, 511n41
Keinan, G., 531n34
Keller, J., 491n56
Kelloway, E. K., 556n24, 558n60
Kelly, E., 495n8
Keltner, D., 530n6
Kemp, C., 507n101, 550n4
Kendall, L., 532n51
Kennedy, J. C., 521n88
Kenward, K., 541n94
Kepes, S., 497n47
Keran, C. M., 540n58
Kerr, N. L., 495n72
Kerr, S., 529n91, 553n72
Kersting, M., 503n13
Kessler, S. R., 515n106
Ketchen, D. J., 553n66
Keyes, V., 544n159
Khazon, S., 532n59
Kiburz, K. M., 539n51
Kidder, D. L., 537n158
Kieszczynska, U., 519n52
Kiiver, H. M., 539n43
Kim, B. H., 554n93
Kim, J. K., 494n59
Kim, M. U., 528n65
Kim, R., 545n13
Kim, S. L., 511n5
King, E. B., 497n45, 497n53, 514n69, 526n19
King, K., 511n6
King, W. C., 547n40

Kinicki, A. J., 517n11, 521n108, 523n15, 523n17, 532n52, 532n61, 540n62
Kinkade, K. M., 515n105
Kinman, G., 501n52
Kirkman, B. L., 523n5
Kirkpatrick, D. L., 516n126
Kirkpatrick, S. A., 550n6
Kisamore, J. L., 505n62
Kish-Gephart, J. J., 535n130
Kjaer, T. W., 545n11
Klaas, B. S., 557n29
Klahr, D., 495n68
Klehe, U.-C., 500n35
Klein, H. J., 512nn14–16, 513n39, 532n44, 532n65, 533n70
Klein, K. J., 526n9
Klein, S. R., 496n30
Kleiner, C., 529n85
Kleingeld, A., 548n64, 548n80
Kleinmann, M., 504n27, 511n45
Klimoski, R. J., 509n6, 528n72
Klineberg, S. L., 498n57
Klion, R., 501n56, 506n70
Klotz, A. C., 502n76, 527n44
Kluemper, D. H., 551n28
Kluger, A. N., 507n90, 521n94, 522n125
Knapp, D. J., 490n48
Knight, P. A., 546n29
Knoll, K., 528n56
Koh, C., 521n88
Kolbe, M., 494n53, 527n38
Kolomitro, K., 513n43, 513n52
Konar, E., 519n41
König, C. J., 511n45, 548n83
Koopman, J., 494n59
Koppes, L. L., 489n4, 489nn13–14, 489n18, 489n20, 489n22
Korabik, K., 530n8, 555n111
Korshunov, K. S., 545n13
Kossek, F. R., 539n46
Kostadinov, V., 544n160
Kostek, J. A., 556n7
Kotter, J. P., 524n44
Kozlowski, S. W. J., 513n51, 513n55, 514n61, 517n132, 519n53, 525n1, 525n4, 525n7, 526n9, 526n12, 554n93
Kraatz, M. S., 537n162
Kraiger, K., 512n27, 513n34, 513nn36–37, 513n54, 514n62, 517n133
Kram, K. E., 515n102
Kramer, J., 536n147
Kramer, R. M., 535n126
Kramer, S. J., 548n78
Kramer, W. S., 554n95
Kraut, A. I., 492n78
Kravitz, D. A., 497n44, 498n57
Kreiner, G. E., 543n128, 543n137, 544n138, 544n141, 544n148
Kreiss, D., 496n19
Kristof-Brown, A. L., 524n32
Krivkovich, A., 519n41
Krome, L. R., 522n119
Kroon, B., 553n77
Kruger, J., 549n92
Kuehl, K. S., 541n92
Kulik, C. T., 514n64, 514n67, 514n72
Kulkari, M., 524n46
Kulkarni, M., 509n3
Kuncel, N. R., 505n63
Kung, M.-C., 509n13
Kuo, T. H., 546n28
Kuruvilla, S., 558n58
Kwang, T., 492n6
Kwong, J. Y. Y., 519n57, 519n60

Lacerenza, C. N., 526n18
Laczo, R. M., 500n31
Ladd, R. T., 558n61
Laginess, A. J., 518n35
Lam, C. F., 533n86
Lam, K. C. H., 549n93
Lam, S. S., 535n118
Lam, T. C. M., 513n43, 513n52
Lambert, D., 542n111
Lambert, L. S., 535n122
Lamm, E., 549n103
Lance, C. E., 521n87
Landay, K., 553n82
Landen, D. D., 498n68
Landis, R. S., 493n31, 533n87
Landy, F. J., 489n15, 489n23, 490n25, 499n8, 510n28
Lang, J., 503n13
Lang, J. W. B., 503n13
Lange, D., 552n62
Langevin, A. M., 500n37
Lapierre, L. M., 543n136
Laran, J., 549n90
Larcher, K., 545n14
Lasswell, H., 536n140
Latham, G. P., 508n116, 547nn49–51, 547n56, 548n58, 548n62, 558nn66–68
Latham, M. E., 529n79, 529n89
Lau, C. L. L., 553n66
Law, K. S., 535n118
Lawler, E. E., III, 522n126, 529n86
Lawrence, T. B., 523n22
Layne, L. A., 498n68
Le, H., 503n14
Leas, K., 511n47
Leavitt, K., 492n22, 518n36
LeBlanc, M. M., 535n135
LeBreton, J. M., 501n61
Ledford, G. E., Jr., 522n126, 529n86
Lee, D.-Y., 549n95
Lee, H. J., 501n53
Lee, I. H., 545n12
Lee, J., 521n95
Lee, J. J., 492n18
Lee, K., 530n14
Lee, M., 514n81
Lee, T. W., 500n39, 549n95
Lee, Y., 519n41
Lefkowitz, J., 490n37, 495n76, 556nn2–3, 557n32
Leidner, D., 528n56
Leiter, M. P., 533n80
Leiva, P. I., 505n53
Lemmon, G., 554n108
LeNoble, C. A., 524n31
Lentz, E., 515n105
LePine, J. A., 527n33, 528n54, 528n70, 529nn80–81, 529n87, 534n104, 538nn19–20
LePine, M. A., 538nn19–20
Lerner, J. S., 530n6
Lester, P. B., 493n38
Levashina, J., 507n91, 508n111
Leventhal, G. S., 534n94
Levine, E. L., 499nn5–6, 500n29, 530n12
Levine, J. D., 499n22
Levine, J. M., 526n24
Levine, N., 514n69
Levitt, S. D., 555n120

Levy, P. E., 521n101, 522n111, 522n114, 536n150
Lewin, K., 524n43
Lezotte, D. V., 507n102
Li, A., 536n149, 542n106, 554n91
Li, C., 525n55
Li, J., 539n43
Li, M., 541n86
Li, N., 520n64
Liao, H., 529n78
Lichtenstein, N., 559n82
Liden, R. C., 550n10, 551n25, 551nn30–31, 552n40, 552n57, 552n61, 553n65
Lider, M., 491n63
Lievens, F., 499n17, 504n31, 506n83, 508n125, 509n7, 509n13
Lilienfeld, S. O., 494n62
Lim, V. K. G., 549n88
Lima, L., 515n105
Lin, J. H., 550n111
Lin, S.-H. (J.), 552n49
Lin, Y., 541n86
Lindsey, A., 497n45, 497n53, 514n69
Linnenluecke, M., 491n66
Lisco, C. C., 558n50
Litwiller, B., 493n25
Liu, A., 541n81
Liu, H., 542n96
Liu, R., 501n50
Liu, S., 542n101, 543n129
Liu, Y., 492nn20–21, 536n146
Liverpool, P. R., 536n144
Livingston, B. A., 542n109
Livingstone, L. P., 500n43
Llorens, S., 546n27
Lobel, J. A., 541n78
Locke, E. A., 529n79, 529n89, 547nn49–51, 547n56, 548n58, 548n62, 550n6
Lockwood, A., 542n111
Lofquist, L. H., 532n53
Logan, J., 545n13
Lombardo, M. M., 515n98
Lombardo, T., 497n32
London, M., 518n18, 520n80, 521n103
Long, M., 541n94
Long, S. R., 501n47
Lootens, H., 540n60
Lopez, Y. P., 536n155
Lopina, E. C., 544nn143–145
Lord, R. G., 550n10, 552n40, 553n65, 553n67, 553n70
Lou, H. C., 545n11
Louckx, F., 544n147
Lounsbury, J. W., 520n66
Lovecraft, H. P., 541n84
Lowe, K. B., 554n104
Lowman, R. L., 492n80
Lu, C. Q., 543n136
Lu, L., 543n136
Luan, S., 530n7
Lucas, J. A., 498n55
Luchman, J., 502n73
Luciano, M. M., 554n99
Lueke, S. B., 511n43
Luhmann, M., 540n65
Luke, J., 493n37
Luksyte, A., 549n102
Luo, Z., 542n107
Luong, A., 494n48
Luria, G., 520n65
Luthans, F., 538nn27–28, 538n29
Lynch, W., 501n47
Lyness, K. S., 555n112, 555nn114–115
Lyons, B. D., 550n8
Lyons, B. J., 501n45
Lyra Health, 537n3
Lytle, A. L., 558n52
Lyubomirsky, S., 531n25
Lyubovnikova, J., 526n10

Macan, T. H., 508n111, 509n8
Macey, W. H., 523nn11–12, 523n18, 524n35, 533n77
Machin, M. A., 516n119
Mackay, M. M., 533n87
MacKenzie, S. B., 500n33, 552n47, 553n74
MacKenzie, W. I., 506n80
Mackey, J. D., 553nn85–86
MacKinnon, D. W., 490n43
MacLachlan, M., 495n3
Madey, S., 509n5
Madison, G., 546nn25–26
Madrid, H., 508n115
Mael, F. A., 506n85, 507n89
Magnusson, P. K. E., 546nn25–26
Magnusson Hanson, L. L., 539n43
Maher, C. P., 515n105
Mahoney, J. J., 507n93
Mainiero, L. A., 515n92, 515n95
Maldagen-Youngjohn, R., 550n8
Malm, K., 499n1
Malos, S. B., 518n21
Manapragada, A., 549n99
Manson, T. M., 505n62
Manzione, G., 491n57
Marantz, Henig, R., 518n32
Marco-Pallarés, J., 545n14
Margenau, J. M., 558n56
Margolis, A., 507n100
Markant, D. B., 513n56
Marks, M. A., 526nn15–16, 526n22, 527n32, 528n64, 528n67, 554n98, 554n100
Marks, M. L., 524n48, 525n52, 541n83
Marler, L. E., 521n92
Marlow, S. L., 526n18
Marquardt, M., 523n7, 523n10
Marr, B., 493n30
Marsh, S. M., 509n6
Marshall, N. J., 546n15
Martin, B. O., 513n43, 513n52
Martin, D. L., 507n99
Martin, J. E., 558n56
Martin, R., 551n29, 553n71
Martin, S. L., 510n23
Martinko, M. J., 553n86
Martins, L. L., 523n3
Martocchio, J. J., 501n44, 504n38
Marwick, A., 496n19
Mas-Herrero, E., 545n14
Maslach, C., 528n51, 533n80
Maslow, A. H., 546n19
Massaro, S., 494n56
Masuda, A. D., 543n122
Mathieu, J. E., 525n2, 525n5, 526n15, 526n22, 526n26, 527nn32–33, 528n67, 529n85, 554nn99–100
Matta, F. K., 552n49
Matthews, R. A., 542n110, 542n114, 543n127, 549n85, 553n68
Mattke, S., 542n96
Maurer, S. D., 508n118
Maurer, T. J., 507n107
May, D. R., 552n51
Mayer, D. M., 534n106
Mayer, K., 547n48

Mayer, R. C., 528n53, 528n55
Mayer, R. E., 513n38
Mayer, S., 503n7
Maynard, D. C., 549n98
Maynard, M. T., 529n85
McAbee, S. T., 493n31
McAllister, C. P., 553n85
McBride, T., 490n54
McCall, M. W., 511n7
McCarthy, J. M., 494n59, 509n13, 543n135
McCauley, C. D., 515n98
McCausland, T., 497n45, 497n53
McClean Parks, J., 537n158
McClean, S. T., 494n59
McCleary-Gaddy, A., 496n14
McClelland, D. C., 550n7
McClurg, L. N., 556n17
McCord, M. A., 537n10, 538n12
McCormick, B. W., 504n23
McCormick, E. J., 490n35, 499n19, 500n27
McCrae, R. R., 504n30, 504n47
4McDaniel, M. A., 493n26, 497nn46–47, 505n54, 506n79, 506n81, 508n118, 508n123, 512n25
McDonald, N., 545n2
McFarland, L. A., 505n60
McHenry, B. J., 522n119
McIlveen, P., 493n37
McIntyre, R. M., 527n39
McKay, P. F., 501n57
McKee, D., 521n92
McKee-Ryan, F. M., 521n108, 532n52, 540n62
McKersie, S. J., 553n68
McKinney, N., 557n31
McLendon, C. L., 528n52
McManus, M. A., 500n38
McNall, L. A., 543n122
McNally, J., 528n55
McNamara, G., 494n58
McPhail, S. M., 494n47
McWha, I., 556n4
Mecham, R. C., 490n35
Medkik, N., 514n73
Medsker, G. J., 530n97
Meeks, M. D., 549n103
Meier, K. J., 517n6
Meier, L. L., 542nn103–105
Meijer, E., 505n52
Meiksins, P., 558n71
Meindl, J. R., 552n39, 553n69
Meinert, D., 525n60
Melchers, K. G., 504n27
Mellor, D., 495n74
Mellor, S., 558n54
Melzer, A., 513n40
Memili, E., 538n30
Mencin, A., 495n1
Menting, C., 553n77
Mercer, 522n123
Merckelbach, H., 505n52
Mesch, D. J., 539n50
Mesmer-Magnus, J. R., 528n68
Metcalf, J., 513nn57–58
Meurs, J. A., 536n147
Meuser, J. D., 550n10, 552n40, 553n65
Meyer, C. J., 558n52
Meyer, H. H., 518n20
Meyer, J. P., 532nn66–67, 533nn68-70
Meyer, R., 532n59
Mhatre, K. H., 538n28
Miake-Lye, I. M., 546n15
Miao, C., 531n30
Michalska, P., 540n74
Michel, A., 542n103
Michel, J. S., 539n46, 543n119
Mickel, A. E., 546n22
Mierke, J., 536n17
Miles, D., 496n25
Miles, E. W., 547n40
Miller, B. K., 547n41
Miller, K., 552n45
Miller, T., 544n159
Mills, M. J., 490n39, 498n64, 498n66, 502n77, 533n81, 535n114, 543n124
Miloslavic, S. A., 534n110
Min, S. W., 526n25
Minkov, M., 523n4
Mintzberg, H., 536n145
Miraglia, M., 501n48
Mishra, V., 519n52
Mitchell, J. L., 500n27
Mitchell, R., 550n111
Mitchell, T. R., 500n39, 547n50, 548n74, 549n95
Mobley, W. H., 557n38
Mohammed, S., 528n59, 528n71
Molleston, J. L., 557n38
Molloy, J. C., 511n2, 532n65
Momen, N. C., 539n43
Momm, T. D., 536n147
Mone, E. M., 518n18
Monge, P., 526n17
Montes, S. D., 537n160
Montgomery, D., 541n92
Moody, J., 510n26
Moon, H., 514n79, 529n82, 558n51
Moore, B. A., 541n76
Moore, D. A., 544n152
Moore, O. A., 511n8
Moorehead-Slaughter, O., 495n75
Moorman, R. H., 547n43
Morath, R. A., 507n89
Moray, N. P., 501n55
Moreira, M., 534n96
Moreland, R. L., 526n24
Moreno-Velazquez, I., 543n136
Morgan, H., 520n83
Morganson, V. J., 542n114, 543n127
Morgeson, F. P., 499n5, 499n10, 499n21, 500n30, 504n48, 505n58, 505n64, 506n79, 507n91, 508n111, 538n23, 548nn71-72, 554n94
Morrison, A., 515n105
Morrison, C. L., 511n6
Morrison, E. W., 521n98, 521n100
Morrison, R., 549n105
Morrison, R. F., 519n53
Morrissey, T. W., 543n133
Mortensen, M., 529n93
Moscardo, G., 516n112
Moser, K., 520n70, 540n63
Mosing, M. A., 546n25
Mosley, E., 522nn128–131
Motala, A., 546n15
Motowidlo, S. J., 508n121
Motro, D., 518n37
Mount, M. K., 504n23, 504n28, 504n33, 504n41, 504n46, 505n49, 505n63, 520n75, 532n55
Mousaid, S., 544n147
Moye, N., 517n9
Muchinsky, P. M., 489n7, 490n46, 511n46, 548n75
Muchiri, M. K., 553n75
Mudgett, B. O., 521n106

Mueller, J. S., 527n41
Mueller-Hanson, R. A., 502n73
Muller-Camen, M., 496n25
Mullins, M. E., 503n1
Mumford, M. D., 507n92
Münsterberg, H., 490n30
Muntean, C. I., 550n112
Munyon, T. P., 536n148
Muris, P., 505n52
Muros, J. P., 514n60
Murphy, K. R., 490n52, 503n6, 503n12, 504n48, 505n58, 505n64, 511n41, 517n2, 517n16, 520n62, 522n121
Murphy, L. R., 542n98
Murphy, S. E., 555n109
Murray, H. A., 490n43
Murray, M. M., 494n56

Nachreiner, F., 538n22
Nadeau, M-C, 519n41
Náfrádi, B., 539n43
Naglieri, J. A., 507n100
Nagorny, L., 500n25
Nahrgang, J. D., 516n124, 527n40, 538n23, 548n71, 550n9
Nakamura, J., 546nn24–26
Nam, K. A., 514n81
Nandkeolyar, A. K., 554n91
Naquin, C. E., 525n6
Narayanan, V. K., 539n49
Nath, R., 539n49
National Safety Council, 538n9
Naumann, S. E., 523n13
NCW Risk Management, 537n6
Neal, A., 538nn13–15
Neale, M. A., 557n47
Nease, A. A., 521n106
Nee, M. T., 503n1
Neiminen, L., 503n5
Nelson, B., 534n97
Nelson, J. K., 498n58, 502n73
Neuman, G. A., 540n53
Newcomb, M. D., 544n158
Newman, D. A., 510n35, 531n32
Newton, P. E., 503n2
Ng, K. Y., 521n88, 533n88, 534n100, 558n51
Ng, L. C., 526n19
Ng, T. W. H., 525n51, 532n45, 537n165
Nguyen, B., 549n86
Nickels, B. J., 507n88
Nicklin, J. M., 543n122, 546n35
Nief, R., 490n54
Nielsen, K., 547n47
Nir, D., 522n125
Nishiyama, K., 539n41
Noam, Y., 501n62
Noble-Tolla, M., 519n41
Noe, R. A., 511n2, 513n36, 513n39, 513n47, 529n76
Nohe, C., 542n103
Nolan, K. P., 508n126
Norenzayan, A., 492n3
Normand, J., 507n93
North, M. S., 497n41
Northcraft, G. B., 521n104
Norton, M. I., 492nn10–11
Notz, W. W., 557n48
Nübold, A., 495n66, 552n53
Nyberg, A. J., 500n41
Nystrom, P. C., 528n57

O'Boyle, E. H., Jr., 495n74, 505n54, 529n77, 531n31
O'Brien, K. E., 515n106
Odgers, C. L., 494n64
Odle-Dusseau, H., 501n56, 506nn70–72
O'Driscoll, M., 543n136
O'Driscoll, T., 490n51
Offerman, L. R., 554n105
Ogbonnaya, C., 547n47
Ogińska-Bulik, N., 540n74
Oh, I.-S., 503n14, 503n17, 504n28, 505nn49–50, 510n33, 511n8
Oke, A., 552n59
O'Keeffe, J., 497n42
Olafsen, A. H., 546n36
Oldham, G. R., 548nn66–67
O'Leary, M., 529n93
O'Leary, R. S., 522n122
Olekalns, M., 558n50
Olivé, G., 545n14
Ollander-Krane, R., 522n121
Olson, R., 541n92
Olson-Buchanan, J. B., 557n30
O'Neil, D. A., 554n106
Ones, D. S., 496n24, 501n60, 505n49, 505n61, 506nn71
Ørbæk, P., 539n34
Ordioni, J., 550n109
Ordóñez, L. D., 548n63, 548n65
Oreg, S., 524n41
O'Reilly, J., 521n95
Organ, D. W., 531n23, 534n107, 534n109, 534n111
Organisation for Economic Co-operation and Development, 496n20
Orman, D., 542n98
Ortman, J. M., 496n17
Osburn, H. G., 502n78
Osicki, M., 509n3
Österberg, K., 539n34
Ostroff, C., 493n28, 523n15, 523n17, 524n37
Oswald, A. J., 531n20
Oswald, F. L., 499n22, 506n68
Otgaar, H., 505n52
O'Toole, L. J., 517n6
Outtz, J. L., 510n27, 511n41
Overton, R. C., 507n97
Owler, K., 549n105
Özbilgin, M., 496n15
Ozminkowski, R. J., 501n47

Paauwe, J., 517n3
Padilla, A., 554nn89–90
Pagon, M., 543n136
Pal, R., 545n10
Palmer, A., 502n74
Pan, X., 541n81
Panchal, N., 541n94
Paoletti, J., 526n19
Papper, E. M., 530n97
Paradise, A., 511n6
Parise, S., 512n12
Pariyothorn, M. M., 489n2, 547n55
Parker, H. M., 516n110
Parks, K. M., 541n95
Parks, L., 546n21
Passarelli, A. M., 494n57
Passmore, J., 516n110
Patel, C., 491n65
Patel, P. C., 527n46, 535n128
Paterson, N. L., 512n13
Patterson, F., 508n125
Patton, G. K., 531n23, 532n58, 532n64
Paul, K. I., 540n63
Payne, R., 540n64

Payne, S. C., 489n2, 532n57, 536n155, 541n79, 547n55
Pearlman, K., 490n53, 499n7, 500n32, 507n98
Pearson, C. M., 535n132
Pearson, J. M., 549n89
Peccei, R., 524n40
Pecchia, L., 494n56
Pedersen, N. L., 546nn25–26
Pedigo, P., 523n9
Peetz, J., 549n91
Pega, F., 539n43
Peiró, J. M., 538n26, 549n97
Peluchette, J. V., 549n104
Pendry, L. F., 514n70
Peng, A. C., 530n11
Peng, J., 541n86
Peng, W., 550n111
Pentland, A., 493n29
Perera, H. N., 493n37
Perrewé, P. L., 501n54, 536n146
Perry, J. L., 514n66, 514n71
Peters, L. H., 518n34
Peterson, A. L., 541n76
Peterson, D. B., 516nn108–109, 516n114
Peterson, M. M., 558n56
Peterson, N. G., 499n18, 500n24
Peterson, S. J., 517n11, 552n62
Petrenko, O. V., 526n25
Peyrefitte, J., 518n39
Pfeffer, J., 491n68
Pfeiffer, K. A., 550n111
Phillips, J. S., 553n67
Phillips, K. W., 495n7
Philpot, J. W., 558n53
Piccini, P., 545n11
Piccolo, R. F., 527n33, 550n11
Pick, D., 500n25
Pickles, M., 495n69, 543n117
Pickren, W., 489n14
Pidd, K., 544n160
Pieper, K. F., 502n78
Pierce, C. A., 493n27
Pierce, J. L., 535n114, 540n57, 553n76
Pirak, M., 505n66
Pitariu, H., 543n136
Place, A., 544n153
Plester, B., 549n105
Plitnick, B., 546n15
Plowman, D. A., 524n46
Ployhart, R. E., 497n44, 500n41, 503n18, 506n80, 507n101, 509n1, 509n14, 511n5
Pocock, B., 559nn83-84
Podlesny, J. A., 506n77
Podsakoff, N. P., 534n105, 534n109, 538nn19–20
Podsakoff, P. M., 500n33, 534n105, 534n109, 552n47, 553n74
Poelmans, S. A., 543n136
Polansek, T., 559n75
Polin, B., 512n14, 512n16
Pollack, J. M., 531n31
Polman, E., 528n51
Portelli, M., 513n50
Porter, C. M., 492n16
Porter, C. O. L. H., 529n82, 533n88, 534n100, 553n72
Porter, M. E., 496n23
Poster, W. R., 502n66
Posthuma, R. A., 533n90
Postlethwaite, B. E., 504n23, 527n44
Poteet, M. L., 515n105
Powell, G. N., 543n116
Prati, M. L., 536n146
Pratt, M. G., 493n43, 523nn20–21
Priem, R. L., 528n57
Prien, E. P., 500n32
Priesemuth, M., 554n88
Priest, H. A., 530nn94-95
Prieto, J. M., 529n74
Prieto, L. C., 490n26
Prifitera, A., 507n100
Primoff, E. S., 499n4
Primps, S. B., 540n55
Pritchard, R. D., 499n1, 517n17, 548n61
Probst, T. M., 501n53
Prokopowicz, P., 525n55
Proto, E., 531n20
Pruitt, D. G., 556n20
Prussia, G. E., 517n11, 521n108
Prüss-Üstün, A. M., 539n43
Pulakos, E. D., 502n73, 503n1, 508n117, 517n9, 518n25, 522n112, 522nn121–122
Punnett, B. J., 514n76
Pursell, E. D., 508n116
Purvanova, R. K., 516n108, 526n14
Purvis, K. L., 519n43
Putka, D. J., 510n25
Pyburn, K. M., 497n44

Qian, S., 531n30
Quade, M. J., 526n25
Quaintance, M. K., 499n20, 503n20, 503n22
Quick, J. C., 542n98
Quinn, R. E., 523n25
Quiñones, M. A., 507n96, 514n68, 521n106

Rabenu, E., 517nn13–15
Rae, M., 541n94
Rafaeli, A., 523nn20–21
Ramaswami, A., 531n33
Ramsay, S., 535n131
Rao, M. S., 523n1
Rapp, A. A., 535n116
Rapp, T. L., 529n85, 535n116
Rasch, R., 514n60
Rauschenberger, J. M., 511n47
Raven, B., 550n12
Raver, J. L., 521n95, 535n128
Raymark, P. H., 500n28, 506n72, 521n89
Rea, M. S., 546n15
Reagans, R. E., 514n74
Reb, J., 505n55, 530n7
Reddock, C., 503n16
Ree, M. J., 504nn25–26
Rees, L., 531n17
Reeves, C. J., 504n23
Rehbein, K., 491n65
Reichard, R. J., 538n28
Reichman, W., 495n4
Reiley, P. J., 551n14
Reilly, R. R., 507n90
Reiter-Palmon, R., 492n19
Rentsch, J. R., 519nn49–50
RepresentUs, 552n58
Restubog, S. L. D., 535n123
Reynolds, D., 493n33
Reynolds, S. J., 495n77
Rhodes, S. R., 501n44
Riba, J., 545n14
Rich, B. L., 505n50
Rich, G. A., 500n33, 552n47
Richards, J., 490n55
Richardson, K. M., 541n91, 541n93
Richey, B., 557n31

Ridley, M., 545n5
Riforgiate, S., 507n105
Riggs, B. S., 553n72
Riketta, M., 532n60, 533n76
Riordan, C. M., 540n69
Ripollés, P., 545n14
Risen, J. L., 492nn10–11
Rivera, K. D., 544n139
Robbins, S. B., 503n14
Roberson, L., 514n64, 514n67, 514n72
Roberson, Q. M., 496n12, 529n79, 529n89, 534n102
Robertson, I. T., 508n123
Robie, C., 505n65, 520n61, 520n77
Robin, M., 552n57
Robinson, K., 519n41
Robinson, N., 519n41
Robinson, R. K., 497n38
Robinson, S. L., 523n22, 537n159, 537n162
Roch, S. G., 519n44, 519n52
Roche, A., 544n160
Rochford, K. C., 494n57
Rode, J. C., 531n33
Rodell, J. B., 530n15
Rodriguez, B., 547n46
Rodriguez-Fornells, A., 545n14
Roe, R. A., 533n72
Roehling, M. V., 538n18
Rogelberg, S. G., 493n44, 494n48, 494n54, 544nn143–145
Rohlman, D. S., 541n92
Rollag, K., 512n12
Roman, P. M., 545n163, 545n165
Ronen, S., 540n55
Rooney, M., 519n41
Rose, D. S., 494n52, 520n78, 520n80, 520n82, 522n110
Rosen, B., 535n115
Rosen, C. C., 494n59, 520n64, 536n150
Rosen, H., 556n6
Rosen, K. R., 510n18
Rosen, S., 521n91
Rosenthal, R., 493n23
Rosette, A. S., 555n110
Rossi, M. E., 530n12
Rotenberry, P. F., 508n124
Roth, P. L., 497n49, 503n14, 504n39, 505n50, 506n72, 506n84, 510n33, 519n43, 548n61
Rothbard, N. P., 533n85
Rothstein, H. R., 493n26, 541n93
Rotundo, M., 501n59
Rousseau, D. M., 526n8, 536n151, 536nn153-154, 536n157, 537n159, 537n162, 537nn166–167, 543n126
Rout, L., 522n120
Rowe, L. J., 528n62
Rowland, D., 525n61
Roy, I., 525n3
Rubin, G. J., 501n50
Rubin, R. S., 518n26
Ruddy, T. M., 554n99
Rudman, L. A., 519n43
Rudolph, C. W., 518n35, 520n63
Rugulies, R., 539n43
Rumsey, M. G., 511n49, 551n22
Rupp, D. E., 491n72, 497n43, 502n71, 556n4
Russ-Eft, D. F., 513n53
Russek, L. N., 531n37
Russell, C. J., 507n90
Russell, J. S., 522n118
Russo, J. M., 539n38
Ruth, P. L., 508n114
Ryan, A. M., 502n74, 509n14
Ryan, R. M., 546nn32–33, 546n36
Rynes, S. L., 491n71, 491n73, 502n75, 546n21

Saari, L. M., 508n116
Sabella, M. J., 528n64
Sackett, P. R., 491n67, 500n31, 500n34, 500n36, 501n60, 503n19, 505n59, 506n69, 506n74, 506n83, 514n60
Sager, C. E., 500n24
Saha, M., 545n10
Saks, A. M., 512n13, 512n19, 518n18, 533n83
Salamatov, V., 543n136
Salanova, M., 533n78, 546n27
Salas, E., 490n27, 512n28, 512n30, 513n33, 513n51, 514n75, 516n109, 516n128, 525n5, 526n18, 526nn28–29, 527n39, 527n49, 528n61, 528n63, 529n73, 529n84, 530nn94–95, 554n95
Salgado, J. F., 505n67, 510n30
Salimpoor, V. N., 545n14
Salyards, S. D., 507n93
Samtani, A., 493nn39–41
Samudio, D. C., 511n47
Sanchez, J. I., 499nn5–7, 499n17, 500n32, 514n73, 543n136
Sanders, K., 491n73
Sanders, M. G., 507n99
Santuzzi, A. M., 497n43, 541n90
Sarinopoulos, I., 494n58
Sarpy, S. A., 538nn11–12
Sauer, J. B., 515n105
Saul, J. R., 527n33
Savani, K., 530n11
Savitz, A. W., 497n31
Sayre, G. M., 531n29
Scandura, T. A., 492nn20–21
Schalk, R., 537n167
Schaufeli, W. B., 533n78, 533n80, 533n82, 538n22
Schaumberg, R. L., 530n10
Scheibe, S., 540n52
Schein, E. H., 490n34, 512n10, 512n17, 523n14, 523n19
Schewe, A. F., 531n28
Schiavone, M., 556n14
Schiemann, W. A., 517n8
Schilpzand, P., 518n36
Schippmann, J. S., 500n32, 504n39
Schleicher, D. J., 520n61, 520n77, 532n42, 551n33
Schmidt, A. M., 547n54, 548n77
Schmidt, F. L., 490n36, 490n41, 493n23, 506n71, 506n73, 508n118, 510n29, 510n31, 511nn41–42
Schminke, M., 533n91, 535n124
Schmit, J. M., 539n38
Schmit, M. J., 500n28, 507n100
Schmitt, N., 503n1, 503n5, 503n8, 504n48, 505n58, 505n64, 508n117, 510n28, 557n46

Schneider, B., 523nn11–12, 523n18, 524nn33–35, 533n77
Schneider, F. W., 520n71
Schneider, P. B., 536n147
Schneider, S., 497n32
Schneider, W. G., 557n46
Schoenfeldt, L. F., 506n86
Scholer, A. A., 548n57
Schoorman, F. D., 528n53, 528n55
Schouten, M. E., 526n27
Schriesheim, C. A., 492nn20–21, 532n52, 552n43, 557n37
Schroeder, A. N., 518n29
Schroeder, J., 492nn10–11
Schuler, H., 509n12
Schulte, B., 549n94
Schumacher, S., 504n27
Schumm, J. A., 541n82
Schuster, L., 550n111
Schwab, K., 496n23
Schwartz, J., 525n3
Schwartz, N. D., 507n94
Schweinsberg, M., 531n18
Schweitzer, M. E., 492nn10–11, 548n63, 548n65
Schwind, K. M., 527n40
Schyns, B., 524n41
Scott, B. A., 502n72, 504n42, 505n50, 528n54, 543n123, 552n49
Scott, J. C., 507n102, 556n4
Scott, K. L., 535n123
Scott, K. S., 501n58
Scott, W. D., 490n28
Scullen, S. E., 518n28
Seabright, M. A., 535n124
Searle, B. J., 538n21
Sebastiano, A., 524n40
Sederburg, M. E., 494n48
Sedikides, C., 540n67
Seeds, M. A., 493n46
Segal, D. R., 511n48
Segall, D. O., 507n98
Segers, M. S. R., 521n102
Seibert, S. E., 555n124
Semmer, N. K., 542nn104–105
Semuels, A., 524n47
Sendanyoye, J., 525n53
Senders, J. W., 501n55
Sendjaya, S., 552n57
Sendra, C. C., 506n87
Seung Jin, H., 550n111
Severance, L., 556n21
Sgroi, D., 531n20
Shadach, E., 531n34
Shadish, W. R., 492n13
Shaffer, J. A., 507n108, 554n91
Shahani-Denning, C., 508n110
Shane, S., 555n121
Shanman, R. M., 546n15
Shao, P., 542n106
Sharf, J. C., 497n48
Shaw, J. C., 505n50
Shaw, S. D., 503n2
Sheldon, O. J., 522n109
Shen, C., 543n129
Shepard, W., 507n98
Sherf, E. N., 521n100
Shi, J., 542n101, 551n32
Shih, H.-L., 531n17
Shihadeh, M., 506n87
Shima, S., 543n136
Shimada, K., 533n84
Shimazu, A., 533n84
Shipp, A. J., 524n36, 532n57, 535n115
Shockley, K. M., 530n12, 539n44, 539n47, 539n51, 542n113, 543n131
Shore, L. M., 520n68, 535n129, 551n27, 556n17
Shore, T. H., 520n68
Shostak, A. B., 556n5
Shuffler, M. L., 512n28, 512n30, 513n33, 516n109, 516n128, 526n21, 527n49, 554n95
Shultz, K. S., 492n19
Sidle, S. D., 494n52
Simmering, M., 521n92
Simon, H. A., 495n68
Simon, S. K., 537n165
Simoni, A. S., 543n136
Simons, R., 545n2
Simons, T., 534n102
Sims, D. E., 530nn94-95
Sinar, E. F., 509n13
Singh, S. N., 545n10
Sitzmann, T., 514nn62–63, 516n127, 517n129
Siu, O. L., 543n136
Sivanathan, N., 535n135
Sivasubramaniam, N., 526n13
Sjöberg, A., 558n59
Skarlicki, D. P., 504n43, 534n95, 558nn67–68
Slaughter, J. E., 505n53, 510n21
Sluss, D. M., 544n141
Smart, B., 518n27
Smith, C., 496n10
Smith, C. E., 517n10
Smith, C. S., 539n36
Smith, E. M., 517n132
Smith, F. J., 557n36
Smith, M. A., 505n62
Smith, P. C., 532n51
Smith, T. J., 540n58
Smith-Crowe, K., 538nn11–12
Smither, J. W., 519n47, 520n80, 521n103
Smoak, V. J., 491n75
Snell, A. F., 521n101
Snyder, L. A., 493n25
Society for Human Resource Management, 515n91, 515nn93–94
Society for Industrial and Organizational Psychology, 491n64, 492n81
Solamon, J. M., 507n107
Solansky, S. T., 524n46
Solinger, O. N., 533n72
Solloway, M. R., 546n15
Soltis, S. M., 509n9
Soman, D., 548n79
Sonenshein, S., 496n27
Song, Z., 540n62
Sonnenstuhl, W. J., 545n161
Sonnentag, S., 502n80, 514n59, 537nn4–5, 546n31
Sonntag, K., 542n103
Sørensen, K., 539n43
Sovern, H. S., 546n29
Soyars, M., 511n6
Spahn, D. R., 494n53, 527n38
Spector, P. E., 501n59, 531n24, 532n62, 534n103, 535n119, 543n136
Speer, A. B., 506n87
Spell, C. S., 514n66, 514n71, 527n47
Spence, J. R., 519nn54–55
Spencer, C. C., 520n74
Spencer, S., 502n71
Sperry, L., 516n111
Spicer, A., 491n65
Spieler, I., 540n52

Spiller, W. E., 558n53
Spitzmüller, C., 544n143, 544n145
Spreitzer, G. M., 533n86, 539n45
Spurk, D., 504n34, 504n40, 504nn44–45
Staats, B. R., 492n18
Stadler, M. J., 512n13
Stagl, K. C., 530nn94–95
Stagner, R., 556n6, 556n22
Stahl, G. K., 514n77
Stamov-Roßnagel, C., 540n52
Stanisavljevic, J., 513n42
Stanley, T. D., 557n33
Stansbury, J. A., 550n110, 550n113
Stanton, J. M., 493n32, 494n49, 494n54
Starikova, I., 519n41
Starke, F. A., 557n48
Statista.com, 511n1
Staw, B. M., 530n16
Steel, P., 548nn81–83, 549n86
Steele, L. M., 493n25
Steele, P., 523n5, 535n134
Steele-Johnson, D., 502n78
Steelman, L. A., 521n101, 541n95
Steers, R. M., 501n44
Steiberg, R. C., 500n40
Steiner, D. D., 501n63
Steinhauer, J., 500n26
Stepanek, M., 546n16
Stephen, A. T., 549n90
Stephens, N. M., 514n74
Stern, P. C., 496n26
Sternberg, R. J., 503n11
Stetzer, M. W., 522n119
Steverson, B., 546n15
Stewart, G. L., 507n106, 507n109, 529n75
Stierwalt, S., 498n56
Stock, M. S., 540n56
Stoeveska, V., 559n81
Stokes, G. S., 507n92
Stone, D. L., 506n76
Stone, N. J., 508n114
Stoneburner, C., 518n24
Stone-Romero, E. F., 492n7, 492n15, 506n76
Story, P. A., 531n31
Strait, L. B., 494n64
Streicher, K. N., 539n43
Streitfeld, D., 524nn26–27
Strickler, L. J., 510n36
Stuebing, K. K., 548n61
Sturman, M. C., 502n79
Su, P., 553n66
Suazo, M. M., 534n113
Sue, D. W., 535n133
Sulsky, L. M., 519n46, 519n48, 519n51
Summers, L., 520n79
Sumpter, D. M., 515n83
Sun, L., 554n87
Sung, S. Y., 513n31
Suphan, A., 538nn31–32
Surface, E. A., 507n99, 512n29, 513n35, 520n67
Sutton, A. W., 519n58
Sutton, K. L., 512n16
Sverke, M., 558nn58–59
Swaen, G. M. H., 539n33
Sweet, S., 558n71
Swider, B. W., 507n106, 507n109
Switzer, F. S., III, 504n39, 505n50, 518n29
Sydell, E. J., 493n46
Szkudlarek, B., 515n83

Takemoto-Chock, N. K., 545n7
Tamkins, M. M., 523n15, 523n17
Tan, R. Y., 514n64, 514n67, 514n72
Tannenbaum, S. I., 513n36, 516n123, 525n5
Taras, V., 523n5
Tate, B. W., 554n90
Tay, L., 546n17
Taylor, F. W., 490n29
Taylor, J., 546n16
Taylor, L. R., 507n97
Taylor, P. J., 513n53
Taylor, S. G., 551n28
Taylor, S. L., 546n15
Taylor, S. N., 520nn85–86
Taylor, W. D., 493n25
Tedeschi, R. G., 541n80
Tehrani, N., 535n127
Telang, F., 545n13
Tenbrink, A. P., 506n87
ten Brummelhuis, L. L., 501n45, 533n85
Tepper, B. J., 535n122, 553n84
ter Hoeven, C. L., 501n45
Terris, W., 510n23
Tesluk, P. E., 491n77, 504n43, 511n8, 538nn11–12
Tesser, A., 521n91
Tetrick, L. E., 501n54, 538n26, 541n87, 551n27, 556n17, 558n57
Texas A&M University, 515n84
Thacker, J. W., 513n44, 513n46, 513n49
Thanos, P. K., 545n13
Thatcher, S. M. B., 527nn46–47
Theeboom, T., 516n116
Thomas, G., 551n29
Thomas, R., 519n41
Thomason, S., 519n40
Thompson, A., 531n22, 531n26
Thompson, B. J., 540n56
Thompson, C. A., 558n53
Thompson, J. C., 494n56
Thompson, L. F., 507n99, 556n4
Thompson, P. S., 534n112
Thompson, R. J., 541n79
Thoresen, C. J., 504n38, 531n23, 532n58, 532n64
Thornton, G. C., 520n68
Thoroughgood, C. N., 554n90
Tiedens, L., 519n43
Timmreck, C. W., 520n79
Tindall, M., 514n75
Tippins, N. T., 507n98
Todd, S. Y., 509n2
Tomasi, D., 545n13
Tominey, E., 540n66
Tomprou, M., 537n166
Tompson, H. B., 511n6
Tonidandel, S., 507n96
Topakas, A., 551n29
Tornow, W. W., 520n84
Tost, L. P., 555n110
Toth, A. A., 495n74
Tourangeau, R., 494n51
Towler, A. J., 516n108
Tracey, J. B., 516n123
Travis, D. V., 524n46
Treadway, D. C., 536n142, 536n146, 536n148
Trevino, L. K., 535n130
Trice, H. M., 523n16
Tripp, T. M., 535n126
Trombley, P. Q., 545n13
Troth, A., 535n131
Trougakos, J. P., 494n59, 502nn68–69

Troxel, W. M., 546n16
Truslow, C. M., 506n77
Truxillo, D. M., 509n11, 541n92, 549n97
Tsai, H. Y., 545n12
Tubré, T. C., 538n24
Tuckey, M. R., 538n21
Tuckman, B. W., 526n23
Turner, M. E., 528n66
Turner, N., 535n135
Turner, S., 496n10
Turnley, W. H., 502n76, 534n113, 537n161
Tyler, C. L., 557n31
Tyler, K., 516n115
Tynan, R. O., 525n6
Tziner, A., 517n13, 517n15

Uggerslev, K. L., 519n51
Ugrin, J. C., 549n89
Uhlmann, E. L., 492n22
Uhrich, B., 533n85
Ujita, Y., 539n43
Ullén, F., 546nn25–26
United Food & Commercial Workers Local 400, 559n76
United Nations, 495n6
U.S. Bureau of Manpower Utilization, 490n32
U.S. Department of Labor, 555n116, 558n65
U.S. Employment Service, 490n32
U.S. Equal Employment Opportunity Commission, 497n39
Uzzi, B., 492n17

Vacharkulksemsuk, T., 531n36
Valle, M., 545n14
van Amelsvoort, L. G. P. M., 539n33
Van Buren, M., 513n41
Vancouver, J. B., 521n98
van Dam, K., 524n41
Vandenberg, R. J., 556n17
Van den Bossche, P., 521n102
van den Brandt, P. A., 539n33
van der Rijt, J., 521n102
Van Der Vegt, G. S., 526n20
VanDeVeer, C., 497n51
VandeWalle, D., 521n96
Van De Water, T. J., 489n16
van de Wiel, M. W. J., 521n102
van Dierendonck, D., 552n57
van Dijk, H., 527n31
Van Durme, Y., 525n3
van Dyck, C., 514n59
Van Dyck, S. E., 543n134
van Eerde, W., 548n84
van Engen, M. L., 527n31, 555n113
Van Hasselt, M., 544n159
Van Hooft, E. A., 493nn39–41
Van Hoye, G., 509n7, 540n60
Van Iddekinge, C. H., 503n14, 505n50, 506n72, 509n13, 510n25
van Ittersum, K., 522n119
van Jaarsveld, D., 502n66
VanKatwyk, P., 511n8
Van Keer, E., 504n31
van Kleef, G. A., 555n117
van Knippenberg, D., 525n2, 526n26, 527n31
Van Maanen, J., 512n10, 512n17
Van Mierlo, H., 548n64, 548n80
Van Olffen, W., 533n72
Van Quaquebeke, N., 552n53
van Riemsdijk, M., 491n73
Vanroelen, C., 544n147
Van Rooy, D. L., 500n40
van Stolk, C., 546n16
van Vianen, A. E. M., 516n116
van Woerkom, M., 553n77
Vasey, J., 499n8
Vaughn, E. D., 493n46
Vecchio, R. P., 555n123
Veiga, J. F., 539n48
Velasquez, R., 507n100
Venette, S., 494n55
Venkataramani, V., 551n33
Verdi, B., 556nn10–11
Vickers, M., 511n6
Vidyarthi, P. R., 551n31
Vigen, T., 494n65
Vigoda-Gadot, E., 536n139
Villado, A. J., 508n130, 516n125, 524n38
Villanova, P., 518n39, 520n76
Vinchur, A. J., 489n4, 504n39
Viswesvaran, C., 505n61, 506n71, 549n99
Viteles, M. S., 490n31, 490n38
Volini, E., 525n3
Volkow, N. D., 545n3, 545n13
Voydanoff, P., 543n120
Vroom, V. H., 547n45

Wacker, J., 494n53, 527n38
Wageman, R., 556n128
Wagner, D. T., 502n72, 527n40, 539n35, 549n88
Wagner, S. H., 552n54
Wainer, H., 507n95
Waldman, D. A., 554n96
Walker, A., 536n156
Walker, R. M., 517n6
Wallace, C., 504n36
Wallace, J. C., 538n16
Wallace, S. R., 499n3
Waller, M. J., 494n53, 527n38
Walsh, G., 502n65
Walsh, J., 540n54
Walter, F., 526n20
Waltz, P. R., 497n43
Walumbwa, F. O., 552n46, 552n50, 552n52, 552n59
Wanberg, C. R., 493nn39–41, 504n32, 515n104, 540nn61–62, 540n68, 540nn70–71
Wanek, J. E., 506n69
Wang, D., 512n18, 554n96
Wang, G., 505n49
Wang, G. J., 545n13
Wang, K., 502n64
Wang, M., 492n79, 494n61, 494n63, 542n101, 551n32
Wang, P., 542n107
Wang, Q., 534n108
Wang, S., 501n47
Wang, X. M. W., 519n60
Wang, Y.-D., 531n21
Wang, Z., 541n81, 541n86, 542n107
Warner, J. L., 520n74
Warner, M. E., 543n133
Warr, P. B., 517n130, 532n50
Warrenfeltz, R., 515n96
Wasserman, R., 493n35
Watola, D. J., 554n93
Watrous-Rodriguez, K. M., 496n29
Watson, I., 526n19
Wayne, J. H., 542n99, 542n110
Wayne, S. J., 537n164, 551n27, 554n108

Wazeter, D. L., 558n69
Weatherbee, T. G., 536n137
Weaver, S. J., 512n28, 512n30, 513n33, 516n109, 516n128
Weber, K., 497n31
Webster, R. K., 501n50
Weekley, J. A., 500n41, 507n101, 518n33
Wegmeyer, L. J., 506n87
Weir, T., 554n103
Weiss, D. J., 532n53
Weiss, H. M., 502n68, 512n21, 530n4
Weiss, P., 540n65
Weldon, E., 529n79, 529n89
Wellman, N., 550n9
Welsh, D. H. B., 538n30
Welsh, E. T., 515n104
Werner, J. M., 518n23
Wernsing, T., 552n46, 552n52
Wesson, M. J., 512n20, 533n88, 534n100
West, B. J., 529n82
West, M. A., 526n10
Westerberg, C., 490n54
Westman, M., 531n34, 542n106
Weyhrauch, W. S., 508nn112–113, 508n120
Wheeler, J. L., 504n25
Wherry, R. J., 499n2
Whetzel, D. L., 493n26, 506n81, 508n118, 508n124
White, F. A., 498n58
White, M., 496n18
Whiting, S. W., 534n105
Whitman, M. V., 553n68
Whitmore, H., 541n94
Widerszal-Bazyl, M., 543n136
Wiemann, S., 506n74
Wiggenhorn, W., 511nn3–4
Wiggins, J. G., 556n9
Wilcox, K., 549n90
Wilder-Smith, A., 491n61
Wildman, J. L., 514n75
Wiley, J. W., 525n50, 525n58, 525nn64–65
Wilhelmy, A., 493n45
Wilk, S. L., 503n19
Wilkinson, M., 516n113
Willaby, H. W., 558n52
Williams, C. R., 500n43, 520n61
Williams, E. A., 492nn20–21, 526n21
Williams, F., 508n128
Williams, K. D., 529n88
Williams, K. M., 499n11
Williams, M., 519n43
Williams, R. E., 517n16
Williams, S. A. S., 496n11
Willness, C. R., 509n5
Wilson, M. A., 499n9
Winefield, A. H., 538n21
Winefield, H. R., 538n21
Winkler, S., 511n45
Winn, B., 550n111
Winters, M.-F., 496n13
Wise, R. A., 545n3
Wisher, R. A., 514n62
Witzki, A. H., 536n147
Woehr, D. J., 509n2, 519n52, 521n90, 550n8
Wolfe, A. W., 544n146
Wolff, S. B., 529n90
Wong, K. F. E., 519n57, 519n60
Woo, S. E., 492n16
Wood, A. M., 540n67, 545n8
Wood, L., 519n58
Woodruff, T. J., 539n43
Woods, S. A., 516n117
Woolley, A., 529n93
Woolum, A. H., 518n36
Workman, K., 516n124
World Health Organization, 491n62
Wren, D. A., 489n17
Wright, J. A., 540n53
Wright, P. M., 495n73
Wu, B., 521n108
Wu, J., 501n61
Wu, X., 541n81
Wurtz, O., 514n80

Xavier, L. F., 514n75

Yammarino, F. J., 553n75
Yan, T., 494n51
Yang, C., 531n21
Yang, J., 543n129
Yang, Y. K., 545n12
Yates, M. D., 559n80
Yeatts, D. E., 527n36, 527n42
Yeh, T. L., 545n12
Yip, J. A., 531n18
Yoo, T. Y., 511n46
Yoon, S., 494n59
Yost, E., 489n19
Young, S. F., 521n81
Youngblood, S. A., 557n38
Youssef-Morgan, C. M., 538n27
Yukl, G., 551n13, 553n80

Zabel, K. L., 502n74
Zaccaro, S. J., 526nn15–16, 526n22, 527n32, 528n64, 528n67, 550nn4–5, 554n98, 554n100
Zacher, H., 553n78
Zagenczyk, T. J., 535n123
Zajac, E. J., 524n39
Zakon, R. H., 490n49
Zalesny, M. D., 557n38
Zapata, C. P., 551n18
Zatorre, R. J., 545n14
Zatzick, C. D., 540n54, 556n18
Zayas, V., 519n42
Zedeck, S., 490n45, 500n34, 500n36, 511n41
Zelin, A., 491n63
Zhan, Y., 524n37, 542n101
Zhang, H., 513n48
Zhang, M., 530n8
Zhang, S., 543n129
Zhang, X., 520n64
Zhang, Y., 503n6, 543n129
Zhang, Z., 540n68, 540n71, 554n96
Zhao, H., 537n164, 555n124
Zhao, H. H., 520n64
Zhao, K., 530n8
Zhao, P., 503nn15–16
Zhou, J., 529n78
Zhou, L., 551n32
Zhu, J., 540n68
Zickar, M. J., 489n1, 489n5, 507n97, 556nn7–8
Zieky, M. J., 510n38
Zimmerman, K. L., 498n63
Zimmerman, R. D., 504n37, 516n127
Zion Market Research, 491n60
Zohar, D., 537n10, 538n12
Zubcsek, P. P., 549n90
Zweig, D., 537n160

Subject Index

Page numbers in **bold** indicate where the entry is defined in the margin.

Aarons, Gregory, 280
abilities, definition, 98. *See also* KSAOs (knowledge, skills, abilities, other personal characteristics)
ability tests, 132–135
absenteeism, 107, 334–335
absorption, 338
academic intelligence, 132
academic tests
computerized adaptive testing (CAT), **148,** 149
COVID-19 and, 184
accidents, 109, 223
achievement (trait approach to leadership), 429
acquiescence bonds, 335
acquisition, **286,** 287
ACT (academic standardized test), 184
action processes (teams), 305, 307
active learning approaches, 206–209, *209*
active management-by-exception (transactional leadership), 438–439
Actors Equity, 72
actual criteria
conceptual criteria *vs.,* 89–90, *90*
definition, **90**
adaptive behavior, **112,** 112–113
adhocracy, 274
ad hoc teams, **296**
adjourning (five stage model of group development), 300
administration, leadership *vs.,* 426
administrative performance management, 234
adverse impact, **75**
affect, attitudes, and behavior at work, 323–357
affect, **325,** 336
behavior, 343–348
broaden-and-build theory of positive emotions, **329,** 329–330, *331*
emotions, **325,** 325–329, *326*
good *vs.* bad archetype, 324
job attitudes, 331–339, *333, 335, 337* (*See also* jobs)
moods, **325**
organizational justice, *339,* 339–343
organizational politics, 348–351
psychological contract, **351,** 351–356, *353, 355*
affiliation (trait approach to leadership), 429
affinity index, 37
affirmative action
definition, **79**
hiring practices and, 79–82
AFL-CIO, 485
Africa, environmental context of work and, 67
after-action reviews (AARs), 224
age issues
Age Discrimination in Employment Act (ADEA, 1967), 73–74, 135
diversity and demographics of workplace, 64
"reverse discrimination," 73
agentic leadership style, 451
agreeableness (personality factor), 137, 138
Aids in Selecting Salesmen (Bureau of Salesmanship Research), 10
Airbnb, 396
alcohol abuse in workplace, 387–389
ALDI, 171
alienated union members, 479
alignment, 230–231
alternative dispute resolution, 474
altruism, 343
Amalgamated Beef Packers, 461
Amazon, 29, 275, 287
American Civil Rights Institute, 81
American Federation of Teachers, 459
American Psychological Association (APA)
code of ethics, 53–55, 458
Industrial and Business Psychology (Division 14), 13–14
pre-World War II history of, 5, 8, 11
Society for Industrial and Organizational Psychology (SIOP), 19, *20,* **22,** *22,* 63, 458
on stress at work, 360
American Rescue Plan Act (ARPA), 83
Americans with Disabilities Act (1990), 14, 74–75, 104, 363, 387
analysis of research methods, 46–50, *49*
anesthesia (research example), 43–44
Angelou, Maya, 448
anger, 326–327, *327*
Annan, Kofi, 486
Apple, 336–337
applicability, job selection and, *159,* 159–161
applied psychology
definition, 3
inception of, 9–10
See also I-O psychology discipline
appraisal. *See* performance appraisal
apprentice training, **480,** 480–481
APT*Metrics,* 150
arbitration, **468,** 468–469, 473–474, 477–478
archival research, **34,** 34–35
Aristotle, 366
Armed Services Vocational Aptitude Battery (ASVAB), **15,** 24, 148, 190
Army, U.S.
Army Alpha, **8**
Army Beta, **8**
Army General Classification Test (AGCT), **12**
Center for Army Profession & Leadership (CAPL), 428 (*See also* military, U.S.)
arousal, self-efficacy and, 407

artifacts, observable, 271–272, *272,* 273
Ash, Mary Kay, 230
assessment centers, **157**
assumptions, 271–272, *272*
AT&T, 157
Attention Deficit Hyperactivity Disorder (ADHD), 74
attributed charisma (transformational leadership), 437–438
attributes (worker-oriented procedure), 98. *See also* work analysis
attribution theory of leadership, 443–444
Australia, organizational citizenship behavior and, 345
authentic leadership, **441**
authority differentiation, 302
authorization cards, **463**
autism spectrum, 363
autoethnography, 53
automaticity, 198
autonomy, 399–401, 410

backup behaviors, 307
Bakke v. University of California (1978), 80
balanced processing, 441
banding, **187**
base rate, **174**
basic assumptions, 271–272, *272*
behavior
  action processes of teams, 305, 307
  adaptive behavior, **112,** 112–113
  backup behaviors, 307
  behavioral approach (leadership), **430**
  behavioral criteria, **225**
  behaviorally anchored rating scales (BARS), 239, **242,** 242–243
  behavioral observation training, **247**
  behavioral research on union/management relations, 475–479, *477, 479*
  behavioral sampling, 130
  behavior description interview, **154**
  behavior modeling, **206**
  citizenship behavior, **113,** 114
  counterproductive work behavior, **110, 345,** 345–348
  deviant work behavior, 110, 270
  Global Leadership and Organizational Behavior Effectiveness (GLOBE), 449–451
  Johns Hopkins behavioral checklist, 243
  organizational behavior and faking, 140–141
  organizational behavior and I-O psychology overlap, 3
  organizational citizenship behavior, **343,** 343–345
  organization development and, 288
  practice behaviors, 208
  safety behaviors for physical stressors, 362–363
  "union citizenship behaviors," 464
  See also affect, attitudes, and behavior at work
Bell, Suzanne T., 304
Beloit College Mindset List, 16
benchmarking, **188,** 189
bias
  criterion contamination and, 91
  hindsight bias, 139
  in peer assessment, 250
  performance management rating errors and biases, 244–246
Biden, Joe, 431
big data, 36–39
Big 5 personality theory, **136,** 136–138
Bingham, Walter Van Dyke, 9–10, 12
biodata inventories, **145,** *145,* 145–147
biological-based theory of motivation
  definition and overview, **394,** 394–395
  synthesis and application of work motivation theories, 412–415
BIPOC (Black, Indigenous, and People of Color), context of work and, 66. *See also* diversity
Black Disciples (street gang), 453
bona fide occupational qualification (BFOQ), **71,** 72
boundary theory, **382**
Brenner, Joshua, 189
broaden-and-build theory of positive emotion, **329,** 329–330, *331*
Bryan, W. L., 5
budgeting game, 350
Buffett, Warren, 431, 439
bullying, 347–349, 366
Bureau of Labor Statistics, 34, 111
Bureau of Salesmanship Research, 9–10
burnout, 338, **364**
Bush, George H. W., 14, 74
business games, **204,** 204–205
business skills, 217
Butz, Earl, 437

call centers, 111
"can do" factors, 182, 315, 392, 393
career-related stressors
  job search, 373
  stressors, definition and overview, **360,** 360–361
  unemployment, 372–373
cartoons, 273
categorical variables, **46**
Cattell, James, 10
causality, 49–50
Center for Army Profession & Leadership (U.S. Army), 428. *See also* military, U.S.
Center for Creative Leadership, 195–196
Centers for Disease Control and Prevention, 5151
Centiment, 29
centralization, **61**
central-tendency error, **245**
certification election, **464**
chain of command, **60,** 60–61
challenge stressors, **363**
change
  change agents, 279
  stress of, 360, 375
  workplace change (1994–2018), 15–17
Chappel, Kate and Tom, 274
Cheaper by the Dozen (Gilbreth family), 7
cheating, 160
chief executive officers (CEOs), 442, 443
chief information officers (CIO), 17
chief learning officers, 194–195
child labor, **84,** 84–85
China
  cultural dimensions of, 267

politeness and, 342
textile industry and organizational change, 279
Chipotle, 296
Chlystek v. Donovan (2013), 237
Churchill, Winston, 350
cigarette smoking (research example), 49
citizenship behavior, **113,** 114
civic virtue, 344
Civil Rights Act
1957, 14
1991, 14
1964, 70–73, 75, 451
Section 106, 133
Title VII, 14–15, 70–73, 75
classification, **190**
Clinton, Bill, 14–15, 80
coal mining accidents, 223
Coburg Banks, 222
coefficient of determination, **181**
coefficient of equivalence, 121–122
coefficient of non-determination, **181**
coefficient of stability, 121
coercive power, 432
cognitive ability, 132–134, 185–186
coin flipping, randomness of, 183
collaborative culture, 274
collective bargaining, **466,** 466–467. *See also* labor contracts
collective efficacy, **309**
collective nouns of occupations/professions, 316
collectivism
cultural differences and, 268–269
definition, 265
success attributed to teams *vs.* individuals, 292
work-nonwork balance and, 380
college admission, 179–184, *180, 182*
College Board, 184
college faculty unionization, 476–477, *477*
colluders, 447–448
Colorado Fuel and Iron Company, 472
Colorado National Guard, 472
commitment, teamwork and, 300
commitment bonds, 336
Commonsense Talent Management (Hunt), 235
communal leadership style, 451
communication
communication performance management, 234
cultural values and, 268
interpersonal processes (teams), 305, 307–310
intrapersonal/interpersonal skills (managerial effectiveness), 217
language of subject matter experts, 95
of organizational change, 279
See also culture and organizational change and development
competence, self-determination theory and, 399–401
competency modeling, **104,** 104–105
competition culture, 275
compressed workweeks, **371**
computer-based training, **201,** 201–204
computerized adaptive testing (CAT), **148,** 149
conceptual criteria
actual criteria *vs.,* 89–90, *90*
definition, **89**
conclusions from research, analysis of, 51–53
concurrent criterion-related validity, 126, *127*
confidence building, motivation and, 308–309
confidentiality of research participants, 54
conflict management
cultural values and, 269
teamwork and, 307–308
conformers, 447
Congress, U.S.
Civil Rights Act passage, 14–15
I-O psychology, pre-World War II history, 6
Conley, Chip, 396
Connerly, Wardell, 81
conscientiousness (organizational citizenship behavior), 343
conscientiousness (personality factor), 136, 137, 140–141
conscious rating, 247–249
consideration factor (behavioral approach to leadership), 430
constructs
construct sampling, 130
construct validity, **124,** 124–126, *125*
definition, **123**
distal and proximal constructs, *413,* 413–415
content validity, **127,** 127–129
context of work, 59–86
context, definition, 60
environmental context, 67–69
legal context and workplace discrimination, 69–80, *78*
legal context and workplace health and safety, 82–85
social context, 62–66, *63, 65*
structural context, 60–61
See also legal context of work
contingency approach, **433,** 433–435
contingent reward (transactional leadership), 438
continuance component, 336
contrast error, **244,** 245
controlling culture, 275
conventional arbitration, **468**
convergent validity coefficients, 124
coordination behaviors, 305
core job dimensions, 410
corporate social responsibility
definition, **69**
triple bottom line and, *69*
correlation coefficient
correlation *vs.* causation, 49–50, 51
definition, **47**
depiction of, 47–49, *49*
traditional use of, 37
counterproductive work behavior, **110, 345,** 345–348
courtesy, 343
COVID-19
college admissions and, 184
employment interview practices, 161
Experience Age and effect of, 17–18, 19
Families First Coronavirus Response Act (FFCRA), 83
focus groups about, 44
health and safety psychological contracts, 352
holistic research needed for, 52

leadership during pandemic, 434
onboarding and, 197
overqualification and work motivation, 420
performance management challenges, 233
person-environment fit, 277
presenteeism (working while sick), 108
union impact during pandemic, 485
virtual instructor-led training and e-learning, 202
working from home, 330, 370, 382
workplace stress and, 360, 374, 382, 386
creative culture, 274
creative intelligence, 132
creative teams, **295**
criteria
actual criteria, **90**
conceptual criteria *vs.* actual criteria, **89,** 89–90, **90,** *90*
criterion contamination, **91,** *91,* 91–93
criterion cutoff, **176**
criterion deficiency, **91,** *91,* 91–93
criterion deficiency, relevance, and contamination, **91,** *91,* 91–93
criterion relevance, **91,** *91,* 91–93
criterion variables, 46, **47**
definition, **88**
for performance management process, 231–232, *232,* 238
See also decision making standards
criterion-related validity
overview, **126,** 126–127, *127*
predictor cutoff, **172,** *172,* 172–173, *173,* 176
critical incidents, **242**
Cronbach's alpha coefficient, 122
cross-cultural issues, 264–269
dimensions of, 264–266, 267
diversity training, **210,** 210–212
environmental context of work and diversity, 67
expatriate training, 212–213, *213*
of leadership, 449–451
organizational citizenship behavior and, 345
politeness, 342
values in Western *vs.* non-Western cultures, 266–269, *268*
work-nonwork balance and, 380
See also individual names of countries
cross-training, **316,** 316–317, *317*
crowdsourced performance review, 259, 260
cultural tightness/looseness, 266
culture and organizational change and development, 263–290
Drucker on, 264
national culture, 264–269, *268* (*See also* cross-cultural issues)
organizational change, 278–287, *281, 284*
organizational climate and culture, 269–276, *272, 274* (*See also* organizational culture)
organization development (OD), 14, **287,** 287–289
perceptions of fit, 276–278
cyberaggression, **348**
cyberloafing, 417

"dark side" of leadership, 446–448, *447*
dark triad, **138,** 138–139, 446
data collection
methods and sources of, 41–44
research online services, 29
for work analysis, 99–102, *101*
See also research methods in I-O psychology
data mining
definition, **36**
practice of, 37–39
sources and characteristics of, 36–37
Davidow, Chuck, 171
daylight saving time, 368
debriefing of research participants, 54
deception, protection from, 54
decision making standards, 87–117
conceptual criteria *vs.* actual criteria, **89,** 89–90, **90,** *90*
criteria for, **88**
criterion deficiency, relevance, and contamination, **91,** *91,* 91–93
cultural values and, 269
decision making in teams, 313
leadership and, 446
for online reviews, 89
performance criteria and, 105–116, *115*
procedural justice and, 341
work analysis and, 93–105, *97, 101* (*See also* work analysis)
See also criteria; leadership
declarative knowledge, **197,** 198
dedication, 338
deductive method, **27,** 100
deep acting, 112, 113
defamation, 237
Deloitte, 64
departmentalization, **60**
Department of Agriculture, U.S., 51
Department of Commerce, U.S., 34, 39
Department of Defense (U.S.) Polygraph Institute, 143
Department of Labor, U.S.
Bureau of Labor Statistics, 34, 111
data mining by, 37
on importance of organizational learning, 194
Occupational Safety and Health Act (1970), 82
Office of Apprenticeship Training, Employer, and Labor Services (OATELS), 480
dependent variables, **46**
description, as goal of science, 26
descriptive norms, 270
design of research studies, 28–29
development, **194**
developmental performance management, 234
deviant work behavior, 110, 270
counterproductive work behavior, **345,** 345–348
workplace bullying, 347
devoted union members, 479
direct observation, 99–102, *101*
dirty work, 383–386
disability, definition, 74
Disney, 62, 214
disparate impact, 75, 77
disparate treatment, **76**
display rules, 110–112
distal constructs, *413,* 413–415
distributive bargaining, 466–467
distributive justice, **341**
divergent validity coefficients, 124

diversity
  definition, **64**
  diversity training, **210,** 210–212
  equity, inclusion, and, 64–66
  gender and, 81, 134, 187, 190, 246, 344, 345, 451–452
  of leadership, 451–452
  race and, 80, 81, 111, 187, 190
  sexual harassment and, **72,** 200, 214–215, 216
  in team composition, 303–305
  typology of organizational diversity initiatives, *65*
documentation performance management, 236
dominance (TRIAD/Tracking Roles In And Across Domains), 302–303
downsizing, **282,** 282–285, *284*
Drucker, Peter, 264
drug abuse in workplace, 387–389
drug testing, **147,** 147–148
Dunleavy, Eric M., 77
Dunning-Kruger effect, **251,** 256–257
dyadic sensitivity, 313
dynamic performance criteria, **115,** *115,* 115–116

Earnest, David R., 422
e-business, 15
eco-friendly business practices, 68–69
Edison, Thomas, 5, 421
Educational Testing Service (ETS), 184
efficiency studies
  Hawthorne studies, **10,** 10–11
  I-O psychology inception and, 5, 6
ego-based motivation, 255
Ehrhart, Mark G., 280
e-learning, 201, 202
electroencephalography (EEG), 45–46
emic perspective, **41**
emotion
  broaden-and-build theory of positive emotion, **329,** 329–330, *331*
  complexity of, 325–326
  dual threshold model of workplace anger, **326,** 326–327, *327*
  emotional contagion, **328,** 329
  emotional intelligence, **328**
  emotional labor, **110,** 110–113, **328**
  emotional stability (personality factor), 137, 138
  emotion management by team members, 309
  emotion regulation, **328**
  emotions, definition, **325**
empirical keying (biodata scoring), 146
empirical research cycle, *26*
employees
  employee assistance programs (EAPs), **388**
  employee-comparison performance rating methods, 239, 240
  employee engagement, **338,** 338–339
  productivity of, 34, 35
  theft by, 109
  turnover of, 33, 61, 107, 334–335
  work behavior of (*See* decision making standards)
  See also performance management
employment tests, historical background of, 13
enactive mastery, 407
environmental context of work
  overview, 67–69
  person-environment fit, **276,** 277
  sensory processing disorders and, 363 (*See also* workplace health and well-being)
Equal Employment Opportunity Commission (EEOC)
  Americans with Disabilities Act (1990), 74
  discrimination determined by, 76–78
  employment discrimination statistics, *78*
  inception of, 70
  on sexual harassment, 72–73, 200, 214–215
  Uniform Guidelines on Employee Selection Procedures, 78, 79
  website of, 78
equity
  definition, **64**
  diversity, inclusion, and, 64–66
  equality *vs.,* 64
  equity sensitivity, **403**
  equity theory, definition, **401**
  equity theory and work motivation, 401–403, *402,* 412–415, *414, 416*
  organizational justice, **339,** *339,* 339–343
  predictor overview and evaluation, 158–161, *159*
equivalent-form reliability, **121,** 121–122
errors
  criterion contamination and, 91
  error-management training, **207,** 207–208
  performance management rating errors and biases, 244–246
e-socialization, 196–197
espoused values, 271–272, *272*
ethics
  corporate social responsibility, **69,** *69*
  of data mining, 39
  for research, 53–55
ethnography
  autoethnography, 53
  definition and overview, **40,** 40–41
etic perspective, **41**
Europe/European Union
  environmental context of work and, 67
  European Commission, 39
  International Standard of Occupational Classifications and EurOccupations, 102
  See also individual names of countries
evaluation
  evaluation criteria of training programs, 224–225
  teamwork and, 300
  of work analysis methods, 104
  See also performance management
executive coaching, **221,** 221–222
expatriates, **212,** 212–213, *213*
expectancy theory
  definition and overview, **403,** 403–406, *406*
  expectancy, **404**
  synthesis and application of work motivation theories, 412–415, *414,* 415
Experience Age (2019–present), 17–18, 19

expertise, 198–199
expertise game, 350
expert power (power and influence approach to leadership), 432
explanation, as goal of science, 26
explosive strength (physical ability), 134
external validity, **28**
extra-role behaviors, 114
extraversion, 125, 137, 138
extrinsic motivation, 393

Facebook, 29, 142, 168
faces of I-O psychology
  Bell, 304
  Brenner, 189
  Dunleavy, 77
  Earnest, 422
  Ehrhart, 280
  Fink, 38
  Houston, 111
  Howes, 340
  Hunt, 235
  Lee, 218
  Park, 378
  Scott, 150
  Wolfe, 428
face validity, 128, 170
fact-finding, **468**
Fair Labor Standards Act (FLSA, 1938), 84–85
fairness. *See* equity
faking, **140,** 140–142, 146, 150
false negatives, **178,** 178–179, 186, 187
false positives, **178,** 178–179, 186, 187
Families First Coronavirus Response Act (FFCRA), 83
Family and Medical Leave Act (1993), 14–15, 82–83, 382
family and work, balancing. *See* work-nonwork balance
fast food industry, organizational strategy and, 166–167
faultlines, **308**
Federal Bureau of Investigation (FBI), 143
Federal Mediation and Conciliation Service (FMCS), 467
feedback
  giving, 254–255
  in performance management process, 231
  reaction to, 256–257
  seeking, 255–256
  survey feedback as organization development, 288–289
  task feedback, 410
  360° feedback, **252,** 252–254, *253, 254,* 260
  understanding, 257
feedforward interview, 259
felt dispensability, 318
femininity-centered cultures, 265
Ferrill v. Parker Group, Inc. (1999), 72
fidelity (research and simulation), 28, 154
Fiedler's contingency model, **433,** 433–434
field experiments, 30
Fields, Mark, 264
"file drawer effect," 36, 55
final-offer arbitration, **468,** 468–469
financial issues
  budgeting game, 350
  executive coaching fees, 222
  monetary incentives for surveys, 43
  of offshoring, 484
  of organizational learning, 194, 225
  of organizational strategy and staffing, 160, 170
  personnel selection and, *159,* 159–161
  of sexual harassment, 214
  unions on wages, 460–461, 475
fine motor skills, 135
Fink, Alexis A., 38
Finland, environmental context of work, 68
five-factor model of personality, 136–138
five stage model of group development, **299,** 299–300
fixed-pie perception, 468
flexibility, 274
flexible work arrangements, 369–371, *371*
flexplace, **370**
flextime, **370**
flow theory
  definition and overview, 398–399, **399,** *399*
  synthesis and application of work motivation theories, 412–415, *414, 416*
focus, internal *vs.* external, 274
focus groups, **44**
Food and Drug Administration, U.S., 485
forced-distribution method, 240–242, *241*
Ford, Henry, 275
Forest Service, U.S., 44
formalization, **61**
forming (five stage model of group development), 299–300
"4/40" work schedule, 371
frame-of-reference training, **246,** 246–247
free riding, 318
Freud, Sigmund, 377
Froehle, Craig, 64
Fulbright, Gil, 442
full-range leadership theory, **436,** 436–440, *440*
fun at work, 421, 422
Functional Job Analysis (FJA), **96**
functional magnetic resonance imaging (fMRI), 45–46
functional turnover, 107
funemployment, 372

gamification, **421,** 422
"garbage in, garbage out," 36
Gates, Bill, 254
gender
  American Civil Rights Institute, 81
  leadership and, 451–452
  organizational citizenship behavior and, 344, 345
  organizational strategy, staffing, and, 187, 190
  performance management rating errors and biases, 246
  physical ability assessment and, 134
  See also diversity; sexual harassment
generalizability, **26**
generalization *vs.* maintenance (organizational learning), 224
Genetic Information Nondiscrimination Act of 2008 (GINA), **395**

genetics, motivation and, 394
Germany, environmental context of work, 67
"Getting Ready for Your Next Job" measure, 373
g (general mental ability)
  definition, **132**
  organizational learning and, 198
  teamwork and, 303
  validity generalization, 185–186
Gilbreth, Frank, 7
Gilbreth, Lillian Moller, 7, 93
Glassdoor, 89, 273
global job satisfaction, 332
Global Leadership and Organizational Behavior Effectiveness (GLOBE), 449–451
goals
  goal orientation, **408**
  goal specification by teams, 305
  organizational strategy and staffing for, 166–167
  See also goal-setting theory; work motivation
goal-setting theory
  definition and overview, **406,** 406–409
  synthesis and application of work motivation theories, 412–415, *414, 416*
good *vs.* bad archetype, 324
graphic performance rating scales, 239, *239,* 240
Great Man Theory, 429
Greece, cultural dimensions of, 267
grievance, 472–474, **473**
grievance arbitration, **473**
Griggs v. Duke Power Company (1971), 76
gross body coordination (physical ability), 134
gross motor skills, 135
groups. *See* teams and teamwork
groupthink, **312**
Grutter v. Bollinger (2003), 81–82
guilt, 325, 380

halo errors, **244,** 244–245
Hamilton (musical), 72
Hamm, Mia, 295
Handbook of Industrial and Organizational Psychology, 458
hand gestures, 212, *213*
happiness, 327
HARKing (hypothesizing after results are known), **55**
"harmful help," 307
Harvard University, 10
Hawthorne effect, 11
Hawthorne studies, **10,** 10–11, 13–14
head hunters, 169
healthcare work. *See* medical field
Heraclitus of Ephesus, 375
hierarchy (controlling culture), 275
Hierarchy of Controls (NIOSH), *361,* 361–362
hierarchy of needs. *See* Maslow's hierarchy of needs
high fidelity research design, 28
high-fidelity simulation, 154
Highlights for Children (magazine), 324
hindrance stressors, **364**
hindsight bias, 139
hiring practices
  affirmative action and, 79–82
  interview questions and discrimination, 71
  Occupational Information Network (O*NET) for, 102
  preferential selection, 67, 79
  recruitment, **168,** 168–170, 278
  See also psychological assessments
history of I-O psychology, 1–24
  early years (1900–1916), 5–8
  Experience Age (2019–present), 17–18, 19
  government intervention (1964–1993), 14–15
  industrial *vs.* organizational aspects of, 3, 4
  Information Age (1994–2018), 15–17
  interwar years (1919–1940), 9–11
  I-O psychology, definition, **3**
  mandate of I-O psychology, 23–24
  overview, 2–5
  science and practice, modern-day, 18–23, *20, 22*
  social media and, 15–17
  specialization in field (1946–1963), 13–14
  timeline, *9–13*
  World War I (1917–1918), 7–9
holistic research approach, 52
"Holy Grail," 50
home, working from, 330, 382
honeymoon-hangover effect, **332,** 332–334
Hong Kong, organizational citizenship behavior and, 345
Hoover, Herbert, 439
horizontal job cuts, 282–285
horn error, 245
hospitality industry, organizational strategy and, 170
hostile-environment harassment, 72, **73**
hostile takeover, 286
Houston, Lawrence, III, 111
Howes, John C., 340, 381
Howes, Satoris S. "Tori," 257, 381
Huffington, Arianna, 431
humanitarian work psychology, **62,** 62–63, *63*
human relations movement, 13–14
human resources. *See* decision making standards; employees; jobs; performance management
human universal patter of inter-relationships, 138
Hunt, Steven T., 235
hybrid keying (biodata scoring), 146

"I Am the Very Model of a Scientist-Practitioner" (Sackett), 19, *20*
IBM, 295
Iceland, unions in, 461
idealized influence, 438
identification bonds, 336
ideology and union commitment, 479
idiosyncratic deals, **382**
image-based motivation, 255
impasse
  definition, **465**
  response to, 469–472
  See also labor contracts
implicit leadership theory, **443,** 443–444
impression management, 140, 169, 248
inbox assessment, 156
inclusion, **64,** 64–65

Increasing Efficiency in Business (Scott), 6
independent variables, **46**
India, Union Carbide disaster, 374
individualism
  cultural differences and, 268–269
  definition, 265
  success attribute to teams *vs.* individuals, 292
individualized consideration, 438
inductive method, **27,** 100
indulgence, 266
industrial psychology, term origin of, 5
inference, 125. *See also* validity
Influencing Men in Business (Scott), 6
informational justice, 341–343
informed consent, 54
initiating structure factor (behavioral approach to leadership), 430
injunctive norms, 270
in-/out-groups, 210, 435
inspirational motivation, 438
instrumental bonds, 336
instrumentality, **404**
instrumental motivation, 255
instrumental union commitment, 479
integrative bargaining, 466–467
integrators, 330, 382
integrity tests, **142,** 142–143
intellectual stimulation, 438
intelligence and intelligence testing
  Armed Services Vocational Aptitude Battery (ASVAB), **15**
  Army Alpha and Army Beta, **8**
  Army General Classification Test (AGCT), **12**
  personality *vs.,* 138
  types of, 132–133
  See also g (general mental ability); psychological assessments
intelligent tutoring systems, **203**
interactional justice, **341,** 341–343
interactive multimedia training, **203,** 203–204
interest arbitration, **468**
inter-/intra-role conflict, 365
internal-consistency reliability, **122**
internalized moral perspective, 441
internal validity, **28**
International Agency for Research on Cancer (IARC), 369
International Brotherhood of Teamsters, 461
International Coach Federation, 221
International Labour Organization (ILO), 84–85, 286
International Standard of Occupational Classifications (Europe), 102
internet and technology
  early history of internet, 15–17
  information and communication technology (ICT) after work hours, 378
  observational research with internet, 44
  volume of data on internet, 37
  workplace telepressure, 376
  See also social media
interpersonal justice, 341–343
interpersonal processes (teams), 305, 307–310
inter-rater reliability, **122,** 122–123
Interstate Commerce Commission (CC), 6
interviews
  employment interviews, 151–154, *154,* 161
  feedforward interview, 259
  work analysis and, 99–102, *101*
intrapersonal/interpersonal skills (managerial effectiveness), 217
intrinsic motivation, 393
investigation (socialization process of teams), 301
I-O psychology discipline
  humanitarian work psychology, **62,** 62–63, *63*
  inception of term, 14
  industrial psychology term, 5
  licensing of I-O psychologists, 22–23
  mandate of I-O psychology, 23–24
  overview, 2–3
  professional affiliations, 21–22, *22* (*See also* American Psychological Association (APA))
  pro-social I-O psychology, 62–63
  as science, 26, 280
  scientist-practitioner model, 18–21, *20*
  Society for Industrial and Organizational Psychology (SIOP), 19, *20,* **22,** *22,* 63, 458
  union/management relations and role of, 480–483, *481, 483*
  unions' distrust of, 458–459, *459*
  See also faces of I-O psychology; history of I-O psychology; research methods in I-O psychology
Iraq War, qualitative research on, 40
Irving, Jessica, 171
issue-by-issue arbitration, **469**

James, LeBron, 392
James, Wilhelm, 7
Japan
  environmental context of work and, 67, 68
  karoshi (death from overwork), 369
  organizational citizenship behavior and, 345
jobs
  definition, 16, **96**
  downsizing of, **282,** 282–285
  employee engagement, **338,** 338–339
  ethnographers, 40–41
  Functional Job Analysis (FJA), **96**
  job attitudes, overview, 331
  job characteristic model, **410,** 410–411
  job crafting, **410**
  job demands-resource model, **364**
  Job Descriptive Index, 332
  job enrichment, **410**
  job facet satisfaction, 332
  job families, tasks, positions and, *97*
  job family, **96**
  job incumbents, 94–95
  job satisfaction, **331,** 331–335, *333*
  job search, 373
  person-job fit, **276**
  work commitment, **335,** 335–337, *336, 337*
  See also employees; I-O psychology discipline; medical field; performance management; service jobs; work analysis
Jobvite, 168
Johns Hopkins, 243
Johnson, Lyndon, 70

Joie de Vivre Hospitality, 396
Jordan, Michael, 392
Jorgenson, Dale O., 131
Journal of Applied Psychology, 9, 35

karoshi (death from overwork), 369
Keller, Helen, 302
Kellogg Company, 370
Kenya, politeness and, 342
knocker-uppers, 17
knowledge
  definition, 98
  knowledge, skills, abilities (KSAs), 187, 202
  knowledge compilation, **197**
  shared mental model, **310,** 310–312, *311, 312*
  of teammates, 311
  See also KSAOs (knowledge, skills, abilities, other personal characteristics)
Kotter, John, 281, *281*
KSAOs (knowledge, skills, abilities, other personal characteristics)
  definition, 94, **98**
  organizational learning for, 194
  for organizational strategy and staffing, 166–167
  overqualification and work motivation, 420
  personnel selection for teams, 314
  task analysis, **200**
  teamwork and level of analysis, 292
  thinking, doing, feeling of team members, 317
  for work analytic information, 103–105
Kuder-Richardson 20 (KR20), 122

laboratory (true) experiments, 30–32
labor contracts, 465–474
  arbitration, **468,** 468–469
  collective bargaining, **466,** 466–467
  definition and overview, **465,** *465,* 465–466
  fact-finding, **468**
  grievance, 472–474, **473**
  impasse, definition, **465**
  impasse response, 469–472
  mediation, **467,** 467–468
labor strike, **469,** 469–472
laissez-faire leadership, **439**
leaderless group discussion (LGD), 156
leader-member exchange theory, **435,** 435–436
leadership, 425–456
  authentic leadership, **441**
  behavioral approach, **430**
  contingency approach, **433,** 433–435
  convergence among approaches to, 445–446
  cross-cultural issues of, 449–451
  cultural values and, 268
  "dark side" of, 446–448, *447*
  diversity issues of, 451–452
  entrepreneurship and, **453,** 453–454
  full-range leadership theory, **436,** 436–440, *440*
  implicit leadership theory, **443,** 443–444
  labor relations and I-O psychology role in leadership development, 480–481
  leader-member exchange theory, **435,** 435–436
  leadership skills, 217
  motivation and, 429, 430, 435, 438, 445, 451, 454–455
  organization development and, 288
  overview, 426–427, 455
  power and influence approach, 431–433, **432,** *432*
  servant leadership, **441,** 441–442
  strategic leadership, **443**
  substitutes for leadership, **444,** 444–445
  in teams, 448–449
  theoretical approaches, overview, 427
  trait approach, **427,** 427–430
Leadership and Organization Change for Implementation (LOCI), 280
"learned helplessness," 307
learning
  definition, **197**
  learning criteria, **224,** 224–225
  learning goal orientation, 408
  learning process and task performance, 197–199
Learn Stuff, 417
Lee, Sandra L., 218
legal context of work, 69–85
  affirmative action, 79–82
  Age Discrimination in Employment Act (ADEA, 1967), 73–74, 135
  American Rescue Plan Act (ARPA), 83
  Americans with Disabilities Act (1990), 14, 74–75, 104, 363, 387
  child labor, **84,** 84–85
  Civil Rights Act, 14, 70–73, 75, 133, 451
  cultural values and, 268
  determining unfair discrimination, 75–82, *78*
  Fair Labor Standards Act (FLSA, 1938), 84–85
  Families First Coronavirus Response Act (FFCRA), 83
  Family and Medical Leave Act (FMLA, 1993), 14–15, 82–83, 382
  I-O psychology and government intervention (1964–1993), 14–15
  labor union formation and, 463–464, *464* (*See also* union/management relations)
  licensure of I-O psychologists, **23**
  Occupational Safety and Health Act (1970), 82
  overview, 69
  performance appraisal and, 237–238, *238*
  See also diversity; union/management relations
legitimate power, 432
leniency errors, **245**
letters of recommendation, 158
level of analysis, **36, 292,** 292–294, *293*
Lewin, Kurt, 279–281, *281*
LGBTQIA2S+ (Lesbian, Gay, Bisexual, Transgender, Queer and/or Questioning, Intersex, Asexual, Two-Spirit), context of work and, 66. *See also* diversity
licensure, **23**
Lincoln, Abraham, 426
linkage analysis, **98,** 98–99

LinkedIn, 168
LMX (leader-member exchange theory), 435–436
lockout, **471**
long-term orientation, 266
Lovecraft, H. P., 375
low fidelity research design, 28
Ludlow Massacre, 472
Lyness, Karen, 452

Ma, Jack, 392
Maasai tribe, politeness and, 342
Machiavelli, Niccolò, 138
Machiavellianism, 138
macro-/meso-/micro-level research, 294
maintenance (socialization process of teams), 301
maintenance *vs.* generalization (organizational learning), 224
management
  development of, **215,** 215–222, *219*
  leadership *vs.,* 426
  managerial work analysis, 103
  See also union/management relations
Martin v. PGA Tour (2001), 75
Mary Kay Cosmetics, 230
masculinity-centered cultures, 265
Maslow's hierarchy of needs
  definition and overview, **395,** 395–396, *397*
  synthesis and application of work motivation theories, 412–415, *414, 416*
mating theories of recruiting, 169
maximum performance, **106**
Mayo, Elton, 13–14
McBride, Tom, 16
McDonald's, 68
measurement of research methods, 46–50, *49*
Mechanical Turk (Amazon), 29
mediation, **467,** 467–468
medical field
  COVID-19 as dirty work, 386
  interactive multimedia training, **203,** 203–204
  Johns Hopkins behavioral checklist, 243
  multiteam systems and, 297
  organizational strategy and staffing for, 166–167
  person-environment fit, 277
mental models, 198
mentoring relationships
  mentors and protégés, definition, **217**
  overview, 217–221, *219*
  power distance and, 220
mergers and acquisitions
  organizational change and, 286, 287
  as stressful change process, 375
"mesearch research," 53, 381
meta-analysis, **35,** 35–36
meta-cognition, 198–199
Mexico, environmental context of work, 67
Meyer, Steven A., 131
Middle Eastern cultures
  communication in, 269
  leadership and, 450–451
military, U.S.
  Armed Services Vocational Aptitude Battery (ASVAB), **15,** 24, 148, 190
  Army Alpha and Army Beta, 8
  Army General Classification Test (AGCT), 12
  classification, **190**
  computerized adaptive testing (CAT), **148,** 149
  Iraq War and qualitative research, 40
  leadership studied by, 427
  My Next Move for Veterans (website), 102
  team decision making and, 292
  textile industry and organizational change, 279
  World War I recruitment and, 8–9
  World War II recruitment and, 12–13
Minnesota Satisfaction Questionnaire, 332, *333*
misrepresentation, 237–238, *238*
mission analysis (by teams), 305
mistakes, learning from, 207–208
mixed method research design, 52
Modi, Narendra, 431
monitoring behaviors, 307
Monster.com, 102
moods
  definition, **325**
  mood of team members, 309
  See also affect, attitudes, and behavior at work
Mosley, Eric, 260
motivation. *See* work motivation
motor skills, 135
Muchinsky, Paul, 95, 412
multimethod approach, 52
multiphenomenon research approach, 52
multiple correlation, **179**
multisource feedback (MSF), 252–254, *253, 254*
multistakeholder perspective, 52
multiteam teams, **297,** 297–298, 449
mum effect, 254
Musk, Elon, 256, 431

narcissism, 138–139, 446
NASA, 21, 304
Natera, 218
national culture. *See* cross-cultural issues; *individual names of countries*
National Education Association, 461
National Institute for Occupational Safety and Health (NIOSH), 82, *361,* 361–362
National Labor Relations Act (NLRA), **463,** 463–464, *464,* 469, 470
National Labor Relations Board (NLRB), **463**
negative leniency, 245
negative spillover, 377
negligence, 237
Nepal, environmental context of work, 68
nepotism, **67,** 68
networking, internal/external, 33
neuroscience, 45–46
New York State Psychological Association, 459
Nguyen, Kenny, 437
Nief, Ron, 16
Nixon, Richard, 437
Noland, Kenneth, 60
non-computer-based training methods, 204–206
non-experiment, **33,** 33–34
nonprofit organizations, 62

non-unionized companies, union influence on, 474–475
Nooyi, Indra, 230
norms
  cultural tightness/looseness, 266
  definition, **270**
  normative component (commitment), 336
  norming (five stage model of group development), 299–300
  norming within-group, 133–134
North Carolina, Fair Labor Standards Act (FLSA, 1938) and, 84

objective performance criteria, **105,** 105–106
observable artifacts, 271–272, *272,* 273
observation, **43,** 43–44
occupational health. *See* workplace health and well-being
Occupational Information Network (O*NET), **100,** 100–102, *101*
Occupational Safety and Health Act (1970), 82
Occupational Safety and Health Administration (OSHA), 485
occupations/professions, collective nouns of, 316
Office of Apprenticeship Training, Employer, and Labor Services (OATELS), 480
Office of Strategic Service, U.S. (OSS), 12
The Office (television show), 385
offshoring
  definition and overview, 282–285, **283**
  labor unions and, 484
Ohio State University, 430
Old Spice, 296
onboarding
  definition, **196**
  organizational strategy, 167, 197
  person-organization fit and, 278
online reviews, 89
online testing, 149–150
on-the-job training, **195,** 195–196
openness to experience (personality factor), 136, 137, 308
open shops, **462**
operationalization, **123**
organizational analysis, **199**
organizational behavior
  faking and, 140–141
  I-O psychology and overlap with, 3
  See also behavior
organizational change, 278–287
  change agents, 279
  definition, **278**
  downsizing, outsourcing, and offshoring, 282–285, *284*
  labor relations and I-O psychology role in, 482–483, *483*
  mergers and acquisitions, 286, 287
  organizational adaptation to work complexity, 319–320
  overcoming resistance to, 279–282, *281*
  overview, 278–279
organizational citizenship behavior
  definition and overview, **343,** 343–345
  as "union citizenship behaviors," 464
organizational climate
  competing values of, 272–276, *274*
  definition, **269**
  norms and, **270**
  See also organizational culture
organizational culture
  definition, **270**
  evaluation of training programs and, 225
  layers of, 270–272, *272*
  stressful change processes and, 375
organizational justice, **339,** *339,* 339–343, 402
organizational learning and training, 193–227
  active learning approaches, 206–209, *209*
  apprentice training, **480,** 480–481
  assessing training needs, 199–200
  behavioral observation training, **247**
  cross-training, **316,** 316–317, *317*
  evaluation criteria of training programs, 224–225
  formal *vs.* informal, 195–197
  frame-of-reference training, **246,** 246–247
  importance of, 194–195
  labor relations and I-O psychology role in, *480,* 480–481
  learning-by-doing, 116
  learning process and task performance, 197–199
  management development, **215,** 215–222, *219*
  methods and techniques of training, 201–206
  on-the-job training, **195,** 195–196
  rater training, 246–247
  special training topics, 210–215, *211, 213*
  training, definition, **194**
  training for teams, 316–317, *317*
  training needs assessment, **199,** 199–200
  transfer of training, **223,** 223–224
  work analytic information for, 103
organizational maintenance, 234–236
organizational merger, **286,** 287
organizational neuroscience, 45–46
organizational politics, **348,** 348–351
organizational records, **41,** 41–42
organizational socialization, **196,** 196–197
organizational strategy and staffing, 165–191
  accomplishing goals with, 166–167
  cutoff score determination, 186–187
  human perspective of, 179–183, *180, 182*
  personnel selection, **172,** *172,* 172–176, *173, 175*
  personnel selection and financial issues, *159,* 159–161
  placement and classification, **190**
  recruitment, **168,** 168–170
  rejection letters, 170, 171
  selection decisions, 176–179, *177,* 194
  test utility and organizational efficiency, 188
  validity generalization, **184,** 184–186, *185*
  See also performance management; psychological assessments; teams and teamwork; union/management relations

organization development (OD), 14, **287,** 287–289
orientation programs, 196
"other characteristics," definition, 98. *See also* KSAOs (knowledge, skills, abilities, other personal characteristics)
outsourcing, 282–285, **283**
overqualification, 419, 420
overt integrity tests, 142–143

pacing, 418–419
paired-comparison method (performance management), 240
pandemic. *See* COVID-19
parent companies, 286
Park, YoungAh, 378
passive learning, 207
passive management-by-exception (transactional leadership), 439
Patinkin, Sheldon, 318
peer assessment (performance), **249,** 249–251, 319
peer nomination, 249, **250**
peer ranking, 249, **250**
peer ratings, 249, **250**
People, Data, and Things (task dimensions), 96–98
PepsiCo, 377
perceptions of fit, 276–278
perceptual speed abilities, 198
performance, motivation and, 392–394. *See also* work motivation
performance accomplishments, self-efficacy and, 407
performance appraisal
  definition, **230**
  documentation performance management and, 236
  legal issues of, 237–238, *238*
  reaction to, 258
  See also performance management
performance criteria (decision making standards), 105–116
  absenteeism, 107
  accidents, 109
  adaptive behavior, **112,** 112–113
  citizenship behavior, **113**
  counterproductive work behavior, **110**
  emotional labor, **110,** 110–112, 113
  objective performance criteria, **105**
  objective *vs.* subjective performance criteria, 105–106
  presenteeism, 107–108
  production, 106
  sales, 106
  subjective performance criteria, **105**
  theft by employees, 109–110
  turnover (tenure), 107
performance goal orientation, 408
performance management, 229–261
  after-action reviews (AARs), 224
  alignment and, 230–231
  crowdsourced performance review, 259, 260
  definition, **230**
  feedback and, 254–257
  future of, 259
  job satisfaction and, 334–335 (*See also* affect, attitudes, and behavior at work)
  legal issues of performance appraisal, 237–238, *238*
  peer assessment, **249,** 249–251
  performance appraisal, **230**
  performance appraisal in teams, 317–319
  performance appraisal reaction, 258
  performance rating scales, *239,* 239–243, *241*
  process of, 231–232, *232,* 233, 238
  purposes of performance management systems, 234–236
  rater motivation, **247,** 247–249
  rater training, 246–247
  rating errors and biases, 244–246
  self-assessment, **251**
  360° feedback, **252,** 252–254, *253, 254,* 260
performing (five stage model of group development), 299–300
personality
  definition, 136
  extraversion, 125
  intelligence *vs.,* 138
  inventories, 136–143
  personality-based integrity test, 143
  task conflict and group performance, 308
  of team members, 315
Personality-Related Position Requirements Form, 103
personal protective equipment (PPE), 362
person analysis, **200**
person-environment fit, **276,** 277
person-job fit, **276**
Personnel Psychology (journal), 131
personnel selection
  definition and overview, **172,** *172,* 172–176, *173, 175*
  financial issues of, *159,* 159–161
  labor relations and I-O psychology role in, 480
  for teams, 314–315
  See also hiring practices; organizational strategy and staffing; performance management; psychological assessments; teams and teamwork
person-organization fit, **276,** 276–278
person-vocation fit, **276**
persuasion, self-efficacy and, 407
PGA of America, 75
physical ability, 134
physical distancing, 17–18
physical stressors
  Hierarchy of Controls (NIOSH), *361,* 361–362
  safety behaviors for, 362–363
  stressors, definition and overview, **360,** 360–361
pinboys, 17
placement, **190**
Planet Champion (McDonald's), 68
planning fallacy, **418**
politeness, 342
political skill, 350–351
polygraph, **143**
position, **96**
Position Analysis Questionnaire (PAQ), **100,** *101*
positive leniency, 245
positive spillover, 377
Post-Traumatic Stress Disorder (PTSD), 74
Powell, Colin, 306
power and influence approach, 431–433, **432,** *432*
power distance, 220, 265

power (trait approach to leadership), 429
practical intelligence, 132
practice behaviors, 208
predictive criterion-related validity, 126, *127*
predictors
  base rate, **174**
  causality and, 50
  definition, 120
  development of, 130–132
  prediction as goal of science, 26
  predictor cutoff, **172,** *172,* 172–173, *173,* 186–187 (*See also* organizational strategy and staffing)
  predictor variables, 46, **47**
  reliability, **121,** 121–123
  reliability and validity inter-relatedness, 129, **129**
  selection ratio, **173,** 173–174, *175*
  unstructured interviews and, 153
  validity, **123,** 123–129, *125, 127*
preferential selection, 67, 79
presenteeism, 107–108
primacy effect, 244
primary research methods
  definition, **30**
  types of, 30–34
The Principles of Scientific Management (Taylor), 6
privacy
  biodata inventories and, 146, 147
  of research participants, 54
privilege walk exercise, 211, *211*
problem-resolution teams, **295**
proceduralization, 198
procedural justice, **341**
procedural knowledge, **198**
Professional and Managerial Position Questionnaire, 103
programmed instruction, **203**
Project A (Armed Services Vocational Aptitude Battery, ASVAB), 15
Project INCUBATE (Veteran Transition Project), 62
Prolific, 29
pro-social behavior, 343–345
pro-social I-O psychology, 62–63
prospecting theories of recruiting, 169
protected classes, **70**
protégés, **217,** 217–221, *219*
proximal constructs, *413,* 413–415
proximity principle, 33
psychological assessments, 119–163
  ability tests, 132–135
  assessment centers, **157**
  biodata inventories, **145,** *145,* 145–147
  computerized adaptive testing (CAT), **148,** 149
  drug testing, **147,** 147–148
  g (general mental ability), **132,** 185–186
  interviews, 151–154, *154*
  letters of recommendation, 158
  online testing, 149–150
  personality inventories, 136–143
  predictor development and, 130–132
  predictor quality and, 121–129, *125, 127, 129*
  predictors, definition, 120
  predictors, overview and evaluation, 158–161, *159*
  situational judgment tests, **144,** 144–145, *145*
  union/management relations and, 458–459
  work samples and situational exercises, **154,** 154–156, **156**
  See also predictors; testing
psychological capital, **366**
psychological contract, **351,** 351–356, *353, 355*
Psychological Corporation, 10
Psychology and Industrial Efficiency (Münsterberg), 7
psychology disciplines
  applied psychology, 3, 9–10
  clinical psychology, 3
  humanitarian work psychology, **62,** 62–63, *63*
  industrial psychology, term origin, 5
  social psychology, 199
  See also I-O psychology discipline
The Psychology of Advertising (Scott), 6
psychometric, definition, **121**
psychomotor ability, 135, 198
psychopathy, 139, 446

qChange, 340
QC Mart, 447
qualitative research, 39–41
  data collection for, 39–41
  definition, **39**
quantitative variables, **46**
quasi-experiments
  definition, **32**
  self-reflective job titles (research example), 32, 46, 51
questionnaires
  definition, **42**
  offering incentives for, 43
  Position Analysis Questionnaire (PAQ), **100,** *101*
  survey feedback as organization development, 288–289
  work analysis and, 99–102, *101*
quid pro quo harassment, 72
quotas, 79–80

race
  affirmative action and, 80
  American Civil Rights Institute, 81
  organizational strategy, staffing, and, 187, 190
  service expectations of Blacks and Whites, 111
  See also diversity
Ramesses II (pharaoh of ancient Egypt), 476
randomization, **30**
random selection, 183
"rank and yank," 241–242
rank-order method, 240
rater error training, **246**
rater motivation, **247,** 247–249
rater training, 246–247
rational keying (biodata scoring), 146
reaction criteria, **224**
Reagan, Ronald, 143
reasonable accommodation, 74, 104, 363
recency effect, 244
recruitment, **168,** 168–170, 278. *See also* organizational strategy and staffing
Red for Ed (teacher strikes), 470
reduction-in-force, 282–285
referent power, 432
rejection and rejection letters, 170, 171, 392

relatedness, self-determination theory and, 399–401
relational contracts, 352
relational transparency, 441
reliability, **121,** 121–123, 129
remembrance (socialization process of teams), 301
RepresentUs, 442
research design, **28,** 28–29
research methods in I-O psychology, 25–57
  conclusions from research, 51–53
  design of research study, 28–29
  empirical research cycle, overview, *26*
  ethical issues, 53–55
  holistic research approach, 52
  measurement and analysis, 46–50, *49*
  methods/sources of data collection, 41–44
  organizational neuroscience, 45–46
  overview, 26–27
  primary research methods, 30–34
  qualitative research, 39–41
  research, definition, **26**
  secondary research methods, 34–39
  statement of research problem, 27
  "WEIRD" participants, 29
resocialization (socialization process of teams), 301
restraint, 266
results criteria, **225**
reward power (power and influence approach to leadership), 431
right-to-work laws, 462, *462,* 463
rituals, 30–31
rival camps game, 350
R (multiple correlation), 179
role playing, **205,** 206
role stressors
  role ambiguity, **365**
  role conflict, **365**
  role overload, **365**
  roles, definition, **364**
  stressors, definition and overview, **360,** 360–361
Roosevelt, Theodore, 7

sabotage, **471**
Sackett, Paul, 19, *20*
sadness, 325–326
safety behaviors
  for physical stressors, 362–363
  safety compliance, **363**
  safety participation, **363**
SAT (academic standardized test), 184
Saturday Night Live (television show), 329
scatterplots, 48, *49*
science
  I-O psychology as, 26, 280
  leadership studied by, 427
scientific management, 6, 93
scientist-practitioner gap, **20**
scientist-practitioner model, **19**
Scott, John C., 150
Scott, Walter Dill, 6, 8
search firms, 169
secondary research methods
  definition, **34**
  types of, 34–39
Second Life, 466
segmenters, 330, 382
selection decisions, 176–179, *177,* 194
selection ratio, **173,** 173–174, *175*
self-assessment (performance), **251,** 259
self-awareness (authentic leadership), 441
self-awareness (intrapersonal skills), 217
self-determination theory
  definition and overview, **399,** 399–401
  synthesis and application of work motivation theories, 412–415, *414, 416*
self-efficacy, **208,** 208–209, **407**
self-evaluation reaction, 208
self-knowledge, 211
self-leadership, 445
self-monitoring, 208
self-reflective job titles (research example), 32, 46, 51
self-regulation (definition), **409**
self-regulation theories, **409**
self-regulatory training, **208,** 208–209
self-similarity principle, 33
sensory/perceptual ability, 135
sensory processing disorders, 363
serial position errors, **244**
servant leadership, **441,** 441–442
service jobs
  display rules in, 110–112
  sexual harassment and, 214
  workplace incivility and, 346
set point theory, 334
70:20:10 Model for Learning and Development, 195–196
sexual harassment
  definition, **72**
  training programs, 200, 214–215
  workplace romance and, 216
shame, 325
shared attitudes and beliefs, 311
shared leadership, **448,** 448–449
shared mental model, **310,** 310–312, *311, 312*
Sherrill, Patrick Henry, 374
shift work, **367,** 367–369
short-term orientation, 266
similar-to-me effect, 244
Singapore, environmental context of work, 68
situational exercises, **156**
situational interview, **153,** 154, *154*
situational judgment test (SJT), **144,** 144–145, *145*
situational stress tests (World War II), 12
skills
  acquisition of, 197–199
  definition, 98 (*See also* KSAOs (knowledge, skills, abilities, other personal characteristics))
  political skill, 350–351
  skill differentiation, 302
  skill variety job characteristics model, 410
  See also organizational behavior; organizational learning
"slactivism" *vs.* activism, 66
sleep, work and, 35
sociability (TRIAD/Tracking Roles In And Across Domains), 302–303
social context of work, 62–66, *63, 65*
social distancing *vs.* physical distancing, 17–18
social information processing theory, 443–444
socialization, 196–197, **300,** 300–301, *301*

social loafing, **318**
social media
assessing personality via Facebook, 142
criteria for online reviews, 89
crowdsourcing and performance reviews, 260
cyberbullying and, 349
cyberloafing, 417
Information Age and, 15–17
leaders and their use of Twitter, 431
as new "water cooler," 273
for recruitment, 168
research and "WEIRD" participants, 29
"slactivism" *vs.* activism, 66
social media teams, 296
social stressors from, 367
union information and organizing, 466
Web 2.0 and, 15, 16
workplace romance and, 216
social psychology, 199
social recognition, 260
social stressors
bullying and, 366
psychological capital for, **366**
from social media, 367
stressors, definition and overview, **360,** 360–361
social validity, 170
Society for Human Resource Management (SHRM), 216
Society for Industrial and Organizational Psychology (SIOP)
definition, **22**
"I Am the Very Model of a Scientist-Practitioner" (Sackett), 19, *20*
membership in, *22*
on United Nations Global Compact, 63, 458
Socratic Method, 207
"The Song of a Consultant" (Meyer and Jorgenson), 131
spacing, 418–419
span of control, **61**
specialization, **60,** 61
special training topics, 210–215, *211, 213*
spillover, 377
split-half reliability, 122
sports, team *vs.* individual, 295
sportsmanship, 344
spurious correlation, **51**
staff validity, 313
stamina (physical ability), 134
STAR framework (Situation, Task, Action, Results), 155
star performers, 315
Star Wars Episode V (film), 393
statement of research problems, 27
static strength (physical ability), 134
statistical methods. *See* organizational strategy and staffing; predictors; research methods in I-O psychology
stigma
definition, **384**
of dirty work, 383–386
storming (five stage model of group development), 299–300
strategic leadership, **443**
strategic performance management, 234
strategy formulation and planning, 306
stressors, **360,** 360–361. *See also* workplace health and well-being
strike, etymology of, 470
structural context of work, 60–61
structured interviews, **152**
study preregistration, **55**
subjective performance criteria, **105,** 105–106
subject matter experts (SME), **94,** 94–95
substance abuse
alcohol and drug abuse in workplace, 387–389
definition, **387**
psychological assessment and, 147–148
substitutes for leadership, **444,** 444–445
succession planning, 234–236. **234**
"sucker" effect, 318
supervisors, 94–95
Supreme Court, U.S. *See individual names of cases*
surface acting, 112, 113
surveys. *See* questionnaires
sustainability, 68–69
Sweden, cultural dimensions of, 267
Sweet Revenge, 346
Switzerland, Swiss Administration on data mining, 39

Taco Bell, 296
tactical teams, **296**
Taft-Hartley Act (1947), 462
Taiwan, politeness and, 342
talent acquisition, 167
talent analytics, 38
Taproot Foundation, 62
target companies, 286
tasks
definition, **96**
learning process and task performance, 197–199
positions, jobs, job families, and, *97*
STAR framework (Situation, Task, Action, Results), 155
subtasks, 418–419
task analysis, **200**
task conflict, 307–308
task feedback, 410
task identity/signification/feedback and job characteristics model, 410
task orientation (TRIAD/Tracking Roles In And Across Domains), 302–303
task-oriented procedure, **96**
task-related knowledge, 311
task-related stressors, 360–361, 363–364
task-specific information, 310–311
taskwork skills, 314
by team members, 294 (*See also* teams and teamwork)
for work analytic procedures, 96–99
tattoos (research example), 31
"Taxonomies of Human Performance," 100
taxonomy, **99**
Taylor, Frederick W., 6, 93, 458
teams and teamwork, 291–321
collectivism *vs.* individualism, 265, 268–269, 292
defining characteristics of teams, 294, 295
leadership and, 448–449

level of analysis, **292,** 292–294, *293*
norms and, **270**
organizational adaptation to work complexity, 319–320
performance appraisal in teams, 317–319
personnel selection for teams, 314–315
star performers, 315
team building and organization development, 288
team cognition, **310,** 310–313, *311, 312*
team cohesion, **309**
team informity, 313
team life cycle, 299–301, *301*
team processes, **305,** 305–310
teams, definition, **294**
team structure and composition, 302–305, *303*
teamwork skills, 314
training for teams, 316–317, *317*
types of teams, 295–298
technology and work. *See* internet and technology; social media
teleworkers, 330, **370,** 382
temporal stability, 302
terrorists (suspected), interrogation of, 55
Tesla, 275
testing
ability tests, 132–135
academic standardized tests, 184
Armed Services Vocational Aptitude Battery (ASVAB), **15,** 24, 148, 190
Army Alpha and Army Beta, **8**
computerized adaptive testing (CAT), **148,** 149
drug testing, **147,** 147–148
historical background, 12, 13
integrity tests, **142,** 142–143
intelligence test types, 132–133
of intelligence *vs.* personality, 138
online testing, 149–150
situational judgment tests, **144,** 144–145, *145*
test-retest reliability, **121**
utility, **188**
Texas A&M University, 214
textile industry, organizational change in, 279
Thatcher, Margaret, 433
theft by employees
integrity tests and, **142,** 142–143
performance criteria and, 109–110
theory
definition, **27**
testing, 39
The Theory of Advertising (Scott), 6
The Prince (Machiavelli), 138
"Therblig," 93
thermodynamics of revenge, **346,** 346–347
360° feedback, **252,** 252–254, *253, 254,* 260
TikTok, 296
time issues
past *vs.* present characteristics of predictors, 130–132
temporal stability, 302
time-and-motion studies, 93
work hours, historical perspective, 460
work motivation and impact of, 416–419
work schedule-related stressors, 367–371, *371*
Titchener, Edward, 5
Title VII, Civil Rights Act (1964), 14–15, 70–73, 75
Tom's of Maine, 274, *274*
top-grading, **241,** 241–242
total-package arbitration, **469**
training, **194**. *See also* organizational learning and training
trait approach (leadership), **427,** 427–430
transactional contracts, 352
transactional leadership
definition and overview, **438,** 438–440
strategic leadership and, 443
transfer of training, **223,** 223–224
transformational leadership
authentic leadership and, 441
"dark side" of, 446
definition and overview, **436,** 436–438
employee satisfaction and, 440
strategic leadership and, 443
substitutes for leadership and, 445
transition processes (teams), 305–306
traumatic events
examples and outcomes, 374
stressors, definition and overview, **360,** 360–361
TRIAD (Tracking Roles In And Across Domains), 302–303, *303*
triple bottom line, *69*
true experiments, **30,** 30–32
true negatives, **177**
true positives, **177**
trust, 309–310
turnover (tenure)
job satisfaction and, 334–335
non-experiment study of, 33
performance criteria (decision making standards), 107
specialization of work and, 61
Twain, Mark, 441
Twitter, 168, 431
two-factor theory
definition and overview, **397,** 397–398
synthesis and application of work motivation theories, 412–415, *414*
typical performance, **106**
Tyson Foods, 485

Uber, 195
uncertainty avoidance, 265–266
unemployment, long-term impact of, 40
Uniform Guidelines on Employee Selection Procedures (EEOC), 78, 79
Union Carbide, 374
"union citizenship behaviors," 464
union/management relations, 457–487
behavioral research on, 475–479, *477, 479*
formation of labor unions, 463–464, *464*
future of unions, 484–486
I-O psychology profession and role in, 458–459, *459,* 480–483, *481, 483*
labor contracts, *465,* 465–474
labor union representation in other countries, 461, 486

non-unionized companies and, 474–475
union-busting, **458,** 458–459
union commitment, **478,** 478–479, *479*
union/non-union wage differential, **475**
unions, definition and overview, **459,** 459–461, *461*
unions as organizations, 461–462, *462*
union shops, **462**
United Auto Workers, 485
United Food and Commercial Workers (UFCW) International Union, 485
United Nations Global Compact, 63, *63,* 458
United States
cultural dimensions of, 267
environmental context of work and, 67, 68
organizational citizenship behavior and, 345
See also military, U.S.; *individual names of agencies*
United Steelworkers, 461, 483
UNITE-HIRE, 485
unity of command, **61**
University of California, 79
University of Michigan, 80–82
University of Texas, 214
unstructured interviews, **152,** 153
utility, **188**

vacation time, cultural values and, 267
valence, **405**
validity
construct validity, **124,** 124–126, *125*
content validity, **127,** 127–129
criterion-related validity, **126,** 126–127, *127*
definition, **123**
predictor overview and evaluation, 158–161, *159*
reliability and inter-relatedness to, 129
validity generalization, **184,** 184–186, *185*
values
culture and, 266–269
decision making and, 88
environmental context of work and, 67
espoused values, 271–272, *272*
organizational climate and competing values, 272–276, *274*
shared attitudes and beliefs, 311
Van Buren, Martin, 439
variables
definition, **46**
types of, 46–47
See also predictors; research methods in I-O psychology
Venezuela, environmental context of work, 68
vertical job cuts, 282–285
Veteran Transition Project, 62
vicarious experience, self-efficacy and, 407
Victoria (queen of England), 439
vigor, 338
virtual instructor-led training, 202
virtual reality training, **204**
virtual teams, **297,** 298
"vitality curve," 241–242
Viteles, Morris, 11, 21
volume/velocity/variety of big data, 37
voluntary turnover, 107

web-based testing, 149–150
"WEIRD" (Western, Education, Industrialized, Rich, Democratic) participants, 29
wellness programs for stress management, 376–377
Wells Fargo, 405
Western cultural values
leadership and, 450–451
non-Western *vs.,* 266–269, *267,* 383
See also cross-cultural issues; *individual names of countries*
Western Electric Company, 10
whistleblower laws, **82**
"Who am I?" exercise, 210
Whole Foods, 287
wildcat strike, 469
Wilde, Oscar, 419
"will do" factors, 182, 315, 392, 393
withdrawal behavior, 334–335
within-group norming, 133–134
Wolfe, Melissa, 428
workaholism, 338
work analysis, 93–105
application of, 103–104
collecting information for, 99–102, *101*
competency modeling and, **104,** 104–105
content validation *vs.,* 128
definition and overview, **93,** 93–94
evaluating methods of, 104
managerial, 103
procedures for, 96–99, *97*
sources of work information for, 94–95
work analysts, 94–95
work commitment, **335,** 335–337, *336, 337*
worker-oriented procedure, **98,** 98–99
work-family enrichment, **380,** 380–382
work-family interventions, **382,** 382–383
working from home, 330, 370, 382
work motivation, 391–424
biological-based theory of motivation, **394,** 394–395
confidence building and, 308–309
direction, intensity, and persistence in, 392–393
equity theory, **401,** 401–403, *402*
expectancy theory, **403,** 403–406, *406*
flow theory, 398–399, **399,** *399*
fun at work and, 421, 422
goal-setting theory, **406,** 406–409
intrinsic and extrinsic motivation, 393
job characteristic model, **410,** 410–411
leadership and, 429, 430, 435, 438, 445, 451, 454–455
Maslow's hierarchy of needs, **395,** 395–396, *397*
overqualification and, 419, 420
performance and, 392–394
rater motivation, **247,** 247–249
for seeking feedback, 255–256
self-determination theory, **399,** 399–401
theories, overview, 394

theories, synthesis and application, 412–415, *414, 416*
time and impact on, 416–419
two-factor theory, **397,** 397–398
work-nonwork balance
cultural values and, 380
work-family balance/conflict, 377–380
work-family enrichment, **380,** 380–382
work-family interventions, **382,** 382–383
work schedule and, 370–371
workplace bullying, 347
workplace discrimination. *See* legal context of work
workplace health and well-being, 359–390
alcohol and drug abuse in workplace, 387–389
balancing work and nonwork, 377–383
career-related stressors, 372–373
child labor, **84,** 84–85
COVID pandemic and, 360, 374, 382, 386
definition, **360**
Family and Medical Leave Act (FMLA, 1993), 82–83
Occupational Safety and Health Act (1970), 82
physical stressors, *361,* 361–363
role stressors, 364–365
social stressors, 366, 367
stigma of dirty work, 383–386
stressful change processes, 375
stress-management interventions and wellness programs, 376–377
stressors, definition and overview, **360,** 360–361
task-related stressors, 363–364
traumatic events, 374
work schedule-related stressors, 367–371, *368, 371*
workplace incivility, 346, **348**
workplace romance, 216
workplace telepressure, 376
work samples, **154,** 154–156
work schedule-related stressors
flexible work arrangements, 369–371, *371*
karoshi (death from overwork), 369
shift work, **367,** 367–369
stressors, definition and overview, **360,** 360–361
work slowdown, **471**
World Health Organization (WHO), 17, 369
Wundt, Wilhelm, 5

Yerkes, Robert, 8
Yousafzai, Malala, 426

Zambia, environmental context of work, 68